THE WESTERN HERITAGE, SINCE 1300

Tenth Edition

AP* EDITION

Donald Kagan

YALE UNIVERSITY

Steven Ozment

HARVARD UNIVERSITY

Frank M. Turner

YALE UNIVERSITY

Prentice Hall

Boston   Columbus   Indianapolis   New York   San Francisco   Upper Saddle River
Amsterdam   Cape Town   Dubai   London   Madrid   Milan   Munich   Paris   Montréal   Toronto
Delhi   Mexico City   São Paulo   Sydney   Hong Kong   Seoul   Singapore   Taipei   Tokyo

VP, Editorial Director: Craig Campanella
Publisher: Charlyce Jones Owen
Editorial Project Manager: Rob DeGeorge
Senior Production Project Manager: Lynn Savino Wendel
Editorial Assistant: Maureen Diana
Senior Managing Editor: Ann Marie McCarthy
Director of Marketing: Brandy Dawson
Senior Marketing Manager: Maureen Prado Roberts
Marketing Assistant: Marissa O'Brien
Operations Specialist: Christina Amato
Senior Art Director: Maria Lange
Text and Cover Designer: Liz Harasymczuk

AV Project Manager: Mirella Signoretto
Manager, Visual Research: Beth Brenzel
Manager, Rights and Permissions: Zina Arabia
Image Permission Coordinator: Michelina Viscusi
Manager, Cover Visual Research & Permissions: Karen Sanatar
Media Director: Brian Hyland
Lead Media Project Manager: Sarah Kinney
Supplements Editor: Emsal Hasan
Composition/Full-Service Project Management: Rebecca Dunn, Prepare, Inc.
Printer/Binder: Courier Kendallville
Cover Printer: Lehigh-Phoenix Color

This book was set in 10/12 Trump Mediaeval

Credits and acknowledgments borrowed from other sources and reproduced, with permission, in this textbook appear on appropriate page within text.

Cover photo credit: Jean Auguse Dominique Ingres (1780–1867), "Napoleon on His Imperial Throne", 1806. Oil on canavans, 259 × 162 cm. Musee des Beaux-Arts, Rennes. Photograph © Erich Lessing/Art Resource, NY.

Library of Congress Cataloging-in-Publication Data

Kagan, Donald
    The Western Heritage : since 1300 : AP version / Donald Kagan, Steven Ozment, Frank M. Turner.—10th ed.
      p. cm.
    Includes bibliographical references and index.
    ISBN 978-0-13-136761-6 (student edition)—ISBN 978-0-13-136927-6 (teacher edtion)
    1. Civilization, Western—History—Textbooks. I. Ozment, Steven E. II. Turner, Frank M. (Frank Miller), 1994 III. Title.
    CB245.K28 2010
    909'.09821—dc22

                              2009041876

10 9 8 7 6 5 4 3 2 1

Prentice Hall
is an imprint of

www.pearsonhighered.com

Student edition

ISBN 10:0-13-136761-7
ISBN 13:978-0-13-136761-6

CONTENTS

iii

11   The Age of Reformation   317

PART 6
Global Conflict, Cold War, and New Directions,
1939– 2008

▼▲ **COMPARE AND CONNECT**
The Munich Settlement   **908**

■ **ENCOUNTERING THE PAST**
Rosie the Riveter and American Women
in the War Effort   **917**

A Closer ▶ LOOK THE VICHY REGIME
                     IN FRANCE   **930**

▼▲ **COMPARE AND CONNECT**
The Soviet Union and the United States
Draw the Lines of the Cold War   **944**

■ **ENCOUNTERING THE PAST**
Rock Music and Political Protest   **966**

A Closer ▶ LOOK COLLAPSE OF THE
                  BERLIN WALL   **970**

▼▲ **COMPARE AND CONNECT**
Margaret Thatcher and Tony Blair Debate Government's Social Responsibility for Welfare   **994**

■ **ENCOUNTERING THE PAST**
Toys from Europe Conquer the United States   **1003**

A Closer ▶ LOOK   THE COPENHAGEN OPERA HOUSE   **1012**

DOCUMENTS

MAPS

USING *THE WESTERN HERITAGE, SINCE 1300*

When writing about history, historians use maps, tables, graphs, and visuals to help their readers understand the past. What follows is an explanation of how to use the historian's tools that are contained in this book.

READING THE TEXTBOOK

Text

Whether it is a biography or an article, or a survey of European history such as this textbook, the text is the historian's basic tool for discussing the past. Historians write about the past using narration and analysis. Narration is the story line of history. It describes what happened in the past, who did it, and where and when it occurred. Narration is also used to describe how people in the past lived, how they passed their daily lives and even, when the historical evidence makes it possible for us to know, what they thought, felt, feared, or desired. Using analysis, historians explain why they think events in the past happened the way they did and offer an explanation for the story of history.

Maps

Maps are important historical tools. They show how geography has affected history and concisely summarize complex relationships and events. Knowing how to read and interpret a map is important to understanding history. Map 13–1 shows the first three major wars of Louis XIV. It has three features to help you read it: a caption, a legend, and a scale. The *caption* explains the historical significance of the map: Between 1667 and 1697 Louis XIV engaged in three wars that resulted in territorial changes in Europe. The *legend* appears in the top left corner of the map. It provides a key to what the colors of the different territorial changes were after each war. The solid red line represents the French boundary in 1648 before the start of the first of the three wars. Cities are marked with a dot. Using the legend, the reader can see what territory became part of France and Spain at the conclusion of each war by the colors used. The *scale* tells us how to estimate the distance between points on the map easily. Some maps also show the topography of the region—its mountains, rivers, and lakes. This helps us understand how geography influenced history.

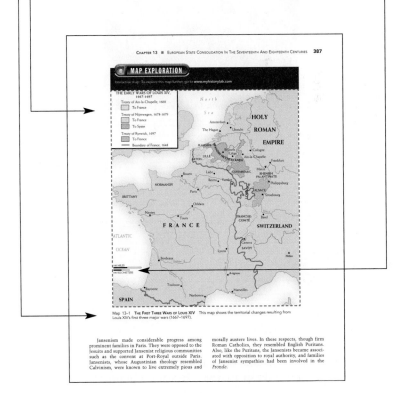

Map Explorations

Many of the maps in each chapter are provided in a useful interactive version on the text's **MyHistoryLab** web site (www.myhistorylab.com). These maps are easily identified by a bar along the top of the map as in Map 13–1. The interactive versions help to focus on the main information in the map and are an excellent resource for strengthening map reading and comprehension skills.

Visuals

Visual images embedded throughout the text provide as much insight into European history as the written word. Within photographs and pieces of fine art lies emotional and historical meaning. Captions provide valuable information, such as in the following example. When studying the image, consider questions such as: "Who are these people?"; "How were they feeling?"; "What event motivated this photograph or painting?"; and "What can be learned from the backdrop surrounding the focal point?" Such analysis allows for a fuller understanding of the people of the West.

Primary Source Documents

Like maps and visuals, primary source documents are essential to the study of history. In each chapter, there are three to four primary sources that illuminate the time, events, or people being discussed in the chapter. The questions that are included with the documents provide an opportunity to learn to analyze and think critically about what these sources tell us about the past.

Study Aids

An outline, a list of key topics, and *an introduction* are included at the beginning of each chapter. Together these features provide a succinct overview of each chapter and a road map for study and review.

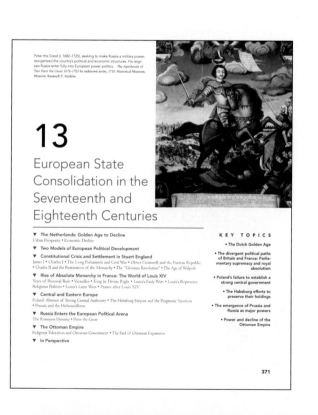

Chronologies follow each major section in a chapter, listing significant events and their dates.

> **CHAPTER 22 ■ THE AGE OF NATION-STATES 673**
>
> Bismarck's spectacular successes overwhelmed the liberal opposition in the Prussian Parliament. The liberals were split between those who prized liberalism and those who supported unification. In the end, nationalism proved more attractive. In 1866, the Prussian Parliament retroactively approved the military budget that it had rejected earlier. Bismarck had crushed the Prussian liberals by making the monarchy and the army the most popular institutions in the country. The drive toward German national unification had achieved its domestic Prussian political goal.
>
> **The Franco-Prussian War and the German Empire (1870–1871)**
>
> Bismarck now wanted to complete unification by bringing the states of southern Germany—Bavaria, Wurtemberg, Baden, and Hesse Darmstadt—into the newly established confederation. Spain gave him the excuse. In 1868, a military coup deposed the corrupt Bourbon queen of Spain, Isabella II (r. 1833–1868). To replace her, the Spaniards chose Prince Leopold of Hohenzollern-Sigmaringen, a Catholic cousin of William I of Prussia. On June 19, 1870, Leopold accepted the Spanish crown with Prussian blessings. Bismarck knew that France would object strongly to a Hohenzollern Spain.
>
> On July 2, the Spanish government announced Leopold's acceptance, and the French reacted as expected. France sent its ambassador, Count Vincent Benedetti (1817–1900), to consult with William I, who was vacationing at Bad Ems. They discussed the matter at several meetings. On July 12, Leopold's father renounced his son's candidacy for the Spanish throne, fearing the issue would cause war between Prussia and France. William was relieved that conflict had been avoided, and he had not had to order Leopold to renounce the Spanish throne.
>
> There the matter might have rested had it not been for the impetuosity of the French and the guile of Bismarck. On July 13, the French government instructed Benedetti to ask William for assurances he would tolerate no future Spanish candidacy for Leopold. The king refused but said he might take the question under further consideration. Later that day he sent Bismarck, who was in Berlin, a telegram reporting the substance of the meeting. The peaceful resolution of the controversy had disappointed the chancellor, who desperately wanted a war with France to complete unification. The king's telegram gave him a new opportunity to provoke war. Bismarck released an edited version of the dispatch. The revised Ems telegram made it appear that William had insulted the French ambassador. The idea was to goad France into declaring war.
>
> The French government fell for Bismarck's bait and declared war on July 19. Napoleon III was sick and not eager for war, but his government believed victory
>
> | GERMAN AND ITALIAN UNIFICATION | |
> | --- | --- |
> | 1854 | Crimean War opens |
> | 1855 | Cavour leads Piedmont into the war on the side of France and England |
> | 1856 | Treaty of Paris concludes the Crimean War |
> | 1858 (January 14) | Attempt to assassinate Napoleon III |
> | 1858 (July 20) | Secret conference between Napoleon III and Cavour at Plombières |
> | 1859 | War of Piedmont and France against Austria |
> | 1860 | Garibaldi lands his forces in Sicily and invades southern Italy |
> | 1861 (March 17) | Proclamation of the Kingdom of Italy |
> | 1861 (June 6) | Death of Cavour |
> | 1862 | Bismarck becomes prime minister of Prussia |
> | 1864 | Danish War |
> | 1865 | Convention of Gastein |
> | 1866 | Austro-Prussian War |
> | 1866 | Austria cedes Venetia to Italy |
> | 1867 | North German Confederation formed |
> | 1870 (June 19–July 12) | Crisis over Hohenzollern candidacy for the Spanish throne |
> | 1870 (July 13) | Bismarck publishes the edited Ems dispatch |
> | 1870 (July 19) | France declares war on Prussia |
> | 1870 (September 1) | France defeated at Sedan and Napoleon III captured |
> | 1870 (September 4) | French Republic proclaimed |
> | 1870 (October 2) | Italian state annexes Rome |
> | 1871 (January 18) | Proclamation of the German Empire at Versailles |
> | 1871 (March 28–May 28) | Paris Commune |
> | 1871 (May 23) | Treaty of Frankfurt ratified between France and Germany |
>
> over the North German Confederation would renew popular support for the empire. Once the conflict erupted, the southern German states, honoring treaties of 1866, joined Prussia against France, whose defeat was not long in coming. On September 1, at the Battle of Sedan, the Germans not only beat the French army but also captured Napoleon III. By late September, Paris was besieged; it finally capitulated on January 28, 1871.

Glossary

Significant historical terms are listed alphabetically and defined in a glossary at the end of the book.

> # GLOSSARY
>
> **absolutism** Term applied to strong centralized continental monarchies that attempted to make royal power dominant over aristocracies and other regional authorities.
>
> **Acropolis** [ACK-row-po-lis] The religious and civic center of Athens. It is the site of the Parthenon.
>
> **Act of Supremacy** The declaration by Parliament in 1534 that Henry VIII, not the pope, was the head of the church in England.
>
> **agape** [AG-a-pay] Meaning "love feast." A common meal that was part of the central ritual of early Christian worship.
>
> **agora** [AG-o-rah] The Greek marketplace and civic center. It was the heart of the social life of the *polis*.
>
> **Agricultural Revolution** The innovations in farm production that began in the eighteenth century and led to a scientific and mechanized agriculture.
>
> **Albigensians** [Al-bi-GEN-see-uns] Thirteenth-century advocates of a dualist religion. They took their name from the city of Albi in southern France. Also called *Cathars*.
>
> **Anabaptists** Protestants who insisted that only adult baptism conformed to Scripture.
>
> **anarchism** The theory that government and social institutions are oppressive and unnecessary and society should be based on voluntary cooperation among individuals.
>
> **Anschluss** [AHN-shluz] Meaning "union." The annexation of Austria by Germany in March 1938.
>
> **anti-Semitism** Prejudice, hostility, or legal discrimination against Jews.
>
> **apartheid** [a-PAR-tid] An official policy of segregation, assignment of peoples to distinct regions, and other forms of social, political, and economic discrimination based on race associated primarily with South Africa.
>
> **apostolic primacy** The doctrine that the popes are the direct successors to the Apostle Peter and as such heads of the church.
>
> **Apostolic Succession** The Christian doctrine that the powers given by Jesus to his original disciples have been handed down from bishop to bishop through ordination.
>
> **appeasement** The Anglo-French policy of making concessions to Germany in the 1930s to avoid a crisis that would lead to war. It assumed that Germany had real grievances and Hitler's aims were limited and ultimately acceptable.
>
> **Areopagus** The governing council of Athens, originally open only to the nobility. It was named after the hill on which it met.
>
> **arete** [AH-ray-tay] Manliness, courage, and the excellence appropriate to a hero. It was considered the highest virtue of Homeric society.
>
> **Arianism** [AIR-ee-an-ism] The belief formulated by Arius of Alexandria (ca. 280–336 C.E.) that Jesus was a created being, neither fully man nor fully God, but something in between. It did away with the doctrine of the Trinity.
>
> **aristocratic resurgence** Term applied to the eighteenth-century aristocratic efforts to resist the expanding power of European monarchies.
>
> **Arminians** [are-MIN-ee-ans] A group within the Church of England who rejected Puritanism and the Calvinist doctrine of predestination in favor of free will and an elaborate liturgy.
>
> **Asia Minor** Modern Turkey. Also called *Anatolia*.
>
> **asiento** [ah-SEE-ehn-tow] The contract to furnish slaves to the Spanish colonies.
>
> **assignats** [as-seen-YAHNTS] Government bonds based on the value of confiscated church lands issued during the early French Revolution.
>
> **Atomists** School of ancient Greek philosophy founded in the fifth century B.C.E. by Leucippus of Miletus and Democritus of Abdera. It held that the world consists of innumerable, tiny, solid, indivisible, and unchangeable particles called *atoms*.
>
> **Attica** [AT-tick-a] The region of Greece where Athens is located.
>
> **Augsburg** [AWGS-berg] **Confession** The definitive statement of Lutheran belief made in 1530.
>
> **Augustus** [AW-gust-us] The title given to Octavian in 27 B.C.E. and borne thereafter by all Roman emperors. It was a semireligious title that implied veneration, majesty, and holiness.
>
> **Ausgleich** [AWS-glike] Meaning "compromise." The agreement between the Habsburg Emperor and the Hungarians to give Hungary considerable administrative autonomy in 1867. It created the Dual Monarchy, or Austria-Hungary.
>
> **autocracy** [AW-to-kra-see] Government in which the ruler has absolute power.
>
> **Axis** The alliance between Nazi Germany and fascist Italy. Also called the *Pact of Steel*.
>
> **banalities** Exactions that the lord of a manor could make on his tenants.
>
> **baroque** [bah-ROWK] A style of art marked by heavy and dramatic ornamentation and curved rather than straight lines that flourished between 1550 and 1750. It was especially associated with the Catholic Counter-Reformation.
>
> **Beguines** [bi-GEENS] Lay sisterhoods not bound by the rules of a religious order.
>
> **benefice** Church offices granted by the ruler of a state or the pope to an individual. It also meant *fief* in the Middle Ages.
>
> **G-1**

SPECIAL FEATURES

"A Closer Look"

In this special feature one illustration per chapter is examined and analyzed using leader lines to point out important and historically significant details. These examples serve as a guide to analyzing and interpreting visual sources to more fully understand the Western heritage. An interactive version of this feature is available on the *MyHistoryLab* web site (www.myhistorylab.com.)

> **CHAPTER 19 ■ THE AGE OF NAPOLEON AND THE TRIUMPH OF ROMANTICISM 565**
>
> **A Closer ▶ LOOK**
>
> ### THE CORONATION OF NAPOLEON
>
> JACQUES-LOUIS DAVID recorded the elaborate coronation of Napoleon in a monumental painting that revealed the enormous political and religious tensions of that event, which involved the kind of ritual and ceremony associated with the monarchy of the ancient regime.
>
> Napoleon's mother sits in a balcony-like setting she presides over her son's establishment of a new reigning dynasty in France and across Europe, through the placement of relatives on various thrones.
>
> Napoleon is about to place a crown on the head of his wife Josephine whom he will later divorce because she and he were unable to conceive an heir for his new dynasty. He would then marry the daughter of the Habsburg emperor.
>
> Jacques-Louis David (1748–1825), *Consecration of the Emperor Napoleon I and Coronation of Empress Josephine, 1806–07*. Louvre, Paris. Bridgeman-Giraudon/Art Resource, NY
>
> To examine this image in an interactive fashion, please go to www.myhistorylab.com
>
> **myhistorylab**
>
> To the right sits Pope Pius VII who observes the event but is not a real participant. Napoleon and the pope had signed a Concordat that restored much of the standing but by no means all of the prerevolutionary authority of the Roman Catholic Church in France. The pope understood that at that moment in France as well as throughout Europe his authority was largely subject to the wishes of the French emperor.

"Encountering the Past"

Each chapter includes an essay on a significant issue of everyday life or popular culture. These essays explore a variety of subjects, including gladiatorial bouts and medieval games, smoking in early modern Europe, and the politics of rock music in the late twentieth century. These thirty essays, each of which includes an illustration and study questions, expand *The Western Heritage*'s rich coverage of social and cultural history.

THE ARRIVAL OF PENNY POSTAGE

ENCOUNTERING *THE* *Past*

WHILE THE ARMIES of the great powers were redrawing the map of Europe during the middle of the nineteenth century, new forms of administration were drawing people closer together. One of the most important of these innovations was the development of postal systems for delivering mail inexpensively. The British government took the lead.

Sending letters and newspapers through the mail had become increasingly expensive, and the British postal service ran large deficits. Other countries had similar problems. At that time the weight of the item to be mailed and the distance over which it had to be carried determined how much it cost to mail it. Furthermore, the person receiving the letter or packet, not the sender, had to pay the postage. Many officials had the privilege of franking their letters and thus paying nothing. The system encouraged resentment and schemes to avoid paying postage. Some people could not afford the postage on letters sent to them. Others put symbols on the outside of a letter, so the recipient could refuse to accept the letter but still "get the message."

Rowland Hill (1775–1879), an English reformer, proposed a simple new procedure in 1837. The price of postage would be lowered, would be uniform for most letters and newspapers regardless of distance, and would be prepaid by the sender. Franking by government officials would also end.

In 1840, the system, known as the Uniform Penny Post, began. Within two years the volume of British mail grew from approximately 75 million items to 196.5 million and, by 1849, to 329 million. The reduced cost of postage meant almost everyone could afford to send letters and postcards. It also led to a huge increase in the size of the government workforce. In Britain and most other countries, the number of postal workers was soon rivaled only by the number of soldiers and sailors.

Hill had also suggested a small, self-adhesive stamp be attached to a letter to indicate the postage had been paid. The first such stamp bore only the words POSTAGE ONE PENNY. It paid for letters up to one half ounce. A two-

penny stamp was used for letters that weighed an ounce.

Other nations soon issued their own stamps. It soon became as important for governments to prevent the forging of postage stamps as currency. Consequently, stamps were printed from engraved steel plates to which small changes were made from time to time. Those changes, introduced to prevent fraud or to commemorate famous people and events, together with the sheer number of national postal systems with their own stamps, gave rise to the hobby of stamp collecting.

The rise of the modern postal system also fostered international cooperation. A treaty signed in Berne, Switzerland, in 1874, established what became the Universal Postal Union, which is still functioning. It mandates that the postage paid in the sender's nation assures delivery of a letter or package anywhere in the world.

Source: M. J. Daunton, "Rowland Hill and the Penny Post," *History Today*, August 1985, "Post, and Postal Service," *Encyclopedia Britannica*, 11th ed.

What changes did Rowland Hill introduce into the British postal service?

How did those changes affect the quantity of mail and the size of the government workforce?

With the new British postal system, the volume of mail vastly increased as did the number of postal workers involved in sorting and delivering it. Image Works/Mary Evans Picture Library Ltd.

685

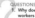

**C O M P A R E
A N D
C O N N E C T**

Andrew Ure and John Ruskin Debate the Conditions of Factory Production

THE FACTORY WAS itself as much an invention of the Industrial Revolution as were the new machines the factory often housed. The factory required a new organization of labor. It also made possible the production of vast new quantities of manufactured goods. From its inception the factory system provoked both praise and criticism. Andrew Ure saw much positive good arising from factory production whereas John Ruskin became a vehement critic. How might the women of Todmorden (see page 635) have replied to both writers?

QUESTIONS

1. Why does Ure emphasize the willingness of workers to be employed in factories?
2. How does Ure portray the factory system as creating the possibility of new abundance?
3. How does Ruskin see the use of machinery reducing workers to a machine?

4. Is Ruskin's criticism of the division of labor a correct analysis or simply a well-crafted metaphorical criticism?
5. How might Ure have replied to Ruskin?

I. Andrew Ure Praises the Factory System

Andrew Ure (1778–1857) was a Scottish physician and a great proponent of the benefits of the factory system. In 1835 he published The Philosophy of Manufactures, *which went through many editions from then until late in the century. He saw factories as increasing productivity and also providing a healthier environment than agricultural work or mining.*

The term Factory, in technology, designates the combined operation of many orders of work—people, adult and young, in tending with assiduous skill a system of productive machines continuously impelled by a central power. This definition includes such organizations as cotton-mills, flax-mills, silk-mills, woolen-mills, and certain engineering works. . . . I conceive that this title, in its strictest sense, involves the idea of a vast automaton, composed of various mechanical and intellectual organs, acting in uninterrupted concert for the production of a common object, all of them being subordinated to a self-regulated moving force. . . .

In its precise acceptation, the Factory system is of recent origin, and may claim England for its birthplace. . . .

When the first water-frames for spinning cotton were erected at Cromford, in the romantic valley of the Derwent, about sixty years ago, mankind were little aware of the mighty revolution which the new system of labor was destined by Providence to achieve, not only

in the structure of British society, but in the fortunes of the world at large.

Arkwright alone had the sagacity to discern, and the boldness to predict in glowing language, how vastly productive human industry would become, when no longer proportioned in its results to muscular effort, which is by its nature fitful and capricious, but when made to consist in the task of guiding the work of mechanical fingers and arms, regularly impelled with great velocity by some indefatigable physical power. . . .

In my recent tour, continued during several months, through the manufacturing districts, I have seen tens of thousands of old, young, and middle-aged of both sexes, many of them too feeble to get their daily bread by any of the former modes of industry, earning abundant food, raiment, and domestic accommodation, without perspiring at a single pore, screened meanwhile from the summer's sun and the winter's frost, in apartments more airy and salubrious than those of the metropolis, in which our legislative and fashionable aristocracies assemble. In those spacious halls the benignant power of steam summons around him his myriads of willing menials, and assigns to each the regulated task, substituting for painful muscular effort on their part, the energies of his own gigantic arm, and demanding in return only attention and dexterity to correct such little aberrations as casually occur in his workmanship. . . . Such is the factory system, replete with prodigies in mechanics and political economy, which promises, in its future growth,

628

"Compare and Connect"

This engaging feature juxtaposes two or more documents in which an important question is debated or a comparison between a document and an illustration is presented. Each feature contains three to five questions on each of the documents, one of which asks students to make connections between and among the viewpoints presented in the feature. These features are intended to encourage debate of different points of view in class, to enhance reading skills, to focus on evaluating differing viewpoints, and to analyze documentary and visual evidence. An interactive version of this feature is available on the **MyHistoryLab** web site (www.myhistorylab.com).

"The West & The World"

This feature, found at the end of each part, focuses on four subjects that compare Western institutions with those in other parts of the world or discuss how developments in the West have influenced other cultures.

THE WEST & THE WORLD

The Abolition of Slavery in the Transatlantic Economy

ONE OF THE most important developments during the age of Enlightenment and revolution was the opening of a crusade to abolish chattel slavery in the transatlantic economy. The antislavery movement constituted the greatest and most extensive achievement of liberal reformers during the eighteenth and nineteenth centuries. Indeed, it marked the first time in the history of the world that a society actually tried to abolish slavery. This achievement came as the result of the impact of Christian ethics, Enlightenment ideals, slave revolts, revolutionary wars in America and Europe, civil war in the United States, and economic dislocation in the slave economies themselves. In 1750, almost no one seriously questioned the existence of slavery, but, by 1888, the institution no longer existed in the transatlantic economy.

Chattel slavery—the ownership of one human being by another—had existed in the West as well as elsewhere in the world since ancient times and had received intellectual and religious justification throughout the history of the West. Both Plato and Aristotle provided arguments for slavery based on the assertion that persons in bondage were intended by nature to be slaves. Christian writers similarly accommodated themselves to the institution. They contended that the most harmful form of slavery was the enslavement of the soul to sin rather than the enslavement of the physical body. They also argued that genuine freedom was realized through one's relationship to God and that problems relating to the injustices of inequality would be solved in the hereafter. Christian scholastic thinkers in the Middle Ages portrayed slavery as part of the natural and necessary hierarchy of the universe.

Slavery Spreads to the Americas

Although a vast slave trade existed throughout the Mediterranean world through the end of the Middle Ages, slavery was no longer a dominant institution on the European continent or within the European economy. The European encounter with America at the end of the fifteenth century radically transformed this situation. The American continent and the West Indies presented opportunities for achieving great wealth, but a major

labor shortage existed in these regions. Eventually slavery provided the means to resolve this labor shortage.

The establishment and maintenance of slavery in the transatlantic economy drew Europeans and Americans into various relationships with Africa. About the same time as the encounter with America, Europeans made contact with areas of West Africa where slavery already existed. This region became the chief source of slaves imported into the Americas. Four centuries later, during the antislavery movement, Europeans would seek to change the African economy by ending its dependence on the slave trade. Those efforts led to the penetration of Africa by European traders, missionaries, and finally colonial forces and administrators.

Although at one time or another slaves labored throughout the Americas, the system of slavery became primarily identified with the plantation economy stretching from Maryland south to Brazil, where tropical products, initially primarily sugar, were produced by slave labor. This plantation economy existed from approximately the late sixteenth through the late nineteenth centuries. The slaves on whose labor this economy was based included Native Americans enslaved within both the Spanish Empire and North America, and Africans forcibly imported into the Americas. Consequently, the slaves were virtually always of a different race from their masters. Race itself soon became part of the justification for the social hierarchy of the plantation world. In and of itself, the fact of slavery in the Americas was not unusual to the Western experience or to that of other societies in Africa or Asia. Slavery had existed at most times and places in human history. Far more unusual in the history of the West, and for that matter in the experience of all other societies that had held and continued to hold slaves, was the emergence after 1760 of an international movement to abolish chattel slavery in the transatlantic economy.

The Crusade Against Slavery

The eighteenth-century crusade against slavery originated in a profound change in the religious and intellectual outlooks on slavery among small but influential groups in

655

CORRELATION OF *THE WESTERN HERITAGE* TO THE AP* TOPIC OUTLINE FOR EUROPEAN HISTORY

Upon publication, this text was correlated to the College Board's European History Course Description dated May 2010, May 2011. We continually monitor the College Board's AP* Course Description for updates to exam topic. For the most current AP* Exam Topic correlation for this textbook, visit PearsonSchool.com/AdvancedCorrelation

1. INTELLECTUAL AND CULTURAL HISTORY	
Changes in religious thought and institutions	Chapter 9: pp. 267–276 Chapter 11: pp. 317–350 Chapter 19: pp. 604–607 Chapter 24: pp. 760–762 Chapter 30: pp. 989–990, 1006–1009
Secularization of learning and culture	Chapter 10: pp. 287–296 Chapter 14: pp. 417–428, 431–438 Chapter 17: pp. 514–520 Chapter 24: pp. 757–760, 762–764
Scientific and technological developments and their consequences	Chapter 10: pp. 303–304 Chapter 14: pp. 417–438 Chapter 15: pp. 455–467 Chapter 24: pp. 754–764 Chapter 30: pp. 1008–1011
Major trends in literature and the arts	Chapter 10: pp. 287–296 Chapter 11: pp. 345–347 Chapter 14: pp. 438–441 Chapter 17: pp. 510–514, 530–533 Chapter 19: pp. 599–605 Chapter 24: pp. 765–771 Chapter 27: p. 887 Chapter 30: pp. 1004–1006
Intellectual and cultural developments and their relationship to social values and political events	Chapter 9: pp. 267–276 Chapter 10: pp. 283–285, 287–291, 298–299, 303–305 Chapter 11: pp. 318–345 Chapter 12: pp. 351–358 Chapter 14: pp. 417–429, 431–438 Chapter 16: pp. 497–501 Chapter 17: pp. 508–543 Chapter 18: p. 571 Chapter 19: pp. 597–599, 607–611 Chapter 20: pp. 615–643 Chapter 21: pp. 662–678 Chapter 22: pp. 690–696, 704–706, 709 Chapter 24: pp. 752–780 Chapter 30: pp. 997–1004

Developments in social, economic, and political thought, including ideologies characterized as "isms," such as socialism, liberalism, nationalism	Chapter 10: pp. 287–291, 303–305 Chapter 14: pp. 417–428 Chapter 16: pp. 497–501 Chapter 17: pp. 508–530 Chapter 18: p. 571 Chapter 19: pp. 588–590, 597–611 Chapter 20: pp. 615–622 Chapter 21: pp. 651–654, 662–669 Chapter 22: pp. 690–696, 704–706, 709 Chapter 23: pp. 732–748 Chapter 24: pp. 754–760, 770–780 Chapter 25: pp. 785, 791–797 Chapter 27: pp. 870–874, 878–879, 882–884, 888–895 Chapter 29: pp. 978–980 Chapter 30: pp. 997–1004
Developments in literacy, education, and communication	Chapter 10: pp. 283–285, 287–291, 303–305 Chapter 11: pp. 318–319, 340–342 Chapter 14: pp. 422–424, 427–429 Chapter 17: pp. 510–513, 520, 527–531 Chapter 19: pp. 598–599, 610–611 Chapter 20: pp. 625, 629, 637–639 Chapter 23: pp. 718–721, 727–728, 733, 735 Chapter 24: pp. 752–756, 760, 763–764 Chapter 30: pp. 997–1001, 1008–1011
The diffusion of new intellectual concepts among different social groups	Chapter 9: pp. 273–274 Chapter 10: pp.303–304 Chapter 11: pp. 318–320, 325–328, 331–336 Chapter 12: pp. 351–354 Chapter 15: pp. 460–461 Chapter 16: pp. 497–501 Chapter 17: pp. 510–511 Chapter 18: pp. 550–555, 557, 560–566, 570–573 Chapter 19: pp. 588–591, 606–607 Chapter 20: pp. 623–627, 632–637 Chapter 21: pp. 651–654, 663–670 Chapter 22: pp. 700–701 Chapter 23: pp. 736–739 Chapter 24: pp. 773–779 Chapter 25: p. 817 Chapter 27: pp. 873, 886 Chapter 29: p. 956 Chapter 30: pp. 1000–1003
Changes in elite and popular culture, such as the development of new attitudes toward religion, the family, work, and ritual	Chapter 9: pp. 260–276 Chapter 10: pp. 289–291 Chapter 11: pp. 318–320, 339–345 Chapter 14: pp. 428–429, 431–438 Chapter 15: pp. 460–461, 468 Chapter 17: pp. 510–518 Chapter 19: pp. 606–607 Chapter 21: pp. 646–659 Chapter 23: pp. 720–723, 728–732 Chapter 24: pp. 754, 575, 763–764, 777–779 Chapter 30: pp. 989–990, 993–997, 999–1002, 1006–1008
Impact of global expansion on European culture	Chapter 9: pp. 257–262, 278–279 Chapter 10: pp. 305–313 Chapter 11: pp. 380–381 Chapter 12: p. 358 Chapter 16: pp. 476–501 Chapter 19: pp. 608–611 Chapter 25: pp. 785–793, 817–821 Chapter 29: pp. 947–949, 952–962, 978–981 Chapter 30: pp. 898–990

2. POLITICAL AND DIPLOMATIC HISTORY

The rise and functioning of the modern state in its various forms	Chapter 10: pp. 283–287, 299–303 Chapter 11: pp. 334–336 Chapter 12: pp. 363–368, 374 Chapter 13: pp. 380–413 Chapter 17: pp. 533–543 Chapter 18: pp. 550–563, 575–576 Chapter 19: pp. 588–590, 594–597 Chapter 20: pp. 615–642 Chapter 21: pp. 687–713 Chapter 23: pp. 740–748 Chapter 27: pp. 872–879 Chapter 30: pp. 1011–1016
Relations between Europe and other parts of the world: colonialism, imperialism, decolonization, and global interdependence	Chapter 10: pp. 305–313 Chapter 16: pp. 476–507 Chapter 19: pp. 608–611 Chapter 20: pp. 630–636 Chapter 25: pp. 785–829 Chapter 30: pp. 941–950, 952–953, 955, 956–964, 978–981
The evolution of political elites and the development of political parties, ideologies, and other forms of mass politics	Chapter 10: pp. 283–287, 297–303 Chapter 11: pp. 331–334 Chapter 15: pp. 446–449 Chapter 16: pp. 497–501 Chapter 18: pp. 550–563, 564–566, 569–573 Chapter 20: pp. 615–617, 624–627, 630–642 Chapter 21: pp. 650–654, 666–677 Chapter 23: pp. 736–748 Chapter 26: pp. 849–853 Chapter 27: pp. 878–897 Chapter 29: pp. 978–979 Chapter 30: pp. 1002–1004
The extension and limitation of rights and liberties (personal, civic, economic, and political); majority and minority political persecutions	Chapter 9: pp. 260–262 Chapter 11: pp. 325–328 Chapter 12: pp. 351–358, 371–374 Chapter 13: pp. 385–388, 392–397 Chapter 14: pp. 437–438 Chapter 15: p. 471 Chapter 16: pp. 483–492, 495–496 Chapter 17: pp. 535–540 Chapter 18: pp. 547–578 Chapter 19: pp. 583–584, 588–589 Chapter 20: pp. 622–628, 635–642 Chapter 21: pp. 669–677 Chapter 22: pp. 696–697, 700–704, 706–713 Chapter 23: pp. 735–737, 739, 741–748 Chapter 24: pp. 773–779 Chapter 25: pp. 801, 804–807, 812–814 Chapter 26: pp. 849–853 Chapter 27: pp. 870–897 Chapter 28: pp. 922–933 Chapter 29: pp. 922–933 Chapter 30: pp. 974–981
The growth and changing forms of nationalism	Chapter 9: pp. 262-268 Chapter 18: pp. 550–557, 564–566, 576–578 Chapter 19: pp. 583–584, 588–594, 607–608 Chapter 20: pp. 615–643 Chapter 21: pp. 669–678 Chapter 22: pp. 690–713 Chapter 24: pp. 773–775 Chapter 27: pp. 878–889, 894–897 Chapter 29: pp. 958–962, 973–975, 978–983

3. SOCIAL AND ECONOMIC HISTORY

WHAT IS THE WESTERN HERITAGE?

This book invites students and instructors to explore the Western Heritage. What is that heritage? The Western Heritage emerges from an evolved and evolving story of human actions and interactions, peaceful and violent, that arose in the eastern Mediterranean, then spread across the western Mediterranean into northern Europe, and eventually to the American continents, and in their broadest impact, to the peoples of Africa and Asia as well.

The Western Heritage as a distinct portion of world history descends from the ancient Greeks. They saw their own political life based on open discussion of law and policy as different from that of Mesopotamia, Persia, and Egypt, where kings ruled without regard to public opinion. The Greeks invented the concept of citizenship, defining it as engagement in some form of self-government. Furthermore, through their literature and philosophy, the Greeks established the conviction, which became characteristic of the West, that reason can shape and analyze physical nature, politics, and morality.

The city of Rome, spreading its authority through military conquest across the Mediterranean world, embraced Greek literature and philosophy. Through their conquests and imposition of their law, the Romans created the Western world as a vast empire stretching from Egypt and Syria in the east to Britain in the west. Although the Roman Republic, governed by a Senate and popular political institutions, gave way after civil wars to the autocratic rule of the Roman Empire, the idea of a free republic of engaged citizens governed by public law and constitutional arrangements limiting political authority survived centuries of arbitrary rule by emperors. As in the rest of the world, the Greeks, the Romans, and virtually all other ancient peoples excluded women and slaves from political life and tolerated considerable social inequality.

In the early fourth century C.E., the Emperor Constantine reorganized the Roman Empire in two fundamental ways that reshaped the West. First, he moved the imperial capital from Rome to Constantinople (Istanbul), establishing separate emperors in the East and West. Thereafter, large portions of the Western empire became subject to the rulers of Germanic tribes. In the confusion of these times, most of the texts embodying ancient philosophy, literature, and history became lost in the West, and for centuries Western Europeans were intellectually severed from that ancient heritage, which would later be recovered in a series of renaissances, or cultural rebirths, beginning in the eighth century.

Constantine's second fateful major reshaping of the West was his recognition of Christianity as the official religion of the empire. Christianity had grown out of the ancient monotheistic religion of the Hebrew people living in ancient Palestine. With the ministry of Jesus of Nazareth and the spread of his teachings by the Apostle Paul, Christianity had established itself as one of many religions in the empire. Because Christianity was monotheistic, Constantine's official embrace of it led to the eradication of pagan polytheism. Thereafter, the West became more or less coterminous with Latin Christianity, or that portion of the Christian Church acknowledging the Bishop of Rome as its head.

As the emperors' rule broke down, bishops became the effective political rulers in many parts of Western Europe. But the Christian Church in the West never governed without negotiation or conflict with secular rulers, and religious law never replaced secular law. Nor could secular rulers govern if they ignored the influence of the church. Hence from the fourth century C.E. to the present day, rival claims to political and moral authority between ecclesiastical and political officials have characterized the West.

In the seventh century the Christian West faced a new challenge from the rise of Islam. This new monotheistic religion originating in the teachings of the prophet Muhammad arose on the Arabian Peninsula and spread through rapid conquests across North Africa and eventually into Spain, turning the Mediterranean into what one historian has termed "a Muslim lake." Between the eleventh and the thirteenth centuries, Christians attempted to reclaim the Holy Land from Muslim control in church-inspired military crusades that still resonate negatively in the Islamic world.

It was, however, in the Muslim world that most of the texts of ancient Greek and Latin learning survived and were studied, while intellectual life languished in the West. Commencing in the twelfth century, knowledge of those texts began to work its way back into Western Europe. By the fourteenth century, European thinkers redefined themselves and their intellectual ambitions by recovering the literature and science from the ancient world, reuniting Europe with its Graeco-Roman past.

From the twelfth through the eighteenth centuries, a new European political system slowly arose based on centralized monarchies characterized by large armies, navies, and bureaucracies loyal to the monarch, and by

In his painting *The School of Athens*, the great Italian Renaissance painter Raphael portrayed the ancient Greek philosopher Plato and his student, Aristotle, engaged in debate. Plato, who points to the heavens, believed in a set of ideal truths that exist in their own realm distinct from the earth. Aristotle urged that all philosophy must be in touch with lived reality and confirms this position by pointing to the earth. Such debate has characterized the intellectual, political, and social experience of the West. Indeed, the very concept of "Western Civilization" has itself been subject to debate, criticism, and change over the centuries.
© Scala/Art Resource, NY

the capacity to raise revenues. Whatever the personal ambitions of individual rulers, for the most part these monarchies recognized both the political role of local or national assemblies drawn from the propertied elites and the binding power of constitutional law on themselves. Also, in each of these monarchies, church officials and church law played important roles in public life. The monarchies, their military, and their expanding commercial economies became the basis for the extension of European and Western influence around the globe.

In the late fifteenth and early sixteenth centuries, two transforming events occurred. The first was the European discovery and conquest of the American continents, thus opening the Americas to Western institutions, religion, and economic exploitation. Over time the labor shortages of the Americas led to the forced migration of millions of Africans as slaves to the "New World." By the mid-seventeenth century, the West consequently embraced the entire transatlantic world and its multiracial societies.

Second, shortly after the American encounter, a religious schism erupted within Latin Christianity. Reformers rejecting both many medieval Christian doctrines as unbiblical and the primacy of the Pope in Rome established Protestant churches across much of northern Europe. As a consequence, for almost two centuries religious warfare between Protestants and Roman Catholics overwhelmed the continent as monarchies chose to defend one side or the other. This religious turmoil meant that the Europeans who conquered and settled the Americas carried with them particularly

The Winged Victory of Samothrace. This is one of the great masterpieces of Hellenistic sculpture. It appears to be the work of the Rhodian sculptor Pythokritos, about 200 B.C.E. The statue stood in the Sanctuary of the Great Gods on the Aegean island of Samothrace on a base made in the shape of a ship's prow. The goddess is seen as landing on the ship to crown its victorious commander and crew. *The Nike of Samothrace*, goddess of victory. Marble figure (190 B.C.E.) from Rhodos, Greece. Height 328 cm, MA 2369, Louvre, Dpt. des Antiquités Grecques/Romaines, Paris, France. Photograph © Erich Lessing/Art Resource, NY

Introduction

The West Before 1300

▼ **Early Humans and Their Culture**
The Paleolithic Age • The Neolithic Age

▼ **Early Civilizations to about 1000 B.C.E.**
Mesopotamian Civilization • Egyptian Civilization • Palestine and the Religion of the Israelites

▼ **The Greeks**
The *Polis* • Greek Political Philosophy and the Crisis of the *Polis* • The Empire of Alexander the Great

▼ **Rome**
The Republic and Expansion in the Mediterranean • From Republic to Empire • The Principate and the Empire • Christianity • Decline and Fall of the Roman Empire

▼ **Europe Enters the Middle Ages**
The Byzantine Empire • The Rise of Islam • New Importance of the Christian Church • Charlemagne • Feudal and Manorial Society

▼ **Church and State in the High Middle Ages**
The Division of Christendom • The Rise of Towns • The Crusades • The Rise of New Monarchies • Universities and Scholasticism

▼ **In Perspective**

HISTORY, IN ITS two senses—as the events of the past that make up the human experience on earth and as the written record of those events—is a subject of both interest and importance. We naturally want to know how we came to be who we are and how the world we live in came to be what it is. But beyond its intrinsic interest, history provides crucial insight into present human behavior. To understand who we are now, we need to know the record of the past and to try to understand the people and forces that shaped it.

For hundreds of thousands of years after the human species emerged, people lived by hunting, fishing, and collecting wild plants. Only some 10,000 years ago did they learn to cultivate plants, herd animals, and make airtight pottery for storage. These discoveries transformed them from gatherers to producers and allowed them to grow in number and to lead a settled life. About 5,000 years ago humans learned how to control the waters of great river valleys, making possible much richer harvests and supporting a further increase in population. The peoples of these river valley societies created the earliest civilizations. They invented writing, which, among other things, enabled them to keep inventories of food and other resources. They discovered the secret of smelting metal to make tools and weapons of bronze far superior to the stone implements of earlier times. They came together in towns and cities, where industry and commerce flourished. Complex religions took form, and social divisions increased. Kings—considered to be representatives of the gods or to be themselves divine—emerged as rulers, assisted by priests and defended by well-organized armies.

▼ Early Humans and Their Culture

Scientists estimate that the earth may be as many as 6 billion years old and that creatures very much like humans may have appeared 3 to 5 million years ago. Our own species, **Homo sapiens**, probably emerged some 200,000 years ago, and the earliest remains of fully modern humans date to about 90,000 years ago.

Humans, unlike other animals, are cultural beings. **Culture** may be defined as the ways of living built up by a group and passed on from one generation to another. It includes behavior, material things, ideas, institutions, and beliefs.

The Paleolithic Age

During the earliest period in human experience, the Paleolithic (from Greek, "old stone") Age, which lasted from the earliest use of stone tools some 1,000,000 years ago to about 10,000 B.C.E., people were hunters, fishers, and gatherers, but not producers, of food. They learned to make and use increasingly sophisticated tools of stone and of perishable materials like wood; they learned to make and control fire; and they acquired language and the ability to use it to pass on what they learned. Evidence of Paleolithic culture has been found in Europe, Asia, and Africa.

Evidence suggests human life in the Paleolithic Age was probably characterized by a division of labor by sex. The men engaged in hunting, fishing, making tools and weapons, and fighting against other families, clans, and tribes. The women, less mobile because of childbearing, gathered nuts, berries, and wild grains, wove baskets, and made clothing. Women gathering food probably discovered how to plant and care for seeds. This knowledge eventually made possible the coming of the Age of Agriculture—the Neolithic revolution.

The Neolithic Age

Some 10,000 years ago, parts of what we now call the Middle East began to shift from a hunter-gatherer culture to a settled agricultural one. Because the shift to agriculture coincided with advances in stone tool technology, this period is called the Neolithic (from Greek,

In Chauvet cave, near Avignon, France, Paleolithic artists decorated the walls with exquisite drawings of animals.   Ministere de la Culture et de la Communication. Direction Régionale des affaires Culturelles de Rhone—Alpes. Service Régional de l'Archéologie

"new stone") Age. The important invention of pottery made it possible to store surplus liquid and dry foods. Cloth came to be made from flax and wool. Crops required constant care from planting to harvest, and so the Neolithic people built permanent buildings, usually in clusters near the best fields.

Neolithic agricultural villages and herding cultures gradually replaced Paleolithic culture in much of the world. Then, beginning first about 4,000 years before the Christian era in the valley of the Tigris and Euphrates Rivers in the region called Mesopotamia (modern Iraq), later in the valley of the Nile River in Egypt, and somewhat later still in the Indus Valley in India and the Yellow River basin in China, another major shift occurred. This shift was marked by the appearance of urban centers, the mastery of smelting and with it the techniques for making metal tools and weapons, and the invention of writing. These traits—urbanism, metallurgy, and writing—are defining characteristics of the form of human culture called *civilization*. At about the time the earliest civilizations were emerging, someone discovered how to smelt tin and copper to make a stronger and more useful material—bronze. The importance of this technological development is reflected in the term ***Bronze Age***.

▼ Early Civilizations to about 1000 B.C.E.

Mesopotamian Civilization

The first civilization appears to have arisen in the valley of the Tigris and Euphrates Rivers, the area the Greeks and the Romans called Mesopotamia, where the rich alluvial plains made possible the production of unprecedented food surpluses (see Map I–1). Its founders, the Sumerians, controlled the southern part of the valley (Sumer) close to the head of the Persian Gulf by the dawn of history, around 3000 B.C.E. While the Sumerians were fighting with their neighbors and among themselves for supremacy in the south, immediately upstream from them a people speaking a Semitic language

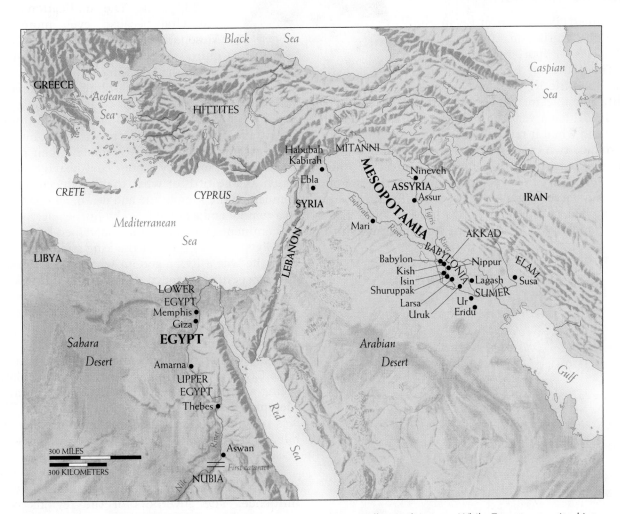

Map I–1 **THE ANCIENT NEAR EAST** There were two ancient river valley civilizations. While Egypt was united into a single state, Mesopotamia was long divided into a number of city-states.

(that is, a language in the same family as Arabic and Hebrew) established themselves. Making their capital at Akkad, near a later city known to us as Babylon, they soon absorbed Sumerian culture.

Despite a brief Sumerian resurgence about 2100 B.C.E., internal dissensions and an invasion by a Semitic people called the Amorites put an end to the Sumerians as an identifiable group. About 1900 B.C.E., the Amorites gained control of the region, establishing their capital at Babylon. Toward 1600 B.C.E., the Babylonian kingdom fell apart under the impact of invasions from the north and east by the Hittites and the Kassites. The Hittites were only a raiding party who plundered what they could and then withdrew to their home in Asia Minor. The Kassites stayed and ruled Mesopotamia for five centuries.

Egyptian Civilization

While a great civilization arose in the valley of the Tigris and Euphrates, another, no less important, emerged in Egypt. The center of Egyptian civilization was the Nile River. The Nile alone made life possible in the almost rainless desert that surrounded it. Each year the river flooded and covered the land, and when it receded, it left a fertile mud that could produce two crops a year. The construction and maintenance of irrigation ditches to preserve the river's water, with careful planning and organization of planting and harvesting, produced agricultural prosperity unmatched in the ancient world. The Nile also served as a highway connecting the long, narrow coun-

This statue of Gudea, city ruler of Lagash after the fall of the Akkadian empire, shows him as a pious Sumerian ruler. It was carved of very hard imported black stone. A brief historical inscription is visible on his cloak. Gudea built a major temple to a local deity at Lagash, Ningirsu, and describes the work, step by step, in one of the longest Sumerian poems known today. Gudea. Statue from Telloh. 2140 B.C.E. Iraq Museum. Baghdad, Iraq. Copyright Scala/Art Resource, NY

try and encouraging its unification. Nature helped protect and isolate the ancient Egyptians from outsiders. The cataracts, the sea, and the desert made it difficult for foreigners to reach Egypt for either friendly or hostile purposes.

The more-than-3,000-year span of ancient Egyptian history is traditionally divided into thirty-one royal dynasties. The first was founded by Menes, the unifier of Upper and Lower Egypt; the last was established by Alexander the Great, who conquered Egypt in 332 B.C.E. The unification of Egypt was vital because, even more than in Mesopotamia, the entire river valley required the central control of irrigation.

In the Old Kingdom (2700–2200 B.C.E.), royal power was absolute. The pharaoh, as he was later called (the term originally meant "great house" or "palace"), governed his kingdom through his family and appointed officials removable at his pleasure. The peasants were carefully regulated, their movement was limited, and they were taxed heavily, perhaps as much as one fifth of what they produced. Luxury accompanied the king in life and death, and he was raised to a remote and exalted level by his people. Such power and eminence cannot be long sustained by force alone. The Egyptians worked for the king and obeyed him because he was a living god on whom their lives, safety, and prosperity depended. He was the direct source of law and justice, and so no law codes were needed. In such a world, government was merely one aspect of religion, and religion dominated Egyptian life.

By the time of the Third Dynasty (ca. 2125–2027 B.C.E.), the pharaohs had achieved full supremacy over all of Egypt, imposing internal peace and order and overseeing a period of great prosperity. The capital was at Memphis in Upper Egypt, just above the delta. The king was regarded not as a mere representative of the gods but as a god himself. The land was his own personal possession, and the people were his servants.

The power of the kings of the Old Kingdom waned as priests and nobles gained more independence and influence. The governors of the regions of Egypt (called nomes) gained hereditary claim to their offices,

---

KEY EVENTS AND PEOPLE IN MESOPOTAMIAN HISTORY

ca. 3500 B.C.E.	Development of Sumerian cities, especially Uruk
ca. 2800–2370 B.C.E.	Early Dynastic period of Sumerian city-states
ca. 2370 B.C.E.	Sargon establishes Akkadian dynasty and empire
ca. 2125–2027 B.C.E.	Third Dynasty of Ur
ca. 2000–1800 B.C.E.	Establishment of Amorites in Mesopotamia
ca. 1792–1750 B.C.E.	Reign of Hammurabi
ca. 1550 B.C.E.	Establishment of Kassite Dynasty at Babylon

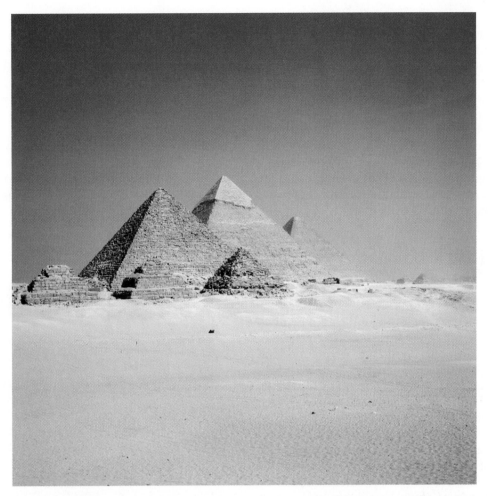

The three largest pyramids of Egypt, located at Giza, near Cairo, are the colossal tombs of pharaohs of the Fourth Dynasty (ca. 2640–2510 B.C.E.): Khufu (right), Khafre (center), and Menkaure (left). The small pyramids and tombs at their bases were those of the pharaohs' queens and officials.   Dorling Kindersley Media Library/Geoff Brightling © Dorling Kindersley

and their families acquired large estates. About 2200 B.C.E., the Old Kingdom collapsed and gave way to the decentralization and disorder of the First Intermediate Period (ca. 2200–2052 B.C.E.). Finally, the nomarchs (governors) of Thebes in Upper Egypt gained control of the country and established the Middle Kingdom about 2052 B.C.E. The rulers of the Twelfth Dynasty restored the pharaoh's power over the whole of Egypt, though they did not completely control the nobles who ruled the nomes. Still, they brought order, peace, and prosperity to a troubled land. They encouraged trade and extended Egyptian power and influence northward toward Palestine and southward toward Ethiopia.

The Middle Kingdom disintegrated in the Thirteenth Dynasty, giving way, with the resurgence of the power of the local nobility, to the Second Intermediate Period. About 1700 B.C.E., Egypt suffered an invasion. Tradition speaks of a people called the Hyksos who came from the east and conquered the Nile Delta. They

seem to have been a collection of Semitic peoples from the area of Palestine and Syria at the eastern end of the Mediterranean. Egyptian nationalism reasserted itself about 1575 B.C.E., when a dynasty from Thebes drove out the Hyksos and reunited Egypt, beginning the New Kingdom (or Empire) Period.

MAJOR PERIODS IN ANCIENT EGYPTIAN HISTORY (DYNASTIES IN ROMAN NUMERALS)

3100–2700 B.C.E.	Early Dynastic Period (I–II)
2700–2200 B.C.E.	Old Kingdom (III–VI)
2200–2052 B.C.E.	First Intermediate Period (VII–XI)
2052–1630 B.C.E.	Middle Kingdom (XII–XIII)
1630–1550 B.C.E.	Second Intermediate Period (XIV–XVII)
1550–1075 B.C.E.	New Kingdom (XVIII–XX)

In reaction to the humiliation of the Second Intermediate Period, the pharaohs of the Eighteenth Dynasty created an absolute government based on a powerful army and an Egyptian empire extending far beyond the Nile Valley. They pushed the southern frontier back a long way and extended Egyptian power into Palestine and Syria and beyond the upper Euphrates River. They were not checked until they came into conflict with the powerful Hittite empire of Asia Minor. In the struggle that ensued between 1400 and 1200 B.C.E., both powers were weakened. Although Egypt survived, it again became the victim of foreign invasion and rule, falling under the sway of one foreign empire after another.

Palestine and the Religion of the Israelites

None of the powerful kingdoms we have described has had as much influence on the future of Western civilization as the small stretch of land on the eastern shore of the Mediterranean between Syria and Egypt, the land called Palestine for much of its history (see Map I–2). The three great religions of the modern world outside the Far East—Judaism, Christianity, and Islam—trace their origins, at least in part, to the people who arrived there a little before 1200 B.C.E. and to the book that recounts their experiences, the Hebrew Bible.

The history of the Israelites must be pieced together from various sources. They are mentioned only rarely in the records of their neighbors, and so we must rely chiefly on their own account, the Bible. This is not a history in our sense, but a complicated collection of historical narrative, wisdom literature, poetry, law, and religious witness. Scholars of an earlier time tended to discard it as a historical source, but the most recent trend is to take it seriously while using it with caution.

According to tradition, the patriarch Abraham came from Ur in Mesopotamia about 1900 B.C.E. and wandered west to tend his flocks in the land of the Canaanites. Some of his people settled there and others wandered into Egypt, perhaps with the Hyksos. By the thirteenth century B.C.E., led by Moses, they had left Egypt and wandered in the desert until they reached Canaan. They established a united kingdom that reached its peak under David and Solomon in the tenth century B.C.E. The sons of Solomon did not maintain the unity of the kingdom, and it split into two parts: Israel in the north and Judah, with its capital at Jerusalem, in the south.

The rise of great empires to the east brought disaster to the Israelites. The northern kingdom fell to the Assyrians in 722 B.C.E., and its people—the ten lost tribes of tradition—were scattered and lost forever. Only the kingdom of Judah remained, and hereafter we may call the Israelites Jews. In 586 B.C.E., Judah was defeated by the Babylonian king Nebuchadnezzar II. He destroyed the great temple built by Solomon and took thousands of hostages to Babylon. When the Persians defeated Babylonia, they ended this Babylonian Captivity of the Jews and allowed them to return to their homeland. After that the area of the old kingdom of the Jews in Palestine was dominated by foreign peoples for some 2,500 years until the establishment of the state of Israel in 1948 C.E.

The fate of this small nation would be of little interest were it not for its unique religious achievement. The great contribution of the Jews is the idea of monotheism,

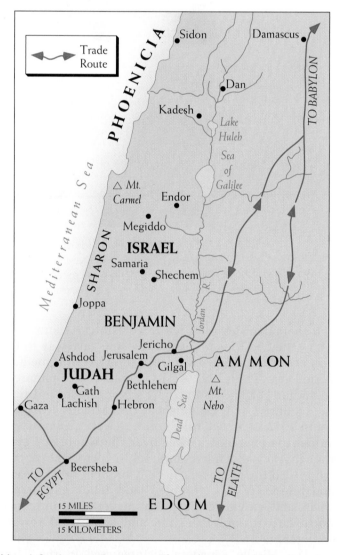

Map I–2 **ANCIENT PALESTINE** The Hebrews established a unified kingdom in Palestine under Kings David and Solomon in the tenth century B.C.E. After the death of Solomon, however, the kingdom was divided into two parts—Israel in the north and Judah, with its capital, Jerusalem, in the south. Along the coast, especially to the north, were the great commercial cities of the Phoenicians, such as Sidon and Tyre.

the existence of one universal God, the creator and ruler of the universe. Some scholars believe that a form of monotheism may have originated with the Egyptian pharaoh Akhenaton (r. 1367–1350 B.C.E.), although too little is known about his ideas and practices to be certain. Only in the Old Testament do we find the first unquestioned proof of monotheistic belief. This idea may be as old as Moses, as the Jewish tradition asserts, and it certainly dates as far back as the prophets of the eighth century B.C.E.

The Jewish God is neither a natural force nor like human beings or any other creatures. He is so elevated that those who believe in him are forbidden to picture him in any form. The faith of the Jews derives special strength from their belief that God made a covenant with Abraham, an agreement that Abraham's progeny would be a chosen people who would be rewarded for following his commandments and the law he revealed to Moses.

An essential ingredient of Jewish religious thought is the powerful ethical element it introduces. God is a severe but just judge. Ritual and sacrifice are not enough to achieve his approval. People must be righteous, and God himself appears to be bound to act righteously. The Jewish prophetic tradition was a powerful ethical force. The prophets constantly criticized any falling away from the law and the path of righteousness. The prophets placed God in history, blaming the misfortunes of the Jews on God's righteous and necessary intervention to punish them for their misdeeds, but the prophets also promised the redemption of the Jews if they repented. The prophetic tradition expected the redemption to come in the form of a Messiah (deliverer). Christianity, emerging from this tradition, maintains that Jesus of Nazareth was that Messiah.

Jewish religious ideas influenced the future development of the West, both directly and indirectly. The Jews' belief in an all-powerful creator, righteous himself and demanding righteousness and obedience from humankind, a universal God who is the father and ruler of all peoples, is a critical part of the Western heritage. (See "The Second Isaiah Defines Hebrew Monotheism," page xlii.)

▼ The Greeks

Western civilization as a distinct culture began with the Greeks. Greek-speaking people from the north settled the lands surrounding the Aegean Sea in the second millennium B.C.E. They established a style of life and formed ideas, values, and institutions that spread far beyond the Aegean corner of the Mediterranean Sea. They later influenced and shaped Roman society. Preserved and adapted by the Romans, Greek culture powerfully influenced the society of western Europe in the High Middle Ages and dominated the Byzantine Empire in the same period.

The Greeks of the Classical Age (500–400 B.C.E.) inherited and adapted many important elements of their culture from earlier civilizations (see Map I–3, page xliii). The Minoan civilization (ca. 2900–1150 B.C.E.), with its center on the island of Crete, was literate. Its records reveal a palace-centered organization ruled by a king who was served by an extensive bureaucracy that kept remarkably detailed records. This sort of organization is typical of what we find in the Near East but is nothing like what is found among the Greeks. The Minoans powerfully influenced the Mycenaeans, a Greek-speaking people who dominated the mainland of Greece and the islands of the Aegean in the latter part of the Bronze Age (ca. 1600–1150 B.C.E.). Mycenaean civilization collapsed and gave way to a period often called the Greek Dark Ages (ca. 1150–750 B.C.E.). During this time, a new Hellenic culture, influenced by the Mycenaean world, but essentially independent of it, took shape. (See "Husband and Wife in Homer's Troy," page xliv)

The "Trojan Horse," depicted on a seventh-century B.C.E. Greek vase. According to legend, the Greeks finally defeated Troy by pretending to abandon their siege of the city, leaving a giant wooden horse behind. Soldiers hidden in the horse opened the gates of the city to their compatriots after the Trojans had brought it within their walls. Note the wheels on the horse and the Greek soldiers holding weapons and armor who are hiding inside it.   Greek 10th–6th centuries B.C.E. Trojan Horse and Greek Soldiers. Relief from neck of an earthenware amphora (640 B.C.E.) from Mykanos, overall ht. 120 cm. Archeological Museum, Mykonos, Greece. Art Resource, NY © Photography by Erich Lessing

THE SECOND ISAIAH DEFINES HEBREW MONOTHEISM

The strongest statement of Hebrew monotheism is found in these words of the anonymous prophet whom we call the Second Isaiah. He wrote during the Hebrew exile in Babylonia, 597–539 B.C.E.

How is the deity in this passage different from the deities of the Mesopotamian and Egyptian societies? Are there any similarities? Many peoples have claimed that a single god was the greatest and the ruler over all others. What is there in this selection that claims a different status for the Hebrew deity?

42

5 Thus says God, the Lord
   who created the heavens and stretched them
    out,
   who spread forth the earth and what comes
    from it,
   who gives breath to the people upon it and
    spirit to those who walk in it:
6 I am the Lord, I have called you in
    righteousness,
   I have taken you by the hand and kept you;
   I have given you as a covenant to the people, a
    light to the nations,
7 to open the eyes that are blind,
   to bring out the prisoners from the dungeon,
   from the prison those who sit in darkness.
8 I am the Lord, that is my name;
   my glory I give to no other,
   nor my praise to graven images.
9 Behold, the former things have come to pass,
    and new things I now declare;
   before they spring forth I tell you of them."

44

6 Thus says the Lord, the King of Israel and his
   Redeemer, the Lord of hosts:
   "I am the first and I am the last; besides me
    there is no god.
7 Who is like me? Let him proclaim it,
   let him declare and set it forth before me.
   Who has announced of old the things to come?
   Let them tell us what is yet to be.
8 Fear not, nor be afraid;

have I not told you from of old and declared it?
And you are my witnesses!
Is there a God besides me?
There is no Rock; I know not any."

49

22 Thus says the Lord God:
   "Behold, I will lift up my hand to the nations,
   and raise my signal to the peoples;
   and they shall bring your sons in their bosom,
   and your daughters shall be carried on their
    shoulders
23 Kings shall be your foster fathers,
   and their queens your nursing mothers.
   With their faces to the ground they shall bow
    down to you,
   and lick the dust of your feet.
   Then you will know that I am the Lord;
   those who wait for me shall not be put to
    shame."
24 Can the prey be taken from the mighty, or the
   captives of a tyrant be rescued?
25 Surely, thus says the Lord:
   "Even the captives of the mighty shall be
    taken, and the prey of the tyrant be rescued,
   for I will contend with those who contend
    with you
   and I will save your children.
26 I will make your oppressors eat their own flesh,
   and they shall be drunk with their own blood
    as with wine.
   Then all flesh shall know
   that I am the Lord your Savior,
   and your Redeemer, the Mighty One of Jacob."

Bible, Revised Standard Version (New York: Division of Christian Education, National Council of Churches, 1952).

Map I–3 **THE AEGEAN AREA IN THE BRONZE AGE** The Bronze Age in the Aegean area lasted from about 1900 to about 1100 B.C.E. Its culture on Crete is called Minoan and was at its height about 1900–1400 B.C.E. Bronze Age Helladic culture on the mainland flourished from about 1600–1200 B.C.E.

At some time in their history, the Greeks of the ancient world founded cities on every shore of the Mediterranean Sea. Pushing through the Dardanelles, they placed many settlements on the coasts of the Black Sea in southern Russia and as far east as the approaches to the Caucasus Mountains. The center of Greek life, however, was always the Aegean Sea and the lands in and around it. This location at the eastern end of the Mediterranean very early put the Greeks in touch with the more advanced civilizations of the Near East.

The *Polis*

The characteristic Greek institution was the ***polis*** (plural, *poleis*). The common translation of that word as "city-state" is misleading, for it says both too much and too little. All Greek *poleis* began as little more than agricultural villages or towns and many stayed that way, and so the word *city* is inappropriate. All of them were states, in the sense of being independent political units, but they were much more than that. The *polis* was thought of as a community of relatives. All its citizens,

HUSBAND AND WIFE IN HOMER'S TROY

Homer's poems provide a picture of early Greek ideas and institutions. In the Iliad, *the poet tells of the return from the battle of the Trojan hero Hector. He is greeted by his loving, "warm, generous wife," Andromache, who is carrying their baby son. Hector reaches for the boy, who is frightened to tears by the plume on his father's helmet. The father removes the helmet and prays that his son will grow up to be called "a better man than his father . . . a joy to his mother's heart." The rest of the scene reveals the character of their marriage and the division of responsibility between men and women in their world.*

How does Homer depict the feelings of husband and wife toward one another? What are the tasks of the aristocratic woman revealed in this passage? What can be learned about the attitude toward death and duty?

So Hector prayed
and placed his son in the arms of his loving wife.
Andromache pressed the child to her scented
   breast,
smiling through her tears. Her husband noticed,
and filled with pity now, Hector stroked her gently,
trying to reassure her, repeating her name:
"Andromache,
dear one; why so desperate? Why so much grief
   for me?
No man will hurl me down to Death, against my
   fate.
And fate? No one alive has ever escaped it,
neither brave man nor coward, I tell you—
it's born with us the day that we are born.
So please go home and tend to your own tasks,

the distaff and the loom, and keep the women
working hard as well. As for the fighting,
men will see to that, all who were born in Troy
but I most of all."
Hector aflash in arms
took up his horsehair-crested helmet once again.
And his loving wife went home, turning, glancing
back again and again and weeping live warm tears.
She quickly reached the sturdy house of Hector,
man-killing Hector, and found her women
   gathered there inside
and stirred them all to a high pitch of mourning.
So in his house they raised the dirges for the dead,
for Hector still alive, his people were so convinced
that never again would he come home from battle,
never escape the Argives' rage and bloody hands.

From *The Iliad by Homer*, translated by Robert Fagles, copyright © 1990 by Robert Fagles. Used by permission of Viking Penguin, a division of Penguin Putnam Inc.

who were theoretically descended from a common ancestor, belonged to subgroups, such as fighting brotherhoods (phratries), clans, and tribes, and worshipped the gods in common ceremonies.

Originally, the word *polis* referred only to a citadel, an elevated, defensible rock to which the farmers of the neighboring area could retreat in case of attack. The Acropolis in Athens and the hill called Acrocorinth in Corinth are examples. For some time such high places and the adjacent farms comprised the *polis*. Availability of farmland and of a natural fortress determined its location. *Poleis* were placed either well inland or far enough away from the sea to avoid pirate raids. Only later and gradually did the agora appear. It grew to be not only a marketplace, but also a civic center and the heart of the Greeks' remarkable social life, which was distinguished by conversation and argument carried on in the open air.

By the time the *polis* was in full flower, between ca. 750 and 700 B.C.E., true monarchy had disappeared in Greece. Kings survived in some places, but they were almost always ceremonial figures without power. The original form of the *polis* was an aristocratic republic dominated by the nobility through its council of nobles and its monopoly of the magistracies.

From the middle of the eighth century B.C.E. until well into the sixth, the Greeks vastly expanded their territory, their wealth, and their contacts with other peoples in a burst of colonizing activity that placed *poleis* from Spain to the Black Sea. A century earlier, a few Greeks had established trading posts in Syria. There they had learned new techniques in the arts and crafts and much more from the older civilizations of the Near East. About 750 B.C.E., they borrowed a writing system from one of the Semitic scripts and added vowels to create the first true alphabet. The new Greek alphabet was easier to learn than any earlier writing system and made possible the widely literate society of classical Greece. Furthermore, by confronting Greeks with the differences between themselves and the new peoples they met, colonization gave the Greeks a sense of cultural identity. It also fostered a Panhellenic ("all-Greek") spirit that led to the establishment of several common religious festivals.

Like most other ancient peoples, the Greeks believed in many gods, and religion played an important part in their lives. A great part of Greek art and literature was closely connected with religion, as was the life of the *polis* in general. The Greek pantheon consisted of the twelve gods who lived on Mount Olympus and who therefore were known as Olympians. Each *polis* had one of the Olympians as its guardian deity and worshipped the god in its own special way, but all the gods were worshipped by all Greeks. In the eighth and seventh centuries B.C.E., common shrines were established at Olympia for the worship of Zeus, at Delphi for Apollo, at the Isthmus of Corinth for Poseidon, and at Nemea once again for Zeus. Each *polis* held athletic contests in honor of its god, to which all Greeks were invited and for which a sacred truce was declared.

The somewhat cold religion of the Olympian gods did little to attend to human fears, hopes, and passions. For these needs, the Greeks turned to other deities and rites. Of these the most popular was Dionysus, a god of nature and fertility, of the grapevine and drunkenness, and of sexual abandon. In some of his rites, the god was followed by maenads, female devotees who cavorted by night, ate raw flesh, and were reputed to tear to pieces any creature they came across.

The heart of Greek life was the *polis*. Generalization about the *polis* becomes difficult not long after its appearance. Although the states had much in common, some of them developed in unique ways. Sparta and Athens, which became the two most powerful Greek states, had especially different characters.

Sparta About 725 B.C.E., Sparta conquered its western neighbor, Messenia, and reduced its population to the status of serfs, or helots. Almost a century later, the helots revolted. After the revolt had been put down, the Spartans were forced to reconsider their way of life. They could not expect to keep down the helots, who outnumbered them by perhaps ten to one, and still maintain the old free and easy habits typical of

most Greeks. To maintain domination over the helots, the Spartans introduced fundamental reforms that turned their city permanently into a military academy and camp.

The Spartan reforms are attributed to the legendary figure Lycurgus. The new system that emerged late in the sixth century B.C.E. exerted direct control over each Spartan from birth until old age. Officials of the state decided which infants were physically fit to survive. At the age of seven, the Spartan boy was taken from his mother and turned over to young instructors who trained him in athletics and the military arts. At twenty, the Spartan youth was enrolled in the army and lived in barracks with his companions until the age of thirty. If married, he could visit his wife only infrequently and even then by stealth. At thirty, he became a full citizen. He took his simple meals at a public mess in the company of fifteen comrades. Military service was required until the age of sixty.

Women were also educated to subordinate themselves wholly to the ideal of service to Sparta. They were not given military training, but they were required to devote their children to the service of the *polis*. Nothing in Sparta was allowed to interfere with the only ambition permitted to a Spartan: to win glory and the respect of his peers by bravery in war.

The Spartan constitution was mixed, containing elements of monarchy, oligarchy, and democracy. There were two kings with very limited power. The oligarchic element was represented by a council of elders who had important judicial functions. The Spartan assembly consisted of all males over thirty. In addition, there was a board of five annually elected ephors who controlled foreign policy, oversaw the generalship of the kings on campaign, presided over the assembly, and guarded against rebellions by the helots. Most Greeks admired the Spartan state for its unmatched stability and also for its ability to mold its citizens into a single pattern, subordinated to an ideal.

Athens The life and politics of Athens developed in a direction very different from that of Sparta. In the seventh century B.C.E., Athens was a typical aristocratic *polis*. The aristocrats held the most and best land and dominated religious and political life. The state was governed by the Areopagus, a council of nobles deriving its name from the hill where it held its sessions. Toward the close of the century, economic hardship caused political conflict in Athens.

Tradition has it that in the year 594 B.C.E. the Athenians gave Solon extraordinary powers to legislate and revise the constitution. He carried out a series of economic reforms that restructured debts and credit. Solon also significantly changed the constitution. All male adults whose fathers were citizens were citizens, too, and to their number he added immigrant craftsmen. All

The Acropolis was both the religious and civic center of Athens. In its final form it is the work of Pericles and his successors in the late fifth century B.C.E. This photograph shows the Parthenon and to its left the Erechtheum.   Meredith Pillon, Greek National Tourism Organization

citizens were divided into four classes according to wealth. He established a Council of Four Hundred, apparently to check the power of the Areopagus. Finally, he established a popular assembly. In 546 B.C.E., the constitution of Solon was overthrown by Pisistratus, who established his own rule. Despite this period of tyranny, however, the principle of a somewhat democratically governed *polis* had been established, and later leaders would build upon that foundation.

Hippias, the son of Pisistratus, was deposed in 510 B.C.E., and the government of Athens underwent another series of reforms. These were undertaken by Clisthenes, who may be regarded as the real founder of Athenian democracy. He made the **deme**, the equivalent of a small town in the country or a ward in the city, the basic unit of civic life. Henceforth, enrollment in the *deme* replaced enrollment in the phratry (clan brotherhood, where tradition and noble birth dominated) as evidence of citizenship. He also further extended the classes of people who might become citizens. He established a Council of Five Hundred, which dealt with foreign policy and finances. Final authority in all things rested with the assembly composed of all adult male citizens. Debate was free and open. Any adult Athenian male could submit legislation, offer amendments, or argue the merits of any question. The reforms of Clisthenes nurtured strong patriotism among the Athenians. The freedom of their constitution also allowed them to achieve very considerable economic prosperity.

Whether a Greek citizen lived in Sparta, Athens, or another of the many *poleis*, he knew that his way of life was different from that of people who lived under the great monarchs of the East. The Greeks were determined to preserve the way of life of the *polis*. In 490 B.C.E., Darius, the king of Persia, (r. 521–485 B.C.E.) attempted to restore the tyrant Hippias in Athens. The Athenians, led by Miltiades, (ca. 550–487 B.C.E.) resisted and won a victory at Marathon (490 B.C.E.). This victory preserved Athenian freedom and instilled in the Athenians a sense of confidence and pride in their *polis*. In 480 B.C.E., the Persians under Xerxes (r. 485–465 B.C.E.) again attempted to conquer Greece. The Greek cities responded by forming a defensive league among themselves. Sparta as leader of the land forces held off the Persians at the Battle of Thermopylae. The Athenians led Greek naval forces to a great victory over Persia at Salamis.

In the half century after the defeat of the Persians, two important developments occurred among the Greeks. First, under the leadership of Pericles (ca. 494–429 B.C.E.), the constitution of Athens became even more democratic. Every decision of the state had to be approved by the popular assembly, a collection of the people themselves, not their representatives. Most officials were selected by lot without regard to class. There was no standing army, no police force, and no way to coerce the people. Yet even in democratic Athens, as in all the other Greek states, participation in government was denied to slaves, resident aliens, and women.

The Peloponnesian War   The second development was the division of the Greek world into two spheres of influence, dominated by Sparta and Athens. Sparta led a relatively loose alliance, but the Athenian alliance quickly developed into an empire in which most of Athens' allies made financial payments in place of military service. The Athenians used the money not only for

A Greek hoplite attacks a Persian soldier. The contrast between the Greek's metal body armor, large shield, and long spear and the Persian's cloth and leather garments indicates one reason the Greeks won. This Attic vase was found on Rhodes and dates from ca. 475 B.C.E.   The Metropolitan Museum of Art, Rogers Fund, 1906 (06.1021.117) Photograph © 1986. The Metropolitan Museum of Art

defense but for their own purposes as well. Increasingly, Athens controlled the policy of the alliance and used it to increase its own wealth, power, and glory. For many years, intense rivalry and occasional conflict occurred between the two cities and their respective allies. Then, in 431 B.C.E., a great conflict—the Peloponnesian War, recorded brilliantly in the history of Thucydides (ca. 460–400 B.C.E.)—began between them. This devastating conflict ended in 404 B.C.E. with the defeat of Athens. After this war, Greek prosperity and confidence were never again fully restored.

The long Peloponnesian War and the struggles accompanying the several attempts at hegemony brought results that undermined the foundations of the *polis*. By ravaging farmland, destroying crops and houses, interfering with commerce, and using up reserve funds, the warring armies and navies did severe and usually lasting damage to the economic well-being that made civic life possible. Civil strife and class conflict, encouraged by the pressure of want and disease as well as by the availability of help from foreign armies, were an even more terrible legacy than poverty. As time passed, people abandoned patriotism, morality, and even family to the

interests of faction. The wars of the fourth century B.C.E. only intensified these developments. Democratic revolutions, accompanied by confiscations of property, executions, exiles, and even great atrocities, were answered with similar actions by victorious aristocratic oligarchs. Such upheavals left permanent scars and damaged the family feeling, the sense of community, and the commitment to the common good required for life in the *polis*.

Greek Political Philosophy and the Crisis of the *Polis*

The decay of healthy political life in the *polis* gave rise to ideas in political philosophy that have influenced Western thought ever since. Probably the most complicated response to the crisis of the *polis* in the fourth century B.C.E. may be found in the life and teachings of Socrates (469–399 B.C.E.). He went into the Athenian marketplace and questioned and cross-examined people who were supposed to know something about politics. These included poets, craftsmen, and politicians. The result was always the same. Those he questioned might have technical information and skills, but they seldom had any substantial knowledge of the fundamental principles of human behavior. It is understandable that Athenians so exposed should be angry with their examiner, and it is not surprising that they thought Socrates was undermining the beliefs and values of the *polis*. Socrates' unconcealed contempt for democracy, which seemingly relied on ignorant amateurs to make important political decisions, created further hostility.

Yet despite this contempt, Socrates still believed that the *polis* had a legitimate claim on the loyalty and obedience of the citizen. He demonstrated this in the most convincing fashion. In 399 B.C.E., he was condemned to death by an Athenian jury on the charges of bringing new gods into the city and of corrupting the youth. He was given a chance to escape, but in the dialogue *Crito*, written by his disciple Plato, we are told of his refusal because of his veneration of the laws of the city. Socrates recognized the difficulties of political life in the *polis* and criticized its shortcomings. He turned away from active political life, but he did not abandon the idea of the *polis*. He fought as a soldier in its defense, obeyed its laws, and sought to put its values on a sound foundation of reason.

Plato (429–347 B.C.E.) was by far the most important of Socrates' associates and is a perfect example of the pupil who becomes greater than his master. He was the first systematic philosopher and therefore the first to place political ideas in their full philosophical context. He presented his philosophy in the format of dialogues. In 386 B.C.E., he founded the Academy, a center of philosophical investigation. As a school for training statesmen and citizens, it had a powerful impact on Greek thought that lasted until it was closed by the Roman emperor Justinian in the sixth century C.E.

Like Socrates, Plato believed in the *polis* and its values. Its virtues were order, harmony, and justice, and one of its main objects was to produce good people. He accepted Socrates' doctrine of the identity of virtue and knowledge and made it plain what he regarded as genuine knowledge. It was *episteme*, science as a body of true and unchanging wisdom open to only a few philosophers, whose training, character, and intellect allowed them to see reality. Only such people were qualified to rule. They themselves would prefer the life of pure contemplation but would accept their political responsibility and take their turn as philosopher kings. The training of such rulers, which Plato outlined in the *Republic*, required a specialization of function and a subordination of the individual to the community even greater than that at Sparta.

For Plato, justice in society meant that each person should do only that one thing to which his nature is best suited. Plato saw quite clearly that the Athenian *polis* of his day suffered from terrible internal stress, class struggle, and factional divisions. For Plato, the way to harmony was to destroy the causes of that strife: private property, the family, or anything else that stood between the individual citizen and his complete loyalty and devotion to the *polis*. (See "Plato on the Role of Women in His Utopian Republic.")

Aristotle (384–322 B.C.E.) was a pupil of Plato and owed much to the thought of his master, but his very different experience and cast of mind led him in some new directions. In 336 B.C.E., he founded his own school in Athens, the Lyceum, or the Peripatos, as it was also called from the covered walk within it. The Lyceum was a very different place from the Academy. Its members took little interest in mathematics and were concerned with gathering, ordering, and analyzing all human knowledge. The range of subjects treated is astonishing, including logic, physics, astronomy, biology, ethics, rhetoric, literary criticism, and politics.

In each field, Aristotle's method was the same. He began with observation of the empirical evidence, which in some cases was physical and in others was common opinion. To this body of information he applied reason and discovered inconsistencies or difficulties. He then introduced metaphysical principles to explain the problems or to reconcile the inconsistencies. His view on all subjects, like Plato's, was teleological; that is, both philosophers recognized purposes apart from and greater than the will of the individual human being in nature and in social life. Plato's purposes, however, were contained in the Ideas or Forms—transcendental concepts outside the experience of most people. For Aristotle, the purposes of

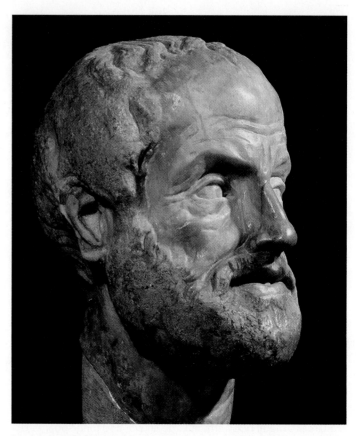

Marble head of Aristotle. Louvre, Dept. des Antiquities Grecques/Romaines, Paris, France. © Photograph by Erich Lessing/Art Resource, NY

most things could be easily inferred by observation of their behavior in the world. Aristotle's most striking characteristics were his moderation and common sense. His theory of knowledge finds room for both reason and experience. His metaphysics gives meaning and reality to both mind and body. His ethics aims at the good life, which is the contemplative life, but recognizes the necessity for moderate wealth, comfort, and pleasure.

THE RISE OF MACEDON

359–336 B.C.E.	Reign of Philip II
338 B.C.E.	Battle of Chaeronea; Philip conquers Greece
338 B.C.E.	Founding of League of Corinth
336–323 B.C.E.	Reign of Alexander III, the Great
334 B.C.E.	Alexander invades Asia
333 B.C.E.	Battle of Issus
331 B.C.E.	Battle of Gaugamela
330 B.C.E.	Fall of Persepolis
327 B.C.E.	Alexander reaches Indus Valley
323 B.C.E.	Death of Alexander

PLATO ON THE ROLE OF WOMEN IN HIS UTOPIAN REPUBLIC

The Greek invention of reasoned intellectual analysis of all things led the philosopher Plato to consider the problem of justice, which is the subject of his most famous dialogue, the Republic. *This leads him to sketch out a utopian state in which justice may be found and where the most radical arrangements may be necessary. These include the equality of the sexes and the destruction of the family in favor of the practice of men having wives and children in common. In the following excerpts, he argues for the fundamental equality of men and women and that women are no less appropriate as Guardians—leaders of the state—than men.*

What are Plato's reasons for treating men and women the same? What objections could be raised to that practice? Would that policy, even if appropriate in Plato's utopia, also be suitable to conditions in the real world of classical Athens? In the world of today?

"If, then, we use the women for the same things as the men, they must also be taught the same things."

"Yes."

"Now music and gymnastics were given to the men."

"Yes."

"Then these two arts, and what has to do with war, must be assigned to the women also, and they must be used in the same ways."

"On the basis of what you say," he said, "it's likely."

"Perhaps," I said, "compared to what is habitual, many of the things now being said would look ridiculous if they were to be done as is said."

"Indeed they would," he said.

"Well," I said, "since we've started to speak, we mustn't be afraid of all the jokes—of whatever kind—the wits might make if such a change took place in gymnastic, in music and, not the least, in the bearing of arms and the riding of horses."

"Then," I said, "if either the class of men or that of women show its superiority in some art or other practice, then we'll say that that art must be assigned to it. But if they look as though they differ in this alone, that the female bears and the male mounts, we'll assert that it has not thereby yet been proved that a woman differs from a man with respect to what we're talking about; rather, we'll still suppose that our guardians and their women must practice the same things."

"And rightly," he said.

"Therefore, my friend, there is no practice of a city's governors which belongs to woman because she's woman, or to man because he's man; but the natures are scattered alike among both animals; and woman participates according to nature in all practices, and man in all, but in all of them woman is weaker than man."

"Certainly."

"So, shall we assign all of them to men and none to women?"

"How could we?"

"For I suppose there is, as we shall assert, one woman apt at medicine and another not, one woman apt at music and another unmusical by nature."

"Of course."

"And isn't there then also one apt at gymnastic and at war, and another unwarlike and no lover of gymnastic?"

"I suppose so."

"And what about this? Is there a lover of wisdom and a hater of wisdom? And one who is spirited and another without spirit?"

"Yes, there are these too."

"There is, therefore one woman fit for guarding and another not, or wasn't it a nature of this sort we also selected for the men fit for guarding?"

"Certainly, that was it."

From *The Republic of Plato*, 2nd ed., trans. by Allan Bloom. Copyright © 1968 by Allan Bloom. Preface to paperback edition, © 1991 by Allan Bloom, pp. 130–134. Reprinted by permission of Basic Books, a member of Perseus Books, L.L.C.

Characteristically, Aristotle was less interested in the best state—the Platonic utopia that required philosophers to rule it—than in the best state practically possible, one that would combine justice with stability. The constitution for that state he called *politeia*, not the best constitution, but the next best, the one most suited to and most possible for most states. Its quality was moderation, and it naturally gave power to neither the rich nor the poor but to the middle class, which must also be the most numerous. The middle class possessed many virtues. Because of its moderate wealth, it was free of the arrogance of the rich and the malice of the poor. Aristotle combined the practical analysis of political and economic realities with the moral and political purposes of the traditional defenders of the *polis*. The result was a passionate confidence in the virtues of moderation and of the middle class and the proposal of a constitution that would give them power. It is ironic that the ablest defense of the *polis* came toward its demise.

The Empire of Alexander the Great

What finally brought the collapse of the independent political life of the Greek *poleis* was their conquest by the kingdom of Macedon in the middle of the fourth century B.C.E. The Macedonians inhabited the land to the north of Thessaly and until the fourth century B.C.E. played no great part in Greek affairs. Macedon possessed no *poleis* but was governed by a king chosen partly by descent and partly by the approval of the army. Under Philip II (r. 359–336 B.C.E.), the Macedonians developed a powerful army. Beginning about 355 B.C.E., Philip moved that army steadily against the various Greek cities. Years of fighting and diplomatic maneuvering followed, but no Greek *polis*, including Athens, was able or willing to mount an effective resistance. Finally, in 338 B.C.E., at the Battle of Chaeronea the Macedonian monarchy defeated an alliance of Greek cities. This defeat ended Greek freedom and autonomy.

In 336 B.C.E., Philip II was assassinated. His successor, Alexander the Great (r. 336–323 B.C.E.), was one of the most extraordinary figures of antiquity. During the next ten years, Alexander led the army of Macedonia across Asia as far as the Indus River (see Map I–4). On the way, he conquered Asia Minor, Syria, Palestine, Egypt, Persia, and Mesopotamia. Alexander was filled with plans for the consolidation and organization of his empire, for geographical exploration, and for building new cities, roads, and harbors. These plans were never carried out because in June 323 B.C.E., he died of fever at the age of thirty-three. He left no real successor, and his generals fought over the lands he had conquered.

The conquests of Alexander and the establishment of successor kingdoms in Macedon, Mesopotamia, and

This sculpture of Alexander the Great, king of Macedon and conqueror of the Persian Empire, was made in the second century B.C.E. and found at the ancient city of Magnesia in Asia Minor. Alexander's conquests spread Greek culture far from its homeland, laying the foundation of the Hellenistic world.   Statue from Magnesia ad Sipylum. Archeological Museum, Istanbul, Turkey. Erich Lessing/Art Resource, NY

Egypt put an end once and for all to the central role of the *polis* in Greek life. At the same time, his conquests spread Greek culture widely throughout the eastern Mediterranean, laying the foundation for the Hellenistic civilization that succeeded the civilization of classical Greece.

Deprived of control of their foreign affairs and with their important internal arrangements determined by a

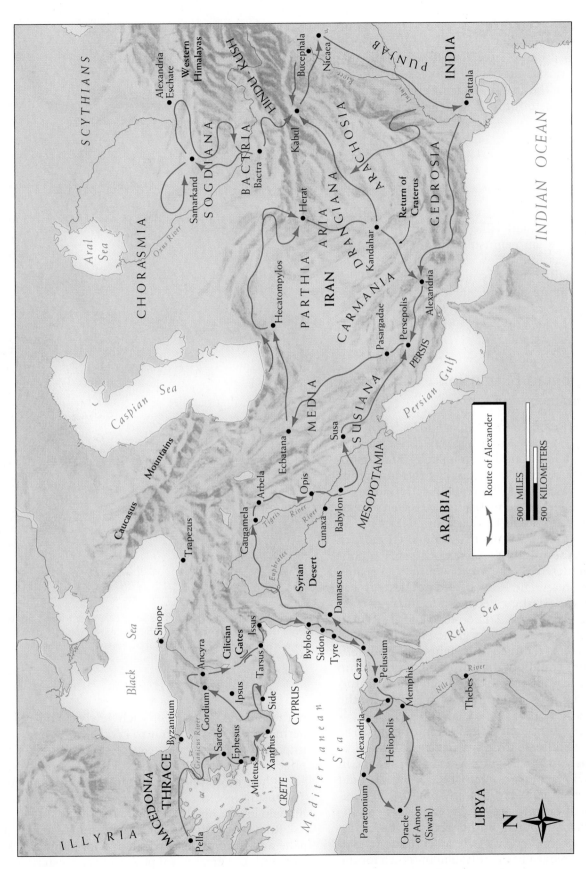

Map I–4 **Alexander's Campaigns** The route taken by Alexander the Great in his conquest of the Persian Empire, 334–323 B.C.E. Starting from the Macedonian capital at Pella, he reached the Indus Valley before being turned back by his own restive troops. He died of fever in Mesopotamia.

li

foreign monarchy, the postclassical Greek cities lost the kind of political freedom that was basic to the old outlook. As time passed, they changed from sovereign states to municipalities merged in military empires. It was not by the cities of Greece but by a city on the Italian peninsula that the future course of civilization in the West would be determined.

▼ Rome

The political achievement of the Romans was one of the most remarkable in human history. The descendants of the inhabitants of a small village in central Italy governed the entire Italian peninsula and then the entire Mediterranean coastline. They conquered most of the Near East and finally much of continental Europe. They ruled this vast empire under a single government that provided peace and prosperity for centuries. Never before or since has that area been united, and rarely, if ever, has it enjoyed a stable peace.

The Republic and Expansion in the Mediterranean

From its foundation in 753 B.C.E. until 509 B.C.E., Rome was governed by kings (see Map I–5). In 509 B.C.E., tradition tells us, the republic replaced the monarchy after a revolution led by noble families incensed by the outrageous behavior of the last kings. The republican form of government, dominated by the institution of the aristocratic Senate, endured for almost five centuries.

By 265 B.C.E., the Romans had conquered most of central and southern Italy and had established a policy toward conquered peoples that would be repeated in many other areas. The Romans did not destroy any of the Latin cities or their people, nor did they treat them all alike. Some near Rome received full Roman citizenship; others farther away gained municipal status. Their citizens retained the rights of local self-government and could obtain full Roman citizenship if they moved to Rome. They followed Rome in foreign policy and provided soldiers to serve in the Roman legions.

Still other states became allies of Rome on the basis of treaties, which differed from city to city. All the allies supplied troops to the army, in which they fought in auxiliary battalions under Roman officers, but they did not pay taxes to Rome. Finally, on some of the conquered land the Romans placed colonies, permanent settlements of veteran soldiers in the territory of recently defeated enemies. The colonists retained their Roman citizenship and enjoyed home rule, and in return for the land they had been given they served as a permanent garrison to deter or suppress rebellion. The Romans did

Map I–5 **Ancient Italy** This map of ancient Italy and its neighbors before the expansion of Rome shows major cities and towns as well as several geographical regions and the locations of some of the Italic and non-Italic peoples.

not regard the status given each newly conquered city as permanent. They held out to loyal allies the prospect of improving their status, even of achieving the ultimate prize, full Roman citizenship. In doing so, the Romans gave their allies a stake in Rome's future and success. The result, in general, was that most of Rome's allies remained loyal even when put to the severest test.

Rome's acquisition of coastal territory and its expansion to the toe of the Italian boot brought it face to face with the great naval power of the western Mediterranean, Carthage, located near what is now the modern city of Tunis. Rome and Carthage engaged in two great

THE PUNIC WARS

264–241 B.C.E.	First Punic War
238 B.C.E.	Rome seizes Sardinia and Corsica
221 B.C.E.	Hannibal takes command of Punic army in Spain
218–202 B.C.E.	Second Punic War
216 B.C.E.	Battle of Cannae
209 B.C.E.	Scipio takes New Carthage
202 B.C.E.	Battle of Zama
149–146 B.C.E.	Third Punic War
146 B.C.E.	Destruction of Carthage

conflicts, the First and Second Punic Wars (264–241 B.C.E. and 218–202 B.C.E.). At very considerable cost, Rome emerged victorious and thereafter ruled virtually all the western Mediterranean. After the defeat of Carthage, the attention of Rome moved toward the eastern Mediterranean and the successor kingdoms of Alexander's brief empire. By 168 B.C.E., after a series of military interventions in Macedon, the Romans effectively governed Greece as a kind of protectorate.

Roman expansion in Italy and overseas was accomplished without a grand general plan. The new territories were acquired as a result of wars that the Romans believed were either defensive or preventive. Foreign policy was aimed at providing security for Rome on Rome's terms, but these terms were often unacceptable to other nations and led to continued conflict. The various conquests of territory overseas presented new political problems to Rome. Instead of following the policy pursued in Italy, the Romans made Sicily, Spain, Sardinia, and Corsica into provinces. The new populations were neither Roman citizens nor allies; they were subjects who did not serve in the army but paid tribute instead. The old practice of extending citizenship and with it loyalty to Rome stopped at the borders of Italy.

These conquests changed both Roman political and cultural life. Roman expansion overseas brought about close and continued association with the Greeks. Many Romans admired Greek art, literature, and philosophy but held Greek politics in contempt. Before long, the education of the Roman upper classes was bilingual. The Romans also often imitated the forms of Greek literature. Roman religion was influenced by the Greeks almost from the beginning because the Romans had early in their history identified their own gods with Greek equivalents and incorporated Greek mythology into their own. The Romans also drew heavily upon Greek philosophy. They always adapted Greek culture to their own particular needs. It was commonplace in antiquity to think that while Rome had conquered Greece militarily, Greece had conquered Rome culturally.

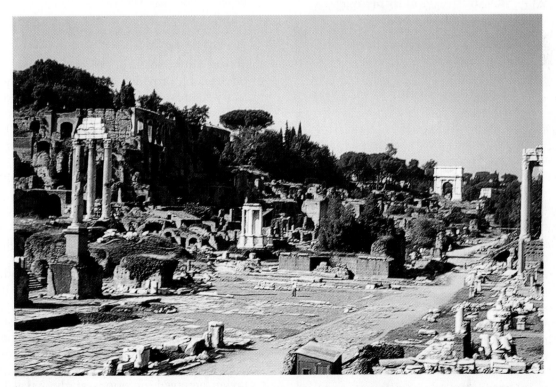

Ruins of the Roman Forum. From the earliest days of the city, the Forum was the center of Roman life. Augustus had it rebuilt, and it was frequently rebuilt and refurbished by his successors, so most of the surviving buildings date to the imperial period. Italian Government Tourist Board

From Republic to Empire

The political and economic problems raised by the overseas conquests eventually undermined the constitution of the republic. During the Punic Wars, much of the farmland in Italy was damaged and even more was bought up by wealthy nobles. Returning veterans found themselves without land and often settled in the city of Rome or other urban areas. The people of Rome became sharply divided into rich and poor, landed and landless, privileged and deprived. By 133 B.C.E. many Roman political leaders believed this issue had to be addressed, but there was no agreement on the method.

Between 133 and 121 B.C.E., two brothers, Tiberius and Gaius Gracchus, tried to carry out a program of limited land redistribution. The Gracchi met intense and violent opposition. Both were assassinated as the wealthy landowning classes moved to protect their interests. For a century after their deaths, political and military turmoil prevailed in the republic. The people who gained power were generals who had armies at their disposal and whose conquests made them popular. For example, Marius (ca. 157–86 B.C.E.) defeated Roman enemies in North Africa and for a time dominated politics. Sulla (ca. 138–78 B.C.E.) established a dictatorship

Lictors, pictured here, attended the chief Roman magistrates when they appeared in public. The axe carried by one of the lictors and the bound bundle of staffs carried by the others symbolize both the power of Roman magistrates to inflict corporal punishment on Roman citizens and the limits on that power. The bound staffs symbolize the right of citizens within the city of Rome not to be punished without a trial. The axe symbolizes the power of the magistrates, as commanders of the army, to put anyone to death without a trial outside the city walls. Alinari/Art Resource, NY

THE FALL OF THE ROMAN REPUBLIC

133 B.C.E.	Tribunate of Tiberius Gracchus
123–122 B.C.E.	Tribunate of Gaius Gracchus
111–105 B.C.E.	Jugurthine War
104–100 B.C.E.	Consecutive consulships of Marius
90–88 B.C.E.	War against the Italian allies
88 B.C.E.	Sulla's march on Rome
82 B.C.E.	Sulla assumes dictatorship
71 B.C.E.	Crassus crushes rebellion of Spartacus
71 B.C.E.	Pompey defeats Sertorius in Spain
70 B.C.E.	Consulship of Crassus and Pompey
60 B.C.E.	Formation of First Triumvirate
58–50 B.C.E.	Caesar in Gaul
53 B.C.E.	Crassus killed in Battle of Carrhae
49 B.C.E.	Caesar crosses Rubicon; civil war begins
48 B.C.E.	Pompey defeated at Pharsalus; killed in Egypt
46–44 B.C.E.	Caesar's dictatorship
45 B.C.E.	End of civil war
43 B.C.E.	Formation of Second Triumvirate
42 B.C.E.	Triumvirs defeat Brutus and Cassius at Philippi
31 B.C.E.	Octavian and Agrippa defeat Antony at Actium

for a time after a series of military victories. The success of one general provided an example to other ambitious military figures. The unequal distribution of wealth and land meant there were always plenty of men willing to serve in the armies of ambitious generals. The Senate in Rome no longer really controlled Roman armies.

By the middle of the first century B.C.E., two generals were contending for domination, Gnaeus Pompey (106–48 B.C.E.) and Julius Caesar (100–44 B.C.E.). Pompey had won fame by ridding the Mediterranean of pirates. Somewhat later, Caesar conquered most of Gaul. For a time they tried to share political influence, but by 49 B.C.E. all cooperation had ceased. In that year Caesar, his career and life in jeopardy, defied the Roman Senate by leading his army out of his province across the Rubicon River (see Map I–6). In the civil war that followed, Caesar defeated the forces of Pompey and the Senate. Until his assassination in 44 B.C.E., Caesar virtually governed Rome alone. After his death, his nephew Octavian (63 B.C.E.–C.E. 14) rallied Caesar's forces. By 31 B.C.E., after years of ruthless civil war, Octavian emerged victorious at the naval battle of Actium. At the age of thirty-two, Octavian stood as the absolute master of the Mediterranean world.

Map I–6 **THE CIVIL WARS OF THE LATE ROMAN REPUBLIC** This map shows the extent of the territory controlled by Rome at the time of Caesar's death and the sites of the major battles of the civil wars of the late republic.

The Principate and the Empire

Octavian was well aware of the fate of his uncle. He knew that it was dangerous to flaunt unprecedented powers and to disregard all republican tradition. He created a political structure that had republican trappings and the appearance of sharing power with the Senate and the people of Rome. Yet in reality the government of Octavian, like that of his successors, was a monarchy. Octavian was simply called by the unofficial title of "first citizen," which in Latin is *princeps*. The Senate also heaped upon him other important political powers and honors. Among them was the semireligious title "Augustus," which carried implications of veneration, majesty, and holiness. From

this time on, historians speak of Rome's first emperor as Augustus and of his regime as the Principate. The union of political and military power in the hands of the *princeps* made it possible for him to install rational, efficient, and stable government in the provinces for the first time.

The Augustan period was one of great prosperity. Augustus had brought in the wealth by the conquest of Egypt during the civil wars (see Map I–7, page lvi). The great increase in commerce and industry made possible general peace and a vast program of public works. Finally, there was a strong return to successful small farming on the part of Augustus's resettled veterans.

The high point of Roman culture came in the last century of the republic and during the Principate of

Map I–7 **PROVINCES OF THE ROMAN EMPIRE TO 117 C.E.** The growth of the empire to its greatest extent is here shown in three stages—at the death of Augustus in 14 C.E., at the death of Nerva in 98, and at the death of Trajan in 117. The division into provinces is also shown. The insert shows the main roads that tied the far-flung empire together.

MAJOR ROADS OF THE ROMAN EMPIRE

Rome

500 MILES
500 KILOMETERS

Caspian Sea

PARTHIAN EMPIRE

Persian Gulf

ARMENIA

ASSYRIA

MESOPOTAMIA

Tigris R.

Euphrates R.

ARABIA

CAPPADOCIA

PONTUS

ASIA

BITHYNIA

GALATIA

CILICIA

ARABIA PETRAEA

Red Sea

PISIDIA

LYCIA

CYPRUS

PALESTINE
Jerusalem

EGYPT

Black Sea

Byzantium

LOWER MOESIA

THRACE

CRETE I.

Mediterranean Sea

LIBYA

SARMATIA

DACIA

UPPER MOESIA

MACEDONIA

GREECE

ILLYRIA

ACHAEA

CYRENAICA

N

PANNONIA (SUP.)

PANNONIA (INF.)

DALMATIA

Danube R.

NORICUM

RHAETIA

Alps Mts.

CISALPINE GAUL

Rome

ITALY

SICILY

SARDINIA

Carthage

AFRICA

NUMIDIA

AFRICA

500 MILES
500 KILOMETERS

GERMANIA

GERMANIA (SUP.)

GERMANIA (INF.)

Cologne

NARBONENSIS

LUGDUNENSIS

GAUL

AQUITANIA

CORSICA

BALEARIC ISLANDS

MAURETANIA

BRITAIN

Wall of Antoninus
Wall of Hadrian

North Sea

TARRACONENSIS

LUSITANIA

BAETICA

ATLANTIC OCEAN

HIBERNIA

14 C.E. – Death of Augustus

14–98 C.E. – Acquisitions, Augustus to Trajan

98–117 C.E. – Acquisitions during the Reign of Trajan

A panel from the *Ara Pacis* (*Altar of Peace*). The altar was dedicated in 9 B.C.E. It was part of a propaganda campaign—involving poetry, architecture, myth, and history—that Augustus undertook to promote himself as the savior of Rome and the restorer of peace. This panel shows the goddess Earth and her children with cattle, sheep, and other symbols of agricultural wealth.   Italian Government Tourist Board

Augustus. The towering literary figure of the late republic was Cicero (106–43 B.C.E.), who delivered his famous orations in the law courts and in the Senate. Together with a considerable body of his private letters, these orations provide us with a clearer and fuller insight into his mind than into that of any other figure in antiquity. He also wrote treatises on rhetoric, ethics, and politics that put Greek philosophical ideas into Latin terminology and at the same time changed them to suit Roman conditions and values. He believed in a world governed by divine and natural law that human reason could perceive and human institutions reflect. His literary style, as well as his values and ideas, was an important legacy for the Middle Ages and, as reinterpreted, for the Renaissance.

Whereas Cicero was the last great voice of the republic, Vergil (70–19 B.C.E.) was the most important of the Augustan poets. Vergil's greatest work is the *Aeneid*, a long national epic. He glorified the civic greatness represented by Augustus and the peace and prosperity that he had brought to Rome.

The central problem for Augustus's successors was the position of the ruler and his relationship to the ruled. Augustus tried to cloak the monarchical nature of his government, but his successors soon abandoned all pretense. The rulers came to be called ***imperator***—from which comes our word *emperor*—as well as *Caesar*. The

latter title signified connection with the imperial house; the former indicated the military power on which everything was based. Because Augustus ostensibly was only the "first citizen" of a restored republic and his powers theoretically were voted him by the Senate and the people, he could not legally name his successor. He plainly designated his heirs, however, by lavishing favors on them and by giving them a share in the imperial power and responsibility.

The genius of the Augustan settlement lay in its capacity to enlist the active cooperation of the upper classes and their effective organ, the Senate. The election of magistrates was taken from the assemblies and given to the Senate, which became the major center for legislation and also exercised important judicial functions. Some emperors, like Vespasian, took pains to maintain, increase, and display the prestige and dignity of the Senate; others, like Caligula, Nero, and Domitian, degraded the Senate and paraded their own despotic power, but from the first the Senate's powers were illusory. Its true function was to be a legislative and administrative extension of the emperor's rule.

The provinces flourished economically and generally accepted Roman rule easily (see Map I–7). In the eastern provinces, the emperor was worshipped as a god, and even in Italy most emperors were deified after death as long as the imperial cult established by Augustus continued. Imperial policy was usually a happy combination of an attempt to unify the empire and its various peoples with a respect for local customs and differences. Roman citizenship was spread ever more widely, and by 212 C.E. almost every inhabitant of the empire was a citizen. Latin became the language of the western provinces. Although the east remained essentially Greek in language and culture, even it adopted many aspects of Roman life.

The army played an important role in the spread of Roman culture and the spiritual unification of the empire. The legionnaires married local women and frequently settled in the province of their service when their term was over.

From an administrative and cultural standpoint, the empire was a collection of cities and towns and had little to do with the countryside. Roman policy during the Principate was to raise urban centers to the status of Roman municipalities with the rights and privileges attached to them. A typical municipal charter left much responsibility in the hands of local councils and magistrates elected from the local aristocracy. Moreover, the holding of a magistracy, and later a seat on the council, carried Roman citizenship with it. Therefore, the Romans enlisted the upper classes of the provinces in their own government, spread Roman law and culture, and won the loyalty of the influential people.

Seen from the harsh perspective of human history, the first two centuries of the Roman Empire deserve their reputation as a "golden age." By the second century, however, troubles had arisen that foreshadowed the difficult times ahead. The literary efforts of the time reveal a flight from the present, reality, and the public realm to the past, romance, and private pursuits. Some of the same aspects may be seen in everyday life, especially in the decline of vitality in local government. (See "Juvenal on Life in Rome.")

In the first century, members of the upper classes vied with one another for election to municipal office and for the honor of doing service to their communities. By the second century, much of their zeal had disappeared. It became necessary for the emperors to intervene to correct abuses in local affairs and even to force unwilling members of the ruling classes to accept public office. The reluctance to serve was caused largely by the imperial practice of holding magistrates and councilmen personally and collectively responsible for the revenues due. There were even some instances of magistrates fleeing to avoid their offices, a practice that became widespread in later centuries.

All these difficulties reflected the presence of more basic problems. The prosperity brought by the end of civil war and the influx of wealth from the East, especially Egypt, could not sustain itself beyond the first half of the second century. There also appears to have been a decline in population for reasons that remain mysterious. The cost of government kept rising as the emperors were required (1) to maintain a costly standing army, (2) to keep the people in Rome happy with subsidized food and public entertainment ("bread and circuses"), (3) to pay an increasingly numerous bureaucracy, and (4) to wage expensive wars to defend the frontiers against dangerous and determined barbarian enemies. The ever-increasing need for money compelled the emperors to raise taxes, to press hard on their subjects, and to bring on inflation by debasing the coinage. These elements were to bring on the desperate crises that ultimately destroyed the empire.

Christianity

The peace, stability, and prosperity of the first two centuries of the Roman Empire provided essential conditions for the rise of Christianity as one of the world's great religions and as the single most important cultural force in the future of Western civilization. Despite certain problems in regard to the historical character of the Gospels, there is no reason to doubt that Jesus was born in the province of Judaea in the time of Augustus and that he was a most effective teacher in the tradition of the Jewish prophets. Jesus had success and won a considerable following, especially among the poor. This success caused much suspicion among the upper classes. His message of love, charity, and humility, as seen in the Sermon on the Mount, and his criticism of the current Jewish religious practices provoked hostility within the religious establishment.

Jesus was put to death by Roman soldiers in Jerusalem probably in 30 C.E.. His followers believed that he was resurrected on the third day after his death, and that belief became a critical element in the religion that they propagated throughout the Roman Empire and beyond. Through the early missionary work of Paul of Tarsus, the Christian faith was carried beyond the area of Palestine to virtually all the eastern Mediterranean world and to Rome itself. Christianity had its greatest success in the cities and among the poor and uneducated. (See "Mark Describes the Resurrection of Jesus," page lx.)

The future of Christianity depended on its communities finding an organization that would preserve unity within the group and help protect it against enemies outside. At first, the churches had little formal organization. By the second century C.E., however, the Christians of each city tended to accept the authority and leadership of a bishop. In time, bishops extended their authority over the Christian communities in outlying towns and the countryside. The power and authority of

JUVENAL ON LIFE IN ROME

The satirical poet Juvenal lived and worked in Rome in the late first and early second centuries C.E. His poems present a vivid picture of the material and cultural world of the Romans of his time. In the following passages, he tells of the discomforts and dangers of life in the city, both indoors and out.

According to Juvenal, what dangers awaited pedestrians in the Rome of his day? Who had responsibility for the condition of Rome? If the situation was as bad as he says, why was nothing done about it? Why did people choose to live in Rome at all and especially in the conditions he describes?

Who, in Praeneste's cool, or the wooded Volsinian
    uplands,
Who, on Tivoli's heights, or a small town like
    Gabii, say,
Fears the collapse of his house? But Rome is
    supported on pipestems,
Matchsticks; it's cheaper, so, for the landlord to
    shore up his ruins,
Patch up the old cracked walls, and notify all the
    tenants
They can sleep secure, though the beams are in
    ruins above them.
No, the place to live is out there, where no cry of
    Fire!
Sounds the alarm of the night, with a neighbor
    yelling for water,
Moving his chattels and goods, and the whole
    third story is smoking.

Look at other things, the various dangers of
    nighttime.
How high it is to the cornice that breaks, and a
    chunk beats my brains out,
Or some slob heaves a jar, broken or cracked, from
    a window.
Bang! It comes down with a crash and proves its
    weight on the sidewalk.
You are a thoughtless fool, unmindful of sudden
    disaster,
If you don't make your will before you go out to
    have dinner.
There are as many deaths in the night as there are
    open windows
Where you pass by; if you're wise, you will pray,
    in your wretched devotions,
People may be content with no more than
    emptying slop jars.

From Juvenal, *The Satires of Juvenal*, trans. by Rolfe Humphries (Bloomington: Indiana University Press, 1958], pp. 40, 43.

the bishops were soon enhanced by the doctrine of Apostolic Succession, which asserted that the powers that Jesus had given his original disciples were passed on from bishop to bishop by ordination.

The new faith soon incurred the distrust of the pagan world and of the imperial government, but in the first two centuries there was comparatively little official persecution. Division within the Christian church during these years was a greater threat. The great majority of Christians held to what even then were traditional, simple, conservative beliefs. This body of majority opinion and the Church that enshrined it came to be called *Catholic*, which means "universal." Its doctrines were deemed orthodox, whereas those holding contrary opinions were deemed heretics.

By the end of the second century, an orthodox canon had been shaped that included the Old Testament, the Gospels, and the Epistles of Paul, among other writings. The orthodox declared the Church itself to be the depository of Christian teaching and the bishops to be its receivers. They also drew up creeds, brief statements of faith to which true Christians should adhere.

By the end of the second century, an orthodox Christian—that is, a member of the Catholic church—was required to accept its creed, its canon of holy writings, and the authority of the bishops. During this same time, the Church in Rome and its bishop came to have special prominence; by 200 C.E., Rome was the most important center of Christianity.

MARK DESCRIBES THE RESURRECTION OF JESUS

Belief that Jesus rose from the dead after his Crucifixion (about 30 C.E.) was and is central to traditional Christian doctrine. The record of the Resurrection in the Gospel of Mark, written a generation later (toward 70 C.E.), is the earliest we have. The significance to most Christian groups revolves about the assurance given them that death and the grave are not final and that, instead, salvation for a future life is possible. The appeal of these views was to be nearly universal in the West during the Middle Ages. The church was commonly thought to be the means of implementing the promise of salvation—hence the enormous importance of the church's sacramental system, its rules, and its clergy.

Why are the stories of miracles such as the one described here important for the growth of Christianity? What is special and important about this miracle? Why is it important in the story that days passed between the death of Jesus and the opening of the tomb? Why might the early Christians believe this story? Why was belief in the resurrection important for Christianity in the centuries immediately after the life of Jesus? Is it still important today?

And when evening had come, since it was the day of Preparation, that is, the day before the sabbath, Joseph of Arimathea, a respected member of the council, who was also himself looking for the kingdom of God, took courage and went to Pilate, and asked for the body of Jesus. And Pilate wondered if he were already dead; and summoning the centurion, he asked him whether he was already dead. And when he learned from the centurion that he was dead, he granted the body to Joseph. And he brought a linen shroud, and taking him down, wrapped him in the linen shroud, and laid him in a tomb which had been hewn out of the rock; and he rolled a stone against the door of the tomb. Mary Magdalene and Mary the mother of Jesus saw where he was laid.

And when the sabbath was past, Mary Magdalene, and Mary the mother of James, and Salome, bought spices, so that they might go and anoint him. And very early on the first day of the week they went to the tomb when the sun had risen. And they were saying to one another, "Who will roll away the stone for us from the door of the tomb?" And looking up, they saw that the stone was rolled back; for it was very large. And entering the tomb, they saw a young man sitting on the right side, dressed in a white robe; and they were amazed. And he said to them, "Do not be amazed; you seek Jesus of Nazareth, who was crucified. He has risen, he is not here, see the place where they laid him. But go, tell his disciples and Peter that he is going before you to Galilee; there you will see him, as he told you." And they went out and fled from the tomb; for trembling and astonishment had come upon them; and they said nothing to any one, for they were afraid.

Gospel of Mark 15:42–47; 16:1–8, Revised Standard Version of the Bible (New York: Thomas Nelson and Sons, 1946, 1952).

Decline and Fall of the Roman Empire

By the time that the Christian religion had firmly established itself, the Roman Empire had entered a period of turmoil and instability known as the "crisis of the third century." There were massive external pressures on Rome's frontiers. The Persians pressed from the east and German tribes endangered the frontiers on the west and north. As the empire moved forces to fight one enemy, the frontier weakened in other areas.

The Roman army was no longer composed of citizens but rather of slaves, gladiators, barbarians, and brigands conscripted to fight. The emperors in this century and later were almost wholly dependent on the army for their authority. The military expenses put great pressure on the economy. Because the em-

A mosaic from Carthage illustrating aspects of life on the manorial estate of a certain Julian in the province of Africa. His housing, provisions, and entertainment appear to have been opulent. Social boundaries hardened in the late empire, and large fortified estates like this increasingly dominated social and economic life. *Musée Nationale du Bardo*

pire was impoverished, with no system of credit financing, the emperors compelled the people to provide food, supplies, money, and labor. The upper classes in the cities were made to serve as administrators without pay and to meet deficits in revenue from their own pockets. The changes in the army, the tax system, and administrative procedures undermined both the authority and the morale of the traditional ruling classes in the empire.

Toward the end of the third century, the emperor Diocletian (r. 284–305 C.E.) responded to these difficulties by dividing the empire into four separate administrative units, each with its own ruler and capital. This political reorganization did not prove to be particularly effective. The emperor Constantine (r. 306–337 C.E.) reunited the empire, but only temporarily. In 330 C.E., he established his capital at Constantinople in the East. Fragmentation and the shifting of the capital meant that by the close of the fourth century the empire consisted of eastern and western halves virtually independent of each other. Constantinople became the center of a vital and flourishing culture that we call *Byzantine* and that lasted until the fifteenth century.

Indeed, when we contemplate the decline and fall of the Roman Empire in the fourth and fifth centuries, we are speaking only of the West. There, life became increasingly rural as barbarian invasions continued and grew in intensity. The villa, a fortified country estate, became the basic unit of life. There, **coloni**, small

landholders who were original settlers, gave their services to the local magnate in return for economic assistance and protection. Many cities shrank to no more than tiny walled fortresses ruled by military commanders and bishops. The failure of the central imperial authority to maintain the roads and the constant danger from robber bands sharply curtailed trade and communications. These circumstances forced greater self-reliance and a more primitive style of life. The only institution providing a high degree of unity was the Christian church.

The new central position of the Christian church was closely connected with the political and cultural turmoil of the third and fourth centuries. During these centuries, many people turned to various kinds of religions, Christianity among them, as traditional political institutions collapsed. Christianity offered converts a rich and attractive philosophy of life. It possessed a god who had suffered, died, and was resurrected, mystical and sacred rites, a moral code, a strong sense of community, the spiritual equality of male and female, rich and poor, a close, personal relationship with the deity, and the promise of immortality. The Church had an efficient organization. And its doctrines of love and the brotherhood of all humankind under a loving and forgiving God were deeply attractive.

Christianity prospered during the third century, but it also encountered new dangers. About the middle of the century, a brief official persecution occurred. In 303, Diocletian launched the most serious persecution the Church had yet experienced. In both cases, persecution backfired and created new sympathy for Christianity.

In 312, Constantine became a champion of the new faith in hopes that the Christian God would bring victory to his military forces. After he won the important Battle of the Milvian Bridge, his support of the Christian cause was unfailing. Although he did not outlaw pagan rituals or abolish the cult of emperor worship, Constantine did go far beyond simply tolerating Christianity by granting various official privileges to the Church. With one exception, the successors of Constantine in the fourth century favored Christianity. In 394, the emperor Theodosius (r. 379–395) forbade the celebration of pagan cults and abolished the pagan religious calendar. At the death of Theodosius, Christianity had become the official religion of the Roman Empire.

The establishment of Christianity as the state religion did not put an end to the troubles of Christians and their church. Instead, it created new ones and complicated some that were old. First, the favored position of the Church attracted converts for the wrong reasons. Second, the problem of the relationship between Church and state arose, presenting the possibility that Christianity

Empress Theodora and her attendants. The union of political and spiritual authority in the person of the empress is shown by the depiction on Theodora's mantle of three magi carrying gifts to the Virgin and Jesus.   Early Christian Mosaic. San Vitale, Ravenna, Italy. Copyright Scala/Art Resource, NY

would become completely subordinate to the state, as religion had been in the classical world and in earlier civilizations.

The position and the influence of the Christian church became strong during the very decades when the political structures of the Roman Empire began to crumble under waves of barbarian invasions from northern and eastern Europe (see Map I–8). In 378, German tribes handily defeated the Roman armies led by the emperor Valens (r. 364–378) at the Battle of Adrianople. Thereafter, the Romans passively permitted settlement after settlement of barbarians within the very heart of the Western empire. In 410 the Visigoths sacked Rome itself.

In 476, the traditional date for the fall of the Roman Empire, the Western emperor Romulus Augustulus (r. 475–476) was deposed and replaced by the barbarian Odoacer (ca. 434–493), who ruled as king of the Romans. By the end of the fifth century, power in western Europe had passed decisively from the hands of the Roman emperors to those of barbarian chieftains. The Ostrogoths settled in Italy, the Visigoths in Spain, the Franks in northern Gaul and Spain, the Vandals in Africa and the Mediterranean, and the Angles and Saxons in England.

▼ Europe Enters the Middle Ages

Barbarians were now the Western masters, but they were masters who also were willing to learn from the people they had conquered. Although the barbarians were militarily superior, the Romans retained their cultural strength. This accommodation of cultures was assisted by the fact that the Visigoths, the Ostrogoths, and the Vandals had entered the West as people already partly Christianized by missionaries. All things considered, reconciliation and a gradual interpenetration of two strong cultures—a creative tension—marked the period of the Germanic invasions. The stronger culture was the Roman, and it became dominant in a later fusion.

The political collapse of western Europe, and with it the end of the political and economic unity between East and West that had characterized the Roman Empire, marked the beginning of the European Middle Ages. The early Middle Ages (476–1000) saw the birth of a distinctive western European culture. It was a period of recovery from the collapse of Roman civilization, a time of forced experimentation with new ideas and institutions. Western European culture, as we know it today, was born of a unique, inventive mix of surviving Graeco-Roman, new Germanic, and evolving Christian tradi-

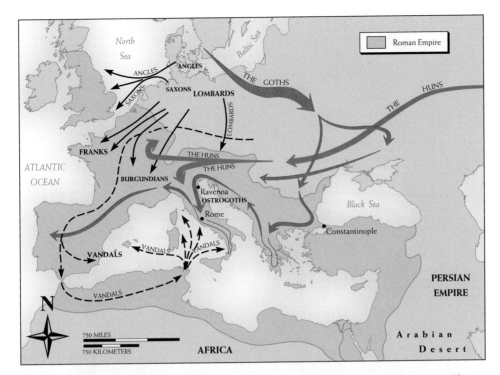

Map I–8   **BARBARIAN MIGRATIONS INTO THE WEST IN THE FOURTH AND FIFTH CENTURIES**   The forceful intrusion of Germanic and non-Germanic barbarians into the Roman Empire from the last quarter of the fourth century through the fifth century made for a constantly changing pattern of movement and relations. The map shows the major routes taken by the usually unwelcome newcomers and the areas most deeply affected by main groups.

tions. Experimentation was required because of the pressure of the invasions, the local political turmoil and economic stagnation, the replacement of paganism by Christianity, and the new problem posed to Europe from the Mediterranean world by the rise of a new, militant religion, Islam.

The Byzantine Empire

As western Europe succumbed to the Germanic invasions, imperial power shifted to the Byzantine Empire, that is, the eastern part of the Roman Empire, with its capital in Constantinople. Between 324 and 1453 the empire passed from an early period of expansion and splendor to a time of contraction and splintering, to final catastrophic defeat.

Between 324 and 632, the empire saw its greatest territorial expansion and its political and cultural golden age. Under Justinian (527–565); Roman law was collated and revised so that it could henceforth aid the growth of central government. Constantinople, with a population of 350,000, became the cultural crossroads of Asian and European civilization.

In the centuries after Justinian, however, Islamic armies progressively besieged the empire. Emperor Leo

III (717–741) successfully repulsed them, but at the same time he created a new problem with western Christians by forbidding images to exist in eastern churches. The ensuing controversy contributed to a major schism between western (Roman Catholic) and eastern (Byzantine) Christianity.

In 1071, the Seljuk Turks overran the eastern provinces of the empire, and western Christians sacked Constantinople in 1204. These events sowed the seeds of the empire's demise, which came finally in the fifteenth century at the hands of the Ottoman Turks, who captured Constantinople in 1453.

The Rise of Islam

Muhammad (570–632), the founder of Islam, received his call to be "the Prophet" at age forty. The name of his religion, Islam, means "submission" (to Allah). Its adherents, called Muslims, which means "submissive" or "surrendering," obey the will of Allah as revealed in the Qur'an, a series of revelations received by Muhammad over a period of time and compiled by his successors. Islam recognizes Jesus Christ as a prophet sent by God, but not one as great as Muhammad and not God's son as the Christians believe. Islam is uncompromisingly monotheistic.

١٢٨

Muslims are enjoined to live by the divine law, or *Shari'a*, and have a right to have disputes settled by an arbiter of the *Shari'a*. Here we see a husband complaining about his wife before the state-appointed judge, or *qadi*. The wife, backed up by two other women, points an accusing finger at the husband. In such cases, the first duty of the *qadi*, who should be a learned person of faith, is to try to effect a reconciliation before the husband divorces his wife, or the wife herself seeks a divorce. Cliche Bibliothèque Nationale de France, Paris

Among the things required of the faithful are prayer five times each day, generous almsgiving, and fasting during the daylight hours for one month each year. Another requirement is a pilgrimage to the holy city of Mecca, in what is now Saudi Arabia, at least once during one's lifetime. By its ability to forge a common Arab culture and its willingness to impose it by force, Islam became a spiritual force capable of uniting the Arab tribes in a true Arab empire.

By the middle of the eighth century, Muslims had conquered the southern and eastern Mediterranean coastline and occupied parts of Spain, which they controlled or strongly influenced until the fifteenth century (see Map I–9). In addition, their armies had pushed north and east through Mesopotamia and Persia and beyond.

Assaulted on both their eastern and their western frontiers, and everywhere challenged in the Mediterranean, Europeans developed a lasting fear and suspicion of Muslims. In 732, an army led by Charles Martel (d. 741), the ruler of the Franks, defeated a raiding party of Arabs at Poitiers. This victory ended the threat of Arab expansion into western Europe by way of Spain. Nonetheless, from the end of the seventh century to the middle of the eleventh century, the Mediterranean remained something of a Muslim lake. Although trade was not entirely cut off during these centuries, it was significantly reduced and was carried on in keen awareness of Muslim dominance.

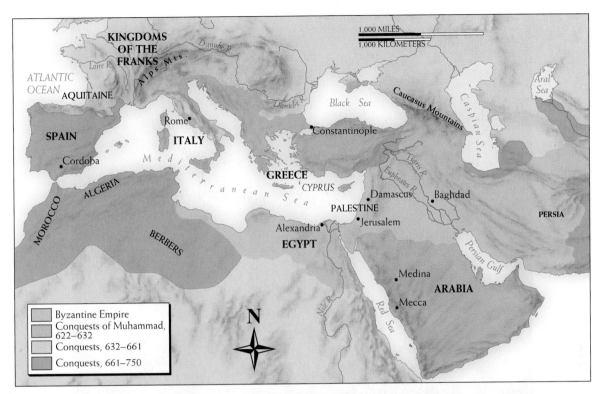

Map I–9 **MUSLIM CONQUESTS AND DOMINATION OF THE MEDITERRANEAN TO ABOUT 750 C.E.** The rapid spread of Islam (both as a religion and as a political-military power) is shown here. Within 125 years of Muhammad's rise, Muslims came to dominate Spain and all areas south and east of the Mediterranean.

New Importance of the Christian Church

When trade wanes, cities decline, and with them those cultural centers that enable a society to look and live beyond itself. The Arab invasions and domination of the Mediterranean during a crucial period of the early Middle Ages contributed to the conditions for the birth of western Europe as a distinctive cultural and social entity. As western shipping in the Mediterranean declined, so too did coastal urban centers. People who would otherwise have been engaged in trade-related work in the cities moved in large numbers to interior regions, where they worked on the farms of the great landholders. The domains of these landholders became the basic social and political units of society, and local barter economies sprang up within them.

The functions of the Christian church also became more important. Local bishops and cathedral chapters filled the vacuum of authority left by the removal of Roman governors. The local cathedral became the center of urban life, and the local bishop became the highest authority for those who remained in the cities. At this time, the Church alone possessed an effective hierarchical administration scattered throughout the old empire and staffed by the best-educated minds in Europe. The Church also strengthened itself through the institution of monasticism. Embracing the biblical

"counsels of perfection" (chastity, poverty, and obedience), the monastic life became the purest form of Christian religious practice in the Middle Ages. The ideal of monasticism as the model for a superior Christian life eventually evolved into a belief in the general superiority of the clergy and the mission of the Church over the laity and the state.

In addition to this distinctly moral and spiritual claim to superiority, the bishops of Rome made a separate claim to superiority within the Church; they had always opposed intervention by the secular state in Church matters. As early as the fifth and sixth centuries, they took advantage of imperial weakness and distraction to develop the doctrine of "papal primacy" for their own defense. This teaching in time raised the Roman pontiff to an unassailable supremacy within the Church when it came to defining orthodox Church doctrine and practice. It also put the pope in a position to make important secular claims that caused repeated conflicts between Church and state in the Middle Ages.

Charlemagne

The chief political characteristic of the Middle Ages was the absence of central political authority. The most persistent problem of medieval political history was the

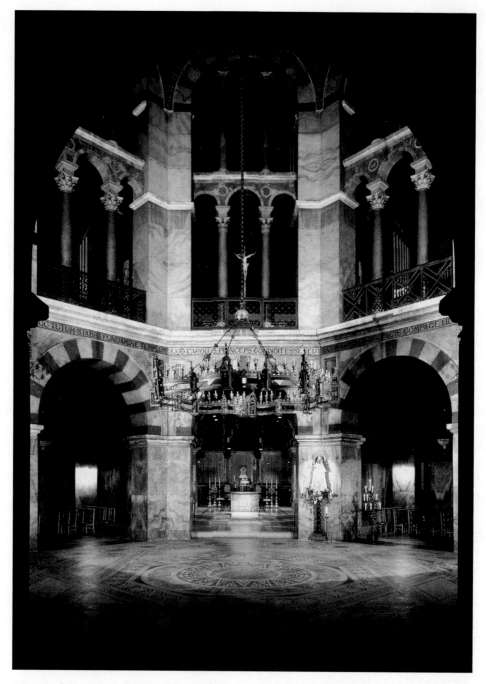

Interior of the Palace Chapel of Charlemagne, Aachen.   French Government Tourist Office

competing claims of the "one" and the "many"—on one hand, the king, who struggled for a centralized government in a particular area and transregional loyalty from his subjects, and on the other, powerful local magnates who strove to preserve their regional autonomy and purely local customs.

Between the sixth and eleventh centuries, only one figure achieved a significant degree of centralized political authority over a substantial region of Europe. This was the Frankish king Charlemagne (r. 768–814), whose kingdom loosely embraced modern France, Bel-

gium, Holland, Switzerland, almost the whole of western Germany, much of Italy, a portion of Spain, and the island of Corsica (see Map I–10). Charlemagne carefully developed strong political ties with local nobles and with the Church, which regarded him as its protector. On Christmas Day, 800, Pope Leo III (r. 795–816) crowned Charlemagne emperor. With this papal act there came into being what would come to be known in the tenth century as the Holy Roman Empire, a revival, based in Germany, of the old Roman Empire in the West.

Map I–10 **THE EMPIRE OF CHARLEMAGNE TO 814** Building on the successes of his predecessors, Charlemagne greatly increased the Frankish domains. Such traditional enemies as the Saxons and the Lombards fell under his sway.

Charlemagne governed his kingdom through counts, of whom there were perhaps as many as 250. They were strategically located within the administrative districts into which the kingdom was divided. The counts often were local magnates who already possessed the arms and the self-interest to enforce the rule of a generous king. These counts served Charlemagne well, but they were never completely loyal and he never wholly controlled their political behavior.

Charlemagne accumulated great wealth in the form of loot and land from conquered tribes. He used a large part of this booty to attract Europe's best scholars to his capital at Aachen (Aix-la-Chapelle). He intended them to use their learning in the classics and Christian writings to upgrade the administrative skills of the clerics and officials who staffed the royal bureaucracy. Through these efforts, a modest rebirth of antiquity occurred in the palace school as scholars collected, studied, and preserved ancient manuscripts.

Charlemagne's empire and the cultural revival it nurtured lasted for a relatively short time. After the death of his son and successor, Louis the Pious (r. 814–840), the kingdom was divided into three equal parts by the Treaty of Verdun (843): a middle section (Lotharingia, embracing roughly modern Holland, Belgium, Switzerland, Alsace-Lorraine, and Italy); a western part (roughly modern France); and an eastern part (roughly modern Germany). Long-term loyalty to a single monarch by the nobles of various regions proved unattainable. Potential monarchs fought each other, and nobles looked out for their own interests. The papacy lost prestige as it cast its lot first with one monarch and then with another in an effort to preserve a major political role for itself.

On top of all these troubles, the late ninth and tenth centuries saw successive waves of attacks by the Vikings from Scandinavia, the Magyars from the eastern European plains, and the Muslims in the south. Local populations became more dependent than ever before on local strongmen to protect them. This brute fact of life provided the essential precondition for the maturation of feudal society.

Feudal and Manorial Society

The early Middle Ages were a time of fragmentation and decentralization, with the weaker seeking the protection of the stronger. The term **feudal society** refers to the social, political, military, and economic system that emerged in response to these conditions. A feudal society is one in which a regional prince or a local lord is dominant and the highest virtues are those of mutual trust and fidelity. In a feudal society what people most need is the firm assurance that others can be depended on in time of dire need.

The two chief institutions of feudal society were vassalage and the fief. *Vassalage* involved "fealty" to a lord. To swear fealty was to promise to refrain from any action that might in any way threaten the lord's well-being and to perform for him on his request personal services, the most important of which was military aid. In return, the lord agreed to protect the vassal from physical harm and to stand as his advocate in public court. After fealty was sworn, the lord provided for the vassal's physical maintenance by the bestowal of a fief. The **fief** was the physical or material wherewithal to meet the vassal's military and other obligations. It could take the form of liquid wealth or, more commonly, a grant of real property. Feudalism could lead to a very confused set of relationships, because often one person was the vassal of more than one lord. And as the centuries passed, personal loyalty and service became quite secondary to the acquisition of property.

The social and economic equivalents of the dependency relationships of feudalism on local levels were the manor and serfdom. It is important to realize, however, that the manorial system existed in many places where feudalism never became well developed. Village farms, normally owned by a local landlord, were called *manors*. Here peasants labored as farmers under a lord,

---

MAJOR POLITICAL AND RELIGIOUS DEVELOPMENTS OF THE EARLY MIDDLE AGES

313	Emperor Constantine issues the *Edict of Milan*
325	Council of Nicaea defines Christian doctrine
410	Rome invaded by Visigoths under Alaric
413–426	Saint Augustine writes *City of God*
451	Council of Chalcedon further defines Christian doctrine
451–453	Europe invaded by the Huns under Attila
476	Barbarian Odoacer deposes Western emperor and rules as king of the Romans
489–493	Theodoric establishes kingdom of Ostrogoths in Italy
529	Saint Benedict founds monastery at Monte Cassino
533	Justinian codifies Roman law
622	Muhammad's flight from Mecca (*Hegira*)
732	Charles Martel defeats Muslims at Poitiers
754	Pope Stephen II and Pepin III ally

---

who gave them small plots of land and tenements in exchange for their services and a portion of their crops. Some of the peasants were free and owned certain lands themselves. They had specific legal rights even if they surrendered their land and services to a landlord in exchange for his support and protection. On the other hand, peasants who entered the service of a lord without any real property to bargain with ended up as unfree **serfs**. All serfs owed labor of several days a week to their lords and were also subject to so-called dues in kind: firewood for cutting the lord's wood, sheep for grazing their sheep on the lord's land, and the like. The discontent of many serfs is witnessed by the high number of recorded escapes.

▼ Church and State in the High Middle Ages

What are known as the High Middle Ages (ca. 1000–1300) mark a period of political expansion and consolidation and of intellectual flowering that followed Europe's deep difficulties during the ninth and tenth centuries. This period saw the borders of western Europe secured against foreign invaders. These centuries also saw the emergence of "national" monarchies in France, England, and Germany. Parliaments and popular assemblies, representing the interests of the landed nobility, the clergy, and townspeople, appeared at the same time to secure local rights and cus-

Benedictine monks at choir. The reform movement that began at the Benedictine monastery at Cluny in northern France in the tenth century spread throughout the Church and was ultimately responsible for the reassertion of papal authority. Courtesy of the Trustees of the British Library

toms against the claims of the developing monarchies. During these centuries, there was also a great revival of trade and commerce, the growth of towns, and the emergence of a "new rich" merchant class, the ancestors of modern capitalists.

The High Middle Ages were also the time when the Western church, now centered on the pope in Rome, established itself as an authority independent of monarchical secular government. This occurred during the Investiture Struggle of the late eleventh and the twelfth centuries. The fortunes of both the empire and the papacy had begun to revive after the dark period of the late ninth and early tenth centuries. The Ottonians, successors to the Franks in Germany, now carried the title of Holy Roman Emperor, and they produced some able leaders.

About the same time, the Church began to undergo a series of internal reforms sponsored by clerics influenced by the monastery of Cluny (founded 910) in France. The Cluny reformers demanded a higher moral standard from the clergy and asserted a sharp separation of Church and state. Previously, emperors and other political rulers often had controlled the appointment of bishops and other high Church officials.

Under Pope Gregory VII (r. 1073–1085), the papacy declared its independence from such lay control of Church offices. Henceforth, bishops were to be installed in their offices by high ecclesiastical authority as empowered by the pope and none other. For almost fifty years controversy raged, until the Concordat of Worms in 1122 provided that the pope or his representative would invest all bishops with the spiritual signs of their office and the emperor or his representative would invest them only with lands. Thereafter, the clergy were more independent of the state than ever before, and the papacy began to assert itself as an independent political power.

The Division of Christendom

Also in this period Christendom became firmly divided into Eastern and Western churches, the result of a long-developing conflict over Church practice and doctrine rooted in the early Middle Ages. From the start, there had been a difference in language (Greek in the East, Latin in the West) and culture. The Eastern patriarchs (rulers of the Church) also had a strong mystical orientation to the next world that caused them to submit more passively than Western popes to secular control of the Church (Caesaro-papism, "Caesar acting as pope"). Contrary to the evolving Western tradition of universal clerical celibacy, the Eastern church permitted the marriage of parish priests, while strictly forbidding bishops to marry. The Eastern church used leavened bread in the Eucharist, contrary to the Western custom of using unleavened bread. The Eastern church objected to the Western church's description of the Holy Spirit as proceeding from the Son as well as from the Father and opposed the Western church's use of icons and images in worship.

Beyond these issues was a major conflict over Church authority. The Eastern church put more stress on the authority of the Bible and of the ecumenical councils of the Church than on papal or Roman primacy. The Roman popes claimed a special primacy of authority on the basis of the apostle Peter's commission from Jesus in Matthew 16:18 ("Thou art Peter, and upon this rock I will build my church"). These claims were completely unacceptable to the East, where the independence and autonomy of national churches was preferred. This basic issue of authority in matters of faith lay behind the mutual excommunication of Pope Nicholas I and Patriarch Photius in the ninth century and that of Pope Leo IX and Patriarch Michael Cerularius in 1054.

The Rise of Towns

Western Europe had little international commerce and even less urban culture during the centuries following the collapse of the Roman Empire. By comparison with previous centuries, western Europe had become an isolated, agricultural society. This is one reason some historians refer to the centuries between 500 and 1000 as a comparative "dark age." By the late tenth century, thanks to improved climate, agricultural production, and the end of Viking invasions, the population had begun to grow rapidly. The increased numbers of people made possible the rebirth of the old Roman towns and the creation of many new ones. The great seaports of Italy had weathered the early Middle Ages better than any other western cities, maintaining vibrant urban cultures. Even in the darkest times, Venice, Pisa, and Genoa traded with Constantinople and the port cities of Palestine, Syria, and Egypt. The Venetians were especially successful merchants throughout the eastern world; their commercial success approached domination there after the First Crusade (1095) opened the Mediterranean to still greater western shipping.

The term **bourgeois**, or *burgher*, first appeared in the eleventh century as a negative description of the newly powerful townspeople. In the popular imagination, they were a new addition to the traditional social ranks of knight (or noble), cleric, and serf. Initially, the term designated the merchant groups who created the *bourgs*, or new market towns, as bases for their commercial operations in and around the old Roman towns. Because the burghers' sole business was trade and banking, the clergy condemned their work as usurious and immoral. The nobility also looked askance at their new wealth and mobility. Because the merchants departed from traditional ways of making money, that is, by owning and cultivating land, they seemed to pose a threat to political and social order.

The common people, by contrast, admired the merchants. They saw their commercial success as providing new economic opportunity for themselves. The new towns became magnets for ambitious and skilled peasants, who both gained their freedom from serfdom there and found new vocations. Lucky peasants experienced a heretofore unknown social mobility, and the diligent and successful among them even became gentlemen.

The merchants for their part resented the laws and customs of traditional society, which gave the nobility and the clergy special privileges. By allowing the nobility and the clergy to subject all others to their notions of morality and work, traditional law and custom impeded the new course of urban life and threatened its future development. Wherever merchants settled, they lobbied for the freedom necessary to pursue successful commerce. In doing so, they had the broad support of townspeople. They opposed tolls, tariffs, and other petty regulations that restricted trade and dampened commercial activity.

THE CAROLINGIAN MANOR

■■

A capitulary from the reign of Charlemagne known as "De Villis" itemizes what the king received from his royal manors or village estates. It is a testimony both to Carolingian administrative ability and domination over the countryside.

What gave the lord the right to absolutely everything? (Has anything been overlooked?) How did the stewards and workers share in the manorial life? Was the arrangment a good deal for them as well as for the lord?

That each steward shall make an annual statement of all our income: an account of our lands cultivated by the oxen which our ploughmen drive and of our lands which the tenants of farms ought to plough; an account of the pigs, of the rents, of the obligations and fines; of the game taken in our forests without our permission; of the various compositions; of the mills, of the forest, of the fields, of the bridges, and ships: of the free-men and the hundreds who are under obligations to our treasury; of markets, vineyards, and those who owe wine to us; of the hay, fire-wood, torches, planks, and other kinds of lumber; of the wastelands; of the vegetables, millet, panic; of the wool, flax, and hemp; of the fruits of the trees, of the nut trees, larger and smaller; of the grafted trees of all kinds; of the gardens; of the turnips; of the fishponds; of the hides, skins, and horns; of the honey, wax; of the fat, tallow and soap; of the mulberry wine, cooked wine, mead, vinegar; beer, wine new and old; of the new grain and the old; of the hens and eggs; of the geese; the number of fishermen, smiths [workers in metal], swordmakers, and shoemakers; of the bins and boxes; of the turners and saddlers; of the forges and mines, that is iron and other mines; of the lead mines; of the tributaries; of the colts and fillies; they shall make all these known to us, set forth separately and in order, at Christmas, in order that we may know what and how much of each thing we have.

In each of our estates our stewards are to have as many cow-houses, piggeries, sheep-folds, stables for goats, as possible, and they ought never to be without these.

They must provide with the greatest care that whatever is prepared or made with the hands, that is, lard, smoked meat, salt meat, partially salted meat, wine, vinegar, mulberry wine, cooked wine, garns, mustard, cheese, butter, malt beer, mead, honey, wax, flour, all should be prepared and made with the greatest cleanliness.

That each steward on each of our domains shall always have, for the sake of ornament, swans, peacocks, pheasants, ducks, pigeons, partridges, turtle-doves.

That in each of our estates, the chambers shall be provided with counterpanes, cushions, pillows, bed-clothes, coverings for the tables and benches; vessels of brass, lead, iron and wood; andirons, chains, pothooks, adzes, axes, augers, cutlasses and all other kinds of tools, so that it shall never be necessary to go elsewhere for them, or to borrow them. And the weapons, which are carried against the enemy, shall be well cared for, so as to keep them in good condition.

For our women's work they are to give at the proper time, as has been ordered, the materials, that is the linen, wool, woad, vermilion, madder, wool-combs, teasels, soap grease, vessels and the other objects which are necessary.

Of the food-products other than meat, two-thirds shall be sent each year for our own use, that is of the vegetables, fish, cheese, butter, honey, mustard, vinegar, millet, panic, dried and green herbs, radishes, and in addition of the wax, soap and other small products.

That each steward shall have in his district good workmen, namely, blacksmiths, goldsmiths, silversmiths, shoemakers, turners, carpenters, sword-makers, fishermen, foilers, soapmakers, men who know how to make beer cider, berry, and all the other kinds of beverages, bakers to make pastry for our table, net-makers who know how to make nets for hunting, fishing and fowling, and the other who are too numerous to be designated.

Translations and Reprints from the Original Sources of European History, Vol. 3 (Philadelphia: Department of History, University of Pennsylvania, 1909), pp. 2–4.

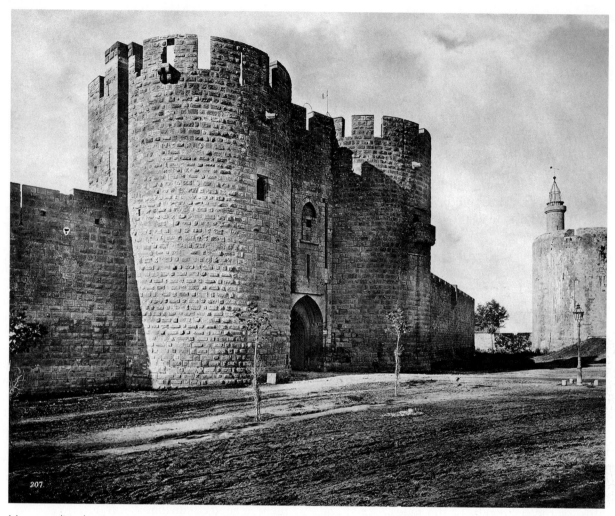

Many medieval towns were entirely enclosed by walls for protection. Here is the walled town of Aigues-Mortes in southern France. French Government Tourist Office

Whether they were wealthy merchants or struggling artisans, townspeople wanted a government in which traders and craftsmen determined policy. Policy made by secular and ecclesiastical overlords was calculated to control and exploit the towns rather than nurture and expand commerce. Such desire brought towns into conflict with the norms of static agricultural society. Merchant guilds and protective associations sprang up in the eleventh century, followed in the twelfth by guilds of craftsmen (drapers, haberdashers, furriers, hosiers, goldsmiths, and so on). These organizations worked to advance the business interest of both merchants and craftsmen as well as to enhance the personal well-being of their members.

During the High and later Middle Ages, towns also formed independent communes and allied with kings against the landed nobility. In this way, townspeople became a force in the breakup of traditional feudal society.

The Crusades

If an index of popular piety and support for the pope in the High Middle Ages is needed, the Crusades amply provide it (see Map I–11). In 1095, Pope Urban II proclaimed the First Crusade at the Council of Clermont in France. Participants in this Crusade to liberate the Holy Land from Muslim control were promised a plenary indulgence should they die in battle, that is, a complete remission of the penance required of them for their mortal sins and hence release from suffering for these sins in purgatory. To rescue Jerusalem, which had been in non-Christian hands since the seventh century, three great armies—tens of thousands of crusaders, gathered from France, Germany, and Italy—converged on the Middle East. Jerusalem fell to them on July 15, 1099. By the middle of the next century, however, Jerusalem had again fallen into Arab hands. Other Crusades attempted to duplicate the feat of the first but with little success.

Frederick I Barbarossa (r. 1152–1190) established the Hohenstaufen dynasty, which succeeded the Ottonians. He set out to reassert the power of the Holy Roman emperors after the setbacks suffered during the investiture controversy, a long conflict with the Church over the right of rulers to appoint high clergy to their offices. Frederick's efforts, however, led only to new and even fiercer disputes between the emperor and the pope.

In the thirteenth century, that conflict became a bitter, deadly feud. Popes excommunicated Emperor Frederick II (r. 1215–1250) no fewer than four times, and the emperor's reign ended in humiliation and defeat at the hands of the German princes. Thereafter, Germany was a politically primitive land by comparison with other major European countries. The victorious papacy now launched itself into European politics on a grand scale, particularly during the reign of Pope Innocent IV (r. 1243–1254). As a consequence, the papacy became vulnerable to new criticism from religious reformers and royal apologists alike, who did not believe such political self-aggrandizement was a proper mission for the Church.

The Emerging Contours of Europe By about 1300, then, the political contours of Europe as they would exist for the next two centuries were relatively clear. England and France had reasonably strong and stable central monarchies that competed economically and politically. The Holy Roman emperors presided rather than ruled over the other German princes, leaving the empire disunited. The papacy made and to some extent still enforced its own claims to what amounted to monarchical power. On the Italian peninsula, independent city-states composed of central urban areas and extensive surrounding countryside were the chief political units. There was an Arab presence on the Iberian Peninsula and strong Arab influence over Mediterranean trade. In the eastern Mediterranean, the Byzantine Empire remained intact. Europe had not experienced such widespread political stability since the demise of central Roman authority in the fourth century.

Universities and Scholasticism

During the two centuries before 1300, an important intellectual flowering had occurred that complemented the achievements in trade, urbanization, and politics. Thanks largely to Spanish Muslim scholars, the logical works of Aristotle, the writings of Euclid and Ptolemy, the basic works of Greek physicians and Arab mathematicians, and the larger texts of Roman law became available to Western scholars in the early twelfth century. Muslim scholars preserved these works, translated portions of the Greek tracts into Latin, and wrote extensive, thought-provoking commentaries on the ancient texts. This renaissance of ancient knowledge, in turn, led to the rise of universities in Europe.

The first important Western university was founded at Bologna in 1158 and specialized in law. The University of Paris, which specialized in theology, followed in 1200. Oxford, Cambridge, and, much later, Heidelberg were among Paris's imitators. All these universities required a foundation in the liberal arts for further study in the higher sciences of medicine, theology, and law. The arts program consisted of the *trivium* (grammar, rhetoric, and logic) and the *quadrivium* (arithmetic, geometry, astronomy, and music).

By the late twelfth century, enough of the works of Aristotle had penetrated Europe through Arab sources to influence European thought and education deeply. Logic and dialectic (the art of logical investigation), tools for bringing discipline to knowledge and thought, rapidly triumphed in importance over the other liberal arts. Within the Scholastic program of study, the student read the traditional authorities in his field, formed short summaries of their teaching, elaborated arguments pro and con, and then drew his own modest conclusions.

Scholasticism had its critics even in the twelfth century. Some, anticipating the later Renaissance Humanists, believed Scholastics emphasized logic to the detriment of eloquence and relevance. Other critics feared that as theologians began to adopt the logic and metaphysics of Aristotle, a threat would arise to biblical and traditional theological authority with dire consequences for the Church.

In Perspective

The roots of Western civilization may be found in the experience and culture of the Greeks. Yet Greek civilization itself was richly nourished by older, magnificent civilizations to the south and east, especially in Mesopotamia and Egypt. In the valley of the Tigris and Euphrates rivers (Mesopotamia), and soon after in the valley of the Nile in Egypt, human beings moved from a life in agricultural villages, using tools of wood, bone, shell, and stone, into a much richer and more varied social organization that we call civilization.

Greek civilization arose after the destruction of the Bronze Age cultures on Crete and the Greek mainland before 1000 B.C.E. It took a turn sharply different from its predecessors in Egypt and western Asia. It was based on the independent existence of hundreds of city-states,

In this engraving, a teacher at the University of Paris leads fellow scholars in a discussion. As shown here, all of the students wore the scholar's cap and gown.   CORBIS

called *poleis*, which retained their autonomy for hundreds of years before being incorporated into larger units. These cities attained a degree of self-government, broad political participation, and individual freedom never achieved before that time. They also introduced a new way of thinking that looked on the world as the product of natural forces to be understood by the sense and human reason, unaided by reference to supernatural forces. The result was the invention of science and philosophy as we know them.

Hellenistic culture was a mixture of Greek elements combined with some elements from the native peoples. It was without the particularism of the Hel-

lenic world, and anyone speaking Greek could move comfortably from city to city and find a familiar and common culture. This was the world that succumbed to the Roman conquest in the last two centuries before the Christian era.

The Romans were tough farmers who began as inhabitants of a small town on the Tiber River in west-central Italy. After deposing their king in about 500 B.C.E., they invented a republican constitution and a code of law that provided a solid foundation for a stable and effective political order. From 264 until well into the first century B.C.E., the Romans extended their conquests overseas until they had conquered the

STUDENT LIFE AT THE UNIVERSITY OF PARIS

As the following account by Jacques de Vitry makes clear, not all students at the University of Paris in the thirteenth century were there to gain knowledge. Students fought constantly and subjected each other to ethnic insults and slurs.

Why were students from different lands so prejudiced against one another? Does the rivalry of faculty members appear to have been as intense as that among students? What are the student criticisms of the faculty? Do they sound credible?

Almost all the students at Paris, foreigners and natives, did absolutely nothing except learn or hear something new. Some studied merely to acquire knowledge, which is curiosity; others to acquire fame, which is vanity; others still for the sake of gain, which is cupidity and the vice of simony. Very few studied for their own edification, or that of others. They wrangled and disputed not merely about the various sects or about some discussions; but the differences between the countries also caused dissensions, hatreds and virulent animosities among them, and they impudently uttered all kinds of affronts and insults against one another.

They affirmed that the English were drunkards and had tails; the sons of France proud, effeminate and carefully adorned like women. They said that the Germans were furious and obscene at their feasts; the Normans, vain and boastful; the Poitevins, traitors and always adventurers. The Burgundians they considered vulgar and stupid. The Bretons were reputed to be fickle and changeable, and were often reproached for the death of Arthur. The Lombards were called avaricious, vicious and cowardly; the Romans, seditious, turbulent and slanderous; the Sicilians, tyrannical and cruel; the inhabitants of Brabant, men of blood, incendiaries, brigands and ravishers; the Flemish, fickle, prodigal, gluttonous, yielding as butter, and slothful. After such insults from words they often came to blows.

I will not speak of those logicians [professors of logic and dialectic] before whose eyes flitted constantly "the lice of Egypt," that is to say, all the sophistical subtleties, so that no one could comprehend their eloquent discourses in which, as says Isaiah, "there is no wisdom." As to the doctors of theology, "seated in Moses' seat," they were swollen with learning, but their charity was not edifying. Teaching and not practicing, they have "become as sounding brass or a tinkling cymbal," or like a canal of stone, always dry, which ought to carry water to "the bed of spices." They not only hated one another, but by their flatteries they enticed away the students of others; each one seeking his own glory, but caring not a whit about the welfare of souls.

Translations and Reprints from the Original Sources of European History, Vol. 2 (Philadelphia: Department of History, University of Pennsylvania, 1902), pp. 19–20.

Carthaginians in the west and defeated all the great Hellenistic powers, dominating the shores of the Mediterranean and lands well beyond.

The Romans were fine engineers and road builders, but in art, literature, and philosophy they had barely made a start when they came into contact with the advanced Greek civilization of the Hellenistic world. In these areas, the Romans became eager students, and as the Roman poet Horace put it, "Captive Greece took Rome captive."

By the fifth century C.E., the Roman Empire in the West had collapsed and was shared among different Germanic tribes, although the eastern portion of the empire, with its capital at Constantinople, survived for a thousand years more. Before Rome's fall, the empire had abandoned paganism and had adopted Christianity as its official religion. The heritage that the ancient world passed on to its medieval successor in western Europe was a combination of cultural traditions including those coming from Egypt,

Mesopotamia, Israel, Greece, Rome, and the German tribes that destroyed the Roman Empire.

In western Europe, the centuries between 476 and 1300 saw both the decline of European classical civilization and the birth of a new European civilization. Beginning in the fifth century, barbarian invasions separated western Europe culturally from its classical past. Although some important works and concepts survived from antiquity, and the Christian church preserved major features of Roman government, the West would be recovering its classical heritage for centuries in "renaissances" that stretched into the sixteenth century. Out of the mixture of barbarian and surviving (or recovered) classical culture, a distinct Western culture was born. With the help of the Christian church, the Franks, under Charlemagne, created a new imperial tradition and shaped basic Western political and social institutions for centuries to come.

The Middle Ages also saw the lasting division of Christendom into Eastern and Western branches. As two different Christian churches evolved, bitter conflict ensued between popes and patriarchs. Constantinople far exceeded any city in the West in population and culture. Serving as both a buffer against Persian, Arab, and Turkish invasions of the West and as a major repository of classical learning and science for Western scholars, the Byzantine Empire did much to make the birth of western Europe possible. Another cultural and religious rival of the West, Islam, also saw its golden age during these same centuries. Like the Byzantine world, the Muslim world also proved a major conduit of ancient scholarship into the West, especially through Muslim Spain. Despite examples of coexistence and even friendship, however, Western and Arabic cultures were too different, their peoples too estranged and suspicious of one another, to coexist without hostility.

After 1000, the growth of Mediterranean trade revived old cities and occasioned the creation of new ones. The Crusades aided and abetted this development. One invaluable result of the new wealth of towns was a patronage of education and culture unseen since Roman times. Western Europe's first universities appeared in the eleventh century. Their numbers steadily expanded over the next four centuries: twenty universities by 1300 and seventy by 1500. Not only did Scholasticism flourish, but a new literature, art, and architecture developed as well, reflecting both a new human vitality and the reshaping of society and politics. For all this growth, western Europeans had no one to thank as much as the new class of merchants, whose greed, daring, and ambition had made it all possible.

REVIEW QUESTIONS

1. How was life during the Paleolithic Age different from that in the Neolithic Age? Present the broad outlines of the history of the earliest civilizations in Mesopotamia and Egypt. What was the significance of Hebrew monotheism for the future of Western civilization?

2. Define the concept of the *polis*. Compare the basic political, social, and economic institutions of Athens and Sparta around 500 B.C.E. Why did Sparta develop its unique form of government?

3. Discuss Rome's expansion to 265 B.C.E. What were some of the problems that plagued the republic in the last century? To what extent was the republic destroyed by ambitious generals who loved power more than Rome itself?

4. What solutions did Augustus provide for the problems that had plagued the Roman republic? How was the Roman Empire organized, and why did it function smoothly?

5. Trace the history of Christianity to the coronation of Charlemagne in 800. What distinctive features characterized the early Church? What role did the Church play in the world after the fall of the western Roman Empire?

6. What were some of the conditions that gave rise to feudal society? What are the essential characteristics of feudal society?

7. Trace the development of national monarchies in England and France in the High Middle Ages. How did the experience of those two countries differ from that of the Holy Roman Empire in the same period?

SUGGESTED READINGS

E. Amt, ed., *Women's Lives in Medieval Europe: A Sourcebook* (1993). Outstanding collection of sources.

A. Andrewes, *The Greeks* (1967). A thoughtful general survey.

E. Badian, *Roman Imperialism in the Late Republic*, 2nd ed. (1968).

G. Barraclough, *The Medieval Papacy* (1968). Brief, comprehensive, with pictures.

A. H. Bernstein, *Tiberius Sempronius Gracchus: Tradition and Apostasy* (1978). A new interpretation of Tiberius's place in Roman politics.

P. Brown, *Augustine of Hippo* (1967). Late antiquity seen through the biography of its greatest Christian thinker.

P. Brown, *The World of Late Antiquity, A.D. 150–750* (1971). A brilliant and readable essay.

Virginia Burrus, ed., *A Peoples' History of Christianity*, II (2005). Substantial and accessible.

G. Cawkwell, *Philip of Macedon* (1978). A keen analysis of an important career.

R. H. C. Davis, *A History of Medieval Europe: From Constantine to St. Louis* (1972). Unsurpassed in clarity.

E. R. Dodds, *The Greeks and the Irrational* (1955). An excellent account of the role of the supernatural in Greek life and thought.

R. Drews, *The Coming of the Greeks* (1988). A fine study of the arrival of the Greeks as part of the movement of Indo-European peoples.

G. Duby, *The Three Orders: Feudal Society Imagined*, trans. by A. Goldhammer (1981). Large, comprehensive, authoritative.

R. M. Errington, *The Dawn of Empire: Rome's Rise to Power* (1972). An account of Rome's conquest of the Mediterranean.

R. Fawtier, *The Capetian Kings of France*, trans. by L. Butler and R. J. Adam (1972). Detailed standard account.

A. Ferrill, *Caligula: Emperor of Rome* (1991). A biography of the monstrous young emperor.

H. Fichtenau, *The Carolingian Empire: The Age of Charlemagne*, trans. by P. Munz (1964). Strong on political history.

J. V. A. Fine, *The Early Medieval Balkans: Sixth to Twelfth Centuries* (1983). Insight into ethnic divisions.

M. I. Finley, *World of Odysseus*, rev. ed. (1965). A fascinating attempt to reconstruct Homeric society.

W. G. Forrest, *The Emergence of Greek Democracy* (1966). A lively interpretation of Greek social and political developments in the archaic period.

J. R. L. Fox, *Alexander the Great* (1973). An imaginative account that does more justice to the Persian side of the problem than is usual.

H. Frankfort et al., *Before Philosophy* (1949). A brilliant examination of the mind of ancient man from the Stone Age to the Greeks.

M. Grant, *The Fall of the Roman Empire* (1990). A lively, well-written account.

P. Green, *Xerxes at Salamis* (1970). A lively and stimulating history of the Persian wars.

E. S. Gruen, *The Last Generation of the Roman Republic* (1973). An interesting but controversial interpretation of the fall of the republic.

W. W. Hallo and W. K. Simpson, *The Ancient Near East: A History* (1971). A fine survey of Egyptian and Mesopotamian history.

V. D. Hanson, *The Western Way of War* (1989). A brilliant and lively discussion of the rise and character of the hoplite phalanx and its influence on Greek society.

C. H. Haskins, *The Rise of the Universities* (1972). A minor classic.

D. Herlihy, *Medieval Households* (1985). Survey of antiquity and the Middle Ages.

A. Hourani, *A History of the Arab People* (1991). Readable, comprehensive overview.

S. Isager and J. E. Skydsgaard, *Ancient Greek Agriculture. An Introduction* (1993). A new study of a fundamental subject.

D. Kagan, ed., *The End of the Roman Empire: Decline or Transformation?* 3rd ed. (1992). A collection of essays discussing the problem of the decline and fall of the Roman Empire.

D. Kagan, *The Great Dialogue: A History of Greek Political Thought from Homer to Polybius* (1965). A discussion of the relationship between the Greek historical experience and political theory.

D. Kagan, *The Outbreak of the Peloponnesian War* (1969). A study of the period from the foundation of the Delian League to the coming of the Peloponnesian War that argues that the war could have been avoided.

H. D. F. Kitto, *The Greeks* (1951). A personal and illuminating interpretation of Greek culture.

D. Knowles, *Christian Monasticism* (1969). Sweeping survey with helpful photographs.

D. Krueger, ed. *Byzantine Christianity* (2006).

J. Leclercq, *The Love of Learning and the Desire for God: A Study of Monastic Culture*, trans. by C. Misrahi (1962). Lucid, delightful, absorbing account of the ideals of monks.

K. Leyser, *Medieval Germany and Its Neighbors, 900–1250* (1982). Basic and authoritative.

R. Macmullen, *Soldier and Civilian in the Later Roman Empire* (1963). A study of the growing militarization of the whole society of the late empire.

R. Macmullen, *Corruption and the Decline of Rome* (1988). A study that examines the importance of changes in ethical ideas and behavior.

E. Mâle, *The Gothic Image: Religious Art in France in the Thirteenth Century* (1913). An enduring classic.

C. Mango, *Byzantium: The Empire of New Rome* (1982). Perhaps the most readable account.

P. B. Manville, *The Origins of Citizenship in Ancient Athens* (1990). An examination of the origins of the concept of citizenship in the time of Solon of Athens.

R. W. Mathison, *Roman Aristocrats in Barbarian Gaul: Strategies for Survival* (1993). An unusual slant on the late empire.

R. Meiggs, *The Athenian Empire* (1972). A fine study of the rise and fall of the empire, making excellent use of inscriptions.

J. B. Morrall, *Political Thought in Medieval Times* (1962). Readable and illuminating account.

P. Munz, *The Age of Charlemagne* (1971). Penetrating social history.

J. Oates, *Babylon*, rev. ed. (1986). An introduction to the history and archaeology of Babylonia revised to make use of newly discovered evidence.

H. M. Orlinsky, *Ancient Israel* (1960). Chiefly a political survey.

H. Pirenne, *Medieval Cities: Their Origins and the Revival of Trade*, trans. by F. D. Halsey (1970). A minor classic.

J. J. Pollitt, *Art and Experience in Classical Greece* (1972). A brilliant interpretation of the place of art in fifth-century Greece.

J. N. Postgate, *Early Mesopotamia* (1992). An excellent study of Mesopotamian economy and society from the earliest times to about 1500 B.C.E., helpfully illustrated with drawings, pictures, and translated documents.

S. Reynolds, *Kingdoms and Communities in Western Europe, 900–1300* (1984). For the medieval origins of Western political and cultural traditions.

V. Rudich, *Political Dissidence Under Nero, The Price of Dissimulation* (1993). A brilliant exposition of the lives and thoughts of political dissidents in the early empire.

S. Runciman, *Byzantine Civilization* (1970). Succinct, comprehensive account by a master.

H. H. Scullard, *A History of the Roman World from 753 to 146 B.C.*, 3rd ed. (1961). An unusually fine narrative history with useful critical notes.

J. Riley-Smith, *The Crusades: A Short History* (1987). Up-to-date, lucid, and readable.

R. W. Southern, *The Making of the Middle Ages* (1973). Originally published in 1953, but still a fresh account by an imaginative historian.

C. Stephenson, *Medieval Feudalism* (1969). Excellent short introduction.

B. Stock, *The Implications of Literacy* (1983). How the ability to read changed medieval society.

R. Syme, *The Roman Revolution* (1960). A brilliant study of Augustus, his supporters, and their rise to power.

W. W. Tarn and G. T. Griffith, *Hellenistic Civilization* (1961). A survey of Hellenistic history and culture.

L. R. Taylor, *Party Politics in the Age of Caesar* (1949). A fascinating analysis of Roman political theory.

B. Tierney, *The Crisis of Church and State 1050–1300* (1964). Very useful collection and interpretation of primary sources on key Church-state conflicts.

Christopher Tyerman, *Fighting for Christendom* (2004). Brief and accessible.

G. Vernadsky, *A History of Russia, I–IV* (1946–1963). A graspable magisterial survey.

R. D. Weigel, *Lepidus: The Tarnished Triumvir* (1992). A biography of the less famous partner of Mark Antony and Augustus.

L. White, Jr., *Medieval Technology and Social Change* (1962). Often fascinating account of the way primitive technology changed life.

J. A. Wilson, *Culture of Ancient Egypt* (1956). A fascinating interpretation of the civilization of ancient Egypt.

For additional learning resources related to this chapter, please go to www.myhistorylab.com

PEARSON
myhistorylab

A procession of flagellants at Tournai in Flanders in 1349, marching with the crucified Christ and scourging themselves in imitation of his suffering.   © ARPL/HIP/The Image Works

9

The Late Middle Ages: Social and Political Breakdown (1300–1453)

▼ **The Black Death**
Preconditions and Causes of the Plague • Popular Remedies • Social and Economic Consequences • New Conflicts and Opportunities

▼ **The Hundred Years' War and the Rise of National Sentiment**
The Causes of the War • Progress of the War

▼ **Ecclesiastical Breakdown and Revival: The Late Medieval Church**
The Thirteenth-Century Papacy • Boniface VIII and Philip the Fair • The Avignon Papacy (1309–1377) • John Wycliffe and John Huss • The Great Schism (1378–1417) and the Conciliar Movement to 1449

▼ **Medieval Russia**
Politics and Society • Mongol Rule (1243–1480)

▼ **In Perspective**

THE LATE MIDDLE Ages saw almost unprecedented political, social, and ecclesiastical calamity. Bubonic plague, known to contemporaries as the Black Death, swept over almost all of Europe between 1348 and 1350 leaving as much as two fifths of the population dead and transforming many pious Christians into believers in the omnipotence of death. France and England grappled with each other in a bitter conflict known as the Hundred Years' War (1337–1453), an exercise in seemingly willful self-destruction that was made even more terrible in its later stages by the introduction of gunpowder and the invention of heavy artillery. A schism emerged within the church, which lasted thirty-nine years (1378–1417) and led, by 1409, to the election of three competing popes and colleges of cardinals. In 1453, the Turks marched seemingly invincibly through Constantinople and toward the West. As their political and religious institutions buckled, disease, bandits, and wolves ravaged their cities, and Islamic armies gathered at their borders, Europeans beheld what seemed to be the imminent total collapse of Western civilization.

It was against this background that such scholars as Marsilius of Padua, William of Ockham, and Lorenzo Valla produced lasting criticisms of medieval assumptions about the nature of God, humankind, and society. Kings worked through parliaments and clergy through councils to limit the pope's temporal power. The notion, derived from Roman law, that a secular ruler is accountable to the body he or she governs had already found expression in documents like the Magna Carta. It came increasingly to carry the force of accepted principle, and conciliarists, who advocated the judicial superiority of church councils over popes, now sought to extend it to papal accountability to the church.

Viewed in terms of their three great calamities—war, plague, and schism—the fourteenth and fifteenth centuries were years in which politics resisted wisdom, nature strained mercy, and the church was less than faithful to its flock.

▼ The Black Death

The virulent plague known as the Black Death struck fourteenth-century Europe when it was already suffering from overpopulation and malnutrition.

Preconditions and Causes of the Plague

In the fourteenth century, nine tenths of the population worked the land. The three-field system of crop production increased the amount of arable land and with it the food supply. As that supply grew, however, so did the population. It is estimated that Europe's population doubled between the years 1000 and 1300 and began thereafter to outstrip food production. There were now more people than there was food to feed them or jobs to employ them, and the average European faced the probability of extreme hunger at least once during his or her expected thirty-five-year life span.

Between 1315 and 1317, crop failures produced the greatest famine of the Middle Ages. Densely populated urban areas such as the industrial towns of the Netherlands suffered greatly. Decades of overpopulation, economic depression, famine, and bad health progressively weakened Europe's population and made it highly vul-

strengthen church

nerable to a virulent bubonic plague that struck with full force in 1348.

The **Black Death**, so called by contemporaries because of the way it discolored the body, followed the trade routes from Asia into Europe. Rats, or more precisely, the fleas the rats bore, on ships from the Black Sea area most likely brought it to Western Europe. Appearing in Constantinople in 1346 and Sicily in late 1347, it entered Europe through the ports of Venice, Genoa, and Pisa in 1348. From there it swept rapidly through Spain and southern France and into northern Europe. Areas that lay outside the major trade routes, like Bohemia, appear to have remained virtually unaffected. Bubonic plague made numerous reappearances in succeeding decades. (See Map 9–1.)

sign from god
turn to indulgences

Popular Remedies

The plague often reached a victim's lungs during the course of the disease. From the lungs, the victim's sneezing and wheezing spread it from person to person. Physicians had little understanding of these processes, so even the most rudimentary preventive measures against the disease were lacking. Contemporaries could neither explain the plague nor defend themselves against it. To them, the Black Death was a catastrophe with no apparent explanation and against which there was no known defense. Throughout much of Western Europe, it inspired an obsession with death and dying and a deep pessimism that endured long after the plague years. (See "Encountering the Past: Dealing with Death," page 261.) *mass hysteria*

Popular wisdom held that a corruption in the atmosphere caused the disease. Some blamed poisonous fumes released by earthquakes. Many wore aromatic amulets as a remedy. According to the contemporary observations of Giovanni Boccaccio, an Italian who recorded the reactions in his *Decameron* (1353), some sought a remedy in moderation and a temperate life, others gave themselves over entirely to their passions (sexual promiscuity ran high within the stricken areas), and still others, "the most sound, perhaps, in judgment," chose flight and seclusion as the best medicine. *whip themselves*

One extreme reaction was processions of flagellants, religious fanatics who beat themselves in ritual penance, believing such action would bring divine intervention. The terror the flagellants created—and their dirty, bleeding bodies may have spread the disease—became so socially disruptive and threatening that the church finally outlawed such processions.

In some places, Jews were cast as scapegoats. Centuries of Christian propaganda had bred hatred toward Jews, as had their role as society's moneylenders. Pogroms occurred in several cities, sometimes incited by the flagellants.

MAP EXPLORATION

Interactive map: To explore this map further, go to www.myhistorylab.com

Extent of the Plague
at Specific Dates

Cities and Regions
Struck by the Plague

Cities and Regions Partially
Spared by the Plague

Bergen

*North
Sea*

Durham

Nottingham
York   Lincoln
Northampton
Cambridge

Dublin

Chester   Yarmouth
Leicester
Kilkenny   Oxford   Norwich
London
Bristol   Canterbury
Weymouth   Bruges
Calais
Southampton   Amiens

*ATLANTIC
OCEAN*

Angers

Paris

Wisby

Moscow

Lübeck   Rostock
Hamburg   Danzig
Bremen   Thorn
Magdeburg   **1350
Osnabrück   June 30**
Erfurt
Cologne   **1349
Dec. 31**
Liège   **1349
Frankfurt   June 30**
Würzburg
Strasbourg   Nuremberg

Colmar
St. Gall
Basel
Lucerne   Zurich

Verona
Milan   Venice
Bordeaux   Avignon   Genoa   Bologna   Ferrara
Montpellier   Florence
Toulouse   Pisa   Ancona
BÉARN   Narbonne   Marseilles   Siena   Perugia
Huesca   Lerida   *CORSICA*   Rome
Saragossa
Teruel   Barcelona
Valencia   *IVIZA*   *MINORCA*   *SARDINIA*
MAJORCA

Almeria   Algiers
300 MILES

300 KILOMETERS

**1350
Dec. 31**

Kiev

Caffa

Vienna

**1348
Dec. 31**

**1348
June 30**

Sebenico
Ragusa

*Black
Sea*

Adriatic Sea

Naples

**1347
Dec. 31**   Constantinople

Athens

Messina   **1347
Dec. 31**
SICILY
Agrigento   Syracuse
Tunis

*Mediterranean
Sea*   *CRETE*

**1348
June 30**

**1347
Dec. 31**

Map 9–1 **SPREAD OF THE BLACK DEATH**   Apparently introduced by seaborne rats from Black Sea areas where plague-infested rodents had long been known, the Black Death brought huge human, social, and economic consequences. One of the lower estimates of Europeans dying is 25 million. The map charts the plague's spread in the mid-fourteenth century. Generally following trade routes, the plague reached Scandinavia by 1350, and some believe it then went on to Iceland and even Greenland. Areas off the main trade routes were largely spared.

2/3 Europe population

The Prince of the World, a sandstone sculpture, vividly portrays the transitory nature of life. When viewers look behind the attractive young prince, they discover his beauty to be only skin deep. His body, like every human body, is filled with death, here symbolized by worms and flesh-eating frogs. A serpect spirals up his left leg and enters his back, an allusion to the biblical teaching that the wages of sin are death. Stadt Nürnberg

fear of the DEVIL greater than love for God

Social and Economic Consequences

Whole villages vanished in the wake of the plague. Among the social and economic consequences of such high depopulation were a shrunken labor supply and a decline in the value of the estates of the nobility.

work force decline

Farms Decline As the number of farm laborers decreased, wages increased and those of skilled artisans soared. Many serfs chose to commute their labor services into money payments and pursue more interesting and rewarding jobs in skilled craft industries in the cities. Agricultural prices fell because of waning demand, and the price of luxury and manufactured goods— the work of skilled artisans—rose. The noble landholders suffered the greatest decline in power. They were forced to pay more for finished products and for farm labor, while receiving a smaller return on their agricultural produce. Everywhere rents declined after the plague.

revolts calmed quickly

Peasants Revolt To recoup their losses, some landowners converted arable land to sheep pasture, substituting more profitable wool production for labor-intensive grains. Others abandoned the farms, leasing them to the highest bidder. Landowners also sought to reverse their misfortune by new repressive legislation that forced peasants to stay on their farms while freezing their wages at low levels. In 1351, the English Parliament passed a Statute of Laborers, which limited wages to pre-plague levels and restricted the ability of peasants to leave their masters' land. Opposition to such legislation sparked the English peasants' revolt in 1381. In France the direct tax on the peasantry, the *taille*, was increased, and opposition to it helped ignite the French peasant uprising known as the Jacquerie.

Cities Rebound Although the plague hit urban populations hard, the cities and their skilled industries came in time to prosper from its effects. Cities had always protected their own interests, passing legislation as they grew to regulate competition from rural areas and to control immigration. After the plague, the reach of such laws extended beyond the cities to include the surrounding lands of nobles and landlords, many of whom now peacefully integrated into urban life.

The omnipresence of death also whetted the appetite for goods that only skilled industries could produce. Expensive clothes and jewelry, furs from the north, and silks from the south were in great demand in

DEALING WITH DEATH

DEATH WAS ALL too familiar in the late Middle Ages, and not just in the time of the plague, when both princes and the simple folk buried their children in the same communal pits. In popular art and literature, the living and the dead embraced in the "Dance of Death," reminding rich and poor, young and old, of their mortality. In the fourteenth century, death divided the Middle Ages from the Renaissance: On one side of the divide was an overpopulated medieval society devastated by the four horsemen of the Apocalypse, while on the other side, a newly disciplined Renaissance society learned to forestall famine, plague, war, and conquest, by abstinence, late marriage, birth control, and diplomacy.

Yet death rates in the past were three times those of the modern West and life expectancy only half as long. Life was a progressive dying, and death a promise of everlasting life. In sixteenth-century Florence, fully a third of newborns died in infancy. In seventeenth-century England, infant mortality was 2 percent on the day of birth, 4 percent at the first week, 9 percent by the first month, and 13 percent at the end of the first year.

Almost everyone by their teens and adulthood suffered from some chronic illness (tuberculosis), debilitating condition (arthritis, gout), or life-threatening infection (streptococci) that pitted them in a personal battle with death.

In Renaissance Italy, Lorenzo de' Medici, duke of Urbino (d. 1519), was plagued with leg ulcers and syphilis in his early twenties. At twenty-five, he received a head wound that was treated by trephination, or by boring holes in his skull. He also developed an abscessed foot that never healed. At twenty-six, he fell prey to chills, fever, diarrhea, vomiting, joint pains, and

A caricature of physicians (early sixteenth century). A physician carries a uroscope (for collecting and examining urine); discolored urine signaled an immediate need for bleeding. The physician/surgeon wears surgical shoes and his assistant carries a flail—a comment on the risks of medical services. Hacker Art Books Inc.

anorexia, and was dead at twenty-seven. His physicians identified the cause of death as a catarrhal phlegm, or tuberculosis, that caused "suffocation of the heart."

In Reformation Germany, at thirty-nine, Elector Frederick III the Wise of Saxony (d. 1525), Luther's protector, spent the last year of his life enclosed in his favorite residence. When his strength permitted, he rolled about the castle on a specially made stool with wheels. Cursed with kidney stones, he died from a septic infection and kidney failure when the stones became too many and too large to pass through his urethra. An autopsy discovered stones "almost two finger joints long and spiked."

Those who suffered from such afflictions found themselves, in the words of a sixteenth-century merchant, "between God and the physicians," a precarious position for the chronically ill in any age. The clergy and the physicians profited greatly from the age's great mortality. People feared both dying and dying out of God's grace. Together, the physician and the priest prepared the way to a good temporal death, while the priest guided the dead through purgatory and into heaven, assisted by the laity's purchase of indulgences and commemorative masses. Like the physicians' bleedings and herbal remedies, the church's sacraments and commemorations both exploited and eased the feared passage into eternity that every Christian soul had to make.

Source: Bruce Gordon and Peter Marshall, eds. *The Place of the Dead: Death and Remembrance in Late Medieval and Early Modern Europe* (Cambridge: Cambridge University Press, 2008), chaps. 2, 14; Ann C. Carmichael, "The Health Status of Florentines in the Fifteenth Century," in M. Tetel et al., eds. *Life and Death in Fifteenth-Century Florence* (Durham: Duke University Press, 1989), chap. 3.

How do illness and death shape history and culture?

How effective were the physicians and the clergy in the face of everyday afflictions? Why did people bother with them?

This illustration from the *Canon of Medicine* by the Persian physician and philosopher Avicenna (980–1037), whose Arabic name was Ibn Sina, shows him visiting the homes of rich patients. In the High Middle Ages, the *Canon of Medicine* was the standard medical textbook in the Middle East and Europe.

Biblioteca Universitaria, Bologna, Italy. Scala/Art Resource, NY

Spain growing

sans and trade guilds grew steadily in the late Middle Ages, along with the demand for their goods and services. The merchant and patrician classes found it increasingly difficult to maintain their traditional dominance and grudgingly gave guild masters a voice in city government. As the guilds won political power, they encouraged restrictive legislation to protect local industries. The restrictions, in turn, caused conflict between master artisans, who wanted to keep their numbers low and expand their industries at a snail's pace, and the many journeymen, who were eager to rise to the rank of master. To the long-existing conflict between the guilds and the ruling urban patriciate was now added one within the guilds themselves.

Also, after 1350, the results of the plague put two traditional "containers" of monarchy—the landed nobility and the church—on the defensive. Kings now exploited growing national sentiment in an effort to centralize their governments and economies. At the same time, the battles of the Hundred Years' War demonstrated the military superiority of paid professional armies over the traditional noble cavalry, thus bringing the latter's future role into question. The plague also killed many members of the clergy—perhaps one third of the German clergy fell victim as they dutifully ministered to the sick and dying. This reduction in clerical ranks occurred in the same century that saw the pope move from Rome to Avignon in southeast France (1309–1377) and the Great Schism (1378–1417) divide the Church into warring factions.

the decades after the plague. Initially this new demand could not be met. The basic unit of urban industry, the master and his apprentices (usually one or two), purposely kept its numbers low, jealously guarding its privileges. The first wave of plague turned this already restricted supply of skilled artisans into a shortage almost overnight. As a result, the prices of manufactured and luxury items rose to new heights, which, in turn, encouraged workers to migrate from the countryside to the city and learn the skills of artisans. Townspeople profited coming and going. As wealth poured into the cities and per capita income rose, the prices of agricultural products from the countryside, now less in demand, declined.

The church also gained and lost. It suffered as a landholder and was politically weakened, yet it also received new revenues from the vastly increased demand for religious services for the dead and the dying, along with new gifts and bequests.

New Conflicts and Opportunities

By increasing the importance of skilled artisans, the plague contributed to new social conflicts within the cities. The economic and political power of local arti-

France and England

▼ The Hundred Years' War and the Rise of National Sentiment

Medieval governments were by no means all-powerful and secure. The rivalry of petty lords kept localities in turmoil, and dynastic rivalries could plunge entire lands into war, especially when power was being transferred to a new ruler—and woe to the ruling dynasty that failed to produce a male heir.

To field the armies and collect the revenues that made their existence possible, late medieval rulers depended on carefully negotiated alliances among a wide range of lesser powers. Like kings and queens in earlier centuries, they, too, practiced the art of feudal government, but on a grander scale and with greater sophistication. To maintain the order they required, the Norman kings of England and the Capetian kings of France fine-tuned traditional feudal relationships by stressing the duties of lesser to higher

rise of secularism

powers and the unquestioning loyalty noble vassals owed to the king. The result was a degree of centralized royal power unseen before in these lands and a growing national consciousness that together equipped both France and England for international warfare.

break down of tradition and feudalism

The Causes of the War

The conflict that came to be known as the Hundred Years' War began in May 1337 and lasted until October 1453. The English king Edward III (r. 1327–1377), the grandson of Philip the Fair of France (r. 1285–1314), may have started the war by asserting a claim to the French throne after the French king Charles IV (r. 1322–1328), the last of Philip the Fair's surviving sons, died without a male heir. The French barons had no intention of placing the then fifteen-year-old Edward on the French throne. They chose instead the first cousin of Charles IV, Philip VI of Valois (r. 1328–1350), the first of a new French dynasty that would rule into the sixteenth century.

But there was, of course, more to the war than just an English king's assertion of a claim to the French throne. England and France were then emergent territorial powers in too close proximity to one another. Edward was actually a vassal of Philip VI, holding several sizable French territories as fiefs from the king of France, a relationship that went back to the days of the Norman conquest. English possession of any French land was repugnant to the French because it threatened the royal policy of centralization. England and France also quarreled over control of Flanders, which, although a French fief, was subject to political influence from England because its principal industry, the manufacture of cloth, depended on supplies of imported English wool. Compounding these frictions was a long history of prejudice and animosity between the French and English people, who constantly confronted one another on the high seas and in ports. Taken together, these various factors made the Hundred Years' War a struggle for national identity as well as for control of territory.

bigger but less mighty

French Weakness   France had three times the population of England, was far the wealthier of the two countries, and fought on its own soil. Yet, for most of the conflict, until after 1415, the major battles ended in often stunning English victories. (See Map 9–2, page 264.) The primary reason for these French failures was internal disunity caused by endemic social conflicts. Unlike England, fourteenth-century France was still struggling to make the transition from a splintered feudal society to a centralized "modern" state.

Desperate to raise money for the war, French kings resorted to such financial policies as depreciating the currency and borrowing heavily from Italian bankers, which aggravated internal conflicts. In 1355, in a bid to secure funds, the king turned to the **Estates General**, a representative council of townspeople, clergy, and nobles. Although it levied taxes at the king's request, its independent members also exploited the king's plight to broaden their own regional sovereignty, thereby deepening territorial divisions.

France's defeats also reflected English military superiority. The English infantry was more disciplined than the French, and English archers carried a formidable weapon, the longbow, capable of firing six arrows a minute with enough force to pierce an inch of wood or the armor of a knight at two hundred yards.

Edward III pays homage to his feudal lord Philip VI of France. Legally, Edward was a vassal of the king of France.   Archives Snark International/Art Resource, NY

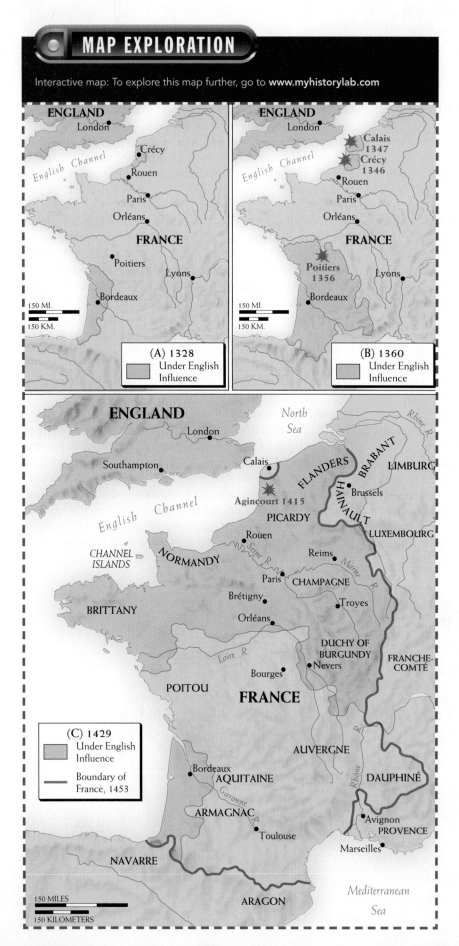

MAP EXPLORATION

Interactive map: To explore this map further, go to **www.myhistorylab.com**

ENGLAND
London
Crécy
Rouen
Paris
Orléans
FRANCE
Poitiers
Lyons
Bordeaux
English Channel
150 MI.
150 KM.

(A) 1328
Under English Influence

ENGLAND
London
English Channel
Calais 1347
Crécy 1346
Rouen
Paris
Orléans
FRANCE
Poitiers 1356
Lyons
Bordeaux
150 MI.
150 KM.

(B) 1360
Under English Influence

ENGLAND
London
Southampton
North Sea
Calais
FLANDERS
BRABANT
LIMBURG
Rhine R.
Brussels
HAINAULT
Agincourt 1415
LUXEMBOURG
PICARDY
English Channel
Rouen
CHANNEL ISLANDS
NORMANDY
Seine R.
Reims
Marne R.
BRITTANY
Paris
CHAMPAGNE
Brétigny
Troyes
Orléans
Loire R.
DUCHY OF BURGUNDY
FRANCHE-COMTÉ
POITOU
Bourges
Nevers
FRANCE
AUVERGNE
Bordeaux
AQUITAINE
DAUPHINÉ
Garonne R.
Rhône R.
Avignon
PROVENCE
ARMAGNAC
Toulouse
Marseilles
NAVARRE
ARAGON
Mediterranean Sea

(C) 1429
Under English Influence
Boundary of France, 1453

150 MILES
150 KILOMETERS

Map 9–2 **THE HUNDRED YEARS' WAR**
The Hundred Years' War went on intermittently from the late 1330s until 1453. These maps show the remarkable English territorial gains up to the sudden and decisive turning of the tide of battle in favor of the French by the forces of Joan of Arc in 1429.

Finally, French weakness during the Hundred Years' War was due, in no small degree, to the comparative mediocrity of its royal leadership. English kings were far shrewder.   *Italy lack of unity*

Progress of the War

The war had three major stages of development, each ending with a seemingly decisive victory by one or the other side.

The Conflict During the Reign of Edward III

In the first stage of the war, Edward embargoed English wool to Flanders, sparking urban rebellions by merchants and the trade guilds. Inspired by a rich merchant, Jacob van Artevelde, the Flemish cities, led by Ghent, revolted against the French and in 1340 signed an alliance with England acknowledging Edward as king of France. On June 23 of that same year, in the first great battle of the war, Edward defeated the French fleet in the Bay of Sluys, but his subsequent effort to invade France by way of Flanders failed.

In 1346, Edward attacked Normandy and, after a series of easy victories that culminated at the Battle of Crécy, seized the port of Calais (which the English would retain until 1558). Exhaustion of both sides and the onset of the Black Death forced a truce in late 1347, as the war entered a brief lull. In 1356, near Poitiers, the English won their greatest victory, routing France's noble cavalry and taking the French king, John II the Good (r. 1350–1364), captive back to England. A complete breakdown of political order in France followed.

Power in France now lay with the Estates General. Led by the powerful merchants of Paris under Etienne Marcel, that body took advantage of royal weakness, demanding and receiving rights similar to those the Magna Carta had granted to the English privileged classes. Yet, unlike the English Parliament, which represented the interests of a comparatively unified English nobility, the French Estates General was too divided to be an instrument for effective government.

To secure their rights, the French privileged classes forced the peasantry to pay ever-increasing taxes and to repair their war-damaged properties without compensation. This bullying became more than the peasants could bear, and they rose up in several regions in a series of bloody rebellions known as the **Jacquerie** in 1358 (after the peasant revolutionary popularly known as Jacques Bonhomme, or "simple Jack"). The nobility quickly put down the revolt, matching the rebels atrocity for atrocity.

On May 9, 1360, another milestone of the war was reached when England forced the Peace of Brétigny-Calais on the French. This agreement declared an end to Edward's vassalage to the king of France and affirmed his sovereignty over English territories in France (including Gascony, Guyenne, Poitou, and Calais). France

also agreed to pay a ransom of 3 million gold crowns to win King John the Good's release. In return, Edward simply renounced his claim to the French throne.

Such a partition was unrealistic, and sober observers on both sides knew it could not last. France struck back in the late 1360s and, by the time of Edward's death in 1377, had beaten the English back to coastal enclaves and the territory around Bordeaux.

French Defeat and the Treaty of Troyes

After Edward's death the English war effort lessened, partly because of domestic problems within England. During the reign of Richard II (r. 1377–1399), England had its own version of the Jacquerie. In June 1381, long-oppressed peasants and artisans joined in a great revolt of the underprivileged classes under the leadership of John Ball, a secular priest, and Wat Tyler, a journeyman. As in France, the revolt was brutally crushed within the year, but it left the country divided for decades.

England recommenced the war under Henry V (r. 1413–1422), who took advantage of internal French turmoil created by the rise to power of the duchy of Burgundy. With France deeply divided, Henry V struck hard in Normandy. Happy to see the rest of France besieged, the Burgundians foolishly watched from the sidelines while Henry's army routed the French at Agincourt on October 25, 1415. In the years thereafter, belatedly recognizing that the defeat of France would leave them easy prey for the English, the Burgundians closed ranks with French royal forces. The renewed French unity, loose as it was, promised to bring eventual victory over the English, but it was shattered in September 1419 when the duke of Burgundy was assassinated. The duke's son and heir, determined to avenge his father's death, joined forces with the English.

France now became Henry V's for the taking—at least in the short run. The Treaty of Troyes in 1420 disinherited the legitimate heir to the French throne and proclaimed Henry V the successor to the French king, Charles VI. When Henry and Charles died within months of one another in 1422, the infant Henry VI of England was proclaimed in Paris to be king of both France and England. The dream of Edward III that had set the war in motion—to make the ruler of England the ruler also of France—seemed to have been realized.

The son of Charles VI went into retreat in Bourges, where, on the death of his father, he became Charles VII to most of the French people, who ignored the Treaty of Troyes. Displaying unprecedented national feeling inspired by the remarkable Joan of Arc, they soon rallied to his cause and united in an ultimately victorious coalition.

Joan of Arc and the War's Conclusion

Joan of Arc (1412–1431), a peasant from Domrémy in Lorraine in eastern France, presented herself to Charles VII in March

A contemporary portrait of Joan of Arc (1412–1431). Anonymous, 15th century. "Joan of Arc." Franco-Flemish miniature. Archives Nationales, Paris, France. Photograph copyright Bridgeman-Giraudon/Art Resource, NY

Within a few months of the liberation of Orléans, Charles VII received his crown in Rheims, ending the nine-year "disinheritance" prescribed by the Treaty of Troyes. The king now forgot his liberator as quickly as he had embraced her. When the Burgundians captured Joan in May 1430, he might have secured her release but did little to help her. The Burgundians and the English wanted her publicly discredited, believing this would also discredit Charles VII and demoralize French resistance. She was turned over to the Inquisition in English-held Rouen. The inquisitors there broke the courageous "Maid of Orléans" after ten weeks of interrogation, and she was executed as a relapsed heretic on May 30, 1431. Twenty-five years later, in 1456, Charles reopened her trial, as the French state and church moved to get on history's side. She was now declared innocent of all the charges against her. In 1920, the Roman Catholic Church declared her a saint.

In 1435, the duke of Burgundy made peace with Charles, allowing France to force the English back. By 1453, when the war ended, the English held only their coastal enclave of Calais.

The Hundred Years' War, with sixty-eight years of nominal peace and forty-four of hot war, had lasting political and social consequences. It devastated France, but it also awakened French nationalism and hastened

1429, declaring that the King of Heaven had called her to deliver besieged Orléans from the English. Charles was skeptical, but being in retreat from what seemed to be a hopeless war, he was also willing to try anything to reverse French fortunes. The deliverance of Orléans, a city key to the control of the territory south of the Loire River, would be a godsend. Charles's desperation overcame his skepticism, and he gave Joan his leave.

Circumstances worked perfectly to her advantage. The English force, already exhausted by a six-month siege, was at the point of withdrawal when Joan arrived with fresh French troops. After repulsing the English from Orléans, the French enjoyed a succession of victories they popularly attributed to Joan. She did deserve much of this credit, but not because she was a military genius. She rather gave the French something military experts could not: an enraged sense of national identity and destiny.

THE HUNDRED YEARS' WAR (1337–1453)

1340	English victory at Bay of Sluys
1346	English victory at Crécy and seizure of Calais
1347	Black Death strikes
1356	English victory at Poitiers
1358	Jacquerie disrupts France
1360	Peace of Brétigny-Calais recognizes English holdings in France
1381	English peasants revolt
1415	English victory at Agincourt
1420	Treaty of Troyes recognizes the English king as heir to the French throne
1422	Henry VI proclaimed king of both England and France
1429	Joan of Arc leads French to victory at Orléans
1431	Joan of Arc executed as a heretic
1453	War ends; English retain only Calais

the transition there from a feudal monarchy to a centralized state. It saw Burgundy become a major European political power. It also encouraged the English, in response to the seesawing allegiance of the Netherlands throughout the conflict, to develop their own clothing industry and foreign markets. In both France and England, the burden of the on-again, off-again war fell most heavily on the peasantry, who were forced to support it with taxes and services.

▼ Ecclesiastical Breakdown and Revival: The Late Medieval Church

decline in church authority

At first glance, the popes may appear to have been in a favorable position in the latter thirteenth century. Frederick II had been vanquished and imperial pressure on Rome had been removed. (See Chapter 8.) The French king, Louis IX, was an enthusiastic supporter of the church, as evidenced by his two disastrous Crusades, which won him sainthood. Although it lasted only seven years, a reunion of the Eastern church with Rome was proclaimed by the Council of Lyons in 1274, when the Western church took advantage of Byzantine emperor Michael VII Palaeologus's (r. 1261–1282) request for aid against the Turks. But despite these positive events, the church's position was less favorable than it appeared.

The Thirteenth-Century Papacy

salvation by faith alone or predestination

As early as the reign of Pope Innocent III (r. 1198–1216), when papal power reached its height, there were ominous developments. Innocent had elaborated the doctrine of papal **plenitude of power** and on that authority had declared saints, disposed of *benefices*, and created a centralized papal monarchy with a clearly political mission. Innocent's transformation of the papacy into a great secular power weakened the church spiritually even as it strengthened it politically. Thereafter, the church as a papal monarchy increasingly parted company with the church as the "body of the faithful." It was against this perceived "papal church" and in the name of the "true Christian church" that both reformers and heretics protested until the Protestant Reformation.

What Innocent began, his successors perfected. Under Urban IV (r. 1261–1264), the papacy established its own law court, the *Rota Romana*, which tightened and centralized the church's legal proceedings. The latter half of the thirteenth century saw an elaboration of the system of clerical taxation; what had begun in the twelfth century as an emergency measure to raise funds for the Crusades became a fixed institution. In the same period, papal power to determine appointments to many major and minor church offices—the "reservation of *benefices*"—was greatly broadened. The thirteenth-century papacy became a powerful political institution governed by its own law and courts, serviced by an efficient international bureaucracy, and preoccupied with secular goals.

Papal centralization of the church undermined both diocesan authority and popular support. Rome's interests, not local needs, came to control church appointments, policies, and discipline. Discontented lower clergy appealed to the higher authority of Rome against the discipline of local bishops. In the second half of the thirteenth century, bishops and abbots protested such undercutting of their power. To its critics, the church in Rome was hardly more than a legalized, "fiscalized," bureaucratic institution. As early as the late twelfth century, heretical movements of Cathars and Waldensians had appealed to the biblical ideal of simplicity and separation from the world. Other reformers who were unquestionably loyal to the church, such as Saint Francis of Assisi, also protested perceived materialism in official religion.

challenge theology (study of religion)

Political Fragmentation More than internal religious disunity was undermining the thirteenth-century church. The demise of imperial power meant the papacy in Rome was no longer the leader of anti-imperial (Guelf, or propapal) sentiment in Italy. Instead of being the center of Italian resistance to the emperor, popes now found themselves on the defensive against their old allies. That was the ironic price the papacy paid to vanquish the Hohenstaufens.

Rulers with a stake in Italian politics now directed the intrigue formerly aimed at the emperor toward the College of Cardinals. For example, Charles of Anjou, the French king of Naples and Sicily (r. 1266–1285), managed to create a French-Sicilian faction within the college. Such efforts to control the decisions of the college led Pope Gregory X (r. 1271–1276) to establish the practice of sequestering the cardinals immediately upon the death of the pope. The purpose of this so-called conclave of cardinals was to minimize political influence on the election of new popes, but the college became so politicized that it proved to be of little avail.

In 1294, such a conclave, in frustration after a deadlock of more than two years, chose a saintly, but inept, hermit as Pope Celestine V. Celestine abdicated under suspicious circumstances after only a few weeks in office. He also died under suspicious circumstances; his successor's critics later argued that the powers behind the papal throne had murdered him to ensure the survival of the papal office. Celestine's tragicomic reign shocked the Cardinals into electing his opposite, Pope Boniface VIII (r. 1294–1303), a nobleman and a skilled politician. His pontificate, however, would mark the beginning of the end of papal pretensions to great-power status.

JOAN OF ARC REFUSES TO RECANT HER BELIEFS

■■

Joan of Arc, threatened with torture, refused to recant her beliefs and instead defended the instructions she had received from the voices that spoke to her. Here is a part of her self-defense from the contemporary trial record.

Do the judges appear to have made up their minds about Joan in advance? How does this judicial process, which was based on intensive interrogation of the accused, differ from a trial today? Why was Joan deemed heretical and not insane when she acknowledged hearing voices?

On Wednesday, May 9th of the same year [1431], Joan was brought into the great tower of the castle of Rouen before us the said judges and in the presence of the reverend father, lord abbot of St. Cormeille de Compiegne, of masters Jean de Châtillon and Guillaume Erart, doctors of sacred theology, of André Marguerie and Nicolas de Venderos, archdeacons of the church of Rouen, of William Haiton, bachelor of theology, Aubert Morel, licentiate in canon law, Nicolas Loiseleur, canon of the cathedral of Rouen, and master Jean Massieu.

And Joan was required and admonished to speak the truth on many different points contained in her trial which she had denied or to which she had given false replies, whereas we possessed certain information, proofs, and vehement presumptions upon them. Many of the points were read and explained to her, and she was told that if she did not confess them truthfully she would be put to the torture, the instruments of which were shown to her all ready in the tower. There were also present by our instruction men ready to put her to the torture in order to restore her to the way and knowledge of truth, and by this means to procure the salvation of her body and soul which by her lying inventions she exposed to such grave perils.

To which the said Joan answered in this manner: "Truly if you were to tear me limb from limb and separate my soul from my body, I would not tell you anything more and if I did say anything, I should afterwards declare that you had compelled me to say it by force." Then she said that on Holy Cross Day last she received comfort from St. Gabriel, she firmly believes it was St. Gabriel. She knew by her voices whether she should submit to the Church, since the clergy were pressing her hard to submit. Her voices told her that if she desired Our Lord to aid her, she must wait upon Him in all her doings. She said that Our Lord has always been the master of her doings, and the Enemy never had power over them. She asked her voices if she would be burned and they answered that she must wait upon God, and He would aid her.

W. P. Barrett, *The Trial of Jeanne D'Arc* (New York: Gotham House, 1932), pp. 303–304.

Boniface VIII and Philip the Fair

Boniface came to rule when England and France were maturing as nation-states. In England, a long tradition of consultation between the king and powerful members of English society evolved into formal parliaments during the reigns of Henry III (r. 1216–1272) and Edward I (r. 1272–1307), and these meetings helped create a unified kingdom. The reign of the French king Philip IV the Fair (r. 1285–1314) saw France become an efficient, centralized monarchy. Philip was no Saint Louis, but a ruthless politician. He was determined to end England's continental holdings, control wealthy Flanders, and establish French hegemony within the Holy Roman Empire.

Boniface had the further misfortune of bringing to the papal throne memories of the way earlier popes had brought kings and emperors to their knees. Painfully he was to discover that the papal monarchy of the early thirteenth century was no match for the new political powers of the late thirteenth century.

vernacular-common langvage of people spoken

The Royal Challenge to Papal Authority France and England were on the brink of all-out war when Boniface became pope in 1294. Only Edward I's preoccupation with rebellion in Scotland, which the French encouraged, prevented him from invading France and starting the Hundred Years' War a half century earlier than it did start. As both countries mobilized for war, they used the pretext of preparing for a Crusade to tax the clergy heavily. In 1215, Pope Innocent III had decreed that the clergy were to pay no taxes to rulers without papal consent. Viewing English and French taxation of the clergy as an assault on traditional clerical rights, Boniface took a strong stand against it. On February 5, 1296, he issued a bull, *Clericis laicos,* which forbade lay taxation of the clergy without papal approval and revoked all previous papal dispensations in this regard. *Latin popular langvage*

In England, Edward I retaliated by denying the clergy the right to be heard in royal court, in effect removing from them the protection of the king. But Philip the Fair struck back with a vengeance: In August 1296, he forbade the exportation of money from France to Rome, thereby denying the papacy the revenues it needed to operate. Boniface had no choice but to come to terms quickly with Philip. He conceded Philip the right to tax the French clergy "during an emergency," and, not coincidentally, he canonized Louis IX in the same year.

Boniface was then also under siege by powerful Italian enemies, whom Philip did not fail to patronize. A noble family (the Colonnas), rivals of Boniface's family (the Gaetani) and radical followers of Saint Francis of Assisi (the Spiritual Franciscans), were seeking to invalidate Boniface's election as pope on the grounds that Celestine V had been forced to resign the office. Charges of heresy, simony, and even the murder of Celestine were hurled against Boniface.

Boniface's fortunes appeared to revive in 1300, a "Jubilee year." During such a year, all Catholics who visited Rome and fulfilled certain conditions had the penalties for their unrepented sins remitted. Tens of thousands of pilgrims flocked to Rome, and Boniface, heady with this display of popular religiosity, reinserted himself into international politics. He championed Scottish resistance to England, for which he received a firm rebuke from an outraged Edward I and from Parliament.

But once again a confrontation with the king of France proved the more costly. Philip seemed to be eager for another fight with the pope. He arrested Boniface's Parisian legate, Bernard Saisset, the bishop of Pamiers and also a powerful secular lord, whose independence Philip had opposed. Accused of heresy and treason, Saisset was tried and convicted in the king's court. Thereafter, Philip demanded that Boniface recognize the process against Saisset, something Boniface could do only if he was prepared to surrender his jurisdiction over the French episco-

Pope Boniface VIII (r. 1294–1303), depicted here, opposed the taxation of the clergy by the kings of France and England and issued one of the strongest declarations of papal authority over rulers, the bull *Unam Sanctam.* This statue is in the Museo Civico, Bologna, Italy. Statue of Pope Boniface VIII. Museo Civico, Bologna. Scala/Art Resource, NY

pate. Boniface could not sidestep this challenge, and he acted swiftly to champion Saisset as a defender of clerical political independence within France. He demanded Saisset's unconditional release, revoked all previous agreements with Philip regarding clerical taxation, and ordered the French bishops to convene in Rome within a year. A bull, *Ausculta fili,* or "Listen, My Son," was sent to Philip

Who Runs the World:
Priests or Princes?

IN ONE OF the boldest papal bulls in the history of Christianity, Pope Boniface VIII declared the temporal authority of rulers to be subject to papal authority. Behind that ideology lay a long, bitter dispute between the papacy and the kings of France and England. Despite the strained scholastic arguments from each side's apologists, the issue was paramount and kingdoms were at stake. The debaters were Giles of Rome, a philosopher and papal adviser, and John of Paris, a French Dominican and Aristotle expert. Quoting ecclesiastical authorities, Giles defended a papal theocracy, while John made the royal case for secular authority.

QUESTIONS

1. Are the arguments pro and con logical and transparent?

2. How is history invoked to support their positions?

3. Which of the two seems to have the better authorities behind his arguments?

I. Giles of Rome, *On Ecclesiastical Power* (1301)

Hugh of St. Victor . . . declares that the spiritual power has to institute the earthly power and to judge it if it has not been good . . . We can clearly prove from the order of the universe that the church is set above nations and kingdoms [Jeremias 1:10] . . . It is the law of divinity that the lowest are led to the highest through intermediaries . . . At Romans 13 . . . the Apostle, having said that there is no power except from God, immediately added: "And those that are, are ordained of God." If then there are two swords [governments], one spiritual, the other temporal, as can be gathered from the words of the Gospel, "Behold, here are two swords" (Luke 22:38), [to which] the Lord at once added, "It is enough" because these two swords suffice for the church, [then] it follows that these two swords, these two powers and authorities, are [both] from God, since there is no power except from God. But, therefore they must be rightly ordered since, what is from God must be ordered. [And] they would not be so ordered unless one sword was led by the other and one was under the other since, as Dionysius said, the law of divinity which God gave to all created things requires this . . . Therefore the temporal sword, as being inferior, is led by the spiritual sword, as being superior, and the one is set below the other as an inferior below a superior.

It may be said that kings and princes ought to be subject spiritually but not temporally . . . But those who speak thus have not grasped the force of the argument. For if kings and princes were only spiritually subject to the church, one sword would not be below the other, nor temporalities below spiritualities; there would be no order in the powers, the lowest would not be led to the highest through intermediaries. If they *are* ordered, the temporal sword must be below the spiritual, and [royal] kingdoms below the vicar of Christ, and that by law . . . [then] the vicar of Christ must hold dominion over temporal affairs.

II. John of Paris, *Treatise on Royal and Papal Power* (1302–1303)

It is easy to see which is first in dignity, the kingship or the priesthood . . . A kingdom is ordered to this end, that an assembled multitude may live virtuously . . . and it is further ordered to a higher end which is the enjoyment of God; and responsibility for this end belongs to Christ, whose ministers and vicars are the priests. Therefore, the priestly power is of greater dignity than the secular and this is commonly conceded . . .

But if the priest is greater in himself than the prince and is greater in dignity, it does not follow that he is greater in all respects. For the lesser secular power is not related to the greater spiritual power as having its origin from it or being derived from it as the power of a proconsul is related to that of the emperor, which is greater in

Mongol Rule (1243–1480)

In the thirteenth century, Mongol, or Tatar, armies swept through China, much of the Islamic world, and Russia. These were steppe peoples with strongholds in the south, whence they raided the north, devastating Russia and compelling the obedience of Moscow for a while. Ghengis Khan (1155–1227) invaded Russia in 1223, and Kiev fell to his grandson Batu Khan in 1240. Russian cities became dependent, tribute-paying principalities of the segment of the Mongol Empire known as the *Golden Horde* (the Tatar words for the color of Batu Khan's tent). Geographically, the Golden Horde included the steppe region of what is today southern Russia and its capital at Sarai on the lower Volga. The conquerors stationed their own officials in all the principal Russian towns to oversee taxation and the conscription of Russians into Tatar armies. The Mongols filled their harems with Russian women and sold Russians who resisted into slavery in foreign lands. Russian women—under the influence of Islam, which became the religion of the Golden Horde—began to wear veils and lead more secluded lives. This forced integration of Mongol and Russian created further cultural divisions between Russia and the West. The Mongols, however, left Russian political and religious institutions largely intact and, thanks to their far-flung trade, brought most Russians greater prosperity. Princes of Moscow collected tribute for their overlords and grew wealthy under Mongol rule. As that rule weakened, the Moscow princes took control of the territory surrounding the city in what was called "the gathering of the Russian Land." Gradually the principality of Moscow expanded through land purchases, colonization, and conquest. In 1380, Grand Duke Dimitri of Moscow (r. 1350–1389) defeated Tatar forces at Kulikov Meadow, a victory that marked the beginning of the decline of the Mongol hegemony. Another century would pass, however, before Ivan III, the Great (d. 1505), would bring all of northern Russia under Moscow's control and end Mongol rule (1480). Moscow replaced Kiev as the political and religious center of Russia. After Constantinople fell to the Turks in 1453, the city became, in Russian eyes, the "third Rome."

In Perspective

Plague, war, and schism convulsed much of late medieval Europe throughout the fourteenth and into the fifteenth centuries. Two fifths of the population, particularly along the major trade routes, died from plague in the fourteenth century. War and famine continued to take untold numbers after the plague had passed. Revolts erupted in town and countryside as ordinary people attempted to defend their traditional communal rights and privileges against the new autocratic territorial regimes. Even God's house seemed to be in shambles in 1409, when three popes came to rule simultaneously.

There is, however, another side to the late Middle Ages. By the end of the fifteenth century, the population losses were rapidly being made up. Between 1300 and 1500, education had become far more accessible, especially to lay people. The number of universities increased from twenty to seventy, and the rise in the number of residential colleges was even more impressive, especially in France, where sixty-three were built. The fourteenth century saw the birth of humanism, and the fifteenth century gave us the printing press. Most impressive were the artistic and cultural achievements of the Italian Renaissance during the fifteenth century. The later Middle Ages were thus a period of growth and creativity, as well as one of waning and decline.

AP* TEST PREP

1. Which social group suffered the greatest decline in power as a result of the plague?
   a. noble landholders
   b. urban elites
   c. peasants
   d. clergy
   e. artisans

2. The Statute of Laborers, enacted in the aftermath of the plague,
   a. guaranteed a minimum wage for artisans.
   b. barred laborers from moving from one city to another.
   c. governed working conditions in early factories.
   d. barred laborers from moving from one profession to another.
   e. limited wages to preplague levels.

3. In the mid–fourteenth century, France had
   a. about the same population as England but was much poorer.
   b. twice the population of England but was much poorer.
   c. half the population of England.
   d. a smaller army than England but was much richer.
   e. three times the population of England and was much richer.

4. What papal doctrine contributed to the transformation of the papacy into a great secular power?
   a. papal primacy

   b. plenitude of power
   c. Petrine doctrine
   d. papal infallibility
   e. Donation of Constantine

5. The writings of John Wycliffe inspired the
   a. Jacquerie.
   b. Levelers.
   c. Hussites.
   d. Lollards.
   e. Ciompi.

6. As a result of the Black Death, it is estimated that the population of Western Europe was reduced by
   a. 40 percent.
   b. 50 percent.
   c. 60 percent.
   d. 70 percent.
   e. 80 percent.

7. The basic argument of the conciliarists was that
   a. church councils working with the pope were best suited to lead the faithful.
   b. church councils guided and directed by a non-schismatic pope would be best.
   c. church legislation could be decided only through a series of regionally sponsored councils.
   d. church councils, guided by the Holy Spirit, had greater authority than popes.
   e. the primitive church had been governed by church councils.

8. All of the following contributed to the outbreak of the Hundred Years' War *except*
   a. the proximity of England and France.
   b. Edward III of England's control of French territories.
   c. religious differences.
   d. a quarrel over Flanders.
   e. a history of prejudice and animosity between the two peoples.

9. The French Estates General was a representative council of
   a. townspeople, clergy, and nobles.
   b. landowners.
   c. high clergy and royal officials.
   d. lawyers and advocates.
   e. nobles and their allies.

10. Joan of Arc gave the French
   a. a sense of national identity and destiny.
   b. a skilled military leader.
   c. new allies within the church.
   d. hope, but no immediate success.
   e. access to a vast peasant army.

11. According to *Unam Sanctum*,
   a. temporal authorities were subject to the spiritual power of the church.
   b. temporal and spiritual authorities enjoyed equal power.
   c. states should control their own churches, but ultimate authority resided in the papacy.
   d. all state churches should be dissolved.
   e. all power on earth emanated from the papacy.

12. *Boyars* were
   a. peasants.
   b. slaves.
   c. army officers.
   d. nobles.
   e. wealthy landowners.

13. In his *Defender of the Peace*, Marsilius of Padua stressed
   a. the independence of the papacy.
   b. the independent origins and autonomy of secular governments.
   c. the role of the church in preventing war.
   d. the need for a unified Christendom.
   e. the valor and righteousness of Pope John XXII.

14. All of the following are true of the Lollards *except* that they
   a. preached in the vernacular.
   b. disseminated translations of Holy Scripture.
   c. came from every social class.
   d. could be put to death for their beliefs after 1401.
   e. believed that Christ was a man, not the son of God.

15. The establishment of two competing popes in 1378 is known as the
   a. Babylonian Captivity.
   b. Conciliar Controversy.
   c. Division of Christendom.
   d. Great Schism.
   e. Malbourg Divide.

16. Advocates of conciliar theory sought to create a church in which
   a. lawyers played a central role.
   b. a representative council regulated the actions of the pope.
   c. each nation-state had its own church.
   d. the pope was the head of a council that served at his discretion.
   e. men and women had equal status.

17. In the fourteenth century, agricultural laborers made up _____ percent of the population.
   a. 50
   b. 40
   c. 90
   d. 75
   e. 25

18. As a result of the Black Death,
    a. skilled artisans found little demand for their products.
    b. noble landowners gained increased control over serfs.
    c. women's status and rights increased.
    d. cities became ghost towns, never to return to their former glory.
    e. wages for farm laborers and artisans increased.

19. Which of the following groups gained new political power in the late Middle Ages?
    a. urban patricians
    b. merchant elites
    c. noble landowners
    d. trade guilds
    e. high-ranking clergy

20. One explanation for France's defeats in the first two phases of the Hundred Years' War is
    a. France's relatively small population.
    b. France's relatively decentralized state.
    c. the absence of large urban centers in France.
    d. the unwillingness of French kings to spend money on large armies.
    e. popular opposition in France to the war.

DOCUMENT-BASED QUESTION

Directions: Construct a valid essay that directly addresses the central issue of the following question. Use facts from the documents provided and from the chapter to prove the position you take in your thesis statement.

How did Europeans respond to the plague that struck Europe in 1347? What does their response tell us about their understanding of disease and its spread?

Document A

A procession of flagellants at Tournai in Flanders in 1349.

Document B

Map 9–1 **SPREAD OF THE BLACK DEATH.**

Document C

Source: Giovanni Boccaccio, poet and humanist, describes the ravages of the Black Death, *The Decameron.*

In Florence, despite all that human wisdom and forethought could devise to avert it, even as the cleansing of the city from many impurities by officials appointed for the purpose, the refusal of entrance to all sick folk, and the adoption of many precautions for the preservation of health; despite also humble supplications to God, and often repeated both in public procession and otherwise by the devout; towards the beginning of the spring of the said year [1348] the doleful effects of the pestilence began to be horribly apparent by the symptoms that [appeared] as if miraculous.

Which maladies seemed to set entirely at naught both the art of the physician and the virtues of physic; indeed, whether it was that the disorder was of a nature to defy such treatment, or that the physicians were at fault . . . and, being in ignorance of its source, failed to apply the proper remedies; in either case, . . . almost all died within three days of the appearance of the said symptoms.

Document D

A caricature of physicians.

Document E

Source: Robert of Avesbury reports on a procession of flagellants through the streets of London in 1349.

About Michaelmas 1349 over six hundred men came to London from Flanders, mostly of Zeeland and Holland origin. Sometimes at St. Paul's and sometimes at other points in the city they made two daily public appearances wearing cloths from the thighs to the ankles, but otherwise stripped bare. Each wore a cap marked with a red cross in front and behind. Each had in his right hand a scourge with three tails. Each tail had a knot and through the middle of it there were sometimes sharp nails fixed. They marched naked in a file one behind the other and whipped themselves with these scourges on their naked and bleeding bodies. Four of them would chant in their native tongue and another four would chant in response like a litany. Thrice they would all cast themselves on the ground in this sort of procession, stretching out their hands like the arms of the cross. The singing would go on and, the one who was in the rear of those thus prostrate acting first, each of them in turn would step over the others and give one stroke with his scourge to the man lying under him. This went on from the first to the last until each of them had observed the ritual to the full tale of those on the ground. Then each put on his customary garments and always wearing their caps and carrying their whips in their hands they retired to their lodgings. It is said that every night they performed the same Penance.

For more on the plague and its impact, see pages 258–261.

10

Renaissance and Discovery

▼ **The Renaissance in Italy (1375–1527)**
The Italian City-State • Humanism • Renaissance Art • Slavery in the Renaissance

▼ **Italy's Political Decline: The French Invasions (1494–1527)**
Charles VIII's March Through Italy • Pope Alexander VI and the Borgia Family • Pope Julius II • Niccolò Machiavelli

▼ **Revival of Monarchy in Northern Europe**
France • Spain • England • The Holy Roman Empire

▼ **The Northern Renaissance**
The Printing Press • Erasmus • Humanism and Reform

▼ **Voyages of Discovery and the New Empires in the West and East**
The Portuguese Chart the Course • The Spanish Voyages of Columbus • The Spanish Empire in the New World • The Church in Spanish America • The Economy of Exploitation • The Impact on Europe

▼ **In Perspective**

KEY TOPICS

- **The politics, culture, and art of the Italian Renaissance**

- **Political struggle and foreign intervention in Italy**

- **The powerful new monarchies of northern Europe**

- **The thought and culture of the northern Renaissance**

IF THE LATE Middle Ages saw unprecedented chaos, it also witnessed a rebirth that would continue into the seventeenth century. Two modern Dutch scholars have employed the same word (*Herfsttij*, or "harvesttide") with different connotations to describe the period. Johan Huizinga has used the word to mean a "waning" or "decline," and Heiko Oberman has used it to mean a "harvest." If something was dying away, some ripe fruit was also being gathered and seed grain was being sown. The late Middle Ages was a time of creative fragmentation.

By the late fifteenth century, Europe was recovering well from two of the three crises of the late Middle Ages: the demographic and the political. The great losses in population were being replenished, and able monarchs and rulers were imposing a new political order. However, a solution to the religious crisis would have to await the Reformation and Counter-Reformation of the sixteenth century.

Although the opposite would be true in the sixteenth and seventeenth centuries, the city-states of Italy survived the century and a half between 1300 and 1450 better than the territorial states of northern Europe. This was due to Italy's strategic location between East and West and its lucrative Eurasian trade. Great wealth gave rulers and merchants the ability to work their will on both society and culture. They became patrons of government, education, and the arts, always as much for their own self-aggrandizement as out of benevolence, for whether a patron was a family, a firm, a government, or the church, endowments enhanced their reputation and power. The result of such patronage was a cultural Renaissance in Italian cities unmatched elsewhere.

With the fall of Constantinople to the Turks in 1453, Italy's once unlimited trading empire began to shrink. City-state soon turned against city-state, and by the 1490s, French armies invaded Italy. Within a quarter century, Italy's great Renaissance had peaked.

The fifteenth century also saw an unprecedented scholarly renaissance. Italian and northern humanists made a full recovery of classical knowledge and languages and set in motion educational reforms and cultural changes that would spread throughout Europe in the fifteenth and sixteenth centuries. In the process the Italian humanists invented, for all practical purposes, critical historical scholarship, while exploiting a new fifteenth-century invention, the "divine art" of printing with movable type.

In this period the vernacular—the local language—began to take its place alongside Latin, the international language, as a widely used literary and political means of communication. In addition, European states progressively superseded the church as the community of highest allegiance, as patriotism and incipient nationalism seized hearts and minds as strongly as religion. Nations henceforth "transcended" themselves not by journeys to Rome, but by competitive voyages to the Far East and the Americas, as the age of global exploration opened.

For Europe, the late fifteenth and sixteenth centuries were a period of unprecedented expansion and experimentation. Permanent colonies were established within the Americas, and the exploitation of the New World's human and mineral resources began. Imported American gold and silver spurred scientific invention and a new weapons industry. The new bullion also helped create the international traffic in African slaves as rival African tribes eagerly sold their captives to the Portuguese. Transported in ever-increasing numbers, these slaves worked the mines and plantations of the New World as replacements for American natives, whose population declined precipitously following the conquest.

The period also saw social engineering and political planning on a large scale, as newly centralized governments began to put long-range economic policies into practice, a development that came to be called mercantilism.

upperclass – elite movement
reconnection

▼ The Renaissance in Italy (1375–1527)

rebirth of the classical world

A nineteenth-century Swiss historian famously described the Renaissance as the "prototype of the modern world." In his *Civilization of the Renaissance in Italy* (1860), Jacob Burckhardt argued that the revival of ancient learning in fourteenth- and fifteenth-century Italy gave rise to new secular and scientific values. This was the period in which people began to adopt a rational and statistical approach to reality and to rediscover the worth and creativity of the individual. The result, in Burckhardt's words, was the gradual release of the "full, whole nature of man."

Most scholars today find Burckhardt's description exaggerated and accuse him of overlooking the continuity between the Middle Ages and the Renaissance. His critics especially point to the still strongly Christian character of Renaissance humanism. Earlier "renaissances," such as that of the twelfth century, had also seen the revival of the ancient classics, new interest in the Latin language and Greek science, and an appreciation of the worth and creativity of individuals.

Despite the exaggeration and bias of Burckhardt's portrayal, most scholars agree that the **Renaissance** (which means "rebirth" in French) was a time of transition from medieval to modern times. Medieval Europe, especially before the twelfth century, had been a fragmented feudal society with an agricultural economy, and the church largely dominated its thought and culture. Renaissance Europe, especially after the fourteenth century, was characterized by growing national consciousness and political centralization, an urban economy based on organized commerce and capitalism, and growing lay and secular control of thought and culture, including religion.

Italy between 1375 and 1527, a century and a half of cultural creativity, most strikingly reveals the distinctive features of the Renaissance. Two events coincide with the beginning of this period: the deaths of Petrarch, considered the "father" of humanism, in 1374 and that of Giovanni Boccaccio, author of the *Decameron*, in 1375. Thereafter, Florentine humanist culture spread throughout Italy and into northern Europe. Scholars have coined the term *civic humanism* to describe this apparent coalescence of humanism and civic reform.

This creative expansion, however, appeared to reach an abrupt end in 1527, when Spanish-imperial soldiers looted and torched Rome, recalling Rome's sacking by the Visigoths and Vandals in antiquity. At this time, French king Francis I and the Holy Roman Emperor Charles V had made Italy the battleground for their mutual dynastic claims to Burgundy and parts of Italy. Pope Clement VIII (r. 1523–1534) had incurred the emperor's wrath by taking the side of the French. However, the infamous sack of Rome in 1527 appears to have been less the result of a breach of papal loyalty than of the anger and boredom of

Spanish-imperial soldiers poorly provisioned and paid by the emperor. Their looting and sacking have since marked the beginning of the end of the cultured Italian Renaissance.   *Bubonic Plague cause of Renaissance*

The Italian City-State

Renaissance society first took distinctive shape within the merchant cities of late medieval Italy. Italy had always had a cultural advantage over the rest of Europe because its geography made it the natural gateway between East and West. Venice, Genoa, and Pisa had traded uninterruptedly with the Near East throughout the Middle Ages, maintaining vibrant urban societies by virtue of such trade. When commerce revived on a large scale in the eleventh century, Italian merchants had quickly mastered the business skills of organization, bookkeeping, scouting new markets, and securing monopolies. During the thirteenth and fourteenth centuries, trade-rich cities became powerful city-states, dominating the political and economic life of the surrounding countryside. By the fifteenth century, the great Italian cities were the bankers for much of Europe.

Growth of City-States   The endemic warfare between pope and emperor and the Guelf (propapal) and Ghibelline (proimperial) factions assisted the growth of Italian cities and urban culture. Either of these factions might successfully have subdued the cities had they permitted each other to concentrate on doing so. Instead, they chose to weaken one another, which strengthened the merchant oligarchies of the cities. Unlike the great cities of northern Europe, which kings and territorial princes dominated, the great Italian cities remained free to expand on their own. Becoming independent states, they absorbed the surrounding countryside, assimilating the local nobility in a unique urban meld of old and new rich. Five such major competitive states evolved: the duchy of Milan the republics of Florence and Venice, the Papal States, and the kingdom of Naples. (See Map 10–1.)

Social strife and competition for political power became so intense within the cities that most evolved into despotisms just to survive. A notable exception was Venice, which was ruled by a successful merchant oligarchy. The Venetian government operated through a patrician senate of three hundred members and a ruthless judicial body. The latter, known as the Council of Ten, was quick to anticipate and suppress all rival groups.

Social Class and Conflict   Florence was the most striking example of social division and anarchy. Four distinguishable social groups existed within the city. There was the old rich, or *grandi*, the nobles and merchants who traditionally ruled the city. The emergent newly rich merchant class, capitalists and bankers

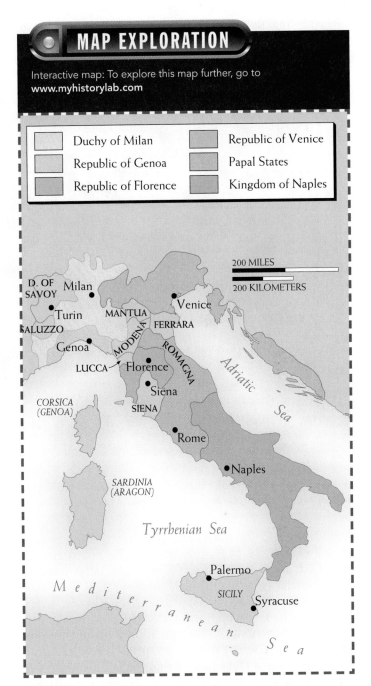

MAP EXPLORATION

Interactive map: To explore this map further, go to www.myhistorylab.com

☐ Duchy of Milan   ☐ Republic of Venice
☐ Republic of Genoa   ☐ Papal States
☐ Republic of Florence   ☐ Kingdom of Naples

Map 10–1   **RENAISSANCE ITALY**   The city-states of Renaissance Italy were self-contained principalities whose internal strife was monitored by their despots and whose external aggression was long successfully controlled by treaty.

known as the *popolo grosso*, or "fat people," formed a second group. In the late thirteenth and early fourteenth centuries, they began to challenge the old rich for political powers. Then there were the middle-burgher ranks of guild masters, shop owners, and professionals, the smaller businesspeople who, in Florence, as elsewhere, tended to side with the new rich against the conservative policies of the old rich. Finally, there was the

Florentine women doing needlework, spinning, and weaving. These activities took up much of a woman's time and contributed to the elegance of dress for which Florentine men and women were famed. Palazzo Schifanoia, Ferrara. Alinari/Art Resource, NY

popolo minuto, or the "little people," the lower economic classes. In 1457, one third of the population of Florence, about 30,000 people, was officially listed as paupers, that is, as having no wealth at all.

These social divisions produced conflict at every level of society, to which was added the ever-present fear of foreign intrigue. In 1378, a great uprising of the poor, known as the Ciompi Revolt, occurred. It resulted from a combination of three factors that made life unbearable for those at the bottom of society: the feuding between the old rich and the new rich; the social anarchy created when the Black Death cut the city's population almost in half; and the collapse of the great banking houses of Bardi and Peruzzi, which left the poor more vulnerable than ever. The Ciompi Revolt established a chaotic four-year reign of power by the lower Florentine classes. True stability did not return to Florence until the ascent to power of the Florentine banker and statesman, Cosimo de' Medici (1389–1464) in 1434.

Despotism and Diplomacy Cosimo de' Medici was the wealthiest Florentine and a natural statesman. He controlled the city internally from behind the scenes, manipulating the constitution and influencing elections.

A council, first of six and later of eight members, known as the *Signoria,* governed the city. These men were chosen from the most powerful guilds, namely, those representing the major clothing industries (cloth, wool, fur, and silk) and such other groups as bankers, judges, and doctors. Through informal, cordial relations with the electors, Cosimo was able to keep councilors loyal to him in the *Signoria.* From his position as the head of the Office of Public Debt, he favored congenial factions. His grandson, Lorenzo the Magnificent (1449–1492; r. 1478–1492), ruled Florence in almost totalitarian fashion during the last, chaotic quarter of the fifteenth century. The assassination of his brother in 1478 by a rival family, the Pazzi, who had long plotted with the pope against the Medicis, made Lorenzo a cautious and determined ruler.

Despotism elsewhere was even less subtle. To prevent internal social conflict and foreign intrigue from paralyzing their cities, the dominant groups cooperated to install hired strongmen, or despots. Known as a *podestà,* the despot's sole purpose was to maintain law and order. He held executive, military, and judicial authority, and his mandate was direct and simple: to permit, by whatever means required, the normal flow of business activity without which neither the old rich and new rich, nor the poor of a city, could long survive, much less prosper. Because despots could not count on the loyalty of the divided populace, they operated through mercenary armies obtained through military brokers known as **condottieri.**

It was a hazardous job. Not only was a despot subject to dismissal by the oligarchies that hired him, he was also a popular object of assassination attempts. The spoils of success, however, were great. In Milan, it was as despots that the Visconti family came to power in 1278 and the Sforza family in 1450, both ruling without constitutional restraints or serious political competition.

Mercifully, the political turbulence and warfare of the times also gave birth to the art of diplomacy. Through their diplomats, the various city-states stayed abreast of foreign military developments and, when shrewd enough, gained power and advantage over their enemies without

art
language
history
philosophy
writing

CHAPTER 10 ■ RENAISSANCE AND DISCOVERY **287**

actually going to war. Most city-states established resident embassies in the fifteenth century for that very purpose. Their ambassadors not only represented them in ceremonies and at negotiations, they also became their watchful eyes and ears at rival courts.

Whether within the comparatively tranquil republic of Venice, the strong-arm democracy of Florence, or the undisguised despotism of Milan, the disciplined Italian city proved a congenial climate for an unprecedented flowering of thought and culture. Italian Renaissance culture was promoted as vigorously by despots as by republicans and as enthusiastically by secularized popes as by the more spiritually minded. Such widespread support occurred because the main requirement for patronage of the arts and letters was the one thing that Italian cities of the High Renaissance had in abundance: great wealth.

Humanism   human worth - dignity

Scholars still debate the meaning of the term *humanism*. Some see the Italian Renaissance as Burckhardt did, as the birth of modernity, driven by an un-Christian philosophy that stressed the dignity of humankind, individualism, and secular values. Others argue that the humanists were actually the champions of Catholic Christianity, opposing the pagan teaching of Aristotle and the Scholasticism his writings nurtured. For still others, humanism was a neutral form of historical scholarship adopted to promote above all a sense of civic responsibility and political liberty.   Greek / Roman culture

A leading scholar, Paul O. Kristeller, accused all of the above of dealing more with the secondary effects of humanism than with its essence. Humanism was not a philosophy or a value system, but an educational program built on rhetoric and scholarship for their own sake.

Each of these definitions has some truth. **Humanism** was the scholarly study of the Latin and Greek classics and of the ancient Church Fathers, both for its own sake and in the hope of reviving respected ancient norms and values. Humanists advocated the **studia humanitatis**, a liberal arts program of study embracing grammar, rhetoric, poetry, history, politics, and moral philosophy. Not only were these subjects considered a joy in themselves, they also celebrated the dignity of humankind and prepared people for a life of virtuous action. The Florentine Leonardo Bruni (ca. 1370–1444) first gave the name *humanitas*, or "humanity," to the learning that resulted from such scholarly pursuits. Bruni was a star student of Manuel Chrysoloras (ca. 1355–1415), the Byzantine scholar who opened the world of Greek scholarship to Italian humanists when he taught at Florence between 1397 and 1403.

The first humanists were orators and poets. They wrote original literature in both classical and vernacular languages, inspired by and modeled on the newly discovered works of the ancients. They also taught rhetoric within the universities. When humanists were not employed as teachers of rhetoric, princely and papal courts sought their talents as secretaries, speechwriters, and diplomats.

The study of classical and Christian antiquity had existed before the Italian Renaissance. There were memorable recoveries of ancient civilization during the Carolingian renaissance of the ninth century, within the cathedral school of Chartres in the twelfth century, during the great Aristotelian revival in Paris in the thirteenth century, and among the Augustinians in the early fourteenth century. These precedents, however, only partially compare with the achievements of the Italian Renaissance of the fourteenth and fifteenth centuries. The latter was far more secular and lay-dominated, had much broader interests, was blessed with far more recovered manuscripts, and its scholars possessed far superior technical skills than those who had delivered the earlier "rebirths" of antiquity.

Unlike their Scholastic rivals, humanists were less bound to recent tradition; nor did they focus all their attention on summarizing and comparing the views of recognized authorities. Their most respected sources were classical and biblical, not medieval philosophers and theologians. Avidly searching out manuscript collections, Italian humanists made the full riches of Greek and Latin antiquity available to contemporary scholars. So great was their achievement that there is a kernel of truth in their assertion that the period between themselves and classical civilization was a "dark middle age."

Petrarch, Dante, and Boccaccio   Francesco Petrarch (1304–1374) was the "father of humanism." He left the legal profession to pursue letters and poetry. Most of his life was spent in and around Avignon. He was involved in a popular revolt in Rome (1347–1349) and, in his later years, he served the Visconti family in Milan.

Petrarch celebrated ancient Rome in his *Letters to the Ancient Dead*, fancied personal letters to Cicero, Livy, Vergil, and Horace. He also wrote a Latin epic poem (*Africa*, a poetic historical tribute to the Roman general Scipio Africanus) and biographies of famous Roman men (*Lives of Illustrious Men*). His most famous contemporary work was a collection of highly introspective love sonnets to a certain Laura, a married woman he admired romantically from a safe distance.

His critical textual studies, elitism, and contempt for the learning of the Scholastics were features many later humanists also shared. As with many later humanists, Classical and Christian values coexist uneasily in his work. Medieval Christian values can be seen in his imagined dialogues with Saint Augustine and in tracts he wrote to defend the personal immortality of the soul against the Aristotelians.

Petrarch was, however, far more secular in orientation than his famous near-contemporary Dante

THE RENAISSANCE GARDEN

IN THE MIDDLE Ages and early Renaissance, few possessions were as prized, or as vital, as a garden. Within that enclosed space grew both ornamental and medicinal flowers and herbs. The more common kitchen garden existed in every manor, castle, monastery, guildhall, and small household. In addition to their large, elaborate gardens, the rich also had orchards and vineyards to grow the fruit from which they made sweet drinks and wine. Behind their shops and guildhalls, apothecaries and barber-surgeons cultivated the curative flowers and herbs from which they concocted the medicines of their trades. Beyond manor and guildhall walls, small householders and cottagers hoed the small, narrow plots behind their houses in which they grew the basic herbs and vegetables of their diet. Although the grandeur and variety of a garden reflected the prestige of its owner, every garden's main purpose was to serve the immediate needs of the household.

Versatility and pungency distinguished the most popular flowers and herbs. The violet was admired for its beauty, fragrance, and utility. Medieval people put violets in baths, oils, and syrups, prizing its soft scent and healing power as well as its ability to color, flavor, and garnish dishes. Nonetheless, subtlety and delicacy were not as important to the medieval palate as they are to ours. An herb or flower was only as good as its impact on the senses. Potent scents and flavors were loved for their ability to bring an otherwise starchy and lackluster meal to life. Fruit, although it was the main ingredient for sweet drinks, rarely appeared on a medieval plate, and vegetables were only slightly more common. Cabbage, lentils, peas, beans, onions, leeks, beets, and parsnips were the most often served vegetables at the medieval table, made palatable by heavy application of the sharpest and bitterest spices.

Beyond its practical function as a source of food and medicine, the medieval garden was a space of social and religious significance. In Christian history, gardens represented sacred places on earth. During the Middle Ages and early Renaissance, it was not the sprawling paradise of the Garden of Eden that captured the imagination, but rather the closed garden of the Bible's Song of Songs (4:12): "A garden enclosed is my sister, my spouse; a spring shut up, a fountain sealed." Such sensuous imagery symbolized the soul's union with God, Christ's union with the Catholic Church, and the bond of love between a man and a woman.

Although enclosed behind walls, fences, or hedges to protect them as vital food sources, gardens were also the private places of dreamers and lovers. Pleasure gardens bloomed around the homes of the wealthy. There, amid grottoes and fountains, lovers breathed the warm scents of roses and lilies and pursued the romantic trysts popularized in court poetry. The stories of courtly love were cautionary as well as titillating, for as the catechism reminded every medieval Christian, the garden was also a place of temptation and lost innocence.

What kinds of gardens existed in the Middle Ages and early Renaissance? How did religion give meaning to gardens?

A wealthy man oversees apple picking at harvest time in a fifteenth-century French orchard. In the town below, individual house gardens can be seen. Protective fences, made of woven sticks, keep out predatory animals. In the right foreground, a boar can be seen overturning an apple barrel. **The British Library**

Teresa McClean, *Medieval English Gardens* (New York: Viking Press, 1980), pp. 64, 133; Marilyn Stokstad and Jerry Stannard, *Gardens of the Middle Ages* (Lawrence, KS: Spencer Museum, 1983), pp. 19–21, 61.

Alighieri (1265–1321), whose *Vita Nuova* and *Divine Comedy* form, with Petrarch's sonnets, the cornerstones of Italian vernacular literature. Petrarch's student and friend Giovanni Boccaccio (1313–1375) was also a pioneer of humanist studies. His *Decameron*—one hundred often bawdy tales told by three men and seven women in a safe country retreat away from the plague that ravaged Florence in 1348 (see Chapter 9)—is both a stinging social commentary (it exposes sexual and economic misconduct) and a sympathetic look at human behavior. An avid collector of manuscripts, Boccaccio also assembled an encyclopedia of Greek and Roman mythology.

Educational Reforms and Goals Humanists delighted in taking their mastery of ancient languages directly to the past, refusing to be slaves to later tradition. Such an attitude not only made them innovative educators, but also kept them constantly in search of new sources of information. In the search, they assembled magnificent manuscript collections, treating them as potent medicines for the ills of contemporary society, and capable of enlightening the minds of any who would immerse themselves in them.

The goal of humanist studies was wisdom eloquently spoken, both knowledge of the good and the ability to move others to desire it. Learning was not meant to remain abstract and unpracticed. "It is better to will the good than to know the truth," Petrarch taught, and it became a motto of many later humanists, who, like Petrarch, believed learning ennobled people. Pietro Paolo Vergerio (1349–1420), the author of the most influential Renaissance tract on education (*On the Morals That Befit a Free Man*), left a classic summary of the humanist concept of a liberal education:

We call those studies liberal which are worthy of a free man; those studies by which we attain and practice virtue and wisdom; that education which calls forth, trains, and develops those highest gifts of body and mind which ennoble men and which are rightly judged to rank next in dignity to virtue only, for to a vulgar temper, gain and pleasure are the one aim of existence, to a lofty nature, moral worth and fame.[1]

The ideal of a useful education and well-rounded people inspired far-reaching reforms in traditional education. The Roman orator Quintilian's (ca. 35–100) *Education of the Orator*, the complete text of which was discovered in 1416, became the basic classical guide for the humanist revision of the traditional curriculum. Vittorino da Feltre (d. 1446) exemplified the ideals of humanist teaching. Not only did he have his students read the difficult works of Pliny, Ptolemy, Terence, Plautus, Livy, and Plutarch, he also subjected them to vigorous physical exercise and games. Still another contemporary educator, Guarino da Verona (d. 1460), the rector of the new University of Ferrara and another student of Greek scholar Manuel Chrysoloras, streamlined the study of classical languages.

Despite the grinding scholarly process of acquiring ancient knowledge, humanistic studies were not confined to the classroom. As Baldassare Castiglione's (1478–1529) *Book of the Courtier* illustrates, the rediscovered knowledge of the past was both a model and a challenge to the present. Written as a practical guide for the nobility at the court of Urbino, a small duchy in central Italy, it embodies the highest ideals of Italian humanism. The successful courtier is said to be one who knows how to integrate knowledge of ancient languages and history with athletic, military, and musical skills, while at the same time practicing good manners and exhibiting a high moral character.

Privileged, educated noblewomen also promoted the new education and culture at royal courts. Among them was Christine de Pisan (1363?–1434), the Italian-born daughter of the physician and astrologer of French king Charles V. She became an expert in classical, French, and Italian languages and literature. Married at fifteen and the widowed mother of three at twenty-seven, she wrote lyric poetry to support herself and was much read throughout the courts of Europe. Her most famous work, *The Treasure of the City of Ladies*, is a chronicle of the accomplishments of the great women of history. (See "Christine de Pisan Instructs Women on How to Handle Their Husbands," page 290.)

The Florentine "Academy" and the Revival of Platonism Of all the important recoveries of the past made during the Italian Renaissance, none stands out more than the revival of Greek studies—especially the works of Plato—in fifteenth-century Florence. Many factors combined to bring this revival about. A foundation, already mentioned above, was laid in 1397 when the city invited Manuel Chrysoloras to come from Constantinople to promote Greek learning. A half century later (1439), the ecumenical Council of Ferrara-Florence, convened to negotiate the reunion of the Eastern and Western churches, opened the door for many Greek scholars and manuscripts to pour into the West. After the fall of Constantinople to the Turks in 1453, many Greek scholars fled to Florence for refuge. This was the background against which the Florentine Platonic Academy evolved under the patronage of Cosimo de' Medici and the supervision of Marsilio Ficino (1433–1499) and Pico della Mirandola (1463–1494).

Renaissance thinkers were especially attracted to the Platonic tradition and to those Church Fathers who tried to synthesize Platonic philosophy with Christian teaching. The so-called Florentine Academy was actually not a formal school, but an informal gathering of influential Florentine humanists devoted to the revival of the works of Plato and the Neoplatonists: Plotinus, Proclus,

---

[1]Cited by De Lamar Jensen, *Renaissance Europe: Age of Recovery and Reconciliation* (Lexington, MA: D. C. Health, 1981), p. 111.

CHRISTINE DE PISAN INSTRUCTS WOMEN ON HOW TO HANDLE THEIR HUSBANDS

Renowned Renaissance noblewoman Christine de Pisan has the modern reputation of being perhaps the first feminist, and her book, The Treasure of the City of Ladies *(also known as* The Book of Three Virtues*), has been described as the Renaissance woman's survival manual. Here she gives advice to the wives of artisans.*

How does Christine de Pisan's image of husband and wife compare with other medieval views? Would the church question her advice? As a noblewoman commenting on the married life of artisans, does her high social standing influence her advice? Would she give similar advice to women of her own social class?

All wives of artisans should be very painstaking and diligent if they wish to have the necessities of life. They should encourage their husbands or their workmen to get to work early in the morning and work until late. . . . [And] the wife herself should [also] be involved in the work to the extent that she knows all about it, so that she may know how to oversee his workers if her husband is absent, and to reprove them if they do not do well. . . . And when customers come to her husband and try to drive a hard bargain, she ought to warn him solicitously to take care that he does not make a bad deal. She should advise him to be chary of giving too much credit if he does not know precisely where and to whom it is going, for in this way many come to poverty. . . .

In addition, she ought to keep her husband's love as much as she can, to this end: that he will stay at home more willingly and that he may not have any reason to join the foolish crowds of other young men in taverns and indulge in unnecessary and extravagant expense, as many tradesmen do, especially in Paris. By treating him kindly she should protect him as well as she can from this. It is said that three things drive a man from his home: a quarrelsome wife, a smoking fireplace, and a leaking roof. She too ought to stay at home gladly and not go off every day traipsing hither and yon gossiping with

Christine de Pisan, who has the modern reputation of being the first European feminist, presents her internationally famous book *The Treasure of the City of Ladies*, also known as *The Book of Three Virtues*, to Isabella of Bavaria amid her ladies in waiting. Historical Picture Archive/CORBIS/Bettmann

the neighbours and visiting her chums to find out what everyone is doing. That is done by slovenly housewives roaming about the town in groups. Nor should she go off on these pilgrimages got up for no good reason and involving a lot of needless expense.

From *The Treasure of the City of Ladies* by Christine de Pisan, trans. by Sarah Lawson (New York: Penguin, 1985), pp. 167–168. Copyright © Sarah Lawson, 1985. Reproduced by permission of Penguin Books Ltd.

Porphyry, and Dionysius the Areopagite. To this end, Ficino edited and published the complete works of Plato.

The appeal of **Platonism** lay in its flattering view of human nature. It distinguished between an eternal sphere of being and the perishable world in which humans actually lived. Human reason was believed to have preexisted in this pristine world and still to commune with it, a theory supported by human knowledge of eternal mathematical and moral truths.

Strong Platonic influence is evident in Pico's *Oration on the Dignity of Man*, perhaps the most famous Renaissance statement on the nature of humankind. (See "Compare & Connect: Is the "Renaissance Man" a Myth?" page 292.) Pico wrote the *Oration* as an introduction to his pretentious collection of nine hundred theses. Published in Rome in December 1486, the theses were intended to serve as the basis for a public debate on all of life's important topics. The *Oration* drew on Platonic teaching to depict humans as the only creatures in the world who possessed the freedom to be whatever they chose, able at will to rise to the height of angels or just as quickly to wallow with pigs.

Critical Work of the Humanists: Lorenzo Valla

Because they were guided by scholarly ideals of philological accuracy and historical truth, the humanists could become critics of tradition even when that was not their intention. Dispassionate critical scholarship shook long-standing foundations, not the least of which were those of the medieval church.

The work of Lorenzo Valla (1406–1457), author of the standard Renaissance text on Latin philology, the *Elegances of the Latin Language* (1444), reveals the explosive character of the new learning. Although a good Catholic, Valla became a hero to later Protestant reformers. His popularity among them stemmed from his exposé of the *Donation of Constantine* (see Chapter 6) and his defense of predestination against the advocates of free will.

The fraudulent *Donation*, written in the eighth century, purported to be a grant of vast territories that the Roman emperor Constantine (r. 307–337) donated to the pope. Valla did not intend the exposé of the *Donation* to have the devastating force that Protestants later attributed to it. He only proved in a careful, scholarly way what others had long suspected. Using textual analysis and historical logic, Valla demonstrated that the document was filled with anachronistic terms, such as *fief*, and contained information that could not have existed in a fourth-century document. In the same dispassionate way, he also pointed out errors in the Latin Vulgate, still the authorized version of the Bible for the Western church.

Such discoveries did not make Valla any less loyal to the church, nor did they prevent his faithful fulfillment of the office of apostolic secretary in Rome under Pope Nicholas V (r. 1447–1455). Nonetheless, historical humanistic criticism of this type also served those less loyal to the medieval church. Young humanists formed the first identifiable group of Martin Luther's supporters.

Civic Humanism A basic humanist criticism of Scholastic education was that much of its content was useless. Education, humanists believed, should promote individual virtue and public service, hence the designation, **civic humanism**. The most striking examples of this were found in Florence, where three humanists served as chancellors of the city: Coluccio Salutati (1331–1406), Leonardo Bruni (ca. 1370–1444), and Poggio Bracciolini (1380–1459). Each used his rhetorical skills to rally the Florentines against the aggression of Naples and Milan. Bruni and Poggio wrote adulatory histories of the city. Another accomplished humanist scholar, Leon Battista Alberti (1402–1472), was a noted Florentine architect and builder. However, many modern scholars doubt that humanistic scholarship really accounted for such civic activity and rather view the three famous humanist chancellors of Florence as men who simply wanted to exercise power.

Toward the end of the Renaissance, many humanists became cliquish and snobbish, an intellectual elite more concerned with narrow scholarly interests and writing pure, classical Latin than with revitalizing civic and social life. In reaction to this elitist trend, the humanist historians Niccolò Machiavelli (1469–1527) and Francesco Guicciardini (1483–1540) wrote in Italian and made contemporary history their primary source and subject matter. Here, arguably, we can see the two sides of humanism: deep scholarship and practical politics.

2-31. feit Renaissance

Renaissance Art

In Renaissance Italy, as in Reformation Europe, the values and interests of the laity were no longer subordinated to those of the clergy. In education, culture, and religion, the laity assumed a leading role and established models for the clergy to emulate. This development was due in part to the church's loss of international power during the great crises of the late Middle Ages. The rise of national sentiment and the emergence of national bureaucracies staffed by laymen, not clerics, and the rapid growth of lay education over the fourteenth and fifteenth centuries also encouraged it. Medieval Christian values were adjusted to a more this-worldly spirit.

This new perspective on life is prominent in the painting and sculpture of the High Renaissance (1450–1527), when art and sculpture reached their full maturity. Whereas medieval art tended to be abstract and formulaic, Renaissance art emphatically embraced the natural world and human emotions. Renaissance artists gave their works a rational, even mathematical, order—perfect symmetry and proportionality reflecting a belief in the harmony of the universe.

Is the "Renaissance Man" a Myth?

AS SEVERAL ILLUSTRATIONS in this chapter attest, the great artists of the Renaissance (Raphael, Leonardo da Vinci, Albrecht Dürer) romanticized their human subjects and made them larger than life. Not only was the iconic "Renaissance man" perfectly proportioned physically, he was also effective in what he undertook, endowed with the divine freedom and power to be and to do whatever he chose.

QUESTIONS

1. Who or what are Pico's and Dürer's glorified humans? Is the vaunted "Renaissance Man" real or fictional?

2. What is one to make of an era fixated on the perfect body and mind?

3. Is Martin Luther's rejoinder (the bondage of the human will) truer to life, or religious misanthropy?

I. Pico della Mirandola, *Oration on the Dignity of Man* (ca. 1486)

One of the most eloquent descriptions of the Renaissance image of human beings comes from the Italian humanist Pico della Mirandola (1463–1494). In his famed Oration on the Dignity of Man *(ca. 1486), Pico describes humans as free to become whatever they choose.*

Pico's "Renaissance Man" stands in stark contrast to the devout Christian pilgrim of the Middle Ages. The latter found himself always at the crossroads of heaven and hell, in constant fear of sin, death, and the devil, regularly confessing his sins and receiving forgiveness in an unending penitential cycle. Had the Middle Ages misjudged human nature? Was there a great transformation in human nature between the Middle Ages and the Renaissance?

The best of artisans [God] ordained that that creature (man) to whom He had been able to give nothing proper to himself should have joint possession of whatever had been peculiar to each of the different kinds of being. He therefore took man as a creature of indeterminate nature and, assigning him a place in the middle of the world, addressed him thus: "Neither a fixed abode nor a form that is thine alone nor any function peculiar to thyself have we given thee, Adam, to the end that according to thy longing and according to thy judgment thou mayest have and possess what abode, what form, and what functions thou thyself shalt desire. The nature of all other beings is limited and constrained within the bounds of laws prescribed by Us. Thou, constrained by no limits, in accordance with thine own free will, in whose hand We have placed thee,

shall ordain for thyself the limits of thy nature. We have set thee at the world's center that thou mayest from thence more easily observe whatever is in the world. We have made thee neither of heaven nor of earth, neither mortal nor immortal, so that with freedom of choice and with honor, as though the maker and molder of thyself, thou mayest fashion thyself in whatever shape thou shalt prefer. Thou shalt have the power to degenerate into the lower forms of life, which are brutish. Thou shalt have the power, out of thy soul's judgment, to be reborn into the higher forms, which are divine." O supreme generosity of God the Father, O highest and most marvelous felicity of man! To him it is granted to have whatever he chooses, to be whatever he wills.

Source: Giovanni Pico della Mirandola, *Oration on the Dignity of Man*, in *The Renaissance Philosophy of Man*, ed. by E. Cassirer et al. (Chicago: Phoenix Books, 1961), pp. 224–225.

II. Albrecht Dürer

In 1500, Albrecht Dürer, then 28, painted the most famous self-portrait of the European Renaissance and Reformation, one that celebrated his own beauty and genius by imposing his face on a portrayal of Christ, a work of art that has been called "the birth of the modern artist."

Fourteen years later (1514), on the occasion of his mother's death, Dürer engraved another famous image of himself, only now as a man in deep depression, or melancholy, his mind darkened and his creativity throttled.

In this self-portrait he is neither effective nor handsome, much less heroic and divine, not a self-portrait of a Renaissance man.

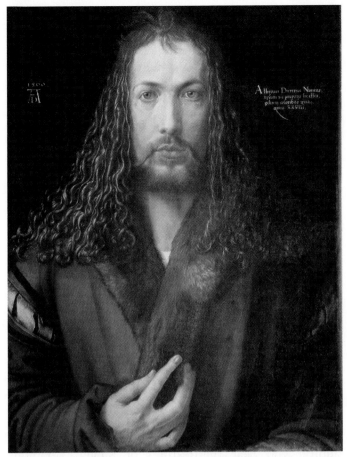

Albrecht Dürer (1471–1528). *Self-portrait at Age 28 with Fur Coat*. 1500. Oil on wood, 67 × 49 cm. Alte Pinakothek, Munich, Germany. Photograph © Scala/Art Resource, NY

Albrecht Dürer. *Melencolia I*. 1514. Engraving. 23.8 × 18.9 cm. Courtesy of the Library of Congress.

III. Martin Luther, *The Bondage of the Will* (1525)

The greater challenge to the Renaissance man came from Martin Luther, who met his "Pico" in the northern humanist Desiderius Erasmus. Like Pico, Erasmus, flying in the face of Reformation theology, conceived free will to be "a power of the human will by which a man may apply himself to those things that lead to eternal salvation, or turn away from the same." Of such thinking, Luther made short-shift.

It is in the highest degree wholesome and necessary for a Christian to know whether or not his will has anything to do in matters pertaining to salvation . . . We need to have in mind a clear-cut distinction between God's power and ours and God's work and ours, if we would live a godly life . . . The will, be it God's or man's, does what it does, good or bad, under no compulsion, but just as it wants or pleases, as if totally free . . . Wise men know what experience of life proves, that no man's purposes ever go forward as planned, but events overtake all men contrary to their expectation. . . Who among us always lives and behaves as he should? But duty and doctrine are not therefore condemned, rather they condemn us.

God has promised His grace to the humbled, that is, to those who mourn over and despair of themselves. But a man cannot be thoroughly humbled till he realizes that his salvation is utterly beyond his own powers, counsels, efforts, will and works, and depends absolutely on the will, counsel, pleasure, and work of Another: GOD ALONE. As long as he is persuaded that he can make even the smallest contribution to his salvation, he . . . does not utterly despair of himself, and so is not humbled before God, but plans for himself a position, an occasion, a work, which shall bring him final salvation. But he who [no longer] doubts that his destiny depends entirely only on the will of God . . . waits for God to work in him, and such a man is very near to grace for his salvation. So if we want to drop this term ("free will") altogether, which would be the safest and most Christian thing to do, we may, still in good faith, teach people to use it to credit man with 'free will' in respect not of what is above him, but of what is below him . . . However, with regard to God and in all that bears on salvation or damnation, he has no 'free will' but is a captive, prisoner and bond-slave, either to the will of God, or to the will of Satan.

Source: Martin Luther, *On the Bondage of the Will*, ed. by J. I Packer and O. R. Johnston (Westwood, NJ: Fleming H. Fevell Co., 1957), pp. 79, 81, 83, 87, 100, 104, 107, 137.

Combining the painterly qualities of all the Renaissance masters, Raphael created scenes of tender beauty and subjects sublime in both flesh and spirit. Musée du Louvre, Paris/Giraudon, Paris/SuperStock

Renaissance artists were helped by the development of new technical skills during the fifteenth century. In addition to the availability of oil paints, two special techniques gave them an edge: the use of shading to enhance naturalness (**chiaroscuro**) and the adjustment of the size of figures to give the viewer a feeling of continuity with the painting (*linear perspective*). These techniques enabled the artist to portray space realistically and to paint a more natural world. The result, compared to their flat Byzantine and Gothic counterparts, was a three-dimensional canvas filled with energy and life.

Giotto (1266–1336), the father of Renaissance painting, signaled the new direction. An admirer of Saint Francis of Assisi, whose love of nature he shared, Giotto painted a more natural world. Though still filled with religious seriousness, his work was no longer an abstract and unnatural depiction of the world. The painter Masaccio (1401–1428) and the sculptor Donatello (1386–1466) also portrayed the world around them literally and naturally. The great masters of the High

Renaissance, Leonardo da Vinci (1452–1519), Raphael (1483–1520), and Michelangelo Buonarroti (1475–1564), reached the heights of such painting.

Leonardo da Vinci A true master of many skills, Leonardo exhibited the Renaissance ideal of the universal person. One of the greatest painters of all time, he also advised Italian princes and the French king Francis I (r. 1515–1547) on military engineering. He advocated scientific experimentation, dissected corpses to learn anatomy, and was a self-taught botanist. His inventive mind foresaw such modern machines as airplanes and submarines. The variety of his interests was so great that it could shorten his attention span. His great skill in conveying inner moods through complex facial expression is apparent not only in his most famous painting, the *Mona Lisa*, but in his self-portrait as well.

Raphael A man of great kindness and a painter of great sensitivity, Raphael was loved by his contemporaries as much for his person as for his work. He is most famous for his tender madonnas and the great fresco in the Vatican, *The School of Athens*, a virtually perfect example of Renaissance technique. It depicts Plato and Aristotle surrounded by other great philosophers and scientists of antiquity who bear the features of Raphael's famous contemporaries.

TMNT

Michelangelo The melancholy genius Michelangelo also excelled in a variety of arts and crafts. His eighteen-foot sculpture of David, which long stood majestically in the great square of Florence, is a perfect example of Renaissance devotion to harmony, symmetry, and proportion, all serving the glorification of the human form. Four different popes commissioned works by Michelangelo. The frescoes in the Vatican's Sistine Chapel are the most famous, painted during the pontificate of Pope Julius II (r. 1503–1513), who also set Michelangelo to work on his own magnificent tomb. The Sistine frescoes originally covered 10,000 square feet and involved 343 figures, over half of which exceeded ten feet in height, but it is their originality and perfection as works of art that impress one most. This labor of love and piety took four years to complete.

His later works are more complex and suggest deep personal changes. They mark, artistically and philosophically, the passing of High Renaissance painting and the advent of a new style known as **mannerism**, which reached its peak in the late sixteenth and early seventeenth centuries. A reaction to the simplicity and symmetry of High Renaissance art, which also had a parallel in contemporary music and literature, mannerism made room for the strange and the abnormal, giving freer reign to the individual perceptions and feelings of the artist, who now felt free to paint, compose, or write in a "mannered," or "affected," way. Tintoretto (d. 1594) and El Greco (d. 1614) are mannerism's supreme representatives.

A Closer ▶ LOOK

LEONARDO PLOTS THE PERFECT MAN

VITRUVIAN MAN BY Leonardo da Vinci, c. 1490. The name "Vitruvian" is taken from that of a first-century C.E. Roman architect and engineer, Marcus Pollio Vitruvius, who used squares and circles to demonstrate the human body's symmetry and proportionality. According to Vitruvius:

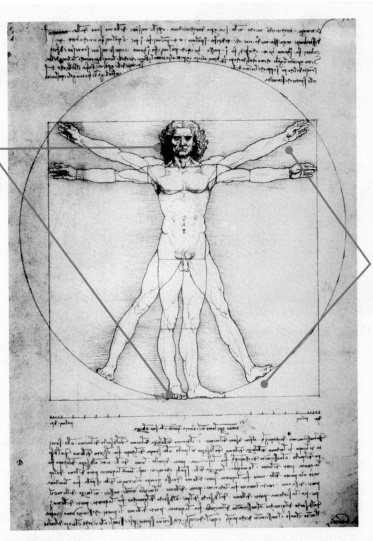

And just as the human body yields a circular outline, so too a square figure may be found from it. For if we measure the distance from the soles of the feet to the top of the head, and then apply that measure to the outstretched arms, the breadth will be found to be the same as the height.

Leonardo, like most artists of his time, shared this classical ideal of human perfection even in his gloomiest etchings and paintings. With few exceptions, the great painters of the age wanted to portray men and women in a more than human beauty and glory. Even the rabbits of the German painter Albrecht Dürer, who shared this ideal, were superior to any rabbit one might see in the wild.

If a man be placed flat on his back, with his hands and feet extended, and a pair of compasses centered at his navel, the fingers and toes of his two hands and feet will touch the circumference of a circle described therefrom.

CORBIS/Bettmann

To examine this image in an interactive fashion, please go to www.myhistorylab.com

myhistorylab

Marilyn Stokstad and David Cateforis, *Art History* (New York: Pearson, 2005), p. 651.

Michelangelo's Scene from the Last Judgment. The High Italian Renaissance obsession with the beefy, pumped up, heroic body finds expression in this detail of a fresco in Michelangelo's rendering of the *Last Judgment* in the Sistine Chapel.   Nippon Television Network Corporation

decline of serfs

Slavery in the Renaissance

Throughout Renaissance Italy, slavery flourished as extravagantly as art and culture. A thriving western slave market existed as early as the twelfth century, when the Spanish sold Muslim slaves captured in raids and war to wealthy Italians and other buyers. Contemporaries looked on such slavery as a merciful act, since their captors would otherwise have killed the captives. In addition to widespread household or domestic slavery, collective plantation slavery, following East Asian models, also developed in the eastern Mediterranean during the High Middle Ages. In the savannas of Sudan and the Venetian estates on the islands of Cyprus and Crete, gangs of slaves cut sugarcane, setting the model for later slave plantations in the Mediterranean and the New World.

MAJOR POLITICAL EVENTS OF THE ITALIAN RENAISSANCE (1375–1527)

1378–1382	The Ciompi Revolt in Florence
1434	Medici rule in Florence established by Cosimo de' Medici
1454–1455	Treaty of Lodi allies Milan, Naples, and Florence (in effect until 1494)
1494	Charles VIII of France invades Italy
1494–1498	Savonarola controls Florence
1495	League of Venice unites Venice, Milan, the Papal States, the Holy Roman Empire, and Spain against France
1499	Louis XII invades Milan (the second French invasion of Italy)
1500	The Borgias conquer Romagna
1512–1513	The Holy League (Pope Julius II, Ferdinand of Aragon, Emperor Maximilian, and Venice) defeats the French
1513	Machiavelli writes *The Prince*
1515	Francis I leads the third French invasion of Italy
1516	Concordat of Bologna between France and the papacy
1527	Sack of Rome by imperial soldiers

After the Black Death (1348–1350) reduced the supply of laborers everywhere in Western Europe, the demand for slaves soared. Slaves were imported from Africa, the Balkans, Constantinople, Cyprus, Crete, and the lands surrounding the Black Sea. Taken randomly from conquered people, they consisted of many races: Tatars, Circassians, Greeks, Russians, Georgians, and Iranians as well as Asians and Africans. According to one source, "By the end of the fourteenth century, there was hardly a well-to-do household in Tuscany without at least one slave: brides brought them [to their marriages] as part of their dowry, doctors accepted them from their patients in lieu of fees—and it was not unusual to find them even in the service of a priest."[2]

Owners had complete dominion over their slaves; in Italian law, this meant the "[power] to have, hold, sell, alienate, exchange, enjoy, rent or unrent, dispose of in [their] will[s], judge soul and body, and do with in perpetuity whatsoever may please [them] and [their] heirs and no man may gainsay [them]."[3] A strong, young, healthy slave cost the equivalent of the wages paid a free servant over several years. Considering the lifetime of free service thereafter, slaves were well worth the price.

[2]Iris Origo, *The Merchant of Prato: Francesco di Marco Datini, 1335–1410* (New York: David Godine, 1986), pp. 90–91.
[3]Origo, *The Merchant of Prato*, p. 209.

Tatars and Africans appear to have been the worst treated, but as in ancient Greece and Rome, slaves at this time were generally accepted as family members and integrated into households. Not a few women slaves became mothers of their masters' children. Fathers often adopted children of such unions and raised them as their legitimate heirs. It was also in the interest of their owners to keep slaves healthy and happy; otherwise they would be of little use and even become a threat. Slaves nonetheless remained a foreign and suspected presence in Italian society; they were, as all knew, uprooted and resentful people.

acquire power through money not just monarchs

▼ Italy's Political Decline: The French Invasions (1494–1527)

As a land of autonomous city-states, Italy had always relied on internal cooperation for its peace and safety from foreign invasion—especially by the Turks. Such cooperation was maintained during the second half of the fifteenth century, thanks to a political alliance known as the Treaty of Lodi (1454–1455). Its terms brought Milan and Naples, long traditional enemies, into the alliance with Florence. These three stood together for decades against Venice, which frequently joined the Papal States to maintain an internal balance of power. However, when a foreign enemy threatened Italy, the five states could also present a united front.

Around 1490, after the rise to power of the Milanese despot Ludovico il Moro, hostilities between Milan and Naples resumed. The peace that the Treaty of Lodi made possible ended in 1494 when Naples, supported by Florence and the Borgia Pope Alexander VI (r. 1492–1503), threatened Milan. Ludovico made a fatal response to these new political alignments: He appealed to the French for aid. French kings had ruled Naples from 1266 to 1442 before being driven out by Duke Alfonso of Sicily. Breaking a wise Italian rule, Ludovico invited the French to reenter Italy and revive their dynastic claim to Naples. In his haste to check rival Naples, Ludovico did not recognize sufficiently that France also had dynastic claims to Milan. Nor did he foresee how insatiable the French appetite for new territory would become once French armies had crossed the Alps and encamped in Italy.

Charles VIII's March Through Italy

The French king Louis XI had resisted the temptation to invade Italy while nonetheless keeping French dynastic claims in Italy alive. His successor, Charles VIII (r. 1483–1498), an eager youth in his twenties, responded to Ludovico's call with lightning speed. Within five months, he had crossed the Alps (August 1494) and raced as conqueror through Florence and the Papal States into Naples.

As Charles approached Florence, its Florentine ruler, Piero de' Medici, who was allied with Naples against Milan, tried to placate the French king by handing over Pisa and other Florentine possessions. Such appeasement only brought about Piero's exile by a citizenry that was being revolutionized by a radical Dominican preacher named Girolamo Savonarola (1452–1498). Savonarola convinced the fearful Florentines that the French king's arrival was a long-delayed and fully justified divine vengeance on their immorality.

That allowed Charles to enter Florence without resistance. Between Savonarola's fatal flattery and the payment of a large ransom, the city escaped destruction. After Charles's departure, Savonarola exercised virtual rule over Florence for four years. In the end, the Florentines proved not to be the stuff theocracies are made of. Savonarola's moral rigor and antipapal policies made it impossible for him to survive indefinitely in Italy. After the Italian cities reunited and ousted the French invader, whom Savonarola had praised as a godsend, Savonarola's days were numbered. In May 1498, he was imprisoned and executed.

Charles's lightning march through Italy also struck terror in non-Italian hearts. Ferdinand of Aragon (r. 1479–1516), who had hoped to expand his own possessions in Italy from his base in Sicily, now found himself vulnerable to a French-Italian axis. In response he created a new counteralliance—the League of Venice. Formed in March 1495, the League brought Venice, the Papal States, and Emperor Maximilian I (r. 1493–1519) together with Ferdinand against the French. The stage was now set for a conflict between France and Spain that would not end until 1559.

Ludovico il Moro meanwhile recognized that he had sown the wind. Having desired a French invasion only as long as it weakened his enemies, he now saw a whirlwind of events he had himself created threaten Milan. In reaction, he joined the League of Venice, which was now strong enough to send Charles into retreat and to end the menace he posed to Italy.

Pope Alexander VI and the Borgia Family

The French returned to Italy under Charles's successor, Louis XII (r. 1498–1515). This time a new Italian ally, the Borgia pope, Alexander VI, assisted them. Probably the most corrupt pope who ever sat on the papal throne, he openly promoted the political careers of Cesare and Lucrezia Borgia, the children he had had before he became pope. He placed papal policy in tandem with the efforts of his powerful family to secure a political base in Romagna in north central Italy.

In Romagna, several principalities had fallen away from the church during the Avignon papacy. Venice, the pope's ally within the League of Venice, continued to contest the Papal States for their loyalty. Seeing that a French alliance would allow him to reestablish control over the region, Alexander took steps to secure French favor. He annulled Louis XII's marriage to Charles VIII's sister so Louis could marry Charles's widow, Anne of Brittany—a popular political move designed to keep Brittany French. The pope also bestowed a cardinal's hat on the archbishop of Rouen, Louis's favorite cleric. Most important, Alexander agreed to abandon the League of Venice, a withdrawal of support that made the league too weak to resist a French reconquest of Milan. In exchange, Cesare Borgia received the sister of the king of Navarre, Charlotte d'Albret, in marriage, a union that enhanced Borgia military strength. Cesare also received land grants from Louis XII and the promise of French military aid in Romagna.

All in all it was a scandalous trade-off, but one that made it possible for both the French king and the pope to realize their ambitions within Italy. Louis invaded Milan in August 1499. Ludovico il Moro, who had originally opened the Pandora's box of French invasion, spent his last years languishing in a French prison. In 1500, Louis and Ferdinand of Aragon divided Naples between them, and the pope and Cesare Borgia conquered the cities of Romagna without opposition. Alexander's victorious son was given the title "duke of Romagna."

Pope Julius II

Cardinal Giuliano della Rovere, a strong opponent of the Borgia family, succeeded Alexander VI as Pope Julius II (r. 1503–1513). He suppressed the Borgias and placed their newly conquered lands in Romagna under papal jurisdiction. Julius raised the Renaissance papacy to its peak of military prowess and diplomatic intrigue, gaining him the title of "warrior pope." Shocked, as were other contemporaries, by this thoroughly secular papacy, the humanist Erasmus (1466?–1536), who had witnessed in disbelief a bullfight in the papal palace during a visit to Rome, wrote a popular anonymous satire entitled *Julius Excluded from Heaven*. This humorous account purported to describe the pope's unsuccessful efforts to convince Saint Peter that he was worthy of admission to heaven.

Assisted by his powerful allies, Pope Julius drove the Venetians out of Romagna in 1509 and fully secured the Papal States. Having realized this long-sought papal goal, Julius turned to the second major undertaking of his pontificate: ridding Italy of his former ally, the French invader. Julius, Ferdinand of Aragon, and Venice formed a second Holy League in October 1511 and were joined by Emperor Maximilian I and the Swiss. In 1512, the league had the French in full retreat, and the Swiss defeated them in 1513 at Novara.

The French were nothing if not persistent. They invaded Italy a third time under Louis's successor, Fran-cis I (r. 1515–1547). This time French armies massacred Swiss soldiers of the Holy League at Marignano in September 1515, avenging the earlier defeat at Novara. The victory won the Concordat of Bologna from the pope in August 1516, an agreement that gave the French king control over the French clergy in exchange for French recognition of the pope's superiority over church councils and his right to collect annates in France. This concordat helped keep France Catholic after the outbreak of the Protestant Reformation, but the new French entry into Italy set the stage for the first of four major wars with Spain in the first half of the sixteenth century: the Habsburg-Valois wars, none of which France won.

Niccolò Machiavelli

The foreign invasions made a shambles of Italy. The same period that saw Italy's cultural peak in the work of Leonardo, Raphael, and Michelangelo also witnessed Italy's political tragedy. One who watched as French, Spanish, and German armies wreaked havoc on Italy was Niccolò Machiavelli (1469–1527). The more he saw, the more convinced he became that Italian political unity and independence were ends that justified any means.

A humanist and a careful student of ancient Rome, Machiavelli was impressed by the way Roman rulers and citizens had then defended their homeland. They possessed *virtù*, the ability to act decisively and heroically for the good of their country. Stories of ancient Roman patriotism and self-sacrifice were Machiavelli's favorites, and he lamented the absence of such traits among his compatriots. Such romanticizing of the Roman past exaggerated both ancient virtue and contemporary failings. His Florentine contemporary, Francesco Guicciardini (1483–1540), a more sober historian less given to idealizing antiquity, wrote truer chronicles of Florentine and Italian history.

Machiavelli also held republican ideals, which he did not want to see vanish from Italy. He believed a strong and determined people could struggle successfully with fortune. He scolded the Italian people for the self-destruction their own internal feuding was causing. He wanted an end to that behavior above all, so a reunited Italy could drive all foreign armies out.

His fellow citizens were not up to such a challenge. The juxtaposition of what Machiavelli believed the ancient Romans had been, with the failure of his contemporaries to attain such high ideals, made him the famous cynic whose name—in the epithet "Machiavellian"—has become synonymous with ruthless political expediency. Only a strongman, he concluded, could impose order on so divided and selfish a people; the salvation of Italy required, for the present, cunning dictators.

second Medici pope, Clement VII (r. 1523–1534), watched helplessly as the army of Emperor Charles V sacked Rome in 1527, also the year of Machiavelli's death.

▼ Revival of Monarchy in Northern Europe

After 1450, the emergence of truly sovereign rulers set in motion a shift from divided feudal monarchy to unified national monarchies. Dynastic and chivalric ideals of feudal monarchy did not, however, vanish. Territorial princes remained on the scene and representative bodies persisted and even grew in influence. Still, in the late fifteenth and early sixteenth centuries, the old problem of the one and the many was now progressively decided in favor of national monarchs.

The feudal monarchy of the High Middle Ages was characterized by the division of the basic powers of government between the king and his semiautonomous vassals. The nobility and the towns then acted with varying degrees of unity and success through evolving representative assemblies, such as the English Parliament, the French Estates General, and the Spanish *Cortés*, to thwart the centralization of royal power into a united nation. But after the Hundred Years' War and the Great Schism in the church, the nobility and the clergy were in decline and less able to block growing national monarchies.

The increasingly important towns now began to ally with the king. Loyal, business-wise townspeople, not the nobility and the clergy, increasingly staffed royal offices and became the king's lawyers, bookkeepers, military tacticians, and foreign diplomats. This new alliance between king and town broke the bonds of feudal society and made possible the rise of sovereign states.

In a sovereign state, the powers of taxation, war making, and law enforcement no longer belong to semiautonomous vassals but are concentrated in the monarch and exercised by his or her chosen agents. Taxes, wars, and laws become national, rather than merely regional, matters. Only as monarchs became able to act independently of the nobility and representative assemblies could they overcome the decentralization that impeded nation building. Ferdinand and Isabella of Spain rarely called the *Cortés* into session. The French Estates General met irregularly, mostly in time of crisis, but was never essential to royal governance. Henry VII (r. 1485–1509) of England managed to raise revenues without going begging to Parliament, which had voted him customs revenues for life in 1485. Brilliant theorists, from Marsilius of Padua in the fourteenth century to Machiavelli in the fifteenth to Jean Bodin (1530–1596) in the sixteenth, emphatically defended the sovereign rights of monarchy.

Santi di Tito's portrait of Machiavelli, perhaps the most famous Italian political theorist, who advised Renaissance princes to practice artful deception and inspire fear in their subjects if they wished to be successful.   Scala/Art Resource, NY

It has been argued that Machiavelli wrote *The Prince* in 1513 as a cynical satire on the way rulers actually do behave and not as a serious recommendation of unprincipled despotic rule. To take his advocacy of tyranny literally, it is argued, contradicts both his earlier works and his own strong family tradition of republican service. But Machiavelli seems to have been in earnest when he advised rulers to discover the advantages of fraud and brutality, at least as a temporary means to the higher end of a unified Italy. He apparently hoped to see a strong ruler emerge from the Medici family, which had captured the papacy in 1513 with the pontificate of Leo X (r. 1513–1521). At the same time, the Medici family retained control over the powerful territorial state of Florence. The situation was similar to that of Machiavelli's hero Cesare Borgia and his father Pope Alexander VI, who had earlier brought factious Romagna to heel by combining secular family goals with religious policy. *The Prince* was pointedly dedicated to Lorenzo de' Medici, duke of Urbino and grandson of Lorenzo the Magnificent.

Whatever Machiavelli's hopes may have been, the Medicis were not destined to be Italy's deliverers. The

The many were, of course, never totally subjugated to the one. But in the last half of the fifteenth century, rulers demonstrated that the law was their creature. They appointed civil servants whose vision was no longer merely local or regional. In Castile they were the *corregidores*, in England the justices of the peace, and in France bailiffs operating through well-drilled lieutenants. These royal ministers and agents could become closely attached to the localities they administered in the ruler's name, and regions were able to secure congenial royal appointments. Throughout England, for example, local magnates served as representatives of the Tudor dynasty that seized the throne in 1485. Nonetheless, these new executives remained royal executives, bureaucrats whose outlook was now "national" and whose loyalty was to the "state."

Monarchies also began to create standing national armies in the fifteenth century. The noble cavalry receded as the infantry and the artillery became the backbone of royal armies. Mercenary soldiers were recruited from Switzerland and Germany to form the major part of the "king's army." Professional soldiers who fought for pay and booty proved far more efficient than feudal vassals who fought simply for honor's sake. Monarchs who failed to meet their payrolls, however, now faced a new danger of mutiny and banditry by foreign troops.

The growing cost of warfare in the fifteenth and sixteenth centuries increased the monarch's need for new national sources of income. The great obstacle was the stubborn belief of the highest social classes that they were immune from government taxation. The nobility guarded their properties and traditional rights and despised taxation as an insult and a humiliation. Royal revenues accordingly had to grow at the expense of those least able to resist and least able to pay.

The monarchs had several options when it came to raising money. As feudal lords, they could collect rents from their royal domains. They could also levy national taxes on basic food and clothing, such as the salt tax (**gabelle**) in France and the 10 percent sales tax (*alcabala*) on commercial transactions in Spain. The rulers could also levy direct taxes on the peasantry, which they did through agreeable representative assemblies of the privileged classes in which the peasantry did not sit. The *taille*, which the French kings independently determined from year to year after the Estates General was suspended in 1484, was such a tax. Innovative fund-raising devices in the fifteenth century included the sale of public offices and the issuance of high-interest government bonds. Rulers still did not levy taxes on the powerful nobility, but instead, they borrowed from rich nobles and the great bankers of Italy and Germany. In money matters, the privileged classes remained as much the kings' creditors and competitors as their subjects.

France

Charles VII (r. 1422–1461) was a king made great by those who served him. His ministers created a permanent professional army, which—thanks initially to the inspiration of Joan of Arc—drove the English out of France. In addition, the enterprise of an independent merchant banker named Jacques Coeur helped develop a strong economy, diplomatic corps, and national administration during Charles's reign. These sturdy tools in turn enabled Charles's son and successor, the ruthless Louis XI (r. 1461–1483), to make France a great power.

French nation building had two political cornerstones in the fifteenth century. The first was the collapse of the English Empire in France following the Hundred Years' War. The second was the defeat of Charles the Bold (r. 1467–1477) and his duchy of Burgundy. Perhaps Europe's strongest political power in the mid-fifteenth century, Burgundy aspired to dwarf both France and the Holy Roman Empire as the leader of a dominant middle kingdom, which it might have done had not the continental powers joined to prevent it. When Charles the Bold died in defeat in a battle at Nancy in 1477, the dream of a Burgundian Empire died with him. Louis XI and Habsburg emperor Maximilian I divided the conquered Burgundian lands between them, with the treaty-wise Habsburgs getting the better part. The dissolution of Burgundy ended its constant intrigue against the French king and left Louis XI free to secure the monarchy. Between the newly acquired Burgundian lands and his own inheritance the king was able to end his reign with a kingdom almost twice the size of that he had inherited. Louis successfully harnessed the nobility, expanded the trade and industry that Jacques Cœur so carefully had nurtured, created a national postal system, and even established a lucrative silk industry.

A strong nation is a two-edged sword. Because Louis's successors inherited a secure and efficient government, they felt free to pursue what proved ultimately to be a bad foreign policy. Conquests in Italy in the 1490s and a long series of losing wars with the Habsburgs in the first half of the sixteenth century left France, by the mid-sixteenth century, once again a defeated nation almost as divided as it had been during the Hundred Years' War.

Spain

Both Castile and Aragon had been poorly ruled and divided kingdoms in the mid-fifteenth century, but the union of Isabella of Castile (r. 1474–1504) and Ferdinand of Aragon (r. 1479–1516) changed that situation. The two future sovereigns married in 1469, despite strong protests from neighboring Portugal and France, both of which foresaw the formidable European power the marriage would create. Castile was by far the richer and more populous of the two, having an estimated 5 million inhabitants to Aragon's population of under 1 million. Castile was also distinguished by its lucrative sheep-farming industry, run by a government-backed organization called the *Mesta*, another example of a developing centralized economic planning. Although the marriage of Ferdinand and Isabella dynastically united the two kingdoms, they remained constitutionally separated. Each retained its respective government agencies—separate laws, armies, coinage, and taxation—and cultural traditions.

Ferdinand and Isabella could do together what neither was able to accomplish alone: subdue their realms, secure their borders, venture abroad militarily, and Christianize the whole of Spain. Between 1482 and 1492 they conquered the Moors in Granada. Naples became a Spanish possession in 1504. By 1512, Ferdinand had secured his northern borders by conquering the kingdom of Navarre. Internally, the Spanish king and queen won the allegiance of the *Hermandad,* a powerful league of cities and towns that served them against stubborn noble landowners. The crown also extended its authority over the wealthy chivalric orders, further limiting the power of the nobility.

Spain had long been remarkable among European lands as a place where three religions—Islam, Judaism, and Christianity—coexisted with a certain degree of toleration. That toleration was to end dramatically under Ferdinand and Isabella, who made Spain the prime exemplar of state-controlled religion.

Ferdinand and Isabella exercised almost total control over the Spanish church as they placed religion in the service of national unity. They appointed the higher clergy and the officers of the Inquisition. The latter, run by Tomás de Torquemada (d. 1498), Isabella's confessor, was a key national agency established in 1479 to monitor the activity of converted Jews (*conversos*) and Muslims (*Moriscos*) in Spain. In 1492, the Jews were exiled and their properties confiscated. In 1502, nonconverting Moors in Granada were driven into exile by Cardinal Francisco Jiménez de Cisneros (1437–1517), under whom Spanish spiritual life was successfully conformed. This was a major reason why Spain remained a loyal Catholic country throughout the sixteenth century and provided a secure base of operation for the European Counter-Reformation.

Despite a certain internal narrowness, Ferdinand and Isabella were rulers with wide horizons. They contracted anti-French marriage alliances that came to determine a large part of European history in the sixteenth century. In 1496, their eldest daughter, Joanna, later known as "the Mad," married Archduke Philip, the son of Emperor Maximilian I. The fruit of this union, Charles I, was the first to rule over a united Spain; because of his inheritance and election as emperor in 1519, his empire almost equaled in size that of Charlemagne. A second daughter, Catherine of Aragon, wed Arthur, the son of the English king Henry VII. After Arthur's premature death, she was betrothed to his brother, the future King Henry VIII (r. 1509–1547), whom she married eight years later, in 1509. The failure of this marriage became the key factor in the emergence of the Anglican church and the English Reformation.

The new power of Spain was also revealed in Ferdinand and Isabella's promotion of overseas exploration. They sponsored the Genoese adventurer Christopher Columbus (1451–1506), who arrived at the islands of the Caribbean while sailing west in search of a shorter route to the spice markets of the Far East. This patronage led to the creation of the Spanish Empire in Mexico and Peru, whose gold and silver mines helped make Spain Europe's dominant power in the sixteenth century.

England

The latter half of the fifteenth century was a period of especially difficult political trial for the English. Following the Hundred Years' War, civil warfare broke out between two rival branches of the royal family: the House of York and the House of Lancaster. The roots of the war lay in succession irregularities after the forced deposition of the erratic king Richard II (r. 1377–1399). This conflict, known to us today as the Wars of the Roses (because York's symbol, according to legend, was a white rose and Lancaster's a red rose), kept England in turmoil from 1455 to 1485.

The duke of York and his supporters in the prosperous southern towns challenged the Lancastrian monarchy of Henry VI (r. 1422–1461). In 1461, Edward IV (r. 1461–1483), son of the duke of York, seized power and instituted a strong-arm rule that lasted more than twenty years; it was only briefly interrupted, in 1470–1471, by Henry VI's short-lived restoration. Assisted by able ministers, Edward effectively increased the power and finances of the monarchy.

His brother, Richard III (r. 1483–1485), usurped the throne from Edward's son, and after Richard's death, the new Tudor dynasty portrayed him as an unprincipled villain who had also murdered Edward's sons in the Tower of London to secure his hold on the throne. Shakespeare's *Richard III* is the best-known version of this characterization—unjust according to some. Be that as it may, Richard's reign saw the growth of support for the exiled Lancastrian Henry Tudor, who returned to England to defeat Richard on Bosworth Field in August 1485.

Henry Tudor ruled as Henry VII (r. 1485–1509), the first of the new Tudor dynasty that would dominate England throughout the sixteenth century. To bring the rival royal families together and to make the hereditary claim of his offspring to the throne uncontestable, Henry married Edward IV's daughter, Elizabeth of York.

He succeeded in disciplining the English nobility through a special instrument of the royal will known as the Court of Star Chamber. Created with the sanction of Parliament in 1487, the court was intended to end the perversion of English justice by "over-mighty subjects," that is, powerful nobles who used intimidation and bribery to win favorable verdicts in court cases. In the Court of Star Chamber, the king's councilors sat as judges, and such tactics did not sway them. The result was a more equitable court system.

It was also a court more amenable to the royal will. Henry shrewdly used English law to further the ends of the monarchy. He managed to confiscate lands and fortunes of nobles with such success that he was able to govern without dependence on Parliament for royal funds, always a cornerstone of a strong monarchy. In these ways, Henry began to shape a monarchy that would develop into one of early modern Europe's most exemplary governments during the reign of his granddaughter, Elizabeth I (r. 1558–1603).

The Holy Roman Empire

Germany and Italy were the striking exceptions to the steady development of politically centralized lands in the last half of the fifteenth century. Unlike England, France, and Spain, the Holy Roman Empire saw the many thoroughly repulse the one. In Germany, territorial rulers and cities resisted every effort at national consolidation and unity. As in Carolingian times, rulers continued to partition their kingdoms, however small, among their sons. By the late fifteenth century, Germany was hopelessly divided into some three hundred autonomous political entities.

The princes and the cities did work together to create the machinery of law and order, if not of union, within the divided empire. Emperor Charles IV (r. 1346–1378) and the major German territorial rulers reached an agreement in 1356 known as the **Golden Bull**. It established a seven-member electoral college consisting of the archbishops of Mainz, Trier, and Cologne; the duke of Saxony; the margrave of Brandenburg; the count Palatine; and the king of Bohemia. This group also functioned as an administrative body. They elected the emperor and, in cooperation with him, provided what transregional unity and administration existed.

The figure of the emperor gave the empire a single ruler in law if not in fact. The conditions of his rule and the extent of his powers over his subjects, especially the seven electors, were renegotiated with every imperial election. Therefore, the rights of the many (the princes) were always balanced against the power of the one (the emperor).

In the fifteenth century, an effort was made to control incessant feuding by the creation of an imperial diet known as the *Reichstag*. This was a national assembly

This portrait of Katharina, by Albrecht Dürer, provides evidence of African slavery in Europe during the sixteenth century. Katharina was in the service of one João Bradao, a Portuguese economic minister living in Antwerp, then the financial center of Europe. Dürer became friends with Bradao during his stay in the Low Countries in the winter of 1520–1521.   Albrecht Dürer (1471–1528), *Portrait of the Moorish Woman Katharina*. Drawing. Uffizi Florence, Italy. Photograph © Foto Marburg/Art Resource, NY

of the seven electors, the nonelectoral princes, and representatives from the sixty-five imperial free cities. The cities were the weakest of the three bodies represented in the diet. During such an assembly in Worms in 1495, the members won from Emperor Maximilian I an imperial ban on private warfare, the creation of a Supreme Court of Justice to enforce internal peace, and an imperial Council of Regency to coordinate imperial and internal German policy. The emperor only grudgingly conceded the latter because it gave the princes a share in executive power.

These reforms were still a poor substitute for true national unity. In the sixteenth and seventeenth centuries, the territorial princes became virtually sovereign rulers in their various domains. Such disunity aided religious dissent and conflict. It was in the cities and territories of still feudal, fractionalized, backward Germany that the Protestant Reformation broke out in the sixteenth century.

▼ The Northern Renaissance

The scholarly works of northern humanists created a climate favorable to religious and educational reforms on the eve of the Reformation. Northern humanism was initially stimulated by the importation of Italian learning through such varied intermediaries as students who had studied in Italy, merchants who traded there, and the Brothers of the Common Life. This last was an influential lay religious movement that began in the Netherlands and permitted men and women to live a shared religious life without making formal vows of poverty, chastity, and obedience.

The northern humanists, however, developed their own distinctive culture. They tended to come from more diverse social backgrounds and to be more devoted to religious reforms than their Italian counterparts. They were also more willing to write for lay audiences as well as for a narrow intelligentsia. Thanks to the invention of printing with movable type, it became possible for humanists to convey their educational ideals to laypeople and clerics

alike. Printing gave new power and influence to elites in both church and state, who now could popularize their viewpoints freely and widely.

The Printing Press

A variety of forces converged in the fourteenth and fifteenth centuries to give rise to the invention of the printing press. Since the days of Charlemagne, kings and princes had encouraged schools and literacy to help provide educated bureaucrats to staff the offices of their kingdoms. Without people who could read, think critically, and write reliable reports, no kingdom, large or small, could be properly governed. By the fifteenth century, a new literate lay public had been created, thanks to the enormous expansion of schools and universities during the late Middle Ages.

The invention of a cheap way to manufacture paper also helped make books economical and broaden their content. Manuscript books had been inscribed on vellum, a cumbersome and expensive medium (170 calfskins or 300 sheepskins were required to make a single vellum Bible.) Single-sheet woodcuts had long been printed. The process involved carving words and pictures on a block of wood, inking it, and then stamping out as many copies as possible before the wood deteriorated. The end product was much like a cheap modern poster.

In response to the demand for books that the expansion of lay education and literacy created, Johann Gutenberg (d. 1468) invented printing with movable type in the mid-fifteenth century in the German city of Mainz, the center of printing for the whole of Western Europe. Thereafter, books were rapidly and handsomely produced on topics both profound and practical and were intended for ordinary lay readers, scholars, and clerics alike. Especially popular in the early decades of print were books of piety and religion, calendars and almanacs, and how-to books (for example, on childrearing, making brandies and liquors, curing animals, and farming).

The new technology proved enormously profitable to printers, whose numbers exploded. By 1500, within just fifty years of Gutenberg's press, printing presses operated in at least sixty German cities and in more than two hundred cities throughout Europe. The printing press was a boon to the careers of humanists, who now gained international audiences.

Literacy deeply affected people everywhere, nurturing self-esteem and a critical frame of mind. By standardizing texts, the print revolution made anyone who could read an instant authority. Rulers in church and state now had to deal with a less credulous

The printing press made possible the diffusion of Renaissance learning, but no book stimulated thought more at this time than did the Bible. With Gutenberg's publication of a printed Bible in 1454, scholars gained access to a dependable, standardized text, so Scripture could be discussed and debated as never before.
This item is reproduced by permission of The Huntington Library, San Marino, California

and less docile laity. Print was also a powerful tool for political and religious propaganda. Kings could now indoctrinate people as never before, and clergymen found themselves able to mass-produce both indulgences and pamphlets.

Erasmus   North

The far-reaching influence of Desiderius Erasmus (1466?–1536), the most famous northern humanist, illustrates the impact of the printing press. Through his printed works, Erasmus gained fame both as an educational and as a religious reformer. A lifelong Catholic, Erasmus, through his life and work, made clear that many loyal Catholics wanted major reforms in the church long before the Reformation made them a reality.

When patronage was scarce (authors received no royalties and had to rely on private patrons for their livelihood), Erasmus earned his living by tutoring well-to-do youths. He prepared short Latin dialogues for his students, intended to teach them how to speak and live well, inculcating good manners and language by internalizing what they read.

These dialogues were entitled *Colloquies*. In consecutive editions, they grew in number and length, including anticlerical dialogues and satires on religious dogmatism and superstition. Erasmus also collected ancient and contemporary proverbs, which appeared under the title *Adages*. Beginning with 800 examples, the final edition included more than 5,000. Among the locutions the *Adages* popularized are such common expressions as "Leave no stone unturned" and "Where there is smoke, there is fire."

Erasmus aspired to unite classical ideals of humanity and civic virtue with the Christian ideals of love and piety. He believed disciplined study of the classics and the Bible, if begun early enough, was the best way to reform individuals and society. He summarized his own beliefs with the phrase *philosophia Christi*, a simple, ethical piety in imitation of Christ. He set this ideal in stark contrast to what he believed to be the dogmatic, ceremonial, and bullying religious practices of the later Middle Ages. What most offended him about the Scholastics, both the old authorities of the Middle Ages and the new Protestant ones, was their letting dogma and argument overshadow Christian piety and practice.

Erasmus was a true idealist, who expected more from people than the age's theologians believed them capable of doing. To promote what he deemed to be the essence of Christianity, he made ancient Christian sources available in their original versions, believing that if people would only imbibe the pure sources of the faith, they would recover the moral and religious health the New Testament promises. To this end, Erasmus edited the works of the Church Fathers and produced a Greek edition of the New Testament (1516), later adding a new Latin translation of the latter (1519). Martin Luther used both of those works when he translated the New Testament into German in 1522.

These various enterprises did not please the church authorities. They remained unhappy with Erasmus's "improvements" on the Vulgate, Christendom's Bible for over a thousand years, and his popular anticlerical writings. At one point in the mid-sixteenth century, all of Erasmus's works were on the church's *Index of Forbidden Books*. Luther also condemned Erasmus for his views on the freedom of human will. Still, Erasmus's works put sturdy tools of reform in the hands of both Protestant and Catholic reformers. Already in the 1520s, there was a popular saying: "Erasmus laid the egg that Luther hatched."

Humanism and Reform

In Germany, England, France, and Spain, humanism stirred both educational and religious reform.

Germany   Rudolf Agricola (1443–1485), the "father of German humanism," spent ten years in Italy and introduced Italian learning to Germany when he returned. Conrad Celtis (d. 1508), the first German poet laureate, and Ulrich von Hutten (1488–1523), a fiery knight, gave German humanism a nationalist coloring hostile to non-German cultures, particularly Roman culture. Von Hutten especially illustrates the union of humanism, German nationalism, and Luther's religious reform. A poet who admired Erasmus, he attacked indulgences and published an edition of Valla's exposé of the *Donation of Constantine*. He died in 1523, the victim of a hopeless knights' revolt against the princes.

The controversy that brought von Hutten onto the historical stage and unified reform-minded German humanists was the Reuchlin affair. Johann Reuchlin (1455–1522) was Europe's foremost Christian authority on Hebrew and Jewish learning. He wrote the first reliable Hebrew grammar by a Christian scholar and was attracted to Jewish mysticism. Around 1506, supported by the Dominican order in Cologne, a Christian who had converted from Judaism began a movement to suppress Jewish writings. When this man, whose name was Pfefferkorn, attacked Reuchlin, many German humanists, in the name of academic freedom and good scholarship—not for any pro-Jewish sentiment—rushed to Reuchlin's defense. The controversy lasted for years and produced one of the great satires of the period, the *Letters of Obscure Men* (1515), a merciless satire of monks and Scholastics to which von Hutten contributed. When Martin Luther came under attack in 1517 for his famous ninety-five theses against indulgences, many German humanists saw a repetition of the Scholastic attack on Reuchlin and rushed to his side.

England Italian learning came to England by way of English scholars and merchants and visiting Italian prelates. Lectures by William Grocyn (d. 1519) and Thomas Linacre (d. 1524) at Oxford and those of Erasmus at Cambridge marked the scholarly maturation of English humanism. John Colet (1467–1519), dean of Saint Paul's Cathedral, patronized humanist studies for the young and promoted religious reform.

Thomas More (1478–1535), a close friend of Erasmus, is the best-known English humanist. His *Utopia* (1516), a conservative criticism of contemporary society, rivals the plays of Shakespeare as the most read sixteenth-century English work. *Utopia* depicted an imaginary society based on reason and tolerance that overcame social and political injustice by holding all property and goods in common and requiring everyone to earn their bread by their own work.

More became one of Henry VIII's most trusted diplomats. His repudiation of the Act of Supremacy (1534), which made the king of England head of the English church in place of the pope (see Chapter 11), and his refusal to recognize the king's marriage to Anne Boleyn, however, led to his execution in July 1535. Although More remained Catholic, humanism in England, as also in Germany, helped prepare the way for the English Reformation.

France The French invasions of Italy made it possible for Italian learning to penetrate France, stirring both educational and religious reform. Guillaume Budé (1468–1540), an accomplished Greek scholar, and Jacques Lefèvre d'Etaples (1454–1536), a biblical authority, were the leaders of French humanism. Lefèvre's scholarly works exemplified the new critical scholarship and influenced Martin Luther. Guillaume Briçonnet (1470–1533), the bishop of Meaux, and Marguerite d'Angoulême (1492–1549), sister of King Francis I, the future queen of Navarre, and a successful spiritual writer in her own right, cultivated a generation of young reform-minded humanists. The future Protestant reformer John Calvin was a product of this native reform circle.

Spain Whereas in England, France, and Germany humanism prepared the way for Protestant reforms, in Spain it entered the service of the Catholic Church. Here the key figure was Francisco Jiménez de Cisneros (1437–1517), a confessor to Queen Isabella and, after 1508, the "Grand Inquisitor"—a position that allowed him to enforce the strictest religious orthodoxy. Jiménez founded the University of Alcalá near Madrid in 1509, printed a Greek edition of the New Testament, and translated many religious tracts designed to reform clerical life and better direct lay piety. His great achievement, taking fifteen years to complete, was the *Complutensian Polyglot Bible*, a six-volume work that placed the Hebrew, Greek, and Latin versions of the Bible in parallel columns. Such scholarly projects and internal church reforms joined with the repressive measures of Ferdinand and Isabella to keep Spain strictly Catholic throughout the Age of Reformation.

▼ Voyages of Discovery and the New Empires in the West and East

The discovery of the Americas dramatically expanded the horizons of Europeans, both geographically and intellectually. Knowledge of the New World's inhabitants and the exploitation of its mineral and human wealth set new cultural and economic forces in motion throughout Western Europe.

Beginning with the voyages of the Portuguese and Spanish in the fifteenth century, commercial supremacy progressively shifted from the Mediterranean and Baltic seas to the Atlantic seaboard, setting the stage for global expansion. (See Map 10–2, page 306.)

The Portuguese Chart the Course

Seventy-seven years before Columbus, who sailed under the flag of Spain, set foot in the Americas, Prince Henry "the Navigator" (1394–1460), brother of the king of Portugal, captured the North African Muslim city of Ceuta. His motives were mercenary and religious, both a quest for gold and spices and the pious work of saving the souls of Muslims and pagans who had no knowledge of Christ. Thus began the Portuguese exploration of the African coast, first in search of gold and slaves, and then by century's end, of a sea route around Africa to Asia's spice markets. Pepper and cloves topped the list of spices, as they both preserved and enhanced the dull diet of most Europeans. Initially the catch of raiders, African slaves were soon taken by Portuguese traders in direct commerce with tribal chiefs, who readily swapped captives for horses, grain, and finished goods (cloth and brassware). Over the second half of the fifteenth century, Portuguese ships delivered 150,000 slaves to Europe.

Before there was a sea route to the East, Europeans could only get spices through the Venetians, who bought or bartered them from Muslim merchants in Egypt and the Ottoman Empire. The Portuguese resolved to beat this powerful Venetian-Muslim monopoly by sailing directly to the source. Overland routes to India and China had long existed, but their transit had become too difficult and unprofitable by the fifteenth century. The route by sea posed a different obstacle and risk: fear of the unknown, making the first voyages of exploration slow and tentative. Venturing down the African coast, the

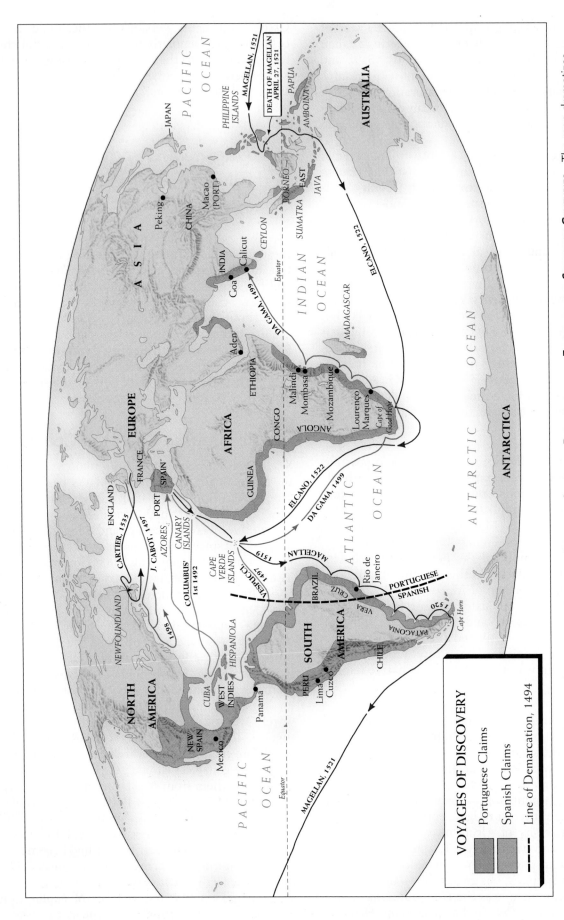

Map 10–2 **European Voyages of Discovery and the Colonial Claims of Spain and Portugal in the Fifteenth and Sixteenth Centuries** The map dramatizes Europe's global expansion in the fifteenth and sixteenth centuries.

VOYAGES OF DISCOVERY

Portuguese Claims

Spanish Claims

- - - Line of Demarcation, 1494

Portuguese ships were turned out into the deep ocean by every protruding cape, and the farther out they sailed to round them, the greater the sailors' fear that the winds would not return them to land. Each cape rounded became a victory and a lesson, giving the crews the skills they needed to cross the oceans to the Americas and East Asia.

In addition to spice markets, the voyagers also gained new allies against Western Europe's archenemies, the Muslims. In 1455, a self-interested pope granted the Portuguese explorers all the spoils of war—land, goods, and slaves—from the coast of Guinea in West Africa to the Indies in East Asia. The church expected exploration to lead to mass conversions, a Christian coup as well as a mercantile advantage. The explorers also kept an eye out for a legendary Eastern Christian ruler known as Prester John.

Bartholomew Dias (ca. 1450–1500) pioneered the eastern Portuguese Empire after safely rounding the Cape of Good Hope at the tip of Africa in 1487. A decade later, in 1498, Vasco da Gama (1469–1525) stood on the shores of India. When he returned to Portugal, he carried a cargo of spices worth sixty times the cost of the voyage. Later, the Portuguese established colonies in Goa and Calcutta on the coast of India, whence they challenged the Arabs and the Venetians for control of the spice trade.

The Portuguese had concentrated their explorations on the Indian Ocean. The Spanish turned west, believing they could find a shorter route to the East Indies by sailing across the Atlantic. Instead, Christopher Columbus (1451–1506) discovered the Americas.

The Spanish Voyages of Columbus

Thirty-three days after departing the Canary Islands, on October 12, 1492, Columbus landed in San Salvador (Watlings Island) in the eastern Bahamas. Thinking he was in the East Indies, he mistook his first landfall as an outer island of Japan. The error was understandable given the information he relied on, namely, Marco Polo's thirteenth-century account of his years in China and Martin Behaim's spherical map of the presumed world. That map showed only ocean and Cipangu (Japan) between the west coast of Europe and the east coast of Asia. (See Martin Behaim's map, page 308.) Not until his third voyage to the Caribbean in 1498 did Columbus realize that Cuba was not Japan and South America was not China.

Naked, friendly natives met Columbus and his crew on the beaches of the New World. They were Taino Indians, who spoke a variant of a language known as Arawak. Believing the island on which he landed to be the East Indies, Columbus called these people Indians, a name that stuck with Europeans even after they realized he had actually discovered a new continent. The natives' generosity amazed Columbus, as they freely gave his men all the corn, yams, and sexual favors they desired. "They

never say no," Columbus marveled. He also observed how easily the Spanish could enslave them.

On the heels of Columbus, Amerigo Vespucci (1451–1512), after whom America is named, and Ferdinand Magellan (1480–1521) explored the coastline of South America. Their travels proved that the new lands Columbus had discovered were an entirely unknown continent that opened on the still greater Pacific Ocean. Magellan, who was continuing the search for a westward route to the Indies, made it all the way around South America and across the Pacific to the Philippines, where he was killed in a skirmish with the inhabitants. The remnants of his squadron eventually sailed on to Spain, making them the first sailors to circumnavigate the globe.

Intended and Unintended Consequences Columbus's first voyage marked the beginning of more than three centuries of a vast Spanish empire in the Americas. What began as voyages of discovery became expeditions of conquest, not unlike the warfare Christian Aragon and Castile waged against Islamic Moors. Those wars had just ended in 1492, and their conclusion imbued the early Spanish explorers with a zeal for conquering and converting non-Christian peoples.

Much to the benefit of Spain, the voyages of discovery created Europe's largest and longest surviving trading bloc and spurred other European countries to undertake their own colonial ventures. The wealth extracted from its American possessions financed Spain's commanding role in the religious and political wars of the sixteenth and seventeenth centuries, while fueling a Europe-wide economic expansion.

European expansion also had a profound biological impact. Europeans introduced numerous new species of fruits, vegetables, and animals into the Americas and brought American species back to Europe. European expansion also spread European diseases. Vast numbers of Native Americans died from measles and smallpox epidemics, while Europeans died from a virulent form of syphilis that may have originated in the Americas.

For the Native Americans, the voyages of discovery were the beginning of a long history of conquest, disease, and slave labor they could neither evade nor survive. In both South and North America, Spanish rule left a lasting imprint of Roman Catholicism, economic dependency, and hierarchical social structure, all still visible today. (See Chapter 18.)

The Spanish Empire in the New World

When the first Spanish explorers arrived, the Aztec Empire dominated Mesoamerica, which stretches from Central Mexico to Guatemala, and the Inca Empire dominated Andean South America. Both were rich, and their conquest promised the Spanish the possibility of acquiring large quantities of gold.

What Columbus knew of the world in 1492 was contained in this map by the Nuremberg geographer Martin Behaim, creator of the first spherical globe of the earth. The ocean section of Behaim's globe is reproduced here. Departing the Canary Islands (in the second section from the right), Columbus expected his first major landfall to be Japan (Cipangu, in the second section from the left). When he landed at San Salvador, he thought he was on the outer island of Japan. Thus, when he arrived in Cuba, he thought he was in Japan.   From *Admiral of the Ocean Sea* by Samuel Eliot Morison. Copyright © 1942 by Samuel Eliot Morison; Copyright © renewed 1970 by Samuel Eliot Morison. By permission of Little, Brown and Company, (Inc.)

The Aztecs in Mexico   The forebears of the Aztecs had arrived in the Valley of Mexico early in the twelfth century, where they lived as a subservient people. In 1428, however, they began a period of imperial expansion. By the time of Spanish conquest, the Aztecs ruled almost all of central Mexico from their capital Tenochtitlán (modern-day Mexico City). The Aztecs demanded heavy tribute in goods and labor from their subjects and, believing the gods must literally be fed with human blood to guarantee sunshine and fertility, they also took thousands of captives each year for human sacrifice. These policies bred resentment and fear among the subject peoples.

In 1519, Hernán Cortés (1485–1547) landed in Mexico with about five hundred men and a few horses. He opened communication with Moctezuma II (1466–1520), the Aztec emperor. Moctezuma may initially have believed Cortés to be the god Quetzalcoatl, who, according to leg-

end, had been driven away centuries earlier but had promised to return. Whatever the reason, Moctezuma hesitated to confront Cortés, attempting at first to appease him with gold, which only whetted Spanish appetites. Cortés forged alliances with the Aztecs' subject peoples, most importantly, with Tlaxcala, an independent state and traditional enemy of the Aztecs. His forces then marched on Tenochtitlán, where Moctezuma welcomed him. Cortés soon seized Moctezuma, who died in unexplained circumstances. The Aztecs' wary acceptance of the Spaniards turned to open hostility. The Spaniards were driven from Tenochtitlán and were nearly wiped out, but they returned and laid siege to the city. The Aztecs, under their last ruler, Cuauhtemoc (ca. 1495–1525), resisted fiercely but were finally defeated in 1521. Cortés razed Tenochtitlán, building his own capital over its ruins, and proclaimed the Aztec Empire to be New Spain.

Armored Spanish soldiers, under the command of Pedro de Alvarado (d. 1541) and bearing crossbows, engage unprotected and crudely armed Aztecs, who are nonetheless portrayed as larger than life by Spanish artist Diego Duran (sixteenth century).   Codex Duran: Pedro de Alvarado (c. 1485–1541), companion-at-arms of Hernando Cortés (1845–1547) besieged by Aztec warriors (vellum) by Diego Duran (16th Century), Codex Duran, Historia De Las Indias (16th century). Biblioteca Nacional, Madrid, Spain. The Bridgeman Art Library International Ltd.

The Incas in Peru   The second great Native American civilization the Spanish conquered was that of the Incas in the highlands of Peru. Like the Aztecs, the Incas also began to expand rapidly in the fifteenth century and, by the time of the Spanish conquest, controlled an enormous empire. Unlike the Aztecs, who extracted tribute from their subject peoples, the Incas compelled their subjects to work for the state on a regular basis.

In 1532, largely inspired by Cortés's example in Mexico, Francisco Pizarro (c. 1478–1541) landed on the western coast of South America with about two hundred men to take on the Inca Empire. Pizarro lured Atahualpa (ca. 1500–1533), the Inca ruler, into a conference and then seized him, killing hundreds of Atahualpa's followers in the process. The imprisoned Atahualpa tried to ransom himself with a hoard of gold, but instead of releasing him, Pizarro executed him in 1533. The Spaniards then captured Cuzco, the Inca capital, but Inca resistance did not end until the 1570s.

The conquests of Mexico and Peru are among the most dramatic and brutal events in modern history. Small military forces armed with advanced weapons subdued, in a remarkably brief time, two powerful peoples. The spread of European diseases, especially smallpox, among the Native Americans also aided the conquest. But beyond the drama and bloodshed, these conquests, as well as those of other Native American peoples, marked a fundamental turning point. Whole civilizations with long histories and enormous social,

architectural, and technological achievements were destroyed. Native American cultures endured, accommodating themselves to European dominance, but there was never any doubt about which culture had the upper hand. In that sense, the Spanish conquests of the early sixteenth century marked the beginning of the transformation of South America into Latin America.

The Church in Spanish America

Roman Catholic priests had accompanied the earliest explorers and the conquerors of the Native Americans. Steeped with the social and religious ideals of Christian humanism, these first clergy members believed they could foster Erasmus's concept of the "philosophy of Christ" in the New World. They were filled with zeal not only to convert the inhabitants to Christianity, but also to bring to them European learning and civilization.

Tension, however, existed between the early Spanish conquerors and the mendicant friars who sought to minister to the Native Americans. Without conquest, the church could not convert the Native Americans, but the priests often deplored the harsh conditions imposed on the native peoples. By far the most effective and outspoken clerical critic of the Spanish conquerors was Bartolomé de Las Casas (1474–1566), a Dominican. He contended that conquest was not necessary for conversion. One result of his campaign was new royal regulations to protect the Indians after 1550.

Another result of Las Casas's criticism was the emergence of the "Black Legend," according to which all Spanish treatment of the Native Americans was unprincipled and inhumane. (See "A Defense of American Natives," page 310.) Those who created this view of Spanish behavior drew heavily on Las Casas's writings. Although substantially true, the "Black Legend" exaggerated the case against Spain. Certainly the rulers of the native empires—as the Aztec demands for sacrificial victims attest—had often themselves been exceedingly cruel to their subjects.

By the end of the sixteenth century, the church in Spanish America had become largely an institution upholding the colonial status quo. Although individual priests defended the communal rights of Indian peoples, the colonial church prospered as the Spanish elite prospered by exploiting the resources and peoples of the New World. The church became a great landowner through crown grants and bequests from Catholics who died in the New World. The monasteries took on an economic as well as a spiritual life of their own. Whatever its concern for the spiritual welfare of the Native Americans, the church remained one of the indications that Spanish

A DEFENSE OF AMERICAN NATIVES

Bartolomé de Las Casas (1474–1566), a Dominican missionary to the New World, describes the native people of the islands of the Caribbean and their systematic slaughter by the Spanish.

Is Las Casas romanticizing the American natives? Does he truly respect their native culture and beliefs?

This infinite multitude of people was so created by God that they were without fraud . . . or malice. . . . Toward the Spaniards whom they serve, patient, meek, and peaceful, [they] lay aside all contentious and tumultuous thoughts, and live without any hatred or desire of revenge. The people are most delicate and tender, enjoying such a feeble constitution of body as does not permit them to endure labour. . . . The[ir] nation [the West Indies] is very poor and indigent, possessing little, and by reason that they gape not after temporal goods, [being] neither proud nor ambitious. Their diet is such that the most holy hermit cannot feed more sparingly in the wildernesse. They go naked . . . and a poor shag mantle . . . is their greatest and their warmest covering. They lie upon mats; only those who have larger fortunes lie upon a kind of net which is tied at the four corners and so fasten'd to the roof, which the Indians in their natural language call *Hamecks* [hammocks]. They are of a very apprehensive and docile wit, and capable of all good learning, and very apt to receive our Religion, which when they have but once tasted [it], they are carried [off] with a very ardent and zealous desire to make further progress in it; so that I

have heard divers Spaniards confess that they had nothing else to hinder them from enjoying heaven, but the ignorance of the true God.

To these quiet Lambs, endued with such blessed qualities, came the Spaniards like most cruel Tygres, Wolves, and Lions . . . for these forty years, minding nothing else but the slaughter of these unfortunate wretches . . . [whom] they have so cruelly and inhumanely butchered, [so] that of three millions of people which Hispaniola [modern Haiti and the Dominican Republic] itself did contain, there are left remaining alive scarce three hundred persons. And the island of Cuba . . . lies wholly desert, untilled and ruined. The islands of St. John and Jamaica lie waste and desolate. The Lycayan islands neighboring to the north upon Cuba and Hispaniola . . . are now totally unpeopled and destroyed; the inhabitants thereof amounting to above 500,000 souls, partly killed, and partly forced away to work in other places. . . . Other islands there were near the island of St. John, more than thirty in number, which were totally made desert. All which islands . . . lie now altogether solitary without any people or inhabitant.

Bartolomé de Las Casas, *The Tears of the Indians*, trans. by John Phillips (1656), from reprint of original edition (Stanford, CA: Academic Reprints, n.d.), pp. 2–4.

America was a conquered world. Those who spoke for the church did not challenge Spanish domination or any but the most extreme modes of Spanish economic exploitation. By the end of the colonial era in the late eighteenth century, the Roman Catholic Church had become one of the most conservative forces in Latin America.

The Economy of Exploitation

From the beginning, both the Native Americans and their lands were drawn into the Atlantic economy and the world of competitive European commercialism. For the Indians of Latin America and, somewhat later, the black peoples of Africa, that drive for gain meant forced labor.

The colonial economy of Latin America had three major components: mining, agriculture, and shipping. Each involved labor, servitude, and the intertwining of the New World economy with that of Spain.

Mining The early ***conquistadores***, or "conquerors," were primarily interested in gold, but by the mid-sixteenth century, silver mining provided the chief source of metallic wealth. The great mining centers were Potosí in Peru and somewhat smaller sites in northern Mexico. The Spanish crown received one fifth (the *quinto*) of all mining revenues. For this reason, the crown maintained a monopoly over the production and sale of mercury, required in the silver-smelting process. Exploring for silver continued throughout the colonial era. Its production by forced labor for the benefit of Spaniards and the Spanish crown epitomized the wholly extractive economy that stood at the foundation of colonial life.

Agriculture The major rural and agricultural institution of the Spanish colonies was the **hacienda**, a large landed estate owned by persons originally born in Spain (*peninsulares*) or persons of Spanish descent born in America (*creoles*). Laborers on the *hacienda* were usually subject in some legal way to the owner and were rarely free to move from working for one landowner to another.

The *hacienda* economy produced two major products: foodstuffs for mining areas and urban centers and leather goods used in mining machinery. Both farming and ranching were subordinate to the mining economy.

In the West Indies, the basic agricultural unit was the plantation. In Cuba, Hispaniola, Puerto Rico, and other islands, the labor of black slaves from Africa produced sugar to supply an almost insatiable demand for the product in Europe.

A final major area of economic activity in the Spanish colonies was urban service occupations, including government offices, the legal profession, and shipping. Those who worked in these occupations were either *peninsulares* or *creoles*, with the former dominating more often than not.

Labor Servitude All of this extractive and exploitive economic activity required labor, and the Spanish in the New World decided early that the native population would supply it. A series of social devices was used to draw them into the new economic life the Spanish imposed.

The first of these was the **encomienda**, a formal grant of the right to the labor of a specific number of Indians, usually a few hundred, but sometimes thousands, for a particular period of time. The *encomienda* was in decline by the mid-sixteenth century because the Spanish monarchs feared its holders might become too powerful. There were also humanitarian objections to this particular kind of exploitation of the Indians.

The passing of the *encomienda* led to a new arrangement of labor servitude: the *repartimiento*. This device required adult male Indians to devote a certain number of days of labor annually to Spanish economic enterprises. In the mines of Peru, the *repartimiento* was known as the *mita*, the Inca term for their labor tax. *Repartimiento* service was often harsh, and some Indians did not survive their stint. The limitation on labor time led some Spanish managers to abuse their workers on the assumption that fresh workers would soon replace them.

The eventual shortage of workers and the crown's pressure against extreme versions of forced labor led to the use of free labor. The freedom, however, was more in appearance than reality. Free Indian laborers were required to purchase goods from the landowner or mine owner, to whom they became forever indebted. This form of exploitation, known as *debt peonage*, continued in Latin America long after the nineteenth-century wars of liberation.

Black slavery was the final mode of forced or subservient labor in the New World. Both the Spanish and the Portuguese had earlier used African slaves in Europe. The sugar plantations of the West Indies and Brazil now became the major center of black slavery.

The conquest, the forced labor of the economy of exploitation, and the introduction of European diseases had devastating demographic consequences for the Native Americans. For centuries, Europeans had lived in a far more complex human and animal environment than Native Americans did. They had frequent contact with different ethnic and racial groups and with a variety of domestic animals. Such interaction helped them develop strong immune systems that enabled them to survive measles, smallpox, and typhoid. Native Americans, by contrast, grew up in a simpler and more sterile environment and were defenseless against these diseases. Within a generation, the native population of New Spain (Mexico) was reduced to an estimated 8 percent of its numbers, from 25 million to 2 million.

The Impact on Europe

Among contemporary European intellectuals, Columbus's discovery increased skepticism about the wisdom of the ancients. If traditional knowledge about the world had been so wrong geographically, how trustworthy was it on other matters? For many, Columbus's discovery demonstrated the folly of relying on any fixed body of presumed authoritative knowledge. Both in Europe and in the New World, there were those who condemned the explorers' treatment of American natives, as more was learned about their cruelty. (See "Montaigne on 'Cannibals' in Foreign Lands," page 312.) Three centuries later, however, on the third centenary of Columbus's discovery (1792), the great thinkers of the age lionized Columbus for having opened up new possibilities for civilization and morality. By establishing new commercial contacts among different peoples of the world, Columbus was said to have made cooperation, civility, and peace among them indispensable. Enlightenment thinkers drew parallels between the discovery of America and the invention of the printing press—both portrayed as world-historical events opening new eras in communication and globalization, an early multicultural experiment.[4]

---

[4]Cf. Anthony Pagden, "The Impact of the New World on the Old: The History of an Idea," *Renaissance and Modern Studies* 30 (1986): pp. 1–11.

MONTAIGNE ON "CANNIBALS" IN FOREIGN LANDS

The French philosopher Michel de Montaigne (1533–1592) had seen a Brazilian native in Rouen in 1562, who was alleged to be a cannibal. The experience gave rise to an essay on the subject of what constitutes a "savage." Montaigne concluded that no people on earth were more barbarous than Europeans, who take natives of other lands captive.

Is Montaigne romanticizing the New World natives? Is he being too hard on Europeans? Had the Aztecs or Incas had the ability to discover and occupy Europe, would they have enslaved and exploited Europeans?

Now, to return to my subject, I think there is nothing barbarous and savage in that nation [Brazil], from what I have been told . . . Each man calls barbarism whatever is not his own practice; for indeed it seems we have no other test of truth and reason than the example and pattern of the opinions and customs of the country we live in. There [we] always [find] the perfect religion, the perfect government, the perfect and accomplished manners in all things. Those [foreign] people are wild, just as we call wild the fruits that Nature has produced by herself and in her normal course; where really it is those that we have changed artificially and led astray from the common order that we should rather call wild. The former retain alive and vigorous their genuine virtues and properties, which we have debased in the latter by adapting them to gratify our corrupted taste. And yet for all that, the savor and delicacy of some uncultivated fruits of those countries is quite as excellent, even to our taste, as that of our own. It is not reasonable that [our human] art should win the place of honor over our great and powerful mother Nature. We have so overloaded the beauty and richness of her works by our inventions that we have quite smoth-

ered her. Yet wherever her purity shines forth, she wonderfully puts to shame our vain and frivolous attempts: "Ivy comes readier without our care;/In lonely caves the arbutus grows more fair;/No art with artless bird song can compare."[1] All our efforts cannot even succeed in reproducing the nest of the tiniest little bird, its contexture, its beauty and convenience; or even the web of the puny spider. All things, says Plato,[2] are produced by nature, by fortune, or by art; the greatest and most beautiful by one or the other of the first two, the least and most imperfect by the last.

These nations, then, seem to me "barbarous" in this sense, that they have been fashioned very little by the human mind, and are still very close to their original naturalness. The laws of nature still rule them, very little corrupted by ours; and they are in such a state of purity that I am sometimes vexed that they were unknown earlier, in the days when there were men able to judge them better than we.

[1]Propertius 1.11.10.
[2]Laws 10.

From *The Complete Essays of Montaigne*, trans. by Donald M. Frame (Stanford, CA: Stanford University Press, 1958), pp. 153–154.

On the material side, the influx of spices and precious metals into Europe from the new Portuguese and Spanish Empires was a mixed blessing. It contributed to a steady rise in prices during the sixteenth century that created an inflation rate estimated at 2 percent a year. The new supply of bullion from the Americas joined with enlarged European production to increase greatly the amount of coinage in circulation, and this increase, in turn, fed inflation. Fortunately, the increase in prices was by and large spread over a long period and was not sudden. Prices doubled in Spain by 1550, quadrupled by 1600. In Luther's Wittenberg in Germany, the cost of basic food and clothing increased almost 100 percent between 1519 and 1540. Generally, wages and rents remained well behind the rise in prices.

The new wealth enabled governments and private entrepreneurs to sponsor basic research and expansion in the printing, shipping, mining, textile, and weapons industries. There is also evidence of large-scale government planning in such ventures as the French silk industry and the Habsburg-Fugger development of mines in Austria and Hungary.

In the thirteenth and fourteenth centuries, capitalist institutions and practices had already begun to develop in the rich Italian cities (for example, the Florentine banking houses of Bardi and Peruzzi). Those who owned the means of production, either privately or corporately, were clearly distinguished from the workers who operated them. Wherever possible, entrepreneurs created monopolies in basic goods. High interest was charged on loans—actual, if not legal, usury. The "capitalist" virtues of thrift, industry, and orderly planning were everywhere in evidence—all intended to permit the free and efficient accumulation of wealth.

The late fifteenth and the sixteenth centuries saw the maturation of this type of capitalism together with its attendant social problems. The Medicis of Florence grew rich as bankers of the pope, as did the Fuggers of Augsburg, who bankrolled Habsburg rulers. The Fuggers lent Charles I of Spain more than 500,000 florins to buy his election as the Holy Roman Emperor in 1519 and boasted they had created the emperor. The new wealth and industrial expansion also raised the expectations of the poor and the ambitious and heightened the reactionary tendencies of the wealthy. This effect, in turn, aggravated the traditional social divisions between the clergy and the laity, the urban patriciate and the guilds, and the landed nobility and the agrarian peasantry.

These divisions indirectly prepared the way for the Reformation as well, by making many people critical of traditional institutions and open to new ideas—especially those that seemed to promise greater freedom and a chance at a better life.

In Perspective

As it recovered from national wars during the late Middle Ages, Europe saw the establishment of permanent centralized states and regional governments. The foundations of modern France, Spain, England, Germany, and Italy were laid at this time. As rulers imposed their will on regions outside their immediate domains, the "one" progressively took control of the "many," and previously divided lands came together as nations.

Thanks to the work of Byzantine and Islamic scholars, ancient Greek science and scholarship found its way into the West in these centuries. Europeans had been separated from their classical cultural heritage for almost eight centuries. No other world civilization had experienced such a disjunction from its cultural past. The discovery of classical civilization occasioned a rebirth of intellectual and artistic activity in both southern and northern Europe. One result was the splendor of the Italian Renaissance, whose scholarship, painting, and sculpture remain among Western Europe's most impressive achievements.

Ancient learning was not the only discovery of the era. New political unity spurred both royal greed and national ambition. By the late fifteenth century, Europeans were in a position to venture far away to the shores of Africa, the southern and eastern coasts of Asia, and the New World of the Americas. European discovery was not the only outcome of these voyages: The exploitation of the peoples and lands of the New World revealed a dark side of Western civilization. Some penalties were paid even then. The influx of New World gold and silver created new human and economic problems on the European mainland. Some Europeans even began to question their civilization's traditional values.

AP* TEST PREP

1. Which country took the lead in exploration in the fifteenth century?
   a. Portugal
   b. Spain
   c. England
   d. France
   e. Austria

2. Renaissance society first took on its distinctive shape in the
   a. large towns of England and Scotland.
   b. city-states of southern France.
   c. papal states.
   d. principalities of northern Germany.
   e. merchant cities of Italy.

3. Erasmus wanted to
   a. lead a revolt against the Catholic Church.
   b. return Europe to the days of the Roman Empire.
   c. elevate the Classics above all other literature.
   d. unite Classical and Christian ideals.
   e. put an end to all social hierarchy.

4. The writings of Las Casas contributed to the emergence of
   a. a new kind of fanatical conquistador.
   b. an organized opposition to European expansion.
   c. the Black Legend.
   d. large-scale Indian revolts in the New World.
   e. a new European consensus about the immorality of conquest.

5. The *encomienda* was
   a. a large estate in the New World.
   b. a charter granting the right to found a colony.
   c. the forced transfer of criminals from Spain to the New World.
   d. a grant of the right to the labor of a specific number of Indians.
   e. a church council designed to deal with New World conflicts.

6. Unified national monarchies began to emerge in Europe largely because monarchs
   a. appointed civil servants.
   b. controlled peasant rebellions.
   c. gained greater financial independence from the nobility.
   d. weakened the European trade system.
   e. had fought in the Crusades.

7. The word *Renaissance* means
   a. "flowering."
   b. "genius."
   c. "eruption."
   d. "new day."
   e. "rebirth."

8. Boccaccio pioneered humanist studies as the author of
   a. *Decameron.*
   b. *Oration on the Dignity of Man.*
   c. *Elegances of the Latin Language.*
   d. *Letters to the Ancient Dead.*
   e. *Book of the Courtier.*

9. The great Italian cities were
   a. dominated by kings.
   b. ruled by foreign princes.
   c. kept out of the lucrative trade with the East.
   d. free to expand on their own.
   e. dominated by territorial princes.

10. The Medici family ruled fifteenth-century
    a. Florence.
    b. Milan.
    c. Venice.
    d. Naples.
    e. Rome.

11. The *studia humanitatis* included all of the following *except*
    a. rhetoric.
    b. grammar.
    c. painting.
    d. history.
    e. politics.

12. *The Treasure of the City of Ladies* exemplifies Italian humanist literature for its
    a. classical verse style.
    b. practical virtue.
    c. attention to critical reasoning.

d. Platonic idealism.
e. attack on Christian hypocrisy.

13. Charles VIII's successful march from Florence to Naples in 1494 inspired
    a. the League of Venice.
    b. the Holy League.
    c. the Golden Bull.
    d. the Council of Pisa.
    e. the Carbonari.

14. The first European explorer to round the Cape of Good Hope was
    a. Vasco de Gama.
    b. Bartholomew Dias.
    c. Henry the Navigator.
    d. Ferdinand Magellan.
    e. Amerigo Vespucci.

15. Tomás de Torquemada oversaw Ferdinand and Isabella's campaign to
    a. establish the *repartimiento* system.
    b. promote overseas exploration.
    c. develop Castille's lucrative sheep farming industry.
    d. negotiate treaties with Portugal.
    e. monitor converted Jews and Muslims.

16. Compared to Italian humanists, northern humanists were more devoted to _____ reforms.
    a. political
    b. social
    c. intellectual
    d. religious
    e. linguistic

17. The Portuguese drive to find a sea route to the East was motivated by a desire to gain access to
    a. iron ore.
    b. spices.
    c. grain.
    d. timber.
    e. cloth.

18. The author of *Utopia* was
    a. Thomas Cranmer.
    b. Thomas Paine.
    c. Thomas Wolsey.
    d. Thomas More.
    e. Thomas Cromwell.

19. The Spanish conquest of the Aztecs was aided by
    a. the numerical superiority of the Europeans.
    b. the superior food supplies of the Europeans.
    c. alliances between the Europeans and the Aztecs' subject peoples.
    d. the resistance of the Europeans to New World diseases.
    e. mass conversions to Christianity among the Aztecs.

20. The early *conquistadores* were primarily interested in
    a. gold.
    b. land.
    c. making converts to Christianity.
    d. obtaining slaves.
    e. exploration and discovery for their own sake.

DOCUMENT-BASED QUESTION

Directions: Construct a valid essay that directly addresses the central issue of the following question. Use facts from the documents provided and from the chapter to prove the position you take in your thesis statement.

How did fifteenth- and sixteenth-century Europeans see the inhabitants of the New World? How did knowledge of New World peoples shape Europeans' vision of themselves?

Document A

Martin Behaim's map of the world, the basis for Columbus's assumptions about global geography.

Document B

Armored Spanish soldiers face Aztec warriors.

Document C

Source: Montaigne, author and philosopher, reflects on the nature of "barbarism," *The Complete Essays of Montaigne.*

Now, to return to my subject, I think there is nothing barbarous and savage in that nation [Brazil], from what I have been told . . . . Each man calls barbarism whatever is not in his own practice; for indeed it seems we have no other test of truth and reason than the example and pattern of the opinions and customs of the country we live in. There [we] always [find] the perfect religion, the perfect government, the perfect and accomplished manners in all things. Those [foreign] people are wild, just as we call the fruits that Nature has produced by herself and in her normal course; where really it is those that we have changed artificially and led astray from the common order that we should call wild. The former retain alive and vigorous their genuine virtues and proprieties, which we debased the latter by adapting them to gratify our corrupted taste . . . . It is not reason-able that [our human] art should win the place of honor over our great and powerful mother nature.

Document D

Source: Christopher Columbus describes his first voyage to the New World.

The people of this island and of all the other islands which I have found and of which I have information, all go naked, men and women, as their mothers bore them . . . . They have no iron or steel or weapons, nor are they fitted to use them. This is not because they are not well built and of handsome stature, but because they are very marvelously timorous . . . . They refuse nothing that they possess, if it be asked of them; on the contrary, they invite any one to share it and display as much love as if they would give their hearts . . . . They do not hold any creed nor are they idolaters; but they all believe that power and good are in the heavens and were very firmly convinced that I, with these ships and men, came from the heavens.

Document E

Source: Dominican friar Bartholomew de Las Casas describes the inhabitants of the New World.

God has created all these numberless people to be quite the simplest, without malice or duplicity, most obedient, most faithful to their natural lord, and to the Christians, whom they serve; the most humble, most patient, most peaceful, and calm, without strife nor tumults; not wrangling, nor querulous, as free from uproar, hate and desire of revenge, as any in the world . . . .

They are likewise of a clean, unspoiled, and vivacious intellect, very capable, and receptive to every good doctrine; most prompt to accept our Holy Catholic Faith, to be endowed with virtuous customs; and they have as little difficulty with such things as any people created by God in the world.

For more on European encounters with peoples of the New World, see pages 307–312.

Painted on the eve of the Reformation, Matthias Grunewald's (ca. 1480–1528) *Crucifixion* shows a Christ who takes all the sins of the world into his own body, as his mother, Mary Magdalene, and John the Baptist share the pain of his afflictions.   Musée Unterlinden, Colmar, France/SuperStock

11

The Age of Reformation

KEY TOPICS

• The social and religious background of the Reformation

• Martin Luther's challenge to the church and the course of the Reformation in Germany

• The Reformation in Switzerland, France, and England

• Transitions in family life between medieval and modern times

IN THE SECOND decade of the sixteenth century, a long-building, powerful religious movement began in Saxony in Germany and spread rapidly throughout northern Europe, deeply affecting society and politics, as well as the spiritual lives of men and women. Attacking what they believed to be burdensome superstitions that robbed people of both their money and their peace of mind, Protestant reformers led a broad revolt against the medieval church. In a short time, hundreds of thousands of people from all social classes set aside the beliefs of centuries and adopted a more simplified religious practice.

The Protestant Reformation challenged aspects of the Renaissance, especially its tendency to follow classical sources in glorifying human nature and its loyalty to traditional religion. Protestants were more impressed by the human potential for evil than by the inclination to do good. They encouraged parents, teachers, and magistrates to be firm disciplinarians, but they also embraced many Renaissance values, especially educational reforms and the training of students in ancient languages. Like the Italian humanists, the Protestant reformers prized the tools that allowed them to go directly to the original sources. For the reformers, however, this meant the study of the Hebrew and Greek scriptures, enabling them to root their challenges to traditional authority and institutions in biblical antiquity.

▼ Society and Religion

The Protestant **Reformation** occurred at a time of sharp conflict between the emerging nation-states of Europe bent on conformity and centralization within their realms and the self-governing towns and villages long accustomed to running their own affairs. Since the late fourteenth century, the territorial ruler's law and custom had progressively overridden local law and custom almost everywhere. The towns remained keenly sensitive to the loss of traditional rights and freedoms. Many townspeople and village folk perceived in the religious revolt an ally in their struggle to remain politically free and independent.

Social and Political Conflict

The Reformation broke out first in the free imperial cities of Germany and Switzerland, and the basic tenets of Lutheran and Zwinglian Protestantism remained visible in subsequent Protestant movements. There were about sixty-five free imperial cities, each a small kingdom unto itself. Most had Protestant movements but with mixed success and duration. Some quickly turned Protestant and remained so. Some were Protestant only for a short time. Still others developed mixed confessions. Frowning on sectarianism and aggressive proselytizing, they made it possible for Catholics and Protestants to live side by side with appropriate barriers between them.

A seeming life-and-death struggle with higher princely or royal authority was not the only conflict late medieval cities were experiencing. They also coped with deep social and political divisions. Certain groups favored the Reformation more than others. In many places, guilds whose members were economically prospering and socially rising were in the forefront of the Reformation. The printers' guild is a prominent example. Its members were literate, sophisticated about the world, and belonged to a rapidly growing industry. They also had an economic stake in fanning religious conflict with Protestant propaganda, which many, of course, also sincerely believed. Guilds with a history of opposition to reigning governmental authority also stood out among early Protestant supporters, regardless of education level. Evidence also suggests that people who felt pushed around and bullied by either local or distant authority—a guild by an autocratic local government, or a city or region by a powerful prince or king—often perceived an ally in the Protestant movement.

Social and political experience naturally influenced religious change in town and countryside. A Protestant sermon or pamphlet praising religious freedom seemed directly relevant, for example, to the townspeople of German and Swiss cities who faced incorporation into the territory of a powerful local prince, who looked on them as his subjects rather than as free citizens. When Martin Luther and his followers, who wrote, preached, and sang about a priesthood of all believers, scorned the authority of ecclesiastical landlords and ridiculed papal laws as arbitrary human inventions, they touched political as well as religious nerves. This was also true in the villages and in the towns. Like city dwellers, the peasants on the land also heard in the Protestant sermon and pamphlet a promise of political liberation, even a degree of social betterment. More than the townspeople, the peasants found their traditional liberties—from fishing and hunting rights to representation at local diets—progressively being chipped away by the secular and ecclesiastical landlords of the age.

Popular Religious Movements and Criticism of the Church

The Protestant Reformation could also not have occurred without the monumental challenges to the medieval church during its "exile" in Avignon, the Great Schism, the Conciliar period, and the Renaissance papacy. For sizable numbers of people in future Protestant lands, the medieval church had ceased to provide a viable foundation for religious piety. Many intellectuals and laypeople felt a sense of spiritual crisis. At the Diet of Worms in 1521 (see page 323), the German nobility presented the emperor with a list of 102 "oppressive [church] burdens and abuses" said to be corrupting the care of German souls. Between the secular pretensions of the papacy and the dry teaching of Scholastic theologians, laity and clerics alike began to seek a more heartfelt, idealistic, and—often, in the eyes of the pope—heretical religious piety. The late Middle Ages were marked by independent lay and clerical efforts to reform local religious practice and by widespread experimentation with new religious forms.

A variety of factors contributed to the growing lay criticism of the church. Urban laypeople were increasingly knowledgeable about the world around them and about the rulers who controlled their lives. They traveled widely—as soldiers, pilgrims, explorers, and traders. New postal systems and the printing press increased the information at their disposal. A new age of books and libraries raised literacy and heightened curiosity. Laypeople were able to shape the cultural life of their communities.

From the Albigensians, Waldensians, Beguines, and Beghards in the thirteenth century to the Lollards and Hussites in the fifteenth, lay religious movements shared a common goal of religious simplicity in the imitation of Jesus. Almost everywhere, the laity was inspired by ideals of apostolic poverty in religion. A simple religion of love and self-sacrifice like that of Jesus and the first disciples seemed to be the ideal. To that end, the laity sought a more egalitarian church—one that gave the members as well as the head of the church a voice—and also a more spiritual church—one that lived manifestly according to its New Testament model.

The Modern Devotion   One of the more constructive lay religious movements in northern Europe on the eve of the Reformation was that of the Brothers of the Common Life, also known as the Modern Devotion, a kind of boarding school for reform-minded laity. The brothers fostered religious life outside formal church offices and apart from formal religious vows—a lay religious life of prayer and study without surrendering the world. Centered at Zwolle and Deventer in the Netherlands, the brother and (less numerous) sister houses of the Modern Devotion spread rapidly throughout northern Europe and influenced parts of southern Europe as well. In these houses clerics and laity shared a common life, stressing individual piety and practical religion. Lay members were not expected to take special religious vows or to wear a special religious dress, nor did they abandon their ordinary secular vocations.

The brothers were also educators. They worked as copyists, sponsored many religious and some classical publications, ran hospices for poor students, and conducted schools for the young—especially boys preparing for the priesthood or a monastic vocation. As youths, the future philosopher Nicholas of Cusa, the humanist and Hebraist Johannes Reuchlin, and Desiderius Erasmus, the proclaimed "prince of the humanists," were looked after by these brothers. Erasmus later formulated his own "philosophy of Christ" after what he had learned there. Thomas à Kempis (d. 1471) summarized the philosophy of the brothers in what became the most popular religious book of the period, the *Imitation of Christ*. This semimystical guide to the inner life was intended primarily for monks and nuns but was also widely read by laity who wanted to pursue the ascetic life.

The Modern Devotion has been seen as the source of humanist, Protestant, and Catholic reform movements in the sixteenth century. Some scholars, however, believe it represented an individualistic approach to religion, indifferent and even hostile to the sacramental piety of the church and papal authority. It was, in truth, a conservative movement. The brothers retained the old clerical doctrines and values but placed them within the new framework of an active common life. Their practices clearly met a need for a more personal piety and a more informed religious life. Their movement appeared at a time when the laity was demanding good preaching in the **vernacular** and taking the initiative to endow special funds for preaching in cities and towns to ensure it.

Lay Control over Religious Life   On the eve of the Reformation, Rome's international network of church offices, which had unified Europe religiously during the Middle Ages, was falling apart in many areas. This collapse was hurried along by a growing sense of regional identity, an increasingly competent local secular administration, and a newly emerging nationalism. The long-entrenched *benefice* system of the medieval church had permitted important ecclesiastical posts to be sold to the highest bidders and had often failed to enforce the requirement that priests and bishops had to live in their parishes and dioceses. Such a system threatened a vibrant, lay spiritual life. The substitutes hired by nonresident holders of *benefices* frequently lived elsewhere, preferably in Rome. They milked the revenues of their offices, performed their clerical chores mechanically, if they did them at all, and had neither firsthand knowledge of, nor much sympathy for, local spiritual needs and problems. Rare was the late medieval German town that did not have complaints about the maladministration, concubinage, or financial greed of its clergy—especially the higher clergy (bishops, abbots, and prelates).

Communities loudly protested the financial and spiritual abuses of the medieval church long before Luther published his famous summary of economic grievances in a treatise entitled *Address to the Christian Nobility of the German Nation* (1520). The sale of indulgences, in particular, had been repeatedly attacked before Luther came on the scene. On the eve of the Reformation, this practice had expanded to permit people to buy release from time in purgatory for both themselves and their deceased loved ones. Rulers and magistrates had little objection to their sale and might even encourage it, as long as a generous portion of the income the sales generated remained in the local coffers. Yet when an indulgence was offered primarily for the benefit of distant interests, as with the sale of indulgences to raise money for a new Saint Peter's basilica in Rome that Luther protested, resistance arose also for strictly financial reasons: their sale drained away local revenues.

The sale of indulgences would not end until rulers found new ways to profit from religion and the laity discovered more effective remedies for religious anxiety. The Reformation provided the former by sanctioning the secular dissolution of monasteries and the confiscation of ecclesiastical properties. It promised the latter in its new theology of justification by faith in God and a life of self-sacrificial service to one's neighbor.

City governments also undertook to improve local religious life on the eve of the Reformation by endowing preacherships. These positions, supported by *benefices*, made possible the hiring of well-trained pastors who provided regular preaching and pastoral care beyond the performance of the Mass. These preacherships often became platforms for Protestants.

Magistrates also carefully restricted the growth of ecclesiastical properties and clerical privileges. During the Middle Ages, canon and civil law had recognized special clerical rights in both property and person. Because they were holy places of "sacral peace" and asylum, churches and monasteries were exempted from the taxes and laws that affected others. Law also deemed it inappropriate for holy persons (clergy) to burden themselves with such "dirty jobs" as military service, compulsory labor, standing watch at city gates, and other ordinary civic obligations. Nor was it thought right that the laity should sit in judgment on those who were their shepherds and intermediaries with God. The clergy, accordingly, came to enjoy an immunity from the jurisdiction of civil courts.

Already on the eve of the Reformation, measures were passed to restrict these clerical privileges and to end their abuses. Governments grew tired of church interference in what to them were strictly secular political spheres of competence and authority. Secular authorities accordingly began to scrutinize the church's acquisition of new properties, finding ways to get around its right of asylum when it interrupted the administration of justice, and generally bringing the clergy under local tax codes.

▼ Martin Luther and the German Reformation to 1525

Unlike England and France, late medieval Germany lacked the political unity to enforce "national" religious reforms during the late Middle Ages. There were no lasting Statutes of Provisors and Praemunire, as in England, nor a Pragmatic Sanction of Bourges, as in France, limiting papal jurisdiction and taxation on a national scale. What had happened on a unified national level in England and France occurred only locally and piecemeal within German territories and towns. As popular resentment of clerical immunities and ecclesiastical abuses spread among German cities and towns, an unorganized "national" opposition to Rome formed. German humanists had long given voice to such criticism, and by 1517 it was pervasive enough to provide a solid foundation for Martin Luther's protest of indulgences and the theology that legitimated them.

The son of a successful Thüringian miner, Luther (1483–1546) was educated in Mansfeld, Magdeburg (where the Brothers of the Common Life had been his teachers) and Eisenach. Between 1501 and 1505, he attended the University of Erfurt, where the nominalist teachings of William of Ockham and Gabriel Biel (d. 1495) prevailed. (See Chapter 8.) After receiving his master-of-arts degree in 1505, Luther registered with the law faculty in accordance with his parents' wishes. But he never began the study of law. To the disappointment of his family, he instead entered the Order of the Hermits of Saint Augustine in Erfurt on July 17, 1505. That decision had apparently been building for some time and was resolved during a lightning storm in which a young Luther, terrified and crying out to Saint Anne for assistance (she was the patron saint of travelers in distress), promised to enter a monastery if he escaped death.

Ordained in 1507, Luther pursued a traditional course of study. In 1510, he journeyed to Rome on the business of his order, finding there justification for the many criticisms of the church he had heard in Germany. In 1511, he moved to the Augustinian monastery in Wittenberg, where he earned his doctorate in theology in 1512, thereafter, to become a leader within the monastery, the new university, and the spiritual life of the city.

Justification by Faith Alone

Luther was especially plagued by the disproportion between his own sense of sinfulness and the perfect righteousness God required for salvation, according to traditional church teaching. Luther came to despise the phrase "righteousness of God," because it demanded of him a perfection neither he nor any other human being could attain. His insight into the meaning of "justification by faith alone" (*sola fide*) was a gradual process between 1513 and 1518. The righteousness that God demands, he concluded, did not result from charitable acts and religious ceremonies but was given in full measure to any and all who believe in and trust Jesus Christ as their perfect righteousness satisfying to God.

The medieval church had always taught that salvation was a joint venture, a combination of divine mercy and human good works, what God alone could do and what man was expected to do in return. Luther also believed that faith without charitable service to one's neighbor was dead. The Christian did not fulfill all the due obligations of a Christian life by simply saying, "I believe," and thereafter did as he pleased. The issue was not whether good works should be done, but how those works should be regarded. It was unbiblical, Luther argued, to treat works as contributing to one's eternal salvation, something only an almighty God could bestow. He also believed that the church's conditioning of salvation on

A Closer ▶ LOOK

A SAINT AT PEACE IN THE GRASP OF TEMPTATION

MARTIN SCHONGAUER (c. 1430–1491), the best engraver in the Upper Rhine, portrays the devil's temptation of St. Anthony in the wilderness as a robust physical attack by demons rather than the traditional melancholic introspection.

Unlike the saint, the demons look perplexed and disbelieving, as their every thrust fails to penetrate.

Although the demons are all over him, Anthony remains untouched. The artist's remarkably distinct lines keep saint and demons apart, reinforcing the saint's inner peace and serenity.

This rendering of faith as serenity amid the most brutal assault anticipates Martin Luther's great hymn of the Reformation: "A Mighty Fortress Is Our God," in which it is said that "one little word" (belief in Christ) slays the devil and his minions.

To examine this image in an interactive fashion, please go to www.myhistorylab.com

National Gallery of Art, Washington, DC

PEARSON
myhistorylab

good works left many Christians only counting their merits and demerits, unable to act selflessly, and struggling to maintain inner peace of mind.

Good works were expected over a lifetime, Luther taught, but not because they earned salvation. The believer who is bound to Christ by faith already possesses God's perfect righteousness. It is this knowledge of faith that sets narcissistic souls free to serve their neighbors selflessly. Such service is ethical, not soteriological—a good work, not a saving work. Inspired by the security faith conveys, such works belong to one's neighbor, who needs help, not to God in heaven, who has everything. God is pleased when those who believe in him do good works, and he expects his people always to do them, but he does not take those works into account when he is merciful and bestows eternal life, which would make God a puppet of man.

The Attack on Indulgences

An **indulgence** was a remission of the temporal penalty imposed on penitents by priests as a "work of satisfaction" for their confessed mortal sins. According to medieval theology, after the priest absolved a penitent of guilt for sin, the penitent still remained under an eternal penalty, a punishment God justly imposed. Priestly absolution, however, was said to transform this eternal penalty into a temporal penalty, a manageable "work of satisfaction" a penitent might perform here and now by prayers, fasting, almsgiving, retreats, and/or pilgrimages. Penitents who defaulted on such prescribed works of satisfaction could expect to suffer for them in purgatory for an indefinite period of time before entering heaven.

Indulgences were originally given to Crusaders who could not complete their penances because they had fallen in battle. By the late Middle Ages, indulgences had become an aid to laypeople made genuinely anxious by their fear of a future suffering in purgatory for neglected penances or unrepented sins. In 1343, Pope Clement VI (r. 1342–1352) proclaimed the existence of a "treasury of merit," an infinite reservoir of good works in the church's possession that could be dispensed at the pope's discretion. On the basis of this alleged treasury, the church sold "letters of indulgence," which made good on the works of satisfaction owed by penitents. In 1476, Pope Sixtus IV (r. 1471–1484) extended indulgences to the unrepented sins of all Christians in purgatory.

By Luther's time, indulgences were regularly dispensed for small cash payments, modest sums that were regarded as a good work of almsgiving. Indulgence preachers presented them to the laity as remitting not only their own future punishments, but also those of dead relatives presumed still to be suffering in purgatory.

In 1517, Pope Leo X (r. 1513–1521) revived a plenary Jubilee Indulgence that had first been issued by Pope Julius II (r. 1503–1513), the proceeds of which were to rebuild St. Peter's Basilica in Rome. Such an indulgence promised for-

A contemporary caricature depicts John Tetzel, the famous indulgence preacher. The last lines of the jingle read, "As soon as gold in the basin rings, right then the soul to Heaven springs." It was Tetzel's preaching that spurred Luther to publish his ninety-five theses. Courtesy Stiftung Luthergedenkstaten in Sachsen-Anhalt/Lutherhalle, Wittenberg giveness of all outstanding unrepented sins upon the completion of certain acts. That indulgence was subsequently preached on the borders of Saxony in the territories of the future Archbishop Albrecht of Mainz, who was much in need of revenues because of the large debts he had incurred to gain a papal dispensation to hold three ecclesiastical appointments at one and the same time.

The selling of the indulgence became a joint venture by Albrecht, the Augsburg banking house of Fugger, and Pope Leo X, with half the proceeds going to the pope and half to Albrecht and his creditors. The famous indulgence preacher John Tetzel (d. 1519) was enlisted to preach the indulgence in Albrecht's territories. A seasoned professional, he knew how to stir ordinary people to action. As he exhorted on one occasion,

Don't you hear the voices of your dead parents and other relatives crying out, "Have mercy on us, for we suffer great punishment and pain. From this you could release us with a few alms. . . . We have created you, fed you, cared for you, and left you our temporal goods. Why do you treat us so cruelly and leave us to suffer in the flames, when it takes only a little to save us?"[1]

When Luther posted his ninety-five theses against indulgences on the door of Castle Church in Wittenberg (October 31, 1517), he protested especially the impression Tetzel created that indulgences remitted sins and released unrepentant sinners from punishment in purgatory. Luther believed these claims went far beyond the traditional practice and seemed to make salvation something that could be bought and sold.

Election of Charles V

The ninety-five theses were embraced by Nuremberg humanists, who translated and widely circulated them. This made Luther a central figure in an already organized national German cultural movement against foreign influence and competition, particularly on the part of the Italians. In October, he was summoned before the general of the Dominican order in Augsburg to answer for his criticism of the church. Yet as sanctions were being prepared against him, Emperor Maximilian I died (January 12, 1519)—a fortunate event for the budding Reformation, because it turned attention away from heresy in Saxony to the contest for a new emperor.

In that contest, the pope backed the French king, Francis I. However, Charles I of Spain, a youth of nineteen, successfully succeeded his grandfather as Emperor Charles V. (See Map 11–1, page 324.) Charles was blessed by both the long tradition of the Habsburg imperial rule and a massive Fugger campaign chest that secured the votes of the seven imperial **electors**. The most prominent among the seven was Frederick the Wise, Luther's lord and protector. Frederick took great pride in

his new University of Wittenberg, and he was not about to let any harm come to his famous court preacher.

In exchange for their votes, the electors wrung new concessions from the Spanish favorable to the Germans. Before becoming emperor, Charles I agreed to revive the German-based Imperial Supreme Court and the Council of Regency and also promised to consult with a diet of the empire on all major domestic and foreign affairs affecting the empire. These measures also helped the development of the Reformation by preventing unilateral imperial action against the Germans.

Luther's Excommunication and the Diet of Worms

In the same month in which Charles was elected emperor, Luther debated the Ingolstadt professor John Eck in Leipzig (June 27, 1519). During this contest, Luther challenged the infallibility of the pope and the inerrancy of church councils, appealing, for the first time, to the

AETHERNA IPSE SVAE MENTIS SIMVLACHRA LVTHERVS
EXPRIMIT·AT VVLTVS CERA LVCAE OCCIDVOS
·M·D·X·X·

In 1520, Luther's first portrait, shown here, depicted him as a tough, steely-eyed monk. Afraid that this portrayal might convey defiance rather than reform to Emperor Charles V, Elector Frederick the Wise of Saxony, Luther's protector, ordered court painter Lucas Cranach to soften the image. The result was a Luther placed within a traditional monk's niche reading an open Bible, a reformer, unlike the one depicted here, who was prepared to listen as well as to instruct. Martin Luther as a monk, 1521. © Foto Marburg/Art Resource, NY

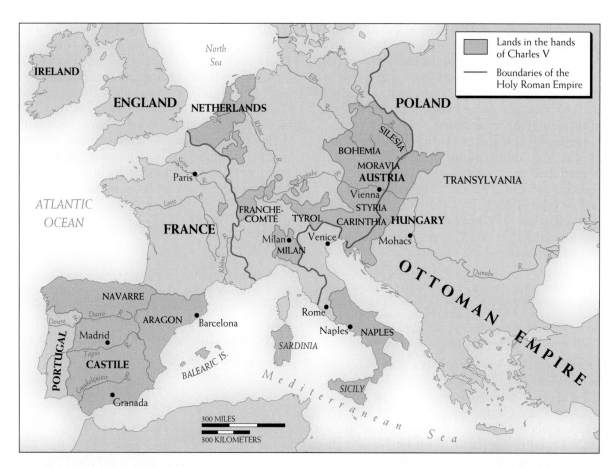

Map 11–1 **THE EMPIRE OF CHARLES V** Dynastic marriages and simple chance concentrated into Charles's hands rule over the lands shown here, plus Spain's overseas possessions. Crowns and titles rained down on him; his election in 1519 as emperor gave him new distractions and responsibilities.

sovereign authority of Scripture alone. He burned all his bridges to the old church when he further defended certain teachings of John Huss, who had been condemned to death for heresy at the Council of Constance.

In 1520, Luther signaled his new direction with three famous pamphlets. The *Address to the Christian Nobility of the German Nation* urged the German princes to force reforms on the Roman church, especially to curtail its political and economic power in Germany. The *Babylonian Captivity of the Church* attacked the traditional seven sacraments, arguing that only two, baptism and the Eucharist, were unquestionably biblical, and it exalted the authority of Scripture, church councils, and secular princes over that of the pope. The eloquent *Freedom of a Christian* summarized the new teaching of salvation by faith alone.

On June 15, 1520, Leo's papal bull *Exsurge Domine* ("Arise, O Lord") condemned Luther for heresy and gave him sixty days to retract. The final bull of excommunication was issued on January 3, 1521.

In April 1521, Luther presented his views before the Diet of Worms, over which the newly elected Emperor Charles V presided. Ordered to recant, Luther declared that to do so would be to act against Scripture, reason, and his conscience. On May 26, 1521, he was placed under the imperial ban, which made him an "outlaw" to secular as well as religious authority. For his own protection, friends disguised and hid him in Wartburg Castle at the instruction of Elector Frederick. There, he spent almost a year, from April 1521 to March 1522. During his stay, he translated the New Testament into German using Erasmus's new Greek text and Latin translation, while overseeing by correspondence the first steps of the Reformation in Wittenberg.

Imperial Distractions: War with France and the Turks

The Reformation was greatly helped in these early years by the emperor's war with France and the advance of the Ottoman Turks into eastern Europe. Against both adversaries Charles V, who remained a Spanish king with dynastic responsibilities in Spain and Austria, needed loyal German troops, to which end he sought friendly relations with the German princes. Between 1521 and 1559, Spain (the Habsburg dynasty) and France (the Valois dynasty) fought four major wars over disputed territories within Italy and along their respective borders.

Thus preoccupied, the emperor agreed through his representatives at the German Diet of Speyer (1526) that each German territory was free to enforce the Edict of Worms (1521) against Luther "so as to be able to answer in good conscience to God and the emperor." That concession in effect gave the German princes, who five years earlier had refused to publish the emperor's condemnation of Luther, territorial sovereignty in religious matters. It also bought the Reformation time to put down deep roots in Germany and Switzerland. In addition, Speyer proved to be a true precedent for the final settlement of the religious conflict in the empire. Later, the Peace of Augsburg (1555) would enshrine regional princely control over religion in imperial law.

How the Reformation Spread

In the late 1520s and 1530s, the Reformation passed from the free hands of the theologians and pamphleteers into the firmer ones of the magistrates and princes. In many cities, the latter quickly mandated new religious reforms. Many rulers had themselves worked for decades to bring about basic church reforms, and they welcomed Lutheran preachers as new allies. Reform now ceased to be merely slogans and was transformed into laws all townspeople had to obey.

The elector of Saxony and the prince of Hesse, the two most powerful German Protestant rulers, led the politicization of religious reform within their territories. Like the urban magistrates, the German princes recognized the political and economic opportunities offered them by the demise of the Roman Catholic Church in their lands. Soon they were pushing Protestant faith and politics onto their neighbors. In the 1530s, German Protestant lands formed a powerful defensive alliance, the Schmaldkaldic League, and prepared for war with the Catholic emperor.

The Peasants' Revolt

In its first decade, the Reformation suffered more from internal division than from imperial interference. By 1525, Luther had become almost as much an object of protest within Germany as was the pope. Original allies, sympathizers, and fellow travelers increasingly declared their independence from Wittenberg.

Like the German humanists, the German peasantry also had at first believed Luther to be an ally. Since the late fifteenth century, the peasantry had opposed the efforts of their secular and ecclesiastical lords to override their traditional laws and customs and to subject them to new territorial regulations and taxes. Peasant leaders, several of whom had been Lutherans, saw in Luther's teaching about Christian freedom and his criticism of monastic landowners a point of view close to their own. They openly solicited

The punishment of a peasant leader in a village near Heilbronn. After the defeat of rebellious peasants in and around the city of Heilbronn, Jacob Rorbach, a well-to-do peasant leader from a nearby village, was tied to a stake and slowly roasted to death.
Courtesy of the Library of Congress

Luther's support of their alleged "Christian" political and economic rights, including a revolutionary demand of release from serfdom.

Luther had initially sympathized with the peasants, condemning the tyranny of the princes and urging them to meet the just demands of the peasants. Lutheran pamphleteers made Karsthans (Hans with a hoe), the burly, hard-working peasant who earned his bread by the sweat of his brow, a model of the honest life God wanted all people to live. The Lutherans, however, were not social revolutionaries and they saw no hope for their movement if it became intertwined with a peasant revolution. When the peasants revolted against their landlords in 1524–1525, invoking Luther's name, Luther predictably condemned them as "un-Christian" and urged the princes to crush the revolt mercilessly. Tens of thousands of peasants (estimates run between 70,000 and 100,000) died by the time the revolt was suppressed.

For Luther, the freedom of the Christian lay in inner spiritual release from guilt and anxiety, not in revolutionary politics. Had the reformers joined the peasants' revolt, Luther would have contradicted his own teaching and likely shared the fate of former Lutherans who died as leaders of peasant revolts. In that scenario the

A Raw Deal for the Common Man, or His Just Desserts?

BEGINNING IN THE late fifteenth century, German feudal lords, both secular and ecclesiastical, increased labor and crop quotas on their peasant tenants, while restricting their freedoms and overriding their customary laws as well. In 1525 massive revolts occurred in southern Germany, in what became the largest social uprising before the French Revolution. Among those responding directly to the revolt were two highly respected authorities: Wittenberg theologian Martin Luther and Nuremberg artist Albrecht Dürer.

QUESTIONS

1. **What is there in Luther's religious teaching that might have led the peasants to think he would support their revolt? What personal interest might he have had in turning them his way? What does he advise them to do to address their grievances properly?**

2. **Does Dürer's 1527 sketch of a "Memorial to the Peasants' Revolt," depicting a peasant sitting** atop a chicken coop with a sword thrust through his back, suggest a greater sympathy for the peasants? Or can it be read as agreement with Luther that the peasants received their just desserts for rebelling against lawful authority?

3. **Does Dürer's monument support or condemn the rebellious peasants?**

I. Martin Luther, *An Admonition to Peace* (1525)

ON STOPPING THE WAR

This matter is great and perilous, concerning both the kingdom of God and the kingdom of the world; if this rebellion gets the upper hand, both kingdoms will be destroyed and there will be neither world government nor Word of God; there will rather result the permanent destruction of all of Germany, therefore, it is necessary . . . to speak boldly . . . Since there is nothing Christian on either side and nothing Christian is at issue between you . . . let yourselves be advised and attack these matters with justice, not with force or strife, and do not start an endless bloodshed in Germany!

We have no one on earth to thank for this mischievous rebellion, except you lords and princes, especially you blind bishops and mad priests and monks . . . In your government you do nothing but flay and rob your subjects in order that you may lead a life of splendor and pride, until the poor common folk can bear it no longer . . .

[As for] the peasants, they must take the name and title of a people who fight because they will not and ought not endure wrong or evil, according to the teaching of nature. You should have <u>that</u> name, and let the name of Christ alone . . . [As for your so-called 'Christian' demands for] freedom of game, birds, fish, wood, forests, labor services, tithes, imposts, excises, and release from the death tax, these I leave to the lawyers, for they are things that do not concern a Christian who is a martyr on this earth . . . Let the name of Christian alone and act in some other name, as men and women who want human and natural rights.

Sources: *A Sincere Admonition to Peace,* cited by Ozment, *Age of Reform,* p. 283 [first paragraph]; cited by Steven Ozment, *The Age of Reform* (New Haven, CT:, Yale University Press, 1980), pp. 280–282, [second and third paragraphs].

II. Martin Luther, *Against the Robbing and Murdering Peasants* (1525)

FINAL WORDS

[The princes] should have no mercy on obstinate, hardened, blinded peasants who refuse to listen to reason. Let everyone, as he is able, strike, hew, stab, and slay, as though among mad dogs, so that by doing so he may show mercy to those [non-rebelling peasants] who have been ruined, put to flight, and led astray by these rebelling peasants [so that] peace and safety may return . . .

Source: Ozment, *The Age of Reform,* p. 284.

III. *An Open Letter Concerning the Hard Book Against the Peasants* (1525)

FINAL WORDS

Suppose I were to break into a man's house, rape his wife and daughters, break open his coffers, take his money, set a sword to his breast and say: 'If you will not put up with this, I shall run you through, for you are a godless wretch.' Then if a crowd gathered and were about to kill me for doing this, or if the judge ordered my head off, suppose I were to cry out: 'But Christ teaches that you are to be merciful and not kill me.' What would people say then? Well, that is exactly what my peasants and their advocates are doing now. The kingdom of this world is nothing else than the servant of God's wrath upon the wicked and it is a real precursor of hell and everlasting death. It should not be merciful, but strict, severe, and wrathful in the fulfillment of its works and duty. Its tool is not a wreath or roses or a flower of love, but a naked sword.

From the start I had two fears. If the peasants became lords, the devil would become abbot; if these tyrants became lords, the devil's dam would become abbess. Therefore I wanted to do two things: quiet the peasants and instruct the lords. The peasants were unwilling, and now they have their reward. The lords will not hear, and they shall have their reward also.

Sources: An Open Letter Concerning the Hard Book Against the peasants, cited by Ozment, Age of Reform, p. 286-287 [first paragraph]; Ozment, *The Age of Reform*, p. 287, [second and third paragraph].

IV. Albrecht Dürer, *Memorial to the Peasants' Revolt* (1527)

Dürer's "Memorial to the Peasants," drawn in 1527, the year before his death, appeared in a book devoted to 'perspective in art.' Fearing that Protestant iconoclasm (destruction of icons) and the coming of religious wars would remove decorative art from the churches, his book was to be a primer for artists who in the aftermath of such destruction would have to learn the art of painting all over again. The sketch shows a peasant sitting atop a chicken coop with a sword thrust through his back, the classic iconography of betrayal.

At this time Dürer's peers, friends, and associates condemned the Peasants' Revolt as strongly as Luther. During the war Dürer painted portraits of the Fuggers, the great merchant family the peasants despised, and also Margrave Casimir of Brandenburg-Ansbach, a brutal slayer of peasants and Anabaptists. Within this context might Dürer's slain rebellious peasant, like Luther's, have gotten his just due?

Source: Joseph Leo Koerner, *The Moment of Self-Portraiture in Renaissance Art* (Chicago: Chicago University Press, 1993), p. 235.

10.

The caption reads: "He who wants to commemorate his victory over the rebellious peasants might use to that end a structure such as I portray here." Illustration from Jane Campbell Hutchinson, *Albrecht Dürer: A Biography* (Princeton, NJ: Princeton University Press, 1990)

327

German Reformation would not have survived beyond the 1520s. Still, many critics believe that Luther's decision ended the promise of the Reformation as a social and moral force in history.

▼ The Reformation Elsewhere

Although the German Reformation was the first, Switzerland and France had their own independent church reform movements almost simultaneously with Germany's. From them developed new churches as prominent and lasting as the Lutheran.

A Catholic Portrayal of Martin Luther Tempting Christ (1547). Reformation propaganda often portrayed the pope as the Antichrist or the devil. Here Catholic propaganda turns the tables on the Protestant reformers by portraying a figure of Martin Luther as the devil (note the monstrous feet and tail under his academic robes). Re-creating the biblical scene of Christ being tempted by the devil in the wilderness, the figure of Luther asks Christ to transform stone into bread, to which temptation Christ responds by saying that humans do not live by bread alone.   Versucung Christi, 1547, Gemälde, Bonn, Rheinisches Landesmuseum, Inv. Nr. 58.3

Zwingli and the Swiss Reformation

Switzerland was a loose confederacy of thirteen autonomous *cantons*, or states, and their allied areas. (See Map 11–2.) Some cantons became Protestant, some remained Catholic, and a few others managed to effect a compromise. There were two main preconditions of the Swiss Reformation. First was the growth of national sentiment occasioned by popular opposition to foreign mercenary service. (Providing mercenaries for Europe's warring nations was a major source of Switzerland's livelihood.) Second was a desire for church reform that had persisted in Switzerland since the councils of Constance (1414–1417) and Basel (1431–1449).

The Reformation in Zurich   Ulrich Zwingli (1484–1531), the leader of the Swiss Reformation, had been humanistically educated. He credited Erasmus over Luther with having set him on the path to reform. He served as a chaplain with Swiss mercenaries who were on the losing side in the disastrous Battle of Marignano in Italy in 1515. Thereafter he became an eloquent critic of Swiss mercenary service, believing it threatened both the political sovereignty and the moral fiber of the Swiss confederacy. By 1518, Zwingli was also widely known for his opposition to the sale of indulgences and to religious superstition.

In 1519, he competed for the post of people's priest in the main church of Zurich. His candidacy was initially questioned after he acknowledged fornicating with a barber's daughter, who had since delivered a child. Zwingli successfully minimized the affair, claiming the woman in question had been a skilled seducer, and denying any paternity as she had had affairs with other men as well. Zwingli's conduct was not so scandalous to contemporaries, who sympathized with the plight of a celibate clergy. One of Zwingli's first acts as a reformer was to petition for an end to clerical celibacy and for the right of clergy legally to marry, a practice accepted in all Protestant lands.

From his new position as people's priest in Zurich, Zwingli engineered the Swiss Reformation. In March 1522, he was party to the breaking of the Lenten fast—then an act of protest analogous to burning one's national flag today. Zwingli's reform guideline was simple and effective: Whatever lacked literal support in Scripture was to be neither believed nor practiced. As had also happened with Luther, that test soon raised questions about such honored traditional teachings and practices as fasting, transubstantiation, the worship of saints, pilgrimages, purgatory, clerical celibacy, and certain sacraments. A disputation held on January 29, 1523, concluded with the city government's sanction of Zwingli's Scripture test. (See "Zwingli Lists the Errors of the Roman Church," page 330.) Thereafter Zurich became the center of the Swiss Reformation. The new regime imposed a harsh discipline that made the city one of the first examples of puritanical Protestantism.

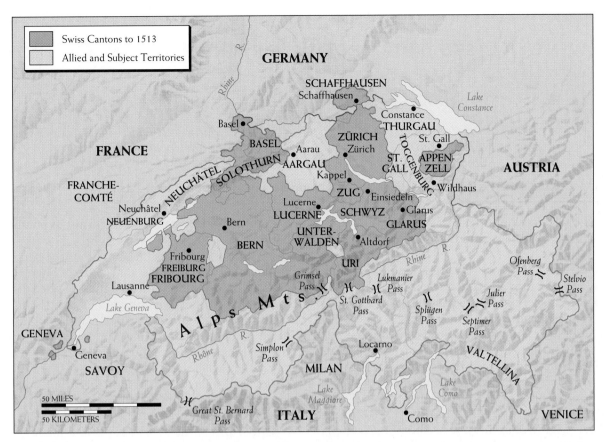

Map 11–2   **THE SWISS CONFEDERATION**   Although nominally still a part of the Holy Roman Empire, Switzerland grew from a loose defensive union of the central "forest cantons" in the thirteenth century into a fiercely independent association of regions with different languages, histories, and, finally, religions.

The Marburg Colloquy   Landgrave Philip of Hesse (1504–1567) sought to unite Swiss and German Protestants in a mutual defense pact. However, Luther's and Zwingli's bitter theological differences, especially over the nature of Christ's presence in the Eucharist, spoiled his efforts. Zwingli favored a symbolic interpretation of Christ's words, "This is my body." Christ, he argued, was spiritually, not bodily, present in the bread and wine of the Eucharist. Luther, to the contrary, insisted that Christ's human nature was such that it shared the properties of his divine nature. Hence, where Christ was spiritually present, he could also be bodily present, for such was his special human nature. Luther wanted no part of an abstract, spiritualized Christ, while Zwingli feared Luther was still mired in medieval sacramental theology.

Philip of Hesse brought the two Protestant leaders together in his castle in Marburg in early October 1529, to work out their differences. However, the effort proved to be in vain. Luther left thinking Zwingli a dangerous fanatic, forevermore to paint him black. Although cooperation between the two Protestant sides did not cease altogether, the disagreement splintered the Protestant movement theologically and politically.

Separate defense leagues formed, and semi-Zwinglian theological views came to be embodied in the non-Lutheran *Tetrapolitan Confession* prepared by the Strasbourg reformers Martin Bucer and Caspar Hedio in 1530.

Swiss Civil Wars   As the Swiss cantons divided themselves between Protestantism and Catholicism, civil wars erupted. There were two major battles, both at Kappel, one in June 1529 and a second in October 1531. The first ended in a Protestant victory, which forced the Catholic cantons to break their foreign alliances and to recognize the rights of Swiss Protestants. After the second battle, Zwingli lay wounded on the battlefield, and when discovered, he was unceremoniously executed, his remains thereafter hacked into pieces and scattered to the four winds so his followers would have no relics to console and inspire them. The subsequent treaty confirmed the right of each canton to determine its own religion. Heinrich Bullinger (1504–1575), Zwingli's protégé and later son-in-law, became the new leader of the Swiss Reformation and guided its development into an established religion, eventually to merge with Calvinism.

ZWINGLI LISTS THE ERRORS OF THE ROMAN CHURCH

Prior to the first Zurich Disputation (1523), which effectively introduced the Protestant Reformation in Zurich, the reformer Zwingli prepared such a summary of the errors of the Roman Church known as the Sixty-Seven Articles. *Here are some of them.*

How do Zwingli's basic religious views compare with those of Martin Luther?

All who consider other teachings equal to or higher than the Gospel err, and they do not know what the Gospel is.

In the faith rests our salvation, and in unbelief our damnation; for all truth is clear in Christ.

In the Gospel one learns that human doctrines and decrees do not aid in salvation.

That Christ, having sacrificed himself once, is to eternity a certain and valid sacrifice for the sins of all faithful, wherefrom it follows that the Mass is not a sacrifice, but is a remembrance of the sacrifice and assurance of the salvation which Christ has given us.

That God desires to give us all things in his name, whence it follows that outside of this life we need no [intercession of the saints or any] mediator except himself.

That no Christian is bound to do those things which God has not decreed, therefore one may eat at all times all food, where from one learns that the decree about cheese and butter is a Roman swindle.

That no special person can impose the ban upon anyone, but the Church, that is, the congregation of those among whom the one to be banned dwells, together with their watchman, i.e., the pastor.

All that the spiritual so-called state [i.e., the papal church] claims to have of power and protection belongs to the lay [i.e., the secular magistracy], if they wish to be Christians.

Greater offence I know not than that one does not allow priests to have wives, but permits them to hire prostitutes.

Christ has borne all our pains and labor. Hence whoever assigns to works of penance what belongs to Christ errs and slanders God.

The true divine Scriptures know naught about purgatory after this life.

The Scriptures know no priests except those who proclaim the word of God.

Ulrich Zwingli (1484–1531), *Selected Works*, ed. by Samuel M. Jackson (Philadelphia: University of Pennsylvania Press, 1972), pp. 111–117.

Anabaptists and Radical Protestants

The moderate pace and seemingly low ethical results of the Lutheran and Zwinglian reformations discontented many people, among them some of the original followers of Luther and Zwingli. These were devout fundamentalist Protestants who desired a more rapid and thorough implementation of Apostolic Christianity. They accused the reform movements that went before them of having gone only halfway. The most important of these radical groups were the **Anabaptists**, the sixteenth-century ancestors of the modern Mennonites and Amish. The Anabaptists were especially distinguished by their rejection of infant baptism and their insistence on only adult baptism, as was the case with Jesus, who was baptized as an adult. (The term *Anabaptism* derives from the Greek word meaning "to rebaptize.") Only a thoughtful consenting adult, able to understand the Scriptures and what the biblical way of life required, could enter the covenant of faith.

Although Luther and Zwingli also taught that believers must believe for themselves (Luther called it the "priesthood of all believers"), they retained the historical practice of infant baptism, despite the absence of any clear biblical mandate. They argued that the congregation "believed for the infant," stood in his or her place, and pledged to raise the baptized infant in the faith. Here, the communal nature and responsibility of the church was deemed to be more basic to Christianity than the radical individualism the Anabaptists asserted.

Conrad Grebel and the Swiss Brethren Conrad Grebel (1498–1526), with whom Anabaptism originated, performed the first adult rebaptism in Zurich in January 1525. Initially a co-worker of Zwingli's and an even greater biblical literalist, Grebel broke openly with him.

In a religious disputation in October 1523, Zwingli supported the city government's plea for a peaceful, gradual removal of resented traditional religious practices—not the rush to perfection the Anabaptists demand.

The alternative of the Swiss Brethren, as Grebel's group came to be called, was embodied in the *Schleitheim Confession* of 1527. This document distinguished Anabaptists not only by their practice of adult baptism, but also by their pacifism, refusal to swear oaths, and nonparticipation in the offices of secular government. By both choice and coercion, Anabaptists physically separated from established society to form a more perfect communion modeled on the first Christians. Because of the close connection between religious and civic life in the sixteenth century, the political authorities also viewed such separatism as a threat to basic social bonds, even as a form of sedition.

The Anabaptist Reign in Münster At first, Anabaptism drew adherents from all social classes. As Lutherans and Zwinglians joined with Catholics in opposition and persecuted them within the cities, however, a more rural, agrarian class came to make up the great majority of Anabaptists. In 1529, rebaptism became a capital offense within the Holy Roman Empire. At least 1,000 and perhaps as many as 5,000 men and women were executed for rebaptizing themselves as adults between 1525 and 1618.

Brutal measures were universally applied against nonconformists after Anabaptist extremists came to power in the German city of Münster in 1534–1535. Led by two Dutch emigrants, a baker, Jan Matthys of Haarlem, and a tailor, Jan Beukelsz of Leiden, the Anabaptists in Münster forced Lutherans and Catholics in the city either to convert or to emigrate. After their departure, the city was blockaded by besieging armies. Under such pressures, Münster was transformed into an Old Testament theocracy, replete with charismatic leaders and the practice of polygamy. The latter was implemented as a measure of social control to deal with the many recently widowed and deserted women left behind in the city. Women opposed to the practice were allowed to leave polygymous marriages.

These developments shocked the outside world, and Protestant and Catholic armies united to crush the radicals. The skeletons of their leaders long hung in public view as a warning to all who would so offend traditional Christian sensitivities. After this episode, moderate, pacifistic Anabaptism became the norm among most nonconformists. Menno Simons (1496–1561), the founder of the Mennonites, set an example of non-provocative separatist Anabaptism, which became the historical form in which Anabaptist sects survived down to the present.

Spiritualists Another diverse and highly individualistic group of Protestant dissenters was the Spiritualists. These were mostly isolated individuals distinguished by their disdain for external, institutional religion. They believed the only religious authority was the Spirit of God, which spoke not in some past revelation, but here and now in the heart and mind of every listening individual. Among them were several renegade Lutherans. Thomas Müntzer (d. 1525), who had close contacts with Anabaptist leaders in Germany and Switzerland, died as a leader of a peasants' revolt in Frankenhausen, Germany. Sebastian Franck (d. 1541), a critic of all dogmatic religion, proclaimed the religious autonomy and freedom of every individual soul. Caspar Schwenckfeld (d. 1561) was a prolific writer and wanderer after whom the Schwenckfeldian Church is named.

Antitrinitarians A final group of persecuted radical Protestants also destined for prominence in the modern world was the Antitrinitarians. These were exponents of a commonsense, rational, and ethical religion. Prominent among them were the Spaniard Michael Servetus (1511–1553), executed in 1553 in Geneva at the encouragement of John Calvin for "blasphemies against the Holy Trinity." The Italians, Lelio (d. 1562) and Faustus Sozzini (d. 1604), the founders of Socinianism, also stand out. These thinkers were the strongest opponents of Calvinism, especially its belief in original sin and **predestination**, and have a deserved reputation as defenders of religious toleration.

John Calvin and the Genevan Reformation

In the second half of the sixteenth century, Calvinism replaced Lutheranism as the dominant Protestant force in Europe. Calvinism was the religious ideology that inspired or accompanied massive political resistance in France, the Netherlands, and Scotland. During the reign of Elector Frederick III (r. 1559–1576) Calvinism established itself within the geographical region of the Palatinate, the German state in the Rhineland in which the Thirty Years' War, the worst of the wars of religion, would break out in 1618. Calvinists believed strongly in both divine predestination and the individual's responsibility to reorder society according to God's plan. They were determined to transform society so men and women lived their lives externally as they professed to believe internally and were presumably destined to live eternally.

The namesake of Calvinism and its perfect embodiment, John Calvin (1509–1564), was born into a well-to-do French family, the son of the secretary to the bishop of Noyon. At age twelve, he received church *benefices* that financed the best possible education at Parisian colleges and a law degree. In the 1520s, he identified with the French reform party. Although he would finally reject this group as ineffectual compromisers, its members contributed much to his intellectual preparation as a religious reformer.

A portrait of the young John Calvin. Bibliothèque Publique et Universitaire, Geneva

It was probably in the spring of 1534 that Calvin experienced that conversion to Protestantism by which he said his "long stubborn heart" was "made teachable" by God. His own hard experience became a personal model of reform by which he would measure the recalcitrant citizenry of Geneva. His mature theology stressed the sovereignty of God's will over all creation and the necessity of humankind's conformity to it. In May 1534, he dramatically surrendered the *benefices* that had educated him and joined the budding Reformation in Geneva.

Political Revolt and Religious Reform in Geneva

Whereas in Saxony religious reform paved the way for a political revolution against the emperor, in Geneva a political revolution against the local prince-bishop laid the foundation for the religious change. Genevans revolted against their resident prince-bishop in the late 1520s, and the city council assumed his legal and political powers in 1527.

In late 1533, the Protestant city of Bern dispatched two reformers to Geneva: Guillaume Farel (1489–1565) and Antoine Froment (1508–1581). In the summer of 1535, after much internal turmoil, the Protestants triumphed, and the traditional Mass and

other religious practices were removed. On May 21, 1536, Geneva voted officially to adopt the Reformation: "to live according to the Gospel and the Word of God . . . without any more Masses, statues, idols, or other papal abuses."

Calvin arrived in Geneva after these events, in July 1536. He was actually en route to a scholarly refuge in Strasbourg, in flight from the persecution of Protestants in France, when warring between France and Spain forced him to turn sharply south to Geneva. Farel persuaded him to stay in the city and assist the Reformation, threatening Calvin with divine vengeance if he turned away from this task.

Calvin drew up articles for the governance of the new church, as well as a catechism to guide and discipline the people. Both were presented for approval to the city councils in early 1537. Because of the strong measures they proposed to govern Geneva's moral life, many suspected the reformers were intent on creating a "new papacy." Opponents feared Calvin and Farel were going too far too fast. Geneva's powerful Protestant ally, Bern, which had adopted a more moderate Protestant reform, pressured Geneva's magistrates to restore traditional religious ceremonies and holidays that Calvin and Farel had abolished. When the reformers opposed these actions, they were exiled from the city.

Calvin went to Strasbourg, a model Protestant city, where he became pastor to French exiles and wrote biblical commentaries. He also produced a second edition of his masterful *Institutes of the Christian Religion*, which many consider the definitive theological statement of the Protestant faith. Most importantly, he learned from the Strasbourg reformer Martin Bucer how to achieve his goals.

Calvin's Geneva In 1540, Geneva elected officials both favorable to Calvin and determined to establish full Genevan political and religious independence from Bern. They knew Calvin would be a valuable ally in that undertaking and invited him to return. This he did in September 1540, never to leave the city again. Within months of his return, the city implemented new ecclesiastical ordinances that provided for cooperation between the magistrates and the clergy in matters of internal discipline.

Following the Strasbourg model, the Genevan Church was organized into four offices: (1) pastors, of whom there were five; (2) teachers or doctors to instruct the populace in, and to defend, true doctrine; (3) elders, a group of twelve laypeople chosen by and from the Genevan councils and empowered to "oversee the life of everybody"; and (4) deacons to dispense church goods and services to the poor and the sick.

The controversial doctrine of predestination was at the center of Calvin's theology as justification by faith was at Luther's. Both doctrines have been criticized,

Luther's for seeming to deny the believer's need to do good works and Calvin's for seeming to deny the existence of human free will. Luther believed works were a mark of a true Christian, even though they did not make him such or save him. Calvin did not discuss predestination until the end of his great theological work, the *Institutes of the Christian Religion*. Explaining why he delayed its discussion, he described predestination as a doctrine only for mature Christians. Whereas it offended nonbelievers, true Christians might take consolation from it. For true believers, predestination recognized that the world and all who dwell in it are in God's hands from eternity to eternity, regardless of all else. When the world seems utterly godless and the devil to be its only lord, the true Christian takes consolation from the knowledge that his present life and future destiny are determined irrevocably by a loving and ever-lasting God. By believing that, and living as the Bible instructed them to do, Calvinists found consoling, presumptive evidence that they were among God's elect.

Possessed of such assurance, Calvinists turned their energies to transforming society spiritually and morally. Faith, Calvin taught, did not sit idly in the mind but conformed one's every action to God's law. The "elect" should at least live in a manifestly God-pleasing way if they are truly God's "elect." In the attempted realization of that goal, Calvin spared no effort. The consistory, or Geneva's regulatory court, became his instrument of power. Composed of the elders and the pastors and presided over by one of the city's chief magistrates that body implemented the strictest moral discipline.

Among the personal conflicts in Geneva that gave Calvin the reputation of a stern moralist, none proved more damaging than his role in the capture and execution in 1553 of the Spanish physician and amateur theologian Michael Servetus, who had already been condemned by the Inquisition for heresy. He died at the stake in Protestant Geneva for denying the doctrine of the Trinity, a subject on which he had written a book scandalous to church authorities.

After 1555, Geneva became home to thousands of exiled Protestants who had been driven out of France, England, and Scotland. Refugees numbering more than 5,000, most of them utterly loyal to Calvin, made up more than one third of Geneva's population. All of Geneva's magistrates were now devout Calvinists, greatly strengthening Calvin's position in the city.

To the thousands of persecuted Protestants who flocked to Geneva in mid-century, the city was a beacon and a refuge, Europe's only free city. During Calvin's lifetime, Geneva also gained the reputation of being a "woman's paradise" because its laws severely punished men who beat their wives, behavior deemed unbefitting a true Calvinist Christian.

▼ Political Consolidation of the Lutheran Reformation

By 1530, the Reformation was in Europe to stay. It would, however, take several decades and major attempts to eradicate it, before all would recognize this fact. With the political triumph of Lutheranism in the empire by the 1550s, Protestant movements elsewhere gained a new lease on life.

The Diet of Augsburg

Charles V devoted most of his first decade as emperor to the pursuit of politics and military campaigns outside the empire, particularly in Spain and Italy. In 1530, he returned to the empire to direct the Diet of Augsburg. This assembly of Protestant and Catholic representatives had been called to address the growing religious division within the empire in the wake of the Reformation's success. With its terms dictated by the Catholic emperor, the diet adjourned with a blunt and unrealistic order to all Lutherans to revert to Catholicism.

The Reformation was by this time too firmly established for that to occur. In February 1531, the Lutherans responded with the formation of their own defensive alliance, the Schmalkaldic League. The league took as its banner the **Augsburg Confession**, a moderate statement of Protestant beliefs that had been spurned by the emperor at the Diet of Augsburg. In 1538, Luther drew up a more strongly worded Protestant confession known as the *Schmalkaldic Articles*. Under the leadership of Landgrave Philip of Hesse and Elector John Frederick of Saxony, the league achieved a stalemate with the emperor, who was again distracted by renewed war with France and the ever-resilient Turks.

The Expansion of the Reformation

In the 1530s, German Lutherans formed regional consistories, judicial bodies composed of theologians and lawyers, which oversaw and administered the new Protestant churches and replaced the old Catholic episcopates. Educational reforms provided for compulsory primary education, schools for girls, a humanist revision of the traditional curriculum, and instruction of the laity in the new religion.

The Reformation also entrenched itself elsewhere. Introduced into Denmark by King Christian II (r. 1513–1523), Lutheranism thrived there under Frederick I (r. 1523–1533), who joined the Schmalkaldic League. Under Christian III (r. 1536–1559), Lutheranism became the official state religion.

In Sweden, King Gustavus Vasa (r. 1523–1560), supported by a Swedish nobility greedy for church lands, embraced Lutheranism, confiscated church property, and subjected the clergy to royal authority at the Diet of Vesteras (1527).

In politically splintered Poland, Lutherans, Anabaptists, Calvinists, and even Antitrinitarians found room to practice their beliefs. Primarily because of the absence of a central political authority, Poland became a model of religious pluralism and toleration in the second half of the sixteenth century.

Reaction Against Protestants

Charles V made abortive efforts in 1540–1541 to enforce a compromise between Protestants and Catholics. As these and other conciliar efforts failed, he turned to a military solution. In 1547, imperial armies crushed the Protestant Schmalkaldic League, defeating and capturing John Frederick of Saxony and Philip of Hesse.

The emperor established puppet rulers in Saxony and Hesse and issued an imperial law mandating that Protestants everywhere readopt old Catholic beliefs and practices. Protestants were granted a few cosmetic concessions, for example, clerical marriage (with papal approval of individual cases) and communion in both bread and wine. Many Protestant leaders went into exile. In Germany, the city of Magdeburg became a refuge for persecuted Protestants and the center of Lutheran resistance.

The Peace of Augsburg

The Reformation was too entrenched by 1547 to be ended even by brute force. Maurice of Saxony, handpicked by Charles V to rule Saxony, had recognized the inevitable and shifted his allegiance to the Lutherans. Confronted by fierce resistance and weary from three decades of war, the emperor was forced to relent. After a defeat by Protestant armies in 1552, Charles reinstated the Protestant leaders and guaranteed Lutherans religious freedoms in the Peace of Passau (August 1552). With this declaration, he effectively surrendered his lifelong quest for European religious unity.

The Peace of Augsburg in September 1555 made the division of Christendom permanent. This agreement recognized in law what had already been well established in practice: *Cuius regio, eius religio,* meaning the ruler of a land would determine its religion. Lutherans were permitted to retain all church lands forcibly seized before 1552. An "ecclesiastical reservation" was added, however, that was intended to prevent high Catholic prelates who converted to Protestantism from taking their lands, titles, and privileges with them. People discontented with the religion of their region were permitted to migrate to another.

The Peace of Augsburg did not extend official recognition to Calvinism and Anabaptism as legal forms of Christian belief and practice. Anabaptists had long adjusted to such exclusion by forming their own separatist communities. Calvinists, however, were not separatists. They remained determined to secure the right to worship publicly as they pleased, and to shape society according to their own religious convictions. While Anabaptists retreated and Lutherans enjoyed the security of an established religion, Calvinists organized to lead national revolutions throughout northern Europe in the second half of the sixteenth century.

▼ The English Reformation to 1553

Late medieval England had a well-earned reputation for maintaining the rights of the crown against the pope. Edward I (r. 1272–1307) had rejected efforts by Pope Boniface VIII to prevent secular taxation of the clergy. Statutes of Provisors and Praemunire passed in the mid-fourteenth century laid a foundation for curtailing payments and judicial appeals to Rome rejecting papal appointments in England. Lollardy, humanism, and widespread anticlerical sentiments prepared the way for Protestant ideas, which entered England in the early sixteenth century.

The Preconditions of Reform

In the early 1520s, future English reformers met in Cambridge to discuss Lutheran writings smuggled into England by merchants and scholars. One of these future reformers was William Tyndale (ca. 1492–1536), who translated the New Testament into English in 1524–1525 while in Germany. Printed in Cologne and Worms, Tyndale's New Testament began to circulate in England in 1526.

Cardinal Thomas Wolsey (ca. 1475–1530), the chief minister of King Henry VIII (r. 1509–1547), and Sir Thomas More (1478–1535), Wolsey's successor, guided royal opposition to incipient English Protestantism. The king himself defended the seven sacraments against Luther, receiving as a reward the title "Defender of the Faith" from Pope Leo X. Following Luther's intemperate reply to Henry's amateur theological attack, More wrote a lengthy *Response to Luther* in 1523.

The King's Affair

Lollardy and humanism may have provided some native seeds for religious reform, but it was Henry's unhappy marriage to Catherine of Aragon (d. 1536) and obsession to get a male heir that broke the soil and allowed the seeds to take root. In 1509, Henry had married Catherine, the daughter of Ferdinand and Isabella of Spain and the aunt of Emperor Charles V. By 1527, the union had produced only one surviving child, a daughter, Mary. Although women could inherit the throne, Henry fretted over the political consequences of leaving only a female heir. In this period, people believed it unnatural for women to rule over men. At best a woman ruler foreshadowed a contested reign, at worst turmoil and revolution. By the end of the century, Elizabeth's strong rule would expose such fears as greatly exaggerated.

Henry came even to believe that God had cursed his union with Catherine, who had many miscarriages and stillbirths. The reason lay in Catherine's previous marriage to Henry's brother Arthur. After Arthur's premature death, Henry's father, Henry VII, betrothed her to Henry to keep the English alliance with Spain intact. The two were wed in 1509, a few days before Henry VIII received his crown. Because marriage to the wife of one's brother was prohibited by both canon and biblical law (see Leviticus 18:16, 20:21), the marriage had required a special dispensation from Pope Julius II.

By 1527, Henry was also thoroughly enamored of Anne Boleyn, one of Catherine's ladies-in-waiting. He determined to put Catherine aside and take Anne as his wife. This he could not do in Catholic England, however, without a papal annulment of the marriage to Catherine. Therein lay a special problem. 1527 was also the year when imperial soldiers fighting in Italy mutinied and sacked Rome. Pope Clement VII was then a prisoner of Emperor Charles V, who also happened to be Catherine's nephew, and he was not about to encourage the pope to annul the royal marriage. Even if such coercion had not existed, it would have been virtually impossible for the pope to grant an annulment of a marriage that not only had survived for eighteen years but had also been made possible in the first place by a special papal dispensation.

Cardinal Wolsey, who aspired to become pope, was placed in charge of securing the royal annulment. Lord Chancellor since 1515 and papal legate-at-large since 1518, Wolsey had long been Henry's heavy and the object of much popular resentment. When he failed to secure the annulment through no fault of his own, he was dismissed in disgrace in 1529. Thomas Cranmer (1489–1556) and Thomas Cromwell (1485–1540), both of whom harbored Lutheran sympathies, thereafter became the king's closest advisers. Finding the way to a papal annulment closed, Henry's new advisers struck a different course: Why not simply declare the king supreme in English spiritual affairs as he was in English temporal affairs? Then the king could settle the king's affair himself.

The "Reformation Parliament"

In 1529, Parliament convened for what would be a seven-year session that earned it the title of the "Reformation Parliament." During this period, it passed a flood of legislation that harassed, and finally placed royal reins on, the clergy. In so doing, it established a precedent that would remain a feature of English government: Whenever fundamental changes are made in religion, the monarch must consult with and work through Parliament. In January 1531, the Convocation (a legislative assembly representing the English clergy) publicly recognized Henry as head of the church in England "as far as the law of Christ allows." In 1532, Parliament published official grievances against the church, ranging from alleged indifference to the needs of the laity to an excessive number of religious holidays. In the same year, Parliament passed the Submission of the Clergy, which effectively placed canon law under royal control and thereby the clergy under royal jurisdiction.

ANNO · ÆTATIS ·   · SVÆ · XLIX ·

Hans Holbein the Younger (1497–1543) was the most famous portrait painter of the Reformation. Here he portrays a seemingly almighty Henry VIII.   © Scala / Art Resource

In January 1533, Henry wed the pregnant Anne Boleyn, with Thomas Cranmer officiating. In February 1533, Parliament made the king the highest court of appeal for all English subjects. In March 1533, Cranmer became archbishop of Canterbury and led the Convocation in invalidating the king's marriage to Catherine. In 1534, Parliament ended all payments by the English clergy and laity to Rome and gave Henry sole jurisdiction over high ecclesiastical appointments. The Act of Succession in the same year made Anne Boleyn's children legitimate heirs to the throne, and the **Act of Supremacy** declared Henry "the only supreme head in earth of the Church of England."

When Thomas More and John Fisher, bishop of Rochester, refused to recognize the Act of Succession and the Act of Supremacy, Henry had them executed, making clear his determination to have his way regardless of the cost. In 1536 and 1538, Parliament dissolved England's monasteries and nunneries.

Wives of Henry VIII

Henry's domestic life lacked the consistency of his political life. In 1536, Anne Boleyn was executed for alleged treason and adultery, and her daughter Elizabeth, like Elizabeth's half sister Mary before her, was declared illegitimate by her father. Henry had four more marriages. His third wife, Jane Seymour, died in 1537 shortly after giving birth to the future Edward VI. Henry wed Anne of Cleves sight unseen on the advice of Cromwell, the purpose being to create by the marriage an alliance with the Protestant princes of Germany. Neither the alliance nor the marriage proved worth the trouble; the marriage was annulled by Parliament, and Cromwell was dismissed and executed. Catherine Howard, Henry's fifth wife, was beheaded for adultery in 1542. His last wife, Catherine Parr, a patron of humanists and reformers, for whom Henry was the third husband, survived him to marry still a fourth time—obviously she was a match for the English king.

The King's Religious Conservatism

Henry's boldness in politics and domestic affairs did not extend to religion. True, because of Henry's actions, the pope had ceased to be head of the English church and English Bibles were placed in English churches, but despite the break with Rome, Henry remained decidedly conservative in his religious beliefs. With the Ten Articles of 1536, he made only mild concessions to Protestant tenets. Otherwise Catholic doctrine was maintained in a country filled with Protestant sentiment. Despite his many wives and amorous adventures, Henry forbade the English clergy to marry and threatened to execute clergy who were caught twice in concubinage.

Angered by the growing popularity of Protestant views, even among his chief advisers, Henry struck directly at them in the Six Articles of 1539. These reaffirmed transubstantiation, denied the Eucharistic cup to the laity, declared celibate vows inviolable, provided for private Masses, and ordered the continuation of oral confession. Protestants referred to the articles as the "whip with six stings," a clear warning from the king that religious reform would not race ahead in England during his reign. Although William Tyndale's English New Testament grew into the Coverdale Bible (1535) and the Great Bible (1539), and the latter was mandated for every English parish, England had to await Henry's death before it could become a genuinely Protestant country.

The Protestant Reformation under Edward VI

When Henry died in 1547, his son and successor, Edward VI (d. 1553), was only ten years old. Edward reigned under the successive regencies of Edward Seymour, who became the duke of Somerset (1547–1550), and the earl of Warwick, who became known as the duke of Northumberland (1550–1553). During this time, England enacted Protestant Reformation. The new king and Somerset cor-

MAIN EVENTS OF THE ENGLISH REFORMATION	
1529	Reformation Parliament convenes
1532	Parliament passes the Submission of the Clergy
1533	Henry VIII weds Anne Boleyn; Convocation invalidates marriage to Catherine of Aragon
1534	Act of Succession makes Anne Boleyn's children legitimate heirs to the English throne
1534	Act of Supremacy declares Henry VIII "the only supreme head of the Church of England"
1535	Thomas More executed for opposition to Acts of Succession and Supremacy
1535	Publication of Coverdale Bible
1539	Henry VIII imposes the Six Articles
1547	Edward VI succeeds to the throne under protectorships of Somerset and Northumberland
1549	First Act of Uniformity imposes *Book of Common Prayer* on English churches
1553–1558	Mary Tudor restores Catholic doctrine
1558–1603	Elizabeth I fashions an Anglican religious settlement

responded directly with John Calvin. During Somerset's regency, Henry's Six Articles and laws against Protestant heresy were repealed, and clerical marriage and communion with cup were sanctioned.

In 1547, the chantries, places where endowed Masses had traditionally been said for the dead, were dissolved. In 1549, the Act of Uniformity imposed Thomas Cranmer's *Book of Common Prayer* on all English churches. Images and altars were removed from the churches in 1550. After Charles V's victory over the German princes in 1547, German Protestant leaders had fled to England for refuge. Several of these refugees, with Martin Bucer prominent among them, now directly assisted the completion of the English Reformation.

The Second Act of Uniformity, passed in 1552, imposed a revised *Book of Common Prayer* on all English churches. A forty-two-article confession of faith, also written by Thomas Cranmer, set forth a moderate Protestant doctrine. It taught justification by faith and the supremacy of Holy Scripture, denied transubstantiation (although not the real presence), and recognized only two sacraments.

All these changes were short-lived, however. In 1553, Catherine of Aragon's daughter succeeded Edward (who had died in his teens) to the throne as Mary I (d. 1558) and restored Catholic doctrine and practice with a single-mindedness rivaling that of her father. It was not until the reign of Anne Boleyn's daughter, Elizabeth I (r. 1558–1603), that England worked out a lasting religious settlement.

▼ Catholic Reform and Counter-Reformation

The Protestant Reformation did not take the medieval church completely by surprise. There were many internal criticisms and efforts at reform before there was a Counter-Reformation in reaction to Protestant successes.

Sources of Catholic Reform

Before the Reformation began, ambitious proposals had been made for church reform. But sixteenth-century popes, ever mindful of how the councils of Constance and Basel had stripped the pope of his traditional powers, squelched such efforts to change the laws and institutions of the church.

Despite such papal foot-dragging, the old church was not without its reformers. Many new religious orders also sprang up in the sixteenth century to lead a broad revival of piety within the church. The first of these orders was the Theatines, founded in 1524 to groom devout and reform-minded leaders at the higher levels of the church hierarchy. One of the co-founders was Bishop Gian Pietro Carafa, who would be Pope Paul IV (r. 1555–1559). Another new order, whose mission pointed in the opposite direction, was the Capuchins. Recognized by the pope in 1528, they sought to return to the original ideals of Saint Francis and became popular among the ordinary people to whom they directed their ministry. The Somaschi, who became active in the mid-1520s, and the Barnabites, founded in 1530, worked to repair the moral, spiritual, and physical damage done to people in war-torn Italy.

For women, there was the influential new order of Ursulines. Founded in 1535, it established convents in Italy and France for the religious education of girls from all social classes. Another new order, the Oratorians, officially recognized in 1575, was an elite group of clerics devoted to the promotion of religious literature and church music. Among their members was the great hymnist and musician Giovanni Perluigi da Palestrina (1526–1594).

In addition to these lay and clerical movements, the mystical piety of medieval monasticism was revived and popularized by two Spanish mystics, Saint Teresa of Avila (1515–1582) and Saint John of the Cross (1542–1591).

Ignatius of Loyola and the Jesuits

Of the various reform groups, none was more instrumental in the success of the Counter-Reformation than the Society of Jesus, the new order of Jesuits. Organized by Ignatius of Loyola in the 1530s, the church recognized it in 1540. The society grew within a century from its original ten members to more than 15,000 members scattered throughout the world, with thriving missions in India, Japan, and the Americas.

The founder of the Jesuits, Ignatius of Loyola (1491–1556), was a heroic figure. A dashing courtier and *soldiero* in his youth, he began his spiritual pilgrimage in 1521 after he had been seriously wounded during a battle with the French. During a lengthy and painful convalescence, he passed the time by reading Christian classics. So impressed was he with the heroic self-sacrifice of the church's saints and their methods of overcoming mental anguish and pain that he underwent a profound religious conversion. Henceforth, he, too, would serve the church as a soldier of Christ.

After recuperating, Ignatius applied the lessons he had learned during his convalescence to a program of religious and moral self-discipline that came to be embodied in the *Spiritual Exercises.* This psychologically perceptive devotional guide contained mental and emotional exercises designed to teach one absolute spiritual self-mastery over one's feelings. It taught that a person could shape his or her own behavior—even create a new religious self—through disciplined study and regular practice.

Whereas in Jesuit eyes Protestants had distinguished themselves by disobedience and religious

MAP EXPLORATION

Interactive map: To explore this map further, go to www.myhistorylab.com

- Lutheran
- Anglican
- Calvinist Control or Influence
- Anabaptist
- Roman Catholic
- Eastern Border of Western Christianity

300 MILES
300 KILOMETERS

Map 11–3 **THE RELIGIOUS SITUATION ABOUT 1560** By 1560, Luther, Zwingli, and Loyola were dead, Calvin was near the end of his life, the English break from Rome was complete, and the last session of the Council of Trent was about to assemble. This map shows "religious geography" of western Europe at the time.

innovation, the exercises of Ignatius were intended to teach good Catholics to deny themselves and submit without question to higher church authority and spiritual direction. Perfect discipline and self-control were the essential conditions of such obedience. To these were added the enthusiasm of traditional spirituality and mysticism and uncompromising loyalty to the church's cause. This potent combination helped counter the Reformation and win many Protestants

back to the Catholic fold, especially in Austria and parts of Germany. (See Map 11–3.)

The Council of Trent (1545–1563)

The broad success of the Reformation and the insistence of the Emperor Charles V forced Pope Paul III (r. 1534–1549) to call a general council of the church to lovers." Both Romeo and Juliet, denied a marriage by their warring families, die tragic deaths. Romeo, believing Juliet to be dead when she has merely taken a sleeping potion, poisons himself. When Juliet awakes to find Romeo dead, she kills herself with his dagger.

Shakespeare's works struck universal human themes, many of which were deeply rooted in contemporary religious traditions. His plays were immensely popular with both the playgoers and the play readers of Elizabethan England. Still today, the works of no other dramatist from his age are performed in theaters or on film more regularly than his.

In Perspective

During the early Middle Ages, Christendom had been divided into Western and Eastern churches with irreconcilable theological differences. When, in 1517, Martin Luther posted ninety-five theses questioning the selling of indulgences and the traditional sacrament of penance that lay behind them, he created a division within Western Christendom itself—an internal division between Protestants and Catholics.

The Lutheran protest came at a time of political and social discontent with the church. Not only princes and magistrates but many ordinary people as well resented traditional clerical rights and privileges. The clergy were exempted from many secular laws and taxes while remaining powerful landowners whose personal lifestyles were not all that different from those of the laity. Spiritual and secular protest combined to make the Protestant Reformation a successful assault on the old church. In town after town and region after region within Protestant lands, the major institutions and practices of traditional piety were transformed.

It soon became clear, however, that the division would not stop with the Lutherans. Making Scripture the only arbiter in religion had opened a Pandora's box. People proved to have different ideas about what Scripture taught. Indeed, there seemed to be as many points of view as there were readers. Rapidly, the Reformation created Lutheran, Zwinglian, Anabaptist, Spiritualist, Calvinist, and Anglican versions of biblical religion—a splintering of Protestantism that has endured and increased until today.

Catholics had been pursuing reform before the Reformation broke out in Germany, although without papal enthusiasm and certainly not along clear Protestant lines. When major reforms finally came in the Catholic Church around the mid-sixteenth century, they were doctrinally reactionary, but administratively and spiritually flexible. The church enforced strict obedience and conformity to its teaching, but it also provided the laity with a better educated and disciplined clergy. For laity who wanted a deeper and more individual piety, experimentation with proven spiritual practices was now permitted. By century's end, such measures had countered, and in some areas even spectacularly reversed, Protestant gains.

After the Reformation, pluralism steadily became a fact of Western religious life. It did so at first only by sheer force, since no one religious body was then prepared to concede the validity of alternative Christian beliefs and practices. During the sixteenth and seventeenth centuries, only those groups that fought doggedly for their faith gained the right to practice it freely. Despite these struggles, religious pluralism endured. Never again would there be only a Catholic Christian Church in Europe.

AP* TEST PREP

1. The Peace of Augsburg
   a. extended legal recognition to Calvinists.
   b. asserted regional princely control over religion.
   c. made Lutheranism the state religion of Denmark.
   d. made Lutheranism the state religion of Sweden.
   e. established Jesuit control over the papacy.

2. Between 1500 and 1800, European men married in their
   a. forties.
   b. mid- to late-teens.
   c. mid- to late-twenties.
   d. mid- to late-thirties.
   d. early teens.

3. Cervantes's most famous work is
   a. *Moll Flanders.*
   b. *Valencia.*
   c. *Under a Spanish Sky.*
   d. *The Tale of Tomas Gatito.*
   e. *Don Quixote.*

4. Which factor was *not* related to the emergence of the Protestant Reformation?
   a. the Renaissance papacy
   b. the Great Schism
   c. the Conciliar period
   d. the Spanish Inquisition
   e. the printing press

5. Pope Leo X's Jubilee Indulgence was meant to raise funds to
   a. assemble an army to defend the papal states.
   b. combat the Reformation.

   c.   launch a new crusade.
   d.   rebuild St. Peter's Basilica in Rome.
   e.   increase pay for clergy.

6. The Marburg Colloquy sought to
   a.   unite Spanish and Italian Catholics.
   b.   unite Swiss and German Protestants.
   c.   establish a new Catholic council system.
   d.   establish religious tolerance throughout Europe.
   e.   outlaw Calvinism in Britain.

7. Ignatius of Loyola organized the Jesuit order to encourage
   a.   a brotherhood of Christ.
   b.   an end to simony in the papal Curia.
   c.   religious innovation and piety.
   d.   religious and moral self-discipline.
   e.   religious toleration and peace.

8. Which of the following occurred *first*?
   a.   Diet of Worms
   b.   Marburg Colloquy
   c.   Diet of Augsburg
   d.   Council of Trent
   e.   Peace of Westphalia

9. Which of the following practices did Zwingli *not* question and repudiate in the course of his reforms?
   a.   worship of saints
   b.   transubstantiation
   c.   pilgrimages
   d.   clerical celibacy
   e.   church attendance

10. Reform efforts of the Council of Trent included all of the following *except*
   a.   several doctrinal concessions to the reformers.
   b.   creation of new seminaries.
   c.   reform of the office of bishop.
   d.   machinery to control the morality of churchmen.
   e.   steps to curtail the selling of church offices.

11. The Reformation broke out first in
   a.   the prosperous ports of Holland.
   b.   London and other important English cities.
   c.   the French countryside.
   d.   Austria.
   e.   the free imperial cities of Germany and Switzerland.

12. Northern European rulers and magistrates attacked the sale of indulgences primarily as
   a.   a medieval superstition.
   b.   a corruption of faith.
   c.   a drain on local revenues.
   d.   an overextension of papal authority.
   e.   an overextension of imperial authority.

13. In houses of the Modern Devotion,
   a.   clerics developed a sense of their separateness from the laity.
   b.   clerics and laity shared a common religious life.
   c.   the authority of the pope was rejected.
   d.   laity refused to admit clerics as members.
   e.   the papacy trained young men to fight heresy.

14. The *benefice* system
   a.   allowed important ecclesiastical posts to be sold to the highest bidder.
   b.   distributed charity throughout Europe.
   c.   allowed poor men and women to become nuns and monks.
   d.   was first developed in houses of the Modern Devotion.
   e.   was supported by most lay Catholics.

15. Thomas à Kempis was known as
   a.   the author of the *Imitation of Christ*.
   b.   a peasant revolt leader burnt at the stake.
   c.   a Swiss reform leader.
   d.   author of *Address to the Christian Nobility of the German Nation*.
   e.   a nobleman providing safe harbor to Lutherans.

16. Luther believed in all of the following *except*
   a.   salvation by faith alone.
   b.   the priesthood of all believers.
   c.   the sovereign authority of scripture.
   d.   the unimportance of good works.
   e.   the need for social and political hierarchy.

17. The Anabaptists were
   a.   embraced by the Lutherans.
   b.   embraced by Zwinglians.
   c.   convinced that all babies should be baptized at birth.
   d.   convinced that they had not really broken from the Catholic church.
   e.   seen as a threat to good order by the political authorities.

18. According to the doctrine of predestination,
   a.   God has foreordained who will be saved and who will be damned.
   b.   Christians must set salvation as their only goal before it can be achieved.
   c.   theological doctrine must begin with ends and then work back to means.
   d.   only men are capable of salvation.
   e.   divorce is a mortal sin.

19. Preacherships were endowed by
    a. monarchs.
    b. city governments.
    c. papal bulls.
    d. monastic orders.
    e. urban laypeople.

20. Protestant reformers tended to do all of the following *except*
    a. favor clerical marriage.
    b. encourage basic education.
    c. oppose monasticism.
    d. see marriage as degraded state.
    e. oppose the celibate life.

DOCUMENT-BASED QUESTION

Directions: Construct a valid essay that directly addresses the central issue of the following question. Use facts from the documents provided and from the chapter to prove the position you take in your thesis statement.

Why was Luther so adamantly opposed to Indulgences? What role did this issue play in sparking the Reformation?

Document A

Source: Erasmus depicts the exclusion of Pope Julius II from heaven.

Julius: What's the trouble here? Won't the gates open? I believe the lock has been changed, or else it's jammed.

Genius [Julius's guardian angel]: Better check to see if you've brought the right key. The one for the treasury won't open this door, you know. But why didn't you bring both keys? This is the key of power, not of knowledge.

Julius: Why, Hell, this is the only one I've ever used! I've never seen what good the other one was when I've had this one.

Genius: Me neither, certainly, except that meanwhile we're locked out.

Julius: I'm losing my temper. I'm going to beat on the gate. Hey there! Somebody open this door instantly! What's the matter, nobody here? What's holding up the doorman? Asleep, I suppose; probably drunk.

Document B

Caricature of John Tetzel, the famous indulgence preacher. (The text includes the lines, "As soon as gold in the basin rings, right then the soul to Heaven springs.")

Document C

ÆTHERNA IPSE SVAE MENTIS SIMVLACHRA LVTHERVS
EXPRIMIT·AT VVLTVS CERA LVCAE OCCIDVOS·

·M·D·X·X·

Portrait of Martin Luther (1520)

Document D

Source: Luther's Ninety-five Theses.

5. The pope has neither the will nor the power to remit any penalties beyond those imposed either at his own discretion or by canon law.

6. The pope himself cannot remit guilt, but only declare and confirm that it has been remitted by God. . . .

21. Hence those who preach indulgences are in error when they say that a man is absolved and saved from every penalty by the pope's indulgences.

27. There is no divine authority for preaching that the soul flies out of purgatory immediately the money chinks in the bottom of the chest.

36. Any Christian whatsoever, who is truly repentant, enjoys plenary remission from penalty and guilt, and this is given to him by God without letters of indulgence.

62. The true treasure of the church is the Holy Gospel of the glory and the grace of God.

For more on the German Reformation, see pages 319–325.

The massacre of worshipping Protestants at Vassy, France (March 1, 1562), which began the French wars of religion. An engraving by an unidentified seventeenth-century artist.   The Granger Collection

12

The Age of Religious Wars

▼ **Renewed Religious Struggle**

▼ **The French Wars of Religion (1562–1598)**
Appeal of Calvinism • Catherine de Médicis and the Guises • The Rise to Power of Henry of Navarre • The Edict of Nantes

▼ **Imperial Spain and Philip II (r. 1556–1598)**
Pillars of Spanish Power • The Revolt in the Netherlands

▼ **England and Spain (1553–1603)**
Mary I (r. 1553–1558) • Elizabeth I (r. 1558–1603)

▼ **The Thirty Years' War (1618–1648)**
Preconditions for War • Four Periods of War • The Treaty of Westphalia

▼ **In Perspective**

THE LATE SIXTEENTH and the first half of the seventeenth centuries are described as the Age of Religious Wars because of the bloody conflict of Protestants and Catholics across Europe. Both genuine religious conflict and bitter dynastic rivalries fueled the wars. In France, the Netherlands, England, and Scotland in the second half of the sixteenth century, Calvinists fought Catholic rulers for the right to govern their own territories and to practice their chosen religion openly. In the first half of the seventeenth century, Lutherans, Calvinists, and Catholics marched against one another in central and northern Europe during the Thirty Years' War. By the mid-seventeenth century, English Puritans had successfully revolted against the Stuart monarchy and the Anglican Church. (See Chapter 13.)

▼ Renewed Religious Struggle

During the first half of the sixteenth century, religious conflict had been confined to central Europe and was primarily a struggle by Lutherans and Zwinglians to secure rights and freedoms for themselves. In the second half of the century, the focus shifted to Western Europe—to France, the Netherlands, England, and Scotland—and became a struggle by Calvinists for recognition. After the Peace of Augsburg (1555) and acceptance of the principle that a region's ruler determined its religion (*cuius regio, eius religio*), Lutheranism became a legal religion in the Holy Roman Empire. The Peace of Augsburg did not, however, extend recognition to non-Lutheran Protestants. Anabaptists and other sectarians continued to be scorned as heretics and anarchists, and Calvinists were not strong enough to gain legal standing.

Outside the empire, the struggle for religious freedom had intensified in most countries. After the Council of Trent adjourned in 1563, Catholics began a Jesuit-led international counteroffensive against Protestants. At the time of John Calvin's death in 1564, Geneva had become both a refuge for Europe's persecuted Protestants and an international school for Protestant resistance, producing leaders equal to the new Catholic challenge.

Genevan Calvinism and Catholicism as revived by the Council of Trent were two equally dogmatic, aggressive, and irreconcilable church systems. Calvinists may have looked like "new papists" to critics when they dominated cities like Geneva. Yet when, as minorities, they found their civil and religious rights denied, they became firebrands and revolutionaries. Calvinism adopted an organization that magnified regional and local religious authority. Boards of **presbyters**, or elders, represented the individual congregations of Calvinists, directly shaping policy.

By contrast, the **Counter-Reformation** sponsored a centralized episcopal church system hierarchically arranged from pope to parish priest and stressing unquestioning obedience to the person at the top. The high clergy—the pope and his bishops—not the synods of local churches, were supreme. Calvinism proved attractive to proponents of political decentralization who opposed such hierarchical rule, in principle, whereas the Roman Catholic Church, an institution also devoted to one head and one law, found absolute monarchy congenial.

The opposition between the two religions may be seen in their respective art and architecture. The Catholic Counter-Reformation found the baroque style congenial. A successor to mannerism, **baroque** presented life in a grandiose, three-dimensional display of raw energy. The great baroque artists Peter Paul Rubens (1571–1640) and Gianlorenzo Bernini (1598–1680) were Catholics. By contrast, the works of prominent Protestant artists were restrained, as can be seen in the gentle, searching portraits of the Dutch Mennonite, Rembrandt van Rijn (1606–1669). (See the juxtaposition of Bavarian Catholic and Palatine Calvinist churches.)

As religious wars engulfed Europe, the intellectuals perceived the wisdom of religious pluralism and toleration more quickly than did the politicians. A new skepticism, relativism, and individualism in religion became respectable in the sixteenth and seventeenth centuries. (See Chapter 14.) Sebastian Castellio's (1515–1563) pithy

censure of John Calvin for his role in the execution of the Antitrinitarian Michael Servetus summarized a growing sentiment: "To kill a man is not to defend a doctrine, but to kill a man."[1] The French essayist Michel de Montaigne (1533–1592) asked in scorn of the dogmatic mind, "What do I know?" The Lutheran Valentin Weigel (1533–1588), surveying a half century of religious strife in Germany, advised people to look within themselves for religious truth and no longer to churches and creeds.

Such skeptical views gained currency in larger political circles only at the cost of painful experience. Religious strife and civil war were best held in check where rulers tended to subordinate theological doctrine to political unity, urging tolerance, moderation, and compromise—even indifference—in religious matters. Rulers of this kind came to be known as ***politiques***, and the most successful among them was Elizabeth I of England. By contrast, Mary I of England, Philip II of Spain, and Oliver Cromwell, all of whom took their religion with the utmost seriousness and refused any compromise, did not, in the end, achieve their political goals.

The wars of religion were both internal national conflicts and truly international wars. Catholic and Protestant subjects struggled against one another for control of the crown of France, the Netherlands, and England. The Catholic governments of France and Spain conspired and finally sent armies against Protestant regimes in England and the Netherlands. The outbreak of the Thirty Years' War in 1618 made the international dimension of the religious conflict especially clear; before it ended in 1648, the war drew every major European nation directly or indirectly into its deadly net.

▼ The French Wars of Religion (1562–1598)

French Protestants are known as **Huguenots**, a term derived from Besançon Hugues, the leader of Geneva's political revolt against the House of Savoy in the 1520s, which had been a prelude to that city's Calvinist Reformation. Huguenots were already under surveillance in France in the early 1520s when Lutheran writings and doctrines began to circulate in Paris. The capture of the French king Francis I by the forces of Emperor Charles V at the Battle of Pavia in 1525 provided a motive for the first wave of Protestant persecution in France. The French government hoped thereby to pacify the Habsburg victor, a fierce opponent of German Protestants, and to win their king's swift release.

A second major crackdown came a decade later. When Protestants plastered Paris and other cities with anti-Catholic placards on October 18, 1534, mass arrests

[1] *Contra libellum Calvini* (N.P., 1562), p. E2a.

A Closer ▷ LOOK

BAROQUE AND PLAIN CHURCH: ARCHITECTURAL REFLECTIONS OF BELIEF

CONTRAST AN eighteenth-century Catholic baroque church in Ottobeuren, Bavaria, and a seventeenth-century Calvinist plain church in the Palatinate. The Catholic church pops with sculptures, paintings, and ornamentation, while the Calvinist church has been stripped of every possible decoration.

Decorated altars dominate the interior of the Catholic church and make the sacrifice of the Eucharist in the Mass the center of worship. The intent is to inspire worshippers to self-transcendence.

Vanni/Art Resource, NY

The open Bible and raised pulpit dominate the Protestant church. The intent is to keep worshippers' attention on God's word and their own immortal souls and to prevent any form of decoration from distracting them.

To examine this image in an interactive fashion, please go to www.myhistorylab.com

German National Museum, Nuremberg, Germany

of suspected Protestants followed. The government re-taliation drove John Calvin and other members of the French reform party into exile. In 1540, the Edict of Fontainebleau subjected French Protestants to the Inqui-sition. Henry II (r. 1547–1559) established new measures against Protestants in the Edict of Chateaubriand in 1551. Save for a few brief interludes, the French monar-chy remained a staunch foe of the Protestants until the ascension to the throne of Henry IV of Navarre in 1589.

The Habsburg-Valois wars (see Chapter 11) had ended with the Treaty of Cateau-Cambrésis in 1559, after which Europe experienced a moment of peace. The same year, however, marked the beginning of internal French conflict and a shift of the European balance of power away from France to Spain. The shift began with an accident. During a tournament held to celebrate the marriage of his thirteen-year-old daughter to Philip II, the son of Charles V and heir to the Spanish Habsburg lands, the French king, Henry II, was mortally wounded when a lance pierced his visor. This unforeseen event brought to the throne his sickly fifteen-year-old son, Francis II, who died after reigning only a year (1559–1560). With the monarchy weakened, three pow-erful families saw their chance to control France and began to compete for the young king's ear: the Bourbons, whose power lay in the south and west; the Mont-morency-Chatillons, who controlled the center of France; and the strongest among them, the Guises, who were dominant in eastern France.

The Guises had little trouble establishing firm con-trol over the young king. Francis, duke of Guise, had been Henry II's general and his brothers, Charles and Louis, were cardinals of the church. Mary Stuart, Queen of Scots, the eighteen-year-old widow of Francis II, was their niece. Throughout the latter half of the sixteenth century, the name "Guise" remained interchangeable with militant, reactionary Catholicism.

The Bourbon and Montmorency-Chatillon families, in contrast, developed strong Huguenot sympathies, largely for political reasons. The Bourbon Louis I, prince of Condé (d. 1569), and the Montmorency-Chatillon ad-miral Gaspard de Coligny (1519–1572) became the polit-ical leaders of the French Protestant resistance. They collaborated early in an abortive plot to kidnap Francis II from his Guise advisers in the Conspiracy of Amboise in 1560. Calvin, who considered such tactics a disgrace to the Reformation, condemned this conspiracy.

Appeal of Calvinism

Often for different reasons, ambitious aristocrats and discontented townspeople joined Calvinist churches in opposing the Guise-dominated French monarchy. In 1561, more than 2,000 Huguenot congregations existed throughout France. Yet Huguenots were a majority of the population in only two regions: Dauphiné and Languedoc. Although they made up only about one fif-teenth of the population, Huguenots held important ge-ographic areas and were heavily represented among the more powerful segments of French society. A good two fifths of the French aristocracy became Huguenots. Many apparently hoped to establish within France a principle of territorial sovereignty akin to what the Peace of Augsburg had secured within the Holy Roman Empire. Calvinism thus served the forces of political decentralization.

John Calvin and Theodore Beza sought to advance their cause by currying favor with powerful aristocrats. Beza converted Jeanne d'Albert, the mother of the future Henry IV. The prince of Condé was apparently convert-ed in 1558 under the influence of his Calvinist wife. For many aristocrats—Condé probably among them—Calvinist religious convictions proved useful to their political goals.

The military organization of Condé and Coligny progressively merged with the religious organization of the French Huguenot churches, creating a potent com-bination that benefited both political and religious dissi-dents. Calvinism justified and inspired political resistance, while the resistance made Calvinism a vi-able religion in Catholic France. Each side had much to gain from the other. The confluence of secular and reli-gious motives, although beneficial to aristocratic resis-tance and the Calvinist religion alike, cast suspicion on the religious appeal of Calvinism. Clearly, religious con-viction was neither the only, nor always the main, rea-son for becoming a Calvinist in France in the second half of the sixteenth century.

Catherine de Médicis and the Guises

Following Francis II's death in 1560, the queen mother, Catherine de Médicis (1519–1589) became regent for her minor son, Charles IX (r. 1560–1574). At a meeting in Poissy, she tried unsuccessfully to reconcile the Protes-tant and Catholic factions. Fearing the power and guile of the Guises, Catherine, whose first concern was al-ways to preserve the monarchy, sought allies among the Protestants. In 1562, after conversations with Beza and Coligny, she issued the January Edict, which granted Protestants freedom to worship publicly outside towns—although only privately within them—and to hold synods. In March 1562, this royal toleration came to an abrupt end when the duke of Guise surprised a Protestant congregation at Vassy in Champagne and massacred many worshippers. That event marked the beginning of the French wars of religion.

Had Condé and the Huguenot armies rushed imme-diately to the queen's side after this attack, Protestants might well have secured an alliance with the crown. The queen mother's fear of Guise power was great. Condé's hesitation, however, placed the young king and the

Catherine de Médicis (1519–1589) exercised power in France during the reigns of her three sons, Francis II (r. 1559–1560), Charles IX (r. 1560–1574), and Henry III (r. 1574–1589). Getty Images, Inc.–Liaison

queen mother, against their deepest wishes, under firm Guise control. Cooperation with the Guises became the only alternative to capitulation to the Protestants.

The Peace of Saint-Germain-en-Laye

During the first French war of religion, fought between April 1562 and March 1563, the duke of Guise was assassinated. It was a measure of the international character of the struggle in France that troops from Hesse and the Palatinate fought alongside the Huguenots. A brief resumption of hostilities in 1567–1568 was followed by the bloodiest of all the conflicts, between September 1568 and August 1570. In this period, Condé was killed, and Huguenot leadership passed to Coligny. This was actually a blessing in disguise for the Protestants, because Coligny was far the better military strategist. In the peace of Saint-Germain-en-Laye (1570), which ended the third war, the crown, acknowledging the power of the Protestant nobility, granted the Huguenots religious freedoms within their territories and the right to fortify their cities.

Perpetually caught between fanatical Huguenot and Guise extremes, Queen Catherine had always sought to balance one side against the other. Like the Guises, she wanted a Catholic France, but she feared a Guise-dominated monarchy. After the Peace of Saint-Germain-en-Laye, the crown tilted manifestly toward the Bourbon faction and the Huguenots, and Coligny became Charles IX's most trusted adviser. Unknown to the king, Catherine began to plot with the Guises against the ascendant Protestants. As she had earlier sought Protestant support when Guise power threatened to subdue the monarchy, she now sought Guise support as Protestant influence grew.

There was reason for Catherine to fear Coligny's hold on the king. Louis of Nassau, the leader of Protestant resistance to Philip II in the Netherlands, had gained Coligny's ear. Coligny used his influence to win the king of France over to a planned French invasion of the Netherlands to support the Dutch Protestants. This would have placed France squarely on a collision course with mighty Spain. Catherine recognized far better than her son that France stood little chance in such a contest. News of the stunning Spanish victory over the Turks at Lepanto in October 1571 had sobered Catherine and her advisors.

The Saint Bartholomew's Day Massacre

When Catherine lent her support to the infamous Saint Bartholomew's Day Massacre of Protestants, she did so out of a far less reasoned judgment. Her decision appears to have been made in near panic. On August 22, 1572, four days after the Huguenot Henry of Navarre had married the king's sister, Marguerite of Valois—still another sign of growing Protestant power—Coligny was struck down, although not killed, by an assassin's bullet. Catherine had apparently been party to this Guise plot to eliminate Coligny. After its failure, she feared both the king's reaction to her complicity with the Guises and Coligny's response. Catherine convinced Charles that a Huguenot coup was afoot, inspired by Coligny, and that only the swift execution of Protestant leaders could save the crown from a Protestant attack on Paris.

On Saint Bartholomew's Day, August 24, 1572, Coligny and 3,000 fellow Huguenots were butchered in Paris. Within three days coordinated attacks across France killed an estimated 20,000 Huguenots. It is a date that has ever since lived in infamy for Protestants.

Pope Gregory XIII and Philip II of Spain reportedly greeted the news of the Protestant massacre with special religious celebrations. Philip had good reason to rejoice. By throwing France into civil war, the massacre ended any planned French opposition to his efforts to subdue his rebellious subjects in the Netherlands. But the massacre of thousands of Protestants also gave the discerning Catholic world cause for new alarm. The event changed the nature of the struggle between Protestants and Catholics both within and beyond the borders of France. It was thereafter no longer an internal contest between Guise and Bourbon factions for French political influence, nor was it simply a Huguenot campaign to win basic religious freedoms. Henceforth, in Protestant eyes, it became an international struggle for sheer survival against an adversary whose cruelty justified any means of resistance.

Protestant Resistance Theory Only as Protestants faced suppression and sure defeat did they begin to sanction active political resistance. At first, they tried to practice the biblical precept of obedient subjection to worldly authority (Romans 13:1). Luther had only grudgingly approved resistance to the emperor after the Diet of Augsburg in 1530. In 1550, Lutherans in Magdeburg had published an influential defense of the right of lower authorities to oppose the emperor's order that all Lutherans return to the Catholic fold.

Calvin, who never faced the specter of total political defeat after his return to Geneva in September 1540, had always condemned willful disobedience and rebellion against lawfully constituted governments as unChristian. Yet he also taught that lower magistrates, as part of the lawfully constituted government, had the right and duty to oppose tyrannical higher authority.

The exiled Scots reformer John Knox (1513–1572), who had seen Mary of Guise, the Regent of Scotland, and Mary I of England crush his cause, laid the groundwork for later Calvinist resistance. In his famous *First Blast of the Trumpet against the Terrible Regiment of Women* (1558), he declared that the removal of a heathen tyrant was not only permissible, but also a Christian duty. He had the Catholic queen of England in mind.

After the great massacre of French Protestants on Saint Bartholomew's Day 1572, Calvinists everywhere came to appreciate the need for an active defense of their religious rights. Classical Huguenot theories of resistance appeared in three major works of the 1570s. The first was the *Franco-Gallia* of François Hotman (1573), a humanist argument that the representative Estates General of France historically held higher authority than the French king. The second was Theodore Beza's *On the Right of Magistrates over Their Subjects* (1574), which, going beyond Calvin's views, justified the correction and even the overthrow of tyrannical rulers by lower authorities. (See "Theodore Beza Defends the Right to Resist Tyranny.") Finally, Philippe du Plessis Mornay's *Defense of Liberty against Tyrants* (1579) admonished princes, nobles, and magistrates beneath the king, as guardians of the rights of the body politic, to take up arms against tyranny in other lands.

The Rise to Power of Henry of Navarre

Henry III (r. 1574–1589) was the last of Henry II's sons to wear the French crown. He found the monarchy wedged between a radical Catholic League, formed in 1576 by Henry of Guise, and vengeful Huguenots. Neither group would have been reluctant to assassinate a ruler they considered heretical and a tyrant. Like the queen mother, Henry sought to steer a middle course. In this effort, he received support from a growing body of neutral Catholics and Huguenots, who put the political survival of France above its religious unity. Such *politiques* were prepared to compromise religious creeds to save the nation.

The Peace of Beaulieu in May 1576 granted the Huguenots almost complete religious and civil freedom. France, however, was not ready then for such sweeping toleration. Within seven months of the Peace, the Catholic League forced Henry to return to the illusory quest for absolute religious unity in France. In October 1577, the king truncated the Peace of Beaulieu and once again limited areas of permitted Huguenot worship. Thereafter, Huguenot and Catholic factions returned to their accustomed anarchical military solutions. The Protestants were led by Henry of Navarre, a legal heir to the French throne by virtue of his descent in a direct male line from St. Louis IX (d. 1270).

In the mid-1580s, the Catholic League, with Spanish support, became dominant in Paris. In what came to be known as the Day of the Barricades, Henry III attempted to rout the league with a surprise attack in 1588. The effort failed, and the king had to flee Paris. Forced by his weakened position into unkingly guerrilla tactics, and also emboldened by news of the English victory over the Spanish Armada in 1588, Henry had both the duke and the cardinal of Guise assassinated. These murders sent France reeling once again. Led by still another Guise brother, the Catholic League reacted with a fury that matched the earlier Huguenot response to the Massacre of Saint Bartholomew's Day. The king was now forced to strike an alliance with the Protestant Henry of Navarre in April 1589.

As the two Henrys prepared to attack the Guise stronghold of Paris, however, an enraged Dominican friar killed Henry III. Thereupon, the Bourbon Huguenot Henry of Navarre succeeded the childless Valois king to the French throne as Henry IV (r. 1589–1610). Pope Sixtus V and Philip II were aghast at the sudden prospect of a Protestant France. They had always wanted France to be religiously Catholic and politically weak, and they now acted to achieve that end. Spain rushed troops to support the besieged Catholic League. Philip II apparently even hoped to place his eldest daughter, Isabella, the granddaughter of Henry II and Catherine de Médicis, on the French throne.

Direct Spanish intervention in the affairs of France seemed only to strengthen Henry IV's grasp on the crown. The French people viewed his right to hereditary succession more seriously than his Protestantism. Henry was also widely liked. Notoriously informal in dress and manner—which made him especially popular with the soldiers—Henry also had the wit and charm to neutralize the strongest enemy in a face-to-face confrontation. He came to the throne as a *politique*, long weary with religious

THEODORE BEZA DEFENDS THE RIGHT TO RESIST TYRANNY

One of the oldest problems in political and social theory has been that of knowing when resistance to repression in matters of conscience is justified. Since Luther's day, Protestant reformers, although accused by their Catholic critics of fomenting social division and revolution, had urged their followers to strict obedience to established political authority. After the 1572 massacre of Saint Bartholomew's Day, however, Protestant pampheteers urged Protestants to resist tyrants and persecutors with armed force. Here, in 1574, Theodore Beza points out the obligation of rulers to their subjects and the latter's right to resist rulers who fail to meet the conditions of their office.

It is apparent that there is a mutual obligation between the king and the officers of a kingdom; that the government of the kingdom is not in the hands of the king in its entirety, but only the sovereign degree; that each of the officers has a share in accord with his degree; and that there are definite conditions on either side. If these conditions are not observed by the inferior officers, it is the part of the sovereign to dismiss and punish them. . . . If the king, hereditary or elective, clearly goes back on the conditions without which he would not have been recognized and acknowledged, can there be any doubt that the lesser magistrates of the kingdom, of the cities, and of the provinces, the administration of which they have received from the sovereignty itself, are free of their oath, at least to the extent that they are entitled to resist flagrant oppression of the realm which they swore to defend and protect according to their office and their particular jurisdiction? . . .

We must now speak of the third class of subjects, which though admittedly subject to the sovereign in a certain respect, is, in another respect, and in cases of necessity the protector of the rights of the sovereignty itself, and is established to hold the sovereign to his duty, and even, if need be, to constrain and punish him. . . . The people is prior to all the magistrates, and does not exist for them, but they for it. . . . Whenever law and equity prevailed, nations neither created nor accepted kings except upon definite conditions. From this it follows that when kings flagrantly violate these terms, these who have the power to give them their authority have no less power to deprive them of it.

Hotman, Beza, and Mornay, trans. and ed. by Julian H. Franklin, *Constitutionalism and Resistance in the Sixteenth Century: Three Treatises* (New York: Pegasus, 1969), pp. 111–114.

strife and fully prepared to place political peace above absolute religious unity. He believed a royal policy of tolerant Catholicism would be the best way to achieve such peace. On July 25, 1593, he publicly abandoned the Protestant faith and embraced the traditional and majority religion of his country. "Paris is worth a Mass," he is reported to have said.

It was, in fact, a decision he had made only after a long period of personal agonizing. The Huguenots were horrified, and Pope Clement VIII was skeptical of Henry's sincerity, but most of the French church and people, having known internal strife too long, rallied to his side. By 1596, the Catholic League was dispersed, its ties with Spain were broken, and the wars of religion in France, to all intents, had ground to a close.

The Edict of Nantes

On April 13, 1598, Henry IV's famous Edict of Nantes proclaimed a formal religious settlement. The following month, on May 2, 1598, the Treaty of Vervins ended hostilities between France and Spain.

In 1591, Henry IV had already assured the Huguenots of at least qualified religious freedoms. The Edict of Nantes made good that promise. It recognized minority religious rights within what was to remain an officially Catholic country. This religious truce—and it was never more than that—granted the Huguenots, who by this time numbered well over a million, freedom of public worship, the right of assembly, admission to public offices and universities, and permission to maintain

Henry IV of France (r. 1589–1610) on horseback, painted in 1594. *Réunion des Musées Nationaux/Art Resource, NY*

fortified towns. They were to exercise most of the new freedoms, however, within their own towns and territories. Concession of the right to fortify their towns revealed the continuing distrust between French Protestants and Catholics. As significant as it was, the edict only transformed a long hot war between irreconcilable enemies into a long cold war. To its critics, it had only created a state within a state.

A Catholic fanatic assassinated Henry IV in May 1610. Although he is best remembered for the Edict of Nantes, Henry IV's political and economic policies were equally important. They laid the foundations for the transformation of France into the absolute state it would become under Cardinal Richelieu and Louis XIV. (See Chapter 13.) Ironically, in pursuit of the political and religious unity that had escaped Henry IV, Louis XIV, calling for "one king, one law, one faith," would revoke the Edict of Nantes in 1685, an action that forced France and Europe to learn again by bitter experience the hard lessons of the wars of religion.

▼ Imperial Spain and Philip II (r. 1556–1598)

Pillars of Spanish Power

Until the English defeated the mighty Spanish Armada in 1588, no one person stood larger in the second half of the sixteenth century than Philip II of Spain. Philip was heir to the intensely Catholic and militarily supreme western Habsburg kingdom. His father, Charles V, had given the eastern Habsburg lands of Austria, Bohemia, and Hungary to Philip's uncle, the emperor Ferdinand I (r. 1558–1564). These lands, together with the imperial title, remained in the possession of the Austrian branch of the family until 1918.

New World Riches Populous and wealthy Castile gave Philip a solid home base. The regular arrival in Seville of bullion from the Spanish colonies in the New World provided additional wealth. In the 1540s, great silver mines had been opened in Potosí in present-day Bolivia and in Zacatecas in Mexico. These provided the great sums needed to pay the king's bankers and mercenaries. He nonetheless never managed to erase the debts his father left or to finance his own foreign adventures fully. He later contributed to the bankruptcy of the Fuggers when, at the end of his life, he defaulted on his enormous debts.

Increased Population The new American wealth brought dramatic social change to the peoples of Europe during the second half of the sixteenth century. As Europe became richer, it was also becoming more populous. In the economically and politically active towns of France, England, and the Netherlands, populations had tripled and quadrupled by the early seventeenth century. Europe's population exceeded 70 million by 1600.

The combination of increased wealth and population triggered inflation. A steady 2-percent-a-year rise in prices in much of Europe had serious cumulative effects by the mid-sixteenth century. There were more people and more coinage in circulation than before, but less food and fewer jobs; wages stagnated while prices doubled and tripled in much of Europe.

MAIN EVENTS OF THE FRENCH WARS OF RELIGION

1559	Treaty of Cateau-Cambrésis ends Habsburg-Valois wars
1559	Francis II succeeds to French throne under regency of his mother, Catherine de Médicis
1560	Conspiracy of Amboise fails
1562	Protestant worshippers massacred at Vassy in Champagne by the duke of Guise
1572	The Saint Bartholomew's Day Massacre leaves thousands of Protestants dead
1589	Assassination of Henry III brings the Huguenot Henry of Navarre to throne as Henry IV
1593	Henry IV embraces Catholicism
1598	Henry IV grants Huguenots religious and civil freedoms in the Edict of Nantes
1610	Henry IV assassinated

This was especially the case in Spain. Because the new wealth was concentrated in the hands of a few, the traditional gap between the haves—the propertied, privileged, and educated classes—and the have-nots widened. Nowhere did the unprivileged suffer more than in Spain, where the Castilian peasantry, the backbone of Philip II's great empire, became the most heavily taxed people of Europe. Those whose labor contributed most to making possible Spanish hegemony in Europe in the second half of the sixteenth century prospered least from it.

Efficient Bureaucracy and Military   A subjugated peasantry and wealth from the New World were not the only pillars of Spanish strength. Philip II shrewdly organized the lesser nobility into a loyal and efficient national bureaucracy. A reclusive man, he managed his kingdom by pen and paper rather than by personal presence. He was also a learned and pious Catholic, although some popes suspected he used religion as much for political as for devotional purposes. That he was a generous patron of the arts and culture can be seen in his unique retreat outside Madrid, the Escorial, a combination palace, church, tomb, and monastery. Philip also knew personal sorrows: His mad and treacherous son, Don Carlos, died under suspicious circumstances in 1568—some contemporaries suspected that Philip had him quietly executed—only three months before the death of his queen.

Supremacy in the Mediterranean   During the first half of Philip's reign, attention focused almost exclusively on the Mediterranean and the Turkish threat. By history, geography, and choice, Spain had traditionally been Catholic Europe's champion against Islam. During the

1560s, the Turks advanced deep into Austria, and their fleets dominated the Mediterranean. Between 1568 and 1570, armies under Philip's half brother, Don John of Austria (1547–1578), the illegitimate son of Charles V, suppressed and dispersed the Moors in Granada.

In May 1571, a Holy League of Spain, Venice, Genoa, and the pope, again under Don John's command, formed to check Turkish belligerence in the Mediterranean. In the largest naval battle of the sixteenth century, Don John's fleet engaged the Ottoman navy under Ali Pasha off Lepanto in the Gulf of Corinth on October 7, 1571. Before the engagement ended, over a third of the Turkish fleet had been sunk or captured, and 30,000 Turks had died. However, the resilient Ottomans still maintained their base in Cyprus and would soon rebuild their fleet and regain control of the eastern Mediterranean. For the moment, however, the Mediterranean belonged to Spain, and the Europeans were left to fight each other. Philip's armies also suppressed resistance in neighboring Portugal, when Philip inherited the throne of that kingdom in 1580. The union with Portugal not only enhanced Spanish sea power, but it also brought Portugal's overseas empire in Africa, India, and Brazil into the Spanish orbit.

The Revolt in the Netherlands

The spectacular Spanish military success in southern Europe was not repeated in northern Europe. When Philip attempted to impose his will within the Netherlands and on England and France, he learned the lessons of defeat. The resistance of the Netherlands especially proved the undoing of Spanish dreams of world empire. (See Map 12–1, page 360.)

Cardinal Granvelle   The Netherlands was the richest area not only of Philip's Hapsburg kingdom, but of Europe as well. In 1559, Philip departed the Netherlands for Spain, never again to return. His half sister, Margaret of Parma, assisted by a special council of state, became regent in his place. The council was headed by the extremely able Antoine Perrenot (1517–1586), known after 1561 as Cardinal Granvelle, who hoped to check Protestant gains by internal church reforms. He planned to break down the traditional local autonomy of the seventeen Netherlands provinces by stages and establish in its place a centralized royal government directed from Madrid. A politically docile and religiously uniform country was the goal.

The merchant towns of the Netherlands were, however, Europe's most independent; many, like magnificent Antwerp, were also Calvinist strongholds. By tradition and habit, the people of the Netherlands were far more disposed to variety and toleration than to obedient conformity and hierarchical order. Two members of the council of state led a stubborn opposition to the

Map 12–1 THE NETHERLANDS DURING THE REFORMATION   The northern and southern provinces of the Netherlands. The former, the United Provinces, were mostly Protestant in the second half of the sixteenth century; the southern Spanish Netherlands made peace with Spain and remained largely Catholic.

Spanish overlords, who now attempted to reimpose their traditional rule with a vengeance. They were the Count of Egmont (1522–1568) and William of Nassau, the Prince of Orange (1533–1584), known as "the Silent" because of his small circle of confidants.

Like other successful rulers in this period, William of Orange placed the political autonomy and well-being of the Netherlands above religious creeds. He personally was successively a confessed Catholic, Lutheran, and Calvinist. In 1561, he married Anne of Saxony, the daughter of the Lutheran elector Maurice and the granddaughter of the late landgrave Philip of Hesse. He maintained his Catholic practices until 1567, the year he turned Lutheran. After the Saint Bartholomew's Day

Massacre (1572), Orange (as he was called) became an avowed Calvinist.

In 1561, Cardinal Granvelle proceeded with his planned ecclesiastical reorganization of the Netherlands. It was intended to tighten the control of the Catholic hierarchy over the country and to accelerate its consolidation as a Spanish ward. Organizing the Dutch nobility in opposition, Orange and Egmont succeeded in gaining Granvelle's removal from office in 1564. Aristocratic control of the country after Granvelle's departure, however, proved woefully inefficient. Popular unrest grew, especially among urban artisans, who joined the congregations of radical Calvinist preachers in large numbers.

The Compromise   The year 1564 also saw the first fusion of political and religious opposition to Regent Margaret's government. This opposition resulted from Philip II's unwise insistence on trying to enforce the decrees of the Council of Trent throughout the Netherlands. William of Orange's younger brother, Louis of Nassau, who had been raised a Lutheran, led the opposition with support from the Calvinist-inclined lesser nobility and townspeople. A national covenant called the *Compromise* was drawn up, a solemn pledge to resist the decrees of Trent and the Inquisition. Grievances were loudly and persistently voiced. When Regent Margaret's government spurned the protesters as "beggars" in 1566, Calvinists rioted throughout the country. Louis called for aid from French Huguenots and German Lutherans, and a full-scale rebellion against the Spanish regency appeared imminent.

The Duke of Alba   The rebellion failed to materialize, however, because the higher nobility of the Netherlands would not support it. Their shock at Calvinist iconoclasm and anarchy was as great as their resentment of Granvelle's more subtle repression. Philip, determined to make an example of the Protestant rebels, dispatched the duke of Alba to suppress the revolt. His army of 10,000 journeyed northward from Milan in 1567 in a show of combined Spanish and papal might. A special tribunal, known to the Spanish as the Council of Troubles and among the Netherlanders as the Council of Blood, reigned over the land. Before Alba's reign of terror ended, the counts of Egmont and Horn and several thousand suspected heretics were publicly executed.

The Spanish levied new taxes, forcing the Netherlands to pay for the suppression of its own revolt. One, the "tenth penny," a 10 percent sales tax, met such resistance from merchants and artisans that it could not be collected in some areas even after reduction to 3 percent. Combined persecution and taxation sent tens of thousands fleeing from the Netherlands during Alba's six-year rule, a man more hated than Granvelle or the radical Calvinists had ever been.

Resistance and Unification   William of Orange was an exile in Germany during these turbulent years. He now emerged as the leader of a broad movement for the independence of the Netherlands from Spain. The northern, Calvinist-inclined provinces of Holland, Zeeland, and Utrecht, of which Orange was the *Stadholder*, or governor, became his base. As in France, political resistance in the Netherlands gained both organization and inspiration by merging with Calvinism.

The early victories of the resistance attest to the popular character of the revolt. A case in point is the capture of the port city of Brill by the "Sea Beggars," an international group of anti-Spanish exiles and criminals, among them many Englishmen. William of Orange did not hesitate to enlist their services. Their brazen piracy, however, had forced Queen Elizabeth to disassociate herself from them and to bar their ships from English ports. In 1572, the Beggars captured Brill and other seaports in Zeeland and Holland. Mixing with the native population, they quickly sparked rebellions against Alba in town after town and spread

The Milch Cow, a sixteenth-century satirical painting depicting the Netherlands as a cow in whom all the great powers of Europe have an interest. Elizabeth of England is feeding her (England had long-standing commercial ties with Flanders); Philip II of Spain is attempting to ride her (Spain was trying to reassert its control over the entire area); William of Orange is trying to milk her (he was the leader of the anti-Spanish rebellion); and the king of France holds her tail (France hoped to profit from the rebellion at Spain's expense).   The "Milch Cow." Rijksmuseum, Amsterdam the resistance southward. In 1574, the people of Leiden heroically resisted a long Spanish siege. The Dutch opened the dikes and flooded their country to repulse the hated Spanish. The faltering Alba had by that time ceded power to Don Luis de Requesens, who replaced him as commander of the Spanish forces in the Netherlands in November 1573.

The Pacification of Ghent The greatest atrocity of the war came after Requesens's death in 1576. Spanish mercenaries, leaderless and unpaid, ran amok in Antwerp on November 4, 1576, leaving 7,000 people dead in the streets. The event came to be known as the Spanish Fury.

These atrocities accomplished in just four days what neither religion nor patriotism had previously been able to do. The ten largely Catholic southern provinces (what is roughly modern Belgium) now came together with the seven largely Protestant northern provinces (what is roughly the modern Netherlands) in unified opposition to Spain. This union, known as the Pacification of Ghent, was accomplished on November 8, 1576. It declared internal regional sovereignty in matters of religion, a key clause that permitted political cooperation among the signatories, who were not agreed over religion. It was a Netherlands version of the territorial settlement of religious differences brought about in the Holy Roman Empire in 1555 by the Peace of Augsburg. Four provinces initially held out, but they soon made the resistance unanimous by joining the all-embracing Union of Brussels in January 1577. For the next two years, the Spanish faced a unified and determined Netherlands.

Don John, the victor over the Turks at Lepanto in 1571, had taken command of Spanish land forces in November 1576. He now experienced his first defeat. Confronted by unified Netherlands' resistance, he signed the humiliating Perpetual Edict in February 1577, which provided for the removal of all Spanish troops from the Netherlands within twenty days. The withdrawal gave the country to William of Orange and effectively ended, for the time being, whatever plans Philip may have had for using the Netherlands as a staging area for an invasion of England.

The Union of Arras and the Union of Utrecht The Spanish, however, were nothing if not persistent. Don John and Alexander Farnese of Parma, the Regent Margaret's son, revived Spanish power in the southern provinces, where fear of Calvinist extremism had moved the leaders to break the Union of Brussels. In January 1579, the southern provinces formed the Union of Arras and soon made peace with Spain. These provinces later served the cause of the Counter-Reformation. The northern provinces responded by forming the Union of Utrecht.

Netherlands Independence Seizing what now appeared to be a last opportunity to break the back of Netherlands' resistance, Philip II declared William of Orange an outlaw and placed a bounty of 25,000 crowns on his head. The act predictably stiffened the resistance of the northern provinces. In a famous defiant speech to the Estates General of Holland in December 1580, known as the Apology, Orange publicly denounced Philip as a heathen tyrant whom the Netherlands need no longer obey.

On July 22, 1581, the member provinces of the Union of Utrecht met in The Hague and formally declared Philip no longer their ruler. They turned instead to the French duke of Alençon, the youngest son of Catherine de Médicis. The southern provinces had also earlier looked to him as a possible middle way between Spanish and Calvinist overlordship. All the northern provinces save Holland and Zeeland (which distrusted him almost as much as they did Philip II) accepted Alençon as their "sovereign" but with the clear understanding that he would be only a titular ruler. Yet Alençon, an ambitious failure, saw this as his one chance at greatness. When he rashly attempted to take actual control of the provinces in 1583, he was deposed and returned to France.

Spanish efforts to reconquer the Netherlands continued into the 1580s. William of Orange, assassinated in July 1584, was succeeded by his seventeen-year-old son, Maurice (1567–1625), who, with the assistance of England and France, continued the Dutch resistance. Fortunately for the Netherlands, Philip II began now to meddle directly in French and English affairs. He signed a secret treaty with the Guises (the Treaty of Joinville in December 1584) and sent armies under Alexander Farnese into France in 1590. Hostilities with the English, who openly aided the Dutch rebels, also increased. Gradually, they built to a climax in 1588, when Philip's great Armada was defeated in the English Channel.

These new fronts overextended Spain's resources, thus strengthening the Netherlands. Spanish preoccupation with France and England now permitted the northern provinces to drive out all Spanish soldiers by 1593. In 1596, France and England formally recognized their independence. Peace was not, however, concluded with Spain until 1609, when the Twelve Years' Truce gave the northern provinces virtual independence. Full recognition came with the Peace of Westphalia in 1648.

▼ England and Spain (1553–1603)

Before Edward VI died in 1553, he agreed to a device to make Lady Jane Grey, the teenage daughter of a powerful Protestant nobleman and the granddaughter, on her mother's side, of Henry VIII's younger sister Mary, his successor in place of the Catholic Mary Tudor

KING JAMES I DEFENDS POPULAR RECREATION AGAINST THE PURITANS

The English Puritans believed in strict observance of the Sabbath, disapproving any sports, games, or general social conviviality on Sunday. James I thought these strictures prevented many Roman Catholics from joining the Church of England. In 1618, he ordered the clergy of the Church of England to read the Book of Sports from their pulpits. In this declaration, he permitted people to engage in certain sports and games after church services. His hope was to allow innocent recreations on Sunday while encouraging people to attend the Church of England. Despite the king's good intentions, the order offended the Puritans. The clergy resisted his order and he had to withdraw it.

What motives of state might have led James I to issue this declaration? How does he attempt to make it favorable to the Church of England? Why might so many clergy have refused to read this statement to their congregations?

With our own ears we heard the general complaint of our people, that they were barred from all lawful recreation and exercise upon the Sunday's afternoon, after the ending of all divine service, which cannot but produce two evils: the one the hindering of the conversion of many [Roman Catholic subjects], whom their priests will take occasion hereby to vex, persuading them that no honest mirth or recreation is lawful or tolerable in our religion, which cannot but breed a great discontentment in our people's hearts, especially as such as are peradventure upon the point of turning [to the Church of England]: the other inconvenience is, that this prohibition barreth the common and meaner sort of people from using such exercises as may make their bodies more able for war, when we or our successors shall have occasion to use them; and in place thereof sets up filthy tipplings and drunkenness, and breeds a number of idle and discontented speeches in their ale-houses. For when shall the common people have leave to exercise, if not upon the Sundays and holy days, seeing they must apply their labor and win their living in all working days? . . .

[A]s for our good people's lawful recreation, our pleasure likewise is, that after the end of divine service our good people be not disturbed, . . . or discouraged from any lawful recreation, such as dancing, either men or women; archery for men, leaping, vaulting, or any other such harmless recreation, or from having of Hay-games, Whitsun-ales, and Morris-dances; and the setting up of May-poles and other sports therewith used; . . . but withal we do here account still as prohibited all unlawful games to be used upon Sundays only, as bear and bull-baitings . . . and at all times in the meaner sort of people by law prohibited, bowling.

And likewise we bar from this benefit and liberty all such known as recusants [Roman Catholics], either men or women, as will abstain from coming to church or divine service, being therefore unworthy of any lawful recreation after the said service, that will not first come to the church and serve God; prohibiting in like sort the said recreations to any that, though [they] conform in religion [i.e., members of the Church of England], are not present in the church at the service of God, before their going to the said recreations.

From Henry Bettenson, ed., *Documents of the Christian Church*, 2nd ed. (London: Oxford University Press, 1963), pp. 400–403. By permission of Oxford University Press.

pensive, but his subjects considered the peace a sign of pro-Catholic sentiment. James's unsuccessful attempt to relax penal laws against Catholics further increased suspicions, as did his wise hesitancy in 1618 to rush English troops to the aid of German Protestants at the outbreak of the Thirty Years' War. His failed efforts to arrange a marriage between his son Charles and a Spanish princess, and then Charles's marriage in 1625 to Henrietta Marie, the Catholic daughter of Henry IV of France, further increased religious concern. In 1624,

EARLY CONTROVERSY OVER TOBACCO AND SMOKING

SMOKING TODAY IS widely condemned throughout the West, but the controversy over tobacco goes back to the earliest European encounter with the plant, which was native to the Americas.

Christopher Columbus on his first voyage in 1492 saw Native Americans smoking tobacco. Later, the first Spanish missionaries associated smoking with pagan religious practices and tried to stop Native Americans from using tobacco. Once tobacco reached Europe in the late sixteenth century, more opposition to smoking arose (although—ironically—some physicians thought it might cure diseases of the lungs and internal organs). As early as 1610, Sir Francis Bacon (1561–1626) noted that smokers found it difficult to stop smoking. The Christian clergy throughout Europe denounced smoking as immoral, and Muslim clerics condemned the practice as contrary to Islam when it spread to the Ottoman Empire. Nonetheless, smoking tobacco in pipes became popular.

The chief British critic of the new practice was none other than King James I (r. 1603–1625). While he defended Sunday sports against Puritan critics who believed any amusements on the Sabbath were sinful, he detested smoking. In 1604, he published his *Counterblaste to Tobacco* in which he declared, "Have you not reason then to be ashamed, and to forbear this filthy novelty . . .? In your abuse thereof sinning against God, harming yourselves in person . . . and taking thereby the marks . . . of vanity upon you. . . . A custom loathsome to the eye, hateful to the nose, harmful to the brain, dangerous to the lungs, and the black stinking fume thereof, nearest resembling the horrible Stygian smoke of the pit that is bottomless."[1]

To discourage smoking, James's government put a high tax on tobacco. Yet when a brisk trade in smuggled tobacco developed, the government decided to lower the tax to a level where people would not seek to evade it. In 1614, James created a royal monopoly to import tobacco into England, which created a steady government revenue that the increasingly unpopular king badly needed. James, like governments to the present day, may also have regarded this policy as a tax on sin. By 1619, James approved the incorporation of a company of clay pipe makers in London, and 40,000 pounds of tobacco arrived from Virginia the next year. Other European governments would also find tobacco a significant source of tax revenue. Often they would tax tobacco and at the same time attempt to regulate its use, especially among the young.

Which groups in Europe in the sixteenth and seventeenth centuries opposed the habit of smoking tobacco?

Why did the English government under King James I modify its opposition to tobacco?

[1] *A Counterblaste to Tobacco* (1604), reprinted by the Rodale Press, London, 1954, p. 36.

Practically from the moment of its introduction into Europe tobacco smoking was controversial. Here a court jester is portrayed as exhaling rabbits from a pipe as three pipe-smoking gentlemen look on.
© Christel Gerstenberg/Corbis

shortly before James's death, England again went to war against Spain, largely in response to parliamentary pressures.

Charles I

Parliament had favored the war with Spain but would not adequately finance it because its members distrusted the monarchy. Unable to gain adequate funds from Parliament, Charles I (r. 1625–1649), like his father, resorted to extraparliamentary measures. These included levying new tariffs and duties, attempting to collect discontinued taxes, and subjecting English property owners to a so-called forced loan (a tax theoretically to be repaid) and then imprisoning those who refused to pay. All these actions, as well as quartering troops in private homes, challenged local political influence of nobles and landowners.

King CHARLES the FIRST in the HOUSE of COMMONS, demanding the FIVE impeached MEMBERS to be delivered up to his AUTHORITY.

One of the key moments in the conflict between Charles I and Parliament occurred in January 1642 when Charles personally arrived at the House of Commons intent on arresting five members who had been responsible for opposing him. They had already escaped. Thereafter Charles departed London to raise his army. The event was subsequently often portrayed in English art. The present illustration is from an eighteenth-century engraving.
The Granger Collection, New York

When Parliament met in 1628, its members would grant new funds only if Charles recognized the Petition of Right. This document required that henceforth there should be no forced loans or taxation without the consent of Parliament, that no freeman should be imprisoned without due cause, and that troops should not be billeted in private homes. Charles agreed to the petition, but whether he would keep his word was doubtful. The next year after further disputes, Charles dissolved Parliament and did not recall it until 1640.

Years of Personal Rule To conserve his limited resources, Charles made peace with France in 1629 and Spain in 1630, again rousing fears that he was too friendly to Roman Catholic powers. To allow Charles to rule without renegotiating financial arrangements with Parliament, his chief adviser Thomas Wentworth (1593–1641; after 1640, earl of Strafford), imposed strict efficiency and administrative centralization in the government and exploited every legal fund-raising device, enforcing previously neglected laws and extending existing taxes into new areas.

Charles might have ruled indefinitely without Parliament had not his religious policies provoked war with Scotland. James I had allowed a wide variety of religious observances in England, Scotland, and Ireland; by contrast, Charles hoped to impose religious conformity at least within England and Scotland. In 1637, Charles and his high-church Archbishop William Laud (1573–1645), against the opposition of both the English Puritans and the Presbyterian Scots, tried to impose on Scotland the English episcopal system and a prayer book almost identical to the Anglican Book of Common Prayer.

The Scots rebelled, and Charles, with insufficient resources for war, was forced in 1640 to call Parliament. It refused even to consider funds for war until the king agreed to redress a long list of political and religious grievances. The king, in response, immediately dissolved that Parliament—hence its name, the Short Parliament (April–May 1640). When the Scots defeated an English army at the Battle of Newburn in the summer of 1640, Charles reconvened Parliament—this time on its terms—for a long and fateful duration.

The Long Parliament and Civil War

The landowners and the merchant classes represented in Parliament had long resented the king's financial measures and paternalistic rule. The Puritans in Parliament resented his religious policies and distrusted the influence of his Roman Catholic wife. What became known as the Long Parliament (1640–1660) thus acted with widespread support and general unanimity when it convened in November 1640.

The House of Commons impeached both Strafford and Laud. Both were executed—Strafford in 1641, Laud in 1645. Parliament abolished the courts that had enforced royal policy and prohibited the levying of new taxes without its consent. Finally, Parliament resolved that no more than three years should elapse between its meetings and that the king could not dissolve it without its own consent.

Parliament, however, was sharply divided over religion. Both moderate Puritans (the Presbyterians) and more extreme Puritans (the Independents) wanted to abolish bishops and the Book of Common Prayer. Yet religious conservatives in both houses of Parliament were determined to preserve the Church of England in its current form.

These divisions intensified in October 1641, when Parliament was asked to raise funds for an army to suppress the rebellion in Scotland. Charles's opponents argued that he could not be trusted with an army and that Parliament should become the commander-in-chief of English armed forces. In January 1642, Charles invaded Parliament, intending to arrest certain of his opponents, but they escaped. The king then left London and began to raise an army. Shocked, a majority of the House of Commons passed the Militia Ordinance, which gave Parliament authority to raise an army of its own. The die was now cast. For the next four years (1642–1646), civil war engulfed England with the king's supporters known as Cavaliers and the parliamentary opposition as Roundheads.

Oliver Cromwell and the Puritan Republic

Two factors led finally to Parliament's victory. The first was an alliance with Scotland in 1643 that committed Parliament to a Presbyterian system of church government. The second was the reorganization of the parliamentary army under Oliver Cromwell (1599–1658), a country squire of iron discipline and strong, independent religious sentiment. Cromwell and his "godly men" were willing to tolerate an established majority church, but only if it permitted Protestant dissenters to worship outside it.

Defeated militarily by June 1645, Charles for the next several years tried to take advantage of divisions within Parliament, but Cromwell and his army foiled him. Members who might have been sympathetic to the monarch were expelled from Parliament in December 1648. After a trial by a special court, Charles was executed on January 30, 1649, as a public criminal. Parliament then abolished the monarchy, the House of Lords, and the Anglican Church.

From 1649 to 1660, England became officially a Puritan republic, although Cromwell dominated it. His army brutally conquered Scotland and Ireland, where his radically Protestant army carried out numerous atrocities against Irish Catholics. As a national leader, however, Cromwell, proved to be no politician. When in 1653, the House of Commons wanted to disband his expensive army of 50,000 men, Cromwell instead disbanded Parliament. He ruled thereafter as Lord Protector.

Oliver Cromwell's New Model Army defeated the royalists in the English Civil War. After the execution of Charles I in 1649, Cromwell dominated the short-lived English republic, conquered Ireland and Scotland, and ruled as Lord Protector from 1653 until his death in 1658. Dorling Kindersley Media Library. The Wallace Collection, London

Cromwell's military dictatorship, however, proved no more effective than Charles's rule and became just as harsh and hated. People deeply resented his Puritan prohibitions of drunkenness, theatergoing, and dancing. Political liberty vanished in the name of religious conformity. When Cromwell died in 1658, the English were ready by 1660 to restore both the Anglican Church and the monarchy.

Charles II and the Restoration of the Monarchy

After negotiations with the army, Charles II (r. 1660–1685) returned to England amid great rejoicing. A man of considerable charm and political skill, Charles set a refreshing new tone after eleven years of somber Puritanism. England returned to the status quo of 1642, with a hereditary monarch, a Parliament of Lords and Commons that met only when the king summoned it, and the Anglican Church, with its bishops and prayer book, supreme in religion.

The king, however, had secret Catholic sympathies and favored religious toleration. He wanted to allow loyal Catholics and Puritans to worship freely. Yet ultraroyalists in Parliament between 1661 and 1665, through a series of laws known as the Clarendon Code, excluded

ENGLAND IN THE SEVENTEENTH CENTURY

1603	James VI of Scotland becomes James I of England
1604	Hampton Court conference
1611	Publication of the authorized, or King James, version of the English Bible
1625	Charles I becomes English monarch
1628	Petition of Right
1629	Charles I dissolves Parliament and embarks on eleven years of personal rule
1640	April–May, Short Parliament; November, Long Parliament convenes
1642	Outbreak of the Civil War
1645	Charles I defeated at Naseby
1648	Pride's Purge
1649	Charles I executed
1649–1660	Various attempts at a Puritan Commonwealth
1660	Charles II restored to the English throne
1670	Secret Treaty of Dover between France and England
1672	Parliament passes the Test Act
1678	Popish Plot
1685	James II becomes king of England
1688	"Glorious Revolution"
1689	William and Mary proclaimed English monarchs
1701	Acts of Settlement provides for Hanoverian succession
1702–1714	Reign of Queen Anne, the last of the Stuarts
1707	Act of Union between England and Scotland
1713	Treaty of Utrecht ends the War of the Spanish Succession
1714	George I becomes king of Great Britain and establishes the Hanoverian dynasty
1721–1742	Robert Walpole dominates British politics
1727	George II becomes king of Great Britain

Roman Catholics, Presbyterians, and Independents from the official religious and political life of the nation.

In 1670 by the Treaty of Dover, England and France formally allied against the Dutch, their chief commercial competitor. In a secret portion of this treaty, Charles pledged to announce his conversion to Catholicism as soon as conditions in England permitted this to happen. In return for this announcement (which Charles never made), Louis XIV promised to pay Charles a substantial subsidy. In an attempt to unite the English people behind the war with Holland, and as a sign of good faith to Louis XIV, Charles is-sued a Declaration of Indulgence in 1672, suspending all laws against Roman Catholics and non-Anglican Protestants. Parliament refused to fund the war, however, until Charles rescinded the measure. After he did so, Parliament passed the Test Act requiring all civil and military officials of the crown to swear an oath against the doctrine of transubstantiation—which no loyal Roman Catholic could honestly do. Parliament had aimed the Test Act largely at the king's brother, James, duke of York, heir to the throne and a recent, devout convert to Catholicism.

In 1678, a notorious liar named Titus Oates swore before a magistrate that Charles's Catholic wife, through her physician, was plotting with Jesuits and Irishmen to kill the king so James could assume the throne. Parliament believed Oates. In the ensuing hysteria, known as the Popish Plot, several innocent people were tried and executed. Riding the crest of anti-Catholic sentiment and led by the earl of Shaftesbury (1621–1683), opposition members of Parliament, called Whigs, made an unsuccessful effort to exclude James from succession to the throne.

More suspicious than ever of Parliament, Charles II turned again to increased customs duties and the assistance of Louis XIV for extra income. By these means, he was able to rule from 1681 to 1685 without recalling Parliament. In those years, Charles drove Shaftesbury into exile, executed several Whig leaders for treason, and bullied local corporations into electing members of Parliament submissive to the royal will. When Charles died in 1685 (after a deathbed conversion to Catholicism), he left James the prospect of a Parliament filled with royal friends.

The "Glorious Revolution"

When James II (r. 1685–1688) became king, he immediately demanded the repeal of the Test Act. When Parliament balked, he dissolved it and proceeded to appoint Catholics to high positions in both his court and the army. In 1687, he issued another Declaration of Indulgence suspending all religious tests and permitting free worship. In June 1688, James imprisoned seven Anglican bishops who had refused to publicize his suspension of laws against the Catholics. Each of these actions represented a direct royal attack on the local authority of nobles, landowners, the church, and other corporate bodies whose members believed they possessed particular legal privileges. James not only sought to aid his fellow Roman Catholics but also to pursue absolutist policies similar to those of Louis XIV whom he deeply admired.

The English had hoped that James would be succeeded by Mary (r. 1689–1694), his Protestant eldest daughter. She was the wife of William III of Orange, the leader of European opposition to Louis XIV. But on June 20, James II's Catholic second wife gave birth to a son. There was now a Catholic male heir to the throne. The Parliamentary opposition invited William to invade

England to preserve its "traditional liberties," that is, the Anglican Church and parliamentary government.

William of Orange arrived with his army in November 1688 and was received with considerable popular support. James fled to France, and Parliament, in 1689, proclaimed William III and Mary II the new monarchs, thus completing the "**Glorious Revolution**." William and Mary, in turn, recognized a Bill of Rights that limited the powers of the monarchy and guaranteed the civil liberties of the English privileged classes. Henceforth, England's monarchs would be subject to law and would rule by the consent of Parliament, which was to be called into session every three years. The Bill of Rights also prohibited Roman Catholics from occupying the English throne. The Toleration Act of 1689 permitted worship by all Protestants and outlawed only Roman Catholics and those who denied the Christian doctrine of the Trinity. It did not, however, extend full political rights to persons outside the Church of England.

As will be seen more fully in the next chapter, in 1690 John Locke published his *Second Treatise of Civil Government*, which defended the idea that government resided in the consent of the governed. This view directly opposed Tory support for absolutism as well as absolutist political thought on the continent. (See "Compare & Connect: The Debate over the Origin and Character of Political Authority," pages 394–395.)

The Revolution of 1688 has traditionally been seen as a relatively peaceful event. Recent scholarship, however, has disclosed considerable resistance in both Scotland and Ireland, which resulted in significant loss of life. Conversely events in England itself now appear driven not only by the long recognized actions of the political elite, but also by a genuinely popular resistance to James II. Furthermore, the political results of the revolution went well beyond the assertion of parliamentary authority. In one area of government policy after another the reign of William and Mary marked important new departures for Britain. These included not only the aforementioned embrace of moderate religious toleration, but also a turn to policies favoring more modern economic activity resembling that of the Netherlands and a redirection of foreign policy toward direct opposition to France whereas both Charles II and James II had sought to imitate French absolutism and to pursue close relationships with Louis XIV.

The parliamentary measure closing this century of strife was the Act of Settlement (1701), which provided for the English crown to go to the Protestant House of Hanover in Germany if Queen Anne (r. 1702–1714), the second daughter of James II and the heir to the childless William III, died without issue. Thus, at Anne's death in 1714, the Elector of Hanover became King George I of Great Britain (r. 1714–1727) since England and Scotland had been combined in an Act of Union in 1707.

The Age of Walpole

George I almost immediately confronted a challenge to his title. James Edward Stuart (1688–1766), the Catholic son of James II, landed in Scotland in December 1715, but met defeat less than two months later.

Despite the victory over the Stuart pretender, the political situation after 1715 remained in flux until Sir Robert Walpole (1676–1745) took over the helm of government. Walpole's ascendancy from 1721 to 1742 was based on royal support, his ability to handle the House of Commons, and his

Sir Robert Walpole (1676–1745), far left, is shown talking with the Speaker of the House of Commons. Walpole, who dominated British political life from 1721 to 1742, is considered the first prime minister of Britain. Mansell/TimePix/Getty Images, Inc.

control of government patronage. Walpole maintained peace abroad and promoted the status quo at home. Britain's foreign trade spread from New England to India. Because the central government refrained from interfering with the local political influence of nobles and other landowners, they were willing to serve as local government administrators, judges, and military commanders, and to collect and pay the taxes to support a powerful military force, particularly a strong navy. As a result, Great Britain became not only a European power of the first order but eventually a world power as well.

The power of the British monarchs and their ministers had real limits. Parliament could not wholly ignore popular pressure. Even with the extensive use of patronage, many members of Parliament maintained independent views. Newspapers and public debate flourished. Free speech could be exercised, as could freedom of association. There was no large standing army. There existed significant religious toleration. Walpole's enemies could and did openly oppose his policies, which would not have been possible on the Continent. Consequently, the English state combined considerable military power with both religious and political liberty. British political life became the model for all progressive Europeans who questioned the absolutist political developments of the Continent. Furthermore, many of the political values that had emerged in the British Isles during the seventeenth century also took deep root among their North American colonies.

▼ Rise of Absolute Monarchy in France: The World of Louis XIV

Historians once portrayed Louis XIV's reign (r. 1643–1715) as a time when the French monarchy exerted far-reaching, direct control of the nation at all levels. A somewhat different picture has now emerged.

The French monarchy, which had faced numerous challenges from strong, well-armed nobles and discontented Protestants during the first half of the seventeenth century, only gradually achieved the firm authority for which it became renowned later in the century. The groundwork for Louis XIV's absolutism had been laid by two powerful chief ministers, Cardinal Richelieu (1585–1642) under Louis XIII (r. 1610–1643), and then by Cardinal Mazarin (1602–1661). Both Richelieu and Mazarin attempted to impose direct royal administration on France. Richelieu had also circumscribed many of the political privileges Henry IV had extended to French Protestants in the Edict of Nantes (1598). The centralizing policies of Richelieu and then of Mazarin, however, finally provoked a series of widespread rebellions among French nobles between 1649 and 1652 known as the *Fronde* (after the slingshots used by street boys).

Though unsuccessful, these rebellions convinced Louis XIV and his advisors that heavy-handed policies could endanger the throne. Thereafter Louis would concentrate unprecedented authority in the monarchy, but he would be more subtle than his predecessors. His genius was to make the monarchy the most important and powerful political institution in France while also assuring the nobles and other wealthy groups of their social standing and influence on the local level. Rather than destroying existing local social and political institutions, Louis largely worked through them. Nevertheless, the king was clearly the senior partner in the relationship.

Years of Personal Rule

On the death of Mazarin in 1661, Louis XIV assumed personal control of the government at the age of twenty-three. He appointed no single chief minister. Rebellious nobles would now be challenging the king directly; they could not claim to be resisting only a bad minister.

Louis XIV of France came to symbolize absolute monarchy though such government was not as absolute as the term implied. This state portrait was intended to convey the grandeur of the king and of his authority. The portrait was brought into royal council meetings when the king himself was absent.   Hyacinthe Rigaud (1659–1743), *Portrait of Louis XIV*. Louvre, Paris, France. Dorling Kindersley Media Library/Max Alexander. © Dorling Kindersley, courtesy of l'Etablissement public du musée et du domaine national de Versailles

Louis devoted enormous personal energy to his political tasks. He ruled through councils that controlled foreign affairs, the army, domestic administration, and economic regulations. Each day he spent hours with the ministers of these councils, whom he chose from families long in royal service or from among people just beginning to rise in the social structure. Unlike the more ancient noble families, the latter had no real or potential power bases in the provinces and depended solely on the king for their standing in both government and society.

Louis made sure, however, that the nobility and other major social groups would benefit from the growth of his own authority. Although he controlled foreign affairs and limited the influence of noble institutions on the monarchy, he never tried to abolish those institutions or limit their local authority. The crown, for example, usually conferred informally with regional judicial bodies, called **parlements**, before making rulings that would affect them. Likewise, the crown would rarely enact economic regulations without consulting local opinion. Louis did, however, clash with the Parlement of Paris, which had the right to register royal laws. In 1673, he curtailed its power by requiring it to register laws before raising any questions about them. Many regional parlements and other authorities, however, had long resented the power of that Parisian body and thus supported the monarch.

Versailles

Louis and his advisors became masters of propaganda and political image creation. Louis never missed an opportunity to impress the grandeur of his crown on the French people but most especially on the French nobility. He did so by the manipulation of symbols. For example, when the *dauphin* (the heir to the French throne) was born in 1662, Louis appeared for the celebration dressed as a Roman emperor. He also dominated the nobility by demonstrating that he could outspend them and create a greater social display than the strongest nobles in the land.

The central element of the image of the monarchy was the palace of Versailles, which, when completed, was the largest secular structure in Europe. More than any other monarch of the day, Louis XIV used the physical setting of his court to exert political control. Versailles, built between 1676 and 1708 on the outskirts of Paris, became Louis's permanent residence after 1682. It was a temple to royalty, designed and decorated to proclaim the glory of the Sun King, as Louis was known. A spectacular estate with magnificent fountains and gardens, it housed thousands of the more important nobles, royal officials, and servants. The stables alone could hold 12,000 horses. Some nobles paid for their own residence at the palace, thus depleting their resources; others required royal patronage to remain in residence. In either case they became dependent on the monarch. Although it consumed over half Louis's annual revenues, Versailles paid significant political dividends.

Because Louis ruled personally, he was himself the chief source of favors and patronage in France. To emphasize his prominence, he organized life at court around every aspect of his own daily routine. Elaborate etiquette governed every detail of life at Versailles. Moments near the king were important to most court nobles because they were effectively excluded from the real business of government. The king's rising and dressing were times of rare intimacy, when nobles could whisper their special requests in his ear. Fortunate nobles held his night candle when he went to his bed.

Some nobles, of course, avoided Versailles. They managed their estates and cultivated their local influence. Many others were simply too poor to cut a figure at court. All the nobility understood, however, that Louis, unlike Richelieu and Mazarin, would not threaten their local social standing. Louis supported France's traditional social structure and the social privileges of the nobility. Yet even the most powerful nobles knew they could strike only a modest figure when compared to the Sun King.

King by Divine Right

An important source for Louis's concept of royal authority was his devout tutor, the political theorist Bishop Jacques-Bénigne Bossuet (1627–1704). Bossuet defended what he called the "divine right of kings" and cited examples of Old Testament rulers divinely appointed by and answerable only to God. Medieval popes had insisted that only God could judge a pope; so Bossuet argued that only God could judge the king. Although kings might be duty bound to reflect God's will in their rule, yet as God's regents on earth they could not be bound to the dictates of mere nobles and parliaments. Such assumptions lay behind Louis XIV's alleged declaration: *"L'état, c'est moi"* ("I am the state"). (See "Compare & Connect: The Debate over the Origin and Character of Political Authority," pages 394–395.)

Despite these claims, Louis's rule did not exert the oppressive control over the daily lives of his subjects that police states would do in the nineteenth and twentieth centuries. His absolutism functioned primarily in the classic areas of European state action—the making of war and peace, the regulation of religion, and the oversight of economic activity. Even at the height of his power, local institutions, some controlled by townspeople and others by nobles, retained their administrative authority. The king and his ministers supported the social and financial privileges of these local elites. In contrast to the Stuart kings of England, however, Louis firmly prevented them from interfering with his authority on the national level. This system would endure until a financial crisis demoralized the French monarchy in the 1780s.

A Closer ▷ LOOK

VERSAILLES

LOUIS XIV CONSTRUCTED his great palace at Versailles, as painted here in 1668 by Pierre Patel the Elder (1605–1676), to demonstrate the new centralized power he sought to embody in the French monarchy.

The central building is the hunting lodge his father Louis XIII had built earlier in the century. Its interior and that of the wings added to it were decorated with themes from mythology presenting Louis XIV as the "Sun King" around whom all his kingdom revolved.

The outer wings, extending from the front of the central structure, housed governmental offices.

The gardens and ponds behind the main structure were the sites of elaborate entertainment, concerts, and fireworks.

Pierre Patel, *Perspective View of Versailles*. Chateaux de Versailles et de Trianon, Versailles, France. Photo copyright Bridgeman-Giraudon/ Art Resource, NY

To examine this image in an interactive fashion, please go to www.myhistorylab.com

PEARSON
myhistorylab

Louis's Early Wars

By the late 1660s, France was superior to any other European nation in population, administrative bureaucracy, army, and national unity. Because of the economic policies of Jean-Baptiste Colbert (1619–1683), his most brilliant minister, Louis could afford to raise and maintain a large and powerful army. His enemies and some later historians claimed that Louis wished to dominate all of Europe, but it would appear that his chief military and foreign policy goal was to achieve secure international boundaries for France. He was particularly concerned to secure its northern borders along the Spanish Netherlands, the Franche-Comté, Alsace, and Lorraine from which foreign armies had invaded France and could easily do so again. Louis was also determined to frustrate Habsburg ambitions that endangered France and, as part of that goal, sought to secure his southern borders toward Spain. Whether reacting to external events or pursuing his own ambitions, Louis's pursuit of French interests threatened and terrified neighboring states and led them to form coalitions against France.

FRANCE FROM LOUIS XIV TO CARDINAL FLEURY

Year	Event
1643	Louis ascends the French throne at the age of five
1643–1661	Cardinal Mazarin directs the French government
1648	Peace of Westphalia
1649–1652	The *Fronde* revolt
1653	The pope declares Jansenism a heresy
1660	Papal ban on Jansenists enforced in France
1661	Louis commences personal rule
1667–1668	War of Devolution
1670	Secret Treaty of Dover between France and Great Britain
1672–1679	French war against the Netherlands
1685	Louis revokes the Edict of Nantes
1688–1697	War of the League of Augsburg
1701	Outbreak of the War of the Spanish Succession
1713	Treaty of Utrecht between France and Great Britain
1714	Treaty of Rastatt between France and the Empire and Holland
1715	Death of Louis XIV
1715–1720	Regency of the duke of Orléans in France
1720	Mississippi Bubble bursts in France
1726–1743	Cardinal Fleury serves as Louis XV's chief minister

The early wars of Louis XIV included conflicts with Spain and the United Netherlands. The first was the War of the Devolution in which Louis supported the alleged right of his first wife, Marie Thérèse, to inherit the Spanish Netherlands. He contended that through complex legal arrangements they should have "devolved" upon her, hence the name of the war. In 1667, Louis's armies invaded Flanders and the Franche-Comté. He was repulsed by the Triple Alliance of England, Sweden, and the United Provinces. By the Treaty of Aix-la-Chapelle (1668), he gained control of certain towns bordering the Spanish Netherlands. (See Map 13–1.)

In 1670, with the secret Treaty of Dover, England and France became allies against the Dutch. Louis invaded the Netherlands again in 1672. The Prince of Orange, the future William III of England, forged an alliance with the Holy Roman Emperor, Spain, Lorraine, and Brandenburg against Louis, now regarded as a menace to the whole of western Europe, Catholic and Protestant alike. The war ended inconclusively with the Peace of Nijmwegen, signed with different parties in successive years (1678, 1679). France gained more territory, including the Franche-Comté.

Louis's Repressive Religious Policies

Like Richelieu before him, Louis believed that political unity and stability required religious conformity. To that end he carried out repressive actions against both Roman Catholics and Protestants.

Suppression of the Jansenists The French crown and the French Roman Catholic church had long jealously guarded their ecclesiastical independence or "Gallican Liberties" from papal authority in Rome. However, after the conversion to Roman Catholicism of Henry IV in 1593, the Jesuits, fiercely loyal to the authority of the Pope, had monopolized the education of French upper-class men, and their devout students promoted the religious reforms and doctrines of the Council of Trent. As a measure of their success, Jesuits served as confessors to Henry IV, Louis XIII, and Louis XIV.

A Roman Catholic religious movement known as *Jansenism* arose in the 1630s in opposition to the theology and the political influence of the Jesuits. Jansenists adhered to the teachings of St. Augustine (354–430) that had also influenced many Protestant doctrines. Serious and uncompromising, they particularly opposed Jesuit teachings about free will. They believed with Augustine that original sin had so corrupted humankind that individuals could by their own effort do nothing good nor contribute anything to their own salvation. The namesake of the movement, Cornelius Jansen (d. 1638), was a Flemish theologian and the bishop of Ypres. His posthumously published *Augustinus* (1640) assailed Jesuit teaching on grace and salvation as morally lax.

MAP EXPLORATION

Interactive map: To explore this map further, go to www.myhistorylab.com

THE EARLY WARS OF LOUIS XIV,
1667–1697

Treaty of Aix-la-Chapelle, 1668
  ☐ To France

Treaty of Nijmwegen, 1678–1679
  ☐ To France
  ☐ To Spain

Treaty of Ryswick, 1697
  ☐ To France
  —— Boundary of France, 1648

Map 13–1 **THE FIRST THREE WARS OF LOUIS XIV** This map shows the territorial changes resulting from Louis XIV's first three major wars (1667–1697).

Jansenism made considerable progress among prominent families in Paris. They were opposed to the Jesuits and supported Jansenist religious communities such as the convent at Port-Royal outside Paris. Jansenists, whose Augustinian theology resembled Calvinism, were known to live extremely pious and morally austere lives. In these respects, though firm Roman Catholics, they resembled English Puritans. Also, like the Puritans, the Jansenists became associated with opposition to royal authority, and families of Jansenist sympathies had been involved in the *Fronde*.

The Debate over the Origin and Character of Political Authority

DURING THE SECOND half of the seventeenth century a profound dispute occurred among European political philosophers over the origin and character of political authority. Some political philosophers, here illustrated by the French bishop Jacques-Bénigne Bossuet, contended that monarchs governed absolutely by virtue of authority derived from God. Other philosophers, here illustrated by the English writer John Locke, contended that political authority originated in the consent of the governed and that such authority was inherently limited in its scope.

QUESTIONS

1. Why might Bossuet have wished to make such extravagant claims for absolute royal power? How might these claims be transferred to any form of government?

2. How does Bossuet's argument for absolute royal authority lead also to the need for a single uniform religion in France?

3. Why does Locke find an absolute monarch in conflict with his subjects and they with him?

4. How do Locke's views serve to provide a foundation for parliamentary government?

5. How might subjects governed according to Bossuet's and Locke's principles relate differently to their monarchs and to the officials of monarchs administering their local communities?

I. Bishop Bossuet Defends the Divine Right of Kings

The revolutions of the seventeenth century caused many to fear anarchy far more than tyranny, among them the influential French bishop Jacques-Bénigne Bossuet (1627–1704), the leader of French Catholicism in the second half of the seventeenth century. Louis XIV made him court preacher and tutor to his son, for whom Bossuet wrote a celebrated universal history. In the following excerpt, Bossuet defends the divine right and absolute power of kings. He depicts kings as embracing in their person the whole body of the state and the will of the people they govern and, as such, as being immune from judgment by any mere mortal.

The royal power is absolute. . . . The prince need render account of his acts to no one. "I counsel thee to keep the king's commandment, and that in regard of the oath of God. Be not hasty to go out of his sight; stand not on an evil thing for he doeth whatsoever pleaseth him. Where the word of a king is, there is power; and who may say unto him, What doest thou? Whoso keepeth the commandment shall feel no evil thing" [Eccles. 8:2–5]. Without this absolute authority the king could neither do good nor repress evil. It is necessary that his power be such that no one can hope

to escape him, and finally, the only protection of individuals against the public authority should be their innocence. This confirms the teaching of St. Paul: "Wilt thou then not be afraid of the power? Do that which is good" [Rom. 13:3].

God is infinite, God is all. The prince, as prince, is not regarded as a private person: he is a public personage, all the state is in him; the will of all the people is included in his. As all perfection and all strength are united in God, so all the power of individuals is united in the person of the prince. What grandeur that a single man should embody so much! . . .

Behold an immense people united in a single person; behold this holy power, paternal and absolute; behold the secret cause which governs the whole body of the state, contained in a single head: you see the image of God in the king, and you have the idea of royal majesty. God is holiness itself, goodness itself, and power itself. In these things lies the majesty of God. In the image of these things lies the majesty of the prince.

Source: From *Politics Drawn from the Very Words of Holy Scripture*, as quoted in James Harvey Robinson, ed., *Readings in European History*, Vol. 2 (Boston: Athenaeum, 1906), pp. 275–276.

II. John Locke Denounces the Idea of Absolute Monarchy

John Locke (1632–1704) was the most important English philosopher of the late seventeenth century. As will be seen in Chapter 14 he wrote on a wide variety of subjects including both political philosophy and religious toleration. In 1690 he published his second Treatise of Civil Government. *In this work he defended limitations on government and rooted political authority in the consent of the governed. He drafted the treatise in the late 1670s in response to Tory assertions of absolute monarchy set forth by supporters of Charles II. The treatise was published in the wake of the Revolution of 1688 and was read at the time as a justification of that event. Locke's thought would almost a century later influence the American Declaration of Independence. In the passages below Locke explains that under absolute monarchy citizens must submit to an authority from which they can make no appeal. Consequently, there is a necessary conflict between citizens and the absolute monarchy. It was to escape such conflict and to secure property and liberty that human beings had left the state of nature to found civil society.*

Man being born . . . with a title to perfect freedom, and an uncontrolled enjoyment of all the rights and privileges of the law of nature, equally with any other man, or number of men in the world, hath by nature a power, not only to preserve his property, that is, his life, liberty and estate, against the injuries and attempts of other men; but to judge of, and punish the breaches of that law in others, as he is persuaded the offence deserve . . . [T]here and there only is political society, where every one of the members hath quitted this natural power, resigned it up into the hands of the community in all cases that excludes him not from appealing for protection to the law established by it. And thus all private judgment of every particular member being excluded, the community comes to be umpire, by settled standing rules, indifferent, and the same to all parties; and by men having authority from the community, for the execution of those rules, decides all the differences that may happen between any members of that society concerning any matter of right . . .

Whenever therefore any number of men are so united into one society, as to quit every one his executive power of the law of nature, and to resign it to the public, there and there only is a political, or civil society. . . .

Hence it is evident, that absolute monarchy, which by some men is counted the only government in the world, is indeed inconsistent with civil society, and so can be no form of civil government at all; for the end of civil society, being to avoid, and remedy those inconveniencies of the state of nature, which necessarily follow from every man's being judge in his own case, by setting up a known authority, to which every one of that society may appeal upon any injury received, or controversy that may arise, and which every one of the society ought to obey; whereever any persons are, who have not such an authority to appeal to, for the decision of any difference between them, there those persons are still in the state of nature; and so is every absolute prince, in respect of those who are under his dominion.

For he being supposed to have all, both legislative and executive power in himself alone, there is no judge to be found, no appeal lies open to any one, who may fairly, and indifferently, and with authority decide, and from whose decision relief and redress may be expected of any injury or inconveniency, that may be suffered from the prince, or by his order: so that such a man, however intitled, czar, or grand seignior, or how you please, is as much in the state of nature, with all under his dominion, as he is with the rest of mankind: for where-ever any two men are, who have no standing rule, and common judge to appeal to on earth, for the determination of controversies of right betwixt them, there they are still in the state of nature, and under all the inconveniencies of it . . .

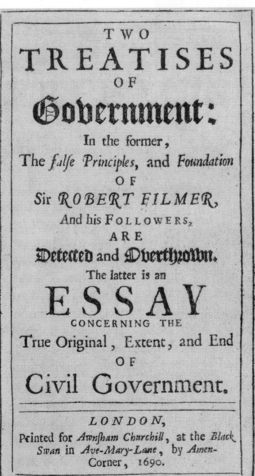

TWO

TREATISES

OF

Government:

In the former,

The *false Principles*, and *Foundation*

O F

Sir *ROBERT FILMER*,

And his FOLLOWERS,

A R E

Detected and Overthrown.

The latter is an

ESSAY

CONCERNING THE

True Original, Extent, and End

O F

Civil Government.

───────────

LONDON,

Printed for *Awnsham Churchill*, at the *Black Swan* in *Ave-Mary-Lane*, by *Amen-Corner*, 1690.

Title page from *Two Treatises of Government* by John Locke, London, 1690. Courtesy of the Library of Congress (Rosenwald Collection, Rare Book and Special Collections Division)

Source: John Locke, *Of Civil Government*, paragraphs 87, 89, 90, 91 in *Two Treatises of Government*, a new ed. (London: 1824), pp. 179–183.

Françoise d'Aubigne, Madame de Maintenon (1635–1719), a mistress to Louis XIV, secretly married him after his first wife's death. The deeply pious Maintenon influenced Louis's policy to make Roman Catholicism France's only religion. Pierre Mignard (1612–1695), *Portrait of Francoise d'Aubigne, Marquise de Maintenon (1635–1719), mistress and second wife of Louis XIV*, c. 1694. Oil on canvas, 128 × 97 cm. Inv.: MV 3637. Chateaux de Versailles et de Trianon, Versailles. Bridgeman-Giraudon/Art Resource, NY

On May 31, 1653, Pope Innocent X declared heretical five Jansenist theological propositions on grace and salvation. In 1656, the pope banned Jansen's *Augustinus*. In 1660, Louis permitted the papal bull banning Jansenism to be enforced in France. He also eventually closed down the Port-Royal community. Thereafter, Jansenists either retracted their views or went underground. In l713, Pope Clement XI issued the bull *Unigenitus*, which again extensively condemned Jansenist teaching. The now aged Louis XIV ordered the French church to accept the bull despite internal ecclesiastical opposition.

The theological issues surrounding Jansenism were complex. By persecuting the Jansenists, however, Louis XIV turned his back on the long tradition of protecting the Gallican Liberties of the French Church and fostered within the French Church a core of opposition to royal authority. This had long-term political significance. During the eighteenth century after the death of Louis XIV, the Parlement of Paris and other French judicial bodies would reassert their authority in opposition to the monarchy. These courts were sympathetic to the Jansenists because of their common resis-

tance to royal authority. Jansenism, because of its austere morality, then also came to embody a set of religious and moral values that contrasted with what eighteenth-century public opinion saw as the corruption of the mid-eighteenth-century French royal court.

Revocation of the Edict of Nantes After the Edict of Nantes in 1598, relations between the Catholic majority (nine tenths of the French population) and the Protestant minority had remained hostile. There were about 1.75 million Huguenots in France in the 1660s (out of an overall population of around 18 million), but their numbers were declining. The French Catholic church had long supported their persecution as both pious and patriotic.

After the Peace of Nijmwegen, Louis launched a methodical campaign against the Huguenots in an effort to unify France religiously. He was also influenced in this policy by his mistress who became his second wife Madame de Maintenon (1635–1719), a deeply pious Catholic who drew Louis toward a much more devout religious observance. Louis hounded Huguenots out of public life, banning them from government office and excluding them from such professions as printing and medicine. He used financial incentives to encourage them to convert to Catholicism. In 1681, he bullied them by quartering troops in their towns. Finally, in October 1685, Louis revoked the Edict of Nantes, and extensive religious repression followed. Protestant churches and schools were closed, Protestant ministers exiled, nonconverting laity were condemned to be galley slaves, and Protestant children were baptized by Catholic priests. (See "Louis XIV Revokes the Edict of Nantes.")

The revocation was a major blunder. Henceforth, Protestants across Europe considered Louis a fanatic who must be resisted at all costs. More than a quarter million people, many of whom were highly skilled, left France. They formed new communities abroad and joined the resistance to Louis in England, Germany, Holland, and the New World. As a result of the revocation of the Edict of Nantes and the ongoing persecution of Jansenists, France became a symbol of religious repression in contrast to England's reputation for moderate, if not complete, religious toleration.

Louis's Later Wars

The League of Augsburg and the Nine Years' War
After the Treaty of Nijmwegen in 1678–1679, Louis maintained his army at full strength and restlessly probed beyond his borders. In 1681 his forces occupied the free city of Strasbourg on the Rhine River, prompting new defensive coalitions to form against him. One of these, the League of Augsburg, grew to include England, Spain, Sweden, the United Provinces, and the major German states. It also had the support of the

LOUIS XIV REVOKES THE EDICT OF NANTES

Believing a country could not be governed by one king and one law unless it was also under one religious system, Louis XIV stunned much of Europe in October 1685, by revoking the Edict of Nantes, which had protected the religious freedoms and civil rights of French Protestants since 1598. Years of serious, often violent, persecution of French Protestants followed this revocation. Consequently, after 1685 in the minds of many Europeans political absolutism was associated with intolerance and religious persecution. Paradoxically, Pope Innocent XI (1676–1689) opposed Louis XIV's revocation of the Edict of Nantes because he understood that this act and other aspects of Louis's ecclesiastical policy were intended as political measures to allow his government to dominate the Roman Catholic Church in France.

Compare this document to the one on page 404 in which the elector of Brandenburg welcomes displaced French Protestants into his domains.

What specific actions does this declaration order against Protestants? Does it offer any incentives for Protestants to convert to Catholicism? How does this declaration compare with the English Test Act?

Art. 1. Know that we . . . with our certain knowledge, full power and royal authority, have by this present, perpetual and irrevocable edict, suppressed and revoked the edict of the aforesaid king our grandfather, given at Nantes in the month of April, 1598, in all its extent . . . together with all the concessions made by [this] and other edicts, declarations, and decrees, to the people of the so-called Reformed religion, of whatever nature they be . . . and in consequence we desire . . . that all the temples of the people of the aforesaid so-called Reformed religion situated in our kingdom . . . should be demolished forthwith.

Art. 2. We forbid our subjects of the so-called Reformed religion to assemble any more for public worship of the above-mentioned religion. . . .

Art. 3. We likewise forbid all lords, of whatever rank they may be, to carry out heretical services in houses and fiefs . . . the penalty for . . . the said worship being confiscation of their body and possessions.

Art. 4. We order all ministers of the aforesaid so-called Reformed religion who do not wish to be converted and to embrace the Catholic, Apostolic, and Roman religion, to depart from our kingdom and the lands subject to us within fifteen days from the publication of our present edict . . . on pain of the galleys.

Art. 5. We desire that those among the said [Reformed] ministers who shall be converted [to the Catholic religion] shall continue to enjoy during their life, and their wives shall enjoy after their death as long as they remain widows, the same exemptions from taxation and billeting of soldiers, which they enjoyed while they fulfilled the function of ministers. . . .

Art. 8. With regard to children who shall be born to those of the aforesaid so-called Reformed religion, we desire that they be baptized by their parish priests. We command the fathers and mothers to send them to the churches for that purpose, on penalty of a fine of 500 livres or more if they fail to do so; and afterwards, the children shall be brought up in the Catholic, Apostolic, and Roman religion. . . .

Art. 10. All our subjects of the so-called Reformed religion, with their wives and children, are to be strongly and repeatedly prohibited from leaving our aforesaid kingdom . . . or of taking out . . . their possessions and effects. . . .

The members of the so-called Reformed religion, while awaiting God's pleasure to enlighten them like the others, can live in the towns and districts of our kingdom . . . and continue their occupation there, and enjoy their possessions . . . on condition . . . that they do not make public profession of [their religion].

S. Z. Ehler and John B. Morrall, eds. and trans., *Church and State Through the Centuries: A Collection of Historic Documents* (New York: Biblo and Tannen, 1967), pp. 209–213. Reprinted by permission of Biblo and Tannen Booksellers and Publishers.

Map 13–2 **EUROPE IN 1714** The War of the Spanish Succession ended a year before the death of Louis XIV. The Bourbons had secured the Spanish throne, but Spain had forfeited its possessions in Flanders and Italy.

Habsburg emperor Leopold I (r. 1658–1705). Between 1689 and 1697, the League and France battled each other in the Nine Years' War, while England and France struggled to control North America.

The Peace of Ryswick, signed in September 1697, which ended the war, secured Holland's borders and thwarted Louis's expansion into Germany.

War of the Spanish Succession On November 1, 1700, the last Habsburg king of Spain, Charles II (r. 1665–1700), died without direct heirs. Before his death, negotiations had begun among the nations involved to partition his inheritance in a way that would preserve the existing balance of power. Charles II, however, left his entire inheritance to Louis's grandson Philip of Anjou, who became Philip V of Spain (r. 1700–1746).

Spain and the vast trade with its American empire appeared to have fallen to France. In September 1701, England, Holland, and the Holy Roman Empire formed the Grand Alliance to preserve the balance of power by once and for all securing Flanders as a neutral barrier between Holland and France and by gaining for the emperor, who was also a Habsburg, his fair share of the Spanish inheritance. Louis soon increased the political stakes by recognizing the Stuart claim to the English throne.

In 1701 the War of the Spanish Succession (1701–1714) began, and it soon enveloped western Europe. France for the first time in Louis's reign went to war with inadequate finances, a poorly equipped army, and mediocre generals. The English, in contrast, had advanced weaponry (flintlock rifles, paper cartridges, and ring bayonets) and superior tactics (thin, maneuverable troop columns rather than the traditional deep ones). John Churchill, the Duke of Marlborough (1650–1722), bested Louis's soldiers in every major engagement, although French arms triumphed in Spain. After 1709 the war became a bloody stalemate.

France finally made peace with England at Utrecht in July 1713, and with Holland and the emperor at Rastatt in March 1714. Philip V remained king of Spain, but England got Gibraltar and the island of Minorca, making it a Mediterranean power. (See Map 13–2.) Louis also recognized the right of the House of Hanover to the English throne.

France After Louis XIV

Despite its military reverses in the War of the Spanish Succession, France remained a great power. It was less strong in 1715 than in 1680, but it still possessed the largest European population, an advanced, if troubled, economy, and the administrative structure bequeathed it by Louis XIV. Moreover, even if France and its resources had been drained by the last of Louis's wars, the other major states of Europe were similarly debilitated.

The impending collapse of John Law's bank triggered a financial panic throughout France. Desperate investors, such as those shown here in the city of Rennes, sought to exchange their paper currency for gold and silver before the banks' supply of precious metals was exhausted. Collection Musée de Bretagne, Rennes

Louis XIV was succeeded by his five-year-old great-grandson Louis XV (r. 1715–1774). The young boy's uncle, the duke of Orléans, became regent and remained so until his death in 1720. The regency, marked by financial and moral scandals, further undermined the faltering prestige of the monarchy.

John Law and the Mississippi Bubble The duke of Orléans was a gambler, and for a time he turned over the financial management of the kingdom to John Law (1671–1729), a Scottish mathematician and fellow gambler. Law believed an increase in the paper-money supply would stimulate France's economic recovery. With the permission of the regent, he established a bank in Paris that issued paper money. Law then organized a monopoly, called the Mississippi Company, on trading privileges with the French colony of Louisiana in North America.

The Mississippi Company also took over the management of the French national debt. The company issued shares of its own stock in exchange for government bonds, which had fallen sharply in value. To redeem large quantities of bonds, Law encouraged speculation in the Mississippi Company stock. In 1719, the price of the stock rose handsomely. Smart investors, however, took their profits by selling their stock in exchange for paper money from Law's bank, which they then sought to exchange for gold. The bank, however, lacked enough gold to redeem all the paper money brought to it.

In February 1720, all gold payments were halted in France. Soon thereafter, Law himself fled the country. The Mississippi Bubble, as the affair was called, had burst. The fiasco brought disgrace on the government that had sponsored Law. The Mississippi Company was later reorganized and functioned profitably, but fear of paper money and speculation marked French economic life for decades.

Renewed Authority of the Parlements The duke of Orléans made a second decision that also lessened the power of the monarchy. He attempted to draw the French nobility once again into the decision-making processes of the government. He set up a system of councils on which nobles were to serve along with bureaucrats. The years of idle noble domestication at Versailles, however, had worked too well, and the nobility seemed to lack both the talent and the desire to govern. The experiment failed. Despite this failure, the great French nobles did not surrender their ancient ambition to assert their rights, privileges, and local influence over those of the monarchy. The chief feature of eighteenth-century French political life was the attempt of the nobility to use its authority to limit the power of the monarchy. The most effective instrument in this process was the previously mentioned *parlements*, or courts dominated by the nobility.

The duke of Orléans reversed the previously noted policy of Louis XIV and formally approved the reinstitution of the full power of the Parlement of Paris to allow

Under Louis XV (r. 1715–1774) France suffered major defeats in Europe and around the world and lost most of its North American empire. Louis himself was an ineffective ruler, and during his reign, the monarchy encountered numerous challenges from the French aristocracy.   CORBIS/Bettmann

or disallow laws. Moreover, throughout the eighteenth century that and other local *parlements* also succeeded in identifying their authority and resistance to the monarchy with wider public opinion. This situation meant that until the revolution in 1789, the *parlements* became natural centers not only for aristocratic, but also for popular resistance to royal authority. In a vast transformation from the days of Louis XIV, the *parlements* rather than the monarchy would come to be seen as more nearly representing the nation.

By 1726, the general political direction of the nation had come under the authority of Cardinal Fleury (1653–1743). He worked to maintain the authority of the monarchy, including ongoing repression of the Jansenists, while continuing to preserve the local interests of the French nobility. Like Walpole in Britain, he pursued economic prosperity at home and peace abroad. Again like Walpole, after 1740, Fleury could not prevent France from entering a worldwide colonial conflict. (See Chapter 17.)

▼ Central and Eastern Europe

Central and eastern Europe were economically much less advanced than western Europe. Except for the Baltic ports, the economy was agrarian. There were fewer cities and many more large estates worked by serfs. The states

in this region did not possess overseas empires; nor did they engage in extensive overseas trade of any kind, except for supplying grain to western Europe—grain, more often than not, carried on western European ships.

During the sixteenth and early seventeenth centuries, the political authorities in this region, which lay largely east of the Elbe River, were weak. The almost constant warfare of the seventeenth century had led to a habit of temporary and shifting political loyalties with princes and aristocracies of small states refusing to subordinate themselves to central monarchical authorities.

During the last half of the seventeenth century, however, three strong dynasties, whose rulers aspired to the absolutism then being constructed in France, emerged in central and eastern Europe. After the Peace of Westphalia in 1648, the Austrian Habsburgs recognized the basic weakness of the position of the Holy Roman Emperor and started to consolidate their power outside Germany. At the same time, Prussia under the Hohenzollern dynasty emerged as a factor in north German politics and as a major challenger to the Habsburg domination of Germany. Most important, Russia under the Romanov dynasty at the opening of the eighteenth century became a military and naval power of the first order. These three monarchies would dominate central and eastern Europe until the close of World War I in 1918. By contrast, Poland during the eighteenth century became the single most conspicuous example in Europe of a land that failed to establish a viable centralized government.

Poland: Absence of Strong Central Authority

In no other part of Europe was the failure to maintain a competitive political position as complete as in Poland. In 1683 King John III Sobieski (r. 1674–1696) had led a Polish army to rescue Vienna from a Turkish siege. Following that spectacular effort, however, Poland became a byword for the dangers of aristocratic independence.

The Polish monarchy was elective, but the deep distrust and divisions among the nobility usually prevented their electing a king from among themselves. Sobieski was a notable exception. Most of the Polish monarchs were foreigners and the tools of foreign powers. The Polish nobles did have a central legislative body called the **Sejm**, or diet. It included only nobles and specifically excluded representatives from corporate bodies, such as the towns. The diet, however, had a practice known as the *liberum veto*, whereby the staunch opposition of any single member, who might have been bribed by a foreign power, could require the body to disband. Such opposition, termed "exploding the diet," was most often the work of a group of dissatisfied nobles rather than of one person. Nonetheless, the requirement of unanimity was a major stumbling block

In 1683 the Ottomans laid siege to Vienna. Only the arrival of Polish forces under King John III Sobieski (r. 1674–1696) saved the Habsburg capital.   Dagli Orti/Picture Desk, Inc./Kobal Collection

to effective government. The price of this noble liberty would eventually be the disappearance of Poland from the map of Europe in the late eighteenth century.

The Habsburg Empire and the Pragmatic Sanction

The close of the Thirty Years' War marked a fundamental turning point in the history of the Austrian Habsburgs. Previously, in alliance with their Spanish cousins, they had hoped to bring all of Germany under their control and back to the Catholic fold. In this they had failed, and the decline of Spanish power meant that the Austrian Habsburgs were on their own. (See Map 13–3, page 402.)

After 1648, the Habsburg family retained a firm hold on the title of Holy Roman Emperor, but the power of the emperor depended less on the force of arms than on the cooperation he could elicit from the various political bodies in the empire. These included large German units (such as Saxony, Hanover, Bavaria, and Brandenburg) and scores of small German cities, bishoprics, principalities, and territories of independent knights. While establishing their new dominance among the German states, the Habsburgs also began to consolidate their power and influence within their hereditary possessions outside the Holy Roman Empire, which included the Crown of Saint Wenceslas, encompassing the kingdom of Bohemia (in the modern Czech Republic) and the duchies of Moravia

and Silesia; and the Crown of Saint Stephen, which ruled Hungary, Croatia, and Transylvania. Much of Hungary was only liberated from the Turks at the end of the seventeenth century (1699).

Through the Treaty of Rastatt in 1714, the Habsburgs further extended their domains, receiving the former Spanish (thereafter Austrian) Netherlands and Lombardy in northern Italy. Thereafter, the Habsburgs' power and influence would be based primarily on their territories outside of Germany.

In each of their many territories the Habsburgs ruled by virtue of a different title—king, archduke, duke—and they needed the cooperation of the local nobility, which was not always forthcoming. They repeatedly had to bargain with nobles in one part of Europe to maintain their position in another. Their domains were so geographically diverse and the people who lived in them of so many different languages and customs that almost no grounds existed on which to unify them politically. Even Roman Catholicism proved ineffective as a common bond, particularly in Hungary, where many Magyar nobles were Calvinist and seemed ever ready to rebel. Over the years the Habsburg rulers established various central councils to chart common policies for their far-flung domains. Virtually all of these bodies, however, dealt with only a portion of the Habsburg holdings.

Despite these internal difficulties, Leopold I (r. 1658–1705) managed to resist the advances of the

Map 13–3 **THE AUSTRIAN HABSBURG EMPIRE, 1521–1772** The empire had three main units—Austria, Bohemia, and Hungary. Expansion was mainly eastward: eastern Hungary from the Ottomans (seventeenth century) and Galicia from Poland (1772). Meantime, Silesia was lost after 1740, but the Habsburgs remained Holy Roman Emperors.

Ottoman Empire into central Europe, which included a siege of Vienna in 1683, and to thwart the aggression of Louis XIV. He achieved Ottoman recognition of his sovereignty over Hungary in 1699 and extended his territorial holdings over much of the Balkan Peninsula and western Romania. These conquests allowed the Habsburgs to hope to develop Mediterranean trade through the port of Trieste on the northern coast of the Adriatic Sea and helped compensate for their loss of effective power over the Holy Roman Empire. Strength in the East gave them greater political leverage in Germany. Joseph I (r. 1705–1711) continued Leopold's policies.

When Charles VI (r. 1711–1740) succeeded Joseph, a new problem was added to the chronic one of territorial diversity. He had no male heir, and there was only the weakest of precedents for a female ruler of the Habsburg domains. Charles feared that on his death the Austrian Habsburg lands might fall prey to the surrounding powers, as had those of the Spanish Habsburgs in 1700. He was determined to prevent that disaster and to provide his domains with the semblance of legal unity. To those ends, he devoted most of his reign to seeking the approval of his family, the estates of his realms, and the major foreign powers for a document called the ***Pragmatic Sanction***.

This instrument provided the legal basis for a single line of inheritance within the Habsburg dynasty through Charles VI's daughter Maria Theresa (r. 1740–1780). Other members of the Habsburg family recognized her as the rightful heir. After extracting various

AUSTRIA AND PRUSSIA IN THE LATE SEVENTEENTH AND EARLY EIGHTEENTH CENTURIES	
1640–1688	Reign of Frederick William, the Great Elector
1658–1705	Leopold I rules Austria and resists the Turkish invasions
1683	Turkish siege of Vienna
1688–1713	Reign of Frederick I of Prussia
1699	Peace treaty between Turks and Habsburgs
1711–1740	Charles VI rules Austria and secures agreement to the Pragmatic Sanction
1713–1740	Frederick William I builds up the military power of Prussia
1740	Maria Theresa succeeds to the Habsburg throne
1740	Frederick II violates the Pragmatic Sanction by invading Silesia

concessions from Charles, the nobles of the various Habsburg domains and the other European rulers also recognized her. Consequently, when Charles VI died in October 1740, he believed that he had secured legal unity for the Habsburg Empire and a safe succession for his daughter. He had indeed established a permanent line of succession and the basis for future legal bonds within the Habsburg holdings. Despite the Pragmatic Sanction, however, his failure to provide his daughter with a strong army or a full treasury left her inheritance open to foreign aggression. Less than two months after his death, the fragility of the foreign agreements became apparent. In December 1740, Frederick II of Prussia invaded the Habsburg province of Silesia in eastern Germany. Maria Theresa had to fight for her inheritance.

Prussia and the Hohenzollerns

The rise of Prussia occurred within the German power vacuum created by the Peace of Westphalia. It is the story of the extraordinary Hohenzollern family, which had ruled Brandenburg since 1417. Through inheritance the family had acquired the duchy of Cleves, and the counties of Mark and Ravensburg in 1614, East Prussia in 1618, and Pomerania in 1648. (See Map 13–4.) Except for Pomerania, none of these lands shared a border with Brandenburg. East Prussia lay inside Poland and outside the authority of the Holy Roman Emperor. All of the territories lacked good natural resources, and many of them were devastated during the Thirty Years' War. Still, by the late seventeenth century, the geographically scattered Hohenzollern holdings represented a block of territory within the Holy Roman Empire, second in size only to that of the Habsburgs.

The person who began to forge these areas into a modern state was Frederick William (r. 1640–1688), who became known as the Great Elector. He established himself and his successors as the central uniting power by breaking the local noble estates, organizing a royal bureaucracy, and building a strong army. (See "The Great Elector Welcomes Protestant Refugees from France," page 404.)

Between 1655 and 1660, Sweden and Poland fought each other across the Great Elector's holdings in Pomerania and East Prussia. Frederick William had neither an adequate army nor the tax revenues to confront this threat. In 1655, the Brandenburg estates refused to grant him new taxes; however, he proceeded to collect them by military force. In 1659, a different grant of taxes, originally made in 1653, elapsed; Frederick William continued to collect them as well as those he had imposed by his own authority. He used the money to build an army, which allowed him to continue to enforce his will without the approval of the nobility. Similar coercion took place against the nobles in his other territories.

There was, however, a political and social trade-off between the Elector and his various nobles. In exchange for their obedience to the Hohenzollerns, the **Junkers**, or German noble landlords, received the right to demand obedience from their serfs. Frederick William also tended to choose as the local administrators of the tax structure men who would normally have been members of the

Map 13–4 **EXPANSION OF BRANDEBURG-PRUSSIA** In the seventeenth century Brandenburg-Prussia expanded mainly by acquiring dynastic titles in geographically separated lands. In the eighteenth century it expanded through aggression to the east, seizing Silesia in 1740 and various parts of Poland in 1772, 1793, and 1795.

THE GREAT ELECTOR WELCOMES PROTESTANT REFUGEES FROM FRANCE

■■

The Hohenzollern dynasty of Brandenburg–Prussia pursued a policy of religious toler-ation. The family itself was Calvinist, whereas most of its subjects were Lutherans. When Louis XIV of France revoked the Edict of Nantes in 1685, Frederick William, the Great Elector, seized the opportunity to invite French Protestants into his realms. As his proclamation indicates, he wanted to attract persons with productive skills who could aid the economic development of his domains.

In reading this document, do you believe religious or economic concerns more nearly led the elector of Brandenburg to welcome the French Protestants? What specific privi-leges did the elector extend to them? To what extent were these privileges a welcoming measure, and to what extent were they inducements to emigrate to Brandenburg? In what kind of economic activity does the elector expect the French refugees to engage?

We, Friedrich Wilhelm, by Grace of God Margrave of Brandenburg . . . Do hereby proclaim and make known to all and sundry that since the cruel perse-cutions and rigorous ill-treatment in which Our co-religionists of the Evangelical-Reformed faith have for some time past been subjected in the Kingdom of France, have caused many families to remove themselves and to betake themselves out of the said Kingdom into other lands, We now . . . have been moved graciously to offer them through this Edict . . . a secure and free refuge in all Our Lands and Provinces. . . .

Since Our Lands are not only well and amply en-dowed with all things necessary to support life, but also very well-suited to the reestablishment of all kinds of manufactures and trade and traffic by land and water, We permit, indeed, to those settling therein free choice to establish themselves where it is most convenient for their profession and way of living. . . .

The personal property which they bring with them, including merchandise and other wares, is to be totally exempt from any taxes, customs dues, licenses, or other imposts of any description, and not detained in any way. . . .

As soon as these Our French co-religionists of the Evangelical-Reformed faith have settled in any town or village, they shall be admitted to the domiciliary rights and craft freedoms customary there, gratis and without payments of any fee; and shall be entitled to the benefits, rights, and privileges enjoyed by Our other, native, subjects, residing there. . . .

Not only are those who wish to establish manu-facture of cloth, stuffs, hats, or other objects in which they are skilled to enjoy all necessary free-doms, privileges and facilities, but also provision is to be made for them to be assisted and helped as far as possible with money and anything else which they need to realize their intention. . . .

Those who settle in the country and wish to maintain themselves by agriculture are to be given a certain plot of land to bring under cultivation and provided with whatever they need to establish themselves initially. . . .

From C. A. Macartney, ed., *The Habsburg and Hohenzollern Dynasties in the Seventeenth and Eighteenth Centuries* (New York: Walker, 1970), pp. 270–273.

noble branch of the old parliament. He thus co-opted po-tential opponents into his service. The taxes fell most heavily on the backs of the peasants and the urban classes. As the years passed, *Junkers* increasingly dominated the army officer corps, and this situation became even more pronounced during the eighteenth century. All officials and army officers took an oath of loyalty directly to the Elector. The army and the Elector thus came to embody the otherwise absent unity of the state. The army made Prussia a valuable potential ally.

Yet even with the considerable accomplishments of the Great Elector, the house of Hohenzollern did not possess a crown. The achievement of a royal title was one of the few state-building accomplishments of Frederick I (r. 1688–1713). This son of the Great Elector was the least "Prussian" of his family during these crucial years. He built palaces, founded Halle University (1694), patronized the arts, and lived luxuriously. In the War of the Spanish Succession, he put his army at the disposal of the Habsburg Holy Roman Emperor Leopold I. In exchange, the emperor permitted Frederick to assume the title of "King in Prussia" in 1701.

His successor, Frederick William I (r. 1713–1740), was both the most eccentric monarch to rule the Hohenzollern domains and one of the most effective. He organized the bureaucracy along military lines. The discipline that he applied to the army was fanatical. The Prussian military grew from about 39,000 in 1713 to over 80,000 in 1740, making it the third or fourth largest army in Europe. Prussia's population, in contrast, ranked thirteenth in size. Separate laws applied to the army and to civilians. Laws, customs, and royal attention made the officer corps the highest social class of the state. Military service thus attracted the sons of *Junkers*. In this fashion the army, the *Junker* nobility, and the monarchy became forged into a single political entity. Military priorities and values dominated Prussian government, society, and daily life as in no other state in Europe. It has often been said that whereas other states possessed armies, the Prussian army possessed its state.

Although Frederick William I built the best army in Europe, he avoided conflict. His army was a symbol of Prussian power and unity, not an instrument for foreign adventures or aggression. At his death in 1740, he passed to his son Frederick II later known as Frederick the Great (r. 1740–1786), this superb military machine, but not the wisdom to refrain from using it. Almost immediately on coming to the throne, Frederick II upset the Pragmatic Sanction and invaded Silesia. He thus crystallized the Austrian-Prussian rivalry for the control of Germany that would dominate central European affairs for over a century.

▼ Russia Enters the European Political Arena

The emergence of Russia in the late seventeenth century as an active European power was a wholly new factor in European politics. Previously, Russia had been considered part of Europe only by courtesy. Before 1673, it did not send permanent ambassadors to western Europe, though it had sent various diplomatic missions since the fifteenth century. Geographically and politically, it lay on the periphery. Hemmed in by Sweden on the Baltic and by the Ottoman Empire on the Black Sea, Russia had no warm-water ports. Its chief outlet for trade to the West was Archangel on the White Sea, which was ice free for only part of the year.

The Romanov Dynasty

The reign of Ivan IV (r. 1533–1584), later known as Ivan the Terrible, had commenced well but ended badly. About midway in his reign he underwent a personality change that led him to move from a program of sensible reform of law, government, and the army toward violent personal tyranny. A period known as the "Time of Troubles" followed upon his death. In 1613, hoping to end the uncertainty, an assembly of nobles elected as tsar a seventeen-year-old boy named Michael Romanov (r. 1613–1645). Thus began the dynasty that ruled Russia until 1917.

Michael Romanov and his two successors, Aleksei (r. 1654–1676) and Theodore II (r. 1676–1682), brought stability and modest bureaucratic centralization to Russia. The country remained, however, weak and impoverished. After years of turmoil, the *boyars*, the old nobility, still largely controlled the bureaucracy. Furthermore, the government and the tsars faced the danger of mutiny from the *streltsy*, or guards of the Moscow garrison.

Peter the Great

In 1682, another boy—ten years old at the time—ascended the fragile Russian throne as co-ruler with his half brother. His name was Peter (r. 1682–1725), and Russia would never be the same after him. He and the sickly Ivan V had come to power on the shoulders of the *streltsy*, who expected to be rewarded for their support. Violence and bloodshed had surrounded the disputed succession. Matters became even more confused when the boys' sister, Sophia, was named regent. Peter's followers overthrew her in 1689. From that date onward, Peter ruled personally, although in theory he shared the crown until Ivan died in 1696. The dangers and turmoil of his youth convinced Peter of two things: First, the power of the tsar must be made secure from the jealousy of the *boyars* and the greed of the *streltsy*; second, Russian military power must be increased. In both respects, he self-consciously resembled Louis XIV of France, who had experienced the turmoil of the *Fronde* during his youth and resolved to establish a strong monarchy safe from the nobility and defended by a powerful army.

Northwestern Europe, particularly the military resources of the maritime powers, fascinated Peter I, who eventually became known as Peter the Great. In 1697, he made a famous visit in transparent disguise to western Europe. There he dined and talked with the great and the powerful, who considered this almost seven-foot-tall ruler crude. He spent his happiest moments on the trip inspecting shipyards, docks, and the manufacture of military hardware in England and the Netherlands. An imitator of the first order, Peter returned to Moscow determined to copy what he had seen abroad, for he knew warfare would be necessary to make Russia a great power. Yet he understood his goal would require him to confront the long-standing power and traditions of the Russian nobles.

Taming the *Streltsy* and *Boyars* In 1698, while Peter was abroad, the *streltsy* had rebelled. On his return, Peter brutally suppressed the revolt with private tortures and public executions, in which Peter's own ministers took part. Approximately a thousand of the rebels were put to death, and their corpses remained on public display to discourage disloyalty.

The new military establishment that Peter built would serve the tsar and not itself. He introduced effective and ruthless policies of conscription, drafting an unprecedented 130,000 soldiers during the first decade of the eighteenth century and almost 300,000 troops by the end of his reign. He had adopted policies for the officer corps and general military discipline patterned on those of West European armies.

Peter also made a sustained attack on the *boyars* and their attachment to traditional Russian culture. After his European journey, he personally shaved the long beards of the court *boyars* and sheared off the customary long hand-covering sleeves of their shirts and coats, which had made them the butt of jokes among other European courts. Peter became highly skilled at balancing one group off against another while never completely excluding any as he set about to organize Russian government and military forces along the lines of the more powerful European states.

Developing a Navy In the mid-1690s, Peter oversaw the construction of ships to protect his interests in the Black Sea against the Ottoman Empire. In 1695, he began a war with the Ottomans and captured Azov on the Black Sea in 1696.[1] Part of the reason for Peter's trip to western Europe in 1697 was to learn how to build still better warships, this time for combat on the Baltic. The construction of a Baltic fleet was essential in Peter's struggles with Sweden that over the years accounted for many of his major steps toward westernizing his realm.

Russian Expansion in the Baltic: The Great Northern War

Following the end of the Thirty Years' War in 1648, Sweden had consolidated its control of the Baltic, thus preventing Russian possession of a port on that sea and permitting Polish and German access to the sea only on Swedish terms. The Swedes also had one of the better armies in Europe. Sweden's economy, however, based primarily on the export of iron, was not strong enough to ensure continued political success.

In 1697, Charles XII (r. 1697–1718) came to the Swedish throne. He was headstrong, to say the least, and perhaps insane. In 1700, Peter the Great began a drive to the west against Swedish territory to gain a foothold on the Baltic. In the resulting Great Northern War (1700–1721), Charles XII led a vigorous and often brilliant campaign, defeating the Russians at the Battle of Narva (1700). As the conflict dragged on, however, Peter was able to strengthen his forces. By 1709, he decisively defeated the Swedes at the Battle of Poltava in Ukraine. Thereafter, the Swedes could maintain only a holding action against their enemies. Charles himself sought refuge in Turkey and did not return to Sweden until 1714. He was killed under uncertain circumstances four years later while fighting the Danes in Norway. When the Great Northern War came to a close in 1721, the Peace of Nystad confirmed the Russian conquest of Estonia, Livonia, and part of Finland. Henceforth, Russia possessed ice-free ports and a permanent influence on European affairs.

Founding St. Petersburg At one point, the domestic and foreign policies of Peter the Great intersected. This was at the site on the Gulf of Finland where he founded his new capital city of St. Petersburg in 1703. There he built government structures and compelled the *boyars* to construct town houses. He thus imitated those European monarchs who had copied Louis XIV by constructing smaller versions of Versailles. The founding of St. Petersburg went beyond establishing a central imperial court, however; it symbolized a new Western orientation of Russia and Peter's determination to hold his position on the Baltic coast. Moreover, he and his successors employed architects from western Europe for many of the most prominent buildings in and around the city. Consequently, St. Petersburg looked different from the old capital Moscow and other Russian cities.

The Case of Peter's Son Aleksei Peter's son Aleksei had been born to his first wife whom he had divorced in 1698. Peter was jealous of the young man, who had never demonstrated strong intelligence or ambition. (See "Peter the Great Tells His Son to Acquire Military Skills," page 407.) By 1716, Peter was becoming convinced that his opponents looked to Aleksei as a focus for their possible sedition while Russia remained at war with Sweden. There was some truth to these concerns because the next year Aleksei went to Vienna where he attempted to enter into a vague conspiracy with the Habsburg emperor Charles VI. Compromised by this trip, Aleksei then returned to Russia surrounded by rumors and suspicions.

Peter, who was investigating official corruption, realized his son might become a rallying point for those he accused. Early in 1718, when Aleksei reappeared in St. Petersburg, the tsar began to look into his son's

---

[1]Although Peter had to return Azov to the Ottomans in 1711, its recapture became a goal of Russian foreign policy. See Chapter 18.

PETER THE GREAT TELLS HIS SON TO ACQUIRE MILITARY SKILLS

Enormous hostility existed between Peter the Great and his son Aleksei. Peter believed his son was not prepared to inherit the throne. In October 1715, he composed a long letter to Aleksei in which he berated him for refusing to take military matters seriously. The letter indicates how an early eighteenth-century ruler saw the conduct of warfare as a fundamental part of the role of a monarch. Peter also points to Louis XIV of France as a role model. Peter and Aleksei did not reach an agreement. Aleksei died under mysterious circumstances in 1718, with Peter possibly responsible for his death.

How did Peter use the recent war with Sweden to argue for the necessity of his son acquiring military skills? What concept of leadership does Peter attempt to communicate to his son? Why did Peter see military prowess as the most important ability in a ruler?

You cannot be ignorant of what is known to all the world, to what degree our people groaned under the oppression of the Swede before the beginning of the present war. . . . You know what it has cost us in the beginning of this war . . . to make ourselves experienced in the art of war, and to put a stop to those advantages which our implacable enemies obtained over us. . . .

But you even will not so much as hear warlike exercises mentioned: though it was by them that we broke through that obscurity in which we were involved, and that we make ourselves known to nations, whose esteem we share at present.

I do not exhort you to make war without lawful reasons: I only desire you to apply yourself to learn the art of it: for it is impossible to govern well without knowing the rules and discipline of it, was it for no other end than for the defense of the country. . . .

You mistake, if you think it is enough for a prince to have good generals to act under his order. Everyone looks upon the head; they study its inclinations and conform themselves to them: all the world own this. . . .

You have no inclination to learn war. You do not apply yourself to it, and consequently you will never learn it: And how then can you command others, and judge of the reward which those deserve who do their duty, or punish others who fail of it? You will do nothing, nor judge of anything but by the assent and help of others, like a young bird that holds up his bill to be fed. . . .

If you think there are some, whose affairs do not fail of success, though they do not go to war themselves; it is true: But they do not go themselves, yet they have an inclination for it, and understand it.

For instance, the late King of France did not always take the field in person; but it is known to what degree he loved war, and what glorious exploits he performed in it, which make his campaigns to be called the theatre and school of the world. His inclinations were not confined solely to military affairs, he also loved mechanics, manufacture and other establishment, which rendered his kingdom more flourishing than any other whatsoever.

From Friedrich C. Weber, *The Present State of Russia* (London, 1722), 2, pp. 97–100; P. F. Riley, *The Global Experience*, 3rd ed., Vol. 2, © 1998. Reprinted by permission of Prentice Hall, Inc., Upper Saddle River, NJ.

Peter the Great built St. Petersburg on the Gulf of Finland to provide Russia with better contact with western Europe. He moved Russia's capital there from Moscow in 1712. This is an eighteenth-century view of the city.   The Granger Collection

Vûe des bords de la Neva en descendant la riviere entre le Palais d'hyver de Sa Majesté Imperiale & les batimens de l'Academie des Sciences

RISE OF RUSSIAN POWER

1533–1584	Reign of Ivan the Terrible
1584–1613	"Time of Troubles"
1613	Michael Romanov becomes tsar
1682	Peter the Great, age ten, becomes tsar
1689	Peter assumes personal rule
1696	Russia captures Azov on the Black Sea from the Turks
1697	European tour of Peter the Great
1698	Peter returns to Russia to put down the revolt of the *streltsy*
1700	The Great Northern War opens between Russia and Sweden; Russia defeated at Narva by Swedish army of Charles XII
1703	St. Petersburg founded
1709	Russia defeats Sweden at the Battle of Poltava
1718	Charles XII of Sweden dies
1718	Aleksei, son of Peter the Great, dies in prison under mysterious circumstances
1721	Peace of Nystad ends the Great Northern War
1721	Peter establishes a synod for the Russian church
1722	Peter issues the Table of Ranks
1725	Peter dies, leaving an uncertain succession

relationships with Charles VI. Peter discovered that had Aleksei and Charles VI succeeded in organizing a conspiracy, many Russian nobles, officials, and churchmen might have joined them. During this six-month investigation, Peter personally interrogated Aleksei, who was eventually condemned to death and died under mysterious circumstances on June 26, 1718.

Reforms of Peter the Great's Final Years   The interrogations surrounding Aleksei had revealed greater degrees of court opposition than Peter had suspected. Recognizing he could not eliminate his opponents the way he had attacked the *streltsy* in 1698, Peter undertook radical administrative reforms designed to bring the nobility and the Russian Orthodox Church more closely under the authority of persons loyal to the tsar.

Administrative Colleges   In December 1717, while his son was returning to Russia, Peter reorganized his domestic administration to sustain his own personal authority and to fight rampant corruption. To achieve this goal, Peter looked to Swedish institutions called *colleges*—bureaus of several persons operating according to written instructions rather than departments headed by a single minister. He created eight of these colleges to oversee matters such as the collection of taxes, foreign relations, war, and economic affairs. Each college was to receive advice from a foreigner. Peter divided the members of these colleges between nobles and persons he was certain would be personally loyal to himself.

DOCUMENT-BASED QUESTION

Directions: Construct a valid essay that directly addresses the central issue of the following question. Use facts from the documents provided and from the chapter to prove the position you take in your thesis statement.

In Louis XIV's view, what were the qualities of an effective monarch? In his opinion, what were the main obstacles to absolute rule?

Document A

Source: Cardinal Richelieu offers advice to Louis XIV's predecessor, Louis XIII, "On the Nobility."

It is a very common fault on the part of those born into the nobility to use violence against the common people to whom God seems to have given arms for earning a living rather than for defending themselves. It is very important to stop such disorders by a constant sternness which will make the weakest of yours, although disarmed, as secure in the shelter of your laws as those who are armed.

The nobility had demonstrated, in the recent war, that it inherited the virtue of its ancestors; it is now necessary to discipline the nobles so that they may preserve their former reputation and usefully serve the state. Men who are injurious to the public are not useful to the state; it is certain that nobility which does not serve in war is not only useless, but a burden to the state, and can be compared to a body which supports a paralyzed arm. . . .

As gentry they merit being well treated when they do well, but it is necessary to be severe with them when they fail to do the things their birth binds them to do. . . .

Document B

Perspective view of Versailles.

Document C

Source: Louis XIV revokes the Edict of Nantes, *Church and State through the Centuries*.

Art. 1. We desire . . . that all the temples of the people of the aforesaid so-called Reformed religion. . . .be demolished forthwith.

Art. 2. We forbid our subjects of the so-called Reformed religion to assemble any more for public worship of the above-mentioned religion. . . .

Art. 3. We likewise forbid all lords, of whatever rank they may be, to carry out heretical services in houses and fiefs. . . .

Art. 4. We order all ministers of the aforesaid so-called Reformed religion . . . to depart from our kingdom. . . .

Art. 10. The members of the so-called Reformed religion, while awaiting God's pleasure to enlighten them . . . can live in the towns and districts of our kingdom . . . . on condition . . . that they do not make public profession of [their religion].

Document D

Source: Louis XIV, *Memoirs for the Instruction of the Dauphin*.

But kings must learn not to permit their servants to become too powerful. . . . I am not saying that we should not for our own interest and grandeur wish that our greatness is shared by those in our good graces, but we must carefully guard against their excess. My advice to guarantee this consists of three principle observations. The first is that you must know your affairs completely, because a king who does not know them is always dependent on those who serve him. . . .The second, that you divide your confidence among many, so that each of those you have entrusted will check the elevation of his rival, ensuring that the jealousy of one will bridle the ambition of the other. And the third, that even though you admit a small number of persons into your secret affairs or into your casual conversations, never permit anyone to imagine that they have the power to speak as they please. . . .

For more on the reign of Louis XIV, see pages 389–397.

The great Dutch artist Rembrandt van Rijn (1606–1669) recorded the contemporary life of the United Provinces of the Netherlands during its golden age. The new sciences including medicine made much progress in the Netherlands, which was a center for publishing and instrument making and known for its religious toleration. *The Anatomy Lesson of Dr. Tulp* (1632) presents the dissection of a cadaver of an executed criminal by the noted Dutch physician Dr. Nicolass Tulp who stands on the right surrounded by other members of the Amsterdam guild of surgeons. Such dissections were a controversial part of new emerging medical education with only one a year permitted in Amsterdam. The dramatic use of light and darkness is characteristic of the painting of the baroque style.
Rembrandt van Rijn (1606–1669). *The Anatomy Lesson of Dr. Tulp.* Mauritshuis, The Hague, The Netherlands. SCALA/Art Resource, NY

New Directions in Thought and Culture in the Sixteenth and Seventeenth Centuries

▼ **The Scientific Revolution**
Nicolaus Copernicus Rejects an Earth-Centered Universe • Tycho Brahe and Johannes Kepler Make New Scientific Observations • Galileo Galilei Argues for a Universe of Mathematical Laws • Isaac Newton Discovers the Laws of Gravitation

▼ **Philosophy Responds to Changing Science**
Nature as Mechanism • Francis Bacon: The Empirical Method • René Descartes: The Method of Rational Deduction • Thomas Hobbes: Apologist for Absolute Government • John Locke: Defender of Moderate Liberty and Toleration

▼ **The New Institutions of Expanding Natural Knowledge**

▼ **Women in the World of the Scientific Revolution**

▼ **The New Science and Religious Faith**
The Case of Galileo • Blaise Pascal: Reason and Faith • The English Approach to Science and Religion

▼ **Continuing Superstition**
Witch Hunts and Panic • Village Origins • Influence of the Clergy • Who Were the Witches? • End of the Witch Hunts

▼ **Baroque Art**

▼ **In Perspective**

THE SIXTEENTH AND seventeenth centuries witnessed a sweeping change in the scientific view of the universe. An earth-centered picture gave way to one in which the earth was only another planet orbiting about the sun. The sun itself became one of millions of stars. This transformation of humankind's perception of its place in the larger scheme of things led to a profound rethinking of moral and religious matters, as well as of scientific theory. Faith and reason needed new modes of reconciliation, as did faith and science. The new ideas and methods of science, usually termed *natural philosophy* at the time, challenged those modes of thought associated with late medieval times: Scholasticism and Aristotelian philosophy.

The impact of the new science that explored the realm of the stars through the newly invented telescope and the world of microorganisms through the newly invented microscope must be viewed in the context of two other factors that simultaneously challenged traditional modes of European thought and culture in the sixteenth and seventeenth centuries. The first of these was the Reformation, which permanently divided the religious unity of central and western Europe and fostered decades of warfare and theological dispute. Although by no means a complete break with medieval thought, the theology of the Reformation did question many ideas associated with medieval Christianity and society. The second factor was the cultural impact of Europe's encounter with the New World of the Americas. The interaction with the Americas meant that Europeans directly or indirectly acquired knowledge of new peoples, plants, and animals wholly different from their own and about which Europeans in neither ancient nor medieval times had any information. Consequently, new uncertainties and unfamiliar vistas confronted many Europeans as they considered their souls, geographical knowledge, and physical nature.

Side by side with this new knowledge and science, however, came a new wave of superstition and persecution. The changing world of religion, politics, and knowledge also created profound fear and anxiety among both the simple and the learned, resulting in the worst witch hunts in European history.

▼ The Scientific Revolution

The process that established the new view of the universe is normally termed the **scientific revolution**. The revolution-in-science metaphor must be used carefully, however. Not everything associated with the "new" science was necessarily new. Sixteenth- and seventeenth-century natural philosophers were often reexamining and rethinking theories and data from the ancient world and the late Middle Ages. Moreover, the word *revolution* normally denotes rapid, collective political change involving many people. The scientific revolution was not rapid. It was a complex movement with many false starts and brilliant people suggesting wrong as well as useful ideas. Nor did it involve more than a few hundred people who labored in widely separated

studies and crude laboratories located in Poland, Italy, Denmark, Bohemia, France, and Great Britain. Furthermore, the achievements of the new science were not simply the function of isolated brilliant scientific minds. The leading figures of the scientific revolution often drew on the aid of artisans and craftspeople to help them construct new instruments for experimentation and to carry out those experiments. Thus, the scientific revolution involved older knowledge as well as new discoveries. Additionally, because the practice of science involves social activity as well as knowledge, the revolution also saw the establishment of new social institutions to support the emerging scientific enterprise.

Natural knowledge was only in the process of becoming science as we know it today during the era of the scientific revolution. In fact the word *scientist*, which was only coined in the 1830s, did not yet exist in the seventeenth century, nor did anything resembling the modern scientific career. Individuals devoted to natural philosophy might work in universities or in the court of a prince or even in their own homes and workshops. Only in the second half of the seventeenth century did formal societies and academies devoted to the pursuit of natural philosophy come into existence. Even then the entire process of the pursuit of natural knowledge was a largely informal one.

Yet by the close of the seventeenth century, the new scientific concepts and the methods of their construction were so impressive that they set the standard for assessing the validity of knowledge in the Western world. From the early seventeenth century through the end of the twentieth century, science achieved greater cultural authority in the Western world than any other form of intellectual activity, and the authority and application of scientific knowledge became one of the defining characteristics of modern Western civilization.

Although new knowledge emerged in many areas during the sixteenth and seventeenth centuries, including medicine, chemistry, and natural history, the scientific achievements that most captured the learned imagination and persuaded people of the cultural power of natural knowledge were those that occurred in astronomy.

Nicolaus Copernicus Rejects an Earth-Centered Universe

Nicolaus Copernicus (1473–1543) was a Polish priest and an astronomer who enjoyed a high reputation during his life, but who was not known for strikingly original or unorthodox thought. He had been educated first at the University of Kraków in Poland and later in Italy. In 1543, the year of his death, Copernicus published *On the Revolutions of the Heavenly Spheres*, which has been described as "a revolution-making rather than a

Thomas Hobbes: Apologist for Absolute Government

Nowhere did the impact of the methods of the new science so deeply affect political thought as in the thought of Thomas Hobbes (1588–1679), the most original political philosopher of the seventeenth century.

An urbane and much-traveled man, Hobbes enthusiastically supported the new scientific movement. During the 1630s, he visited Paris, where he came to know Descartes, and Italy, where he spent time with Galileo. He took special interest in the works of William Harvey (1578–1657), who was famous for his discovery of the circulation of blood through the body. Hobbes was also a superb classicist. His earliest published work was the first English translation of Thucydides' *History of the Peloponnesian War* and is still being reprinted today. Part of Hobbes's dark view of human nature would appear to derive from Thucydides' historical analysis.

Hobbes had written works of political philosophy before the English Civil War, but the turmoil of that struggle led him in 1651 to publish his influential work *Leviathan*. His aim was to provide a rigorous philosophical justification for a strong central political authority. Hobbes portrayed human beings and society in a thoroughly materialistic and mechanical way. He traced all psychological processes to bare sensation and regarded all human motivations as egoistical, intended to increase pleasure and minimize pain. According to his analysis, human reasoning penetrated to no deeper reality or wisdom than those physical sensations. Consequently, for Hobbes, unlike both previous Christian and ancient philosophers, human beings exist only to meet the needs of daily life, not for higher spiritual ends or for any larger moral purpose. Only a sovereign commonwealth established by a contract between the ruler and the ruled could enable human beings to meet those needs by limiting the free exercise of the natural human pursuit of self-interest with all its potential for conflict.

According to Hobbes human beings in their natural state are inclined to a "perpetual and restless desire" for power. Because all people want and, in their natural state, possess a natural right to everything, their equality breeds enmity, competition, diffidence, and perpetual quarreling—"a war of every man against every man," as Hobbes put it in a famous summary.

In such condition there is no place for industry, because the fruit thereof is uncertain; and consequently no culture of the Earth; no navigation nor use of the commodities that may be imported by sea; no commodious building; no instruments of moving and removing such things as require much force; no knowledge of the face of the Earth; no account of time; no arts; no letters; no society; and, which is worst of all, continual fear and danger of violent death; and the life of man solitary, poor, nasty, brutish, and short.[7]

[7]Thomas Hobbes, *Leviathan*, Parts I and II, ed. by H. W. Schneider (Indianapolis: Bobbs-Merrill, 1958), pp. 86, 106–107.

The famous title page illustration for Hobbes's *Leviathan*. The ruler is pictured as absolute lord of his lands, but note that the ruler incorporates the mass of individuals whose self-interests are best served by their willing consent to accept him and cooperate with him. Courtesy of the Library of Congress

As seen in this passage, Hobbes, contrary to Aristotle and Christian thinkers like Thomas Aquinas (1225–1274), rejected the view that human beings are naturally sociable. Rather, they are self-centered creatures who lack a master. Thus, whereas earlier and later philosophers saw the original human state as a paradise from which humankind had fallen, Hobbes saw it as a state of natural, inevitable conflict in which neither safety, security, nor any final authority existed. Human beings in this state of nature were constantly haunted by fear of destruction and death.

Human beings escaped this terrible state of nature, according to Hobbes, only by entering into a particular kind of political contract according to which they agreed to live in a commonwealth tightly ruled by a recognized sovereign. This contract obliged every person, for the sake of peace and self-defense, to agree to set aside personal rights to all things and to be content with as much liberty against others as he or she would allow others against himself or herself. All agreed to live according to a secularized version of the golden rule, "Do not that to another which you would not have done to yourself."[8]

Because, however, words and promises are insufficient to guarantee this agreement, the contract also established the coercive use of force by the sovereign to compel compliance. Believing the dangers of anarchy to be always greater than those of tyranny, Hobbes thought that rulers should be absolute and unlimited in their power, once established as authority. Hobbes's political philosophy has no room for protest in the name of individual conscience or for individual appeal to some other legitimate authority beyond the sovereign. In a reply to critics of his position on sovereign authority, Hobbes pointed out the alternative:

The greatest [unhappiness] that in any form of government can possibly happen to the people in general is scarce sensible in respect of the miseries and horrible calamities that accompany a civil war or that dissolute condition of masterless men, without subjection to laws and a coercive power to tie their hands from rapine and revenge.[9]

The specific structure of this absolute government was not of enormous concern to Hobbes. He believed absolute authority might be lodged in either a monarch or a legislative body, but once that person or body had been granted authority, there existed no argument for appeal. For all practical purposes, obedience to the Hobbesian sovereign was absolute.

Hobbes's argument for an absolute political authority that could assure order aroused sharp opposition. Monarchists objected to his willingness to assign sovereign authority to a legislature. Republicans rejected his willingness to accept a monarchical authority. Many Christian writers, including those who supported the divine right of kings, furiously criticized his materialist arguments for an absolute political authority. Other Christian writers attacked his refusal to recognize the authority of either God or the church as standing beside or above his secular sovereign. The religious critique of Hobbes meant that his thought had little immediate practical impact, but his ideas influenced philosophical literature from the late seventeenth century onward.

John Locke: Defender of Moderate Liberty and Toleration

Locke (1632–1704) proved to be the most influential philosophical and political thinker of the seventeenth century. Although he was less original than Hobbes, his political

[8]Hobbes, *Leviathan*, Parts I and II, p. 130.
[9]Hobbes, *Leviathan*, Parts I and II, p. 152.

writings became a major source of criticism of absolutism and provided a foundation for later liberal political philosophy in both Europe and America. His philosophical works dealing with human knowledge became the most important work of psychology for the eighteenth century.

Locke's family had Puritan sympathies, and during the English Civil War his father had fought for the parliamentary forces against the Stuart monarchy. Although a highly intellectual person who was well read in all the major seventeenth-century natural philosophers, Locke became deeply involved with the tumultuous politics of the English Restoration period. He was a close associate of Anthony Ashley Cooper, the earl of Shaftesbury (1621–1683), considered by his contemporaries to be a radical in both religion and politics. Shaftesbury organized an unsuccessful rebellion against Charles II in 1682, after which both he and Locke, who lived with him, were forced to flee to Holland.

During his years of association with Shaftesbury and the opposition to Charles II, Locke wrote two treatises on government that were eventually published in 1690. In the first of these, he rejected arguments for absolute gov-

John Locke (1632–1704), defender of the rights of the people against rulers who think their power absolute. *John Locke (1632–1704).* By courtesy of the National Portrait Gallery, London ernment that based political authority on the patriarchal model of fathers ruling over a family. After the publication of this treatise, no major political philosopher again appealed to the patriarchal model. In that regard, though not widely read today, Locke's *First Treatise of Government* proved enormously important by clearing the philosophical decks, so to speak, of a long-standing traditional argument that could not stand up to rigorous analysis.

In his *Second Treatise of Government*, Locke presented an extended argument for a government that must necessarily be both responsible for and responsive to the concerns of the governed. Locke portrayed the natural human state as one of perfect freedom and equality in which everyone enjoyed, in an unregulated fashion, the natural rights of life, liberty, and property. Locke, contrary to Hobbes, regarded human beings in their natural state as creatures of reason and basic goodwill rather than of uncontrolled passion and selfishness. For Locke, human beings possess a strong capacity for dwelling more or less peacefully in society before they enter a political contract. What they experience in the state of nature is not a state of war, but a condition of competition and modest conflict that requires a political authority to sort out problems rather than to impose sovereign authority. They enter into the contract to form political society to secure and preserve the rights, liberty, and property that they already possess prior to the existence of political authority. In this respect, government exists to protect the best achievements and liberty of the state of nature, not to overcome them. Thus, by its very foundation, Locke's government is one of limited authority. (See "John Locke Denounces the Idea of Absolute Monarchy" in the previous chapter, page 395).

The conflict that Hobbes believed characterized the state of nature emerged for Locke only when rulers failed to preserve people's natural freedom and attempted to enslave them by absolute rule. The relationship between rulers and the governed is that of trust, and if the rulers betray that trust, the governed have the right to replace them. In this regard, Locke's position resembled that of Thomas Aquinas, who also permitted rebellion when government violated laws of nature.

In his *Letter Concerning Toleration* (1689), Locke used the premises of the as yet unpublished *Second Treatise* to defend extensive religious toleration among Christians, which he saw as an answer to the destructive religious conflict of the past two centuries. To make his case for toleration, Locke claimed that each individual was required to work out his or her own religious salvation and these efforts might lead various people to join different religious groups. For its part, government existed by its very nature to preserve property, not to make religious decisions for its citizens. Governments that attempted to impose religious uniformity thus misunderstood their real purpose. Moreover, government-imposed religious uniformity could not achieve real religious ends, because assent to religious truth must be freely given by the individual's conscience rather than by force. Consequently, Locke urged a wide degree of religious toleration among differing voluntary Christian groups. He did not, however, extend toleration to Roman Catholics, whom he believed to have given allegiance to a foreign prince (i.e., the pope), to non-Christians, or to atheists, whom he believed could not be trusted to keep their word. Despite these limitations, Locke's *Letter Concerning Toleration* established a powerful foundation for the future extension of toleration, religious liberty, and the separation of church and state. His vision of such expansive toleration was partially realized in England after 1688 and most fully in the United States after the American Revolution.

Finally, just as Newton had set forth laws of astronomy and gravitation, Locke hoped to elucidate the basic structures of human thought. He did so in the most immediately influential of his books, his *Essay Concerning Human Understanding* (1690), which became the major work of European psychology during the eighteenth century. There, Locke portrayed a person's mind at birth as a blank tablet whose content would be determined by sense experience. His vision of the mind has been aptly compared to an early version of behaviorism. It was a reformer's psychology, which contended that the human condition could be improved by changing the environment.

Locke's view of psychology rejected the Christian understanding of original sin, yet he believed his psychology had preserved religious knowledge. He thought such knowledge came through divine revelation in Scripture and also from the conclusions that human reason could draw from observing nature. He hoped this

---

MAJOR WORKS OF THE SCIENTIFIC REVOLUTION

1543	*On the Revolutions of the Heavenly Spheres* (Copernicus)
1605	*The Advancement of Learning* (Bacon)
1609	*The New Astronomy* (Kepler)
1610	*The Starry Messenger* (Galileo)
1620	*Novum Organum* (Bacon)
1632	*Dialogue on the Two Chief World Systems* (Galileo)
1637	*Discourse on Method* (Descartes)
1651	*Leviathan* (Hobbes)
1687	*Principia Mathematica* (Newton)
1689	*Letter Concerning Toleration* (Locke)
1690	*An Essay Concerning Human Understanding* (Locke)
1690	*Treatises of Government* (Locke)

interpretation of religious knowledge would prevent human beings from falling into what he regarded as fanaticism arising from the claims of alleged private revelations and irrationality arising from superstition. For Locke, reason and revelation were compatible and together could sustain a moderate religious faith that would avoid religious conflict.

▼ The New Institutions of Expanding Natural Knowledge

One of the most fundamental features of the expansion of science was the emerging idea that *genuinely new knowledge* about nature and humankind could be discovered. In the late Middle Ages, the recovery of Aristotle and the rise of humanistic learning looked back to the ancients to rediscover the kind of knowledge that later Europeans needed. Luther and other Reformers had seen themselves as recovering a better understanding of the original Christian message. By contrast, the proponents of the new natural knowledge and the new philosophy sought to pursue what Bacon called the advancement of learning. New knowledge would be continuously created. This outlook required new institutions.

The expansion of natural knowledge had powerful social implications. Both the new science and the philosophical outlook associated with it opposed Scholasticism and Aristotelianism. These were not simply disembodied philosophical outlooks, but ways of approaching the world of knowledge most scholars in the universities of

Colbert was Louis XIV's most influential minister. He sought to expand the economic life of France and to associate the monarchy with the emerging new science from which he hoped might flow new inventions and productive technology. Here he is portrayed presenting members of the French Academy of Science to the monarch. On the founding of the French Academy. Henri Testelin (1616–1695). (after Le Brun). Minister of Finance Colbert presenting the members of the Royal Academy of Science (founded in 1667) to Louis XIV. Study for a tapestry. Photo: Gerard Blot. Chateaux de Versailles et de Trianon, Versailles, France. Reunion des Musées Nationaux/Art Resource, NY

the day still believed in. Such scholars had a clear, vested interest in preserving those traditional outlooks. As they saw it, they were defending the ancients against the moderns. Not surprisingly, the advanced thinkers of the seventeenth century often criticized the universities. For example, in his *Discourse on Method*, Descartes was highly critical of the education he had received. Hobbes filled the *Leviathan* with caustic remarks about the kind of learning then dominating schools and universities, and Locke advocated educational reform.

Some of the criticism of universities was exaggerated. Medical faculties, on the whole, welcomed the advancement of learning in their fields of study. Most of the natural philosophers had themselves received their education at universities. Moreover, however slowly new ideas might penetrate universities, the expanding world of natural knowledge would be taught to future generations. With that diffusion of science into the universities came new supporters of scientific knowledge beyond the small group of natural philosophers themselves. Universities also provided much of the physical and financial support for teaching and investigating natural philosophy and employed many scientists, the most important of whom was Newton himself. University support of science did, however, vary according to country, with the Italian universities being far more supportive than the French.

Yet because of the reluctance of universities to rapidly assimilate the new science, its pioneers quickly understood that they required a framework for cooperating and sharing of information that went beyond existing intellectual institutions. Consequently, they and their supporters established what have been termed "institutions of sharing" that allowed information and ideas associated with the new science to be gathered, exchanged, and debated.[10] The most famous of these institutions was the Royal Society of London, founded in 1660, whose members consciously saw themselves as following the path Bacon had laid out almost a half century earlier. The Royal Society had been preceded by the Academy of Experiments in Florence in 1657 and was followed by the French Academy of Science in 1666. Germany only slowly overcame the destruction of the Thirty Years' War, and the Berlin Academy of Science was not founded until 1700. In addition to these major institutions, the new science was discussed and experiments were carried out in many local societies and academies.

These societies met regularly to hear papers and observe experiments. One of the reasons many early experiments achieved

[10]Lewis Pyenson and Susan Sheets-Pyenson, *Servants of Nature: A History of Scientific Institutions, Enterprises, and Sensibilities* (New York: W. W. Norton, 1999), p. 75.

credibility was that they had been observed by persons of social respectability who belonged to one or more of the societies and who, because of their social standing, were presumed to be truthful witnesses of what they had observed. These groups also published information relating to natural philosophy and often organized libraries for their members. Perhaps most important, they attempted to separate the discussion and exploration of natural philosophy from the religious and political conflicts of the day. They intended science to exemplify an arena for the polite exchange of ideas and for civil disagreement and debate. This particular function of science as fostering civility became one of its major attractions.

The activities of the societies also constituted a kind of crossroads between their own members always drawn from the literate classes, and people outside the elite classes, whose skills and practical knowledge might be important for advancing the new science. The latter included craftspeople who could manufacture scientific instruments, sailors whose travels had taken them to foreign parts and who might report on the plants and animals they had seen there, and workers who had practical knowledge of problems in the countryside. In this respect, the expansion of the European economy and the drive toward empires contributed to the growth of the scientific endeavor by bringing back to Europe specimens and experiences that required classification, analysis, and observation.

In good Baconian fashion, the members of the societies presented science as an enterprise that could aid the goals of government and the growth of the economy. For example, mathematicians portrayed themselves as being useful for solving surveying and other engineering problems and for improving armaments. Furthermore, people who had ideas for improving production, navigation, or military artillery might seek the support of the associated societies. In the English context, these people became known as *projectors* and were often regarded as people simply eager to sell their often improbable ideas to the highest bidder. Nonetheless, their activities brought the new science and technology before a wider public. (See "Compare & Connect: Descartes and Swift Debate the Scientific Enterprise" pages 432–433.)

The work, publications, and interaction of the scientific societies with both the government and private business established a distinct role and presence for scientific knowledge in European social life. By 1700, that presence was relatively modest, but it would grow steadily during the coming decades. The groups associated with the new science saw themselves as championing modern practical achievements of applied knowledge and urging religious toleration, mutual forbearance, and political liberty. Such people would form the social base for the eighteenth-century movement known as the **Enlightenment**.

▼ Women in the World of the Scientific Revolution

The absence of women in the emergence of the new science of the seventeenth century has been a matter of much historical speculation. What characteristics of early modern European intellectual and cultural life worked against extensive contributions by women? Why have we heard so little of the activity by women that did actually occur in regard to the new science?

The same factors that had long excluded women from participating in most intellectual life continued to exclude them from working in the emerging natural philosophy. Traditionally, the institutions of European intellectual life had all but excluded women. Both monasteries and universities had been institutions associated with celibate male clerical culture. Except for a few exceptions in Italy, women had not been admitted to either medieval or early modern European universities; they would continue to be excluded from them until the end of the nineteenth century. Women could and did exercise influence over princely courts where natural philosophers, such as Galileo, sought patronage, but they usually did not determine those patronage decisions or benefit from them. Queen Christina of Sweden (r. 1632–1654), who brought René Descartes to Stockholm to provide the regulations for a new science

Margaret Cavendish, who wrote widely on scientific subjects, was the most accomplished woman associated with the new science in seventeenth-century England. ImageWorks/Mary Evans Picture Library Ltd.

academy, was an exception. When various scientific societies were founded, women were not admitted to membership. In that regard, there were virtually no social spaces that might have permitted women to pursue science easily.

Yet a few isolated women from two different social settings did manage to engage in the new scientific activity—noblewomen and women from the artisan class. In both cases, they could do so only through their husbands or male relatives.

The social standing of certain noblewomen allowed them to command the attention of ambitious natural philosophers who were part of their husband's social circle. Margaret Cavendish (1623–1673) actually made significant contributions to the scientific literature of the day. As a girl she had been privately tutored and become widely read. Her marriage to the duke of Newcastle introduced her into a circle of natural philosophers. She understood the new science, quarreled with the ideas of Descartes and Hobbes, and criticized the Royal Society for being more interested in novel scientific instruments than in solving practical problems. Her most important works were *Observations Upon Experimental Philosophy* (1666) and *Grounds of Natural Philosophy* (1668). She was the only woman in the seventeenth century to be allowed to visit a meeting of the Royal Society of London. (See "Margaret Cavendish Questions the Fascination with Scientific Instruments.")

MARGARET CAVENDISH QUESTIONS THE FASCINATION WITH SCIENTIFIC INSTRUMENTS

Margaret Cavendish, duchess of Newcastle, was the most scientifically informed woman of seventeenth-century England. She read widely in natural philosophy and had many acquaintances who were involved in the new science. Although she was enthusiastic about the promise of science, she also frequently criticized some of its leading proponents, including Descartes and Hobbes. She was skeptical of the activities of the newly established Royal Society of London, which she was once permitted to visit. She believed some of its members had become overly enthusiastic about experimentation and new scientific instruments for their own sakes and had begun to ignore the practical questions that she thought science should address. In this respect, her criticism of the Royal Society and its experiments is a Baconian one. She thought the society had replaced scholastic speculation with experimental speculation and that both kinds of speculation ignored important problems of immediate utility.

Why might Margaret Cavendish think that the experiments which were reported about new optical instruments dealt with superficial wonders? Why does she contrast experimental philosophy with the beneficial arts? Do you find a feminist perspective in her comparison of the men of the Royal Society with boys playing with bubbles?

Art has intoxicated so many men's brains, and wholly imployed their thoughts and bodily actions about phaenomena, or the exterior figure of objects, as all better Arts and Studies are laid aside. ... But though there be numerous Books written of the wonder of these [experimental optical] Glasses, yet I cannot perceive any such; at best, they are but superficial wonders, as I may call them. But could Experimental Philosophers find out more beneficial Arts then our Fore-fathers have done, either for the better increase of Vegetables and brute Animals to nourish our bodies, or better and commodious contrivances in the Art of Architecture to build us houses, or for the advancing of trade and traffick . . . it would not only be worth their labour, but of as much praise as could be given to them: But, as Boys that play with watry Bubbles . . . are worthy of reproof rather than praise, for wasting their time with useless sports; so those that addict themselves to unprofitable Arts, spend more time than they reap benefit thereby.

From Margaret Cavendish, *Observations Upon Experimental Philosophy*, to which is added, *The Description of a New Blazing World* (London, 1666), pp. 10–11, as quoted in Anna Battigelli, *Margaret Cavendish and the Exiles of the Mind* (Lexington: University of Kentucky Press, 1998), p. 94.

Women associated with artisan crafts actually achieved greater freedom to pursue the new sciences than did noblewomen. Traditionally, women had worked in artisan workshops, often with their husbands, and might take over the business when their spouse died. In Germany, much study of astronomy occurred in these settings, with women assisting their fathers or husbands. One German female astronomer, Maria Cunitz, published a book on astronomy that many people thought her husband had written until he added a preface supporting her sole authorship. Elisabetha and Johannes Hevelius constituted a wife-and-husband astronomical team, as did Maria Winkelmann and her husband Gottfried Kirch. In each case, the wife served as the assistant to an artisan astronomer. Although Winkelmann discovered a comet in 1702, it was not until 1930 that the discovery was ascribed to her rather than to her husband. Nonetheless, contemporary philosophers did recognize her abilities and understanding of astronomy. Winkelmann had worked jointly with her husband who was the official astronomer of the Berlin Academy of Sciences and was responsible for an official calendar the academy published. When her husband died in 1710, Winkelmann applied for permission to continue the work, basing her application for the post on the guild's tradition of allowing women to continue their husbands' work, in this case the completion of observations required to create an accurate calendar. After much debate, the academy formally rejected her application on the grounds of her gender, although its members knew of her ability and previous accomplishments. Years later, she returned to the Berlin Academy as an assistant to her son, who had been appointed astronomer. Again, the academy insisted that she leave, forcing her to abandon astronomy. She died in 1720.

Such policies of exclusion, however, did not altogether prevent women from acquiring knowledge about scientific endeavors. Margaret Cavendish had composed a *Description of a New World, Called the Blazing World* (1666) to introduce women to the new science. Other examples of scientific writings for a female audience were Bernard de Fontenelle's *Conversations on the Plurality of Worlds* and Francesco Algarotti's *Newtonianism for Ladies* (1737). During the 1730s, Emilie du Châtelet (1706–1749) aided Voltaire in his composition of an important French popularization of Newton's science. Her knowledge of mathematics was more extensive than his and crucial to his completing his book. She also translated Newton's *Principia* into French, an accomplishment made possible only by her exceptional understanding of advanced mathematics.

Still, with few exceptions, women were barred from science and medicine until the late nineteenth century, and not until the twentieth century did they enter these fields in significant numbers. Not only did the institutions of science exclude them, but also, the ideas associated with medical practice, philosophy, and biology suggested that women and their minds were essentially different from, and inferior to, men. By the early eighteenth century, despite isolated precedents of women pursuing natural knowledge, reading scientific literature, and engaging socially with natural philosophers, it had become a fundamental assumption of European intellectual life that the pursuit of knowledge about nature was a male vocation.

▼ The New Science and Religious Faith

For many contemporaries, the new science posed a potential challenge to religion. Three major issues were at stake. First, certain theories and discoveries did not agree with biblical statements about the heavens. Second, who would decide conflicts between religion and science—church authorities or the natural philosophers? Finally, for many religious thinkers, the new science seemed to replace a universe of spiritual meaning and significance with a purely materialistic one. Yet most of the natural philosophers genuinely saw their work as supporting religious belief by contributing to a deeper knowledge of the divine. Their efforts and those of their supporters to reconcile faith and the new science constituted a fundamental factor in the spread of science and its widespread acceptance in educated European circles. The process was not an easy one.

The Case of Galileo

The condemnation of Galileo by Roman Catholic authorities in 1633 is the single most famous incident of conflict between modern science and religious institutions. For centuries it was interpreted as exemplifying the forces of religion smothering scientific knowledge. More recent research has modified that picture.

The condemnation of Copernicanism and of Galileo occurred at a particularly difficult moment in the history of the Roman Catholic Church. In response to Protestant emphasis on private interpretation of Scripture, the Council of Trent (1545–1563) had stated that only the church itself possessed the authority to interpret the Bible. Furthermore, after the Council, the Roman Catholic Church had adopted a more literalist mode of reading the Bible in response to the Protestant emphasis on the authority of Scripture. Galileo's championing of Copernicanism took place in this particular climate of opinion and practice when the Roman Catholic Church, on the one hand, could not surrender the interpretation of the Bible to a layman and, on the other, had difficulty moving beyond a literal reading of the Bible, lest the Protestants accuse it of abandoning Scripture.

In a *Letter to the Grand Duchess Christina* (1615), Galileo, as a layman, had published his own views about how scripture should be interpreted to accommodate the new science. (See "Galileo Discusses the Relationship of Science to the Bible," page 434.) To certain

Descartes and Swift Debate the Scientific Enterprise

THROUGHOUT THE SEVENTEENTH and eighteenth centuries various writers asserted that the growth of natural knowledge held the promise of improving the human situation. Others, who did not dispute the truth or correctness of the new natural knowledge, nonetheless questioned whether it could actually improve the human situation. In these two documents the French philosopher René Descartes upholds the former position while many decades later the English satirist Jonathan Swift questions the usefulness of the new natural knowledge pursued by the Royal Society of London and by implication by other European scientific academies.

QUESTIONS

1. How does Descartes compare the usefulness of science with previous speculative philosophy?

2. What, if any, limits does he place on the extension of scientific knowledge?

3. Why might Swift have so emphasized what he saw as the impracticality of science?

4. How might Swift's presentation be seen as manifesting jealousy of a literary figure toward the growing influence of science?

5. How does Swift's passage serve as an effort to refute the promise of science championed by Bacon and Descartes?

I. Descartes Explores the Promise of Expanding Natural Knowledge

In 1637, Descartes published his Discourse on Method. *He wrote against what he believed to be the useless speculations of scholastic philosophy. He championed the careful investigation of physical nature on the grounds that it would expand the scope of human knowledge beyond anything previously achieved and, in doing so, make human beings the masters of nature. This passage contains much of the broad intellectual and cultural argument that led to the ever-growing influence and authority of science from the seventeenth century onward.*

My speculations were indeed truly pleasing to me; but I recognize that other men have theirs, which perhaps please them even more. As soon, however, as I had acquired some general notions regarding physics, and on beginning to make trial of them in various special difficulties had observed how far they can carry us and how much they differ from the principles hitherto employed, I believed that I could not keep them hidden without grievously sinning against the law which lays us under obligation to promote, as far as in us lies, the general good of all mankind. For they led me to see that it is possible to obtain knowledge highly useful in life, and that in place of the speculative philosophy taught in the Schools we can have a practical philosophy, by means of which, knowing the force and the actions of fire, water, air, and of the stars, of the heavens, and of all the bodies that surround us—knowing them as distinctly as we know the various crafts of the artisans—we may in the same fashion employ them in all the uses for which they are suited, thus rendering ourselves the masters and possessors of nature. This is to be desired, not only with a view to the invention of an infinity of arts by which we would be enabled to enjoy without heavy labor the fruits of the earth and all its conveniences, but above all for the preservation of health, which is, without doubt, of all blessings in this life, the first of all goods and the foundation on which the others rest. For the mind is so dependent on the temper and disposition of the bodily organisms that if any means can ever be found to render men wiser and more capable than they have hitherto been, I believe that it is in the science of medicine that the means must be sought. . . . With no wish to depreciate it, I am yet sure there is no one, even of those engaged in the profession, who does not admit that all we know is almost nothing in comparison with what remains to be discovered; and that we could be freed from innumerable maladies, both of body and of mind, and even perhaps from the infirmities of age, if we had sufficient knowledge of their causes and of the remedies provided by nature.

Source: From René Descartes, *Discourse on Method*, in Norman Kemp Smith, ed., *Descartes's Philosophical Writings* (New York: The Modern Library, 1958), pp. 130–131. Reprinted by permission of Macmillan Press Ltd.

During the eighteenth century farm women normally worked in the home and performed such tasks as churning butter as well as caring for children. As time passed tasks such as making butter were mechanized and women were displaced from such work. Francis Wheatley (RA) (1747–1801) *Morning*, signed and dated 1799, oil on canvas, 17½ × 21½ in. (44.5 × 54.5 cm), Yale Center for British Art, Paul Mellon Collection, USA/Bridgeman Art Library (B1977.14.120)

15

Society and Economy Under the Old Regime in the Eighteenth Century

▼ **Major Features of Life in the Old Regime**
Maintenance of Tradition • Hierarchy and Privilege

▼ **The Aristocracy**
Varieties of Aristocratic Privilege • Aristocratic Resurgence

▼ **The Land and Its Tillers**
Peasants and Serfs • Aristocratic Domination of the Countryside: The English Game Laws

▼ **Family Structures and the Family Economy**
Households • The Family Economy • Women and the Family Economy • Children and the World of the Family Economy

▼ **The Revolution in Agriculture**
New Crops and New Methods • Expansion of the Population

▼ **The Industrial Revolution of the Eighteenth Century**
A Revolution in Consumption • Industrial Leadership of Great Britain • New Methods of Textile Production • The Steam Engine • Iron Production • The Impact of the Agricultural and Industrial Revolutions on Working Women

▼ **The Growth of Cities**
Patterns of Preindustrial Urbanization • Urban Classes • The Urban Riot

▼ **The Jewish Population: The Age of the Ghetto**

▼ **In Perspective**

DURING THE FRENCH Revolution and the turmoil that upheaval spawned, it became customary to refer to the patterns of social, political, and economic relationships that had existed in France before 1789 as the *ancien régime*, or the **Old Regime**. The term has come to be applied generally to the life and institutions of pre-revolutionary Europe. Politically, on the continent, though not in Great Britain, it meant the rule of theoretically absolute monarchies with growing bureaucracies and aristocratically led armies. Economically, a scarcity of food, the predominance of agriculture, slow transport, a low level of iron production, comparatively unsophisticated financial institutions, and, in some cases, competitive commercial overseas empires characterized the Old Regime. Socially, men and women living during the period saw themselves less as individuals than as members of distinct corporate bodies that possessed certain privileges or rights as a group.

Tradition, hierarchy, a corporate feeling, and privilege were the chief social characteristics of the Old Regime. Yet it was by no means a static society. Change and innovation were fermenting in its midst. Farming became more commercialized, and both food production and the size of the population increased. The early stages of the Industrial Revolution made more consumer goods available, and domestic consumption expanded throughout the century. The colonies in the Americas provided strong demand for European goods and manufactures. Merchants in seaports and other cities were expanding their businesses. By preparing their states for war, European governments put new demands on the resources and the economic organizations of their nations. The spirit of rationality that had been so important to the scientific revolution of the seventeenth century continued to manifest itself in the economic life of the eighteenth century. The Old Regime itself fostered the changes that eventually transformed it into a different kind of society.

▼ Major Features of Life in the Old Regime

Socially, pre-revolutionary Europe was based on (1) aristocratic elites possessing a wide variety of inherited legal privileges; (2) established churches intimately related to the state and the aristocracy; (3) an urban labor force usually organized into guilds; and (4) a rural peasantry subject to high taxes and feudal dues. Of course, the men and women living during this period did not know it was the Old Regime. Most of them earned their livelihoods and passed their lives as their forebearers had done for generations before them and as they expected their children to do after them.

Maintenance of Tradition

During the eighteenth century, the past weighed more heavily on people's minds than did the future. Few persons outside the government bureaucracies, the expanding merchant groups, and the movement for reform called the Enlightenment (see Chapter 17) considered change or innovation desirable. This was especially true of social relationships. Both nobles and peasants, for different reasons, repeatedly called for the restoration of traditional, or customary, rights. The nobles asserted what they considered their ancient rights against the intrusion of the expanding monarchical bureaucracies. The peasants, through petitions and revolts, called for the revival or the maintenance of the customary manorial rights that allowed them access to particular lands, courts, or grievance procedures.

Except for the early industrial development in Britain and the accompanying expansion of personal consumption, the eighteenth-century economy was also predominantly traditional. The quality and quantity of the grain harvest remained the most important fact of life for most of the population and the gravest concern for governments.

Hierarchy and Privilege

Closely related to this traditional social and economic outlook was the hierarchical structure of the society. The medieval sense of rank and degree not only persisted, but also became more rigid during the century. In several continental cities, sumptuary laws regulating the dress of the different classes remained on the books. These laws forbade persons in one class or occupation from wearing clothes like those worn by their social superiors. The laws, which sought to make the social hierarchy easily visible, were largely ineffective by this time. What really enforced the hierarchy was the corporate nature of social relationships.

Each state or society was considered a community composed of numerous smaller communities. Eighteenth-century Europeans did not enjoy what Americans regard as "individual rights." Instead, a person enjoyed such rights and privileges as were guaranteed to the particular communities or groups of which she or he was a part. The "community" might include the village, the municipality, the nobility, the church, the guild, a university, or the parish. In turn, each of these bodies enjoyed certain privileges, some great and some small. The privileges might involve exemption from taxation or from some especially humiliating punishment, the right to practice a trade or craft, the right of one's children to pursue a particular occupation, or, for the church, the right to collect the tithe.

▼ The Aristocracy

The eighteenth century was the great age of the aristocracy. The nobility constituted approximately 1 to 5 percent of the population of any given country. Yet in every country, it was the single wealthiest sector of the population, had the widest degree of social, political, and economic power, and set the tone of polite society. In most countries, the nobility had their own separate house in the parliament, estates, or diet. Only nobles had any kind of representation in Hungary and Poland. Land continued to provide the aristocracy with its largest source of income, but aristocrats did not merely own estates: Their influence was felt throughout social and economic life. In much of Europe, however, manual labor was regarded as beneath a noble. In Spain, it was assumed that even the poorer nobles would lead lives of idleness. In other nations, however, the nobility often fostered economic innovation and embraced the commercial spirit. Such willingness to change helped protect the nobility's wealth and, in both Great Britain and France, gave them common interest with the commercial classes who were also eager to see the economy grow and protect their property.

Varieties of Aristocratic Privilege

To be an aristocrat was a matter of birth and legal privilege. This much the aristocracy had in common across the Continent. In almost every other respect, they differed markedly from country to country.

British Nobility   The smallest, wealthiest, best defined, and most socially responsible aristocracy resided in Great Britain. It consisted of about four hundred families, and the eldest male members of each family sat in the House of Lords. Through the corruptions of the electoral system, these families also controlled many seats in the House of Commons. The estates of the British nobility ranged from a few thousand to 50,000 acres, from which they received rents. The nobles owned about one fourth of all the arable land in the country. Increasingly, the British aristocracy invested its wealth in commerce, canals, urban real estate, mines, and even industrial ventures. Because only the eldest son inherited the title (called a "peerage"), the right to sit in the House of Lords, and the land, younger sons moved into commerce, the army, the professions, and the church. British landowners in both houses of Parliament levied taxes and also paid them. They had few significant legal privileges, but their direct or indirect control of local government gave them immense political power and social influence. The aristocracy dominated the society and politics of the English counties. Their country houses, many of which were built in the eighteenth century, were the centers of local society.

French Nobility   The situation of the continental nobilities was less clear-cut. In France, the approximately 400,000 nobles were divided between nobles "of the sword," or those whose nobility was derived from military service, and those "of the robe," who had acquired their titles either by serving in the bureaucracy or by having purchased them. The two groups had quarreled in the past but often cooperated during the eighteenth century to defend their common privileges.

The French nobles were also divided between those who held office or favor with the royal court at Versailles and those who did not. The court nobility reaped the immense wealth that could be gained from holding high office. The nobles' hold on such offices intensified during the century. By the late 1780s, appointments to the church, the army, and the bureaucracy, as well as other profitable positions, tended to go to the nobles already established in court circles. Whereas these well-connected aristocrats were rich, the provincial nobility, called *hobereaux*, were often little better off than wealthy peasants.

Despite differences in rank, origin, and wealth, certain hereditary privileges set all French aristocrats apart from the rest of society. They were exempt from many taxes. For example, most French nobles did not pay the *taille*, or land tax, the basic tax of the Old Regime. The nobles were technically liable for payment of the **vingtième**, or the "twentieth," which resembled an income tax, but they rarely had to pay it in full. The nobles were not liable for the royal **corvées**, or forced labor on public works, which fell on the peasants. In addition to these exemptions, French nobles could collect feudal dues from their tenants and enjoyed exclusive hunting and fishing privileges.

Eastern European Nobilities   East of the Elbe River, the character of the nobility became even more complicated and repressive. Throughout the area, the military traditions of the aristocracy remained important. In Poland, there were thousands of nobles, or *szlachta*, who were entirely exempt from taxes after 1741. Until 1768, these Polish aristocrats possessed the right of life and death over their serfs. Most of the Polish nobility were relatively poor. A few rich nobles who had immense estates exercised political power in the fragile Polish state.

In Austria and Hungary, the nobility continued to possess broad judicial powers over the peasantry through their manorial courts. They also enjoyed various degrees of exemption from taxation. The wealthiest of them, Prince Esterhazy of Hungary, owned 10 million acres of land.

In Prussia, after the accession of Frederick the Great in 1740, the position of the Junker nobles became much stronger. Frederick's various wars required their full support. He drew his officers almost wholly from the Junker

A Closer ▶ LOOK

AN ARISTOCRATIC COUPLE

PORTRAITS, SUCH AS this one of the English landowner, *Robert Andrews and His Wife*, by Thomas Gainsborough (1728–1788), contain many clues to the aristocratic dominance of landed society.

Andrews's gun and dog indicate his exclusive right to hunt game on his land.

His wife's sitting against the expanse of his landed estate suggests the character of their legal relationship, whereby he could have controlled her property, which would have thus become an extension of his.

© National Gallery, London

To examine this image in an interactive fashion, please go to www.myhistorylab.com

myhistorylab

The market price of the wheat raised on his estate (known in England as corn) would have been protected by various import laws enacted by the English Parliament whose membership was dominated by landowners such as Andrews himself.

class. Nobles also increasingly made up the bureaucracy. As in other parts of eastern Europe, the Prussian nobles had extensive judicial authority over the serfs.

In Russia, the eighteenth century saw what amounted to the creation of the nobility. Peter the Great's (r. 1682–1725) linking of state service and noble social status through the Table of Ranks (1722) established among Russian nobles a self-conscious class identity that had not previously existed. Thereafter, they were determined to resist compulsory state service. In 1736, Empress Anna (r. 1730–1740) reduced such service to twenty-five years. In 1762, Peter III (r. 1762) exempted the greatest nobles entirely from compulsory service. In 1785, in the Charter of the Nobility, Catherine the Great (r. 1762–1796) legally defined the rights and privileges of noble men and women in exchange for the assurance that the nobility would serve the state voluntarily. Noble privileges included the right of transmitting noble status to a nobleman's wife and children, the judicial protection of noble rights and property, considerable power over the serfs, and exemption from personal taxes.

Aristocratic Resurgence

The Russian Charter of the Nobility constituted one aspect of the broader European-wide development termed the *aristocratic resurgence*. This was the nobility's reaction to the threat to their social position and privileges that they felt from the expanding power of the monarchies. This resurgence took several forms in the eighteenth century.

First, all nobilities tried to preserve their exclusiveness by making it more difficult to become a noble. Second, they pushed to reserve appointments to the officer corps of the armies, the senior posts in the bureaucracies and government ministries, and the upper ranks of the church exclusively for nobles. By doing this, they hoped to resist the encroaching power of the monarchies.

Third, the nobles attempted to use the authority of existing aristocratically controlled institutions against the power of the monarchies. These institutions included the British Parliament, the French courts, or *parlements*, and the local aristocratic estates and provincial diets in Germany and the Habsburg Empire.

Fourth, the nobility sought to improve its financial position by gaining further exemptions from taxation or by collecting higher rents or long-forgotten feudal dues from the peasantry. The nobility tried to shore up its position by various appeals to traditional and often ancient privileges that had lapsed over time. This aristocratic challenge to the monarchies was a fundamental political fact of the day and a potentially disruptive one.

▼ The Land and Its Tillers

Land was the economic basis of eighteenth-century life and the foundation of the status and power of the nobility. Well over three fourths of all Europeans lived in the country, and few of them ever traveled more than a few miles from their birthplace. Except for the nobility and the wealthier nonaristocratic landowners, most people who dwelled on the land were poor, and in many regions, desperately poor. They lived in various states of economic

and social dependency, exploitation, and vulnerability. (See "Two Eighteenth-Century Writers Contemplate the Effects of Different Economic Structures," pages 458–459.)

Peasants and Serfs

Rural social dependency related directly to the land. The nature of the dependency differed sharply for free peasants, such as English tenants and most French cultivators, and for the serfs of Germany, Austria, and Russia, who were legally bound to a particular plot of land and a particular lord. Yet everywhere, the class that owned most of the land also controlled the local government and the courts. For example, in Great Britain, all farmers and smaller tenants had the legal rights of English citizens. The justices of the peace, however, who presided over the county courts and who could call out the local militia, were always substantial landowners, as were the members of Parliament, who made the laws. In eastern Europe, the landowners presided over the manorial courts. On the Continent, the burden of taxation fell on the tillers of the soil.

Obligations of Peasants The power of the landlord increased as one moved across Europe from west to east. Most French peasants owned some land, but there were a few serfs in eastern France. Nearly all French peasants were subject to certain feudal dues, called *banalités*. These included the required use-for-payment of the lord's, or **seigneur's**, mill to grind grain and his oven to bake bread. The seigneur could also require a certain number of days each year of the peasant's labor. This practice of forced labor was termed the *corvée*. Because French peasants rarely possessed enough land to support their families, they had to rent more land from the seigneur and were also subject to feudal dues attached to those plots. In Prussia and Austria, despite attempts by the monarchies late in the century to improve the lot of the serfs, the landlords continued to exercise almost complete control over them. In many of the Habsburg lands, law and custom required the serfs to provide service, or **robot**, to the lords.

Serfs were worst off in Russia. There, nobles reckoned their wealth by the number of "souls," or male serfs, they owned rather than the size of their acreage. Russian landlords, in effect, regarded serfs merely as economic commodities. They could demand as many as six days a week of labor, known as *barshchina*, from the serfs. Like Prussian and Austrian landlords, they enjoyed the right to punish their serfs. On their own authority, Russian landlords could even exile a serf to Siberia. Serfs had no legal recourse against the orders and whims of their lords. There was little difference between Russian serfdom and slavery.

In southeastern Europe, where the Ottoman Empire held sway, peasants were free, though landlords tried to

Eighteenth-century France had some of the best roads in the world, but they were often built with forced labor. French peasants were required to work part of each year on such projects. This system, called the *corvée*, was not abolished until the French Revolution in 1789.   Joseph Vernet, *Construction of a Road*. Louvre, Paris, France. Bridgeman-Giraudon/Art Resource, NY

landowners' political cooperation. Russia experienced vast peasant unrest, with well over fifty peasant revolts between 1762 and 1769. These culminated in Pugachev's Rebellion between 1773 and 1775, when Emelyan Pugachev (1726–1775) promised the serfs land of their own and freedom from their lords. All of southern Russia was in turmoil until the government brutally suppressed the rebellion. Thereafter, any thought of improving the condition of the serfs was set aside for a generation.

Pugachev's was the largest peasant uprising of the eighteenth century, but smaller peasant revolts or disturbances took place in Bohemia in 1775, in Transylvania in 1784, in Moravia in 1786, and in Austria in 1789. There were almost no revolts in Western Europe, but England experienced many rural riots. Rural rebellions were violent, but the peasants and serfs normally directed their wrath against property rather than per-

exert authority in every way. The domain of the landlords was termed a *çift*. The landlord was often an absentee who managed the estate through an overseer. During the seventeenth and eighteenth centuries, these landlords, like those elsewhere in Europe, often became more commercially oriented and turned to the production of crops, such as cotton, vegetables, potatoes, and maize, that they could sell in the market.

A scarcity of labor rather than the recognition of their legal rights supported the independence of the southeastern European peasants. A peasant might migrate from one landlord to another. Because the second landlord needed the peasant's labor, he had no reason to return him to the original landlord. During the seventeenth and eighteenth centuries, however, disorder originating in Constantinople (now Istanbul), the capital, spilled over into the Balkan Peninsula. In this climate, landlords increased their authority by offering their peasants protection from bandits or rebels who might destroy peasant villages. As in medieval times, the manor house or armed enclosure of a local landlord became the peasants' refuge. These landlords also owned all the housing and tools the peasants needed to work the land and also furnished their seed grain. Consequently, despite legal independence, Balkan peasants under the Ottoman Empire became largely dependent on the landlords, though never to the extent of serfs in eastern Europe or Russia.

Peasant Rebellions The Russian monarchy itself contributed to the further degradation of the serfs. Peter the Great gave whole villages to favored nobles. Later in the century, Catherine the Great confirmed the authority of the nobles over their serfs in exchange for the

Emelyan Pugachev (1726–1775) led the largest peasant revolt in Russian history. In this contemporary propaganda picture he is shown in chains. An inscription in Russian and German was printed below the picture decrying the evils of revolution and insurrection.   Bildarchiv Preussischer Kulturbesitz

sons. The rebels usually sought to reassert traditional or customary rights against practices that they perceived as innovations. Their targets were carefully chosen and included unfair pricing, onerous new or increased feudal dues, changes in methods of payment or land use, unjust officials, or extraordinarily brutal overseers and landlords. Peasant revolts were thus conservative in nature.

Aristocratic Domination of the Countryside: The English Game Laws

One of the clearest examples of aristocratic domination of the countryside and of aristocratic manipulation of the law to its own advantage was the English legislation on hunting.

Between 1671 and 1831, English landowners had the exclusive legal right to hunt game animals, including, in particular, hares, partridges, pheasants, and moor fowl. Similar legislation covered other animals such as deer, the killing of which by an unauthorized person became a capital offense in the eighteenth century. By law, only persons owning a particular amount of landed property could hunt these animals. Excluded from the right to hunt were all persons renting land, wealthy city merchants who did not own land, and poor people in cities, villages, and the countryside. The poor were excluded because the elite believed that allowing them to enjoy the sport of hunting would undermine their work habits. The city merchants were excluded because the landed gentry in Parliament wanted to demonstrate visibly and legally the superiority of landed wealth over commercial wealth. Thus, the various game laws upheld the superior status of the aristocracy and the landed gentry.

The game laws were a prime example of legislation related directly to economic and social status. The gentry who benefited from the laws and whose parliamentary representatives had passed them also served as the local justices of the peace who enforced the laws and punished their violation. The justices of the peace could levy fines and even have poachers impressed into the army. Gentry could also take civil legal action against wealthier poachers, such as rich farmers who rented land, and thus saddle them with immense legal fees. The gentry also employed gamekeepers to protect game from poachers. The gamekeepers were known to kill the dogs belonging to people suspected of poaching. By the middle of the century, gamekeepers had devised guns to shoot poachers who tripped their hidden levers.

A small industry arose to circumvent the game laws, however. Many poor people living either on an estate or in a nearby village would kill game for food. They believed the game actually belonged to the community, and this poaching increased during hard times. Poaching was thus one way for the poor to find food.

Even more important was the black market in game animals that the demand in the cities for this kind of luxury meat sustained. This created the possibility of poaching for profit, and indeed, poaching technically meant stealing or killing game for sale. Local people from both the countryside and the villages would steal the game and then sell it to intermediaries called *higglers.* Later, coachmen took over this function. The higglers and the coachmen would smuggle the game into the cities, where poulterers would sell it at a premium price. Everyone involved made a bit of money along the way. During the second half of the century, English aristocrats began to construct large game preserves. The rural poor, who had lost their rights to communal land as a result of its enclosure by the large landowners, resented these preserves, which soon became hunting grounds to organized gangs of poachers.

Penalties against poaching increased in the 1790s after the outbreak of the French Revolution, but so did the amount of poaching as the economic hardships increased. Britain's participation in the wars of the era put a greater burden on poor people as the demand for food in English cities grew along with their population. By the 1820s, both landowners and reformers called for a change in the law. In 1831, Parliament rewrote the game laws, retaining the landowners' possession of the game, but permitting them to allow other people to hunt it. Poaching continued, but the exclusive right of the landed classes to hunt game had ended.

▼ Family Structures and the Family Economy

In preindustrial Europe, the household was the basic unit of production and consumption. Few productive establishments employed more than a handful of people not belonging to the family of the owner, and those rare exceptions were in cities. Most Europeans, however, lived in rural areas. There, as well as in small towns and cities, the household mode of organization predominated on farms, in artisans' workshops, and in small merchants' shops. With that mode of economic organization, there developed what is known as the **family economy**. Its structure, as described here, had prevailed over most of Europe for centuries.

Households

What was a household in the preindustrial Europe of the Old Regime? There were two basic models, one characterizing northwestern Europe and the other eastern Europe.

Northwestern Europe In northwestern Europe, the household almost invariably consisted of a married couple, their children through their early teenage

During the seventeenth century the French Le Nain brothers painted scenes of French peasant life. Although the images softened many of the harsh realities of peasant existence, the clothing and the interiors were based on actual models and convey the character of the life of better-off French peasants whose lives would have continued very much the same into the eighteenth century.   Erich Lessing/Art Resource, NY

Those young men and women who had left home would eventually marry and form their own independent households. This practice of moving away from home is known as *neolocalism.* These young people married relatively late. Men were usually over twenty-six, and women over twenty-three. The new couple usually had children as soon after marriage as possible. Frequently, the woman was already pregnant at marriage. Family and community pressure often compelled the man to marry her. In any case, premarital sexual relations were common. The new couple would soon employ a servant, who, together with their growing children, would undertake whatever form of livelihood the household used to support itself.

The word *servant* in this context does not refer to someone looking after the needs of wealthy people. Rather, in preindustrial Europe, a servant was a person—either male or female—who was hired, often under a clear contract, to work for the head of the household in exchange for room, board, and wages. The servant was usually young and by no means always socially inferior to his or her employer. Normally, the servant was an integral part of the household and ate with the family.

Young men and women became servants when their labor was no longer needed in their parents' household or when they could earn more money for their family outside the parental household. Being a servant for several years—often as many as eight or ten years—allowed young people to acquire the productive skills and the monetary savings necessary to begin their own household. These years spent as servants largely account for the late age of marriage in northwestern Europe.

Eastern Europe   As one moved eastward across the Continent, the structure of the household and the pattern of marriage changed. In eastern Europe, both men and women usually married before the age of twenty. Consequently, children were born to much younger parents. Often—especially among Russian serfs—wives were older than their husbands. Eastern European households were generally larger than those in the West. Frequently a rural Russian household consisted of more than nine, and pos-

years, and their servants. Except for the few wealthy people, households usually consisted of not more than five or six members. Furthermore, in these households, more than two generations of a family rarely lived under the same roof. High mortality and late marriage prevented a formation of families of three generations or more. In other words, grandparents rarely lived in the same household as their grandchildren, and families consisted of parents and children. The family structure of northwestern Europe was thus nuclear rather than extended.

Historians used to assume that before industrialization Europeans lived in extended familial settings, with several generations living together in a household. Demographic investigation has now sharply reversed this picture. Children lived with their parents only until their early teens. Then they normally left home, usually to enter the workforce of young servants who lived and worked in another household. A child of a skilled artisan might remain with his or her parents to learn a valuable skill; but only rarely would more than one child do so, because children earned more working outside the home.

sibly more than twenty, members, with three or perhaps even four generations of the same family living together. Early marriage made this situation more likely. In Russia, marrying involved not starting a new household, but remaining in and expanding one already established.

The landholding structure in eastern Europe accounts, at least in part, for these patterns of marriage and the family. The lords of the manor who owned land wanted to ensure that it would be cultivated, so they could receive their rents. Thus, in Poland, for example, landlords might forbid marriage between their own serfs and those from another estate. They might also require widows and widowers to remarry to assure adequate labor for a particular plot of land. Polish landlords also frowned on the hiring of free laborers—the equivalent of servants in the West—to help cultivate land. The landlords preferred to use other serfs. This practice inhibited the formation of independent households. In Russia, landlords ordered the families of young people in their villages to arrange marriages within a short set time. These lords discouraged single-generation family households because the death or serious illness of one person in such a household might mean the land assigned to it would go out of cultivation.

The Family Economy

Throughout Europe, most people worked within the family economy. That is to say, the household was the basic unit of production and consumption. Almost everyone lived within a household of some kind because it was virtually impossible for ordinary people to support themselves independently. Indeed, except for members of religious orders, people living outside a household were viewed with great suspicion. They were considered potentially criminal, disruptive, or at least dependent on the charity of others. Everywhere beggars met deep hostility.

Depending on their ages and skills, everyone in the household worked. The need to survive poor harvests or economic slumps meant that no one could be idle. Within this family economy, all goods and income produced went to the benefit of the household rather than to the individual family member. On a farm, much of the effort went directly into raising food or producing other agricultural goods that could be exchanged for food. Few Western Europeans, however, had enough land to support their household from farming alone. Thus, one or more family members might work elsewhere and send wages home; for example, the father and older children might work as harvesters, fishermen, or engage in other labor either in the neighborhood or farther from home. If the father was such a migrant worker, his wife and their younger children would have to work the family farm. This was not an uncommon pattern.

The family economy also dominated the life of skilled urban artisans. The father was usually the chief artisan. He normally employed one or more servants but would expect his children to work in the enterprise also. He usually trained his eldest child in the trade. His wife often sold his wares or opened a small shop of her own. Wives of merchants also frequently ran their husbands' businesses, especially when the husband traveled to purchase new goods. In any case, everyone in the family was involved. If business was poor, family members would look for employment elsewhere—not to support themselves as individuals, but to ensure the survival of the family unit.

In Western Europe, the death of a father often brought disaster to the household. The continuing economic life of the family usually depended on his land or skills. The widow might take on the farm or the business, or his children might do so. The widow usually sought to remarry quickly to restore the labor and skills of a male to the household and to prevent herself from becoming dependent on relatives or charity.

The high mortality rate of the time meant that many households were reconstituted second-family groups that included stepchildren. Because of the advanced age of the widow or economic hard times, however, some households might simply dissolve. The widow became dependent on charity or relatives. The children became similarly dependent or entered the workforce as servants earlier than they would have otherwise. In other cases, the situation could be so desperate that they would resort to crime or to begging. The personal, emotional, and economic vulnerability of the family cannot be overemphasized.

In Eastern Europe, the family economy functioned in the context of serfdom and landlord domination. Peasants clearly thought in terms of their families and expanding the land available for cultivation. The village structure may have mitigated the pressures of the family economy, as did the multigenerational family. Dependence on the available land was the chief fact of life. There were many fewer artisan and merchant households, and there was far less geographical mobility than in Western Europe.

Women and the Family Economy

The family economy established many of the chief constraints on the lives and personal experiences of women in preindustrial society. Most of the historical research that has been undertaken on this subject relates to Western Europe. There, a woman's life experience was largely the function of her capacity to establish and maintain a household. For women, marriage was an economic necessity, as well as an institution that fulfilled sexual and psychological needs. Outside a household, a woman's life was vulnerable and precarious. Some women became economically independent, but they were the exception. Normally, unless she were an aristocrat or a member of a religious order, a woman probably could not support herself solely by her own efforts. Consequently, a woman devoted much of her life first to maintaining her parents' household and then to devising some means of getting her own household to live in as an adult. Bearing and rearing children were usually subordinate to these goals.

By the age of seven, a girl would have begun to help with the household work. On a farm, this might mean looking after chickens, watering the animals, or carrying food to the adults working the land. In an urban artisan's household, she would do light work, perhaps cleaning or carrying, and later sewing or weaving. The girl would remain in her parents' home as long as she made a real contribution to the family enterprise or as long as her labor elsewhere was not more remunerative to the family.

An artisan's daughter might not leave home until marriage, because at home she could learn increasingly valuable skills associated with the trade. The situation was different for the much larger number of girls growing up on farms. Their parents and brothers could often do all the necessary farm work, and a girl's labor at home quickly became of little value to her family. She would then leave home, usually between the age of twelve and fourteen years. She might take up residence on another farm, but more likely she would migrate to a nearby town or city. She would rarely travel more than thirty miles from her parents' household. She would then normally become a servant, once again living in a household, but this time in the household of an employer. Having left home, the young woman's chief goal was to accumulate enough capital for a dowry. Her savings would make her eligible for marriage, because they would allow her to make the necessary contribution to form a household with her husband. Marriage within the family economy was a joint economic undertaking, and the wife was expected to make an immediate contribution of capital to establish the household. A young woman might well work for ten years or more to accumulate a dowry. This practice meant that marriage was usually postponed until her mid- to late twenties.

Within marriage, earning enough money or producing enough farm goods to ensure an adequate food supply dominated women's concerns. Domestic duties, childbearing, and child rearing were subordinate to economic pressures. Consequently, couples tried to limit the number of children they had, usually through the practice of *coitus interruptus*, the withdrawal of the male before ejaculation.

The work of married women differed markedly between city and country and was in many ways a function of their husbands' occupations. If the peasant household had enough land to support itself, the wife spent much of her time literally carrying things for her husband—water, food, seed, harvested grain, and the like. Such landholdings, however, were few. If the husband had to do work besides farming, such as fishing or migrant labor, the wife might actually be in charge of the farm and do the plowing, planting, and harvesting. In the city, the wife of an artisan or a merchant might be in charge of the household finances and help manage the business. When her husband died, she might take over the business and perhaps hire an artisan. Finally, if economic disaster struck the family, it was usually the wife who organized what Olwen Hufton has called the "economy of expedients,"[1] within which family members might be sent off to find work elsewhere or even to beg in the streets.

Despite all this economic activity, women found many occupations and professions closed to them because they were female. They labored with less education than men, because in such a society women at all levels of life consistently found fewer opportunities for education than did men. They often received lower wages than men for the same work. The mechanization of agriculture and the textile industries, which will be discussed later in this chapter, made these disabilities worse.

Children and the World of the Family Economy

For women of all social ranks, childbirth meant fear and vulnerability. Contagious diseases endangered both mother and child. Puerperal fever was frequent, as were other infections from unsterilized medical instruments. Not all midwives were skillful practitioners. Furthermore, most mothers gave birth in conditions of immense poverty and wretched housing. Assuming both mother and child survived, the mother might nurse the infant, but often the child would be sent to a wet nurse. The wealthy may have done this for convenience, but economic necessity dictated it for the poor. The structures and customs of the family economy did not permit a woman to devote herself entirely to rearing a child. The wet-nursing industry was well organized, with urban children being frequently transported to wet nurses in the country, where they would remain for months or even years.

The birth of a child was not always welcome. The child might represent another economic burden on an already hard-pressed household, or it might be illegitimate. The number of illegitimate births seems to have increased during the eighteenth century, possibly because increased migration of the population led to fleeting romances.

[1] Olwen Hufton, "Women and the Family Economy in Eighteenth-Century France," *French Historical Studies* 9 (1976), p. 19.

Through at least the end of the seventeenth century, unwanted or illegitimate births could lead to infanticide, especially among the poor. The parents might smother the infant or expose it to the elements. These practices were one result of both the ignorance and the prejudice surrounding contraception.

The late seventeenth and the early eighteenth centuries saw a new interest in preserving the lives of abandoned children. Although foundling hospitals established to care for abandoned children had existed before, their size and number expanded during these years. Two of the most famous were the Paris Foundling Hospital (1670) and the London Foundling Hospital (1739). Such hospitals cared for thousands of children, and the demand for their services increased during the eighteenth century. For example, early in the century, an average of 1,700 children a year were admitted to the Paris Foundling Hospital. In the peak year of 1772, however, that number rose to 7,676 children. Not all of those children came from Paris. Many had been brought to the city from the provinces, where local foundling homes and hospitals were overburdened. The London Foundling Hospital lacked the income to deal with all the children brought to it. In the middle of the eighteenth century, the hospital found itself compelled to choose children for admission by a lottery system.

Sadness and tragedy surrounded abandoned children. Most of them were illegitimate infants from across the social spectrum. Many, however, were left with the foundling hospitals because their parents could not support them. There was a close relationship between rising food prices and increasing numbers of abandoned children in Paris. Parents would sometimes leave personal tokens or saints' medals on the abandoned baby in the vain hope they might one day be able to reclaim the child. Few children were reclaimed. Leaving a child at a foundling hospital did not guarantee its survival. In Paris, only about 10 percent of all abandoned children lived to the age of ten.

Despite all of these perils of early childhood, children did grow up and come of age across Europe. The world of the child may not have received the kind of attention it does today, but during the eighteenth century, the seeds of that modern sensibility were sown. Particularly among the upper classes, new interest arose in educating children. In most areas, education remained firmly in the hands of the churches. As economic skills became more demanding, literacy became more valuable, and literacy rates rose during the century. Yet most Europeans remained illiterate. Not until the late nineteenth century was the world of childhood inextricably linked to the process of education. Then children would be reared to become members of a national citizenry. In the Old Regime, they were reared to make their contribution to the economy of their parents' family and then to set up their own households.

▼ The Revolution in Agriculture

Thus far, this chapter has examined those groups that sought stability and that, except for certain members of the nobility, resisted change. Other groups, however, wished to pursue significant new directions in social and economic life. The remainder of the chapter considers those forces and developments that would transform European life during the next century. These developments first appeared in agriculture.

The main goal of traditional peasant society was a stability that would ensure the local food supply. Despite differences in rural customs across Europe, the tillers resisted changes that might endanger the sure supply of food, which they generally believed traditional methods of cultivation would provide. The food supply was never certain, and the farther east one traveled, the more uncertain it became. Failure of the harvest meant not only hardship, but also death from either outright starvation or malnutrition. People living in the countryside often had more difficulty finding food than did city dwellers, whose local government usually stored reserve supplies of grain.

Poor harvests also played havoc with prices. Smaller supplies or larger demand raised grain prices. Even small increases in the cost of food could exert heavy pressure on peasant or artisan families. If prices increased sharply, many of those families fell back on poor relief from their local government or the church.

Historians now believe that during the eighteenth century bread prices slowly but steadily rose, spurred largely by population growth. Since bread was their main food, this inflation put pressure on the poor. Prices rose faster than urban wages and brought no appreciable advantage to the small peasant producer. However, the

The English agricultural improver Jethro Tull devised this seed drill, which increased wheat crops by planting seed deep in the soil rather than just casting it randomly on the surface. Image Works/Mary Evans Picture Library Ltd.

rise in grain prices benefited landowners and those wealthier peasants who had surplus grain to sell.

The rising grain prices gave landlords an opportunity to improve their incomes and lifestyle. To achieve those ends, landlords in Western Europe began a series of innovations in farm production that became known as the **Agricultural Revolution**. Landlords commercialized agriculture and thereby challenged the traditional peasant ways of production. Peasant revolts and disturbances often resulted. The governments of Europe, hungry for new taxes and dependent on the goodwill of the nobility, used their armies and militias to smash peasants who defended traditional practices.

New Crops and New Methods

The drive to improve agricultural production began during the sixteenth and seventeenth centuries in the Low Countries, where the pressures of the growing population and the shortage of land required changes in cultivation. Dutch landlords and farmers devised better ways to build dikes and to drain land, so they could farm more land. They also experimented with new crops, such as clover and turnips, that would increase the supply of animal fodder and restore the soil. These improvements became so famous that early in the seventeenth century English landlords hired Cornelius Vermuyden, a Dutch engineer, to drain thousands of acres of land around Cambridge.

English landlords provided the most striking examples of eighteenth-century agricultural improvement. They originated almost no genuinely new farming methods, but they popularized ideas developed in the previous century either in the Low Countries or in England. Some of these landlords and agricultural innovators became famous. For example, Jethro Tull (1674–1741) was willing to conduct experiments himself and to finance the experiments of others. Many of his ideas, such as the rejection of manure as fertilizer, were wrong. Others, however, such as using iron plows to turn the earth more deeply and planting wheat by a drill rather than by just casting seeds, were excellent. His methods permitted land to be cultivated for longer periods without having to leave it fallow.

Charles "Turnip" Townsend (1674–1738) encouraged other important innovations. He learned from the Dutch how to cultivate sandy soil with fertilizers. He also instituted crop rotation, using wheat, turnips, barley, and clover. This new system of rotation replaced the fallow field with one sown with a crop that both restored nutrients to the soil and supplied animal fodder. The additional fodder meant that more livestock could be raised. These fodders allowed animals to be fed during the winter and assured a year-round supply of meat. The larger number of animals increased the quantity of manure available as fertilizer for the grain crops.

Consequently, in the long run, both animals and human beings had more food.

A third British agricultural improver was Robert Bakewell (1725–1795), who pioneered new methods of animal breeding that produced more and better animals and more milk and meat. These and other innovations received widespread discussion in the works of Arthur Young (1741–1820), who edited the *Annals of Agriculture*. In 1793, he became secretary of the British Board of Agriculture. Young traveled widely across Europe, and his books are among the most important documents of life during the late eighteenth century.

Enclosure Replaces Open-Field Method   Many of the agricultural innovations, which were adopted only slowly, were incompatible with the existing organization of land in England. Small cultivators who lived in village communities still farmed most of the soil. Each farmer tilled an assortment of unconnected strips. The two- or three-field systems of rotation left large portions of land fallow and unproductive each year. Animals grazed on the common land in the summer and on the stubble of the harvest in the winter. Until at least the mid-eighteenth century, the whole community decided what crops to plant. The entire system discouraged improvement and favored the poorer farmers, who needed the common land and stubble fields for their animals. The village method precluded expanding pastureland to raise more animals that would, in turn, produce more manure for fertilizer. Thus, the methods of traditional production aimed at a steady, but not a growing, supply of food.

In 1700, approximately half the arable land in England was farmed by this open-field method. By the second half of the century, the rising price of wheat encouraged landlords to consolidate or enclose their lands to increase production. The **enclosures** were intended to use land more rationally and to achieve greater commercial profits. The process involved the fencing of common lands, the reclamation of previously untilled waste, and the transformation of strips into block fields. These procedures brought turmoil to the economic and social life of the countryside. Riots often ensued.

Because many English farmers either owned their strips or rented them in a manner that amounted to ownership, the larger landlords usually resorted to parliamentary acts to legalize the enclosure of the land, which they owned but rented to the farmers. Because the large landowners controlled Parliament, such measures passed easily. Between 1761 and 1792, almost 500,000 acres were enclosed through acts of Parliament, compared with 75,000 acres between 1727 and 1760. In 1801, a general enclosure act streamlined the process.

The enclosures were controversial at the time and have remained so among historians. They permitted the extension of both farming and innovation and thus increased food production on larger agricultural units. They also disrupted small traditional communities; they forced off the land independent farmers, who had needed the common pasturage, and poor cottage dwellers, who had lived on the reclaimed wasteland. The enclosures, however, did not depopulate the countryside. In some counties where the enclosures took place, the population increased. New soil had come into production, and services that supported farming also expanded.

The enclosures did not create the labor force for the British Industrial Revolution. What the enclosures most conspicuously displayed was the introduction of the entrepreneurial or capitalistic attitude of the urban merchant into the countryside. This commercialization of agriculture, which spread from Britain slowly across the Continent during the next century, strained the paternal relationship between the governing and governed classes. Previously, landlords had often looked after the welfare of the lower orders through price controls or waivers of rent during hard times. As the landlords became increasingly concerned about profits, they began to leave the peasants to the mercy of the marketplace.

Limited Improvements in Eastern Europe Improving agriculture tended to characterize farm production west of the Elbe River. Dutch farming was efficient. In France, despite the efforts of the government to improve agriculture, enclosures were restricted. Yet many people in France wanted to improve agricultural methods. These new procedures benefited the ruling classes because better agriculture increased their incomes and assured a larger food supply, which discouraged social unrest. (See "Compare & Connect: Two Eighteenth-Century Writers Contemplate the Effects of Different Economic Structures," pages 458–459.)

In Prussia, Austria, Poland, and Russia, agricultural improvement was limited. Nothing in the relationship of the serfs to their lords encouraged innovation. In eastern Europe, the chief method of increasing production was to bring previously untilled lands under the plow. The landlords or their agents, and not the villages, normally directed farm management. By extending tillage, the great landlords sought to squeeze more labor from their serfs, rather than greater productivity from the soil. Eastern European landlords, like their western counterparts, sought to increase their profits, but they were less ambitious and successful. The only significant nutritional gain they achieved was the introduction of maize and the potato. Livestock production did not increase significantly.

Expansion of the Population

The population explosion with which the entire world must contend today had its origins in the eighteenth century. Before that time, Europe's population had experienced dramatic increases, but plagues, wars, or famine had redressed the balance. Beginning in the second quarter of the eighteenth century, the population began to increase steadily. The need to feed this population caused food prices to rise, which spurred agricultural innovation. The need to provide everyday consumer goods for the expanding numbers of people fueled the demand side of the Industrial Revolution.

In 1700, Europe's population, excluding the European provinces of the Ottoman Empire, was probably between 100 million and 120 million people. By 1800, the figures had risen to almost 190 million and by 1850, to 260 million. The population of England and Wales rose from 6 million in 1750 to more than 10 million in 1800. France grew from 18 million in 1715 to about 26 million in 1789. Russia's population increased from 19 million in 1722 to 29 million in 1766. Such extraordinary sustained growth put new demands on all resources and considerable pressure on the existing social organization.

The population expansion occurred across the Continent in both the country and the cities. Only a limited consensus exists among scholars about the causes of this growth. The death rate clearly declined. There were fewer wars and epidemics in the eighteenth century. Hygiene and sanitation also improved. Better medical knowledge and techniques, however, did not contribute much to the decline in deaths. The more important medical advances came after the initial population explosion and would not have affected it directly.

Instead, changes in the food supply itself may have allowed population growth to be sustained. Improved and expanding grain production made one contribution. Another and even more important change was the cultivation of the potato. This tuber was a product of the New World and came into widespread European production during the eighteenth century. (See "The West & The World," page 505.) On a single acre, a peasant family could grow enough potatoes to feed itself for an entire year. This more certain food supply enabled more children to survive to adulthood and rear children of their own.

The impact of the population explosion can hardly be overestimated. It created new demands for food, goods, jobs, and services. It provided a new pool of labor. Traditional modes of production and living had to be revised. More people lived in the countryside than could find employment there. Migration increased. There were also more people who might become socially and politically discontented. Because the population growth fed on itself, these pressures and demands continued to increase. The society and the social practices of the Old Regime literally outgrew their traditional bounds.

Two Eighteenth-Century Writers Contemplate the Effects of Different Economic Structures

AMONG EIGHTEENTH-CENTURY public officials and commentators there existed a broad agreement that European economic life needed to be reorganized and stimulated to achieve greater productivity and wealth. These writers also understood that different modes of productive activity resulted in very different kinds of society. In these two documents a French writer bemoans problems of French agriculture and landholding while a Scottish writer praises the wealth and good society that flow from growing commerce and refinement of both mechanical and liberal arts.

QUESTIONS

1. Why does Turgot favor those farmers who can make investments in the land they rent from a proprietor?

2. What are the structures of the métayer system? Why did it lead to poor investments and lower harvests?

3. Why does Hume link industry and the arts?

4. How does he see a commercial, improving economy producing important intellectual outlooks and social skills?

5. What benefits to agriculture might Hume have assigned to prosperous cities, and what benefits might Turgot have seen agriculture contributing to urban life?

I. Turgot Decries French Landholding

During the eighteenth century, many observers became keenly aware that different kinds of landholding led to different attitudes toward work and to different levels of production and wealth. Robert Jacques Turgot (1727–1781), who later became finance minister of France, analyzed these differences in an effort to reform French agriculture. He was especially concerned with arrangements that encouraged long-term investment. The métayer *system Turgot discusses was an arrangement whereby landowners had land farmed by peasants who received part of the harvest as payment for working the land, but the peasant had no long-term interest in improving the land. Virtually all observers regarded the system as inefficient.*

1. What really distinguishes the area of large-scale farming from the areas of small-scale production is that in the former areas the proprietors find farmers who provide them with a permanent revenue from the land and who buy from them the right to cultivate it for a certain number of years. These farmers undertake all the expenses of cultivation, the ploughing, the sowing and the stocking of the farm with cattle, animals and tools. They are really agricultural entrepreneurs, who possess, like the entrepreneurs in all other branches of commerce, considerable funds, which they employ in the cultivation of land. . . .

They have not only the brawn but also the wealth to devote to agriculture. They have to work, but unlike workers, they do not have to earn their living by the sweat of their brow, but by the lucrative employment of their capital, just as the ship owners of Nantes and Bordeaux employ theirs in maritime commerce.

2. *Métayer* System The areas of small-scale farming, that is to say at least four-sevenths of the kingdom, are those where there are no agricultural entrepreneurs, where a proprietor who wishes to develop his land cannot find anyone to cultivate it except wretched peasants who have no resources other than their labor, where he is obliged to make, at his own expense, all the advances necessary for tillage, beasts, tools, sowing, even to the extent of advancing to his *métayer* the wherewithal to feed himself until the first harvest, where consequently a proprietor who did not have any property other than his estate would be obliged to allow it to lie fallow.

After having deducted the costs of sowing and feudal dues with which the property is burdened, the proprietor shares with the *métayer* what remains of the profits, in accordance with the agreement they have concluded. The proprietor runs all the risks of harvest failure and any loss of cattle: he is the real entrepreneur. The *métayer* is nothing more than a mere workman, a farm hand to whom the proprietor surrenders a share of his profits instead of paying wages. But in his work the proprietor enjoys none of the advantages of the farmer who, working on his own behalf, works carefully and diligently; the proprietor is obliged to entrust all his advances to a man who may be negligent or a scoundrel and is answerable for nothing.

This *métayer*, accustomed to the most miserable existence and without the hope and even the desire to obtain a better living for himself, cultivates badly and neglects to employ the land for valuable and profitable production; by preference he occupies himself in cultivating those things whose growth is less troublesome and which provide him with more foodstuffs, such as buckwheat and chestnuts which do not require any attention. He does not worry very much about his livelihood; he knows that if the harvest fails, his master will be obliged to feed him in order not to see his land neglected.

Source: From *Œuvres, et documents les concernant*, by A. M. R. Turgot, ed. by F. Schelle, 5 vols. (Paris, 1914), Vol. II, pp. 448–450; *Documents of European Economic History*, as quoted and trans. by S. Pollard and C. Holmes (Edward Arnold, 1968), pp. 38–39.

This is the detail of a 1739 map by Louis Bretez, a member of the Academy of Painting and Sculpture, showing an aerial view of the city of Paris. The primary function of the map was to reestablish Paris as the universal model of a capital city. Library of Congress

II. David Hume Praises Luxury and the Refinement of the Arts

David Hume (1711–1776) was a Scottish philosopher, historian, and economic commentator. He was deeply committed to the modernization of the Scottish and wider European economy through the growth of commerce and the fostering of improved means of mechanical production. In this essay published in 1752 he outlined the beneficial social consequence he saw resulting from commercial wealth and new mechanical inventions. He believed such economic activity not only increased riches but also produced a population capable of providing a national defense. He was quite concerned to demonstrate that luxury and the economy that fostered it would not lead to moral decay.

In times when industry and the arts flourish, men are kept in perpetual occupation, and enjoy, as their reward, the occupation itself, as well as those pleasures which are the fruit of their labour. The mind acquires new vigour; enlarges its powers and faculties; and by an assiduity in honest industry, both satisfies its natural appetites, and prevents the growth of unnatural ones, which commonly spring up, when nourished by ease and idleness. . . .

Another advantage of industry and of refinements in the mechanical arts, is, that they commonly produce some refinements in the liberal; nor can one be carried to perfection, without being accompanied, in some degree, with the other. . . .

The more these refined arts advance, the more sociable men become . . . They flock into cities; love to receive and communicate knowledge; to show their wit or their breeding; their taste in conversation or living, in clothes or furniture. Curiosity allures the wise; vanity the foolish, and pleasure both. Particular clubs and societies are everywhere formed: Both sexes meet in an easy and sociable manner: and the tempers of men, as well as their behaviour, refine apace. So that, beside the improvements which they receive from knowledge and the liberal arts, it is impossible but they must feel an encrease of humanity, from the very habit of conversing together, and contributing to each other's pleasure and entertainment. Thus *industry, knowledge,* and *humanity,* are linked together by an indissoluble chain, and are found, from experience as well as reason, to be peculiar to the more polished, and, what are commonly denominated, the more luxurious ages. . . .

But industry, knowledge, and humanity are not advantageous in private life alone: They diffuse their beneficial influence on the *public,* and render the government as great and flourishing as they make individuals happy and prosperous. The encrease and consumption of all the commodities . . . are advantageous to society; because . . . they are a kind of *storehouse* of labour, which, in the exigencies of state, may be turned to the public service. In a nation, where there is no demand for such superfluities, men sink into indolence, lose all enjoyment of life, and are useless to the public, which cannot maintain or support its fleets and armies, from the industry of such slothful members.

Source: David Hume, "Of Refinement in the Arts (1752)," in *Essays: Moral, Political and Literary* (Indianapolis, IN: Liberty Classics, 1985), pp. 270–272.

▼ The Industrial Revolution of the Eighteenth Century

The second half of the eighteenth century witnessed the beginning of the industrialization of the European economy. That achievement of sustained economic growth is termed the **Industrial Revolution**. Previously, the economy of a province or a country might grow, but growth soon reached a plateau. Since the late eighteenth century, however, the economy of Europe has managed to expand at an almost uninterrupted pace. Depressions and recessions have been temporary, and even during such economic downturns, the Western economy has continued to grow.

At considerable social cost, industrialization made possible the production of more goods and services than ever before in human history. Industrialization in Europe eventually overcame the economy of scarcity. The new means of production demanded new kinds of skills, new discipline in work, and a large labor force. The goods produced met immediate consumer demand and also created new demands. In the long run, industrialization raised the standard of living and overcame the poverty that most Europeans, who lived during the eighteenth century and earlier, had taken for granted. It gave human beings greater control over nature than they had ever known before; yet by the mid-nineteenth century, industrialism would also cause new and unanticipated problems with the environment.

During the eighteenth century, people did not call these economic developments a *revolution*. That term came to be applied to the British economic phenomena only after the French Revolution. Then continental writers observed that what had taken place in Britain was the economic equivalent of the political events in France, hence an Industrial Revolution. It was revolutionary less in its speed, which was on the whole rather slow, than in its implications for the future of European society.

A Revolution in Consumption

The most familiar side of the Industrial Revolution was the invention of new machinery, the establishment of factories, and the creation of a new kind of workforce. Recent studies, however, have emphasized the demand side of the process and the vast increase in both the desire and the possibility of consuming goods and services that arose in the early eighteenth century.

The inventions of the Industrial Revolution increased the supply of consumer goods as never before in history. The supply of goods was only one side of the economic equation, however. An unprecedented demand for the humble goods of everyday life created the supply. Those goods included clothing, buttons, toys, china, furniture, rugs, kitchen utensils, candlesticks, brassware, silverware, pewterware, glassware, watches, jewelry, soap, beer, wines, and foodstuffs. It was the ever-increasing demand for these goods that sparked the ingenuity of designers and inventors. Furthermore, consumer demand seemed unlimited. (See "David Hume Praises Luxury and the Refinement of the Arts," page 459.)

Many social factors helped establish the markets for these consumer goods. During the seventeenth century, the Dutch had enjoyed enormous prosperity and had led the way in new forms of consumption. For reasons that are still not clear, during the eighteenth century, first the English and then the people on the Continent came to have more disposable income. This wealth may have resulted from the improvements in agriculture. Those incomes allowed people to buy consumer goods that previous generations had inherited or did not possess. What is key to this change in consumption is that it depended primarily on expanding the various domestic markets in Europe.

This revolution, if that is not too strong a term, in consumption was not automatic. People became persuaded that they needed or wanted new consumer goods. Often, entrepreneurs caused it to happen by developing new methods of marketing. For example, the English porcelain manufacturer

Consumption of all forms of consumer goods increased greatly in the eighteenth century. This engraving illustrates a shop, probably in Paris. Here women, working apparently for a woman manager, are making dresses and hats to meet the demands of the fashion trade. As the document on page 454 demonstrates, some women writers urged more such employment opportunities for women. Bildarchiv Preussischer Kulturbesitz

Josiah Wedgwood (1730–1795) first attempted to find customers among the royal family and the aristocracy. Once he had gained their business with luxury goods, he then produced a less expensive version of the chinaware for middle-class customers. He also used advertising, opened showrooms in London, and sent salespeople all over Britain with samples and catalogs of his wares. On the Continent, his salespeople used bilingual catalogs. There seemed to be no limit to the markets for consumer goods that social emulation on the one hand and advertising on the other could stimulate.

Furthermore, the process of change in style itself became institutionalized. New fashions and inventions were always better than old ones. If new kinds of goods could be produced, there usually was a market for them. If one product did not find a market, its failure provided a lesson for how to develop a different new product.

This expansion of consumption quietly, but steadily, challenged the social assumptions of the day. Fashion publications made all levels of society aware of new styles. Clothing fashions could be copied. Servants could begin to dress well if not luxuriously. Changes in the consumption of food and drink demanded new kinds of dishware for the home. Tea and coffee became staples. The brewing industry became fully commercialized. Those developments entailed the need for new kinds of cups and mugs and many more of them.

There would always be critics of this consumer economy. The vision of luxury and comfort it offered contrasted with the asceticism of ancient Sparta and contemporary Christian ethics. Yet, the ever-increasing consumption and production of the goods of everyday life became hallmarks of modern Western society from the eighteenth century to our own day. It would be difficult to overestimate the importance of the desire for consumer goods and the higher standard of living that they made possible in Western history after the eighteenth century. The presence and accessibility of such goods became the hallmark of a nation's prosperity. It was the absence of such consumer goods, as well as of civil liberties, that during the 1980s led to such deep discontent with the communist regimes in Eastern Europe and the former Soviet Union.

Industrial Leadership of Great Britain

Great Britain was the home of the Industrial Revolution and, until the middle of the nineteenth century, remained the industrial leader of Europe. Several factors contributed to the early start in Britain.

Great Britain took the lead in the **consumer revolution** that expanded the demand for goods that could be efficiently supplied. London was the largest city in Europe. It was the center of a world of fashion and taste to which hundreds of thousands, if not millions, of British citizens were exposed each year. In London, these people learned to want the consumer goods they saw on vis-

its for business and pleasure. Newspapers thrived in Britain during the eighteenth century, and the advertising they printed increased consumer wants. The social structure of Britain encouraged people to imitate the lifestyles of their social superiors. It seems to have been in Britain that a world of fashion first developed that led people to want to accumulate goods. In addition to the domestic consumer demand, the British economy benefited from demand from the colonies in North America.

Britain was also the single largest free-trade area in Europe. The British had good roads and waterways without internal tolls or other trade barriers. The country had rich deposits of coal and iron ore. Its political structure was stable, and property was absolutely secure. The sound systems of banking and public credit established a stable climate for investment. Taxation in Britain was heavy, but it was efficiently and fairly collected, largely from indirect taxes. Furthermore, British taxes received legal approval through Parliament, with all social classes and all regions of the nation paying the same taxes. In contrast to the Continent, there was no pattern of privileged tax exemptions.

Finally, British society was mobile by the standards of the time. Persons who had money or could earn it could rise socially. The British aristocracy would receive into its ranks people who had amassed large fortunes. Even persons of wealth who did not join the aristocracy could enjoy their riches, receive social recognition, and exert political influence. No one of these factors preordained the British advance toward industrialism. Together, however, when added to the progressive state of British agriculture, they provided the nation with the marginal advantage to create a new mode of economic production.

New Methods of Textile Production

The industry that pioneered the Industrial Revolution and met the growing consumer demand was the production of textiles for clothing. Textile production is the key example of industrialism emerging to supply the demands of an ever-growing market for everyday goods. Furthermore, it illustrates the surprising fact that much of the earliest industrial change took place not in cities, but in the countryside.

Although the eighteenth-century economy was primarily agricultural, manufacturing also permeated rural areas. The peasant family living in a one- or two-room cottage, rather than the factory, was the basic unit of production. The same peasants who tilled the land in spring and summer often spun thread or wove textiles in the winter.

Under what is termed the **domestic**, or putting-out, **system of textile production**, agents of urban textile merchants took wool or other unfinished fibers to the homes of peasants, who spun it into thread. The agent then transported the thread to other peasants, who wove it into the finished product. The merchant sold the wares. In thousands of peasant cottages from Ireland to

MANCHESTER'S CALICO PRINTERS PROTEST THE USE OF NEW MACHINERY

The introduction of the new machines associated with the Industrial Revolution stirred much protest. With machines able to duplicate the skills of laborers, workers feared the loss of jobs and the resulting loss of status when their chief means of livelihood lay in their possession of those displaced and now mechanized skills. The following letter was sent anonymously to a Manchester manufacturer by English workers. It shows the outrage of those workers, the intimidation they were willing to use as threats, and their own economic fears.

How might new machines adversely affect the livelihood of workers? Did the workers have other complaints against Mr. Taylor in addition to the introduction of new machinery? How have these workers reached an agreement to protect the interests of James Hobson? How do the workers combine the threat of violent actions with claims that other actions they have taken are legal?

Mr. Taylor, If you dont discharge James Hobson from the House of Correction we will burn your House about your Ears for we have sworn to stand by one another and you must immediately give over any more Mashen Work for we are determined there shall be no more of them made use of in the Trade and it will be madness for you to contend with the Trade as we are combined by Oath to fix Prices we can afford to pay him a Guinea Week and not hurt the fund if you was to keep him there till Dumsday therefore mind you comply with the above or by God we will keep our Words with you we will make some rare Bunfires in this Countey and at your Peril to call any more Meetings mind that we will make the Mosney Pepel shake in their Shoes we are determined to destroy all Sorts of Masheens for Printing in the Kingdom for there is more hands then is work for so no more from the ingerd Gurnemen Rember we are a great number sworn nor you must not advertise the Men that you say run away from you when your il Usage was the Cause of their going we will punish you for that our Meetings are legal for we want nothing but what is honest and to work for selvs and familers and you want to starve us but it is better for you and a few more which we have marked to die then such a Number of Pore Men and their famerles to be starved.

London Gazette, 1786, p. 36, as reprinted in Douglas Hay, ed., *Albion's Fatal Tree* (New York: Pantheon Books, 1975), p. 318.

Austria, there stood a spinning wheel or a hand loom. Sometimes the spinners or weavers owned their own equipment, but more often than not by the middle of the century, the merchant capitalist owned the machinery as well as the raw material.

The domestic system of textile production was a basic feature of this family economy and would continue to be so in Britain and on the Continent well into the nineteenth century. By the mid-eighteenth century, however, production bottlenecks had developed within the domestic system. The demand for cotton textiles was growing more rapidly than production, especially in Britain, which had a large domestic and North American market for these goods. Inventors devised some of the most famous machines of the early Industrial Revolution to meet consumer demand for cotton textiles.

The Spinning Jenny   Cotton textile weavers had the technical capacity to produce the quantity of fabric demanded. The spinners, however, did not have the equipment to produce as much thread as the weavers needed. John Kay's invention of the flying shuttle, which increased the productivity of the weavers, had created this imbalance during the 1730s. Thereafter, manufacturers and merchants offered prizes for the invention of a machine to eliminate this bottleneck.

About 1765, James Hargreaves (d. 1778) invented the **spinning jenny**. Initially, this machine allowed 16 spindles of thread to be spun, but by the close of the century, it could operate 120 spindles.

The Water Frame   The spinning jenny broke the bottleneck between the productive capacity of the

James Hargreaves's spinning jenny permitted the spinning of numerous spindles of thread on a single machine. AKG London Ltd.

spinners and the weavers, but it was still a piece of machinery used in the cottage. The invention that took cotton textile manufacture out of the home and put it into the factory was Richard Arkwright's (1732–1792) **water frame**, patented in 1769. This was a water-powered device designed to permit the production of a purely cotton fabric, rather than a cotton fabric containing linen fiber for durability. Eventually Arkwright lost his patent rights, and other manufacturers used his invention freely. As a result, many factories sprang up in the countryside near streams that provided the necessary water power. From the 1780s onward, the cotton industry could meet an ever-expanding demand. Cotton output increased by 800 percent between 1780 and 1800. By 1815, cotton composed 40 percent of the value of British domestic exports and by 1830, just over 50 percent.

The Industrial Revolution had commenced in earnest by the 1780s, but the full economic and social ramifications of this unleashing of human productive capacity were not really felt until the early nineteenth century. The expansion of industry and the incorporation of new inventions often occurred slowly. For example, Edmund Cartwright (1743–1822) invented the power loom for machine weaving in the late 1780s. Yet not until the 1830s were there more power-loom weavers than hand-loom weavers in Britain. Nor did all the social ramifications of industrialism appear immediately. The first cotton mills used water power, were located in the country, and rarely employed more than two dozen workers. Not until the late-century application of the steam engine, perfected by James Watt (1736–1819) in 1769, to run textile machinery could factories easily be located in or near urban centers. The

steam engine not only vastly increased and regularized the available energy, but also made possible the combination of urbanization and industrialization.

The Steam Engine

More than any other invention, the steam engine permitted industrialization to grow on itself and to expand into one area of production after another. This machine provided for the first time in human history a steady and essentially unlimited source of inanimate power. Unlike engines powered by water or wind, the steam engine, driven by burning coal, provided a portable source of industrial power that did not fail or falter as the seasons of the year changed. Unlike human or animal power, the steam engine depended on mineral energy that never tired. Finally, the steam engine could be applied to many industrial and, eventually, transportation uses.

Thomas Newcomen (1663–1729) in the early eighteenth century had invented the first practical engine to use steam power. When the steam that had been induced into the cylinder condensed, it caused the piston of this device to fall. The Newcomen machine was large and inefficient in its use of energy because both the condenser and the cylinder were heated, and practically untransportable. Despite these problems, English mine operators used the Newcomen machines to pump water out of coal and tin mines. By the third quarter of the eighteenth century, almost a hundred Newcomen machines were operating in the mining districts of England.

During the 1760s, James Watt, a Scottish engineer and machine maker, began to experiment with a model of a Newcomen machine at the University of Glasgow. He gradually understood that separating the condenser from the piston and the cylinder would achieve much greater efficiency. In 1769, he patented his new invention, but transforming his idea into a practical application presented difficulties. His design required precise metalwork. Watt soon found a partner in Matthew Boulton (1728–1809), a successful toy and button manufacturer in Birmingham, the city with the most skilled metalworkers in Britain. Watt and Boulton, in turn, consulted with John Wilkinson (1728–1808), a cannon manufacturer, to drill the precise metal cylinders Watt's design required. In 1776, the Watt steam engine found its first commercial application pumping water from mines in Cornwall.

The use of the steam engine spread slowly because until 1800 Watt retained the exclusive patent rights. He was also reluctant to make further changes to permit the engine to operate more rapidly. Boulton eventually persuaded him to make modifications and improvements that allowed the engines to be used not only for pumping, but also for running cotton mills. By the early nineteenth century, the steam engine had become the prime mover for all industry. With its application to ships and then to wagons on iron rails, the steam engine also revolutionized transportation.

Iron Production

The manufacture of high-quality iron has been basic to modern industrial development. Iron is the chief element of all heavy industry and of land or sea transport. Most productive machinery itself is also manufactured from iron. During the early eighteenth century, British ironmakers produced somewhat less than 25,000 tons of iron annually. Three factors held back the production. First, charcoal rather than coke was used to smelt the ore. Charcoal, derived from wood, was becoming scarce as forests in Britain diminished, and it does not burn at as high a temperature as coke, derived from coal. Second, until the perfection of the steam engine, furnaces could not achieve high enough blasts. Finally, the demand for iron was limited. The elimination of the first two problems also eliminated the third.

Eventually, British ironmakers began to use coke, and the steam engine provided new power for the blast furnaces. Coke was an abundant fuel because of Britain's large coal deposits. The steam engine both improved iron production and increased the demand for iron.

In 1784, Henry Cort (1740–1800) introduced a new puddling process, that is, a new method for melting and stirring molten ore. Cort's process allowed the removal

During the eighteenth century, most goods were produced in small workshops, such as this iron forge painted by Joseph Wright of Derby (1734–1797), or in the homes of artisans. Not until very late in the century, with the early stages of industrialization, did a few factories appear. In the small early workshops, it would not have been uncommon for the family of the owner to visit, as portrayed in this painting. *The Iron Forge*, 1772 (oil on canvas) by Joseph Wright of Derby (1734–1797). Broadlands Trust, Hampshire, UK/Bridgeman Art Library, London

---

MAJOR INVENTIONS IN THE TEXTILE-MANUFACTURING REVOLUTION

1733	John Kay's flying shuttle
1765	James Hargreaves's spinning jenny (patented 1770)
1769	James Watt's steam engine patent
1769	Richard Arkwright's water frame patent
1787	Edmund Cartwright's power loom

---

of more slag (the impurities that bubbled to the top of the molten metal) and thus the production of purer iron. Cort also developed a rolling mill that continuously shaped the still-molten metal into bars, rails, or other forms. Previously, the metal had to be pounded into these forms.

All these innovations achieved a better, more versatile, cheaper product. The demand for iron consequently grew. By the early nineteenth century, the British produced over a million tons annually. The lower cost of iron, in turn, lowered the cost of steam engines and allowed them to be used more widely.

The Impact of the Agricultural and Industrial Revolutions on Working Women

The transformation of agriculture and industry led to a series of seemingly modest changes that, taken collectively, diminished the importance and the role of those women already in the workforce.

Women had been an important part of traditional European agriculture. They worked in and often were permitted to glean the grain left over after the general harvest. Women also managed industries like milking and cheese production. However, primarily in Western Europe, increasing commercialization and mechanization eroded these traditional roles. Machinery operated by men displaced the work of women in the field and their skills in dairying and home industry, particularly in Britain. Even nonmechanized labor came to favor men. For example, during the late eighteenth century, heavy scythes wielded by men replaced the lighter sickles that women had used to harvest grain. Moreover, the drive to maximize profits led landlords to enclose lands and curtail customary rights like gleaning.

This transformation of farming constricted women's ability to earn their living from the land. Women came to be viewed as opponents of agricultural improvement because these improvements hurt them economically. As a result, proponents of the new agriculture often demeaned the role of women in farming and their related work. Indeed, the vast literature on agricultural improvement specifically advocated removing women from the agricultural workforce.

A similar process took place in textile manufacturing, where mechanization deprived many women of one of their most traditional means of earning income. Before mechanization thousands of women worked at spinning wheels to produce thread that hand-loom weavers, who were often their husbands, then wove. The earlier, small spinning jennies did not immediately disrupt this situation because women could use them in the loft of a home, but the larger ones required a factory setting where men often ran the machinery. As a result, most women spinners were put out of work, and those women who did move into the factory labor force performed less skilled work than men. In the long run, however, the mechanization of spinning left many other women without one of their most traditional means of earning income.

Many working women, displaced from spinning thread or from farming, slowly turned to cottage industries, such as knitting, button making, straw plaiting, bonnet making, or glove stitching, that invariably earned them less than their former occupations had. In later generations, women who earlier would have been spinners or farm workers moved directly into cottage industries. The work and skills these occupations involved were considered inferior; and because it paid so poorly, women who did this work might become prostitutes or engage in other criminal activity. Consequently, the reputations and social standing of many working women suffered.

Among women who did not work in the cottage industries, thousands became domestic servants in the homes of landed or commercial families. During the nineteenth century, such domestic service became the largest area of female employment. It was far more respectable than the cottage industries but was isolated from the technologically advanced world of factory manufacture or transport.

By the end of the eighteenth century, the work and workplaces of men and women were becoming increasingly separate and distinct. In this respect, many people, such as the English writer Priscilla Wakefield (1750–1832), believed the kinds of employment open to women had narrowed. Wakefield called for new occupations for women. (See "Priscilla Wakefield Demands More Occupations for Women," on page 466.)

This shift in female employment, or what one historian has termed "this defamation of women workers,"[2] produced several long-term results. First, women's work,

whether in cottage industries or domestic service, became associated with the home rather than with places where men worked. Second, the laboring life of most women was removed from the new technologies in farming, transportation, and manufacturing. Woman's work thus appeared traditional, and people assumed women could do only such work. Third, during the nineteenth and early twentieth centuries, Europeans also assumed most women worked only to supplement a husband's income. Finally, because the work women did was considered marginal and only as supplementing a male income, men were paid much more than women. Most people associate the Industrial Revolution with factories, but for many working women, these revolutions led to a life located more in homes than ever before. Indeed, in the nineteenth century, one, though only one, motive behind efforts to restrict the hours and improve the conditions of women in factories was the belief that it was bad for them to be there in the first place. The larger picture of the relationship of the new industrial workplace to family life will be addressed in Chapter 21.

▼ The Growth of Cities

Remarkable changes occurred in the pattern of city growth between 1500 and 1800. In 1500, within Europe (excluding Hungary and Russia) 156 cities had a population greater than 10,000. Only four of those cities— Paris, Milan, Venice, and Naples—had populations larger than 100,000. By 1800, 363 cities had 10,000 or more inhabitants, and 17 of them had populations larger than 100,000. The percentage of the European population living in urban areas had risen from just over 5 percent to just over 9 percent. A major shift in urban concentration from southern, Mediterranean Europe to the north had also occurred.

Patterns of Preindustrial Urbanization

The eighteenth century witnessed a considerable growth of towns, closely related to the tumult of the day and the revolutions with which the century closed. London grew from about 700,000 inhabitants in 1700 to almost 1 million in 1800. By the time of the French Revolution, Paris had more than 500,000 inhabitants. Berlin's population tripled during the century, reaching 170,000 in 1800. Warsaw had 30,000 inhabitants in 1730, but almost 120,000 in 1794. St. Petersburg, founded in 1703, numbered more than 250,000 inhabitants a century later. The number of smaller cities with 20,000 to 50,000 people also increased considerably. This urban growth must, however, be kept in perspective. Even in France and Great Britain, probably somewhat less than 20 percent of the population lived in cities. And the town of 10,000 inhabitants was much more common than the giant urban center.

<hr>

[2]Deborah Valenze, *The First Industrial Woman* (New York: Oxford University Press, 1995), p. 183.

PRISCILLA WAKEFIELD DEMANDS MORE OCCUPATIONS FOR WOMEN

At the end of the eighteenth century, Priscilla Wakefield was one of several English women writers who began to demand a wider life for women. She was concerned that women found themselves able to pursue only occupations that paid poorly. They were often excluded from work because of their alleged physical weakness. She also believed women should receive equal wages for equal work. These issues reflected a narrowing of opportunities for women that had occurred in England during the second half of the eighteenth century. As a result of the mechanization of both agriculture and the textile industry, many found traditional occupations were closing to women. Wakefield is thus addressing a general question of opportunities available to women and more recent developments. Many of the issues she raised have yet to be adequately addressed.

What arguments were used at the end of the eighteenth century to limit the kinds of employment that women might enter? Why did women receive less pay than men for similar or the same work? What occupations traditionally filled by men does Wakefield believe women might also pursue?

Another heavy discouragement to the industry of women, is the inequality of the reward of their labor, compared with that of men; an injustice which pervades every species of employment performed by both sexes.

In employments which depend on bodily strength, the distinction is just; for it cannot be pretended that the generality of women can earn as much as men, when the produce of their labor is the result of corporeal exertion; but it is a subject of great regret, that this inequality should prevail even where an equal share of skill and application is exerted. Male stay-makers, mantua-makers, and hair-dressers, are better paid than female artists of the same professions; but surely it will never be urged as an apology for this disproportion, that women are not as capable of making stays, gowns, dressing hair, and similar arts, as men; if they are not superior to them, it can only be accounted for upon this principle, that the prices they receive for their labor are not sufficient to repay them for the expense of qualifying themselves for their business; and that they sink under the mortification of being regarded as artisans of inferior estimation. . . .

Besides these employments which are commonly performed by women, and those already shown to be suitable for such persons as are above the condition of hard labor, there are some professions and trades customarily in the hands of men, which might be conveniently exercised by either sex. Watchmaking requiring more ingenuity than strength, seems peculiarly adapted to women; as do many parts of the business of stationer, particularly, ruling account books or making pens. The compounding of medicines in an apothecary's shop, requires no other talents than care and exactness; and if opening a vein occasionally be an indispensable requisite, a woman may acquire the capacity of doing it, for those of her own sex at least, without any reasonable objection. . . . Pastry and confectionery appear particularly consonant to the habits of women, though generally performed by men; perhaps the heat of the ovens, and the strength requisite to fill and empty them, may render male assistants necessary; but certain women are most eligible to mix up the ingredients, and prepare the various kinds of cakes for baking. Light turnery and toy-making depend more upon dexterity and invention than force, and are therefore suitable work for women and children. . . .

Farming, as far as respects the theory, is commensurate with the powers of the female mind: nor is the practice of inspecting agricultural processes incompatible with the delicacy of their frames if their constitution be good.

Priscilla Wakefield, *Reflections on the Present Condition of the Female Sex* (1798) (London, 1817), pp. 125–127, as quoted in Bridget Hill, ed., *Eighteenth-Century Women: An Anthology* (London: George Allen & Unwin, 1984), pp. 227–228.

These raw figures conceal significant changes that took place in how cities grew and how the population redistributed itself. The major urban development of the sixteenth century had been followed by a leveling off, and even a decline, in the seventeenth. New growth began in the early eighteenth century and accelerated during the late eighteenth and the early nineteenth centuries.

Between 1500 and 1750, major urban expansion took place within already established and generally already large cities. After 1750, the pattern changed with the birth of new cities and the rapid growth of older, smaller cities.

Growth of Capitals and Ports In particular, between 1600 and 1750, the cities that grew most vigorously were capitals and ports. This situation reflects the success of monarchical state building during those years and the consequent burgeoning of bureaucracies, armies, courts, and other groups who lived in the capitals. The growth of port cities, in turn, reflects the expansion of European overseas trade—especially, that of the Atlantic routes. Except for Manchester in England and Lyons in France, the new urban conglomerates were nonindustrial cities.

Furthermore, between 1600 and 1750, cities with populations of fewer than 40,000 inhabitants declined. These included older landlocked trading centers, medieval industrial cities, and ecclesiastical centers. They contributed less to the new political regimes, and the expansion of the putting-out system transferred production from medieval cities to the countryside because rural labor was cheaper than urban labor.

The Emergence of New Cities and the Growth of Small Towns In the mid-eighteenth century, a new pattern emerged. The rate of growth of existing large cities declined, new cities emerged, and existing smaller cities grew. Several factors were at work in the process, which Jan De Vries has termed "an urban growth from below."[3] First was the general overall population increase. Second, the early stages of the Industrial Revolution, particularly in Britain, occurred in the countryside and fostered the growth of smaller towns and cities located near factories. Factory organization itself led to new concentrations of population.

Cities also grew as a result of the new prosperity of European agriculture, even where there was little industrialization. Improved agricultural production promoted the growth of nearby market towns and other urban centers that served agriculture or allowed more prosperous farmers to have access to consumer goods and recreation. This new pattern of urban growth—new cities and the expansion of smaller existing ones—would continue into the nineteenth century.

[3]Jan De Vries, "Patterns of Urbanization in Pre-Industrial Europe, 1500–1800," in H. Schmal, ed., *Patterns of Urbanization since 1500* (London: Croom Helm, 1981), p. 103.

Urban Classes

Social divisions were as marked in eighteenth-century cities as they were in nineteenth-century industrial centers. The urban rich were often visibly segregated from the urban poor. Aristocrats and the upper middle class lived in fashionable town houses, often constructed around newly laid-out green squares. The poorest town dwellers usually congregated along the rivers. Small merchants and artisans lived above their shops. Whole families might live in a single room. Modern sanitary facilities were unknown. Pure water was rare. Cattle, pigs, goats, and other animals roamed the streets. All reports on the cities of Europe during this period emphasize both the striking grace and beauty of the dwellings of the wealthy and the dirt, filth, and stench that filled the streets. (See "Encountering the Past: Water, Washing, and Bathing," page 468.)

Poverty was not just an urban problem; it was usually worse in the countryside. In the city, however, poverty was more visible in the form of crime, prostitution, vagrancy, begging, and alcoholism. Many a young man or woman from the countryside migrated to the nearest city to seek a better life, only to discover poor housing, little food, disease, degradation, and finally death. It did not require the Industrial Revolution and the urban factories to make the cities into hellholes for the poor and the dispossessed. The full darkness of London life during the mid-century "gin age," when consumption of that liquor blinded and killed many poor people, is evident in the engravings of William Hogarth (1697–1764).

Also contrasting with the serenity of the aristocratic and upper-commercial-class lifestyle were the public executions that took place all over Europe, the breaking of men and women on instruments of torture in Paris, and the public floggings in Russia. Brutality condoned and carried out by the ruling classes was a fact of everyday life.

The Upper Classes At the top of the urban social structure stood a generally small group of nobles, large merchants, bankers, financiers, clergy, and government officials. These upper-class men controlled the political and economic affairs of the town. Normally, they constituted a self-appointed and self-electing oligarchy that governed the city through its corporation or city council. Some form of royal charter usually gave the city corporation its authority and the power to select its own members. In a few cities on the Continent, artisan guilds controlled the corporations, but generally, the local nobility and the wealthiest commercial people dominated the councils.

The Middle Class Another group in the city was the prosperous, but not always immensely wealthy, merchants, trades people, bankers, and professional people. They were the most dynamic element of the urban

WATER, WASHING, AND BATHING

BEFORE THE LATE nineteenth century, clean water was scarce in Europe. Except for the few households and institutions that had their own wells, water had to be carried from a public fountain or public well. Drought in summer and freezing in winter could lead to shortages.

Governments made little effort to provide water. Everyone assumed that people required little water for their personal use—less than 7.5 liters per day, according to one eighteenth-century commentator. (The average American uses 210 liters per day.) Commerce and agriculture used much more water than individuals: to power mills in the cloth and dye trades, and to quench the thirst of work animals and irrigate fields.

Attitudes toward personal appearance also determined the use of water. In the Middle Ages, public bathhouses were not uncommon. The appearance of the body—cleanliness—was believed to reflect the state of the soul, and townspeople and aristocrats bathed fairly often. However, during the Renaissance and the Reformation, the quality and condition of clothing, not bodily cleanliness, were thought to mirror the soul. Clean clothes also revealed a person's social status—clothes made the man and the woman.

Moreover, from the late Middle Ages through the end of the eighteenth century, etiquette and medical manuals advised people to wash only those parts of their bodies that could be seen in public—the hands, the face, the neck, and the feet. All forms of public bathing were associated with immoral behavior—public bathing meant public nudity, and prostitutes frequented bathhouses.

The switch from woolen to linen clothing accompanied the decline in bathing. By the sixteenth century, easily washable linen clothing had begun to replace woolen garments in much of Western Europe. Clean linen shirts or blouses allowed persons who had not bathed to appear clean. Possession of large quantities of freshly laundered linens was a sign of high social status.

Appearance thus became more important than bodily hygiene. Medical opinion supported these practices. Physicians believed odors or *miasma* (bad air), such as might be found in soiled linens—along with lice, fleas, and other vermin—caused disease. One should therefore change one's shirt every few days but avoid baths, which might let the bad air enter the body through the open pores. Consequently, in an age in which there were practically no personal bathtubs, thousands of shirts were washed each week, almost always by female laundresses, in every city.

Attitudes toward bathing only began to change toward the middle of the eighteenth century when writers argued that frequent bathing might lead to greater health. Large public baths, such as had been known in the ancient world and were a fixture of the Ottoman Empire, revived during the nineteenth century, and the germ theory of disease led health authorities to urge people to bathe often to rid their bodies of germs. The great water projects of the nineteenth century (see Chapter 23) would assure vast quantities of water for personal hygiene.

Source: Daniel Roche, *The Culture of Clothing: Dress and Fashion in the "Ancien Regime"* (Cambridge: Cambridge University Press, 1994); Georges Vigarello, *Concepts of Cleanliness: Changing Attitudes in France since the Middle Ages* (Cambridge: Cambridge University Press, 1988); Alain Corbin, *The Foul and the Fragrant: Odor and the French Social Imagination* (Cambridge, MA: Harvard University Press, 1988).

Why did bathing become less frequent after the late Middle Ages? How did the use of linen clothing contribute to this change?

In the eighteenth century washing linen clothing by hand was a major task of women servants. J. B. S. Chardin, *The Washerwoman*. Nationalmuseum med Prins Eugens Waldemarsudde. Photo: The National Museum of Fine Arts population and made up the middle class, or bourgeoisie. The concept of the middle class was much less clear-cut than that of the nobility. The middle class itself was and would remain diverse and divided, with persons employed in the professions often resentful of those who drew their incomes from commerce. Less wealthy members of the middle class of whatever occupation resented wealthier members who might be connected to the nobility through social or business relationships.

The middle class had less wealth than most nobles, but more than urban artisans. Middle-class people lived in the cities and towns, and their sources of income had little or nothing to do with the land. In one way or another, they all benefited from expanding trade and commerce, whether as merchants, lawyers, or small-factory owners. Theirs was a world in which earning and saving of money enabled rapid social mobility and change in lifestyle. They saw themselves as willing to put their capital and energy to work, whereas they portrayed the nobility as idle. The members of the middle class tended to be economically aggressive and socially ambitious. People often made fun of them for these characteristics and were jealous of their success. The middle class normally supported reform, change, and economic growth. They also wanted more rational regulations for trade and commerce, as did some progressive aristocrats.

The middle class was made up of people whose lives fostered the revolution in consumption. On one hand, as owners of factories and of wholesale and retail businesses, they produced and sold goods for the expanding consumer market; on the other hand, members of the middle class were among the chief consumers. It was to their homes that the vast array of new consumer goods made their way. They were also the people whose social values most fully embraced the commercial spirit. They might not enjoy the titles or privileges of the nobility, but they could enjoy material comfort and prosperity. It was this style of life that less well-off people could emulate as they sought to acquire consumer goods for themselves.

During the eighteenth century, the relationship between the middle class and the aristocracy was complicated. On one hand, the nobles, especially in England and France, increasingly embraced the commercial spirit associated with the middle class by improving their estates and investing in cities. On the other

hand, wealthy members of the middle class often tried to imitate the lifestyle of the nobility by purchasing landed estates. The aspirations of the middle class for social mobility, however, conflicted with the determination of the nobles to maintain and reassert their own privileges and to protect their own wealth. Middle-class commercial figures—traders, bankers, manufacturers, and lawyers—often found their pursuit of profit and prestige blocked by the privileges of the nobility and its social exclusiveness, by the inefficiency of monarchical bureaucracies dominated by the nobility, or by aristocrats who controlled patronage and government contracts.

The bourgeoisie was not rising to challenge the nobility; rather, both were seeking to increase their existing political power and social prestige. The tensions that arose between the nobles and the middle class during the eighteenth century normally involved issues of power sharing or access to political influence, rather than clashes over values or goals associated with class.

The middle class in the cities also feared the lower urban classes as much as they envied the nobility. The lower orders were a potentially violent element in society, a threat to property, and, in their poverty, a drain on national resources. The lower classes, however, were much more varied than either the city aristocracy or the middle class cared to admit.

Artisans Shopkeepers, artisans, and wage earners were the single largest group in any city. They were grocers, butchers, fishmongers, carpenters, cabinetmakers, smiths, printers, hand-loom weavers, and tailors, to give a few examples. They had their own culture, values, and institutions. Like the peasants, they were, in many

This engraving illustrates a metalworking shop such as might have been found in almost any town of significance in Europe. Most of the people employed in the shop probably belonged to the same family. Note that two women are also working. The wife may very well have been the person in charge of keeping the accounts of the business. The two younger boys might be children of the owner or apprentices in the trade, or both. The Granger Collection, New York respects, conservative. Their economic position was vulnerable. If a poor harvest raised the price of food, their own businesses suffered. These urban classes also contributed to the revolution in consumption, however. They could buy more goods than ever before, and, to the extent their incomes permitted, many of them sought to copy the domestic consumption of the middle class.

The lives of these artisans and shopkeepers centered on their work and their neighborhoods. They usually lived near or at their place of employment. Most of them worked in shops with fewer than a half dozen other artisans. Their primary institution had historically been the guild, but by the eighteenth century, the guilds rarely exercised the influence their predecessors had in medieval or early modern Europe.

Nevertheless, the guilds were not to be ignored. They played a conservative role. Rather than seeking economic growth or innovation, they tried to preserve the jobs and skills of their members. In many countries, the guilds still determined who could pursue a craft. To lessen competition, they attempted to prevent too many people from learning a particular skill.

The guilds also provided a framework for social and economic advancement. At an early age, a boy might become an apprentice to learn a craft or trade. After several years, he would be made a journeyman. Still later, if successful and competent, he might become a master. The artisan could also receive social benefits from the guilds, including aid for his family during sickness or the promise of admission for his son. The guilds were the chief protection for artisans against the workings of the commercial market. They were particularly strong in central Europe.

The Urban Riot

The artisan class, with its generally conservative outlook, maintained a rather fine sense of social and economic justice based largely on traditional practices. If they felt that what was economically "just" had been offended, artisans frequently manifested their displeasure by rioting. The most sensitive area was the price of bread, the staple food of the poor. If a baker or a grain merchant announced a price that was considered unjustly high, a riot might well ensue. Artisan leaders would confiscate the bread or grain and sell it for what the urban crowd considered a "just price." They would then give the money paid for the grain or bread to the baker or merchant.

The danger of bread riots restrained the greed of merchants. Such disturbances represented a collective method of imposing the "just price" in place of the price the commercial marketplace set. Thus, bread and food riots, which occurred throughout Europe, were not irrational acts of screaming, hungry people, but highly ritualized social phenomena of the Old Regime and its economy of scarcity.

Other kinds of riots also characterized eighteenth-century society and politics. The riot was a way in which people who were excluded in every other way from the political processes could make their will known. Sometimes religious bigotry led to urban riots. For example, in 1753, London Protestant mobs compelled the government to withdraw an act to legalize Jewish naturalization. In 1780, the same rabidly Protestant spirit manifested itself in the Gordon riots. Lord George Gordon (1751–1793) had raised the specter of an imaginary Catholic plot after the government relieved military recruits from having to take specifically anti-Catholic oaths.

In these riots and in food riots, violence was normally directed against property rather than people. The rioters themselves were not disreputable people but usually small shopkeepers, freeholders, artisans, and wage earners. They usually wanted only to restore a traditional right or practice that seemed endangered. Nevertheless, their actions could cause considerable turmoil and destruction.

During the last half of the century, urban riots increasingly involved political ends. Though often simultaneous with economic disturbances, the political riot always had nonartisan leadership or instigators. In fact, an eighteenth-century "crowd" was often the tool of the upper classes. In Paris, the aristocratic *Parlement* often urged crowd action in its disputes with the monarchy. In Geneva, middle-class citizens supported artisan riots against the local oligarchy. In Great Britain in 1792, the government incited mobs to attack English sympathizers of the French Revolution. Such outbursts indicate that the crowd or mob had entered the European political and social arena well before the revolution in France.

▼ The Jewish Population: The Age of the Ghetto

Although the small Jewish communities of Amsterdam and other Western European cities became famous for their intellectual life and financial institutions, most European Jews lived in Eastern Europe. In the eighteenth century and thereafter, the Jewish population of Europe was concentrated in Poland, Lithuania, and Ukraine, where no fewer than 3 million Jews dwelled. Perhaps 150,000 Jews lived in the Habsburg lands, primarily Bohemia, around 1760. Fewer than 100,000 Jews lived in Germany. France had approximately 40,000 Jews. England and Holland, each had a Jewish population of fewer than 10,000. There were even smaller groups of Jews elsewhere.

In 1762, Catherine the Great of Russia specifically excluded Jews from a manifesto that welcomed foreigners to settle in Russia. She relaxed the exclusion a few years later, but Jews during her reign often felt they needed assurances of imperial protection for their livelihoods and religious practices against the ordinances of local officials. (See "Belorussian Jews Petition Catherine

During the Old Regime, European Jews were separated from non-Jews, typically in districts known as ghettos. Relegated to the least desirable section of a city or to rural villages, most lived in poverty. This watercolor painting depicts a street in Kazimlesz, the Jewish quarter of Kraków, Poland. Judaica Collection, Max Berger, Vienna, Austria. Photograph © Erich Lessing/Art Resource, NY

the Great," page 472.) After the first partition of Poland of 1772, discussed in Chapter 17, the Russian Empire included a large Jewish population, and the number of Jews in Prussia and under Austrian rule also increased.

Jews dwelled in most nations without enjoying the rights and privileges that other subjects had unless monarchs specifically granted them to Jews. Jews were regarded as a kind of resident alien whose residence might well be temporary or changed at the whim of rulers.

No matter where they dwelled, Old Regime Jews lived apart in separate communities from non-Jewish Europeans. These communities might be distinct districts of cities, known as **ghettos**, or in primarily Jewish villages in the countryside. Jews were also treated as a distinct people religiously and legally. In Poland for much of the century, they were virtually self-governing. In other areas, they lived under the burden of discriminatory legislation. Except in England, Jews could not and did not mix in the mainstream of the societies in which they dwelled. This period, which may be said to have begun with the expulsion of the Jews from Spain at the end of the fifteenth century, is known as the age of the ghetto, or separate community.

During the seventeenth century, a few Jews had helped finance the wars of major rulers. These financiers often became close to the rulers and were known as "court Jews." Perhaps the most famous was Samuel

Oppenheimer (1630–1703), who helped the Habsburgs finance their struggle against the Turks and the defense of Vienna. However, these loans were often not repaid. The court Jews and their financial abilities became famous. They tended to marry among themselves.

Most European Jews, however, lived in poverty. They occupied the most undesirable sections of cities or poor villages. Some were small-time moneylenders, but most worked at the lowest occupations. Their religious beliefs, rituals, and community set them apart. Virtually all laws and social institutions kept them socially inferior to and apart from their Christian neighbors.

Under the Old Regime, it is important to emphasize that this discrimination was based on religious separateness. Jews who converted to Christianity were welcomed, even if not always warmly, into the major political and social institutions of Gentile European society. Until the last two decades of the eighteenth century, in every part of Europe, however, those Jews who remained loyal to their faith were subject to various religious, civil, and social disabilities. They could not pursue the professions freely, they often could not change residence without official permission, and they were excluded from the political structures of the nations in which they lived. Jews could be expelled from their homes, and their property could be confiscated. They could be required to listen to sermons that insulted their religion. Their children could be taken away from them and given Christian instruction. They knew their non-Jewish neighbors might suddenly turn against them and kill them.

In subsequent chapters, it will be shown how the end of the Old Regime brought major changes in the lives of European Jews and in their relationship to the larger culture.

In Perspective

Near the close of the eighteenth century, European society was on the brink of a new era. That society had remained traditional and corporate largely because of an economy of scarcity. Beginning in the eighteenth century, however, the commercial spirit and the values of the marketplace, although not new, were permitted fuller play

BELORUSSIAN JEWS PETITION CATHERINE THE GREAT

In the 1780s, through military expansion, Empress Catherine the Great of Russia (see Chapter 17) annexed Belorussia, bringing a new Jewish minority under her imperial government. In response to her decree, governing many aspects of the region's law and economy, Belorussian Jews petitioned the empress to protect certain of their traditional rights regarding the distillation and sale of spirits. They also petitioned for protection in court and for the right to retain their own traditional practices and courts for matters relating to their own community. The petition indicates how in Russia, as elsewhere in Europe, Jews were treated as a people apart. It also illustrates how Jews, like other minorities in Old Regime Europe, sought both to receive the protection of monarchies against arbitrary local officials and to maintain long-standing social practices. The document reveals the Jews' dependence on the goodwill of the non-Jewish community.

How do the petitioners attempt to appeal to long-standing custom to defend their interests? How does the petition suggest that Jewish law and practice, distinct from the rest of the society, governed Jewish social life? In the context of this petition, which non-Jewish authorities may actually or potentially influence Jewish life?

2.

According to an ancient custom, when the squires built a new village, they summoned the Jews to reside there and gave them certain privileges for several years and then permanent liberty to distill spirits, brew beer and mead, and sell these drinks. On this basis, the Jews built houses and distillation plants at considerable expense. . . . A new decree of Her Imperial Majesty . . . reserved [this right] to the squires. . . . But a decree of the governor-general of Belorussia has now forbidden the squires to farm out distillation in their villages to Jews, even if the squires want to do this. As a result, the poor Jews who built houses in small villages and promoted both this trade and distillation have been deprived of these and left completely impoverished. But until all the Jewish people are totally ruined, the Jewish merchants suffer restraints equally with the poor rural Jews, since their law obliges them to assist all who share their religious faith. They therefore request an imperial decree authorizing the squire, if he wishes, to farm out distillation to Jews in rural areas.

3.

Although, with Her Imperial Majesty's permission, Jews may be elected as officials . . . , Jews are allotted fewer votes than other people and hence no Jew can ever attain office. Consequently, Jews have no one to defend them in courts and find themselves in a desperate situation—given their fear and ignorance of Russian—in case of misfortune, even if innocent. To consummate all the good already bestowed, Jews dare to petition that an equal number of electors be required from Jews as from others (or, at least, that in matters involving Jews and non-Jews, a representative from the Jewish community hold equal rights with non-Jews, be present to accompany Jews in court, and attend the interrogation of Jews). But cases involving only Jews (except for promissory notes and debts) should be handled solely in Jewish courts, because Jews assume obligations among themselves, make agreements and conclude all kinds of deals in the Jewish language and in accordance with Jewish rites and laws (which are not known to others). Moreover, those who transgress their laws and order should be judged in Jewish courts. [Similarly, preserve intact all their customs and holidays in the spirit of their faith, as is mercifully assured in the imperial manifesto.]

than ever before in European history. The newly unleashed commercial spirit led increasingly to a conception of human beings as individuals rather than as members of communities. In particular, that spirit manifested itself in the Agricultural and Industrial Revolutions, as well as in the drive toward greater consumption. Together, those two vast changes in production overcame most of the scarcity that had haunted Europe and the West generally. The accompanying changes in landholding and production would transform the European social structure.

The expansion of population further stimululated change. More people meant more labor, more energy, and more minds contributing to the creation and solution of social difficulties. Cities had to accommodate expanding populations. Corporate groups, such as the guilds, had to confront the existence of a larger labor force. New wealth meant that birth would eventually become less and less a determining factor in social relationships, except for the social roles assigned to the two sexes. Class structure and social hierarchy remained, but the boundaries became more blurred.

Finally, the conflicting ambitions of monarchs, the nobility, and the middle class generated innovation. In the pursuit of new revenues, the monarchs interfered with the privileges of the nobles. In the name of ancient rights, the nobles attempted to secure and expand their existing social privileges. The middle class, in all of its diversity, was growing wealthier from trade, commerce, and the practice of the professions. Its members wanted social prestige and influence equal to their wealth. They resented privileges, frowned on hierarchy, and rejected tradition.

All these factors meant the society of the eighteenth century stood at the close of one era in European history and at the opening of another.

AP* TEST PREP

1. James Watt is primarily remembered as the inventor of the
   a. spinning wheel.
   b. spinning jenny.
   c. steam engine.
   d. flying shuttle.
   e. rolling mill.

2. By 1800, London's inhabitants numbered
   a. over 100,000.
   b. just about 250,000.
   c. just above 500,000.
   d. almost 1 million.
   e. just about 250 million.

3. The immediate effect upon women by the industrialization of spinning was to
   a. push women into domestic labor.
   b. advance their standing as skilled workers.
   c. embolden women to assert their rights.
   d. disrupt their domain as primary child-care providers.
   e. give women greater control in guilds.

4. Raising grain prices in the eighteenth century did all of the following *except*
   a. put pressure on the poor.
   b. stimulate a series of agricultural innovations.
   c. benefit landowners.
   d. give advantages to small peasant producers.
   e. put pressure on city dwellers.

5. Peasants resisted enclosure laws largely because the laws
   a. forced large numbers of peasants off the land.
   b. led to malnutrition and low birthrates.
   c. prohibited the use of new technologies.
   d. disrupted community life and traditional practices.
   e. revealed class bias.

6. The Russian Charter of the Nobility exemplified aristocratic resurgence by
   a. resisting the encroachment of monarchical control over traditional privileges.
   b. curtailing the social advancement of the newly emboldened commercial classes.
   c. successfully suppressing peasant uprisings.
   d. unifying the interests of the nobility with the landed gentry.
   e. unifying the interests of the nobility with the Church.

7. *Banalités* were
   a. peasant land tenure rights.
   b. monarchical decrees.
   c. peasant feudal dues for use privileges.
   d. peasant service requirements for labor.
   e. aristocratic service requirements at court.

8. The relative independence of southeastern European peasants in the seventeenth and eighteenth centuries can be attributed to
   a. a culture of *noblesse oblige*.
   b. a culture of work for hire.
   c. scarcity of labor.
   d. intermarriage between landholders and workers.
   e. early recognition of rights.

9. Servants in preindustrial Western European households
   a. were always young people of inferior status.
   b. used the position to acquire a productive skill and some savings.

c. were always women.
d. could be afforded by only the wealthiest classes.
e. were often abused.

10. In Eastern Europe, landlords asserted their interest in keeping land cultivated by
    a. traveling broadly to learn new technologies.
    b. hiring free laborers.
    c. investing in international ventures.
    d. ordering serfs to arrange early marriages for their children.
    e. planting clover and adopting the three-field system.

11. An artisan's daughter might not leave home until marriage because she
    a. would be concerned for her physical safety.
    b. had to have her marriage arranged for her.
    c. could learn increasingly valuable skills associated with the trade at home.
    d. required the local lord's permission.
    e. did not need a dowry.

12. Foundling hospitals grew importance for all the following reasons *except*
    a. an increase in food prices.
    b. ignorance and prejudice regarding contraception.
    c. illegitimate births across the social spectrum.
    d. increased migration.
    e. little interest in preserving the lives of abandoned children.

13. Over the course of the eighteenth century, disposable income
    a. rose in England but fell on the Continent.
    b. fell throughout Europe.
    c. rose only in central Europe.
    d. rose only in France.
    e. rose throughout Europe.

14. The single largest group in eighteenth-century cities was/were
    a. shopkeepers, artisans, and wage earners.
    b. the middle class.
    c. the unemployed.
    d. merchants.
    e. foreigners.

15. Sumptuary laws
    a. regulated regional trade.
    b. barred women from certain professions.
    c. established guidelines for midwives.
    d. were largely abolished in the eighteenth century.
    e. regulated the dress of different social classes.

16. French nobles were divided between those "of the robe" and those
    a. "of the sword."
    b. "of the crown."
    c. "of the land."
    d. "of the blood."
    e. "of the church."

17. In eighteenth-century Britain, all of the following were excluded from the right to hunt *except*
    a. the poor.
    b. all persons renting land.
    c. city merchants.
    d. large landowners.
    e. clergy.

18. The economic basis of eighteenth-century life was
    a. regional trade.
    b. international trade.
    c. the land.
    d. manufacturing.
    e. heavy industry.

19. In the Old Regime, Jews
    a. were always discriminated against.
    b. were welcomed into gentile society upon conversion to Christianity.
    c. were forced into ghettos.
    d. were always prohibited from participating in financial institutions.
    e. were bestowed with rights to practice their religion but were excluded from political life.

20. The British Industrial Revolution was aided by all of the following *except*
    a. a large free trade area.
    b. an absence of royal monopolies.
    c. flourishing newspapers.
    d. relatively fair taxation.
    e. rich deposits of coal and iron ore.

DOCUMENT-BASED QUESTION

Directions: Construct a valid essay that directly addresses the central issue of the following question. Use facts from the documents provided and from the chapter to prove the position you take in your thesis statement.

What role did women play in the eighteenth-century economy? Do you agree or disagree with the assertion that eighteenth-century women were limited to the domestic sphere?

Document A

Francis Wheatly's painting *Morning*.

Document B

An eighteenth-century French dress and hat shop.

Document C

J. B. S. Chardin's painting *The Washerwoman*.

Document D

Source: Priscilla Wakefield demands more occupations for women, *Reflections on the Present Condition of the Female Sex.*

Another heavy discouragement to the industry of women, is the inequality of the reward of their labor, compared with that of men; an injustice which pervades every species of employment performed by both sexes.

In employments which depend on bodily strength, the distinction is just; for it cannot be pretended that the generality of women can earn as much as men, when the produce of their labor is the result of corporeal exertion; but it is a subject of great regret, that this inequality should prevail even where an equal share of skill and application is exerted. Besides these employments which are commonly performed by women, and those already shown to be suitable for such persons as are above the condition of hard labor, there are some professions and trades customarily in the hands of men, which might be conveniently exercised by either sex.

For more on women and work in the eighteenth century, see pages 453–454, 460, 464–466, 469.

new inventions, cotton-textiles, population boom 6-10 mill, consumerism, banking, free trade, army, naval fleets land, labor, capitolism, social nobility, consumer rev manufac goods

newspapers, print culture

General James Wolfe was mortally wounded during his victory over the French at Quebec in 1759. This painting by the American artist Benjamin West (1738–1820) became famous for portraying the dying Wolfe and the officers around him in poses modeled after classical statues. Getty Images Inc.— Hulton Archive Photos

16

The Transatlantic Economy, Trade Wars, and Colonial Rebellion

▼ **Periods of European Overseas Empires**

▼ **Mercantile Empires**
Mercantilist Goals • French–British Rivalry

▼ **The Spanish Colonial System**
Colonial Government • Trade Regulation • Colonial Reform under the Spanish Bourbon Monarchs

▼ **Black African Slavery, the Plantation System, and the Atlantic Economy**
The African Presence in the Americas • Slavery and the Transatlantic Economy
• The Experience of Slavery

▼ **Mid-Eighteenth-Century Wars**
The War of Jenkins's Ear • The War of the Austrian Succession (1740–1748) • The "Diplomatic Revolution" of 1756 • The Seven Years' War (1756–1763)

▼ **The American Revolution and Europe**
Resistance to the Imperial Search for Revenue • The Crisis and Independence • American Political Ideas
• Events in Great Britain • Broader Impact of the American Revolution

▼ **In Perspective**

THE MID-EIGHTEENTH century witnessed a renewal of European warfare on a worldwide scale. The conflict involved two separate, but interrelated, rivalries. Austria and Prussia fought for dominance in central Europe while Great Britain and France dueled for commercial and colonial supremacy. The wars were long, extensive, and costly in both effort and money. They resulted in a new balance of power on the Continent and on the high seas. Prussia emerged as a great power, and Great Britain gained a world empire.

The expense of these wars led every major European government after the Peace of Paris of 1763 to reconstruct its policies of taxation and finance. Among the results of these policies were the American Revolution, an enlightened absolutism on the Continent, a continuing financial crisis for the French monarchy, and a reform of the Spanish Empire in South America.

▼ Periods of European Overseas Empires

Since the Renaissance, European contacts with the rest of the world have gone through four distinct stages. The first was that of the European discovery, exploration, initial conquest, and settlement of the New World. This phase also witnessed the penetration of Southeast Asian markets by Portugal and the Netherlands, which established major imperial outposts and influence in the region. This period closed by the end of the seventeenth century. (See Chapter 10.)

The second era—that of the mercantile empires, which are largely the concern of this chapter—was one of colonial trade rivalry among Spain, France, and Great Britain. Although during the sixteenth and seventeenth centuries differing motives had led to the establishment of overseas European empires, by the eighteenth century they generally existed to foster trade and commerce. These commercial goals, however, often sparked intense rivalry and conflict in key imperial trouble spots. As a result, the various imperial ventures led to the creation of large navies and a series of major naval wars at the mid-century—wars that in turn became linked to warfare on the European continent. The Anglo-French side of the contest has often been compared to a second Hundred Years' War, with theaters of conflict in Europe, the Americas, West Africa, and India.

A fundamental element in these first two periods of European imperial ventures in the Americas was the presence of slavery. By the eighteenth century, the slave population of the New World consisted almost entirely of a black population that had either recently been forcibly imported from Africa or born to slaves whose forebearers had been forcibly imported from Africa. Both the forced migration of so many people from one continent to another and the mid-Atlantic **plantation economies** that such slave labor supported were unprecedented in history. The creation in the Americas of this slave-based plantation economy led directly to over three centuries of extensive involvement by Europeans and white Americans in the slave trade with Africa—particularly, with the societies of West Africa. In turn, on the American continent the slave trade created extensive communities of Africans from the Chesapeake region of Maryland and Virginia south to Brazil. The Africans brought to the American experience

not only their labor, but also their languages, customs, and ethnic associations. The Atlantic economy and the societies that arose in the Americas were, consequently, the creation of both Europeans and Africans while, as a result of the Spanish conquest, Native Americans were pressed toward the margins of those societies. In this respect from the sixteenth century onward Africans became a significant factor in the forging of the Western Heritage as commodities in the slave trade that enriched western European economies and as laborers in the New World plantation economy, the wealth and products of which enriched the daily life of peoples in Europe and European settlers and their descendants in the Americas.

Finally, during the second period, both the British colonies of the North American seaboard and the Spanish colonies of Mexico and Central and South America emancipated themselves from European control. This era

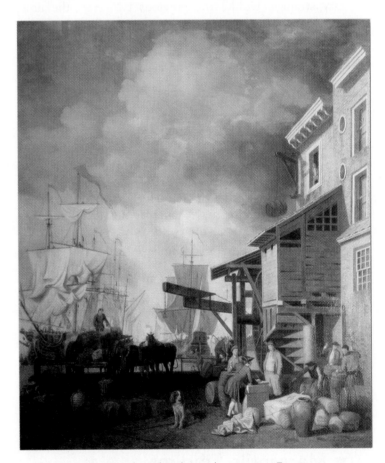

During the seventeenth and eighteenth centuries, European maritime nations established overseas empires and set up trading monopolies within them in an effort to magnify their economic strength. As this painting of the Old Custom House Quay in London suggests, trade from these empires and the tariffs imposed on it were expected to generate revenue for the home country. But behind many of the goods carried in the great sailing ships in the harbor and landed on these docks lay the labor of African slaves working on the plantations of North and South America. Samuel Scott "Old Custom House Quay" Collection. V & A Images, The Victoria and Albert Museum, London of independence, part of which is discussed in this chapter and part in Chapter 20, may be said to have closed during the 1820s. This same revolutionary era witnessed the beginning of the antislavery movement that extended through the third quarter of the nineteenth century. (See "The West and the World: The Abolition of Slavery in the Transatlantic Economy," p. 681.)

The third stage of European contact with the non-European world occurred in the nineteenth century. During that period, European governments largely turned from their involvement in the Americas and carved out new formal empires involving the direct European administration of indigenous peoples in Africa and Asia. Those nineteenth-century empires also included new areas of European settlement, such as Australia, New Zealand, South Africa, and Algeria. The bases of these empires were trade, national honor, Christian missionary enterprise, and military strategy. Unlike the previous two eras, the nineteenth-century empires were based on formally free labor forces though they still involved much harsh treatment of non-white indigenous populations. (See Chapter 25.)

The last period of the European empire occurred during the mid- and late twentieth century, with the decolonization of peoples who had previously lived under European colonial rule. (See Chapter 29.)

During the four-and-one-half centuries before decolonization, Europeans exerted political, military, and economic dominance over much of the rest of the world that was far disproportional to the geographical size or population of Europe. Europeans frequently treated other peoples as social, intellectual, economic, and racial inferiors. Europeans ravaged existing cultures because of greed, religious zeal, or political ambition. These actions are major facts of both European and world history and remain significant factors in the contemporary relationship between Europe and its former colonies, as well as between the United States and those former colonies. What allowed the Europeans initially to exert such influence and domination for so long over so much of the world was not any innate cultural superiority, but a technological supremacy related to naval power and gunpowder. Ships and guns allowed the Europeans to exercise their will almost wherever they chose.

▼ Mercantile Empires

Navies and merchant shipping were the keystones of the mercantile empires that were meant to bring profit to a nation rather than to provide areas for settlement. The Treaty of Utrecht (1713) established the boundaries of empire during the first half of the eighteenth century.

Except for Brazil, which Portugal governed, and Dutch Guiana, Spain controlled all of mainland South America. In North America, it ruled Florida, Mexico, California, and the Southwest. The Spanish also governed Central America and the islands of Cuba, Puerto Rico, Trinidad, and the eastern part of Hispaniola that is today the Dominican Republic.

The British Empire consisted of the colonies along the North Atlantic seaboard, Nova Scotia, Newfoundland, Bermuda, Jamaica, and Barbados. Britain also possessed a few trading stations on the Indian subcontinent.

The French domains covered the Saint Lawrence River valley and the Ohio and Mississippi River valleys. They included the West Indian islands of Saint Domingue (modern Haiti on the western part of Hispaniola), Guadeloupe, and Martinique, and also stations in India and on the West Coast of Africa. To the French and British merchant communities, India appeared as a vast potential market for European goods, as well as the source of calico cloth and spices that were in much demand in Europe.

The Dutch controlled Surinam, or Dutch Guiana, in South America, Cape Colony in what is today South Africa, and trading stations in West Africa, Sri Lanka, and Bengal in India. Most importantly, they also controlled the trade with Java in what is now Indonesia. The Dutch had opened these markets largely in the seventeenth century and had created a vast trading empire far larger in extent, wealth, and importance than the geographical size of the United Netherlands would have led one to expect. The Dutch had been daring sailors and they made important technological innovations in sailing.

All of these powers and the Danes also possessed numerous smaller islands in the Caribbean. In the eighteenth century, the major rivalries existed among the Spanish, the French, and the British.

Mercantilist Goals

If any formal economic theory lay behind the conduct of eighteenth-century empires, it was **mercantilism**, that practical creed of hard-headed businesspeople. The terms *mercantilism* and *mercantile system* were invented by later opponents and critics of the system whereby governments heavily regulated trade and commerce in hope of increasing national wealth. Economic writers believed this system necessary for a nation to gain a favorable trade balance of gold and silver bullion. They regarded bullion as the measure of a country's wealth, and a nation was truly wealthy only if it amassed more bullion than its rivals.

The mercantilist statesmen and traders regarded the world as an arena of scarce resources and economic limitations. Mercantilist thinking assumed that only modest levels of economic growth were possible. Such thinking predated the expansion of agricultural and later industrial productivity discussed in the previous chapter. Before such sustained economic growth began, the wealth of one nation was assumed to grow or increase largely at the direct expense of another nation. That is to say, the wealth of one state might expand only if its armies or navies conquered the domestic or colonial territory of another state and thus gained the productive capacity of that area, or if a state expanded its trading monopoly over new territory, or if, by smuggling, it could intrude on the trading monopoly of another state.

From beginning to end, the economic well-being of the home country was the primary concern of mercantilist writers. Colonies existed to provide markets and natural resources for the industries of the home country. In turn, the home country was to protect and administer the colonies. Both sides assumed the colonies were the inferior partner in the relationship. The home country and its colonies were to trade exclusively with each other. To that end, governments tried to forge trade-tight systems of national commerce through navigation laws, tariffs, bounties to encourage production, and prohibitions against trading with the subjects of other monarchs. National monopoly was the ruling principle.

Mercantilist ideas had always been neater on paper than in practice. By the early eighteenth century, mercantilist assumptions were far removed from the economic realities of the colonies. The colonial and home markets simply did not mesh. Spain could not produce enough goods for South America. Economic production in the British North American colonies challenged English manufacturing and led to British attempts to limit certain colonial industries, such as iron and hat making.

Colonists of different countries wished to trade with each other. English colonists could buy sugar more cheaply from the French West Indies than from English suppliers. The traders and merchants of one nation always hoped to break the monopoly of another. For all these reasons, the eighteenth century became what one historian many years ago termed the "golden age of smugglers."[1] Governments could not effectively control their subjects' activities. Clashes among colonists could and did bring about conflict between European governments.

French–British Rivalry

Major flash points existed between France and Britain in North America. Their colonists quarreled endlessly with each other over the coveted regions of the lower Saint Lawrence River valley, upper New England, and, later, the Ohio River valley. Other rivalries arose over fishing rights, the fur trade, and alliances with Native Americans.

The heart of the eighteenth-century colonial rivalry in the Americas, however, lay in the West Indies. These tropical islands, close to the American continents, were the jewels of empire. The West Indies plantations raised tobacco, cotton, indigo, coffee, and, above all, sugar, for which there existed huge markets in Europe. These commodities were becoming part of

daily life, especially in Western Europe. They represented one aspect of those major changes in consumption that marked eighteenth-century European culture. Sugar in particular had become a staple rather than a luxury. It was used in coffee, tea, and cocoa, for making candy and preserving fruits, and in the brewing industry. There seemed no limit to its uses, no limit to consumer demand for it, and, for a time, almost no limit to the riches it might bring to plantation owners. Only slave labor allowed the profitable cultivation of these products during the seventeenth and eighteenth centuries. (See "Encountering the Past: Sugar Enters the Western Diet," page 485.)

India was another area of French–British rivalry. In India, both France and Britain traded through privileged chartered companies that enjoyed a legal monopoly. The East India Company was the English institution; the French equivalent was the *Compagnie des Indes*. The trade of India and Asia figured only marginally in the economics of early eighteenth-century empire. Nevertheless, enterprising Europeans always hoped to develop profitable commerce with India. Others regarded India as a springboard into the even larger potential market of China. The original European footholds in India were trading posts called *factories*. They existed through privileges granted by various Indian governments that in theory were themselves subject to the decaying Mughal Empire, which exercised little effective authority.

Two circumstances in the mid-eighteenth century changed this situation in India. First, the administration and government of several Indian states had decayed. Second, Joseph Dupleix (1697–1763) for the French and Robert Clive (1725–1774) for the British saw the developing power vacuum as providing opportunities for expanding the control of their respective companies. To maintain their own security and to expand their privileges, each of the two companies began in effect to take over the government of some of the regions. Each group of Europeans hoped to checkmate the other.

The Dutch maintained their extensive commercial empire further to the east in what today is Indonesia. By the eighteenth century, the other European powers more or less acknowledged Dutch predominance in that region.

▼ The Spanish Colonial System

Spanish control of its American Empire involved a system of government and a system of monopolistic trade regulation. Both were more rigid in appearance than in practice. Actual government was often informal, and the trade monopoly was frequently breached. Until the mid-eighteenth century, the primary purpose of the Spanish Empire was to supply Spain with the precious metals mined in the New World.

[1]Walter Dorn, *Competition for Empire, 1740–1763* (New York: Harper, 1940), p. 266.

Colonial Government

Because Queen Isabella of Castile (r. 1474–1504) had commissioned Columbus, the technical legal link between the New World and Spain was the crown of Castile. Its powers both at home and in America were subject to few limitations. The Castilian monarch assigned the government of America to the Council of the Indies, which, with the monarch, nominated the viceroys of New Spain (Mexico) and Peru. These viceroys served as the chief executives in the New World and carried out the laws issued by the Council of the Indies.

Each of the viceroyalties was divided into several subordinate judicial councils, known as *audiencias.* There was also a variety of local officers, the most important of which were the *corregidores,* who presided over municipal councils. All of these officers represented a vast array of patronage, which the monarchy usually bestowed on persons born in Spain. Virtually all power flowed from the top of this political structure downward; in effect, local initiative or self-government scarcely existed.

Trade Regulation

The colonial political structures functioned largely to support Spanish commercial self-interests. The *Casa de Contratación* (House of Trade) in Seville regulated all trade with the New World. Cádiz was the only port authorized for use in the American trade. The *Casa* was the most influential institution of the Spanish Empire. Its members worked closely with the *Consulado* (Merchant Guild) of Seville and other groups involved with American commerce in Cádiz.

A complicated system of trade and bullion fleets administered from Seville maintained Spain's trade monopoly. Each year, a fleet of commercial vessels (the *flota*), controlled by Seville merchants and escorted by warships, carried merchandise from Spain to a few specified ports in America, including Portobello, Veracruz, and Cartagena on the Atlantic coast. There were no authorized ports on the Pacific Coast. Areas far to the south, such as Buenos Aires on the Río de la Plata, received goods only after the shipments had been unloaded at one of the authorized ports. After selling their wares, the ships were loaded with silver and gold bullion; they usually spent the winter in heavily fortified Caribbean ports and then sailed back to Spain. The *flota* system always worked imperfectly, but trade outside it was illegal. Regulations prohibited the Spanish colonists within the American Empire from establishing direct trade with each other and from building their own shipping and commercial industry. Foreign merchants were also forbidden to breach the Spanish monopoly. Spanish ships continued to transport precious metals and coins from the Americas to Spain through the early nineteenth century. Modern day treasure hunters still occasionally discover troves of precious metal from shipwrecked vessels of the colonial Spanish Empire.

Colonial Reform under the Spanish Bourbon Monarchs

A crucial change occurred in the Spanish colonial system in the early eighteenth century. The War of the Spanish Succession (1701–1714) and the Treaty of Utrecht (1713) replaced the Spanish Habsburgs with the Bourbons of France on the Spanish throne. Philip V (r. 1700–1746) and his successors tried to use French administrative skills to reassert the imperial trade monopoly, which had decayed under the last Spanish Habsburgs, and thus to improve the domestic economy and revive Spanish power in Europe.

Under Philip V, Spanish coastal patrol vessels tried to suppress smuggling in American waters. (See "Buccaneers Prowl the High Seas.") An incident arising from this policy led to war with England in 1739, the year in which Philip established the viceroyalty of New Granada in the area that today includes Venezuela, Colombia, and Ecuador. The goal was to strengthen the royal government there.

The great mid-century wars exposed the vulnerability of the Spanish empire to naval attack and economic penetration. As an ally of France, Spain emerged as one of the defeated powers in 1763. Government circles then became convinced that the colonial system had to be reformed.

Charles III (r. 1759–1788), the most important of the imperial reformers, attempted to reassert Spain's control of the empire. Like his Bourbon predecessors, Charles emphasized royal ministers rather than councils. Thus, the role of both the Council of the Indies and the *Casa de Contratación* diminished. After 1765, Charles abolished the monopolies of Seville and Cádiz and permitted other Spanish cities to trade with America. He also opened more South American and Caribbean ports to trade and authorized commerce between Spanish ports in America. In 1776, he organized a fourth viceroyalty in the region of Río de la Plata, which included much of present-day Argentina, Uruguay, Paraguay, and Bolivia. (See Map 16–1, page 482.)

To increase the efficiency of tax collection and end bureaucratic corruption, Charles III introduced the institution of the *intendant* into the Spanish Empire. These loyal, royal bureaucrats were patterned on the domestic French *intendants* made so famous and effective as agents of French royal administration under the absolutism of Louis XIV.

The late-eighteenth-century Bourbon reforms did stimulate the imperial Spanish economy. Trade expanded and became more varied. These reforms, however, also brought the empire more fully under direct Spanish control. Many **peninsulares** (persons born in Spain) entered

BUCCANEERS PROWL THE HIGH SEAS

Piracy was a major problem for transatlantic trade. There was often a fine line between freewheeling buccaneering pirates operating for their own gain and privateers who in effect worked for various European governments that wanted to penetrate the commercial monopoly of the Spanish Empire. Alexander Exquemelin was a ship's surgeon who for a time plied his trade on board a pirate ship and then later settled in Holland. His account of those days emphasizes the careful code of conduct among the pirates themselves and the harshness of their behavior toward both those on ships they captured and poor farmers and fishermen whom they robbed and virtually enslaved.

How did the restrictive commercial policy of the Spanish Empire encourage piracy and privateering? Was there a code of honor among the pirates? What kinds of people may have suffered most from piracy? To what extent did pirates have any respect for individual freedom? How romantic was the real world of pirates?

When a buccaneer is going to sea he sends word to all who wish to sail with him. When all are ready, they go on board, each bringing what he needs in the way of weapons, powder, and shot.

On the ship, they first discuss where to go and get food supplies. . . . The meat is either [salted] pork or turtle. . . . Sometimes they go and plunder the Spaniards' *corrales*, which are pens where they keep perhaps a thousand head of tame hogs. The rovers. . . find the house of the farmer. . . [whom] unless he gives them as many hogs as they demand, they hang. . . without mercy. . . .

When a ship has been captured, the men decide whether the captain should keep it or not: if the prize is better than their own vessel, they take it and set fire to the other. When a ship is robbed, nobody must plunder and keep the loot to himself. Everything taken. . . must be shared. . . , without any man enjoying a penny more than his fair share. To prevent deceit, before the booty is distributed everyone has to swear an oath on the Bible that he has not kept for himself so much as the value of a

sixpence. . . . And should any man be found to have made a false oath, he would be banished from the rovers, and never be allowed in their company. . . .

When they have captured a ship, the buccaneers set the prisoners on shore as soon as possible, apart from two or three whom they keep to do the cooking and other work they themselves do not care for, releasing these men after two or three years.

The rovers frequently put in for fresh supplies at some island or other, often . . . lying off the south coast of Cuba. . . . Everyone goes ashore and sets up his tent, and they take turns to go on marauding expeditions in their canoes. They take prisoner. . . poor men who catch and set turtles for a living, to provide for their wives and children. Once captured, these men have to catch turtle for the rovers as long as they remain on the island. Should the rovers intend to cruise along a coast where turtle abound, they take the fishermen along with them. The poor fellows may be compelled to stay away from their wives and families four or five years, with no news whether they are alive or dead.

Alexander O. Exquemelin, *The Buccaneers of America*, trans. by Alexis Brown (Baltimore, MD: Penguin Books, 1969), pp. 70–72.

the New World to fill new posts, which were often the most profitable jobs in the region. Expanding trade brought more Spanish merchants to Latin America. The economy remained export oriented, and their economic life was still organized to benefit Spain. As a result of these policies, the **creoles** (persons of European descent born in the Spanish colonies) came to feel they were sec-

ond-class subjects. In time, their resentment would provide a major source of the discontent leading to the wars of independence in the early nineteenth century. The imperial reforms of Charles III were the Spanish equivalent of the new colonial measures the British government undertook after 1763, which, as will be seen later in this chapter, led to the American Revolution.

MAP EXPLORATION

Interactive map: To explore this map further, go to www.myhistorylab.com

DISPUTED BY
ENGLAND,
RUSSIA,
AND SPAIN

VICEROYALTY
OF
NEW SPAIN

Rio Grande

EFFECTIVE FRONTIER OF
SPANISH SETTLEMENT

Gulf of Mexico

A T L A N T I C

O C E A N

Mexico
City
Veracruz

Santo Domingo

Caribbean Sea

Cartagena   Caracas
Portobelo

VICEROYALTY OF
NEW GRANADA

Bogotá   Separated From
Viceroyalty of
Peru,
1717, 1739

Quito

GUIANA

Amazon R.

VICEROYALTY
OF
PERU

VICEROYALTY
OF
BRAZIL

Pernambuco

Lima

Bahia

P A C I F I C

O C E A N

Portosi

São Paulo

VICEROYALTY
OF
LA PLATA
Separated From the
Viceroyalty of Peru,
1776

Rio de Janeiro

Santiago

AUDIENCIA
OF CHILE

Buenos
Aires

Claimed but not
settled by Spain

Map 16–1   **VICEROYALTIES IN LATIN AMERICA IN 1780**   The late eighteenth-century viceroyalties in Latin America display the effort of the Spanish Bourbon monarchy to establish more direct control of the colonies. They sought this control through the introduction of more royal officials and by establishing more governmental districts.

The Silver Mines of Potosí. The Spanish had discovered precious metals in their South American Empire early in the sixteenth century. The silver mines of Potosi were worked by conscripted Indian laborers under extremely harsh conditions. These mines provided Spain with a vast treasure in silver from the sixteenth through the eighteenth century.   Hispanic Society of America

▼ Black African Slavery, the Plantation System, and the Atlantic Economy

Within various parts of Europe itself, slavery had existed since ancient times. Before the eighteenth century, little or no moral or religious stigma was attached to slave owning or slave trading. It had a continuous existence in the Mediterranean world, where only the sources of slaves changed over the centuries. After the conquest of Constantinople in 1453, the Ottoman Empire forbade the exportation of white slaves from regions under its control. The Portuguese then began to import African slaves into the Iberian Peninsula from the Canary Islands and West Africa. Black slaves from Africa were also not uncommon in other parts of the Mediterranean, and a few found their way into northern Europe. There they might be used as personal servants or displayed because of the novelty of their color in royal courts or in wealthy homes.

Yet, from the sixteenth century onward, first within the West Indies and the Spanish and Portuguese settlements in South America and then in the British colonies on the South Atlantic seaboard of North America, slave labor became a fundamental social and economic factor. The development of those plantation economies based on slave labor led to unprecedented interaction between the peoples of Europe and Africa and between the European settlers in the Americas and Africa. From that point onward, Africa and Africans were drawn into the Western experience as never before in history.

The African Presence in the Americas

Once they had encountered and begun to settle the New World, the Spanish and Portuguese faced a severe shortage of labor. They and most of the French and English settlers who came later had no intention of undertaking manual work themselves. At first, they used Native Americans as laborers, but during the sixteenth century as well as afterward, disease killed hundreds of thousands of the native population. As a result, labor soon became scarce. The Spanish and Portuguese then turned to the labor of imported African slaves. Settlers in the English colonies of North America during the seventeenth century turned more slowly to slavery, with the largest number coming to the Chesapeake Bay region of Virginia and Maryland and then later into the low country of the Carolinas. Which African peoples became sold into slavery during any given decade largely depended on internal African warfare and state-building. This remained the case until the end of the transatlantic slave trade in the nineteenth century.

The major sources for slaves were slave markets on the West African Coast from Senegambia to Angola. Slavery and an extensive slave trade had existed in West Africa for centuries. Just as particular social and economic conditions in Europe had led to the voyages of exploration and settlement, political and military conditions in Africa and warfare among various African nations similarly created a supply of slaves that certain African

This eighteenth-century print shows bound African captives being forced to a slaving port. It was largely African middlemen who captured slaves in the interior and marched them to the coast. North Wind Picture Archives

societies were willing to sell to Europeans. European slave traders did not confront a passive situation in West Africa over which they exercised their will by force and commerce. Rather, they encountered dynamic African societies working out their own internal historic power relationships and rivalries in which Africans sold and acquired other Africans from different regions and nations as slaves.

The West Indies, Brazil, and Sugar

To grasp the full impact of the forced immigration of Africans to the Americas, we must take into account both regions and the entire picture of the transatlantic economy. Far more slaves were imported into the West Indies and Brazil than into North America. Although citizens of the United States mark the beginning of slavery in 1619 with the arrival of African slaves on a Dutch ship in Jamestown, Virginia, over a century of slave trading in the West Indies and South America had preceded that event. Indeed, by the late sixteenth century, Africans had become a major social presence in the West Indies and in the major cities of both Spanish and Portuguese South America. Their presence and influence in these regions would grow over the centuries. African labor and African immigrant slave communities were the most prominent social features of these regions, making the development of their economies and cultures what one historian has described as "a Euro-African phenomenon."[2] In these places, African slaves equaled or more generally surpassed the numbers of white European settlers in what soon constituted multiracial societies. Someone passing through the marketplace of these towns and cities would have heard a vast number of African, as well as European, languages. Although Na-

tive American labor continued to be exploited on the South American continent, it was increasingly a marginal presence in the ever-expanding African slave-based plantation economy of the Atlantic seaboard, the Caribbean, and offshore islands.

Within much of Spanish South America, the numbers of slaves declined during the late seventeenth century, and slavery became somewhat less fundamental there than elsewhere. Slavery continued to expand its influence, however, in Brazil and in the Caribbean through the spreading cultivation of sugar to meet the demand of the European market. By the close of the seventeenth century, the Caribbean islands were the world center for the production of sugar and the chief supplier for the ever-growing demand for it. The opening of new areas of cultivation and other economic enterprises required additional slaves during the eighteenth century, a period of major slave importation. The growing prosperity of sugar islands that had begun to be exploited in the late seventeenth century, as well as the new sugar, coffee, and tobacco regions of Brazil, where gold mining also required additional slaves, accounts for this increase in slave commerce and allowed higher prices to be paid for slaves. In Brazil, the West Indies, and the southern British colonies, prosperity and slavery went hand in hand.

A vast increase in the number of Africans brought as slaves to the Americas occurred during the eighteenth century, with most arriving in the Caribbean or Brazil. Early in the century, as many as 20,000 new Africans a year arrived in the West Indies as slaves. By 1725, it has been estimated that almost 90 percent of the population of Jamaica consisted of black slaves. After the midcentury, the numbers were even larger. The influx of new Africans in most areas—even in the British colonies—meant the numbers of new forced immigrants outnumbered the slaves of African descent already present.

---

[2]John Thornton, *Africa and the Africans in the Making of the Atlantic World, 1400–1800*, 2nd ed. (Cambridge: Cambridge University Press, 1998), p. 140.

SUGAR ENTERS THE WESTERN DIET

BEFORE THE EUROPEAN discovery of the Americas, sugar was a luxury product that only the wealthy could afford. Because it requires subtropical temperatures and heavy rainfall, sugarcane could not be grown in Europe. Sugar had to be imported, at great expense, from the Arab world or from the Spanish and Portuguese islands off the coast of Africa, which were too arid for the plant to flourish.

The Caribbean, however, is ideal for sugarcane. Columbus carried it to the New World in 1493, and within about a decade sugar was being cultivated—by slaves—on Santo Domingo.

Yet, sugar production did not begin to soar until Britain and France established themselves in the Caribbean in the seventeenth century and the demand for sugar began to grow in Europe, first slowly and then insatiably. By the eighteenth century, the small British and French islands in the Caribbean where sugar was produced by African slave labor had become some of the most valuable real estate on earth.

Whereas the North American colonies imported Caribbean molasses to make rum, Europeans desired sugar to sweeten other foods. Sugar, the largest colonial import into Britain, embodied the mercantile policy of a closed economic system. It was raised in British colonies, paid for by British exports, shipped on British ships, insured by British firms, refined in British cities, and consumed on British tables.

The voracious demand for sugar as a sweetener was tied up with three other tropical products—coffee, tea, and chocolate—that European consumers began to drink in enormous quantities in the seventeenth and eighteenth centuries. Each of these beverages is a stimulant, which helps explain their popularity, but by themselves they taste bitter. Sugar made them palatable to European consumers. The demand for sugar and these drinks became mutually reinforcing. As the markets for coffee, chocolate, and especially tea grew in England and the English colonies, so did the demand for sugar.

As the production of sugar rose, its price fell. The cheaper sugar became, the more of it Europeans consumed. By the end of the eighteenth century, tea with sugar was cheaper than beer or milk, and it had become the most popular drink among the British poor (while remaining an elegant drink for the wealthy). Moreover, because sugar had originally been a luxury item, people felt they were improving their standard of living if they consumed more of it.

During the nineteenth century, sugar consumption continued to expand, and sugar became even cheaper when free-trade policies reduced protective import duties and when the French began to manufacture it from sugar beets, which could easily be grown in Europe. Nineteenth-century Westerners developed the custom of ending a meal with dessert, food usually sweetened with sugar.

Source: Sidney Mintz, *Sweetness and Power: The Place of Sugar in Modern History* (New York: Penguin Books, 1985).

How did the colonization of the Americas affect the European demand for sugar?

Why did sugar consumption increase so rapidly in Europe during the eighteenth and nineteenth centuries?

Sugar was both raised and processed on plantations such as this one in Brazil. Library of Congress

A Closer ▷ LOOK

A SUGAR PLANTATION IN THE WEST INDIES

WEST INDIES SUGAR plantations, owned by Europeans who often stayed only long enough to make their fortunes, were located on the remarkably beautiful islands of the Caribbean that today attract thousands of tourists. Employing slave laborers imported from Africa, the sugar plantations combined agricultural production of sugarcane and the industrial processing of it into sugar for export to Europe. The latter involved slaves working with dangerous machinery often near fires and hot metal equipment used in the distillation process.

The production of sugar from the cane occurred in structures near the sugarcane fields themselves. Note the aqueducts carrying water to power some machinery.

Plantation owners generally lived on high windswept areas of their estates while slaves dwelled in quite humble housing near the areas of sugarcane cultivation or the grazing of animals used for food and sugar production.

The Granger Collection, New York

Raw sugarcane from the nearby fields was placed between the vertical crushers to extract juice to be distilled into sugar crystals elsewhere on the plantation in cauldrons over fires.

Animal power was used to move the crushers until the late eighteenth century when on some plantations steam engines replaced horses or mules.

To examine this image in an interactive fashion, please go to www.myhistorylab.com

Denis Diderot, *Encyclopedie, ou, Dictionnaire Raisonné des Sciences, des Arts et des Métiers*. Recueil de Planches, sur les Sciences. (Paris, 1762), vol. 1. Special Collections, University of Virginia Library

PEARSON
myhistorylab

Newly imported African slaves were needed because the fertility rate of the earlier slave population was low and the death rate high from disease, overwork, and malnutrition. The West Indies proved to be a particularly difficult region in which to secure a stable, self-reproducing slave population. The conditions for slaves there led to high rates of mortality with new slaves coming primarily from the ongoing slave trade. A similar situation prevailed in Brazil. Restocking through the slave trade meant the slave population of those areas consisted of African-born persons rather than of persons of African descent. Consequently, one of the key factors in the social life of many of the areas of American slavery during the eighteenth century was the presence of persons newly arrived from Africa, carrying with them African languages, religion, culture, and local African ethnic identities that they would infuse into the already existing slave communities. Thus, the eighteenth century witnessed an enormous new African presence throughout the Americas.

Slavery and the Transatlantic Economy

Different nations dominated the slave trade in different periods. During the sixteenth century, the Portuguese and the Spanish were most involved. The Dutch supplanted them during most of the seventeenth century. Thereafter, during the late seventeenth and eighteenth centuries, the English were the chief slave traders. French traders also participated in the trade.

Slavery touched most of the economy of the transatlantic world. (See Map 16–2, page 490.) Colonial trade followed roughly a geographic triangle. European goods—often guns—were carried to Africa to be exchanged for slaves, who were then taken to the West Indies, where they were traded for sugar and other tropical products, which were then shipped to Europe. Not all ships covered all three legs of the triangle. Another major trade pattern existed between New England and the West Indies with New England fish, rum, or lumber being traded for sugar. At various times, the prosperity of such cities as Amsterdam, Liverpool, England, and Nantes, France, rested largely on the slave trade. Cities in the British North American colonies, such as Newport, Rhode Island, profited from slavery sometimes by trading in slaves, but more often by supplying other goods to the West Indian market. All the shippers who handled cotton, tobacco, and sugar depended on slavery, though they might not have had direct contact with the institution, as did all the manufacturers and merchants who produced finished products for the consumer market.

As had been the case during previous centuries, eighteenth-century political turmoil in Africa, such as the civil wars in the Kingdom of Kongo (modern Angola and Republic of Congo), increased the supply of slaves during

that period. These Kongo wars had originated in a dispute over succession to the throne in the late seventeenth century and continued into the eighteenth. Some captives were simply sold to European slave traders calling at ports along the West African coast. Other African leaders conducted slave raids, so their captives could be sold to finance the purchase of more weapons. Similar political unrest and turmoil in the Gold Coast area (modern Ghana) during the eighteenth century increased the supply of African captives to be sold into American slavery. Consequently, warfare in West Africa, often far into the interior, and the economic development of the American Atlantic seaboard were closely related.

The Experience of Slavery

The Portuguese, Spanish, Dutch, French, and English slave traders forcibly transported several million (perhaps more than 9 million; the exact numbers are disputed) Africans to the New World—the largest forced intercontinental migration in human history. During the first four centuries of settlement, far more black slaves came involuntarily to the New World than did free European settlers or European indentured servants. The conditions of slaves' passage across the Atlantic were wretched. Quarters were unspeakably cramped, food was bad, disease was rampant. Many Africans died during the crossing. (See "Compare & Connect: The Atlantic Passage," pages 488–489.) There were always more African men than women transported, so it was difficult to preserve traditional African extended family structures. During the passage and later, many Africans attempted to re-create such structures among themselves, even if they were not actually related by direct family ties.

In the Americas, the slave population was divided among new Africans recently arrived, old Africans who had lived there for some years, and creoles who were the descendants of earlier generations of African slaves. Plantation owners preferred the two latter groups, who were already accustomed to the life of slavery. They sold for higher prices. The newly arrived Africans were subjected to a process known as *seasoning*, during which they were prepared for the laborious discipline of slavery and made to understand that they were no longer free. The process might involve receiving new names, acquiring new work skills, and learning, to some extent, the local European language. Some newly arrived Africans worked in a kind of apprentice relationship to an older African slave of similar ethnic background. Other slaves were broken into slave labor through work on field gangs. Occasionally, plantation owners preferred to buy younger Africans, whom they thought might be more easily acculturated to the labor conditions of the Americas. Generally, North American

The Atlantic Passage

SLAVERY LAY AT the core of the eighteenth-century transatlantic economy. At the heart of slavery lay the forced transportation in slave ships across the Atlantic of millions of Africans to the Americas. The frightening and horrific character of the Atlantic Passage became widely known through the memoirs of sailors and slave trade captains. Later the groups who after the mid-eighteenth century sought the abolition of slavery made known the inhumanity of the passage through published attacks on the slave trade and by providing illustrations of slave ships such as that of the *Brooks*.

QUESTIONS

1. Who are the various people described in this document who in one way or another were involved in or profited from the slave trade?

2. What dangers did the Africans face on the voyage?

3. What contemporary attitudes could have led this captain to treat and think of his human cargo simply as goods to be transported?

4. How might the publication of the interior compartments of a slave ship have served the cause of antislavery? How and why might this illustration of a slave ship have proved more persuasive in rousing antislavery sentiment than a prose description?

5. How would this illustration and the description of the Atlantic Passage have contrasted with contemporary illustrations and memoirs of victorious naval battles on the high seas?

I. A Slave Trader Describes the Atlantic Passage

During 1693 and 1694, Captain Thomas Phillips carried slaves from Africa to Barbados on the ship Hannibal. *The financial backer of the voyage was the Royal African Company of London, which held an English crown monopoly on slave trading. Phillips sailed to the west coast of Africa, where he purchased the Africans who were sold into slavery by an African king. Then he set sail westward.*

Having bought my complement of 700 slaves, 480 men and 220 women, and finish'd all my business at Whidaw [on the Gold Coast of Africa], I took my leave of the old king and his *cappasheirs* [attendants], and parted, with many affectionate expressions on both sides, being forced to promise him that I would return again the next year, with several things he desired me to bring from England. . . . I set sail the 27th of July in the morning, accompany'd with the East-India Merchant, who had bought 650 slaves, for the Island of St. Thomas. . . from which we took our departure on August 25th and set sail for Barbadoes.

We spent in our passage from St. Thomas to Barbadoes two months eleven days, from the 25th of August to the 4th of November following: in which time there happened such sickness and mortality among my poor men and Negroes. Of the first we buried 14, and of the last 320, which was a great detriment to our voyage, the Royal African Company losing ten pounds by every slave that died, and the owners of the ship ten pounds ten shillings, being the freight agreed on to be paid by the charter-party for every Negro delivered alive ashore to the African Company's agents at Barbadoes. . . . The loss in all amounted to near 6500 pounds sterling.

The distemper which my men as well as the blacks mostly died of was the white flux, which was so violent and inveterate that no medicine would in the least check it, so that when any of our men were seized with it, we esteemed him a dead man, as he generally proved. . . .

The Negroes are so incident to [subject to] the smallpox that few ships that carry them escape without it, and sometimes it makes vast havoc and destruction among them. But tho' we had 100 at a time sick of it, and that it went thro' the ship, yet we lost not above a dozen by it. All the assistance we gave the diseased was only as much water as they desir'd to drink, and some palm-oil to annoint their sores, and they would generally recover without any other helps but what kind nature gave them. . . .

But what the smallpox spar'd, the flux swept off, to our great regret, after all our pains and care to give them their messes in due order and season, keeping their lodg-

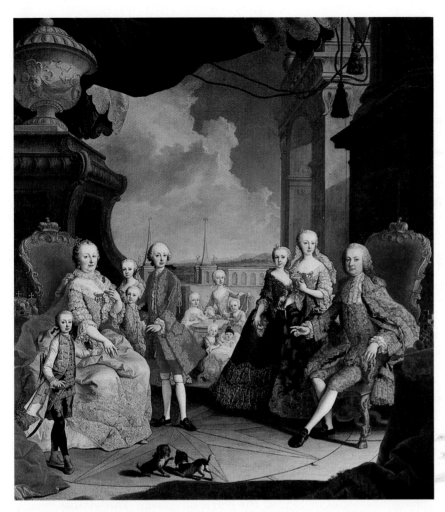

Maria Theresa of Austria provided the leadership that saved the Habsburg Empire from possible disintegration after the Prussian invasion of Silesia in 1740.
Martin van Meytens: *Kaiserin Maria Theresia mit ihrer Familie auf der Schloßterasse von Schobrunn.* Kunsthistorisches Museum, Vienna, Austria

granting new privileges to the nobility. Most significantly, the empress recognized Hungary as the most important of her crowns and promised the Magyar nobility local autonomy. She thus preserved the Habsburg state, but at considerable cost to the power of the central monarchy.

Hungary would continue to be, as it had been in the past, a particularly troublesome area in the Habsburg Empire. When the monarchy was strong and secure, it could ignore guarantees made to Hungary. When the monarchy was threatened, or when the Magyars could stir up enough opposition, the Habsburgs promised new concessions.

France Draws Great Britain into the War   The war over the Austrian succession and the British–Spanish commercial conflict could have remained separate disputes. What united them was the role of France. Just as British merchant interests had pushed Sir Robert Walpole into war, aggressive court aristocrats compelled the elderly Cardinal Fleury (1653–1743), first minister of Louis XV (r. 1715–1774), to abandon his planned naval attack on British trade and instead to support the Prussian aggression against Austria, the traditional enemy of France. This was among the more fateful decisions in French history.

In the first place, aid to Prussia consolidated a new and powerful state in Germany. That new power could, and indeed later did, endanger France. Second, the French move against Austria brought Great Britain into the continental war, as Britain sought to make sure the Low Countries remained in the friendly hands of Austria, not France. In 1744, the British–French conflict expanded beyond the Continent when France supported Spain against Britain in the New World. As a result, French military and economic resources were badly divided. France could not bring sufficient strength to the colonial struggle. Having chosen to continue the old struggle with Austria, France lost the struggle for the future against Great Britain. The war ended in a stalemate in 1748 with the Treaty of Aix-la-Chapelle. Prussia retained Silesia, and Spain renewed Britain's privilege from the Treaty of Utrecht (1713) to import slaves into the Spanish colonies.

The "Diplomatic Revolution" of 1756

Although the Treaty of Aix-la-Chapelle had brought peace in Europe, France and Great Britain continued to struggle unofficially in the Ohio River valley and in upper New England. These clashes were the prelude to what is known in American history as the French and Indian War, which formally erupted in the summer of 1755.

Before war commenced again in Europe, however, a dramatic shift of alliances took place, in part, as a result of the events in North America. The British king, George II (r. 1727–1760), who was also the Elector of Hanover in Germany, thought the French might attack Hanover in response to the conflict in America. In January 1756, Britain and Prussia signed the Convention of Westminster, a defensive alliance aimed at preventing the entry of foreign troops into the German states. Whereas George II feared a French attack on Hanover, Frederick II feared an alliance of Russia and Austria. The convention meant that Great Britain, the ally of Austria since the wars of Louis XIV, had now joined forces with Austria's major eighteenth-century enemy.

Maria Theresa was despondent over this development. It delighted her foreign minister, Prince Wenzel Anton Kaunitz (1711–1794), however. He had long hoped for an alliance with France to help dismember Prussia. The Convention of Westminster made possible this alliance, which would have been unthinkable a few years earlier. France was agreeable because Frederick had not consulted with its ministers before coming to his understanding with Britain. So, in May 1756, France and Austria signed a defensive alliance. Kaunitz had succeeded in completely reversing the direction that French foreign policy had followed since the sixteenth century. France would now fight to restore Austrian supremacy in central Europe.

The Seven Years' War (1756–1763)

Once again, however, Frederick II precipitated a European war that extended into a colonial theater.

Frederick the Great Opens Hostilities   In August 1756, Frederick II opened what would become the Seven Years' War by invading Saxony. Frederick considered this to be a preemptive strike against a conspiracy by Saxony, Austria, and France to destroy Prussian power. He regarded the invasion as a continuation of the defensive strategy of the Convention of Westminster. The invasion itself, however, created the very destructive alliance that Frederick feared. In the spring of 1757, France and Austria made a new alliance dedicated to the destruction of Prussia. Sweden, Russia, and many of the smaller German states joined them.

Two factors in addition to Frederick's stubborn leadership (it was after this war that he came to be called Frederick the Great) saved Prussia. First, Britain furnished considerable financial aid. Second, in 1762, Empress Elizabeth of Russia (r. 1741–1762) died. Her successor was Tsar Peter III (he was murdered the same year), whose admiration for Frederick was boundless. He immediately made peace with Prussia, thus relieving Frederick of one enemy and allowing him to hold off Austria and France. The Treaty of Hubertusburg of 1763 ended the continental conflict with no significant changes in prewar borders. Silesia remained Prussian, and Prussia clearly stood among the ranks of the great powers.

William Pitt's Strategy for Winning North America
The survival of Prussia was less impressive to the rest of Europe than were the victories of Great Britain in every theater of conflict. The architect of these victories was William Pitt the Elder (1708–1778), a person of colossal ego and administrative genius. Although he had previously criticized British involvement with the Continent, once he became secretary of state in charge of the war in 1757, he pumped huge sums into the coffers of Frederick the Great. He regarded the German conflict as a way to divert French resources and attention from the

colonial struggle. He later boasted of having won America on the plains of Germany.

North America was the center of Pitt's real concern. Put simply, he wanted all of North America east of the Mississippi for Great Britain, and that was what he won. He sent more than 40,000 regular English and colonial troops against the French in Canada. Never had so many soldiers been devoted to colonial warfare. He achieved unprecedented cooperation with the American colonies, whose leaders realized they might finally defeat their French neighbors.

The French government was unwilling and unable to direct similar resources against the English in America. Their military administration was corrupt, the military and political commands in Canada were divided, and France could not adequately supply its North American forces. In September 1759, on the Plains of Abraham, overlooking the valley of the Saint Lawrence River at Quebec City, the British army under James Wolfe defeated the French under Louis Joseph de Montcalm. The French Empire in Canada was ending.

Pitt's colonial vision, however, extended beyond the Saint Lawrence valley and the Great Lakes basin. The major islands of the French West Indies fell to British fleets. Income from the sale of captured sugar helped finance the British war effort. British slave interests captured the bulk of the French slave trade. Between 1755 and 1760, the value of the French colonial trade fell by more than 80 percent. In India, the British forces under the command of Robert Clive defeated France's Indian allies in 1757 at the Battle of Plassey. This victory opened the way for the eventual conquest of Bengal in northeast India and later of all of India by the British East India Company. (See Chapter 25.) Never had Great Britain or any other European power experienced such a complete worldwide military victory.

CONFLICTS OF THE MID-EIGHTEENTH CENTURY

1713	Treaty of Utrecht
1739	Outbreak of War of Jenkins's Ear between England and Spain
1740	War of the Austrian Succession commences
1748	Treaty of Aix-la-Chapelle
1756	Convention of Westminster between England and Prussia
1756	Seven Years' War opens
1757	Battle of Plassey
1759	British forces capture Quebec
1763	Treaty of Hubertusburg
1763	Treaty of Paris

This scene, painted by artist Edward Penny, shows Robert Clive receiving a sum of money from Siraj-ud-daulah, the Mughal Nawab of Bengal, for injured officers and soldiers at Plassey. Clive's victory in 1757 at the Battle of Plassey brought English domination of the Indian subcontinent for almost two centuries. Clive had won the battle largely through bribing many of the Nawab's troops and potential allies.   Erich Lessing © The Trustees of the British Museum/Art Resource, NY

The Treaty of Paris of 1763   The Treaty of Paris of 1763 reflected somewhat less of a victory than Britain had won on the battlefield. Pitt was no longer in office. George III (r. 1760–1820) and Pitt had quarreled over policy, and the minister had departed. His replacement was the earl of Bute (1713–1792), a favorite of the new monarch. Bute was responsible for the peace settlement. Britain received all of Canada, the Ohio River valley, and the eastern half of the Mississippi River valley. Britain returned Pondicherry and Chandernagore in India and the West Indian sugar islands of Guadeloupe and Martinique to the French.

The Seven Years' War had been a vast worldwide conflict. Tens of thousands of soldiers and sailors had been killed or wounded. Major battles had been fought around the globe. At great internal sacrifice, Prussia had permanently wrested Silesia from Austria and had turned the Holy Roman Empire into an empty shell. Habsburg power now depended largely on the Hungarian domains. France, though still having sources of colonial income, was no longer a great colonial power. The Spanish Empire remained largely intact, but the British were still determined to penetrate its markets.

In India, the British East India Company continued to impose its own authority on the decaying indigenous governments. The ramifications of that situation would extend until the mid-twentieth century. In North America, the British government faced the task of organizing its new territories. From this time until World War II, Great Britain was a world power, not just a European one.

The quarter century of warfare also caused a long series of domestic crises among the European powers. Defeat convinced many in France of the necessity for political and administrative reform. The financial burdens of the wars had astounded all contemporaries. Every power had to increase its revenues to pay its war debt and finance its preparation for the next combat. Nowhere did this search for revenue lead to more far-ranging consequences than in the British colonies in North America.

▼ The American Revolution and Europe

The revolt of the British colonies in North America was an event in both transatlantic and European history. It marked the beginning of the end of European colonial domination of the American continents. The colonial American revolt that led eventually to revolution erupted from problems of revenue collection common to all the major powers after the Seven Years' War. The War of the American Revolution also continued the conflict between France and Great Britain. The French support of the Americans deepened the existing financial and administrative difficulties of the French monarchy.

Resistance to the Imperial Search for Revenue

After the Treaty of Paris of 1763, the British government faced two imperial problems. The first was the sheer cost of maintaining their empire, which the British felt they could no longer carry alone. The national debt had risen considerably, as had domestic taxation. Since the American colonies had been the chief beneficiaries of the conflict, the British felt it was rational for the colonies henceforth to bear part of the cost of their protection and administration. The second problem was the vast expanse of new territory in North America that the British had to organize. This included all the land from the mouth of the Saint Lawrence River to the Mississippi River, with its French settlers and, more importantly, its Native Americans. (See Map 16–3, page 496.)

The British drive for revenue began in 1764 with the passage of the Sugar Act under the ministry of George Grenville (1712–1770). The measure attempted to produce more revenue from imports into the colonies by

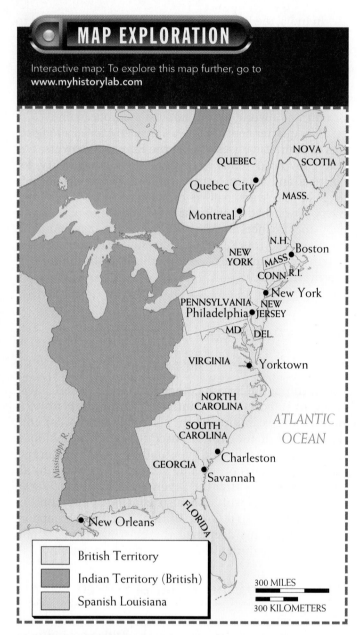

MAP EXPLORATION

Interactive map: To explore this map further, go to
www.myhistorylab.com

Map 16–3 NORTH AMERICA IN 1763 In the year of the victory over France, the English colonies lay along the Atlantic seaboard. The difficulties of organizing authority over the previous French territory in Canada and west of the Appalachian Mountains would contribute to the coming of the American Revolution.

the rigorous collection of what was actually a lower tax. Smugglers who violated the law were to be tried in admiralty courts without juries. The next year, Parliament passed the Stamp Act, which put a tax on legal documents and other items such as newspapers. The British considered these taxes legal, because Parliament had approved the decision to collect them, and fair, because the money was to be spent in the colonies.

The Americans responded that they alone, through their colonial assemblies, had the right to tax themselves and that they were not represented in Parliament.

Furthermore, the expenditure in the colonies of the revenue Parliament levied did not reassure the colonists. They feared that if their colonial government was financed from outside, they would lose control over it. In October 1765, the Stamp Act Congress met in America and drew up a protest to the crown. There was much disorder in the colonies, particularly in Massachusetts, roused by groups known as the Sons of Liberty. The colonists agreed to refuse to import British goods. In 1766, Parliament repealed the Stamp Act, but through the Declaratory Act said it had the power to legislate for the colonies.

The Stamp Act crisis set the pattern for the next ten years. Parliament, under the leadership of a royal minister, would approve revenue or administrative legislation. The Americans would then resist by reasoned argument, economic pressure, and violence. Then the British would repeal the legislation, and the process would begin again. Each time, tempers on both sides became more frayed and positions more irreconcilable. With each clash, the Americans more fully developed their own thinking about political liberty.

The Crisis and Independence

In 1767, Charles Townshend (1725–1767), as Chancellor of the Exchequer, the British finance minister, led Parliament to pass a series of revenue acts relating to colonial imports. The colonists again resisted. The ministry sent over its own customs agents to administer the laws. To protect these new officers, the British sent troops to Boston in 1768. The obvious tensions resulted. In March 1770, the Boston Massacre, in which British troops killed five citizens, took place. That same year, Parliament repealed all of the Townshend duties except the one on tea.

In May 1773, Parliament passed a new law relating to the sale of tea by the East India Company. The measure permitted the direct importation of tea into the American colonies. It actually lowered the price of tea while retaining the tax imposed without the colonists' consent. In some cities, the colonists refused to permit the unloading of the tea; in Boston, a shipload of tea was thrown into the harbor.

The British ministry of Lord North (1732–1792) was determined to assert the authority of Parliament over the colonies. During 1774, Parliament passed a series of laws known in American history as the **Intolerable Acts**. These measures closed the port of Boston, reorganized the government of Massachusetts, allowed troops to be quartered in private homes, and removed the trials of royal customs officials to England. The same year, the Quebec Act extended the boundaries of Quebec to include the Ohio River valley. The Americans regarded the Quebec Act as an attempt to prevent their mode of self-government from spreading beyond the Appalachian Mountains.

During these years, citizens critical of British policy had established committees of correspondence throughout the colonies. They made the various sections of the eastern seaboard aware of common problems and encouraged united action. In September 1774, these committees organized the First Continental Congress in Philadelphia. This body hoped to persuade Parliament to restore self-government in the colonies and abandon its direct supervision of colonial affairs. Conciliation, however, was not forthcoming. By April 1775, the Battles of Lexington and Concord had been fought. In June, the colonists suffered defeat at the Battle of Bunker Hill. Despite that defeat, the colonial assemblies began to meet under their own authority rather than under that of the king.

The Second Continental Congress gathered in May 1775. It still sought conciliation with Britain, but the pressure of events led it to begin to conduct the government of the colonies. By August 1775, George III had declared the colonies in rebellion. During the winter, Thomas Paine's (1737–1809) pamphlet *Common Sense* galvanized public opinion in favor of separation from Great Britain. A colonial army and navy were organized. In April 1776, the Continental Congress opened American ports to the trade of all nations. On July 4, 1776, the Continental Congress adopted the Declaration of Independence. Thereafter, the War of the American Revolution continued until 1781, when the forces of George Washington defeated those of Lord Cornwallis at Yorktown. Early in 1778, however, the war had widened into a European conflict when Benjamin Franklin (1706–1790) persuaded the French government to support the rebellion. In 1779, the Spanish also joined the war against Britain. The 1783 Treaty of Paris concluded the conflict, and the thirteen American colonies finally established their independence.

American Political Ideas

The political ideas of the American colonists had largely arisen out of the struggle of the seventeenth-century English aristocrats and gentry against the absolutism of the Stuart monarchs. The American colonists looked to the English Revolution of 1688 as having established many of their own fundamental political liberties, as well as those of the English. The colonists claimed that, through the measures imposed from 1763 to 1776, George III and the British Parliament were attacking those liberties and dissolving the bonds of moral and political allegiance that had formerly united the two peoples. Consequently, the colonists employed a theory that had developed to justify an aristocratic rebellion to support their own popular revolution.

These Whig political ideas, largely derived from the writings of John Locke, were, however, only a part of the English ideological heritage that affected the Americans. Throughout the eighteenth century, they had become

Many Americans fiercely objected to the British Parliament's attempts to tax the colonies. This print of a British tax collector being tarred and feathered warned officials of what could happen to them if they tried to collect these taxes.   Philip Dawe (c. 1750–c.1785), *The Bostonians Paying the Excise-Man or Tarring & Feathering.* London, 1774. Colored Engraving. The Gilder Lehman Collection on deposit at the Pierpont Morgan Library. GL 4961.01. Photography: Joseph Zehavi. The Pierpont Morgan Library/Art Resource, NY

familiar with a series of British political writers called the **Commonwealthmen**, who held republican political ideas that had their intellectual roots in the most radical thought of the Puritan revolution. During the early eighteenth century, these writers, the most influential of whom were John Trenchard (1662–1723) and Thomas Gordon (d. 1750) in *Cato's Letters* (1720–1723), had relentlessly criticized the government patronage and parliamentary management of Sir Robert Walpole and his successors. They argued that such government was corrupt and it undermined liberty. They regarded much parliamentary taxation as simply a means of financing political corruption. They also considered standing armies instruments of tyranny. In Great Britain, this republican political tradition had only a marginal impact. The writers were largely ignored because most British subjects regarded themselves as the freest people in the world. Three thousand miles away, however, colonists read the radical books and pamphlets and often accepted them at face value. The policy of Great Britain toward America following the Treaty of Paris of 1763 and certain political events in Britain had made many colonists believe the worst fears of the Commonwealthmen were coming true. All of these events coincided with the accession of George III to the throne.

Events in Great Britain

George III believed that a few powerful Whig families and the ministries they controlled had bullied and dominated his two immediate royal predecessors. George III also believed he should have ministers of his own choice and Parliament should function under royal, rather than aristocratic, management. When George appointed the Earl of Bute as his first minister after William Pitt resigned in 1761, he ignored the great Whig families that had run the country since 1715. The king sought the aid of politicians whom the Whigs hated. Moreover, he tried to use the same kind of patronage techniques Walpole developed to control of the House of Commons.

Between 1761 and 1770, George tried one minister after another, but each, in turn, failed to gain enough support from the various factions in the House of Commons. Finally, in 1770, he turned to Lord North, who remained the king's first minister until 1782. The Whig families and other political spokespersons claimed that George III was attempting to impose a tyranny. What they meant was that the king was attempting to curb the power of a particular group of the aristocracy. George III certainly was seeking to restore more royal influence to the government of Great Britain, but he was not trying to make himself a tyrant.

The Challenge of John Wilkes Then, in 1763 began the affair of John Wilkes (1725–1797). This London political radical and member of Parliament published a newspaper called *The North Briton*. In issue number 45, Wilkes strongly criticized Lord Bute's handling of the peace negotiations with France. Wilkes was arrested under the authority of a general warrant issued by the secretary of state. He pleaded the privileges of a member of Parliament and was released. The courts also later ruled that the vague kind of general warrant by which he had been arrested was illegal. The House of Commons, however, ruled that issue number 45 of *The North Briton* constituted libel, and it expelled Wilkes. He soon fled the country and was outlawed. Throughout these procedures Wilkes enjoyed widespread support.

In 1768, Wilkes returned to England and was reelected to Parliament, but the House of Commons, under the influence of George III's friends, refused to seat him. He was elected three more times. After the fourth election, the House of Commons simply ignored the results and seated the government-supported candidate. As had happened earlier, large, unruly demonstrations of shopkeepers, artisans, and small-property owners supported Wilkes as did aristocratic politicians who wished to humiliate George III. "Wilkes and Liberty" became the slogan of political radicals and many noble opponents of the monarch. Wilkes was finally seated in 1774, after having become the lord mayor of London.

The American colonists followed these developments closely. Events in Britain confirmed their fears about a monarchical and parliamentary conspiracy against liberty. The king, as their Whig friends told them, was behaving like a tyrant. The Wilkes affair displayed the arbitrary power of the monarch, the corruption of the House of Commons, and the contempt of both for popular electors. That same monarch and Parliament were attempting to overturn the traditional relationship of Great Britain to its colonies by imposing parliamentary taxes. The same government had then landed troops in Boston, changed the government of Massachusetts, and undermined the traditional right of jury trial. All of these events fulfilled too exactly the portrait of political tyranny that had developed over the years in the minds of articulate colonists.

Movement for Parliamentary Reform The political influences between America and Britain operated both ways. The colonial demand for no taxation without representation and the criticism of the adequacy of the British system of representation struck at the core of the eighteenth-century British political structure. British subjects at home who were no more directly represented in the House of Commons than were the Americans could adopt the colonial arguments. The colonial questioning of the tax-levying authority of the House of Commons was related to the protest of John Wilkes. Both the Americans and Wilkes were challenging the power of the monarch and the authority of Parliament. Moreover, both the colonial leaders and Wilkes appealed over the head of legally constituted political authorities to popular opinion and popular demonstrations. Both were protesting the power of a largely self-selected aristocratic political body. The British ministry was fully aware of these broader political implications of the American troubles.

The American colonists also demonstrated to Europe how a politically restive people in the Old Regime could fight tyranny and protect political liberty. They established revolutionary, but orderly, political bodies that could function outside the existing political framework: the congress and the convention. These began with the Stamp Act Congress of 1765 and culminated in the Constitutional Convention of 1787. The legitimacy of these congresses and conventions lay not in existing law, but in the alleged consent of the governed. This approach represented a new way to found a government.

Toward the end of the War of the American Revolution, calls for parliamentary reform arose in Britain itself. The method proposed for changing the system was the extra-legal Association Movement.

The Yorkshire Association Movement

By the close of the 1770s, many in Britain resented the mismanagement of the American war, the high taxes, and Lord North's ministry. In northern England in 1778, Christopher Wyvil (1740–1822), a landowner and retired clergyman, organized the Yorkshire Association Movement. Property owners, or freeholders, of Yorkshire met in a mass meeting to demand moderate changes in the corrupt system of parliamentary elections. They organized corresponding societies elsewhere. They intended that the association examine, and suggest reforms for, the entire government. The Association Movement was thus a popular attempt to establish an extra-legal institution to reform the government. (See "Major Cartwright Calls for the Reform of Parliament," page 500.)

The movement collapsed during the early 1780s because its supporters, unlike Wilkes and the American rebels, were not willing to appeal for broad popular support. Nonetheless, the agitation of the Association Movement provided many people with experience in political protest. Several of its younger figures lived to raise the issue of parliamentary reform after 1815.

Parliament was not insensitive to the demands of the Association Movement. In April 1780, the Commons passed a resolution that called for lessening the power of the crown. In 1782, Parliament adopted a measure for "economical" reform, which abolished some patronage at the disposal of the monarch. These actions, however, did not prevent George III from appointing a minister of his own choice. In 1783, shifts in Parliament obliged Lord North to form a ministry with Charles James Fox (1749–1806), a longtime critic of George III. The monarch was most unhappy with the arrangement.

In 1783, the king approached William Pitt the Younger (1759–1806), son of the victorious war minister, to manage the House of Commons. During the election of 1784, Pitt received immense patronage support from the crown and constructed a House of Commons favorable to the monarch. Thereafter, Pitt sought to formulate trade policies that would give his ministry broad popularity. In 1785, he attempted one measure of modest parliamentary reform. When it failed, the young prime minister, who had been only twenty-four at the time of his appointment, abandoned the cause of reform.

By the mid-1780s, George III had achieved part of what he had sought since 1761. He had reasserted the influence of the monarchy in political affairs. It proved a temporary victory, because his own mental illness, which would eventually require a regency, weakened the royal power.

The surrender of Lord Cornwallis's British army at Yorktown, Virginia, in 1781 to American and French forces under George Washington ended Britain's hopes of suppressing the American Revolution. John Trumbull (American 1756–1843), *The Surrender of Lord Cornwallis at Yorktown, 19 October 1781,* 1787–c. 1828. Oil on canvas, 53.3 × 77.8 × 1.9 cm (21 × 30 ⅝ × ¾ in.) 1832.4. Yale University Art Gallery, Trumbull Collection

---

EVENTS IN BRITAIN AND AMERICA RELATING TO THE AMERICAN REVOLUTION

1760	George III becomes king
1763	Treaty of Paris concludes the Seven Years' War
1763	John Wilkes publishes issue number 45 of *The North Briton*
1764	Sugar Act
1765	Stamp Act
1766	Stamp Act repealed and Declaratory Act passed
1767	Townshend Acts
1768	Parliament refuses to seat John Wilkes after his election
1770	Lord North becomes George III's chief minister
1770	Boston Massacre
1773	Boston Tea Party
1774	Intolerable Acts
1774	First Continental Congress
1775	Second Continental Congress
1776	Declaration of Independence
1778	France enters the war on the side of America
1778	Yorkshire Association Movement founded
1781	British forces surrender at Yorktown
1783	Treaty of Paris concludes War of the American Revolution

MAJOR CARTWRIGHT CALLS FOR THE REFORM OF PARLIAMENT

During the American Revolution there were many demands in England to reform Parliament. In this pamphlet of 1777, Major John Cartwright demands that many more English citizens be allowed to vote for members of the House of Commons. He also heaps contempt on the opponents of reform. Note how he declares that no political authority in Britain has the power to establish the unjust situation he describes.

What does Cartwright mean by "corruption"? How does he believe Britain has been deprived of its liberties? Why does he prefer an annual election of Parliament to elections every seven years? How does he illustrate the wrongful state of representation under the present system?

Suffering as we do, from a deep parliamentary corruption, it is no time to tamper with silly correctives, and trifle away the life of public freedom: but we must go to the bottom of the stinking sore and cleanse it thoroughly: we must once more infuse into the constitution the vivifying spirit of liberty and expel the very last dregs of this poison. *Annual parliaments* with an *equal representation of the commons* are the only specifics in this case: and they would effect a radial cure. That a house of commons, formed as ours is, should maintain septennial elections [i.e., elections every seven years], and laugh at every other idea is no wonder. The wonder is, that the British nation which, but the other day, was the greatest nation on earth, should be so easily laughed out of its liberties. . . .

Those who now claim the *exclusive* right of sending to parliament the 513 representatives for about six million souls (amongst whom are one million five hundred thousand males, *competent as electors*) consist of about two hundred and fourteen thousand persons; and 254 of these representatives are elected by 5,723. . . . Their pretended rights are many of them, derived from *royal favour*; some from antient usage and prescription; and some indeed from act of parliament; but neither the most authentic acts of royalty, nor precedent, nor prescription, nor even parliament can establish any flagrant injustice; much less can they strip one million two hundred and eighty-six thousand of an inalienable right, to vest it in a number amounting to only one-seventh of that multitude. . . .

From *Legislative Rights of the Commonality Vindicated*, by John Carwright (1740–1824), in *The English Radical Tradition*, 1763–1914 (London: Adam and Charles Black, 1966), pp. 32–33.

The cost of his years of dominance had been high, however. On both sides of the Atlantic, the issue of popular sovereignty had been widely discussed. The American colonies had been lost. Economically, this loss did not prove disastrous. British trade with America after independence actually increased.

Broader Impact of the American Revolution

The Americans—through their state constitutions, the Articles of Confederation, and the federal Constitution adopted in 1788—had demonstrated to Europe the possibility of government without kings and hereditary

nobilities. They had established the example of a nation in which written documents based on popular consent and popular sovereignty—rather than on divine law, natural law, tradition, or the will of kings—were the highest political and legal authority. The political novelty of these assertions should not be ignored.

As the crisis with Britain unfolded during the 1760s and 1770s, the American colonists had come to see themselves first as preserving traditional English liberties against the tyrannical crown and corrupt Parliament and then as developing a whole new sense of liberty. By the mid-1770s, the colonists had rejected monarchical government and embraced republican political ideals. They would govern themselves through elected assemblies without any monarchical authority.

Once a constitution was adopted, they would insist on a Bill of Rights specifically protecting a whole series of civil liberties. The Americans would reject the aristocratic social hierarchy that had existed in the colonies. They would embrace democratic ideals—even if the franchise remained limited. They would assert the equality of white male citizens not only before the law, but also in ordinary social relations. They would reject social status based on birth and inheritance and assert the necessity of the liberty for all citizens to improve their social standing and economic lot by engaging in free commercial activity. They did not free their slaves, nor did they address issues of the rights of women or of Native Americans. Yet in making their revolution, the American colonists of the eighteenth century produced a society more free than any the world had ever seen and one that would eventually expand the circle of political and social liberty. In all these respects, the American Revolution was a genuinely radical movement, whose influence would widen as Americans moved across the continent and as other peoples began to question traditional modes of European government.

In Perspective

During the sixteenth and seventeenth centuries, the West European maritime powers established extensive commercial, mercantile empires in North and South America. The point of these empires was to extract wealth and to establish commercial advantage for the colonial power. Spain had the largest of these empires, but by the end of the seventeenth century, Britain and France had also each established a major American presence. As a vast plantation economy emerged, significant portions of these American empires became economically dependent on slave labor, drawn from the forced importation of Africans. Through this large slave labor force, African linguistic, social, and religious influences became major cultural factors in these regions.

During the eighteenth century, the great European powers engaged in warfare over their American empires and over their power in India. These colonial wars became entangled in dynastic wars in central and eastern Europe and resulted in worldwide mid-century European conflict.

In the New World, Britain, France, and Spain battled for commercial dominance. France and Britain also clashed in India. By the third quarter of the century, Britain had ousted France from its major holdings in North America and from any significant presence in India. Spain, though no longer a military power of the first order, had managed to maintain its vast colonial empire in Latin America and much of its monopoly over the region's trade.

On the Continent, France, Austria, and Prussia collided over conflicting territorial and dynastic ambitions. Britain used the continental wars to divert France from the colonial arena. With British aid, Prussia had emerged in 1763 as a major continental power. Austria had lost territory to Prussia, while France had accumulated a vast debt.

The mid-century conflicts, in turn, led to major changes in all the European states. Each of the monarchies needed more money and tried to govern itself more efficiently. This problem led Britain to attempt to tax the North American colonies, which led to a revolution and the colonies' independence. Already deeply in debt, the French monarchy aided the Americans, fell into a deeper financial crisis, and soon clashed sharply with the nobility as royal ministers tried to find new revenues. That clash eventually unleashed the French Revolution. Spain moved to administer its Latin American empire more efficiently, which increased revolutionary discontent in the early nineteenth century. In preparation for future wars, the rulers of Prussia, Austria, and Russia pursued a mode of activist government known as Enlightened Absolutism (see Chapter 17). In that regard, the mid-eighteenth-century wars set in motion most of the major political developments of the next half century.

AP* TEST PREP

1. John Wilkes was
   a. a popular elected member of the House of Commons and Lord Mayor of London.
   b. a Son of Liberty.
   c. the leader of the Yorkshire Movement.
   d. a general in the Seven Years' War.
   e. a slave who fought in the Continental Army.

2. When English Whigs accused George III of becoming a tyrant, they were complaining of
   a. his corruption of office and personal lifestyle.
   b. his refusal to work with Parliament.
   c. his dependence on the military authority of Lord North.
   d. his refusal to acknowledge the authority of a portion of the aristocracy.
   e. his determination to subdue the colonies.

3. The *Flota* system describes
   a. Spanish efforts to fight piracy.
   b. the intercolony trade system in the West Indies.
   c. the strict exchange of Spanish goods in the colonies for a return of New World bullion.
   d. the shipbuilding industry in Cádiz.
   e. the Spanish slave triangle.

4. Among the imperial reformers, Charles III stood out for
   a. supporting legislative councils.
   b. abolishing the monopolies of Seville and Cádiz.
   c. closing off commerce between Spanish and American ports.
   d. relieving serfs of certain taxes.
   e. asserting humanitarian rights for slaves and indentured servants.

5. The advent of the commercial slave trade in the Americas can be marked by
   a. the arrival of a Dutch slave ship in Jamestown in 1619.
   b. the arrival of Christopher Columbus at Hispaniola.
   c. the development of sugar plantations in the West Indies.
   d. the *encomienda* system in Latin America.
   e. the development of tobacco plantations in North America.

6. Inhabitants of the New World who were born in Spain were known as
   a. *cajuns.*
   b. *creoles.*
   c. *mulattos.*
   d. *mistisos.*
   e. *peninsulares.*

7. The Saint Lawrence River Valley and the Ohio and Mississippi River Valleys were part of the _____ overseas empire.
   a. French
   b. British
   c. Dutch
   d. Spanish
   e. Russian

8. The process by which newly arrived Africans were prepared for slavery in the New World was known as
   a. hazing.
   b. chopping.
   c. unmanning.
   d. sorting.
   e. seasoning.

9. Black slaves had the fewest legal protections in
   a. Spanish areas.
   b. Portuguese areas.
   c. French areas.
   d. British areas.
   e. Dutch areas.

10. Thomas Paine is most famous for having written
    a. *The Rights of Free Men.*
    b. *A Response to the Intolerable Acts.*
    c. *Common Sense.*
    d. *An Almanac for the Americas.*
    e. *The Republican.*

11. Mercantilists regarded _____ as a measure of a nation's wealth.
    a. bullion
    b. the volume of trade
    c. the size of the army
    d. the amount of land under cultivation
    e. population

12. By 1725, it has been estimated that _____ percent of the population of Jamaica consisted of black slaves.
    a. 20
    b. 40
    c. 60
    d. 80
    e. 90

13. After the American Revolution, British trade with her former colonies
    a. stopped altogether.
    b. increased.
    c. decreased slowly.
    d. remained the same.
    e. decreased rapidly.

14. The Englishman who boasted of having won America on the plains of Germany was
    a. George III.
    b. William Pitt the Elder.
    c. Robert Clive.
    d. Robert Jenkins.
    e. Robert Walpole.

15. The early success of the British East India Company can be attributed to
    a. quinine.
    b. English demand for spices.
    c. exploding bullets.
    d. the acquisition of Pondicherry from the French.
    e. the vacuum created by the administrative and governmental decay of several Indian states.

16. The Seven Years' War pitted Prussia, Sweden, and Russia against Austria and
    a. France.
    b. Spain.
    c. Portugal.
    d. Italy.
    e. Britain.

17. Colonial reform in the Spanish colonies took place under the
    a. Spanish Habsburgs.
    b. Castilians.
    c. Argonese.
    d. Bourbons.
    e. Chatas.

18. The British Parliament passed the Sugar Act in 1764 reasoning that
    a. sugar prices needed to be controlled.
    b. it would be cheaper to start sugar plantations in India.
    c. the colonies were becoming too powerful and independent.
    d. sugar beet producers in England needed protection.
    e. colonists should share the cost of their own protection and administration.

19. All the following were part of the British Empire *except*
    a. Nova Scotia.
    b. Jamaica.
    c. Cuba.
    d. Bermuda.
    e. Newfoundland.

20. Mercantilists believed that a home country and its colonies should
    a. have little contact.
    b. concentrate on developing the military potential of the colony.
    c. work toward the eventual independence of that colony.
    d. develop separate economic systems.
    e. trade exclusively with each other.

DOCUMENT-BASED QUESTION

Directions: Construct a valid essay that directly addresses the central issue of the following question. Use facts from the documents provided and from the chapter to prove the position you take in your thesis statement.

Why was it so difficult for the Spanish to control their New World empire? Why was it so tempting for landowners, merchants, and traders to try to evade government oversight and regulation?

Document A

Brazilian sugar plantation.

Document B

The silver mines of Potosi.

Document C

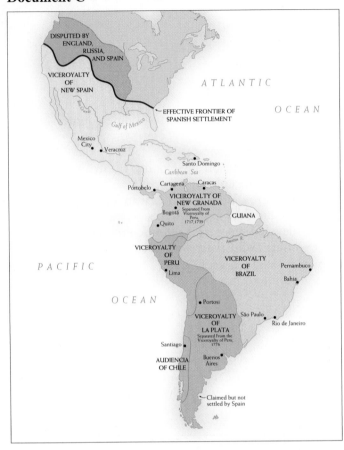

Map 16–1 **Viceroyalties in Latin America in 1780.**

Document D

Source: Visitors describe the Portobello fair, a fair that was the chief means of facilitating the official trade between the western coast of South America and Spain, *A Voyage to South America.*

The town of Portobello, so thinly inhabited, by reason of its noxious air, the scarcity of provisions, and the soil, becomes at the time of the [Spanish] galleons one of the most populous places in South America. . . .

The ships are no sooner moored in the harbor, than the first work is, to erect, in the square, a tent made of the ship's sails, for receiving cargo. . . .

Whilst the seamen and European traders are thus employed, the land is covered with droves of mules from Panama, each drove consists of about a hundred, loaded with chests of gold and silver. . . .

. . . in the presence of the commodore of the galleons, and the president of Panama, . . . the prices of the several kinds of merchandizes are settled. . . . The purchases and sales, likewise the exchanges of money, are transacted by brokers, both from Spain and Peru.

Document E

Source: A description of piracy in the Caribbean, *The Buccaneers of America.*

When a buccaneer is going to sea he sends word to all who wish to sail with him. When all are ready, they go on board, each bringing what he needs in the way of weapons, powder, and shot. . . .

When a ship has been captured, the men decide whether the captain should keep it or not: if the prize is better than their own vessel, they take it and set fire to the other. When a ship is robbed, nobody must plunder and keep the loot for himself. Everything taken . . . must be shared . . . , without any man enjoying a penny more than his fair share.

For more on the Spanish colonial system, see pages 479–486.

The Columbian Exchange: Disease, Animals, and Agriculture

THE EUROPEAN ENCOUNTER with the Americas produced remarkable ecological transformations that have shaped the world to the present moment. The same ships that carried Europeans and Africans to the New World also transported animals, plants, and germs that had never before appeared in the Americas. There was a similar transport back to Europe and Africa. Alfred Crosby, the leading historian of the process, has named this cross-continental flow "the Columbian exchange."

Diseases Enter the Americas

With the exception of a few ships that had gone astray or, in the case of the Vikings that had gone in search of new lands, the American continents had been biologically separated from Europe, Africa, and Asia for tens of thousands of years. In the Americas no native animals could serve as major beasts of burden except for the llama, which could not transport more than about a hundred pounds. Nor did animals constitute a major source of protein for Native Americans, whose diets consisted largely of maize, beans, peppers, yams, and potatoes. At the same time, the American continents included areas of vast grassland without grazing animals that would have transformed those plants into animal protein. Moreover, it also appears that native peoples had lived on the long-isolated American continents without experiencing major epidemics.

By the second voyage of Columbus (1493), that picture began to change in remarkable ways. On his return voyage to Hispaniola and other islands of the Caribbean, Columbus brought a number of animals and plants that were previously unknown to the New World. The men on all his voyages and those on subsequent European voyages also carried diseases novel to the Americas.

The diseases thus transported by Europeans ultimately accounted for the conquest of the people of the Americas as much as the advanced European weaponry. Much controversy surrounds the question of the actual size of the populations of Native Americans in the Caribbean islands, Mexico, Peru, and the North Atlantic coast. All

Nothing so destroyed the life of the Native Americans whom the Spanish encountered as the introduction of smallpox. With no immune defenses to this new disease, millions of Native Americans died of smallpox during the sixteenth and seventeenth centuries. The Granger Collection

accounts present those populations as quite significant, with those of Mexico in particular numbering many millions. Yet in the first two centuries after the encounter, wherever Europeans went either as settlers or as conquerors, extremely large numbers of Native Americans died from diseases they had never before encountered. The most deadly such disease was smallpox, which destroyed millions of people. Beyond the devastation wrought by that disease, bubonic plague, typhoid, typhus, influenza, measles, chicken pox, whooping cough, malaria, and diphtheria produced deadly results in more localized epidemics. For example, an unknown disease, but quite possibly typhus, caused major losses among the Native Americans of New England between approximately 1616 and 1619.

Native Americans appear to have been highly susceptible to these diseases because, with no earlier exposure, they lacked immunity. Wherever such outbreaks are recorded, Europeans either contracted or died from them at a much lower rate than the Native Americans. These diseases would continue to victimize Native Americans at a higher rate than Americans of European descent through the end of the nineteenth century when smallpox and measles still killed large numbers of the Plains Indian peoples of North America.

Although many historical and medical questions still surround the subject, it appears almost certain that syphilis, which became a rampant venereal disease in Europe at the close of the fifteenth century and eventually spread around the globe, originated in the New World. It seems to have been an entirely new disease, spawned through a mutation when the causal agent for yaws migrated from the Americas to new climatic settings in Europe. Until the discovery of penicillin in the 1940s, syphilis remained a major concern of public health throughout the world.

Animals and Agriculture

The introduction of European livestock to the Americas quite simply revolutionized the agriculture of two continents. The most important new animals were pigs, cattle, horses, goats, and sheep. Once transported to the New World, these animals multiplied at unprecedented rates. The place where this first occurred was in the islands of the Caribbean, during the first forty years of Spanish settlement and exploitation. This situation established the foundation for the later Spanish conquest of both Mexico and Peru by providing the Spanish with strong breeds of animals, especially horses, acclimated to the Americas when they set out to conquer the mainland of South America.

The horse became first the animal of the conquest and then the animal of colonial Latin American cul-

ture. Native Americans had no experience with such large animals who would obey the will of a human rider. The mounted Spanish horseman struck fear into these people, and for good reason. After the conquest, however, the Americas from Mexico southward became the largest horse-breeding region of the world, with ranches raising thousands of animals. Horses became relatively cheap, and even Native Americans could acquire them. By the nineteenth century, the possession of horses would allow the Plains Indians of North America to resist the advance of their white conquerors.

The flourishing of pigs, cattle, and sheep allowed a vast economic exploitation of the Americas. These animals produced enormous quantities of hides and wool. Their presence in such large numbers also meant the

Within one year of Columbus's encounter with the Americas, the event had been captured in this woodcut (c. 1493). Columbus's several voyages, and those of later Europeans as well, introduced not only European warfare but also began a vast ecological exchange of plants, animals, and diseases between the Old and New Worlds. Courtesy of the Library of Congress

Americas from the sixteenth century through the present would support a diet more plentiful in animal protein than anywhere else in the world.

Europeans also brought their own plants to the New World, including peaches, oranges, grapes, melons, bananas, rice, onions, radishes, and various green vegetables. Socially, for three centuries the most significant of these was sugarcane, whose cultivation created the major demand for slavery throughout the transatlantic plantation economy. Nutritionally, European wheat would, over the course of time, allow the Americas not only to feed themselves, but also to export large amounts of grain throughout the world. This American production of wheat on the vast plains of the two continents contrasted sharply with the difficulty Europeans faced raising grain in the northern and northeastern parts of the Continent, particularly in Russia.

No significant animals from the Americas, except the turkey, actually came to be raised in Europe. The Americas did send to Europe, however, a series of plants that eventually changed the European diet: maize, potatoes, sweet potatoes, peppers, beans, manioc (tapioca), peanuts, squash, pumpkin, pineapple, cocoa, and tomatoes. All of these, to a greater or lesser degree, eventually entered the diet of Europeans and of European settlers and their descendants in the Americas. Maize and the potato, however, had the most transforming impact. Each of these two crops became a major staple in European farming, as well as in the European diet. Both crops grow rapidly, supplying food quickly and steadily if not attacked by disease. Tobacco, we should note, originated in the Americas, too.

Maize was established as a crop in Spain within thirty years of the country's encounter with the New World. A century and a half later it was commonplace in the Spanish diet, and its cultivation had spread to Italy and France. Maize produced more grain for the seed and farming effort than wheat did. Throughout Europe, maize was associated primarily with fodder for animals. As early as the eighteenth century, travelers noted the presence of polenta in the peasant diet, and other forms of maize dishes, such as fried mush, spread.

The potato established its European presence more slowly than maize. The Spanish encountered the potato only when Pizarro conquered Peru, where it was a major part of the Native American food supply. It was adopted slowly by Europeans because it needed to be raised in climates more temperate than that of Spain and the Mediterranean. It appears to have become a major peasant food in Scotland, Ireland, and parts of Germany during the eighteenth century. It became more widely cultivated elsewhere in Europe only after new strains of the plant were imported from Chile in the late nineteenth century. In the middle of the seventeenth century, Irish peasants were urged to cultivate the potato as a major source of cheap nutrition that could grow in quantity on a small plot. The food shortages arising from the wars of Louis XIV and then during the eighteenth century led farmers in northern Europe to adopt the potato for similar reasons. It was nutrient insurance against failure of the grain harvest. There is good reason to believe the cultivation of the potato was one of the major causes of the population increase in eighteenth- and nineteenth-century Europe. It was the quintessential food of the poor.

Many tragedies arose from the encounter between the people of the Americas and those of Europe, as well as from the forging of new nations and civilizations in the Americas. Yet, one of the last chapters of those tragedies to arise as a direct fallout of the Columbian exchange three centuries earlier was the Irish famine of the 1840s. Irish peasants had become almost wholly dependent on the potato as a source of food. In the middle of the 1840s, an American parasite infected the Irish potato crop. The result of the failure of the crop was the death of hundreds of thousands of Irish peasants and the migration of still more hundreds of thousands to the Americas and elsewhere in the world.

Define the Columbian exchange. What was the impact of European diseases on the Americas? Why was the impact so profound? Why could so many European crops grow well in the Americas? What was the cultural impact of animals taken from Europe to the Americas? How did food from the Americas change the diet of Europe and then later, as Europeans immigrated, the diet of the entire world?

The salon of Madame Marie Thérèse Geoffrin (1699–1777) was one of the most important Parisian gathering spots for Enlightenment writers during the middle of the eighteenth century. Well-connected women such as Madame Geoffrin were instrumental in helping the philosophes they patronized to bring their ideas to the attention of influential people in French society and politics.   Chateaux de Malmaison et Bois-Preau, Rueil-Malmaison. Bridgeman-Giraudon/Art Resource, NY

17

The Age of Enlightenment: Eighteenth-Century Thought

▼ **Formative Influences on the Enlightenment**
Ideas of Newton and Locke • The Example of British Toleration and Political Stability
• The Emergence of a Print Culture

▼ **The Philosophes**
Voltaire—First Among the Philosophes

▼ **The Enlightenment and Religion**
Deism • Toleration • Radical Enlightenment Criticism of Christianity • Jewish Thinkers in the Age of Enlightenment • Islam in Enlightenment Thought

▼ **The Enlightenment and Society**
The *Encyclopedia*: Freedom and Economic Improvement • Beccaria and Reform of Criminal Law • The Physiocrats and Economic Freedom • Adam Smith on Economic Growth and Social Progress

▼ **Political Thought of the Philosophes**
Montesquieu and *Spirit of the Laws* • Rousseau: A Radical Critique of Modern Society • Enlightened Critics of European Empires

▼ **Women in the Thought and Practice of the Enlightenment**

▼ **Rococo and Neoclassical Styles in Eighteenth-Century Art**

▼ **Enlightened Absolutism**
Frederick the Great of Prussia • Joseph II of Austria • Catherine the Great of Russia • The Partition of Poland • The End of the Eighteenth Century in Central and Eastern Europe

▼ **In Perspective**

KEY TOPICS

• The intellectual and social background of the Enlightenment

• The philosophes of the Enlightenment and their agenda of intellectual and political reform

• Enlightenment writers' attitude toward religion

• The philosophes' political thought

• Efforts of "enlightened" monarchs in central and eastern Europe to increase the economic and military strength of their domains

• The partition of Poland by Prussia, Russia, and Austria

D URING THE EIGHTEENTH century, the conviction began to spread throughout the expanding literate sectors of European society that economic improvement and political reform were both possible and desirable. This attitude is now commonplace, but it came into its own only after 1700. It represents one of the primary continuing intellectual inheritances from that age. The movement of people and ideas that fostered such thinking is called the Enlightenment.

Inspired by the scientific revolution and prepared to challenge traditional intellectual and ecclesiastical authority, Enlightenment writers believed that human beings can comprehend the operation of physical nature and mold it to achieve material and moral improvement, economic growth, and administrative reform. They advocated agricultural improvement, commercial society, expanding consumption, and the application of innovative rational methods to traditional social and economic practices. The rationality of the physical universe became a standard against which they measured and criticized the customs and traditions of society. In religious matters they generally advocated a policy of toleration that opposed the claims to exclusive religious privilege of state-supported established churches whether Roman Catholic or Protestant. As the criticisms of Enlightenment writers penetrated every corner of contemporary society, politics, and religious opinion, the spirit of innovation and improvement came to characterize modern Europe and Western society.

Some of the ideas and outlooks of the Enlightenment had a direct impact on rulers in central and eastern Europe. These rulers, whose policies became known by the term *enlightened absolutism*, sought to centralize their authority so as to reform their countries. They often attempted to restructure religious institutions and to sponsor economic growth. Although they frequently associated themselves with the Enlightenment, many of their military and foreign policies were in direct opposition to enlightened ideals. Nonetheless, both the Enlightenment writers and these monarchs were forces for modernization in European life.

▼ Formative Influences on the Enlightenment

The Newtonian worldview, the political stability and commercial prosperity of Great Britain after 1688, the need for administrative and economic reform in France after the wars of Louis XIV, and the consolidation of what is known as a *print culture* were the chief factors that fostered the ideas of the Enlightenment and the call for reform throughout Europe.

Ideas of Newton and Locke

Isaac Newton (1642–1727) and John Locke (1632–1704) were the major intellectual forerunners of the Enlightenment. The achievements of the Scientific Revolution from Copernicus to Newton had persuaded natural philosophers and then many other writers that traditions of thought inherited from both the ancient and medieval Christian worlds were incorrect or confused and needed to be challenged. Newton's formulation of the law of universal gravitation exemplified the newly perceived power of the human mind. Newtonian physics had portrayed a pattern of mechanical and mathematical rationality in the physical world. During the eighteenth century, thinkers from a variety of backgrounds began to apply this insight to society. If nature was rational, they reasoned, society, too, should be organized rationally. Furthermore, Newton had encouraged natural philosophers to approach the study of nature directly and to avoid metaphysics and supernaturalism. He had insisted on the use of empirical experience to check rational speculation. This emphasis on concrete experience became a key feature of Enlightenment thought.

As explained in Chapter 14, Newton's success in physics had inspired his fellow countryman John Locke to explain human psychology in terms of experience. In *An Essay Concerning Human Understanding* (1690), Locke argued that all humans enter the world a **tabula rasa**, or blank page. Personality is the product of the sensations that impinge on an individual from the external world throughout his or her life. Thus, experience, and only experience, shapes character. This essentially behaviorist theory implied that human nature is changeable and can be molded by modifying the surrounding physical and social environment. Locke's was thus a reformer's psychology that suggested the possibility of improving the human condition. Locke's psychology also, in effect, rejected the Christian doctrine that sin permanently flawed human beings. By contrast, Locke's thought implied that human beings need not wait for the grace of God or other divine aid to better their lives. They can take charge of their own destiny.

The Example of British Toleration and Political Stability

Newton's physics and Locke's psychology provided the theoretical basis for a reformist approach to society. The domestic stability of Great Britain after the Revolution of 1688 furnished a living example of a society in which, to many contemporaries, enlightened reforms appeared to benefit everyone. England permitted religious toleration to all except Unitarians and Roman Catholics, and even they were not actively persecuted. Relative freedom of the press and free speech prevailed. The authority of the monarchy was limited, and political sovereignty resided in Parliament. The courts protected citizens from arbitrary government action. The army was small. Furthermore, the domestic economic life of Great Britain displayed far less regulation than that of France or other continental nations, and English commerce flourished. As reformist observers on the Continent noted, these liberal policies had produced neither disorder nor instability, but rather economic prosperity, political stability, and a loyal citizenry.

Printing shops were the productive centers for the book trade and newspaper publishing that spread the ideas of the Enlightenment. The Granger Collection

This view may have been idealized, but England was nonetheless significantly freer than any other European nation at the time. Many writers of the continental Enlightenment contrasted what they regarded as the wise, progressive features of English life with the absence of religious toleration, the extensive literary censorship, the possibility of arbitrary arrest, the overregulation of the economy, and the influence of aristocratic military values in their own nations and most particularly in France.

The Emergence of a Print Culture

The Enlightenment flourished in a *print culture*, that is, a culture in which books, journals, newspapers, and pamphlets had achieved a status of their own. In the past, print culture had deeply influenced the intellectual and religious movements associated with Renaissance humanism, the Reformation, and the Counter-Reformation. During the seventeenth century, a lively world of publication had arisen, which many governments sought to censor. During the eighteenth century, the volume of printed material—books, journals, magazines, and daily newspapers—increased sharply throughout Europe, notably in Britain. Prose came to be valued as highly as poetry, and the novel emerged as a distinct literary genre.

One of the driving forces behind this expansion of printed materials was the increase in literacy that occurred across Europe. Significantly more people especially in the urban centers of Western and central Europe could read. As a result, the printed word became the chief vehicle for communicating information and ideas and would remain so until the electronic revolution of our own day.

A growing concern with everyday life and material concerns—with secular as opposed to religious issues—accompanied this expansion of printed forms. Toward the end of the seventeenth century, half the books published in Paris were religious; by the 1780s, only about 10 percent were. Novels often came to provide the moral and social instruction that books of piety once furnished. An English journal observed unhappily in 1790: "Novels spring into existence like insects on the banks of the Nile; and, if we may be indulged in another comparison, cover the shelves of circulating libraries, as locusts crowd the fields of Asia. Their great and growing number is a serious evil; for, in general, they exhibit delusive views of human life; and while they amuse, frequently they poison the mind."[1] People may have thus criticized the moral influence of the novel but did not deny its influence.

Books were not inexpensive in the eighteenth century, but they, and the ideas they conveyed, circulated in a variety of ways to reach a broad public. Private and public libraries, as the previous quotation noted, grew in number, allowing single copies to reach many readers. Authors might also publish the same material in different formats. The English essayist, critic, and dictionary author Samuel Johnson (1709–1784), for example, published as books a collection of essays that had first appeared in newspapers or journals. The number of the latter publications also expanded throughout the century.

Within both aristocratic and middle-class society, people were increasingly expected to be familiar with books and secular ideas. Popular publications, such as *The Spectator*, begun in 1711 by Joseph Addison (1672–1719) and Richard Steele (1672–1729), fostered the value of polite conversation and the reading of books. Coffeehouses became centers for discussing writ-

[1]Quoted T. C. W. Blanning, *The Culture of Power and the Power of Culture: Old Regime Europe 1660–1789* (Oxford: Oxford University Press, 2002), p. 151.

ing and ideas. (See "Encountering the Past: Coffeehouses and Enlightenment," page 512.) The lodges of Freemasons, the meeting places for members of a movement that began in Britain and spread to the Continent, provided another site for discussing secular ideas in secular books.

The expanding market for printed matter allowed writers to earn a living from their work for the first time, making authorship an occupation. Parisian ladies who hosted fashionable salons sought out popular writers. Some writers, notably Alexander Pope (1688–1744) in England and Voltaire in France, grew wealthy, providing an example for their young colleagues. In a challenge to older aristocratic values, status for authors in this new print culture was based on merit and commercial competition, not heredity and patronage.

A division, however, soon emerged between high and low literary culture. Successful authors of the Enlightenment addressed themselves to monarchs, nobles, the upper middle classes, and professional groups, and they were read and accepted in these upper levels of society. Other aspiring authors found social and economic disappointment. They lived marginally, writing professionally for whatever newspaper or journal that would pay for their work. Many of these lesser writers grew resentful, blaming a corrupt society for their lack of success. From their anger, they often espoused radical ideas or took moderate Enlightenment ideas to radical extremes, transmitting them in this embittered form to their often lower-class audience.

An expanding, literate public and the growing influence of secular printed materials created a new and increasingly influential social force called *public opinion*. This force—the collective effect on political and social life of views circulated in print and discussed in the home, the workplace, and centers of leisure—seems not to have existed before the middle of the eighteenth century. Books and newspapers could have thousands of readers, who in effect supported the writers whose works they bought, as they discussed their ideas and circulated them widely. The writers, in turn, had to answer only to their readers. The result changed the cultural and political climate in Europe. In 1775, a new member of the French Academy declared:

A tribunal has arisen independent of all powers and that all powers respect, that appreciates all talents, that pronounces on all people of merit. And in an enlightened century, in a century in which each citizen can speak to the entire nation by way of print, those who have a talent for instructing men and a gift for moving them—in a word, men of letters—are, amid the public dispersed, what the orators of Rome and Athens were in the middle of the public assembled.[2]

Governments could no longer operate wholly in secret or with disregard to the larger public sphere. They, as well as their critics, had to explain and discuss their views and policies openly.

Continental European governments sensed the political power of the new print culture. They regulated the book trade, censored books and newspapers, confiscated offending titles, and imprisoned offending authors. The eventual, but never in the eighteenth nor in most of the nineteenth century expansion of freedom of the press represented also an expansion of the print culture—with its independent readers, authors, and publishers—and the challenge it posed to traditional intellectual, social, and political authorities.

▼ The Philosophes

The writers and critics who flourished in the expanding print culture and who took the lead in forging the new attitudes favorable to change, championed reform, and advocated toleration were known as the **philosophes**. Not usually philosophers in a formal sense, but rather usually literary figures, economists, or historians, these figures sought rather to apply the rules of reason, criticism, and common sense to nearly all the major institutions, economic practices, and exclusivist religious policies of the day. The most famous of their number included Voltaire, Montesquieu, Diderot, D'Alembert, Rousseau, Hume, Gibbon, Smith, Lessing, and Kant.

A few of these philosophes, particularly those in Germany, were university professors. Most, however, were free agents who might be found in London coffeehouses, Edinburgh drinking spots, the salons of fashionable Parisian ladies, the country houses of reform-minded nobles, or the courts of the most powerful monarchs on the Continent. In eastern Europe, they were often royal bureaucrats. They were not an organized group; they disagreed on many issues and did not necessarily like or respect each other. Their relationship to one another and to lesser figures of the same turn of mind has been compared with that of a family, which, despite quarrels and tensions, preserves a basic unity. Another historian has portrayed the unity of the Enlightenment across many different local cultures as that of "eighteenth-century thinkers who saw themselves as members of a wider intellectual movement, dedicated to understanding and publicizing the cause of human betterment on this earth."[3]

The philosophes drew the bulk of their readership from the prosperous commercial and professional urban classes. These people as well as forward-looking aristocrats discussed the reformers' writings and ideas in local philosophical societies, Freemason lodges, and clubs. These

[2]Chrétien-Guillaume Malesherbes, as quoted in Roger Chartier, *The Cultural Origins of the French Revolution*, trans. by Lydia G. Cochran (Durham, NC: Duke University Press, 1991), pp. 30–31.

[3]Peter Gay, *The Enlightenment: An Interpretation*, Vol. 1 (New York: Knopf, 1967), p. 4; John Robertson, *The Case for the Enlightenment: Scotland and Napes 1680–1760* (Cambridge: 2005), p. 377.

COFFEEHOUSES AND ENLIGHTENMENT

THE IDEAS OF the Enlightenment not only spread through books and journals. They also took on a life of their own in public discussions in what was a new popular institution of European social life—the coffeehouse.

Coffee, originally imported into Europe from the Ottoman Empire, is the chief Turkish contribution to the Western diet. Coffeehouses had long existed in the Muslim world, encouraged by the Islamic prohibition on alcoholic drink. The first European coffeehouse appeared in Venice in the 1640s, and the first coffeehouse in Vienna opened its doors in 1683 with coffee left behind when the Turks abandoned their siege of the city.

By the middle of the eighteenth century, thousands of coffeehouses dotted European cities and towns. Customers were attracted to them in part because the coffeehouses did not serve alcoholic beverages, which made unruly behavior less likely than in taverns. (The practice of tipping began in the coffeehouses of London. The word *tips* originated as an acronym for "to insure prompt service.")

Throughout Europe, the coffeehouse provided a social arena for the open, spontaneous discussion of events, politics, literature, and ideas—but only for men (respectable women did not enter coffeehouses). By furnishing copies of newspapers and other journals, the proprietors of coffeehouses linked their customers to the growing print culture just as today's Internet cafés link customers to the World Wide Web. In London coffeehouses, members of the Royal Society and other men associated with the new science mixed with merchants and bankers. Some London coffeehouse proprietors invited learned persons to lecture, usually for a fee, on Newtonian physics, the mechanical philosophy, ethics, and the relationship of science and religion. One historian has described these lecturers as "the philosophical brotherhood of the coffeehouses."[1]

In France the philosophes, such as Voltaire, Rousseau, and Diderot, looked to the café as a place to meet other writers. By 1743, a German commented, "A coffeehouse is like a political stock exchange, where the most gallant and wittiest heads of every estate come together. They engage in wide-ranging and edifying talk, issue well-founded judgments on matters concerning the political and the scholarly world, converse sagaciously about the most secret news from all courts and states, and unveil the most hidden truths."[2]

One irony, however, should be noted about the eighteenth-century European coffeehouses. Although they provided one of the chief locations for the public discussion of the ideas of the Enlightenment, which fostered greater liberty of thought in Europe, the coffee and sugar consumed in these establishments were cultivated by slave labor on plantations in the Caribbean and Brazil. The coffeehouse was one of many institutions of European life that was connected to the transatlantic plantation slave economy.

How did coffeehouses help spread the ideas of the Enlightenment?

How was the consumption of coffee related to the transatlantic slave trade?

Business, science, religion, and politics were discussed in London coffeehouses such as this. Permission of the Trustees of the British Museum

[1]Larry Stewart, *The Rise of Public Science, Rhetoric Technology, and Natural Philosophy in Newtonian Britain, 1660–1750* (Cambridge: Cambridge University Press, 1992), p. 145.

[2]Quoted in James Van Horn Melton, *The Rise of the Public in Enlightenment Europe* (Cambridge: Cambridge University Press, 2001), p. 243.

readers had enough income to buy and the leisure to read the philosophes' works. Although the writers of the Enlightenment did not consciously champion the goals or causes of the middle class, they did provide an intellectual ferment and a major source of ideas that could be used to undermine existing social practices and political structures based on aristocratic privilege. They taught their contemporaries, including reform-minded aristocrats, how to pose pointed, critical questions. Moreover, the philosophes generally supported the expansion of trade, the improvement of agriculture and transport, and the invention of new manufacturing machinery that were transforming the society and the economy of the eighteenth century and enlarging the business and commercial classes.

The chief bond among the philosophes was their common desire to reform religion, political thought, society, government, and the economy for the sake of human liberty. As the historian Peter Gay once suggested, this goal included "freedom from arbitrary power, freedom of speech, freedom of trade, freedom to realize one's talents, freedom of aesthetic response, freedom, in a word, of moral man to make his way in the world."[4] Though challenged over the last three centuries, no other single set of ideas has done so much to shape and define the modern Western world.

Voltaire—First Among the Philosophes

By far the most influential of the philosophes was François-Marie Arouet, known to posterity by his pen name Voltaire (1694–1778). During the 1720s, Voltaire had offended first the French monarch and then certain nobles by his politically and socially irreverent poetry and plays. He was arrested and twice briefly imprisoned, in comfortable conditions, in the Bastille, the royal prison-fortress in Paris. In 1726, to escape the wrath of a powerful aristocrat whom he had offended, Voltaire went into exile in England. There he visited its best literary circles, observed its tolerant intellectual and religious climate, relished the freedom he felt in its moderate political atmosphere, and admired its science and economic prosperity. In 1727, he also witnessed the elaborate funeral of Sir Isaac Newton. The next year Voltaire returned to France and, in 1733, published *Letters on the English*, which appeared in French the next year. The book praised the virtues of the English, especially their religious liberty, and implicitly criticized the abuses of French society. The Parlement of Paris condemned the book, and the authorities harassed Voltaire. He moved to Cirey from which, if necessary, he

Statue of Voltaire by Jean-Antoine Houdon (Théâtre Francais, Paris).   Musée Lambinet, Versailles/Giraudon/Art Resource, NY

could easily escape France into what was then the nearby independent duchy of Lorraine. There he lived with Countess Emilie de Chatelet (1706–1749), the brilliant mathematician, discussed in Chapter 14, who became his mistress. In 1738, with her considerable help, he published *Elements of the Philosophy of Newton*, which more than any other single book popularized the thought of Isaac Newton across the continent. In 1749, Madame de Chatelet died.

Shortly thereafter, Voltaire took up residence for three years in Berlin at the court of Frederick the Great of Prussia with whom he had corresponded for several years. The residency ended unhappily with Voltaire fleeing to France. For a time he settled in Switzerland near Geneva but clashed with local conservative Calvinist clergy over his sponsoring plays in the theater in his

[4]Gay, *The Enlightenment*, p. 3.

home. Thereafter he acquired the estate of Ferney, just across the French border, but close enough to flee to Geneva should the French authorities bother him. His extremely popular plays, essays, histories, and stories along with his far-flung correspondence made him the literary dictator of Europe. For the rest of his long life, he turned the venom of his satire and sarcasm against one evil after another in French and European life.

In 1755 a huge earthquake struck Lisbon, Portugal, killing at least 60,000 people. Voltaire wrote a deeply pessimistic poem commemorating the event. Other contemporary writers questioned his pessimism arguing for a more optimistic view of life and nature. In 1759, Voltaire replied in the novel *Candide*, his still widely read satire attacking war, religious persecution, and what he considered unwarranted optimism about the human condition. Like most of the philosophes, Voltaire believed human society could and should be improved, but he was never certain that reform, if achieved, would be permanent. In that respect his thought reflected the broader pessimistic undercurrent of the Enlightenment. As his fellow philosophe Jean d'Alembert wrote, "Barbarism lasts for centuries; it seems that it is our natural element; reason and good taste are only passing."[5]

In his later years, as will be seen in the next section, Voltaire also became a major voice attacking religious persecution and advocating toleration. He died in 1778 in Paris after a triumphal return to that city, which he had not seen for decades.

▼ The Enlightenment and Religion

For many, but not all, philosophes of the eighteenth century, ecclesiastical institutions, especially in their frequently privileged position as official parts of the state, were the chief impediment to human improvement and happiness. Voltaire's cry, "Crush the Infamous Thing," summed up the attitude of a number of philosophes toward the churches and Christianity. Almost all varieties of Christianity, but especially Roman Catholicism, felt their criticism as also did both Judaism and Islam.

The critical philosophes complained that both established and non-established Christian churches hindered the pursuit of a rational life and the scientific study of humanity and nature. Both Roman Catholic and Protestant clergy taught that humans were basically depraved, becoming worthy only through divine grace. According to the doctrine of original sin—either Protestant or Catholic—meaningful improvement in human nature on earth was impossible. Religion thus turned attention away from this world to the world to come. For example, the philosophes argued that the Calvinist doctrine of pre-

destination denied that virtuous behavior in this life could affect the fate of a person's soul after death. Mired in conflicts over obscure doctrines, the churches promoted intolerance and bigotry, inciting torture, war, and other forms of human suffering.

With this attack, the philosophes were challenging not only a set of ideas, but also some of Europe's most powerful institutions. The churches were deeply enmeshed in the power structure of the Old Regime. They owned large amounts of land and collected tithes from peasants before any secular authority collected its taxes. Most clergy were legally exempt from taxes and made only annual voluntary grants to the government. The upper clergy in most countries were relatives or clients of aristocrats. High clerics were actively involved in politics. Bishops served in the British House of Lords and on the Continent, cardinals and bishops advised rulers or were sovereign princes themselves. In Protestant countries, the leading local landowner usually appointed the parish clergyman. In Britain and on the Continent, membership in the state church conferred political and social advantages. Those who did not belong to it were often excluded from political life, the universities, and the professions. Clergy frequently provided intellectual justification for the social and political status quo, and they were active agents of religious and literary censorship.

Deism

The philosophes, although critical of many religious institutions and frequently anticlerical, did not oppose all religion. In Scotland, for example, the enlightened historian William Robertson (1721–1793) was the head of the Scottish Presbyterian Kirk. In England, Anglican clergymen did much to popularize the thought of Newton. In France, several of the leading philosophes were Catholic priests. What the philosophes sought, however, was religion without fanaticism and intolerance, a religious life that would largely substitute human reason for the authority of churches. The Newtonian worldview had convinced many writers that nature was rational. Therefore, the God who had created nature must also be rational, and the religion through which that God was worshipped should be rational. Most of them believed the life of religion and of reason could be combined, giving rise to a a broad set of ideas known as **deism**.

The title of one of the earliest deist works, *Christianity Not Mysterious* (1696) by John Toland (1670–1722), indicates the general tenor of this religious outlook. Toland and later deist writers promoted religion as a natural and rational, rather than a supernatural and mystical, phenomenon. In this respect they differed from Newton and Locke, both of whom regarded themselves as Christians (though not necessarily theologically orthodox ones). Newton believed God could interfere with the natural order, whereas the deists regarded God as a

[5]Jean Le Rond d'Alembert, *Preliminary Discourse to the Encyclopedia of Diderot*, trans. by Richard N. Schwab (Indianapolis: ITT Bobbs-Merrill Educational Publishing, 1985), p. 103.

kind of divine watchmaker who had created the mechanism of nature, set it in motion, and then departed.

The deists' informal creed had two major points. The first was a belief in the existence of God, which they thought the contemplation of nature could empirically justify, and in this respect many Protestant and Roman Catholic writers fully agreed with them. Joseph Addison's poem on the spacious firmament (1712) illustrates this idea:

The spacious firmament on high,
With all the blue ethereal sky,
And spangled heav'n, a shining frame,
Their great Original proclaim:
Th' unwearied Sun, from day to day,
Does his Creator's power display,
And publishes to every land
The work of an Almighty hand.

Because nature provided evidence of a rational God, that deity must also favor rational morality. So the second point in the deists' creed was a belief in life after death, when rewards and punishments would be meted out according to the virtue of the lives people led on this earth.

Deism, Enlightenment writers urged, was empirical, tolerant, reasonable, and capable of encouraging virtuous living. Voltaire once wrote,

The great name of Deist, which is not sufficiently revered, is the only name one ought to take. The only gospel one ought to read is the great book of Nature, written by the hand of God and sealed with his seal. The only religion that ought to be professed is the religion of worshiping God and being a good man.[6]

Deists hoped that wide acceptance of their faith would end rivalry among the various Christian sects and with it religious fanaticism, conflict, and persecution. They also felt deism would remove the need for priests and ministers, who, in their view, were often responsible for fomenting religious differences and denominational hatred. Deistic thought led some contemporaries to believe God had revealed himself in different ways and that many religions might embody divine truth.

There was never a formal or extensive deist movement, but deist ideas spread informally throughout the culture and provided for some people a framework for a nondogmatic religious outlook. Furthermore, in England writers defending the privileges of the Church of England often ascribed deist ideas to quite orthodox English nonconformists who were serious Protestants who simply dissented from the established church. Most deist writers were strongly anticlerical and were for that reason regarded as politically radical, an association that was strengthened by the links between Unitarians and political radicalism. Christian writers often attacked the deists because of this anticlericalism and associated political radi-

calism and thus actually spread their ideas and may have made the movement appear more influential and pervasive than it was. In this respect, religious controversy arising from orthodox writers themselves placed new religious ideas into the public sphere as much or more than the actual publications of unorthodox authors.

Toleration

As discussed in Chapter 14, John Locke had set forth a strong argument for toleration in his *Letter Concerning Toleration* of 1689. Except in England, however, toleration generally remained the exception during most of the eighteenth century. Continuing in Locke's spirit, the philosophes presented religious toleration as a primary social condition for the virtuous life. Again Voltaire took the polemical lead in championing this cause. In 1762, the Roman Catholic political authorities in the city of Toulouse ordered the execution of a Huguenot named Jean Calas, who had been accused of murdering his son to prevent him from converting to Roman Catholicism. Calas was viciously tortured and publicly strangled without ever confessing his guilt. The confession would not have saved his life, but it would have given the Catholics good propaganda to use against Protestants.

Voltaire learned of the case only after Calas's death. He made the dead man's cause his own. In 1763, he published his *Treatise on Tolerance* and hounded the authorities for a new investigation. Finally, in 1765, the judicial decision against the unfortunate man was reversed. For Voltaire, the case illustrated the fruits of religious fanaticism and the need for rational reform of judicial processes. (See "Voltaire Attacks Religious Fanaticism," page 516.)

In 1779, the German playwright and critic Gotthold Lessing (1729–1781) wrote *Nathan the Wise*, a plea for toleration not only of different Christian groups, but also of religious faiths other than Christianity. The premise behind all of these calls for toleration was, in effect, that life on earth and human relationships should not be subordinated to religious zeal that permitted one group of people to persecute, harm, or repress other groups.

Radical Enlightenment Criticism of Christianity

Some philosophes went beyond the formulation of a rational religious alternative to Christianity and the advocacy of toleration to attack the churches and the clergy with vehemence. The Scottish philosopher David Hume (1711–1776), argued in "Of Miracles," a chapter in his *Inquiry into Human Nature* (1748), that no empirical evidence supported the belief in divine miracles central to much of Christianity. For Hume, the greatest miracle was that people believed in miracles. Voltaire repeatedly

[6]Quoted in J. H. Randall, *The Making of the Modern Mind*, rev. ed. (New York: Houghton Mifflin, 1940), p. 292.

VOLTAIRE ATTACKS RELIGIOUS FANATICISM

The chief complaint of the philosophes against Christianity was that over the course of its history it had bred a fanaticism that led people to commit crimes in the name of religion. In this passage from Voltaire's Philosophical Dictionary *(1764), he directly reminds his readers of the intolerance of the Reformation era and indirectly referred to examples of contemporary religious excesses. He argues that the philosophical spirit can overcome fanaticism and foster toleration and more humane religious behavior. Shocking many of his contemporaries, he praises the virtues of Confucianism over those of Christianity.*

What concrete examples of religious fanaticism might Voltaire have had in mind? Why does Voltaire contend that neither religion nor laws can contain religious fanaticism? Why does Voltaire admire the Chinese?

Fanaticism is to superstition what delirium is to fever and rage to anger. The man visited by ecstasies and visions, who takes dreams for realities and his fancies for prophecies, is an enthusiast; the man who supports his madness with murder is a fanatic. . . .

The most detestable example of fanaticism was that of the burghers of Paris who on St. Bartholomew's Night [1572] went about assassinating and butchering all their fellow citizens who did not go to mass, throwing them out of windows, cutting them in pieces.

Once fanaticism has corrupted a mind, the malady is almost incurable. . . . The only remedy for this epidemic malady is the philosophical spirit which, spread gradually, at last tames men's habits and prevents the disease from starting; for once the disease has made any progress, one must flee and wait for the air to clear itself. Laws and religion are not strong enough against the spiritual pest; religion, far from being healthy food for infected brains, turns to poison in them. . . .

Even the law is impotent against these attacks of rage; it is like reading a court decree to a raving maniac. These fellows are certain that the holy spirit with which they are filled is above the law, that their enthusiasm is the only law they must obey.

What can we say to a man who tells you that he would rather obey God than men, and that therefore he is sure to go to heaven for butchering you?

Ordinarily fanatics are guided by rascals, who put the dagger into their hands; these latter resemble that Old Man of the Mountain who is supposed to have made imbeciles taste the joys of paradise and who promised them an eternity of the pleasures of which he had given them a foretaste, on condition that they assassinated all those he would name to them. There is only one religion in the world that has never been sullied by fanaticism, that of the Chinese men of letters. The schools of philosophy were not only free from this pest, they were its remedy; for the effect of philosophy is to make the soul tranquil, and fanaticism is incompatible with tranquility. If our holy religion has so often been corrupted by this infernal delirium, it is the madness of men which is at fault.

Voltaire, *Philosophical Dictionary*, trans. by P. Gay (New York: Basic Books, 1962), pp. 267–269.

questioned the truthfulness of priests and the morality of the Bible. In his *Philosophical Dictionary* (1764), he humorously pointed out inconsistencies in biblical narratives and immoral acts of the biblical heroes. In *The Decline and Fall of the Roman Empire* (1776), Edward Gibbon (1737–1794), the English historian, explained the rise of Christianity in terms of natural causes rather than the influence of miracles and piety. Some of these ideas were new, but many had existed before the Enlightenment in the anti–Roman Catholic polemics of Protestant writers and were brought back into circulation by the philosophes.

A few, but actually very few, philosophes went further than criticism. Baron d'Holbach (1723–1789) and Julien Offray de La Mettrie (1709–1751) embraced positions close to atheism and materialism. Theirs was distinctly a minority position, however. Most of the philosophes sought not the abolition of religion, but its transformation into a humane force that would encourage virtuous living. In the words of the title of a work by the German philosopher Immanuel Kant (1724–1804), they sought to pursue *Religion within the Limits of Reason Alone* (1793).

Jewish Thinkers in the Age of Enlightenment

Despite their emphasis on toleration, the philosophes' criticisms of traditional religion often reflected an implicit contempt not only for Christianity but also, and sometimes more vehemently, for Judaism and, as we see later, for Islam as well. Their attack on the veracity of biblical miracles and biblical history undermined the authority of the Hebrew scriptures as well as the Christian. They often aimed their satirical barbs at personalities from the Hebrew scriptures. Some philosophes characterized Judaism as a more primitive faith than Christianity and one from which philosophical rationalism provided a path of escape. The Enlightenment view of religion thus served in some ways to further stigmatize Jews and Judaism in the eyes of non-Jewish Europeans.

Enlightenment values also, however, allowed certain Jewish intellectuals to rethink the relationship of their communities to the wider European culture from which they had largely lived apart. Two major Jewish writers—one a few decades before the opening of the Enlightenment and one toward the close—entered the larger debate over religion and the place of Jews in European life. These were Baruch Spinoza (1632–1677), who lived in the Netherlands, and Moses Mendelssohn (1729–1786), who lived in Germany. Spinoza set the example for a secularized version of Judaism, and Mendelssohn established the main outlines of an assimilationist position. Although their approaches displayed certain similarities, there were also important differences.

The new science of the mid-seventeenth century deeply influenced Spinoza, the son of a Jewish merchant of Amsterdam. Like his contemporaries, Hobbes and Descartes, he looked to the power of human reason to reconceptualize traditional thought. In that regard his thinking reflected the age of scientific revolution and looked toward the later Enlightenment.

In his *Ethics*, the most famous of his works, Spinoza so closely identified God and nature, or the spiritual and material worlds, that contemporaries condemned him. Many thought he drew God and nature too intimately into a single divine substance, leaving little room for the possibility of a distinctly divine revelation to humankind in scripture. Both Christians and Jews also believed Spinoza's near pantheistic position (the idea that God is not a distinct personality but that everything in the universe is) meant that human beings might not be personally re-

The Dutch Jewish philosopher Baruch Spinoza was deeply influenced by the new science of the mid-seventeenth century. In his writings, Spinoza argued for rationality over traditional spiritual beliefs.   Library of Congress

sponsible for their actions and that there could be no personal, individual immortality of the human soul after death. During his lifetime the controversial character of his writings led both Jews and Protestants to criticize him as an atheist. When he was twenty-four, his own synagogue excommunicated him, and thereafter he lived apart from the Amsterdam Jewish community.

In his *Theologico-Political Treatise* (1670), Spinoza directly anticipated much of the religious criticism of the Enlightenment and its attacks on the power of superstition in human life. Spinoza described the origins of religion in thoroughly naturalistic terms. He believed the Hebrew Bible provided Jews with divine legislation, but not with specially revealed theological knowledge. In this respect, he was calling on both Jews and Christians to use their own reason in religious matters and to read the Bible like other ancient books. Spinoza's extensive rational and historical criticism of the biblical narratives disturbed Christian and Jewish contemporaries who saw him as a writer seeking to lead people away from all religion. He actually argued, however, that the formally organized religious institutions of both Christianity and Judaism led people away from the original teaching of scripture and encouraged them to persecute those who disagreed with the leaders of their respective churches and synagogues.

Because of Spinoza's excommunication from his synagogue, the philosophes considered him a martyr for rationality against superstition. He also symbolized Jews who, through the use of their critical reason, separated themselves from traditional Judaism and attempted to enter mainstream society to pursue a secular existence with little or no regard for their original faith. Consequently, his life and his writings, as one commentator has stated, "made it possible for defenders of the Enlightenment to advocate toleration of Jews while simultaneously holding Judaism in contempt."[7] This stance of championing toleration while condemning Judaism itself would later characterize the outlook of many non-Jewish Europeans regarding the assimilation of Jews into European civic life. It was, however, an outlook that Jewish communities themselves could not welcome without considerable modification.

Moses Mendelsohn, the leading Jewish philosopher of the eighteenth century, was known as the "Jewish Socrates." Writing almost a century after Spinoza, he also advocated the entry of Jews into modern European life. In contrast to Spinoza, however, Mendelsohn argued that a Jew could combine loyalty to Judaism with adherence to rational, Enlightenment values. Mendelsohn could hold this position in part because of the influence of Lessing's arguments for toleration. Indeed, Mendelsohn had been the chief model for Lessing's character *Nathan the Wise*.

Mendelsohn's most influential work was *Jerusalem; or, On Ecclesiastical Power and Judaism* (1783) in which he argued both for extensive religious toleration and for maintaining the religious distinction of Jewish communities. Mendelsohn urged that religious diversity within a nation did not harm loyalty to the government; therefore, governments should be religiously neutral and Jews should enjoy the same civil rights as other subjects. Then, in the spirit of the deists, he presented Judaism as one of many religious paths revealed by God. Jewish law and practice were intended for the moral benefit of Jewish communities; other religions similarly served other people. Consequently, various communities should be permitted to practice their religious faith alongside other religious groups.

Unlike Spinoza, Mendelsohn wished to advocate religious toleration while genuinely sustaining the traditional religious practices and faith of Judaism. Nevertheless, Mendelsohn believed Jewish communities should not have the right to excommunicate their members over differences in theological opinions or even if their members embraced modern secular ideas. He thus sought both toleration of Jews within European society and toleration by Jews of a wider spectrum of opinion within their own communities. His hope was that the rationalism of the Enlightenment would provide the foundation for both types of toleration. Mendelsohn thus set forth a far more extensive vision of religious toleration than had John Locke almost a century earlier. Locke had contended that

while the state should tolerate many different religious communities, each should retain the right of excommunication over its members (see Chapter 14).

Islam in Enlightenment Thought

Unlike Judaism, Islam, except in the Balkan Peninsula, had few adherents in eighteenth-century Europe. Although European merchants traded with the Ottoman Empire or with those parts of South Asia where Islam prevailed, most Europeans came to know what little they did know about the Islamic world and Islam as a religion through books—the religious commentaries of Christian missionaries, histories, and the reports of travelers—that, with rare exceptions, were hostile to Islam and deeply misleading.

Islam continued to be seen as a rival to Christianity. European writers, such as Pascal in his *Pensées* (see Chapter 14), repeated what other Christian critics had said for centuries. They portrayed Islam as a false religion and Muhammad as an impostor and a false prophet because he had not performed miracles. Furthermore, they also attacked Islam as an exceptionally carnal or sexually promiscuous religion because of its teaching that heaven was a place of sensuous delights, its permission for a man to have more than one wife, Muhammad's own polygamy, and the presence of harems in the Islamic world.

Christian authors also ignored the Islamic understanding of the life and mission of Muhammad. They referred to Islam as Muhammadanism, thus implying that Muhammad was divine rather than a human being with whom God had chosen to communicate. Muslims consider the suggestion that Muhammad was divine to be blasphemous.

European universities did endow professorships to study Arabic during the seventeenth century, but these university scholars generally agreed with theological critics that Islam too often embodied religious fanaticism. Even relatively well-informed works based on knowledge of Arabic and Islamic sources, such as Barthélemy d'Herbelot's *Bibliothèque orientale* (*Oriental Library*), a reference book published in 1697, Simon Ockley's *History of the Saracens* (1718), and George Sale's introduction to the first full English translation of the Qur'an (1734), were largely hostile to their subject. All of these books continued to be reprinted and remained influential well into the nineteenth century, demonstrating how little information disinterested Europeans had about Islam.

Enlightenment philosophes spoke with two voices regarding Islam. Voltaire indicated his opinion along with that of many of his contemporaries in the title of his 1742 tragedy *Fanaticism, or Mohammed the Prophet*. Although he sometimes spoke well of the Qur'an, Voltaire declared in a later historical work, "We must suppose that Muhammed, like all enthusiasts, violently impressed by his own ideas, retailed them in good faith, fortified them with fancies, deceived himself in deceiving others, and

---

[7]Steven B. Smith, *Spinoza, Liberalism, and the Question of Jewish Identity* (New Haven, CT: Yale University Press, 1997), p. 166.

Few Europeans visited the Ottoman Empire. What little they knew about it came from reports of travelers and from illustrations such as this 1710 view of Constantinople, the empire's capital.   © Historical Picture Archive/CORBIS

finally sustained with deceit a doctrine he believed to be good."[8] Thus, for Voltaire, Muhammad and Islam in general represented simply one more example of the religious fanaticism he had so often criticized among Christians.

Some Enlightenment writers, however, spoke well of the Islamic faith. The deist John Toland, who opposed prejudice against both Jews and Muslims, contended that Islam derived from early Christian writings and was thus a form of Christianity. These views so offended most of his contemporaries that Toland became known as a "Mohametan" Christian. Edward Gibbon, who blamed Christianity for contributing to the fall of the Roman Empire, wrote with respect of Muhammad's leadership and Islam's success in conquering so vast a territory in the first century of its existence. Other commentators approved of Islam's tolerance and the charitable work of Muslims.

Some philosophes criticized Islam on cultural and political grounds. In *The Persian Letters* (1721), supposedly written by two Muslim Persians visiting Europe, the young philosophe Charles de Montesquieu used Islamic culture as a foil to criticize his own European society. Yet, by the time he wrote his more influential *Spirit of the Laws*

(1748), discussed more fully later in this chapter, Montesquieu associated Islamic society with the passivity that he ascribed to people subject to political despotism. Like other Europeans, Montesquieu believed the excessive influence of Islamic religious leaders prevented the Ottoman Empire from adapting itself to new advances in technology.

One of the most positive commentators on eighteenth-century Islam was a woman. Between 1716 and 1718, Lady Mary Wortley Montagu (1689–1762) lived in Istanbul with her husband, the British ambassador to Turkey. She wrote a series of letters about her experiences there that were published the year after her death. In these *Turkish Embassy Letters*, she praised much about Ottoman society and urged the English to copy the Turkish practice of vaccination against smallpox. Unlike European males, Montagu had access to the private quarters of women in Istanbul. In contrast to the constraints under which English women found themselves, she thought upper-class Turkish women were remarkably free and well treated by their husbands despite having to wear clothing that completely covered them in public. In fact, Montagu thought the anonymity these coverings bestowed allowed Turkish women to move freely about Istanbul. She also considered the magnificent Ottoman architecture better than anything in Western Europe. Montagu repeatedly criticized the misinformation that

[8]Quoted in Theodore Besterman, *Voltaire* (New York: Harcourt, Brace, & World, 1969), p. 409.

prevailed in Europe about the Ottoman Empire and declared that many of the hostile comments about Islam and Islamic morality were simply wrong.

Nevertheless, the European voices demanding fairness and expressing empathy for Islam were rare throughout the eighteenth century. As one historian has commented, "The basic Christian attitude was still what it had been for a millennium: a rejection of the claim of Muslims that Muhammad was a prophet and the Qur'an the word of God, mingled with a memory of periods of fear and conflict, and also, a few thinkers and scholars apart, with legends, usually hostile and often contemptuous."[9]

Muslims were not curious about the Christian West themselves. Only a handful of Muslims from the Ottoman Empire visited Western Europe in the eighteenth century, and no Islamic writers showed much interest in contemporary European authors. The Ulema, the Islamic religious scholars, reinforced these attitudes. They taught that God's revelations to Muhammad meant Islam had replaced Christianity as a religion and therefore there was little for Muslims to learn from Christian culture.

▼ The Enlightenment and Society

The *Encyclopedia:* Freedom and Economic Improvement

The mid-century witnessed the publication of the *Encyclopedia,* one of the greatest monuments of the Enlightenment and its most monumental undertaking in the realm of print culture. Under the heroic leadership of Denis Diderot (1713–1784) and Jean Le Rond d'Alembert (1717–1783), the first volume appeared in 1751. Eventually, numbering seventeen volumes of text and eleven of plates (illustrations), the project was completed in 1772. No other work of the Enlightenment so illustrated the movement's determination to probe life on earth rather than in the religious realm. As one writer in the *Encyclopedia* observed, "Man is the unique point to which we must refer everything, if we wish to interest and please amongst considerations the most

arid and details the most dry."[10] The use of the word *man* in this passage was not simply an accident of language. Most philosophes, as we shall see later in the chapter, were thinking primarily of men, not women, when they framed their reformist ideas.

The *Encyclopedia,* in part a collective plea for freedom of expression, reached fruition only after many attempts to censor it and halt its publication. It was the product of the collective effort of more than a hundred authors, and its editors had at one time or another solicited articles from all the major French philosophes. It included the most advanced critical ideas of the time on religion, government, and philosophy. To avoid official censure, these ideas often had to be hidden in obscure articles or under the cover of irony. The *Encyclopedia* also included numerous important articles and illustrations on manufacturing, canal building, ship construction, and improved agriculture, making it an important source of knowledge about eighteenth-century social and economic life.

Between 14,000 and 16,000 copies of various editions of the *Encyclopedia* were sold before 1789. The project had been designed to secularize learning and to undermine intellectual assumptions that lingered from the Middle Ages and the Reformation. The articles on politics, ethics, and society ignored divine law and concentrated on humanity and its immediate well-being. The Encyclopedists looked to antiquity rather than to the Christian centuries for their intellectual and ethical models. For them, the future welfare of humankind lay not in pleasing God or following divine commandments, but rather in harnessing the power and resources of the earth and in living at peace with one's fellow human beings. The good life lay here and now and was to be achieved through the application of reason to human relationships. The publication of the *Encyclopedia* spread Enlightenment thought more fully over the Continent, penetrating German and Russian intellectual and political circles.

Denis Diderot was the heroic editor of the *Encylopedia* published in seventeen volumes of text and eleven of prints between 1751 and 1772. Through its pages many of the chief ideas of the Enlightenment reached a broad audience of readers. Réunion des Musées Nationaux/Art Resource, NY. Jean-Simon Berthelemy (1743-1811), "Denis Diderot" (1713–1784). Writer and Encyelopaedist. Oil on canvas, 55 x 46 cm. Inv.: P 2082. Photo: Bulloz. Musee de la Ville de Paris, Musee Carnavalet, Paris, France/Art Resource, NY

[9]A. Hourani, *Islam in European Thought* (Cambridge: Cambridge University Press, 1991), p. 136.

[10]Quoted in F. L. Baumer, *Main Currents of Western Thought,* 4th ed. (New Haven, CT: Yale University Press, 1978), p. 374.

Beccaria and Reform of Criminal Law

Although the term did not appear until later, the idea of *social science* originated with the Enlightenment. Philosophes hoped to end human cruelty by discovering social laws and making people aware of them. These concerns are most evident in the philosophes' work on law and prisons.

In 1764, Marquis Cesare Beccaria (1738–1794), an Italian aristocrat and philosophe, published *On Crimes and Punishments*, in which he applied critical analysis to the problem of making punishments both effective and just. He wanted the laws of monarchs and legislatures—that is, positive law—to conform with the rational laws of nature. He rigorously and eloquently attacked both torture and capital punishment. He thought the criminal justice system should ensure a speedy trial and certain punishment and the intent of punishment should be to deter further crime. The purpose of laws was not to impose the will of God or some other ideal of perfection, but to secure the greatest good or happiness for the greatest number of human beings. This utilitarian philosophy based on happiness in this life permeated most Enlightenment writing on practical reforms.

The Physiocrats and Economic Freedom

Economic policy was another area in which the philosophes saw existing legislation and administration preventing the operation of natural social laws. They believed mercantilist legislation (designed to protect a country's trade from external competition) and the regulation of labor by governments and guilds actually hampered the expansion of trade, manufacture, and agriculture. In France, these economic reformers were called the **physiocrats**. Their leading spokespeople were François Quesnay (1694–1774) and Pierre Dupont de Nemours (1739–1817).

The physiocrats believed the primary role of government was to protect property and to permit its owners to use it freely. They argued that agriculture was the basis on which all economic production depended. They favored the consolidation of small peasant holdings into larger, more efficient farms. Here, as elsewhere, the rationalism of the Enlightenment was closely connected to the spirit of improvement that influenced so much of eighteenth-century European economic life.

Adam Smith on Economic Growth and Social Progress

The most important economic work of the Enlightenment was Adam Smith's (1723–1790) *Inquiry into the Nature and Causes of the Wealth of Nations* (1776). Smith, who was for a time a professor at Glasgow University in Scotland, believed economic liberty was the foundation of a natural economic system. As a result, he urged that the mercantile system of England—including the navigation acts governing colonial trade, the bounties the government gave to favored merchants and industries, most tariffs, trading monopolies, and the domestic regulation of labor and manufacture—be abolished. These regulations were intended to preserve the wealth of the nation, to capture wealth from other nations, and to maximize the work available for the nation's laborers. Smith argued, however, that they hindered the expansion of wealth and production. The best way to encourage economic growth, he maintained, was to unleash individuals to pursue their own selfish economic interests. As self-interested individuals sought to enrich themselves by meeting the needs of others in the marketplace, the economy would expand. Consumers would find their wants met as manufacturers and merchants competed for their business.

Mercantilism assumed that the earth's resources were limited and scarce, so one nation could acquire wealth only at the expense of others. Smith's book challenged this assumption. He saw the resources of nature—water, air, soil, and minerals—as boundless. To him, they demanded exploitation for the enrichment and comfort of humankind. In effect, Smith was saying the nations and peoples of Europe need not be poor.

Smith is usually regarded as the founder of **laissez-faire** economic thought and policy, which favors a limited role for the government in economic life. *The Wealth of Nations* was, however, a complex book. Smith was no simple dogmatist. For example, he did not oppose all government activity in the economy. The government, he argued, should provide schools, armies, navies, and roads. It should also undertake certain commercial ventures, such as opening dangerous new trade routes that were economically desirable, but too expensive or risky for private enterprise. The public should in particular support education of those people who occupied the humbler occupations of life. (See "Adam Smith Calls for Government Action to Support the Education of the Poor," page 522.)

Within *The Wealth of Nations*, Smith, like other Scottish thinkers of the day, embraced an important theory of human social and economic development, known as the *four-stage theory*. According to this theory, human societies can be classified as hunting and gathering, pastoral or herding, agricultural, or commercial. The hunters and gatherers have little or no settled life. Pastoral societies are groups of nomads who tend their herds and develop some private property. Agricultural or farming societies are settled and have clear-cut property arrangements. Finally, the commercial state includes advanced cities, the manufacture of numerous items for wide consumption, extensive trade between cities and the countryside, as well as elaborate forms of property and financial arrangements. Smith and other Scottish writers described the passage of human society through these stages as a movement from barbarism to civilization.

ADAM SMITH CALLS FOR GOVERNMENT ACTION TO SUPPORT THE EDUCATION OF THE POOR

Adam Smith in The Wealth of Nations *had argued that the division of labor increased the productive capacity of human beings and hence economic growth and the accumulation of wealth. Smith, however, also recognized that the division of labor might over the course of time take a very heavy toll on the lives of workers involved in repetitive activities of production. In this passage he portrays that human toll and then calls for government action to provide education for the poor. He also believed that the workers should pay for part of their education so that the schoolmaster would be held accountable to paying students.*

What does Smith portray as the results of repetitive work caused by the division of labor? Why does he place so much emphasis on the mental and emotional costs? How does he see this situation as undermining civic interest? What solutions does he propose?

In the progress of the division of labour, the employment of the far greater part of those who live by labour, that is, of the great body of the people, comes to be confined to a few very simple operations, frequently to one or two. But the understandings of the greater part of men are necessarily formed by their ordinary employments. The man whose whole life is spent in performing a few simple operations, of which the effects too are, perhaps, always the same, or very nearly the same, has no occasion to exert his understanding, or to exercise his invention in finding out expedients for removing difficulties which never occur. He naturally loses, therefore, the habit of such exertion, and generally becomes as stupid and ignorant as it is possible for a human creature to become. The torpor of his mind renders him not only incapable of relishing or bear a part in any rational conversation, but of conceiving any generous, noble, or tender sentiment, and consequently of forming any just judgment concerning many even of the ordinary duties of private life. Of the great and extensive interest of his country he is altogether incapable of judging; and unless very particular pains have been taken to render him otherwise, he is equally incapable of defending his country in war. The uniformity of his stationary life naturally corrupts the courage of his mind, and makes him regard with abhorrence the irregular, uncertain, and adventurous life of a soldier. It corrupts even the activity of his body, and render him incapable of exerting his strength with vigour and perseverance, in any other employment than that to which he has been bred. His dexterity at his own particular trade seems, in this manner, to be acquired at the expence of his intellectual, social, and martial virtues. But in every improved and civilized society this is the state into which the labouring poor, that is, the great body of the people, must necessarily fall, unless government takes some pains to prevent it. . . .

The education of the common people requires . . . the attention of the public more than that of people of some rank and fortune . . . [who]are generally eighteen or nineteen years of age before they enter upon that particular business, profession, or trade by which they propose to distinguish themselves in the world. . . .

It is otherwise with the common people. They have little time to spare for education. Their parents can scarce afford to maintain them even in infancy. As soon as they are able to work, they must apply to some trade by which they can earn their subsistence. . . . but though the common people cannot . . . be so well instructed as people of some rank and fortune, the most essential parts of education, however to read, write, and account, can be acquired at so early a period of life, that the greater part even of those who are to be bred to the lowest occupations, have time to acquire them before they can be employed in those occupations. For a very small expence the public can facilitate, can encourage, and can even impose upon almost the whole body of the people, the necessity of acquiring those most essential parts of education.

Adam Smith, *An Inquiry into the Nature and Causes of the Wealth of Nations* (London: T. Nelson and Sons, 1852), pp. 327–328.

The four-stage theory implicitly evaluated the later stages of economic development and the people dwelling in them as higher, more progressive, and more civilized than the earlier ones. A social theorist using this theory could thus quickly look at a society and, on the basis of the state of its economic development and organizations, rank it in terms of the stage it had achieved. In fact, the commercial stage, the highest rank in the theory, described society as it appeared in northwestern Europe. Thus, Smith's theory allowed Europeans to look about the world and always find themselves dwelling at the highest level of human achievement. To Europeans, this outlook helped justify their economic and imperial domination of the world during the following century. They repeatedly portrayed themselves as bringing a higher level of civilization to people elsewhere who, according to the four-stage theory, lived in lower stages of human social and economic development. Europeans thus imbued with the spirit of the Enlightenment presented themselves as carrying out a civilizing mission to the rest of the world. (See Chapter 25.)

▼ Political Thought of the Philosophes

Nowhere was the philosophes' reformist agenda, as well as tensions among themselves, so apparent as in their political thought. Most philosophes were discontented with certain political features of their countries, but French philosophes were especially discontented. There, the corruption around the royal court, the blundering of the bureaucracy, the less-than-glorious mid-century wars, and the power of the church seemed to make all problems worse. Consequently, the most important political thought of the Enlightenment occurred in France. The French philosophes, however, were divided over how to solve their country's problems. Their proposed solutions spanned a wide political spectrum, from aristocratic reform to democracy to absolute monarchy.

Montesquieu and *Spirit of the Laws*

Charles Louis de Secondat, baron de Montesquieu (1689–1755), was a lawyer, a noble of the robe, and a member of a provincial *parlement*. He also belonged to the Bordeaux Academy of Science, before which he presented papers on scientific topics.

Although living comfortably within the bosom of French society, he saw the need for reform. In 1721, as already noted, he published *The Persian Letters* to satirize contemporary institutions. Behind the humor lay the cutting edge of criticism and an exposition of the cruelty and irrationality of European life. About a decade after this volume appeared, Montesquieu, like Voltaire, visited England and deeply admired English institutions.

In his most enduring work, *Spirit of the Laws* (1748), Montesquieu held up the example of the British constitution as the wisest model for regulating the power of government. Montesquieu's *Spirit of the Laws*, perhaps the single most influential book of the century, exhibits the internal tensions of the Enlightenment. In it, Montesquieu pursued an empirical method, taking illustrative examples from the political experience of both ancient and modern nations. From these, he concluded that no single set of political laws could apply to all peoples at all times and in all places. The good political life depended rather on the relationship among many political variables. Whether the best form of government for a country was a monarchy or a republic, for example, depended on that country's size, population, social and religious customs, economic structure, traditions, and climate. Only a careful examination and evaluation of these elements could reveal what mode of government would most benefit a particular people.

For France, Montesquieu favored a monarchical government tempered and limited by various intermediary institutions, including the aristocracy, the towns, and the other corporate bodies that enjoyed liberties the monarch had to respect. These corporate bodies might be said to represent segments of the general population and thus of public opinion. In France, he regarded the aristocratic courts, or *parlements*, as a major example of an intermediary association. Their role was to limit the power of the monarchy and thus to preserve the liberty of its subjects.

In championing these aristocratic bodies and the general oppositional role of the aristocracy, Montesquieu was a political conservative. He adopted this conservatism in the hope of achieving reform, however, for he believed the oppressive and inefficient absolutism of the monarchy accounted for the degradation of French life.

One of Montesquieu's most influential ideas was that of the division of power in government. For his model of a government with authority wisely separated among different branches, he took contemporary Great Britain. There, he believed, executive power resided in the king, legislative power in the Parliament, and judicial power in the courts. He thought any two branches could check and balance the power of the other. His perception of the eighteenth-century British constitution was incorrect because he failed to see how patronage and electoral corruption allowed a handful of powerful aristocrats to dominate the government. Moreover, he was also unaware of the emerging cabinet system, which was slowly making the executive power a creature of the Parliament.

Nevertheless, Montesquieu's analysis illustrated his strong belief that monarchs should be subject to constitutional limits on their power and that a separate legislature, not the monarch, should formulate laws. For this reason, although he set out to defend the political privileges of the

French aristocracy, Montesquieu's ideas have had a profound effect on the constitutional form of liberal democracies for more than two centuries.

Rousseau: A Radical Critique of Modern Society

Jean-Jacques Rousseau (1712–1778) held a different view of the exercise and reform of political power from Montesquieu's. Rousseau was a strange, isolated genius who never felt particularly comfortable with the other philosophes. His own life was troubled. He could form few close friendships. He sired numerous children, whom he abandoned to foundling hospitals. Yet perhaps more than any other writer of the mid-eighteenth century, he transcended the political thought and values of his own time. Rousseau hated the world and the society in which he lived. It seemed to him impossible for human beings living according to the commercial values of his time to achieve moral, virtuous, or sincere lives. In 1750, in his *Discourse on the Moral Effects of the Arts and Sciences*, he contended that the process of civilization and the Enlightenment had corrupted human nature. In 1755, in his *Discourse on the Origin of Inequality*, Rousseau blamed much of the evil in the world on the uneven distribution of property. He contended that human beings in a primeval state of nature had been good, but that as they eventually formed social relations and then social institutions, they had lost that goodness. Society itself was the source of human evil for Rousseau, and one manifestation of that unnatural evil was unequal distribution of property.

In both discourses, Rousseau brilliantly and directly challenged the social fabric of the day. He questioned the concepts of material and intellectual progress and the morality of a society in which commerce, industry, and the preservation of property rights were regarded as among the most important human activities. The other philosophes generally believed life would improve if people could enjoy more of the fruits of the earth or could produce more goods. Rousseau raised the more fundamental questions of what constitutes the good life and how human society can be reshaped to achieve that life. This question

Among the philosophes of the Enlightenment Jean-Jacques Rousseau set forth the most democratic and egalitarian political ideas. This bust was created by the French sculptor Jean-Antoine Houdon after Rousseau's death mask. Réunion des Musées Nationaux/Art Resource, NY

has haunted European social thought ever since the eighteenth century.

Rousseau carried these same concerns into his political thought. His most extensive discussion of politics appeared in *The Social Contract* (1762). Although the book attracted little immediate attention, by the end of the century it was widely read in France. Compared with Montesquieu's *Spirit of the Laws*, *The Social Contract* is an abstract book. It does not propose specific reforms but outlines the kind of political structure that Rousseau believed would overcome the evils of contemporary politics and society.

In the tradition of John Locke, most eighteenth-century political thinkers regarded human beings as individuals and society as a collection of individuals pursuing personal, selfish goals. These writers wished to liberate individuals from the undue bonds of government. Rousseau picked up the stick from the other end. His book opens with the declaration, "All men are born free, but everywhere they are in chains."[11] The rest of the volume is a defense of the chains of a properly organized society over its members.

Rousseau suggested that society is more important than its individual members, because they are what they are only by virtue of their relationship to the larger community. Independent human beings living alone can achieve little. Through their relationship to the larger political community, they become moral creatures capable of significant action. The question then becomes: What kind of community allows people to behave morally? In his two previous discourses, Rousseau had explained that the contemporaneous European society was not such a community; it was merely an aggregate of competing individuals whose chief social goal was to preserve selfish independence despite all potential social bonds and obligations.

Rousseau envisioned a society in which each person could maintain personal freedom while behaving as a loyal member of the larger community. Drawing on the traditions of Plato and Calvin, he defined freedom as obedience to law. In his case, the law to be obeyed was that created by the general will. In a society with virtuous customs and morals in which citizens have adequate information on

[11]Jean-Jacques Rousseau, *The Social Contract and Discourses*, trans. by G. D. H. Cole (New York: Dutton, 1950), p. 3.

important issues, the concept of the general will is normally equivalent to the will of a majority of voting citizens. Democratic participation in decision making would bind the individual citizen to the community. Rousseau believed the general will, thus understood, must always be right and that to obey the general will is to be free. This argument led him to the notorious conclusion that under certain circumstances some people must be forced to be free. Rousseau's politics thus constituted a justification for radical direct democracy and for collective action against individual citizens.

Rousseau had, in effect, attacked the eighteenth-century cult of the individual and the fruits of selfishness. He stood at odds with the commercial spirit that was transforming the society in which he lived. Rousseau would have disapproved of the main thrust of Adam Smith's *Wealth of Nations*, which he may or may not have read, and would no doubt have preferred a study on the virtue of nations. Smith wanted people to be prosperous; Rousseau wanted them to be good even if being good meant they might remain poor. He saw human beings not as independent individuals, but as creatures enmeshed in necessary social relationships. He believed loyalty to the community should be encouraged. As one device to that end, he suggested a properly governed society should decree a civic religion based on the creed of deism. Such a shared religion could, he argued, help unify a society even if it had to be enforced by repressive legislation.

Rousseau had only a marginal impact on his own time. The other philosophes questioned his critique of material improvement. Aristocrats and royal ministers could hardly be expected to welcome his proposal for radical democracy. Too many people were either making or hoping to make money to appreciate his criticism of commercial values. He proved, however, to be a figure to whom later generations returned. Leading figures in the French Revolution were familiar with his writing, and he influenced writers in the nineteenth and twentieth centuries who were critical of the general tenor and direction of Western culture. Rousseau hated much about the emerging modern society in Europe, but he contributed much to modernity by exemplifying for later generations the critic who dared to question the very foundations of social thought and action.

Enlightened Critics of European Empires

Most European thinkers associated with the Enlightenment favored the extension of European empires across the world. Like the Scottish writers who embraced the four-stage theory, they believed that the extension of the political structures and economies of northwestern Europe amounted to the spread of progress and civilization. The Scottish commentators and

their followers were not without their criticisms of European civilization and of excessive economic regulation in contemporary empires, but on the whole, they believed European civilization superior to that of other cultures.

A few Enlightenment voices, however, did criticize the European empires on moral grounds, especially the European conquest of the Americas, the treatment of Native Americans, and the enslavement of Africans on the two American continents. The most important of these critics were Denis Diderot and two German philosophers, Immanuel Kant and Johann Gottlieb Herder (1744–1803). (See "Denis Diderot Condemns European Empires," page 526.)

What ideas allowed these figures from the Enlightenment to criticize their empires? As Sankar Muthu has recently written, "The first and most basic idea is that human beings deserve some modicum of moral and political respect simply because of the fact that they are human."[12] In other words, the Enlightenment critics of their empires argued for a form of shared humanity that the sixteenth-century European conquerors and their successors in the Americas and in other areas of imperial conquest had ignored. Immanuel Kant wrote, "When America, the Negro countries, the Spice Islands, the Cape, and so forth were discovered, they were to them [the Europeans], countries belonging to no one, since they counted the inhabitants as *nothing*."[13] Kant, Diderot, and Herder rejected this dismissive outlook and the harsh policies that had flowed from it. They believed no single definition of human nature could be made the standard throughout the world and then used to dehumanize people whose appearance or culture differed from it.

A second of these critical ideas was the conviction that the people whom Europeans had encountered in the Americas had possessed cultures that should have been respected and understood rather than destroyed. Some Europeans in the early years of the encounter with America had argued that while the native peoples were human, their way of life was too degraded to treat them as the human equals of Europeans. In the late eighteenth century, Herder rejected such a view, "'European culture' is a mere abstraction, an empty concept. Where does or did it actually exist in its entirety? In which nation? In which period? . . . Only a misanthrope could regard European culture as the universal condition of our species. The culture of *man* is not the culture of the *European*; it manifests itself according to time and place in every people."[14] For

[12]Sankar Muthu, *Enlightenment Against Empire* (Princeton, NJ: Princeton University Press, 2003), p. 268. This section draws primarily from this excellent recent book.
[13]Quoted in Muthu, *Enlightenment Against Empire*, p. 267.
[14]Quoted in F. M. Barnard, *Self-Direction and Political Legitimacy: Rousseau and Herder* (Oxford: Clarendon Press, 1988), p. 227.

DENIS DIDEROT CONDEMNS EUROPEAN EMPIRES

Denis Diderot was one of the most prolific writers of the Enlightenment. He is most famous as the editor of the Encyclopedia. *Some of his writings were published without being directly attributed to him. Among these were his contributions to Abbé G. T. Raynal's* History of the Two Indies, *published in various editions after 1772. Diderot's contributions appear to have been made in 1780. Raynal's entire* History *was critical of the European colonial empires that had arisen since the Spanish encounter with the New World. Diderot particularly condemned the inhumane treatment of the native populations of the Americas, the greed all Europeans displayed, and the various forms of forced labor.*

What is the basis for Diderot's view that Europeans have behaved tyrannically? How does he portray the behavior of Europeans in foreign areas? What specific social results does he associate with European greed?

Let the European nations make their own judgment and give themselves the name they deserve. . . . Their explorers arrive in a region of the New World unoccupied by anyone from the Old World, and immediately bury a small strip of metal on which they have engraved these words: *This country belongs to us.* Any why does it belong to you?

. . . You have no right to the natural products of the country where you land, and you claim a right over your fellow-men. Instead of recognizing this man as a brother you only see him as a slave, a beast of burden. Oh my fellow citizens! You think like that and you behave like that; and you have ideas of justice, a morality, a holy religion . . . . in common with whose whom you treat so tyrannically. This reproach should especially be addressed to the Spaniards.

* * *

Beyond the Equator a man is neither English, Dutch, French, Spanish, nor Portuguese. He retains only those principles and prejudices of his native country which justify or excuse his conduct. He crawls when he is weak; he is violent when strong; he is in a hurry to acquire, in a hurry to enjoy, and capable of every crime which will lead him most quickly to his goals. He is a domestic tiger returning to the forest; the thirst for blood takes hold of him once more. This is how all the Europeans, every one of them, indistinctly, have appeared in the countries of the New World. There they have assumed a common frenzy—the thirst for gold.

* * *

The Spaniard, the first to be thrown up by the waves onto the shores of the New World, thought he had no duty to people who did not share his color, customs, or religion. He saw in them only tools for his greed, and he clapped them in irons. These weak men, not used to work, soon died in the foul air of the mines, or in other occupations which were virtually as lethal. Then people called for slaves from Africa. Their number has gone up as more land has been cultivated. The Portuguese, Dutch, English, French, Danes, all the nations, free or subjected, have without remorse sought to increase their fortune in the sweat, blood and despair of these unfortunates. What a horrible system!

From "Extracts from the Histoire des Deux Indes," "6 Principles of Colonisation" (Book 8, Chap. I; IV, 105–8), pgs. 176–177, "7 National Character at Home and Overseas" (Book 9, Chap. I; IV, 233–5), pg. 178, "14 Slavery and Liberty" (Book 11, Chap. 24, V, 275–8), pg. 178 in *Political Writings* by Denis Diderot, trans. by John Hope Mason and Robert Wokler. © Cambridge University Press 1992. Reprinted with the permission of Cambridge University Press.

Herder, human beings living in different societies possessed the capacity as human beings to develop in culturally different fashions. He thus embraced an outlook later known as cultural relativism.

A third idea, closely related to the second, was that human beings may develop distinct cultures possessing intrinsic values that cannot be compared, one to the detriment of another, because each culture possesses deep inner social and linguistic complexities that make any simple comparison impossible. Indeed, Diderot, Kant, and Herder argued that being a human includes the ability to develop a variety of distinctly different cultures.

MAJOR WORKS OF THE ENLIGHTENMENT AND THEIR PUBLICATION DATES

1670	Spinoza's *Theologico-Political Treatise*
1677	Spinoza's *Ethics* (published posthumously)
1687	Newton's *Principia Mathematica*
1690	Locke's *Essay Concerning Human Understanding*
1696	Toland's *Christianity Not Mysterious*
1721	Montesquieu's *Persian Letters*
1733	Voltaire's *Letters on the English*
1738	Voltaire's *Elements of the Philosophy of Newton*
1748	Montesquieu's *Spirit of the Laws*
1748	Hume's *Inquiry into Human Nature*, with the chapter "Of Miracles"
1750	Rousseau's *Discourse on the Moral Effects of the Arts and Sciences*
1751	First volume of the *Encyclopedia*, edited by Diderot
1755	Rousseau's *Discourse on the Origin of Inequality*
1759	Voltaire's *Candide*
1762	Rousseau's *Social Contract* and *Émile*
1763	Voltaire's *Treatise on Tolerance*
1764	Voltaire's *Philosophical Dictionary*
1764	Beccaria's *On Crimes and Punishments*
1776	Gibbon's *Decline and Fall of the Roman Empire*
1776	Smith's *Wealth of Nations*
1779	Lessing's *Nathan the Wise*
1783	Mendelsohn's *Jerusalem; or, On Ecclesiastical Power and Judaism*
1792	Wollstonecraft's *Vindication of the Rights of Woman*
1793	Kant's *Religion within the Limits of Reason Alone*

These arguments critical of empire often involved criticism of New World slavery and were part of the antislavery movement to be discussed in Chapter 20. Whereas the antislavery arguments took strong hold in both Europe and America from the late eighteenth century onward, the arguments critical of empires did not. They remained isolated from the rest of Enlightenment political thought and would not be strongly revived until new anticolonial voices were raised in Europe and the non-European world at the close of the nineteenth century.

▼ Women in the Thought and Practice of the Enlightenment

Women, especially in France, helped significantly to promote the careers of the philosophes. In Paris, the salons of women such as Marie-Thérèse Geoffrin (1699–1777), Julie de Lespinasse (1733–1776), and Claudine de Tencin (1689–1749) gave the philosophes access to useful social and political contacts and a receptive environment in which to circulate their ideas. Association with a fashionable salon brought philosophes increased social status and added luster and respectability to their ideas. Philosophes clearly enjoyed the opportunity to be the center of attention that a salon provided, and their presence at them could boost the sales of their works. The women who organized the salons were well connected to political figures who could help protect the philosophes and secure royal pensions for them. The marquise de Pompadour (1721–1764), the mistress of King Louis XV, played a key role in overcoming efforts to censor the *Encyclopedia*. She also hindered the publication of works attacking the philosophes. Other salon hostesses distributed the writings of the philosophes among their friends. Madame de Tencin promoted Montesquieu's *Spirit of the Laws* in this way.

Despite this help and support from the learned women of Paris, the philosophes were on the whole not strong feminists. Many urged better and broader education for women. They criticized the education women did receive as overly religious, and they tended to reject ascetic views of sexual relations. In general, however, they displayed traditional views toward women and advocated no radical changes in their social condition.

Montesquieu, for example, maintained, in general, that the status of women in a society was the result of climate, the political regime, culture, and women's physiology. He believed women were not naturally inferior to men and should have a wider role in society. He showed himself well aware of the kinds of personal, emotional, and sexual repression European women endured in his day. He sympathetically observed the value placed on women's appearance and the prejudice women met as they aged. In *The Persian Letters*, he included a long exchange about the repression of women in a Persian harem, condemning by implication the restrictions on women in European society. Yet Montesquieu's willingness to consider social change for women in European life had limits. Although in the *Spirit of the Laws* he indicated a belief in the equality of the sexes, he still retained a traditional view of marriage and family and expected men to dominate those institutions. Furthermore, although he supported the right of women to divorce and opposed laws that oppressed them, he upheld the ideal of female chastity.

The views about women expressed in the *Encyclopedia* were less generous than those of Montesquieu. The *Encyclopedia* suggested ways to improve women's lives, but in general, it did not emphasize that the condition of women needed reform. Almost all the contributors were men, and the editors, Diderot and d'Alembert, evidently saw no need to include many articles by women. Most of the articles that dealt with women specifically or discussed women in connection with other subjects often emphasized their physical weakness and inferiority, usually attributed to menstruation or childbearing. Some contributors favored the social equality of women, others opposed it, and still others were indifferent. The articles conveyed a general sense that women were reared to be frivolous and unconcerned with important issues. The Encyclopedists discussed women primarily within a family context—as daughters, wives, and mothers—and presented motherhood as a woman's most important occupation. On sexual behavior, the Encyclopedists upheld an unquestioned double standard.

In contrast to the articles, however, illustrations in the *Encyclopedia* showed women deeply involved in the economic activities of the day. The illustrations also portrayed the activities of lower-class and working-class women, about whom the articles had little to say.

One of the most surprising and influential analyses of the position of women came from Jean-Jacques Rousseau. This most radical of all Enlightenment political theorists urged a traditional and conservative role for women. In his novel *Émile* (1762) (discussed again in Chapter 19), he set forth a radical version of the view that men and women occupy separate spheres. He declared that women should be educated for a position subordinate to men, emphasizing especially women's function in bearing and rearing children. In his vision, there was little else for women to do but make themselves pleasing to men. He portrayed them as weaker and inferior to men in virtually all respects, except perhaps for their capacity for feeling and giving love. He excluded them from political life. Only men were to populate the world of citizenship, political action, and civic virtue. Women were relegated to the domestic sphere. (See "Rousseau Argues for Separate Spheres for Men and Women.") Many of these attitudes were not new—some have roots as ancient as Roman law—but Rousseau's powerful presentation and the influence of his other writings gave them new life in the late eighteenth century. Rousseau deeply influenced many leaders of the French Revolution, who, as shall be seen in the next chapter, often incorporated his view on gender roles in their policies.

Paradoxically, despite these views and despite his own ill treatment of the women who bore his many children, Rousseau achieved a vast following among women in the eighteenth century. He is credited with persuading thousands of upper-class women to breast-feed their own children rather than putting them out to wet nurses. One explanation for this influence is that his writings, although they did not advocate liberating women or expanding their social or economic roles, did stress the im-

Mary Wollstonecraft in her *Vindication of the Rights of Woman* defended equality of women with men on the grounds of men and women sharing the capacity of human reason. CORBIS/Bettmann

portance of their emotions. He portrayed the domestic life and the role of wife and mother as a noble and fulfilling vocation, giving middle- and upper-class women a sense that their daily occupations had a purpose. He assigned them a degree of influence in the domestic sphere that they could not have competing with men outside it.

In 1792, in *A Vindication of the Rights of Woman*, Mary Wollstonecraft (1759–1797) brought Rousseau before the judgment of the rational Enlightenment ideal of progressive knowledge. The immediate incentive for this essay was her opposition to certain policies of the French Revolution, unfavorable to women, that Rousseau had inspired. Wollstonecraft (who, like so many women of her day, died of puerperal fever, a form of blood poisoning caused by unsanitary conditions during childbirth) accused Rousseau and others after him who upheld traditional roles for women of attempting to narrow women's vision and limit their experience. She argued that to confine women to the separate domestic sphere because of supposed limitations of their physiology was to make them the sensual slaves of men. Confined in this separate sphere, they were the victims of male tyranny, their obedience was blind, and they could never achieve their own moral or intellectual identity.

ROUSSEAU ARGUES FOR SEPARATE SPHERES FOR MEN AND WOMEN

■■

Rousseau published Émile, *a novel about education, in 1762. In it, he made one of the strongest and most influential arguments of the eighteenth century for distinct social roles for men and women. Furthermore, he portrayed women as fundamentally subordinate to men. In the next document, Mary Wollstonecraft, a contemporary, presents a rebuttal.*

How does Rousseau move from the physical differences between men and women to an argument for distinct social roles and social spheres? What would be the proper kinds of social activities for women in Rousseau's vision? What kind of education would he think appropriate for women?

There is no parity between the two sexes in regard to the consequences of sex. The male is male only at certain moments. The female is female her whole life or at least during her whole youth. Everything constantly recalls her sex to her; and, to fulfill its functions well, she needs a constitution which corresponds to it. She needs care during her pregnancy; she needs rest at the time of childbirth; she needs a soft and sedentary life to suckle her children; she needs patience and gentleness, a zeal and an affection that nothing can rebuff in order to raise her children. She serves as the link between them and their father; she alone makes him love them and gives him the confidence to call them his own. How much tenderness and care is required to maintain the union of the whole family! And, finally, all this must come not from virtues but from tastes, or else the human species would soon be extinguished.

The strictness of the relative duties of the two sexes is not and cannot be the same. When woman complains on this score about unjust man-made inequality, she is wrong. This inequality is not a human institution—or, at least, it is the work not of prejudice but of reason. It is up to the sex that nature has charged with the bearing of children to be responsible for them to the other sex. Doubtless it is not permitted to anyone to violate his faith, and every unfaithful husband who deprives his wife of the only reward of the austere duties of her sex is an unjust and barbarous man. But the unfaithful woman does more; she dissolves the family and breaks all the bonds of nature. . . .

Once it is demonstrated that man and woman are not and ought not be constituted in the same way in either character or temperament, it follows that they ought not to have the same education. In following nature's directions, man and woman ought to act in concert, but they ought not to do the same things. The goal of their labors is common, but their labors themselves are different, and consequently so are the tastes directing them. . . .

The good constitution of children initially depends on that of their mothers. The first education of men depends on the care of women. Men's morals, their passions, their tastes, their pleasures, their very happiness also depend on women. Thus the whole education of women ought to relate to men. To please men, to be useful to them, to make herself loved and honored by them, to raise them when young, to care for them when grown, to counsel them, to console them, to make their lives agreeable and sweet—these are the duties of women at all times, and they ought to be taught from childhood. So long as one does not return to this principle, one will deviate from the goal, and all the precepts taught to women will be of no use for their happiness or for ours.

From *Émile* or *On Education* by Jean-Jacques Rousseau by Allan Bloom, trans. Copyright © 1979 by Basic Books, Inc. Reprinted by permission of Basic Books, member of Perseus Books, L.L.C.

Denying good education to women would impede the progress of all humanity. With these arguments, Wollstonecraft was demanding for women the kind of liberty that male writers of the Enlightenment had been championing for men for more than a century. In doing so, she placed herself among the philosophes and broadened the agenda of the Enlightenment to include the rights of women as well as those of men. (See "Mary Wollstonecraft Criticizes Rousseau's View of Women.")

▼ Rococo and Neoclassical Styles in Eighteenth-Century Art

Two contrasting styles dominated eighteenth-century European art and architecture. The Rococo style embraced lavish, often lighthearted decoration with an emphasis on pastel colors and the play of light. Neoclassicism embodied a return to figurative and architectural models drawn from the Renaissance and the ancient world. The Rococo became associated with the aristocracies of the Old Regime while Neoclassicism recalled ancient republican values that implicitly criticized the Old Regime and, toward the end of the century, was embraced by the French Revolution and Napoleon.

Rococo architecture and decoration originated in early eighteenth-century France. After Louis XIV's death in 1715, the Regent Philippe d'Orleans (1674–1723) and the French aristocracy spent less time at Versailles and began to enjoy the diversions of Paris. There, wealthy French aristocrats built houses known as *hôtels*. Their designers compensated for the relatively small scale and nondescript exteriors of these mansions with interiors that were elaborately decorated and painted in light colors to make the rooms seem brighter and more spacious. It was in such aristocratic urban settings that fashionable Parisian hostesses held the salons the philosophes attended. Louis XV also liked Rococo art, and he had both Madame de Pompadour and other mistresses painted, sometimes in compromising poses, by Rococo artists, especially Francois Boucher (1700–1770). Consequently Rococo also became known as the Style of Louis XV, suggesting a social and political world more accommodating to the French aristocracy and less religiously austere than that of Louis XIV.

Beyond such domestic and personally intimate settings in France, the Rococo style spread across Europe and was adapted to many public buildings and churches. One of the most spectacular Rococo spaces was the Imperial Hall (*Kaisarsaal*) built in Würzburg, Bavaria, to the design of Balthasar Neumann (1687–1753) with ceilings painted with scenes from Greek mythology by the Venetian Gian Battista Tiepolo (1696–1770).

The paintings associated with Rococo art often portrayed the aristocracy, and particularly the French aristocracy, at play. Artists depicted what were known as *fêtes galantes* or scenes of elegant parties in lush gardens. The paintings showed not reality, but an idealized landscape with carefree men and women pursuing a life of leisure, romance, and seduction. Among the most prominent of such artists was Jean-Antoine Watteau (1684–1721) in

Jean-Antoine Watteau, *Embarkation for Cythera*, (1717). Oil on canvas. 129 × 194 cm. Louvre, Paris, France/ Giraudon-Bridgeman Art Library

MARY WOLLSTONECRAFT CRITICIZES ROUSSEAU'S VIEW OF WOMEN

Mary Wollstonecraft published A Vindication of the Rights of Woman *in 1792, thirty years after Rousseau's* Émile *had appeared. In this pioneering feminist work, she criticizes and rejects Rousseau's argument for distinct and separate spheres for men and women. She portrays that argument as defending the continued bondage of women to men and as hindering the wider education of the entire human race.*

What criticisms does Wollstonecraft direct against Rousseau's views? Why does Wollstonecraft emphasize a new kind of education for women?

The most perfect education . . . is such an exercise of the understanding as is best calculated to strengthen the body and form the heart. Or, in other words, to enable the individual to attain such habits of virtue as will render it independent. In fact, it is a farce to call any being virtuous whose virtues do not result from the exercise of its own reason. This was Rousseau's opinion respecting men: I extend it to women. . . .

I may be accused of arrogance; still I must declare what I firmly believe, that all the writers who have written on the subject of female education and manners from Rousseau to Dr. Gregory [a Scottish physician], have contributed to render women more artificial, weak characters, than they would otherwise have been; and, consequently, more useless members of society. . . .

Strengthen the female mind by enlarging it, and there will be an end to blind obedience; but, as blind obedience is ever sought for by power, tyrants and sensualists are in the right when they endeavour to keep women in the dark, because the former only wants slaves, and the latter a plaything. The sensualist, indeed, has been the most dangerous of tyrants, and women have been duped by their lovers, as princes by their ministers, whilst dreaming that they reigned over them. . . .

Rousseau declares that a woman should never, for a moment, feel herself independent, that she should be governed by fear to exercise her natural cunning, and made a coquettish slave in order to render her a more alluring object of desire, a sweeter companion to man, whenever he chooses to relax himself. He carries the arguments, which he pretends to draw from the indications of nature, still further, and insinuates that truth and fortitude, the cornerstones of all human virtue, should be cultivated with certain restrictions, because, with respect to the female character, obedience is the grand lesson which ought to be impressed with unrelenting rigour.

What nonsense! When will a great man arise with sufficient strength of mind to put away the fumes which pride and sensuality have thus spread over the subject! If women are by nature inferior to men, their virtues must be the same in quality, if not in degree, or virtue is a relative idea; consequently, their conduct should be founded on the same principles, and have the same aim.

Connected with man as daughters, wives, and mothers, their moral character may be estimated by their manner of fulfilling those simple duties; but the end, the grand end of their exertions should be to unfold their own faculties and acquire the dignity of conscious virtue. . . .

But avoiding . . . any direct comparison of the two sexes collectively, or frankly acknowledging the inferiority of women according to the present appearance of things, I shall only insist that men have increased that inferiority till women are almost sunk below the standard of rational creatures. Let their faculties have room to unfold, and their virtues to gain strength, and then determine where the whole sex must stand in the intellectual scale. . . .

I . . . will venture to assert, that till women are more rationally educated, the progress of human virtue and improvement in knowledge must receive continual checks. . . .

The mother, who wishes to give true dignity of character to her daughter, must, regardless of the sneers of ignorance, proceed on a plan diametrically opposite to that which Rousseau has recommended with all the deluding charms of eloquence and philosophical sophistry: for his eloquence renders absurdities plausible, and his dogmatic conclusions puzzle, without convincing, those who have not ability to refute them.

From Mary Wollstonecraft, *A Vindication of the Rights of Woman,* ed. by Carol H. Poston (New York: W.W. Norton, 1975), pp. 21, 22, 24–26, 35, 40, 41.

whose *Pilgrimage to Isle of Cithera* young lovers embark to pay homage to the goddess Venus. Other artists such as Boucher and Jean-Honoré Fragonard (1732–1806) produced works filled with female nudes and with men and women in sexually suggestive poses.

As the eighteenth century wore on, the way of life illustrated in Rococo paintings and of more popular prints produced from them convinced many people in France that the monarchy, the court, and the aristocracy were frivolous and decadent. In reality, as seen in Chapter 15, many French and European aristocrats were hardworking and disciplined, and Louis XVI, who succeeded Louis XV in 1774, was a well-intentioned, pious, and highly moral monarch. Nonetheless, the lighthearted carelessness of Rococo art increased hostility toward the political and social elites of the Old Regime.

Contemporaries, moreover, did not have to wait for the tumult of the French Revolution to view art that directly criticized the society Rococo art portrayed. The mid-eighteenth century witnessed a new admiration for the art of the ancient world. In 1755, Johann Joachim Winckelmann (1717–1768), a German archaeologist, published *Thoughts on the Imitation of Greek Works in Painting and Sculpture*, followed in 1764 by *The History of Ancient Art*. In both works he either directly or in-

directly contrasted the superficiality of the Rococo with the seriousness of ancient art and architecture. His books and the simultaneous rediscovery and partial excavation of the ancient Roman cities of Pompeii and Herculaneum in southern Italy fostered the rise of *Neoclassicism* in art and architecture. This movement constituted a return to themes, topics, and styles drawn from antiquity itself and from the Renaissance appeal to antiquity.

The popularity of the city of Rome as a destination for artists and aristocratic tourists contributed to the rise of Neoclassicism. European aristocrats who came to Italy in the mid-eighteenth century on what was called "the Grand Tour" increasingly admired both the ancient and Renaissance art that was on view there and the Neoclassical works that contemporary artists were producing there. Not only did these wealthy and influential travelers purchase paintings and statues to bring home with them, but they also commissioned architects to rebuild their own houses and public buildings in Neoclassical style.

Figures in Neoclassical paintings rarely suggest movement and often seem to stand still in a kind of tableau illustrating a moral theme. These paintings were didactic rather than emotional or playful. Their

The color, the light, and the elaborate decorative details associated with Rococo style are splendidly exemplified in the Imperial Hall (Kaisarsaal) built in Würzburg, Bavaria, according to the design of Balthasar Neumann (1687–1753). Art Resource, N.Y.

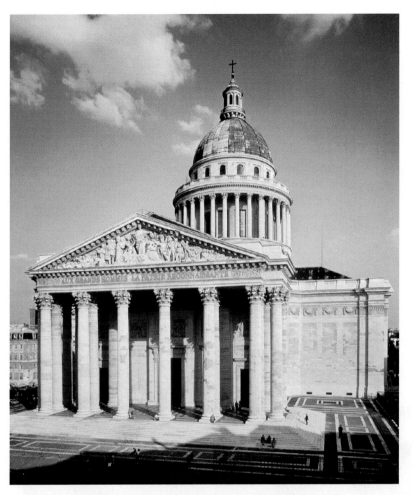

The Pantheon in Paris (construction commencing 1758) embodied the Neoclassical style used for a Jesuit church. After the French Revolution it became a national monument where famous figures of the Enlightenment and Revolution were buried. The bodies of both Voltaire and Rousseau were transferred there during the 1790s. Jacques Germain Soufflot (1713–1780), Facade of the Pantheon (formerly Church of Ste. Genevieve), 1757. Pantheon, Paris, France. © Bridgeman-Giraudon/Art Resource, NY

subject matter was usually concerned with public life or public morals, rather than depicting intimate family life, daily routine, or the leisure activity favored by Rococo painters.

Many Neoclassical painters used scenes of heroism and self-sacrifice from ancient history to draw contemporary moral and political lessons. Such scenes provided a sharp moral contrast to the works of Watteau or Boucher in which lovers seek only pleasure and escape from care.

Other Neoclassical artists intended their paintings to be a form of direct political criticism. Jacques-Louis David (1748–1825), the foremost French Neoclassical painter, used ancient republican themes in the 1780s to emphasize the corruption of French monarchical government. His *Oath of the Horatii* in 1784 illustrates a scene, derived from the ancient Roman historian Livy, of soldiers taking an oath to die for the Roman Republic.

The painting also portrays the concept of separate spheres for men and women. The brothers are taking the oath to defend the republic with their lives. The women in the scene appear emotional and incapable of entering the masculine civic life of the republic. David painted many similar scenes from the ancient Roman Republic and later became an artistic champion of the French Revolution and Napoleon (who, ironically, made him a baron).

The philosophes themselves became the subjects of Neoclassical artists. The French sculptor Jean-Antoine Houdon (1741–1828) produced numerous portraits in stone of leading philosophes including Voltaire and Rousseau as well as American admirers of the Enlightenment such as Benjamin Franklin (1706–1790) and Thomas Jefferson (1743–1826). Such statues furnished a gallery of writers who had criticized the Old Regime or embodied modern republican values.

Even religious structures built in the Neoclassical style were, by the end of the century, transformed to monuments to the Enlightenment and Revolution. Modeled on its ancient pagan namesake in Rome, the Pantheon in Paris was begun in 1758 as a Jesuit church. During the French Revolution, the new government transformed it into a national monument where the remains of French heroes could be interred. Voltaire's remains were placed there in 1791 and Rousseau's in 1794.

▼ Enlightened Absolutism

Most of the philosophes favored neither Montesquieu's reformed and revived aristocracy nor Rousseau's democracy as a solution to contemporary political problems. Like other thoughtful people of the day in other stations and occupations, they looked to the existing monarchies. Because of his personal clash with aristocrats as a young writer and his general distrust of democratic ideas, Voltaire was a strong monarchist. In 1759, he published a *History of the Russian Empire under Peter the Great*, which declared, "Peter was born, and Russia was formed."[15] Voltaire and other philosophes, such as Diderot, who visited Catherine II of Russia, and the physiocrats, some of whom were ministers to Louis XV and Louis XVI, did not wish to limit the power of monarchs. Rather, they sought to use that power to rationalize economic and political structures and liberate intellectual life. Most

---

[15]Quoted in Larry Wolff, *Inventing Eastern Europe: The Map of Civilization on the Mind of the Enlightenment* (Palo Alto, CA: Stanford University Press, 1994), p. 200.

A Closer ▷ LOOK

AN EIGHTEENTH-CENTURY ARTIST APPEALS TO THE ANCIENT WORLD

JACQUES-LOUIS DAVID completed *The Oath of the Horatii* in 1784. Like many of his other works, it used themes from the supposedly morally austere ancient Roman Republic to criticize the political life of his own day. David intended the painting to contrast ancient civic virtue with the luxurious aristocratic culture of contemporary France.

The Horatii take an oath their father administers to protect the Roman Republic against enemies even if it means sacrificing their own lives. One of these enemies is romantically involved with one of their sisters in the right of the painting. Patriotism must be upheld over other relationships.

The sharp division of the painting with a male world on the left and a female world on the right illustrates how eighteenth-century republican thinkers, such as Rousseau, excluded women from civic life and political participation.

The sisters and mother of the Horatii weep in a separate part of the scene. The emotion of the women and their uncertain political loyalty suggest that civic virtue pertains only to men.

To examine this image in an interactive fashion, please go to www.myhistorylab.com

myhistorylab

Jacques-Louis David, *The Oath of the Horatii.* 1784–1785.© Réunion des Musees Nationaux, Paris, France/Art Resource, NY philosophes were not opposed to power if they could find a way to use it for their own purposes or if they could profit in one way or another from their personal relationships to strong monarchs. For this reason, it is important not to see Enlightenment political thought only as a source of modern liberal outlooks.

During the last third of the century, some observers believed that several European rulers had embraced many of the reforms the philosophes advocated. Historians use the term *enlightened absolutism* for this form of monarchical government in which the central absolutist administration was strengthened and rationalized at the cost of other, lesser centers of political power, such as the aristocracy, the church, and the parliaments or diets that had survived from the Middle Ages. The monarchs most closely associated with it are Frederick II (r. 1740–1786) of Prussia, Joseph II of Austria (r. 1765–1790), and Catherine II (r. 1762–1796) of Russia. Each had complicated relationships with the community of enlightened writers.

Frederick II corresponded with the philosophes, gave Voltaire and other philosophes places at his court, and even wrote history, political tracts, literary criticism, and music. Catherine II, adept at what would later be called public relations, consciously sought to create the image of being an enlightened ruler. She read and cited the works of the philosophes, subsidized Diderot, and corresponded with Voltaire, lavishing compliments on him, all in the hope that she would receive favorable comments from them, as she indeed did. Joseph II continued numerous initiatives begun by his mother, Maria Theresa (r. 1740–1780). He imposed a series of religious, legal, and social reforms that contemporaries believed he had derived from the philosophes' suggestions.

The relationship between these rulers and the writers of the Enlightenment was, however, more complicated than these appearances suggest. The humanitarian and liberating zeal of the Enlightenment writers was only part of what motivated the policies of the rulers. Frederick II, Joseph II, and Catherine II were also determined to play major diplomatic and military roles in Europe. In no small measure, they adopted Enlightenment policies favoring the rational economic and social integration of their realms because these policies also increased their military strength and political power. As explained in Chapter 13, all the major European states had emerged from the Seven Years' War knowing they would need stronger armies for future wars and increased revenues to finance these armies. The search for new revenues and internal political support was one of the incentives prompting the "enlightened" reforms of the monarchs of Russia, Prussia, and Austria. Consequently, they and their advisers used rationality to pursue goals most philosophes admired, and also to further what some philosophes considered irrational militarism. The flattery of monarchs could bend the opinions of a philosophe. For example, Voltaire, who had written against war, could praise the military expansion of Catherine's Russia because it appeared in his mind to bring civilization to peoples he regarded as uncivilized and because he enjoyed being known as a literary confidant of the empress.

Frederick the Great of Prussia

More than any other ruler of the age, Frederick the Great of Prussia embodied enlightened absolutism. Drawing upon the accomplishments of his Hohenzollern forebearers, he forged a state that commanded the loyalty of the military, the junker nobility, the Lutheran clergy, a growing bureaucracy recruited from an educated middle class, and university professors. Because the authority of the Prussian monarchy and the military were so strong and because the nobles, bureaucracy, clergy, and professors were so loyal, Frederick had the confidence to permit a more open discussion of Enlightenment ideas and to put into effect more Enlightenment values, such as extensive religious toleration, than any other continental ruler. Consequently, in marked contrast to France, Prussians sympathetic to the Enlightenment tended to support the state rather than criticize it.

Promotion Through Merit Reflecting an important change in the European view of the ruler, Frederick frequently described himself as "the first servant of the State" contending that his own personal and dynastic interests should always be subordinate to the good of his subjects. Like earlier Hohenzollern rulers, he protected the local social and political interests of the Prussian nobility as well as their role in the army, but he also required nobles who sought positions in his well-paid bureaucracy to qualify for those jobs by merit. By 1770, a Prussian Civil Service Commission oversaw the education and examinations required for all major government appointments. Frederick thus made it clear that merit rather than privilege of birth would determine who served the Prussian state.

During his reign Frederick created few new nobles, and those persons whom he did ennoble earned their titles by merit, for having served the king and the state well. This policy of ennobling only for merit and Frederick's protecting the nobility's local social interests and leadership of the army meant that Prussia did not experience the conflicts between the aristocracy and the monarchy that troubled other eighteenth-century European states.

Frederick felt comfortable in the intellectual life of his day and personally participated in the culture of the Enlightenment. He favored the Prussian universities and allowed professors wide latitude to discuss new ideas. In turn, Prussian professors were virtually unanimous in their praise and support of Frederick.

Frederick II of Prussia became known as Frederick the Great after his victories in the Seven Years' Wars. This portrait of 1763 shows him at the time of those triumphs when he had permanently secured the position of Prussia as a major European power. He was equally interested in the economic development of Prussia. Erich Lessing/Art Resource, NY

that province from the Habsburgs in the 1740s. (See Chapter 13.) He even stated that he would be willing to build mosques for Turks should they move into his country. His religious toleration won the strong support of philosophers, such as Immanuel Kant and Moses Mendelsohn. Frederick nonetheless tended to appoint Protestants to most key positions in the bureaucracy and army.

Administrative and Economic Reforms Frederick also ordered a new codification of Prussian law, which was completed after his death. His objective was to rationalize the existing legal system and make it more efficient, eliminating regional peculiarities, reducing aristocratic influence, abolishing torture, and limiting the number of capital crimes. The other enlightened monarchs shared this concern for legal reform, which they saw as a way to extend and strengthen royal power.

The mid-century wars had inflicted considerable economic damage on Prussia. Thereafter, Frederick used the power of the state to foster economic growth. He continued the long-standing Hohenzollern policy of importing workers from outside Prussia. He sought to develop Prussian agriculture. Under state supervision, swamps were drained, new crops introduced, and peasants encouraged and sometimes compelled to migrate where they were needed. For the first time in Prussia, potatoes and turnips became important crops. Frederick also established a land-mortgage credit association to help landowners raise money for agricultural improvements. Despite these efforts, however, most Prussians did not prosper under Frederick's reign, and the burden of taxation, reflecting his protection of the interests of the nobles, fell disproportionately on peasants and townspeople.

Because the Prussian state required academic training for appointment to positions of authority, nobles attended the universities. There they studied with middle-class Prussians who were training to serve the state either as Protestant clergy or bureaucrats. Consequently, nobles, clergy, and bureaucrats in Prussia shared a similar educational background that combined a moderate exposure to Enlightenment ideas with broadly shared religious values and loyalty to the state.

Religious Toleration No single policy so associated Frederick with the Enlightenment as that of full religious toleration. Continuing the Hohenzollern policy of toleration for foreign workers who brought important skills into Prussia, Frederick allowed Catholics and Jews to settle in his predominantly Lutheran country, and he protected the Catholics living in Silesia after he conquered

Joseph II of Austria

No eighteenth-century ruler so embodied rational, impersonal force as did the emperor Joseph II of Austria. He was the son of Maria Theresa and co-ruler with her from 1765 to 1780. Thereafter, he ruled alone until his death in 1790. Joseph was an austere and humorless person. During much of his life, he slept on straw and ate little but boiled beef. He prided himself on a narrow, passionless rationality, which he sought to impose by his own will on the various Habsburg domains. Despite his personal eccentricities and cold personality, Joseph II sincerely wished to improve the lot of his people. He was much less a political opportunist and cynic than either Frederick the Great of Prussia or Catherine the Great of Russia. Nonetheless, the ultimate result of his well-intentioned efforts was a series of aristocratic and peasant rebellions extending from Hungary to the Austrian Netherlands.

Centralization of Authority

As explained in Chapter 13, of all the rising states of the eighteenth century, Austria was the most diverse in its people and problems. The historian Robert Palmer likened the Habsburg domains to "a vast holding company."[16] The Habsburgs never succeeded in creating either a unified administrative structure or a strong aristocratic loyalty to the dynasty. To preserve the monarchy during the War of the Austrian Succession (1740–1748), Maria Theresa had guaranteed the aristocracy considerable independence, especially in Hungary.

During and after the conflict, however, she took steps to strengthen the power of the crown outside of Hungary, building more of a bureaucracy than had previous Habsburg rulers. In Austria and Bohemia, the empress imposed a much more efficient system of tax collection that extracted funds even from the clergy and the nobles. She also established central councils to deal with governmental problems. To assure her government a supply of educated officials, she sought to bring all educational institutions into the service of the crown and expanded primary education on the local level.

Maria Theresa was concerned about the welfare of the peasants and serfs. She brought them some relief by expanding the authority of the royal bureaucracy over the local power of the nobility and limiting the amount of labor, or *robot*, landowners could demand from peasants. Her motives were less humanitarian than to assure a good pool from which to draw military recruits. In these policies and in her desire to stimulate prosperity and military strength by royal initiative, Maria Theresa anticipated the policies of her son.

Joseph II was more determined than his mother, and his projected reforms were more wide ranging. He aimed to extend his territories at the expense of Poland, Bavaria, and the Ottoman Empire. His greatest ambition, however, was to increase the authority of the Habsburg emperor over his various realms. He sought to overcome the pluralism of the Habsburg holdings by imposing central authority on areas of political and social life in which Maria Theresa had wisely chosen not to interfere.

In particular, Joseph sought to reduce Hungarian autonomy. To avoid having to guarantee Hungary's existing privileges or extend new ones at the time of his coronation, he refused to have himself crowned king of Hungary and even had the Crown of Saint Stephen, symbol of the Hungarian state, sent to the Imperial Treasury in Vienna. He reorganized local government in Hungary to increase the authority of his own officials. He also required the use of German in all governmental matters.

[16]Robert R. Palmer, *The Age of Democratic Revolution*, Vol. 1 (Princeton, NJ: Princeton University Press, 1959), p. 103.

Ecclesiastical Policies

Another target of Joseph's royal absolutism was the church. Since the reign of Charles V (r. 1510–1558), the Habsburgs had been the most important dynastic champions of Roman Catholicism. Maria Theresa was devout, but she had not allowed the church to limit her authority. Although she had attempted to discourage certain of the more extreme modes of Roman Catholic popular religious piety, such as public flagellation, she was adamantly opposed to religious toleration. (See "Compare & Connect: Maria Theresa and Joseph II of Austria Debate Toleration," pages 538–539)

Joseph II was also a practicing Catholic, but based on both Enlightenment values and pragmatic politics, he favored a policy of toleration. In October 1781, Joseph extended freedom of worship to Lutherans, Calvinists, and the Greek Orthodox. They were permitted to have their own places of worship, to sponsor schools, to enter skilled trades, and to hold academic appointments and positions in the public service. Joseph also granted the right of private worship to Jews and relaxed the financial and social burdens imposed on them, though he did not give Jews full equality with other Habsburg subjects.

Above all, Joseph sought to bring the Roman Catholic Church directly under royal control. He forbade the bishops of his realms to communicate directly with the pope. Since he considered religious orders that did not run schools or hospitals to be unproductive, he dissolved more than six hundred monasteries, confiscated their lands, and used some of their revenue to found new parishes in areas where there was a shortage of priests. He also reorganized the training of priests. The emperor believed that the traditional Roman Catholic seminaries, which were run by the various dioceses, instilled in priests too great a loyalty to the papacy and too little concern for their future parishioners. They were, therefore, replaced by eight general seminaries under government supervision whose training emphasized parish duties. In effect, Joseph's policies made Roman Catholic priests the employees of the state, ending the influence of the Roman Catholic Church as an independent institution in Habsburg lands. In many respects, his ecclesiastical policies, known as *Josephinism*, prefigured those of the French Revolution.

Economic and Agrarian Reform

Like Frederick of Prussia, Joseph sought to improve the economic life of his domains. He abolished many internal tariffs, encouraged road building, and improved river transport. He personally inspected farms and manufacturing districts. Joseph also reconstructed the judicial system to make laws more uniform and rational and to lessen the influence of local landlords. All of these improvements were expected to bring new unity to the state and more taxes into the imperial coffers in Vienna.

Joseph's policies toward serfdom and the land were a far-reaching extension of those Maria Theresa had

Maria Theresa and Joseph II of Austria Debate Toleration

THE ISSUE OF religious toleration was widely debated throughout the age of Enlightenment. Many rulers feared that their domains would be overcome by religious turmoil and potential political unrest if their subjects could pursue religious freedom. The issue divided the Empress Maria Theresa and her son Joseph II who since 1765 had been co-rulers of the Austrian Empire. In 1777 they exchanged important letters setting forth their sharply differing views of the subject.

Joseph believed some religious toleration should be introduced into the Habsburg realms. Maria Theresa refused to consider toleration. The toleration of Protestants that is in dispute related only to Lutherans and Calvinists. Maria Theresa died in 1780; the next year Joseph issued an edict of toleration.

QUESTIONS

1. How does Joseph define toleration, and why does Maria Theresa believe it is the same as religious indifference?

2. Why does Maria Theresa fear that toleration will bring about political as well as religious turmoil?

3. Why does Maria Theresa think that Joseph's belief in toleration has come from Joseph's acquaintance with wicked books?

I. Joseph to Maria Theresa, July 20, 1777

It is only the word "toleration" which has caused the misunderstanding. You have taken it in quite a different meaning [from mine expressed in an earlier letter]. God preserve me from thinking it a matter of indifference whether the citizens turn Protestant or remain Catholic, still less, whether they cleave to, or at least observe, the cult which they have inherited from their fathers! I would give all I possess if all the Protestants of your states would go over to Catholicism.

The word "toleration," as I understand it, means only that I would employ any person, without distinction of religion, in purely temporal matters, allow them to own property, practice trades, be citizens, if they were qualified and if this would be of advantage to the State and its industry. Those who, unfortunately, adhere to a false faith, are far further from being converted if they remain in their own country than if they migrate into another, in which they can hear and see the convincing truths of the Catholic faith. Similarly, the undisturbed practice of their religion makes them far

better subjects and causes them to avoid irreligion, which is a far greater danger to our Catholics than if one lets them see others practice their religion unimpeded.

II. Maria Theresa to Joseph, Late July 1777

Without a dominant religion? Toleration, indifference are precisely the true means of undermining everything, taking away every foundation; we others will then be the greatest losers. . . . He is no friend of humanity, as the popular phrase is, who allows everyone his own thoughts. I am speaking only in the political sense, not as a Christian, nothing is so necessary and salutary as religion. Will you allow everyone to fashion his own religion as he pleases? No fixed cult, no subordination to the Church—what will then become of us? The result will not be quiet and contentment; its outcome will be the rule of the stronger and more unhappy times like those which we have already seen. A manifesto by you to this effect can produce the utmost distress and make you responsible for many thousands of souls. And what are my own sufferings, when I see you entangled in opinions so erroneous? What is at stake is not only the welfare of the State but your own salvation. . . . Turning your eyes and ears everywhere, mingling your spirit of contradiction with the simultaneous desire to create something, you are ruining yourself and dragging the Monarchy down with you into the abyss. . . . I only wish to live so long as I can hope to descend to my ancestors with the consolation that my son will be as great, as religious as his forebearer, that he will return from his erroneous views, from those wicked books whose authors parade their cleverness at the expense of all that is most holy and most worthy of respect in the world, who want to introduce an imaginary freedom which can never exist and which degenerates into license and into complete revolution.

Source: As quoted in C. A. Macartney, ed., *The Habsburg and Hohenzollern Dynasties in the Seventeenth and Eighteenth Centuries* (New York: Walker, 1970), pp. 151–153. Reprinted by permission of Walker and Co.

An eighteenth-century scroll of the biblical Book of Esther. According to the story, Queen Esther, who was married to King Ahasuerus of Persia, was responsible for thwarting a plan to annihilate all Jews in the Persian Empire. Unbeknownst to the king when they married, Esther, herself, was Jewish. The vizier, Haman the Agagite, devised this genocidal plan and the king ordered him to be hanged for his role in it.   Courtesy of the Library of Congress initiated. During his reign, he introduced reforms that touched the very heart of the rural social structure. He did not abolish the authority of landlords over their peasants, but he did seek to make that authority more moderate and subject to the oversight of royal officials. He abolished serfdom as a legally sanctioned state of servitude. He granted peasants a wide array of personal freedoms, including the right to marry, to engage in skilled work, and to have their children learn a skill without having to secure the landlord's permission.

Joseph reformed the procedures of the manorial courts and opened avenues of appeal to royal officials. He also encouraged landlords to change land leases, so that peasants could more easily inherit land or transfer it to other peasants. His goal in all of these efforts to reduce traditional burdens on peasants was to make them more productive and industrious farmers.

Near the end of his reign, Joseph proposed a new and daring system of land taxation. He decreed in 1789 that all proprietors of the land were to be taxed regardless of social status. No longer were the peasants alone to bear the burden of taxation. He commuted *robot* into a monetary tax, only part of which was to go to the landlord, the rest reverting to the state. Angry nobles blocked the implementation of this decree, and it died with Joseph in

1790. This and other of Joseph's earlier measures, however, brought turmoil throughout the Habsburg realms. Peasants revolted over disagreements with landlords about their newly granted rights. The nobles of the various Habsburg realms protested the taxation scheme. The Magyars resisted Joseph's centralization measures in Hungary and forced him to rescind them.

Joseph was succeeded by his brother Leopold II (r. 1790–1792). Although sympathetic to Joseph's goals, Leopold was forced to repeal many of the most controversial decrees, such as that on taxation. In other areas, Leopold considered his brother's policies simply wrong. For example, he returned political and administrative power to local nobles because he thought it expedient for them to have a voice in government. Still, he did not repudiate his brother's program wholesale. He retained, in particular, Joseph's religious policies and maintained as much political centralization as he thought possible.

Catherine the Great of Russia

Joseph II never grasped the practical necessity of forging political constituencies to support his policies. Catherine II, who had been born a German princess, but who became empress of Russia, understood only too well the fragility of the Romanov dynasty's base of power.

After the death of Peter the Great in 1725, the court nobles and the army repeatedly determined the Russian succession. As a result, the crown fell primarily into the hands of people with little talent. Peter's wife, Catherine I, ruled for two years (1725–1727) and was succeeded for three years by Peter's grandson, Peter II. In 1730, the crown devolved on Anna, a niece of Peter the Great. During 1740 and 1741, a child named Ivan VI, who was less than a year old, was the nominal ruler. Finally, in 1741, Peter the Great's daughter Elizabeth came to the throne. She held the title of empress until 1762, but her reign was not notable for new political departures or sound administration. Her court was a shambles of political and romantic intrigue. Much of the power the tsar possessed at the opening of the century had vanished.

At her death in 1762, Elizabeth was succeeded by her nephew Peter III. He was a weak ruler whom many contemporaries considered mad. He immediately exempted the nobles from compulsory military service and then rapidly made peace with Frederick the Great, for whom he held unbounded admiration. That decision probably saved Prussia from military defeat in the Seven Years' War. The one positive feature of this unbalanced creature's life was his marriage in 1745 to a young German princess born in the small duchy of Anhalt Zerbst. This was the future Catherine the Great.

For almost twenty years, Catherine lived in misery and frequent danger at the court of Elizabeth. During that

RUSSIA FROM PETER THE GREAT THROUGH CATHERINE THE GREAT

1725	Death of Peter the Great
1725–1727	Catherine I
1727–1730	Peter II
1730–1741	Anna
1740–1741	Ivan VI
1741–1762	Elizabeth
1762	Peter III
1762	Catherine II (the Great) becomes empress
1767	Legislative commission summoned
1769	War with Turkey begins
1773–1775	Pugachev's Rebellion
1772	First Partition of Poland
1774	Treaty of Kuchuk-Kainardji ends war with Turkey
1775	Reorganization of local government
1783	Russia annexes Crimea
1785	Catherine issues the Charter of the Nobility
1793	Second Partition of Poland
1795	Third Partition of Poland
1796	Death of Catherine the Great

Catherine the Great ascended to the Russian throne after the murder of her husband. She tried initially to enact major reforms, but she never intended to abandon absolutism. She assured nobles of their rights and by the end of her reign had imposed press censorship.   The Granger Collection

time, she befriended important nobles and read widely the books of the philosophes. She was a shrewd person whose experience in a court crawling with rumors, intrigue, and conspiracy had taught her how to survive. She exhibited neither love nor fidelity toward her demented husband. A few months after his accession as tsar, Peter was deposed and murdered with Catherine's approval, if not her aid, and she was immediately proclaimed empress.

Catherine's familiarity with the Enlightenment and the general culture of Western Europe convinced her Russia was backward and that it needed major reforms to remain a great power. She understood that any significant reform must have a wide base of political and social support, especially since she had assumed the throne through a palace coup. In 1767, she summoned a legislative commission to advise her on revising the law and government of Russia. There were more than five hundred delegates, drawn from all sectors of Russian life. Before the commission convened, Catherine issued a set of instructions, partly written by herself. They contained many ideas drawn from the political writings of the philosophes. The commission considered the instructions as well as other ideas and complaints its members raised.

Russian law, however, was not revised for more than half a century. In 1768, Catherine dismissed the commission before several of its key committees had reported. Yet the meeting had not been useless, for it had gathered a vast amount of information about the conditions of local administration and economic life throughout Russia. The inconclusive debates and the absence of programs from the delegates themselves suggested that most Russians saw no alternative to an autocratic monarchy, and Catherine had no intention of departing from absolutism.

Limited Administrative Reform Catherine carried out limited reforms on her own authority. She gave strong support to the rights and local power of the nobility. In 1775, she reorganized local government to solve problems the legislative commission had brought to light. She put most local offices in the hands of nobles rather than creating a royal bureaucracy. In 1785, Catherine issued the Charter of the Nobility, which guaranteed nobles many rights and privileges. In part, the empress had to favor the nobles because they could topple her from the throne. Moreover, Russia's educated class was too small to provide an independent bureaucracy, and the treasury could not afford an army strictly loyal to the crown. So Catherine wisely made a virtue of necessity. She strengthened the stability of her crown by making convenient friends with her nobles.

Economic Growth Part of Catherine's program was to continue the economic development begun under Peter the Great. She attempted to suppress internal barriers to trade. Exports of grain, flax, furs, and naval stores grew dramatically. She also favored the expansion of the small Russian urban middle class that was so vital to trade. Through all of these departures, Catherine tried to maintain ties of friendship and correspondence with the philosophes. She knew that if she treated them kindly, they would be sufficiently flattered to give her a progressive reputation throughout Europe.

Territorial Expansion Catherine's limited administrative reforms and her policy of economic growth had a counterpart in the diplomatic sphere. The Russian drive for warm-water ports continued. (See Map 17–1, page 542.) This goal required warfare with the Turks. In 1769, as a result of a minor Russian incursion, the Ottoman Empire declared war on Russia. The Russians responded with a series of strikingly successful military moves.

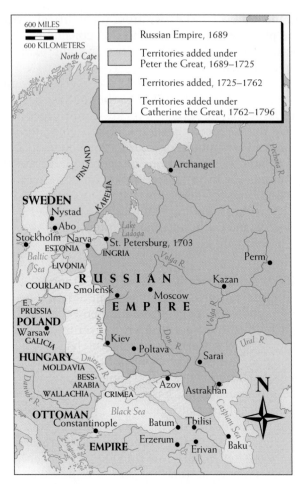

Map 17–1 **EXPANSION OF RUSSIA, 1689–1796** The overriding territorial aim of the two most powerful Russian monarchs of the eighteenth century, Peter the Great (in the first quarter of the century) and Catherine the Great (in the last half of the century), was to secure navigable outlets to the sea both in the north and the south for Russia's vast empire; hence Peter's push to the Baltic Sea and Catherine's to the Black Sea. Russia also expanded into Central Asia and Siberia during this time period.

During 1769 and 1770, the Russian fleet sailed all the way from the Baltic Sea into the eastern Mediterranean. The Russian army won several major victories that by 1771 gave Russia control of Ottoman provinces on the Danube River and the Crimean coast of the Black Sea. The conflict dragged on until 1774, when the Treaty of Kuchuk-Kainardji gave Russia a direct outlet on the Black Sea, free navigation rights in its waters, and free access through the Bosporus. Crimea became an independent state, which Catherine painlessly annexed in 1783. Finally, under this treaty Catherine, as empress of Russia, was made the protector of the Orthodox Christians living in the Ottoman Empire. In the future this would cause conflict with France whose monarch had previously been recognized as the protector of Roman Catholic Christians in the empire.

The Partition of Poland

The Russian military successes increased Catherine's domestic political support, but they made the other states of eastern Europe uneasy. These anxieties were overcome by an extraordinary division of Polish territory known as the First Partition of Poland.

The Russian victories along the Danube River were most unwelcome to Austria, which also harbored ambitions of territorial expansion in that direction. At the same time, the Ottoman Empire was pressing Prussia for aid against Russia. Frederick the Great made a proposal to Russia and Austria that would give each something it wanted, prevent conflict among the powers, and save appearances. After long, complicated secret negotiations, Russia agreed to abandon the conquered Danubian provinces. In compensation, it received a large portion of Polish territory with almost 2 million inhabitants. As a reward for remaining neutral, Prussia annexed most of the territory between East Prussia and Prussia proper. This land allowed Frederick to unite two previously separate sections of his realm. Finally, Austria took Galicia in southern Poland, with its important salt mines, and other Polish territory with more than 2.5 million inhabitants. (See Map 17–2.)

In September 1772, the helpless Polish aristocracy, paying the price for maintaining internal liberties at the expense of developing a strong central government, ratified this seizure of nearly one third of Polish territory. The loss was not necessarily fatal to Poland's continued existence, and it inspired a revival of national feeling. Attempts were made to strengthen the Polish state and reform its feeble central government, but they proved to be too little and too late. Poland was no match for its stronger, more ambitious neighbors. The partition of Poland clearly demonstrated that any nation without a strong monarchy, bureaucracy, and army could no longer compete within the European state system. It also demonstrated that the major powers in eastern Europe were prepared to settle their own rivalries at the expense of such a weak state. If Polish territory had not been available to ease tensions, international rivalries might have led to warfare among Russia, Austria, and Prussia.

As shall be seen in Chapter 18, the wars and social upheaval that followed the outbreak of the French Revolution gave Russia and Prussia an excuse to partition Poland again in 1793, and Russia, Prussia, and Austria partitioned it a third time in 1795, removing it from the map of Europe for more than a century. Each time, the great powers contended they were saving themselves, and by implication the rest of Europe, from Polish anarchy. The fact was that Poland's political weakness left it vulnerable to plunderous aggression by its more powerful neighbors.

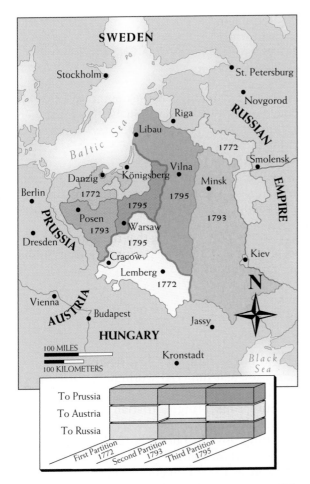

Map 17–2   PARTITIONS OF POLAND, 1772, 1793, AND 1795.
The callous eradication of Poland from the map displayed eighteenth-century power politics at its most extreme. Poland, without a strong central government, fell victim to the strong absolute monarchies of central and eastern Europe.

The End of the Eighteenth Century in Central and Eastern Europe

During the last two decades of the eighteenth century, all three regimes based on enlightened absolutism became more conservative and politically repressive. In Prussia and Austria, the innovations of the rulers stirred resistance among the nobility. In Russia, fear of peasant unrest was the chief factor.

Frederick the Great of Prussia grew remote during his old age, leaving the aristocracy to fill important military and administrative posts. A reaction to Enlightenment ideas also set in among Prussian Lutheran writers.

In Austria, Joseph II's plans to restructure society and administration in his realms provoked growing frustration and political unrest, with the nobility calling for an end to innovation. In response, Joseph turned increasingly to censorship and his secret police.

Russia faced a peasant uprising, the Pugachev Rebellion, between 1773 and 1775, and Catherine the Great never fully recovered from the fears of social and political upheaval that it raised. Once the French Revolution broke out in 1789, the Russian empress censored books based on Enlightenment thought and sent offensive authors into Siberian exile.

By the close of the century, fear of, and hostility to, change permeated the ruling classes of central and eastern Europe. This reaction had begun before 1789, but the events in France bolstered and sustained it for almost half a century. Paradoxically, nowhere did the humanity and liberalism of the Enlightenment encounter greater rejection than in those states that had been governed by "enlightened" rulers.

In Perspective

The writers of the Enlightenment, known as *philosophes*, charted a major new path in modern European and Western thought. They operated within a print culture that made public opinion into a distinct, cultural force. Admiring Newton and the achievements of physical science, they tried to apply reason and the principles of science to the cause of social reform. They also believed that passions and feelings are essential parts of human nature. Throughout their writings they championed reasonable moderation in social life. More than any other previous group of Western thinkers, they opposed the authority of the established churches and especially of Roman Catholicism. Most of them championed some form of religious toleration. They also sought to achieve a science of society that could discover how to maximize human productivity and material happiness. The great dissenter among them was Rousseau, who also wished to reform society, but in the name of virtue rather than material happiness.

The political influence of these writers was diverse and far-reaching. The founding fathers of the American republic looked to them for political guidance, as did moderate liberal reformers throughout Europe, especially within royal bureaucracies. The autocratic rulers of eastern Europe consulted the philosophes in the hope that Enlightenment ideas might allow them to rule more efficiently. The revolutionaries in France would honor them. This diverse assortment of followers illustrates the diverse character of the philosophes themselves. It also shows that Enlightenment thought cannot be reduced to a single formula. Rather, it should be seen as an outlook that championed change and reform, giving central place to humans and their welfare on earth rather than to God and the hereafter.

AP* TEST PREP

1. The most important intellectual forerunners of the Enlightenment included
   a. Bacon and Galileo.
   b. Newton and Galileo.
   c. Newton and Locke.
   d. Descartes and Bacon.
   e. Copernicus and Galileo.

2. According to Locke, human personality is the result of
   a. conditions in the womb.
   b. race, class, and climate.
   c. appetites and aversions.
   d. original sin.
   e. individual physical and social conditions.

3. The most significant factor explaining the emergence of the novel was
   a. technological improvements to printing.
   b. widespread literacy.
   c. renewed interest in piety and moral guidance.
   d. aristocratic patronage.
   e. court manners and tastes.

4. Voltaire was known as a
   a. philatelist.
   b. physician.
   c. parliamentarian.
   d. *philosophe.*
   e. physiocrat.

5. *Philosophes* were largely
   a. antireligion.
   b. republican.
   c. against intolerance.
   d. anti-Catholic.
   e. antideist.

6. The author of *Religion within the Limits of Reason Alone* was
   a. Kant.
   b. Locke.
   c. Hume.
   d. Lessing.
   e. Spinoza.

7. Which Enlightenment thinker was condemned for too closely identifying God and nature in his *Ethics?*
   a. Hume
   b. Spinoza
   c. Mendelsohn
   d. Kant
   e. Lessing

8. *The Social Contract* is one of the best-known works of
   a. Spinoza.
   b. Rousseau.
   c. Voltaire.
   d. Diderot.
   e. Montesquieu.

9. To escape official censure, some articles in the *Encyclopedia* had to be published
   a. under the cover of irony.
   b. in Latin.
   c. outside of France.
   d. without reference to religion or government.
   e. with an exclusive concentration on areas of practical knowledge such as ship construction.

10. The philosophy proposing that the purpose of law is to secure the greatest happiness for the greatest number is
    a. rationalism.
    b. Platonism.
    c. materialism.
    d. humanism.
    e. utilitarianism.

11. Which of the following justifications for European economic and imperial world domination relied on Adam Smith's philosophy?
    a. Europeans bring Christian ethics to a savage people.
    b. Europeans introduce civilizing influences like law and medicine.
    c. Mercantilism reflects the advancement of manufacture, trade, and property relations.
    d. Only the best survive the competition for survival.
    e. European commerce represents the fourth and, by implication, final stage of human development.

12. Most philosophers favored
    a. democracy.
    b. monarchy.
    c. oligarchy.
    d. anarchy.
    e. dictatorship.

13. The popularity of travel to Rome contributed to the rise of
    a. neoclassicism.
    b. rococo.
    c. realism.
    d. romanticism.
    e. idealism.

14. Montesquieu's unique contribution to political philosophy was the idea of
    a. popular sovereignty.
    b. religious toleration.
    c. separation of powers.
    d. adoption of the British cabinet system.
    e. the star chamber.

15. Rousseau believed that men and women
    a. should not mingle until the age of eighteen.
    b. were equal in all things.
    c. should receive the same education.
    d. were different species.
    e. should inhabit separate spheres.

16. The effect of the frivolity of rococo was to
    a. impugn all aristocrats as morally lax and unserious in purpose.
    b. ingratiate the nobility to the monarchy.
    c. incite outrage at the papacy.
    d. enrage nationalist sentiments.
    e. demean women as physiologically and morally weaker than men.

17. One clear sign of the Enlightenment shared by eighteenth-century monarchs was the
    a. institution of government checks and balances.
    b. patronage of academies of science.
    c. bestowal of privileges on the basis of merit rather than social station.
    d. redistribution of land ownership.
    e. patronage of *philosophes*.

18. Monarchs most closely associated with enlightened absolutism include all of the following *except*
    a. Frederick II.
    b. Louis XV.
    c. Catherine the Great.
    d. Joseph II.
    e. Maria Theresa.

19. Mary Wollstonecraft argued that
    a. women were prepared to participate politically and economically with men.
    b. women's emotional natures made them morally superior to men.
    c. women needed relief from domestic drudgery.
    d. women's liberation depends on birth control.
    e. the whole of humanity would not achieve true moral progress without advancing women's education.

20. The annexation of Crimea in 1783 provided Russia with direct access to the
    a. Black Sea.
    b. Caspian Sea.
    c. Aegean Sea.
    d. Baltic Sea.
    e. Mediterranean Sea.

DOCUMENT-BASED QUESTION

Directions: Construct a valid essay that directly addresses the central issue of the following question. Use facts from the documents provided and from the chapter to prove the position you take in your thesis statement.

Speculate on the relationship between the means through which Enlightenment thought spread and the actual content of Enlightenment thought. How were the values of the Enlightenment reflected in the spaces where ideas were discussed and the vehicles that were used to disseminate them?

Document A

The salon of Madame Geoffrin.

Document B

An eighteenth-century print shop.

Document C

An eighteenth-century coffeehouse.

Document D

Source: Immanuel Kant defines Enlightenment, "What Is Enlightenment?"

Enlightenment is man's emergence from his self-imposed nonage. Nonage is the inability to use one's own understanding without another's guidance. . . . Dare to know! (*Sapere aude*) "Have the courage to use your own understanding," is therefore the motto of the Enlightenment. . . .

. . . given freedom, enlightenment is almost inevitable. There will always be a few independent thinkers, even among the self-appointed guardians of the multitude. Once such men have thrown off the yoke of nonage, they will spread about them the spirit of a reasonable appreciation of man's value and of this duty to think for himself. . . .

This enlightenment requires nothing but freedom—and the most innocent of all that may be called "freedom": freedom to make public use of one's reason in all matters.

Document E

Source: The Encyclopédie.

It cannot be denied that, since the revival of letters among us, we owe partly to dictionaries the general enlightenment that has spread in society and the germ of science that is gradually preparing men's minds for more profound knowledge. How valuable would it not be, then to have a book of this kind that one could consult on all subjects and that would serve as much to guide those who have the courage to work at the instruction of others as to enlighten those who only instruct themselves!

For more on the spread of the Enlightenment, see pages 509–513, 520–521, 527.

On July 14, 1789, crowds stormed the Bastille, a prison in Paris. This event, whose only practical effect was to free a few prisoners, marked the first time the populace of Paris redirected the course of the revolution. Anonymous, France, eighteenth century, *Siege of the Bastille, 14 July, 1789.* Musée de la Ville de Paris, Musée Carnavalet, Paris, France. Bridgeman—Giraudon/Art Resource, NY

18

The French Revolution

KEY TOPICS

• **The financial crisis that impelled the French monarchy to call the Estates General**

• **The transformation of the Estates General into the National Assembly, the Declaration of the Rights of Man and Citizen, and the reconstruction of the political and ecclesiastical institutions of France**

• **The second revolution, the end of the monarchy, and the turn to more radical reforms**

• **The war between France and the rest of Europe**

• **The Reign of Terror, the Thermidorian Reaction, and the establishment of the Directory**

IN THE SPRING of 1789 political turmoil soon resulting in revolution erupted in France. The events of that year marked the beginning of a new political order in France and eventually throughout the West. The French Revolution brought to the foreground the principles of civic equality and popular sovereignty that challenged the major political and social institutions of Europe and that in evolving forms have continued to shape and reshape Western political and social life to the present day. During the 1790s the forces the revolution unleashed would cause small-town provincial lawyers and Parisian street orators to exercise more influence over the fate of the Continent than aristocrats, royal ministers, or monarchs. Citizen armies commanded by people of low birth and filled by conscripted village youths would defeat armies composed of professional soldiers led by officers of noble birth. The king and queen of France, as well as thousands of French peasants and shopkeepers, would be executed. The existence of the Roman Catholic faith in France and indeed of Christianity itself would be challenged. Finally Europe would embark on almost a quarter century of war that would eventually extend across the continent and result in millions of casualties.

▼ The Crisis of the French Monarchy

Although the French Revolution would shatter many of the political, social, and ecclesiastical structures of Europe, its origins lay in a much more mundane problem. By the late 1780s, the French royal government could not command sufficient taxes to finance itself. The monarchy's unsuccessful search for adequate revenues led it into ongoing conflicts with aristocratic and ecclesiastical institutions. Eventually, the resulting deadlock was so complete that Louis XVI and his ministers were required to summon the French Estates General, which had not met since 1614. Once the deputies to that body gathered, a new set of issues and problems quickly emerged that led to the revolution itself. Yet, none of this would have occurred if the monarchy had not reached a state of financial crisis that meant it could no longer function within the limits and practices of existing political institutions.

The Monarchy Seeks New Taxes

The French monarchy emerged from the Seven Years' War (1756–1763) defeated, deeply in debt, and unable thereafter to put its finances on a sound basis. French support of the American revolt against Great Britain further deepened the financial difficulties of the government. On the eve of the revolution, the interest and payments on the royal debt amounted to just over one half of the entire budget. Given the economic vitality of France, the debt was neither overly large nor disproportionate to the debts of other European powers. The problem lay with the inability of the royal government to tap the nation's wealth through taxes to service and repay the debt. Paradoxically, France was a rich nation with an impoverished government.

The debt was symptomatic of the failure of the late-eighteenth-century French monarchy to come to terms with the political power of aristocratic institutions and, in particular, the *parlements*. As explained in Chapter 13, French absolutism had always involved a process of ongoing negotiation between the monarchy and local aristocratic interests. This process had become more difficult after the death of Louis XIV (r. 1643–1715) when the aristocracy had sought to reclaim parts of the influence it had lost. Nonetheless, for the first half of the century, the monarchy had retained most of its authority.

For twenty-five years after the Seven Years' War, however, a standoff occurred between the monarchy and the aristocracy, as one royal minister after another attempted to devise new tax schemes that would tap the wealth of the nobility, only to be confronted by opposition from both the *Parlement* of Paris and provincial *parlements*. Both Louis XV (r. 1715–1774) and Louis XVI (r. 1774–1792) lacked the character, resolution, and political skills to resolve the dispute. In place of a consistent policy for dealing with the growing debt and aristocratic resistance to change, the monarchy hesitated, retreated, and even lied.

In 1770, Louis XV appointed René Maupeou (1714–1792) as chancellor. The new minister was determined to break the *parlements* and increase taxes on the nobility. He abolished the *parlements* and exiled their members to different parts of the country. He then began an ambitious program to make the administration more efficient. What ultimately doomed Maupeou's policy was

Well-meaning, but weak and vacillating, Louis XVI (r. 1774–1792) stumbled from concession to concession until he finally lost all power to save his throne. Joseph Siffred Duplessis (1725–1802), *Louis XVI*. Versailles, France. Photograph copyright Bridgeman—Giraudon/Art Resource, NY

19

The Age of Napoleon and the Triumph of Romanticism

KEY TOPICS

- Napoleon's rise, his coronation as emperor, and his administrative reforms

- Napoleon's conquests, the creation of a French Empire, and Britain's enduring resistance

- The invasion of Russia and Napoleon's decline

- The reestablishment of a European order at the Congress of Vienna

- Romanticism and the reaction to the Enlightenment

- Islam and Romanticism

 Defense

 Prosecution

BY THE LATE 1790s, the French people, especially property owners, who now included the peasants, longed for stability. The Directory was not providing it. Only the army was able to take charge of the nation as a symbol of both order and the popular values of the revolution. The most politically astute general was Napoleon Bonaparte, who had been a radical during the early revolution, a victorious commander in Italy, and a supporter of the repression of revolutionary disturbances after Thermidor. *strong beliefs / break rules*

Once in power, Napoleon consolidated many of the achievements of the revolution. He also repudiated much of it by establishing an empire. Thereafter, his ambitions drew France into wars of conquest and liberation across the Continent. For over a decade, Europe was at war, with only brief periods of armed truce. Through his conquests Napoleon spread many of the ideas and institutions of the revolution and overturned much of the old political and social order. He also provoked popular nationalism in opposition to French domination. This new force and the great alliances that opposed France eventually defeated Napoleon.

Throughout these Napoleonic years, new ideas and sensibilities, known by the term *Romanticism*, grew across Europe. Many of the ideas had originated in the eighteenth century, but they flourished in the turmoil of the French Revolution and the Napoleonic Wars. The revolution spurred the imagination of poets, painters, and philosophers. Some Romantic ideas, such as nationalism, supported the revolution; others, such as the emphasis on history and religion, opposed its values.

▼ The Rise of Napoleon Bonaparte

The chief threat to the Directory came from royalists, who hoped to restore the Bourbon monarchy by legal means. Many of the *émigrés* had returned to France. Their plans for a restoration drew support from devout Catholics and from those citizens disgusted by the excesses of the revolution. Monarchy promised stability. The spring elections of 1797 replaced most incumbents with constitutional monarchists and their sympathizers, thus giving them a majority in the national legislature.

To preserve the republic and prevent a peaceful restoration of the Bourbons, the antimonarchist Directory staged a *coup d'état* on 18 Fructidor (September 4, 1797). They put their own supporters into the legislative seats their opponents had won. They then imposed censorship and exiled some of their enemies. At the request of the Directors, Napoleon Bonaparte, the general in charge of the French invasion of Italy, had sent a subordinate to Paris to guarantee the success of the coup. In 1797, as in 1795, the army and Bonaparte had saved the day for the government installed in the wake of the Thermidorian Reaction.

Napoleon Bonaparte was born in 1769 to a poor family of lesser nobles at Ajaccio, on the Mediterranean island of Corsica. Because France had annexed Corsica in 1768, he went to French schools and, in 1785, obtained a commission as a French artillery officer. He favored the revolution and was a fiery Jacobin. In 1793, he played a leading role in recovering the port of Toulon from the British. As a reward for his service, he was appointed a brigadier general. During the Thermidorian Reaction, his defense of the new regime on 13 Vendémiaire won him a command in Italy.

Jacobins - radical & formed wake of revolution, lead Reign of Terror

Early Military Victories *3rd Estate*

By 1795, French arms and diplomacy had shattered the enemy coalition, but France's annexation of Belgium guaranteed continued fighting with Britain and Austria. The invasion of Italy aimed to deprive Austria of its rich northern Italian province of Lombardy. In a series of lightning victories, Bonaparte crushed the Austrian and Sardinian armies. On his own initiative, and against the wishes of the government in Paris, he concluded the Treaty of Campo Formio in October 1797. The treaty took Austria out of the war and crowned Napoleon's campaign with success. Before long, France dominated all of Italy and Switzerland.

In November 1797, the triumphant Bonaparte returned to Paris as a hero and to confront France's only remaining enemy, Britain. He judged it impossible to cross the Channel and invade England at that time. Instead, he chose to attack British interests through the eastern Mediterranean by capturing Egypt from the Ottoman Empire. By this strategy, he hoped to drive the British fleet from the Mediterranean, cut off British communications with India, damage British trade, and threaten the British Empire.

Napoleon easily overran Egypt, but the invasion was a failure. Admiral Horatio Nelson (1758–1805) destroyed the French fleet at Abukir on August 1, 1798. The French army was cut off from France. To make matters worse, the situation in Europe was deteriorating. The invasion of Egypt had alarmed Russia, which had its own ambitions in the Near East. The Russians, the Austrians, and the Ottomans joined Britain to form the Second Coalition against France. In 1799, the Russian and Austrian armies defeated the French in Italy and Switzerland and threatened to invade France.

Napoleon's venture into Egypt in 1798 and 1799 marked the first major Western European assault on the Ottoman Empire. It occurred less than a quarter century after Russia, under Catherine the Great, had taken control of the Crimea in the Treaty of Kuchuk-Kainardji. (See Chapter 17.) Significantly, British, not Ottoman forces, drove the French out of Egypt. As shall be seen in Chapter 22, after Napoleon's invasion, the Ottoman Empire realized that it had to reform itself if it was to resist other European encroachments.

The Constitution of the Year VIII

Economic troubles and the dangerous international situation eroded the Directory's fragile support. One of the Directors, the Abbé Siéyès (1748–1836), proposed a new constitution. The author of the pamphlet *What Is the Third Estate?* (1789) now wanted an executive body independent of the whims of electoral politics, a government based on the principle of "confidence from below, power from above." The change would require another *coup d'état* with military support. News of France's misfortunes had reached Napoleon in Egypt. Without orders and leaving his army behind, he returned to France in October 1799 to popular acclaim. Soon he joined Siéyès. On 19 Brumaire (November 10, 1799), his troops ensured the success of the coup.

Siéyès appears to have thought that Napoleon could be used and then dismissed, but he misjudged his man. The proposed constitution divided executive authority among three consuls. Bonaparte quickly pushed Siéyès aside, and in December 1799, he issued the Constitution of the Year VIII. Behind a screen of universal male suffrage that suggested democratic principles, a complicated system of checks and balances that appealed to republican theory, and a Council of State that evoked memories of Louis XIV, the new constitution established the rule of one man—the First Consul, Bonaparte. To find an appropriate historical analogy, we must go back to Caesar and Augustus in ancient Rome, and to the Greek tyrants of the sixth century B.C.E. The career of Bonaparte, however, pointed forward to the dictators of the twentieth century. He was the first modern political figure to use the rhetoric of revolution and nationalism, to back it with military force, and to combine these elements into a mighty weapon of imperial expansion in the service of his own power.

▼ The Consulate in France (1799–1804)

The **Consulate** in effect ended the revolution in France. The leading elements of the Third Estate—that is, officials, landowners, doctors, lawyers, and financiers—had achieved most of their goals by 1799. They had abolished hereditary privilege, and the careers thus opened to talent allowed them to achieve wealth, status, and security for their property. The peasants were also satisfied. They had gained the land they had always wanted and had destroyed oppressive feudal privileges. The newly established dominant classes had little or no desire to share their new privileges with the lower social orders. Bonaparte seemed just the person to give them security. When he submitted his constitution to the voters in a plebiscite, they overwhelmingly approved it.

Suppressing Foreign Enemies and Domestic Opposition

Throughout much of the 1790s, the pressures of warfare, particularly conscription, had accounted for much French internal instability. Bonaparte justified the public's confidence in himself by making peace with France's enemies. Russia had already left the Second Coalition. A campaign in Italy brought another victory over Austria at Marengo in 1800. The Treaty of Lunéville early in 1801 took Austria out of the war. Britain was now alone and, in 1802, concluded the Treaty of Amiens, which brought peace to Europe.

Bonaparte also restored peace and order at home. He used generosity, flattery, and bribery to win over enemies. He issued a general amnesty and employed men from all political factions. He required only that they be loyal to him. Men who had been radicals during the Reign of Terror, or who had fled the Terror and favored constitutional monarchy, or who had been high officials under Louis XVI occupied some of the highest offices.

Bonaparte, however, ruthlessly suppressed opposition. He established a highly centralized administration in which prefects responsible to the government in Paris managed all departments. He employed secret police. He stamped out the royalist rebellion in the west and made the rule of Paris effective in Brittany and the Vendée for the first time in years.

Napoleon also used and invented opportunities to destroy his enemies. A plot on his life in 1804 provided an excuse to attack the Jacobins, though it was the work of the royalists. Also in 1804, he violated the sovereignty of the German state of Baden to seize and execute the Bourbon duke of Enghien (1772–1804). The duke was accused of participation in a royalist plot, though Bonaparte knew him to be innocent. The action was a flagrant violation of international law and of due process. Charles Maurice de Talleyrand-Périgord (1754–1838), Bonaparte's foreign minister, later termed the act "worse than a crime—a blunder" because it provoked foreign opposition. It was popular with the former Jacobins, however, for it seemed to preclude the possibility of a Bourbon restoration. The executioner of a Bourbon was not likely to restore the royal family. The execution also seems to have put an end to royalist plots.

Concordat with the Roman Catholic Church

No single set of revolutionary policies had aroused as much domestic opposition as those regarding the French Catholic Church; nor were there any other policies to which fierce supporters of the revolution seemed so attached. When the French armies had invaded Italy, they had driven Pope Pius VI (r. 1775–1799) from Rome, and he eventually died in exile in France. In 1801, to the shock and dismay of his anticlerical supporters, Napoleon concluded a concordat with Pope Pius VII (r. 1800–1823). The agreement was possible because Pius VII, before becoming pope, had written that Christianity was compatible with the ideals of equality and democracy. The concordat gave Napoleon what he most wanted. The agreement required both the refractory clergy and those who had accepted the revolution to resign. Their replacements received their spiritual investiture from the pope, but the state named the bishops and paid their salaries and the salary of one priest in each parish. In return, the church gave up its claims to its confiscated property.

The concordat declared, "Catholicism is the religion of the great majority of French citizens." This was merely a statement of fact and fell far short of what the pope had wanted: religious dominance for the Roman Catholic Church. The clergy had to swear an oath of loyalty to the state. The Organic Articles of 1802, which the government issued on its own authority without consulting the pope, established the supremacy of state over church. Similar laws were applied to the Protestant and Jewish communities, reducing still further the privileged position of the Catholic Church.

The Napoleonic Code

In 1802, a plebiscite ratified Napoleon as consul for life, and he soon produced another constitution that granted him what amounted to full power. He thereafter set about reforming and codifying French law. The result was the Civil Code of 1804, usually known as the Napoleonic Code.

The Napoleonic Code safeguarded all forms of property and tried to secure French society against internal challenges. All the privileges based on birth that the revolution had overthrown remained abolished.

The conservative attitudes toward labor and women that had emerged during the revolution also received full support. Workers' organizations remained forbidden, and workers had fewer rights than their employers. Fathers were granted extensive control over their children and husbands over their wives. However, primogeniture—the right of an eldest son to inherit most or all of his parents' property—remained abolished, and property was distributed among all children, males and females, but married women needed their husbands' consent to dispose of their own property. Divorce remained more difficult for women than for men. Before this code, French law had differed from region to region. That confused set of laws had given women opportunities to protect their interests. The universality of the Napoleonic Code ended that.

Establishing a Dynasty

In 1804, Bonaparte seized on a bomb attack on his life to make himself emperor. He argued that establishing a dynasty would make the new regime secure and make further attempts on his life useless. Another new constitution declared Napoleon Bonaparte Emperor of the French, instead of First Consul of the Republic. A plebiscite also overwhelmingly ratified this constitution.

To conclude the drama, Napoleon invited Pope Pius VII to Notre Dame to take part in the coronation. At the last minute, however, the pope agreed that Napoleon should crown himself. The emperor would not allow anyone to think his power and authority depended on the church. Henceforth, he was called Napoleon I.

▼ Napoleon's Empire (1804–1814)

Between his coronation as emperor and his final defeat at Waterloo (1815), Napoleon conquered most of Europe. France's victories changed the map of the Continent. The wars put an end to the Old Regime and its feudal trappings throughout Western Europe and forced the eastern European states to reorganize themselves to resist Napoleon's armies.

Everywhere, Napoleon's advance unleashed the powerful force of nationalism, discussed more fully in Chapter 20. His weapon was the militarily mobilized French nation, one of the achievements of the revolution. Napoleon could put 700,000 men under arms at one time, risk 100,000 troops in a single battle, endure heavy losses, and fight again. He could conscript citizen soldiers in unprecedented numbers, thanks to their loyalty to the nation and to him. No single enemy could match such resources. Even coalitions were unsuccessful, until Napoleon's mistakes led to his own defeat.

Conquering an Empire

The Peace of Amiens (1802) between France and Great Britain was merely a truce. Napoleon's unlimited ambitions shattered any hope that it might last. He sent an army to restore the rebellious colony of Haiti to French rule. This move aroused British fears that he was planning a new French empire in America, because Spain had restored Louisiana to France in 1801. More serious were his interventions in the Dutch Republic, Italy, and Switzerland and his reorganization of Germany. The Treaty of Campo Formio had required a redistribution of territories along the Rhine River, and the petty princes of the region engaged in a scramble to enlarge their holdings. Among the results were the reduction of Austrian influence and the emergence of fewer, but larger, German states in the West, all dependent on Napoleon.

British Naval Supremacy   Alarmed by these developments, the British issued an ultimatum. When Napoleon ignored it, Britain declared war in May 1803. William Pitt the Younger returned to office as prime minister in 1804 and began to construct the Third Coalition. By August 1805, he had persuaded Russia

A Closer ▷LOOK

THE CORONATION OF NAPOLEON

JACQUES-LOUIS DAVID recorded the elaborate coronation of Napoleon in a monumental painting that revealed the enormous political and religious tensions of that event, which involved the kind of ritual and ceremony associated with the monarchy of the ancient regime.

Napoleon's mother sits in a balcony-like setting and presides over her son's establishment of a new reigning dynasty in France and across Europe, through the placement of relatives on various thrones.

Napoleon is about to place a crown on the head of his wife Josephine whom he will later divorce because she and he were unable to conceive an heir for his new dynasty. He would then marry the daughter of the Habsburg emperor.

Jacques-Louis David (1748–1825), *Consecration of the Emperor Napoleon I and Coronation of Empress Josephine*, 1806–07. Louvre, Paris. Bridgeman—Giraudon/Art Resource, NY

To examine this image in an interactive fashion, please go to www.myhistorylab.com

myhistorylab

To the right sits Pope Pius VII who observes the event but is not a real participant. Napoleon and the pope had signed a Concordat that restored much of the standing but by no means all of the prerevolutionary authority of the Roman Catholic Church in France. The pope understood that at that moment in France as well as throughout Europe his authority was largely subject to the wishes of the French emperor.

In this early-nineteenth-century cartoon, England, personified by a caricature of William Pitt, and France, personified by a caricature of Napoleon, are carving out their areas of interest around the globe. *Bildarchiv Preussischer Kulturbesitz*

and Austria to move once more against France. A great naval victory soon raised the fortunes of the allies. On October 21, 1805, the British admiral Lord Nelson destroyed the combined French and Spanish fleets at the Battle of Trafalgar off the Spanish coast. Nelson died in the battle, but the British lost no ships. Trafalgar ended all French hope of invading Britain and guaranteed British control of the seas for the rest of the war. (See "Encountering the Past: Sailors and Canned Food.")

Napoleonic Victories in Central Europe On land the story was different. Even before Trafalgar, Napoleon had marched to the Danube River to attack his continental enemies. In mid-October he forced an Austrian army to surrender at Ulm and occupied Vienna. On December 2, 1805, in perhaps his greatest victory, Napoleon defeated the combined Austrian and Russian forces at Austerlitz. The Treaty of Pressburg that followed won major concessions from Austria. The Austrians withdrew from Italy and left Napoleon in control of everything north of Rome. He was recognized as king of Italy.

Napoleon also made extensive political changes in Germany. In July 1806, he organized the Confederation of the Rhine, which included most of the western German princes. Their withdrawal from the Holy Roman Empire led Francis II to dissolve that ancient political body and henceforth to call himself Emperor Francis I of Austria.

Prussia, which had remained neutral up to this point, now foolishly went to war against France. Napoleon's forces quickly crushed the famous Prussian army at Jena and Auerstädt on October 14, 1806. Two weeks later, Napoleon was in Berlin. There, on November 21, he issued the Berlin Decrees, forbidding his allies from importing British goods. On June 13, 1807, Napoleon defeated the Russians at Friedland and occu-

pied East Prussia. The French emperor was master of all Germany.

Treaty of Tilsit Unable to fight another battle and unwilling to retreat into Russia, Tsar Alexander I (r. 1801–1825) was ready to make peace. He and Napoleon met on a raft in the Niemen River while the two armies and the nervous king of Prussia watched from the bank. On July 7, 1807, they signed the Treaty of Tilsit, which confirmed France's gains. Prussia lost half its territory. Only the support of Alexander saved it from extinction. Prussia openly and Russia secretly became allies of Napoleon.

Napoleon organized conquered Europe much like the estate of a Corsican family. The great French Empire was ruled directly by the head of the clan, Napoleon. On its borders lay satellite states ruled by members of his family. His stepson ruled Italy for him, and three of his brothers and his brother-in-law were made kings of other conquered states. Napoleon denied a kingdom only to his brother Lucien, of whose wife he disapproved. The French emperor expected his relatives to take orders without question. When they failed to do so, he rebuked and even punished them. This establishment of the Napoleonic family as the collective sovereigns of Europe provoked political opposition that needed only encouragement and assistance to flare up into serious resistance.

The Continental System

After the Treaty of Tilsit, such assistance could come only from Britain, and Napoleon knew he must defeat the British before he could feel safe. Unable to compete with the British navy, he continued the economic warfare the Berlin Decrees had begun. He planned to cut off all British trade with the European continent and thus to cripple British commercial and financial power. He hoped to cause domestic unrest and drive Britain from the war. The Milan Decree of 1807 went further and attempted to stop neutral nations from trading with Britain. (See Map 19–1, page 588.)

Despite initial drops in exports and domestic unrest, the British economy survived. British control of the seas assured access to the growing markets of North and South America and of the eastern Mediterranean. At the same time, the Continental System badly hurt the European economies. Napoleon rejected advice to turn his empire into a free-trade area. Such a policy would have been both popular and helpful. Instead, his tariff policies favored France, increased the resentment of foreign merchants, and made them less willing to enforce the system and more ready to engage in smuggling. It was, in part, to prevent smuggling that Napoleon invaded Spain in 1808. The resulting peninsular campaign in Spain and Portugal helped bring on his ruin.

SAILORS AND CANNED FOOD

IN 1803, DURING the Napoleonic wars, the French navy undertook a secret experiment—provisioning a few of its naval vessels involved in long overseas voyages or blockades with food preserved by the then novel process of canning. The results were excellent: The crews thrived and the French government ordered more canned goods.

Until the discovery of canning, the chief methods for preserving food were drying, salting, pickling, smoking, fermenting, and condensing. Most of these techniques are still used, but they strongly alter the taste of food and destroy some of its nutritive value. Although vitamins were unknown in the eighteenth century, military authorities did know that something in fresh fruit and vegetables kept their men healthy. In the 1790s, the French government offered a reward to anyone who could invent a method of preserving food that would make it both nearer in taste and texture to fresh products and more nourishing for sailors and soldiers who often suffered from scurvy and malnutrition from their rations of dried bread and salted meat. The desired food would allow naval vessels to stay at sea longer without having to put into port for fresh food and armies to campaign without having to live off the land.

Nicholas Appert, a French chef, was determined to produce preserved food that would be both tasty and healthful. In 1795, he established what amounted to a small food preservation laboratory on the outskirts of Paris. He eventually discovered that if he filled glass jars with fresh vegetables, fruit, soups, or meat, added water or a sauce, sealed the jars with tight stoppers, and then cooked them in a hot water bath, the result was a tasty preserved food that lasted indefinitely as long as the jars remained sealed. Although Appert did not know it, one reason the food remained unspoiled was that his process killed any microbes in it.

Although many fine French foods are still canned in jars, the process quickly took a new turn in Great Britain where the navy as well as food producers were interested in it. Appert published a book on his method in 1810, and by 1813 an English company began canning in tins, which were less expensive and more durable than glass jars. Soon other canning companies appeared in Europe, including those that produced canned sardines. By mid-century, millions of people, particularly in Western Europe and North America, were eating canned food. By 1900, canned goods had become what they remain today—part of everyday life around the world. The basic process used in canning is still the one Appert devised in the 1790s.

Source: Sue Shephard, *Pickled, Potted, and Canned: How the Art and Science of Food Processing Changed the World* (New York: Simon & Schuster, 2000).

What advantages did canning have over other methods of preserving food?

Why was the military interested in it?

How did canning become a part of everyday life?

Nicholas Appert (1749–1841) invented canning as a way of preserving food nutritiously. Canned food could be transported over long distances without spoiling.
Private Collection/Bridgeman Art Library

Map 19–1 **THE CONTINENTAL SYSTEM, 1806–1810** Napoleon hoped to cut off all British trade with the European continent and thereby drive the British from the war.

▼ European Response to the Empire

Wherever Napoleon ruled, he imposed the Napoleonic Code and abolished hereditary social distinctions. Feudal privileges disappeared, and the peasants were freed from serfdom and manorial dues. In the towns, the guilds and the local oligarchies that had been dominant for centuries were dissolved or deprived of their power. The established churches lost their traditional independence and were made subordinate to the state. Toleration replaced monopoly of religion by an established church. Despite these reforms, however, it was always clear that Napoleon's policies were intended first for his own glory and that of France. The Continental System demonstrated that Napoleon's rule was intended to enrich France, rather than Europe generally. Consequently, before long, the conquered states and peoples grew restive. (See "Napoleon Advises His Brother to Rule Constitutionally.")

German Nationalism and Prussian Reform

The German response to Napoleon's success was particularly interesting and important. There had never been a unified German state. The great German writers of the Enlightenment, such as Immanuel Kant and Gotthold Lessing, were neither deeply politically engaged nor nationalistic.

At the beginning of the nineteenth century, the Romantic Movement had begun to take hold. One of its basic features in Germany was the emergence of nationalism, which went through two distinct stages there. Initially, nationalistic writers emphasized the unique and admirable qualities of German culture, which, they argued, arose from the history of the German people. Such cultural nationalism prevailed until Napoleon's humiliation of Prussia at Jena in 1806.

At that point many German intellectuals began to urge resistance to Napoleon on the basis of German nationalism. The French conquest endangered the independence and achievements of all German-speaking people. Many nationalists also criticized the German

NAPOLEON ADVISES HIS BROTHER TO RULE CONSTITUTIONALLY

As Napoleon swept through Europe, he set his relatives on the thrones of various conquered kingdoms and then imposed written constitutions on them. In this letter of November 1807, Napoleon sent his brother Jerome (1784–1860) a constitution for the Kingdom of Westphalia in Germany. The letter shows how Napoleon spread the political ideas and institutions of the French Revolution across Europe. Napoleon ignored, however, the nationalistic resentment that French conquest aroused, even when that conquest brought more liberal political institutions. Such nationalism would contribute to his downfall.

What benefits does Napoleon believe his conquest and subsequent rule by his brother will bring to their new subjects? Why does he believe that these, rather than military victory, will achieve new loyalty? How does Napoleon suggest playing off the resentment of the upper classes to consolidate power? What is the relationship between having a written constitution such as Napoleon is sending his brother and the power of public opinion that he mentions toward the close of the letter?

I enclose the constitution for your Kingdom. You must faithfully observe it. I am concerned for the happiness of your subjects, not only as it affects your reputation, and my own, but also for its influence on the whole European situation.

Don't listen to those who say that your subjects are so accustomed to slavery that they will feel no gratitude for the benefits you give them. There is more intelligence in the Kingdom of Westphalia than they would have you believe; and your throne will never be firmly established except upon the trust and affection of the common people. What German opinion impatiently demands is that men of no rank, but of marked ability, shall have an equal claim upon your favour and your employment, and that every trace of serfdom, or of a feudal hierarchy between the sovereign and the lowest class of his subjects shall be done away with. The benefits of the Code Napoleon, public trial, and the introduction of juries, will be the leading features of your Government. And to tell you the truth, I count more upon their effects, for the extension and consolidation of your rule, than upon the most resounding victories. I want your subjects to enjoy a degree of liberty, equality, and prosperity hitherto unknown to the German people. . . . Such a method of government will be a stronger barrier between you and Prussia than the Elbe, the fortresses, and the protection of France. What people will want to return under the arbitrary Prussian rule, once it has tasted the benefits of a wise and liberal administration? In Germany, as in France, Italy, and Spain, people long for equality and liberalism. I have been managing the affairs of Europe long enough now to know that the burden of the privileged classes was resented everywhere. Rule constitutionally. Even if reason, and the enlightenment of the age, were not sufficient cause, it would be good policy for one in your position; and you will find that the backing of public opinion gives you a great natural advantage over the absolute kings who are your neighbors.

From J. M. Thompson, ed., *Napoleon's Letters* (London: Dent, 1954), pp. 190–191, as quoted in Maurice Hutt, ed., *Napoleon* (Englewood Cliffs, NJ: Prentice Hall, 1972), p. 34.

princes, who ruled selfishly and inefficiently and who seemed ever ready to lick Napoleon's boots. Only a people united through its language and culture could resist the French onslaught. No less important in forging a German national sentiment was the example of France itself, which had attained greatness by enlisting the active support of the entire people in the patriotic cause. Henceforth, many Germans sought to solve their internal political problems by attempting to establish a unified German state, reformed to harness the energies of the entire people.

After Tilsit, only Prussia could arouse such patriotic feelings. Elsewhere German rulers were either under Napoleon's thumb or collaborating with him. Defeated, humiliated, and diminished, Prussia continued to resist, however feebly. To Prussia fled German nationalists from other states, calling for reforms and unification that King Frederick William III (r. 1797–1840) and the Junker nobility in fact feared and hated. Reforms came about despite such opposition because the defeat at Jena had shown that the Prussian state had to change to survive.

The Prussian administrative and social reforms were the work of Baron vom Stein (1757–1831) and Prince von Hardenberg (1750–1822). Neither of these reformers intended to reduce the autocratic power of the Prussian monarch or to end the dominance of the Junkers, who formed the bulwark of the state and of the officer corps. Rather, they wanted to fight French power with their own version of the French weapons. As Hardenberg declared,

Our objective, our guiding principle, must be a revolution in the better sense, a revolution leading directly to the great goal, the elevation of humanity through the wisdom of those in authority . . . Democratic rules of conduct in a monarchical administration, such is the formula . . . which will conform most comfortably with the spirit of the age.[1]

Although the reforms came from the top, they wrought important changes in Prussian society.

Stein's reforms broke the Junker monopoly of landholding. Serfdom was abolished. However, unlike in the western German states where all remnants of serfdom simply disappeared, in Prussia the Junkers ensured that vestiges of the system survived. Former Prussian serfs were free to leave the land if they chose, but those who stayed had to continue to perform manorial labor. They could obtain the ownership of the land they worked only if they forfeited a third of it to the lord. The result was that Junker holdings grew larger. Some peasants went to the cities to find work, others became agricultural laborers, and some did actually become small freeholding farmers. In Prussia and elsewhere, serfdom had ended, but the rise in the numbers of landless laborers created new social problems.

Military reforms sought to increase the supply of soldiers and to improve their quality. Jena had shown that an army of free patriots commanded by officers chosen on merit rather than by birth could defeat an army of serfs and mercenaries commanded by incompetent nobles. To remedy the situation, the Prussian reformers abolished inhumane military punishments, sought to inspire patriotic feelings in the soldiers,

opened the officer corps to commoners, gave promotions on the basis of merit, and organized war colleges that developed new theories of strategy and tactics.

These reforms soon enabled Prussia to regain its former power. Because Napoleon strictly limited the size of its army to 42,000 men, however, Prussia could not introduce universal conscription until it broke with Napoleon in 1813. Before that date, the Prussians evaded the limit by training one group each year, putting them into the reserves, and then training a new group the same size. Prussia could thus boast an army of 270,000 by 1814.

The Wars of Liberation

Spain   In Spain more than elsewhere in Europe, national resistance to France had deep social roots. Spain had achieved political unity as early as the sixteenth century. The Spanish peasants were devoted to the ruling dynasty and especially to the Roman Catholic Church. France and Spain had been allies since 1796. In 1807, however, a French army came into the Iberian Peninsula to force Portugal to abandon its traditional alliance with Britain. The army stayed in Spain to protect lines of supply and communication. Napoleon used a revolt that broke out in Madrid in 1808 as a pretext to depose the Spanish Bourbons and to place his brother Joseph (1768–1844) on the Spanish throne. Attacks on the privileges of the church increased public outrage. Many members of the upper classes were prepared to collaborate with Napoleon, but the peasants, urged on by the lower clergy and the monks, rebelled.

In Spain, Napoleon faced a new kind of warfare. Guerrilla bands cut lines of communication, killed stragglers, destroyed isolated units, and then disappeared into the mountains. The British landed an army under Sir Arthur Wellesley (1769–1852), later the duke of Wellington, to support the Spanish insurgents. Thus began the long peninsular campaign that would drain French strength from elsewhere in Europe and hasten Napoleon's eventual defeat. (See "Compare & Connect: The Experience of War in the Napoleonic Age," pages 592–593.)

Austria   The French troubles in Spain encouraged the Austrians to renew the war in 1809. Since their defeat at Austerlitz, they had sought a war of revenge. The Austrians counted on Napoleon's distraction in Spain, French war weariness, and aid from other German princes. Napoleon was fully in command in France, however, and the German princes did not move. The French army marched swiftly into Austria and won the Battle of Wagram. The resulting Peace of Schönbrunn deprived Austria of much territory and 3.5 million subjects.

[1]Quoted in Geoffrey Brunn, *Europe and the French Imperium* (New York: Harper & Row, 1938), p. 174.

Another spoil of victory was the Austrian archduchess Marie Louise (1791–1847), daughter of Emperor Francis I. Napoleon's wife, Josephine de Beauharnais (1763–1814), was forty-six and had borne him no children. His dynastic ambitions, as well as the desire for a royal marriage, led him to divorce Josephine and marry the eighteen-year-old Marie Louise. Napoleon had also considered marrying the sister of Tsar Alexander, but had received a polite rebuff.

The Invasion of Russia

The failure of Napoleon's marriage negotiations with Russia emphasized the shakiness of the Franco-Russian alliance concluded at Tilsit. Russian nobles disliked the alliance because of the liberal politics of France and because the Continental System prohibited timber sales to Britain. Only French aid in gaining Constantinople could justify the alliance in their eyes, but Napoleon gave them no help against the Ottoman Empire. The organization of the Polish Duchy of Warsaw as a Napoleonic satellite on the Russian doorstep and its enlargement with Austrian territory in 1809 after the Battle of Wagram angered Alexander. Napoleon's annexation of Holland in violation of the Treaty of Tilsit, his recognition of the French marshal Bernadotte (1763–1844) as the future King Charles XIV of Sweden, and his marriage to Marie Louise further disturbed the tsar. At the end of 1810, Russia withdrew from the Continental System and began to prepare for war. (See Map 19–2.)

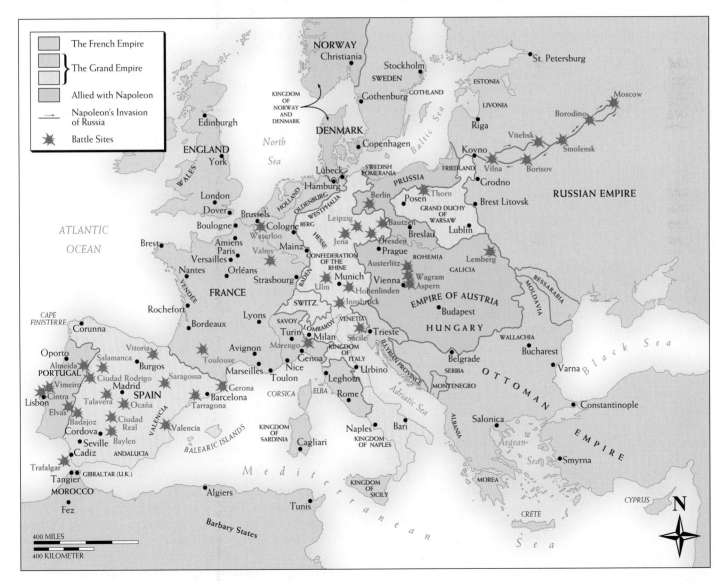

Map 19–2 NAPOLEONIC EUROPE IN LATE 1812   By mid-1812 the areas shown in peach were incorporated into France, and most of the rest of Europe was directly controlled by or allied with Napoleon. But Russia had withdrawn from the failing Continental System, and the decline of Napoleon was about to begin.

COMPARE AND CONNECT

The Experience of War in the Napoleonic Age

THE NAPOLEONIC WARS spread violence across Europe. Different participants, writers, and artists portrayed the experience of war differently. William Napier reported his own heroism in a quite matter-of-fact manner. The German poet and historian Ernest Moritz Arndt recalled moments of intense nationalistic patriotism. The Spanish painter Goya portrayed a moment of enormous brutality suffered by the Spanish at the hands of French troops.

QUESTIONS

1. What were Napier's expectations of his men? Of his officers? Of himself?
2. Why does Arndt claim each of these various groups wanted war?
3. How does Arndt suggest the possibility of a united nation that did not yet actually exist?
4. How does Goya portray Spaniards as victims of harsh, unmerciful military violence?
5. How do Napier's memoir, Arndt's call to arms, and Goya's painting illustrate different points of view and ways of interpreting the violence of modern warfare?

I. A Commander Recalls an Incident in Spain

William Napier, a British officer during the Napoleonic Wars and later a distinguished leader in the British army, describes his experiences in a battle that took place in Spain during 1811.

I arrived [with two companies] just in time to save Captain Dobbs, 52nd, and two men who were cut off from their regiment. The French were gathering fast about us, we could scarcely retreat, and Dobbs agreed with me that boldness would be our best chance; so we called upon the men to follow, and, jumping over a wall which had given us cover, charged the enemy with a shout which sent the nearest back. . . .

Only the two men of the 52nd followed us, and we four arrived unsupported at a second wall, close to a considerable body of French, who rallied and began to close upon us. Their fire was very violent, but the wall gave cover. I was, however, stung by the backwardness of my men, and told Dobbs I would save him or lose my life by bringing up the two companies; he entreated me not, saying I could not make two paces from the wall and live. Yet I did go back to the first wall, escaped the fire, and, reproaching the men gave them the word again, and returned to Dobbs, who was now upon the point of being taken; but again I returned alone! The sol-

diers had indeed crossed the wall in their front, but kept edging away to the right to avoid the heavy fire. Being now maddened by this second failure, I made another attempt, but I had not made ten paces when a shot struck my spine, and the enemy very ungenerously continued to fire at me when I was down. I escaped death by dragging myself by my hands—for my lower extremities were paralyzed—towards a small heap of stones which was in the midst of the field, and thus covering my head and shoulders. . . . However, Captain Lloyd and my company, and some of the 52nd, came up at that moment, and the French were driven away.

Source: Quoted in H. A. Bruce, *Life of Sir William Napier* (London: John Murray, 1864), 1, pp. 55–57.

II. A German Writer Describes the War of Liberation

The German resistance to Napoleon as his army retreated from Moscow in 1813 was the first time in modern German history that people from virtually all German-speaking lands cooperated together. Ernest Moritz Arndt (1769–1860) described the excitement of that moment in a passage frequently reprinted in German history textbooks for more than a century.

Fired with enthusiasm, the people rose, "with God for King and Fatherland." Among the Prussians there was only one voice, one feeling, one anger and one love, to save the Fatherland and to free Germany. . . . War, war, sounded the cry from the Carpathians to the Baltic, from the Niemen to the Elbe. War! cried the nobleman and landed proprietor who had become impoverished. War! that peasant who was driving his last horse to death. . . . War! the citizen who was growing exhausted from quartering soldiers and paying taxes. War! the widow who was sending her only son to the front. War! the young girl who, with tears of pride and pain, was leaving her betrothed. . . . Even young women, under all sorts of disguises, rushed to arms; all wanted to drill, arm themselves and fight and die for the Fatherland. . . .

The most beautiful thing about all this holy zeal and happy confusion was . . . that the one great feeling for the Fatherland, its freedom and honor, swallowed all other feelings, caused all other considerations and relationships to be forgotten.

Source: Louis L., Snyder, trans., *Documents of German History*. Copyright © 1958 by Rutgers, the State University. Reprinted by permission of Rutgers University Press.

III. Francisco Goya, *The Third of May, 1808* (painted 1814–1815)

Napoleon had begun to send troops into Spain in 1807 after the king of Spain had agreed to aid France against Portugal, which was assisting Britain. By early 1808 Spain had essentially become an occupied nation. On May 2, riots took place in Madrid between French troops, many of whom were Islamic soldiers whom Napoleon had recruited in Egypt, and Spanish civilians. In response to that resistance the French general Murat ordered the execution of numerous citizens of Madrid, which occurred the night of May 2 and 3. The events of these two days marked the opening of the Spanish effort to rid their peninsula of French rule.

After the restoration of the Spanish monarchy, Francisco Goya (1745–1828) depicted the savagery of those executions in the most memorable war painting of the Napoleonic era, The Third of May, 1808. *There is one group of humble Spaniards who have already been shot, another in the process of execution, and a third group, some of whom are hiding their eyes, who will be the next victims.*

The painting illustrates two forces of Napoleonic warfare confronting each other: the professional solider and the guerilla (a term coined during the Spanish resistance of this era). The guerilla must fight with what few resources he finds at his command and with few advanced weapons. By contrast, in this painting the well-disciplined soldiers, equipped with modern rifles, carry out the execution by the light of large technologically advanced lanterns fueled by either gas or oil with which Napoleon equipped his troops. Goya succeeds in making ordinary people and very poor clergy not only the victims, but also symbolic heroes of the national war of liberation.

Goya y Lucientes, Francisco de Goya, recorded Napoleon's troops executing Spanish guerilla fighters who had rebelled against the French occupation in *The Third of May, 1808.* Francisco de Goya, *Los fusilamientos del 3 de Mayo, 1808*. 1814. Oil on canvas, 8'60" × 11'40". © Museo Nacional del Prado, Madrid

Napoleon was determined to end the Russian military threat. He amassed an army of more than 600,000 men, including a core of Frenchmen and more than 400,000 other soldiers drawn from the rest of his empire. He intended the usual short campaign crowned by a decisive battle, but the Russians retreated before his advance. His vast superiority in numbers—the Russians had only about 160,000 troops—made it foolish for them to risk a battle. Instead they followed a "scorched-earth" policy, destroying all food and supplies as they retreated. The so-called Grand Army of Napoleon could not live off the country, and the expanse of Russia made supply lines too long to maintain. Terrible rains, fierce heat, shortages of food and water, and the courage of the Russian rear guard eroded the morale of Napoleon's army. Napoleon's advisers urged him to abandon the venture, but he feared an unsuccessful campaign would undermine his position in the empire and in France. He pinned his faith on the Russians' unwillingness to abandon Moscow without a fight.

In September 1812, Russian public opinion forced the army to give Napoleon the battle he wanted despite the canny Russian general Mikhail Kutuzov's (1745–1813) wish to let the Russian winter defeat the invader. At Borodino, not far west of Moscow, the bloodiest battle of the Napoleonic era cost the French 30,000 casualties and the Russians almost twice as many. Yet the Russian army was not destroyed. Napoleon won nothing substantial, and the battle was regarded as a defeat for him.

Fires set by the Russians soon engulfed Moscow and left Napoleon far from home with a badly diminished army lacking adequate supplies as winter came to a vast and unfriendly country. After capturing the burned city, Napoleon addressed several peace offers to Alexander, but the tsar ignored them. By October, what was left of the Grand Army was forced to retreat. By December, Napoleon realized the Russian fiasco would encourage plots against him at home. He returned to Paris, leaving the remnants of his army to struggle westward. Perhaps only 100,000 of the original 600,000 survived their ordeal.

European Coalition

Even as the news of the disaster reached the West, the final defeat of Napoleon was far from certain. He was able to put down his opponents in Paris and raise another 350,000 men. Neither the Prussians nor the Austrians were eager to risk another contest with Napoleon, and even the Russians hesitated. The Austrian foreign minister, Prince Klemens von Metternich (1773–1859), would have been glad to make a negotiated peace that would leave Napoleon on the throne of a shrunken and chastened France rather than see Russia dominate

Europe. Napoleon might have negotiated a reasonable settlement had he been willing to make concessions that would have split his jealous opponents. He would not consider that solution, however. As he explained to Metternich,

Your sovereigns born on the throne can let themselves be beaten twenty times and return to their capitals. I cannot do this because I am an upstart soldier. My domination will not survive the day when I cease to be strong, and therefore feared.[2]

In 1813, patriotic pressure and national ambition brought together the last and most powerful coalition against Napoleon. The Russians drove westward, and Prussia and then Austria joined them. Vast amounts of British money assisted them. From Spain, Wellington marched his army into France. Napoleon's new army was inexperienced and poorly equipped. His generals had lost confidence in him and were tired. The emperor himself was worn out and sick. Still, he waged a skillful campaign in central Europe and defeated the allies at Dresden. In October, however, the combined armies of the enemy decisively defeated him at Leipzig in what the Germans called the Battle of the Nations. In March 1814, the allied armies marched into Paris. A few days later, Napoleon abdicated and went into exile on the island of Elba, off the coast of central Italy. (See "The Experience of War in the Napoleonic Age," pages 592–593.)

▼ The Congress of Vienna and the European Settlement

Fear of Napoleon and hostility to his ambitions had held the victorious coalition together. As soon as he was removed, the allies pursued their separate ambitions. The key person in achieving eventual agreement among them was Robert Stewart, Viscount Castlereagh (1769–1822), the British foreign secretary. Even before the victorious armies had entered Paris, he brought about the signing of the Treaty of Chaumont on March 9, 1814. It provided for the restoration of the Bourbons to the French throne and the contraction of France to its frontiers of 1792. Even more importantly, Britain, Austria, Russia, and Prussia agreed to form a Quadruple Alliance for twenty years to preserve whatever settlement they agreed on. Remaining problems—and there were many—and final details were left for a conference to be held at Vienna.

[2]Quoted in Felix Markham, *Napoleon and the Awakening of Europe* (New York: Macmillan, 1965), pp. 115–116.

LE CONGRÈS.

In this political cartoon of the Congress of Vienna, Tallyrand simply watches which way the wind is blowing, Castlereagh hesitates, while the monarchs of Russia, Prussia, and Austria form the dance of the Holy Alliance. The king of Saxony holds on to his crown and the republic of Geneva pays homage to the kingdom of Sardinia.   Bildarchiv Preussischer Kulturbesitz

Territorial Adjustments

The Congress of Vienna assembled in September 1814, but did not conclude its work until November 1815. Although a glittering array of heads of state attended the gathering, the four great powers conducted the important work of the conference. The only full session of the congress met to ratify the arrangements the big four made. The easiest problem the great powers faced was France. All the victors agreed that no single state should be allowed to dominate Europe, and all were determined to prevent France from doing so again. The restoration of the French Bourbon monarchy, which was temporarily popular, and a nonvindictive boundary settlement were designed to keep France calm and satisfied.

The powers also strengthened the states around France's borders to serve as barriers to renewed French expansion. They established the kingdom of the Netherlands, which included Belgium and Luxembourg, in the north and added the important port of Genoa to strengthen Piedmont in the south. Prussia was given important new territories along the Rhine River to deter French aggression in the West. Austria gained full control of northern Italy to prevent a repetition of Napoleon's conquests there. As for the rest of Germany, most of Napoleon's territorial arrangements were left untouched. The venerable Holy Roman Empire, which had been dissolved in 1806, was not revived. (See Map 19–3.) In all these areas, the

Map 19–3 **THE GERMAN STATES AFTER 1815**   As noted, the German states were also recognized.

congress established the rule of legitimate monarchs and rejected any hint of the republican and democratic policies that had flowed from the French Revolution.

On these matters agreement was not difficult, but the settlement of eastern Europe sharply divided the victors. Alexander I of Russia wanted all of Poland under his rule. Prussia was willing to give it to him in return for all of Saxony, which had been allied with Napoleon. Austria, however, was unwilling to surrender its share of Poland or to see Prussian power grow or Russia penetrate deeper into central Europe. The Polish-Saxon question almost caused a new war among the victors, but defeated France provided a way out. The wily Talleyrand, now representing France at Vienna, suggested the weight of France added to that of Britain and Austria might bring Alexander to his senses. When news of a secret treaty among the three leaked out, the tsar agreed to become ruler of a smaller Poland, and Prussia settled for only part of Saxony. Thereafter, France was included as a fifth great power in all deliberations.

The Hundred Days and the Quadruple Alliance

Napoleon's return from Elba on March 1, 1815, further united the victors. The French army was still loyal to the former emperor, and many of the French people preferred his rule to that of the restored Bourbons. The coalition seemed to be dissolving in Vienna. Napoleon seized the opportunity, escaped to France, and soon regained power. He promised a liberal constitution and a peaceful foreign policy. The allies were not convinced. They declared Napoleon an outlaw (a new device under international law) and sent their armies to crush him. Wellington, with the crucial help of the Prussians under Field Marshal von Blücher (1742–1819), defeated Napoleon at Waterloo in Belgium on June 18, 1815. Napoleon again abdicated and was exiled on Saint Helena, a tiny Atlantic island off the coast of Africa, where he died in 1821.

The Hundred Days, as the period of Napoleon's return is called, frightened the great powers and made the peace settlement harsher for France. In addition to some minor territorial adjustments, the victors imposed a war indemnity and an army of occupation on France. Alexander proposed a Holy Alliance, whereby the monarchs promised to act together in accordance with Christian principles. Austria and Prussia signed, but Castlereagh thought it absurd, and England abstained. The tsar, who was then embracing mysticism, believed his proposal a valuable tool for international relations. The Holy Alliance soon became a symbol of extreme political reaction.

England, Austria, Prussia, and Russia renewed the Quadruple Alliance on November 20, 1815. Henceforth, it was as much a coalition for maintaining peace as for pursuing victory over France. A coalition for such a purpose had never existed in European diplomacy before. It represented an important new departure in European affairs. Unlike eighteenth-century diplomacy, certain powers were determined to prevent war. The statesmen at Vienna had seen the armies of the French Revolution and Napoleon overturning the political and social order of much of the Continent. Their nations had experienced unprecedented destruction and had had to raise enormous military forces. They knew war affected not just professional armies and navies, but entire civilian populations as well. They were determined to prevent any more such upheaval and destruction.

Consequently, the chief aims of the Congress of Vienna were to prevent a recurrence of the Napoleonic nightmare and to arrange a lasting peace. The leaders of Europe had learned that a treaty should secure not victory, but peace. The diplomats aimed to establish a framework for stability, rather than to punish France. The great powers sought to ensure that each of them would respect the Vienna settlement and not use force to change it.

The Congress of Vienna achieved its goals. France accepted the new situation without undue resentment, in part because the new international order recognized it as a great power. The victorious powers settled difficult problems reasonably. They established a new legal framework whereby treaties were made between states rather than between monarchs. The treaties remained in place when a monarch died. Furthermore, during the quarter century of warfare, European leaders had come to calculate the nature of political and economic power in new ways that went beyond the simple vision of gaining a favorable balance of trade that had caused so many eighteenth-century wars. They took into account their natural resources and economies, their systems of education, and the possibility that general growth in agriculture, commerce, and industry would benefit all states and not one at the expense of others.

The congress has been criticized for failing to recognize and provide for the great forces that would stir the nineteenth century—nationalism and democracy. Such criticism is inappropriate. At the time nationalist pressures were relatively rare; the general desire was for peace. The settlement, like all such agreements, aimed to solve past ills, and in that it succeeded. The statesmen at Vienna would have had to have a super-human ability to have anticipated future problems or to have yielded to forces of which they disapproved and that they believed threatened international peace and stability. The measure of the suc-

MAP EXPLORATION

Interactive map: To explore this map further, go to **www.myhistorylab.com**

Map 19–4   **EUROPE 1815, AFTER THE CONGRESS OF VIENNA**   The Congress of Vienna achieved the post-Napoleonic territorial adjustments shown on the map. The most notable arrangements dealt with areas along France's borders (the Netherlands, Prussia, Switzerland, and Piedmont) and in Poland and northern Italy.

cess of the Vienna settlement is that it remained essentially intact for almost half a century and prevented general war for a hundred years. (See Map 19–4.)

▼ The Romantic Movement

The years of the French Revolution and the conquests of Napoleon saw the emergence of a new and important intellectual movement throughout Europe. **Romanticism**,

in its various manifestations, was a reaction against much of the thought of the Enlightenment. Romantic writers and artists saw the imagination or some such intuitive intellectual faculty supplementing reason as a means to perceive and understand the world. Many of them urged a revival of Christianity, so that it would once again permeate Europe as it had during the Middle Ages. Unlike the philosophes, the Romantics liked the art, literature, and architecture of medieval times. They were also deeply interested in folklore, folk songs, and fairy tales. Dreams,

NAPOLEONIC EUROPE

1797	Napoleon concludes the Treaty of Campo Formio
1798	Nelson defeats the French navy in the harbor of Abukir in Egypt
1799	Consulate established in France
1801	Concordat between France and the papacy
1802	Treaty of Amiens
1803	War renewed between France and Britain
1804	Execution of Duke d'Enghien
1804	Napoleonic Civil Code issued
1804	Napoleon crowned as emperor
1805 (October 21)	Nelson defeats French and Spanish fleet at Trafalgar
1805 (December 2)	Austerlitz
1806	Jena
1806	Continental System established by Berlin Decrees
1807	Friedland
1807	Treaty of Tilsit; Russia becomes an ally of Napoleon
1808	Beginning of Spanish resistance to Napoleonic domination
1809	Wagram
1809	Napoleon marries Archduchess Marie Louise of Austria
1812	Invasion of Russia and French defeat at Borodino
1813	Leipzig (Battle of the Nations)
1814 (March)	Treaty of Chaumont establishes Quadruple Alliance
1814 (September)	Congress of Vienna convenes
1815 (March 1)	Napoleon returns from Elba
1815 (June 18)	Waterloo
1815 (September 26)	Holy Alliance formed at Congress of Vienna
1815 (November 20)	Quadruple Alliance renewed at Congress of Vienna
1821	Napoleon dies on Saint Helena

hallucinations, sleepwalking, and other phenomena that suggested the existence of a world beyond that of empirical observation, sensory data, and discursive reasoning fascinated the Romantics.

▼ Romantic Questioning of the Supremacy of Reason

The Romantic Movement had roots in the individualism of the Renaissance, Protestant devotion and personal piety, sentimental novels of the eighteenth century, and dramatic German poetry of the **Sturm und Drang** (literally, "storm and stress") movement, which rejected the influence of French rationalism on German literature. However, two writers who were also closely related to the Enlightenment provided the immediate intellectual foundations for Romanticism: Jean-Jacques Rousseau and Immanuel Kant raised questions about whether the rationalism so dear to the philosophes was sufficient to explain human nature and be the bedrock principle for organizing human society.

Rousseau and Education

We already pointed out in Chapter 17 that Jean-Jacques Rousseau, though sharing in the reformist spirit of the Enlightenment, opposed many of its other facets. Rousseau's conviction that society and material prosperity had corrupted human nature profoundly influenced Romantic writers.

Rousseau set forth his view on how the individual could develop to lead a good and happy life uncorrupted by society in his novel *Émile* (1762), a work that was for a long time far more influential than *The Social Contract*. (See Chapter 17.) In *Émile*, Rousseau stressed the difference between children and adults. He distinguished the stages of human maturation and urged that children be raised with maximum individual freedom. Each child should be allowed to grow freely, like a plant, and to learn by trial and error what reality is and how best to deal with it. The parent or teacher would help most by providing the basic necessities of life and warding off what was manifestly harmful. Beyond that, the adult should stay completely out of the way, like a gardener who waters and weeds a garden but otherwise lets nature take its course. As noted in Chapter 17, Rousseau thought that, because of their physical differences, men and women would naturally grow into social roles with different spheres of activity.

Rousseau also thought that adults should allow the child's sentiments, as well as its reason, to flourish. To Romantic writers, this concept of human development vindicated the rights of nature over those of artificial society. They thought such a form of open education would eventually lead to a natural society. In its fully developed form, this view of life led the Romantics to value the uniqueness of each individual and to explore childhood in great detail. Like Rousseau, the Romantics saw humankind, nature, and society as organically interrelated.

Kant and Reason

Immanuel Kant (1724–1804) wrote the two greatest philosophical works of the late eighteenth century: *The Critique of Pure Reason* (1781) and *The Critique of Practical Reason* (1788). He sought to accept the rationalism of the Enlightenment and to still preserve a belief in human freedom, immortality, and the existence of God. Against Locke and other philosophers who saw knowledge rooted in sensory experience alone, Kant argued for the subjective character of human knowledge. For Kant, the human mind does not simply reflect the world around it like a passive mirror; rather, the mind actively imposes on the world of sensory experience "forms of sensibility" and "categories of understanding." The mind itself generates these categories. In other words, the human mind perceives the world as it does because of its own internal mental categories. This meant that human perceptions are as much the product of the mind's own activity as of sensory experience.

Kant found the sphere of reality that was accessible to pure reason to be limited. He believed, however, that beyond the phenomenal world of sensory experience, over which "pure reason" was master, there existed what he called the "noumenal" world. This world is a sphere of moral and aesthetic reality known by "practical reason" and conscience. Kant thought all human beings possess an innate sense of moral duty or an awareness of what he called a **categorical imperative**. This term refers to an inner command to act in every situation as one would have all other people always act in the same situation. Kant regarded the existence of this imperative of conscience as incontrovertible proof of humankind's natural freedom. On the basis of humankind's moral sense, Kant postulated the existence of God, eternal life, and future rewards and punishments. He believed that reason alone could not prove these transcendental truths. Still, he was convinced they were realities to which every reasonable person could attest.

To many Romantic writers, Kantian philosophy refuted the narrow rationality of the Enlightenment. Whether they called it "practical reason," "fancy," "imagination," "intuition," or simply "feeling," the Romantics believed that the human mind had the power to penetrate beyond the limits of largely passive human understanding as set forth by Hobbes, Locke, and Hume. Most Romantics also believed poets and artists possess these powers in abundance. Other Romantic writers appealed to the limits of human reason to set forth new religious ideas or political thought that were often at odds with Enlightenment writers.

▼ Romantic Literature

The term *Romantic* appeared in English and French literature as early as the seventeenth century. Neoclassical writers then used the word to describe literature they considered unreal, sentimental, or excessively fanciful. In the eighteenth century, the English writer Thomas Warton (1728–1790) associated Romantic literature with medieval romances. In Germany, a major center of the Romantic literary movement, Johann Gottfried Herder (1744–1803) used the terms *Romantic* and *Gothic* interchangeably. In both England and Germany, the term came to be applied to all literature that did not observe classical forms and rules and gave free play to the imagination.

As an alternative to such dependence on the classical forms, August Wilhelm von Schlegel (1767–1845) praised the "Romantic" literature of Dante, Petrarch, Boccaccio, Shakespeare, the Arthurian legends, Cervantes, and Calderón. According to Schlegel, Romantic literature was to classical literature what the organic and living were to the merely mechanical. He set forth his views in *Lectures on Dramatic Art and Literature* (1809–1811).

The Romantic Movement had peaked in Germany and England before it became a major force in France under the leadership of Madame de Staël (1766–1817) and Victor Hugo (1802–1885). (See "Madame de Staël Describes the New Romantic Literature of Germany," page 600.) So influential was the classical tradition in France that not until 1816 did a French writer openly declare himself a Romantic. That was Henri Beyle (1783–1842), who wrote under the pseudonym Stendhal. He praised Shakespeare and criticized his own countryman, the seventeenth-century classical dramatist Jean Racine (1639–1699).

The English Romantic Writers

The English Romantics believed poetry was enhanced by freely following the creative impulses of the mind. In this belief, they directly opposed Lockean psychology, which regarded the mind as a passive receptor and poetry as a mechanical exercise of "wit" following prescribed rules. For Samuel Taylor Coleridge (1772–1834), the artist's imagination was God at work in the mind. As Coleridge expressed his views, the imagination was "a repetition in the finite mind of the eternal act of creation in the infinite I AM." Poetry

MADAME DE STAËL DESCRIBES THE NEW ROMANTIC LITERATURE OF GERMANY

Anne-Louise-Germaine de Staël, known generally as Madame de Staël, was the daughter of Jacques Necker, the finance minister of Louis XVI. She was also the friend of major French political liberals and a critic of Napoleonic absolutism. More importantly for European literary life, Madame de Staël visited Germany, read the emerging German Romantic literature, and introduced it to both French- and English-speaking Europe in her book Concerning Germany *(1813). In the passage that follows, she endorses the new literature then emerging in Germany. She points to the novelty of this Romantic poetry and then relates it to a new appreciation of Christianity and the Middle Ages. The Christian features she associates with the poetry represent one strain among many of the religious revival that followed the de-Christianizing religious policies of the French Revolution.*

How does de Staël characterize the new Romantic school of poetry? Why does she contrast it with the literature that had its roots in ancient Greece and Rome? Why does she believe the new literature will continue to grow? What is the relationship of the Middle Ages to the new poetry and other examples of the fine arts touched by Romantic sensibilities?

The word *romantic* has been lately introduced in Germany, to designate that kind of poetry which is derived from the songs of the Troubadours; that which owes its birth to the union of chivalry and Christianity. If we do not admit that the empire of literature has been divided between paganism and Christianity, the north and the south, antiquity and the middle ages, chivalry and the institutions of Greece and Rome, we shall never succeed in forming a philosophical judgment of ancient and of modern taste.

Some French critics have asserted that German literature is still in its infancy; this opinion is entirely false: men who are best skilled in the knowledge of languages, and the works of the ancients, are certainly not ignorant of the defects and advantages attached to the species of literature which they either adopt or reject; but their character, their habits, and their modes of reasoning, have led them to prefer that which is founded on the recollection of chivalry, on the wonders of the middle ages, to that which has for its basis the mythology of the Greeks. The literature of romance is alone capable of further improvement, because, being rooted in our own soil, that alone can continue to grow and acquire fresh life: it expresses our religion; it recalls our history; its origin is ancient, although not of classical antiquity. Classic poetry, before it comes home to us, must pass through our recollections of paganism; that of the Germans is the Christian era of the fine arts; it employs our personal impressions to excite strong and vivid emotions; the genius by which it is inspired addresses itself immediately to our hearts; of all phantoms at once the most powerful and the most terrible. . . .

The new school maintains the same system in the fine arts as in literature, and affirms that Christianity is the source of all modern genius; the writers of this school also characterize, in a new manner, all that in Gothic architecture agrees with the religious sentiments of Christians. It does not follow however from this, that the moderns can and ought to construct Gothic churches; . . . it is only of consequence to us, in the present silence of genius, to lay aside the contempt which has been thrown on all the conceptions of the middle ages.

From Madame De Staël, *Concerning Germany* (London, John Murray, 1814) as quoted in Howard E. Hugo, ed., *The Romantic Reader* (Viking, 1957), pp. 64–66.

thus could not be considered idle play. Rather, it was the highest of human acts, humankind's self-fulfillment in a transcendental world.

Coleridge was the master of Gothic poems of the supernatural, such as "The Rime of the Ancient Mariner," which relates the story of a sailor cursed for killing an albatross. The poem treats the subject as a crime against nature and God and raises the issues of guilt, punishment, and the redemptive possibilities of humility and penance. At the end of the poem, the mariner discovers the unity and beauty of all things. Having repented, he is delivered from his awful curse, which has been symbolized by the dead albatross hung around his neck:

O happy living things! no tongue
Their beauty might declare:
A spring of love gushed from my heart,
And I blessed them unaware . . .
The self-same moment I could pray;
And from my neck so free
The Albatross fell off, and sank
Like lead into the sea.

Wordsworth　William Wordsworth (1770–1850) was Coleridge's closest friend. Together they published *Lyrical Ballads* in 1798 as a manifesto of a new poetry that rejected the rules of eighteenth-century criticism. Among Wordsworth's most important later poems is his "Ode on Intimations of Immortality" (1803), written in part to console Coleridge, who was suffering a deep personal crisis. Its subject is the loss of poetic vision, something Wordsworth also felt then in himself. Nature, which he had worshipped, no longer spoke freely to him, and he feared it might never speak to him again:

There was a time when meadow, grove, and stream,
The earth, and every common sight,
To me did seem
Appareled in celestial light,
The glory and the freshness of a dream.
It is not now as it hath been of yore—
Turn whereso'er I may,
By night or day,
The things which I have seen I now can
see no more.

He had lost what he believed all human beings lose in the necessary process of maturation: their childlike vision and closeness to spiritual reality. For both Wordsworth and Coleridge, childhood was the bright period of creative imagination. Wordsworth held a theory of the soul's preexistence in a celestial state before its creation. The child, being closer in time to its eternal origin and undistracted by worldly experience, recollects the supernatural world much more easily. Aging and urban living corrupt and deaden the imagination, making one's inner feelings and the beauty of nature less important. In his book-length poem *The Prelude* (1850), Wordsworth presented a long autobiographical account of the growth of the poet's mind.

Lord Byron　A true rebel among the Romantic poets was Lord Byron (1788–1824). In Britain, even most of the other Romantic writers distrusted and disliked him. He had little sympathy for their views of the imagination. Outside England, however, Byron was regarded as the embodiment of the new person the French Revolution had created. He rejected the old traditions (he was divorced and famous for his many love affairs) and championed the cause of personal liberty. Byron was outrageously skeptical and mocking, even of his own beliefs. In *Childe Harold's Pilgrimage* (1812), he created a brooding, melancholy Romantic hero. In *Don Juan* (1819), he wrote with ribald humor, acknowledged nature's cruelty as well as its beauty, and even expressed admiration for urban life.

The German Romantic Writers

Much Romantic poetry was also written on the Continent, but almost all major German Romantics wrote at least one novel. Romantic novels often were highly sentimental and borrowed material from medieval romances. The characters of Romantic novels were treated as symbols of the larger truth of life. Purely realistic description was avoided. The first German Romantic novel was Ludwig Tieck's (1773–1853) *William Lovell* (1793–1795). It contrasts the young Lovell, whose life is built on love and imagination, with those who live by cold reason alone and who thus become easy prey to unbelief, misanthropy, and egoism. As the novel rambles to its conclusion, a mixture of philosophy, materialism, and skepticism, administered to him by two women he naively loves, destroys Lovell.

Schlegel　Friedrich Schlegel (1767–1845) wrote the progressive early Romantic novel *Lucinde* (1799) that attacked prejudices against women as capable of being little more than lovers and domestics. Schlegel's novel reveals the ability of the Romantics to become involved in the social issues of their day. He depicted Lucinde as the perfect friend and companion, as well as the unsurpassed lover, of the hero. Like other early Romantic novels, the work shocked contemporary morals by frankly discussing sexual activity and by describing Lucinde as equal to the male hero.

PUBLICATION DATES OF MAJOR ROMANTIC WORKS

1762   Rousseau's *Émile*

1774   Goethe's *Sorrows of Young Werther*

1781   Kant's *Critique of Pure Reason**

1788   Kant's *Critique of Practical Reason**

1798   Wordsworth and Coleridge's *Lyrical Ballads*

1799   Schlegel's *Lucinde*

1799   Schleiermacher's *Speeches on Religion to Its Cultured Despisers*

1802   Chateaubriand's *Genius of Christianity*

1806   Hegel's *Phenomenology of Mind*

1808   Goethe's *Faust, Part I*

1812   Byron's *Childe Harold's Pilgrimage*

1819   Byron's *Don Juan*

1825   Scott's *Tales of the Crusaders*

1841   Carlyle's *On Heroes and Hero-Worship*

*Kant's books were not themselves part of the Romantic Movement, but they were fundamental to later Romantic writers.

Goethe   Towering above all of these German writers stood Johann Wolfgang von Goethe (1749–1832). Perhaps the greatest German writer of modern times, Goethe defies easy classification. Part of his literary production fits into the Romantic mold, and part of it was a condemnation of Romantic excesses. The book that made his early reputation was *The Sorrows of Young Werther*, published in 1774. This novel, like many in the eighteenth century, is a series of letters. The hero falls in love with Lotte, who is married to another man. The letters explore their relationship with the sentimentalism that was characteristic of the age. Eventually Werther and Lotte part, but in his grief, Werther takes his own life. This novel became popular throughout Europe. Romantic authors admired its emphasis on feeling and on living outside the bounds of polite society.

Goethe's masterpiece was *Faust*, a long dramatic poem. Part I, published in 1808, tells the story of Faust, who makes a pact with the devil—he will exchange his soul for greater knowledge than other human beings possess. As the story progresses, Faust seduces a young woman named Gretchen. She dies but is received into heaven as the grief-stricken Faust realizes he must continue to live.

In Part II, completed in 1832, Faust is taken through a series of adventures involving witches and mythological characters. At the conclusion, however, he dedicates his life, or what remains of it, to the improvement of humankind. He feels this goal will allow him to overcome the restless striving that induced him to make the pact with the devil. That new knowledge breaks the pact. Faust dies and is received by angels.

▼ Romantic Art

The art of the Romantic Era, like its poetry and philosophy, stood largely in reaction to that of the eighteenth century. Whereas the Rococo artists had looked to Renaissance models and Neo-Classical painters to the art of the ancient world, Romantic painters often portrayed scenes from medieval life. For them, the Middle Ages represented the social stability and religious reverence that was disappearing from their own era.

The Cult of the Middle Ages and Neo-Gothicism

Like many early Romantic artists, the English landscape painter John Constable (1776–1837) was politically conservative. In *Salisbury Cathedral from the Meadows*, he portrayed a stable world in which neither political turmoil nor industrial development challenged the traditional dominance of the church and the landed classes. Although the clouds and sky in the painting depict a severe storm, the works of both nature and humankind present a powerful sense of enduring order. The trees clearly have withstood this storm as they have withstood others for many years. The cathedral, built in the Middle Ages, has also stood majestically intact for centuries. Like many English conservatives of his day, Constable saw the church and the British constitution as intimately related. Religious institutions were barriers to political radicalism. In his private letters, Constable associated liberal reformers with the devil, leading some scholars to suggest that the lightning striking the back roof of the cathedral symbolizes those evil forces and that the rainbow, arching over the entire scene and giving it a sacramental nature, indicates God's blessing for the traditional order of nature and society.

Constable and other Romantics tended to idealize rural life because they believed it was connected to the medieval past and was opposed to the increasingly urban, industrializing, commercial society that was developing around them. In fact, the rural landscape and rustic society that Constable depicted in his paintings had already largely disappeared from England.

John Constable's *Salisbury Cathedral from the Meadows* displays the appeal of Romantic art to both medieval monuments and the sublime power of nature.   Art Resource, NY. © The National Gallery, London

Medieval structures not only appeared in Romantic painting. The Neo-Gothic revival in architecture also dotted the European landscape with modern imitations of them. Many medieval cathedrals were restored during this era, and new churches were designed to resemble their medieval forerunners. The British Houses of Parliament built in 1836–1837 were the most famous public buildings in the Neo-Gothic style, but town halls, schools, and even railroad stations were designed to look like medieval buildings, while aristocratic country houses were rebuilt to resemble medieval castles.

The single most remarkable nineteenth-century Neo-Gothic structure was the castle of Neuschwanstein constructed between 1869 and 1886 on a mountain in southern Germany by King Ludwig II of Bavaria (r.

1864–1886). The cost of this castle, the interior of which was never completed, almost bankrupted the Bavarian monarchy.

Nature and the Sublime

Beyond their attraction to history, Romantic artists also sought to portray nature in all of its majestic power as no previous generation of European artists had ever done. Moreover, like Romantic poets, the artists of the era were drawn toward the mysterious and unruly side of nature rather than toward the rational Newtonian order that had prevailed during the Enlightenment. Their works often sought to portray what they and others termed *the sublime*—that is, subjects from nature that aroused strong emotions, such as fear, dread, and

At the castle of Neuschwanstein King Ludwig II of Bavaria erected the most extensive Neo-Gothic monument of central Europe.   Josaf Beck/Getty Images, Inc.—Taxi

awe, and raised questions about whether and how much we control our lives. Painters often traveled to remote areas such as the Scottish Highlands, the mountains of Wales, or the Swiss Alps to portray unruly and danger-ous scenes from nature that would immediately grip and engage the viewer's emotions.

Romantics saw nature as a set of infinite forces that overwhelmed the smallness of humankind. For example, in 1824, the German artist Caspar David Friedrich (1774–1840) in *The Polar Sea* painted the plight of a ship trapped and crushed by the force of a vast polar ice field. In direct contrast to eighteenth-century artists' portrayal of sunny Enlightenment, Friedrich also painted numerous scenes in which human beings stand shrouded in the mys-terious darkness of night where moonlight and torches cast only fitful illumination.

An artist who similarly understood the power of na-ture but also depicted the forces of the new industrial-ism that was challenging them was Joseph Mallord William Turner (1775–1851) whose painting *Rain, Steam and Speed—The Great Western Railway* of 1844 illustrated the recently invented railway engine barrel-

ing through an enveloping storm. In this scene the new technology is both part of the natural world and strong enough to dominate it.

Friedrich's and Turner's paintings taken together symbolize the contradictory forces affecting Romantic artists—the sense of the power, awe, and mastery of nature coupled with the sense that the advance of in-dustry represented a new kind of awesome human power that could challenge or even surpass the forces of nature itself.

▼ Religion in the Romantic Period

During the Middle Ages, the foundation of religion had been the authority of the church. The Reformation lead-ers had appealed to the authority of the Bible. Then, many Enlightenment writers attempted to derive reli-gion from the rational nature revealed by Newtonian physics. Other Enlightenment figures attacked religion in general and Christianity in particular. Romantic reli-gious thinkers, in contrast, sought the foundations of

Caspar David Friedrich's *The Polar Sea* illustrated the power of nature to diminish the creations of humankind as seen in the wrecked ship on the right of the painting.   Kunsthalle, Hamburg, Germany/A.K.G., Berlin/SuperStock

Joseph Mallord William Turner's *Rain, Steam, and Speed—The Great Western Railway* captured the tensions many Europeans felt between their natural environment and the new technology of the industrial age.   Joseph Mallord William Turner, 1775–1851, *Rain, Steam, and Speed—The Great Western Railway 1844*. Oil on canvas, 90.8 × 121.9. © The National Gallery, London

religion in the inner emotions of humankind. Reacting to the anticlericalism of both the Enlightenment and the French Revolution, these thinkers also saw religious faith, experience, and institutions as central to human life. Their forerunners were the mystics of Western Christianity. One of the first great examples of a religion characterized by Romantic impulses—Methodism—arose in mid-eighteenth-century England during the Enlightenment itself and became one of the most powerful forces in transatlantic religion during the nineteenth century.

Methodism

Methodism originated in the middle of the eighteenth century as a revolt against deism and rationalism in the Church of England. The Methodist revival formed an important part of the background of English Romanticism. The leader of the Methodist movement was John Wesley (1703–1791). His mother, Susannah Wesley, who bore eighteen children, had carefully supervised his education and religious development.

While at Oxford University studying to be an Anglican priest, Wesley organized a religious group known as the Holy Club. He soon left England for missionary work in the new colony of Georgia in America, where he arrived in 1735. While he was crossing the Atlantic, a group of German Moravians on the ship deeply impressed him with their unshakable faith and confidence during a storm. Wesley, who had despaired of his life, concluded they knew far better than he the meaning of justification by faith. When he returned to England in 1738, Wesley began to worship with Moravians in London. There, in 1739, he underwent a conversion experience that he described in the words, "My heart felt strangely warmed." From that point on, he felt assured of his own salvation.

Wesley discovered he could not preach his version of Christian conversion and practical piety in Anglican church pulpits. Therefore, late in 1739, he began to preach in the open fields near the cities and towns of western England. Thousands of humble people responded to his message of repentance and good works. Soon he and his brother Charles (1707–1788), who be-

John Wesley (1703–1791) was the founder of Methodism. He emphasized the role of emotional experience in Christian conversion.
CORBIS/Bettmann

came famous for his hymns, began to organize Methodist societies. By the late eighteenth century, the Methodists had become a separate church. They ordained their own clergy and sent missionaries to America, where they eventually achieved their greatest success and influence.

Methodism stressed inward, heartfelt religion and the possibility of Christian perfection in this life. John Wesley described Christianity as "an inward principle . . . the image of God impressed on a created spirit, a fountain of peace and love springing up into everlasting life."[3] True Christians were those who were "saved in this world from all sin, from all unrighteousness . . . and now in such a sense perfect as not to commit sin and . . . freed from evil thoughts and evil tempers."[4]

Many people, weary of the dry rationalism that derived from deism, found Wesley's ideal relevant to their own lives. The Methodist preachers emphasized the role of enthusiastic, emotional experience as part of Christian conversion. After Wesley, religious revivals became highly emotional in style and content.

New Directions in Continental Religion

Similar religious developments based on feeling appeared on the Continent. After the Thermidorian Reaction, a strong Roman Catholic revival took place in France. Its followers disapproved of both the religious policy of the revolution and the anticlericalism of the Enlightenment. The most important book to express these sentiments was *The Genius of Christianity* (1802) by Viscount François René de Chateaubriand (1768–1848). In this work, which became known as the "bible of Romanticism," Chateaubriand argued that the essence of religion is "passion." The foundation of faith in the church was the emotion that its teachings and sacraments inspired in the heart of the Christian.

Against the Newtonian view of the world and of a rational God, the Romantics found God immanent in nature. No one stated the Romantic religious ideal more eloquently or with greater impact on the modern world than Friedrich Schleiermacher (1768–1834). In 1799, he published *Speeches on Religion to Its Cultured Despisers.* It was a response to Lutheran orthodoxy, on the one hand, and to Enlightenment rationalism, on the other. The advocates of both were the "cultured despisers" of real, or heartfelt, religion. According to Schleiermacher, religion was neither dogma nor a system of ethics. It was an intuition or feeling of absolute dependence on an infinite reality. Religious institutions, doctrines, and moral activity

expressed that primal religious feeling only in a secondary, or indirect, way.

Although Schleiermacher considered Christianity the "religion of religions," he also believed every world religion was unique in its expression of the primal intuition of the infinite in the finite. He thus turned against the universal natural religion of the Enlightenment, which he termed "a name applied to loose, unconnected impulses," and defended the meaningfulness of the numerous world religions. Every such religion was seen to be a unique version of the emotional experience of dependence on an infinite being. In so arguing, Schleiermacher interpreted the religions of the world in the same way that other Romantic writers interpreted the variety of unique peoples and cultures.

▼ Romantic Views of Nationalism and History

A distinctive feature of Romanticism, especially in Germany, was its glorification of both the individual person and individual cultures. Behind these views lay the philosophy of German idealism, which understood the world as the creation of subjective egos. J. G. Fichte (1762–1814), an important German philosopher and nationalist, identified the individual ego with the Absolute that underlies all existing things. According to him and similar philosophers, the world is truly the creation of humankind. The world is as it is because especially strong persons conceive of it in a particular way and impose their wills on the world and other people. Napoleon served as the contemporary example of such a great person. This philosophy has ever since served to justify the glorification of great persons and their actions in overriding all opposition to their will and desires.

Herder and Culture

In addition to this philosophy, the influence of new historical studies lay behind the German glorification of individual cultures. German Romantic writers went in search of their own past in reaction to the copying of French manners in eighteenth-century Germany, the impact of the French Revolution, and the imperialism of Napoleon. An early leader in this effort was Johann Gottfried Herder (1744–1803), already discussed in Chapter 17, as a critic of European colonialism. Herder resented French cultural dominance in Germany. In 1778, he published an influential essay entitled "On the Knowing and Feelings of the Human Soul." In it, he vigorously rejected the mechanical explanation of nature so popular with Enlightenment writers. He saw human

---

[3]Quoted in Albert C. Outler, ed., *John Wesley: A Representative Collection of His Writings* (New York: Oxford University Press, 1964), p. 220.

[4]Outler, *John Wesley*, p. 220.

beings and societies as developing organically, like plants, over time. Human beings were different at different times and places.

Herder revived German folk culture by urging the collection and preservation of distinctive German songs and sayings. His most important followers in this work were the Grimm brothers, Jakob (1785–1863) and Wilhelm (1786–1859), famous for their collection of fairy tales. Believing each language and culture were the unique expression of a people, Herder opposed both the concept and the use of a "common" language, such as French, and "universal" institutions, such as those Napoleon had imposed on Europe. These, he believed, were forms of tyranny over the individuality of a people. Herder's writings led to a broad revival of interest in history and philosophy. Although initially directed toward identifying German origins, such work soon expanded to embrace other world cultures. Eventually the ability of the Romantic imagination to be at home in any age or culture spurred the study of non-Western religion, comparative literature, and philology.

Hegel and History

The most important philosopher of history in the Romantic period was the German Georg Wilhelm Friedrich Hegel (1770–1831). He is one of the most complicated and significant philosophers in the history of Western civilization.

Hegel believed ideas develop in an evolutionary fashion that involves conflict. At any given time, a predominant set of ideas, which he termed the **thesis**, holds sway. Conflicting ideas, which Hegel termed the **antithesis**, challenge the thesis. As these patterns of thought clash, a **synthesis** emerges that eventually becomes the new thesis. Then the process begins all over again. Periods of world history receive their character from the patterns of thought that predominate during them. (See "Hegel Explains the Role of Great Men in History.")

Several important philosophical conclusions followed from this analysis. One of the most significant was the belief that all periods of history have been of almost equal value because each was, by definition, necessary to the achievements of those that came later. Also, all cultures are valuable because each contributes to the necessary clash of values and ideas that allows humankind to develop. Hegel discussed these concepts in *The Phenomenology of Mind* (1806), *Lectures on the Philosophy of History* (1822–1831), and other works, many of which were published only after his death. During his lifetime, his ideas became widely known through his university lectures at Berlin.

Islam, the Middle East, and Romanticism

The new religious, literary, and historical sensibilities of the Romantic period modified the European understanding of both Islam and the Arab world while at the same time preserving long-standing attitudes.

The energized Christianity associated with Methodist-like forms of Protestantism, on the one hand, and Chateaubriand's emotional Roman Catholicism, on the other, renewed the traditional sense of necessary conflict between Christianity and Islam. Chateaubriand wrote a travelogue of his journey from Paris to Jerusalem in 1811. A decade later, when he was a member of the French parliament, he invoked the concept of a crusade against the Muslim world in a speech on the danger posed by the Barbary pirates of North Africa.

Indeed, the medieval Crusades against Islam fired the Romantic imagination. Nostalgic European artists painted from a Western standpoint the great moments of the Crusades including the bloody capture of Jerusalem. Stories from those conflicts filled historical novels such as *Tales of the Crusaders* (1825) by Sir Walter Scott (1771–1832). Although they presented heroic images of Muslim warriors, these paintings and novels ignored the havoc that the crusaders had visited on the peoples of the Middle East.

The general nineteenth-century association of nationalistic aspirations with Romanticism also cast the Ottoman Empire and with it Islam in an unfavorable political light. Romantic poets and intellectuals championed the cause of the Greek Revolution (see Chapter 20) and revived older charges of Ottoman despotism.

By contrast, other Romantic sensibilities induced Europeans to see the Muslim world in a more positive fashion. The Romantic emphasis on the value of literature drawn from different cultures and ages allowed many nineteenth-century European readers to enjoy the stories from *The Thousand and One Nights*, which first appeared in English in 1778 from a French translation. As poets across Europe rejected classicism in literature in favor of folk stories and fairy tales, they saw the *Arabian Nights* as mysterious and exotic. In 1859, Edward FitzGerald (1809–1883) published his highly popular translation of the *Rubáiyát of Omar Khayyám* of Nishapur, a Persian poet of the twelfth century.

Herder's and Hegel's concepts of history gave both the Arab peoples and Islam distinct roles in history. For Herder, Arab culture was one of the numerous communities that composed the human race and manifested the human spirit. The Prophet Muhammad, while giving voice to the ancient spirit of the Arab people, had drawn them from a polytheistic faith to a great monotheistic vision. For Hegel, Islam represented an important stage of

HEGEL EXPLAINS THE ROLE OF GREAT MEN IN HISTORY

Hegel believed that behind the development of human history from one period to the next lay the mind and purpose of what he termed the World-Spirit, *a concept somewhat like the Christian God. Hegel thought particular heroes from the past (such as Caesar) and in the present (such as Napoleon) were the unconscious instruments of that spirit. In this passage from his lectures on the philosophy of history, Hegel explained how these heroes could change history. All these concepts are characteristic of the Romantic belief that human beings and human history are always intimately connected with larger, spiritual forces at work in the world. The passage also reflects the widespread belief of the time that the world of civic or political action pertained to men and that of the domestic sphere belonged to women.*

How might the career of Napoleon have inspired this passage? What are the antidemocratic implications of this passage? In this passage, do great men make history or do historical developments make great men? Why do you think Hegel does not associate this power of shaping history with women as well as men? In that regard, note how he relates history with political developments rather than with those of the private social sphere.

Such are all great historical men—whose own particular aims involve those large issues which are the will of the World-Spirit. They may be called Heroes, inasmuch as they have derived their purposes and their vocation, not from the calm, regular course of things, sanctioned by the existing order, but from a concealed fount—one which has not attained to phenomenal, present existence—from that inner Spirit, still hidden beneath the surface, which, impinging on the outer world as on a shell, bursts it in pieces, because it is another kernel than that which belonged to the shell in question. They are men, therefore, who appear to draw the impulse of their life from themselves; and whose deeds have produced a condition of things and a complex of historical relations which appear to be only their interest, and their work.

Such individuals had no consciousness of the general Idea they were unfolding, while prosecuting those aims of theirs; on the contrary, they were practical, political men. But at the same time they were thinking men, who had an insight into the requirements of the time—what was ripe for development. This was the very Truth for their age, for their world; the species next in order, so to speak, and which was already formed in the womb of time. It was theirs to know this nascent principle; the necessary, directly sequent step in progress, which their world was to take; to make this their aim, and to expend their energy in promoting it. World historical men—the Heroes of an epoch—must, therefore, be recognized as its clear-sighted ones; their deeds, their words are the best of that time.

From G. W. F. Hegel, *The Philosophy of History*, trans. by J. Sibree (New York: Dover, 1956), pp. 30–31. Reprinted by permission.

When Napoleon invaded Egypt in 1799, he met stiff resistance. On July 25, however, the French won a decisive victory. This painting of that battle by Baron Antoine Gros (1771–1835) emphasizes French heroism and Muslim defeat. Such an outlook was typical of European views of Arabs and the Islamic world. Antoine Jean Gros (1771–1835). Detail, *Battle of Aboukir, July 25, 1799*, c. 1806. Oil on canvas. Chateaux de Versailles et de Trianon, Versailles, France. Bridgeman—Giraudon/Art Resource, NY

the development of the world spirit. However, Hegel believed Islam had fulfilled its role in history and no longer had any significant part to play. These outlooks, which penetrated much nineteenth-century intellectual life, made it easy for Europeans to believe that Islam could, for all practical purposes, be ignored or reduced to a spent historical force.

The British historian and social commentator Thomas Carlyle (1795–1881) attributed new, positive qualities to Muhammad himself. Carlyle disliked the Enlightenment's disparagement of religion and spiritual values. He was also drawn to German theories of history. In his book *On Heroes and Hero-Worship* (1841), Carlyle presented Muhammad as the embodiment of the hero as prophet. He repudiated the traditional Christian and general Enlightenment view of Muhammad as an impostor. (See Chapter 17.) To Carlyle, Muhammad was straightforward and sincere. Carlyle's understanding of religion was similar to Schleiermacher's, and thus in his pages,

Muhammad appeared as a person who had experienced God subjectively and had communicated a sense of the divine to others. Although friendly to Muhammad from a historical standpoint, Carlyle nonetheless saw him as one of many great religious figures and not, as Muslims believed, as the last of the prophets through whom God had spoken.

The person whose actions in the long run did perhaps the most to reshape the idea of both Islam and the Middle East in the European imagination was Napoleon himself. With his Egyptian expedition of 1798, the first European military invasion of the Near East since the Crusades, the study of the Arab world became an important activity within French intellectual life. For his invasion of Egypt to succeed, Napoleon believed he must make it clear he had no intention of destroying Islam but rather sought to liberate Egypt from the military clique that governed the country in the name of the Ottoman Empire. To that end, he took with him scholars of Arabic and Islamic culture whom he urged to converse with the most educated people they could meet. Napoleon personally met with the local Islamic leaders and had all of his speeches and proclamations translated into classical Arabic. Such cultural sensitivity and the serious efforts of the French scholars to learn Arabic and study the Qur'an impressed Egyptian scholars. (When the French sought to levy new taxes, however, the Egyptians' enthusiasm waned.)

It was on this expedition that the famous Rosetta Stone was discovered. Now housed in the British Museum, it eventually led to the decipherment of ancient Egypt's hieroglyphic writing. Napoleon's scholars also published a twenty-three volume *Description of Egypt* (1809–1828), which concentrated largely on ancient Egypt. Their approach suggested the history of the Ottoman Empire needed to be related first to the larger context of Egyptian history and that Islam, although enormously important, was only part of a larger cultural story. The implication was that if Egypt and Islam were to be understood, it would be through European—if not necessarily Christian—categories of thought.

Two cultural effects in the West of Napoleon's invasion were an increase in the number of European visitors to the Middle East and a demand for architecture based on ancient Egyptian models. Perhaps the most famous example of this fad is the Washington Monument in Washington, D.C., which is modeled after ancient Egyptian obelisks.

In Perspective

Romantic ideas made a major contribution to the emergence of nationalism, which proved to be one of the strongest motivating forces of the nineteenth and twentieth centuries. The writers of the Enlightenment had generally championed a cosmopolitan outlook on the world. By contrast, the Romantic thinkers emphasized the individuality and worth of each separate people and culture. A people or a nation was defined by a common language, history, and customs and by the possession of a historical homeland. This cultural nationalism gradually became transformed into a political creed. It came to be widely believed that every people, ethnic group, or nation should constitute a separate political entity and that only when it so existed could the nation be secure in its own character.

France under the revolutionary government and Napoleon had demonstrated the power of nationhood. Other peoples came to desire similar strength and confidence. Napoleon's toppling of ancient political struc-

tures, such as the Holy Roman Empire, proved the need for new political organization in Europe. By 1815, only a few Europeans aspired to this, but as time passed, peoples from Ireland to Ukraine came to share these yearnings. The Congress of Vienna could ignore such feelings, but for the rest of the nineteenth century, as shall be seen in subsequent chapters, statesmen had to confront the growing power these feelings had unleashed.

AP* TEST PREP

1. Representatives in the national legislature saved the antimonarchist Directory from certain end
   a. by executing Gracchus Babeuf.
   b. by squabbling with each other and dividing their votes.
   c. by enacting the treaties of Basel.
   d. by staging a *coup d'état*.
   e. by appealing to the peasants.

2. Napoleon's Concordat with the Catholic Church accomplished all of the following *except*
   a. giving the French state the right to name bishops.
   b. declaring Catholicism the religion of the majority of French citizens.
   c. requiring refractory clergy to resign.
   d. requiring clergy to swear an oath of loyalty to the state.
   e. establishing Roman Catholicism as the only legitimate religion in France.

3. The Continental System was designed to
   a. funnel taxes from conquered territories back to France.
   b. establish French political control of Europe.
   c. cut off British trade with the rest of Europe.
   d. establish supply lines for Napoleon's far-flung forces.
   e. provoke France into a trade war with the Dutch.

4. Napoleon invaded Ottoman Egypt to
   a. obtain antiquities to enhance his empire.
   b. prevent the British fleet from communicating with India and damage trade.
   c. wrest the Crimea from the Russians.
   d. thwart Ottoman incursions into the southern flank of Europe.
   e. establish a base for re-creating the Alexandrian Empire for France.

5. Constable and other Romantics tended to idealize
   a. ancient Greece.
   b. reason.
   c. city life.
   d. rural life.
   e. the future.

6. John Wesley was the leader of the
   a. English romantic movement.
   b. Methodist movement.
   c. English Catholic revival.
   d. Charter movement.
   e. English neoclassical movement.

7. All of the following is true about the Battle of Trafalgar *except*
   a. the British lost only three ships.
   b. Lord Nelson died in battle.
   c. the battle ended all French hope of invading Britain.
   d. the battle guaranteed British control of the seas.
   e. the battle was fought off the Spanish coast.

8. Napoleon's real reason for establishing the Bonapartist dynasty in 1804 was
   a. the need to publicly demonstrate supremacy over the church in France.
   b. the need to demonstrate supremacy over the pope.
   c. because it represented a natural expression of his ambition.
   d. the need to gain the support of the nobility.
   e. the need to gain the support of the peasantry.

9. Which statement best describes Napoleon's treatment of the relatives he placed in control of European kingdoms?
   a. He generally allowed them to make decisions.
   b. He cared little for what they did.
   c. He gave them orders and expected them to be carried out.
   d. He gave them considerable autonomy but expected to be consulted on important decisions.
   e. He placed them only in unimportant kingdoms.

10. Among the greatest difficulties Napoleon's armies faced in Spain were
    a. outbreaks of typhoid and malaria.
    b. Italian troops.
    c. Portuguese troops.
    d. lack of supplies.
    e. guerrilla bands.

11. Mikhail Kutuzov's strategy to defeat Naopoleon's 600,000-strong army involved
    a. an alliance with Prussia.
    b. reliance on swifter troops.
    c. reliance on the loyalty of the peasantry.
    d. guerilla tactics.
    e. "scorched-earth" policy.

12. The Congress of Vienna pursued a program that included all of the following *except*
    a. exclusion of France from deliberations.
    b. Austrian control over northern Italy.
    c. restoration of the Bourbon monarchy.
    d. a nonvindictive boundary settlement with France.
    e. establishment of the kingdom of the Netherlands.

13. The Quadruple Alliance included all of the following *except*
    a. Spain.
    b. Britain.
    c. Prussia.
    d. Russia.
    e. Austria.

14. The romantic movement had roots in all of the following *except*
    a. the individualism of the Renaissance.
    b. the neoclassicism of the eighteenth century.
    c. Protestant devotion and personal piety.
    d. the sentimental novels of the eighteenth century.
    e. dramatic German poetry.

15. Perhaps one of the greatest results from Napoleon's campaign in Egypt was
    a. renewed interest in the Crusades.
    b. a fresh attitude toward Muslims.
    c. discovery of the Rosetta Stone.
    d. discovery of the Code of Hammurabi.
    e. Muslim interest in Europeans.

16. The author of *Lucinde* who shocked readers for depicting a female character as an equal to men was
    a. Mary Shelley.
    b. Lord Byron.
    c. Schlegel.
    d. Goethe.
    e. Wordsworth.

17. Kant's categorical imperative refers to
    a. the necessity of democracy for peace.
    b. an inner command to act in every situation as one would have others do in the same situation.
    c. a mathematical means by which to deduce the existence of God.
    d. the superiority of the sentiments to discover the Good.
    e. the necessity of education for democracy.

18. After Prussia's defeat at Jena, many German intellectuals urged
    a. resistance to Napoleon on the basis of German nationalism.

CHAPTER 19 ■ THE AGE OF NAPOLEON AND THE TRIUMPH OF ROMANTICISM

b. acceptance of Napoleon's rule on the basis of republicanism.

c. resistance to Napoleon on the basis of a shared culture.

d. limited acceptance of Napoleon's rule.

e. sweeping reforms to the army.

19. As a result of the Treaty of Tilsit (1807), which of the following became an ally of Napoleon?

a. Austria

b. Prussia

c. Britain

d. Spain

e. the Ottoman Empire

20. Methodism developed a particular view of faith that

a. was to be heartfelt and guide the believer to salvation in this world.

b. revealed a heightened emotional connection to the sacraments.

c. demonstrated an awareness of the infinity of God in nature.

d. was to be expressed in communal living.

e. required a new asceticism.

DOCUMENT-BASED QUESTION

Directions: Construct a valid essay that directly addresses the central issue of the following question. Use facts from the documents provided and from the chapter to prove the position you take in your thesis statement.

What do the following documents tell us about the Romantics' views of nature and history? What about religion?

Document A

Source: Madame de Staël describes the new romantic literature of Germany, *Concerning Germany.*

The literature of romance is alone capable of further improvement, because, being rooted in our own soil, that alone can continue to grow and acquire fresh life: it expresses our religion; it recalls our history; its origin is ancient, although not of classical antiquity. . . .

The new school maintains the same system in the fine arts as in literature, and affirms that Christianity is the source of all modern genius; the writers of this school also characterize, in a new manner, all that in Gothic architecture agrees with the religious sentiments of Christians. It does not follow however, from this, that the moderns can and ought to construct Goth-

ic churches; . . . it is only of consequence to us, in the present silence of genius, to lay aside the contempt which has been thrown on all the conceptions of the middle ages.

Document B

John Constable's *Salisbury Cathedral.*

Document C

Caspar David Frieddrich's *The Polar Sea.*

Document D

Joseph Turner's *Rain, Steam, and Speed.*

Document E

Source: Chateaubriand on "Gothic churches," Western Civilization Documents CD-ROM 20.7.

Although "Everything ought to be put in its place" is a trivial truth which carries force by its constant repetition, nevertheless without accepting it one cannot, after all, have anything perfect. The Greeks would not have appreciated an Egyptian temple at Athens any more than the Egyptians would a Greek temple at Memphis. The two buildings in exchanging place would have lost their main beauty, that is to say their relationship with the institutions and practices of the people. We can apply the same reflection to old Christian edifices. It is pertinent to remark that, even in this century of unbelief, poets and novelists, by a natural return to the customs of our ancestors, like to introduce . . . Gothic temples into their fictions; so great is the charm of memories linked with religion and the history of our country. Nations do not discard their ancient customs as people do their old clothes.

For more on the romantic movement, see pages 597–606 of this chapter.

position. During the 1820s, Britain had become unenthusiastic about a political role that placed it in opposition to all change. For its own commercial reasons, it favored independence for Latin America. Popular pressures at home led the British aristocratic leadership to enact a moderate reform bill in 1832. Thereafter, Britain would be viewed as the leading liberal state in Europe and one that would support nationalistic causes.

AP* TEST PREP

1. The vast majority of nationalists believed all of the following *except*
   a. legitimate monarchies provide a basis for political unity.
   b. "multinational state" is an oxymoron.
   c. popular sovereignty should prevail.
   d. language is the primary determinant of nationhood.
   e. folk culture and history provide a connection to national legitimacy.

2. All of the following national groups sought independence from their host states *except* the
   a. Irish.
   b. Poles.
   c. Greeks.
   d. Czechs.
   e. Romani.

3. The author who associated nationhood with the divine order of things was
   a. Burke.
   b. Constant.
   c. Mazzini.
   d. Hegel.
   e. Herder.

4. Nineteenth-century liberalism is associated with all of the following *except*
   a. religious toleration.
   b. free press.
   c. representation.
   d. democracy.
   e. individualism.

5. The pillars of nineteenth-century conservatism include all of the following *except*
   a. legitimate monarchies.
   b. traditional privileges.
   c. landed aristocracies.
   d. written constitutions.
   e. social hierarchy.

6. The Decembrist Revolt was led by
   a. junior officers.
   b. Russian socialists.

   c. leaders of the emerging middle class.
   d. angry peasants.
   e. cabinet ministers.

7. Nicholas I saw serfdom as
   a. a great evil that required immediate action.
   b. part of the natural order of society.
   c. the basis of Russian prosperity.
   d. a great evil, but too dangerous to reform.
   e. consistent with Christian teachings.

8. In the French elections of 1830, the liberals
   a. saw their power diminish.
   b. suffered an unprecedented defeat.
   c. won a stunning victory.
   d. were not represented on the ballot.
   e. saw their chances of gaining power slip.

9. The real goal of early-nineteenth-century political liberals was
   a. mass democracy.
   b. the end of monarchy.
   c. free education for all.
   d. the end of poverty.
   e. political reform based on private property.

10. In July 1819, Metternich suppressed student organizations with the
    a. Carlsbad Decrees.
    b. Council of State.
    c. Six Acts.
    d. Charter.
    e. Protocol of Troppau.

11. The Cato Street Conspiracy was
    a. a plot to blow up the cabinet.
    b. the acts of local magistrates to suppress the Manchester reform movement.
    c. a ring of radical newspapers with the *Political Register* to incite social unrest.
    d. a group of Whig members of Parliament organizing to overthrow the crown.
    e. a group of Tory members of Parliament organizing to raise tariffs.

12. The Russians established a special relationship with independent Serbia for all of the following reasons *except*
    a. its shared Slavic population.
    b. the shared affinity for the Eastern Orthodox Church.
    c. access to Mediterranean trade.
    d. the new leader, Milos Obrenovitch, was a cousin of the tsar.
    e. continuation of its expansion policy in the region.

13. The two liberators of South America from Spain were
    a. Simon Bolívar and Miguel Hidalgo y Costilla.

b. Miguel Hidalgo y Costilla and Augustín de Iturbide.
c. Augustín de Iturbide and Simon Bolívar.
d. Simon Bolívar and San Martín.
e. San Martín and Augustín de Iturbide.

14. France formally recognized Haitian independence in
    a. 1789.
    b. 1793.
    c. 1804.
    d. 1820.
    e. 1827.

15. The wars of independence in South America were led by
    a. *peninsulares.*
    b. *creoles.*
    c. *mestízos.*
    d. *mulattos.*
    e. maroons.

16. What power lost territory and prestige as a result of the Greek Revolution of 1821?
    a. France
    b. Britain
    c. the Ottoman Empire
    d. Austria
    e. Russia

17. The Great Reform Bill of 1832 finally passed because
    a. of fears of mob violence.
    b. new elections were held for the House of Commons.

c. the king threatened to alter the structure of the House of Lords.
d. of the Peterloo Massacre.
e. a plebicite demonstrated widespread popular support of the bill.

18. The purpose of the Catholic Emancipation Act was to
    a. protect Irish Catholics from Protestant armies in Northern Ireland.
    b. allow Catholics seats in Parliament.
    c. free Creoles to become government officials in British-controlled Latin America.
    d. revoke Catholic privileges in the armed forces.
    e. provide positions for Catholics in the armed forces.

19. Under Metternich's leadership in the early 1820s, Austria moved to suppress revolutions in
    a. Belgium and Hungary.
    b. Italy and the Balkans.
    c. Prussia and the Balkans.
    d. Spain and Italy.
    e. Hungary and Prussia.

20. Charles X's reign was associated with all of the following *except*
    a. divine right and primogeniture.
    b. capture of Algiers.
    c. coup d'état.
    d. alliance with the middle class.
    e. dissolution of the Chamber of Deputies.

DOCUMENT-BASED QUESTION

Directions: Construct a valid essay that directly addresses the central issue of the following question. Use facts from the documents provided and from the chapter to prove the position you take in your thesis statement.

What did supporters of the Great Reform Bill of 1832 hope it would accomplish? What did opponents of the bill fear would be its result?

Document A

Eugène Delacroix's *Liberty Leading the People*, a symbolic representation of the 1830 Revolution in France.

Document B

Source: Thomas Macaulay, a member of the House of Commons, defends the Great Reform Bill, *Hansard's Parliamentary Debates.*

[The principle of the ministers] is plain, rational and consistent. It is this – to admit the middle class to a large and direct share in the Representation, without any violent shock to the institutions of our country. . . . I hold it to be clearly expedient, that in a country like this, the right of suffrage should depend on a pecuniary qualification. Every argument . . . which would induce me to oppose Universal Suffrage, induces me to support the measure which is now before us. I oppose Universal Suffrage, because I think it would produce a destructive revolution. I support this measure because I am sure it is our best security against revolution . . . .

Document C

Source: Thomas Macaulay, a member of the House of Commons, satirizes radical politicians.

Awake, arise, the hour is come
For rows and revolutions;
There's no receipt like pike and drum
For crazy constitutions.
Close, close the shop! Break, break the loom!
Desert your hearths and furrows,
And throng in arms to seal the doom
Of England's rotten boroughs. . . .

The peer shall dangle from the gate,
The bishop from his steeple,
Till all recanting, own, the State
Means nothing but the People.

Document D

Source: John Cam Hobhouse recalls Lord John Russell's speech in which the Great Reform Bill was outlined, *Recollections of a Long Life* (1910).

Lord John Russell began his speech at six o'clock. Never shall I forget the astonishment of my neighbors as he developed his plan. Indeed, all the House of Commons seemed perfectly astounded; and when he read the long list of the boroughs to be either wholly or partially disfranchised there was a sort of wild ironical laughter. Baring Wall, turning to me, said, "They are mad! They are mad!" and others made use of similar exclamations - all but Sir Robert Peel; he looked serious and angry, as if he had discovered that the Ministers, by the boldness of their measure, had secured the support of the country. Burdett and I agreed there was every chance of the measure being carried, and that a revolution would be the consequence.

Document E

Source: Thomas Creevey, "Letter to Miss Old on the passing of the Reform Act" (June 5, 1832).

Thank God! I was in at the death of this Conservative plot, and the triumph of the Bill! This is the third great event of my life at which I have been present, and in each of which I have been to a certain extent mixed up - the battle of Waterloo, the battle of Queen Caroline, and the battle of Earl Grey and the English nation for the Reform Bill.

For more on the Great Reform Bill, see pages 639–642 of this chapter.

In 1848 Ana Ipatescu helped to lead Transylvanian revolutionaries against Russian rule. Transylvania is part of present-day Romania. The revolutions of 1848 in eastern Europe were primarily uprisings of nationalist groups. Although generally repressed in the revolutions of that year, subject nationalities would prove a source of political upheaval and unrest in the region throughout the rest of the century, ultimately providing the spark for the outbreak of World War I. The Art Archive/Picture Desk, Inc./Kobal Collection

21

Economic Advance and Social Unrest (1830–1850)

▼ **Toward an Industrial Society**
Population and Migration • Railways

▼ **The Labor Force**
The Emergence of a Wage-Labor Force • Working-Class Political Action: The Example of British Chartism

▼ **Family Structures and the Industrial Revolution**
The Family in the Early Factory System

▼ **Women in the Early Industrial Revolution**
Opportunities and Exploitation in Employment • Changing Expectations in the Working-Class Marriage

▼ **Problems of Crime and Order**
New Police Forces • Prison Reform

▼ **Classical Economics**
Malthus on Population • Ricardo on Wages • Government Policies Based on Classical Economics

▼ **Early Socialism**
Utopian Socialism • Anarchism • Marxism

▼ **1848: Year of Revolutions**
France: The Second Republic and Louis Napoleon • The Habsburg Empire: Nationalism Resisted • Italy: Republicanism Defeated • Germany: Liberalism Frustrated

▼ **In Perspective**

BY 1830, EUROPE was headed toward an industrial society. Only Great Britain had already attained that status, but the pounding of new machinery and the grinding of railway engines soon began to echo across much of the Continent. Yet what characterized the second quarter of the century was not the triumph of industrialism but the final protests of those economic groups who opposed it. Intellectually, the period saw the formulation of the major creeds supporting and criticizing the newly emerging society.

These were years of uncertainty for almost everyone. Even the most confident entrepreneurs knew the trade cycle could bankrupt them within weeks. For the industrial workers and the artisans, unemployment became a haunting and recurring problem. For the peasants, the question was sufficiency of food. It was a period of self-conscious transition that culminated in 1848 with a continent-wide outbreak of revolution. People knew one mode of life was passing, but no one knew what would replace it.

▼ Toward an Industrial Society

The Industrial Revolution had begun in eighteenth-century Great Britain with the advances in textile production described in Chapter 15. Natural resources, adequate capital, native technological skills, a growing food supply, a social structure that allowed considerable mobility, and strong foreign and domestic demand for goods had given Britain an edge in achieving a vast new capacity for production in manufacturing. British factories and recently invented machines allowed producers to furnish customers with a greater number of consumer products of a higher quality and for lower prices than those of any competitors. Also, the French Revolution and the wars of Napoleon had finally destroyed the French Atlantic trade and thus disrupted continental economic life for two decades. The Latin American wars of independence opened the markets of South America to British goods. In North America, both the United States and Canada demanded British products. Through its control of India, Britain commanded the markets of southern Asia. British banks similarly dominated the international financial markets.

The British textile industry was a vast worldwide economic network. For much of its supply of raw cotton, this industry depended on the labor of American slaves, although Britain itself had been trying to end the slave trade since 1807. In turn, the finished textiles were shipped all over the world along sea-lanes the British navy protected. The wealth that Britain gained through textile production and its other industries of iron making, shipbuilding, china production, and the manufacture of other finished goods was invested all over the world, but especially in the United States and Latin America. This enormous activity provided the economic foundation for British dominance of the world scene throughout the nineteenth century.

Despite their economic lag, the continental nations were beginning to make material progress. By the 1830s, in Belgium, France, and Germany, the number of steam engines in use was growing steadily. Exploitation of the coalfields of the Ruhr and the Saar basins had begun. Coke was replacing charcoal in iron and steel production.

Industrial areas on the Continent were generally less concentrated than in Britain; nor did the Continent have large manufacturing districts, such as the British Midlands. Major pockets of production, such as Lyons, Rouen, and Lille in France and Liege in Belgium, did exist in Western Europe, but most continental manufacturing still took place in the countryside. New machines were integrated into the existing domestic system. The slow pace of continental imitation of the British example meant that, at midcentury, peasants and urban artisans remained more important politically than industrial factory workers.

Population and Migration

While the process of industrialization spread, the population of Europe continued to grow on the base of the eighteenth-century population explosion. The number of people in France rose from 32.5 million in 1831 to 35.8 million in 1851. During approximately the same period, the population of Germany rose from 26.5 million to 33.5 million and that of Britain from 16.3 million to 20.8 million. More and more of the people of Europe lived in cities. By midcentury, one half of the population of England and Wales and one quarter of the population of France and Germany had become town dwellers. Eastern Europe, by contrast, remained overwhelmingly rural, with little industrial manufacturing.

The sheer numbers of human beings put considerable pressure on the physical resources of the cities. Migration from the countryside meant that existing housing, water, sewers, food supplies, and lighting were completely inadequate. Slums with indescribable filth grew, and disease, especially cholera, ravaged the population. Crime increased and became a way of life for those who could make a living in no other manner. Human misery and degradation in many early-nineteenth-century cities seemed to have no bounds.

The situation in the countryside was scarcely better. During the first half of the century, the productive use of the land remained the basic fact of life for most Europeans. The enclosures of the late eighteenth century, the land redistribution of the French Revolution, and the emancipation of serfs in Prussia and later in Austria (1848) and Russia (1861) commercialized landholding. Liberal reformers had hoped the legal revolution in ownership would transform peasants into progressive, industrious farmers. Instead, most peasants became conservative landholders without enough land to make agricultural innovations or, oftentimes, even to support themselves.

It is important to note the differing dates of rural emancipation across Europe. In England, France, and the Low Countries, persons living in the countryside could move freely between country and town. In Germany, eastern Europe, and Russia, such migration was difficult until the serfs were emancipated. Even when emancipation did occur, as throughout Germany early in the century, it did not make migration simple. So from Germany eastward, the pace of industrialization was much slower, in part because of the absence of a fluid market for free labor moving to the cities.

The specter of poor harvests still haunted Europe. The worst such experience of the century was the Irish famine of 1845 to 1847. Perhaps as many as half a million Irish peasants with no land or small plots simply starved when disease blighted the potato crop. Hundreds of thousands emigrated. (See "Encountering the Past: The Potato and the Great Hunger in Ireland.") By midcentury, the revolution in landholding led to greater agricultural production. It also resulted in a vast uprooting of people from the countryside into cities and from

Europe into the rest of the world. The countryside thus provided many of the workers for the new factories, as well as people with few economic skills who slowly emigrated to cities in hope of finding work.

Railways

Industrial advance itself had also contributed to this migration. The 1830s and 1840s opened the first great age of railway building. The Stockton and Darlington Line opened in England in 1825. By 1830, another major line had been built between Manchester and Liverpool and had several hundred passengers a day. Belgium had undertaken railway construction by 1835. The first French line opened in 1832, but serious construction came only in the 1840s. Germany entered the railway age in 1835. At midcentury, Britain had 9,797 kilometers of railway, France 2,915, and Germany 5,856. (See Map 21–1.)

Interactive map: To explore this map further, go to **www.myhistorylab.com**

Map 21–1 **EUROPEAN RAILROADS IN 1850** At midcentury Britain had the most extensive rail network, and the most industrialized economy, in Europe, but rail lines were expanding rapidly in France, the German states, and Austria. Southern and eastern Europe had few railways, and the Ottoman Empire had none.

THE POTATO AND THE GREAT HUNGER IN IRELAND

ANY AGRICULTURAL ECONOMY that depends on a single product is in a precarious position. If the people that economy supports also depend on a single source of food, they also stand on the edge of catastrophe—they have nothing to fall back on if their only source of food fails. That kind of catastrophe occurred in Ireland, which was under British rule in the 1840s when the potato crop failed.

During the eighteenth century, almost half of the Irish population came to depend on the potato, which had been brought to Europe from South America in the seventeenth century, as virtually their only food. On less than one acre, an Irish peasant could raise enough potatoes to feed ten other people for a year and pay his rent (few Irish peasants owned their own land).

Before the 1840s, there had been isolated potato failures in parts of Ireland, but never a general failure. Then in 1845, a mysterious blight, caused by a fungus, struck potato crops across Ireland. The potato vines withered in the fields, and potatoes in storage became moldy and inedible. Half the crop was lost. The Irish, with modest aid from the British government, survived, but in 1846 the blight reappeared and destroyed the entire crop. The crop of 1847 was better, but the blight came again in 1848.

This series of Irish potato crop failures was the worst natural disaster to strike nineteenth-century Europe. Without potatoes, Irish tenants could not pay their rent. Landlords drove starving tenants off their farms. Disease spread, and tens of thousands died.

In 1846, in response to the Irish famine, the British government repealed the tariffs on imported grain known as the Corn Laws and enacted a program of public works to employ the dispossessed, but the help was inadequate. Most economists and politicians believed government aid caused more harm than good, and the government was reluctant to provide charity. The 1847 Irish Poor Relief Act required anyone who occupied more than one quarter acre of land to enter a government-run workhouse before receiving poor relief, but the scale of the disaster overwhelmed the workhouses.

To escape the famine, soon known as The Great Hunger, many of the Irish poor emigrated, primarily to the United States and Britain itself. Much of Ireland became depopulated. The census of 1841 counted 8,197,000 people in Ireland; ten years later, death and emigration had cut the population by more than 1.5 million. By 1901, more waves of emigration had reduced it to 4,459,000. The population had still not recovered to prefamine levels at the dawn of the twenty-first century: In 2000, the combined population of the Irish Republic and British-ruled Northern Ireland was only 5,460,000. Alone among the nations of Europe, Ireland has fewer inhabitants today than it did in the nineteenth century.

Source: R. N. Salaman, *The History and Social Influence of the Potato* (Cambridge: Cambridge University Press, 1985); Cecil Woodham-Smith, *The Great Hunger: Ireland 1845–1849* (New York: Harper & Row, 1962).

Why was the failure of the potato crop such a disaster for Ireland?

How did the famine affect the Irish population?

Painter George Frederick Watts's 1850 depiction of a scene set during the Irish Potato Famine. So many people starved during the famine that workhouses could not shelter them all. © Trustees of the Watts Gallery, Compton, Surrey, UK/The Bridgeman Art Library

George Stephenson (1781–1848) invented the locomotive in 1814, but the "Rocket," his improved design shown here, did not win out over other competitors until 1829. In the following two decades the spread of railways transformed the economy of Western Europe. Image Works/Mary Evans Picture Library Ltd.

The railroads, plus canals and improved regular roads, meant people could leave the place of their birth more easily than ever before. The improvement in transportation also allowed cheaper and more rapid passage of raw materials and finished products.

Railways epitomized the character of the industrial economy during the second quarter of the century. They represented investment in capital goods rather than in consumer goods. Consequently, there was a shortage of consumer goods at cheap prices. This favoring of capital over consumer production was one reason the working class was often unable to purchase much for its wages. The railways in and of themselves also brought about still more industrialization. Embodying the most dramatic application of the steam engine, they sharply increased demand for iron and steel and then for a more skilled labor force. The new iron and steel capacity soon permitted the construction of ironclad ships and iron machinery rather than ships and machinery made of wood. These new capital industries led to the formation of vast industrial fortunes that would be invested in still newer enterprises. Industrialism had begun to grow on itself.

▼ The Labor Force

The composition and experience of the early nineteenth-century labor force was varied. No single description could include all the factory workers, urban artisans, domestic craftspeople, household servants, miners, countryside peddlers, farm workers, or railroad workers. Some of the workforce was reasonably well off and enjoyed steady employment and decent wages. Other workers were the "laboring poor," who held jobs, but earned little more than subsistence wages. Then there were those, such as the women and children who worked nearly naked in the mines of Wales, whose conditions of life shocked Europe when a parliamentary report in the 1840s publicized them. Furthermore, the conditions of workers varied from decade to decade and from industry to industry within any particular decade.

Although historians have traditionally emphasized the role and experience of industrial factory workers, only the textile-manufacturing industry became thoroughly mechanized and moved into the factory setting during the first half of the century. Far more of the nonrural, nonagricultural workforce consisted of skilled artisans living in cities or small towns. They were attempting to maintain the value of their skills and control over their trades in the face of changing features of production. All these working people faced possible unemployment, with little or no provision for their security. During their lives, they confronted the dissolution of many of the traditional social ties of custom and community.

The Emergence of a Wage-Labor Force

During the nineteenth century, artisans as well as factory workers eventually came to participate in a wage-labor force in which their labor became a commodity of the labor marketplace. This process has often been termed *proletarianization*. In the process of becoming wage laborers, artisans gradually lost both significant ownership of the means of production, such as tools and equipment, and of control over the conduct of their own trades. The process occurred most rapidly wherever the factory system arose displacing previous skilled labor. The factory owner provided the financial capital to construct the factory, to purchase the machinery, and to secure the raw materials. The factory workers contributed their labor for a wage. The process could also occur outside the factory setting if a new invention, such as a mechanical printing press, could do the work of several artisans within an urban or rural workshop setting.

Factory workers also had to submit to various kinds of factory discipline that was virtually always unpopular and difficult to impose. This discipline meant the demands for a smooth operation of the machinery largely determined working conditions. Closing of factory gates to late workers, fines for such lateness, dismissal for drunkenness, and public scolding of faulty laborers were attempts to create human discipline that would match the mechanical regularity of the cables, wheels, and pistons. The factory worker had no direct say about the quality of the product or its price. (See "Compare & Connect: Andrew Ure and John Ruskin Debate the Conditions of Factory Production," pages 652–653.)

For all the difficulties of workers in factory conditions, however, their economic situation was often better than that of textile workers who resisted the factory mode of production. In particular, English hand-loom weavers, who continued to work in their homes, experienced decades of declining trade and growing poverty in their failing attempt to compete with power looms.

Urban artisans in the nineteenth century entered the wage-labor force more slowly than factory workers, and machinery had little to do with the process. The emergence of factories in and of itself did not harm urban artisans. Many even prospered from the development. For example, the construction and maintenance of the new machines generated major demand for metalworkers, who consequently did well. The actual erection of factories and the expansion of cities benefited all craftspeople in the building trades, such as carpenters, roofers, joiners, and masons. The lower prices for machine-made textiles aided artisans involved in making clothing, such as tailors and hatters, by reducing the costs of their raw materials. Where the urban artisans encountered difficulty and where they found their skills and livelihood threatened was in the organization of production.

In the eighteenth century, a European town or city workplace had usually consisted of a few artisans laboring for a master. They labored first as apprentices and then as journeymen, according to established guild regulations and practices. The master owned the workshop and the larger equipment, and the apprentices and journeymen owned their tools. The journeyman could expect eventually to become a master. This guild system had allowed workers to exercise a considerable degree of control over labor recruitment and training, the pace of production, the quality of the product, and its price. The guild functioned to protect the integrity of the craft and the prosperity of the craftsmen.

In the nineteenth century, it became increasingly difficult for artisans to exercise corporate or guild direction and control over their trades. The legislation of the French Revolution had outlawed such organizations in France. Across Europe, political and economic liberals disapproved of labor and guild organizations and attempted to ban them. These thinkers believed guilds raised the price of both labor and products to the disadvantage of owners of capital and consumers.

Other destructive forces were also at work. The masters often found themselves under increased competitive pressure from larger, more heavily capitalized establishments or from the introduction of machine production into a previously craft-dominated industry. In many workshops masters began to follow a practice, known in France as *confection*, whereby goods, such as shoes, clothing, and furniture, were produced in standard sizes and styles rather than by special orders for individual customers.

This practice increased the division of labor in the workshop. Each artisan produced a smaller part of the more-or-less uniform final product. Thus, less skill was required of each artisan, and the particular skills a worker possessed became less valuable. To increase production and reduce costs, masters also tried to lower the wages they paid for piecework. Those attempts often led to work stoppages or strikes. Migrants from the countryside or small towns into the cities created, in some cases, a surplus of relatively unskilled workers. They were willing to work for lower wages or under less favorable and protected conditions than traditional artisans. This situation made it much more difficult for urban journeymen ever to hope to become masters in charge of their own workshops. Increasingly, these artisans became lifetime wage laborers whose skills were simply bought and sold in the marketplace.

Working-Class Political Action: The Example of British Chartism

By midcentury, such artisans, proud of their skills and frustrated in their social and economic expectations, became the most radical political element in the European working class. From at least the 1830s onward, these artisans took the lead in one country after another in attempting to formulate new ways to protect their social and economic interests.

By the late 1830s, many British workers linked the solution of their economic plight to a program of political reform known as **Chartism**. In 1836, William Lovett (1800–1877) and other London radical artisans formed the London Working Men's Association. In 1838, the group issued the Charter, demanding six specific reforms. The Six Points of the Charter included universal male suffrage, annual election of the House of Commons, the secret ballot, equal electoral districts, and the abolition of property qualifications for and the payment of salaries to members of the House of Commons.

For more than ten years, the Chartists, who were never tightly organized, agitated for their reforms. On three occasions the Charter was presented to Parliament, which refused to pass it. Petitions with millions of signatures were presented to the House of Commons. Strikes were called. The Chartists published a newspaper, the *Northern Star*. Feargus O'Connor (1794–1855), the most important Chartist leader, made speeches

Andrew Ure and John Ruskin Debate the Conditions of Factory Production

THE FACTORY WAS itself as much an invention of the Industrial Revolution as were the new machines the factory often housed. The factory required a new organization of labor. It also made possible the production of vast new quantities of manufactured goods. From its inception the factory system provoked both praise and criticism. Andrew Ure saw much positive good arising from factory production whereas John Ruskin became a vehement critic. How might the women of Todmorden (see page 659) have replied to both writers?

QUESTIONS

1. Why does Ure emphasize the willingness of workers to be employed in factories?

2. How does Ure portray the factory system as creating the possibility of new abundance?

3. How does Ruskin see the use of machinery reducing workers to a machine?

4. Is Ruskin's criticism of the division of labor a correct analysis or simply a well-crafted metaphorical criticism?

5. How might Ure have replied to Ruskin?

I. Andrew Ure Praises the Factory System

Andrew Ure (1778–1857) was a Scottisch physician and a great proponent of the benefits of the factory system. In 1835 he published The Philosophy of Manufactures, *which went through many editions from then until late in the century. He saw factories as increasing productivity and also providing a healthier environment than agricultural work or mining.*

The term Factory, in technology, designates the combined operation of many orders of work—people, adult and young, in tending with assiduous skill a system of productive machines continuously impelled by a central power. This definition includes such organizations as cotton-mills, flax-mills, silk-mills, woolen-mills, and certain engineering works. . . . I conceive that this title, in its strictest sense, involves the idea of a vast automaton, composed of various mechanical and intellectual organs, acting in uninterrupted concert for the production of a common object, all of them being subordinated to a self-regulated moving force. . . .

In its precise acceptation, the Factory system is of recent origin, and may claim England for its birthplace. . . .

When the first water-frames for spinning cotton were erected at Cromford, in the romantic valley of the Derwent, about sixty years ago, mankind were little aware of the mighty revolution which the new system of labor was destined by Providence to achieve, not only in the structure of British society, but in the fortunes of the world at large.

Arkwright alone had the sagacity to discern, and the boldness to predict in glowing language, how vastly productive human industry would become, when no longer proportioned in its results to muscular effort, which is by its nature fitful and capricious, but when made to consist in the task of guiding the work of mechanical fingers and arms, regularly impelled with great velocity by some indefatigable physical power. . . .

In my recent tour, continued during several months, through the manufacturing districts, I have seen tens of thousands of old, young, and middle-aged of both sexes, many of them too feeble to get their daily bread by any of the former modes of industry, earning abundant food, raiment, and domestic accommodation, without perspiring at a single pore, screened meanwhile from the summer's sun and the winter's frost, in apartments more airy and salubrious than those of the metropolis, in which our legislative and fashionable aristocracies assemble. In those spacious halls the benignant power of steam summons around him his myriads of willing menials, and assigns to each the regulated task, substituting for painful muscular effort on their part, the energies of his own gigantic arm, and demanding in return only attention and dexterity to correct such little aberrations as casually occur in his workmanship. . . . Such is the factory system, replete with prodigies in mechanics and political economy, which promises, in its future growth, to become the great minister of civilization to the terraqueous globe, enabling this country, as its heart, to diffuse along with its commerce, the life-blood of science and religion to myriads of people still lying "in the region and shadow of death."

Source: Andrew Ure, *The Philosophy of Manufactures; or, An Exposition of the Scientific, Moral, and Commercial Economy of the Factory System* (London, 1835), pp. 13 ff., as quoted in Mack Walker, ed., *Metternich's Europe* (New York: Walker and Company, 1968), pp. 275–276, 278–279.

II. John Ruskin Decries the Impact of Industrial Production on Workers

The Englishman John Ruskin (1819–1900) was the foremost mid-nineteenth-century critic of art and architecture. He commenced his career interested primarily in painting and then moved to architecture. In the course of that transition he became increasingly sensitive to the working conditions of the craftsmen who constructed the buildings he studied. Over time he became a major social critic of the new industrial order. His earliest statement of social criticism occurred in a chapter entitled "The Nature of Gothic" in his 1851 book The Stones of Venice. *Here Ruskin passionately attacked the mechanical routine of work associated with industrial machinery. He also attacked the concept of increasing work through the division of labor, which had been conceptualized by Adam Smith in* The Wealth of Nations *(1776). Smith had illustrated the division of labor by describing a pin factory. Ruskin here responds to Smith's analysis.*

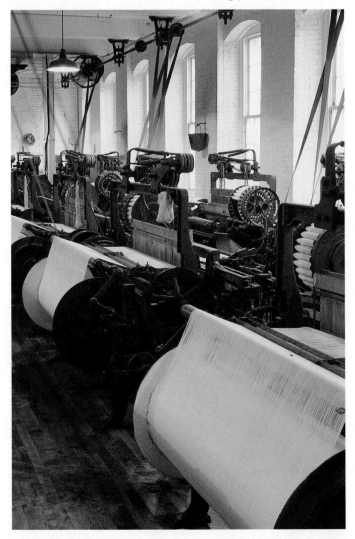

Power looms used in the mass production of textiles during the Industrial Revolution.   Dorling Kindersley Medical Library/David Lyons © Dorling Kindersley. Courtesy of the Boott Cotton Mills Museum, Lowell, Massachusetts

You must either make a tool of the creature, or a man of him. You cannot make both. Men were not intended to work with the accuracy of tools, to be precise and perfect in all their actions. If you will have that precision out of them, and make their fingers measure degrees like cog-wheels, and their arms strike curves like compasses, you must unhumanize them. All the energy of their spirits must be given to make cogs and compasses of themselves. All their attention and strength must go to the accomplishment of the mean act . . . On the other hand, if you will make a man of the working creature, you cannot make a tool. Let him but begin to imagine, to think to try to do anything worth doing; and the engine-turned precision is lost at once. Out come all his roughness, all his dulness, all his incapability; shame upon shame, failure upon failure, pause after pause: but out comes the whole majesty of him also; . . .

It is verily this degradation of the operative into a machine, which, more than any other evil of the times, is leading the mass of the nations everywhere into vain, incoherent, destructive struggling for a freedom of which they cannot explain the nature to themselves. . . . It is not that men are ill read, but that they have no pleasure in the work by which they make their bread, and therefore look to wealth as the only means of pleasure. . . .

It is not, truly speaking, the labour that is divided; but the men:—Divided into mere segments of men—broken into small fragments and crumbs of life; so that all the little piece of intelligence that is left in a man is not enough to make a pin, or a nail, but exhausts itself in making the point of a pin or the head of a nail . . . . And all the evil to which that cry is urging our myriads can be met only in one way: not by teaching nor preaching, for to teach them is but to show them their misery, and to preach to them, if we do nothing more than preach, is to mock at it. It can be met only by a right understanding, on the part of all classes, of what kinds of labour are good for men, raising them, and making them happy; by a determined sacrifice of such convenience, or beauty, or cheapness as is to be got only by the degradation of the workman; and by equally determined demand for the products and results of healthy and ennobling labour.

Source: J. Ruskin, *The Stones of Venice* (New York: Lovell, Coryell, and Co., n.d.), 2, pp. 162, 164, 165–166.

In the 1830s and 1840s, the Chartists circulated petitions throughout Britain demanding political reform. Here the petitions are being taken to Parliament in a vast ceremonious procession. © Museum of London

across Britain. Despite this vast activity, Chartism as a national movement failed. Its ranks were split between those who advocated violence and those who wanted to use peaceful tactics. On the local level, however, the Chartists scored several successes and controlled the city councils in Leeds and Sheffield.

As prosperity returned after the depression of the late 1830s and early 1840s, many working people abandoned the movement. Chartists' demonstrations in 1848 fizzled. Nevertheless, Chartism was the first large-scale European working-class political movement. It had specific goals and largely working-class leadership. Eventually, several of the Six Points became law (for example, the secret ballot was enacted in 1872). Continental working-class observers saw in Chartism the kind of mass movement that workers must eventually adopt if they were to improve their situation.

▼ Family Structures and the Industrial Revolution

It is more difficult to generalize about the European working-class family structure in the age of early industrialism than under the Old Regime. Industrialism developed at different rates across the Continent, and the impact of industrialism cannot be separated from that of migration and urbanization. Furthermore, industrialism did not touch all families directly; the structures and customs of many peasant families changed little for much of the nineteenth century.

Much more is known about the relationships of the new industry to the family in Great Britain than elsewhere. Many of the British developments foreshadowed those in other countries as the factory system spread.

The Family in the Early Factory System

Contrary to what historians and other observers once believed, the adoption of new machinery and factory production did not destroy the working-class family. Before the late-eighteenth-century revolution in textile production in England, the individual family involved in textiles was the chief unit of production. The earliest textile-related inventions, such as the spinning jenny, did not change that situation. As noted in Chapter 15, the new machine was initially simply brought into the home to spin the thread. It was the mechanization of weaving that led to the major change. The father who became a machine weaver was then employed in a factory. His work was thus separated from his home. Although one should not underestimate the changes and pressures in family life that occurred when the father left for the factory, the structure of early English factories allowed the father to preserve certain of his traditional family roles as they had existed before the factory system.

In the domestic system of the family economy, the father and mother had worked with their children in textile production as a family unit. They had trained and disciplined the children within the home setting. Their home life and their economic life were largely the same. Moreover, in the home setting, the wife who worked as a spinner might have earned as much or even more than her husband. Early factory owners and supervisors permitted the father to employ his wife and children as his assistants. Thus, parental training and discipline could be transferred from the home into the early factory. In some cases, in both Britain and France, whole families would move near a new factory so that the family as a unit could work there. Despite those accommodations to family life, family members still had to face the new work discipline of the factory setting. Moreover, women assisting their husbands in the factory often did less skilled work than they had in their homes.

A major shift in this family and factory structure began in the mid-1820s in England and had been more or less completed by the mid-1830s. As spinning and weaving were put under one roof, the size of factories and of the machinery grew. These newer machines required fewer skilled operators, but many relatively unskilled attendants. This became the work of unmarried women and children. Factory owners found these workers would accept lower wages and were less likely than adult men to try to form worker organizations or unions.

Factory wages for the more skilled adult males, however, became sufficiently high to allow some fathers to remove their children from the factory and send them

A Closer > LOOK

THE GREAT EXHIBITION IN LONDON

THE GREAT EXHIBITION of 1851 was held in London to celebrate progress in industry and commerce achieved through the new industrial order. Its organizers invited governments and businesses from around the globe to display the products they manufactured. The organizers generally supported free trade and believed the displays would demonstrate the value of peaceful commerce.

Note the construction of the building known as the Crystal Palace. The structural iron symbolized the possibility of using new kinds of building materials. The vast quantities of glass demonstrated that a once scarce luxury good could now be produced in large quantities for everyday consumption. In the past such structures of iron and glass had been used only for small greenhouses to raise plants on aristocratic estates.

The crowds in the picture and the even larger crowds who actually attended the Great Exhibition demonstrated that, after a quarter century of social turmoil and political discontent in Europe, large numbers of people could gather peacefully in public.

The classical statues to the left were present to show that the new consumer goods industrialism made possible was compatible with an ongoing culture of elite art.

London's Crystal Palace during the International Exhibition of 1851. Victoria & Albert Museum, London, Great Britain/Art Resource, NY

To examine this image in an interactive fashion, please go to www.myhistorylab.com

myhistörylab

to school. The children who were left working in the factories as assistants were often the children of the economically depressed hand-loom weavers. The wives of the skilled operatives also usually no longer worked in the factories. So the original links of the family in the British textile factory that had existed for well over a quarter century largely disappeared. Men were supervising women and children who did not belong to their families.

Concern for Child Labor At this point in the 1830s, workers became concerned about the plight of child laborers because parents were no longer exercising discipline over their own children in the factories. The English Factory Act of 1833 forbade the employment of children under age nine, limited the workday of children aged nine to thirteen to nine hours a day, and required the factory owner to pay for two hours of education a day for these children. The effect was further to divide work and home life. The workday for adults and older teenagers remained twelve hours. Younger children often worked in relays of four or six hours. Consequently, the parental link was thoroughly broken. The education requirement began the process of removing nurturing and training from the home and family to a school, where a teacher rather than the parents was in charge of education.

After passage of the English Factory Act, many British workers demanded shorter workdays for adults. They desired to reunite, in some manner, the workday of adults with that of their children or at least to allow adults to spend more time with their children. In 1847, Parliament mandated a ten-hour workday. By present standards, this was long. At that time, however, it allowed parents and children more hours together as a domestic unit, since their relationship as a work or production unit had ceased wherever the factory system prevailed. By the mid-1840s, in the lives of industrial workers, the roles of men as breadwinners and as fathers and husbands had become distinct in the British textile industry. Furthermore, reformers' concerns about the working conditions of women in factories and in mines arose in part from the relatively new view that the place of women was in the home rather than in an industrial or even agrarian workplace.

Changing Economic Role for the Family What occurred in Britain presents a general pattern for what would happen elsewhere with the spread of industrial capitalism and public education. The European family was passing from being the chief unit of both production and consumption to becoming the chief unit of consumption alone. This development did not mean the end of the family as an economic unit. Parents and children, however, now came to depend on sharing wages often derived from several sources, rather than on sharing work in the home or factory.

Ultimately, the wage economy meant that families were less closely bound together than in the past. Because wages could be sent over long distances to parents, children might now move farther away from home. Once they moved far away, the economic link was, in time, often broken. In contrast, when a family settled in an industrial city, the wage economy might, in that or the next generation, actually discourage children from leaving home as early as they had in the past. Children could find wage employment in the same city and then live at home until they had accumulated enough savings to marry and begin their own household. That situation meant children often remained with their parents longer than in the past.

▼ Women in the Early Industrial Revolution

As noted in Chapter 15, the industrial economy ultimately produced an immense impact on the home and family life of women. First, it eventually took most productive work out of the home and allowed many families to live on the wages of the male spouse. That transformation prepared the way for a new concept of gender-determined roles in the home and in domestic life generally. Women came to be associated with domestic duties, such as housekeeping, food preparation, child rearing and nurturing, and household management, or with poorly paid, largely unskilled cottage industries. Men came to be associated almost exclusively with supporting the family. Children were raised to conform to these expected gender patterns. Previously, this domestic division of labor into separate male and female spheres had prevailed only among the relatively small middle class and the gentry. During the nineteenth century, that division came to characterize the working class as well.

Opportunities and Exploitation in Employment

Because the early Industrial Revolution had begun in textile production, women and their labor were deeply involved from the start. Although both spinning and weaving were still domestic industries, women usually worked in all stages of production. Hand spinning was virtually always a woman's task. At first, when spinning was moved into factories and involved large machines, men often displaced women. Furthermore, the higher wages male cotton-factory workers commanded allowed many married women not to work or to work only to supplement their husbands' wages.

Women in Factories With the next generation of machines in the 1820s, however, unmarried women became a partner in one of the largest cotton factories in Britain at New Lanark, Scotland. Owen was a firm believer in the environmentalist psychology of the Enlightenment that had flowed from the thought of John Locke. If human beings were placed in the correct surroundings, they and their character could be improved. Moreover, Owen saw no incompatibility between creating a humane industrial environment and making a good profit.

At New Lanark, he put his ideas into practice. Workers were provided with good quarters. Recreational possibilities abounded, and the children received an education. There were several churches, although Owen himself was a notorious freethinker on matters of religion and sex. In the factory itself, rewards were given for good work. His plant made a fine profit. Visitors flocked from all over Europe to see what Owen had done through enlightened management.

In numerous articles and pamphlets, as well as in letters to influential people, Owen pleaded for a reorganization of industry based on his own successful model. He envisioned a series of communities shaped like parallelograms in which factory workers and farm workers might live together and produce their goods in cooperation. During the 1820s, Owen sold his New Lanark factory and then went to the United States, where he established the community of New Harmony, Indiana. When quarrels among the members led to the community's failure, he refused to give up his reformist causes. He returned to Britain, where he became the moving force behind the organization of the Grand National Union, an attempt to draw all British trade unions into a single body. It collapsed along with other labor organizations during the early 1830s.

Fourierism   Charles Fourier (1772–1837) was Owen's French intellectual counterpart. He was a commercial salesperson who never succeeded in attracting the same kind of public attention as Owen. He wrote his books and articles and waited at home each day at noon, hoping to meet a patron who would undertake his program. No one ever arrived to meet him. Fourier believed the industrial order ignored the passionate side of human nature. Social discipline ignored all the pleasures that human beings naturally seek.

Fourier advocated the construction of communities, called *phalanxes*, in which liberated living would replace the boredom and dullness of industrial existence. Agrarian rather than industrial production would predominate in these communities. Sexual activity would be relatively free, and marriage was to be reserved only for later life. Fourier also urged that no person be required to perform the same kind of work for the entire day. People would be both happier and more productive if they moved from one task to another. Through his emphasis on the problem of boredom, Fourier isolated one of the key difficulties of modern economic life.

Saint-Simon, Owen, and Fourier expected some existing government to carry out their ideas. They failed to confront the political difficulties their envisioned social transformations would arouse. Other figures paid more attention to the politics of the situation. In 1839, Louis Blanc (1811–1882) published *The Organization of Labor*. Like other socialist writers, this Frenchman demanded an end to competition, but he did not seek a wholly new society. He called for political reform that would give the vote to the working class. Once so empowered, workers could use the vote to turn the political processes to their own economic advantage. A state controlled by a working-class electorate would finance workshops to employ the poor. In time, such workshops might replace private enterprise, and industry would be organized to ensure jobs. Blanc recognized the power of the state to improve life and the conditions of labor. The state itself could become the great employer of labor.

Anarchism

Other writers and activists of the 1840s, however, rejected both industry and the dominance of government. These were the **anarchists**. They are usually included in the socialist tradition, although they do not exactly fit there. Some favored programs of violence and terrorism; others were peaceful. Auguste Blanqui (1805–1881) was a major spokesperson for terror. He spent most of his adult life in jail. Seeking to abolish both capitalism and the state, Blanqui urged the development of a professional revolutionary vanguard to attack capitalist society. His ideas for the new society were vague, but in his call for professional revolutionaries, he foreshadowed Lenin.

Pierre-Joseph Proudhon (1809–1865) represented the other strain of anarchism. In his most famous work *What Is Property?* (1840), Proudhon attacked the banking system, which rarely extended credit to small-property owners or the poor. He wanted credit expanded to allow such people to engage in economic enterprise that would not involve unfair or unearned profits. Society should be organized on the basis of mutualism, which amounted to a system of small businesses and other cooperative enterprises among which there would be peaceful cooperation and exchanges of goods based on mutual recognition of the labor each area of production required. With such a social system, the state as the protector of property would be unnecessary. Later in the century, anarchists would favor a wide variety of cooperative businesses whose point was to favor the community good over that of the individual as well as to afford an essential fairness in exchange. Proudhon's ideas later influenced the French labor movement, which was generally less directly political in its activities than the labor movements in Britain and Germany.

Marxism

quick revolution vs Mensheviks

The mode of socialist thought that eventually exerted more influence over modern European history than any other was **Marxism**. During the late nineteenth century, its ideas permeated the major continental socialist parties. With the Bolshevik Revolution of November 1917, the communist strain of Marxist thought came to dominate the Soviet Union and, after World War II, Eastern Europe and revolutionary movements in the colonial and post-colonial world. With the collapse of the Soviet Union and of the communist governments in Eastern Europe in the last twenty years of the twentieth century, it is difficult for many people to recapture the power that Marx's political and social vision exerted over Europe and other parts of the world for more than a hundred years.

Too often, the history of European socialism has been regarded as a linear development leading naturally or necessarily to the late-nineteenth-century triumph of Marxism within the major socialist political parties. Nothing could be further from the truth. Marxist socialist ideas did eventually triumph over much, though not all, of Europe, but only through competition with other socialist formulas and largely as a result of the political situation in Germany during the last quarter of the nineteenth century. At midcentury, the ideas of Karl Marx were simply one more contribution to a heady mixture of concepts and programs criticizing the emerging industrial capitalist society. Marxism differed from its competitors in its claims to scientific accuracy, its rejection of liberal reform, its harsh criticism of other contemporary socialist platforms, and its call for revolution, though the character of that revolution was not well defined. Furthermore, Marx set the emergence of the industrial workforce in the context of a world historical development from which he drew sweeping political conclusions.

Karl Marx (1818–1883) was born in Germany in the Prussian Rhineland. His family was Jewish, but his father had converted to Lutheranism, and Judaism played no role in his education. Marx's middle-class parents sent him to the University of Berlin, where he became deeply involved in Hegelian philosophy and radical politics. In 1842 and 1843, he edited the radical *Rhineland Gazette* (*Rheinische Zeitung*). Soon the Prussian authorities drove him from his native land. He lived as an exile, first in Paris, then in Brussels, and finally, after 1849, in London.

Partnership with Engels In 1844, Marx met Friedrich Engels (1820–1895), another young middle-class German, whose father owned a textile factory in Manchester, England. The next year Engels published *The Condition of the Working Class in England*, which presented a devastating picture of industrial life. The two men became fast friends. Late in 1847, they were asked to write a pamphlet for a newly organized and ultimately short-lived secret Communist League. *The Communist Manifesto*, published in German, appeared early in 1848. Marx, Engels, and the League had adopted the name *communist* because it was much more self-consciously radical than socialist. Communism implied the outright abolition of private property, rather than a less extensive rearrangement of society. Despite its later vast influence throughout the world, the *Manifesto*, a work of fewer than fifty pages, was at the time of its publication and for many years thereafter just one more political tract. Moreover, neither Marx nor his thought had any effect on the revolutionary events of 1848, which will be discussed more fully later in this chapter.

Sources of Marx's Ideas Marx derived the major ideas of the *Manifesto* and of his later work, including *Capital* (Vol. 1, 1867), from German Hegelianism, French utopian socialism, and British classical economics. Marx applied to concrete historical, social, and economic developments Hegel's abstract philosophical concept that thought develops from the clash of thesis and antithesis into a new intellectual synthesis. For Marx, the conflict between dominant and subordinate social groups led to the emergence of a new dominant social group. These new social relationships, in turn, generated new discontent, conflict, and development. The French utopian socialists had depicted the problems of capitalist society and had raised the issue of property redistribution. Both Hegel and Saint-Simon led Marx to

Karl Marx's socialist philosophy eventually triumphed over most alternative versions of socialism in Europe, but his monumental work became subject to varying interpretations, criticisms, and revisions that continue to this day. Library of Congress

see society and economic conditions as developing through historical stages. The classical economists had produced the analytical tools for an empirical, scientific examination of the industrial capitalist society.

Using the intellectual tools that Hegel, the French utopian socialists, and the British classical economists provided, Marx fashioned a philosophy that gave a special role or function to the new industrial workforce as the single most important driving force of contemporary history. Marx later explained to a friend:

What I did that was new was to prove: (1) that the existence of classes is bound up with particular historical phases in the development of production; (2) that the class struggle necessarily leads to the dictatorship of the proletariat; (3) that this dictatorship itself only constitutes the transition to the abolition of all classes and to a classless society.[3]

In the *Communist Manifesto* and his numerous other writings, Marx equated the fate of the proletariat—that is, the new industrial labor force—with the fate of humanity itself. According to Marx, as the proletariat came to liberate itself from its bondage to the capitalist mode of industrial production, such liberation would eventually amount to the liberation of all humanity. It was this utopian vision of human emancipation, no matter how much the actual later development of the European and world economy failed to conform to Marx's predictions, that drew many people from Europe and elsewhere to embrace much of his thought and to base their political actions on their understanding of his philosophy. Besides this wider vision, however, the details of Marx's argument were also important for later nineteenth-century and twentieth-century European political life.

Revolution Through Class Conflict In the *Communist Manifesto*, Marx and Engels contended that human history must be understood rationally and as a whole. History is the record of humankind's coming to grips with physical nature to produce the goods necessary for survival. That basic productive process determines the structures, values, and ideas of a society. Historically, the organization of the means of production has always involved conflict between the classes that owned and controlled the means of production and the classes that worked for them. That necessary conflict has provided the engine for historical development; it is not an accidental by-product of mismanagement or bad intentions. Thus, piecemeal reforms cannot eliminate the social and economic evils inherent in the very structures of production. To achieve that, a radical social transformation is required. The development of capitalism will make such a revolution inevitable.

In Marx's and Engels's eyes, the class conflict that had characterized previous Western history had become sim-

plified during the early nineteenth century into a struggle between the bourgeoisie and the proletariat, or between the middle class associated with industry and commerce, on the one hand, and the workers, on the other. The character of capitalism itself ensured the sharpening of the struggle. Capitalist production and competition would steadily increase the size of the unpropertied proletariat. Large-scale mechanical production crushed both traditional and smaller industrial producers into the ranks of the proletariat. As the business structures grew larger and larger, the competitive pressures would squeeze out smaller middle-class units. Competition among the few remaining giant concerns would lead to more intense suffering for the proletariat. The process also meant the proletariat itself would continue to expand to include more and more people. As this ever-expanding body of workers suffered increasingly from the competition among the ever-enlarging firms, Marx contended, they would eventually begin to foment revolution. Finally, they would overthrow the few remaining owners of the means of production. For a time, the workers would organize the means of production through a dictatorship of the proletariat. This would eventually give way to a propertyless and classless communist society.

This proletarian revolution was inevitable, according to Marx and Engels. The structure of capitalism required competition and consolidation of enterprise. Although the class conflict involved in the contemporary process resembled that of the past, it differed in one major respect: The struggle between the capitalistic bourgeoisie and the industrial proletariat would culminate in a wholly new society that would be free of class conflict. The victorious proletariat, by its very nature, could not be a new oppressor class: "The proletarian movement is the self-conscious, independent movement of the immense majority, in the interest of the immense majority."[4] The result of the proletarian victory would be "an association in which the free development of each is the condition for the free development of all."[5] The victory of the proletariat over the bourgeoisie would represent the culmination of human history. For the first time in human history, one group of people would not be oppressing another. (See "Karl Marx and Friedrich Engels Describe the Class Struggle," page 668.)

The economic environment of the 1840s had conditioned Marx's analysis. The decade had seen much unemployment and deprivation. During the later part of the century, however, European and American capitalism did not collapse as he had predicted, nor did the middle class become proletarianized. Rather, the industrial system benefited more and more people. Nonetheless,

[3]Albert Fried and Ronald Sanders, eds., *Socialist Thought: A Documentary History* (Garden City, NY: Anchor Doubleday, 1964), p. 295.

[4]Robert C. Tucker, ed., *The Marx-Engels Reader* (New York: W. W. Norton, 1972), p. 353.

[5]Tucker, *The Marx-Engels Reader*, p. 353.

KARL MARX AND FRIEDRICH ENGELS DESCRIBE THE CLASS STRUGGLE

The Communist Manifesto (1848) is arguably the most influential political pamphlet of modern European history. In that relatively brief document, Karl Marx and Friedrich Engels portrayed human history as developing from ancient times to the present through a series of economic class struggles. In the contemporary world, they saw the complex struggles of the past reduced to a head-on economic, political, and social clash between the bourgeoisie, or capital-owning class, and the proletariat, or workers. Both groups had emerged in the course of history. The bourgeoisie had arisen from medieval townsmen asserting their liberty against feudal landowners and then against other groups of aristocrats. In turn, as the bourgeoisie came to dominate the economy and invest their capital in modern industry, they produced the contemporary wage-labor force. Over time this labor force came to see that its interests opposed those of its economic masters. The result was to be the final class conflict of history because, as Marx and Engels argued, the proletariat, unlike any previous group seeking to establish its liberty, was so large that its victory was also the victory of humanity itself.

Whom do Marx and Engels portray as the previous enemies of the bourgeoisie? How did bourgeois economic development and dominance lead to a society based on the "cash nexus"? Why is the bourgeoisie responsible for the emergence of the proletariat? Why is the victory of the proletariat inevitable?

The history of all hitherto existing society is the history of class struggles. . . .

Our epoch, the epoch of the bourgeoisie, possesses, however, this distinctive feature: it has simplified the class antagonisms. Society as a whole is more and more splitting up into two great hostile camps, into two great classes directly facing each other: Bourgeoisie and Proletariat. . . .

Each step in the development of the bourgeoisie was accompanied by a corresponding political advance of that class. . . .

The bourgeoisie, wherever it has gotten the upper hand, has put an end to all feudal, patriarchal, idyllic relations. It has pitilessly torn asunder the motley feudal ties that bound man to his "natural superiors," and has left remaining no other nexus between man and man than naked self-interest, than callous "cash payment." . . .

The proletariat goes through various stages of development. With its birth begins its struggle with the bourgeoisie. . . .

But with the development of industry the proletariat not only increases in number; it becomes concentrated in greater masses, its strength grows, and it feels that strength more. The various interests and conditions of life within the ranks of the proletariat are more and more equalized, in proportion as machinery obliterates all distinctions of labour, and nearly everywhere reduces wages to the same low level. . . .

The bourgeoisie finds itself involved in a constant battle. . . .

Of all the classes that stand face to face with the bourgeoisie today, the proletariat alone is a really revolutionary class. . . .

All previous historical movements were movements of minorities, or in the interest of minorities. The proletarian movement is the self-conscious, independent movement of the immense majority, in the interest of the immense majority. . . .

The advance of industry, whose involuntary promoter is the bourgeoisie, replaces the isolation of the labourers, due to competition, by their revolutionary combination, due to association. The development of Modern Industry, therefore, cuts from under its feet the very foundation on which the bourgeoisie produces and appropriates products. What the bourgeoisie, therefore, produces, above all, is its own grave-diggers. Its fall and the victory of the proletariat are equally inevitable. . . .

The proletarians have nothing to lose but their chains. They have a world to win.

Karl Marx and Friedrich Engels, *The Communist Manifesto*, in Lawrence H. Simon, ed., *Karl Marx, Selected Writings* (Indianapolis: Hackett Publishing Company, Inc, 1994), pp. 158, 159, 160, 161, 165, 166–167, 168, 169, 186. © 1994 International Publishers Co. Reprinted by permission of International Publishers Co., Inc./New York.

within a generation of the publication of the *Communist Manifesto*, Marxism had captured the imagination of many socialists, especially in Germany, and large segments of the working class. Marxist doctrines appeared to be based on the empirical evidence of hard economic fact. Marxism's scientific claim helped spread the ideology as science became more influential during the second half of the century. At its core, however, the attraction of the ideology was its utopian vision of ultimate human liberation, no matter how illiberal or authoritarian the governments that embraced the Marxist vision in the twentieth century were.

▼ 1848: Year of Revolutions

In 1848, a series of liberal and nationalistic revolutions erupted across the Continent. (See Map 21–2.) No single factor caused this general revolutionary groundswell; rather, similar conditions existed in several countries. Severe food shortages had prevailed since 1846. Grain and potato harvests had been poor. The famine in Ireland was simply the worst example of a more widespread situation. The commercial and industrial economy was also depressed. Unemployment was widespread. Systems of poor relief were overburdened. These

Map 21–2 **CENTERS OF REVOLUTION IN 1848–1849** The revolution that toppled the July Monarchy in Paris in 1848 soon spread to Austria and many of the German and Italian states. Yet by the end of 1849, most of these uprisings had been suppressed.

difficulties, added to the wretched living conditions in the cities, heightened the frustration and discontent of the urban artisan and laboring classes.

The dynamic force for change in 1848 originated, however, not with the working classes, but with the political liberals, who were generally drawn from the middle classes. Throughout the Continent, liberals were pushing for their program of a more representative government, civil liberty, and unregulated economic life. The repeal of the English Corn Laws and the example of peaceful agitation by the Anti–Corn Law League encouraged them. The liberals on the Continent wanted to pursue similar peaceful tactics. To put additional pressure on their governments, however, they began to appeal for the support of the urban working classes. The latter, however, wanted improved working and economic conditions, rather than a more liberal government. Moreover, their tactics were frequently violent rather than peaceful. The temporary alliance of liberals and workers in several states overthrew or severely shook the old order; then the allies began to fight each other.

Finally, outside France, nationalism was an important common factor in the uprisings. Germans, Hungarians, Italians, Czechs, and smaller national groups in eastern Europe sought to create national states that would reorganize or replace existing political entities. The Austrian Empire, as usual, was the state nationalism most profoundly endangered. At the same time, various national groups clashed with each other during these revolutions.

The immediate results of the 1848 revolutions were stunning. Never in a single year had Europe known so many major uprisings. The French monarchy fell, and other thrones were shaken. Yet the revolutions proved to be a false spring for progressive Europeans. Without exception, the revolutions failed to establish genuinely liberal or national states. The conservative order proved stronger and more resilient than anyone had expected. Moreover, the liberal middle-class political activists in each country discovered they could no longer push for political reform without also raising the social question. The liberals refused to follow political revolution with social reform and thus isolated themselves from the working classes. Once separated from potential mass support, the liberal revolutions became an easy prey for the armies of the reactionary classes.

France: The Second Republic and Louis Napoleon

As had happened twice before, the revolutionary tinder first blazed in Paris. The liberal political opponents of the corrupt regime of Louis Philippe and his minister Guizot organized a series of political banquets. They used these occasions to criticize the government and de-

mand further admission for them and their middle-class supporters to the political process. The poor harvests of 1846 and 1847 and the resulting high food prices and unemployment brought working-class support to the liberal campaign. On February 21, 1848, the government forbade further banquets. A large one had been scheduled for the next day. On February 22, disgruntled Parisian workers paraded through the streets demanding reform and Guizot's ouster. The next morning the crowds grew, and by afternoon, Guizot had resigned. The crowds erected barricades, and numerous clashes occurred between the citizenry and the municipal guard. On February 24, 1848, Louis Philippe abdicated and fled to England.

The National Assembly and Paris Workers   The liberal opposition, led by the poet Alphonse de Lamartine (1790–1869), organized a provisional government. The liberals intended to call an election for an assembly that would write a republican constitution. The various working-class groups in Paris, however, had other ideas: They wanted a social as well as a political revolution. Led by Louis Blanc, they demanded representation in the cabinet. Blanc and two other radical leaders became ministers. Under their pressure, the provisional government organized national workshops to provide work and relief for thousands of unemployed workers.

On Sunday, April 23, an election based on universal male suffrage chose the new National Assembly. The result was a legislature dominated by moderates and conservatives. In the French provinces, many people resented the Paris radicals and were frightened by their ideas. The church and the local notables still exercised considerable influence. Peasants feared that Parisian socialists would confiscate their small farms. The new conservative National Assembly had little sympathy for the expensive national workshops, which they incorrectly perceived to be socialistic.

Throughout May, government troops and the unemployed workers and artisans of Paris clashed. As a result, the assembly closed the workshops to new entrants and planned to eject many enrolled workers. By late June, barricades again appeared in Paris. On June 24, under orders from the government, General Louis Cavaignac (1802–1857), with troops drawn largely from the conservative countryside, moved to destroy the barricades and quell disturbances. During the next two days, more than four hundred people were killed. Thereafter, troops hunted down another 3,000 persons in street fighting. The drive for social revolution had ended.

Emergence of Louis Napoleon   The so-called June Days confirmed the political predominance of conservative property holders in French life. They wanted a state that was safe for small property. Late in 1848, the election for president confirmed this search for social

During the February days of the French Revolution of 1848, crowds in Paris burned the throne of Louis Philippe.   Bildarchiv Preussischer Kulturbesitz

order. The new president was Louis Napoleon Bonaparte (1808–1873), a nephew of the great emperor. For most of his life, he had been an adventurer living outside of France. Twice he had attempted to lead a coup against the July Monarchy. The disorder of 1848 gave him a new opportunity to enter French political life. After the corruption of Louis Philippe and the turmoil of the early months of the Second Republic, the voters turned to the name of Bonaparte as a source of stability and greatness.

The election of the "Little Napoleon" doomed the Second Republic. Louis Napoleon was dedicated to his own fame rather than to republican institutions. He was the first of the modern dictators who, by playing on unstable politics and social insecurity, changed European life. He quarreled with the National Assembly and claimed that he, rather than they, represented the will of the nation. In 1851, the assembly refused to amend the constitution to allow the president to run for reelection. Consequently, on December 2, 1851, the anniversary of the great Napoleon's victory at Austerlitz, Louis Napoleon

seized power. Troops dispersed the assembly, and the president called for new elections. More than two hundred people died resisting the coup, and more than 26,000 persons were arrested throughout the country. Almost 10,000 persons who opposed the coup were transported to Algeria.

Yet, in the plebiscite of December 21, 1851, more than 7.5 million voters supported the actions of Louis Napoleon and approved a new constitution that consolidated his power. Only about 600,000 citizens dared to vote against him. A year later, in December 1852, an empire was proclaimed, and Louis Napoleon became Emperor Napoleon III. Again a plebiscite approved the action. For the second time in just over fifty years, France had turned from republicanism to Caesarism.

Frenchwomen in 1848   The years between the February Revolution of 1848 and the Napoleonic coup of 1851 saw major feminist activity by Frenchwomen. Especially in Paris, women seized the opportunity of the collapse of the July Monarchy to voice demands for reform of their social conditions. They joined the wide variety of political clubs that emerged in the wake of the revolution. Some of these clubs emphasized women's rights. Some women even tried unsuccessfully to vote in the elections of 1848. Both middle-class and working-class women were involved in these activities. The most radical group of women called themselves the Vesuvians, after the volcano in Italy. They claimed it was time for the demands of women to erupt like pent-up lava. They demanded full domestic household equality between men and women, the right of women to serve in the military, and similarity in dress for both sexes. They also conducted street demonstrations. The radical character of their demands and actions lost them the support of more moderate women.

Certain Parisian women quickly attempted to use for their own cause the liberal freedoms that suddenly had become available. They organized the *Voix des femmes (The Women's Voice)*, a daily newspaper that addressed issues of concern to women. The newspaper insisted that improving the lot of men would not necessarily improve the condition of women. They soon organized a society with the same name as the newspaper. Many of the women involved in the newspaper and society had earlier been involved in Saint-Simonian or Fourierist groups. Members of the *Voix des femmes* group were relatively conservative feminists. They cooperated with male political groups, and they urged the integrity of the family and fidelity in marriage. They furthermore warmly embraced the maternal role for women but tried to use it to raise the importance of women in society. Because motherhood and child rearing are so important to a society, they argued, women must receive better education, economic security, equal civil rights, property rights, and the rights to work and vote. The provisional government made no move to enact these rights, although some members of the assembly supported the women's groups. The emphasis on family and motherhood represented, in part, a defensive strategy to prevent conservative women and men from accusing the advocates of women's rights of seeking to destroy the family and traditional marriage.

The fate of French feminists in 1848 was similar to that of the radical workers. They were thoroughly defeated and their efforts wholly frustrated. Once the elections were held that spring, the new government expressed no sympathy for their causes. The closing of the national workshops adversely affected women workers as well as men and blocked one outlet that women had used to make their needs known. The conservative crackdown on political clubs closed another arena in which women had participated. Women were soon specifically forbidden to participate in political clubs either by themselves or with men. These repressive actions repeated what had happened to politically active Frenchwomen and their organizations in 1793.

THE REVOLUTIONARY CRISIS OF 1848 TO 1851

1848

February 22–24	Revolution in Paris forces the abdication of Louis Philippe
February 26	National workshops established in Paris
March 3	Kossuth attacks the Habsburg domination of Hungary
March 13	Revolution in Vienna
March 15	The Habsburg emperor accepts the Hungarian March Revolution Laws in Berlin
March 18	Frederick William IV of Prussia promises a constitution; revolt against Austria in Milan
March 19	Frederick William IV is forced to salute the corpses of slain revolutionaries in Berlin
March 22	Piedmont declares war on Austria
April 23	Election of the French National Assembly
May 15	Worker protests in Paris lead the National Assembly to close the national workshops
May 17	Habsburg emperor Ferdinand flees from Vienna to Innsbruck
May 18	The Frankfurt Assembly gathers to prepare a German constitution
June 2	Pan-Slavic Congress gathers in Prague
June 17	Austrian troops suppress a Czech revolution in Prague
June 23–26	Troops of the National Assembly suppress a workers' insurrection in Paris
July 24	Austria defeats Piedmont
September 17	General Jellachich invades Hungary
October 31	Vienna falls to General Windischgraetz
November 15	Papal minister Rossi is assassinated in Rome
November 16	Revolution in Rome
November 25	Pope Pius IX flees Rome
December 2	Habsburg Emperor Ferdinand abdicates and Francis Joseph becomes emperor
December 10	Louis Napoleon is elected president of the Second French Republic

1849

January 5	General Windischgraetz occupies Budapest
February 2	The Roman Republic is proclaimed
March 12	War is resumed between Piedmont and Austria
March 23	Piedmont is defeated, and Charles Albert abdicates the crown of Piedmont in favor of Victor Emmanuel II

14. Bobbies were a unique force in that they
    a. only attended to property offenses.
    b. wore special uniforms.
    c. did not carry guns.
    d. were despised by the working class.
    e. were commissioned by private companies.

15. For most of his life, Malthus contended that the effect of rising workers' wages was population increase and that therefore
    a. there would be a need to invest in housing.
    b. crime rates would rise.
    c. the government should begin to promote contraception.
    d. there would be a constant pressure to lower wages.
    e. there would be an enormous strain on the food supply.

16. The author of *The Principles of Morals and Legislation* (1889) was
    a. Ricardo.
    b. Bentham.
    c. Smith.
    d. Fourier.
    e. Owen.

17. The British repealed the Corn Laws in 1846 as a result of
    a. mob violence.
    b. new leadership in Parliament.
    c. pressure from the monarch.
    d. demand for lower prices.
    e. the Irish famine.

18. The dynamic force behind the revolutions of 1848 was the
    a. working poor.
    b. political liberals.
    c. socialists.
    d. Marxists.
    e. landless peasants.

19. The Prussian constitution of 1850 called for all of the following *except*
    a. universal male suffrage.
    b. property ratio to representation.
    c. loyalty oaths to the monarch for the armed forces.
    d. ministers answerable to the monarch.
    e. legislative right to propose laws.

20. The lasting effect of the Vienna Uprising was the
    a. new rights for student groups.
    b. Magyarization of Hungary.
    c. massive investments in sewage and clean water.
    d. trade union rights.
    e. emancipation of serfs.

DOCUMENT-BASED QUESTION

Directions: Construct a valid essay that directly addresses the central issue of the following question. Use facts from the documents provided and from the chapter to prove the position you take in your thesis statement.

On the basis of the evidence provided in the following documents, describe the experiences of women workers during the early Industrial Revolution. What drew women into the factories and mines of Britain?

Document A

Source: Women factory workers explain their opposition to efforts to eliminate women's employment in factories, *The Examiner.*

. . . we have looked with no little anxiety for your opinion on the Factory Bill. . . . You are for doing away with our services in manufacturing altogether. So much the better, if had pointed out any other more eligible and practical employment for the surplus female labour. . . .

We see no way of escape from starvation, but to accept the very tempting offers of the newspapers, held out as bait to us, fairly to ship ourselves off to Van Dieman's Land [Tasmania] on the very delicate errand of husband hunting, and having arrived at the "Land of Goshen" jump ashore, who a "Who wants me?" . . .

Document B

Source: A women miner describes her life, *Parliamentary Papers.*

My cousin looks after my children in the day time. I am very tired when I get home at night. I fall asleep sometimes before I get washed. I am not so strong as I was, and cannot stand my work so well as I used to. I have drawn [filled and hauled coal baskets] till I have hathe skin off me; the belt and chain is worse when we are in the family way. My feller (husband) has beaten me many a times for not being ready. I were not used to it at first, and he had little patience.

I have known many a man beat his drawer. I have known men to take liberties with the drawers, and some of the women have bastards.

Document C

Women working in an early textile factory.

Document D

A female factory worker describes her co-workers.

I saw among my coworkers—the despised factory women—examples of the most extraordinary sacrifices for others. If there was a special emergency in one family, then they chipped in their kreuzers to help. Even though they had worked twelve hours in the factory and many still had an hour's walk home, they mended their own clothes, without ever having been taught how. They took apart their old dresses to fashion new ones from separate pieces, which they sewed at night and on Sundays.

For more on women and the early Industrial Revolution, see pages 654–659 of this chapter.

The Abolition of Slavery in the Transatlantic Economy

ONE OF THE most important developments during the age of Enlightenment and revolution was the opening of a crusade to abolish chattel slavery in the transatlantic economy. The antislavery movement constituted the greatest and most extensive achievement of liberal reformers during the eighteenth and nineteenth centuries. Indeed, it marked the first time in the history of the world that a society actually tried to abolish slavery. This achievement came as the result of the impact of Christian ethics, Enlightenment ideals, slave revolts, revolutionary wars in America and Europe, civil war in the United States, and economic dislocation in the slave economies themselves. In 1750, almost no one seriously questioned the existence of slavery, but, by 1888, the institution no longer existed in the transatlantic economy.

Chattel slavery—the ownership of one human being by another—had existed in the West as well as elsewhere in the world since ancient times and had received intellectual and religious justification throughout the history of the West. Both Plato and Aristotle provided arguments for slavery based on the assertion that persons in bondage were intended by nature to be slaves. Christian writers similarly accommodated themselves to the institution. They contended that the most harmful form of slavery was the enslavement of the soul to sin rather than the enslavement of the physical body. They also argued that genuine freedom was realized through one's relationship to God and that problems relating to the injustices of inequality would be solved in the hereafter. Christian scholastic thinkers in the Middle Ages portrayed slavery as part of the natural and necessary hierarchy of the universe.

Slavery Spreads to the Americas

Although a vast slave trade existed throughout the Mediterranean world through the end of the Middle Ages, slavery was no longer a dominant institution on the European continent or within the European economy. The European encounter with America at the end of the fifteenth century radically transformed this situation. The American continent and the West Indies presented opportunities for achieving great wealth, but a major labor shortage existed in these regions. Eventually slavery provided the means to resolve this labor shortage.

The establishment and maintenance of slavery in the transatlantic economy drew Europeans and Americans into various relationships with Africa. About the same time as the encounter with America, Europeans made contact with areas of West Africa where slavery already existed. This region became the chief source of slaves imported into the Americas. Four centuries later, during the antislavery movement, Europeans would seek to change the African economy by ending its dependence on the slave trade. Those efforts led to the penetration of Africa by European traders, missionaries, and finally colonial forces and administrators.

Although at one time or another slaves labored throughout the Americas, the system of slavery became primarily identified with the plantation economy stretching from Maryland south to Brazil, where tropical products, initially primarily sugar, were produced by slave labor. This plantation economy existed from approximately the late sixteenth through the late nineteenth centuries. The slaves on whose labor this economy was based included Native Americans enslaved within both the Spanish Empire and North America, and Africans forcibly imported into the Americas. Consequently, the slaves were virtually always of a different race from their masters. Race itself soon became part of the justification for the social hierarchy of the plantation world. In and of itself, the fact of slavery in the Americas was not unusual to the Western experience or to that of other societies in Africa or Asia. Slavery had existed at most times and places in human history. Far more unusual in the history of the West, and for that matter in the experience of all other societies that had held and continued to hold slaves, was the emergence after 1760 of an international movement to abolish chattel slavery in the transatlantic economy.

The Crusade Against Slavery

The eighteenth-century crusade against slavery originated in a profound change in the religious and intellectual outlooks on slavery among small but influential groups in both America and Europe. The entire thrust of Enlightenment reasoning to the extent that it challenged or questioned the wisdom of existing institutions gnawed away at the older defenses of slavery, most particularly the concept of an unchanging social hierarchy. Although some writers associated with the Enlightenment, including John Locke, were reluctant to question slavery and even defended it, the general Enlightenment rhetoric of equality stood in sharp contrast to the radical inequality of slavery. Montesquieu sharply satirized slavery in *The Spirit of the Laws* (1748). Similarly, the emphasis of Adam Smith in *The Wealth of Nations* (1776) on free labor and efficiency of free markets undermined defenses of slavery.

Within much eighteenth-century literature, there emerged a tendency to idealize primitive peoples living in cultures very different from those of Europe. Previously such peoples had been regarded as backward and rebellious. Now numerous writers portrayed them as embodying a lost human virtue. This expanding body of literature transformed the way many people thought about slavery and allowed some Europeans to look on African slaves in the Americas as having been betrayed and robbed of an original innocence. Additionally, much eighteenth-century European ethical thinking, as well as later romantic poetry, emphasized empathy and feel-

After 1807, the British Royal Navy patrolled the West African coast attempting to intercept slave-trading ships. In 1846, the British ship HMS *Albatross* captured a Spanish slave ship, the *Albañoz*, and freed the slaves. A British officer depicted the appalling conditions in the slave hold in this watercolor.
The Granger Collection, New York

ing. In such a climate, attitudes toward slavery were transformed. Once considered to be the natural and deserved result of some deficiency in slaves themselves, slavery now grew to be regarded as undeserved and unacceptable. The same kind of ethical thinking led reformers to believe that by working against slavery, for virtually the first time defined as an unmitigated evil, they would realize their own highest ethical character.

Religious movements became the single most important cultural force to foster the antislavery crusade. The evangelical religious revival associated with Methodism and with other forms of Protestant preaching emphasized the conversion experience and the change of heart as a sign of having received salvation. In 1774, John Wesley, the founder of Methodism, attacked slaveholding in *Thoughts on Slavery*. Turning against slaveholding and slave trading by plantation owners and slave traders served to illustrate one clear example of such a change of heart. Some slaveholders and slave traders feared they might be endangering their own salvation by their association with the institution. John Newton, a former slave trader who underwent an evangelical conversion, wrote the hymn "Amazing Grace."

The initial religious protest against slavery originated among English Quakers, a radical Protestant religious group founded by George Fox in the seventeenth century. By the early eighteenth century, it had solidified itself into a small but relatively wealthy sect in England. Members of Quaker congregations at that time actually owned slaves in the West Indies and participated in the transatlantic slave trade. During the Seven Years' War (1756–1763), however, many Quakers experienced economic hardship. Furthermore, the war created other difficulties for the English population as a whole. Certain Quakers decided the presence of the evil of slavery in the world explained these troubles. They then sought to remove this evil from their own lives and that of their congregations and began to take action against the whole system of slavery that characterized the transatlantic economy.

Just as the slave system was a transatlantic affair, so was the crusade against it. Quakers in both Philadelphia and England soon moved against the institution. The most influential of the early antislavery writers was Anthony Benezet, a Philadelphia Quaker, whose most important publications were *Some Considerations on the Keeping of Negroes* (1754) and *A Short Account of That Part of Africa Inhabited by the Negroes* (1762). The latter work emphasized the manner in which the slave trade degraded African society itself. Benezet also drew heavily on Montesquieu. This may not be surprising because Enlightenment writers often admired the English Quakers as exemplifying a religion of tolerance and reason.

By the earliest stages of the American Revolution a small group of reformers, normally spearheaded by

Quakers, had established an antislavery network. They published pamphlets, sermons, and books on the subject. The Society for the Relief of Free Negroes Illegally Held in Bondage, the first antislavery society in the world, was founded in Philadelphia in 1775 and, when reorganized in 1784 as the Pennsylvania Abolition Society, Benjamin Franklin became its president. In 1787, the Committee for the Abolition of the Slave Trade was organized in England. In France, the Société des Amis des Noirs was founded in 1778.

The turmoil of the American Revolution and the founding of the American republic gave these groups the occasion for some of their earliest successes. Emancipation gradually, but nonetheless steadily, spread among the northern states. In 1787, the Continental Congress forbade the presence of slavery in the newly organized Northwest Territory north of the Ohio River. What is important so far as the crusade against slavery is concerned is the disappearance of slavery in approximately half of the new nation and the commitment not to extend it to an important new territory. Despite these American developments, Great Britain became and remained the center for the antislavery movement. In 1772, a decision by the chief justice affirmed that slaves brought into Great Britain could not forcibly be removed. The decision, though of less immediate importance than some thought at the time, gave further impetus to the small but growing group of antislavery reformers.

During the early 1780s, the antislavery reformers in Great Britain decided to work toward ending the slave trade rather than the institution of slavery. The horrors of the slave trade caught the public's attention in 1783 when the captain of the slave ship *Zong* threw more than 130 slaves overboard in order to collect insurance. For the reformers, attacking the trade rather than the institution appeared a less radical and a more achievable reform. To many, the slave trade appeared to be a more obvious crime than the holding of slaves, which seemed a more nearly passive act. Furthermore, attacking slavery itself involved serious issues of property rights that might alienate potential supporters of the abolition of the slave trade. The antislavery groups also believed that if the trade was ended, planters would have to treat their remaining slaves more humanely.

By the end of the 1780s, the English Quakers were joined by evangelical Christians from the Church of England to form the Society for the Abolition of the Slave Trade. The most famous of the new leaders was William Wilberforce who, for the rest of his life, fought the slave trade. Year after year, he introduced a bill to abolish the slave trade. Finally, in 1807, he saw it passed.

Slave Revolts

While the British reformers worked for the abolition of the slave trade, slaves themselves in certain areas took matters into their own hands. The largest emancipation of slaves to occur in the eighteenth century came on the island of Saint Domingue (Haiti), France's wealthiest colony, as a result of the slave revolt of 1794 led by Toussaint L'Ouverture and Jean-Jacques Dessalines. The revolt in Haiti and Haiti's eventual independence in 1804 stood as a warning to slave owners throughout the

The slave revolt on the French island of St. Domingue achieved the largest emancipation of slaves in the eighteenth century. In this print, Toussaint L'Ouverture leads the revolt. CORBIS/Bettmann

West Indies. (See Chapter 20.) There would be other slave revolts such as those in Virginia led by Gabriel Prosser in 1800 and by Nat Turner in 1831, in South Carolina led by Denmark Vesey in 1822, in British-controlled Demarra in 1823 and 1824, and in Jamaica in 1831. Each of these was brutally suppressed.

Economic Pressures

Through the conclusion of the Seven Years' War, the West Indies interest group had been one of the most powerful in the British Parliament. During the second half of the eighteenth century and beyond, new and different economic interest groups began to displace the influence of that group. Within the West Indies themselves the planters were experiencing soil exhaustion and new competition from newly tilled islands controlled by France and other new islands opened for sugar cultivation. Some older plantations were being abandoned while others operated with low profitability. Now with the new islands under cultivation there was a glut of sugar on the market, and as a consequence the price was falling.

Under these conditions some British West Indies planters, for reasons that had nothing to do with religion or humanitarianism, began to favor curtailing the slave trade. Without new slaves, French planters would lack the labor they needed to exploit their islands. During the Napoleonic Wars, the British captured a number of the valuable French islands. In order to protect the planters on the older British West Indies islands, in 1805, the British cabinet issued Orders in Council, which forbade the importation of slaves into the newly acquired French islands. By 1807, the abolition sentiment was strong enough for Parliament to pass Wilberforce's measure prohibiting slave trading from any British port.

The suppression of this trade through the navy became one of the fundamental pillars of nineteenth-century British foreign policy. Throughout the rest of the Napoleonic era the British attempted to draw allies into a policy of forbidding the slave trade. They also attempted unsuccessfully to incorporate the abolition of the slave trade into the settlement of the Congress of Vienna. In addition, the British navy maintained squadrons of ships around the coast of West Africa to halt slave traders. Although the French and Americans also patrolled the West African coast, neither was deeply committed to ending the slave trade. Nonetheless, in 1824, the American Congress made slave trading a capital offense.

The French invasion of Spain in 1808, as discussed in Chapter 21, provided the spark for the Latin American wars of independence. The leaders of these movements had been influenced by the liberal ideas of the Enlightenment and were, thus, generally predisposed to disapprove of slavery. The political groups seeking independence from Spain also sought the support of slaves by promises of emancipation. Furthermore, the newly independent nations needed good relations with Britain to support their economies, and, consequently, most of them very quickly freed their slaves to gain such support. The actual freeing of slaves was gradual and often came some years after the emancipation legislation. Despite the gradual nature of this abolition, slavery would disappear by approximately the middle of the nineteenth century from all of the newly independent nations of Latin America. The great exception was Brazil.

Abolishing Slavery in the New World

British reformers gradually recognized that the abolition of the slave trade had not actually improved the lot of slaves. In 1823, they adopted as a new goal the gradual emancipation of slaves. The chief voices calling for this change were those of William Wilberforce and Thomas Clarkson, who were active in founding the Abolition Society. The savagery with which West Indian planters put down slave revolts in 1823 and 1824 and again in 1831 strengthened the resolve of the antislavery reformers. By 1830, the reformers had abandoned the goal of gradual abolition and demanded the complete abolition of slavery. In 1833, after the passage of the Reform Bill in Great Britain, they achieved that goal when Parliament abolished the right of British subjects to hold slaves. In the British West Indies, 750,000 slaves were freed within a few years.

The other old colonial powers in the New World tended to be much slower in their own abolition of slavery. Portugal did little or nothing about slavery in Brazil, and when that nation became independent of Portugal, its new government continued slavery. Portugal ended slavery elsewhere in its American possessions in 1836; the Swedes, in 1847; the Danes, in 1848; but the Dutch not until 1863. France had witnessed a significant antislavery movement throughout the first half of the century, but slavery was not abolished in its West Indian possessions until the revolution of 1848.

During the first thirty years of the nineteenth century, the institution of slavery revived and achieved strong new footholds in the transatlantic world. These areas were the lower south of the United States for the cultivation of cotton, Brazil for the cultivation of coffee, and Cuba for the cultivation of sugar. World demand for these products made the slave system economically viable in these regions. Consequently, despite the drive to emancipation, which had succeeded in the northern states of the United States, slavery persisted in much of the Caribbean and in most of Latin America.

An antislavery movement had existed in the United States since the end of the eighteenth century, but it took on a new life in the early 1830s. The British abolition of slavery in the West Indies served as an inspiration to a new generation of American antislavery leaders, the most famous of whom was William Lloyd Garrison. He and other American abolitionists raised the question of slavery throughout the 1830s and 1840s. It was, however, the disposition of lands the United States had acquired in the Mexican War of 1847 that placed slavery at the heart of the American political debate. For over a decade the question of slavery sharply divided Americans. The election of Lincoln in 1860 brought those sectional tensions to a head, and the American Civil War erupted in the spring of 1861. In 1863, Lincoln issued the Emancipation Proclamation, which ended slavery in the combatant states. The passage of the Thirteenth Amendment to the American Constitution in 1865 abolished slavery in the United States.

The end of slavery in the United Sates left both Cuba, the most important remaining possession of the Spanish Empire in the Americas, and Brazil with slave economies. In 1868, an insurgency against Spanish colonial policy broke out in Cuba and lasted for ten years. This war disrupted much of the Cuban economy and saw some planters move toward using free labor. The Spanish forces attacked other planters by freeing their slaves. In 1870, the Spanish government passed a measure for gradual emancipation of slaves in both Cuba and Puerto Rico. In subsequent years, the sugar economy collapsed, making slavery unprofitable. Abolitionist agitation grew in Spain, and slavery was abolished in its New World colonies in 1886.

Brazil, under British pressure, had effectively ended the slave trade in 1850, but the question of the abolition of slavery was postponed for many years. In 1871, as a result of abolitionist agitation and because the Emperor Pedro II opposed slavery, a law providing for an extremely gradual abolition of slavery was passed. During the next two decades, abolitionist sentiment grew, and public figures from across the political spectrum voiced opposition to slavery. In 1888, Isabel Christiana, then regent while her father Pedro II was in Europe for medical treatment, signed a law abolishing slavery in Brazil without any form of compensation to the slave owners.

The abolition of slavery in Brazil ended a system of forced labor that had characterized the transatlantic economy for almost four hundred years. Wherever slavery had existed, however, its presence left and would continue to leave long-term consequences for the realization of equality and social justice. The end of slavery, consequently, did not end the problems that slavery created in the transatlantic world.

Africa and the End of Slavery

The transatlantic slave trade itself had adversely affected the life of Africa both through the vast loss of population over the centuries as well as through the undermining of African society through the internal slave trade. Similarly, the crusade against transatlantic slavery had drawn Europeans much more deeply into the affairs of the African continent. The various efforts by antislavery groups began to impact Africa in the first half of the nineteenth century. Their goal was to transform the African economy by substituting new peaceful trade in tropical goods for the slave trade. The reformers hoped to spread both free trade and Christianity into Africa. "Christianity and civilization" and "Christianity and commerce" were popular slogans of the day. Missionaries and traders saw themselves as natural allies in the cause.

The first effort in this direction was the resettlement of black slaves or children of black slaves into Africa. In 1787, the British established a colony of poor free blacks from Britain in Sierra Leone. The effort went badly, but a few years later former slaves once owned by British loyalists in America were settled there. Then former slaves from the Caribbean were brought to Sierra Leone. The colony became relatively successful only after 1807, when the British navy landed slaves rescued from captured slave trading ships. Sierra Leone, though quite small, became a place on the coast of West Africa where Christianity and commerce rather than the slave trade flourished. The French established a smaller experiment at Libreville in Gabon. The most famous and lasting attempt to resettle former black slaves in Africa was the establishment of Liberia by the efforts of the American Colonization Society after 1817. Liberia became an independent republic in 1847. All these efforts to move former slaves back to Africa had only modest success, but they did affect the life of West Africa.

Other antislavery reformers were less interested in establishing outposts for the settlement of former slaves than in transforming the African economy itself. In 1841, the African Civilization Society under the leadership of Thomas Fowell Buxton sent a group of paddle steamers up the Niger River in the hope of creating the basis for new trade with Africa. The goal was to establish free trade between Britain and Africa in which the manufactured goods of the former, most particularly textiles, would be exchanged for tropical agricultural goods produced by Africans. The expedition failed because most of its members died of disease. Yet the impulse to penetrate Africa for purposes of spreading trade and Christianity would continue for the rest of the century.

The antislavery movement marked the first of the intrusions of the European powers well beyond the coast of West Africa into the heart of the continent. After the American Civil War finally halted any large-scale demand for slaves from Africa, the antislavery reformers began to focus on ending the slave trade in East Africa and the Indian Ocean. This drive against slavery and the slave trade in Africa itself became one of the rationales for European interference in Africa during the second half of the nineteenth century and served as one of the foundations for the establishment of the late-century colonial empires.

The crusade against slavery in the transatlantic economy eventually touched most of the world. It radically transformed the economies and societies of both North and South America. It led to a transformation of the African economy and eventually to a significant European presence in the life of African societies. Efforts to eradicate slavery, particularly the efforts by British reformers, caused the spread of the reform movement into Asia. Slavery has not been abolished throughout the world, and antislavery societies still exist, though they receive little publicity. Yet the abolition of slavery in the transatlantic world stands as one of the most permanent achievements of the forces of eighteenth-century Enlightenment and revolution.

What were the justifications of slavery prior to the eighteenth century? What religious and intellectual developments led some Europeans and some Americans to question and criticize the institution of slavery? Why did antislavery reformers first concentrate on the abolition of the slave trade? How did both slavery and antislavery lead Americans and Europeans to become involved with Africa? How did that involvement change between approximately 1600 and 1870?

Giuseppe Garibaldi, the charismatic Italian nationalist leader, can be seen on the right urging on his troops in the rout of Neapolitan forces at Calatafimi, Sicily, in 1860. Bildarchiv Preussischer Kulturbesitz

22

The Age of Nation-States

KEY TOPICS

- Reforms in the Ottoman Empire

- The unification of Italy and Germany

- The shift from empire to republic in France

- The emergence of a dual monarchy in Austria-Hungary

- Reforms in Russia, including the emancipation of the serfs

- The emergence of Great Britain as the exemplary liberal state and its confrontation with Irish nationalists

THE REVOLUTIONS OF 1848 collapsed in defeat for both liberalism and nationalism. In the 1850s, conservative regimes were entrenched across the Continent. Yet only a quarter century later, many of the major goals of early-nineteenth-century liberals and nationalists had been reached. Italy and Germany were each united under conservative constitutional monarchies. The Habsburg emperor accepted constitutional government and recognized the liberties of the Magyars of Hungary. In Russia, the tsar emancipated the serfs. France had become a republic. Liberalism and even democracy flourished in Great Britain. The Ottoman Empire also undertook major reforms.

Paradoxically, most of these developments occurred under conservative political leadership. War and competition with other states compelled some governments to pursue new policies at home as well as abroad. They had to find novel methods to maintain the loyalty of their subjects. Some conservative leaders preferred to carry out a popular policy on their own terms, so that they, rather than the liberals, would receive credit. Other leaders acted as they did because they had no choice.

▼ The Crimean War (1853–1856)

As has so often been true in modern European history, the impetus for change originated in war. The Crimean War (1853–1856) was rooted in the long-standing desire of Russia to extend its influence over the Ottoman Empire. Two disputes led to the conflict. First, as noted in Chapter 17, the Russians had, since the time of Catherine the Great (r. 1762–1796), been given protective oversight of Orthodox Christians in the Empire, and France had similar oversight of Roman Catholics. In 1851, yielding to French pressure, the Ottoman sultan had assigned care of certain holy places in Palestine to Roman Catholics. This decision angered the Russians and damaged Russian prestige. Second, Russia wanted to extend its control over the Ottoman provinces of Moldavia and Walachia (now in Romania). In the summer of 1853, the Russians used their right to protect Orthodox Christians in the Ottoman Empire as the pretext to occupy the two provinces. Shortly thereafter, the Ottoman Empire declared war on Russia.

Of far more significance to the great powers than the protection of Christian sites in Palestine was the fate of the weak Ottoman Empire. The Russian government envisioned the eventual breakup of the empire and hoped to extend its influence at Ottoman expense. Both France and Britain, though recognizing the difficulties of the Ottoman government and using it to their own advantage when the opportunity presented itself, opposed Russian expansion in the eastern Mediterranean, where they had extensive naval and commercial interests. The French emperor Napoleon III (r. 1852–1870) also thought an activist foreign policy would shore up domestic support for his regime.

On March 28, 1854, France and Britain declared war on Russia in alliance with the Ottomans. Much to the disappointment of Tsar Nicholas I, Austria and Prussia remained neutral. The Austrians had their own ambitions in the Balkans, and, for the moment, Prussia followed Austrian leadership.

Both sides conducted the conflict ineptly, a fact that became widely known in Western Europe because the Crimean War was the first to be covered by war correspondents and photographers. The ill-equipped and poorly commanded armies became bogged down along the Crimean coast of the Black Sea. In September 1855, after a long siege, the Russian fortress of Sevastopol finally fell to the French and British. Thereafter, both sides moved to end the war.

Peace Settlement and Long-Term Results

In March 1856, a conference in Paris concluded the Treaty of Paris. This treaty required Russia to surrender territory near the mouth of the Danube River, to recognize the neutrality of the Black Sea, and to renounce its claims to protect Orthodox Christians in the Ottoman Empire. Even before the conference, Austria had forced Russia to withdraw from Moldavia and Walachia. The image of an invincible Russia that had prevailed across Europe since the close of the Napoleonic Wars was shattered.

Also shattered was the Concert of Europe (see Chapter 20), as a means of dealing with international relations on the Continent. Following the successful repression of the 1848 uprisings, the great powers feared revolution less than they had earlier in the century, and, consequently, they displayed much less reverence for the Vienna settlement. As historian Gordon Craig put it, "After 1856, there were more powers willing to fight to overthrow the existing order than there were to take up arms to defend it."[1] As a result, for about twenty-five years after the Crimean War, European affairs were unstable, producing a period of adventurism in foreign policy. While these events reshaped Western Europe, however, the Ottoman Empire over whose fate the Crimean War had been fought undertook reforms. These need to be considered before we return to the events in Europe.

▼ Reforms in the Ottoman Empire

The short-lived Napoleonic invasion of the Ottoman province of Egypt in 1798–1799 (see Chapter 19) sparked a drive for change in the Ottoman Empire. In 1839, under pressure from imperial bureaucrats who had studied in Europe, the sultan issued a decree, called the *Hatt-i Sharif of Gülhane*, that attempted to reorganize the empire's administration and military along European lines. This decree opened what became known as the *Tanzimat* (meaning "reorganization") era of the Ottoman Empire, lasting from 1839 to 1876. The reforms, which were drawn up by administrative councils and not issued arbitrarily by the sultan, liberalized the economy, ended the practice of tax farming, and sought to eliminate corruption. The *Hatt-i Sharif* was particularly

---

[1]*The New Cambridge Modern History*, Vol. 10 (Cambridge: Cambridge University Press, 1967), p. 273.

A Closer ⟩ LOOK

THE CRIMEAN WAR RECALLED

THE WARS OF the third quarter of the nineteenth century brought European armies once again to the foreground in European culture and art. Beginning with the Crimean War (1853–1856) and ending with those of German unification (1870), the armed forces of the various nation-states reforged European political life. Artists might record even the most difficult moments of warfare. Here, Elizabeth Thompson, Lady Butler, portrayed *Roll Call after an Engagement, Crimea*. She completed the work in 1874 two decades after the war, and Queen Victoria purchased it.

The abilities of the aristocratic officers leading the British army had been discredited, so Butler here portrays ordinary troops.

A certain nostalgia for the comradeship of soldiers even under the most difficult circumstances penetrates this scene at a time when Britain had not engaged in a major war for many years.

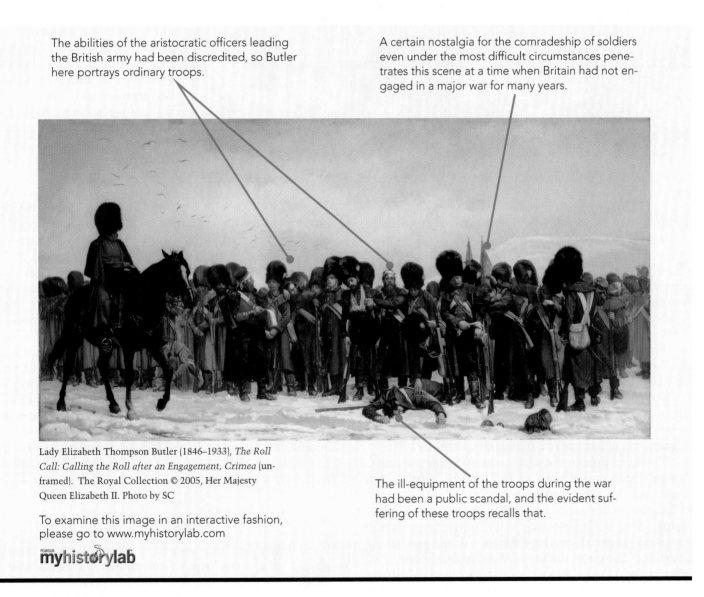

Lady Elizabeth Thompson Butler (1846–1933), *The Roll Call: Calling the Roll after an Engagement, Crimea* (unframed). The Royal Collection © 2005, Her Majesty Queen Elizabeth II. Photo by SC

To examine this image in an interactive fashion, please go to www.myhistorylab.com

myhistorylab

The ill-equipment of the troops during the war had been a public scandal, and the evident suffering of these troops recalls that.

remarkable for extending civic equality to Ottoman subjects regardless of their religion. Muslims, Christians, and Jews were now equal before the law. The empire also made it much easier for Muslims to enter into commercial agreements with non-Muslims, both within the empire and from abroad.

Another reform decree, called the *Hatti-i Hümayun*, was promulgated in 1856 at the close of the Crimean War. Under the influence of Britain and France, it spelled out the rights of non-Muslims more explicitly, giving them equal obligations with Muslims for military service and equal opportunity for state employment and

Ottoman reformers established a parliament in 1877, but the sultan retained most political authority. *Illustrated London News* of April 14, 1877. Mary Evans Picture Library Ltd.

admission to state schools. The decree also abolished torture and allowed foreigners to acquire some forms of property. In time, printing presses and Western-oriented schools appeared in the empire mainly via Christian missionaries, many of whom were Americans. For the first time in its long history, the Ottoman Empire actually sought to copy European legal and military institutions and the secular values flowing from liberalism.

The imperial government took these steps to gain the loyalty of its Christian subjects at a time when nationalism was making increasing inroads among them. In effect, during this reform era the Ottoman government broke down the millet system (see Chapter 13) and sought to define all its citizens as Ottoman subjects rather than as members of particular religious communities.

However, putting these reforms into practice proved difficult. In some regions of the empire, especially in Egypt and Tunis, local rulers were virtually independent of Istanbul. They carried out their own modernizing reforms, often working closely with European powers. In the capital itself, power struggles developed among courtiers, European-oriented administrators and army officers, merchants who prospered from the changes, and the *ulema*, which sought to maintain the rule of Islamic law. Because of these tensions, as well as growing nationalism in various regions, the Ottoman Empire failed to achieve genuine political strength and stability. Many Ottomans questioned the wisdom of Tanzimat and warned that replacing long-standing Islamic institutions with European ones would lead to disaster.

The Balkan wars of the late 1870s, which resulted in either the independence of, or Russian or Austrian dominance over, most of the empire's European holdings, demonstrated the inability of the Ottoman Empire to master its own destiny. (See Chapter 26.) The response to these foreign defeats resulted in greater efforts to modernize the army and the economy and to build railways and telegraphs. In 1876, reformers persuaded the sultan to proclaim an Ottoman constitution on the grounds that European political arrangements as well as technology accounted for European strength. The constitution called for a parliament consisting of an elected chamber of deputies and an appointed senate (these met for the first time in 1877) but left the sultan's power mostly intact. Nonetheless, a new sultan soon rejected even these limited steps toward constitutionalism and dismissed the parliament. In 1908, military officers carried out a revolution against the authority, though not the person, of the sultan. Another group of reformist officers, known as the *Young Turks*, came to the fore with another program to modernize the empire. They were still in charge when World War I broke out, and their decision to enter the war on the side of the Central Powers in November 1914 led to the empire's defeat and collapse. (See Chapter 26.)

One of the underlying themes of all these attempts at reform and modernization from 1839 to 1914 was the increasing secularization of the government, which sought less to question the Islamic foundations of society than to reduce the influence of the Muslim religious authorities on the state.

▼ Italian Unification

Nationalists had long wanted to unite the small, mostly absolutist principalities of the Italian peninsula into a single state. During the first half of the century, however, opinion differed about how to achieve Italian unification.

Romantic Republicans

One approach to the issue was *romantic republicanism*. After the Congress of Vienna, secret republican societies were founded throughout Italy, the most famous of which was the **Carbonari** ("charcoal burners"). They were ineffective.

After the failure of nationalist uprisings in Italy in 1831, the leadership of romantic republican nationalism passed to Giuseppe Mazzini (1805–1872). He became the most important nationalist leader in Europe and brought new fervor to the cause. He once declared, "Nationality is the role assigned by God to a people in the work of humanity. It is its mission, its task on earth, to the end that God's thought may be realized in the world."[2] In 1831, he founded the Young Italy Society to drive Austria from the peninsula and establish an Italian republic.

During the 1830s and 1840s, Mazzini and his fellow republican Giuseppe Garibaldi (1807–1882) led insurrections. Both were involved in the ill-fated Roman Republic of 1849. Throughout the 1850s, they continued to conduct what amounted to guerrilla warfare. Because both men spent much time in exile, they became well known across the Continent and in the United States.

Republican nationalism frightened moderate Italians, who wanted to rid themselves of Austrian domination but not to establish a republic. For a time, these people had hoped the papacy would sponsor unification. That solution became impossible after the experience of Pius IX with the Roman Republic in 1849. Consequently, at midcentury, "Italy" remained a geographical expression rather than a political entity.

Yet by 1860, the Italian peninsula was transformed into a nation-state under a constitutional monarchy. Count Camillo Cavour (1810–1861), the prime minister of Piedmont—not of romantic republicans—made this possible. His method was a force of arms tied to secret diplomacy. The spirit of Machiavelli must have smiled over the enterprise.

Cavour's Policy

Piedmont (officially styled the Kingdom of Sardinia), in northwestern Italy, was the most independent state on the peninsula. The Congress of Vienna had restored the kingdom as a buffer between French and Austrian ambitions. As has been seen, during 1848 and 1849, King Charles Albert of Piedmont, after having promulgated a conservative constitution, twice unsuccessfully fought Austria. After the second defeat, he abdicated in favor of his son, Victor Emmanuel I (r. 1849–1878). In 1852, the new monarch chose Cavour as his prime minister.

A cunning statesman, Cavour had begun political life as a conservative but had gradually moved toward a moderately liberal position. He had made a fortune by investing in railroads, reforming agriculture on his estates, and editing a newspaper. He was deeply im-

Count Camillo Cavour (1810–1861) used an opportunistic alliance with France against Austria and military interventions in the Papal States and southern Italy to secure Italian unification under King Victor Emmanuel II of Piedmont, rather than as the republic that Mazzini and Garibaldi had advocated. © Archivo Iconografico, S.A./CORBIS

bued with the ideas of the Enlightenment, classical economics, and utilitarianism. Cavour was a nationalist of a new breed who had no respect for Mazzini's ideals. A strong monarchist, Cavour rejected republicanism. Economic and material progress, not romantic ideals, required a large, unified state on the Italian peninsula.

Cavour believed that if Italians proved themselves to be efficient and economically progressive, the great powers might decide that Italy could govern itself. As premier, he promoted free trade, railway construction, expansion of credit, and agricultural improvement. He believed that such material and economic bonds, rather than fuzzy romantic yearnings, must unite the Italians. Cavour also recognized the need to capture the loyalties of those Italians who believed in other varieties of nationalism. He thus fostered the Nationalist Society, which established chapters in other Italian states to press for unification under the leadership of Piedmont. Finally, the prime minister believed only French intervention could defeat Austria and unite Italy. The accession of Napoleon III in France seemed to open the way for such aid.

[2]Quoted in William L. Langer, *Political and Social Upheaval, 1832–1852* (New York: Harper Torchbooks, 1969), p. 115.

French Sympathies Cavour used the Crimean War to bring Italy into European politics. In 1855, Piedmont sent 10,000 troops to help France and Britain capture Sebastopol. This small but significant participation in the war allowed Cavour to raise the Italian question at the Paris conference. He left Paris with no diplomatic reward, but his intelligence and political capacity had impressed everyone, especially Napoleon III. During the rest of the decade, he achieved further international respectability for Piedmont by opposing Mazzini, who was still attempting to lead nationalist uprisings. By 1858, Cavour represented a moderate liberal, monarchist alternative to both republicanism and reactionary absolutism in Italy.

Cavour bided his time. Then, in January 1858, an Italian named Felice Orsini attempted to assassinate Napoleon III. The incident heightened the emperor's interest in the Italian issue. He saw himself continuing his more famous uncle's liberation of the peninsula. He also saw Piedmont as a potential ally against Austria. In July 1858, Cavour and Napoleon III met at Plombières in southern France. Riding alone in a carriage, with the emperor at the reins, the two men plotted to provoke a war in Italy that would permit them to defeat Austria. A formal treaty in December 1858 confirmed the agreement.

War with Austria In early 1859, tension grew between Austria and Piedmont as Piedmont mobilized its army. On April 22, Austria demanded that Piedmont demobilize. That allowed Piedmont to claim that Austria was provoking a war. France intervened to aid its ally. On June 4, the Austrians were defeated at Magenta, and on June 24 at Solferino. Meanwhile, revolutions had broken out in Tuscany, Modena, Parma, and the Romagna provinces of the Papal States.

With the Austrians in retreat and the new revolutionary regimes calling for union with Piedmont, Napoleon III feared too extensive a Piedmontese victory. On July 11, he concluded peace with Austria at Villafranca. Piedmont received Lombardy, but Venetia remained under Austrian control. Cavour felt betrayed by France, but the war had driven Austria from most of northern Italy. Later that summer, Parma, Modena, Tuscany, and the Romagna voted to unite with Piedmont. (See Map 22–1.)

Garibaldi's Campaign At this point, the forces of romantic republican nationalism compelled Cavour to pursue the complete unification of northern and southern Italy. In May 1860, Garibaldi landed in Sicily with more than 1,000 troops, who had been outfitted in the north. He captured Palermo and prepared to attack the mainland. By September he controlled the city and kingdom of Naples, probably the most corrupt example of Italian absolutism. For more than two decades Garibaldi had hoped to form a republican Italy, but Cavour forestalled him. He rushed Piedmontese troops south to confront Garibaldi. On the way, they conquered the rest of the Papal States except the area around Rome, which French troops saved for the pope. Garibaldi's nationalism won out over his republicanism, and he accepted Piedmontese domination. In late 1860, Naples and Sicily voted to join the Italian kingdom. In response to the help received from France and Napoleon III's concern over the new large nation-state on his borders, Piedmont ceded Savoy and Nice, where much of the population spoke French, to France. (See "Compare & Connect: Nineteenth Century Nationalism: Two Sides," pages 694–695.)

The New Italian State

In March 1861, Victor Emmanuel II was proclaimed king of Italy. Three months later Cavour died. The new state more than ever needed his skills, because Piedmont had, in effect, not so much united Italy as conquered it. The republicans resented the treatment of Garibaldi. The clericals were appalled at the conquest of the Papal States. In the south, armed resistance against the imposition of Piedmontese-style administration continued until 1866. The economies and societies of north and south Italy were incompatible. The south was rural, poor, and backward. The north was industrializing, and its economy was increasingly linked to that of the rest of Europe. The social structures of the two regions reflected these differences, with large landholders and peasants dominant in the south and an urban working class emerging in the north.

The political framework of the united Italy could not overcome these problems. The constitution, which was that promulgated for Piedmont in 1848, provided for a conservative constitutional monarchy. Parliament consisted of two houses: a senate appointed by the king and a chamber of deputies elected on a narrow franchise. Ministers were responsible to the monarch, not to Parliament. These arrangements did not foster vigorous parliamentary life. Political leaders often simply avoided major problems. In place of efficient, progressive government, such as Cavour had brought to Piedmont, a system called *transformismo* developed. Bribery, favors, or a seat in the cabinet "transformed" political opponents into government supporters. Italian politics became a byword for corruption.

The unification was not complete. Many Italians believed other territories should be added to their nation. The most important of these were Venetia and Rome. The former was gained in 1866 in return for Italy's

Map 22–1 **THE UNIFICATION OF ITALY** Beginning with the association of Sardinia and Piedmont by the Congress of Vienna in 1815, unification was achieved through the expansion of Piedmont between 1859 and 1870. Both Cavour's statesmanship and the campaigns of ardent nationalists played large roles.

Nineteenth Century Nationalism: Two Sides

THE SECOND QUARTER of the nineteenth century witnessed the unification first of Italy and then of Germany. Both processes involved warfare. The Kindom of Sardina conquered and united northern Italy, and then Garibaldi led his "Red Shirts" to conquer the south. Prussia united Germany in a series of wars against Denmark, Austria, and France. These two documents illustrate different justifications for the call to military action for unifying each nation. Garibaldi presents his forces as liberators against tyranny. Treitschke makes an argument for the German annexation of Alsace and Lorraine on the grounds of national security and history.

QUESTIONS

1. How does Garibaldi's manifesto turn the war for unification in southern Italy into a popular campaign?

2. How does Garibaldi portray the struggle for unification as a battle against tyranny?

3. On what grounds does Treitschke base the German claim to Alsace and Lorraine?

4. Why does Treitschke contend it is proper to ignore the wishes of the people involved?

5. How could one nationalist, Garibaldi, see his goal as one of popular liberation while another, Treitschke, see his as reclaiming lost regions of a national homeland? Are these two views compatible or distinctly different?

I. Garibaldi Calls Italians to Act to Unify Their Nation

Garibaldi was the most charismatic figure in the drive for Italian unification. He was the leader of guerrilla military forces known as the Red Shirts. In May 1860 after northern Italy had been united under the Kingdom of Sardinia whose monarch was Victor Emmanuel, Garibaldi landed his force of about a thousand men in Sicily and from there they crossed into southern Italy to conquer the kingdom of Naples and make it part of a united Italian state. Garibaldi was himself a republican, but he reconciled himself to supporting Victor Emmanuel. Before leaving Sicily for the mainland, Garibaldi issued this call to arms demanding that the Italians of southern Italy rise against the kingdom of Naples. The various geographical areas he mentions were located from the south northward to Rome. The Tincino River

lay in northern Italy and Garibaldi is recalling the participation of his troops in the war that unified the north.

Italians! The Sicilians are fighting against the enemies of Italy and for Italy. To help them with money, arms, and especially men, is the duty of every Italian.

Let the Marches, Umbria, Sabine, the Roman Campagna, and the Neapolitan territory rise, so as to divide the enemy's forces.

If the cities do not offer a sufficient basis for insurrection, let the more resolute throw themselves into the open country. A brave man can always find a

General Giuseppe Garibaldi (1807–1882).
Museum of the City of New York/Hulton Archive

weapon. In the name of Heaven, hearken not to the voice of those who cram themselves at well-served tables. Let us arm. Let us fight for our brothers; tomorrow we can fight for ourselves.

A handful of brave men, who have followed me in battles for our country, are advancing with me to the rescue. Italy knows them; they always appear at the hour of danger. Brave and generous companions, they have devoted their lives to their country; they will shed their last drop of blood for it, seeking no other reward than that of a pure conscience.

"Italy and Victor Emmanuel!"—that was our battle-cry when we crossed the Tincino; it will resound into the very depths of Aetna [the volcanic mountain]. As this prophetic battle-cry re-echoes from the hills of Italy to the Tarpeian Mount, the tottering thrones of tyranny will fall to pieces, and the whole country will rise like one man.

Source: "History," *The Annual Register . . . 1860* (London, 1861), p. 221 as quoted in Raymond Phineas Stearns, *Pageant of Europe: Sources and Selections from the Renaissance to the Present Day* (New York: Harcourt, Brace and Company, 1948), pp. 583–584.

II. Heinrich von Treitschke Demands the Annexation of Alsace and Lorraine

The Franco-Prussian War witnessed outbursts of extreme nationalistic rhetoric on both sides. One such voice was that of the German historian Heinrich von Treitschke (1834–1896). In a newspaper article, he demanded the annexation of Alsace and Lorraine from France. He did so even though the population of Alsace wished to remain part of France and German was not the dominant language in the region. He appealed to an earlier time when the region had been German in language and culture, and he asserted that "might makes right" to assure German domination.

The sense of justice to Germany demands the lessening of France. . . .

What is demanded by justice is, at the same time, absolutely necessary for our security. . . .

Every State must seek the guarantees of its own security in itself alone. . . .

In view of our obligation to secure the peace of the world, who will venture to object that the people of Alsace and Lorraine do not want to belong to us? The doctrine of the right of all the branches of the German race to decide on their own destinies, the plausible solution of demagogues without a fatherland, shiver to pieces in presence of the sacred necessity of these great days. These territories are ours by the right of the sword, and

we shall dispose of them in virtue of a higher right—the right of the German nation, which will not permit its lost children to remain strangers to the German Empire. We Germans, who know Germany and France, know better than these unfortunates themselves what is good for the people of Alsace. . . . Against their will we shall restore them to their true selves. We have seen with joyful wonder the undying power of the moral forces of history, manifested far too frequently in the immense changes of these days, to place much confidence in the value of a mere popular disinclination. The spirit of a nation lays hold, not only of the generation which lives beside it, but of those who are before and behind it. We appeal from the mistaken wishes of the men who are there today to the wishes of those who were there before them. We appeal to all those strong German men who once stamped the seal of our German nature on the language and manners, the art and the social life of the Upper Rhine. Before the nineteenth century closes, the world will recognize that . . . we were only obeying the dictates of national honor when we made little account of the preferences of the people who live in Alsace today. . . .

At all times the subjection of a German race to France has been an unhealthy thing; today it is an offence against the reason of History—a vassalship of free men to half-educated barbarians. . . .

There is no perfect identity between the political and national frontier of any European country. Not one of the great Powers, and Germany no more than the rest of them, can ever subscribe to the principle that "language alone decides the formation of States." It would be impossible to carry that principle into effect. . . .

The German territory which we demand is ours by nature and by history. . . . In the tempests of the great Revolution the people of Alsace, like all the citizens of France, learned to forget their past. . . .

Most assuredly, the task of reuniting there the broken links between the ages is one of the heaviest that has ever been imposed upon the political forces of our nation. . . .

The people of Alsace are already beginning to doubt the invincibility of their nation, and at all events to divine the mighty growth of the German Empire. Perverse obstinacy, and a thousand French intrigues creeping in the dark, will make every step on the newly conquered soil difficult for us: but our ultimate success is certain, for on our side fights what is stronger than the lying artifices of the stranger—nature herself and the voice of common blood.

Source: From Heinrich von Treitschke, "What We Demand from France" (1870), in Heinrich von Treitschke, *Germany, France, Russia and Islam* (New York: G. P. Putnam's Sons, 1915), pp. 100, 102, 106, 109, 120, 122, 134–135, 153, 158.

alliance with Prussia in the Austro-Prussian War. French troops continued to guard Rome and the papacy until the troops were withdrawn during the Franco-Prussian War of 1870. The Italian state then annexed Rome and made it the capital. The papacy confined itself to the Vatican and remained hostile to the Italian state until the Lateran Accord of 1929. (See Chapter 27.)

By 1870, only the small province of Trent and the city of Trieste, both ruled by Austria, remained outside Italy. In and of themselves, these areas were not important, and their inhabitants were a mix of Italians, Germans, and Slavs, but they fueled the continued hostility of Italian nationalists toward Austria. The desire to liberate **Italia irredenta**, or "unredeemed Italy," was one reason for the Italian support of the Allies against Austria and Germany during World War I.

▼ German Unification

German unification was the most important political development in Europe between 1848 and 1914. (See Map 22–2.) It transformed the balance of economic, mil-

itary, and international power. Moreover, the way it was created largely determined the character of the new German state. Germany was united by the conservative army, the monarchy, and the prime minister of Prussia, who wanted to outflank Prussian liberals. A unified Germany, which two generations of German liberals had sought, was actually achieved for the most illiberal of reasons.

During the 1850s, German unification seemed remote. The political structure of the German-speaking lands was the German Confederation, which had been established at the Congress of Vienna. It was a loose federation of thirty-nine states of differing size and strength whose appointed representatives met in a central diet in Frankfurt. The two by far strongest states were Austria and Prussia. During the 1850s, Austria presided over the diet of the German Confederation. The major states continued to trade with each other through the *Zollverein* (tariff union), and railways linked their economies. Frederick William IV of Prussia had given up thoughts of unification under Prussian leadership. Austria continued to oppose any union that might lessen its influence. Liberal nation-

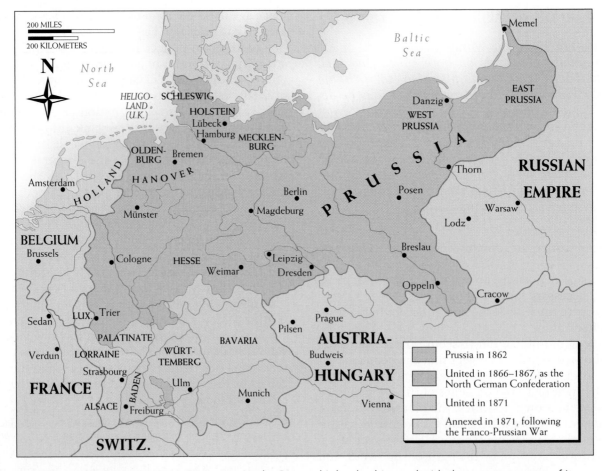

Map 22–2 **THE UNIFICATION OF GERMANY** Under Bismarck's leadership, and with the strong support of its royal house, Prussia used diplomatic and military means, on both the German and international stages, to forcibly unify the German states into a strong national entity.

alists had not recovered from the humiliations of 1848 and 1849, so they could do little or nothing for unification. What quickly overturned this static situation was a series of domestic political changes and problems within Prussia.

In 1858, Frederick William IV was adjudged insane, and his brother William assumed the regency. William I (r. 1861–1888), who became king in his own right in 1861, was less idealistic than his brother and more of a Prussian patriot. In the usual Hohenzollern tradition, his first concern was to strengthen the Prussian army. In 1860, his war minister and chief of staff proposed to enlarge the army, to increase the number of officers, and to extend the period of conscription from two to three years. The Prussian Parliament, created by the Constitution of 1850, refused to approve the necessary taxes. The liberals, who dominated the body, sought to avoid placing additional power in the hands of the monarchy. For two years, monarch and Parliament were deadlocked.

Bismarck

In September 1862, William I turned for help to the person who, more than any other single individual, shaped the next thirty years of European history: Otto von Bismarck (1815–1898). Bismarck came from Junker (noble landlord) stock. He attended a university and displayed an interest in German unification. During the 1840s, he was elected to the provincial diet, where he was so reactionary he disturbed even the king. Yet he had made his mark. From 1851 to 1859, Bismarck served as the Prussian representative to the German Confederation. Later he became Prussian ambassador to Russia and was ambassador to France when William I appointed him prime minister.

Although Bismarck entered public life as a reactionary, he had mellowed into a conservative. He opposed parliamentary government, but not a constitutionalism that preserved a strong monarchy. He understood that Prussia—and later, Germany—must have a strong industrial base. His years in Frankfurt arguing with his Austrian counterpart had hardened his Prussian patriotism. In politics, he was a pragmatist who put more trust in power and action than in ideas. As he declared in his first speech as prime minister, "Germany is not looking to Prussia's liberalism but to her power. . . . The great questions of the day will not be decided by speeches and majority decisions—that was the mistake of 1848–1849—but by iron and blood."[3] Yet this same minister, after having led Prussia into three wars, spent the next nineteen years seeking to preserve peace.

Upon becoming prime minister in 1862, Bismarck immediately moved against the liberal Parliament. He contended that even without new financial levies, the Prussian constitution permitted the government to carry out its functions on the basis of previously granted taxes. Therefore, taxes could be collected and spent despite the parliamentary refusal to vote them. The army and most of the bureaucracy supported this interpretation of the constitution. In 1863, however, new elections sustained the liberal majority in the Parliament. Bismarck had to find a way to attract popular support away from the liberals and toward the monarchy and the army. He, therefore, set about uniting Germany through the conservative institutions of Prussia. In effect, Bismarck embraced the cause of German nationalism as a strategy to enable Prussian conservatives to outflank Prussian liberals.

The Danish War (1864) Bismarck's vision of a united Germany did not include all German-speaking lands. That is to say, he pursued a *kleindeutsch*, or small German, solution to unification. He intended to exclude Austria from any future united German state. This goal required complex diplomacy.

The Schleswig-Holstein problem gave Bismarck the handle for his policy. The kings of Denmark had long ruled these two northern duchies, which had never actually become part of Denmark itself. Their populations were a mixture of Germans and Danes. Holstein, where Germans predominated, belonged to the German Confederation. In 1863, the Danish Parliament moved to incorporate both duchies into Denmark. The smaller states of the German Confederation proposed an all-German war to halt this move. Bismarck, however, wanted Prussia to act alone or only in cooperation with Austria. Together, the two large states easily defeated Denmark in 1864.

The Danish defeat increased Bismarck's personal prestige and strengthened his political hand. Over the next two years, he managed to maneuver Austria into war with Prussia. In August 1865, the two powers negotiated the Convention of Gastein, which put Austria in charge of Holstein and Prussia in charge of Schleswig. Bismarck then mended other diplomatic fences. He had gained Russian sympathy in 1863 by supporting Russia's suppression of a Polish revolt, and he persuaded Napoleon III to promise neutrality in an Austro-Prussian conflict. In April 1866, Bismarck promised Italy Venetia if it attacked Austria in support of Prussia when war broke out. Now Bismarck had to provoke his war.

The Austro-Prussian War (1866) Constant Austro-Prussian tensions had arisen over the administration of Schleswig and Holstein. Bismarck ordered the Prussian forces to be as obnoxious as possible to the Austrians. On June 1, 1866, Austria appealed to the German Confederation to intervene in the dispute. Bismarck claimed that this request violated the 1864 alliance and the

[3]Quoted in Otto Pflanze, *Bismarck and the Development of Germany: The Period of Unification: 1815–1871* (Princeton, NJ: Princeton University Press, 1963), p. 177.

The proclamation of the German Empire in the Hall of Mirrors at Versailles, January 18, 1871, after the defeat of France in the Franco-Prussian War. Kaiser Wilhelm I is standing at the top of the steps under the flags. Bismarck is in the center in a white uniform. Bildarchiv Preussischer Kulturbesitz

Convention of Gastein. The Seven Weeks' War, which resulted in the summer of 1866, led to the decisive defeat of Austria at Königgrätz in Bohemia.

The Treaty of Prague, which ended the conflict on August 23, was lenient toward Austria, which only lost Venetia, ceded as promised to Napoleon III, who in turn ceded it to Italy. Austria refused to give Venetia directly to Italy because the Austrians had crushed the Italians during the war. The treaty permanently excluded the Austrian Habsburgs from German affairs. Prussia had thus established itself as the only major power among the German states.

The North German Confederation In 1867, Prussia annexed Hanover, Hesse Kassel, Nassau, and the city of Frankfurt, all of which had all supported Austria during the war and deposed their rulers. Under Prussian leadership, all Germany north of the Main River now formed the North German Confederation. Each state retained its own local government, but all military forces were under federal control. The president of the federation was the king of Prussia, represented by his chancellor, Bismarck. A legislature consisted of two houses: a federal council, or **Bundesrat**, composed of members appointed by the governments of the states, and a lower house, or **Reichstag**, chosen by universal male suffrage.

Bismarck, the great conservative chancellor, unlike German liberals, actually embraced a democratic franchise because he sensed that the peasants would vote for conservatives Moreover, the *Reichstag* had little real power, because the ministers were responsible only to the monarch. The *Reichstag* could not even originate legislation. The chancellor had to propose all laws. The legislature did have the right to approve military budgets, but these were usually submitted to cover several years at a time. The constitution of the North German Confederation, which, after 1871, became the constitution of the German Empire, possessed some of the appearances, but none of the substance, of liberalism. Germany was, in effect, a military monarchy.

Bismarck's spectacular successes overwhelmed the liberal opposition in the Prussian Parliament. The liberals were split between those who prized liberalism and those who supported unification. In the end, nationalism proved more attractive. In 1866, the Prussian Parliament retroactively approved the military budget that it had rejected earlier. Bismarck had crushed the Prussian liberals by making the monarchy and the army the most popular institutions in the country. The drive toward German national unification had achieved his domestic Prussian political goal.

The Franco-Prussian War and the German Empire (1870–1871)

Bismarck now wanted to complete unification by bringing the states of southern Germany—Bavaria, Wurtemberg, Baden, and Hesse Darmstadt—into the newly established confederation. Spain gave him the excuse. In 1868, a military coup deposed the corrupt Bourbon queen of Spain, Isabella II (r. 1833–1868). To replace her, the Spaniards chose Prince Leopold of Hohenzollern-Sigmaringen, a Catholic cousin of William I of Prussia. On June 19, 1870, Leopold accepted the Spanish crown with Prussian blessings. Bismarck knew that France would object strongly to a Hohenzollern Spain.

On July 2, the Spanish government announced Leopold's acceptance, and the French reacted as expected. France sent its ambassador, Count Vincent Benedetti (1817–1900), to consult with William I, who was vacationing at Bad Ems. They discussed the matter at several meetings. On July 12, Leopold's father renounced his son's candidacy for the Spanish throne, fearing the issue would cause war between Prussia and France. William was relieved that conflict had been avoided, and he had not had to order Leopold to renounce the Spanish throne.

There the matter might have rested had it not been for the impetuosity of the French and the guile of Bismarck. On July 13, the French government instructed Benedetti to ask William for assurances he would tolerate no future Spanish candidacy for Leopold. The king refused but said he might take the question under further consideration. Later that day he sent Bismarck, who was in Berlin, a telegram reporting the substance of the meeting. The peaceful resolution of the controversy had disappointed the chancellor, who desperately wanted a war with France to complete unification. The king's telegram gave him a new opportunity to provoke war. Bismarck released an edited version of the dispatch. The revised Ems telegram made it appear that William had insulted the French ambassador. The idea was to goad France into declaring war.

The French government fell for Bismarck's bait and declared war on July 19. Napoleon III was sick and not eager for war, but his government believed victory

GERMAN AND ITALIAN UNIFICATION	
1854	Crimean War opens
1855	Cavour leads Piedmont into the war on the side of France and England
1856	Treaty of Paris concludes the Crimean War
1858 (January 14)	Attempt to assassinate Napoleon III
1858 (July 20)	Secret conference between Napoleon III and Cavour at Plombières
1859	War of Piedmont and France against Austria
1860	Garibaldi lands his forces in Sicily and invades southern Italy
1861 (March 17)	Proclamation of the Kingdom of Italy
1861 (June 6)	Death of Cavour
1862	Bismarck becomes prime minister of Prussia
1864	Danish War
1865	Convention of Gastein
1866	Austro-Prussian War
1866	Austria cedes Venetia to Italy
1867	North German Confederation formed
1870 (June 19–July 12)	Crisis over Hohenzollern candidacy for the Spanish throne
1870 (July 13)	Bismarck publishes the edited Ems dispatch
1870 (July 19)	France declares war on Prussia
1870 (September 1)	France defeated at Sedan and Napoleon III captured
1870 (September 4)	French Republic proclaimed
1870 (October 2)	Italian state annexes Rome
1871 (January 18)	Proclamation of the German Empire at Versailles
1871 (March 28–May 28)	Paris Commune
1871 (May 23)	Treaty of Frankfurt ratified between France and Germany

over the North German Confederation would renew popular support for the empire. Once the conflict erupted, the southern German states, honoring treaties of 1866, joined Prussia against France, whose defeat was not long in coming. On September 1, at the Battle of Sedan, the Germans not only beat the French army but also captured Napoleon III. By late September, Paris was besieged; it finally capitulated on January 28, 1871.

Ten days earlier, in the Hall of Mirrors at the Palace of Versailles, the German Empire had been proclaimed. The German princes requested William to accept the title of German emperor. The princes remained heads of their respective states within the new empire. Through the peace settlement with France, Germany annexed Alsace and part of Lorraine and forced the French to pay a large indemnity. (See "Heinrich von Treitschke Demands the Annexation of Alsace and Lorraine," page 695.)

Both the fact and the manner of German unification produced long-range effects in Europe. A powerful new state had been created in north central Europe. It was rich in natural resources and talented citizens. Militarily and economically, the German Empire would be far stronger than Prussia had been alone. The unification of Germany was also a blow to European liberalism, because the new state was a conservative creation. Conservative politics were now backed not by a weak Austria or an economically retrograde Russia, but by the strongest state on the Continent.

The two nations most immediately affected by German and Italian unification were France and Austria. The emergence of the two new unified states revealed French and Habsburg weakness. Each had to change. France returned to republican government, and the Habsburgs came to terms with their Magyar subjects.

▼ France: From Liberal Empire to the Third Republic

Historians divide the reign of Napoleon III (r. 1852–1870) into the years of the authoritarian empire and those of the liberal empire. The year of division is 1860. After the coup in December 1851, Napoleon III had controlled the legislature, censored the press, and harassed political dissidents. His support came from the army, property owners, the French Catholic Church, peasants, and businesspeople. They approved the security he ensured for property, his protection of the pope, and his economic program. French victory in the Crimean War had confirmed the emperor's popularity.

From the late 1850s onward, Napoleon III began to modify his policy. In 1860, he concluded a free-trade treaty with Britain and permitted freer debate in the legislature. By the late 1860s, he had relaxed the press laws and permitted labor unions. In 1870, he allowed the leaders of the moderates in the legislature to form a ministry, and he also agreed to a liberal constitution that made the ministers responsible to the legislature.

Napoleon III's liberal concessions sought to shore up domestic support to compensate for his failures in foreign policy. By 1860, he had lost control of the diplomacy of Italian unification. Between 1861 and 1867, he had

supported a disastrous military expedition against Mexico led by Archduke Maximilian of Austria that ended in defeat and Maximilian's execution. In 1866, France had watched passively while Bismarck and Prussia reorganized German affairs. The war of 1870 against Germany had been the French government's last and most disastrous attempt to shore up its foreign policy and secure domestic popularity.

The Second Empire, but not the war, came to an inglorious end with the Battle of Sedan in September 1870. The emperor was captured and then allowed to go to England, where he died in 1873. Shortly after news of Sedan reached Paris, a republic was proclaimed and a government of national defense established. Paris itself was soon under Prussian siege, and the government moved to Bordeaux. Paris finally surrendered in January 1871, but France had been ready to sue for peace long before.

The Paris Commune

The division between the provinces and Paris became sharper after the fighting with Germany stopped. Monarchists dominated the new National Assembly elected in February. For the time being, the assembly gave executive power to Adolphe Thiers (1797–1877), who had been active in French politics since 1830. He negotiated a settlement with Prussia (the Treaty of Frankfurt), which was officially ratified on May 23.

Many Parisians, having suffered during the siege, resented what they regarded as a betrayal by the monarchist National Assembly sitting at Versailles. The Parisians elected a new municipal government, called the *Paris Commune*, which was formally proclaimed on March 28, 1871. The Commune intended to administer Paris separately from the rest of France. Radicals and socialists of all stripes participated in the Commune. In April, the National Assembly surrounded Paris with an army. On May 8, this army bombarded the city. On May 21, it broke through the city's defenses. During the next seven days, the troops killed about 20,000 inhabitants while the communards shot scores of hostages.

The Paris Commune became a legend throughout Europe. Marxists regarded it as a genuine proletarian government that the French bourgeoisie had suppressed. This interpretation is mistaken. The Commune, though of shifting composition, was dominated by petty bourgeois members. The socialism of the Commune had its roots in Blanqui's and Proudhon's anarchism rather than in Marx's concept of class conflict. The Commune wanted not a workers' state, but a nation of relatively independent, radically democratic enclaves. Its suppression thus represented not only the protection of property, but also the triumph of the centralized nation-state. Just as the armies of Piedmont and Prussia had united the small states of Italy and Germany, the army of the

French National Assembly destroyed the particularistic political tendencies of Paris and, by implication, those of any other French community.

The Third Republic

The National Assembly backed into a republican form of government against its will. Its monarchist majority was divided in loyalty between the House of Bourbon and the House of Orléans. They could have surmounted this problem, because the Bourbon claimant, the count of Chambord, had no children and agreed to accept the Orléanist heir as his successor. Chambord refused to become king, however, if France retained the revolutionary tricolor flag. Even the conservative monarchists would not return to the white flag of the Bourbons, which symbolized extreme political reaction.

While the monarchists quarreled among themselves, events marched on. By September 1873, the indemnity had been paid, and the Prussian occupation troops had withdrawn. Thiers was ousted from office because he had displayed clear republican sentiments. The monarchists wanted a more sympathetic executive. They elected as president a conservative army officer, Marshal Patrice MacMahon (1808–1893), who was expected to prepare for a monarchist restoration. In 1875, the National Assembly, still monarchist in sentiment, but unable to find a king, decided to regularize the political system. It adopted a law that provided for a Chamber of Deputies elected by universal male suffrage, a senate chosen indirectly, and a president elected by the two legislative houses. This rather simple republican system had resulted from the bickering and frustration of the monarchists.

After numerous quarrels with the Chamber of Deputies, MacMahon resigned in 1879. His departure meant that dedicated republicans controlled the national government despite lingering opposition from the church, wealthy families, and a part of the army.

The political structure of the Third Republic proved much stronger than many citizens suspected at the time. It survived challenges from persons such as General Georges Boulanger (1837–1891), who would have imposed stronger executive authority. It also survived several scandals, such as those involving sales of awards of the Legion of Honor and widespread corruption of politicians and journalists by a company that tried to construct a canal in Panama, that made its politics appear increasingly sleazy. The institutions of the republic, however, allowed new ministers to replace those whose corruption was exposed.

The Dreyfus Affair

The greatest trauma of the Third Republic occurred over what became known as the *Dreyfus affair*. On December 22, 1894, a French military court found Cap-

---

MAJOR DATES IN THE HISTORY OF THE THIRD FRENCH REPUBLIC

1870	Defeat by Prussia and proclamation of republic
1871	Paris Commune
1873	Prussian occupation troops depart
1873	Marshal MacMahon elected president
1875	Major political institutions of Third Republic organized
1879	MacMahon resigns as president
1894	Captain Dreyfus convicted
1906	Dreyfus's conviction set aside

---

tain Alfred Dreyfus (1859–1935) guilty of passing secret information to the German army. The evidence against him was flimsy and was later revealed to have been forged. Someone in the officer corps had been passing documents to the Germans, and it suited the army investigators to accuse Dreyfus, who was Jewish. After Dreyfus had been sent to Devil's Island, a notorious prison in French Guiana, however, secrets continued to flow to the German army. In 1896, a new head of French counterintelligence reexamined the Dreyfus file and found evidence of forgery. A different officer was implicated, but a military court acquitted him of all charges.

By then the affair had provoked near-hysterical public debate. The army, the French Catholic Church, political conservatives, and vehemently anti-Semitic newspapers contended that Dreyfus was guilty. Such anti-Dreyfus opinion was dominant at the beginning of the affair. In 1898, however, the novelist Émile Zola (1840–1902) published a newspaper article entitled *"J'accuse"* ("I accuse"), in which he contended that the army had denied due process to Dreyfus and had suppressed or forged evidence. Zola was convicted of libel and fled to England to avoid serving a one-year prison sentence. (See "Émile Zola Accuses the Enemies of Dreyfus of Self-Interest and Illegal Actions," page 703.)

Zola was only one of numerous liberals, radicals, and socialists who had begun to demand a new trial for Dreyfus. Although these forces of the political left had come to Dreyfus's support rather slowly, they soon realized his cause could aid their own public image. They portrayed the conservative institutions of the nation as having denied Dreyfus the rights belonging to any citizen of the republic. They also claimed, and properly so, that Dreyfus had been framed to protect the guilty persons, who were still in the army. In August 1898, further evidence of forged material came to light. The officer responsible for those forgeries committed suicide

The prosecution of Captain Alfred Dreyfus, who is shown here standing on the right at his military trial, provoked the most serious crisis of the Third Republic. © Bettman/CORBIS

in jail, but a new military trial again convicted Dreyfus. The president of France immediately pardoned him, however, and eventually, in 1906, a civilian court set aside the results of both military trials.

The Dreyfus case divided France as no issue had done since the Paris Commune. By its conclusion, the conservatives were on the defensive. They had allowed themselves to persecute an innocent person and to manufacture false evidence against him to protect themselves from disclosure. They had also embraced violent anti-Semitism. On the political left, radicals, republicans, and socialists developed an informal alliance, which outlived the Dreyfus case itself. These groups realized that the political left had to support republican institutions to achieve its goals. Nonetheless, the political, religious, and racial divisions and suspicions growing out of the Dreyfus affair continued to divide the Third Republic until France's defeat by Germany in 1940.

▼ The Habsburg Empire

After 1848, the Habsburg Empire was a problem both to itself and for the rest of Europe. An ungenerous critic remarked that a standing army of soldiers, a kneeling army of priests, and a crawling army of informers supported the empire. In the age of national states, liberal institutions, and industrialism, the Habsburg domains remained primarily dynastic, absolutist, and agrarian. The Habsburg response to the revolts of 1848–1849 had been to reassert absolutism. Emperor Francis Joseph (r. 1848–1916) was honest, conscientious, and hardworking, but unimaginative. He reacted to events but rarely commanded them.

The coronation of Francis Joseph of Hungary in 1867 is depicted in this painting. The so-called *Ausgleich*, or Compromise, of 1867 transformed the Habsburg Empire into a dual monarchy in which Austria and Hungary became almost separate states except for defense and foreign affairs. Bildarchiv der Oesterreichischen Nationalbibliothek, Wien

MAJOR DATES IN LATE-NINETEENTH-CENTURY BRITAIN

1867	Second Reform Act
1868	Gladstone becomes prime minister
1869	Disestablishment of Church of Ireland
1870	Education Act and first Irish Land Act
1871	Purchase of army officers' commissions abolished
1871	Religious tests abolished at Oxford and Cambridge
1872	Secret Ballot Act
1874	Disraeli becomes prime minister
1875	Public Health Act and Artisan Dwelling Act
1880	Beginning of Gladstone's second ministry
1881	Second Irish Land Act and Irish Coercion Act
1884	Third Reform Act
1885	Gladstone announces support of Irish home rule
1886	Home Rule Bill defeated and Lord Salisbury becomes the Conservative prime minister
1892	Gladstone begins his third ministry; second Irish Home Rule Bill defeated
1903	Third Irish Land Act
1912	Third Irish Home Rule Bill passed
1914	Provisions of Irish Home Rule Bill suspended because of the outbreak of World War I

home rule issue then split the Liberal Party. In 1886, a group known as the Liberal Unionists joined with the Conservatives to defeat home rule. Gladstone called for a new election, but the Liberals were defeated. They remained divided, and Ireland remained firmly under English administration.

The new Conservative ministry of Lord Salisbury (1830–1903) attempted to reconcile the Irish to British rule through public works and administrative reform. The policy, which was tied to further coercion, had only marginal success. In 1892, Gladstone returned to power. A second Home Rule Bill passed the House of Commons but was defeated in the House of Lords. There the Irish question stood until after the turn of the century. The Conservatives sponsored a land act in 1903 that carried out the final transfer of land to tenant ownership. Ireland became a country of small farms. In 1912, a Liberal ministry passed the third Home Rule Bill. Under the provisions of the House of Lords Act of 1911, which curbed the power of the Lords, the bill had to pass the Commons three times over the Lords' veto to become law. The third passage occurred in the summer of 1914, but the implementation of home rule was suspended for the duration of World War I.

The Irish question affected British politics in a manner not unlike that of the Austrian nationalities problem. Normal British domestic issues could not be resolved because of the political divisions Ireland created. The split of the Liberal Party proved especially harmful to the cause of further social and political reform. People who could agree about reform could not agree about Ireland, and the Irish problem seemed more important. Because the two traditional parties failed to deal with the social questions by the turn of the century, a newly organized Labour Party began to fill the vacuum.

In Perspective

Between 1850 and 1875, the major contours of the political systems that would dominate Europe until World War I had been drawn. These systems and political arrangements solved, as far as such matters can be solved, many of the political problems that had troubled Europeans during the first half of the nineteenth century. On the whole, the concept of the nation-state had triumphed. Support for governments no longer stemmed from loyalty to dynasties, but from citizen participation. Moreover, the unity of nations was now based on ethnic, cultural, linguistic, and historical bonds. The parliamentary governments of Western Europe were different from the autocracies of eastern Europe, but both political systems had been compelled to recognize the force of nationalism and the larger role of citizens in political affairs. Only Russia failed to make such concessions. In Russia the only concession to popular opinion had been the emancipation of the serfs.

Future discontent would arise primarily from the demands of labor to enter the political processes and the unsatisfied aspirations of subject nationalities. These two sources of unrest would trouble Europe for the next forty years and would eventually undermine the political structures created during the late nineteenth century.

AP* TEST PREP

1. The period of reform in the Ottoman Empire that lasted from 1839 to 1876 is known as the
   a. *Tanzimat.*
   b. Era of Self-Strengthening.
   c. New Birth.
   d. *Hatt-i Sharif.*
   e. New Caliphate.

2. The events of the Crimean War shattered all of the following *except*
   a. public opinion of war heroics and commanders.
   b. the aura of Russian invincibility.
   c. the Concert of Europe.
   d. the Ottoman Empire.
   e. Ottoman complacency regarding reform.

3. Victor Emmanuel II was proclaimed king of unified Italy in
   a. 1820.
   b 1848.
   c. 1861.
   d. 1871.
   e. 1893.

4. One of the principle reasons unified Italy had trouble from the beginning was
   a. papal interference.
   b. failed diplomacy with Britain.
   c. Garibaldi's dominance.
   d. incompatibility between northern and southern Italian economies.
   e. inadequate investments in shipping.

5. _____ declared: "Germany is not looking to Prussia's liberalism but to her power."
   a. William I
   b. William II
   c. Joseph II
   d. Frederick William IV
   e. Bismarck

6. The peace settlement concluding the German annexation of Alsace and Lorraine also compelled the French to
   a. restore the republic.
   b. restore the monarchy.
   c. pay an indemnity.
   d. give Venetia to Italy.
   e. give up Corsica.

7. The Ausgleich of 1867 refers to the Austrian
   a. architectural redesign of Vienna.
   b. replacement of poor districts with factories in Vienna.
   c. dual monarchy.
   d. bicameral imperial parliament.
   e. policy of managing nationalist linguistic minorities.

8. Camillo Cavour played an instrumental role in
   a. ending the Crimean War.
   b. settling the Irish question.
   c. the leadership of the Paris Commune.
   d. passage of the Second Reform Act.
   e. the unification of Italy.

9. What German-speaking country did Bismarck intend to exclude from united Germany?
   a. Alsace
   b. Schleswig-Holstein
   c. Bavaria
   d. Saxony
   e. Austria

10. The newly elected French National Assembly of 1871 was dominated by
    a. socialists.
    b. radicals.
    c. monarchists.
    d. liberals.
    e. anarchists.

11. In 1894, Captain Alfred Dreyfus was found guilty of
    a. passing secrets to the Germans.
    b. embezzling funds from the French army.
    c. crimes against humanity.
    d. conducting unauthorized secret talks with Russia.
    e. lying about his religious affiliation.

12. Gladstone's ministry of 1868–1874 witnessed the
    a. culmination of classical British liberalism.
    b. introduction of socialism into British national policy.
    c. complete collapse of liberalism.
    d. high point of British conservatism.
    e. high point of British-Irish relations.

13. The Russian students' group devoted to communal life and peasant uplift was
    a. The People's Will.
    b. Land and Freedom.
    c. Freedom and Bread.
    d. Socialist Land Party.
    e. Zemstvos.

14. Disraeli's efforts at social reform focused on
    a. individualism.
    b. free trade.
    c. family life.
    d. paternalistic legislation.
    e. environmental issues.

15. The Paris Commune was dominated by the
    a. petty bourgeoisie.
    b. communists.
    c. urban poor.
    d. ultra-royalists.
    e. anarchists.

16. The emancipation of serfs in Russia in 1861 was only fully realized in
    a. 1871.
    b. 1876.
    c. 1889.
    d. 1906.
    e. 1916.

17. The correct chronological order of Bismarck's victories that lead to the unification of Germany were
    a. Denmark, Austria, and France.
    b. Austria, Denmark, and France.
    c. France, Denmark, and Austria.
    d. France, Austria, and Denmark.
    e. Austria, France, and Denmark.

18. The *Hatti-i Hümayun*
    a. declared Islam the sole religion of the Ottoman Empire.

b. were a series of modernization efforts.
c. were a series of military reforms.
d. were opposed by European powers.
— e. spelled out more rights of non-Muslim subjects of the Ottoman Empire.

19. Garibaldi led the campaign for control of
 a. northern Italy.
 b. Rome.
 c. Corsica.

— d. Sicily and southern Italy.
 e. Trieste.

20. In the 1860s, Napoleon III did all of the following *except*
 a. sign a free trade treaty with Britain.
 b. permit labor unions.
 c. relax press laws.
 d. permit freer debate in the legislature.
— e. form an alliance with Prussia.

DOCUMENT-BASED QUESTION

Directions: Construct a valid essay that directly addresses the central issue of the following question. Use facts from the documents provided and from the chapter to prove the position you take in your thesis statement.

Compare and contrast the three visions of nineteenth-century nationalism contained in the following documents. How does each author conceive of the nation and national rights?

Document A

Source: The Italian patriot Giuseppe Mazzini defines nationality, *From Absolutism to Revolution.*

The essential characteristics of a nationality are common ideas, common principles and a common purpose. A nation is an association of those who are brought together by language, by given geographical conditions or by the role assigned them by history, who acknowledge the same principles and who march together to the conquest of a single definite goal under the rule of a uniform body of law. . . .

The people must be the basis of nationality; its logically derived and vigorously applied principles its means; the strength of all its strength; the improvement of the life of all and the happiness of the greatest possible number its results; and the accomplishment of the task assigned to it by God its goal. This is what we mean by a nationality.

Document B

Source: The German historian Heinrich von Treitschke demands the annexation of Alsace and Lorraine.

In view of our obligation to secure the peace of the world, who will venture to object that the people of Alsace and Lorraine do not want to belong to us? The doc-

trine of the right of all the branches of the German race to decide on their own destinies, the plausible solution of demagogues without a fatherland, shiver to pieces in the presence of the sacred necessity of these great days. These territories are ours by the right of the sword, and we shall dispose of them in virtue of a higher right—the right of the German nation, which will not permit its lost children to remain strangers to the German Empire. We Germans, who know Germany and France, know better than these unfortunates what is good for the people of Alsace. . . . Against their will we shall restore them to their true selves.

Document C

Source: The English historian Lord Acton condemns nationalism.

The greatest adversary of the rights of nationality is the modern theory of nationality. By making the State and the nation commensurate with each other in theory, it reduces practically to a subject condition all other nationalities that may be within the boundary. . . . According, therefore, to the degree of humanity and civilization in that dominant body which claims all the rights of community, the inferior races are exterminated, or reduced to servitude, or outlawed, or put into a condition of dependence.

There is no principle of change, no phrase of political speculation conceivable, more comprehensive, more subversive, or more arbitrary than this [nationalism]. It is a confutation of democracy, because it sets limits to the exercise of the popular will, and substitutes for it a higher principle.

For more on nineteenth-century nationalism, see Chapters 20 and 22 of this text.

Women Laundry Workers. Although new opportunities opened to them in the late nineteenth century, many working-class women, like these women ironing in a laundry, remained in traditional occupations. As the wine bottle suggests, alcoholism was a problem for women as well as men engaged in tedious work. The painting is by Edgar Degas (1834–1917). Réunion des Musées Nationaux/Art Resource, NY

23

The Building of European Supremacy: Society and Politics to World War I

▼ **Population Trends and Migration**

▼ **The Second Industrial Revolution**
New Industries • Economic Difficulties

▼ **The Middle Classes in Ascendancy**
Social Distinctions Within the Middle Class

▼ **Late-Nineteenth-Century Urban Life**
The Redesign of Cities • Urban Sanitation • Housing Reform and Middle-Class Values

▼ **Varieties of Late-Nineteenth-Century Women's Experiences**
Women's Social Disabilities • New Employment Patterns for Women • Working-Class Women • Poverty and Prostitution • Women of the Middle Class • The Rise of Political Feminism

▼ **Jewish Emancipation**
Differing Degrees of Citizenship • Broadened Opportunities

▼ **Labor, Socialism, and Politics to World War I**
Trade Unionism • Democracy and Political Parties • Karl Marx and the First International • Great Britain: Fabianism and Early Welfare Programs • France: "Opportunism" Rejected • Germany: Social Democrats and Revisionism • Russia: Industrial Development and the Birth of Bolshevism

▼ **In Perspective**

THE GROWTH OF industrialism between 1860 and 1914 increased Europe's productive capacity to unprecedented and unparalleled levels. New steel mills, railways, shipyards, and chemical plants reflected an expanding supply of capital goods in the second half of the nineteenth century. By the first decade of the twentieth century, the age of the automobile, the airplane, the bicycle, the refrigerated ship, the telephone, the radio, the typewriter, and the electric light bulb had dawned. The world's economies, based on the **gold standard**, became increasingly interdependent. European manufactured goods and financial capital flowed into markets all over the globe. In turn, Europeans imported foreign raw materials and foodstuffs. Within Europe itself, the eastern and southern European countries tended to import finished goods from the west and the north and to export agricultural products.

During this half century, European political, economic, and social life assumed many of its current characteristics. Nation-states with large electorates, political parties, and centralized bureaucracies emerged. Business adopted large-scale corporate structures, and the labor force organized itself into trade unions. The number of white-collar workers increased. Western Europe became predominately urban. Socialism strongly affected the political life of all nations. The foundations of the welfare state and of vast military establishments were laid. Taxation increased accordingly.

Europe had also quietly become dependent on the resources and markets of the rest of the world. Changes in the weather in Kansas, Argentina, or New Zealand might now affect the European economy. Before World War I, however, Europe's industrial, military, and financial supremacy concealed that dependency. Many Europeans assumed their supremacy to be natural and permanent, but the twentieth century would reveal it to have been temporary.

▼ Population Trends and Migration

The proportion of Europeans in the world's total population was apparently greater around 1900—estimated at about 20 percent—than ever before or since. The number of Europeans had risen from approximately 266 million in 1850 to 401 million in 1900 and to 447 million in 1910. Thereafter, birth and death rates declined or stabilized in Europe and other developed regions, and population growth began to slow in those areas but not elsewhere. The result has been a persistent demographic differential between the developed and undeveloped world—stable or slowly growing populations in developed countries and large, rapidly growing populations in undeveloped regions—that contributes to the world's present food and resource crisis.

Europe's peoples were on the move in the latter half of the century as never before (see Map 23–1, page 718). The mid-century emancipation of peasants lessened the authority of landlords and made legal movement and migration easier. Railways, steamships, and better roads increased mobility. Cheap land and better wages accompanied economic development in Europe, North America, Latin America, and Australia, enticing people to move from regions where they had little prospect of improving their lives to regions that held or seemed to hold opportunity. In Europe itself the main migration continued to be from the countryside into urban areas. During this era, Europeans also left their own continent in record numbers. Between 1846 and 1932, more than 50 million Europeans left their homelands. The major areas to benefit from this movement were the United States, Canada, Australia, South Africa, Brazil, Algeria, and Argentina. At midcentury, most of the emigrants were from Great Britain (especially Ireland), Germany, and Scandinavia. After 1885, migration from southern and eastern Europe rose. This exodus helped relieve the social and population pressures on the Continent. The outward movement of peoples, in conjunction with Europe's economic and technological superiority, contributed heavily to the Europeanization of the world. Not since the sixteenth century had European civilization had such an impact on other cultures.

▼ The Second Industrial Revolution

During the third quarter of the nineteenth century, the gap that had long existed between British and continental economic development closed. (See Map 23–2, page 719.) The basic heavy industries of Belgium, France, and Germany expanded rapidly. In particular, the growth of the German industry was stunning. German steel production surpassed Britain's in 1893 and was nearly twice that of Britain by the outbreak of World War I. This emergence of an industrial Germany was the major fact of European economic and political life at the turn of the century.

MAJOR DATES OF THE SECOND INDUSTRIAL REVOLUTION

1856–1870	Passage of laws permitting joint stock companies: 1856, Britain; 1863, France; 1870, Prussia
1857	Bessemer process for making steel
1873	Beginning of major economic downturn
1876	Alexander Graham Bell invents the telephone
1879	Edison perfects the electric light bulb
1881	First electric power plant in Britain
1885	Gottlieb Daimler invents the internal combustion engine
1889	Daimler's first automobile
1895	Diesel engine invented
1895	Wireless telegraphy invented
1890s	First major impact of petroleum
1903	Wright brothers make first successful airplane flight
1909	Henry Ford manufactures the Model T

| Emigration from Europe |
| Emigration from Japan |
| Emigration from China |
| Emigration from India |
| Migration from European Russia |

Number of Immigrants		
From Asia		700,000
Main groups		
Chinese	370,000	
Japanese	275,000	
From Canada		2,200,000
From Europe		30,000,000
Main groups		
Germans	5,000,000	
Irish	4,500,000	
Italians	4,500,000	
Poles	2,600,000	
English	2,600,000	
Jews	2,000,000	
From Latin America		900,000

Map 23–1 **PATTERNS OF GLOBAL MIGRATION, 1840–1900** Emigration was a global process by the late nineteenth century, but more immigrants went to the United States than to every other nation combined.

New Industries

Initially, the economic expansion of the third quarter of the century involved the spread of industries similar to those pioneered earlier in Great Britain. In particular, the expansion of railway systems on the Continent spurred economic growth. Thereafter, however, wholly new industries emerged. This latter development is usually termed the *Second Industrial Revolution*. The first Industrial Revolution was associated with textiles, steam, and iron; by contrast, the second was associated with steel, chemicals, electricity, and oil.

In the 1850s, Henry Bessemer (1830–1898), an English engineer, discovered a new process, named after

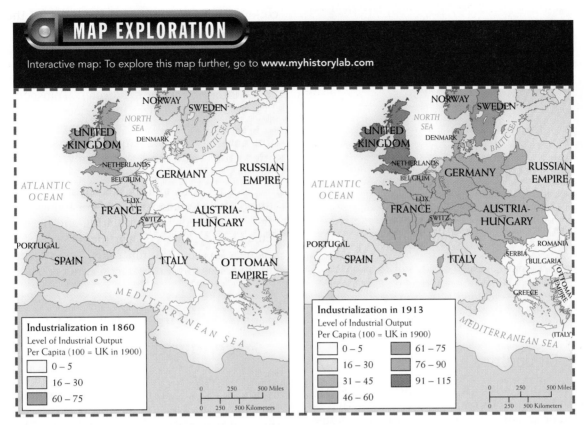

MAP EXPLORATION

Interactive map: To explore this map further, go to **www.myhistorylab.com**

Map 23–2   **EUROPEAN INDUSTRIALIZATION, 1860–1913**   In 1860 Britain was far more industrialized than other European countries. But in the following half century, industrial output rose significantly, if unevenly, across much of Western Europe, especially in the new German Empire. The Balkan states and the Ottoman Empire, however, remained economically backward.

him, for manufacturing steel cheaply in large quantities. In 1860, Great Britain, Belgium, France, and Germany combined produced 125,000 tons of steel. By 1913, the figure had risen to over 32 million tons.

The chemical industry also came of age during this period. The Solway process of alkali production replaced the older Leblanc process, allowing the recovery of more chemical by-products. The new process permitted increased production of sulfuric acid and laundry soap. New dyestuffs and plastics were also developed. Formal scientific research played an important role in this growth of the chemical industry, marking the beginning of a direct link between science and industrial development. As in so many other aspects of the Second Industrial Revolution, Germany was a leader in forging this link, fostering scientific research and education.

The most significant change for industry and, eventually, for everyday life involved the application of electrical energy to production. Electricity was the most versatile and transportable source of power ever discovered. It could be delivered almost anywhere to run either large or small machinery, making the locations of factories more flexible and factory construction more efficient. The first major public power plant was constructed in 1881 in Great Britain. Soon electric poles, lines, and generating stations dotted the European landscape. Homes began to use electric lights. Streetcar and subway systems were electrified.

In 1885, the German engineer Gottlieb Daimler (1834–1900), improving a previous prototype, invented the modern internal combustion engine. By 1889, he had mounted it on a carriage body specifically designed to incorporate a still more improved internal combustion engine, and the automobile was born. France initially took the lead in auto manufacturing, but for many years, the car remained a novelty item that only the wealthy could afford. It was the American, Henry Ford (1863–1947), who later made the automobile accessible to the masses. No single invention so transformed the mobility of large numbers of people, first through the automobile itself and then through trolleys and buses. The automobile industry, furthermore, created a vast new demand for steel and the materials that went into other auto parts and established an ever-growing demand for petroleum products that continues to this day. Then as now, Europe depended on imported supplies of oil. The major oil companies were Standard Oil of the United States, British Shell Oil, and Royal Dutch Petroleum.

458 M. FOURNIER'S "MORS."
The Winner of the Race from Paris
to Berlin. 1901.

The invention and commercialization of automobiles soon led to auto races in Europe and North America. Here Henri Fournier, the winner of the 1901 Paris to Berlin Motor Car Race, sits in his winning racing car manufactured by the Paris-based auto firm of Emile and Louis Mors. Getty Images Inc.–Hulton Archive Photos

Economic Difficulties

Despite the multiplication of new industries, the second half of the nineteenth century was not a period of uninterrupted or smooth economic growth. Both industry and agriculture generally prospered from 1850 to 1873, but in the last quarter of the century, economic advance slowed. Bad weather and foreign competition put grave pressures on European agriculture and caused many European peasants to emigrate to other parts of the world.

As new farming regions developed in the United States, Canada, Argentina, Australia, and New Zealand, products from those areas challenged the market for home-produced European agricultural goods. Refrigerated ships could bring meat and dairy products to Europe from all over the world. Grain could be grown more economically on the plains of North America, Argentina, and Ukraine than it could in Western Europe, and railways and steamships made it easy and cheap to ship it across continents and oceans. These developments lowered the prices of consumer goods, but put great pressure on European agriculture.

Several large banks failed in 1873, and the rate of capital investment slowed. Some industries then entered a two-decade-long period of stagnation that many contemporaries regarded as a depression. Overall, however, the general standard of living in the industrialized nations improved in the second half of the nineteenth century. Both prices and wages, as well as profits, fell, so real wages generally held firm and even rose in some countries. Yet many workers still lived and labored in abysmal conditions. There were pockets of *unemployment* (a word that was coined during this period), and strikes and other forms of labor unrest were

common. These economic difficulties fed the growth of trade unions and socialist political parties.

The new industries produced consumer goods, and expansion in consumer demand brought the economy out of stagnation by the end of the century. (See "Encountering the Past: Bicycles: Transportation, Freedom, and Sport.") Lower food prices eventually allowed all classes to spend more on consumer goods. Urbanization naturally created larger markets. People living in cities simply saw more things they wanted to buy than they would have encountered in the countryside. New forms of retailing and marketing appeared—department stores, chain stores, mail-order catalogs, and advertising—simultaneously stimulating and feeding consumer demand. (See "Paris Department Stores Expand Their Business," page 722.) Imperialism also opened new markets overseas for European consumer goods.

▼ The Middle Classes in Ascendancy

The sixty years before World War I were the age of the middle classes. The London Great Exhibition of 1851 held in the Crystal Palace displayed the products and the new material life they had forged. Thereafter, the middle classes became the arbiter of consumer taste. After the revolutions of 1848, the middle classes ceased to be a revolutionary group. Once the question of social equality and equality of property had been raised, large and small property owners across the Continent moved to protect what they possessed against demands from socialists and other working-class groups.

Social Distinctions Within the Middle Classes

The middle classes, never perfectly homogeneous, grew increasingly diverse. Their most prosperous members—the owners and managers of great businesses and banks—lived in splendor that rivaled, and sometimes exceeded, that of the aristocracy. In Britain some of them, such as W. H. Smith (1825–1891), the owner of railway newsstands, were made members of the House of Lords. The Krupp family of Germany who owned huge steel works in the Rhineland were pillars of the state and were ennobled by the German emperor and received visits from the imperial court.

Only a few hundred families gained such wealth. Beneath them were the comfortable small entrepreneurs and professional people, whose incomes permitted private homes, large quantities of furniture, pianos, pictures, books, journals, education for their children, and vacations. Also in this group were the shopkeepers, schoolteachers, librarians, and others who had either a

BICYCLES: TRANSPORTATION, FREEDOM, AND SPORT

BEFORE THE CAR came the bicycle. Bicycles were the first mass-produced, affordable machines for individual travel. Between 1880 and 1900, they took Europe and North America by storm. For the first time in history, individual men and, significantly, women had a machine that enabled them to travel on their own for work or pleasure. Bicycles had an immense impact on Western society.

The first functioning bicycles had been invented in Germany about 1817, but they were clumsy and dangerous. Made of wood, these machines lacked pedals and tires. They had to be pushed along the ground, and their riders could not control their speed. It took another eighty years for the modern bicycle to take shape. Pedals were introduced in the 1860s. Metal frames, solid rubber tires, and chain drives, which increased speed, appeared in the 1870s. In the 1880s, the ride became much smoother when John Boyd Dunlop, an Irish physician, invented the pneumatic tire, and in France, the Michelin brothers introduced the inner tube. (Before then, the ride was so rough that bicycles were sometimes called "boneshakers.") By the 1890s, the "safety bicycle" with its now familiar triangular frame and chain drive attached to the pedal and back wheel was being mass produced across Europe and North America, and men and women of the working class could afford them. By 1900, male workers of modest means across Europe were riding bicycles to work.

By increasing individual mobility, the bicycle made it easier to get to work, to hold a job farther from home, and to move about one's city or town or reach the countryside. New clothing designs, especially "bloomers," trousers worn under skirts (designed before the bicycle), permitted women to bicycle while maintaining modesty. In the 1890s, feminists like Marie Pognon in France and Susan B. Anthony in the United States hailed the "egalitarian and leveling bicycle" for the freedom it gave women.

By 1914, there were millions of cyclists across the transatlantic world. Europeans and Americans organized cycling clubs with distinctive uniforms. Some of these clubs, such as the English Clarion Cycling Clubs, the French Union Sportive du Parti Socialiste, and the German *Solidaritet*, used cycling trips to spread literature for left-wing causes. Other groups cycled for pleasure. The kinds of touring clubs that now exist for automobiles were first organized for cyclists, as were many of the early European travel guides such as the French *Guides Michelin*, which first appeared in 1900. Then as now, Michelin made tires and stood to sell more of them the more people toured the countryside.

Bicycle racing quickly became a competitive sport. The most famous professional racer in the world was Marshall Walter "Major" Taylor, an African American who raced in both the United States and Europe. Paris and other French cities built velodromes for indoor cycle racing, which was one of the official sports of the first modern Olympics in 1896. In 1903, *L'Auto*, a French sports paper, organized the first Tour de France race to increase its circulation. Six riders raced a 2,500 km-course over nineteen days.

Source: Eugen Weber, *France: Fin de Siècle* (Cambridge, MA: Harvard University Press, 1986), pp. 103–104, 195–206; Will and Terra Hanger, "Bicycles," *History Magazine*, October/November 2001.

Why did bicycles become so popular in Europe in the late nineteenth century?

What advantages did bicycles bring to women?

The bicycle helped liberate women's lives, but as this poster suggests, it also was associated with glamour and fashion. © Archivo Iconografico, S.A./CORBIS

PARIS DEPARTMENT STORES EXPAND THEIR BUSINESS

The department store in Europe and the United States became a major retailing institution in the last half of the nineteenth century. It was one of the reasons for the expansion in late-century consumer demand. This description, written by E. Levasseur in 1907, follows the growth of such stores in Paris and explains why they exerted such economic power. Note how many of their sales techniques stores still use today.

Why should French governments have favored the growth of department stores? Where did these stores stand in the process of economic production and sales? Why was the volume of sales so important? What kinds of people might have benefited from the jobs available in these stores? Why might these stores have hurt small retailers?

It was in the reign of Louis Philippe [1830–1848] that department stores for fashion goods and dresses . . . . began to be distinguished. The type was already one of other notable developments of the Second Empire; it became one of the most important ones of the Third Republic. These stores have increased in number and several of them have become extremely large. Combining in their different departments all articles of clothing, toilet articles, furniture and many other ranges of goods, it is their special object so to combine all commodities as to attract and satisfy customers who will find conveniently together an assortment of a mass of articles corresponding to all their various needs. They attract customers by permanent display, by free entry into the shops, by periodic exhibitions, by special sales, by fixed prices, and by their ability to deliver the goods purchased to customers' homes, in Paris and to the provinces. Turning themselves into direct intermediaries between the producer and the consumer, even producing sometimes some of their articles in their own workshops, buying at lowest prices because of their large orders and because

they are in a position to profit from bargains, working with large sums, and selling to most of their customers for cash only, they can transmit these benefits in lowered selling prices. They can even decide to sell at a loss, as an advertisement or to get rid of out-of-date fashions.

The success of these department stores is only possible thanks to the volume of their business, and this volume needs considerable capital and a very large turnover. Now capital, having become abundant, is freely combined nowadays in large enterprises . . . . [T]he large urban agglomerations, the ease with which goods can be transported by the railways, the diffusion of some comforts to strata below the middle classes, have all favoured these developments. . . .

According to the tax records of 1891, these stores in Paris, numbering 12, employed 1,708 persons and rated their site values at 2,159,000 francs; the largest had then 542 employees. These same stores had, in 1901, 9,784 employees; one of them over 2,000 and another over 1,600; their site value was doubled.

From Sidney Pollard and Colin Holmes, *Documents of European Economic History*, Vol. 3. (London: Edward Arnold, 1972), pp. 95–96.

bit of property or a skill derived from education that provided respectable nonmanual employment.

Finally, there was a wholly new element—"white-collar workers"—who formed the lower middle class, or **petite bourgeoisie**. They included secretaries, retail clerks, and lower-level bureaucrats in business and government. They often had working-class origins and might even belong to unions, but they had middle-class aspirations and consciously sought to distance themselves from a lower-class lifestyle. They pursued

educational opportunities and chances for even the slightest career advancement for themselves and, especially, for their children. Many of them spent much of their disposable income on consumer goods, such as stylish clothing and furniture, that were distinctively middle class in appearance.

Significant tensions and social anxieties marked relations among the various middle-class groups. Small shopkeepers resented the power of the great capitalists, with their department stores and mail-order catalogs.

in Britain, 2 million in Germany, and 977,000 in France), most of Europe's labor force was never unionized in this period. What the unions did represent for workers was a new collective form of association to confront economic difficulties and improve security.

Democracy and Political Parties

Except for Russia, all the major European states adopted broad-based, if not perfectly democratic, electoral systems in the late nineteenth century. Great Britain passed its second voting reform act in 1867 and its third in 1884. Bismarck brought universal male suffrage to the German Empire in 1871. The French Chamber of Deputies was democratically elected. Universal male suffrage was adopted in Switzerland in 1879, in Spain in 1890, in Belgium in 1893, in the Netherlands in 1896, and in Norway in 1898. Italy finally fell into line in 1912. The broadened franchise meant politicians could no longer ignore workers, and discontented groups could now voice their grievances and advocate their programs within the institutions of government rather than from the outside.

The advent of democracy brought organized mass political parties like those already in existence in the United States to Europe for the first time. In the liberal European states with narrow electoral bases, most voters had been people of property who knew what they had at stake in politics. Organization had been minimal. The expansion of the electorate brought into the political process many people whose level of political consciousness, awareness, and interest was low. This electorate had to be organized and taught about power and influence in the liberal democratic state.

The organized political party—with its workers, newspapers, offices, social life, and discipline—was the vehicle that mobilized the new voters. The largest single group in these mass electorates was the working class. The democratization of politics presented the socialists with opportunities and required the traditional ruling classes to vie with the socialists for the support of the new voters.

During these years, socialism as a political ideology and plan of action opposed nationalism. The problems of class were supposed to be transnational, and socialism was supposed to unite the working classes across national borders. European socialists, however, badly underestimated the emotional drawing power of nationalism. Many workers had both socialist and nationalist sympathies, which were rarely in conflict with each other. When the outbreak of war in 1914 did bring them into conflict, however, nationalist feelings prevailed.

The major question for late-century socialist parties throughout Europe was whether revolution or democratic reform would improve the life of the working class. This question sharply divided all socialist parties and especially those whose leadership adhered to the intellectual legacy of Karl Marx. The Bolshevik Revolution of November 1917 would transform socialist debates and actions and render many of the disputes of the late nineteenth and early twentieth centuries moot. During those decades, however, the dispute over whether to achieve socialism through revolution or reform sharply shaped socialist thought, party programs, and political behavior and influenced not only socialism but the larger European political arena as well.

Karl Marx and the First International

Karl Marx himself took into account the new realities that developed during the third quarter of the century. Although he continued to predict the disintegration of capitalism, his practical, public political activity reflected a different approach.

In 1864, a group of British and French trade unionists founded the International Working Men's Association. Known as the First International, its membership encompassed a vast array of radical political types, including socialists, anarchists, and Polish nationalists. In the inaugural address for the First International, Marx approved workers' and trade unions' efforts to reform the conditions of labor within the existing political and economic processes. In his private writings he often criticized such reformist activity, but these writings were not made public until near the end of the century, years after his death.

The violence involved in the rise and suppression of the Paris Commune (see Chapter 22), which Marx had declared a genuine proletarian uprising, cast a pall over socialism throughout Europe. British trade unionists, who received legal protections in 1871, wanted no connection with the events in Paris. The French authorities used the uprising to suppress socialist activity. Under these pressures, the First International held its last European congress in 1873. It soon transferred its offices to the United States, where it was dissolved in 1876.

The short-lived First International had a disproportionately great impact on the future of European socialism. Throughout the late 1860s, the organization gathered statistics, kept labor groups informed of mutual problems, provided a forum to debate socialist doctrine, and extravagantly proclaimed (and overstated) its own influence over contemporary events. From these debates and activities, Marxism emerged as the single most important strand of socialism. Marx and his supporters defeated or drove out anarchists and advocates of other forms of socialism. The apparently scientific character of Marxism made it attractive at a time when science was more influential than at any previous period in European history. Marx's thought deeply impressed German socialists, who were to establish the most powerful socialist party in Europe and became the chief vehicle for preserving and developing it. The full development of German socialism, however, also involved the influence of non-Marxist socialists in Great Britain.

Great Britain: Fabianism and Early Welfare Programs

Neither Marxism nor any other form of socialism made significant progress in Great Britain, the most advanced industrial society of the day. There trade unions grew steadily, and their members normally supported Liberal Party candidates. The "new unionism" of the late 1880s and the 1890s organized the dockworkers, the gas workers, and similar unskilled groups. In 1892, Keir Hardie (1856–1915) became the first independent working man to be elected to Parliament, but the small socialist Independent Labour Party founded a year later remained ineffective. Until 1901, labor's general political activity remained limited. In that year, however, the House of Lords, which also acts as Britain's highest court, through the Taff Vale decision, removed the legal protection previously accorded union funds. The Trades Union Congress responded by launching the Labour Party. In the election of 1906, the fledgling party sent twenty-nine members to Parliament. Their goals as trade unionists, however, did not yet include socialism. In this same period, the British labor movement became more militant. In scores of strikes before the war, workers fought for wages to meet the rising cost of living. The government took a larger role than ever before in mediating these strikes, which in 1911 and 1912 involved the railways, the docks, and the coal mines.

British socialism itself remained primarily the preserve of non-Marxist intellectuals. The **Fabian** Society, founded in 1884, was Britain's most influential socialist group. The society took its name from Q. Fabius Maximus (d. 203 B.C.E.), the Roman general whose tactics against Hannibal involved avoiding direct conflict that might lead to defeat. The name reflected the society's gradualist approach to major social reform. Its leading members were Sidney Webb (1859–1947), Beatrice Webb (1858–1943), H. G. Wells (1866–1946), Graham Wallas (1858–1932), and George Bernard Shaw (1856–1950). Many Fabians were civil servants who believed the problems of industry, the expansion of ownership, and the state direction of production could be solved and achieved gradually, peacefully, and democratically. They sought to educate the country about the rational wisdom of socialism. They were particularly interested in modes of collective ownership on the municipal level, the so-called gas-and-water socialism.

The British government and the Liberal and Conservative parties responded slowly to these pressures. In 1903, Joseph Chamberlain (1836–1914) launched his unsuccessful campaign to match foreign tariffs and to

Beatrice and Sidney Webb. These most influential British Fabian Socialists, shown in a photograph from the late 1920s, wrote many books on governmental and economic matters, served on special parliamentary commissions, and agitated for the enactment of socialist policies. CORBIS/Bettmann

finance social reform through higher import duties. The campaign split the Conservative Party. After 1906, the Liberal Party, led by Sir Henry Campbell-Bannerman (1836–1908) and, after 1908, by Herbert Asquith, pursued a two-pronged policy. Fearful of losing seats in Parliament to the new Labour Party, they restored the former protection of the unions. Then, after 1909, with Chancellor of the Exchequer David Lloyd George (1863–1945) as its guiding light, the Liberal ministry undertook a broad program of social legislation that included establishing labor exchanges, regulating certain trades, such as tailoring and lace making, and passing the National Insurance Act of 1911, which provided unemployment benefits and health care.

The financing of these programs brought the Liberal majority in the House of Commons into conflict with the Conservative-dominated House of Lords. The result was the Parliament Act of 1911, which allowed the Commons to override the legislative veto of the upper chamber. The new taxes and social programs meant that in Britain, the home of nineteenth-century liberalism, the state was taking on an expanded role in the life of its citizens. The early welfare legislation was only marginally satisfactory to labor, many of whose members still thought they could gain more from the direct action of strikes.

France: "Opportunism" Rejected

French socialism was a less united and more politically factionalized movement than socialism in other countries. At the turn of the century, Jean Jaurès (1859–1914) and Jules Guesde (1845–1922) led the two major factions of French socialists. Jaurès believed socialists should cooperate with middle-class Radical ministries to ensure the enactment of needed social legislation. Guesde opposed this policy, arguing that socialists could not, with integrity, support a bourgeois cabinet they were theoretically dedicated to overthrowing. The government's response to the Dreyfus affair brought the quarrel to a head. In 1899, seeking to unite all supporters of Dreyfus, Prime Minister René Waldeck-Rousseau (1846–1904) appointed the socialist Alexander Millerand (1859–1943) to the cabinet.

The Second International had been founded in 1889 in a new effort to unify the various national socialist parties and trade unions. By 1904, the Amsterdam Congress of the Second International debated the issue of *opportunism*, as such participation by socialists in cabinets was termed. The Congress condemned opportunism in France and ordered French socialists to form a single party. Jaurès accepted the decision. Thereafter French socialists began to work together, and by 1914, the recently united Socialist Party had become the second largest group in the Chamber of Deputies. Jaurès was assassinated in 1914 in a Paris cafe at the outbreak of World War I. Thereafter in the patriotism of the war effort, French socialist leaders participated in the wartime cabinet. After the war the French socialist movement split with socialists not again serving in a French cabinet until the Popular Front Government of 1936. (See Chapter 28.)

The French labor movement, with deep roots in anarchism, was uninterested in either politics or socialism. French workers usually voted socialist, but the unions themselves, unlike those in Britain, avoided active political participation. The main labor union, Confédération Générale du Travail, founded in 1895, regarded itself as a rival to the socialist parties. Its leaders sought to improve the workers' conditions through direct action. They embraced the doctrines of **syndicalism**, which had been most persuasively expounded by Georges Sorel (1847–1922) in *Reflections on Violence* (1908). This book enshrined the general strike as a device to unite workers and gain them power. The strike tactic often conflicted with the socialist belief in aiding labor through state action. Strikes were common in France between 1905 and 1914, and the middle-class Radical ministry used troops to suppress them on more than one occasion.

Germany: Social Democrats and Revisionism

The negative judgment the Second International rendered against French socialist participation in bourgeois ministries reflected a policy of permanent hostility to nonsocialist governments that the German Social Democratic Party, or SPD, had already adopted. The organizational success of this party, more than any other single factor, kept Marxist socialism alive during the late nineteenth and early twentieth centuries.

The SDP had been founded in 1875. Its origins lay in the labor agitation of Ferdinand Lasalle (1825–1864), who wanted workers to participate in German politics. Wilhelm Liebknecht (1826–1900) and August Bebel (1840–1913), who were Marxists who opposed reformist politics, soon joined the party. Thus, from its founding, the SPD was divided between those who advocated reform and those who advocated revolution.

GERMANY

Bismarck's Repression of the SPD Twelve years of persecution under Bismarck forged the character of the SPD. The so-called Iron Chancellor believed socialism would undermine German politics and society. He used an assassination attempt on Emperor William I (r. 1861–1888) in 1878, in which the socialists were not involved, to steer antisocialist laws through the *Reichstag*. The measures suppressed the organization, meetings, newspapers, and other public activities of the SPD. Thereafter, to remain a socialist meant to remove oneself from the mainstream of respectable German life and possibly to lose one's job. The antisocialist legislation proved politically counterproductive. From the early 1880s onward, the SPD steadily polled more and more votes in elections to the *Reichstag*.

As simple repression failed to wean German workers from socialist loyalties, Bismarck undertook a program of social welfare legislation. In 1883, the German Empire adopted a health insurance measure. The next year the *Reichstag* enacted accident insurance legislation. Finally, in 1889, Bismarck sponsored a plan for old age and disability pensions. These programs, to which both workers and employers contributed, represented a paternalistic, conservative alternative to socialism. The state itself would organize a system of social security that did not require any change in the system of property holding or politics. Germany became the first major industrial nation to enjoy this kind of welfare program.

The Erfurt Program After forcing Bismarck's resignation mainly because of differences over foreign policy, Emperor William II (r. 1888–1918) allowed the antisocialist legislation to expire, hoping to build new political support among the working class. Even under the repressive laws, members of the SPD could sit in the *Reichstag*. With the repressive measures lifted, the party needed to decide what attitude to assume toward the German Empire.

The answer came in the Erfurt Program of 1891, formulated under the political guidance of Bebel and the ideological tutelage of Karl Kautsky (1854–1938). In good Marxist fashion, the program declared the imminent doom of capitalism and the necessity of socialist ownership of the means of production. The party intended to pursue these goals through legal political participation rather than by revolutionary activity. Kautsky argued that because capitalism by its very nature must collapse, the immediate task for socialists was to improve workers' lives rather than work for revolution, which was inevitable. So, although in theory the SPD was vehemently hostile to the German Empire, in practice the party functioned within its institutions. The SPD members of the *Reichstag* maintained clear political consciences by refusing to enter the cabinet (to which they were not invited anyway) and by refraining for many years from voting in favor of the military budget.

The Debate over Revisionism

The dilemma of the SPD, however, generated the most important challenge within the socialist movement to the orthodox Marxist analysis of capitalism and the socialist revolution. The author of this socialist heresy, Eduard Bernstein (1850–1932), had lived in Britain and was familiar with the Fabians. Bernstein questioned whether Marx and his later orthodox followers, such as Kautsky, had been correct in their pessimistic appraisal of capitalism and the necessity of revolution. In *Evolutionary Socialism* (1899), Bernstein pointed to conditions that did not meet orthodox Marxists' expectations. The standard of living was rising in Europe. Stockholding was making the ownership of capitalist industry more widespread. The middle class was not falling into the ranks of the proletariat and was not identifying its problems with those of the workers. The inner contradictions of capitalism had simply not developed the way Marx had predicted. Moreover, the extension of the franchise to the working class meant that parliamentary methods might achieve revolutionary social change. For Bernstein, social reform through democratic institutions replaced revolution as the path to a humane socialist society. (See "Compare & Connect: Bernstein and Lenin Debate the Character of Tactics of European Socialism," pages, 744–745.)

Bernstein's doctrines, known as **Revisionism**, generated heated debate among German socialists, who finally condemned them. His critics argued that evolution toward social democracy might be possible in liberal, parliamentary Britain, but not in authoritarian, militaristic Germany, with its feeble *Reichstag*. Nonetheless, while still calling for revolution, the SPD pursued a course of action similar to what Bernstein advocated. Its trade union members, prospering within the German economy, did not want revolution. Its grassroots members

wanted to be patriotic Germans as well as good socialists. Its leaders feared anything that might renew the persecution they had experienced under Bismarck.

Consequently, the SPD worked for electoral gains, expansion of its membership, and short-term political and social reform. It prospered and became one of the most important institutions of imperial Germany. Even middle-class Germans voted for it to oppose the illiberal institutions of the empire. In August 1914, after long debate among themselves, the SPD members of the *Reichstag* unanimously voted for the war credits that would finance Germany's participation in World War I.

Russia: Industrial Development and the Birth of Bolshevism

In the 1890s, Russia entered the industrial age and confronted many of the problems that the more advanced nations of the Continent had experienced fifty or seventy-five years earlier. Unlike those other countries, Russia had to deal with political discontent and economic development simultaneously. Russian socialism reflected that peculiar situation.

Witte's Program for Industrial Growth

Tsar Alexander III (r. 1881–1894) and, after him, Nicholas II (r. 1894–1917) were determined that Russia should become an industrial power. Only by doing so, they believed, could the country maintain its position as a great power. Count Sergei Witte (1849–1915) led Russia into the industrial age. After a career in railways and other private business, he was appointed first minister of communications and then finance minister in 1892. Witte, who pursued a policy of planned economic development, protective tariffs, high taxes, putting Russia's currency on the gold standard, and efficiency in government and business, epitomized the nineteenth-century modernizer. He established a strong financial relationship with the French money market, which enabled Russia to finance its modernization program with French loans and which later led to diplomatic cooperation and an alliance between Russia and France.

Witte favored heavy industries. Between 1890 and 1904, the Russian railway system grew from 30,596 to 59,616 kilometers. The 5,000-mile-long Trans-Siberian Railroad was completed in 1903. Coal output more than tripled during the same period. Pig-iron production increased from 928,000 tons in 1890 to 4,641,000 tons in 1913. During the same period, steel production rose from 378,000 to 4,918,000 tons. Textile manufacturing continued to expand and was still the single largest industry. The factory system spread extensively.

Industrialism, however, also brought social discontent to Russia, as it had elsewhere. Landowners felt that foreign capitalists were earning too much of the profit.

The peasants saw their grain exports and tax payments finance development that did not measurably improve their lives. A small, but significant, industrial proletariat emerged. In 1900, Russia had approximately 3 million factory workers. Their working and living conditions were poor. (See "A Russian Social Investigator Describes the Condition of Children in the Moscow Tailoring Trade," page 742.) They enjoyed little state protection, and trade unions were illegal. In 1897, Witte did enact an 11.5-hour workday, but needless to say, discontent and strikes continued.

Similar social and economic problems arose in the countryside. Russian agriculture had not prospered after the emancipation of the serfs in 1861. The peasants remained burdened with redemption payments for the land they farmed, local taxes, excessive national taxes, and falling grain prices. Peasants did not own their land as individuals, but communally through the *mir*, or village. They farmed the land inefficiently through strip farming or by tilling small plots. Many free peasants with too little land to support their families had to work on large estates owned by nobles or for more prosperous peasant farmers, known as **kulaks**. Between 1860 and 1914, the population of European Russia rose from about 50 million to around 103 million people. Land hunger and discontent spread among the peasants and sparked frequent uprisings in the countryside.

New political developments accompanied economic changes. The membership and intellectual roots of the Social Revolutionary Party, founded in 1901, reached back to the Populists of the 1870s. The new party opposed industrialism and looked to the communal life of rural Russia as a model for the future. In 1903, the Constitutional Democratic Party, or Cadets, was formed. This liberal party drew its members from those who participated in local councils called **zemstvos**. Modeling themselves on the liberal parties of Western Europe, the Cadets wanted a constitutional monarchy under a parliamentary regime with civil liberties and economic progress.

Lenin's Early Thought and Career The situation of Russian socialists differed radically from that of socialists in other major European countries. Russia had no representative institutions and only a small working class. The compromises and accommodations achieved elsewhere were meaningless in Russia where socialists believed that in both theory and practice they must be revolutionary. The repressive policies of the tsarist regime required the Russian Social Democratic Party, founded in 1898, to function in exile. The party members greatly admired the German Social Democratic Party and adopted its Marxist ideology.

The leading late-nineteenth-century Russian Marxist was Gregory Plekhanov (1857–1918), who wrote from exile in Switzerland. At the turn of the century, his chief disciple was Vladimir Ilyich Ulyanov (1870–1924),

who later took the name of Lenin. The future leader of the communist revolution was the son of a high bureaucrat. His older brother, while a student in Saint Petersburg, had become involved in radical politics; arrested for participating in a plot against Alexander III, he was executed in 1887. In 1893, Lenin moved to Saint Petersburg, where he studied law. Soon he, too, was drawn to the revolutionary groups among the factory workers. He was arrested in 1895 and exiled to Siberia. In 1900, after his release, Lenin left Russia for the West. He spent most of the next seventeen years in Switzerland.

There, Lenin became deeply involved in the disputes of the exiled Russian Social Democrats. They all considered themselves Marxists, but they differed on what a Marxist revolution would mean for primarily rural Russia and on how to structure their own party. Unlike the backward-looking Social Revolutionaries, the Social Democrats were modernizers who favored industrial development. Looking to Karl Marx's writings, most Russian Social Democrats believed Russia must develop a large proletariat before the Marxist revolution could come. They also hoped to build a mass political party like the German SPD.

Lenin dissented from both these ideas. In *What Is to Be Done?* (1902), he condemned any accommodations, such as those the German SPD practiced. He also criticized trade unionism that settled for short-term reformist gains rather than work for true revolutionary change for the working class. Lenin further rejected the concept of a mass democratic party composed of workers. Instead, he declared that revolutionary consciousness would not arise spontaneously from the working class. Rather, "people who make revolutionary activity their profession" must carry that consciousness to the workers.[3] Only a small, tightly organized elite party could possess the proper dedication to revolution and resist penetration by police spies. The guiding principle of that party should be "the strictest secrecy, the strictest selection of members, and the training of professional revolutionaries."[4] Lenin thus rejected both Kautsky's view that revolution was inevitable and Bernstein's view that democratic means could achieve revolutionary goals. Lenin substituted the small, professional, nondemocratic revolutionary party for Marx's proletariat as the instrument of revolutionary change. (See ""Compare & Connect: Bernstein and Lenin Debate the Character of Tactics of European Socialism," pages, 744–745.)

In 1903, at the London Congress of the Russian Social Democratic Party, Lenin forced a split in the party ranks. He and his followers lost many votes on questions put before the congress, but near its close they mustered a slim majority. Thereafter Lenin's faction assumed the name

---

[3]Quoted in Albert Fried and Ronald Sanders, eds., *Socialist Thought: A Documentary History* (Garden City, NY: Anchor Doubleday, 1964), p. 459.
[4]Fried and Sanders, *Socialist Thought*, p. 468.

A RUSSIAN SOCIAL INVESTIGATOR DESCRIBES THE CONDITION OF CHILDREN IN THE MOSCOW TAILORING TRADE

E.A. Oliunina was a young Russian woman who had been active among union organizers during the Revolution of 1905. Later, as a student at the Higher Women's Courses in Moscow, a school for women's postsecondary education, she began to investigate and to write about child garment workers. The clothes produced by these children might have ended up in Russian department stores that copied those in Paris, described in an earlier document in this chapter.

Why might the parents of these children have allowed them to work in these sweat-shops? Why was alcoholism such a prevalent problem? Why does Oliunina regard schools as the solution to this problem?

Children begin their apprenticeship between the ages of twelve and thirteen, although one can find some ten- and eleven-year-olds working in the shops. . . .

Apprenticeship is generally very hard on children. At the beginning, they suffer enormously, particularly from the physical strain of having to do work well beyond the capacity of their years. They have to live in an environment where the level of morality is very low. Scenes of drunkenness and debauchery induce the boys to smoke and drink at an early age.

For example, in one subcontracting shop that made men's clothes, a fourteen-year-old boy worked together with twelve adults. When I visited there at four o'clock one Tuesday afternoon, the workers were half-drunk. Some were lying under the benches, others in the hallway. The boy was as drunk as the rest of them and lay there with a dare-devil look on his face, dressed only in a pair of longjohns and a dirty, tattered shirt. He had been taught to drink at the age of twelve and could now keep up with the adults.

"Blue Monday" is a custom in most subcontracting shops that manufacture men's clothes.

The whole workshop gets drunk, and work comes to a standstill. The apprentices do nothing but hang around. Many of the workers live in the workshop, so the boys are constantly exposed to all sorts of conversations and scenes. In one shop employing five workers and three boys, "Blue Monday" was a regular ritual. Even the owner himself is prone to alcoholic binges. In these kinds of situations, young girls are in danger of being abused by the owner or his sons. . . .

In Russia, there have been no measures taken to improve the working conditions of apprentices. As I have tried to show, the situation in workshops in no way provides apprentices with adequate training in their trade. The young workers are there only to be exploited. Merely limiting the number of apprentices would not better their position, nor would it eradicate the influx of cheap labor. An incomparably more effective solution would be to replace apprenticeship with a professional educational system and well-established safeguards for child workers. However, the only real solution to the exploitation of unpaid child labor is to introduce a minimum wage for minors.

Quoted in Victoria E. Bonnell, *The Russian Worker: Life and Labor Under the Tsarist Regime* (Berkeley: University of California Press, 1983), pp. 177, 180–181, 182–183.

Bolsheviks, meaning "majority," and the other, more moderate, democratic revolutionary faction came to be known as the **Mensheviks**, or "minority." There was, of course, a considerable public relations advantage to the name *Bolshevik*. (In 1912, the Bolsheviks organized themselves as a separate party.)

A fundamental organizational difference had existed between what in 1903 were the two chief factions of the

In this photograph taken in 1895, Lenin sits at the table among a group of other young Russian radicals from Saint Petersburg. CORBIS/Bettmann

Russian Social Democratic Party. The Mensheviks wanted a party with a mass membership, similar to the German SDP and other West European socialist parties, which would function democratically. The Bolsheviks intended the party to consist of elite professional revolutionaries who would provide centralized leadership for the working class. Lenin believed a mass party functioning in a democratic fashion would seek only to reform workers' wages, hours, and living conditions, whereas he wanted a revolution that would transform Russia.

In 1905, Lenin complemented his organizational theory with a program for revolution in Russia. In *Two Tactics of Social Democracy in the Bourgeois-Democratic Revolution*, he urged the socialist revolution to unite the proletariat and the peasantry. Lenin grasped better than any other revolutionary the profound discontent in the Russian countryside. He believed the tsarist government probably could not suppress an alliance of workers and peasants in rebellion.

Lenin's two principles—an elite party and a dual social revolution—guided later Bolshevik activity. The Bolsheviks ultimately seized power in November 1917, transforming the political landscape of the twentieth century, but they did so only after the turmoil of World War I had undermined support for the tsar and only after other political forces had already toppled the tsarist government in February 1917. Be-

fore World War I, the Bolsheviks constituted the odd man out in European socialist politics; they exerted no significant prewar influence on members of other socialist groups, who, in general, ignored them. For their part, the Bolsheviks responded by scorning the West European socialist parties that worked within their nations' political systems. Between 1900 and the outbreak of World War I, the government of Nicholas II managed to confront political upheaval more or less successfully.

The Revolution of 1905 and Its Aftermath The quarrels among the exiled Russian socialists and Lenin's doctrines had no immediate influence on events in Russia. Industrialization continued to stir resentment. In 1903, Nicholas II dismissed Witte, hoping to quell the criticism. The next year, in response to conflicts over Manchuria and Korea, Russia went to war against Japan, partly in hopes the conflict would rally public opinion to the tsar. Instead, the Russians lost the war, and the government faced an internal political crisis. The Japanese captured Port Arthur, Russia's naval base on the coast of China, early in 1905. A few days later, on January 22, a Russian Orthodox priest named Father George Gapon led several hundred workers to present a petition to the tsar to improve industrial conditions. The petioners did not know that the tsar was not even in Saint Petersburg,

Bernstein and Lenin Debate the Character of Tactics of European Socialism

BY THE CLOSE of the nineteenth century the European Socialist movement found itself sharply divided over its future goals and tactics. On the one side some socialists, here represented by Eduard Bernstein, came to reject many of the ideas of Karl Marx, particularly that of a proletarian revolution, and embraced democratic politics as the best way to realize their goals of the improvement of the life of the working class. Others, a minority at the time, represented here by Lenin, rejected democracy and embraced the concept of violent revolution achieved by a small professional elite rather than by a spontaneous proletarian uprising. In the twentieth century after the 1917 Bolshevik Revolution in Russia, those divisions would play themselves out in an enormously hostile conflict between democratic socialist parties in Western Europe and Communists in the Soviet Union and Communist parties in Western Europe dominated by the Soviet Union. (See Chapters 26 and 27.)

QUESTIONS

1. According to Bernstein, what specific predictions in the *Communist Manifesto* failed to materialize?

2. Why is the advance of democracy important to Bernstein's argument? Why does he renounce the concept of a "dictatorship of the proletariat"?

3. What does Lenin mean by "professional revolutionaries"? Why does Russia need such revolutionaries?

4. How does Lenin reconcile his antidemocratic views to the goal of aiding the working class?

5. How could the ideas of both Bernstein and Lenin be seen as departures from Marx's own thinking?

I. Eduard Bernstein Urges Socialists to Embrace Democracy

Eduard Bernstein was responsible for the emergence of Revisionism within the German Social Democratic Party. He was a dedicated socialist who recognized that Marx's Communist Manifesto *(1848) had not predicted the actual future of the European working classes. Bernstein believed the capitalist system would not suddenly collapse and that socialists should change their tactics to achieve democratic political rights and pursue reform instead of revolution. (Compare this document with the passages from* The Communist Manifesto *in Chapter 21.)*

Social conditions have not developed to such an acute opposition of things and classes as is depicted in the [*Communist*] *Manifesto.* . . . The number of members of the possessing classes is today not smaller but larger. The enormous increase of social wealth is not accompanied by a decreasing number of large capitalists but by an increasing number of capitalists of all degrees. . . .

In all advanced countries we see the privileges of the capitalist bourgeoisie yielding step by step to democratic organizations. . . .

The conquest of political power by the working classes, the expropriation of capitalists, are not ends in themselves but only means for the accomplishment of certain aims and endeavours. . . .

Democracy is in principle the suppression of class government, though it is not yet the actual suppression of classes. . . . The right to vote in a democracy makes its members virtually partners in the community, and this virtual partnership must in the end lead to real partnership. . . .

Universal franchise is, from two sides, the alternative to a violent revolution. But universal suffrage is only a part of democracy, although a part which in time must draw the other parts after it as the magnet attracts to itself the scattered portions of iron. It certainly proceeds more slowly than many would wish, but in spite of that it is at work. And social democracy cannot further this work better than by taking its stand unreserved only the theory of democracy—on the ground of universal suffrage with all the consequences resulting therefrom to its tactics. . . .

By 1900, these strands of thought had become woven into a new fabric. Many of the traditional intellectual signposts were disappearing. Christianity had experienced the most severe intellectual attack in its history. The picture of the physical world prevailing since Newton had undergone major modification. Darwin and Freud had challenged the special place that Western thinkers had assigned to humankind. Writers began to question rationality. The humanitarian ideals of liberalism and socialism gave way to aggressive nationalism. European intellectuals were more daring than ever before, but they were also probably less certain and optimistic.

▼ The New Reading Public

The social context of intellectual life changed in the latter part of the nineteenth century. For the first time in Europe, a mass reading public came into existence as more people than ever before became drawn into the world of print culture. In 1850, about half the population of Western Europe and a much higher proportion of Russians were illiterate. That situation changed during the next half century.

Advances in Primary Education

Literacy on the Continent improved steadily from the 1860s onward as governments financed education. Hungary provided elementary education in 1868, Britain in 1870, Switzerland in 1874, Italy in 1877, and France between 1878 and 1881. The already advanced education system of Prussia was extended throughout the German Empire after 1871. By 1900, in Britain, France, Belgium, the Netherlands, Germany, and Scandinavia, approximately 85 percent or more of the people could read, but Italy, Spain, Russia, Austria-Hungary, and the Balkans still had illiteracy rates of between 30 and 60 percent.

Public education became widespread in Europe during the second half of the nineteenth century and women came to dominate the profession of school teaching, especially at the elementary level. This 1905 photograph shows English schoolchildren going through morning drills. © Hulton-Deutsch Collection/CORBIS

The new primary education in the basic skills of reading, writing, and elementary arithmetic reflected and generated social change. Both liberals and conservatives regarded such minimal training as necessary for orderly political behavior by the newly enfranchised voters. They also hoped that literacy would create a more productive labor force. This side of the educational crusade embodied the Enlightenment faith that right knowledge would lead to right action.

Literacy and its extension, however, soon became a force in its own right. The school-teaching profession grew rapidly in numbers and prestige and, as noted in Chapter 23, became a major area for the employment of women. Those people who learned to read soon discovered that much of the education that led to better jobs and political influence was still open only to those who could afford it. Having created systems of primary education, the major nations had to give further attention to secondary education by the time of World War I. In another generation, the question would become one of democratic university instruction.

Reading Material for the Mass Audience

The expanding literate population created a vast market for new reading material. The number of newspapers, books, magazines, mail-order catalogs, and libraries grew rapidly. Cheap mass-circulation newspapers, such as *Le Petit Journal* of Paris and the *Daily Mail* and *Daily Express* of London, enjoyed their first heyday. Such newspapers carried advertising that alerted readers to the new consumer products available through the Second Industrial Revolution. Other publishers produced newspapers with specialized political or religious viewpoints. The number of monthly and quarterly journals for families, women, and freethinking intellectuals increased. Probably more people with different ideas could get into print in the late nineteenth century than ever before in European history. In addition, more people could read their ideas than ever before.

Because many of the new readers were only marginally literate and still ignorant about many subjects, the books and journals catering to them were often mediocre. The cheap newspapers prospered on stories of sensational crimes and political scandal and on pages of advertising. Religious journals depended on denominational rivalry. A brisk market existed for pornography. Newspapers with editorials on the front page became major factors in the emerging mass politics. The news could be managed, but in central Europe more often by the government censor than by the publisher.

Critics pointed to the low level of public taste, but the new education, the new readers, and the myriad of new books and journals permitted a popularization of knowledge that has become a hallmark of our world.

The new literacy was the intellectual parallel of the railroad and the steamship. People could leave their original intellectual surroundings because literacy is not an end in itself but leads to other skills and other knowledge.

▼ Science at Midcentury

In about 1850, Voltaire (1694–1778) would have felt at home in a general discussion of scientific concepts. The basic Newtonian picture of physical nature that he had popularized still prevailed. Scientists continued to believe that nature operates as a vast machine according to mechanical principles. At midcentury, learned persons regarded the physical world as rational, mechanical, and dependable. Experiment and observation could reveal its laws objectively. Scientific theory purportedly described physical nature as it really existed. Moreover, by 1850, science had a strong institutional life in French and German universities and in new professional societies. William Whewell of Cambridge University had invented the word "scientist" in the early 1830s, and it was in common use by the end of the century. (See "Encountering the Past: The Birth of Science Fiction.")

Comte, Positivism, and the Prestige of Science

During the early nineteenth century, science had continued to establish itself as the model for all human knowledge. The French philosopher Auguste Comte (1798–1857), a late child of the Enlightenment and a onetime follower of Saint-Simon, developed **positivism**, a philosophy of human intellectual development that culminated in science. In *The Positive Philosophy* (1830–1842), Comte argued that human thought had developed in three stages. In the first, or theological, stage, physical nature was explained in terms of the action of divinities or spirits. In the second, or metaphysical, stage, abstract principles were regarded as the operative agencies of nature. In the final, or positive stage, explanations of nature became matters of exact description of phenomena, without recourse to an unobservable operative principle.

Physical science had, in Comte's view, entered the positive stage, and similar thinking should penetrate other areas of analysis. In particular, Comte believed that positive laws of social behavior could be discovered in the same fashion as laws of physical nature. He is, thus, generally regarded as the father of sociology. Works like Comte's helped convince learned Europeans that all knowledge must resemble scientific knowledge.

THE BIRTH OF SCIENCE FICTION

DURING THE RENAISSANCE many European writers composed works about fantasy voyages to distant lands. In the seventeenth century, authors published some two hundred accounts of trips to the moon. Throughout the nineteenth century, other authors told tales of fantastic voyages into space or beneath the earth.

However, the real father of today's works of popular science fiction was Jules Verne (1828–1905). His *Five Weeks in a Balloon* (1863), a tale of a balloon trip across Africa, sold so well that a French publisher immediately gave Verne a contract to write two such stories each year for a magazine. So influential was Verne's image of the future that the United States named its first atomic submarine the *Nautilus* after the vessel the mysterious Captain Nemo commanded in Verne's *Twenty Thousand Leagues under the Sea* (1870).

Verne prided himself on his scientific veracity. He also located his stories in his own age. Readers felt they were experiencing a contemporary adventure.

Toward the turn of the century, science fiction found another master in the English novelist H. G. Wells (1866–1946), who in 1895 published *The Time Machine* in which the characters travel through time. Wells's first success was rapidly followed by *The Island of Dr. Moreau* (1896) about a mad surgeon's inhuman experiments on animals, and *The War of the Worlds* (1898) about a Martian invasion of the earth. Wells invented many of the devices, such as new stars appearing near the solar system, Martians and other planetary creatures unfriendly to humans, machinery that goes astray, and strange diseases, that would become the stock in trade for later science fiction writers.

Verne, Wells, and their many imitators published their stories in cheap illustrated magazines with mass circulations. Consequently, science fiction immediately entered popular culture. Throughout the twentieth century popular movies and television series were made based on the stories of both Verne and Wells. In 1938, when Orson Welles (1915–1985) broadcast Wells's *War of the Worlds* over the radio, many Americans actually believed Martians had landed in New Jersey. The works of Verne and Wells continue to influence the writing of science fiction.

Source: P. Nichols and J. Clute, *The Encyclopedia of Science Fiction* (New York: St. Martin's Press, 1995); Dieter Wuckel and Bruce Cassidy, *The Illustrated History of Science Fiction* (New York: Ungar, 1986); David Kyle, *A Pictorial History of Science Fiction* (London: Hamlyn, 1976).

Why is Jules Verne considered the father of modern science fiction?

What enduring plot devices did H. G. Wells introduce?

Why did science fiction become so popular?

Captain Nemo's submarine confronts a giant octopus in Verne's *Twenty Thousand Leagues under the Sea.* © Bettman/CORBIS

From the mid-nineteenth century onward, the links of science to the technology of the Second Industrial Revolution made the general European public aware of science and technology as never before. The British Fabian socialist Beatrice Webb (1858–1943) recalled this situation from her youth:

Who will deny that the men of science were the leading British intellectuals of that period; that it was they who stood out as men of genius with international reputations; that it was they who were the self-confident militants of the period; that it was they who were routing the theologians, confounding the mystics, imposing their theories on philosophers, their inventions on capitalists, and their discoveries on medical men; whilst they were at the same time snubbing the artists, ignoring the poets, and even casting doubts on the capacity of the politicians?[1]

Her remarks would have applied in every industrialized nation in Europe. Writers spoke of a religion of science that would explain all nature without resorting to supernaturalism. Popularizers, such as Thomas Henry Huxley (1825–1895) in Britain and Ernst Haeckel (1834–1919) in Germany, worked to gain government support of scientific research and to include science in the schools and universities.

Darwin's Theory of Natural Selection

In 1859, Charles Darwin (1809–1882) published *On the Origin of Species*, which carried the mechanical interpretation of physical nature into the world of living things. The book was one of the seminal works of Western thought and earned Darwin the honor of being regarded as the "Newton of biology." Both Darwin and his book have been much misunderstood. He did not originate the concept of evolution, which had been discussed widely before he wrote. What he and Alfred Russel Wallace (1823–1913) did, working independently, was to formulate the principle of natural selection, which explained how species had changed or evolved over time. Earlier writers had believed evolution might occur; Darwin and Wallace explained how it could occur.

Drawing on Malthus, the two scientists contended that more living organisms come into existence than can survive in their environment. Those organisms with a marginal advantage in the struggle for existence live long enough to propagate. This principle of survival of the fittest Darwin called **natural selection**. It was naturalistic and mechanistic, requiring no guiding mind behind the development in organic nature. What neither Darwin nor anyone else in his day could explain was the origin of those chance variations that provided some living things with the marginal chance for survival. Only after 1900, when the work on heredity of the Austrian

monk, Gregor Mendel (1822–1884), received public attention, did the mystery of those variations begin to be unraveled.

Darwin and Wallace's theory represented the triumph of naturalistic explanation, which removed the idea of purpose from organic nature. Eyes were not made for seeing according to the rational wisdom and purpose of God, but had developed mechanistically over time. Thus, the theory of evolution through natural selection not only contradicted the biblical narrative of the Creation but also undermined both the deistic argument for the existence of God from the design of the universe and the whole concept of fixity in nature or the universe at large. The world was a realm of flux. The idea that physical and organic nature might be constantly changing allowed people to believe that society, values, customs, and beliefs should also change.

In 1871, in *The Descent of Man*, Darwin applied the principle of evolution by natural selection to human beings. Darwin was hardly the first person to treat human beings as animals, but he contended that humankind's moral nature and religious sentiments, as well as its physical frame, had developed naturalistically largely in response to the requirements of survival. Neither the origin nor the character of humankind, in Darwin's view, required the existence of a god for their explanation. Not since Copernicus had removed the earth from the center of the universe had the pride of Western human beings received so sharp a blow.

Darwin's theory of evolution by natural selection was controversial from the moment *On the Origin of Species* appeared. It encountered criticism from both the religious and the scientific communities. By the end of the century, scientists widely accepted the concept of evolution, but not yet Darwin's mechanism of natural selection. The acceptance of the latter really dates from the 1920s and 1930s, when Darwin's theory was combined with modern genetics.

Science and Ethics—Social Darwinism

One area in which science came to have a new significance was social thought and ethics. Philosophers applied the concept of the struggle for survival to human social relationships. The phrase "survival of the fittest" predated Darwin and reflected the competitive outlook of classical economics. Darwin's use of the phrase gave it the prestige associated with advanced science.

The most famous advocate of evolutionary ethics was Herbert Spencer (1820–1903), a British philosopher. Spencer, a strong individualist, believed human society progresses through competition. If the weak receive too much protection, the rest of humankind is the loser. In Spencer's work, struggle against one's fellow human beings became a kind of ethical imperative. The concept could be applied to justify not aiding the poor and the

---

[1]Beatrice Webb, *My Apprenticeship* (London: Longmans, Green, 1926), pp. 130–131.

working class or to justify the domination of colonial peoples or to advocate aggressive competition among nations. Evolutionary ethics and similar concepts, all of which are usually termed **Social Darwinism**, often came close to saying that "might makes right."

One of the chief opponents of such thinking was Thomas Henry Huxley, the great defender of Darwin. In 1893, Huxley declared that the physical process of evolution was at odds with human ethical development. The struggle in nature only showed how human beings should not behave. (See "Compare & Connect: The Debate over Social Darwinism." pages 758–759.) Despite Huxley's arguments, the ideas of Social Darwinism continued to influence thought and public policy on both sides of the Atlantic.

▼ Christianity and the Church Under Siege

The nineteenth century was one of the most difficult periods in the history of the organized Christian churches. Many European intellectuals left the faith. The secular, liberal nation-states attacked the influence of the church. The expansion of population and the growth of cities challenged its organizational capacity. Yet during all this turmoil, the Protestant and Catholic churches continued to draw much popular support and personal religious devotion. Furthermore, as will be seen in the next chapter, the same decades marked by skepticism among many European intellectuals saw the burgeoning of the Christian missionary movement around the globe. Nonetheless, what would in the twentieth century become the overwhelmingly secular character of European society, a development that now largely distinguishes Europe from the United States, had its roots in the changes that commenced in the late nineteenth century.

Intellectual Skepticism

The intellectual attack on Christianity challenged its historical credibility, its scientific accuracy, and its morality. The philosophes of the Enlightenment had delighted in pointing out contradictions in the Bible. The historical scholarship of the nineteenth century brought new issues to the foreground.

History In 1835, David Friedrich Strauss (1808–1874) published *The Life of Jesus*, in which he questioned whether the Bible provides any genuine historical evidence about Jesus. Strauss contended the story of Jesus is a myth that arose from the particular social and intellectual conditions of first-century Palestine. Jesus' character and life represent the aspirations of the people of

that time and place, rather than events that actually occurred. Other authors also published skeptical examinations of the life of Jesus.

During the second half of the century, scholars such as Julius Wellhausen (1844–1918) in Germany, Ernst Renan (1823–1892) in France, and Matthew Arnold (1822–1888) in Great Britain contended that human authors had written and revised the books of the Bible with the problems of Jewish society and politics in mind. In the scholarship of these writers the Bible appeared not an inspired book, but one, like the Homeric epics, that had been written by normal human beings in a primitive society. This questioning of the historical validity of the Bible caused more literate men and women to lose faith in Christianity than any other single cause.

Science Science also undermined Christianity and faith in the validity of biblical narratives. This blow was particularly cruel because many eighteenth-century writers had led Christians to believe the scientific examination of nature buttressed their faith. William Paley's (1743–1805) *Natural Theology* (1802) and books by numerous scientists had enshrined that belief. The geology of Charles Lyell (1797–1875) suggested the earth is much older than the biblical records contend. By looking to natural causes to explain floods, mountains, and valleys, Lyell removed the miraculous hand of God from the physical development of the earth. Darwin's theory cast doubt on the Creation. His ideas and those of other writers suggested that the moral nature of humankind can be explained without appeal to God. Finally, anthropologists, psychologists, and sociologists proposed that religious sentiments are just one more set of natural phenomena.

Morality Other intellectuals questioned the morality of Christianity. The issue of immoral biblical stories was again raised. The morality of the Old Testament God, his cruelty and unpredictability, did not fit well with the tolerant, rational values of liberals. They also wondered about the morality of the New Testament God, who would sacrifice for his own satisfaction the only perfect being ever to walk the earth. Many of the clergy began to wonder if they could preach doctrines they felt to be immoral.

From another direction, writers like Friedrich Nietzsche (1844–1900) in Germany portrayed Christianity as a religion that glorified weakness rather than the strength life required. Christianity demanded a useless and debilitating sacrifice of the flesh and spirit, rather than heroic living and daring. Nietzsche once observed, "War and courage have accomplished more great things than love of neighbor."[2]

---

[2]Walter Kaufmann, ed. and trans., *The Portable Nietzsche* (New York: Viking, 1967), p. 159.

The Debate over Social Darwinism

DURING THE LATE-nineteenth and early-twentieth centuries scientists as well as other social commentators debated the question of whether the concept of "survival of the fittest" on which Charles Darwin had based his concept of evolution by natural selection should apply to human society and the competition between nations. Some commentators, such as Herbert Spencer, had advocated generally unbridled economic competition with little or no help to the poor and others who fared badly as a result of such competition. In 1893 T. H. Huxley rejected that view. However, a few years later Karl Pearson, another distinguished British scientist who supported the idea of evolution, argued that Social Darwinism should and did govern the relationships among nations.

QUESTIONS

1. Why does Huxley equate "social progress" with the "ethical process"?

2. In this passage, does Huxley present human society as part of nature or as something that may be separate from nature?

3. How does Pearson connect Darwin's ideas to the concept of human progress?

4. How might Pearson's ideas justify imperial expansion, which will be considered in the next chapter? How could these arguments foster a climate of international violence?

5. How might Huxley's ideas be used to support broadly beneficial social welfare programs enacted to produce national populations healthy enough to compete in the international rivalry envisioned by Pearson?

I. T. H. Huxley Criticizes Evolutionary Ethics

T. H. Huxley (1825–1895) was a British scientist who had been among Darwin's strongest defenders. Huxley, however, became a major critic of Social Darwinism, which attempted to deduce ethical principles from evolutionary processes involving struggle in nature. Drawing a strong distinction between the cosmic process of evolution and the social process of ethical development, he argued in Evolution and Ethics *(1893) that human ethical progress occurs through combating the cosmic process.*

Men in society are undoubtedly subject to the cosmic process. As among other animals, multiplication goes on without cessation, and involves severe competition for the means of support. The struggle for existence tends to eliminate those less fitted to adapt themselves to the circumstances of their existence. The strongest, the most self-assertive, tend to tread down the weaker. But the influence of the cosmic process on the evolution of society is the greater the more rudimentary its civilization. Social progress means a checking of the cosmic process at every step and the substitution for it of another, which may be called the ethical process; the end of which is not the survival of those who may happen to be the fittest, in respect of the whole of the conditions which obtain, but of those who are ethically the best.

As I have already urged, the practice of that which is ethically best—what we call goodness or virtue—involves a course of conduct which, in all respects, is opposed to that which leads to success in the cosmic struggle for existence. In place of ruthless self-assertion it demands self-restraint; in place of thrusting aside, or treading down, all competitors, it requires that the individual shall not merely respect, but shall help his fellows; its influence is directed, not so much to the survival of the fittest, as to the fitting of as many as possible to survive. It repudiates the gladiatorial theory of existence.

It is from neglect of these plain considerations that the fanatical individualism of our time attempts to apply the analogy of cosmic nature to society. . . .

II. Social Darwinism and Imperialism

T. H. Huxley's assault did not end the influence of Social Darwinism. Debates about competition among nations for trade, military superiority, and empire dominated much turn-of-the-twentieth-century political thought. The idea of biological competition became applied to nations and races and produced substantial impact on public opinion and among policymakers. In the selection that follows Karl Pearson (1857–1936), an English scientist, attempts to connect concepts from evolutionary theory—the struggle for survival and the survival of the fittest—to the development of human societies.

The first step towards lightening

"The White Man's Burden"

is through teaching the virtues of cleanliness.

Pears' Soap

is a potent factor in brightening the dark corners of the earth as civilization advances, while amongst the cultured of all nations it holds the highest place—it is the ideal toilet soap.

All sorts of people use it, all sorts of stores sell it.

Racism was often a by-product of Social Darwinist theory. At the turn of the twentieth century, racism permeated many facets of popular life. This ad for Pears' Soap caters to the racist attitudes held by many whites during this time. Library of Congress/*Colliers*, October 4, 1899

Let us understand, once for all, that the ethical progress of society depends, not on imitating the cosmic process, still less in running away from it, but in combating it.

Source: From T. H. Huxley, *Evolution and Ethics* (London: Macmillan & Co., 1893), as quoted in Franklin L. Baumer, *Main Currents of Western Thought: Readings in Western European Intellectual History from the Middle Ages to the Present*, 3rd ed., rev. (New York: Alfred A. Knopf, 1970), pp. 561–562.

History shows me one way, and one way only, in which a state of civilisation has been produced, namely, the struggle of race with race, and the survival of the physically and mentally fitter race. This dependence of progress on the survival of the fitter race, terribly black as it may seem to some of you, gives the struggle for existence its redeeming features; it is the fiery crucible out of which comes the finer metal. You may hope for a time when the sword shall be turned into the ploughshare, when American and German and English traders shall no longer compete in the markets of the world for raw materials, for their food supply, when the white man and the dark shall share the soil between them, and each till it as he lists. But, believe me, when that day comes mankind will no longer progress; there will be nothing to check the fertility of inferior stock; the relentless law of heredity will not be controlled and guided by natural selection. Man will stagnate. . . . The path of progress is strewn with the wreck of nations; traces are everywhere to be seen of the hecatombs of inferior races, and of victims who found not the narrow way to the greater perfection. Yet these dead peoples are, in very truth, the stepping stones on which mankind has arisen to the higher intellectual and deeper emotional life of today.

Source: From Karl Pearson, *National Life from the Standpoint of Science*, 2nd ed. (Cambridge: Cambridge University Press, 1907), pp. 21, 26–27, 64.

These skeptical currents created a climate in which Christianity lost much of its intellectual respectability. Fewer educated people joined the clergy. Many people found they could live with little or no reference to Christianity. The secularism of everyday life proved as harmful to the faith as the direct attacks. This situation was especially prevalent in the cities, which were growing faster than the capacity of the churches to meet the challenge. Whole generations of the urban poor grew up with little or no experience of the church as an institution or of Christianity as a religious faith.

Conflict Between Church and State

The secular states of late-nineteenth-century Europe clashed with both the Protestant and the Roman Catholic churches. Liberals, including those who were religiously observant, disliked the dogma and the political privileges of the established churches. National states were often suspicious of the supranational character of the Roman Catholic Church. The primary area of conflict between the state and the churches, however, was education. Previously, most education in Europe had taken place in church schools. The churches feared that future generations would emerge from the new state-financed schools without any religious teaching. From 1870 through the turn of the century, all the major countries debated religious education.

Great Britain In Great Britain, the Education Act of 1870 provided for state-supported schools run by elected school boards, whereas earlier the government had given small grants to religious schools. The new schools were to be built in areas where the religious denominations did not provide satisfactory education. There was rivalry both between the Anglican church and the state and between the Anglican church and the Nonconformist denominations—that is, those Protestant denominations that were not part of the Church of England. All the churches opposed improvements in education because these increased the costs of church schools. In the Education Act of 1902, the government provided state support for both religious and nonreligious schools but imposed the same educational standards on each.

France The British conflict was calm compared with that in France, which had a dual system of Catholic and public schools. Under the Falloux Law of 1850, the local priest provided religious education in the public schools. The conservative French Catholic Church and the Third French Republic loathed each other. Between 1878 and 1886, a series of educational laws sponsored by Jules Ferry (1832–1893) replaced religious instruction in the public schools with civic training. The number of public schools was expanded, and members of religious orders could no longer teach in them. After the Dreyfus affair, the French Catholic Church again paid a price for its reactionary politics. The Radical government of Pierre Waldeck-Rousseau (1846–1904), drawn from pro-Dreyfus groups, suppressed the religious orders. In 1905, the Napoleonic Concordat was terminated, and church and state were separated.

Germany and the *Kulturkampf* The most extreme and violent church-state conflict occurred in Germany during the 1870s. At unification, the German Catholic hierarchy wanted freedom for the churches guaranteed in the constitution. Bismarck left the matter to the federal states, but he soon felt the Roman Catholic Church and the Catholic Center Party threatened the unity of the German Empire. In 1870 and 1871, he removed the clergy from overseeing local education in Prussia and set education under state direction. This secularization of education represented the beginning of a concerted attack on the Catholic Church in Germany.

The "May Laws" of 1873, which applied to Prussia, but not to the entire German Empire, required priests to be educated in German schools and universities and to pass state examinations. The state could veto the appointments of priests. The legislation abolished the disciplinary power of the pope and the church over the clergy and transferred it to the state. Many of the clergy refused to obey these laws, and by 1876, Bismarck had either arrested or expelled all Catholic bishops from Prussia.

In the end, Bismarck's ***Kulturkampf*** ("cultural struggle") against the Catholic Church failed. By the end of the 1870s, he abandoned his attack. He had gained state control of education and civil laws governing marriage only at the price of provoking Catholic resentment against the German state. The *Kulturkampf* was probably his greatest blunder.

Areas of Religious Revival

The German Catholic resistance to the intrusions of the secular state illustrates the continuing vitality of Christianity during this period of intellectual and political hardship for the church. In Great Britain, both the Anglican church and the Nonconformist denominations expanded and raised vast sums for new churches and schools. In Ireland, the 1870s saw a Catholic devotional revival. In France, after the defeat by Prussia, priests organized special pilgrimages to shrines for thousands of penitents who believed France had been defeated because of their sins. The cult of the miracle of Lourdes grew during these years. Churches of all denominations gave more attention to the urban poor.

In effect, the last half of the nineteenth century witnessed the final great effort to Christianize Europe. It was well organized, well led, and well financed. It failed only because the population of Europe had outstripped the resources of the churches. The vitality of the churches accounts, in part, for the intense hostility of their enemies.

A Closer ▷ LOOK

CONFLICT BETWEEN CHURCH AND STATE IN GERMANY

THE CONFLICT BETWEEN the German imperial government and the German Roman Catholic Church was among the most intense church-state encounters of the late nineteenth century. Here the tumultuous event is somewhat trivialized as Bismarck and the pope are portrayed attempting to checkmate each other.

The chess game is intended to illustrate how Bismarck sought to remove major German church leaders from public life.

Zwischen Berlin und Rom.

The pope has fewer and fewer pieces on the board. Those Bismarck has captured have been placed in the box on the left denoted by an indistinct German word suggesting imprisonment. The German government had sent some Catholic clergy to prison.

The chess piece in the pope's hand is called *Encyclical*, indicating the official statement that the pope could issue against the German government.

To examine this image in an interactive fashion, please go to www.myhistorylab.com

myhistorylab

Bildarchiv Preussischer Kulturbesitz

The Roman Catholic Church and the Modern World

The most striking feature of Christian religious revival was the resilience of the papacy. The brief hope for a liberal pontificate from Pope Pius IX (r. 1846–1878) vanished when he fled the turmoil in Rome in November 1848. In the 1860s, embittered by the process of Italian unification, he launched a counteroffensive against liberalism. In 1864, he issued the *Syllabus of Errors*, which set the Catholic Church squarely against contemporary science, philosophy, and politics.

In 1869, the pope summoned the First Vatican Council. The next year, through the political manipulations of the pontiff and against opposition from many bishops, the council promulgated the dogma of **papal infallibility** when speaking officially on matters of faith and morals. No earlier pope had asserted such centralized authority within the church. The First Vatican Council ended in 1870, when Italian troops occupied Rome at the outbreak of the Franco-Prussian War. Thereafter the territory of the papacy was limited to the Vatican City, and the papacy made no formal accommodation to the Italian state until 1929. Pius IX and many other Roman Catholics believed the Catholic Church could sustain itself in the modern world of nation-states with large electorates only by centering the authority of the church in the papacy itself. The spiritual authority of the papacy became a substitute for its lost political and temporal authority.

Pius IX was succeeded by Leo XIII (r. 1878–1903). Leo, who was sixty-eight years old at the time of his election, sought to make accommodations to the modern age and to address its great social questions. He looked to the philosophy of Thomas Aquinas (1225–1274) to reconcile the claims of faith and reason.

Leo's most important pronouncement on public issues was the encyclical *Rerum Novarum* (1891). In that document, he defended private property, religious education, and religious control of the marriage laws, and he condemned socialism and Marxism, but he also declared that employers should treat their employees justly, pay them proper wages, and permit them to organize labor unions. The pope supported laws to protect workers and urged that modern society be organized in corporate groups that would include people from various classes who would cooperate according to Christian principles. The corporate society, based on medieval social organization, was to be an alternative to both socialism and competitive capitalism. On the basis of Leo XIII's pronouncements, democratic Catholic political parties and Catholic trade unions were founded throughout Europe. (See "Leo XIII Considers the Social Question in European Politics.")

His successor Pius X (r. 1903–1914) hoped to resist modern thought and restore traditional devotional life. Between 1903 and 1907, he condemned Catholic modernism, a movement of modern biblical criticism within the church, and in 1910 he required all priests to take an anti-Modernist oath. The struggle between Catholicism and modern thought was resumed.

Islam and Late-Nineteenth-Century European Thought

The few European thinkers who wrote about Islam in the late nineteenth century discussed it using the same scientific and naturalistic scholarly methods they applied to Christianity and Judaism. They interpreted Islam as a historical phenomenon without any reference to the supernatural, and the Qur'an received the same kind of critical historical analysis that was being directed toward the Bible. Islam, like the other great world religions, was seen as a product of a particular culture. In the works of scholars such as the influential French writer Ernest Renan, Islam was, like Judaism, a manifestation of the ancient Semitic mentality, which had given rise to a powerful monotheistic vision. Renan, and sociologists such as Max Weber, also dismissed Islam as a religion and culture incapable of developing science and closed to new ideas.

However, Renan's views were opposed in a French journal by Jamal al-din Al-Afghani (1839–1897), an Egyptian intellectual, who argued that over time Islam, which had arisen six hundred years after Christianity, would eventually produce cultures as modern as those in Europe. Al-Afghani was one of the rare Islamic writers who directly contested a European thinker.

The European racial and cultural outlooks that denigrated nonwhite peoples and their civilizations were also directed toward the Arab world. European authors who championed white racial superiority looked to India and the Aryan civilization that was supposed to have risen there and later influenced northern European life as the source of Europe's cultural superiority.

Christian missionaries reinforced these anti-Islamic attitudes. They blamed Islam for Arab economic backwardness, for mistreating women, and for condoning slavery. They also often came into conflict with Islamic religious authorities. Because the penalty for abjuring Islam is death, the missionaries made few converts among Muslims. So they turned their efforts to founding schools and hospitals, hoping these Christian foundations would eventually lead some Muslims to Christianity. Few Muslims converted, but these institutions did educate young Arabs in Western science and medicine, and many of their students became leaders in the Middle East. Eventually, as missionary families came to live for long periods of time among Arabs, they became more sympathetic to Arab political aspirations.

Within the Islamic world, and especially in the decaying Ottoman Empire, as political leaders continued to champion Western scientific education and technology, they confronted a variety of responses from religious thinkers. Some of these thinkers sought to combine modern thought with Islam. For example, the Salafi, or the salafiyya movement, believed there was no inherent contradiction between science and Islam. They believed Muhammad had wisely and properly addressed the issues of his day, and a reformed Islamic faith could do so again. The Arab world should cease imitating the West and modernize itself on the basis of a pure, restored Islamic faith. The Salafi emphasized a rational reading of the Qur'an and saw Ottoman decline as the result of Muslim religious error. This outlook, which had originally sought to reconcile Islam with the modern world, eventually led many Muslims in the twentieth century to oppose Western influence.

Other Islamic religious leaders simply rejected the West and modern thought. They included the Mahdist movement in Sudan, the Sanussiya in Libya, and the Wahhabi movement in the Arabian peninsula. Such religious-based opposition was strongest in those portions of the Middle East where the European presence was least direct, which is to say outside of Morocco, Algeria, Egypt, and Tunisia, which for all intents and purposes were under the control of Western powers by 1900, and Turkey, where Ottoman leaders had long been deeply involved with the West.

LEO XIII CONSIDERS THE SOCIAL QUESTION IN EUROPEAN POLITICS

In his 1891 encyclical Rerum Novarum, *Pope Leo XIII provided the Catholic Church's answer to secular calls for social reforms. The pope denied the socialist claim that class conflict is the natural state of affairs. He urged employers to seek just and peaceful relations with workers.*

How does Leo XIII reject the concept of class conflict? What responsibilities does he assign to the rich and to the poor? Are the responsibilities of the two classes equal? What kinds of social reform might emerge from these ideas?

The great mistake that is made in the matter now under consideration is to possess oneself of the idea that class is naturally hostile to class; that rich and poor are intended by Nature to live at war with one another. So irrational and so false is this view that the exact contrary is the truth. . . . Each requires the other; capital cannot do without labour, nor labour without capital. Mutual agreement results in pleasantness and good order; perpetual conflict necessarily produces confusion and outrage. Now, in preventing such strife as this, and in making it impossible, the efficacy of Christianity is marvelous and manifold. . . . Religion teaches the labouring man and the workman to carry out honestly and well all equitable agreements freely made; never to injure capital, or to outrage the person of an employer; never to employ violence in representing his own cause, or to engage in riot or disorder; and to have nothing to do with men of evil principles, who work upon the people with artful promises and raise hopes which usually end in disaster and in repentance when too late. Religion teaches the rich man and the employer that their work people are not their slaves; that they must respect in every man his dignity as a man and as a Christian; that labour is nothing to be ashamed of, if we listen to right reason and to Christian philosophy, but is an honourable employment, enabling a man to sustain his life in an upright and creditable way; and that it is shameful and inhuman to treat men like chattels to make money by, or to look upon them merely as so much muscle or physical power. Thus, again, Religion teaches that, as among the workman's concerns are Religion herself and things spiritual and mental, the employer is bound to see that he has time for the duties of piety; that he be not exposed to corrupting influences and dangerous occasions; and that he be not led away to neglect his home and family or to squander his wages. Then, again, the employer must never tax his work people beyond their strength, nor employ them in work unsuited to their sex or age. His great and principal obligation is to give every one that which is just.

As quoted in F. S. Nitti, *Catholic Socialism*, trans. by Mary Mackintosh (London: S. Sonnenschein, 1895), p. 409.

▼ Toward a Twentieth-Century Frame of Mind

The last quarter of the nineteenth century and the first decade of the twentieth century were the crucible of modern Western thought. Philosophers, scientists, psychologists, and artists began to portray physical reality, human nature, and society in ways different from those of the past. Their new concepts challenged the major presuppositions of mid-nineteenth-century science, rationalism, liberalism, and bourgeois morality.

Science: The Revolution in Physics

The changes in the scientific worldview originated within the scientific community itself. By the late 1870s, discontent existed over the excessive realism of mid-century science. It was thought that many scientists believed their mechanistic models, solid atoms, and absolute time and space actually described the real universe.

In 1883, Ernst Mach (1838–1916) published *The Science of Mechanics*, in which he urged that scientists consider their concepts descriptive not of the physical world, but of the sensations the scientific observer experiences. Scientists could describe only the sensations, not the physical world that underlay those sensations. In line with Mach, the French scientist Henri Poincaré (1854–1912) urged that the theories of scientists be regarded as hypothetical constructs of the human mind rather than as true descriptions of nature. In 1911, Hans Vaihinger (1852–1933) suggested the concepts of science be considered "as if" descriptions of the physical world. By World War I, few scientists believed they could portray the "truth" about physical reality. Rather, they saw themselves as recording the observations of instruments and as offering useful hypothetical or symbolic models of nature.

Marie Curie (1869–1934) and Pierre Curie (1859–1906) were two of the most important figures in the advance of physics and chemistry. Marie was born in Poland but worked in France for most of her life. She is credited with the discovery of radium, for which she was awarded the Nobel Prize in Chemistry in 1911.
The Granger Collection, New York

X Rays and Radiation Discoveries in the laboratory paralleled the philosophical challenge to nineteenth-century science. With those discoveries, the comfortable world of supposedly "complete" nineteenth-century physics vanished forever. In December 1895, Wilhelm Roentgen (1845–1923) published a paper on his discovery of X rays, a form of energy that penetrated various opaque materials. Major steps in the exploration of radioactivity followed within months of the publication of his paper.

In 1896, Henri Becquerel (1852–1908) discovered that uranium emitted a similar form of energy. The next year, J. J. Thomson (1856–1940), at Cambridge University, formulated the theory of the electron. The interior world of the atom had become a new area for human exploration. In 1902, Ernest Rutherford (1871–1937) explained the cause of radiation through the disintegration of the atoms of radioactive materials. Shortly thereafter, he speculated on the immense store of energy present in the atom.

Theories of Quantum Energy, Relativity, and Uncertainty The discovery of radioactivity and discontent with the existing mechanical models led to revolutionary theories in physics. In 1900, Max Planck (1858–1947) pioneered the articulation of the quantum theory of energy, according to which energy is a series of discrete quantities, or packets, rather than a continuous stream. In 1905, Albert Einstein (1879–1955) published his first epoch-making papers on **relativity** in which he contended that time and space exist not separately, but rather as a combined continuum. Moreover, the measurement of time and space depends on the observer as well as on the entities being measured.

In 1927, Werner Heisenberg (1901–1976) set forth his uncertainty principle, according to which the behavior of subatomic particles is a matter of statistical probability rather than of exactly determinable cause and effect. Much that had seemed unquestionable about the physical universe had now become ambiguous.

The mathematical complexity of twentieth-century physics meant science would rarely again be successfully popularized. At the same time, through applied technology and further research in chemistry, physics, and medicine, science affected daily living more than ever before. Scientists from the late nineteenth century onward became the most successful group of Western intellectuals in gaining the financial support of governments and private institutions for the pursuit of their research. They did so by relating the success of science to the economic progress, military security, and the health of their nations. Science, through research, medicine, and technological change, has thus affected modern life more significantly than any other intellectual activity.

AP* TEST PREP

1. Positivism is associated with the idea of
   a. scientific certainty based on mathematical principles.
   b. skepticism.
   c. the greatest good for the greatest number.
   d. competition as the mechanism to achieve progress.
   e. explanation of phenomena based on observation only.

2. Alfred Russel Wallace is remembered for
   a. formulating the principle of natural selection.
   b. his discoveries of Egyptian antiquities.
   c. his research into Indo-European languages.
   d. his work on heredity.
   e. evolutionary ethics.

3. The author noted for distinguishing between the cosmic process of evolution and the social process of ethical development was
   a. Jeremy Bentham.
   b. Auguste Comte.
   c. T. A. Huxley.
   d. David Friedrich Strauss.
   e. William Paley.

4. _____ claimed: "War and Courage have accomplished more great things than love of neighbor."
   a. Charles Lyell
   b. G. B. Shaw
   c. Friederich Nietzsche
   d. George Sorrell
   e. T. H. Huxley

5. Bismarck's *Kulturkampf* describes state action aimed at
   a. wresting secular control over education and marriage.
   b. enforcing a single German language and dialect.
   c. censoring radical newspapers and books.
   d. excluding socialists from political office.
   e. anti-Semitic policies.

6. The 1870s represent a period of
   a. religious revival.
   b. a high point of secularism.
   c. decline of the papacy.
   d. harmony between religion and science.
   e. decline of the Anglican church.

7. Pope Leo XIII's corporatist vision offered
   a. corporate ethics for the industrial age.
   b. aristocratic ethics for the industrial age.
   c. an alternative to both socialism and competitive capitalism.
   d. Christian trade unionism.
   e. Catholic harmony with the secular state.

8. Which literary work uses realism to describe a woman's self-discovery?
   a. *Ghosts*
   b. *Mrs. Warren's Profession*
   c. *Madame Bovary*
   d. *Emma*
   e. *A Doll's House*

9. European missionaries in the Middle East
   a. gained converts among the upper classes.
   b. gained converts among the working classes.
   c. trained young Muslims in Western science and medicine.
   d. trained young Muslims in Western law and ethics.
   e. concentrated their efforts in Iran.

10. The author noted for transforming not only the novel but also the structure of the paragraph was
    a. Thomas Mann.
    b. Marcel Proust.
    c. Virginia Woolf.
    d. G. B. Shaw.
    e. James Joyce.

11. Josephine Butler is best known for her campaign for
    a. better pay for working-class women.
    b. racial equality.
    c. equal legal rights for women and minorities.
    d. the rights of children.
    e. the repeal of the Contagious Diseases Acts.

12. Nietzsche's "Overman" character in *Thus Spake Zarathustra* harkened to
    a. Christian martyrdom.
    b. Talmudic scholarship.
    c. Homeric heroism.
    d. Germanic legend.
    e. Mesopotamian myth.

13. According to authors such as Durkheim and Wallas, human social behavior is determined largely by
    a. cost/benefit rationality.
    b. instinct, habit, and affections.
    c. competition for scarce resources.
    d. sensory experience and memory.
    e. genetic predisposition.

14. Max Planck pioneered the
    a. theory of relativity.
    b. quantum theory of energy.
    c. universal constant theory.
    d. uncertainty principle.
    e. singularity theory.

15. The single most important new departure in early-twentieth-century Western art was
    a. cubism.
    b. postimpressionism.

    c. Dada.
    d. surrealism.
    e. postmodernism.

16. Modernism was *not*
    a. critical of middle-class society.
    b. a major influence on literature.
    c. deeply concerned with social issues.
    d. deeply concerned with aesthetics.
    e. concerned with the creation of new forms.

17. According to Freud, the id
    a. consists of the instinctive drive for physical pleasure.
    b. consists of external moral imperatives.
    c. mediates between the ego and the superego.
    d. is a relatively new component of consciousness.
    e. will one day cease to exist.

18. Proponents of the Wahhabi movement
    a. rejected the West and modern thought.
    b. endorsed Western science but rejected Western society.

    c. hoped to build alliances with Christian fundamentalists.
    d. were most concerned with the development of secular states in the Middle East.
    e. advocated immigration to Europe.

19. Theodore Herzl called for
    a. the creation of a Jewish state outside of Europe.
    b. renewed efforts at Jewish assimilation.
    c. renewed efforts to achieve legal equality for Jews in Europe.
    d. government support for popular anti-Semitism.
    e. the expulsion of Jews from Europe.

20. At the end of the nineteenth century, most scientists
    a. accepted the concept of evolution and natural selection.
    b. accepted natural selection, but not evolution.
    c. rejected evolution and natural evolution.
    d. accepted evolution but not natural selection.
    e. were creationists.

DOCUMENT-BASED QUESTION

Directions: Construct a valid essay that directly addresses the central issue of the following question. Use facts from the documents provided and from the chapter to prove the position you take in your thesis statement.

How did the theory of evolution influence racial thinking in the late nineteenth century?

Document A

Caricature of Darwin.

Document B

Source: The British scientist T. H. Huxley criticizes evolutionary ethics, *Evolution and Ethics.*

As I have urged, the practice of that which is ethically best—what we call goodness or virtue—involves a course of conduct which, in all respects, is opposed to that which leads to success in the cosmic struggle for existence. . . .

It is from neglect of these plain considerations that the fanatical individualism of our time attempts to apply the analogy of cosmic nature to society. . . .

Let us understand, once for all, that the ethical progress of society depends, not on imitating the cosmic process, still less in running away from it, but in combating it.

Document C

Source: Alexis de Tocqueville forecasts the danger of French diplomat and race theorist Count Arthur de Gatineau's racial thought, *Evolution and Ethics.*

Your doctrine is rather a sort of fatalism, of predestination, if you wish, . . . Whether the element of fatality should be introduced into the material order of things, or whether God willed to make different kinds of men so that He imposed special burdens of race on some, withholding from them a capacity for certain feelings, for certain thoughts, for certain habits, for certain qualities—all this has nothing to do with my own concern with the practical consequences of these philosophical

African and Asian culture that explorers or other travelers or researchers had brought home. These exhibitions, like the botanical gardens, zoos and museums of natural history, introduced Western audiences to what they considered to be the exotic features and otherness of non-Western peoples and cultures.

The idea of museums or zoos to display exotic creatures was also extended to human beings in both Europe and the United States. Showmen such as the American P. T. Barnum would exhibit Africans, Asians, and Native Americans. Carl Hagenbeck, a German, brought Polynesians, Sudanese, and Inuits from Canada to live in" native villages" in the Hamburg Zoo. In the thirty years before World War I, the Paris zoo staged over twenty-five such exhibitions. At World's Fairs, millions of Europeans and Americans paid to view native peoples. As late as 1958 the Brussels World's Fair, like that of Leopold II sixty years earlier, boasted a village of Congolese people.

In Perspective

Western imperialism during the nineteenth and early twentieth centuries reshaped the world in ways that still affect us today. The productive capacity, military superiority, and technological prowess first of the European powers and later of the United States allowed those nations to dominate the world as they had never been able to do before. That dominance would last for about a century. Western influence arose from decades of free-trade imperialism in the early nineteenth century that was marked in general by the absence of formal imperial government except for Britain in India and its settler colonies. The New Imperialism began in the 1870s largely as a result of the political changes that had occurred in Europe since the 1850s—the defeat of Russia in the Crimean War, the unification of Italy and Germany, and the defeat of France by Germany in 1870—that upset the balance of power and heightened tensions and competition among the great powers who increasingly sought to reassure themselves and assert their power by expanding into the non-Western world. The New Imperialism thus involved the creation of formal empires as a sign of great power status, the protection of what were seen as vital geo-political interests, an assertion of white racial superiority, and the partition of Africa. All these ideas and events led the European powers into overseas imperial rivalries that contributed to the tensions resulting in the outbreak of World War I in 1914.

Western imperialism found many supporters. Manufacturers and merchants sought markets for their goods and sources of tropical raw materials. Missionaries sought to evangelize the parts of Africa and Asia previously closed to Christianity. Scientists saw the imperial mission as creating networks for research and a new appreciation of their own efforts as supporters of their national governments. Army and navy officers looked to colonial wars as avenues for professional advancement.

For over a century, from the 1830s to the 1940s, the peoples of the non-Western world found themselves generally acted upon by foreign political, economic, and military forces that they could not effectively resist. Many of these non-Western peoples sought to work with Westerners for their own advantage. Indeed, the Western colonial empires could not have functioned without African and Asian collaborators. By the outbreak of World War I, however, discontent was stirring throughout the colonial world, and the leaders of the post–World War II movement for decolonization and independence had begun to emerge.

AP* TEST PREP

1. New Imperialism can be distinguished from previous forms of imperialism by
   a. settling conquered lands.
   b. establishing trading centers.
   c. building roads for moving troops and trade.
   d. exacting tribute.
   e. direct political and administrative control.

2. British free trade policy in the colonies was significant
   a as a means to avoid conquest by force.
   b. as a means to avoid having to establish a formal colonial administration.
   c. as a means to negotiate workers' compensation in England.
   d. as a means to avoid the politics of resentment.
   e. as a means to establish settlements.

3. The English sought to obtain _____ from China.
   a. opium
   b. quinine
   c. indigo
   d. tea
   e. labor

4. In the aftermath of the Opium Wars, Britain exacted all of the following *except*
   a. more open ports.
   b. freer access for missionaries.
   c. control over Hong Kong.
   d. foreign embassies.
   e. exclusive rights to trade.

5. The cause of the Sepoy Rebellion demonstrated
   a British colonial disorganization.
   b. British parliamentary disputes over colonial policy.
   c. British disrespect for Indian beliefs and customs.
   d. British policy of "divide and conquer."
   e. British missionary zeal.

6. The chief British imperial strategy during the nineteenth century was
   a. keeping Prussia out of Africa.
   b. keeping France out of India.
   c. controlling Africa.
   d. civilizing savages.
   e. protecting military and commercial routes to India.

7. The British Crown took political authority over India in
   a. 1773.
   b. 1820.
   c. 1832.
   d. 1858.
   e. 1871.

8. In 1885, Hindus founded the
   a. Hindu Party for Liberated India.
   b. Indian National Congress.
   c. Committee for Indian Liberation.
   d. National Congress of Hindus.
   e. Hindu League.

9. The author associated with the analysis that imperialism results from an excess of goods and capital in a home market was
   a. V. I. Lenin.
   b. Karl Marx.
   c. J. A. Hobson.
   d. Joseph Chamberlain.
   e. T. H. Huxley.

10. A crucial component of the New Imperialism was the need
    a. for new markets.
    b. for testing new technologies.
    c. for a new labor force.
    d. to relieve Europe of an excess population.
    e. to assert national prestige among competing powers.

11. Algeria was administered by
    a. civilian French officials.
    b. Algerians who paid tribute to France.
    c. royal armed forces.
    d. the French Trading Company.
    e. native rulers "advised" by the French.

12. Russian expansion depended on
    a. Prussian and English assistance.
    b. co-opting local elites and leaving local practices intact.
    c. mercenary armies and tribute.
    d. subjugating conquered people to agricultural collectives.
    e. naval prowess.

13. The "Great Game" journalists and fiction writers referred to was
    a. intercontinental car racing.
    b. Cecil Rhodes's ambitions in Africa.
    c. Muslim-Hindu rivalries for British patronage.
    d. Russian-British rivalry over central Asia, especially Afghanistan.
    e. Anglo-French rivalries in North Africa.

14. The Chinese Open Door policy was proposed by
    a. Britain.
    b. Prussia.
    c. France.
    d. the United States.
    e. Russia.

15. French control over Morocco and Italian control over Libya represent
    a. a significant growth of those empires.
    b. major competition between France and Italy.
    c. a unified continental front against British interests.
    d. the weakness of the Ottoman Empire.
    e. significant development of North African natural resources.

16. Egypt came under British control largely because of
    a. Italian failure to conquer Egypt.
    b. Khedive bankruptcy.
    c. the success of the Wahhabi movement.
    d. the English purchase of French shares in the Suez Canal project.
    e. Ottoman requests to help suppress nationalist rebellions there.

17. The "nervous system" of the civilized world described
    a. the printing press.
    b. submarine cables.
    c. naval power.
    d. the system of indirect rule.
    e. electricity.

18. Quinine, derived from cinchona bark, comes from
    a. an African product.
    b. a Peruvian product.
    c. an Indian product.
    d. a North African product.
    e. a Chinese product.

19. The defeat of the Italians at the Battle of Aduwa can be attributed to
    a. interference from the British.
    b. a lack of adequate supplies.
    c. a lack of adequate understanding of the terrain.
    d. Ethiopian access to French weaponry.
    e. disorder in the Italian army.

20. The greatest negative impact on the Amazon rubber tree business came as a result of
   a. smallpox and malaria.
   b. a lack of slave labor.
   c. the extra cost of shipping out of the Amazon.
   d. revolts from indigenous populations.
   e. exportation of rubber tree seeds to Kew Gardens and elsewhere.

DOCUMENT-BASED QUESTION

Directions: Construct a valid essay that directly addresses the central issue of the following question. Use facts from the documents provided and from the chapter to prove the position you take in your thesis statement.

Discuss and analyze the factors that led to European imperialism in the nineteenth century.

Document A

Source: Denis Diderot, eighteenth-century French philosopher, *Supplement au voyage de Bougainville* (1772).

This country belongs to you. Why? Because you have set foot on it? If a Tahitian landed one day on your coast and he engraved on one of your rocks or on the bark of a tree: "This country belongs to the inhabitants of Tahiti," what would you think?

Document B

Source: John Ruskin, British critic, inaugural lecture, Oxford University (1870).

There is a destiny now possible to us, the highest ever set before a nation to be accepted or refused. Will you youths of England make your country again a royal throne of kings, a sceptred isle, for all the world a source of light, a centre of peace; mistress of learning and of the Arts, faithful guardian of time-honoured principles? This is what England must do or perish: she must found colonies as fast and as far as she is able, formed of her most energetic and worthiest men; seizing every piece of fruitful waste ground she can set her feet on, and there teaching these her colonists that their chief virtue is to be fidelity to their country, and their first aim is to advance the power of England by land and sea.

Document C

Source: Lord Cromer, British government agent, "The Government of the Subject Races" (1882).

We need not always enquire too closely what these people, who are all, nationally speaking, more or less in *statu pupillari*, [student status] themselves think is in their own interests . . . it is essential that each special issue should be decided mainly with reference to what, by the light of western knowledge and experience . . . we conscientiously think is best for the subject race.

Document D

Source: Clement Hill, British Foreign Office official, Foreign Office memorandum (December 9, 1884).

The geographical position of the East Coast lays it more within the general area of our foreign policy than that of the West Coast. . . . Our alternative route by the Cape to India may at any time make it important that we should have possession of or at least free access to good harbors. The importance is not less since the French move to Madagascar. Is it not worth considering whether in view of the European race for territories on the West Coast. . . . we might not confine ourselves to securing the utmost possible freedom of trade on that coast, yielding to other Powers the territorial responsibilities and seeking compensation on the East Coast where . . . we are at present, but who can say for how long, without a European rival; where the political future of the country is of real importance to Indian and Imperial interests; where the climate is superior; where commerce is capable of vast extension, and where our influence could be exercised . . . in the extension of civilization, and the consequent extinction of the Slave Trade for which we have so long labored.

Document E

Source: Decree following the proclamation of a Portuguese protectorate over Dahomey, signed by Pinheiro Chagas, Foreign Minister (1886).

The monarch of Dahomey, the terror of all Europeans, shows himself affable and condescending to the Portuguese alone. It was he who asked urgently that our protectorate should be established upon the coast of his kingdom. . . . It is he who appears disposed to accept at our hands the benefits of European civilization, and to this design he has already borne honorable witness by abolishing human sacrifices.

The Portuguese protectorate in Dahomey is the lighted pathway that links this kingdom of darkness with Europe.

Document F

Source: G. W. Steevens, British journalist, *Daily Mail* (June 23, 1897).

Up they came, more and more, new types, new realms at every couple of yards, an anthropological museum—a living gazetteer of the British Empire. With them came their English officers, whom they obey and follow like children. And you begin to understand, as never before, what the Empire amounts to. Not only that we possess all these remote outlandish places . . . but also that all these people are working, not simply under us, but with us—that we send out a boy here and a boy there, and a boy takes hold of the savages of the part he comes to, and teaches them to march and shoot as he tells them, to obey him and believe in him and die for him and the Queen. . . . A plain, stupid, uninspired people, they call us, and yet we are doing this with every kind of savage man there is. And each one of us—you and I, and that man in his shirt-sleeves at the corner—is a working part of this world-shaping force. How small you must feel in face of this stupendous whole, and yet how great to be a unit in it.

Document G

Source: Carl Peters, German author, *Die Gründung von Deutsch-Ostafrika* (The Foundation of German East Africa) (1906).

Manifesto of the Society for German Colonization, April 1884

In the partition of the earth, as it has proceeded from the beginning of the fifteenth century up to our times, the German nation received nothing. All the remaining European culture-bearing peoples possess areas outside our continent where their languages and customs can take firm root and flourish. The moment that the German emigrant leaves the borders of the Reich behind him, he is a stranger sojourning on foreign soil. The German Reich, great in size and strength through its bloodily achieved unity, stands in the leading position among the continental European powers: her sons abroad must adapt themselves to nations which look upon us with either indifference or even hostility. For centuries the great stream of German emigration has been plunging down into foreign races where it is lost sight of. Germandom outside Europe has been undergoing a perpetual national decline. . . .

The Society for German Colonization aims to undertake on its own, in a resolute and sweeping manner, carefully chosen colonization projects and thereby supplement the ranks of organizations with similar tendencies.

Its particular tasks will be:

1. to provide necessary sums of capital for colonization;
2. to seek out and lay claim to suitable districts for colonization;
3. to direct German emigrants to these regions

Document H

Source: Karl Pearson, English author, *National Life from the Standpoint of Science* (1907).

History shows me one way, and one way only, in which a state of civilization has been produced, namely, the struggle of race with race, and the survival of the physically and mentally fitter race.

This dependence of progress on the survival of the fitter race, terribly black as it may seem to some of you, gives the struggle for existence its redeeming features; it is the fiery crucible out of which comes the finer metal. You may hope for a time when the sword shall be turned into the ploughshare, when American and German and English traders shall no longer compete in the markets of the world for raw materials, for their food supply, when the white man and the dark shall share the soil between them, and each till it as he lists. . . . The path of progress is strewn with the wreck of nations; traces are everywhere to be seen of the hecatombs of inferior races, and of victims who found not the narrow way to the greater perfection. Yet these dead peoples are, in very truth, the stepping stones on which mankind has arisen to the higher intellectual and deeper emotional life of today.

For more on early European imperialism, see pages 787–797 of this chapter.

THE WEST & THE WORLD

Imperialism: Ancient and Modern

THE CONCEPT OF "empire" does not win favor today, and the word *imperialism*, derived from it, has carried an increasingly pejorative meaning since it was coined in the nineteenth century. Both words imply forcible domination by a nation or a state that exploits an alien people for its own benefit. Although, in our time, the charge of imperialism arises whenever a large and powerful nation influences weaker ones, exertion of influence alone is not imperialism. To be true to historical experience, one nation's actions toward another are imperialistic only if the dominant nation exerts both political and military control over the weaker one. In that sense, the last great empire in the modern world was the conglomeration of republics and ostensibly independent satellite states dominated by Russia prior to the USSR's collapse, but the Russians and the other imperial powers after World War II took no public pride in their domination. In our day, ruling an "empire" or engaging in "imperialism" is generally considered among the worst acts a nation can commit.

Such views are rare, perhaps unique, in the history of civilization. A major source for this opinion is the Christian religious tradition, especially parts of the New Testament that deprecate power and worldly glory and praise humility. In fact, Christianity was not hostile to power and empire for it took control of the Roman Empire in the fourth century C.E. and has lived comfortably with "empire" until our own century. The rise of democracy and nationalism in the last two centuries may have been more influential in changing attitudes toward imperialism, because these movements exalt the freedom and autonomy of a people. Perhaps the modern disdain for empire building has its principal origins in the extraordinary horror of modern warfare and the historical knowledge that competition for empire has often led to war.

If, however, we are to understand the widespread experience of empire throughout history, we must be alert to the great gap that separates the views of most people throughout history from our current opinions. The earliest empires go back more than 4000 years to the valleys of the Nile and the Tigris-Euphrates, and empires arose later in China, Japan, India, Iran, and Central and South America, among other areas. Typically, they were led by rulers who were believed to be gods or the representatives of gods, or at least were godlike in their ability to rule over many people. To their own people they brought wealth and prosperity, power, and reflected glory, all considered highly desirable. No one appears to have questioned the propriety of conquering another people and taking their lands, property, and persons to benefit the conquerors. Empire seemed to be part of the order of things—good for the rulers, usually bad for the ruled.

The Greeks: Ambiguities of Power

In most respects, the Greeks resembled other ancient peoples in their attitudes toward power, conquest, empire, and the benefits that came with them. Their Olympian gods held sway over earth, heaven, and the underworld because of victorious wars over other deities, and they gloried in their rule. The heroes in the epic poems that formed the Greek system of values won glory and honor through battle, conquest, and rule over other people. They viewed the world as a place of intense competition in which victory and domination, which brought fame and glory, were the highest goals, whereas defeat and subordination brought ignominy and shame.

When the legendary world of aristocratic heroes gave way to the world of city-states (*poleis*), competition was elevated from contests among individuals, households, and clans to contests and wars among *poleis*. In 416 B.C.E., more than a decade after the death of Pericles (c. 490–429 B.C.E.), Athenian spokesmen explained to some Melian officials their view of international relations: "Of the gods we believe, and of men we know, that by a necessity of their nature they always rule wherever they have the power."[1] Although their language was shockingly blunt, it reflected the views of most Greeks.

Yet this was also a dramatic presentation of the morally problematic status of the Athenian Empire. The Athenians' harsh statement would have struck a sympathetic chord among the Greeks. They appreciated power and the security and glory it can bring, but their own historical experience was different from that of other ancient nations. Their culture had been shaped by small autonomous, independent city-states, and they considered freedom natural for people raised in such an environment. Citizens, they believed, should be free in their persons, free to maintain their own constitutions, laws,

[1]Thucydides 5.105

and customs, and their city-states should be free to conduct their own foreign relations and to compete for power and glory. The free, autonomous *polis*, they thought, was greater than the mightiest powers in the world, and the sixth-century B.C.E. poet Phocylides was prepared to compare it to the great Assyrian Empire: "A little *polis* living orderly in a high place is greater than block-headed Nineveh" (Fragment 5).

When *poleis* fought one another, the victor typically took control of a piece of borderland that was usually the source of the dispute. They did not normally enslave the defeated enemy or annex and occupy its land. In these matters, as in many others, the Greeks distinguished themselves from alien peoples who did not speak Greek and were not shaped by the Greek cultural tradition. These people were called barbarians, *barbaroi*, because their speech sounded to the Greeks like "bar bar." Because they had not been raised as people in free communities but lived as subjects to a ruler, they were, it seemed, slaves by nature. To the Greeks, then, dominating and enslaving such people was perfectly acceptable. Greeks, however, viewed themselves as naturally free, as they demonstrated by creating and living in the free institutions of the *polis*. To rule over such people, to deny them their freedom and autonomy, would be wrong—so the Greeks thought, but they did not always act accordingly. The early Spartans, for instance, had changed the status of the conquered Greeks of Laconia and Messenia to *Helots*, or slaves of the state.

The Greeks shared still another belief that interfered with the comfortable acceptance of great power and empire: They thought any good thing amassed by humans to excess, beyond moderation, eventually led to *hubris*, a condition of wanton violence arising from arrogant pride in one's greatness. Those overcome by hubris were thought to have overstepped the limits established for human beings, to have shown contempt for the gods and, thereby, to have incurred *nemesis*, or divine anger and retribution. The great example to the Greeks of the fifth century B.C.E. of the workings of hubris and nemesis was the fate of Xerxes (r. 486–465 B.C.E.), Great King of the Persian Empire. His power became so great, it filled him with a blind arrogance that led him to try to extend his rule over the Greek mainland and thus brought disaster to himself and his people. When, therefore, the Athenians undertook the leadership of a Greek alliance after the Persian War, and that leadership brought them wealth and power and, in fact, turned into what was frankly acknowledged to be an empire, their response was ambiguous and contradictory. These developments were a source of pride and gratification, but also of embarrassment and, to some Athenians, shame.

The Macedonian conquest of the Greek city-states in 338 B.C.E. marked a return to an older attitude toward empire. Alexander the Great (r. 340–323 B.C.E.) conquered the vast Persian Empire, itself the successor of empires that had stretched from the Nile to the Indus valley. The death of Alexander led to its division and eventual absorption by the emergent Roman Empire by the second century B.C.E.

The ancient world was fascinated by the clash of empires that marked its history. The Romans created the grandest of the ancient empires, but they knew theirs had been preceded by others. On the walls of the House of the Faun in Pompeii, there resides an ancient mosaic depicting the Battle of Issus (333 B.C.E.), when the Macedonian Alexander the Great defeated the Persian Empire ruled by Darius III. Alexander appears on the left of the mosaic and Darius appears on his chariot. The mosaic, based on a still more ancient lost painting, probably dates from the second century B.C.E. and was rediscovered in 1831.

Art Resource, NY

The Romans: A Theory of Empire

The Romans had fewer hesitations about the desirability of imperial power than the Greeks. Their culture, which arose from a world of farmers accustomed to hard work, deprivation, and subordination to authority, venerated the military virtues. Roman society valued power, glory, and the responsibilities

The Ottoman Turks began to overrun the Balkans in the mid-1300s. In 1526, Sultan Suleyman the Magnificent destroyed a Hungarian army at the Battle of Mohacs. The Ottoman Empire ruled most of the Balkans until the late nineteenth century. Suleyman I the Magnificent (1494-1566). Sultan Suleyman at the Battles of Mahocs (detail). Lokman, The Military Campaigns of Suleyman the Magnificent. Hunername manuscript. Ottoman dynasty, Istanbul. Topkapi Palace Museum, Istanbul, Turkey. Bridgeman-Giraudon/Art Resource, NY.

of leadership, even domination, without embarrassment. In time, the Romans formulated a theory of empire that claimed Roman rule brought great advantages to its subjects: prosperity, justice, the rule of law, and, most valuable of all, peace. In the words of their great epic poet Virgil (70–19 B.C.E.), it was the Roman practice "to humble the arrogant and be sparing to their subjects."[2] These claims had considerable foundation, and the Romans could not have ruled so vast an empire with a relatively small army for more than half a millennium if their subjects had not enjoyed these benefits. Some of the conquered had a different viewpoint, however. As one British chieftain put it in the first century C.E.: "They make a wilderness and call it peace."[3]

[2]Virgil *Aeneid* 6.850
[3]Tacitus *Agricola* 30

Muslims, Mongols, and Ottomans

The rise of Islam in the seventh century C.E. produced a new kind of empire that derived its energy from religious zeal. Bursting out of Arabia, the Muslim armies swiftly gained control of most of the territory held by the old Persian Empire, North Africa, and Spain.

In the twelfth and thirteenth centuries, the great Mongol Empire, at its height, dominated Eurasia from the Pacific to central Europe, ruling Russia for more than two centuries. As in most ancient empires, the Mongols demanded taxes and military service from the conquered. They also imposed their rule over the mighty and long-standing Chinese Empire, parts of India, and much of the Islamic world before their power declined.

Still another great empire that spanned Europe and Asia was that of the Ottomans, a Turkish people, originally from central Asia. In the fourteenth century, they established a kingdom in Anatolia (Asia Minor) and soon conquered the ancient Byzantine Empire, seizing Constantinople in 1453. In the next century, the Ottoman Empire dominated southeastern Europe, the Black Sea, North Africa from Morocco to Egypt, Palestine, Syria and Arabia, Mesopotamia and Iraq, and Kurdistan and Georgia in the Caucasus. As late as 1683, Ottoman armies threatened to take Vienna and push into western Europe. Over the next two centuries, however, Ottoman power declined as the European national states grew stronger. Russia, in particular, inflicted defeats that left Turkey in the late nineteenth century, "the sick man of Europe."

European Expansion

Europe, divided first by feudalism, then by the emergence of multiple nascent national states, had been the victim of Islamic imperial expansion during the Middle Ages, first at the hands of the Arabs, then the Turks. The crusades had produced small and transitory conquests. It was only in the late 1400s that Europeans began the economic and political expansion that culminated in their command of much of the planet by 1900. The first phase of European expansion involved the "discovery," exploration, conquest, exploitation, and settlement of the Americas. It was made possible by important developments in naval and military technology, the dynamism inherent in early commercial and financial capitalism, and the freedom to compete for wealth and power unleashed by the division into separate states.

Spain and Portugal took the lead, founding empires in Central and South America, sometimes conquering existing empires ruled by native peoples. In Central America, the Aztecs exacted labor and taxes from their subject peoples, using some of them as human sacrifices. In the Andes, the Incas ruled a great empire that also required military service and forced labor from its subjects. Both Native American empires were overthrown by Spain, which then established a vast American empire whose resources, especially gold and silver, formed the basis of the great Spanish Empire in Europe. Portugal exploited the agricultural and mineral riches of Brazil using slaves imported from Africa.

The seventeenth century saw the establishment of European trading posts and then colonies on the Indian subcontinent and in the East Indies, chiefly by the Dutch, British, and French. In North America, Spain held Mexico, Florida, and California. Of more lasting significance were French and British settlements in Canada and what was to become the United States. The British colonies, especially, represented a special kind of European overseas settlement in which concern for commerce was less important than the acquisition of land for farming.

The wars of the eighteenth century ultimately cleared North America and India of French competition, leaving both as British monopolies and important bases of what would become a worldwide British Empire. The largest and most populous empire in the history of the world, it included colonies of one sort or another on all the inhabited continents; "the sun," as the saying went, "never set on the British Empire." Whether European colonialism was profitable for the imperial powers is still controversial, but Great Britain certainly benefited more than the others. Unlike most colonial powers, the British imported great quantities of natural resources from their colonies and carried on a high percentage of their trade with them. Even more singular, the British Empire included such self-governing areas as Canada, Australia, New Zealand, and South Africa, ruled by emigrants from Britain who remained loyal to the mother country and were willing to assist it in wartime. "The jewel in Britain's imperial crown," as another saying went, "was India." With a population of some 300 million, it contained perhaps 80 percent of the empire's subjects and provided much of the imperial profit.

At the height of its power in the mid-nineteenth century, it is remarkable how little money and effort Britain needed to spend to maintain these desired conditions. The cost of its armed services, including its great navy, during these years was only about 2 to 3 percent of its gross national product—a low figure compared with other nations, and incredibly low considering Britain's status as the world's greatest empire. The British army was the smallest among the European powers: By 1880 it numbered fewer than a quarter of a million men—less than half the size of France's and barely a quarter of Russia's.

France returned to its imperial pursuits after its defeat in the Napoleonic Wars, especially in North Africa and Southeast Asia, and in the last quarter of the century, Germany and Italy joined the competition for colonies. The latter part of the century brought the European partition of Africa and the establishment of European economic and political power throughout Asia. Modernized Japan, too, became a colonial power, modeling itself on the imperialist policies of the European powers. (See Chapter 26.)

By the next century, European dominance had created a single global economy and had made events in any corner of the world significant thousands of miles away. The possession of colonies became part of the definition of a great power, and the competition for colonies helped bring on World War I.

European imperialism ultimately rested on the willingness to use force. When anti-British agitation mounted in India after World War I, General Reginald Dyer's troops fired on unarmed Indian demonstrators at Amritsar. More than three hundred Indians were killed. UPI/CORBIS/Bettmann

Toward Decolonization

The weakening of the European colonial powers in World War II began the process of decolonization. The economic value of most colonies had proved to be much smaller than anticipated, and the colonial powers lacked both the capacity and the incentive to restore their former rule. Nationalist movements in the old colonies, moreover, would make such attempts costly and unpleasant. These movements flourished under the banner of national self-determination, self-government, and independence, ideas that came from and were cherished by the European colonial powers themselves. The example of Nazi Germany, moreover, had discredited theories of racial superiority that had justified much of European imperial rule. For European imperialism the handwriting was on the wall, although some colonial powers held on more fiercely than others. The French, for instance, fought at great cost—but in vain—to retain Algeria and Indochina. By the 1970s, a postcolonial world had emerged, and the concept of empire had become unclean. (See Chapter 29.)

What were the major ancient attitudes toward imperialism? What are the major modern attitudes? How do you account for the differences? What justifications and explanations have modern people used in connection with imperialism? Which do you think are the most important? Do you think ancient and modern reasons for imperialism are fundamentally different?

World War I produced unprecedented destruction and loss of life. Rather than a war of rapid movement, much combat occurred along stationary trenches dug in both Western and Eastern Europe. Here, Austro-Hungarian troops fight from trenches on the eastern front wearing gas masks. The use of poison gas was one of the innovations of the war and was generally condemned after the war. National Archives and Records Administration

26

Alliances, War, and a Troubled Peace

▼ **Emergence of the German Empire and the Alliance Systems (1873–1890)**
Bismarck's Leadership • Forging the Triple Entente (1890–1907)

▼ **World War I**
The Road to War (1908–1914) • Sarajevo and the Outbreak of War (June–August 1914) • Strategies and Stalemate: 1914–1917

▼ **The Russian Revolution**
The Provisional Government • Lenin and the Bolsheviks • The Communist Dictatorship

▼ **The End of World War I**
Germany's Last Offensive • The Armistice • The End of the Ottoman Empire

▼ **The Settlement at Paris**
Obstacles the Peacemakers Faced • The Peace • World War I and Colonial Empires • Evaluating the Peace

▼ **In Perspective**

IN THE SUMMER of 1914, the Archduke Francis Ferdinand, heir to the throne of Austria-Hungry, was assassinated in Sarajevo, Bosnia. This act of political violence set off a crisis that concluded with the outbreak of a European war that eventually became a worldwide conflict involving numerous colonies of the European imperial powers and the United States of America. Originally known as the Great War, the First World War witnessed unprecedented loss of life and destruction of property. The war constituted the defining event of the twentieth century from which followed revolution first in Russia and later in Germany and Austria. The Ottoman Empire would also collapse. Thereafter from that time to the present day the vast semicircle of territories commencing in Germany in central Europe then passing through eastern Europe and the Balkans into Turkey and then across northeastern Africa into the Arab peninsula has for almost a century witnessed violent shifts in political power and political ideologies.

Moreover, the deeply flawed peace settlement that ended the First World War planted the seeds of ongoing European international tension, economic dislocation, and conflict. That settlement treated Germany harshly though presumably no more harshly than Germany would have treated its foes if it had been victorious. Despite the severity of the settlement toward Germany, the new international system failed to provide realistic and effective safeguards against a return to power of a vengeful Germany. The withdrawal of the United States into a disdainful isolation from world affairs further destroyed the basis for keeping the peace on which the hopes of Britain and France relied. The economic consequences of the peace settlement produced domestic economic problems that played into the hands of extreme political parties that wished to overturn the post–World War I peace settlement.

The First World War, which produced these extensive ongoing destructive results, originated in the domestic unrest among subject nationalities on the continent and the imperial rivalries among the great powers that built up in the decades after the unification of Germany and Italy. The ferocity of the conflict was the result of the modern armament of European nations made possible by the second Industrial Revolution. The conflict reached its worldwide extent because of the empires created by European states in the nineteenth century and the rise to status of a great power by the United States.

For over two decades after 1871 European diplomats and political leaders through various alliances had been able to contain and resolve those domestic and international tensions while Europe prospered and exerted vast global influence. After 1890, however, Europe witnessed a series of international crises that might have but did not lead to war. It also witnessed important diplomatic realignments. Then in the summer of 1914 the crisis in the Balkans following the assassination of heir to the throne of Austria-Hungry erupted into a conflict of previously unimaginable extent, destruction, and political upheaval that lasted until 1918.

▼ Emergence of the German Empire and the Alliance Systems (1873–1890)

Prussia's victories over Austria and France and its creation of a large, powerful German Empire in 1871 revolutionized European diplomacy. A vast new political unit had united the majority of Germans to form a nation of great and growing population, wealth, industrial capacity, and military power. Its sudden appearance created new problems and upset the balance of power that the Congress of Vienna had forged. Britain and Russia retained their positions, although the Crimean War had weakened the latter.

Austria, however, had been severely weakened, and the forces of nationalism threatened it with disintegration. The Franco-Prussian War and the German annexation of Alsace-Lorraine badly damaged French power and prestige. The French were afraid of their powerful new neighbor as well as resentful of their defeat, their loss of territory, and the loss of France's traditional position as the dominant Western European power.

Bismarck's Leadership

Until 1890, Bismarck continued to guide German policy. After 1871, he insisted Germany was a satisfied power and wanted no further territorial gains, and he meant it. He wanted to avoid a new war that might undo his achievement. He tried to assuage French resentment by pursuing friendly relations and by supporting French colonial aspirations. He also prepared for the worst. If France could not be conciliated, it must be isolated. Bismarck sought to prevent an alliance between France and any other European power—especially Austria or Russia—that would threaten Germany with a war on two fronts.

War in the Balkans Bismarck's first move was to establish the Three Emperors' League in 1873. The League brought together the three great conservative empires of Germany, Austria, and Russia. The league soon collapsed over Austro-Russian rivalry in the Balkans that arose from the Russo-Turkish War that broke out in 1877. The tottering Ottoman Empire was held together chiefly because the European powers could not agree about how to partition it. Ottoman weakness encouraged Serbia and Montenegro to come to the aid of their fellow Slavs in Bosnia and Herzegovina when they revolted against Turkish rule. Soon the rebellion spread to Bulgaria.

Then Russia entered the fray and turned it into a major international crisis. The Russians hoped to pursue their traditional policy of expansion at Ottoman expense and especially to achieve their most cherished goal: control of Constantinople and the Dardanelles. Russian intervention also reflected the influence of the Pan-Slavic movement, which sought to unite all the Slavic peoples, even those under Austrian or Ottoman rule, under the protection of Holy Mother Russia.

The Ottoman Empire was soon forced to sue for peace. The Treaty of San Stefano of March 1878 was a Russian triumph. The Slavic states in the Balkans were freed of Ottoman rule, and Russia itself obtained territory and a large monetary indemnity. The settlement, however, alarmed the other great powers. Austria feared that the Slavic victory and the increase in Russian influence in the Balkans would threaten its own Balkan provinces. The British were alarmed both by the effect of the Russian victory on the European balance of power and by the possibility of Russian control of the Dardanelles, which would make Russia a Mediterranean power and threaten Britain's control of the Suez Canal. Disraeli was determined to resist, and British public opinion supported him. A music-hall song that became popular gave the language a new word for super patriotism: *jingoism*.

We don't want to fight,
But by jingo if we do,
We've got the men,
We've got the ships,
We've got the money too!
The Russians will not have Constantinople!

The Congress of Berlin Britain and Austria forced Russia to agree to an international conference at which the other great powers would review the provisions of San Stefano. The resulting Congress of Berlin met in June and July 1878 under the presidency of Bismarck. The choice of site and presiding officer were a clear recognition of Germany's new importance and of Bismarck's claim that Germany wanted no new territory and sought to preserve the peace.

Bismarck referred to himself as an "honest broker," and the title was justified. He wanted to avoid a war between Russia and Austria into which he feared Germany would be drawn with nothing to gain and much to lose. From the collapsing Ottoman Empire, he wanted nothing. "The Eastern Question," he said, "is not worth the healthy bones of a single Pomeranian musketeer."[1]

The decisions of the congress were a blow to Russian ambitions. Bulgaria, a Russian client, was reduced in size by two thirds and deprived of access to the Aegean Sea. Austria-Hungary was given Bosnia and Herzegovina to "occupy and administer," although those provinces remained formally under Ottoman rule. Britain received Cyprus, and France was encouraged to occupy Tunisia. These territories were compensation for the gains that Russia was permitted to keep. Germany asked for nothing, but still earned Russian resentment. The Russians believed they had saved Prussia in 1807 from complete destruction by Napoleon and had expected German gratitude. They were bitterly disappointed, and the Three Emperors' League was dead.

The Berlin settlement also annoyed the Balkan states. Romania wanted Bessarabia, which Russia kept; Bulgaria wanted the borders of the Treaty of San Stefano; and Greece wanted more Ottoman territory. The major trouble spot, however, was in the south Slavic states of Serbia and Montenegro. They resented the Austrian occupation of Bosnia and Herzegovina, as did many of the natives of those provinces. The south Slavic question, no less than the estrangement between Russia and Germany, was a threat to the peace of Europe.

[1]Quoted in Hajo Holborn, *A History of Modern Germany, 1840–1945* (New York: Knopf, 1969), p. 239.

German Alliances with Russia and Austria For the moment, Bismarck could ignore the Balkans, but he could not ignore the breach in his eastern alliance system. With Russia alienated, he concluded a secret treaty with Austria in 1879. This Dual Alliance provided that Germany and Austria would come to each other's aid if Russia attacked either of them. If another country attacked one of them, each promised at least to maintain neutrality.

The treaty was for five years and was renewed regularly until 1918. As the anchor of German policy, it was criticized at the time, and in retrospect, some have considered it an error. It appeared to tie German fortunes to those of the troubled Austro-Hungarian Empire and thus to borrow trouble for Germany. That is, Germany was much more likely to be drawn into aiding Austria-Hungary than the reverse. In addition, by isolating the Russians, the Dual Alliance pushed them to seek alliances in the West.

Bismarck was fully aware of these dangers but discounted them with good reason. He personally never allowed the alliance to drag Germany into Austria's Balkan quarrels. As he put it, in any alliance there is a horse and a rider, and he meant Germany to be the rider. He made it clear to the Austrians that the alliance was purely defensive and Germany would never be a party to an attack on Russia. "For us," he said, "Balkan questions can never be a motive for war."

Bismarck believed that monarchical, reactionary Russia would not seek an alliance either with republican, revolutionary France or with increasingly democratic Britain. In fact, he expected the Austro-German negotiations to frighten Russia into seeking closer relations with Germany, and he was right. By 1881, he had renewed the Three Emperors' League on a firmer basis. The three powers promised to maintain friendly neutrality in case a fourth power attacked any of them. Other clauses included the right of Austria to annex Bosnia-Herzegovina whenever it wished and the support of all three powers for closing the Dardanelles to all nations in case of war.

The agreement allayed German fears of a Russian-French alliance and Russian fears of a combination of Austria and Britain against it, of Britain's fleet sailing into the Black Sea, and of a hostile combination of Germany and Austria. Most importantly, the agreement reduced the tension in the Balkans between Austria and Russia.

The Triple Alliance In 1882, Italy, ambitious for colonial expansion and angered by the French occupation of Tunisia, asked to join the Dual Alliance. The provisions of its entry were defensive and directed against France. Bismarck's policy was now a complete success. He was allied with three of the great powers and friendly with the other, Great Britain, which held aloof from all alliances. France was isolated and no threat. Bismarck's diplomacy was a great achievement, but an even greater challenge was to maintain this complicated system of secret alliances in the face of the continuing rivalries among Germany's allies. Despite a war in 1885 between Serbia and Bulgaria that again estranged Austria and Russia, Bismarck succeeded.

Although the Three Emperors' League lapsed, the Triple Alliance (Germany, Austria, and Italy) was renewed for another five years. To restore German relations with Russia, Bismarck negotiated the Reinsurance Treaty of 1887, in which both powers promised to remain neutral if either was attacked. All seemed smooth, but a change in the German monarchy upset Bismarck's arrangements. (See "Bismarck Explains His Foreign Policy," page 834.)

In 1888, William II (r. 1888–1918) came to the German throne. He was twenty-nine years old, ambitious, and impetuous. He was imperious by temperament and believed he ruled by divine right. An injury at birth had left him with a withered left arm. He compensated for this disability with vigorous exercise, a military bearing, and an often embarrassingly bombastic rhetoric.

Like many Germans of his generation, William II was filled with a sense of Germany's destiny as the leading power of Europe. He wanted recognition of at least equality with Britain, the land of his mother and of his grandmother, Queen Victoria. To achieve a "place in the sun," he and his contemporaries wanted a navy and colonies like Britain's. These aims, of course, ran counter to Bismarck's limited continental policy. When William argued for a navy as a defense against a British landing in North Germany, Bismarck replied, "If the British should land on our soil, I should have them arrested." This was only one example of the great distance between the young emperor, or kaiser, and his chancellor. In 1890, William used a disagreement over domestic policy to dismiss Bismarck.

As long as Bismarck held power, Germany was secure, and the great European powers remained at peace. Although he made mistakes, there was much to admire in his understanding and management of international relations in the hard world of reality. He had a clear and limited idea of his nation's goals. He resisted pressures for further expansion with few and insignificant exceptions. He understood and used the full range of diplomatic weapons: appeasement and deterrence, threats and promises, secrecy and openness. He understood the needs and hopes of other countries and, where possible, tried to help them satisfy their needs or used those countries to his own advantage. His system of alliances created a stalemate in the Balkans and ensured German security.

During Bismarck's time, Germany was a force for European peace and was increasingly understood to be so. This position would not, of course, have been possible without its great military power. It also required, however, the leadership of a statesman who was willing and able to exercise restraint and who understood what his country needed and what was possible.

Bismarck and the young Kaiser William II meet in 1888. The two disagreed over many issues, and in 1890 William dismissed the aged chancellor. German Information Center

Forging the Triple Entente (1890–1907)

Franco-Russian Alliance Almost immediately after Bismarck's retirement, his system of alliances collapsed. His successor was General Leo von Caprivi (1831–1899), who had once asked, "What kind of jackass will dare to be Bismarck's successor?" Caprivi refused the Russian request to renew the Reinsurance Treaty, in part because he felt incompetent to continue Bismarck's complicated policy and in part because he wished to draw Germany closer to Britain, but Britain remained aloof, and Russia was alienated.

Even Bismarck had assumed that ideological differences would prevent a Franco-Russian alliance. Political isolation and the need for foreign capital, however, drove the Russians toward France. The French, who were even more isolated, encouraged their investors to pour capital into Russia if such investment would help produce security against Germany. In 1894, France and Russia signed a defensive alliance against Germany.

BISMARCK EXPLAINS HIS FOREIGN POLICY

Otto von Bismarck, chancellor of the new German Empire, guided German foreign policy in the years from its establishment of the empire in 1871 until his dismissal from office in 1890. In that period and for another quarter century, Europe was free of war among the great powers. The system of alliances Bismarck took the lead in creating is often given credit for preserving that peace. The following passage from his memoirs, written in his retirement, sets forth in retrospect his intentions in creating this system.

What alliances made up Bismarck's system? How were they meant to preserve the peace? What is Bismarck's stated purpose for avoiding a war in Europe? Were there other reasons too?

The Triple Alliance which I originally sought to conclude after the peace of Frankfurt, and about which I had already sounded Vienna and St. Petersburg, from Meaux, in September 1870, was an alliance of the three emperors with the further idea of bringing into it monarchical Italy. It was designed for the struggle which, as I feared, was before us; between the two European tendencies which Napoleon called Republican and Cossack, and which I, according to our present ideas, should designate on the one side as the system of order on a monarchical basis, and on the other as the social republic to the level of which the antimonarchical development is wont to sink, either slowly or by leaps and bounds, until the conditions thus created become intolerable, and the disappointed populace are ready for a violent return to monarchical institutions in a Cæsarean form. I consider that the task of escaping from this *circulus vitiosus*, or, if possible, of sparing the present generation and their children an entrance into it, ought to be more closely incumbent on the strong existing monarchies, those monarchies which still have a vigorous life, than any rivalry over the fragments of nations which people the Balkan peninsula. If the monarchical governments have no understanding of the necessity for holding together in the interests of political and social order, but make themselves subservient to the chauvinistic impulses of their subjects, I fear that the international revolutionary and social struggles which will have to be fought out will be all the more dangerous, and take such a form that the victory on the part of monarchical order will be more difficult. Since 1871 I have sought for the most certain assurance against those struggles in the alliance of the three emperors, and also in the effort to impart to the monarchical principle in Italy a firm support in that alliance.

Otto von Bismarck, *Reflections and Reminiscences*, ed. by Theodore S. Hamerow (New York: Harper Torchbooks, 1968), pp. 236–237.

Britain and Germany   Britain now became the key to the international situation. Colonial rivalries pitted the British against the Russians in Central Asia and against the French in Africa. (See Chapter 25.) Traditionally, Britain had also opposed Russian control of Constantinople and the Dardanelles and French control of the Low Countries. There was no reason to think Britain would soon become friendly to its traditional rivals or abandon its accustomed friendliness toward the Germans.

Yet within a decade of William II's accession, Germany had become the enemy in British minds. Before the turn of the century, popular British thrillers about imaginary wars portrayed the French as the invader; after the turn of the century, the enemy was usually Germany. This remarkable transformation has often been attributed to economic rivalry between Germany and Britain, in which Germany challenged and even overtook British production in various materials and markets. Certainly, Germany made such gains, and many Britons resented them. Yet the economic problem was not a serious cause of hostility, and it waned during the first decade of the century. The real problem lay in the foreign and naval policies of the German emperor and his ministers.

William II admired Britain's colonial empire and mighty fleet. At first, Germany tried to win the British over to the Triple Alliance, but when Britain clung to its "splendid isolation," German policy changed. The idea was to demonstrate Germany's worth as an ally by withdrawing support and even making trouble for Britain. This odd manner of gaining an ally reflected the kaiser's confused feelings toward Britain, which mixed dislike and jealousy with admiration. Many Germans, especially in the intellectual community, shared these feelings. Like William, they were eager for Germany to pursue a "world policy" rather than Bismarck's limited one that confined German interests to Europe. They, too, saw England as the barrier to German ambitions. Their influence in the schools, the universities, and the press guaranteed popular approval of hostility to Britain.

In Africa, the Germans blocked British attempts to build a railroad from Cape Town to Cairo. They also openly sympathized with the Boers of South Africa in their resistance to British expansion. In 1896, William congratulated Paul Kruger (1825–1904), president of the Boer Transvaal Republic, for repulsing a British raid "without having to appeal to friendly powers [i.e., Germany] for assistance." (See Chapter 25.)

In 1898, William began to realize his dream of a German navy with the passage of a naval law providing for the construction of nineteen battleships. In 1900, a second law doubled that figure. The architect of the new navy was Admiral Alfred von Tirpitz (1849–1930), who openly proclaimed that Germany's naval policy was aimed at Britain. His "risk" theory argued that Germany could build a fleet strong enough, not to defeat the British, but to do enough damage to make the British navy inferior to that of other powers like France or the United States. The theory was, in fact, absurd, because as Germany's fleet became menacing, the British would certainly build enough ships to maintain their advantage, and Britain had greater financial resources than Germany.

The naval policy, therefore, was doomed to failure. Its main results were to waste German resources and to begin a great naval race with Britain. Eventually, the threat the German navy posed so antagonized and alarmed British opinion that the British abandoned their traditional policies of avoiding alliances.

At first, however, Britain was not unduly concerned. The general hostility of world opinion during the Boer War (1899–1902), in which their great empire crushed a rebellion by South African farmers, embarrassed the British, and their isolation no longer seemed so splendid. The Germans had acted with restraint during the war. Between 1898 and 1901, Joseph Chamberlain, the colonial secretary, made several attempts to conclude an alliance with Germany. The Germans, confident that a British alliance with France or Russia was impossible, refused and held out for greater concessions.

The Entente Cordiale   The first breach in Britain's isolation came in 1902, when it concluded an alliance with Japan to defend British interests in the Far East against Russia. Next, Britain abandoned its traditional antagonism toward France and in 1904 concluded a series of agreements with the French, collectively called the Entente Cordiale. It was not a formal treaty and had no military provisions, but it settled all outstanding colonial differences between the two nations. In particular, Britain gave France a free hand in Morocco in return for French recognition of British control over Egypt. The Entente Cordiale was a long step toward aligning the British with Germany's great potential enemy.

Britain's new relationship with France was surprising, but in 1904, hardly anyone believed the British whale and the Russian bear would ever come together. The Russo-Japanese War of 1904–1905 made such a development seem even less likely, because Britain was allied with Russia's enemy, but Britain had behaved with restraint, and their unexpected defeat, which also led to the Russian Revolution of 1905, humiliated the Russians. Although the revolution was put down, it weakened Russia and reduced British apprehensions about Russian power. The British also became concerned that Russia might again drift into the German orbit.

The First Moroccan Crisis   At this point, Germany decided to test the new understanding between Britain and France. In March 1905, Emperor William II landed at Tangier, made a speech in favor of Moroccan independence, and by implication asserted Germany's right to participate in Morocco's destiny. This speech was a challenge to France. Germany's chancellor, Prince Bernhard von Bülow (1849–1929), intended to show France how weak it was. He also hoped to gain colonial concessions.

The Germans demanded an international conference to show their power more dramatically. The conference met in 1906 at Algeciras in Spain. Austria sided with its German ally, but Spain, which also had claims in Morocco, Italy, Russia and the United States, voted with Britain and France. The Germans had overplayed their hand, receiving trivial concessions, and the French position in Morocco was confirmed. German bullying had, moreover, driven Britain and France closer together. In the face of the threat of a German attack on France, Sir Edward Grey (1862–1933), the British foreign secretary, without making a firm commitment, authorized conversations between the British and French general staffs. Their agreements became morally binding as the years passed. By 1914, French and British military and naval plans were so mutually dependent that the two countries were effectively, if not formally, allies.

British Agreement with Russia   Britain's fear of Germany's growing naval power, its concern over German ambitions in the Near East (as represented by the German-sponsored plan to build a railroad from Berlin to Baghdad), and its closer relations with France made it desirable for Britain to become more friendly with France's ally, Russia. With French support, in 1907 the British concluded an agreement with Russia much like the Entente Cordiale with France. It settled Russo-British quarrels in Central Asia and opened the door for wider cooperation. The Triple Entente, an informal, but powerful, association of Britain, France, and Russia, was now ranged against the Triple Alliance. Italy was an unreliable ally, however, which meant two great land powers and Great Britain encircled Germany and Austria-Hungary.

William II and his ministers had turned Bismarck's nightmare of the prospect of a two-front war with France and Russia into a reality. They had made it more horrible by adding Britain to their foes. The equilibrium that Bismarck had worked so hard to achieve was destroyed. Britain would no longer support Austria in restraining Russian ambitions in the Balkans. Germany, increasingly alarmed by a sense of being encircled, was less willing to restrain the Austrians for fear of alienating them, too. In the Dual Alliance of Germany and Austria, the rider was now less clear.

Bismarck had built his alliance system to maintain peace, but the new alliance increased the risk of war and made the Balkans a likely spot for it to break out. Bismarck's diplomacy had left France isolated and impotent. The new arrangement associated France with the two greatest powers in Europe besides Germany. The Germans could rely only on Austria, and Austria's troubles made it less likely to provide aid than to need it.

▼ World War I

The Road to War (1908–1914)

The weak Ottoman Empire still controlled the central strip of the Balkan Peninsula running west from Constantinople to the Adriatic. North and south of it were the independent states of Romania, Serbia, Montenegro, and Greece, as well as Bulgaria, technically still part of the empire, but legally autonomous and practically independent. The Austro-Hungarian Empire included Croatia and Slovenia and, since 1878, had "occupied and administered" Bosnia and Herzegovina.

Except for the Greeks and the Romanians, most of the inhabitants of the Balkans spoke variants of the same Slavic language and felt a cultural and historical kinship with one another. For centuries Austrians, Hungarians, or Turks had ruled them, and the nationalism that characterized late-nineteenth-century Europe made many of them eager for independence. The more radical among them longed for a union of the south Slavic, or Yugoslav, peoples in a single nation. They looked to independent Serbia as the center of the new nation and hoped to detach all the Slavic provinces (especially Bosnia, which bordered on Serbia) from Austria. Serbia

believed its destiny was to unite the Slavs at the expense of Austria, as Piedmont had united the Italians and Prussia the Germans.

In 1908, a group of modernizing reformers called the Young Turks seized power in the Ottoman Empire. Their actions threatened to breathe new life into the empire and to interfere with the plans of the European jackals to pounce on the Ottoman corpse. These events brought on the first of a series of Balkan crises that would eventually lead to war.

The Bosnian Crisis In 1908, the Austrian and Russian governments decided to act quickly before Turkey became strong enough to resist. They struck a bargain in which Russia agreed to support the Austrian annexation of Bosnia and Herzegovina in return for Austrian backing for opening the Dardanelles to Russian warships.

Austria, however, declared the annexation before the Russians could act. The British and French, eager for the favor of the Young Turks, refused to agree to the Russian demand to open the Dardanelles. The Russians were humiliated and furious, but too weak to do anything but protest. The Austrian annexation of Bosnia enraged Russia's "little brothers," the Serbs.

Germany had not been warned in advance of Austria's plans and was unhappy because the action threatened their relations with Russia and Turkey. Germany felt so dependent on the Dual Alliance, however, that it nevertheless assured Austria of its support. Austria had been given a free hand, and to some extent, Vienna was now making German policy. It was a dangerous precedent. Also, the failure of Britain and France to support Russia strained the Triple Entente. This made it harder for them to oppose Russian interests in the future if they were to keep Russian friendship.

The Second Moroccan Crisis The second Moroccan crisis, in 1911, emphasized the French and British need for mutual support. When France sent an army to Morocco, Germany took the opportunity to "protect German interests" there as a means to extort colonial concessions in the French Congo. To add force to their demands, the Germans sent the gunboat *Panther* to the Moroccan port of Agadir, purportedly to protect German citizens there. Once again, as in 1905, the Germans went too far. The *Panther*'s visit to Agadir provoked a strong reaction in Britain. For some time Anglo-German relations had been growing worse, chiefly because the naval race had intensified. In 1907, Germany had built its first dreadnought, a new type of battleship that Britain had launched in 1906. In 1908, Germany had passed still another naval law that accelerated the challenge to British naval supremacy.

These actions threatened Britain's security. Britain had to increase taxes to pay for new armaments just when its liberal government was launching its expensive program

Soon, however, Bethmann-Hollweg realized what he should have known from the first: If Germany attacked France, Britain must fight. Until July 30, his public appeals to Austria for restraint were a sham. Thereafter, he sincerely tried to persuade the Austrians to negotiate and avoid a general war, but it was too late. The Austrians could not turn back without losing their own self-respect and the respect of the Germans.

On July 30, Austria ordered mobilization against Russia. Bethmann-Hollweg resisted the enormous pressure to mobilize, not because he hoped to avoid war, but because he wanted Russia to mobilize against Germany first and appear to be the aggressor. Only in that way could he win the support of the German nation for war, especially the backing of pacifist Social Democrats. His luck was good for a change. The news of Russian general mobilization came only minutes before Germany would have mobilized in any case. Germany then declared war on Russia on August 1. The **Schlieffen Plan** went into effect. The Germans occupied Luxembourg on August 2 and invaded Belgium, which resisted, on August 3—the same day Germany declared war on France. The invasion of Belgium violated the treaty of 1839 in which the British had joined the other powers in guaranteeing Belgian neutrality. This factor undermined sentiment in Britain for neutrality and united the nation against Germany, which then invaded France. On August 4, Britain declared war on Germany.

The Great War had begun. As Sir Edward Grey, the British foreign secretary, put it, the lights were going out all over Europe. They would come on again, but Europe would never be the same.

Although debate on the causes of the war continues, the most common opinion today is that German ambitions for a higher place in the international order under the new kaiser William II led to a new challenge to the status quo. German bullying resulted in a series of crises that led to the final crisis in July 1914, when Germany supported—indeed, pushed—its only reliable ally Austria into a war against Serbia that touched off the world war.

The deeper causes of that war are seen to be Germany's new ambitions to become a world power like Great Britain and to become the dominant power on the European continent. Germany's decision to build a battleship navy threatened Britain's interests and security. In response, the British launched an expensive and unwelcome naval race to maintain their superiority at sea and abandoned their cherished "splendid isolation" and long-standing competitions with France and Russia. In an unprecedented reversal of policy, they made an alliance with Japan and agreements with France and Russia to form the "Triple Entente," which grew from a set of colonial accords to an informal, but visible, check on German ambitions. This new international configuration alarmed Germany, which complained that jealous and hostile forces were "encircling" it. The Germans feared the growing power of the country's enemies,

but Germany did not seriously attempt to ease the tension. Instead, a new arms race ensued, and Germany assumed a rigid stance in the final crisis that ended in war.

Strategies and Stalemate: 1914–1917

Throughout Europe, jubilation greeted the outbreak of war. No general war had been fought since Napoleon, and few understood the horrors of modern warfare. The dominant memory was of Bismarck's swift and decisive campaigns, in which the costs and casualties were light and the rewards great. After years of crises and resentments, war came as a release of tension. The popular press had increased public awareness of, and interest in, foreign affairs and had fanned the flames of patriotism. The prospect of war moved even a rational man of science like Sigmund Freud to say, "My whole libido goes out to Austria-Hungary."

Both sides expected to take the offensive, force a battle on favorable ground, and win a quick victory. The Triple Entente powers—or the Allies, as they called themselves—held superiority in numbers and financial resources, as well as command of the sea. (See Figure 26–1, page 844.) Germany and Austria, the Central Powers, had the advantages of possessing internal lines of communication and having launched their attack first.

Germany's war plan was based on ideas developed by Count Alfred von Schlieffen (1833–1913), chief of the German general staff from 1891 to 1906. (See Map 26–2.) It aimed to outflank the French frontier defenses

Map 26–2 **THE SCHLIEFFEN PLAN OF 1905** Germany's grand strategy for quickly winning the war against France in 1914 is shown by the wheeling arrows on the map. In the original plan, the crushing blows at France were to be followed by the release of troops for use against Russia on Germany's eastern front. The plan, however, was not adequately implemented, and the war on the western front became a long contest in place.

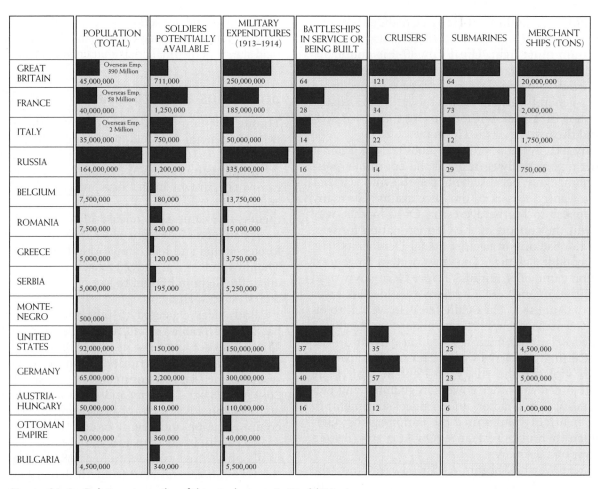

	POPULATION (TOTAL)	SOLDIERS POTENTIALLY AVAILABLE	MILITARY EXPENDITURES (1913–1914)	BATTLESHIPS IN SERVICE OR BEING BUILT	CRUISERS	SUBMARINES	MERCHANT SHIPS (TONS)
GREAT BRITAIN	Overseas Emp. 390 Million 45,000,000	711,000	250,000,000	64	121	64	20,000,000
FRANCE	Overseas Emp. 58 Million 40,000,000	1,250,000	185,000,000	28	34	73	2,000,000
ITALY	Overseas Emp. 2 Million 35,000,000	750,000	50,000,000	14	22	12	1,750,000
RUSSIA	164,000,000	1,200,000	335,000,000	16	14	29	750,000
BELGIUM	7,500,000	180,000	13,750,000				
ROMANIA	7,500,000	420,000	15,000,000				
GREECE	5,000,000	120,000	3,750,000				
SERBIA	5,000,000	195,000	5,250,000				
MONTE-NEGRO	500,000						
UNITED STATES	92,000,000	150,000	150,000,000	37	35	25	4,500,000
GERMANY	65,000,000	2,200,000	300,000,000	40	57	23	5,000,000
AUSTRIA-HUNGARY	50,000,000	810,000	110,000,000	16	12	6	1,000,000
OTTOMAN EMPIRE	20,000,000	360,000	40,000,000				
BULGARIA	4,500,000	340,000	5,500,000				

Figure 26–1   Relative strengths of the combatants in World War I.

by sweeping through Belgium to the Channel and then wheeling to the south and east to envelop the French and crush them against the German fortresses in Lorraine. The secret of success lay in making the right wing of the advancing German army immensely strong and deliberately weakening the left opposite the French frontier. The weakness of the left was meant to draw the French into attacking the wrong place while the war was decided on the German right. In the east, the Germans planned to stand on the defensive against Russia until France had been crushed, a task they thought would take only six weeks.

The apparent risk, besides the violation of Belgian neutrality and the consequent alienation of Britain, lay in weakening the German defenses against a direct attack across the frontier. The strength of German fortresses and the superior firepower of German howitzers made that risk more theoretical than real. The true danger was that the German striking force on the right through Belgium would not be powerful enough to make the swift progress vital to success. The execution of the plan fell to Count Helmuth von Moltke, the nephew of Bismarck's most effective general. Moltke added divisions to the left

wing and even weakened the Russian front for the same purpose. For reasons still debated, the plan failed by a narrow margin.

The War in the West   The French had also put their faith in the offensive, but with less reason than the Germans. They underestimated the numbers and effectiveness of the German reserves and overestimated what the courage and spirit of their own troops could achieve. Courage and spirit could not defeat machine guns and heavy artillery. The French offensive on Germany's western frontier failed totally. This defeat probably was preferable to a partial success, because it released troops for use against the main German army. As a result, the French and the British were able to stop the German advance on Paris at the Battle of the Marne in September 1914. (See Map 26–3, on page 845 and Map 26–4, page 846.)

Thereafter, the nature of the war in the west became one of position instead of movement. Both sides dug in behind a wall of trenches protected by barbed wire that stretched from the North Sea to Switzerland. Strategically placed machine-gun nests made assaults difficult and dangerous. Both sides, nonetheless, attempted

Map 26–3 **WORLD WAR I IN EUROPE** Despite the importance of military action in the Far East, in the Arab world, and at sea, the main theaters of activity in World War I were in the European areas.

World War I in Europe (map labels):

FINLAND

Petrograd (St. Petersburg)

Moscow

Revel · ESTONIA · LATVIA

SUMMER, 1918

DEC., 1917

Minsk · Gomel

RUSSIAN FRONT

RUSSIA

Pinsk

BRUSILOV'S OFFENSIVE AUG., 1916

FARTHEST GERMAN ADVANCE, SUMMER, 1918

SUMMER, 1918

Rostov

Sea of Azov

Kharkov · Poltava

Kiev

UKRAINE

CRIMEA

Odessa

FARTHEST GERMAN ADVANCE, DEC., 1917

DEC., 1917

Galatz

Constantsa

Black Sea

Constantinople

OTTOMAN EMPIRE

Angora

CYPRUS

NORWAY

Christiania

Stockholm · Göteborg

SWEDEN

Baltic Sea

LITHUANIA

Kaunas · Vilna

Suwalki

EAST PRUSSIA

FARTHEST RUSSIAN ADVANCE, 1914.

1914

Memel

Danzig

Warsaw · Brest Litovsk

MAY, 1915

FEB. 1915

FEB. 1915

Lemberg

Cracow · Gorlice

Debrecen

TRANSYLVANIA

Hermannstadt

Jassy

ROMANIA

Bucharest

Varna

BULGARIA

Sofia

Nish

SERBIA

Skopje

MONTE- NEGRO

ALBANIA

1917–18

1916

1915

Strumitsa

GREECE

Dardanelles

Gallipoli, 1915–1916

BALKAN FRONT

DENMARK

Copenhagen

Kiel Canal

Hamburg

Bremen · Berlin

Essen · Leipzig · Dresden

Cologne · Koblenz · Frankfurt

Elbe R.

Oder R.

GERMAN EMPIRE

SILESIA

Breslau

Prague

BOHEMIA

MORAVIA

SLOVAKIA

Budapest

AUSTRIA-HUNGARY

Vienna

Munich

Nuremberg · Mainz · Strasbourg

NETH.

Amsterdam

Brussels

Liège · BELG.

LUX. · Metz

Sedan · Verdun

Toul

Rhine R.

WESTERN FRONT

Ypres · Arras

Compiègne

Versailles · Paris

FRANCE

Belfort

SWITZ. · Berne

Geneva

Clermont-Ferrand

Lyons

Rhône R.

Marseilles

Klagenfurt

TYROL

Caporetto

AUG., 1917

MARCH, 1918

Trieste · Fiume

Agram

Sarajevo

Belgrade

ITALIAN FRONT

Venice

Milan · Turin · Genoa

ITALY

Rome

Naples · Taranto

Adriatic Sea

CORSICA

SARDINIA

SICILY

Mediterranean Sea

UNITED KINGDOM

Aberdeen · Edinburgh

Hull

Yarmouth

London · Dover

Le Havre

North Sea

ATLANTIC OCEAN

SPAIN

N

400 MILES

400 KILOMETERS

Triple Entente

Allies of the Triple Entente

Central Powers

Allies of the Central Powers

Neutral

Battle Lines

845

Map 26–4 **THE WESTERN FRONT, 1914–1918** This map shows the crucial western front in detail.

massive attacks preceded by artillery bombardments of unprecedented and horrible force and duration. Still, the defense was always able to recover and to bring up reserves fast enough to prevent a breakthrough.

Assaults that cost hundreds of thousands of lives produced advances of only hundreds of yards. Even poison gas proved ineffective. In 1916, the British introduced the tank, which eventually proved to be the answer to the machine gun. The Allied command was slow to understand this, however, and until the end of the war, defense was supreme. For three years after its establishment, the western front moved only a few miles in either direction.

The War in the East In the east, the war began auspiciously for the Allies. The Russians advanced into Austrian territory and inflicted heavy casualties, but Russian incompetence and German energy soon reversed the situation. A junior German officer, Erich Ludendorff (1865–1937), under the command of the elderly general

Paul von Hindenburg (1847–1934), destroyed or captured an entire Russian army at the Battle of Tannenberg and defeated another one at the Masurian Lakes. In 1915, the Central Powers pressed their advantage in the east and drove into the Baltic states and Russian Poland, inflicting more than 2 million casualties in a single year.

As the battle lines hardened, both sides sought new allies. Turkey (because of its hostility to Russia) and Bulgaria (the enemy of Serbia) joined the Central Powers. Both sides bid for Italian support with promises of the spoils of victory. Because the Austrians held what the Italians wanted most, the Allies could promise more. In a secret treaty of 1915, they agreed to deliver to Italy after victory most of *Italia irredenta* (i.e., the South Tyrol, Trieste, and some of the Dalmatian Islands), plus colonies in Africa and a share of the Turkish Empire. By the spring of 1915, Italy was engaging Austrian armies. The Italian campaign weakened Austria and diverted some German troops, but the Italian alliance never produced significant results. Romania joined the Allies in 1916 but was quickly defeated and driven from the war.

In the Far East, Japan honored its alliance with Britain and entered the war. The Japanese quickly overran the German colonies in China and the Pacific and used the opportunity to put pressure on China. Both sides also appealed to nationalistic sentiment in areas the enemy held. The Germans supported nationalist movements among the Irish, the Flemings in Belgium, and the Poles and Ukrainians under Russian rule. They even tried to persuade the Turks to lead a Muslim uprising against the British in Egypt and India, and against the French and Italians in North Africa. The Allies made the same appeals with greater success. They sponsored movements of national autonomy for the Czechs, the Slovaks, the south Slavs, and againt the Poles who were under Austrian rule. They also favored a movement of Arab independence from Turkey. Guided by Colonel T. E. Lawrence (1888–1935), this last scheme proved especially successful later in the war.

In 1915, the Allies tried to break the deadlock on the western front by going around it. The idea came chiefly from Winston Churchill (1874–1965), first lord of the British admiralty. He proposed to attack the Dardanelles and capture Constantinople. This policy supposedly would knock Turkey from the war, bring help to the Balkan front, and ease communications with Russia. The plan was daring, but promising, and in its original form, it presented little risk. British naval superiority and the element of surprise might force the straits and capture Constantinople by purely naval action. Even if the scheme failed, the fleet could just sail away.

The success of Churchill's plan depended on timing, speed, and daring leadership, but all of these were lacking. Worse, the execution of the attack was inept and overly cautious. Troops were landed, and as Turkish

British tanks moving toward the Battle of Cambrai in Flanders late in 1917. Tanks were impervious to machine-gun fire. Had they been used in great numbers, they might have broken the stalemate in the west.   Bildarchiv Preussischer Kulturbesitz

resistance continued, the Allied commitment increased. Before the campaign was abandoned, the Allies lost almost 150,000 men and diverted three times that number from more useful occupations.

Return to the West Both sides turned back to the west in 1916. General Erich von Falkenhayn (1861–1922), who had succeeded Moltke in September 1914, attacked the French stronghold of Verdun. His plan was not to break through the French line, but to inflict enormous casualties on the French, who would have to defend Verdun against superior firepower from several directions. He, too, underestimated the superiority of the defense. The French held Verdun with comparatively few men and inflicted almost as many casualties as they suffered. The commander of Verdun, Henri Pétain (1856–1951), became a national hero, and "They shall not pass" became a slogan of national defiance.

The Allies tried to end the impasse by launching a major offensive along the River Somme in July. Aided by a Russian attack in the east that drew off some German strength and by an enormous artillery bombardment, they hoped at last to break through. Once again, the defense was superior. Enormous casualties on both sides brought no result. The war on land dragged on with no end in sight.

The War at Sea As the war continued, control of the sea became more important. The British ignored the distinction between war supplies (which were contraband according to international law) and food or other peaceful cargo (which was not subject to seizure). They imposed a strict blockade meant to starve out the enemy, regardless of international law. The Germans responded with submarine warfare meant to destroy British shipping and starve the British. They declared the waters around the British Isles a war zone, where even neutral ships would not be safe. Both policies were unwelcome to neutrals, and especially to the United States, which conducted extensive trade in the Atlantic. Yet the sinking of neutral ships by German submarines was both more dramatic and more offensive than the British blockade.

In May 1915, a German submarine torpedoed the British liner *Lusitania*. Among the 1,200 who drowned were 118 Americans. President Woodrow Wilson (1856–1924) warned Germany that a repetition would have grave consequences; the Germans desisted for the time being, rather than further anger the United States. This development gave the Allies a considerable advantage. The German fleet that had cost so much money and had caused so much trouble played no significant part in the war. The only major battle it

A Closer ▶ LOOK

THE DEVELOPMENT OF THE ARMORED TANK

WARFARE FREQUENTLY PROVES a source of technological innovation. Such was true of World War I, which witnessed the development of numerous new weapons. Among the most important of these was the tank—an armored vehicle using a caterpillar track rather than wheels for transport. The caterpillar track had been invented in Great Britain but was then purchased by the American Holt tractor company, which devised a caterpillar tractor in the first decade of the century to cultivate areas with either wet or loose earth where a wheeled vehicle would sink into the ground. During World War I the British modified the caterpillar tractor by introducing a heavily armored closed compartment for a crew armed with machine guns. These early slow-moving tanks could drive over trenches, small hills, and rough terrain and through mud and thus bring mobility to the combat zones where trench warfare had made any kind of effective assault on enemy troops difficult. The tank was used primarily by Britain, France, and the United States in relatively small numbers in World War I, but later rapidly moving tanks became one of the major weapons of later twentieth-century warfare.

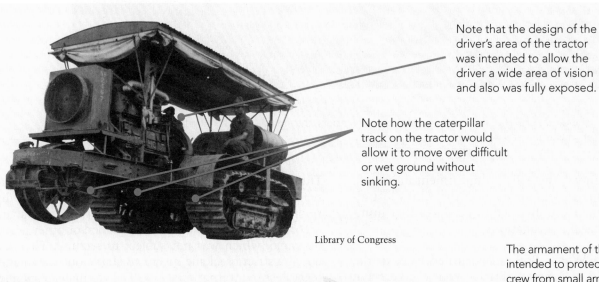

Note that the design of the driver's area of the tractor was intended to allow the driver a wide area of vision and also was fully exposed.

Note how the caterpillar track on the tractor would allow it to move over difficult or wet ground without sinking.

Library of Congress

The armament of the tank was intended to protect the tank crew from small arms fire while the opening on the top permitted the mounting of a machine gun.

The interior of the tank allowed for a small crew working in an extremely hot climate with little or no chance for escape if the tank was hit by a large artillery round or became bogged down in enemy territory.

To examine this image in an interactive fashion, please go to www.myhistorylab.com

Dorling Kindersley Media Library/Andy Crawford/Dorling Kindersley © Imperial War Museum, London

myhistorylab

The use of poison gas (by both sides) during the First World War and its dreadful effects—blinding, asphyxiation, burned lungs—came to symbolize the horrors of modern war. This painting shows a group of British soldiers being guided to the rear after they were blinded by mustard gas on the western front.   John Singer Sargent (1856–1925), *Gassed*, an Oil Study. Private Collection. 1918–1919. Imperial War Museum, London. Negative Number Q1460

fought was at Jutland in 1916. The battle resulted in a standoff and confirmed British domination of the surface of the sea.

America Enters the War   In December 1916, President Woodrow Wilson intervened to try to bring about a negotiated peace. Neither side, however, was willing to renounce war aims that its opponent found acceptable. The war seemed likely to continue until one or both sides reached exhaustion.

Two events early in 1917 changed the situation radically. On February 1, the Germans announced the resumption of unrestricted submarine warfare, which led the United States to break off diplomatic relations. On April 6, the United States declared war on Germany. One of the deterrents to an earlier American intervention had been the presence of the autocratic tsarist Russia among the Allies. Wilson could conceive of the war only as an idealistic crusade "to make the world safe for democracy." That problem was resolved in March 1917 by a revolution in Russia that overthrew the tsarist government.

▼ The Russian Revolution

Many unexpected consequences flowed from World War I reshaping both Europe and the rest of the world in ways that virtually no one could have anticipated in 1910. For the rest of European history in the twentieth century no such unexpected event produced so many long-term results as the revolution that occurred in Russia in 1917. That revolution changed the course of

the war and the future course of Europe by setting a Communist government in charge of a major European state and empire.

The Russian Revolution of 1917, which ultimately produced impacts over the years around the globe, went through two distinct stages. In March of that year the government of Tsar Nicholas II collapsed in the wake of popular demonstrations against the war, its casualties, and the economic and social conditions flowing from Russian participation in the conflict. Then in November a second unforeseen event occurred. The previously largely obscure and ignored Bolshevik Party led by Lenin (see Chapter 23) seized power from the provisional government. The Bolsheviks would quickly take Russia out of the war and then proceed to establish their own domestic Communist Party dictatorship.

No political faction planned or led the March Revolution in Russia. It was the result of the collapse of the monarchy's ability to govern. Although public opinion in Russia had strongly supported the country's entry into the war, the conflict overtaxed Russia's resources and the efficiency of the tsarist government.

Nicholas II was weak and incompetent and suspected of being under the domination of his German wife and the insidious peasant faith healer Rasputin, whom a group of Russian noblemen assassinated in 1916. Military and domestic failures produced massive casualties, widespread hunger, strikes by workers, and disorganization in the army. The peasant discontent that had plagued the countryside before 1914 did not subside during the conflict. In 1915, the tsar took personal command of the armies on the German front, which kept him away from the capital. In his absence, corrupt and

Petrograd munitions workers demonstrating in 1917. Ria-Novosti/Sovfoto/Eastfoto

incompetent ministers increasingly discredited the government even in the eyes of conservative monarchists. All political factions in the Duma, Russia's parliament, were discontented.

The Provisional Government

In early March 1917, strikes and worker demonstrations erupted in Petrograd, as Saint Petersburg had been renamed. The ill-disciplined troops in the city refused to fire on the demonstrators. (See "The Outbreak of the Russian Revolution.") The tsar abdicated on March 15. The government of Russia fell into the hands of members of the Duma, who soon formed a provisional government composed chiefly of Constitutional Democrats (Cadets) with Western sympathies.

At the same time, the various socialist groups, including both Social Revolutionaries and Social Democrats of the Menshevik wing, began to organize soviets, councils of workers and soldiers. Initially, they allowed the provisional government to function without actually supporting it. As relatively orthodox Marxists, the Mensheviks believed that Russia had to have a bourgeois stage of development before it could have a revolution of the proletariat. They were willing to work temporarily with the Constitutional Democrats in a liberal regime, but they became estranged when the Cadets failed to control the army or to purge "reactionaries" from the government.

In this climate, the provisional government decided to remain loyal to Russia's alliances and continue the war. The provisional government thus accepted tsarist foreign policy and associated itself with the main source of domestic suffering and discontent. The collapse of the last Russian offensive in the summer of 1917 sealed its fate. Disillusionment with the war, shortages of food and other necessities at home, and the peasants' demands for land reform undermined the government. This occurred even after the moderate socialist Alexander Kerensky (1881–1970) became prime minister. Moreover, discipline in the army had disintegrated.

THE OUTBREAK OF THE RUSSIAN REVOLUTION

The Russian Revolution of March 1917 started with a series of ill-organized demonstrations in Petrograd. These actions and the ineffectuality of the government's response are described in the memoirs of Maurice Paléologue (1859–1944), the French ambassador.

What elements contributing to the success of the March Revolution emerge from this selection? Why might the army have been unreliable? Why did the two ambassadors think a new ministry should be appointed? What were the grievances of the revolutionaries? Why is there no discussion of the leaders of the revolution? What role did the emperor (tsar) play in these events?

MONDAY, MARCH 12, 1917

At half-past eight this morning, just as I finished dressing, I heard a strange and prolonged din which seemed to come from the Alexander Bridge. I looked out: there was no one on the bridge, which usually presents such a busy scene. But, almost immediately, a disorderly mob carrying red flags appeared at the end which is on the right bank of the Neva, and a regiment came towards it from the opposite side. It looked as if there would be a violent collision, but on the contrary the two bodies coalesced. The army was fraternizing with revolt.

Shortly afterwards, someone came to tell me that the Volhynian regiment of the Guard had mutinied during the night, killed its officers and was parading the city, calling on the people to take part in the revolution and trying to win over the troops who still remain loyal.

At ten o'clock there was a sharp burst of firing, and flames could be seen rising somewhere on the Liteïny Prospekt which is quite close to the embassy. Then silence. Accompanied by my military attaché, Lieutenant-Colonel Lavergne, I went out to see what was happening. Frightened inhabitants were scattering through the streets. There was indescribable confusion at the corner of the Liteïny. Soldiers were helping civilians to erect a barricade. Flames mounted from the Law Courts. The gates of the arsenal burst open with a crash. Suddenly the crack of machine-gun fire split the air: it was the regulars who had just taken up position near the Nevsky Prospekt. The revolutionaries replied. I had seen enough to have no doubt as to what was coming. Under a hail of bullets I returned to the embassy with Lavergne who had walked calmly and slowly to the hottest corner out of sheer bravado.

About half-past eleven I went to the Ministry for Foreign Affairs, picking up Buchanan [the British ambassador to Russia] on the way.

I told Pokrovski [the Russian foreign minister] everything I had just witnessed.

"So it's even more serious than I thought," he said.

But he preserved unruffled composure, flavoured with a touch of skepticism, when he told me of the steps on which the ministers had decided during the night:

"The sitting of the Duma has been prorogued to April and we have sent a telegram to the Emperor, begging him to return at once. With the exception of M. Protopopov [the Minister of the Interior, in charge of the police], my colleagues and I all thought that a dictatorship should be established without delay; it would be conferred upon some general whose prestige with the army is pretty high, General Russky for example."

I argued that, judging by what I saw this morning, the loyalty of the army was already too heavily shaken for our hopes of salvation to be based on the use of the "strong hand," and that the immediate appointment of a ministry inspiring confidence in the Duma seemed to me more essential than ever, as there is not a moment to lose. I reminded Pokrovski that in 1789, 1830, and 1848, three French dynasties were overthrown because they were too late in realizing the significance and strength of the movement against them. I added that in such a grave crisis the representative of allied France had a right to give the Imperial Government advice on a matter of internal politics.

Buchanan endorsed my opinion.

Pokrovski replied that he personally shared our views, but that the presence of Protopopov in the Council of Ministers paralyzed action of any kind.

I asked him:

"Is there no one who can open the Emperor's eyes to the real situation?"

He heaved a despairing sigh.

"The Emperor is blind!"

Deep grief was writ large on the face of the honest man and good citizen whose uprightness, patriotism and disinterestedness I can never sufficiently extol.

From Maurice Paléologue, *An Ambassador's Memoirs* (London: Doubleday & Company, Inc., and Hutchinson Publishing Group, Ltd., 1924), pp. 221–225.

AN EYEWITNESS ACCOUNT OF THE BOLSHEVIKS' SEIZURE OF POWER

John Reed was an American newspaperman who was in Russia during the Revolution of 1917, an enthusiastic convert to Communism, a supporter of the Bolsheviks, and an ardent admirer of Lenin. In the following selections from his account of the Bolshevik revolution he described Lenin's qualities and the part Lenin played in overthrowing the provisional government.

What was the provisional government? How did it come into being? Why was it under pressure in November 1917? Which groups were vying for power? What program gave gave victory to the Bolsheviks?

THURSDAY, OCT. 26/NOV. 8

The Congress was to meet at one o'clock, and long since the great meeting-hall had filled, but by seven there was yet no sign of the presidium. . . . The Bolshevik and Left Social Revolutionary factions were in session in their own rooms. All the livelong afternoon Lenin and Trotzky had fought against compromise. A considerable part of the Bolsheviki were in favour of giving way so far as to create a joint all-Socialist government. "We can't hold on!" they cried. "Too much is against us. We haven't got the men. We will be isolated, and the whole thing will fall." So Kameniev, Riazanov and others.

But Lenin, with Trotzky beside him, stood firm as a rock. "Let the compromisers accept our programme and they can come in! We won't give way an inch. If there are comrades here who haven't the courage and the will to dare what we dare, let him leave with the rest of the cowards and conciliators! Backed by the workers and soldiers we shall go on."

At five minutes past seven came word from the left Socialist Revolutionaries to say that they would remain in the Military Revolutionary Committee. "See!" said Lenin, "They are following.". . .

It was just 8:40 when a thundering wave of cheers announced the entrance of the presidium with Lenin—great Lenin—among them. A short, stocky figure, with a big head set down in his

Lenin and the Bolsheviks

Ever since April, the Bolshevik wing of the Social Democratic Party had been working against the provisional government. The Germans, in their most successful attempt at subversion, had rushed the brilliant Bolshevik leader V. I. Lenin (1870–1924) in a sealed train from his exile in Switzerland across Germany to Petrograd. They hoped he would cause trouble for the revolutionary government.

Lenin saw the opportunity to achieve the political alliance of workers and peasants he had discussed before the war. In speech after speech, he hammered away on the theme of peace, bread, and land. The Bolsheviks demanded that all political power go to the soviets, which they controlled. The failure of the summer offensive encouraged them to attempt a coup, but the effort was a failure. Lenin fled to Finland, and his chief collaborator, Leon Trotsky (1879–1940), was imprisoned.

The failure of a right-wing countercoup gave the Bolsheviks another chance. Trotsky, released from prison, led the powerful Petrograd soviet. Lenin returned in October, insisted to his doubting colleagues that the time was ripe to take power, and by the extraordinary force of his personality persuaded them to act. Trotsky organized the coup that took place on November 6 and concluded with an armed assault on the provisional government. The Bolsheviks, almost as much to their own astonishment as to that of the rest of the world, had come to rule Russia. (See "An Eyewitness Account of the Bolsheviks' Seizure of Power.")

The Communist Dictatorship

The victors moved to fulfill their promises and to assure their own security. The provisional government had decreed an election for late November to select a Constituent Assembly. The Social Revolutionaries won a large majority over the Bolsheviks. When the assembly gathered in Janu-

CHAPTER 26 ■ ALLIANCES, WAR, AND A TROUBLED PEACE 853

shoulders, bald and bulging. Little eyes, a snubbish nose, wide, generous mouth, and heavy chin; clean-shaven now, but already beginning to bristle with the well-known beard of his past and future. Dressed in shabby clothes, his trousers much too long for him. Unimpressive, to be the idol of a mob, loved and revered as perhaps few leaders in history have been. A strange popular leader—a leader purely by virtue of intellect; colourless, humourless, uncompromising and detached, without picturesque idiosyncrasies—but with the power of explaining profound ideas in simple terms, of analysing a concrete situation. And combined with shrewdness, the greatest intellectual audacity.

. . .

Other speakers followed, apparently without any order. A delegate of the coal-miners of the Don Basin called upon the Congress to take measures against Kaledin, who might cut off coal and food from the capital. Several soldiers just arrived from the Front brought the enthusiastic greetings of their regiments.

. . . Now Lenin, gripping the edge of the reading stand, letting his little winking eyes travel over the crowd as he stood there waiting, apparently oblivious to the long-rolling ovation, which lasted several minutes. When it finished, he said simply, "We shall now proceed to construct the Socialist order!" Again that overwhelming human roar.

"The first thing is the adoption of practical measures to realise peace. . . . We shall offer peace to the peoples of all the belligerent countries upon the basis of the Soviet terms—no annexations, no indemnities, and the right of self-determination of peoples. At the same time, according to our promise, we shall publish and repudiate the secret treaties. . . . The question of War and Peace is so clear that I think that I may, without preamble, read the project of a Proclamation to the Peoples of All the Belligerent Countries . . . ."

His great mouth, seeming to smile, opened wide as he spoke; his voice was hoarse—not unpleasantly so, but as if it had hardened that way after years and years of speaking—and went on monotonously, with the effect of being able to go on forever. . . . For emphasis he bent forward slightly. No gestures. And before him, a thousand simple faces looking up in intent adoration . . . .

It was exactly 10:35 when Kameniev asked all in favour of the proclamation to hold up their cards. One delegate dared to raise his hand against, but the sudden sharp outburst around him brought it swiftly down. . . . Unanimous.

At two o'clock the Land Decree was put to vote, with only one against and the peasant delegates were wild with joy. . . . So plunged the Bolsheviki ahead, irresistible, over-riding hesitation and opposition—the only people in Russia who had a definite programme of action while the others talked for eight long months. . . .

From John Reed, *Ten Days That Shook the World* (New York: Boni and Liveright, 1919), pp. 123–129.

ary, it met for only a day before the Red Army, controlled by the Bolsheviks, dispersed it. All other political parties also ceased to function in any meaningful fashion. In November and January, the Bolshevik government nationalized the land and turned it over to its peasant proprietors. Factory workers were put in charge of their plants. The state seized banks and repudiated the debt of the tsarist government. Property of the church reverted to the state.

The Bolshevik government also took Russia out of the war, which they believed benefited only capitalism. They signed an armistice with Germany in December 1917 and in March 1918 accepted the Treaty of Brest-Litovsk, by which Russia yielded Poland, Finland, the Baltic states, and Ukraine. Some territory in the Transcaucasus region went to Turkey. The Bolsheviks also agreed to pay a heavy war indemnity.

These terms were a high price to pay for peace, but Lenin had no choice. Russia was incapable of renewing the war effort, and the Bolsheviks needed time to im-

pose their rule. Moreover, Lenin believed that the war and the Russian example would soon lead to communist revolutions across Europe.

The new Bolshevik government met major domestic resistance. Civil war erupted between Red Russians, who supported the revolution, and **White Russians**, who opposed it. In the summer of 1918, the Bolsheviks murdered the tsar and his family. Loyal army officers continued to fight the revolution and received aid from Allied armies. Under the leadership of Trotsky, however, the Red Army eventually overcame the domestic opposition. By 1921, Lenin and his supporters were in firm control.

▼ The End of World War I

The collapse of Russia and the Treaty of Brest-Litovsk were the zenith of German success. The Germans controlled eastern Europe and its resources, especially food, and by 1918 they were free to concentrate their forces on the western front. These developments would probably have been decisive without American intervention. Still, American troops would not arrive in significant numbers for about a year, and both sides tried to win the war in 1917.

An Allied attempt to break through in the west failed disastrously. Losses were heavy and the French army mutinied. The Austrians, supported by the Germans, defeated the Italians at Caporetto and threatened to overrun northern Italy, until they were checked with the aid of Allied troops. The deadlock continued, but time was running out for the Central Powers.

Germany's Last Offensive

In March 1918, the Germans decided to gamble everything on one last offensive. (This decision was taken chiefly by Ludendorff, second in command to Hindenburg, but the real leader of the army.) The German army reached the Marne again but got no farther. They had no more reserves, and the entire nation was exhausted. In contrast, the arrival of American troops in ever-increasing numbers bolstered the Allies. An Allied counteroffensive proved irresistible. As the exhausted Austrians collapsed in Italy, and Bulgaria and Turkey dropped out of the war, the German high command knew the end was imminent.

Ludendorff was determined to make peace before the German army was thoroughly defeated in the field and to make civilians responsible for ending the war. For some time, he had been the effective ruler of Ger-

---

MAJOR CAMPAIGNS AND EVENTS OF WORLD WAR I

August 1914	Germans attack in West
August–September 1914	First Battle of the Marne
1914	Battles of Tannenberg and the Masurian Lakes
April 1915	British land at Gallipoli, start of Dardanelles campaign
May 1915	Germans sink British ship *Lusitania*
February 1916	Germans attack Verdun
May–June 1916	Battle of Jutland
February 1917	Germans declare unrestricted submarine warfare
March 1917	Russian Revolution
April 1917	United States enters war
November 1917	Bolsheviks seize power in Russia
March 1918	Treaty of Brest-Litovsk
March 1918	German offensive in the West
November 1918	Armistice

---

many under the aegis of the emperor. He now allowed a new government to be established on democratic principles and to seek peace immediately. The new government, under Prince Max of Baden, asked for peace on the basis of the **Fourteen Points** that President Wilson had declared as the American war aims. These were idealistic principles, including self-determination for nationalities, open diplomacy, freedom of the seas, disarmament, and the establishment of the League of Nations to keep the peace. Wilson insisted he would deal only with a democratic German government because he wanted to be sure he was dealing with the German people and not merely their rulers.

The Armistice

The disintegration of the German army forced William II to abdicate on November 9, 1918. The majority branch of the Social Democratic Party proclaimed a republic to prevent their radical Leninist wing from setting up a soviet government. Two days later, this republican, socialist-led government signed the armistice that ended the war by accepting German defeat. The German people were, in general, unaware their army had been defeated and was crumbling. No foreign soldier stood on German soil. Many Germans expected a negotiated and mild settlement. The real peace was different and embittered the Germans. Many of them came to believe Germany had not been defeated but had been tricked by the enemy and betrayed—even stabbed in the back—by republicans and socialists at home.

The victors rejoiced, but they also had much to mourn. The casualties on all sides came to about 10 million dead and twice as many wounded. The economic and financial resources of the European states were badly strained. The victorious Allies, formerly creditors to the world, became debtors to the new American colossus, which the calamities of war had barely touched.

The Great War, as contemporaries called it, the First World War to those who lived through its horrible offspring, lasted more than four years, doing terrible damage. Battle casualties alone counted more than 4 million dead and 8.3 million wounded among the Central Powers and 5.4 million dead and 7 million wounded from their opponents, and millions of civilians died from the war and causes arising from it. Among the casualties also were the German, Austro-Hungarian, Russian, and Turkish Empires. The American intervention in 1917 thrust the United States into European affairs with a vengeance, and the collapse of the Russian autocracy brought the Bolshevik revolution and the reality of a great communist state. Disappointment, resentment, and economic dislocations caused by the war brought various forms of fascism to Italy, Germany, and other countries. The comfortable nineteenth-century assumptions of inevitable progress based on reason, science and technology, indi-

Women munitions workers in England. World War I demanded more from the civilian populations than had previous wars, resulting in important social changes. The demands of the munitions industries and a shortage of men (so many of whom were in uniform) brought many women out of traditional roles at home and into factories and other war-related work.   Getty Images Inc.—Hulton Archive Photos

vidual freedom, democracy, and free enterprise gave way in many places to cynicism, nihilism, dictatorship, statism, official racism, and class warfare. It is widely agreed that the First World War was the mother of the Second and to most of the horrors of the rest of the century.

These kinds of changes affected the colonial peoples the European powers ruled, and overseas empires would never again be as secure as they had seemed before the war. Europe was no longer the center of the world, free to interfere when it wished or to ignore the rest of the world if it chose. The memory of that war lived on to shake the nerve of the victorious Western powers as they faced the new conditions of the postwar world.

The End of the Ottoman Empire

The First World War witnessed the end of the German, Austrian, and Russian Empires in the heart of Europe. The conflict also brought about the collapse of the Ottoman Empire, the ramifications of which also persist to the present day.

At the outbreak of World War I in August 1914, the Ottoman Empire was neutral, but many military offi-

cers, the so-called Young Turks who had taken control of the Ottoman government in 1909, were pro-German. After hesitating for three months, the Turks decided to enter the war on the German side in November 1914. This decision ultimately brought about the end of the Ottoman Empire. Early victories gave way to defeat after defeat at the hands of the Russians and the British, the latter assisted by Arabs from the Arabian peninsula and neighboring lands, most notably Hussein (1856–1931), *sherif* (ruler or emir) of Mecca, the city of Muhammad. The British drove the Ottomans out of Palestine and advanced deep into Mesopotamia, as far north as the oil fields of Mosul in modern Iraq. By October 30, 1918, Turkey was out of the war. In November, an Allied fleet sailed into the harbor of Constantinople and landed troops who occupied the city. The Ottoman government was helpless.

The peace treaty signed in Paris in 1920 between Turkey and the Allies dismembered the Ottoman Empire, placing large parts of it, particularly the areas Arabs inhabited, under the control of Britain and France. In Mesopotamia the British created the state of Iraq, which, along with Palestine, became British mandates. Syria and

The Allies promoted Arab efforts to secure independence from Turkey in an effort to remove Turkey from the war. Delegates to the peace conference of 1919 in Paris included British colonel T. E. Lawrence, who helped lead the rebellion, and representatives from the Middle Eastern region. Prince Feisal, the third son of King Hussein, stands in the foreground of this picture; Colonel T. E. Lawrence is in the middle row, second from the right; and Brigadier General Nuri Pasha Said of Baghdad is second from the left. CORBIS/Bettmann

▼ The Settlement at Paris

The representatives of the victorious states gathered at Versailles and other Parisian suburbs in the first half of 1919. Wilson speaking for the United States, David Lloyd George (1863–1945) for Britain, Georges Clemenceau (1841–1929) for France, and Vittorio Emanuele Orlando (1860–1952) for Italy made up the Big Four. Japan also had an important part in the discussions. The diplomats who met in Paris had a far more difficult task than those who had sat at Vienna a century earlier. Both groups attempted to restore order to the world after long and costly wars. At the earlier conference, however, Metternich and his associates could confine their thoughts to Europe. France had acknowledged defeat and was willing to take part in and uphold the Vienna settlement. The diplomats at Vienna were not much affected by public opinion, and they could draw the new map of Europe along practical lines determined by the realities of power and softened by compromise.

Ataturk (1881–1938), the father of the Turkish Republic, sought to modernize his country by forcing Turks to adopt Western ways, including the Latin alphabet. Here he is shown teaching the alphabet as president in 1928. Turkish Cultural Office

Lebanon became French mandates. (**Mandates** were territories that were legally administered under the auspices of the League of Nations but were in effect ruled as colonies.) A Greek invasion of the Turkish homeland in Anatolia in 1919 provoked a nationalist reaction, bringing the young general Mustafa Kemal (1881–1938), who later took the name Ataturk, meaning "Father of the Turks," to power. He drove the Greeks out of Anatolia and compelled the victorious powers to make a new arrangement sealed by the treaty of Lausanne in 1923. Ataturk abolished the Ottoman sultanate and deposed the last caliph. The new Republic of Turkey abandoned most of the old Ottoman Empire but became fully independent of control by the European powers and sovereign in its Anatolian homeland. Under Ataturk and his successors, Turkey, although its population was overwhelmingly Muslim, became a secular state and a force for stability in the region.

The Arab portions of the old empire, however, were a different story. Divided into a collection of artificial states that had no historical reality, governed or dominated as client regimes by the British and French, they were relatively quiet during the 1920s and 1930s. The weakening of Britain and France during and after the Second World War, however, and their subsequent abandonment of control in the Middle East would create problems in the latter part of the century.

"The Big Four" attending the Paris peace conference in 1919: Vittorio Orlande, premier of Italy; David Lloyd George, prime minister of Great Britain; Georges Clemenceau, premier of France; and Woodrow Wilson, president of the United States (left to right.).   National Archives and Records Administration

Obstacles the Peacemakers Faced

The negotiators at Paris in 1919 were less fortunate. They represented constitutional, generally democratic governments, and public opinion had become a mighty force. Though there were secret sessions, the conference often worked in the full glare of publicity. Nationalism had become almost a secular religion, and Europe's many ethnic groups could not be relied on to remain quiet while the great powers distributed them on the map. Moreover, propaganda and especially the intervention of Woodrow Wilson had transformed World War I into a moral crusade to achieve a peace that would be just as well as secure. (See "Encountering the Past: War Propaganda and the Movies, page 858.") The Fourteen Points set forth the right of nationalities to self-determination as an absolute value, but in fact no one could draw the map of Europe to match ethnic groups perfectly with their homelands. All these elements made compromise difficult.

Wilson's idealism, moreover, came into conflict with the more practical war aims of the victorious pow-

ers and with many of the secret treaties that had been made before and during the war. The British and French people had been told that Germany would be made to pay for the war. Russia had been promised control of Constantinople in return for recognizing the French claim to Alsace-Lorraine and British control of Egypt. Romania had been promised Transylvania at the expense of Hungary.

Some of the agreements contradicted others. Italy and Serbia had competing claims in the Adriatic. During the war, the British had encouraged Arab hopes of an independent Arab state carved out of the Ottoman Empire. Those plans, however, contradicted the Balfour Declaration (1917), in which the British seemed to accept Zionist ideology and to promise the Jews a national home in Palestine. Both of these plans conflicted with an Anglo-French agreement to divide the Near East between themselves.

The continuing national goals of the victors presented further obstacles to an idealistic "peace without victors." France was painfully conscious of its numerical inferiority to Germany and of the low birthrate that

WAR PROPAGANDA AND THE MOVIES: CHARLIE CHAPLIN

THE VAST SCOPE of the First World War required support. As the war stretched on and its costs increased, all the competing nations intensified propaganda campaigns to justify the huge expenditure of lives and resources. Sometimes this took the form of painting the enemy in brutal and lurid colors to provoke hatred, and sometimes it took the form of sympathetic images of patriotism and sacrifice for a noble cause. These efforts, sponsored both by government and private agencies, saturated the lives of everyone—men, women, and even children—while the war lasted.

At first, most of the propaganda came in the form of writing—newspaper articles and pamphlets, justifying the war and demonizing the enemy. Soon, however, verbal efforts gave way to more emotionally powerful visual devices such as posters, cartoons, and caricatures. By the middle of the war, however, the relatively new medium of film became the most powerful weapon of propaganda. Graphically and dramatically, movies showed the enemy as either horrible or ridiculous and one's own soldiers and people as brave and noble. Such images could reach rich and poor, literate and illiterate, young and old, with great emotional effect.

Both sides produced films that became enormously popular, but none more so than those Charlie Chaplin (1889–1977) did for the Allies. Born in England, he came to America as a vaudeville star in 1914 and was already famous when the war broke out. His tragicomic character, the tramp, in many variations, had universal appeal. His wartime films had amazing effects: They helped sell great quantities of Liberty Bonds (which the American government used to help pay for its involvement in the war), raised the morale of civilians, and even eased the miseries of shell-shocked soldiers.

Chaplin's 1918 movie *Shoulder Arms* was his greatest wartime success. It gave a comic picture of the difficulties of basic training for American recruits and portrays the Germans as bumbling fools. In the film, Chaplin's character, exhausted by the rigors of drilling, falls asleep. He wakes up at the front, where he deceives the enemy by pretending to be a tree, captures first a German unit and finally the kaiser, all by himself.

The Germans, too, soon learned the propaganda value of films, which were more completely in the hands of the government than those made in the Allied states. The German army made comedies, melodramas, and newsreels and showed them both to the troops and the civilian public. The German government thought movies so important that even during the freezing, brutal winter of 1917–1918 when fuel supplies were at a premium, it gave movie theaters special priority to use coal and electricity, but there was no German Charlie Chaplin.

What were the purposes of propaganda in the war? What were the advantages of using movies in the war effort?

Charlie Chaplin in *Shoulder Arms*. © Sunset Boulevard/ Corbis Sygma

Keynes's argument had a great effect on the British, who were already suspicious of France and glad of an excuse to withdraw from continental affairs. The decent and respectable position came to be one that supported revision of the treaty in favor of Germany. In the United States, the book fed the traditional tendency toward isolationism and gave powerful weapons to Wilson's enemies. Wilson's own political mistakes helped prevent American ratification of the treaty. Thus, America was out of the League of Nations and not bound to defend France. Britain, therefore, was also free from its obligation to France. France was left to protect itself without adequate means to do so for long.

Many of the attacks on the Treaty of Versailles are unjustified. It was not a Carthaginian peace. Germany was neither dismembered nor ruined. Reparations could be and were scaled down. Until the great world depression of the 1930s, the Germans recovered prosperity. Complaints against the peace should also be measured against the peace that the victorious Germans had imposed on Russia at Brest-Litovsk and their plans for a European settlement if they had won. Both were far more severe than anything enacted at Versailles. The attempt to achieve self-determination for nationalities was less than perfect, but it was the best effort Europe had ever made to do so.

Divisive New Boundaries and Tariff Walls The peace, nevertheless, was unsatisfactory in important ways. The elimination of the Austro-Hungarian Empire, however inevitable, created serious problems. Economically, it was disastrous. New borders and tariff walls separated raw materials from manufacturing areas and producers from their markets. In hard times, this separation created friction and hostility that aggravated other quarrels the peace treaties also created. Poland contained unhappy German, Lithuanian, and Ukrainian minorities, and Czechoslovakia and Yugoslavia were collections of nationalities that did not find it easy to live together. Territorial disputes in Eastern Europe promoted further tension.

Moreover, the peace rested on a victory that Germany did not admit. The Germans felt cheated rather than defeated. The high moral principles the Allies proclaimed undercut the validity of the peace, for it plainly fell far short of those principles.

Failure to Accept Reality Finally, the great weakness of the peace was its failure to accept reality. Germany and Russia must inevitably play an important part in European affairs, yet the settlement and the League of Nations excluded them. Given the many discontented parties, the peace was not self-enforcing, yet no satisfactory machinery to enforce it was established. The League of Nations was never a serious force for this purpose. It was left to France,

with no guarantee of support from Britain and no hope of help from the United States, to defend the new arrangements. Finland, the Baltic states, Poland, Romania, Czechoslovakia, and Yugoslavia were expected to be a barrier to the westward expansion of Russian communism and to help deter a revival of German power. Most of these states, however, would have to rely on France in case of danger, and France was simply not strong enough to protect them if Germany revived.

The tragedy of the Treaty of Versailles was that it was neither conciliatory enough to remove the desire for revision, even at the cost of war, nor harsh enough to make another war impossible. The only hope for a lasting peace was that Germany would remain disarmed while the more obnoxious clauses of the peace treaty were revised. Such a policy required continued attention to the problem, unity among the victors, and farsighted leadership; but none of these was consistently present during the next two decades.

In Perspective

The unification of Germany in 1871 transformed the European international order. For twenty years a series of alliances and an ongoing process of shrewd negotiation on the part of Bismarck had brought a fragile stability to European diplomatic relations. In years after Bismarck was forced from office in 1890, Kaiser Wilhelm and the German military pursued expansively aggressive policies that destabilized European diplomatic relations. Germany became overly dependent upon its alliance with Austria. Britain, France, and Russia by the first decade of the twentieth century had come to forge the very kind of friendly diplomatic understandings that Bismarck had sought to avoid.

The first fifteen years of the twentieth century saw a number of European diplomatic crises related to imperial concerns and rivalries in the Balkan Peninsula. These crises increased distrust between Germany and other European powers and worked to cement the understandings among Britain, France, and Russia. The assassination of Archduke Francis Ferdinand in the summer of 1914 sparked a Balkans crisis that could not be contained. The initial conflict between Serbia and Austria-Hungry soon drew in Russia in support of the former and Germany in support of the latter. Thereafter, the other alliances and understandings of mutual support came into play. The war plans of the various powers quickly led to the most extensive war Europe had experienced in a century.

Other unexpected transformative events followed the military stalemate. In March 1917 revolution overthrew the tsarist government of Russia. The next month the United States entered the war. In November 1917 the Bolsheviks seized power in Russia and rapidly withdrew Russia from the conflict. By November 1918 Germany surrendered. In both Germany and Austria-Hungry the governments that had led their nations into the war had collapsed.

At the Paris Peace Conference of 1919 the victorious allies redrew the map of Europe, rearranged much of the European colonial world, established the League of Nations, and imposed a war guilt clause and high reparations on Germany. The United States refused to ratify the treaty and for two decades largely withdrew from European affairs. The peace settlement itself planted the seeds of ongoing resentment and nationalist unrest in Europe.

AP* TEST PREP

1. The Russian triumph reflected in the Treaty of San Stefano of 1878 threatened
   a. Austrian control in the Balkans.
   b. British access to the Red Sea.
   c. German colonial ambitions.
   d. the Russian labor movement.
   e. French territories in the Mediterranean.

2. Which treaty pushed the Russians into a closer alliance with Germany?
   a. Three Emperors League
   b. Concert of Europe
   c. Treaty of San Stefano
   d. Dual Alliance
   e. Quadruple Alliance

3. The Triple Alliance was composed of
   a. Britain, France, Russia.
   b. Germany, Italy, Austria.
   c. Britain, France, Austria.
   d. Russia, Austria, Germany.
   e. France, Germany, Italy.

4. Bismarck's strength as a leader included all of the following *except*
   a. a clear ideology.
   b. an ability to work with the needs of other countries.
   c. a general resistance to expansionist policies.
   d. an ability to use the full range of diplomatic skills.
   e. an ability to negotiate between various class interests.

5. France and Russia signed a defensive alliance against Germany in 1894 as a consequence of
   a. British meddling in their internal affairs.
   b. Caprivi's refusal to renew the Reinsurance Treaty.
   c. renewed German interest in Alsace.
   d. William II's naval fleet in the Baltic.
   e. Germany colonial expansion in Africa.

6. The breach in British isolation from continental alliances came in 1902 when it
   a. joined the Triple Alliance.
   b. entered into Morocco's bid for independence.
   c. entered into Libya's bid for independence.
   d. concluded an alliance with Japan.
   e. concluded negotiations with the Indian National Congress.

7. World War I was sparked by the assassination of
   a. Otto von Bismarck.
   b. Archduke Francis Ferdinand.
   c. Emperor Franz Joseph II.
   d. Theobald von Bethmann-Hollweg.
   e. Emperor Edward VII.

8. Most inhabitants throughout the Balkans shared the same Slavic language and culture with the exception of these two groups:
   a. Bosnians and Romanians.
   b. Croats and Greeks.
   c. Greeks and Bosnians.
   d. Croats and Romanians.
   e. Greeks and Romanians.

9. In 1914, _____ claimed a decisive war against Russia, if necessary, should be fought "the sooner the better."
   a. William II
   b. William I
   c. Theobald von Bethmann-Hollweg
   d. Conrad von Holzendorf
   e. Helmut von Moltke

10. The failure of the French offensive at the beginning of World War I can be explained as the result of their
    a. preoccupation in Algeria.
    b. execution of the Schlieffen Plan.
    c. underestimation of German courage and spirit.
    d. underestimation of the size and firepower of German troops.
    e. overconfidence in British support.

11. Churchill's initial plan to knock out Turkey from the war was spoiled by
    a. poor execution.
    b. lack of support from the navy.
    c. lack of support from the army.
    d. lack of caution on the part of the officers involved.
    e. superior Turkish military technology.

12. When the tsar abdicated, the Russian government fell into the hands of
    a. reactionary aristocrats.
    b. moderate socialists.
    c. Lenin's allies in Russia.
    d. the Duma.
    e. illiterate peasants.

13. Russia's participation in World War I came to an end with the signing of the Treaty of
    a. Brest-Litovsk.
    b. Saint Petersburg.
    c. Moscow.
    d. Berlin.
    e. Archangel.

14. The advantages of the Triple Entente in World War I included all of the following *except*
    a. superiority of numbers.
    b. superior resources to sustain the domestic population.
    c. superior financial resources.
    d. command of the seas.
    e. internal lines of communication.

15. The most common explanation of the root causes of World War I focuses on
    a. France's failure to accept the results of the Franco-Prussian War.
    b. Britain's refusal to accept Germany's navy.
    c. Germany's ambitions for a higher place in the international order.
    d. Austrian intransigence.
    e. uneven industrialization on the Continent.

16. Lenin made his way into Russia in 1917 with the help of
    a. France.
    b. Spain.
    c. Britain.
    d. Austria.
    e. Germany.

17. Which of the following countries was/were excluded from the Versailles peace conference?
    a. Germany and the Soviet Union.
    b. Japan.
    c. Japan and Italy.
    d. Spain and Italy.
    e. France.

18. Which of the following is *not* a result of the Congress of Berlin of 1878?
    a. Austria-Hungary gained the provinces of Bosnia and Herzegovina.
    b. Germany gained control of Egypt.
    c. Bulgaria was reduced in size.
    d. Britain received Cypress.
    e. France was encouraged to occupy Tunisia.

19. Wilson's Fourteen Points set forth the right of nationalities to
    a. economic independence.
    b. fight defensive war.
    c. self-determination.
    d. ethnic purity.
    e. administer their own colonies.

20. The only major naval battle fought by the Germans in World War I was at
    a. Calais.
    b. Dover.
    c. Ostend.
    d. Jutland.
    e. Bremen.

DOCUMENT-BASED QUESTION

Directions: Construct a valid essay that directly addresses the central issue of the following question. Use facts from the documents provided and from the chapter to prove the position you take in your thesis statement.

In what ways was World War I a "new kind of war"? What role did technology play in making World War I different than previous conflicts?

Document A

John Singer Sargent's *Gassed*.

Document B

French troops advancing on the Western Front.

Document C

British tanks moving toward the Battle of Cambrai in Flanders in 1917.

Document D:

Source: Siegfried Sassoon, "They."

The Bishop tells us: "when the boys come back
They will not be the same; for they'll have fought
In a just cause: they lead the last attack
On Anti-Christ; their comrades' blood has bought
New right to breed an honorable race,
They have challenged Death and dared him face to
    face."

"We're none of us the same!" the boys reply,
"For George lost both his legs; and Bill's stone blind;
Poor Jim's shot through the lungs and like to die;
And Bert's gone syphilitic: you'll not find
A chap who's served that hasn't found *some* change."
And the Bishop said: "The ways of God are strange!"

October 31, 1916

Document E

Source: Anna Eisenmenger describes the impact of the war on her son Karl.

Karl looked very ill. He had no underlinen or socks. His uniform was dirty and in rags. "Mother, I am famished!" he said, and walking straight into the kitchen without waiting for me bring him something he began to devour our rations of bread and jam. "Forgive me, Mother, but we have got into the habit of taking what we can find." He only greeted us very casually and did not notice until much later that Erni, who had come into welcome him on Liesbeth's arm, was wounded. "Hullo! So it's caught you too!" and then, still hurriedly chewing and swallowing: "Well, just wait! We'll pay them out yet, the war profiteers and parasites. We've grown wiser out there in the trenches, far wiser than we were. Everything must be changed, utterly changed."

For more on the experience of World War I, see pages 843–849, 853–855, 858 of this chapter.

This poster shows an idealized Soviet collective farm on which tractors owned by the state have replaced peasant labor. In reality, collectivization provoked fierce resistance and caused famines in which millions of peasants died.   Poster concerning the first Five Year Plan with a photograph of Joseph Stalin (1879–1953), "At the end of the Plan, the basis of collectivisation must be completed," 1932 (colour litho.) by Klutchis (fl. 1932). Deutsches Plakat Museum, Essen, Germany/Archives Charmet/The Bridgeman Art Library

27

The Interwar Years: The Challenge of Dictators and Depression

▼ **After Versailles: Demands for Revision and Enforcement**

▼ **Toward the Great Depression in Europe**
Financial Tailspin • Problems in Agricultural Commodities • Depression and Government Policy in Britain and France

▼ **The Soviet Experiment**
War Communism • The New Economic Policy • The Third International • Stalin versus Trotsky • The Decision for Rapid Industrialization • The Collectivization of Agriculture • The Purges

▼ **The Fascist Experiment in Italy**
The Rise of Mussolini • The Fascists in Power

▼ **German Democracy and Dictatorship**
The Weimar Republic • Depression and Political Deadlock • Hitler Comes to Power • Hitler's Consolidation of Power • Anti-Semitism and the Police State • Racial Ideology and the Lives of Women • Nazi Economic Policy

▼ **Trials of the Successor States in Eastern Europe**
Economic and Ethnic Pressures • Poland: Democracy to Military Rule • Czechoslovakia: A Viable Democratic Experiment • Hungary: Turn to Authoritarianism • Austria: Political Turmoil and Nazi Occupation • Southeastern Europe: Royal Dictatorships

▼ **In Perspective**

DURING THE TWO decades that followed the Paris settlement, Europe saw bold experiments in politics and economic life. Two broad sets of factors accounted for these experiments. First, the war, the Russian Revolution, and the peace treaty had transformed the political face of Europe. New political regimes had emerged in the wake of the collapse of the monarchies of Germany, Austria-Hungary, and Russia. These were the Weimar Republic in Germany, a host of successor states to the Austro-Hungarian and Russian Empires, and the Communist Soviet Union. In Great Britain, most of Ireland established itself as, in effect, an independent nation. These new governments immediately faced the problems of postwar reconstruction, economic dislocation, and nationalistic resentment. Most of these nations also included large groups who questioned the legitimacy of their governments. All the governments and societies of both Western and Eastern Europe believed themselves profoundly threatened by the Soviet Union. The Russian Revolution was thus a pivotal factor in the rise of right-wing and fascist dictators, who often justified their power on the basis of their firm opposition to the "Red Menace" and to the growing popularity of socialism and communism in many European countries during the economic crisis of the 1930s.

Second, beginning in the early twenties, economic dislocations that led to the economic downturn that became known as the Great Depression began to spread across the world. The economic troubles were caused by financial turmoil in the industrialized nations and a collapse of commodity prices that hurt the economies of the countries that exported raw materials. Faced with political instability and economic crisis, governments contrived various responses. The Great Depression itself, which began in 1929, was the most severe downturn capitalist economies had ever experienced. High unemployment, low production, financial instability, and shrinking trade arrived and would not depart. Business and political leaders despaired over the market's seeming inability to resolve the crisis. Marxists and, indeed, many other observers thought the final downfall of capitalism was at hand.

European voters looked for new ways out of the doldrums, and politicians sought to escape the pressures that the Depression had brought on them. One result of the fight for economic security was the establishment of the Nazi dictatorship in Germany. Another was the piecemeal construction of what became known as the mixed economy; that is, governments became directly involved in making economic decisions alongside business and labor. In both cases, most of the political and economic guidelines of nineteenth-century liberalism were abandoned, and so were decency and civility in political life. Authoritarianism and aggression were not the inescapable destiny of Europe. They emerged from the failure to secure alternative modes of democratic political life and stable international relations and from the inability to achieve long-term economic prosperity.

▼ After Versailles: Demands for Revision and Enforcement

The Paris settlement fostered both resentments and discontent. Those resentments counted among the chief political factors in Europe for the next two decades. Germany had been humiliated. The arrangements for reparations led to endless haggling over payments. Many national groups in the successor states of the Austro-Hungarian Empire felt that their rights to self-determination had been violated or ignored. There were strident demands for further border adjustments because significant national minorities, particularly Germans and Magyars, resided outside the national boundaries drawn in Paris. On the other side, the victorious powers, especially France, often believed that the provisions of the treaties were being inadequately enforced. Consequently, throughout the 1920s and into the 1930s, demands either to revise or to enforce the Paris treaties contributed to domestic political turmoil across the Continent. Many political figures were willing to fish in these troubled international waters for a large catch of domestic votes.

▼ Toward the Great Depression in Europe

Along with the move toward political experimentation and the demands for revision of the new international order, there was a widespread yearning to return to the economic prosperity of the prewar years. After 1918, however, it was impossible to restore in the economic realm what American president Warren Harding (1865–1923) would term *normalcy*. During the Great War, Europeans had turned the military and industrial power that they had created during the previous century against themselves. What had been "normal" in economic and social life before 1914 could not be reestablished.

The casualties from the war numbered in the millions. (See Table 27–1.) This represented not only a waste of human life and talent, but also the loss of producers and consumers.

Three factors originating in the 1920s combined to bring about the intense severity and the extended length of the **Great Depression**. First, a financial crisis stemmed directly from the war and the peace settlement. To this was added a crisis in the production and distribution of goods in the world market. These two problems became intertwined in 1929, and in Europe they reached the breaking point in 1931. Finally, both of these difficulties became worse than they might have been because no major Western European coun-

TABLE 27–1   TOTAL CASUALTIES IN THE FIRST WORLD WAR

Country	Dead	Wounded	Total Killed as a Percentage of Population
France	1,398,000	2,000,000	3.4
Belgium	38,000	44,700	0.5
Italy	578,000	947,000	1.6
British Empire	921,000	2,090,000	1.7
Romania	250,000	120,000	3.3
Serbia	278,000	133,000	5.7
Greece	26,000	21,000	0.5
Russia	1,811,000	1,450,000	1.1
Bulgaria	88,000	152,000	1.9
Germany	2,037,000	4,207,000	3.0
Austria-Hungary	1,100,000	3,620,000	1.9
Turkey	804,000	400,000	3.7
United States	114,000	206,000	0.1

Source: Niall Ferguson, *The Pity of War* (New York: Basic Books, 1998).

Financial Tailspin

As one of the chief victors in the war, France was determined to collect reparations from Germany for the destruction the war had caused in northern France. The United States was no less determined that its allies repay the money it had lent them during the war. The European allies also owed debts to each other. German reparations were to provide the means of repaying all these debts. Most of the money that the Allies collected from each other also went to the United States.

The quest for payment of German reparations caused one of the major diplomatic crises of the 1920s; that crisis itself resulted in further economic upheaval. In early 1923 the Allies—France in particular—declared Germany to be in technical default of its reparation payments. On January 11, to ensure receipt of the hard-won reparations, French and Belgian troops occupied the Ruhr mining and manufacturing district. The **Weimar Republic** ordered passive resistance that amounted to a general strike in Germany's largest industrial region. Confronted with this tactic, the French sent technicians and engineers to run the German mines and railroads. France got its way. The Germans paid, but its victory cost France dearly. The British were alienated by the French heavy-handedness and took no part in the occupation. Britain became more suspicious of France and more sympathetic to Germany. The cost of the Ruhr occupation, moreover, vastly increased French as well as German inflation and damaged the French economy.

The political and economic turmoil of the Ruhr invasion led to international attempts to ease the German payment of reparations. At the same time, American investment capital was pouring into Europe. However, by 1928 this investment decreased as American money became diverted into the booming New York stock market. The crash of Wall Street in October 1929—the result of virtually unregulated financial speculation—saw the loss of large amounts of money. Credit sharply contracted in the United States as numerous banks failed. Thereafter, little American capital was available for investment in Europe.

As American credit for Europe began to run out, a major financial crisis struck the Continent. In May 1931 the Kreditanstalt bank in Austria collapsed. The Kreditanstalt was a primary financial institution for much of central and eastern Europe. Its collapse put severe pressure on the German banking system, which was saved only through government guarantees. As the

try or the United States provided strong, responsible economic leadership that might have resulted in some form of cooperation to face the challenge of the Depression.

The French invasion of the German Ruhr (1923) began a crisis that brought strikes and rampant inflation in Germany. Here French troops have commandeered a German locomotive during one of the strikes. UPI/CORBIS/Bettmann

German difficulties increased, U.S. president Herbert Hoover (1874–1964) announced in June 1931 a one-year moratorium on all payments of international debts. The Hoover moratorium was a prelude to the end of reparations. The Lausanne Conference in the summer of 1932 brought, in effect, the era of reparations to a close. The next year the debts owed to the United States were settled either through small token payments or simply through default.

Problems in Agricultural Commodities

In the 1920s the market demand for European goods shrank leaving much of the Continent's productive capacity idle or underused. This problem originated both within and outside Europe. In both instances the difficulty arose from agriculture. Better methods of farming, improved strains of wheat, expanded acreage under the plow, and more extensive transport facilities vastly increased the quantity of grain farmers around the world produced. World wheat prices fell to record lows. Although this helped consumers, it decreased the income of European farmers. At the same time, higher industrial wages raised the cost of the industrial goods that farmers or peasants used. Consequently, they had great difficulty paying off their mortgages and loans for normal operating costs. These problems were especially acute in central and eastern Europe and increased farmers' disillusionment with liberal politics. German farmers, for example, would become prime supporters of the National Socialist Workers Party (Nazis).

Outside Europe similar problems affected other producers of agricultural commodities. The prices they received for their products plummeted. Government-held reserves of raw materials reached record levels. This glut of major world commodities involved wheat, sugar, coffee, rubber, wool, and lard. The people who produced these goods in underdeveloped nations could no longer make enough money to buy goods from industrial Europe. As world credit collapsed, the economic position of these commodity producers worsened. Commodity production had simply outstripped world demand.

The results of the collapse in the agricultural sector of the world economy and the financial turmoil were stagnation and depression for European industry. Coal, iron, and textiles had depended largely on international markets. Unemployment spread from these industries to those producing consumer goods. Persistent unemployment in Great Britain and, to a lesser extent, in Germany during the 1920s had created "soft" domestic markets. The policies of reduced spending with which the governments confronted the Depression further weakened domestic demand. By the early 1930s the Depression was feeding on itself.

Depression and Government Policy in Britain and France

The Depression did not mean absolute economic decline or total unemployment. But the economic downturn spread potential as well as actual insecurity. People in nearly all walks of life feared the loss of their economic security. The Depression also frustrated normal social and economic expectations. Even the employed often seemed to make no progress; and their anxieties created a major source of discontent.

The governments of the late 1920s and the early 1930s were not well suited in either structure or ideology to confront these problems. The electorates demanded action. The governments' responses depended largely on the severity of the Depression in a particular country and on the self-confidence of the nation's political system.

Great Britain and France, which because of their vast empires commanded very large economies, undertook moderate political experiments. In 1924 the Labour Party in Great Britain established itself as a viable governing party by forming a short-lived government. It again formed a ministry in 1929. Under the pressure of the Depression and at the urging of King George V (r. 1910–1936), the Labour prime minister Ramsay MacDonald (1866–1937) organized a National Government, which was a coalition of the Labour, Conservative, and Liberal Parties. It remained in power until 1935, when a Conservative ministry led by Stanley Baldwin (1867–1947) replaced it. (See "John Maynard Keynes Calls for Government Investment to Create Employment.")

The 1920s also saw the establishment of an independent Irish state. On Easter Monday in April 1916, a nationalist uprising occurred in Dublin, the only rebellion of a national group against any government engaged in World War I. The British suppressed the uprising but made martyrs of its leaders by executing several of them. Leadership of the nationalist cause quickly shifted from the Irish Party in Parliament to the extremist **Sinn Fein**, or "Ourselves Alone," movement. In the election of 1918, Sinn Fein won all but four of the Irish parliamentary seats outside Ulster. They refused to go to the Parliament at Westminster. Instead, they constituted themselves into a *Dail Eireann*, or Irish Parliament. On January 21, 1919, they declared Irish independence. Thereafter a civil war broke out between the military wing of Sinn Fein, which became the Irish Republican Army (IRA), and the British army. The conflict ended with a treaty in December 1921, which established the Irish Free State as one of the dominions in the British Commonwealth. The six, predominately Protestant, counties of Ulster, or Northern Ireland, were permitted to remain part of what was now called the United Kingdom of Great Britain and Northern Ireland,

JOHN MAYNARD KEYNES CALLS FOR GOVERNMENT INVESTMENT TO CREATE EMPLOYMENT

Since at least the late nineteenth century, European social critics had questioned whether capitalistic economies could function without major crises that resulted in unemployment and other social disruptions. Virtually all economists, however, believed that given enough time capitalistic economies would correct themselves. Consequently, when the Great Depression struck the worldwide economy, the governments of Western Europe and the United States initially undertook relatively modest actions to address it. They were doing what most economists at the time advocated. Socialists, of course, had long advocated government intervention. In 1936, however, John Maynard Keynes, a prominent British economist, published The General Theory of Employment, Interest and Money. *Keynes, who was not a socialist, believed that the Great Depression demonstrated that economic crises could be so severe that private investment would simply not take place and thus could not generate new economic activity that would revive employment and lift the economy out of depression. In the passage below, Keynes explains that although he believes in individual initiative, there are times it will not occur. Under those conditions he calls for the "socialisation of investment," which was his term for government spending to spark new economic activity that would expand employment. In the second paragraph, he argues that the role of such government investment or spending is to provide employment for those workers whom the private economy cannot employ. Keynes's book did not influence many policies during the Great Depression, but after World War II, many Western governments devised economic policies along the lines he advocated.*

Why does Keynes believe the private economy will not always provide sufficient employment? Why does he call government spending the "socialisation of investment"? How much of his argument is analytical? How much political?

In some respects the foregoing theory is moderately conservative in its implications. For whilst it indicates the vital importance of establishing certain central controls in matters which are now left in the main to individual initiative, there are wide fields of activity which are unaffected. The State will have to exercise a guiding influence on the propensity to consume partly through its scheme of taxation, partly by fixing the rate of interest, and partly, perhaps, in other ways. Furthermore, it seems unlikely that the influence of banking policy on the rate of interest will be sufficient by itself to determine an optimum rate of investment. I conceive, therefore, that a somewhat comprehensive socialisation of investment will prove the only means of securing an approximation to full employment; though this need not exclude all manner of compromises and of devices by which public authority will co-operate with private initiative. But beyond this, no obvious case is made out for a system of State Socialism which would embrace most of the economic life of the community. It is not the ownership of the instruments of production which it is important for the State to assume. If the State is able to determine the aggregate amount of resources devoted to augmenting the instruments and the basic rate of reward to those who own them, it will have accomplished all that is necessary. . . .

To put the matter concretely, I see no reason to suppose that the existing system seriously misemploys the factors of production which are in use. There are, of course, errors of foresight; but these would not be avoided by centralizing decisions. When 9,000,000 men are employed out of 10,000,000 willing and able to work, there is no evidence that the labour of these 9,000,000 men is misdirected. The complaint against the present system is not that these 9,000,000 men ought to be employed on different tasks, but that tasks should be available for the remaining 10,000,000 men. It is in determining the volume, not the direction, of actual employment that the existing system has broken down.

John Maynard Keynes, *The General Theory of Employment, Interest and Money* (London: Macmillan & Co., Ltd., 1960), p. 379.

with provisions for home rule. In the 1920s and 1930s, the Free State gradually severed its ties to Britain. It remained neutral during World War II and declared itself an independent republic in 1949.

The most important French interwar political experiment was the **Popular Front** Ministry, which came to office in 1936. It was composed of Socialists, Radicals, and Communists—the first time that Socialists and Communists had cooperated in a ministry. They did so because they feared right-wing political groups in France and saw the threat of such regimes elsewhere in Europe. Despite fierce resistance from business and conservative groups, the Popular Front enacted major social and economic reforms, including the forty-hour week, paid vacations for workers, and compulsory arbitration of labor disputes. But its parliamentary support gradually faded until its final collapse in October 1938.

The political changes in Britain and France were essentially of domestic significance. But the political experiments of the 1920s and 1930s that reshaped world history and civilization involved the establishment of a Soviet government in Russia, a Fascist regime in Italy, and a Nazi dictatorship in Germany.

▼ The Soviet Experiment

The consolidation of the Bolshevik Revolution in Russia established the most extensive and durable of all twentieth-century authoritarian governments. The Communist Party of the Soviet Union retained power from 1917 until the end of 1991, and its presence influenced the political history of Europe and much of the rest of the world, as did no other single factor. Unlike the Italian Fascists or the German National Socialists, the Bolsheviks seized power violently through revolution. For several years they confronted civil war, and their leaders long felt insecure about their hold on the country. The Communist Party was neither a mass party nor a nationalistic one. Its early membership rarely exceeded more than 1 percent of the Russian population. The Bolsheviks confronted a much less industrialized economy than that in Italy or Germany. They believed in and practiced the collectivization of economic life. The Marxist-Leninist ideology had vastly more international appeal than the nationalism of the Fascists and the racism of the Nazis. Communism was an exportable commodity. The Communists regarded their government and their revolution not as part of the national history of Russia, but as epoch-making events in the history of the world and the development of humanity. (See "Compare & Connect: The Soviets and the Nazis Confront the Issues of Women and the Family," pages 892–893.) Fear of communism and determination to stop its spread became one of the leading political forces in Western Europe and the United States

for most of the rest of the century. Policies flowing from that opposition would influence European and American relationships with much of the rest of the world.

War Communism

Within the Soviet Union the Red Army under the organizational genius of Leon Trotsky (1879–1940) had suppressed internal and foreign military opposition to the new government during the civil war that raged from 1918 to 1920. Within months of the revolution, a new secret police, known as *Cheka*, appeared. Throughout the civil war Lenin (1870–1924) had declared that the Bolshevik Party, as the vanguard of the revolution, was imposing the dictatorship of the proletariat. Political and economic administration became highly centralized. All major decisions flowed from the top in a nondemocratic manner. Under the economic policy of **War Communism**, the revolutionary government confiscated and then operated the banks, the transport facilities, and heavy industry. The state also forcibly requisitioned grain and shipped it from the countryside to feed the army and the urban workers. The Bolsheviks used the need to fight the civil war as justification for suppressing any resistance to these economic policies.

War Communism helped the Red Army defeat its opponents. The revolution had survived and triumphed. The policy, however, generated domestic opposition to the Bolsheviks, who in 1920 numbered only about 600,000. The alliance of workers and peasants forged in 1917 by the Bolsheviks' slogan of "Peace, Bread, and Land" had begun to dissolve. Many Russians were no longer willing to make the sacrifices demanded by the central party bureaucrats. In 1920 and 1921, serious strikes occurred. Peasants were discontented and resisted the requisition of grain. In March 1921, the sailors mutinied at the Kronstadt naval base on the Baltic. The Red Army crushed the rebellion with grave loss of life. Each of these acts of opposition suggested that the proletariat itself was opposing the dictatorship of the proletariat. Also, by late 1920 it had become clear that revolution was not going to sweep across the rest of Europe. For the time being the Soviet Union would constitute a vast island of revolutionary socialism in the larger sea of world capitalism.

The New Economic Policy

Under these difficult conditions Lenin made a strategic retreat. In March 1921, following the Kronstadt mutiny, he outlined the **New Economic Policy**, or NEP. Apart from what he termed "the commanding heights" of banking, heavy industry, transportation, and international commerce, considerable private economic enterprise was allowed. In particular, peasants could farm for

Anxiety over the spread of the Bolshevik revolution was a fundamental factor of European politics during the 1920s and 1930s. Images like this Soviet portrait of Lenin as a heroic revolutionary conjured fears among people in the rest of Europe of a political force determined to overturn their social, political, and economic institutions.   Bildarchiv Preussischer Kulturbesitz

West, before the war, as discussed in Chapter 23, social democratic parties had regarded the Russian Bolsheviks as eccentric, politically marginal Marxist extremists. The Bolshevik victory forced West European social democrats to rethink their position within the world of international socialism. For their part, the Bolsheviks intended to establish themselves as the international leaders of Marxism and regarded reformist social democrats as enemies and rivals.

In 1919, the Soviet communists founded the Third International of the European socialist movement, better known as the *Comintern*. The Comintern worked to make the Bolshevik model of socialism, as Lenin had developed it, the rule for all socialist parties outside the Soviet Union. In 1920, the Comintern imposed its Twenty-one Conditions on any socialist party that wished to join it. These conditions included acknowledging Moscow's leadership, rejecting reformist or revisionist socialism, repudiating previous socialist leaders, and adopting the Communist Party name. In effect, the Comintern sought to destroy democratic socialism, which it accused of having betrayed the working class through reform policies and parliamentary accommodation.

The decision whether to accept these conditions split every major European socialist party. As a result, separate communist and social democratic parties emerged in most countries and they fought each other more intensely than they fought either capitalism or conservative political parties. Their fierce conflict was one of the fundamental features of the interwar European political landscape.

These Comintern polices and the resulting divisions of the socialist parties directly affected the rise of the fascists and the Nazis in Western Europe. It is difficult to overestimate the fears that Soviet political rhetoric and Communist Party activity aroused in Europe during the 1920s and 1930s. Conservative and right-wing political groups manipulated and exaggerated these fears. The presence of separate communist parties in Western Europe meant that right-wing politicians always had a convenient target they could justly accuse of seeking to overthrow the government and to impose Soviet-style political, social, and economic systems in their nations. Furthermore, right-wing politicians also accused the democratic socialists of supporting policies that might facilitate a communist takeover. The divisions between Communists and democratic socialists also meant that right-wing political movements rarely had to confront a united left.

a profit. They would pay taxes like other citizens, but they could sell their surplus grain on the open market. The NEP was consistent with Lenin's earlier conviction that the Russian peasantry held the key to the success of the revolution. After 1921 the countryside did become more stable, and a secure food supply seemed assured for the cities. Similar free enterprise flourished within light industry and the domestic retail trade. By 1927 industrial production had reached its 1913 level. The revolution seemed to have transformed Russia into a land of small farms and privately owned shops and businesses.

The Third International

The onset and consolidation of the Bolshevik revolution in Russia was a transforming event for the history of socialism as well as for Russia and international affairs. The revolution stunned West European socialists. In the

Stalin versus Trotsky

The NEP had caused sharp disputes within the Politburo, the highest governing committee of the Communist Party. The partial return to capitalism seemed to some members nothing less than a betrayal of sound Marxist principles. These frictions increased as Lenin's firm hand disappeared. In 1922 he suffered a stroke and never again dominated party affairs; in 1924 he died. In the ensuing power vacuum, an intense struggle for leadership of the party commenced. Two factions emerged. One was led by Trotsky; the other by Joseph Stalin (1879–1953), who had become general secretary of the party in 1922. Shortly before his death Lenin had criticized both men. He was especially harsh toward Stalin. However, as general secretary Stalin's base of power lay with the party membership and with the daily management of party affairs, he was able to withstand the posthumous criticism of Lenin.

Each faction wanted to control the party and thus also the state, but the struggle was fought over the question of Russia's path toward industrialization and the future of the Communist revolutionary movement. Trotsky, speaking for what became known as the left wing, urged rapid industrialization and looked to voluntary collectivization of farming by poor peasants as a means of increasing agricultural production. He further argued that the revolution in Russia could succeed only if new revolutions took place elsewhere. Russia needed the skills and wealth of other nations to build its own economy. As Trotsky's influence within the party began to wane, he also demanded that party members be permitted to criticize the policies of the government and the party. Trotsky, however, was a latecomer to the advocacy of open discussion. When he had controlled the Red Army, he had been a harsh and unflinching disciplinarian.

A right-wing faction opposed Trotsky. Although its chief ideological voice was that of Nikolai Bukharin (1888–1938), the editor of *Pravda*, the official party paper, Stalin was its true political manipulator. In the mid-1920s this group pressed for the continuation of Lenin's NEP and relatively slow industrialization.

Stalin was the ultimate victor in these intraparty rivalries. Unlike the other early Bolshevik leaders, he had not spent a long exile in Western Europe. He was much less an intellectual and internationalist. He was also much more brutal. His handling of various recalcitrant national groups within Russia after the revolution had shocked even Lenin. Stalin's power lay in his command of bureaucratic and administrative methods. He was neither a brilliant writer nor an effective public speaker; however, he mastered the crucial, if dull, details of party structure, including admission, promotion, and rewards. That mastery meant that he could draw on the support of the lower levels of the party apparatus when he clashed with other leaders.

In the mid-1920s Stalin supported Bukharin's position on economic development. In 1924 he also enunciated, in opposition to Trotsky, the doctrine of "socialism in one country." He urged that socialism could be achieved in Russia alone. Russian success did not depend on the fate of the revolution elsewhere.

Stalin thus nationalized the previously international scope of the Marxist revolution. He cunningly used the apparatus of the party and his control over its Central Committee to edge out Trotsky and his supporters. By 1927 Trotsky had been removed from all his offices, ousted from the party, and exiled to Siberia. In 1929 he was expelled from Russia and eventually moved to Mexico, where he was murdered in 1940 by one of Stalin's agents. With the removal of Trotsky, Stalin was firmly in control of the Soviet state. It remained to be seen what "socialism in one country" would mean in practice.

The Decision for Rapid Industrialization

In 1927 the Party Congress decided to push for rapid industrialization. As implemented through what has been termed "industrialization by political mobilization," this policy marked a sharp departure from the NEP and a rejection of the pockets of relatively free-market operations within the larger Soviet economy.[1]

Stalin's goal was to have the Soviet Union overtake the productive capacity of its enemies, the capitalist nations. This policy required the rapid construction of heavy industries, such as iron, steel, and machine tool making, building electricity-generating stations, and manufacturing tractors. Stalin's organizational vehicle for industrialization was a series of five-year plans, starting in 1928. The State Planning Commission, or *Gosplan*, set goals for production in every area of economic life and attempted to organize the economy to meet them. The task of coordinating all facets of production was immensely complicated. Deliveries of materials from mines or factories had to be assured before the next unit could carry out its part of the plan. Enormous economic disruption occurred as the *Gosplan* built power plants and steel mills and increased the output of mines. The plans consistently favored capital projects over the production of consumer goods. The number of centralized agencies and ministries involved in planning soared, and they often competed with each other.

The rapid expansion of the industrial base created the first genuinely large factory labor force in what had been Russia. Workers were recruited from the countryside and from the urban unemployed. New cities and industrial districts in existing cities arose. Most workers were crowded into shoddy buildings with inadequate sanitation, living space, and nourishment. Their lives were as bad as or worse than anything Marx and Engels had decried in the nineteenth century.

The government and the Communist Party undertook a vast program of propaganda to sell the five-year

[1]Vladimir Andrle, *A Social History of Twentieth-Century Russia* (London: Arnold, 1994), p. 161.

Magnitogorsk was a city that became a monument to Stalin's drive toward rapid industrialization. Located in the Ural Mountains near a vast supply of iron ore, the city became the site of major iron and steel production. It was one of the new industrial cities founded under the Five Year Plans designed to challenge the capitalist production of the Western nations. National Archives and Records Administration

The Collectivization of Agriculture

Agricultural productivity had always been a core problem for the emerging Soviet economy. Under the NEP the government purchased a certain amount of grain at prices it set itself. The rest of the grain was then supposed to be sold at market prices, which were higher than the government-set prices. Many peasant farmers of all degrees of wealth tried to circumvent this system, often by keeping grain off the market in hopes that its price would rise. The scarcity of consumer goods available for purchase in the countryside also encouraged hoarding. With little to buy from what they earned by selling their grain, farmers had little incentive to sell it. Instead, many of them preferred to hoard grain, so that they could sell it in the future when they hoped more consumer goods would be available for them to purchase. The Soviet government, however, needed the grain immediately to feed its expanding urban workforce and to pay for imports from abroad. In 1928 and 1929, as a result of peasants hoarding their grains for better prices, the Soviet government confronted shortfalls of grain on the market and the prospect of food shortages in the cities and social unrest.

Stalin therefore decided to reverse the agricultural policies of the NEP. Toward the end of the 1920s, Soviet economists and party officials devised an explanation for the difficulties they confronted in the agricultural sector. First, they asserted that the traditional peasant holdings were too small to produce enough grain to meet the country's needs. Second, they claimed that a class-enemy was responsible for the hoarding and for what they regarded as speculation in the grain trade. This enemy was the group of relatively prosperous peasants, known as *kulaks*, who numbered somewhat less than 5 percent of the rural population and were often the most productive and efficient farmers. On the basis of these ideas, Stalin decided that Soviet agriculture must be collectivized to produce enough grain for domestic food and foreign export. **Collectivization** —the replacement of private peasant farms with huge state-run and state-owned farms called collectives— would also put the Communist Party firmly in control of

plans to the Russian people and to elicit their cooperation. The government boasted of the sheer size of the plants and new towns being constructed. Such propaganda was necessary because most industrial workers were displaced peasants who had never worked in a factory and often resisted industrial discipline. The party appealed to the idealism of the young in proclaiming its goals of rapidly modernizing the nation. Workers, such as a legendary coal miner named Stakhanov, who exceeded their assigned goals received rewards and publicity.

The results were impressive. Soviet industrial production rose approximately 400 percent between 1928 and 1940. Industries that had never existed in Russia challenged their foreign counterparts. Hundreds of thousands of people populated new industrial cities. The social and human cost of this effort had, however, been appalling.

the farm sector of the economy and free up peasant labor to work in the expanding industrial sector. To carry out this policy, Stalin portrayed the *kulak*s as the fundamental cause of the agricultural problems.

Party officials with troops at their command carried out the initial campaign of dekulakization and collectivization. Usually they would seek first to remove *kulaks* from a village while confiscating their land and would then attempt to coerce the remaining peasants into organizing a collective farm. Enormous turmoil and violence resulted. In March 1930, Stalin called a brief halt to the process, justifying the slowdown on the grounds of "dizziness from success." After the harvest of that year had been secured, however, the drive to collectivize the farms was renewed with vehemence.

Peasants determined to keep their land, often with women in the lead, had sabotaged collectivization by slaughtering millions of livestock between 1929 and 1933. Peasants who resisted were killed outright. Others starved to death on their own farms when all the grain that they had produced was seized. Over 2 million peasants were forcibly removed from their homes and deported to distant areas of the Soviet Union or to prison camps where many died from disease, exposure, and malnutrition. Even if they survived that ordeal, they then had to patch together some kind of life as industrial workers or miners in Siberia or another inhospitable province. Their children were treated as class-enemies and political traitors. Much of the violence of collec-

tivization occurred in Ukraine, where Stalin used the process not only to restructure agricultural production but also to crush any vestiges of Ukrainian nationalism, and many millions of lives were lost as a result.

During the drive toward collectivization, the Communist Party also targeted priests of the Russian Orthodox Church. The Party, atheistic in its ideology, had always opposed religion, but only with collectivization were many rural priests attacked and churches closed or vandalized. Between 1926 and 1937, the number of priests recorded in the Soviet census dropped by more than one half. Rabbis, Catholic priests, Protestant ministers, and mullahs received the same harsh treatment.

By 1937, over 90 percent of Soviet grain production had been collectivized. The violent transformation of Soviet agriculture meant producers on collective farms could no longer decide what crops to produce or how much to sell them for. The government organized Motor-Tractor Stations that supplied the seed and equipment for several collective farms in a region and oversaw the collection and sale of grain. The heads of these stations were Party political operatives, and they determined what payments the farmers eventually received for the grain they had produced. Alongside the state-run collective farms, by the mid-1930s, the government allowed farmers small household plots to grow fruit and vegetables for their families and for local sale. These plots became an important part of Soviet agriculture because peasants tended them so carefully and productively.

Stalin used intimidation and propaganda to support his drive to collectivize Soviet agriculture. Communist Party agitators led groups of peasants such as these to demand the seizure of the farms worked by the better-off and more successful farmers known as *kulaks*. AP/Wide World Photos

At the cost of millions of peasant lives, Stalin and the Communist Party had won the battle of the grain fields, but they had not solved the problem of producing enough food. That difficulty would plague the Soviet Union until its collapse in 1991 and remains a problem for its successor states.

The Purges

In 1933, with turmoil in the countryside and economic dislocation caused by industrialization, Stalin and others in the central Soviet bureaucracy began to fear they were losing control of the country and the party apparatus and that effective rivals to their power and policies might emerge. These apprehensions were largely a figment of Stalin's own paranoia and lust for power, but they resulted in the **Great Purges**, which remain one of the most mysterious and horrendous political events of the twentieth century. Few observers understood the purges at the time, and despite the recent opening of Soviet archives, they have still not been fully comprehended, either inside or outside the former Soviet Union.

The pretext for the onset of the purges was the assassination on December 1, 1934, of Sergei Kirov (1888–1934), the popular party chief of Leningrad and a member of the Politburo. In the wake of the shooting, thousands of people were arrested, and still more were expelled from the party and sent to labor camps. At the time, many thought that opponents of the regime had murdered Kirov, and Stalin routinely accused those whom he attacked of complicity in the crime. Today, many scholars believe that Stalin himself authorized Kirov's assassination because he was afraid of him. The available documentary evidence does not allow us to know for sure whether Stalin was involved, but he quickly used Kirov's death for his own purposes. Under Stalin, the Soviet Communist Party had already shown it could punish dissent within its ranks. The debates of the 1920s within the party and the expulsion of Trotsky had established a clear precedent for exercising firm discipline, and in the confusion surrounding the implementation of the five-year plans, persons accused of sabotage and disloyalty had been executed. The purges, however, went far beyond any of these precedents.

The purges that took place immediately after Kirov's death were just the beginning of a larger and longer process. Between 1936 and 1938, a series of spectacular show trials were held in Moscow. Former high Soviet leaders, including members of the Politburo, such as Bukharin, publicly confessed to political crimes and were convicted and executed. It is still not certain why they made their palpably false confessions, although this seems to have been the kind of ritual confession of faults and shortcomings that had long characterized internal Communist Party life. They had also been interrogated under the most difficult conditions, including torture, and feared for their families' lives. (Stalin regularly arrest-ed the wives, children, siblings, and in-laws of "traitors" and had them shot or sent to die in labor camps.) Other lower-level party members were tried in private and shot. Hundreds of thousands, perhaps millions, of ordinary Soviet citizens received no trial at all and were either executed or deported to slave labor camps where many died. Within the party itself, thousands of members were expelled, and applicants for membership were removed from the rolls. After the civilian party members and leaders had been purged, the prosecutors turned against the government bureaucracy and the Soviet army and navy, convicting and executing thousands of officials and officers, including heroes of the civil war. The exact number of executions, imprisonments, interrogations, and expulsions is unknown, but it ran well into the millions. While the purges went on, no one in the Soviet Union, except Stalin himself, was safe.

The rational explanations of the purges—to the extent that mass murder can ever be rationally explained—probably lie in two directions. First, over the several years the purges lasted, different portions of the party leadership moved against others. Initially, Stalin and the central Moscow leadership used the purges to settle old scores and to discipline and gain more control over lower levels of the party in the far-flung regions of the Soviet Union. In addition to increasing Stalin's authority, these central bureaucratic groups wanted to eliminate any opposition to their own positions or policies. By 1937, however, Stalin seems to have become distrustful of the central party elite, his own supporters, and began to find or pretend to find enemies within its ranks. Moreover, by that date, local communist groups were allowed to designate their own victims with little direction from Moscow. Thereafter, a self-destructive cascade of accusations, imprisonments, and executions occurred throughout the party and within its highest levels. The Communist Party leadership at all levels appeared to be consuming itself in an atmosphere of terror for its own sake. This situation has been termed "centrally authorized chaos."[2]

Second, no matter how much tension and rivalry there were among the different levels and regions of the Communist Party, Stalin's primary motive in the purges was almost certainly fear for his own power and a ruthless determination to preserve and increase it. He and the deputies whom he allowed to survive the purges personally selected certain victims and determined the fate of their families. In effect, the purges created a new Communist Party that was absolutely subservient and loyal to Stalin. The "old Bolsheviks" of the October Revolution in 1917 were among his earliest targets. They and others active in the first years of the revolution knew how far Stalin had moved from Lenin's policies.

[2]J. Arch Getty and Oleg V. Naumov, *The Road to Terror: Stalin and the Self-Destruction of the Bolsheviks, 1932–1939,* trans. by Benjamin Sher (New Haven, CT: Yale University Press, 1999), p. 583.

By the mid-1930s, Stalin's purges had eliminated many leaders and other members from the Soviet Communist Party. This photograph of a meeting of a party congress in 1936 shows a number of the surviving leaders with Stalin, who sits fourth from the right in the front row. To his left is Vyacheslav Molotov, longtime foreign minister. The first person on the left in the front row is Nikita Khruschev, who headed the Soviet Union in the late 1950s and early 1960s.   Itar-Tass/Sovfoto/Eastfoto

New, younger recruits replaced the party members who were executed or expelled. The newcomers knew little about old Russia or the ideals of the original Bolsheviks. They had not been loyal to Lenin, Trotsky, Bukharin, or any other Soviet leader except Stalin himself.

The internal difficulties collectivization and industrialization and his worries about internal opposition caused led Stalin to make an important shift in foreign policy. In 1934, he began to fear the nation might be left isolated against aggression by Nazi Germany. The Soviet Union was not yet strong enough to withstand such an attack. So that year he ordered the Comintern to permit communist parties in other countries to cooperate with noncommunist parties against Nazism and fascism. This reversed the Comintern policy Lenin established as part of the Twenty-One Conditions in 1919. The new Stalinist policy allowed the Popular Front Government in France to come to power.

▼ The Fascist Experiment in Italy

The first authoritarian political experiment in Western Europe that arose in part from fears of the spread of bolshevism beyond the Soviet Union occurred in Italy. The general term *fascist*, which has been used to describe the various right-wing dictatorships that arose between the wars, was derived from the Italian Fascist movement of Benito Mussolini (1883–1945).

While scholars still dispute the exact meaning of ***fascism*** as a political term, the governments regarded as fascist were antidemocratic, anti-Marxist, antiparliamentary, and frequently anti-Semitic. They hoped to hold back the spread of bolshevism, which seemed a real threat at the time. They sought a world that would be safe for the middle class, small businesses, owners of moderate amounts of property, and small farmers. The fascist regimes rejected the political inheritance of the French Revolution and of nineteenth-century liberalism. (See "Mussolini Heaps Contempt on Political Liberalism.") Their adherents believed that normal parliamentary politics and parties sacrificed national honor and greatness to petty party disputes. They wanted to overcome the class conflict of Marxism and the party conflict of liberalism by consolidating the various groups and classes within the nation for great national purposes. As Mussolini declared in 1931, "The fascist conception of the state is all-embracing, and outside of the state no human or spiritual values can exist, let alone be desirable."[3] Fascist governments were usually single-party dictatorships characterized by terrorism

[3]Quoted in Denis Mack Smith, *Italy: A Modern History* (Ann Arbor: University of Michigan Press, 1959), p. 412.

each other. All the political parties except the small Communist Party represented a particular ethnic group rather than the nation of Yugoslavia. The violent clash of nationalities eventually led to a royal dictatorship in 1929 under King Alexander I (r. 1921–1934), himself a Serb. He outlawed political parties and jailed popular politicians. Alexander was assassinated in 1934, but the authoritarian government continued under a regency for his son.

Other royal dictatorships were imposed elsewhere in the Balkans: in Romania by King Carol II (r. 1930–1940) and in Bulgaria by King Boris III (r. 1918–1943). They regarded their own illiberal regimes as preventing the seizure of power by more extreme antiparliamentary movements and as quieting the discontent of the varied nationalities within their borders. In Greece, the parliamentary monarchy floundered amid military coups and calls for a republic. In 1936, General John Metaxas (1871–1941) instituted a dictatorship under King George II (r. 1935–1947) that, for the time being, ended parliamentary life in Greece.

In Perspective

By the mid-1930s, dictators of the right and the left had established themselves across much of Europe. Political tyranny was hardly new to Europe, but several factors combined to give these rulers unique characteristics. They drew their immediate support from well-organized political parties. Except for the Bolsheviks, these were mass parties. The roots of support for the dictators lay in nationalism, the social and economic frustration of the Great Depression, and political ideologies that promised to transform the social and political order. As long as the new rulers seemed successful, they did not lack support. Many citizens believed these leaders had ended the pettiness of everyday politics.

After coming to power, the dictators possessed a practical monopoly over mass communications. Through armies, police forces, and party discipline, they also monopolized terror and coercive power. They could propagandize large populations and compel people to obey them and their followers. Finally, as a result of the second Industrial Revolution, they commanded a vast amount of technology and a capacity for immense destruction. Earlier rulers in Europe may have shared the ruthless ambitions of Hitler, Mussolini, and Stalin, but they had lacked the ready implements of physical force to impose their wills.

Mass political support, the monopoly of police and military power, and technological capacity meant the dictators of the 1930s held more extensive sway over their nations than any other group of rulers who had ever governed on the Continent. Soon the issue would become whether they would be able to maintain peace among themselves and with their democratic neighbors.

AP* TEST PREP

1. Nikolai Bukharin and the right wing of the Communist Party favored
   a. a quick end to the NEP.
   b. relatively slow industrialization.
   c. declaring war on Germany.
   d. pardoning the leaders of the White Russian Army.
   e. total focus on heavy industry.

2. The Bolshevik revolution can be characterized as
   a. a mass movement.
   b. a nationalistic movement.
   c. an industrial movement.
   d. a world historical movement.
   e. a peasant movement.

3. While the term "fascism" is still under dispute, the governments regarded as fascist were all of the following *except*
   a. antiliberal.
   b. anti-Marxist.
   c. antiparliamentary.
   d. anti-small business.
   e. anti-class conflict.

4. Through the Lateran Accord of 1929, Mussolini made peace with
   a. Austria.
   b. Germany.
   c. France.
   d. the Roman Catholic Church.
   e. Greece.

5. The Irish national uprising on Easter Monday 1916
   a. was the only rebellion of a national group against any government in World War I.
   b. was inspired by the national uprising of Hindus in India at the same time.
   c. inspired the Slovaks to rebel against the Czech-controlled government that same year.
   d. ended all emigration to the United States.
   e. concluded with Irish representation at Westminster.

6. The era of reparations came to an end in 1932 as a result of the
   a. Young Conference.
   b. Dawes Conference.
   c. Lausanne Conference.
   d. Kellogg-Briand Conference.
   e. Hoover Plan.

7. The only central European successor state *not* to eventually adopt a self-imposed authoritarian government was
   a. Poland.
   b. Hungary.
   c. Austria.
   d. Germany.
   e. Czechoslovakia.

8. In the 1920s, the effect of worldwide improved wheat farming was
   a. higher wheat prices.
   b. reduced wheat production.
   c. lower cost of industrial goods needed by farmers.
   d. cheaper mortgages so farmers could obtain more land.
   e. decreased agricultural revenues.

9. The Weimar Republic gained stability and self-confidence under the leadership of
   a. Ebert.
   b. Lueger.
   c. Ludendorff.
   d. Stresemann.
   e. Karlstein.

10. A new spirit of hope was brought to Europe by the
    a. Locarno Agreements.
    b. Concord Cordial.
    c. Franco-German Accord.
    d. Briand Agreements.
    e. entry of the United States into the League of Nations.

11. The difficulties of the Great Depression included all of the following *except*
    a. shrinking trade.
    b. colonial independence.
    c. financial instability.
    d. low production.
    e. high unemployment.

12. Which of the following is the most accurate statement about Mussolini?
    a. He was always a nationalist.
    b. He was always a socialist.
    c. He was originally a socialist and became a nationalist during World War I.
    d. He always put the nation before himself.
    e. His political beliefs were animated by anti-Semitism.

13. The Nuremburg laws
    a. gave Hitler unlimited authority.
    b. stripped German Jews of their citizenship.
    c. repudiated reparations.
    d. nullified all of Germany's international treaties.
    e. were strongly opposed by the Nazis.

14. France's Popular Front was a coalition of
    a. right-wing parties.
    b. left-wing parties.
    c. fascists and religious conservatives.
    d. communists and anarchists.
    e. women's groups.

15. Hitler's rise to power was largely the result of
    a. the Nazi party majority in the Reichstag.
    b. a conspiracy of business elites.
    c. lower-middle-class support.
    d. miscalculations by political elites.
    e. Hitler's personal charisma.

16. By late 1921, it was clear only _____ remained loyal to the Dictatorship of the Proletariat.
    a. White Russians
    b. Peasants
    c. *Kulaks*
    d. Proletarians
    e. Bolsheviks

17. The 21 Conditions of the Comintern sought to destroy
    a. Fascism.
    b. Capitalism.
    c. Authoritarianism.
    d. Liberalism.
    e. Democratic Socialism.

18. Stalin's rise to power depended on his
    a. allegiance to Trotsky.
    b. allegiance to Bukharin.
    c. ideological purity.
    d. advocacy of industrialization.
    e. command of the bureaucracy.

19. On what constitutional basis did Hitler issue an Emergency Decree suspending civil liberties?
    a. Article 48
    b. The Hindenburg rule
    c. *Schutzstaffel*
    d. Enabling Act
    e. *Wehrmacht*

20. Gosplan oversaw
    a. the purges of Stalin's enemies.
    b. all Soviet military efforts.
    c. the entire Soviet economy.
    d. the expansion of the Soviet bureaucracy.
    e. the Soviet secret police.

DOCUMENT-BASED QUESTION

Directions: Construct a valid essay that directly addresses the central issue of the following question. Use facts from the documents provided and from the chapter to prove the position you take in your thesis statement.

What were the most important themes of Nazi propaganda? Why did so many Germans find the Nazi message so appealing?

Document A

Source: Joseph Goebbels outlines the key tenets of the Nazis, "Nationalists, Socialists, and Jews."

WHY ARE WE NATIONALISTS?

We are NATIONALISTS because we see in the NATION the only possibility for the protection of the people and the furtherance of our existence. . . .

WE ARE NATIONALISTS BECAUSE WE, AS GERMANS, LOVE GERMANY. And because we love Germany, we demand the protection of the national spirit and we battle against its destroyers.

WHY ARE WE SOCIALISTS?

We are SOCIALISTS because we see in SOCIALISM the only possibility for maintaining our racial existence and through it the reconquest of our political freedom and the rebirth of the German state.

WHY DO WE OPPOSE THE JEWS?

We are ENEMIES OF THE JEWS, because we are fighters for the freedom of the German people. THE JEW IS THE CAUSE AND THE BENEFICIARY OF OUR MISERY.

Document B

Source: A Nazi propaganda message, "Free Germany!"

HITLER is the password of all who believe in Germany's resurrection.

HITLER is the last hope of those who were deprived of everything. . . .

HITLER is the word of deliverance for millions....

HITLER was bequeathed the legacy of two million dead comrades of the World War....

HITLER is the man of the people hated by the enemy because he understands the people and fights for the people.

HITLER is the furious will of Germany's youth. . . . Hence Hitler is the password and the flaming signal of all who wish for a German future.

Document C

Nazi party rally.

Document D

Nazi harassment of German Jewish businesses.

For more on Germany in the 1920s and 1930s, see pages
881–895 of this chapter.

In August 1945, the United States exploded atomic bombs on the Japanese cities of Hiroshima and Nagasaki. A week later Japan surrendered. Without the bombs the United States would almost certainly have had to invade Japan, and tens of thousands of Americans would have been killed. Still, the decision to use the bomb remains controversial.   © CORBIS

28
World War II

KEY TOPICS

• **The origins of World War II**

• **The course of the war**

• **Racism and the Holocaust**

• **The impact of the war on the people of Europe**

• **Relationships among the victorious allies and the preparations for peace**

T HE MORE IDEALISTIC survivors of World War I, especially in the United States and Great Britain, thought of it as "the war to end all wars" and a war "to make the world safe for democracy." Only thus could they justify the slaughter, expense, and upheaval of that terrible conflict. How appalled they would have been had they known that only twenty years after the peace treaties a second great war would break out, more global than the first. In this war, the democracies would be fighting for their lives against militaristic, nationalistic, authoritarian, and totalitarian states in Europe and Asia, and they would be allied with the communist Soviet Union in the struggle. The defeat of the militarists and dictators would not bring the peace they longed for, but the Cold War, in which the European states would become powers of the second class, subordinate to two new superpowers, partially or fully non-European: the Soviet Union and the United States.

▼ Again the Road to War (1933–1939)

World War I and the Versailles treaty had only a marginal relationship to the world depression of the 1930s. In Germany, however, where the reparations settlement had contributed to the vast inflation of 1923, economic and social discontent focused on the Versailles settlement as the cause of all ills. Throughout the late 1920s, Adolf Hitler and the Nazi Party denounced Versailles as the source of all of Germany's troubles. The economic woes of the early 1930s seemed to bear them out. Nationalism and attention to the social question, along with party discipline, had been the sources of Nazi success. They continued to influence Hitler's foreign policy after he became chancellor in January 1933. Moreover, the Nazi destruction of the Weimar constitution and of political opposition meant that Hitler himself totally dominated German foreign policy. Consequently, it is important to know what his goals were and how he planned to achieve them.

Hitler's Goals

From the first expression of his goals in a book written in jail, *Mein Kampf (My Struggle)*, to his last days in the underground bunker in Berlin where he killed himself, Hitler's racial theories and goals were at the center of his thought. He meant to go far beyond Germany's 1914 boundaries, which were the limit of the vision of his predecessors. He meant to bring the entire German people—the *Volk*—understood as a racial group, together into a single nation.

The new Germany would include all the Germanic parts of the old Habsburg Empire, including Austria. This virile and growing nation would need more space to live, or **Lebensraum**, that would be taken from the Slavs, who, according to Nazi theory, were a lesser race, fit only for servitude. The removal of the Jews, another inferior race according to Nazi theory, would purify the new Germany. The plans required the conquest of Poland and Ukraine as the primary areas for German settlement and for providing badly needed food. Neither *Mein Kampf* nor later statements of policy were blueprints for action. Rather, Hitler was a brilliant improviser who exploited opportunities as they arose. He never lost sight of his goal, however, which would almost certainly require a major war. (See "Hitler Describes His Goals in Foreign Policy.")

Germany Rearms When Hitler came to power, Germany was far too weak to permit a direct approach to reach his aims. The first problem he set out to resolve was to shake off the fetters of Versailles and to make Germany a formidable military power. In October 1933, Germany withdrew from an international disarmament conference and also from the League of Nations. Hitler argued that because the other powers had not disarmed as they had promised, it was wrong to keep Germany helpless. These acts alarmed the French but were merely symbolic. In January 1934, Germany signed a nonaggression pact with Poland that was of greater concern to France, for it undermined France's chief means of containing the Germans. At last, in March 1935, Hitler formally renounced the disarmament provisions of the Versailles treaty with the formation of a German air force, and soon he reinstated conscription, which aimed at an army of half a million men.

The League of Nations Fails Growing evidence that the League of Nations could not keep the peace and that collective security was a myth made Hitler's path easier. In September 1931, Japan occupied Manchuria. China appealed to the League of Nations. The league dispatched a commission under a British diplomat, the earl of Lytton (1876–1951). The *Lytton Report* condemned the Japanese for resorting to force, but the powers were unwilling to impose sanctions. Japan withdrew from the League and kept control of Manchuria.

When Hitler announced his decision to rearm Germany, the League formally condemned that action, but it took no steps to prevent it. France and Britain felt unable to object forcefully because they had not carried out their own promises to disarm. Instead, they met with Mussolini in June 1935 to form the so-called Stresa Front, promising to use force to maintain the status quo in Europe. This show of unity was short-lived, however. Britain, desperate to maintain superiority at sea, violated the spirit of the Stresa accords and sacrificed French security needs to make a separate naval agreement with Hitler. The pact allowed him to rebuild the German fleet to 35 percent of the British navy. Hitler had taken a major step toward his goal without provoking serious opposition. Italy's expansionist ambitions in Africa, however, soon brought it into conflict with the Western powers.

Italy Attacks Ethiopia

In October 1935, Mussolini, using a border incident as an excuse, attacked Ethiopia. This attack made the impotence of the League of Nations and the timidity of the Allies clear. Mussolini's purposes were to avenge a humiliating defeat that the Italians had suffered in Ethiopia in 1896, to restore Roman imperial glory, and, perhaps, to distract Italian public opinion from domestic problems.

France and Britain were eager to appease Mussolini to offset the growing power of Germany. They were prepared to allow him the substance of conquest if he would maintain Ethiopia's formal independence. For Mussolini, however, the form was more important than the substance. His attack outraged opinion in the West, and the French and British governments were forced to at least appear to resist.

HITLER DESCRIBES HIS GOALS IN FOREIGN POLICY

From his early career, Hitler had certain long-term general views and goals. They were set forth in his Mein Kampf (My Struggle), *which appeared in 1925 and called for uniting the German* Volk *(people), more land for the Germans, and contempt for such "races" as Slavs and Jews. Here are some of Hitler's views about land.*

On what basic principle is Hitler's policy founded? How does he justify his plans for expansion? Why is he hostile to France and Russia? Why does Hitler claim every man has a right to own farmland? Was that a practical goal for Germany in the 1930s? Could Hitler have achieved his goals without a major war?

The National Socialist movement must strive to eliminate the disproportion between our population and our area—viewing this latter as a source of food as well as a basis for power politics—between our historical past and the hopelessness of our present impotence. . . .

The demand for restoration of the frontiers of 1914 is a political absurdity of such proportions and consequences as to make it seem a crime—quite aside from the fact that the Reich's frontiers in 1914 were anything but logical. For in reality they were neither complete in the sense of embracing the people of German nationality, nor sensible with regard to geomilitary expediency. . . .

As opposed to this, we National Socialists must hold unflinchingly to our aim in foreign policy, namely, to secure for the German people the land and soil to which they are entitled on this earth. . . .

The soil on which some day German generations of peasants can beget powerful sons will sanction the investment of the sons of today, and will some day acquit the responsible statesmen of blood-guilt and sacrifice of the people, even if they are persecuted by their contemporaries. . . .

Much as all of us today recognize the necessity of a reckoning with France, it would remain ineffectual in the long run if it represented the whole of our aim in foreign policy. It can and will achieve meaning only if it offers the rear cover for an enlargement of our people's living space in Europe. . . .

If we speak of soil in Europe today, we can primarily have in mind only Russia and her vassal border states. . . .

See to it that the strength of our nation is founded, not on colonies, but on the soil of our European homeland. Never regard the Reich as secure unless for centuries to come it can give every scion of our people his own parcel of soil. Never forget that the most sacred right on this earth is a man's right to have earth to till with his own hands, and the most sacred sacrifice the blood that a man sheds for this earth.

The League of Nations condemned Italian aggression and, for the first time, voted economic sanctions. It imposed an arms embargo that limited loans and credits to, and imports from, Italy. To avoid alienating Mussolini, however, Britain and France refused to embargo oil, the one economic sanction that could have prevented Italian victory. Even more important, Britain allowed Italian troops and munitions to reach Ethiopia through the Suez Canal. The results of this policy were disastrous. The League of Nations and collective security were discredited, and Mussolini was alienated. He now turned to Germany, and by November 1, 1936, he spoke publicly of a Rome-Berlin **Axis**.

Remilitarization of the Rhineland

The Ethiopian affair also convinced Hitler that the Western powers were too timid to oppose him forcefully. On March 7, 1936, he took his greatest risk yet, sending a small armed force into the demilitarized Rhineland. This was a breach not only of the Versailles treaty, but also of the Locarno Agreements of 1925—agreements Germany had made voluntarily. It also removed a crucial element of French security. France and Britain had every right to resist, and the French especially had a claim to retain the only element of security left to them after the failure of the Allies to guarantee France's defense. Yet neither

This poster supports General Francisco Franco's Nationalists in the bloody Spanish Civil War, which lasted almost three years and claimed hundreds of thousands of lives. Courtesy of the Library of Congress

German force in the Rhineland. As the German general Alfred Jodl (1890–1946) said some years later, "The French covering army would have blown us to bits."[1]

A Germany that was rapidly rearming and had a defensible western frontier presented a completely new problem to the Western powers. Their response was the policy of **appeasement**, based on the assumption that Germany had real grievances and that Hitler's goals were limited and ultimately acceptable. They set out to negotiate and make concessions before a crisis could lead to war.

Behind this approach was the universal dread of another war. Memories of the horrors of the last war were still vivid, and the prospect of aerial bombardment made the thought of a new war even more terrifying. A firmer policy, moreover, would have required rapid rearmament. British leaders especially were reluctant to pursue this path because of the expense and the widespread belief that the arms race had been a major cause of the last war. As Germany armed, the French huddled behind their newly constructed defensive wall, the Maginot Line, and the British hoped for the best.

The Spanish Civil War

The Spanish Civil War, which broke out in July 1936, made the new European alignment that found the Western democracies on one side and the fascist states on the other clearer. (See Map 28–1.) In 1931, the monarchy had collapsed, and Spain became a democratic republic. The new government followed a program of moderate reform that antagonized landowners, the Catholic Church, nationalists, and conservatives without satisfying the demands of peasants, workers, Catalán separatists, or radicals. Elections in February 1936 brought to power a Spanish Popular Front government ranging from republicans of the left to communists and anarchists. The losers, especially the Falangists, the Spanish fascists, would not accept defeat at the polls. In July, General Francisco Franco (1892–1975) led an army from Spanish Morocco against the republic.

Thus began the Spanish Civil War, which lasted almost three years, cost hundreds of thousands of lives, and provided a training ground for World War II. Germany and Italy supported Franco with troops, airplanes,

power did anything but register a feeble protest with the League of Nations. British opinion would not permit support for France, and the French would not act alone. Internal division and a military doctrine that stressed defense and shunned the offensive paralyzed them. A growing pacifism further weakened both countries.

In retrospect, the Allies lost a great opportunity in the Rhineland to stop Hitler before he became a serious menace. The failure of his gamble, taken against his generals' advice, might have led to his overthrow; at the least, it would have made German expansion to the east dangerous if not impossible. Nor is there reason to doubt that the French army could easily have routed the tiny

[1]Quoted in W. L. Shirer, *The Collapse of the Third Republic* (New York: Simon & Schuster, 1969), p. 281.

Map 28–1 THE SPANISH CIVIL WAR, 1936–1939 The purple area on the map shows the large portion of Spain quickly overrun by Franco's insurgent armies during the first year of the war. In the next two years, progress came more slowly for the fascists as the war became a kind of international rehearsal for the coming World War II. Madrid's fall to Franco in the spring of 1939 had been preceded by that of Barcelona a few weeks earlier.

and supplies. The Soviet Union sent equipment and advisers to the republicans. Liberals and leftists from Europe and America volunteered to fight in the republican ranks against fascism.

The civil war, fought on blatantly ideological lines, profoundly affected world politics. It brought Germany and Italy closer together, leading to the Rome-Berlin Axis Pact in 1936. Japan joined the Axis powers in the Anti-Comintern Pact, ostensibly directed against international communism, but really a new and powerful diplomatic alliance. Western Europe, especially France, had a great interest in preventing Spain from falling into the hands of a fascist regime closely allied with Germany and Italy. Appeasement reigned, however. Al-

though international law permitted the sale of weapons and munitions to the legitimate republican government, France and Britain forbade the export of war materials to either side, and the United States passed new neutrality legislation to the same end. When Barcelona fell to Franco early in 1939, the fascists had won effective control of Spain.

Austria and Czechoslovakia

Hitler made good use of his new friendship with Mussolini. He had always planned to annex his native Austria. In 1934, the Nazi Party in Austria assassinated the prime minister and tried to seize power. Mussolini had not yet allied with Hitler and was suspicious of German intentions. He quickly moved an army to the Austrian border, thus preventing German intervention and causing the coup to fail.

In 1938, the new diplomatic situation encouraged Hitler to try again. He perhaps hoped to achieve his goal by propaganda, bullying, and threats, but Austrian chancellor Kurt von Schuschnigg (1897–1977) refused to be intimidated. Schuschnigg announced a plebiscite for March 13, in which the Austrian people themselves could decide whether to unite with Germany. To forestall the plebiscite, Hitler sent his army into Austria on March 12. To his relief, Mussolini did not object, and Hitler rode to Vienna amid the cheers of his Austrian sympathizers.

The **Anschluss**, or union of Germany and Austria, was another clear violation of Versailles. The treaty, however, was now a dead letter, and the West remained passive. The *Anschluss* had great strategic significance, however, because Germany now surrounded Czechoslovakia, one of the bulwarks of French security, on three sides.

In fact, the very existence of Czechoslovakia was an affront to Hitler. It was democratic and pro-Western; it had been created partly to check Germany and was allied both to France and to the Soviet Union. It also contained about 3.5 million Germans who lived in the Sudetenland, near the German border. These Germans had belonged to the dominant nationality group in the old Austro-Hungarian Empire and resented their new minority position. Supported by Hitler and led by Konrad Henlein (1898–1945), they made ever-increasing demands for privileges and autonomy within the Czech state. The Czechs made concessions, but Hitler really wanted to destroy Czechoslovakia. He told Henlein, "We must always demand so much that we can never be satisfied."[2]

As pressure mounted, the Czechs grew nervous. In May 1938, they received false rumors of an imminent attack by Germany and mobilized their army. The French, British, and Russians all warned they would support the Czechs. Hitler, who had not planned an attack at that time, was forced to publicly deny any designs on Czechoslovakia. The humiliation infuriated him, and he planned a military attack on the Czechs. The affair stiffened Czech resistance, but it frightened the French and British. The French, as had become the rule, deferred to British leadership. The British prime minister Neville Chamberlain (1869–1940) was determined not to allow Britain to go to war again. He pressed the Czechs to make concessions to Germany, but no concession was enough.

On September 12, 1938, Hitler made a provocative speech at the Nuremberg Nazi Party rally. His rhetoric led to rioting in the Sudetenland, and the Czechs declared martial law. German intervention seemed imminent. Chamberlain, aged sixty-nine, who had never

flown before, made three flights to Germany between September 15 and September 29 in an attempt to appease Hitler at Czech expense and thus to avoid war. At Hitler's mountain retreat, Berchtesgaden, on September 15, Chamberlain accepted the separation of the Sudetenland from Czechoslovakia, and he and the French premier, Edouard Daladier (1884–1970), forced the Czechs to agree by threatening to abandon them if they did not. A week later, Chamberlain flew yet again to Germany, only to find that Hitler had raised his demands. He wanted cession of the Sudetenland in three days and immediate occupation by the German army.

Munich

Chamberlain returned to England, and France and Britain prepared for war. At Chamberlain's request and at the last moment, Mussolini proposed a conference of Germany, Italy, France, and Britain. It met on September 29 at Munich. Hitler received almost everything he had demanded. (See Map 28–2.) The Sudetenland, the key to Czech security, became part of Germany, thus depriving the Czechs of any chance of self-defense. In return, Hitler agreed to spare the rest of Czechoslovakia. He promised, "I have no more territorial demands to make in Europe." Chamberlain returned to England with the Munich agreement and told a cheering crowd that he had brought "peace with honour. I believe it is peace for our time."

Even in the short run, the appeasement of Hitler at Munich was a failure. Czechoslovakia did not survive. Soon Poland and Hungary tore more territory from it, and the Slovaks demanded a state of their own. Finally, on March 15, 1939, Hitler broke his promise and occupied Prague, putting an end to the Czech state and to illusions that his only goal was to restore Germans to the Reich. Defenders of the appeasers have argued that their policy bought valuable time in which the West could prepare for war, but the appeasers themselves, who thought they were achieving peace, did not make that argument, nor does the evidence support it.

If the French and the British had been willing to attack Germany from the west while the Czechs fought in their own defense, their efforts might have been successful. High officers in the German army were opposed to Hitler's risky policies and might have overthrown him. Even failing such developments, a war begun in October 1938 would have forced Hitler to fight without the friendly neutrality and material assistance of the Soviet Union—and without the resources of Eastern Europe that became available to him as a result of appeasement and Soviet cooperation. If, moreover, the West ever had a chance of concluding an alliance with the Soviet Union against Hitler, the exclusion of the Russians from Munich and the appeasement policy

[2]Quoted in Alan Bullock, *Hitler, a Study in Tyranny* (New York: Harper & Row, 1962), p. 443.

MAP EXPLORATION

Interactive map: To explore this map further, go to
www.myhistorylab.com

CZECHOSLOVAKIA:
- Ceded to Germany, Munich Pact, 1938
- German Protectorate, 1939
- Nominally independent German satellite, 1939
- Acquired by Hungary, 1938–1939

POLAND:
- Annexed by Germany, 1939
- Occupied by Germany, 1939
- Annexed by U.S.S.R., 1939

Map 28–2 **PARTITIONS OF CZECHOSLOVAKIA AND POLAND, 1938–1939**   The immediate background of World War II is found in the complex international drama unfolding on Germany's eastern frontier in 1938 and 1939. Germany's expansion inevitably meant the victimization of Austria, Czechoslovakia, and Poland. With the failure of the Western powers' appeasement policy and the signing of a German-Soviet pact, the stage for the war was set.

helped destroy it. Munich remains an example of short-sighted policy that helped bring on war in disadvantageous circumstances because of the very fear of war and the failure to prepare for it. (See "Compare & Connect: The Munich Settlement," pages 908–909.)

Hitler's occupation of Prague discredited appeasement in Britain. In the summer of 1939, a Gallup poll showed that three quarters of the British public believed it was worth a war to stop Hitler. Though Chamberlain himself had not lost all faith in his policy, he felt he had to respond to public opinion, and he responded to excess.

Poland was the next target of German expansion. In the spring of 1939, the Germans put pressure on Poland to restore the formerly German city of Danzig and to allow a railroad and a highway through the Polish Corridor to connect East Prussia with the rest of Germany. When the Poles would not yield, the usual propaganda

campaign began, and the pressure mounted. On March 31, Chamberlain announced a Franco-British guarantee of Polish independence. Hitler appears to have expected to fight a war with Poland, but not with the Western allies, for he did not take their guarantee seriously. He had come to hold their leaders in contempt. He knew both countries were unprepared for war and that large segments of their populations opposed fighting for Poland.

Moreover, France and Britain had no means to get effective help to the Poles. The French, still dominated by the defensive mentality of the Maginot Line, had no intention of attacking Germany. The only way to defend Poland was to bring Russia into the alliance against Hitler, but a Russian alliance posed many problems. Each side was profoundly suspicious of the other. The French and the British were hostile to communism, and since Stalin's purge of the Red Army, they were skeptical of the

The Munich Settlement

ON SEPTEMBER 29–30, 1938, Germany's dictator Adolf Hitler met with the British prime minister Neville Chamberlain, Italy's dictator Benito Mussolini, and France's prime minister Edouard Daladier to settle the fate of Czechoslovakia. The Czechs were not permitted to take part. It was the height of the Western democracies' effort to appease the dictators and resulted in the partition of Czechoslovakia, and the region called the Sudetenland was handed over to Germany, leaving the Czechs without a viable defense. Although Hitler promised to stop there, he took over the rest of the country without firing a shot on March 15, 1939. The following documents present opposite views on the achievement at Munich.

QUESTIONS

1. Why did Chamberlain think the meeting at Munich was a success for Britain?

2. How would he defend his policy of appeasement?

3. What were Churchill's objections to the Munich agreement?

4. What critique would he make of the appeasement policy?

5. Who do you think was right? Why?

I. Chamberlain's Evaluation

The following is an account of Chamberlain's return to England the day after the conference. He was greeted like a hero at the airport by a big crowd. Later that day he stood outside Number 10 Downing Street where again he read from the document and declared that he had brought back "peace with honour. I believe it is peace for our time."

Various shots of Mrs Chamberlain waving and shaking hands with crowds around Downing Street who are offering their support. M/S as Chamberlain's aeroplane finishes its return journey after the conference, taxis and comes to a stop at Heston. M/S of newsreel cameras filming his return from a roof at the aerodrome. M/S as Chamberlain emerges smiling from the door of a British Airways aeroplane to the cheers of the crowd. He shakes hands with a man waiting for him. L/S of crowds watching.

C/U as he makes a speech on the airfield—"The settlement of the Czech problem, which has now been achieved, is, in my view only the prelude to a larger settlement in which all Europe may find peace" (people cheer at this). "This morning I had another talk with the German Chancellor Herr Hitler and here is the paper which bears his name upon it as well as mine" (he holds paper up and waves it about, people cheer again). "Some of you perhaps have already heard what it contains, but I would just like to read it to you." (He reads—'We, the German Fuhrer and Chancellor and the British Prime Minister, have had a further meeting today and are agreed in recognising that the question of Anglo-German relations is of the first importance for the two countries, and for Europe. We regard the agreement signed last night and the Anglo-German naval agreement, as symbolic of the desire of our two peoples never to go to war with one another again' (everyone cheers) 'We are resolved that the method of consultation shall be the method adopted' (lots of "hear hears") 'to deal with any other questions that may concern our two countries, and we are determined to continue our efforts to remove possible sources of difference and thus to contribute to assure the peace of Europe.'" Everyone cheers and someone shouts "three cheers for Chamberlain" which they all do as he walks away and gets into the car. Everyone waves as he drives away.

Various shots as his car drives through the crowds to Buckingham Palace, people wave as he passes. M/S as King George VI and Queen Elizabeth (later the Queen Mother) come out onto the balcony of the palace with Neville Chamberlain and his wife. L/S as they wave and crowds wave back. L/S of cars and people blocking the street outside the palace.

Source: British Pathe.com Peace Four Power Conference 983.14.

II. Churchill's Response to Munich

In the parliamentary debate that followed the Munich conference at the end of September 1938, Winston Churchill was one of the few critics of what had been accomplished. In the following selections from his speech, he expresses his concerns.

I will begin by saying what everybody would like to ignore or forget but which must nevertheless be stated, namely, that we have sustained a total and unmitigated defeat, and that France has suffered even more than we have . . . .

We really must not waste time after all this long debate upon the difference between the positions reached at Berchtesgaden, at Godesberg and at Munich. They can be very simply epitomized if the House will permit me to vary the metaphor. One pound was demanded at the pistol's point. When it was given, £2 were demanded at the pistol's point. Finally, the dictator consented to take £1 17s. 6d. and the rest in promises of good will for the future. . . .

All is over. Silent, mournful, abandoned, broken, Czechoslovakia recedes into the darkness. She has suffered in every respect by her association with the Western democracies and with the League of Nations, of which she has always been an obedient servant. . . .

We have been reduced in these five years from a position of security so overwhelming and so unchallengeable that we never cared to think about it. We have been reduced from a position where the very word "war" was considered one which could be used only by persons qualifying for a lunatic asylum. We have been reduced

from a position of safety and power—power to do good, power to be generous to a beaten foe, power to make terms with Germany, power to give her proper redress for her grievances, power to stop her arming if we chose, power to take any step in strength or mercy or justice which we thought right—reduced in five years from a position safe and unchallenged to where we stand now. . . .

The responsibility must rest with those who have had the undisputed control of our political affairs. They neither prevented Germany from rearming, nor did they rearm ourselves in time. They quarreled with Italy without saving Ethiopia. They exploited and discredited the vast institution of the League of Nations and they neglected to make alliances and combinations which might have repaired previous errors, and thus they left us in the hour of trial without adequate national defense or effective international security. . . .

We are in the presence of a disaster of the first magnitude which has befallen Great Britain and France. Do not let us blind ourselves to that. It must now be accepted that all the countries of Central and Eastern Europe will make the best terms they can with the triumphant Nazi power. The system of alliances in Central Europe upon which France has relied for her safety has been swept away, and I can see no means by which it can be reconstituted. The road down the Danube Valley to the Black Sea, the road which leads as far as Turkey, has been opened.

Source: "Churchill's Response to Munich" from *Blood, Sweat, and Tears* by Winston S. Churchill (New York: G.P. Putnam's Sons, 1941), pp. 55–56, 58, 60–61. Reproduced with permission of Curtis Brown Ltd., London on behalf of Winston S. Churchill. Copyright Winston S. Churchill. 1941.

Agreement at Munich. On September 29–30, 1938, Hitler met with the leaders of Britain and France at Munich to decide the fate of Czechoslovakia. The Allied leaders abandoned the small democratic nation in a vain attempt to appease Hitler and avoid war. From left to right in the foreground: British Prime Minister Neville Chamberlain, French Prime Minister Edouard Daladier, Adolf Hitler, Benito Mussolini, and Italian Minister of Foreign Affairs (and Mussolini's son-in-law), Count Ciano. National Archives and Records Administration military value of a Russian alliance. Besides, the Russians could not help Poland without being given the right to enter Poland and Romania. Both nations, suspicious of Russian intentions—and with good reason—refused to grant these rights. As a result, Western negotiations for an alliance with Russia made little progress.

The Nazi-Soviet Pact

The Russians had at least equally good reason to hesitate. They resented being left out of the Munich agreement. The low priority that the West gave to negotiations with Russia, compared with the urgency with which Britain and France dealt with Hitler, annoyed them. The Russians feared, rightly, that the Western powers meant them to bear the burden of the war against Germany. As a result, they opened negotiations with Hitler, and on August 23, 1939, the world was shocked to learn of a Nazi-Soviet nonaggression pact.

The secret provisions of the pact, which were easily guessed and soon carried out, divided Poland between the two powers and allowed Russia to occupy the Baltic states and to take Bessarabia from Romania. The most bitter ideological enemies had become allies. Communist parties in the West changed their line overnight from ardently advocating resistance to Hitler to a policy of peace and quiet. Ideology gave way to political and military reality. The West offered the Russians immediate danger without much prospect of gain. Hitler offered Stalin short-term gain without immediate danger. There could be little doubt about Stalin's decision.

The Nazi-Soviet pact sealed the fate of Poland, and the Franco-British commitment guaranteed a general war. On September 1, 1939, the Germans invaded Poland. Two days later, Britain and France declared war on Germany. World War II had begun.

▼ World War II (1939–1945)

World War II was truly global. Fighting took place in Europe, North Africa, and Asia, on the Atlantic and the Pacific Oceans, and in the northern and southern hemispheres. The demand for the fullest exploitation of material and human resources for increased production, the use of blockades, and the intensive bombing of civilian targets made the war of 1939 even more "total"— that is, comprehensive and intense—than that of 1914.

The German Conquest of Europe

The German attack on Poland produced swift success. The new style of "lightning warfare," or **blitzkrieg**, employed fast-moving, massed armored columns supported by airpower. The Poles had few planes and fewer

tanks, and their defense soon collapsed. The speed of the German victory astonished the Russians, who hastened to collect their share of the booty before Hitler could deprive them of it.

On September 17, Russia invaded Poland from the east, dividing the country with the Germans. The Red Army then occupied the encircled Baltic countries. By July 1940, Estonia, Latvia, and Lithuania had become puppet republics within the Soviet Union. In June 1940, the Russians forced Romania to cede Bessarabia. In November 1939, the Russians invaded Finland, but the Finns resisted fiercely for six months. Although they were finally worn down and compelled to yield territory and bases to Russia, the Finns remained independent. Russian expansionism and the poor performance of the Red Army in Finland may well have encouraged Hitler to invade the Soviet Union in June 1941, just twenty-two months after the 1939 treaty.

Until the spring of 1940, the western front was quiet. The French remained behind the Maginot Line while Hitler and Stalin swallowed Poland and the Baltic states. Britain rearmed hastily, and the British navy blockaded

THE COMING OF WORLD WAR II

1919 (June)	The Versailles Treaty
1923 (January)	France occupies the Ruhr
1925 (October)	The Locarno Agreements
1931 (Spring)	Onset of the Great Depression in Europe
1931 (September)	Japan occupies Manchuria
1933 (January)	Hitler comes to power
1933 (October)	Germany withdraws from the League of Nations
1935 (March)	Hitler renounces disarmament, starts an air force, and begins conscription
1935 (October)	Mussolini attacks Ethiopia
1936 (March)	Germany reoccupies and remilitarizes the Rhineland
1936 (July)	Outbreak of the Spanish Civil War
1936 (October)	Formation of the Rome-Berlin Axis
1938 (March)	*Anschluss* with Austria
1938 (September)	The Munich conference and the partition of Czechoslovakia
1939 (March)	Hitler occupies Prague; France and Great Britain guarantee Polish independence
1939 (August)	The Nazi-Soviet pact
1939 (September 1)	Germany invades Poland
1939 (September 3)	Britain and France declare war on Germany

Adolf Hitler receives news of Marshal Pétain's request for an armistice following the fall of Paris in June 1940.   National Archives and Records Administration

Germany. Cynics in the West called it the phony war, or *Sitzkrieg*, but Hitler shattered the stillness in the spring of 1940. In April, without warning and with swift success, the Germans invaded Denmark and Norway. Hitler's northern front was secure, and he now had both air and naval bases closer to Britain. A month later, a combined land and air attack struck Belgium, the Netherlands, and Luxembourg. German airpower and armored divisions were irresistible. The Dutch surrendered in a few days; the Belgians, though aided by the French and the British, gave up less than two weeks later.

The British and French armies in Belgium were forced to flee to the English Channel to seek escape on the beaches of Dunkirk. The heroic efforts of hundreds of Britons manning small boats saved more than 200,000 British and 100,000 French soldiers. Casualties, however, were high, and valuable equipment was abandoned.

The Maginot Line ran from Switzerland to the Belgian frontier. Until 1936, the French had expected the Belgians to continue the fortifications along their German border. After Hitler remilitarized the Rhineland without opposition, the Belgians lost faith in their French alliance and proclaimed their neutrality, leaving the Maginot Line exposed on its left flank. Hitler's swift advance through Belgium, therefore, circumvented France's main line of defense.

The French army, poorly and hesitantly led by aged generals who did not understand how to use tanks and planes, collapsed. Mussolini, eager to claim the spoils of victory when he thought it was safe to do so, invaded southern France on June 10. Less than a week later, the new French government, under the ancient hero of Verdun, Marshal Henri Philippe Pétain (1856–1951), asked for an armistice. In two months Hitler had accomplished what Germany had failed to achieve in four years of bitter fighting in the previous war.

The Battle of Britain

The fall of France left Britain isolated, and Hitler expected the British to come to terms. He was prepared to allow Britain to retain its empire in return for a free hand for Germany on the Continent. The British had never been willing to accept such an arrangement and had fought the long and difficult war against Napoleon to prevent a single power from dominating the Continent. If there was any chance the British would consider such terms, it disappeared when Winston Churchill (1874–1965) replaced Chamberlain as prime minister in May 1940.

Churchill had been an early and forceful critic of Hitler, the Nazis, and the policy of appeasement. He was a descendant and biographer of the duke of Marlborough

(1650–1722), who had fought Louis XIV in the eighteenth century. Churchill's sense of history, his feeling for British greatness, and his hatred of tyranny and love of freedom made him reject any compromise with Hitler. His skill as a speaker and a writer enabled him to inspire the British people with his own courage and determination and to undertake what seemed a hopeless fight. Hitler and his allies, including the Soviet Union, controlled all of Europe. Japan was having its way in Asia. The United States was neutral, dominated by isolationist sentiment, and determined to avoid involvement outside the western hemisphere.

One of Churchill's greatest achievements was establishing a close relationship with the American president Franklin D. Roosevelt (1882–1945). Roosevelt found ways to help the British despite strong political opposition. In 1940 and 1941, before the United States was at war, America sent military supplies, traded badly needed warships for leases on British naval bases, and even convoyed ships across the Atlantic to help the British survive.

As weeks passed and Britain remained defiant, Hitler was forced to contemplate an invasion, and that required control of the air. The first strikes by the German air force (**Luftwaffe**), directed against the airfields and fighter planes in southeast England, began in August 1940. If these attacks had continued, Germany might have gained control of the air and, with it, the chance of a successful invasion.

In early September, however, seeking revenge for some British bombing raids on German cities, the *Luftwaffe* switched its main attacks to London. For two months, it bombed London every night. Much of the city was destroyed, and about 15,000 people were killed. The theories of victory through airpower alone, however, proved false. Casualties were much fewer than expected,

and morale was not shattered. In fact, the bombings united the British people and made them more resolute.

The Royal Air Force (RAF) inflicted heavy losses on the *Luftwaffe*. Aided by the newly developed radar and excellent communications, the British Spitfire and Hurricane fighter planes destroyed more than twice as many enemy planes as the RAF lost. Hitler had lost the Battle of Britain in the air and was forced to abandon his plans for invasion.

The German Attack on Russia

The defeat of Russia and the conquest of the Ukraine to provide *Lebensraum*, or "living space," for the German people had always been a major goal for Hitler. Even before the assault on Britain, he had informed his staff of his intention to attack Russia as soon as conditions were favorable. In December 1940, even while the bombing of England continued, he ordered his generals to prepare to invade Russia by May 15, 1941. (See Map 28–3.) He apparently thought a *blitzkrieg* victory in the east would also destroy the British hope of resistance.

Operation Barbarossa, the code name for the invasion of Russia, was aimed to destroy Russia before winter could set in. Success depended, in part, on an early start, but here Hitler's Italian alliance proved costly. Mussolini was jealous of Hitler's success and annoyed by how the German dictator had treated him. His invasion of France was a fiasco, even though the Germans were simultaneously crushing the main French forces. Hitler did not allow Mussolini to annex French territory in Europe or North Africa. Mussolini instead attacked the British in Egypt and drove them back some sixty miles. Encouraged by this success, he also invaded Greece from his base in Albania (which he had seized in 1939). As he told his son-in-law, Count Ciano: "Hitler always faces me with a fait accompli. This time I am going to pay him back in his own coin. He will find out in the newspapers that I have occupied Greece."[3]

In North Africa, however, the British counterattacked and invaded Libya. The Greeks themselves pushed into Albania. In March 1941, the British sent help to the Greeks, and Hitler was forced to divert his attention to the Balkans and Africa. General Erwin Rommel (1891–1944), later to earn the title of "Desert Fox," went to Africa and soon drove the British back into Egypt. In the Balkans, the German army swiftly occupied Yugoslavia and crushed Greek resistance. The price, however, was a delay of six weeks. The diversion Mussolini's vanity caused proved to be costly the following winter in the Russian campaign.

Operation Barbarossa was launched against Russia on June 22, 1941, and it almost succeeded. Despite their

In August 1941, President Franklin Roosevelt and Prime Minister Winston Churchill met at sea and agreed on a broad program of liberal peace aims, called the Atlantic Charter, in the spirit of Woodrow Wilson's Fourteen Points (see page 933). The Granger Collection

[3]Quoted in Gordon Wright, *The Ordeal of Total War, 1939–1945* (New York: Harper & Row, 1968), pp. 35–36.

Map 28–3 AXIS EUROPE, 1941 On the eve of the German invasion of the Soviet Union, the Germany-Italy Axis bestrode most of Western Europe by annexation, occupation, or alliance—from Norway and Finland in the north to Greece in the south and from Poland to France. Britain, the Soviets, a number of insurgent groups, and, finally, America, had before them the long struggle of conquering this Axis "fortress Europe."

deep suspicion of Germany (and the excuse apologists for the Soviet Union later offered that the Nazi-Soviet pact was meant to give Russia time to prepare), the Russians were taken quite by surprise. Stalin appears to have panicked. He had not fortified his frontier, nor did he order his troops to withdraw when attacked. In the first two days, the Germans destroyed 2,000 Russian planes on the ground. By November, the German army stood at the gates of Leningrad, on the outskirts of Moscow, and on the Don River. Of the 4.5 million troops with which the Russians had begun the fighting,

they had lost 2.5 million; of their 15,000 tanks, only 700 were left. Moscow was in panic, and a German victory seemed imminent.

Yet the Germans could not deliver the final blow. In August, they delayed their advance while Hitler decided strategy. The German general staff wanted to take Moscow before winter. This plan probably would have brought victory. Unlike in Napoleon's time, Moscow was the hub of the Russian transportation system. Hitler, however, diverted a significant force to the south. By the time he was ready to return to the offensive near

Moscow, it was too late. Winter devastated the German army, which was not equipped to face it.

Given precious time, Stalin restored order and built defenses for the city. Even more importantly, troops arrived from Siberia, where they had been placed to check a possible Japanese attack. In November and December, the Russians counterattacked. The *blitzkrieg* had turned into a war of attrition, and the Germans began to have nightmares of duplicating Napoleon's retreat.

Hitler's Plans for Europe

Hitler often spoke of the "new order" that he meant to impose after he had established his **Third Reich** (empire) throughout Europe. The first two German empires were those of Charlemagne in the ninth century and Bismarck in the nineteenth. Hitler predicted that his own would last for a thousand years. If his organization of Germany before the war is a proper guide, he had no single plan of government but relied on intuition and pragmatism. His organization of a conquered Europe had the same patchwork characteristics. Some conquered territory was annexed to Germany, some was not annexed but administered directly by German officials, and other lands were nominally autonomous but ruled by puppet governments.

Hitler's regime was probably unmatched in history for carefully planned terror and inhumanity. His plan of giving *Lebensraum* to the Germans was to be accomplished at the expense of people he deemed to be inferior. Hitler established colonies of Germans in parts of Poland, driving the local people from their land and employing them as cheap, virtually slave labor. He had similar plans on an even greater scale for Russia. The Russians would be driven back to Central Asia and Siberia. Frontier colonies of German war veterans would keep them in check while Germans settled European Russia.

Hitler's long-range plans included germanization as well as colonization. In lands people racially akin to the Germans inhabited, like the Scandinavian countries, the Netherlands, and Switzerland, the German nation would absorb the natives. Such peoples would be reeducated and purged of dissenting elements, but there would be little or no colonization. Hitler even had plans to adopt selected people from the lesser races into the master race. For example, the Nazis planned to bring half a million Ukrainian girls to Germany as servants and find German husbands for them.

Hitler regarded the conquered lands as a source of plunder. From Eastern Europe, he removed everything useful, including entire industries. In Russia and Poland, the Germans simply confiscated the land itself. In the West, the conquered countries had to support the occupying army at a rate several times above the real cost. The Germans used the profits to buy up everything desirable, stripping the conquered peoples of most necessities. The Nazis were frank about their policies. One of Hitler's high officials said, "Whether nations live in prosperity or starve to death interests me only insofar as we need them as slaves for our culture."[4]

Japan and the United States Enter the War

The American government was pro-British. The assistance that Roosevelt gave Britain would have justified a German declaration of war. Hitler, however, held back. The U.S. government might not have overcome isolationist sentiment and entered the war in the Atlantic if war had not been thrust on America in the Pacific.

Since the Japanese conquest of Manchuria in 1931, American policy toward Japan had been suspicious and unfriendly. The outbreak of the war in Europe emboldened the Japanese to accelerate their drive to dominate Asia. They allied themselves with Germany and Italy, made a treaty of neutrality with the Soviet Union, and forced defeated France to give them bases in Indochina. They also continued their war in China and planned to gain control of Malaya and the East Indies (Indonesia) at the expense of beleaguered Britain and the conquered Netherlands. The only barrier to Japanese expansion was the United States.

The Americans had temporized, unwilling to cut off vital supplies of oil and other materials for fear of provoking a Japanese attack on Southeast Asia and the East Indies. The Japanese occupation of Indochina in July 1941 changed that policy, which had already begun to stiffen. The United States froze Japanese assets and cut off oil supplies; the British and Dutch did the same. Japanese plans for expansion could not continue without the conquest of the Indonesian oil fields and Malayan rubber and tin.

In October, a war faction led by General Hideki Tojo (1885–1948) took power in Japan and decided to risk a war rather than yield. On Sunday morning, December 7, 1941, while Japanese representatives were in Washington to discuss a settlement, Japan launched an air attack on Pearl Harbor, Hawaii, the chief American naval base in the Pacific. The technique was similar to the one Japan had used against the Russian fleet at Port Arthur in 1904, and it caught the Americans equally by surprise. The attack destroyed much of the American fleet and many airplanes. The American capacity to wage war in the Pacific was negated for the time being. The next day, the United States and Britain declared war on Japan. Three days later, Germany and Italy declared war on the United States.

---

[4]Quoted in Wright, *The Ordeal of Total War*, p. 117.

The successful Japanese attack on the American base at Pearl Harbor in Hawaii on December 7, 1941, together with simultaneous attacks on other Pacific bases, brought the United States into war against the Axis powers. This picture shows the battleships USS *West Virginia* and USS *Tennessee* in flames as a small boat rescues a man from the water.   U.S. Army Photo

The Tide Turns

The potential power of the United States was enormous, but America was ill prepared for war. The army was tiny, inexperienced, and poorly supplied. American industry was not ready for war. The Japanese swiftly captured Guam, Wake Island, and the Philippine Islands. By the spring of 1942, they had conquered Hong Kong, Malaya, Burma, and the Dutch East Indies. They controlled the southwest Pacific as far as New Guinea and were poised for an attack on Australia. It seemed that nothing could stop them.

In 1942, the Germans also advanced deeper into Russia, while in Africa Rommel drove the British back into Egypt until they stopped him at El Alamein, only seventy miles from Alexandria. Relations between the democracies and their Soviet ally were not close. German submarine warfare was threatening British sup-

plies. The Allies were being thrown back on every front, and the future looked bleak.

The first good news for the Allied cause in the Pacific came in the spring of 1942. A naval battle in the Coral Sea sank many Japanese ships and gave security to Australia. A month later, the United States defeated the Japanese in a fierce air and naval battle off Midway Island. This victory blunted the chance of another assault on Hawaii and did enough damage to halt the Japanese advance. Soon American marines landed on Guadalcanal in the Solomon Islands and began to reverse the momentum of the war. The war in the Pacific was far from over, but the check to Japan allowed the Allies to concentrate their efforts on Europe.

More than twenty nations located all over the world were opposed to the Axis powers. The main combatants, however, were Great Britain, the Soviet Union, and the United States. The two Western democracies

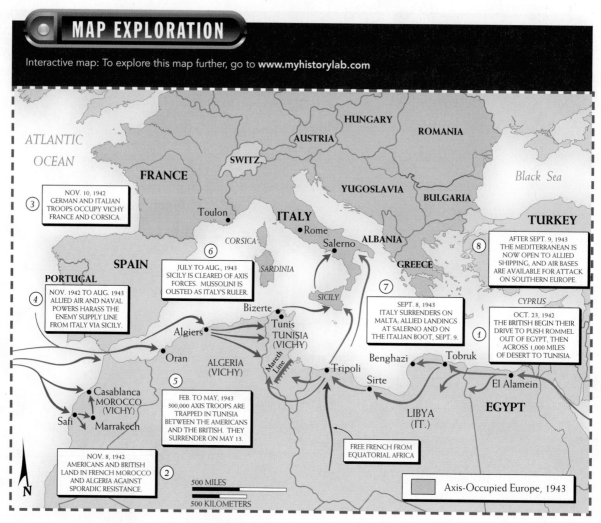

MAP EXPLORATION

Interactive map: To explore this map further, go to www.myhistorylab.com

3 NOV. 10, 1942 GERMAN AND ITALIAN TROOPS OCCUPY VICHY FRANCE AND CORSICA.

4 NOV. 1942 TO AUG. 1943 ALLIED AIR AND NAVAL POWERS HARASS THE ENEMY SUPPLY LINE FROM ITALY VIA SICILY.

6 JULY TO AUG., 1943 SICILY IS CLEARED OF AXIS FORCES. MUSSOLINI IS OUSTED AS ITALY'S RULER.

5 FEB. TO MAY, 1943 300,000 AXIS TROOPS ARE TRAPPED IN TUNISIA BETWEEN THE AMERICANS AND THE BRITISH. THEY SURRENDER ON MAY 13.

2 NOV. 8, 1942 AMERICANS AND BRITISH LAND IN FRENCH MOROCCO AND ALGERIA AGAINST SPORADIC RESISTANCE.

8 AFTER SEPT. 9, 1943 THE MEDITERRANEAN IS NOW OPEN TO ALLIED SHIPPING, AND AIR BASES ARE AVAILABLE FOR ATTACK ON SOUTHERN EUROPE.

7 SEPT. 8, 1943 ITALY SURRENDERS ON MALTA; ALLIED LANDINGS AT SALERNO AND ON THE ITALIAN BOOT, SEPT. 9.

1 OCT. 23, 1942 THE BRITISH BEGIN THEIR DRIVE TO PUSH ROMMEL OUT OF EGYPT, THEN ACROSS 1,000 MILES OF DESERT TO TUNISIA.

FREE FRENCH FROM EQUATORIAL AFRICA

500 MILES

500 KILOMETERS

Axis-Occupied Europe, 1943

Map 28–4 **NORTH AFRICAN CAMPAIGNS, 1942–1945** Control of North Africa would give the Allies access to Europe from the south. The map illustrates this theater of the war from Morocco to Egypt and the Suez Canal.

cooperated to an unprecedented degree, but suspicion between them and the Soviet Union continued. The Russians accepted all the aid they could get. Nevertheless, they did not trust their allies, complained of inadequate help, and demanded that the democracies open a "second front" on the mainland of Europe.

In 1942, American preparation and production were inadequate to invade Europe. German submarines made it dangerous to ship the vast numbers of troops such an invasion needed across the Atlantic. Not until 1944 were conditions right for the invasion, but in the meantime other developments forecast the doom of the Axis. (See "Encountering the Past: Rosie the Riveter and American Women in the War Effort.")

Allied Landings in Africa, Sicily, and Italy In November 1942, an Allied force landed in French North Africa. (See Map 28–4.) Even before that landing, after stopping Rommel at El Alamein, British field marshal Bernard Montgomery (1887–1976) had begun a drive to the west. Now, the Americans pushed eastward through

Morocco and Algeria. The two armies caught the German army between them in Tunisia and crushed it. The Allies now controlled the Mediterranean and could attack southern Europe.

In July and August 1943, the Allies took Sicily. A coup toppled Mussolini, but the Germans occupied Italy. The Allies landed in Italy, and Marshal Pietro Badoglio (1871–1956), the leader of the new Italian government, declared war on Germany. Churchill had spoken of Italy as the "soft underbelly" of the Axis, but the Germans there resisted fiercely. Still, the need to defend Italy weakened the Germans on other fronts.

Battle of Stalingrad The Russian campaign became especially demanding. In the summer of 1942, the Germans resumed the offensive on all fronts but were unable to get far except in the south. (See Map 28–5, page 918.) Their goal was the oil fields near the Caspian Sea. Stalingrad, on the Volga, was a key point on the flank of the German army in the south. Hitler was determined to take the city, and Stalin was equally

ROSIE THE RIVETER AND AMERICAN WOMEN IN THE WAR EFFORT

THE INDUCTION OF millions of men into the armed forces created a demand for new workers, especially in the defense industries. In response, millions of women entered the labor force, some of them taking jobs in defense plants to do work only men usually did. Economic pressures caused by the Great Depression of the 1930s had already brought many more women into the workforce than had been common before. Most came from poor families and worked in white-collar jobs to support themselves or to help their families eke out a living. Even so, the heavy burden of housework and the widespread hostility to women working outside the home kept most women at home.

America's entry into the war changed things quickly. The need for vast amounts of equipment to wage the war called for and attracted new groups to seek work in the many enlarged and new factories. African Americans from the south came to northern and western cities to seek well-paying jobs, and women, too, came forward in greater numbers than ever before. Prejudices of various kinds had kept them from many opportunities, but the needs of war were too important. In October 1942, President Roosevelt made the new situation clear: "In some communities employers dislike to hire women. In others they are reluctant to hire Negroes. We can no longer afford to indulge such prejudice."

Many women changed jobs to work in the defense industries; others entered the workforce for the first time, lured less by wages than by patriotism. Their brothers and boyfriends were risking their lives for their country and its ideals of freedom and democracy. They were eager to do their part to support them, to be, in the words of a current song, the woman "behind the man behind the gun." Another popular song, "Rosie the Riveter," told of a young woman working in an aircraft factory to provide protection for her boyfriend in the Marines. Rosie became one of the best known symbols of the war effort when she appeared on the cover of the *Saturday Evening Post* in a painting by Norman Rockwell. With her rivet gun on her lap she stamps on a copy of Hitler's *Mein Kampf*, the hated symbol of the evil enemy.

How did the war change women's place in American society?

What attitudes did it need to overcome?

Rosie the Riveter was one of the best known symbols of the U.S. war effort in World War II. Printed by permission of the Norman Rockwell Family Agency. Copyright © 1943 the Norman Rockwell Family Entities

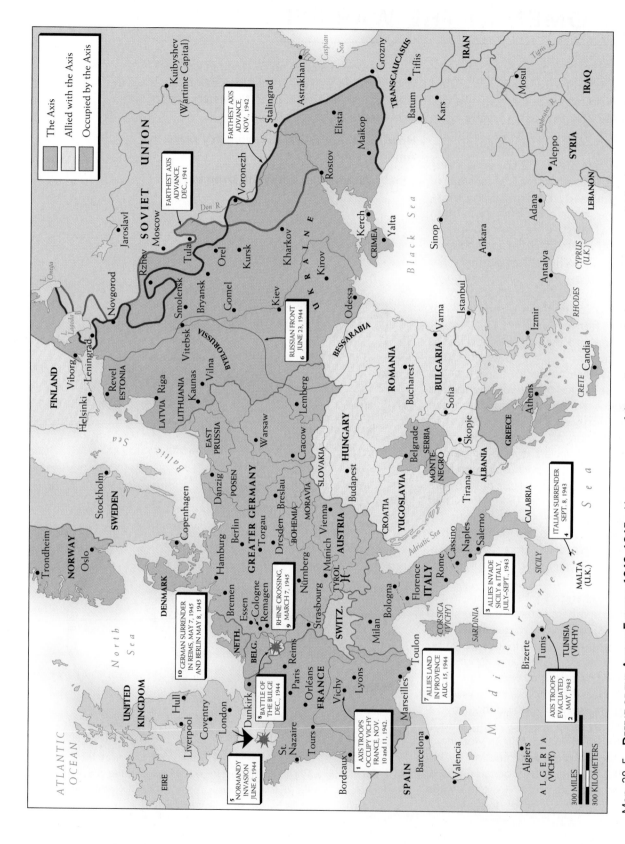

Map 28-5 DEFEAT OF THE AXIS IN EUROPE, 1942–1945 Here are some of the major steps in the progress toward Allied victory against Axis Europe. From the south through Italy, the west through France, and the east through Russia, the Allies gradually conquered the Continent to bring the war in Europe to a close.

The Axis

Allied with the Axis

Occupied by the Axis

FARTHEST AXIS ADVANCE, NOV., 1942

FARTHEST AXIS ADVANCE, DEC., 1941

6 RUSSIAN FRONT JUNE 23, 1944

4 ITALIAN SURRENDER SEPT. 8, 1943

10 GERMAN SURRENDER IN REIMS, MAY 7, 1945 AND BERLIN MAY 8, 1945

RHINE CROSSING, 9 MARCH 7, 1945

3 ALLIES INVADE SICILY & ITALY, JULY–SEPT. 1943

7 ALLIES LAND IN PROVENCE AUG. 15, 1944

8 BATTLE OF THE BULGE DEC., 1944

1 AXIS TROOPS OCCUPY VICHY FRANCE, NOV. 10 and 11, 1942.

5 NORMANDY INVASION JUNE 6, 1944

2 AXIS TROOPS EVACUATED, MAY, 1943

300 MILES

300 KILOMETERS

In the battle of Stalingrad, Russian troops contested every street and building. Although the city was all but destroyed in the fighting and Russian casualties were enormous, the German army in the east never recovered from the defeat it suffered there.   Hulton Archives/Getty Images, Inc.

determined to hold it. The Battle of Stalingrad raged for months with unexampled ferocity. The Russians lost more men in this one battle than the Americans lost in combat during the entire war, but their heroic defense prevailed. Because Hitler again overruled his generals and would not allow a retreat, he lost an entire German army at Stalingrad.

Stalingrad marked the turning point of the Russian campaign. Thereafter, the Americans provided material help. Even more importantly, increased production from their own industry allowed the Russians to gain and keep the offensive. As the Germans' resources dwindled, the Russians inexorably advanced westward.

Strategic Bombing In 1943, the Allies also gained ground in production and logistics. The industrial might of the United States began to come into full force, and new technology and tactics reduced the submarine menace.

In the same year, the American and British air forces began a series of massive bombardments of Germany by night and day. The Americans were more committed to the theory of "precision bombing" of military and industrial targets vital to the enemy war effort, so they flew the day missions. The British considered precision bombing impossible and therefore useless. They preferred indiscriminate "area bombing," which they could do at night, to destroy the morale of the German people. Neither kind of bombing had much effect on the war until 1944, when the Americans introduced long-range fighters

that could protect the bombers and allow accurate missions by day.

By 1945, the Allies could bomb at will. Concentrated attacks on industrial targets, especially communication centers and oil refineries, did extensive damage and helped shorten the war. Terror bombing continued, too, with no useful result. The bombardment of Dresden in February 1945 was especially savage and destructive. It was much debated within the British government and has raised moral questions since. Whatever else it accomplished, the aerial war over Germany took a heavy toll of the German air force and diverted German resources from other military purposes.

The Defeat of Nazi Germany

On June 6, 1944 ("D-Day"), American, British, and Canadian troops landed in force on the coast of Normandy. The "second front" was opened. General Dwight D. Eisenhower (1890–1969), the commander of the Allied armies, faced a difficult problem. The European coast was heavily fortified. Amphibious assaults, moreover, are especially vulnerable to wind and weather. Success depended on meticulous planning, heavy bombing, and feints to mask the point of attack. The German defense was strong, but the Allies established a beachhead and then broke out of it. In mid-August, the Allies also landed in southern France. By the beginning of September, France had been liberated.

The Battle of the Bulge All went smoothly until December, when the Germans launched a counterattack in Belgium and Luxembourg through the Ardennes Forest. Because the Germans pushed forward into the Allied line, this was called the Battle of the Bulge. Although the Allies suffered heavy losses, the Bulge was the last gasp for the Germans in the West. The Allies crossed the Rhine in March 1945, and German resistance crumbled. This time there could be no doubt the Germans had lost the war on the battlefield.

The Capture of Berlin In the east, the Russians swept forward no less swiftly, despite fierce German resistance. By March 1945, they were near Berlin. Because the Allies insisted on unconditional surrender, the Germans fought on until May. Hitler committed suicide in an underground bunker in Berlin on April 30, 1945. The Russians occupied Berlin by agreement with their Western allies. The Third Reich lasted only a dozen years instead of the thousand Hitler had predicted.

American soldiers land at Omaha Beach in Normandy on D-Day, June 6, 1944. Courtesy of the Library of Congress

Fall of the Japanese Empire

The war in Europe ended on May 8, 1945, and by then, victory over Japan was also in sight. The original Japanese attack on the United States had been a calculated risk against the odds. Japan was inherently weaker than the United States. The longer the war lasted, the more American superiority in industrial production and population counted.

Americans Recapture the Pacific Islands In 1943, the American forces, still small in number, began a campaign of "island hopping." They did not try to recapture every Pacific island the Japanese held but selected major bases and strategic sites along the enemy supply line. (See Map 28–6.) Starting from the Solomon Islands, they moved northeast toward Japan itself. By June 1944, they had reached the Mariana Islands, usable as bases to bomb the Japanese in the Philippines, China, and Japan itself.

In October of the same year, the Americans recaptured most of the Philippines and drove the Japanese fleet back into its home waters. In 1945, Iwo Jima and Okinawa fell, despite fierce Japanese resistance that included

kamikaze attacks, suicide missions in which pilots deliberately flew their explosive-filled planes into American warships. From these new bases, closer to Japan, the Americans launched a terrible wave of bombings that destroyed Japanese industry and disabled the Japanese navy. Still the Japanese government, dominated by a military clique, refused to surrender.

Confronted with Japan's determination, the Americans made plans for a frontal assault on the Japanese homeland. They calculated it might cost a million American casualties and even greater losses for the Japanese. At this point, science and technology presented the Americans with another choice.

The Atomic Bomb Since early in the war, a secret program had been in progress. Its staff, many of whom were exiles from Hitler's Europe, was working to use atomic energy for military purposes. On August 6, 1945, an American plane dropped an atomic bomb on the Japanese city of Hiroshima. The city was destroyed, and more than 70,000 of its 200,000 residents were killed. Two days later, the Soviet Union declared war on Japan and invaded Manchuria. The next day, a

Map 28–6 **WORLD WAR II IN THE PACIFIC**   As in Europe, the Pacific war involved Allied recapture of areas that had been quickly taken earlier by the enemy. The enormous area represented by the map shows the initial expansion of Japanese holdings to cover half the Pacific and its islands, as well as huge sections of eastern Asia, and the long struggle to push the Japanese back to their homeland and defeat them by the summer of 1945.

second atomic bomb hit Nagasaki. Even then, the Japanese cabinet was prepared to face an invasion rather than give up.

The unprecedented intervention of Emperor Hirohito (r. 1926–1989) finally forced the government to surrender on August 14 on the condition that Japan retain the emperor. Although the Allies had continued to insist on unconditional surrender, President Harry S. Truman (1884–1972), who had come to office on April 12, 1945, on the death of Franklin D. Roosevelt, accepted the condition. Peace was formally signed aboard the USS *Missouri* in Tokyo Bay on September 2, 1945.

Revulsion at the use of atomic bombs, as well as hindsight arising from the Cold War, have made the decision to use the bomb against Japanese cities controversial. Some have suggested the bombings were unnecessary to win the

war and their main purpose was to frighten the Russians into a more cooperative attitude after the war. Others have emphasized the bureaucratic, almost automatic nature of the decision, once it had been decided to develop the bomb. To the decision makers and their contemporaries, however, matters were simpler. The bomb was a way to end the war swiftly and save American lives. The decision to use it was conscious, not automatic, and required no ulterior motive.

The Cost of War

World War II was the most terrible war in history. Military deaths are estimated at some 15 million, and at least as many civilians were killed. If we include deaths linked indirectly to the war, from disease, hunger, and other causes, the number of victims might reach 40 million. Most of Europe and large parts of Asia were devastated. Yet the end of so terrible a war brought little opportunity to relax. The dawn of the atomic age made people conscious that another major war might extinguish humanity. Everything depended on concluding a stable peace, but even as the fighting ended, conflicts among the victors made the prospects of a lasting peace doubtful.

▼ Racism and the Holocaust

The most horrible aspect of the Nazi rule in Europe arose not from military or economic necessity but from the inhumanity and brutality inherent in Hitler's racial doctrines. These were applied to several groups of people in Eastern Europe.

Hitler considered the Slavs *Untermenschen*, subhuman creatures like beasts who need not be treated as people. In parts of Poland, the upper and professional classes were entirely removed—jailed, deported, or killed. Schools and churches were closed. The Nazis limited marriage to keep down the Polish birthrate and imposed harsh living conditions.

In Russia, things were even worse. Hitler spoke of his Russian campaign as a war of extermination. Heinrich Himmler (1900–1945), head of Hitler's elite SS formations, planned to eliminate 30 million Slavs to make room for Germans; he formed extermination squads for this purpose. Six million Russian prisoners of war and deported civilians may have died under Nazi rule.

Hitler, however, had envisioned a special fate for the Jews. He meant to make all Europe *Judenrein*, or "free of Jews." For a time, he considered sending them to the island of Madagascar. Later, he arrived at the "final solution of the Jewish problem"—extermination. The Nazis built extermination camps in Germany and Poland and used the latest technology to achieve the most efficient means to kill millions of men, women, and children simply because they were Jews. (See "Mass Murder at

World War II resulted in the near-total destruction of the Jews of Europe, victims of the Holocaust spawned by Hitler's racial theories of the superiority and inferiority of particular ethnic groups. Hitler placed special emphasis on the need to exterminate the Jews, to whom he attributed particular wickedness. This picture shows Hungarian Jewish women, after "disinfection" and head shaving, marching to the concentration or death camp at Auschwitz-Birkenau, Poland. Library of Congress/Photo by Bernhard Walter; source: National Archives and Records Administration

Map 28–7 **THE HOLOCAUST** The Nazi policy of ethnic cleansing—targeting Jews, Gypsies, political dissidents, and "social deviants"—began with imprisoning them in concentration camps, but by 1943 the *Endlösung*, or Final Solution, called for the systematic extermination of "undersirables."

The Destruction of the Polish Jewish Community

A large Jewish community had dwelled within Poland for centuries, often in a climate of religious and cultural anti-Semitism. As a result of this anti-Semitism, Polish Jews had long lived in their own villages and later in their own urban neighborhoods. After the late-eighteenth-century partitions of Poland and the Congress of Vienna, most of Poland came under Russian rule. Through the policy of Official Nationalism (see Chapter 21), the nineteenth-century tsars identified loyalty to their government with membership in the Russian Orthodox Church. Other Christian groups, such as Lutherans and Roman Catholics, were often treated with suspicion. Jews were treated worse and were subject to a wide variety of discriminatory legislation. Polish Jews did not experience any of the forms of Jewish emancipation that occurred in Western Europe. (See Chapter 24.)

Language, food, dress, and place of residence as well as religion distinguished Jews from the rest of the Polish population, almost all of whom were Roman Catholics. Hebrew was the Polish Jews' chief written language, and Yiddish their primary spoken language. Many Jews, particularly older ones, wore distinctive dress. They ate food different from that of most Poles. Many Polish Jews also moved to cities, and Jews were regarded as an urban people in a predominantly rural nation. Moreover, Jews were among the poorest people in Poland, often working as self-employed merchants, peddlers, and craftspeople, or in industries, such as textiles, clothing, and paper, that other Poles identified as Jewish-dominated. Few Polish Jews belonged to trade unions. These conditions made them vulnerable during the economic turmoil of the 1920s and especially of the 1930s.

Polish Anti-Semitism Between the Wars

After the restoration of Poland following World War I, Polish leaders were divided about the role of Jews in Polish national life. Jozef Pilsudski (1867–1935), who dominated the interwar era, favored including Jews within the civic definition of the nation, and the constitution allowed Jews to participate in political life. After Pilsudski's death, political groups that equated citizenship with Polish ethnicity and embraced anti-Semitism came to the fore. Their ideology, no less than that of tsarist Russian Orthodoxy, defined Jews as outside the Polish nation.

Belsen," pages 924–925.) The most extensive destruction occurred in Eastern Europe and Russia, but the Nazis and their collaborators in occupied areas of Western Europe, including France, the Netherlands, Italy, and Belgium, also deported Jews from these nations to almost certain death in the east. Before the war was over, perhaps 6 million Jews had died in what has come to be called the **Holocaust**. Only about a million European Jews remained alive, most of them in pitiable condition. (See Map 28–7.)

It is difficult to comprehend the massive Nazi effort to eradicate the Jews of Europe. This destruction took different forms in different regions of the Continent. To explore this central event of twentieth-century European history, we examine the fate of the Polish Jewish community, which before the Second World War was the largest in Europe, consisting of 10 percent of Poland's population.

MASS MURDER AT BELSEN

■■

Hitler's calculated plan to wipe out Europe's Jews, along with millions of other people he considered undesirable for racial and other reasons, was not widely known during the war. Care was taken to keep the mass murders secret. Even when news of them leaked out, many people were reluctant to believe what they heard, and participants in the crimes were naturally not eager to talk about them. Kurt Gerstein, a colonel in the SS, was part of the apparatus of extermination. However, unlike most people involved and at great risk to himself, he tried to tell the world what was taking place. The following is an account of what he saw at the death camp at Belsen in 1942.

What were the reasons for Hitler's policy of exterminating millions of men, women, and children? Why did many Germans take part in the process? Why did so conscientious a man as Colonel Gerstein not resist?

A train arrived from Lemberg [Lvov]. There were forty-five cars containing 6,700 people, 1,450 of whom were already dead. Through the gratings on the windows, children could be seen peering out, terribly pale and frightened, their eyes filled with mortal dread . . . The train entered the station, and two hundred Ukrainians wrenched open the doors and drove the people out of the carriages with their leather whips. Instructions came through a large loudspeaker telling them to remove all their clothing, artificial limbs, glasses, etc. They were to hand over all objects of value at the counter . . . Shoes were to be carefully tied together, for otherwise no one would ever again have been able to find shoes belonging to each other in a pile that was a good eighty feet high. Then the women and girls were sent to the barber who, with two or three strokes of his scissors, cut off all their hair and dropped it into potato sacks. "That's for some special purpose or other on U-Boats, for packing or something like that," I was told by an SS-Unterscharfuhrer . . .

Then the column moved off. Headed by an extremely pretty young girl, they walked along the avenue, all naked, men, women, and children, with artificial limbs removed. I myself was stationed up on the ramp between the [gas] chambers with Captain Wirth.

No matter which political outlook dominated, discrimination against Jews existed throughout the culture and politics of interwar Poland. During those years, the Polish government, supported by spokesmen for the Polish Roman Catholic Church, pursued policies that were anti-Semitic. The Polish government nationalized the matches, salt, tobacco, and alcohol industries and then enacted legislation that discriminated against hiring Jews for these government monopolies. Other laws made it difficult for Jews to observe the Sabbath while keeping their jobs. Regulations requiring businesses to be closed on Sunday meant Jewish shops had to close two days of the week. By the late 1930s, as ethnic nationalism became stronger, the government required businesses to display their owners' names prominently, which made it easy for people to avoid Jewish shops. Because Jews were excluded from the civil service, they moved into law and medicine, which provoked further resentment.

The path of assimilation into the larger culture that many European Jewish leaders had advocated during the nineteenth century hit a dead end in Poland because many Poles refused to regard even secular, assimilated Jews as fellow Poles. Nonetheless, many Jews attempted to embrace the social practices, dress, and language of the Polish majority without actually expecting to be considered Polish. They saw themselves as moving from a traditional style of life to a more modern and Polish one. Jewish newspapers and other magazines began to be published in Polish. Jews took advantage of their right to political participation, but they were divided into different factions and could not agree on how to defend Jewish life and culture in Poland. These divisions made the Jews of Poland more vulnerable when the Second World War broke out in 1939.

Whatever active anti-Semitism existed in Poland before the German invasion of 1939, it was the Nazis who tried to destroy the Polish Jewish community and

Mothers with babies at their breasts came up, hesitated, and entered the chambers of death. At the corner stood a burly SS man with a priest-like voice. "Nothing at all is going to happen to you!" he told the poor wretches. "All you have to do when you get into the chambers is to breathe in deeply. That stretches the lungs. Inhaling is necessary to prevent disease and epidemics." When asked what would be done with them, he replied: "Well, of course, the men will have to work building houses and roads, but the women won't need to work. They can do housework or help in the kitchen, but only if they want to." For some of these poor creatures, this was a small ray of hope that was enough to make them walk the few steps to the chambers without resistance. Most of them knew what was going on. The smell told them what their fate was to be. They went up the small flight of steps and saw everything. Mothers with their babies clasped to their breasts, small children, adults, men, women, all naked; they hesitated, but they entered the chambers of death, thrust forward by the others behind them or by the leather whips of the SS [Storm Troopers]. Most went in without a word . . . Many were saying prayers. I prayed with them. I pressed myself into a corner and cried aloud to my God and theirs. How gladly I should have gone into the chambers with them; how gladly I should have died with them. Then they would have found an SS offi-cer in uniform in their gas chambers; they would have believed it was an accident and the story would have been buried and forgotten. But I could not do that yet. First, I had to make known what I had seen here. The chambers were filling up. Fill them up well—that was Captain Wirth's order. The people were treading on each other's feet. There were 700–800 of them in an area of 270 square feet, in 1,590 cubic feet of space. The SS crushed them together as tightly as they possibly could. The doors closed. Meanwhile, the rest waited out in the open, all naked. "It's done exactly the same way in winter," I was told. "But they may catch their death!" I said. "That's what they're here for," an SS man said . . . The Diesel exhaust gases were intend-ed to kill those unfortunates. But the engine was not working . . . The people in the gas chambers waited, in vain. I heard them weeping, sobbing . . . After 2 hours and 49 minutes, measured by my stop watch, the Diesel started. Up to that moment, men and women had been shut up alive in those four chambers, four times 750 people in four times 1,590 cubic feet of space. Another twenty-five minutes dragged by. Many of those inside were already dead. They could be seen through the small window when the electric light went on for a moment and lit up the inside of the chamber. After twenty-eight minutes, few were left alive. At the end of thirty-two minutes, all were dead.

Saul Friedländer *Pius XII and the Third Reich: A Documentation.* Copyright © 1966 by Alfred A. Knopf, Inc. Copyright © 1964 by Editions du Seuil. Originally published in French under the title *Pie XII et le III Reich, Documents.* Reprinted by permission of Georges Borchardt, Inc., for the author.

Jewish communities elsewhere in Europe that fell under German control. In that respect, the Holocaust constitutes an event driven by German policy within the larger event of the Second World War.

The Nazi Assault on the Jews of Poland

The joint German-Soviet invasion of Poland brought millions of Jews under either German or Soviet authority. By conquering Poland, the Nazi government could carry out the destruction of Jewish communities to an extent far beyond anything possible in Germany itself. From the Nazi standpoint, the destruction of the Polish Jewish community held special importance. Polish Jewry was large and had produced many religious, cultural, and political leaders. It also constituted the single most important source for Jewish emigration beyond Eastern Europe. For the Nazis, Poland was the chief breeding ground for world Jewry.

By late autumn 1939, the Germans had begun to move against Polish Jews. The Nazi government first thought it might herd virtually all the Jews of occupied Europe into the Lublin region of Poland. By early 1940, the Nazis decided to move as many Jews as possible into ghettos, where they would be separated from the rest of the Polish population. The largest ghettos were Lodz and Warsaw, each of which had populations of several hundred thousand. The Nazis moved Jews from all over Poland and, eventually, other occupied regions by rail into these ghettos and then sealed them off with police guards and walls. Jewish councils, which were torn between responsibility to their communities and the need to respond to German orders, administered the ghettos. The Nazis confiscated and sold the personal property and businesses of the Jews who were herded into the ghettos. Jewish laborers were sent out to work as contract labor while their families remained in the ghettos. By 1941, the Polish Jews had lost their civic standing and property. They had been located in segregated communities within Poland where disease was rampant and the food supply meager. Approximately 20 percent of the population of both the Lodz and Warsaw ghettos died of disease and malnourishment.

The German invasion of the Soviet Union in June 1941 made the situation of Jews in Poland even worse. The advancing German forces killed tens of thousands of Jews in the Soviet Union during 1941 and hundreds of thousands more the next year. Bolsheviks and Jews became conflated in German thinking and propaganda. During the second half of 1941, the Nazi government decided to exterminate the Jews of Europe. From late 1941 through 1944, the Germans transported Jews from the ghettos by rail to death camps in Poland, including Kulmhof, Belzen, Sobibor, Treblinka, Birkenau, and Auschwitz. One or more of the camps were in operation from 1941 to 1944, with Auschwitz being the last closed. In these camps, Jews were systematically killed in gas chambers.

By 1945, approximately 90 percent of the pre-1939 Jewish population of Poland had been destroyed. The tiny minority of Polish Jews who had survived faced bitter anti-Semitism under the postwar Soviet-dominated government. Many immigrated to Israel, leaving only a few thousand Jews within the borders of a nation where they had numbered in the millions and where they had created a rich religious, cultural, and political community. The largest Jewish community in Europe had virtually ceased to exist.

Explanations of the Holocaust

As interest in the Holocaust has grown since the 1960s, so has debate about its character and meaning. Was it a unique event of unprecedented and unparalleled evil, or was it one specific instance of a more general human wickedness that has found expression throughout history? Are its roots to be found in flaws in human nature as a whole, or are they unique to the experience of the West or, perhaps, to the German people? Some scholars point to the horrible mass murders committed in the twentieth century by communist regimes under Stalin in the Soviet Union and under Mao in China, each of which killed many more people than did Hitler, as evidence of the more general character of the phenomenon. Others argue that the Holocaust was unique because its goal was the annihilation of a whole people, from infants to the aged, just because of who they were. Some focus on the wickedness personified by Hitler, who was driven by his fixation on the myth of Jewish power and evil.

Perhaps we should think of the problem from the standpoint of two questions: Why were the Jews the main target of Hitler's policy of extermination? How was it possible to carry out such a vast mass murder? Surely, an essential part of an answer to the first question is the persistence of anti-Semitism in Christianity and Western culture, from the Church Fathers to Luther and to the teachings of churches in modern times. Some would combine this religious and historical anti-Semitism with the coming of the Enlightenment and the social sciences, which gave rise to pseudoscientific racial theories that lent a new twist to the old hatred of the Jews. Pseudoscientific racism appears to have been the most powerful influence on Hitler, but it could not have found widespread support without deeply rooted religious and social anti-Semitism.

For example, in at least one instance in Poland, Poles turned against their Jewish neighbors in outbursts of localized anti-Semitic violence. In July 1941, in the town of Jedwabne, in northeast Poland, non-Jewish Poles killed approximately 1,600 of their Jewish fellow townspeople. This horrendous incident suggests that although the Nazis carried out most of the atrocities against the Jews, a climate of either indifference or outright support existed in Poland as well as in other parts of Nazi-occupied Europe. Yet it must also be noted that between 1942 and 1945 the Council for Aid to Jews in Occupied Poland, known as ZEGOTA and sponsored by the Polish government in exile, protected and aided the escape of many thousands of Polish Jews.

MAJOR CAMPAIGNS AND EVENTS OF WORLD WAR II

September 1939	Germany and the Soviet Union invade Poland
November 1939	The Soviet Union invades Finland
April 1940	Germany invades Denmark and Norway
May 1940	Germany invades Belgium, the Netherlands, Luxembourg, and France
June 1940	Fall of France
August 1940	Battle of Britain begins
June 1941	Germany invades the Soviet Union
July 1941	Japan takes Indochina
December 1941	Japan attacks Pearl Harbor; United States enters war against Axis powers
June 1942	Battle of Midway Island
November 1942	Battle of Stalingrad begins
July–August 1943	Allies take Sicily, land in Italy
June 1944	Allies land in Normandy
May 1945	Germany surrenders
August 1945	Atomic bombs dropped on Hiroshima and Nagasaki
September 1945	Japan formally surrenders

2. The secret provision of the Nazi-Soviet Pact
   a. brought Japan into the alliance.
   b. called for Germany to declare war on France in 1939.
   c. called for joint intelligence operations against France and Britain.
   d. involved the direct payment of large sums of money to Stalin.
   e. divided Poland between the two powers.

3. The British routed Rommel at
   a. Cairo.
   b. Alexandria.
   c. Safi.
   d. El Alemain.
   e. Casablanca.

4. Hitler claimed that the German people needed *Lebensraum*, or
   a. a "pure life."
   b. "living space."
   c. "blood and iron."
   d. the "people's religion."
   e. a "pure leader."

5. The firebombing of Dresden took out
   a. industrial targets.
   b. oil refineries.
   c. rail yards.
   d. civilian centers.
   e. communications.

6. The turning point in the Germans' Russian campaign came at the Battle of
   a. the Volga.
   b. Moscow.
   c. Leningrad.
   d. Stalingrad.
   e. the Urals.

7. The American strategy in the Pacific in 1943 was known as
   a. strike and retreat.
   b. total war.
   c. island hopping.
   d. saturation attack.
   e. shock and awe.

8. Peace with Japan was formally signed
   a. aboard the *Enola Gay*.
   b. aboard the USS *Missouri*.
   c. aboard the USS *West Virginia*.
   d. in Okinawa.
   e. in Tokyo.

9. Josef Goebbels was in charge of
   a. concentration camps in Poland.
   b. Nazi propaganda.
   c. coordinating operations in the Soviet Union.
   d. coordinating German economic planning.
   e. military operations in France.

10. The Vichy government was headed by
    a. General Foch.
    b. General Joffre.
    c. Marshal Pétain.
    d. Charles de Gaulle.
    e. Leon Blum.

11. For the broad mass of the British population
    a. the war was a welcome relief from the tensions of the 1930s.
    b. the standard of living declined during the war.
    c. the war had little impact on their lives.
    d. the war was an economic disaster.
    e. the standard of living improved during the war.

12. The United Nations' Lytton Report condemned
    a. Italy's attack on Ethiopia.
    b. Germany's invasion of Poland.
    c. Hitler's rearmament of Germany.
    d. Vichy France.
    e. Japan's invasion of Manchuria.

13. The Big Three included
    a. Britain, France, and the United States.
    b. Germany, Italy, and Japan.
    c. the Soviet Union, France, and Britain.
    d. Britain, the United States, and the Soviet Union.
    e. Germany, Italy, and Spain.

14. The United States and Britain agreed to open a second front in France in 1944 at the _____ conference.
    a. Yalta
    b. Tehran
    c. Potsdam
    d. Moscow
    e. North Atlantic

15. Italian setbacks in North Africa and Greece
    a. forced the Germans to divert troops from the invasion of Russia.
    b. had little impact on the larger course of the war.
    c. were offset by victories in France and Cyprus.
    d. could not be capitalized on by the Allies.
    e. were offset by victories in the Balkans.

16. The Nazi invasion of Russia was code named
    a. Operation Blitzkreig.
    b. Operation Black Bear.
    c. Operation Barbarossa.
    d. Operation East Wing.
    e. Operation Stalingrad.

17. By 1945, the Nazis had exterminated approximately _____ percent of the Jewish population of Poland.
    a. 20
    b. 40
    c. 60
    d. 80
    e. 90

18. The assumptions that Germany had real grievances and that Hitler's goals were limited underlay the policy of
    a. containment.
    b. appeasement.
    c. zero tolerance.
    d. consensus building.
    e. constructive negotiation.

19. The *Anschluss* was
    a. Hitler's policy of mandatory military service for men under 65.
    b. the union of Germany and Austria.
    c. a secret intelligence unit in the German army.
    d. the name for Hitler's broad economic plan.
    e. an anti-Nazi newspaper.

20. The German *blitzkrieg* relied for its success on
    a. huge numbers of infantry.
    b. infantry supported by cavalry.
    c. massed tanks supported by airpower.
    d. bombing raids followed by massed infantry.
    e. massed cavalry.

DOCUMENT-BASED QUESTION

Directions: Construct a valid essay that directly addresses the central issue of the following question. Use facts from the documents provided and from the chapter to prove the position you take in your thesis statement.

What were the arguments for and against appeasement? Why were France and Britain so eager to avoid war?

Document A

Source: Adolf Hitler, "The Misery of the Sudeten Germans is Indescribable" (September 12, 1938).

The misery of the Sudeten Germans is indescribable. It is sought to annihilate them. As human beings they oppressed and scandalously treated in an intolerable fashion. When three and half million members of a people which numbers nearly eighty millions [ethnic Germans] may not sing a song they like simply because it does not please the Czechs. . . . when they are hunted and harried like helpless wild-fowl for every expression of their national sentiment—this may perhaps cause the worthy representatives of our democracies no concern. . . . but I can only say to the representatives of these democracies that this does concern us. . . .

Document B

Source: Winston Churchill responds to the Munich Conference (September 29, 1938, *Blood, Sweat, and Tears*).

We have been reduced in these five years from a position of safety and power. . . . reduced in five years from a position safe and unchallenged to where we stand now. . . .

The responsibility must rest with those who have had the undisputed control of our political affairs. They neither prevented Germany from rearming, nor did they rearm ourselves in time. They quarreled with Italy without saving Ethiopia. They exploited and discredited the vast institution of the League of Nations and they neglected to make alliances and combinations which might have repaired previous errors, and thus they left us in the hour of trial without adequate national defense or effective international security. . . .

Document C

Source: Adolf Hitler, "Czechoslovakia Has Ceased to Exist" (March 15, 1939).

In order to definitely remove this menace to peace [alleged attacks on ethnic Germans] and to create the conditions for a necessary new order in this living space,

I have resolved to allow German troops to march into Bohemia and Moravia. They will disarm the terror gangs and the Czech forces supporting them, and protect the lives of those who are menaced. Thus they will lay the foundations for introducing a fundamental re-ordering of affairs which will be in accordance with a thousand-year history and will satisfy the practical needs of the German and Czech peoples.

Document D

Source: Neville Chamberlain, "I Bitterly Regret What Has Now Occurred" (March 15, 1939).

In a speech which I made at Birmingham on 30th January last I pointed out that we ought to define our aims and attitude, namely our determination to search for peace. I added that I felt it was time now that others should make their contribution to a result which would overflow in benefits to many besides those immediately concerned. It is natural, therefore, that I should bitterly regret what has now occurred. But do not let us on that account be deflected from our course. Let us remember that the desire of all the peoples of the world still remains concentrated on the hopes of peace and a return to the atmosphere of understanding and good will which has so often been disturbed.

For more on the events leading to the outbreak of World War II, see pages 901–910 of this chapter.

A statue of Queen Victoria is removed from the front of the Supreme Court building in Georgetown, former capital of the British colony of Guyana, in February 1970, in preparation for the transition to independence. Decolonization represented as dramatic a transition in world political relations as had the establishment of European empires in the nineteenth-century Victorian age. Bettmann/CORBIS. All rights reserved.

29

The Cold War Era, Decolonization, and the Emergence of a New Europe

KEY TOPICS

• The origins of the Cold War and the division of Europe into Eastern and Western blocs following World War II

• Major moments of Cold War tensions

• Decolonization and the conflicts in Korea and Vietnam

• Polish protests against Soviet domination of Eastern Europe

• *Perestroika* and *glasnost* in the Soviet Union

• The collapse of communism in Eastern Europe and the Soviet Union

• The civil war in Yugoslavia

• The rise of radical political Islamism

SINCE THE END of World War II in 1945, two often interrelated sets of fundamental, international political relationships have shaped the experience of Europe, the United States, and the wider global community. These were the **Cold War** between the United States and the Soviet Union and the long process of **decolonization**, whereby the peoples of those regions of the world formally or informally dominated by European nations and later by the United States have rejected that domination.

From the end of World War II in 1945 until the collapse of communist regimes in Eastern Europe between 1989 and 1991, the Soviet Union and the United States—two nuclear-armed superpowers—confronted each other in a simmering conflict known as the **Cold War**. While it lasted, this conflict dominated global politics and threatened the peace of Europe, which stood divided between the U.S.-dominated North Atlantic Treaty Organization (NATO) and the Soviet-dominated Warsaw Pact.

Decolonization very rapidly became enmeshed with the Cold War. As the nations of Europe retreated from empire, the rivalry between the two superpowers expanded into a contest for dominance in the postcolonial world. Superpower intervention aggravated local conflicts on every continent. In its efforts to limit communism, the United States became embroiled in bitter wars in Korea and Vietnam. The struggle between Israel and the Arab nations likewise became an arena of superpower conflict.

In the almost two decades since the collapse of the Soviet Union, the United States has remained the world's single superpower. It has become symbolically identified as embodying the political, economic, and cultural values of modern Western civilization. In this role, it has replaced Europe as the object of anti-Western resistance. One of the numerous results of this new situation is the clash between the United States and radical political Islamism. The result has been the terrorist attacks on the United States on September 11, 2001, and the subsequent American intervention in Afghanistan and Iraq.

One way to think of the past sixty years is to see the history of Western civilization as entering a new global era. Europe and later the United States had been active across the world scene since the end of the fifteenth century. Europe had created formal and informal regions of empire by the early twentieth century. However, commencing strongly in the 1930s and continuing to the present day, those once colonially dominated areas of the world have actively impacted upon the international relations and domestic politics of many European nations and of the United States rather than remaining regions largely subject to Western economic, political, and military influence. The give and take of political, economic, military, and cultural power has become far more reciprocal between the West and the rest of the global community.

▼ The Emergence of the Cold War

The tense relationship between the United States and the Soviet Union began in the closing months of World War II. Some scholars attribute the hardening of the atmosphere between the two countries to Harry Truman's assumption of the presidency in April 1945, after the death of the more sympathetic Franklin Roosevelt, and to the American possession of an effective atomic bomb. Evidence suggests, however, that Truman was trying to carry Roosevelt's policies forward and that Soviet actions in Eastern Europe had begun to distress Roosevelt himself. Some have also argued that Truman did not use the atomic bomb to try to keep Russia out of the Pacific. On the contrary, he worked hard to ensure Russian intervention against Japan in 1945. In part, the coldness between the Allies arose from the mutual feeling that each had violated previous agreements. The Russians were plainly asserting permanent control of Poland and Romania under puppet communist governments. The United States was taking a harder line about German reparation payments to the Soviet Union.

In retrospect, however, and as more information emerges from the previously closed Soviet archives, it appears unlikely that friendlier styles on either side could have avoided a split that arose from basic differences of ideology and interest. The Soviet Union's attempt to extend its control westward into central Europe and the Balkans and southward into the Middle East continued the general thrust of the foreign policy of tsarist Russia. Britain had traditionally tried to restrain Russian expansion into these areas, and the United States inherited that task as Britain's power waned.

The Americans made no attempt to roll back Soviet power where it existed at the close of World War II. (See Map 29–1, page 942.) At the time, American military forces were the greatest in U.S. history, American industrial power was unmatched in the world, and atomic weapons were an American monopoly. In less than a year from the war's end, the Americans had reduced their forces in Europe from 3.5 million to 500,000. The speed of the withdrawal reflected domestic pressure to "get the boys home" but was also fully in accord with America's peacetime plans and goals, which included support for self-determination, autonomy, and democracy in the political sphere, and free trade, freedom of the seas, no barriers to investment, and an Open Door policy in the economic sphere. These goals reflected American principles and served American interests well. As the strongest, richest nation in the world—the one with the greatest industrial base and the strongest currency—the United States would benefit handsomely from an international order based on such goals.

Although postwar American hostility to colonial empires created tensions with France and Britain, the main conflict lay with the Soviet Union. The growth in France

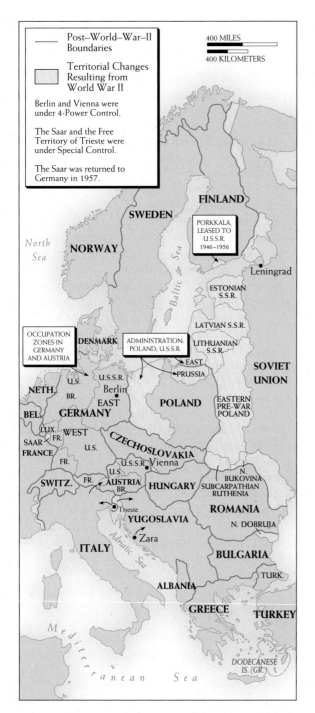

Map 29–1　**TERRITORIAL CHANGES IN EUROPE AFTER WORLD WAR II**
The map shows the shifts in territory that followed the defeat of the Axis. No treaty of peace formally ended the war with Germany.

thus see American resistance to their expansion as a threat to their security and their legitimate aims. They considered American objections to Soviet actions in Poland and other states as an effort to undermine regimes friendly to Russia and to encircle the Soviet Union with hostile neighbors. The Soviets could also use this point of view to justify their own attempts to overthrow regimes friendly to the United States in Western Europe and elsewhere.

Evidence of the new mood of postwar hostility between the former allies was soon apparent. In February 1946, both Stalin and his foreign minister, Vyacheslav Molotov (1890–1986), publicly spoke of the Western democracies as enemies. A month later, Churchill gave a speech in Fulton, Missouri, in which he declared that an "Iron Curtain" had descended on Europe, dividing a free and democratic West from an East under totalitarian rule. He warned against communist subversion and urged Western unity and strength against the new menace. In this atmosphere, difficulties grew.

Containment in American Foreign Policy

The resistance of Americans and Western Europeans to what they increasingly perceived as Soviet intransigence and communist plans for subversion and expansion took a clearer form in 1947. The American policy became known as one of **containment**, the purpose of which was to resist the extension of Soviet expansion and influence in the expectation that eventually the Soviet Union would collapse from internal pressures and the burdens of its foreign oppression. This strategy, which American policymakers devised in the late 1940s, would direct the broad outlines of American foreign policy for the next four decades, until the Soviet Union did collapse from exactly such pressures. Containment marked a major departure in American foreign policy and transformed the international situation during the second half of the twentieth century. The execution of the policy led the United States to enter overseas alliances, to make formal and informal commitments of support to regimes around the world it perceived as being anticommunist, to undertake enormous military expenditures, and to send large amounts of money abroad. In all these respects, the United States assumed unprecedented long-term foreign policy responsibilities. The United States thus became a permanent player in European international relations and in areas of the world where only European nations had been involved earlier in the century. (See "Compare & Connect: The Soviet Union and the United States Draw the Lines of the Cold War." pages 944–945.)

The Truman Doctrine　Since 1944, civil war had been raging in Greece between the royalist government restored by Britain and insurgents supported by the communist countries, chiefly Yugoslavia. In 1947, Britain informed the United States it could no longer financially

and Italy of large popular communist parties taking orders from Moscow led the Americans to believe that Stalin was engaged in a worldwide plot to subvert capitalism and democracy. From the Soviet perspective, extending the borders of the USSR and dominating the formerly independent successor states of Eastern Europe would provide needed security and compensate for the fearful losses the Soviet people had endured in the war. The Soviets could support its Greek allies. On March 12, President Truman asked Congress to provide funds to support Greece and Turkey, which was then under Soviet pressure to yield control of the Dardanelles, and Congress complied. In a speech to Congress that gave these actions much broader significance, the president set forth what came to be called the Truman Doctrine. He advocated a policy of support for "free people who are resisting attempted subjugation by armed minorities or by outside pressures," by implication, anywhere in the world.

The Marshall Plan American aid to Greece and Turkey took the form of military equipment and advisers. For Western Europe, where postwar poverty and hunger fueled the menacing growth of communist parties, the Americans devised the European Recovery Program. Named the **Marshall Plan** after George C. Marshall (1880–1959), the secretary of state who introduced it, this program provided broad economic aid to European states on the sole condition that they work together for their mutual benefit. The Soviet Union and its satellites were invited to participate. Finland and Czechoslovakia were willing to do so, and Poland and Hungary showed interest. The Soviets, however, forbade them to take part.

The Marshall Plan restored prosperity to Western Europe and set the stage for Europe's unprecedented postwar economic growth. In addition to the vast program of American economic aid, the strong Christian Democratic movement that dominated the politics of Italy, France, and West Germany worked to keep communist influence at bay outside the Soviet sphere in Eastern Europe.

Following the declaration of the Truman Doctrine and the announcement of the Marshall Plan, the Soviet Union defined a new era of conflict between the United States and itself. (See "Compare & Connect: The Soviet Union and the United States Draw the Lines of the Cold War." pages 944–945.)

Soviet Domination of Eastern Europe

The Soviet determination to control Eastern Europe had both historical and ideological roots. Western European powers had invaded Russia twice in the nineteenth century (under Napoleon in 1812 and during the Crimean War of 1854–1856) and already twice more in the twentieth century. Tsarist Russia had governed most of Poland from the 1790s to 1915 and had intervened at the request of the Austrian Empire to put down the Hungarian revolution in 1849. Russia's interests in Turkey and the lands around the Black Sea were similarly long-standing. Given this history and the Soviet Union's extraordinary losses in World War II, it is not surprising that Soviet leaders sought to use their Eastern European satellites as a buffer against future invasions.

Stalin may have seen containment as a renewed Western attempt to isolate and encircle the USSR. In Eastern

President Harry Truman greets Secretary of State George Marshall returning from Europe. Truman and Marshall were the architects of American foreign policy during the early years of the Cold War.   Hulton Archive Photos/Getty Images, Inc.

The Soviet Union and the United States Draw the Lines of the Cold War

BETWEEN 1945 AND 1950 the lines of tensions between the United States and the Soviet Union that became known as the Cold War were drawn. Each country quickly came to define the other as its principal enemy on the world scene. These two documents illustrate the manner in which each nation set its conflict with the other into a larger framework of ideological and political rivalry. Much of the rhetoric of these two documents would characterize the Cold War from its inception until the collapse of the Soviet Union.

QUESTIONS

1. How did the Cominform use the terms "democratic" and "imperialist" to its advantage?

2. Why did it see the Marshall Plan as an act of aggression?

3. How did the National Security Council characterize Soviet policy?

4. What were the goals of containment?

5. Why did the Council urge that the Soviet Union always be given opportunity to save face and to back down with dignity?

6. How does each document indicate that both the Soviet Union and the United States regarded their tensions and conflict as part of a wider global political scene?

I. The Cominform Defines Conflict between the Soviet Union and the United States

In 1947, under the leadership of the Soviet Union, the leaders of the Soviet and East European Communist Parties formed the Communist Information Bureau, which became known as the Cominform. It was organized in the wake of the Truman Doctrine and Marshall Plan. In September 1947, the Communist Parties constituting the Cominform issued a statement that set forth their view of the emerging conflict between the Soviet bloc and the United States. In doing so, they not only attacked the United States, but also the democratic socialist parties of Western Europe that the Soviet Union had seen as an enemy since the days of Lenin.

Fundamental changes have taken place in the international situation as a result of the Second World War and in the post-war period.

These changes are characterized by a new disposition of the basic political forces operating in the world arena, by a change in the relations among the victor states in the Second World War, and their realignment.

. . . The Soviet Union and the other democratic countries regarded as their basic war aims the restoration and consolidation of democratic order in Europe, the eradication of fascism and the prevention of the possibility of new aggression on the part of Germany, and the establishment of a lasting all-round cooperation among the nations of Europe. The United States of America, and Britain in agreement with them, set themselves another aim in the war: to rid themselves of competitors on the markets (Germany and Japan and to establish their dominant position. . . .

Thus two camps were formed—the imperialist and anti-democratic camp having as its basic aim the establishment of world domination of American imperialism and the smashing of democracy, and the anti-imperialist and democratic camp having as its basic aim the undermining of imperialism, the consolidation of democracy, and the eradication of the remnants of fascism. . . .

. . . the imperialist camp and its leading force, the United States, are displaying particularly aggressive activity. . . .The Truman-Marshall Plan is only a constituent part . . . of the general plan for the policy of global expansion pursued by the United States in all parts of the World. . . .

To frustrate the plan of imperialist aggression the efforts of all the democratic anti-imperialist forces of Europe are necessary. The right-wing Socialists are traitors to this cause. . . . and primarily the French Socialists and the British Labourites . . . by their servility and sycophancy are helping American capital to achieve its aims, provoking it to resort to extortion and impelling their own countries on to a path of vassal-like dependence on the United States of America.

This imposes a special task on the Communist Parties. They must take into their hands the banner of defense of the national independence and sovereignty of their countries. . . .

The principle danger for the working class today lies in underestimating their own strength and overestimating the strength of the imperialist camp.

Source: United States Senate, 81st Congress, 1st Session, Document No. 48, *North Atlantic Treaty: Documents Relating to the North Atlantic Treaty* (Washington, DC: U. S. Government Printing Office, 1949), pp. 117–120 as quoted in Katharine J. Lualdi, *Sources of the Making of the West: Peoples and Culture* (Boston: Bedford/St. Martin's, 2009), 2, pp. 248–250.

The Allied airlift in action during the Berlin Blockade. Every day for almost a year Western planes supplied the city until Stalin lifted the blockade in May 1949. Art Resource/Bildarchiv Preussischer Kulturbesitz

II. The United States National Security Council Proposes to Contain the Soviet Union

In response to the domination of Eastern Europe by Communist Parties dominated by the Soviet Union and the occupation of these nations by Soviet troops, the United States government in 1950 adopted a policy of "containment" of the Soviet Union. This policy had been debated for many months and had for all practical purposes been in effect since the declaration of the Truman Doctrine in 1947. It was formally set forth after a period of implementation in what became known as the National Security Council Paper 68, arguably the most important statement of American foreign policy of the mid-twentieth century. The paper presented the Soviet Union as a nation determined to pursue an expansionist foreign policy and ideological struggle and as a long-term solution to that challenge proposed a policy of containing the influence of the Soviet Union diplomatically and militarily.

The fundamental design of those who control the Soviet Union and the international communist movement is to retain and solidify their absolute power, first in the Soviet Union and second in the areas now under their control. . . .

The design, therefore, calls for the complete subversion or forcible destruction of the machinery of government and structure of society in the countries of the non-Soviet world and their replacement by an apparatus and structure subservient to and controlled from the Kremlin. . . .

Our overall policy at the present time may be described as one designed to foster a world environment in which the American system can survive and flourish. It therefore rejects the concept of isolation and affirms the necessity of our positive participation in the world community.

This broad intention embraces two subsidiary policies. One is a policy which we would probably pursue even if there were no Soviet threat. It is a policy of attempting to develop a healthy international community. The other is the policy of "containing" the Soviet system. . . .

As for the policy of "containment," it is one which seeks by all means short of war to (1) block further expansion of Soviet power, (2) expose the falsities of Soviet pretensions, (3) induce a retraction of the Kremlin's control and influence, and (4) in general, so foster the seeds of destruction within the Soviet system that the Kremlin is brought at least to the point of modifying its behavior to conform to generally accepted international standards. . . .

One of the most important ingredients of power is military strength. . . . Without superior aggregate military strength . . . a policy of "containment"—which is in effect a policy of calculated and gradual coercion—is no more than a policy of bluff.

At the same time, it is essential to the successful conduct of a policy of "containment" that we always leave open the possibility of negotiation with the USSR . . .

In "containment" it is desirable to exert pressure in a fashion which will avoid so far as possible directly challenging Soviet prestige, to keep open the possibility for the USSR to retreat before pressure with a minimum loss of face and to secure political advantage from the failure of the Kremlin to yield or take advantage of the openings we leave it.

Source: National Security Council, Paper Number 68, *Foreign Relations of the United States* (Washington, DC: U.S. Government Printing Office, 1977), Sections: III, IV, VI. as cited on www.seattleu.edu/artsci/history/us1945/docs/nsc68-1.htm

MAJOR DATES OF EARLY COLD WAR YEARS

1945	Yalta Conference
1945	Founding of the United Nations
1946	Churchill's Iron Curtain speech
1947 (March)	Truman Doctrine regarding Greece and Turkey
1947 (June)	Announcement of Marshall Plan
1948	Communist takeover in Czechoslovakia
1948	Communist takeover in Hungary
1948–1949	Berlin blockade
1949	NATO founded
1949	East and West Germany emerge as separate states
1950–1953	Korean conflict
1955	Warsaw Pact founded

Europe, the Soviet Union found numerous supporters among those segments of the population who had opposed the various right-wing movements in those countries before the war and who had fought the Nazis during the war. In the autumn of 1947, Stalin called a meeting in Warsaw of all communist parties from around the globe. There they organized the Communist Information Bureau (Cominform), a revival of the old Comintern, dedicated to spreading revolutionary communism throughout the world. In Western Europe the establishment of the Cominform officially ended the era of the popular front during which communists had cooperated with noncommunist parties. Hard-liners who supported the Soviet line on every issue replaced communist leaders in the West who favored collaboration and reform.

In February 1948, in Prague, Stalin gave a brutal display of his new policy of bringing the governments of Eastern Europe under direct Soviet control. The communists expelled the democratic members of what had been a coalition government and murdered Jan Masaryk (1886–1948), the foreign minister and son of the founder of Czechoslovakia, Thomas Masaryk. President Edvard Beneš (1884–1948) was forced to resign, and Czechoslovakia was brought fully under Soviet rule. There and elsewhere in Eastern Europe, it was clear there would be no multiparty political system.

During the late 1940s, the Soviet Union required the other subject governments in Eastern Europe to impose Stalinist policies, including one-party political systems, close military cooperation with the Soviet Union, the collectivization of agriculture, Communist Party domination of education, and attacks on the churches. Longtime Communist Party officials were purged and condemned in show trials like those that had taken place in Moscow during the late 1930s. The catalyst for this harsh tightening probably was the success of Marshal Josip (Broz) Tito

(1892–1980), the leader of communist Yugoslavia, in freeing his country from Soviet domination. Stalin wanted to prevent other Eastern European states from following the Yugoslav example.

The Postwar Division of Germany

Soviet actions, especially those in Czechoslovakia, increased the determination of the United States to go ahead with its own arrangements in Germany.

Disagreements over Germany During the war, the Allies had never decided how to treat Germany after its defeat. At first they all agreed it should be dismembered, but they differed on how. By the time of Yalta, Churchill had come to fear Russian control of Eastern and central Europe and began to oppose dismemberment.

The Allies also differed on economic policy. The Russians swiftly dismantled German industry in the eastern zone, but the Americans acted differently in the western zone. They concluded that if they followed the Soviet policy, the United States would have to support Germany economically for the foreseeable future. It would also cause chaos and open the way for communism. They preferred, therefore, to try to make Germany self-sufficient, and this meant restoring, rather than destroying, its industrial capacity. To the Soviets, the restoration of a powerful industrial Germany, even in the western zone only, was frightening. The same difference of approach hampered agreement on reparations. The Soviets claimed the right to the industrial equipment in all the zones, and the Americans resisted their demands.

Berlin Blockade When the Western powers agreed to go forward with a separate constitution for the western sectors of Germany in February 1948, the Soviets walked out of the joint Allied Control Commission. In the summer of that year, the Western powers issued a new currency in their zone. All four powers governed Berlin, though it was well within the Soviet zone. The Soviets feared the new currency, which was circulating in Berlin at better rates than their own currency. They chose to seal the city off by closing all railroads and highways that led from Berlin to West Germany. Their purpose was to drive the Western powers out of Berlin.

The Western allies responded to the Berlin blockade by airlifting supplies to the city for almost a year. In May 1949, the Russians were forced to reopen access to Berlin. The incident, however, was decisive. It increased tensions and suspicions between the opponents and hastened the separation of Germany into two states. West Germany formally became the German Federal Republic in September 1949, and the eastern region became the German Democratic Republic a month later. Ironically, Germany had been dismembered in a way no one had planned or expected. The two Germanys and the di-

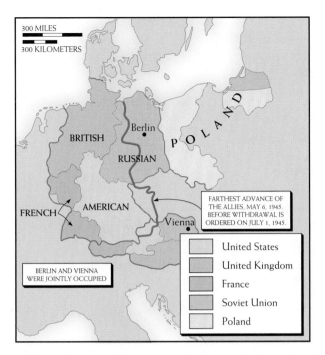

300 MILES

300 KILOMETERS

BRITISH

Berlin

P O L A N D

RUSSIAN

FRENCH

AMERICAN

Vienna

FARTHEST ADVANCE OF
THE ALLIES, MAY 6, 1945,
BEFORE WITHDRAWAL IS
ORDERED ON JULY 1, 1945.

BERLIN AND VIENNA
WERE JOINTLY OCCUPIED

United States

United Kingdom

France

Soviet Union

Poland

Map 29–2 OCCUPIED GERMANY AND AUSTRIA At the war's end, defeated Germany, including Austria, was occupied by the victorious Allies in the several zones shown here. Austria, by prompt agreement, was reestablished as an independent, neutral state, no longer occupied. The German zones hardened into an "East" Germany (the former Soviet zone) and a "West" Germany (the former British, French, and American zones). Berlin, within the Soviet zone, was similarly divided.

vided city of Berlin, isolated within East Germany, would remain central fixtures in the geopolitics of the Cold War until 1989. (See Map 29–2.)

NATO and the Warsaw Pact

Meanwhile, the nations of Western Europe had been drawing closer together. The Marshall Plan encouraged international cooperation. In March 1948, Belgium, the Netherlands, Luxembourg, France, and Britain signed the Treaty of Brussels, providing for cooperation in economic and military matters. In April 1949, these nations joined with Italy, Denmark, Norway, Portugal, and Iceland to sign a treaty with Canada and the United States that formed the North Atlantic Treaty Organization (NATO), which committed its members to mutual assistance if any of them was attacked. The NATO treaty transformed the West into a bloc. A few years later, West Germany, Greece, and Turkey joined the alliance. For the first time in history, the United States was committed to defend allies outside the western hemisphere.

A series of bilateral treaties providing for close ties and mutual assistance in case of attack governed Soviet relations with the states of Eastern Europe. In 1949, these states formed the Council of Mutual Assistance (COMECON) to integrate their economies. Unlike the NATO

states, the Soviets directly dominated the Eastern alliance system through local communist parties controlled from Moscow and the presence of the Red Army. The Warsaw Pact of May 1955, which included Albania, Bulgaria, Czechoslovakia, East Germany, Hungary, Poland, Romania, and the Soviet Union, gave formal recognition to this system. Europe was divided into two unfriendly blocs. The Cold War had taken firm shape in Europe. (See Map 29–3, page 948.)

The strategic interests of the United States and the Soviet Union would not, however, permit the Cold War to be limited to the European continent. Major flash points would erupt around the world during the decades that followed, particularly in the Middle East and Asia. The establishment of a communist government in Cuba after 1959 would bring the conflict to the American hemisphere as well. In each case, the Cold War rivalry transformed what might otherwise have been regional conflicts into superpower strategic concerns.

The Creation of the State of Israel

One of the areas of ongoing regional conflict that became a major point of Cold War rivalry was the Middle East. Following World War I, Great Britain had exercised the chief political influence in the region under various mandates from the League of Nations. After World War II, both the Zionist movement, which sought to establish an independent Jewish state, and Arab nationalists, who sought to achieve self-determination, challenged British authority and influence.

British Balfour Declaration The modern state of Israel was the achievement of the world Zionist movement, founded in 1897 by Theodor Herzl (see Chapter 24) and later led by Chaim Weizmann (1874–1952). In 1917, during World War I, Arthur Balfour (1846–1930), the British foreign secretary, declared that Britain favored establishing a national home for the Jewish people in Palestine, which was then under Ottoman rule. Between the wars, thousands of Jews, mainly from Europe, immigrated to what had become British-ruled Palestine. During this period, the *Yishuv*, or Jewish community in Palestine, developed its own political parties, press, labor unions, and educational system. Arabs already living in Palestine considered the Jewish settlers intruders, and violent conflicts ensued. The British tried, but failed, to mediate these clashes.

This situation might have prevailed longer, except for the outbreak of World War II and Hitler's attempt to exterminate the Jews of Europe. The Nazi persecution united Jews throughout the world behind the Zionist ideal of a Jewish state in Palestine, and it touched the conscience of the United States and other Western powers. It seemed morally right to do something for the Jewish refugees from Nazi concentration camps.

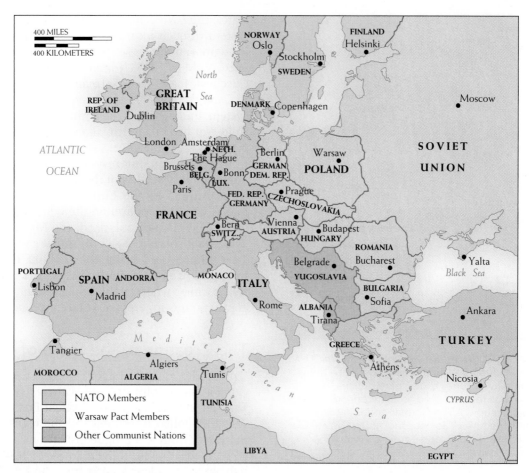

Map 29–3 **MAJOR COLD WAR EUROPEAN ALLIANCE SYSTEMS** The North Atlantic Treaty Organization, which includes both Canada and the United States, stretches as far east as Turkey. By contrast, the Warsaw Pact nations were the contiguous Communist states of Eastern Europe, with the Soviet Union, of course, as the dominant member.

The U.N. Resolution In 1947, the British turned over to the United Nations the problem of the relationship of Arabs and Jews in Palestine. That same year, the United Nations passed a resolution dividing the territory into two states, one Jewish and one Arab. The Arabs in Palestine and the surrounding Arab states resisted this resolution. Not unnaturally, they resented the influx of new settlers. Many Palestinian Arabs were displaced and became refugees themselves.

Israel Declares Independence In May 1948, the British officially withdrew from Palestine, and the Yishuv declared the independence of a new Jewish state called *Israel* on May 14. Two days later, the United States, through the personal intervention of President Truman, recognized the new nation, whose first prime minister was David Ben-Gurion (1886–1973). Almost immediately, Lebanon, Syria, Jordan, Egypt, and Iraq invaded Israel. The fighting continued throughout 1948 and 1949. By the end of its war of independence against the Arabs, Israel had expanded its borders beyond the limits

the United Nations had originally set forth. Jerusalem was divided between Jordan and Israel. By 1949, Israel had secured its existence, but not the acceptance of its Arab neighbors. As long as Egypt, Jordan, Syria, Lebanon, Iraq, and Saudi Arabia, to name those nations closest, withheld diplomatic recognition from Israel, the peace was only an armed truce. (See Map 29–4.)

The Arab-Israeli conflict would inevitably draw in the superpowers. The dispute directly involved Europe because many of the citizens of Israel had emigrated from there, and Europe, like the United States, was highly dependent on oil from Arab countries. Furthermore, both the United States and the Soviet Union believed they had major strategic and economic interests in the region.

By 1949, the United States had established itself as a firm ally of Israel. Gradually, the Soviet Union began to furnish aid to the Arab nations. The bipolar tensions that had settled over Europe were thus transferred to the Middle East. Furthermore, the existence of the state of Israel would become one of the major points of contention

150 MILES

150 KILOMETERS

Mediterranean

Sea

Tripoli

LEBANON
Beirut

Damascus
SYRIA

Sea of Galilee

Haifa
ISRAEL

Tel Aviv
Jaffa
Jerusalem
Amman

Jordan R.

Gaza
Dead Sea

Nile Delta
Port Said
Damietta

El 'Arish
Beersheba

JORDAN

El Mansura
Suez Canal
El Auja

Ismailia

EGYPT
Gida Pass
Mitla Pass

NEGEV

Cairo
Suez
Kuntilla

Helwan
Eilat
Aqaba

Nile R.
Sinai
Peninsula

Gulf of Suez
Mt. Sinai
△

Gulf of Aqaba

**SAUDI
ARABIA**

El Nabq
Sharm El
Sheikh
*TIRAN
ISLAND*

Red

Sea

Golan Heights
West Bank
Gaza Strip
Jordan Water
to the Negev

Map 29–4 ISRAEL AND ITS NEIGHBORS IN 1949 The territories gained by Israel in 1949 did not secure peace in the region. In fact, the disposition of those lands and the Arab refugees who live there has constituted the core of the region's unresolved problems to the present day.

tarily in Korea, following the same principle of containment that directed its actions in Europe.

Between 1910 and 1945, Japan, as an Asian colonial power, had occupied and exploited the formerly independent kingdom of Korea, but at the close of World War II, the United States and the Soviet Union expelled the Japanese and divided Korea into two parts along the thirty-eighth parallel of latitude. Korea was supposed to be reunited. By 1948, however, two separate states had emerged: the Democratic People's Republic of Korea in the north, supported by the Soviet Union, and the Republic of Korea in the south, supported by the United States.

In late June 1950, after border clashes, North Korea invaded South Korea across the thirty-eighth parallel. The United States intervened, at first unilaterally and then under the authority of a UN resolution. Great Britain, Turkey, Australia, and other countries sent token forces. The Korean police action was technically a UN-sponsored venture to halt aggression. (It had been made possible when Stalin ordered the Soviet ambassador to boycott the United Nations when the key vote was taken.) For the United States, the point of the Korean conflict was to contain the spread and halt the aggression of communism.

Late in 1950, the Chinese, responding to the approach of UN forces near their border, sent troops to support North Korea. The American forces had to retreat. The U.S. policymakers believed, mistakenly, that the Chinese, who, since 1949, had been under the communist government of Mao Zedong (1893–1976), were simply Soviet puppets. Accordingly, the Americans viewed the movement of Chinese troops into Korea as another example of communist pressure against a noncommunist state, similar to what had previously happened in Europe. Today it is clear that Mao disliked Stalin and that tension existed between Moscow and the People's Republic of China, but that was little understood at the time.

On June 16, 1953, the Eisenhower administration concluded an armistice ending the Korean War and restoring the border near the thirty-eighth parallel. (See Map 29–5, page 950.) Thousands of American troops, however, are still stationed in Korea. The United States seemed to have successfully applied the lessons of the Cold War it had learned in Europe to Asia. The Korean War confirmed the American government's faith in containment. It also transformed the Cold War into a global rivalry that ranged well beyond Europe.

The formation of NATO and the Korean conflict capped the first round of the Cold War. In 1953, Stalin's death and the armistice in Korea fostered hopes that international tensions might ease. In early 1955, Soviet occupation forces left Austria after that nation accepted neutral status. Later that year, the leaders of France, Great Britain, the Soviet Union, and the United States held a summit conference in Geneva. Nuclear weapons

between the United States and the governments of the various Arab states and later one of the chief complaints of radical political Islamists against the United States.

The Korean War

While early stages of the Cold War took place in Europe and the Arab-Israeli conflict developed in the Middle East, the United States confronted armed aggression in Asia. As part of a UN police action, it intervened mili-

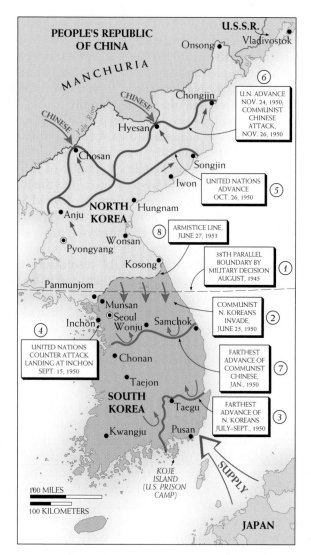

Map 29–5 **KOREA, 1950–1953** This map indicates the major developments in the bitter three-year struggle that followed the North Korean invasion of South Korea in 1950.

and the future of a divided Germany were the chief items on the agenda. Despite public displays of friendliness, the meeting produced few substantial agreements, and the Cold War soon resumed.

▼ The Khrushchev Era in the Soviet Union

No other nation had suffered greater losses or more deprivation during World War II than the Soviet Union. Many Russians had hoped the end of the war would signal a reduction in the scope of the police state and a redirection of the economy away from heavy industry to consumer products. They were disappointed. Stalin did little or nothing to modify the character of the regime he had created. If anything, his determination to cen-

tralize his authority and a desire to undertake a new wave of internal purges continued until his death on March 6, 1953.

For a time, no single leader replaced Stalin. Rather, the *presidium* (the renamed Politburo) pursued a policy of collective leadership. Gradually, however, power and influence began to devolve on Nikita Khrushchev (1894–1971), who had been named party secretary in 1953. Three years later, he became premier. Khrushchev's rise ended collective leadership, but he never commanded the extraordinary powers of Stalin.

Khrushchev's Domestic Policies

The Khrushchev era, which lasted until the autumn of 1964, witnessed a retreat from Stalinism, though not from authoritarianism. Khrushchev sought to reform the Soviet system but to maintain the dominance of the Communist Party. Intellectuals were somewhat freer to express their opinions. Although Boris Pasternak (1890–1960), the author of *Dr. Zhivago* (1957), was not permitted to receive the Nobel prize for literature in 1958, another dissident author, Aleksandr Solzhenitsyn (b. 1918), could publish *One Day in the Life of Ivan Denisovich* (1963), a grim account of life in a Soviet labor camp under Stalin. Khrushchev also made modest efforts to meet the demand for more consumer goods and decentralize economic planning. In agriculture, he removed many of the more restrictive regulations on private cultivation and sought to expand the area available for growing wheat. At first, this program led to record grain production, but inappropriate farming techniques soon reduced yields. The Soviet Union had to import vast quantities of grain each year from the United States and other countries.

The Secret Speech of 1956 In February 1956, Khrushchev made an extraordinary departure from expected practice by directly attacking the policies of the Stalin years. At the Twentieth Congress of the Com-

MAJOR DATES OF THE EARLY KHRUSHCHEV ERA	
1953	Death of Stalin
1955	Austria established as a neutral state
1955	Geneva summit
1956 (February)	Khrushchev's secret speech denouncing Stalin
1956 (Autumn)	Polish crisis
1956 (October)	Suez crisis
1956 (October)	Hungarian uprising
1957	*Sputnik* launched

KHRUSHCHEV DENOUNCES THE CRIMES OF STALIN: THE SECRET SPEECH

In 1956, Khrushchev denounced Stalin in a secret speech to the Party Congress. The New York Times *published a text of that speech, smuggled from Russia.*

What specific actions by Stalin did Khrushchev denounce? Why does Khrushchev pay so much attention to Stalin's creation of the concept of an "enemy of the people"? Why does Khrushchev distinguish between the actions of Stalin and those of Lenin?

Stalin acted not through persuasion, explanation, and patient cooperation with people, but by imposing his concepts and demanding absolute submission to his opinion. Whoever opposed this concept or tried to prove his viewpoint and the correctness of his position was doomed to removal from the leading collective [group] and to subsequent moral and physical annihilation. . . .

Stalin originated the concept of "enemy of the people." This term automatically rendered it unnecessary that the ideological errors of a man or men engaged in a controversy be proved; this term made possible the usage of the most cruel repression violating all norms of revolutionary legality, against anyone who in any way disagreed with Stalin, against those who were only suspected of hostile intent, against those who had bad reputations.

This concept "enemy of the people" actually eliminated the possibility of any kind of ideological fight or the making of one's views known on this or that issue, even those of a practical character. In the main, and in actuality, the only proof of guilt used, against all norms of current legal science, was the "confession" of the accused himself; and, as a subsequent probing proved, "confessions" were acquired through physical pressures against the accused. . . .

Lenin used severe methods only in the most necessary cases, when the exploiting classes were still in existence and were vigorously opposing the revolution, when the struggle for survival was decidedly assuming the sharpest forms, even including civil war.

Stalin, on the other hand, used extreme methods and mass repressions at a time when the revolution was already victorious, when the Soviet State was strengthened, when the exploiting classes were already liquidated and Socialist relations were rooted solidly in all phases of national economy, when our party was politically consolidated and had strengthened itself both numerically and ideologically. It is clear that here Stalin showed in a whole series of cases his intolerance, his brutality and his abuse of power. Instead of proving his political correctness and mobilizing the masses, he often chose the path of repression and physical annihilation, not only against actual enemies, but also against individuals who had not committed any crimes against the party and the Soviet Government.

munist Party, Khrushchev gave a secret speech (later published outside the Soviet Union) in which he denounced Stalin and his crimes against socialist justice during the purges of the 1930s. The speech stunned party circles, but it also opened the way for genuine, if limited, internal criticism of the Soviet government and for many of the changes in intellectual and economic life cited earlier. Gradually, Khrushchev removed the strongest supporters of Stalinist policies from the presidium. By 1958, all of Stalin's former supporters were gone, and none had been executed. (See "Khrushchev Denounces the Crimes of Stalin: The Secret Speech.")

Khrushchev's speech, however, had repercussions well beyond the borders of the Soviet Union. Communist leaders in Eastern Europe took it as a signal that they could govern with greater leeway than before and retreat from Stalinist policies. Indeed, Khrushchev's speech was simply the first of a number of extraordinary events in 1956.

The Three Crises of 1956

The Suez Intervention In July 1956, President Gamal Abdel Nasser (1918–1970) of Egypt nationalized the Suez Canal. Great Britain and France who had controlled the private company that had run the canal feared that this action would close the canal to their supplies of oil in the Persian Gulf. In October 1956, war broke out between Egypt and Israel. The British and French seized the opportunity to intervene militarily; however, the United States refused to support their action. The Soviet Union protested vehemently. The Anglo-French forces had to be withdrawn, and Egypt retained control of the canal.

The Suez intervention proved that without the support of the United States the nations of Western Europe could no longer impose their will on the rest of the world. It also appeared that the United States and the Soviet Union had restrained their allies from undertaking actions that might have resulted in a wider conflict. The fact that neither of the superpowers wanted war constrained both Egypt and the Anglo-French forces.

Polish Efforts Toward Independent Action The autumn of 1956 also saw important developments in Eastern Europe that demonstrated similar limitations on independent action among the Soviet bloc nations. When the prime minister of Poland died, the Polish Communist Party leaders refused to replace him with Moscow's nominee, despite considerable pressure from the Soviets. In the end, Wladyslaw Gomulka (1905–1982) emerged as the new Communist leader of Poland. He was the choice of the Poles, and he proved acceptable to the Soviets because he promised continued economic and military cooperation, and particularly because he continued Polish membership in the Warsaw Pact. Within those limits he halted the collectivization of Polish agriculture and improved relations with the Polish Roman Catholic Church.

The Hungarian Uprising Hungary provided the third trouble spot for the Soviet Union. In late October, demonstrations of sympathy for the Poles in Budapest led to street fighting. The Hungarian communists installed a new ministry headed by former premier Imre Nagy (1896–1958). Nagy was a Communist who sought a more independent position for Hungary. He went much further in his demands than Gomulka and directly appealed for political support from noncommunist groups in Hungary. Nagy called for the removal of Soviet troops and the ultimate neutralization of Hungary. He even called for Hungarian withdrawal from the Warsaw Pact. These demands were wholly unacceptable to the Soviet Union. In early November, Soviet troops invaded Hungary; deposed Nagy, who was later executed; and imposed Janos Kadar (1912–1989) as premier.

The events of 1956 in the Middle East and Eastern Europe solidified the position of the United States and the Soviet Union as superpowers. In different ways and to differing degrees, the two superpowers had demonstrated this new political reality to their allies. The nations of Western Europe would be able to make independent policy among themselves within Europe but were generally curtailed from independent action on the broader international scene. For approximately twenty-five years, the nations of Eastern Europe would be permitted virtually no autonomous actions in either the domestic or the international sphere.

▼ Later Cold War Confrontations

After 1956, the Soviet Union began to talk about "peaceful coexistence" with the United States. With the 1957 launch of *Sputnik*, the first satellite to orbit the earth, the Soviet Union appeared to have achieved an enormous technological superiority over the West. In 1958, the two countries began negotiations toward limiting the testing of nuclear weapons. By 1959, tensions had relaxed sufficiently for Western leaders to visit Moscow and for Khrushchev to tour the United States. A summit meeting was scheduled for May 1960, and President Eisenhower was to go to Moscow.

Just before the Paris Summit Conference, the Soviet Union shot down an American U-2 aircraft that was flying reconnaissance over Soviet territory. Khrushchev demanded an apology from Eisenhower for this air surveillance. Eisenhower accepted full responsibility for the surveillance policy but refused to apologize publicly. Khrushchev then refused to take part in the summit conference, just as the participants arrived in the French capital. The conference, as well as Eisenhower's proposed trip to the Soviet Union, was thus aborted.

The Soviets did not scuttle the summit meeting on the eve of its opening simply because of the American spy flights. They had long been aware of these flights and had other reasons for protesting them when they did. By 1960, the communist world itself had split between the Soviets and the Chinese, who were portraying the Russians as lacking revolutionary zeal. Destroying the summit was, in part, a way to demonstrate the Soviet Union's hard-line attitude toward the capitalist world.

The Berlin Wall

The aborted Paris conference opened the most difficult period of the Cold War. In 1961, the new U.S. president, John F. Kennedy (1917–1963), and Premier Khrushchev met in Vienna with inconclusive results.

Throughout 1961, thousands of refugees from East Germany crossed the border into West Berlin. This outflow of people embarrassed East Germany, hurt its economy, and demonstrated the Soviet Union's inability to control Eastern Europe. Consequently, in August 1961, the East Germans, with Soviet support, erected a concrete wall along the border between East and West Berlin, separating the two parts of the city. Despite speeches and symbolic support from the West, the wall halted the flow of refugees and brought the U.S. commitment to West Germany into doubt.

The Cuban Missile Crisis

The most dangerous days of the Cold War occurred during the Cuban missile crisis of 1962. This event represented another facet of the globalization of the Cold War, on this occasion, into the Americas. Cuba lies less than 100 miles off the Florida coast, and the United States had dominated the island since the Spanish-American War in 1898. In 1957, Fidel Castro (b. 1926) launched an insurgency in Cuba, which toppled the dictatorship of Flugencio Batista (1901–1973) on New Year's Day of 1959. Thereafter Castro established a communist government, and Cuba became an ally of the Soviet Union. These events caused enormous concern within the United States.

MAJOR DATES OF LATER COLD WAR YEARS	
1959	Khrushchev's visit to the United States
1960	Failed Paris Summit
1961	East Germany erects Berlin Wall
1962	Cuban missile crisis
1963	Test Ban Treaty between Soviet Union and the United States
1964	Khrushchev falls from power
1968	Soviet invasion of Czechoslovakia
1972	Strategic Arms Limitation Treaty

In 1962, the Soviet Union secretly began to place nuclear missiles in Cuba. In response, the American government, under President Kennedy, blockaded Cuba, halted the shipment of new missiles, and demanded the removal of existing installations. After a tense week, during which nuclear war seemed a real possibility, the Soviets backed down, and the crisis ended. This adventurism in foreign policy undermined Khrushchev's credibility in the ruling circles of the Soviet Union and caused other non-European communist regimes to question the Soviet commitment to their security and survival. It also increased the influence of the People's Republic of China in communist circles and convinced

During the Cuban missile crisis of 1962, the American ambassador to the United Nations displayed photographs to persuade the world of the threat to the United States less than one hundred miles from its own shores. © CORBIS

Soviet military leaders of the need to strengthen their forces, so that they would be as strong as, or stronger than, those of the United States in any future confrontation.

If the Cuban missile crisis had led to war, the United States could have launched missiles over Europe or from European bases into the Soviet Union. The crisis thus threatened Europe directly, but it was the last major Cold War confrontation to do so. In 1963, the United States and the Soviet Union concluded a nuclear test ban treaty. This agreement marked the beginning of a lessening in the overt tensions between the two powers.

▼ The Brezhenev Era

By 1964, many in the Soviet Communist Party had concluded that Khrushchev had tried to do too much too soon and had done it poorly. On October 16, 1964, Khrushchev was forced to resign. He was replaced by Alexei Kosygin (1904–1980) as premier and Leonid Brezhnev (1906–1982) as party secretary. Brezhnev eventually emerged as the dominant figure.

1968: The Invasion of Czechoslovakia

In 1968, during what became known as the Prague Spring, the government of Czechoslovakia, under Alexander Dubcek (1921–1992), began to experiment with a more liberal communism. Dubcek expanded freedom of discussion and other intellectual rights at a time when the Soviet Union was suppressing them. In the summer of 1968, the Soviet government and its allies in the Warsaw Pact sent troops into Czechoslovakia and replaced Dubcek with communist leaders more to its own liking.

At the time of the invasion, Soviet party chairman Brezhnev, in what came to be termed the *Brezhnev Doctrine*, declared the right of the Soviet Union to interfere in the domestic politics of other communist countries. Whereas the Truman Doctrine of 1947 had supported democratic governments and offered help to resist further communist penetration in Europe, the Brezhnev Doctrine of 1968 sought to sustain the communist governments of Eastern Europe and prevent any liberalization in the region. No further direct Soviet interventions occurred in Eastern Europe after 1968, yet the invasion of Czechoslovakia showed that any attempt at a greater liberalization could trigger Soviet military repression.

In the summer of 1968, Soviet tanks rolled into Czechoslovakia, ending that country's experiment in liberalized communism. This picture shows defiant flag-waving Czechs on a truck rolling past a Soviet tank in the immediate aftermath of the invasion. Hulton Archive Photos/Getty Images, Inc.

The United States and Détente

Foreign policy under Brezhnev combined attempts to reach an accommodation with the United States with continued efforts to expand Soviet influence and maintain Soviet leadership of the communist movement.

Although the Soviet Union sided with North Vietnam in its war with the United States, which is discussed later in this chapter, Soviet support was restrained. Under President Richard Nixon (1969–1974), the United States began a policy of détente with the Soviet Union, and the two countries concluded agreements on trade and on reducing strategic arms. Despite these agreements, Soviet spending on defense, and particularly on its navy, grew, damaging the consumer sectors of the economy.

During Gerald Ford's presidency (1974–1977), both the United States and the Soviet Union along with other European nations signed the Helsinki Accords. The accords recognized the Soviet sphere of influence in Eastern Europe, but they also recognized the human rights of the signers' citizens, which every government, including the Soviet Union, agreed to protect. President Jimmy Carter (1977–1981), a strong advocate of human rights, sought to induce the Soviet Union to comply with this commitment, a policy that cooled relations between the two countries.

Throughout this period of détente, in addition to its military presence in Eastern Europe, the Soviet Union pursued an activist foreign policy around the world. During the 1970s, it financed Cuban military intervention in Angola, Mozambique, and Ethiopia. Soviet funds flowed to the Sandinista forces in Nicaragua and to Vietnam, which permitted the Soviets to use naval bases after North Vietnam conquered the south in 1975. The Soviet Union also provided funds and weapons to various Arab governments for use against Israel.

Each of these actions represented either Soviet support for what it viewed as its own strategic interests or an attempt to weaken the interests of the United States. Even more importantly, following its backing down in the Cuban missile crisis, the Soviet government was determined to build up its military forces. By the early 1980s, the Soviet Union possessed the largest armed force in the world and had achieved virtual nuclear parity with the United States.

The Invasion of Afghanistan

It was at this moment of great military strength in 1979 that the Brezhnev government decided to invade Afghanistan, a strategic decision of enormous long-range consequences for the future of the Soviet Union as well as the United States. Although the Soviet Union already had a presence in Afghanistan, the Brezhnev government, for reasons that remain unclear, determined to send in troops to ensure its influence in central Asia and to install a puppet Afghan government.

The invasion brought a sharp response from the United States. The U.S. Senate refused to ratify a second Strategic Arms Limitation agreement that President Carter had signed earlier that year. The United States also embargoed grain shipments to the Soviet Union, boycotted the 1980 Olympic Games in Moscow, and sent aid to the Afghan rebels through various third parties, as did Pakistan, Saudi Arabia, and other Islamic nations. The U.S. Central Intelligence Agency became directly involved with the Afghan resistance forces, some of whom were radical Muslims. China, which felt threatened by the invasion, also helped the rebels.

Eventually, the Soviet forces bogged down in Afghanistan and could not defeat their guerrilla enemies. The Afghans killed approximately 2,000 Soviet troops a year and inflicted many other casualties. The morale and prestige of the Soviet army plummeted. At first, few Soviets knew about the problems in Afghanistan, but during the 1980s, the military failure became common knowledge in the Soviet Union. Although the Afghan war did not make daily headline news in the Western press, it sapped Soviet strength for ten years and demoralized the Soviet Union not unlike the way the Vietnam conflict did the United States.

Communism and Solidarity in Poland

Events in Poland commencing in 1980—a time when the Soviet government was becoming increasingly rigidified and involved in Afghanistan—challenged both the authority of the Polish Communist Party and the influence of the Soviet Union.

After the events of late 1956, when the Polish Communist Party had accommodated itself to Soviet domination, chronic economic mismanagement and persistent shortages of food and consumer goods plagued Poland for twenty-five years. In 1978, the election of Karol Wojtyla, cardinal archbishop of Kraków, as Pope John Paul II (d. 2005) proved important for Polish resistance to communist control and Soviet domination. An outspoken Polish opponent of communism now occupied a position of authority and enormous public visibility well beyond the reach of Soviet or communist control. The new pope visited his homeland in 1979 and received a tumultuous welcome.

In July 1980, the Polish government raised meat prices, leading to hundreds of protest strikes across the country. On August 14, workers occupied the Lenin shipyard at Gdansk on the Baltic coast. The strike soon spread to other shipyards, transport facilities, and factories connected with the shipbuilding industry. The strikers, led by Lech Walesa (b. 1944), refused to negotiate through any of the government-controlled unions. The Gdansk strike ended on August 31 after the government promised the workers the right to organize an in-

---

MAJOR DATES OF THE BREZHNEV ERA

1974	Solzhenitsyn expelled
1975	Helsinki Accords
1979	Soviet invasion of Afghanistan
1980	U.S. Olympic Games boycott
1981	Martial law declared in Poland in response to Solidarity
1982	Death of Brezhnev

---

dependent union called Solidarity. In September, the head of the Polish Communist Party was replaced, the Polish courts recognized Solidarity as an independent union, and the state-controlled radio broadcast a Roman Catholic mass for the first time in thirty years.

The summer of 1981 saw events that were no less remarkable occur within the Polish Communist Party itself. For the first time in any European communist state, secret elections for the party congress were permitted with real choices among the candidates. A single party continued to govern Poland, but for the time being, the party congress permitted real debate within its ranks.

This extraordinary Polish experiment, however, ended abruptly. In 1981, General Wojciech Jaruzelski (b. 1923) became head of the Polish Communist Party, and the army imposed martial law in December. The leaders of Solidarity were arrested. The Polish military acted to preserve its own position and perhaps to prevent a Soviet invasion similar to the one in Czechoslovakia in 1968. Martial law remained in effect until late in 1983, but the Polish Communist Party could not solve Poland's major economic problems.

Relations with the Reagan Administration

Early in the administration of President Ronald Reagan (1981–1989), the United States relaxed its grain embargo on the Soviet Union and placed less emphasis on human rights. At the same time, however, Reagan intensified Cold War rhetoric, famously describing the Soviet Union as an "evil empire." More importantly, the Reagan administration increased U.S. military spending, slowed arms limitation negotiations, deployed a new missile system in Europe, and proposed the Strategic Defense Initiative (dubbed "Star Wars" by the press), involving a high-technology space-based defense against nuclear attack. The Star Wars proposal, although controversial in the United States, was a major issue in later arms control negotiations with the Soviet Union. Star Wars and the Reagan defense spending forced the Soviet Union to increase its own defense spending when it could ill afford to do so and contributed to the economic problems that helped bring about its collapse. Yet even during Rea-

gan's first term (1981–1985), no major transformation of the Soviet Union seemed to be in the offing.

Meanwhile throughout these four decades of the Cold War between the United States and the Soviet Union, extraordinary events had been occurring in Africa and Asia.

▼ Decolonization: The European Retreat from Empire

The transformation of much of Africa and Asia from colonial domains into independent nations was the most remarkable global political event of the second half of the twentieth century. The numbers of people involved alone reveals the magnitude of the change. At the founding of the United Nations in 1945, approximately one third of the population of the world was subject to the government of colonial powers. Since that time, more than eighty of those then non-self-governing territories have been admitted to UN membership as independent states. (See Map 29–6.)

During the interwar years the European colonial powers had confronted a variety of revolts or nationalist movements, which they had been able to contain either by military force or modest reforms. The war itself and the opportunities it provided to indigenous nationalist movements within Africa, Asia, and the Middle East transformed the situation. World War II drew the military forces of the colonial powers back to Europe. The Japanese overran European possessions in East Asia and demonstrated thus that the European presence there might not be permanent. After the dislocations of the war came the immediate postwar European economic collapse, which left the European colonial powers less able to afford to maintain their military and administrative positions abroad. Consequently, in less than a century after the great nineteenth-century drive toward empire, European imperialists found themselves in retreat around the globe.

The liberal-democratic war aims of the Allies had also undermined colonialism. It was difficult to fight against tyranny in Europe while maintaining colonial dominance abroad. The United States, and in particular Franklin Roosevelt, opposed the continuation of the colonial empires. This policy was, in part, a matter of principle, but it also recognized that both the political and economic interests of the United States were more likely to prosper in a decolonized world. The founding of the United Nations also assured the presence of an international body opposed to colonialism.

The Cold War complicated the process of decolonization. Both the United States and the Soviet Union opposed the old colonial empires, but both also worried about the potential alignment of the new nations and moved to create spheres of influence and, in some cases, alliances with the newly independent states. Certain

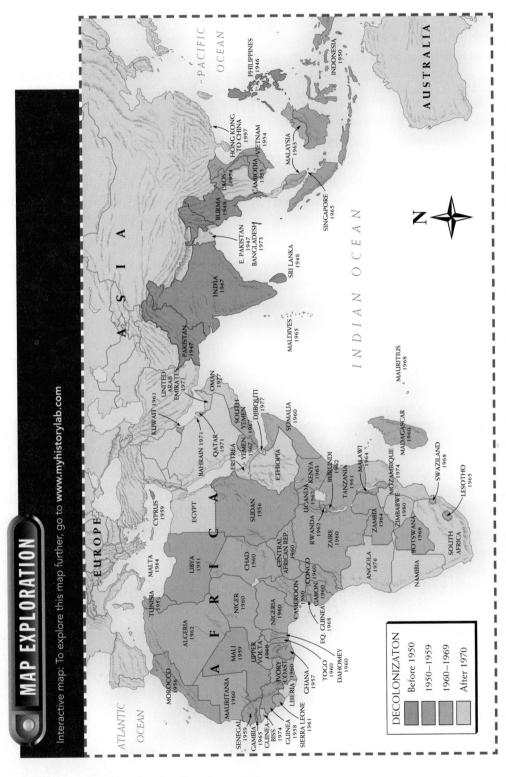

Map 29–6 **DECOLONIZATION SINCE WORLD WAR II** The Western powers' rapid retreat from imperialism after World War II is graphically shown on this outline map covering half the globe—from West Africa to the southwest Pacific.

nations, such as India, fiercely pursued policies of neutrality in hopes of receiving aid and support from both sides.

Major Areas of Colonial Withdrawal

Decolonization was a worldwide event lasting throughout the second half of the twentieth century and beyond. It involved such dramatic moments as the Dutch being forced from the East Indies in 1949 to be replaced by the independent nation of Indonesia, the Belgian withdrawal from the Congo in 1960, the liberation of Portuguese Mozambique and Angola in 1974 and 1975, and the end of all-white rule in Rhodesia (Zimbabwe) in 1979 and most remarkably in South Africa in 1994.

Each of these events was important, especially to the peoples involved, but the two largest colonial empires were the British and the French. Their retreat from empire produced the most far-reaching repercussions not only in former colonial nations, but in both Europe and the United States as well.

India

No anticolonial movement so gripped the imagination of the Western world as that carried out in India under the leadership of Mohandas Gandhi (1869–1948). The British had solidified their rule of India in the mid-eighteenth century extending and consolidating it throughout the nineteenth. (See Chapter 25.) The British administration required the Indians themselves to pay for British rule. India supplied the raw materials for the British cotton mills. Other British policies pushed many Indians to migrate to British possessions in East Asia, Africa, and the Caribbean. For decades, the religious, ethnic, linguistic, and political divisions among Indians permitted the British to dominate the country through a divide-and-rule strategy.

As early as 1885, politically active Hindu Indians founded the Indian National Congress with the goals of modernizing Indian life and liberalizing British policy. Muslims organized the Muslim League in 1887, which for a time cooperated with the National Congress but eventually sought an independent Muslim nation. After World War I, the Indian nationalist movement grew steadily in strength, in part because of British blunders, but more importantly because remarkable leaders pursued effective strategies.

Chief among these leaders was Gandhi, who had studied law in Britain and there began to encounter the ideas of liberal Western thinkers, including the American Henry David Thoreau (1817–1862) from whom he learned the concept of passive resistance. After being called to the bar in London in 1891, he returned briefly to India and then in 1893 went to South Africa where for over twenty years he worked on behalf of Indian immi-

grants. During those years he continued to read widely and became convinced of the power of passive resistance. Gandhi returned to India in 1915 and soon distinguished himself as a leader of Indian nationalism by his insistence on religious toleration. From the 1920s to the mid-1940s, he inspired a growing movement of passive resistance to British rule in India. In 1930, he lead a famous march to break the British salt monopoly by collecting salt from the sea. He was repeatedly arrested and jailed by the British authorities. To embarrass the British during these imprisonments and to gain worldwide publicity, he undertook long protest fasts during which he nearly died. In 1942, during World War II, Gandhi called on the British Government to leave India. In 1947, the British Labor government, weary of the incessant agitation and uncertain of its ability to maintain control in India, decided to do so.

Gandhi became and remains the most famous anticolonial leader of the twentieth century. His career demonstrates how such a leader could use ideas taken from the West against colonial regimes. His use of passive resistance became a model for Dr. Martin

Ghandi led India from colonialism to independence. Part of his appeal was the simplicity of his life and dress. CORBIS/Bettmann

GANDHI EXPLAINS HIS DOCTRINE OF NONVIOLENCE

The most famous device Indian nationalists used against British colonial rule in India was Gandhi's doctrine of nonviolence. He had come to believe in its power during his years in South Africa. Gandhi wrote this description of the meaning of nonviolence during World War II. Yet even while enunciating its meaning, he refused to associate himself with nonviolence in international relations. This reluctance may have stemmed from his recognition that the war against the Axis powers was a war against Nazi racism and Japanese imperialism, both of which were dangerous for colonial peoples of color.

Why does Gandhi see nonviolence as evidence of strength? How does he refrain from extending nonviolence to external relations? How was Gandhi's doctrine transferable to other political movements, such as the American civil rights struggle?

I do believe that, where there is only a choice between cowardice and violence, I would advise violence. . . .

But I believe that non-violence is infinitely superior to violence, forgiveness is more manly than punishment. . . .

Non-violence is the law of our species as violence is the law of the brute. The spirit lies dormant in the brute, and he knows no law but that of physical might. The dignity of man requires obedience to a higher law—to the strength of the spirit.

I have therefore ventured to place before India the ancient law of self-sacrifice. . . .

Non-violence in its dynamic condition means conscious suffering. It does not mean meek submission to the will of the evil-doer, but it means the pitting of one's whole soul against the will of the tyrant. Working under this law of our being, it is possible for a single individual to defy the whole might of an unjust empire to save his honour, his religion, his soul, and lay the foundation for that empire's fall or its regeneration. . . .

I have not the capacity for preaching universal non-violence to the country. I preach, therefore, non-violence restricted strictly for the purpose of winning our freedom and therefore perhaps for preaching the regulation of international relations by non-violent means. But my incapacity must not be mistaken for that of the doctrine of non-violence. I see it with my intellect in all its effulgence. My heart grasps it. But I have not yet the attainments of preaching universal non-violence with effect. . . .

I do justify entire non-violence, and consider it possible in relation between man and man and nation and nation; but it is not "a resignation from all fighting against wickedness." On the contrary, the non-violence of my conception is a more active, more real fighting against wickedness than retaliation whose very nature is to increase wickedness. I contemplate a mental, and therefore a moral, opposition to immoralities. I seek entirely to blunt the edge of the tyrant's sword, not by putting up against it a sharper-edged weapon, but by disappointing his expectations that I should be offering physical resistance. . . .

Non-violence, therefore, presupposes ability to strike. It is a conscious deliberate restraint put upon one's desire for vengeance.

"Gandhi Explains His Doctrine of Non-Violence" from M. K. Gandhi, *Non-Violence in Peace and War* (Navajivan Publishing, 1942). Reprinted by permission of the Navajivan Trust.

Luther King, Jr. (1929–1968) during the civil rights movement in the United States during the late 1950s and 1960s. (See "Gandhi Explains His Doctrine of Nonviolence.")

Gandhi and the Congress Party succeeded in forcing the British from India. However, they did not succeed in creating a single nation. Parallel to Gandhi's drive for an India characterized by diverse religions living in mutual toleration, the Muslim League led by Ali Jinnah (1876–1948) sought a distinctly Muslim state. What occurred in 1947 as the British left India was a partition of the country into the states of India and Pakistan. Intense sectarian warfare and hundreds of thousands of deaths marked the partition. A Hindu extremist assassinated Gandhi himself in 1948. It should also be noted that despite partition a vast Muslim population remained in India. Pakistan was initially a nation of two parts separated geographically by hundreds of miles of Indian territory. In 1971, East Pakistan broke away to become independent Bangladesh. As will be seen later in this chapter, the founding of Pakistan would be important for the emergence of political Islamism.

The partition of India and Pakistan illustrates an often-neglected factor in the process of decolonization. In many colonial regions, the retreat of the colonial powers opened the way for new or renewed conflicts among different ethnic and religious groups within the former colonial empires. For example, since partition, India and Pakistan have disputed the ownership of Kashmir in repeated armed clashes. Another example is the conflict over the former Portuguese colony of East Timor whose people have asserted a right to independence against the government of Indonesia, which occupied it for twenty years after Portugal withdrew in 1975.

Further British Retreat from Empire

The British surrender of India marked the beginning of a long, steady retreat from empire. Generally speaking, the British accepted the loss of empire as inevitable. British decolonization sought first to maintain whatever links were economically and politically possible without conflict. Indeed, during the 1940s and 1950s, the British undertook various development programs in their remaining Asian, African, and Caribbean colonies. These investments paradoxically made the British government and public more aware of the actual costs of empire and may have led both to accept more easily the end of empire. Second, throughout decolonization the British hoped to oversee the creation of institutions in their former colonies that would assure representative self-government once they had departed.

In 1948, Burma and Sri Lanka (formerly Ceylon) became independent. As already observed, the formation of the state of Israel and Arab nationalist movements forced Britain to withdraw from Palestine. During the 1950s, the British tried, belatedly, to prepare their tropical colonies for self-government. Ghana (formerly the Gold Coast) and Nigeria—which became self-governing in 1957 and 1960, respectively—were the major examples of planned decolonization. In other areas, such as Cyprus, Kenya, and Aden (now part of Yemen), the British withdrew under the pressure of militant nationalist movements. In many areas, violence between the British and the forces demanding independence hastened this retreat.

The development of these former colonies in the second half of the twentieth century has followed two distinct paths. In general, political instability and poverty have characterized the history of the independent states in Africa. By contrast, Asia has been an area of overall political stability and remarkable economic growth, challenging the economies of both the United States and Western Europe.

▼ The Turmoil of French Decolonization

Although the British retreat from empire involved violence, at no point did the British "make a stand." Moreover, many groups in Britain, including the leadership of the Labour Party, had long been critical of colonialism. Such was not the case with France. Having been defeated by the Nazis and then liberated by the allied forces, France believed it must reassert its position as a great power. This determination led it into two disastrous attempts to maintain its colonial empire, in Algeria and Vietnam. As will be seen, the situation in Vietnam, because of the intervention of the United States, drew French decolonization directly into the tensions of the Cold War.

France and Algeria

France had conquered the pirate's nest of Algiers in 1830 as Charles X (r. 1824–1830) futilely hoped the invasion would increase support for his monarchy. (See Chapter 20.) In late 1848, the French government made Algeria an integral part of France, establishing three administrative departments that were administered like those in France itself. Over the decades, as France consolidated and extended its position in Algeria, French soldiers and hundreds of thousands of Europeans from France and other Mediterranean countries settled there, primarily in the cities and on small farms. By the close of World War I, approximately 20 percent of the population was of European descent. Collectively these immigrants were termed the *pieds noirs* (meaning "black feet," a derogatory term). The voting structure was set up to give the French settlers as large a voice as the majority Arab Muslim population. The further one moved toward the south away from the coast and into the Sahara Desert, the greater the influence of the French military. Algerian Muslims were not given posts in the administration. Shortly after World War I, the French extended the rights of full French citizenship to Algerian Muslims who had fought in the war, who were literate in French, or who owned land, but this rewarded only a few thousand of them.

During World War II, the forces of Free France dominated Algeria after 1942 while the Vichy regime still governed metropolitan France. The Free French government did little to change the colonial status quo. Moreover, in May 1945, during celebrations of the Allied victory in World War II, a violent clash broke out at Sétif between Muslims and French settlers. Matters rapidly got out of hand, and people on both sides were killed, but the French repressed the Muslims with a considerable loss of life. The Muslims of Algeria saw this incident the same way the Russian working classes viewed Bloody Sunday in 1905. (See Chapter 23.) It robbed the French administration of legitimacy and marked the beginning of conscious Algerian nationalism. Thereafter, many Algerian Muslims supported independence. To placate Muslim opinion, in 1947, the French established a structure for limited political representation of the Muslim population and undertook economic reforms. Not unsurprisingly, these steps proved ineffective.

Algerian nationalists soon founded the National Liberation Front (FLN). In late 1954, insurrections and soon open civil war broke out in Algeria as the FLN undertook highly effective guerrilla warfare. The government of the Fourth French Republic that had been founded in 1945 adamantly declared Algeria an integral part of France and refused to compromise with the insurgents. Thereafter a war lasting until 1962 ground on between the Algerian nationalists and the French. Both sides committed atrocities; hundreds of thousands of Algerians were killed. The war divided France itself with many French citizens, often of left-wing political opinion, objecting to the war, and the French military, still smarting from its defeats in World War II and in Indochina, determined to fight on. The presence of more

than 1 million European settlers in Algeria, who saw any settlement with the nationalists as a betrayal, exacerbated the situation. The French government itself became paralyzed and lost control of the army. There was fear of civil war in France itself or of a military takeover. In Algeria, violence was spreading.

In the midst of this turmoil, General Charles de Gaulle (1890–1970), who had led the Free French forces during World War II and had briefly governed France immediately after the war, reentered French political life largely at the urging of the military. His condition for taking office was the end of the Fourth Republic and the promulgation of a new constitution, which enhanced the power of the president and created the Fifth Republic. The voters ratified this, and de Gaulle became president of France in December 1958. He then undertook a long strategic retreat from Algeria. The process was neither peaceful nor easy. In 1961, for example, it looked as if a group of officers known as the OAS (Organisation Armée Secrète) would attempt a coup in Paris. There were bombings, murders, and attempts on de Gaulle's life. In 1962, however, de Gaulle held a referendum in Algeria on independence, which passed overwhelmingly. Algeria became independent on July 3, 1962.

Once the FLN took over Algeria under the presidency of Mohammed Ben Bella (b. 1919), however, a second factor came into play in French domestic life. Hundreds of thousands of *pied noirs* settlers fled Algeria for France as did many Muslims who had supported the French and

In 1959, Charles de Gaulle as president of the French Republic visited Algiers to great acclaim from its European inhabitants, known as *colons*. By 1962, however, he had sponsored a referendum that led to Algerian independence and the flight of most of those people.   Loomis Dean/Getty Images, Inc.

had good cause to fear reprisals. (Thousands of pro-French Muslims who did not flee were massacred.) The emigration of this latter group marked the beginning of a large, and largely unwelcome, Muslim population in France.

France and Vietnam

One of the reasons for the strong French stand against Algerian independence had been the loss of its south Asian empire in Indochina just before the Algerian insurrection broke out in 1954. Whereas the Algerian drive toward independence essentially involved only France and the populations of Algeria, the Indochina problem eventually drew the United States into war in Vietnam.

In its push for empire, France had occupied Indochina (which contained Laos, Cambodia, and Vietnam) between 1857 and 1893. By 1930, Ho Chi Minh (1892–1969) had turned a nationalist movement against French colonial rule into the Indochina Communist Party, which the French, for a time, succeeded in suppressing. World War II, however, provided new opportunities for Ho Chi Minh and other nationalists as they fought both the Japanese who occupied Indochina in 1941 and the pro-Vichy French colonial administration that collaborated with the Japanese until 1945. The war thus established Ho Chi Minh as a major anticolonial, nationalist leader. He was a communist to be sure, but he had achieved his position in Vietnam during the war without the support of Chinese or Soviet communists.

In September 1945, Ho Chi Minh declared the independence of Vietnam under the Viet Minh, a coalition of nationalists that the communists soon dominated. By 1947, a full-fledged civil war had erupted in Vietnam. (Cambodia and, to a lesser extent, Laos remained quiescent under pro-French or neutralist monarchies.)

Until 1949, the United States displayed minimal concern about the Indochina war. The establishment of the Communist People's Republic of China that year dramatically changed the U.S. outlook. The United States now saw the French colonial war against Ho Chi Minh as an integral part of the Cold War conflict. The U.S. support for France in southeast Asia also served to gain French support for the establishment of NATO. Even though the United States supported the French effort in Vietnam financially, it was not prepared, despite divisions among policymakers, to intervene militarily. In the spring of 1954, during an international conference in Geneva on the future of Vietnam, the French military stronghold of Dien Bien Phu fell to Viet Minh forces after a prolonged siege. France lost the will to continue the struggle, which had become increasingly unpopular with the French people.

By late June, a complicated and unsatisfactory peace accord divided Vietnam at the seventeenth parallel of latitude. North of the parallel, centered in Hanoi, the Viet Minh were in charge; below it, centered in Saigon, the French were in charge. This was to be a temporary border. By 1956, elections were to be held to reunify the country. In effect, the conference attempted to transform a military conflict into a political one.

Vietnam Drawn into the Cold War

Unhappy with these arrangements, the United States, in September 1954, formed the Southeast Asia Treaty Organization (SEATO), a collective security agreement that somewhat resembled the European NATO alliance, but without the integration of military forces or inclusion of all states in the region. Its membership consisted of the United States, Great Britain, France, Australia, New Zealand, Thailand, Pakistan, and the Philippines.

By 1955, American policymakers had begun to think about Indochina, and particularly Vietnam, largely in terms of the Korean example. The U.S. government assumed, incorrectly, that, like the government of North Korea, the government in North Vietnam was basically a communist puppet of the Soviets and the Chinese. That same year, French troops began to withdraw from South Vietnam. As they left, the various Vietnamese political groups began to fight for power among themselves.

The United States stepped into the turmoil in Vietnam with military and economic aid. Among the Vietnamese politicians, it chose to support was Ngo Dinh Diem (1901–1963), a strong noncommunist nationalist who had not collaborated with the French. Because the United States had been publicly and deeply committed

MAJOR DATES IN THE VIETNAM CONFLICT

1945	Ho Chi Minh proclaims Vietnamese independence from French rule
1947–1954	War between France and Vietnam
1950	U.S. financial aid to France
1954	Geneva conference on Southeast Asia opens
1954	French defeat at Dien Bien Phu
1954	Southeast Asia Treaty Organization (SEATO) founded
1955	Diem establishes Republic of Vietnam in the south
1960	Founding of National Liberation Front to overthrow the Diem government
1961	Six hundred American troops and advisers in Vietnam
1963	Diem overthrown and assassinated
1964	Gulf of Tonkin Resolution
1965	Major U.S. troop commitment
1969	Nixon announces policy of Vietnamization
1973	Cease-fire announced
1975	Saigon falls to North Vietnamese troops

to the French, however, Vietnamese nationalists would view any government it supported with suspicion. In October 1955, Diem established a Republic of Vietnam in the territory for which the Geneva conference had made France responsible. Diem announced that the Geneva agreements would not bind his newly established government and that elections would not be held in 1956. The American government, which had not signed the Geneva documents, supported his position.

In 1960, the National Liberation Front was founded, with the goals of overthrowing Diem, unifying the country, reforming the economy, and ousting the Americans. It was anticolonial, nationalist, and communist. Its military arm was called the Viet Cong and was aided by the government of North Vietnam. Diem, a Roman Catholic, also faced mounting criticism from Buddhists and the army. His response to these pressures was further repression and dependence on an ever-smaller group of advisers.

Direct United States Involvement

The Eisenhower and Kennedy administrations continued to support Diem while demanding reforms in his government. The American military presence grew

from about 600 advisers in early 1961 to more than 16,000 troops in late 1963. The political situation in Vietnam became increasingly unstable. On November 1, 1963, an army coup in which the United States was deeply involved overthrew and murdered Diem. The United States hoped a new government in South Vietnam would generate popular support. Thereafter, the United States sought to find a leader who could fulfill that hope. It finally settled on Nguyen Van Thieu (1923–2001), who governed South Vietnam from 1966 to 1975.

President Kennedy was assassinated on November 22, 1963. His successor, Lyndon Johnson (1963–1969), vastly expanded the commitment to South Vietnam. In August 1964, after an attack on an American ship in the Gulf of Tonkin, Johnson authorized the first bombing of North Vietnam. In February 1965, major bombing attacks began. They continued, with only brief pauses, until early in 1973. The land war grew until more than 500,000 Americans were stationed in South Vietnam.

In 1969, President Richard Nixon began a policy known as *Vietnamization*, which involved the gradual withdrawal of American troops from Vietnam while the South Vietnamese army took over the full military

U.S. troops engaged in combat in Vietnam. At the war's peak, more than 500,000 American troops were stationed in South Vietnam. The United States struggled in Vietnam for more than a decade, seriously threatening its commitment to Western Europe. U.S. Army Photo

MAP EXPLORATION

Interactive map: To explore this map further, go
www.myhistorylab.com

Map 29–7 **Vietnam and Its Southeast Asian Neighbors** The map identifies important locations associated with the war in Vietnam.

fected the entire Western world. For a decade after the Cuban missile crisis, Vietnam largely diverted the attention of the United States from Europe. American prestige suffered, and the U.S. policy in Southeast Asia made many Europeans question the wisdom of the American government and its commitment to Western Europe. Many young Europeans and many people in the former colonial world as well as many Americans came to regard the United States not as a protector of liberty, but as an ambitious, aggressive, and cruel power trying to keep colonialism alive after the end of the colonial era. Within the United States, the Vietnam conflict produced enormous divisions and debates over American involvement in the rest of the world that persist to the present day.

▼ The Collapse of European Communism

The withdrawal of Soviet influence from Eastern Europe and the internal collapse of the Soviet Union are the most important European historical events of the second half of the twentieth century. They had virtually no parallel in modern European history. All of the other major governments that had disappeared in Europe earlier in the century had fallen either as the result of domestic revolution brought on by military defeat, as happened in tsarist Russia, Germany, and Austria after World War I and Italy during World War II, or military defeat followed by military occupation, as was the case with Germany after 1945 and the Third Republic in France in 1940. By contrast, the Soviet Union essentially imploded and then divided into separate successor states. There was no foreign invasion, no military defeat, and no internal revolution. Many of the factors leading to the Soviet collapse remain murky, but here is a relatively clear narrative of what occurred.

Under Brezhnev, who governed from 1964 to 1982, the Soviet government became markedly more repressive at home, suggesting a return to Stalinist policies. In 1974, the government expelled Aleksandr Solzhenitsyn. It also began to harass Jewish citizens, creating bureaucratic obstacles for those who wanted to emigrate to Israel. This internal repression gave rise to a dissident movement. Certain Soviet citizens dared to criticize the regime in public and accused the government of violating the human rights provision of the 1975 Helsinki Accords. The dissidents included prominent citizens, such as the Nobel Prize–winning physicist Andrei Sakharov (1921–1989). The Soviet government responded with further repression, placing some opponents in psychiatric hospitals and others under what amounted to house arrest. During the same period the structures of

effort. Peace negotiations had begun in Paris in the spring of 1968, but a cease-fire was not finally arranged until January 1973. American troops left South Vietnam, and North Vietnam released its American prisoners of war. In early 1975, an evacuation of South Vietnamese troops from the northern part of their country turned into a rout when they were attacked by the North Vietnamese. On April 30, 1975, Saigon (renamed Ho Chi Minh City) fell to the Viet Cong and the North Vietnamese army. Vietnam was finally united. (See Map 29–7.)

The U.S. intervention in Vietnam, which grew out of a power vacuum left by French decolonization, af-

President Ronald Reagan and Premier Mikhail Gorbachev confer at a summit meeting in December 1987. AP Wide World Photos

the Communist Party became both rigidified and corrupt, which increasingly demoralized younger Soviet bureaucrats and party members.

Gorbachev Attempts to Reform the Soviet Union

Although economic stagnation, party corruption, and the lingering Afghan war had long been undermining Soviet authority, what brought these forces to a head and began the dramatic collapse of the Soviet Empire was the accession to power of Mikhail S. Gorbachev (b. 1931) in 1985 after both of Brezhnev's two immediate successors, Yuri Andropov (1914–1984) and Konstantin Chernenko (1911–1985), died within thirteen months of each other. In what proved to be the last great attempt to reform the Soviet system, Gorbachev immediately began the most remarkable changes that the Soviet Union had witnessed since the 1920s. These reforms loosed forces that, within seven years, would force him to retire from office and would end both communist rule and the Soviet Union as it had existed since the Bolshevik revolution of 1917. (See "Encountering the Past: Rock Music and Political Protest," page 966.)

Economic *Perestroika* Gorbachev's primary goal was to revive the Russian economy to raise the country's standard of living. Initially, he and his supporters, most of whom he had appointed himself, challenged traditional party and bureaucratic management of the Soviet government and economy. Under the policy of **perestroika**, or "restructuring," they reduced the size and importance of the centralized economic ministries.

During these same years, Gorbachev confronted significant labor discontent. A major strike by coal miners occurred in July 1989 in Siberia. Gorbachev had to settle their grievances quickly, because the economy desperately needed their output. He promised them better wages and wider political liberties.

By early 1990, in a clear abandonment of traditional Marxist ideology, Gorbachev began to advocate private ownership of property and liberalization of the economy toward free market mechanisms. Despite many organizational changes, the Soviet economy remained stagnate and even declined. The failure of Gorbachev's economic policies affected his political policies. To some extent, he pursued bold political reform because he failed to achieve economic progress.

Glasnost Gorbachev allowed an extraordinary public discussion and criticism of Soviet history and Soviet

ROCK MUSIC AND POLITICAL PROTEST

ROCK MUSIC, WHICH epitomizes popular culture throughout the Western world, was a form of entertainment with a loud antiestablishment political message. Rock originated in the United States in the 1950s with African-American musicians and working-class and country music singers. By the early 1960s, rock also included folk singers who used their music to champion the civil rights movement and protest the war in Vietnam.

European rock groups both embraced and transformed American rock music. The most spectacularly successful European group was the Beatles. Though sporting long hair and attracting the politically active young, the Beatles' lyrics were more laid back than political.

During the 1970s, in both the United States and Europe, punk rock groups, with provocative names such as the Sex Pistols, became popular. Punk rock was deeply antiestablishment, but Western society, which was increasingly pluralistic, took punk rock in its stride.

In Eastern Europe and the Soviet Union, however, punk rock was literally revolutionary. There the ever-more radical rock music of the 1970s and 1980s became a major vehicle for social and political criticism. In the face of communist cultural conformity, rock stars symbolized daring and personal heroism. Lyrics openly criticized communist governments, as in this example from "Get Out of Control," sung at a rock concert in Leningrad (now St. Petersburg) in 1986:

We were watched from the days of kindergarten.
Some nice men and kind women
Beat us up. They chose the most painful places
And treated us like animals on the farm.
So we grew up like a disciplined herd.
We sing what they want and live how they want
And we look at them downside up, as if we're
    trapped.
We just watch how they hit us
Get out of control!
Get out of control!
And sing what you want
And not just what is allowed
We have a right to yell![1]

This song became popular throughout Eastern Europe. It revealed how alienated the youth of the region had become from the official culture of the communist regimes. Rock music expressed and helped spread the disaffection that contributed to the collapse of communism throughout Eastern Europe at the end of the 1980s.

How did rock music evolve into an antiestablishment form of entertainment?

Why was rock considered subversive in the Eastern bloc nations?

The Russian rock group Dynamic performs in Moscow in 1987. R. Podemi/
TASS/Sovfoto/Eastfoto

[1]Quoted in Artemy Troitsky, *Back in the USSR: The True Story of Rock in Russia* (Boston: Faber & Faber, 1987), p. 127, as cited in Sabrina P. Ramet, ed., *Social Currents in Eastern Europe: The Sources and Meaning of the Great Transformation* (Durham, NC: Duke University Press, 1991), p. 239.

Communist Party policy. This development was termed *glasnost*, or openness. The contributions to Soviet history of such figures from the 1920s and 1930s as Nikolai Bukharin, whom Stalin had executed in 1938, received official public recognition. Workers were permitted to criticize party officials and the economic plans of the party and the government. Censorship was relaxed and free expression encouraged. Dissidents were released from prison. In the summer of 1988, Gorbachev presided over a party congress that witnessed full debates.

Gorbachev soon applied *perestroika* to the political arena. In 1988, a new constitution permitted openly contested elections. After real political campaigning—a new experience for the Soviet Union—the Congress of People's Deputies was elected in 1989. One of the new members of the congress was Andrei Sakharov, the dissident physicist whom Brezhnev had persecuted. After lively debate, the Supreme Soviet, another elected body—although one the Communist Party dominated—formally elected Gorbachev president in 1989.

The policy of open discussion allowed national minorities within the Soviet Union to demand political autonomy. Throughout its history, the Soviet Union had remained a vast empire of subject peoples. The tsars had conquered some of those groups, Stalin had incorporated others, such as the Baltic states, into the Soviet Union. *Glasnost* quickly brought to the foreground the discontent of all such peoples, no matter how or when they had been subjugated. Gorbachev proved inept in addressing these ethnic complaints. He badly underestimated the unrest that internal national discontent could generate.

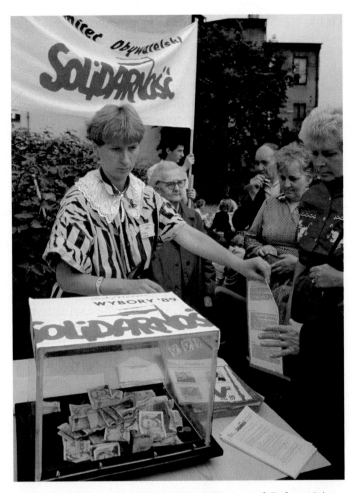

The Polish trade union "Solidarity" in 1989 successfully forced the Polish communist government to hold free elections. In June of that year Solidarity, whose members here are collecting funds for their campaign, won overwhelmingly.   Bernard Bisson/CORBIS/Bettmann

1989: Revolution in Eastern Europe

Solidarity Reemerges in Poland   In the early 1980s, Poland's government relaxed martial law, and it eventually released all the Solidarity prisoners, although Jaruzelski remained president. In 1988, new strikes surprised even the leaders of Solidarity. This time, the communist government could not reimpose control. After consultations between the government and Solidarity, the union was legalized. Lech Walesa again took center stage, as a kind of mediator between the government and the more independent elements of the trade union movement he had founded.

Jaruzelski began some political reforms with the tacit consent of the Soviet Union. He promised free elections to a parliament with increased powers. When elections were held in 1989, the communists lost overwhelmingly to Solidarity candidates. Late in the summer, Jaruzelski, unable to find a communist who could forge a majority coalition in Parliament, turned to Solidarity and appointed the first noncommunist prime minister of Poland since 1945. Gorbachev expressly approved the appointment.

Toward Hungarian Independence   Throughout 1989, as these events unfolded within Poland, one Soviet-dominated state after another in Eastern Europe moved toward independence. Early in the year, the Hungarian government opened its border with Austria, permitting free travel between the two countries. This breach in the Iron Curtain immediately led thousands of East Germans to move through Hungary and Austria to West Germany. In May, Janos Kadar, who had been installed after the Soviet intervention in 1956, was stripped of his position as president of the Hungarian Communist Party. Thousands of Hungarians gave an honorary burial to the body of Imre Nagy, whom Kadar had executed in 1958. The Hungarian Communist Party changed its name to the Socialist Party, permitted other parties to engage openly in politics, and promised free elections by October.

German Reunification   In the autumn of 1989, popular demonstrations erupted in East German cities. Adding to the pressure, Gorbachev told the leaders of the East German Communist Party that the Soviet

Union would not use force to support them. With startling swiftness, the East German government resigned, making way for a younger generation of communist leaders who remained in office for only a few weeks. In November 1989, in one of the most emotional moments in European history since 1945, the government of East Germany ordered the opening of the Berlin Wall. That week, tens of thousands of East Berliners crossed into West Berlin to celebrate, to visit their families, and to shop with money the West German government gave them. Shortly thereafter, free travel began between East and West Germany. (See Map 29–8.)

Within days of these dramatic events, West Germany and the other Western nations faced the issue of German reunification. Helmut Kohl (b. 1930), the chancellor of West Germany, became the leading force in moving toward full unification. Late in 1989, the European Economic Community accepted, in principle, the unification of Germany. By February 1990, some form of reunification had become a foregone conclusion, accepted by the United States, the Soviet Union, Great Britain, and France.

The Velvet Revolution in Czechoslovakia

Revolution in Czechoslovakia rapidly followed the breach of the Berlin Wall. The popular new Czech leader who led the forces against the party was Václav Havel (b. 1936), a playwright of international standing whom the communist government had imprisoned. In December 1989, the tottering communist government, together with the Soviet Union and other Warsaw Pact states, acknowledged that the invasion of 1968 had been a mistake. Shortly thereafter, Havel's group, known as Civic Forum, forced Gustav Husak (b. 1913), who had been president of Czechoslovakia since 1968, to resign. On December 28, 1989, Alexander Dubcek became chairman of the Parliament, and the next day, Havel was elected president.

Violent Revolution in Romania

The only revolution of 1989 that involved significant violence occurred in Romania. There, in mid-December, the forces of President Nicolae Ceausescu (1918–1989), who had governed without opposition since 1965, fired on crowds that were protesting conditions in the country. By December 22, Bucharest was in full revolt. Ceausescu and his wife attempted to flee, but were captured, secretly tried, and shot on December 25.

The Soviet Stance on Revolutionary Developments

None of the revolutions of 1989 could have taken place unless the Soviet Union had refused to intervene militarily, in contrast to 1956 and 1968. As events unfolded, it became clear that Gorbachev would not rescue the old-line communist governments and party leaderships in Eastern Europe. In October 1989, he formally renounced the Brezhnev Doctrine. For the first time since the end of World War II, Eastern Europeans could shape their own political destiny without the fear of Soviet military intervention. Once they realized the Soviets would not act, thousands of ordinary citizens took to the streets to denounce Communist Party domination and assert their desire for democracy. The major question facing the Soviet Union became the peaceful withdrawal of its troops from Eastern Europe. The haphazard nature of that withdrawal and the general poverty to which those troops returned were other factors undermining the Soviet armed forces.

The peaceful character of most of these revolutions was not inevitable. It may, in part, have resulted from the shock with which much of the world responded to the violent repression of pro-democracy protesters in Beijing's Tiananmen Square by the People's Republic of China in May 1989. The Communist Party officials of Eastern Europe and the Soviet Union clearly decided in 1989 that they could not offend world opinion with a similar attack on democratic demonstrators.

The Collapse of the Soviet Union

Gorbachev clearly believed, as his behavior toward Eastern Europe in 1989 showed, that the Soviet Union could no longer afford to support communist governments in that region or intervene to uphold their authority while seeking to restructure its own economy. He also had concluded that the Communist Party in the Soviet Union must restructure itself and its relationship to the Soviet state and society.

Renunciation of Communist Political Monopoly

In early 1990, Gorbachev formally proposed to the Central Committee of the Soviet Communist Party that the party abandon its monopoly of power. After intense debate, the committee abandoned the Leninist position that only a single elite party could act as the vanguard of the revolution and forge a new Soviet society.

New Political Forces

Gorbachev confronted challenges from three major political forces by 1990. One consisted of those groups—considered conservative in the Soviet context—whose members wanted to preserve the influence of the Communist Party and the Soviet army. The country's economic stagnation and political and social turmoil deeply disturbed them. They appeared to control significant groups in the economy and society. During late 1990 and early 1991, Gorbachev, who himself seems to have been disturbed by the nation's turmoil, began to appoint members of these factions to key positions in the government. In other words, he seemed to be making a strategic retreat.

Map 29–8 **THE BORDERS OF GERMANY IN THE TWENTIETH CENTURY**   Map A shows the borders of imperial Germany at the outbreak of World War I. Map B shows the borders of Germany after the Versailles peace settlement. Map C shows the borders of Germany after Hitler's invasion of the Rhineland, the Anschluss with Austria, the Munich Pact, the invasion of Czechoslovakia, and the invasion of Poland. Map D illustrates the division of Germany into the German Federal Republic (West Germany) and the German Democratic Republic (East Germany) in the aftermath of World War II. Map E illustrates the borders of Germany after reunification in 1990.

A Closer ▶ LOOK

COLLAPSE OF THE BERLIN WALL

NO SINGLE STRUCTURE so illustrated the divisions of the Cold War as the Berlin Wall, which was erected in 1961. The most symbolic moment in the collapse of communism across Eastern Europe came in November 1989 when that wall was breached.

R. Bossu/Sygma/CORBIS

The sight of hundreds of Germans standing on top of the wall would have been unthinkable just days before. Armed East German and Soviet guards had for over a quarter century prevented Germans from crossing the wall except at a few heavily guarded checkpoints.

English graffiti had been placed on the wall to ensure that an international television audience, which was largely English-speaking, would understand the aspirations of those people who wanted the wall to come down.

The overwhelmingly youthful crowd indicates the repudiation by the new generation of Germans and Europeans of the Cold War divisions.

To examine this image in an interactive fashion, please go to www.myhistorylab.com

myhistorylab

Gorbachev initiated these moves because he was now facing opposition from a second group—those who wanted much more extensive and rapid change. Their leading spokesman was Boris Yeltsin (1931–2007). He and his supporters wanted to move quickly to a market economy and a more democratic government. Like Gorbachev, Yeltsin had risen through the ranks of the Communist Party and had then become disillusioned with its policies. Throughout the late 1980s, he had been critical of Gorbachev. In 1990, he was elected president of the Russian Republic, the largest and most important of the Soviet Union's constituent republics. In the new political climate, that position gave him a firm political base from which to challenge Gorbachev's authority and increase his own.

The third force that came into play from 1989 onward was growing regional unrest in some of the republics of the Soviet Union. These republics had experienced considerable discontent in the past, but the military and the Communist Party had always managed to repress it. Initially, the greatest unrest came from the three Baltic republics of Estonia, Latvia, and Lithuania, which had been independent states until 1940 when the Soviet Union had occupied

MAJOR EVENTS IN THE REVOLUTIONS OF 1989

January 11	Independent parties permitted in Hungary
April 5	Solidarity legalized in Poland and free elections accepted by government
May 2	Hungary dismantles barriers along its borders
May 8	Janos Kadar removed from office in Hungary
May 17	Polish government recognizes Roman Catholic Church
June 4	Solidarity victory in Polish parliamentary elections
July 25	Solidarity asked to join coalition government
August 24	Solidarity member appointed premier in Poland
October 18	Erich Honecker removed from office in East Germany
October 23	Hungary proclaims itself a republic
October 25	Gorbachev renounces Brezhnev Doctrine
November 9	Berlin Wall opened
November 17	Large antigovernment demonstration in Czechoslovakia crushed by police
November 19	Czechoslovak opposition groups organize into Civic Forum and demand resignation of communist leaders responsible for 1968 invasion
November 24	Czechoslovak communist leadership resigns
December 1	New Czechoslovak communist leaders denounce 1968 invasion; Soviet Union and Warsaw Pact express regret over 1968 invasion
December 3	Czechoslovak government announces ministry with noncommunist members
December 16–17	Massacre of civilians in Timisoara, Romania
December 22	Ceausescu government overthrown in Romania with many casualties
December 25	Announcement of Ceausescu's execution
December 28	Alexander Dubcek elected chairman of Czechoslovak Parliament
December 29	Václav Havel elected president of Czechoslovakia

themselves as national leaders rather than as party stalwarts.

During 1989 and 1990, the parliaments of the Baltic republics tried to decrease Soviet control, and Lithuania actually declared independence. Gorbachev used military force to resist these moves. Discontent also arose in the Soviet Islamic republics in Central Asia and the Caucasus. Riots broke out in Azerbaijan and Tajikistan, where the army was used as a police force against Soviet citizens. Throughout 1990 and 1991, Gorbachev sought to negotiate new constitutional arrangements between the republics and the central government. His failure to effect such arrangements may have been the single most important reason for the rapid collapse of the Soviet Union.

The August 1991 Coup The turning point in all of these events came in August 1991, when the conservative forces that Gorbachev had brought into the government attempted a coup. Troops occupied Moscow, and Gorbachev was placed under house arrest while on vacation in Crimea. The forces of political and economic reaction—led by people who, at the time, were associated with Gorbachev—had at last tried to seize control. The day of the coup, Boris Yeltsin climbed on a tank in front of the Russian Parliament building to denounce the coup and ask the world for help to maintain the Soviet Union's movement toward democracy.

Within two days, the coup collapsed. Gorbachev returned to Moscow, but in humiliation, having been victimized by the groups to whom he had turned for support. One of the largest public demonstrations in Russian history—perhaps even the largest—celebrated the failure of the coup in Moscow. From that point on, Yeltsin steadily became the dominant political figure in the nation. The Communist Party, compromised by its participation in the coup, collapsed as a political force. The constitutional arrangements between the central government and the individual republics were revised. In December 1991, the Soviet Union ceased to exist, Gorbachev left office, and the Commonwealth of Independent States came into being. (See Map 29–9, page 972.)

The collapse of European communism in the Soviet Union and throughout Eastern Europe has closed the era in which Marxism dominated European socialism that began in the 1870s with the German socialists' adoption of Marxist thought. The Bolshevik victory in the Russian Revolution seemed to validate Marxism, and the policies of Lenin and Stalin sought to extend it around the world. Now the Soviet Union and the communist governments of Eastern Europe—heirs to the Bolshevik revolution—have vanished, and the economies they built have collapsed. As a result, Marxist socialism has been discredited, and socialism in general may find itself on the defensive in the future.

them in accord with secret provisions of the Soviet-German nonaggression pact of 1939. That pact with Nazi Germany provided the only seemingly legal basis for the Soviet Union's continued control. In these republics, many local communist leaders began to see

Map 29–9 **THE COMMONWEALTH OF INDEPENDENT STATES** In December 1991, the Soviet Union broke up into its fifteen constituent republics. Eleven of these were loosely joined in the Commonwealth of Independent States. Also shown is the autonomous region of Chechnya, which has waged two bloody wars with Russia in the last decade. Because the borders of Soviet republics were drawn not so much as to promote stability but instability among the many ethnic groups of the Soviet Union, long-simmering disputes flared up once the empire collapsed. The many conflicts Georgia has faced since it regained its independence in 1991 are representative: It fought unsuccessful wars in the early 1990s to keep the breakaway regions of Abkhazia and South Ossetia, both of whose populations were heavily non-Georgian, under its control. In August 2008, when Georgia attempted to reassert its sovereignty over South Ossetia after Russian provocation, it was quickly repulsed by a massive invasion from Russia that resulted in hundreds of fatalities and billions of dollars of damage.

The Yeltsin Decade

Boris Yeltsin emerged as the strongest leader within the new commonwealth. As president of Russia, he was head of the largest and most powerful of the new states. His popularity was high both in Russia and in the commonwealth in 1992, but within a year, he faced serious economic and political problems. The Russian Parliament, most of whom were former communists, opposed Yeltsin personally and his policies of economic and political reform. Relations between the president and Parliament reached an impasse, crippling the government. In September 1993, Yeltsin suspended Parliament, which responded by deposing him. Parliament leaders tried to incite popular uprisings against Yeltsin in Moscow. The military, however, backed Yeltsin, and he surrounded the Parliament building with troops and tanks. On October 4, 1993, after pro-Parliament rioters rampaged through Moscow, Yeltsin ordered the tanks to attack the Parliament building, crushing the opposition.

These actions consolidated Yeltsin's authority. The major Western powers, deeply concerned by the turmoil

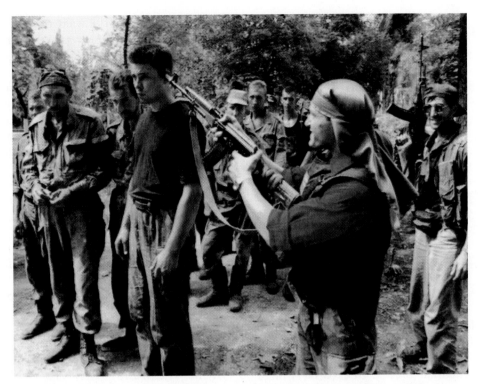

A Chechen fighter points his rifle at the head of a Russian prisoner of war outside the Chechen capital Grozny in August 1996.   Mindaugas Kulbis/AP Wide World Photos

in Russia, supported him. In December 1993, Russians voted for a new Parliament and approved a new constitution. By 1994, the central government found itself at war in the Islamic province of Chechnya in the Caucasus. Under Yeltsin, Russian forces held off a rebel victory, but the war reached no clear conclusion.

During the mid-1990s, to dismantle the Soviet state and economy, former state-owned industries were privatized. This complicated process involved much corruption and opportunism by individuals determined to profit from the emerging economic organization. One result was the creation of a small group of enormously wealthy individuals, whom the press dubbed "the oligarchs." While these people amassed vast wealth, the general Russian economy remained stagnant. In 1998, Russia defaulted on its international debt payments. Political assassinations occurred and have continued to the present time. The economic downturn contributed to further political unrest. In the face of these problems and in declining health, Yeltsin resigned the presidency in a dramatic gesture just as the new century opened. His hand-picked successor was Vladimir Putin (b. 1952), a relatively unknown figure at the time. Putin would lead the Russian Federation in new economic and political directions. Before considering Putin's role, it is necessary to examine the events that occurred during the 1990s in southeastern Europe.

▼ The Collapse of Yugoslavia and Civil War

Yugoslavia was created after World War I. Its borders included seven major national groups—Serbs, Croats, Slovenes, Montenegrins, Macedonians, Bosnians, and Albanians—among whom there have been ethnic disputes for centuries. The Croats and Slovenes are Roman Catholic and use the Latin alphabet. The Serbs, Montenegrins, and Macedonians are Eastern Orthodox and use the Cyrillic alphabet. The Bosnians and Albanians are mostly Muslims. Most members of each group reside in a region with which they are associated historically—Serbia, Croatia, Slovenia, Montenegro, Macedonia, Bosnia-Herzegovina, and Kosovo—and these regions constituted individual republics or autonomous areas within Yugoslavia. Many Serbs, however, lived outside Serbia proper.

Tito (1892–1980) had acted independently of Stalin in the late 1940s and pursued his own foreign policy. To mute ethnic differences, he encouraged a cult of personality around himself and instituted complex political power sharing among these different groups. After his death, economic difficulties undermined the authority of the central government, and Yugoslavia gradually dissolved into civil war.

THE BREAKUP OF YUGOSLAVIA

June 1991	Slovenia declares independence; Croatia declares independence
September 1991	Macedonia declares independence
April 1992	War erupts in Bosnia and Herzegovina after Muslims and Croats vote for independence
April 1992	Serbia and Montenegro proclaim a new Federal Republic of Yugoslavia
November 1995	Peace agreement reached in Dayton, Ohio
March 1998	War breaks out in Kosovo, a province of Serbia
March 1999	NATO bombing of Serbia begins
February 2008	Kosovo declares independence

In the late 1980s, the old ethnic differences came to the foreground again in Yugoslav politics. Nationalist leaders—most notably Slobodan Milosevic (b. 1941–2006) in Serbia and Franjo Tudjman (b. 1922) in Croatia—gained authority. The Serbs contended that Serbia did not exercise sufficient influence in Yugoslavia and that Serbs living in Yugoslavia but outside Serbia encountered systematic discrimination, especially from Croats and Albanians. Ethnic tension and violence resulted. During the summer of 1990, in the wake of the changes in the former Soviet bloc nations, Slovenia and Croatia declared independence from the central Yugoslav government, and several European nations, including, most importantly, Germany, immediately granted them recognition. The full European community soon did likewise.

From this point on, violence escalated. Serbia—concerned about Serbs living in Croatia and about the loss of lands and resources there—was determined to maintain a unitary Yugoslav state that it would dominate. Croatia was equally determined to secure independence. Croatian Serbs demanded safeguards against discrimination and violence, providing the Serbian army with a pretext to move against Croatia. By June 1991, full-fledged war had erupted between the two republics. Serbia accused Croatia of reviving fascism; Croatia accused Serbia of maintaining a Stalinist regime. At its core, however, the conflict was ethnic; as such, it highlights the potential for violent ethnic conflict within the former Soviet Union.

The conflict took a new turn in 1992 when Croatian and Serbian forces determined to divide Bosnia-Herzegovina. The Muslims in Bosnia—who had lived alongside Serbs and Croats for generations—soon became crushed between the opposing forces. The Serbs in particular, pursuing a policy called "ethnic cleansing," a euphemism redolent of some of the worst horrors of World War II, killed or forcibly removed many Bosnian Muslims.

Destruction of Sarajevo. An elderly parishioner walks through the ruins of St. Mary's Roman Catholic Church in Sarajevo. The church was destroyed by Serb shelling in May 1992.
Reuters/CORBIS/ Bettmann

More than any other single event, the unremitting bombardment of Sarajevo, the capital of Bosnia-Herzegovina, brought the violence of the Yugoslav civil war to the attention of the world. The United Nations attempted unsuccessfully to mediate the conflict and imposed sanctions that had little effect. Early in 1994, however, a shell exploded in the marketplace in Sarajevo, killing dozens of people. Thereafter, NATO forced the Serbs to withdraw their artillery from around Sarajevo.

The events of the civil war came to a head in 1995 when NATO forces carried out strategic air strikes. Later that year, under the leadership of the United States, the leaders of the warring forces negotiated a peace agreement in Dayton, Ohio. The agreement was of great complexity but recognized an independent Bosnia. NATO troops, including those from the United States, have enforced the terms of the agreement.

Toward the end of the 1990s, Serbian aggression against ethnic Albanians in the province of Kosovo again drew NATO into Yugoslav affairs. For months, through television and other media, the world watched the Serbian military deport Albanians from Kosovo where Albanians constituted a majority of the population. The tactics closely resembled those the Serbs previously used in Bosnia. There were many casualties, atrocities, and deaths. Early in 1999, NATO again carried out an air campaign and sent troops into Kosovo to safeguard the ethnic Albanians. This air campaign was the largest military action in Europe since the close of World War II. In 2000, a revolution overthrew Slobodan Milosevic. The new Yugoslav government turned the former leader over to the International War Crimes Tribunal at the Hague; however, Milosevic died in 2006 before his trial reached completion.

The disintegration of the former Yugoslavia took still another important turn in February 2008 when Kosovo with its Albanian majority population declared its independence from Serbia. The United States, a majority of the nations composing the European Union, and all Kosovo's neighbors except Serbia have recognized the independence of Kosovo. The Russian Federation, a longtime supporter of Serbia, immediately and strongly condemned the independence of Kosovo. The issue of Kosovo's independence, as will be seen in the next section, led to Russian military actions in the region of the Black Sea later in 2008.

▼ Putin and the Resurgence of Russia

Vladimir Putin, who had become president of the Russian Federation in 2000, immediately moved to establish his position as a national and nationalistic leader of the federation. He vigorously renewed the war against the rebels in Chechnya, which resulted in heavy casualties and enormous destruction there, but also strengthened Putin's political support in Russia itself. The ongoing Chechen war spawned one of the major acts of recent terrorism in Russia. In September 2003, a group of Chechens captured an elementary school in Beslan, a community in the Russian republic of North Ossetia (in the north Caucasus) on the opening day of the term. Approximately 1,200 students, teachers, and parents were held hostage for several days. When government troops stormed the school, approximately 330 of the hostages were killed. By the middle of the decade, however, Russian forces had clearly established the upper hand over the Chechen rebels and the drive toward independence was firmly checked at a very high cost in lives on both sides.

In the wake of the Chechen war and as part of his determination that the central government will dominate Russia's economy and political life, Putin has sought to diminish local autonomy and centralize power in his own hands. The central government has also moved against leading oligarchs and other businessmen with some being imprisoned. Putin used the attacks on these enormously wealthy and economically powerful figures to generate support from the broad Russian public who regard the oligarchs as thieves and one of the causes of the economic hardship of the 1990s. Putin also imprisoned political critics and opponents as well as moving against independent newspapers and television stations.

During Putin's presidency the Russian economy genuinely began to improve. Foreign debts were paid. The Russian ruble came to be regarded as a serious currency. Many more consumer goods were available. Much of this relative prosperity was the result of the oil resources available to the Russian Federation and the rising price of oil on the world market. Under Putin a clear trade-off occurred between political freedom and economic and political stability. In 2008 Putin left the elected presidency at the end of his second four-year term, turning the office over to his own handpicked successor Dmitri Medvedev (b. 1965). At the same time, however, Putin assumed the office of prime minister and clearly remained the chief political figure in the country.

Putin both as president and now prime minister has been determined to use the nation's economic recovery and new wealth to allow Russia to reassert its position as a major power on both the regional and world scene. After the terrorist attacks on the United States in September 2001, Putin supported the American assault on Afghanistan, largely because the Russian government was afraid that Islamic extremism would spread beyond Chechnya to other regions in Russia and to the largely Muslim nations that bordered Russia in Central Asia and the Caucasus. This period of cooperation proved short-lived. Putin became one of the leading voices against the American-led invasion of Iraq and has continued to criticize American policy in the region. Putin has also been sharply critical of the ongoing expansion of NATO, which has embraced nations directly bordering the Russian Federation. His government continued to attempt to exert influence in various new nations, such as the former Soviet republics of Ukraine and Georgia, that came into existence with the collapse of the former Soviet Union. (See "Vladimir Putin Outlines a Vision of the Russian Future.")

This determination to assert Russian domination over recently independent nations once part of the former Soviet Union dramatically displayed itself in August 2008. That month troops of the Russian Federation invaded the republic of Georgia. What had provoked this attack was Georgia's having shortly before sent troops into South Ossetia. Russian troops first drove the Georgians out of South Ossetia, and then continued into Georgia itself. South Ossetia itself a part of the former Soviet Union, had been divided into regions dominated by Russia and Georgia. Georgia sought to assert further influence only to be immediately and overwhelmingly blocked by Russian forces. Russia eventually withdrew after a cease-fire but had succeeded in demonstrating its

power in the region and in creating potential instability in postwar Georgia.

The Russian invasion of Georgia marked a new departure in post–Soviet Russian foreign policy and a resurgence of Russian international influence following the collapse of the Soviet Union nearly twenty years earlier. During that period both the European Union and NATO had moved to expand their memberships by expanding into Eastern Europe and into regions previously dominated by or part of the former Soviet Union. The Russian Federation found itself compelled to watch over these expansions without being able to stop them or otherwise significantly influence them. Discussions had taken place about the possibility of bringing both Ukraine and Georgia into NATO. The United States had indicated support for such inclusion. Putin and other leaders of the Russian Federation had witnessed the manner in which various regions of the former Yugoslavia, most recently Kosovo in February 2008, had broken away from Serbia and established their own independence. The Russia Federation feared the example of Kosovo and the international recognition its independence had achieved might serve as a pattern for potential break-away regions in the Russian Federation. It also feared encirclement by NATO member nations where the United States might

The aftermath of an attack by a Russian warplane on an apartment block in Gori, Georgia, during the conflict in South Ossetia in August 2008. Here a Georgian man cradles the body of a relative killed during the bombing, which killed at least five people.   © Gleb Garanich/Reuters/America LLC

VLADIMIR PUTIN OUTLINES A VISION OF THE RUSSIAN FUTURE

Vladimir Putin served as president of the Russian Federation from 1998 to 2008 when he moved to the office of prime minister. In one of his last presidential speeches he outlined his view of a democratic Russian future as well as his concerns about the relationship of the Russian Federation to NATO. His speech embraced a strong rhetoric of democracy but at the same time placed very considerable limits on the kind of activity and criticism that democratic parties might exercise. Note that he made no provision about who might decide if they were behaving in a fashion dangerous to the national interest. In his own time in office he imprisoned numerous political opponents. Also note his concerns about the future place in the world of the Russian Federation and his strong commitment to expansion of its military defense capacities.

How does Putin seem to embrace democratic reform? What are the limits that he places on democratic activity? How might those limits lead to government interference with the activity of political parties? What are Putin's concerns regarding NATO and the place of the Russian Federation in world affairs?

The desire of millions of our citizens for individual freedom and social justice is what defines the future of Russia's political system. The democratic state should become an effective instrument for civil society's self-organization. . . .

Russia's future political system will be centered on several large political parties that will have to work hard to maintain or affirm their leading positions, be open to change and broaden their dialogue with the voters.

Political parties must not forget their immense responsibility for Russia's future, for the nation's unity and for our country's stable development.

No matter how fierce the political battles and no matter how irreconcilable the differences between parties might be, they are never worth so much as to bring the country to the brink of chaos.

Irresponsible demagogy and attempts to divide society and use foreign help or intervention in domestic political struggles are not only immoral but are illegal. They belittle our people's dignity and undermine our democratic state. . . .

No matter what their differences, all of the different public forces in the country should act in accordance with one simple but essential principle: do nothing that would damage the interests of Russia and its citizens and act only for Russia's good, act in its national interests and in the interest of the prosperity and security of all its people. . . .

It is now clear that the world has entered a new spiral in the arms race. This does not depend on us and it is not we who began it. . . .

NATO itself is expanding and is bringing its military infrastructure ever closer to our borders. We have closed our bases in Cuba and Vietnam, but what have we got in return? New American bases in Romania and Bulgaria, and a new missile defense system with plans to install components of this system in Poland and the Czech Republic soon it seems. . . .

We are effectively being forced into a situation where we have to take measures in response, where we have no choice but to make the necessary decisions. . . .

Russia has a response to these new challenges and it always will. Russia will begin production of new types of weapons over these coming years, the quality of which is just as good and in some cases even surpasses those of other countries.

Validmir Putin, Speech at Expanded Meeting of the State Council on Russia's Development Strategy through 2020, February 8, 2008, President of Russia, Official Web Portal, www.kremlin.ru/eng/text/speeches/2008/02/08/1137_type82912type82913_159643.shtml

locate military bases. The action taken against Georgia served to demonstrate the ability of the Russian Federation to take military action on its borders and to give warning to other nations in the region of its capacity to intervene. At the same time the absence of any effective resistance to Russian actions in Georgia from either the United States or the European Union nations raised doubts about the capacity of either to influence events in the region of the Black Sea. Therefore, though the Russian incursion into Georgia was relatively brief, it demonstrated that the classic issues of European great power politics remain alive in the new Europe. Moreover, the action also demonstrated Russian willingness to take advantage of American involvement in Iraq and Afghanistan to reassert its potential authority in those regions it has dominated since the wars of Catherine the Great in the eighteenth century.

In late 2008 another question suddenly confronted Russia. As one element in the worldwide financial crisis commodity prices dropped sharply. These included the price of oil on the world market. It remains to be seen whether Russia will be able to maintain its economic growth and political resurgence in the face of dropping income from the sale of oil, which has financed its new international influence during the past decade.

▼ The Rise of Radical Political Islamism

On September 11, 2001, Islamic terrorists attacked the United States, crashing hijacked civilian domestic aircraft into the twin towers of the World Trade Center in New York City, the Pentagon in Washington, DC, and a Pennsylvania field with a vast loss of life and property. These events and those flowing from them not only transformed American foreign policy toward the Middle East but have also changed European relations with the United States.

In retrospect, we can see that those attacks were the result of forces that had been affecting not only the United States but the Western world as well for at least a half century. The end of the Cold War has been succeeded by a new political world in which both the United States and the nations of Europe, including the Russian Federation, are endangered by terrorist attacks from nongovernmental or non-state-based organizations. These groups are guided by ideologies in the Islamic world that have filled a political and ideological vacuum left by the end of the Cold War.

Radical Islamism is the term scholars use to describe an interpretation of Islam that came to have a significant impact in the Muslim world during the decades of decolonization. It is only one—and by no means the most popular—interpretation of Islam. The ideas informing radical Islamism extend back to the

1930s and resistance to British rule in Egypt, but for many years, those had little impact on the politics of the Middle East.

Arab Nationalism

Radical Islamism arose primarily in reaction to the secular Arab nationalism that developed in countries like Egypt and Syria in the 1920s and 1930s. Although Arab and other Middle Eastern nationalists, like nineteenth-century modernizers in the Ottoman Empire, believed that the path to independence and strength lay in adopting the technology and imitating the political institutions of the West, these advocates of radical Islam wanted to reject Western ideas and create a society based on a rigorous interpretation of Islam and its teachings. (See Chapter 22.)

In the wake of World War II, many of the foremost leaders of Arab nationalism against Western direct and indirect dominance, such as Gamal Abdul Nasser of Egypt, were sympathetic to socialism or to the Soviet Union. Because socialism and communism were Western ideologies, left-leaning Arab nationalism was no less Western in its orientation than were nationalists friendly to the United States. Moreover, Soviet communism was overtly atheistic and hence doubly offensive to devout Arab Muslims.

Nationalism forged by nondemocratic Middle Eastern governments, usually traditional monarchies or authoritarian regimes dominated by the military, brought different results to the various Arab nations. Oil made Saudi Arabia wealthy and powerful and the small Gulf states, such as Kuwait, rich but not powerful. Other states, such as Jordan, Syria, and Egypt, which lacked oil, remained burdened by large impoverished populations.

Arab governments defining themselves according to the values of nationalism worked out arrangements with local Muslim authorities. For example, the Saudi royal family turned over its educational system to adherents of a rigorist, puritanical form of Islam called *Wahhabism* while modernizing the country's infrastructure. The Egyptian government attempted to play different Islamic groups off against one another. These governments retained the support of prosperous, devout middle-class Muslims while doing little about the plight of the poor. In general, Muslim religious leaders were hostile to the Soviet Union and its influence in the Islamic world.

The Iranian Revolution

The Iranian Revolution of 1979 transformed the Middle East. The Ayatollah Ruhollah Khomeini (1902–1989) managed to unite both the middle and lower classes of a major Middle Eastern nation to overthrow a repressive but a modernizing government that had long cooperated with the United States. For the first time, a religiously dominated government defining itself and its mission in distinctly Islamic, as well as nationalistic, terms took control of a major state. Iran's revolutionary government was a theocracy; that is, there was no separation of religion and government or, in European terms, of church and state. The Iranian constitution gave the clergy, acting on behalf of God, the final say in all matters.

By challenging the Westernization of Iranian society, the Iranian Revolution shocked the world. It also challenged the largely secular presuppositions of Arab nationalists in states such as Egypt, Saudi Arabia, and Algeria that had failed to satisfy the needs of their own underclasses. In the mid-twentieth century, Arabs and other Middle Eastern peoples had turned to nationalism in reaction against European colonial powers. Those who grew up under nationalist leadership and still found themselves politically and economically disadvantaged, however, reacted against nationalism. The Iranian Revolution, which many thought would spread throughout the Islamic world, attracted them.

The Iranian Revolution both embodied and emboldened the forces of what is commonly called Islamic *fundamentalism*, but it is more correctly termed Islamic or Muslim *reformism*. This is the belief that a reformed or pure Islam must be established in the contemporary world. Most adherents of this point of view would emphasize personal piety and religious practice. However, a minority wish to see their states strictly governed the way Iran purports to be by Islamic law or the Shari'a. In fact, the Iranian clergy made numerous compromises to the practical demands of everyday government and the oil industry, but their public message to the world was that Iran is a strict Islamic state hostile to the West in general and the United States—"the Great Satan"—in particular. The Iranian Revolution also opposed the state of Israel on both religious and nationalistic grounds.

The conservative Arab governments feared the Iranian Revolution would challenge their legitimacy. They consequently began to pay much more attention to their own religious authorities and cracked down on radical reformist or fundamentalist Muslims. In Egypt, such actions followed the assassination in 1981 of President Anwar Sadat (b. 1918) by a member of the Muslim Brotherhood.

Afghanistan and Radical Islamism

The Russian invasion of Afghanistan of 1979, discussed earlier in this chapter, introduced a major new component into this already complicated picture, illustrating the convergence of Cold War and Islamist politics. The Soviet Union sought to impose a communist, and hence both Western and atheist, government in Afghanistan. Muslim religious authorities declared *jihad*, literally meaning "a struggle" but commonly interpreted as a religious war, against the Soviet Union. The Afghan resistance to the Soviets thus became simultaneously nationalistic, universalistic, and religious.

Thousands of Muslims, mostly fundamentalist in outlook, arrived in Afghanistan from across the Islamic world to oust the Soviets and their Afghan puppets. Conservative Arab states and the United States supported this effort, which succeeded when all Soviet forces withdrew in 1989. The conservative Arab states saw the Afghan war as an opportunity both to resist Soviet influence and to divert the energies of their own religious extremists. The United States saw the Afghan war as another round in the Cold War. The militant Muslim fundamentalists saw it as a religious struggle against an impious Western power.

The Taliban and Al Qaeda The Soviet withdrawal created a power vacuum in Afghanistan that lasted almost a decade. By 1998, however, rigorist Muslims known as the *Taliban* had seized control of the country. They imposed their own version of Islamic law, which involved strict regimentation of women and public executions, floggings, and mutilations for criminal, religious, and moral offenses. The Taliban also allowed groups of Muslim terrorists known as *Al Qaeda*, which means "Base," to establish training camps in their country. The terrorists who attacked the United States on September 11, 2001, came from these camps.

The ideology of these groups had emerged over several decades from different regions of the Islamic world but had been inculcated in Pakistan. The Pakistani government had long assigned considerable control over education to Islamic schools, or *madrasas*, that taught reformed Islam, rejection of liberal and nationalist secular values, intolerance toward non-Muslims, repudiation of Western culture, hostility to Israel, and hatred of the United States.

***Jihad* Against the United States** Once the *jihad* against the Soviet Union had succeeded, radical Muslims, largely educated in these Pakistani schools, turned their attention to the United States, the other great Western power. The event that brought about this redirection was the Persian Gulf War of 1991. The occasion for that conflict was the invasion of Kuwait by Iraq, under Saddam Hussein (1937–2006). The conservative Arab governments, most importantly Saudi Arabia, not only supported the United States but also permitted it to construct military bases on their territory. Islamic extremists who had fought in Afghanistan, one of whom was Osama Bin Laden (b. 1957), saw the establishment of U.S. bases in Saudi Arabia, which was the home of the prophet Muhammad and contains Islam's two holiest cities, Mecca and Medina, as a new invasion by Western Crusaders. The bases added a new grievance to the already long list of radical Muslim complaints against the United States.

The United States became a target because of its secular public morality, its international wealth and power, its military strength, its ongoing support for Israel, and its adherence to the UN sanctions imposed on Iraq after the Gulf War. Certain Muslim religious authorities declared a

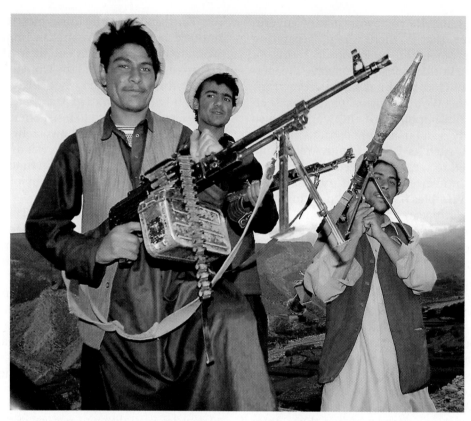

Taliban fighters brandish machine guns and rocket launchers near the Tora Bora mountains in Afghanistan, the site of a major battle with U.S. forces in late 2001. Knut Mueller/Das Fotoarchiv/Peter Arnold, Inc.

jihad against the United States, thus transforming opposition to American policies and culture into a religious war. Through the 1990s, terrorists attacks were directed against targets in or associated with the United States. These included bombings of the World Trade Center in New York City in 1993, of a U.S. army barracks in Saudi Arabia in 1996, of U.S. embassies in East Africa in 1998, and of the USS *Cole* in the Yemeni port of Aden in 2000. These attacks resulted in a considerable loss of life.

▼ A Transformed West

The attacks on the United States on September 11, 2001, transformed and redirected American foreign policy into what the administration of President George W. Bush (b. 1946) termed "a war on terrorism." In late 2001, the United States attacked the Taliban government of Afghanistan, rapidly overthrowing it. The defeat of the Taliban destroyed Al Qaeda's Afghan bases but not its leadership, which survived, although it was dispersed and remains in hiding. By 2008 there was evidence that the Taliban had regrouped and again become active.

Following the Afghan campaign, the Bush administration set forth a policy of preemptive strikes and inter-vention against potential enemies of the United States. The administration argued that the danger of weapons of mass destruction developed by governments such as that of Iraq falling into the hands of international terrorist organizations posed so severe a danger to the security of the United States that the nation could not wait to respond to an attack but must take preemptive action. This argument, which aroused controversy both at home and abroad, marked a major departure from previous United States foreign policy. It is a direct result of the attacks on the United States that occurred on September 11.

In 2002, the Bush administration turned its attention to Saddam Hussein's government in Iraq. Since the defeat of Iraq in 1991 by an international coalition led by the United States, Saddam Hussein, contrary to widespread expectations, had remained in power and had continued to oppress his own people. Throughout the 1990s, the Iraqi government had also resisted the work of United Nations inspectors charged with discovering and destroying weapons of mass destruction found in Iraq or facilities capable of manufacturing such weapons. The Iraqis eventually expelled the United Nations inspectors in 1998, and the United Nations was unable to reinsert them for almost five years.

The United States government adopted a policy of regime change in Iraq during the last years of the Clinton administration (1993—2001) though it did little to carry out that policy. In the wake of the September 11, 2001, attacks, however, the Bush administration determined to overthrow Saddam Hussein and remove any threat from supposed Iraqi weapons of mass destruction. In late 2002 and early 2003, the United States and British governments sought to obtain passage of United Nations Security Council resolutions that would require Iraq to disarm on its own or to be disarmed by military force. These efforts failed. France and Russia threatened to veto the measure, and a majority of the Security Council voted against it. Nonetheless, the United States and Great Britain, backed by token forces or other support from over thirty other nations, invaded Iraq in late March 2003. After three weeks of fighting, the Iraqi army and with it the government of Saddam Hussein collapsed. The announced goals of the invasion, in addition to toppling the Iraqi regime, were to destroy Iraq's capacity to manufacture or deploy weapons of mass destruction and to bring consensual government to the Iraqi people. The latter goal has remained elusive as Iraq has been violently split by deadly internal political conflict.

The invasion of Iraq was undertaken in the face of considerable opposition from France, Germany, and Russia. It also provoked large antiwar demonstrations in the United States and throughout the world. Both the war and the diplomatic difficulties preceding it disrupted the long-standing Atlantic alliance. Moreover, French and German opposition to the war created strains within Europe and particularly within NATO and the European Union, as other European governments either strongly supported or opposed the United States and Britain. As a result, the war in Iraq marked a new and divisive era in relations between the United States and Europe, and between the United States and the rest of the world.

Once the invasion of Iraq had been carried out and the occupation commenced, Al Qaeda terrorists struck in Europe itself. On March 11, 2004, at least 190 people were killed in train bombings in Madrid, Spain. The terrorist attack occurred just before the Spanish election. The Spanish government, which had supported the American invasion of Iraq, unexpectedly lost the election. The new government then soon withdrew Spanish troops from Iraq. The Madrid bombings were the largest act of terrorism against civilians in Europe since World War II. The attack demonstrated that terrorist attacks can directly influence European political processes.

The Iraq war and the bloody insurgency that followed generated enormous controversy. The coalition forces found no weapons of mass destruction in Iraq. Government commissions in the United States and Britain have criticized the intelligence information used to justify the invasion. In 2004, however, President Bush was reelected. In March 2005, thousands of Iraqis braved threats to vote in the first meaningful election held in Iraq since the 1950s; later in October 2005 they would vote to ratify a new constitution. In 2006 Saddam Hussein was tried and executed for crimes against humanity. Meanwhile in May 2005, the British government of Prime Minister Tony Blair was also reelected, though with a much reduced parliamentary majority. However, on July 7, 2005, terrorist bombings struck the London bus and subway system with a considerable loss of life. Once more, as in Spain, terrorism struck a major European city. The British government, unlike the Spanish, continued to retain its armed forces in Iraq.

The Iraq war, which has witnessed the death of more than 4,000 American troops and thousands of Iraqis, continued to cause controversy in the United States and between the United States and its NATO allies. However, in early 2007 the Bush administration increased the number of troops committed to Iraq. The purpose of the increase in troops, called "the surge" in the press, was to bring about greater internal stability in the country and most particularly in Baghdad. Over the months the level of violence did subside. By 2008 the United States under the Bush administration and the Iraq government were negotiating the future status of American troops in Iraq with the goal of significantly reducing their numbers in upcoming years. Somewhat surprisingly, issues of the economy more than those of Middle East involvement dominated the 2008 U.S. presidential campaign. Early in 2009 after assuming the presidency, President Barack Obama undertook a policy to establish an orderly withdrawal of most American combat troops from Iraq by the late summer of 2010.

In Perspective

In 1900, the major European nations dominated the world. Their wealth in terms of manufacturing, investment banking, and consumer demand profoundly influenced the lives of millions of people on every continent. Their military power, particularly their navies, and their colonial administrators controlled most of Africa and much of Asia. Many Europeans were emigrating, especially to the Americas. Wherever Europeans traveled or governed, they could expect that people on other continents would look to Europe as a model for industrial development, accumulation of wealth, and high culture in the arts and sciences. It was the apex of the European era that began at the close of the fifteenth century. In 1900, almost no one could have predicted the enormous human tragedies that would occur in Europe during the next half century or the retreat from world dominance

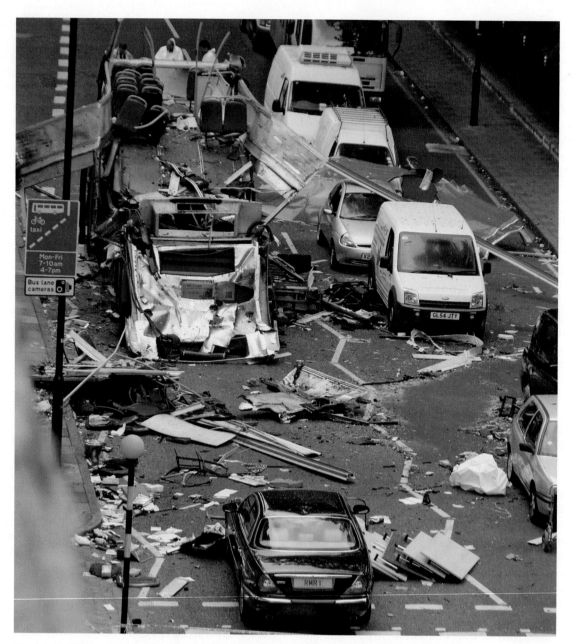

On July 7, 2005, a series of bombs rocked the London transport system with the loss of over fifty lives. This photo shows the remains of a London bus on which a suicide bomber took more than a dozen lives near Russell Square, London. Sion Touhig/CORBIS/Bettmann

that would mark the European experience during the rest of the twentieth century.

World War II resulted in the political collapse of Europe. In the wake of the war, the United States and the Soviet Union emerged as two superpowers, both of them equipped with nuclear weapons. From that time until the collapse of the Soviet Union in 1991, the U.S.–Soviet rivalry dominated world affairs. Local flash points became regions for rivalry and conflict between the two nuclear powers.

While the Cold War profoundly influenced international relations, the process of decolonization spread around the globe. One nation after another in Africa and Asia became free of direct European colonial rule. Scores of new nations emerged. Both the Soviet Union and the United States frequently filled the political, economic, and military vacuum the departure of the European colonial rulers left. This situation led each nation into major military interventions—the United States in Vietnam and the Soviet Union in

Afghanistan—that had significant domestic consequences in each nation.

By the middle of the 1980s, the economy and political structures of the Soviet Union could no longer bear the burden of the Cold War. The effort to reform Soviet structures Mikhail Gorbachev commenced concluded with the surrender of political monopoly by the Soviet Communist Party. Simultaneously the Soviet Union retreated from Eastern Europe, and the states that the Soviet-controlled Communist Party formerly dominated achieved independence. By 1991, the Soviet Union had collapsed internally. The loosely structured Confederation of Independent States replaced it. Many former Soviet republics became completely independent states, some of which were hostile to Russia.

Since the collapse of the Soviet Union, the United States has remained the single superpower. Just after the turn of the new century, the United States suffered a major and unprecedented terrorist attack on its soil. Thereafter, the United States responded with unprecedented intervention in the Middle East. The political structures of that region were themselves the result of the decisions the Western powers took after World War I at the Versailles peace conference in 1919. In that regard, the conflict between the United States and many groups in the Middle East, most prominently radical political Islamists, represents one more chapter in the long, unfolding twentieth-century story of the global interaction between regions of the world European power once dominated and the West. The ongoing ramifications of decolonization have continued in the wake of the end of the Cold War.

AP* TEST PREP

1. All of the following undermined Soviet authority in the early 1980s *except*
   a. economic stagnation.
   b. a surge in the population of Soviet cities.
   c. party corruption.
   d. the Afghan war.
   e. shortages of consumer goods.

2. *Perestroika* means
   a. "restructuring."
   b. "openness."
   c. "renewal."
   d. "freedom."
   e. "new start."

3. Solidarity played a key role in political reform in
   a. Hungary.
   b. Poland.
   c. Romania.
   d. Croatia.
   e. Poland.

4. Vaclav Havel led the opposition to the communist government in
   a. Bulgaria.
   b. Czechoslovakia.
   c. East Germany.
   d. Latvia.
   e. Estonia.

5. After the failure of the August 1991 coup, the dominant political figure in Russia was
   a. Jaruzelski.
   b. Gorbachev.
   c. Putin.
   d. Yeltsin.
   e. Chernov.

6. Putin believes that the dominant force in Russia's economy and political life should be
   a. the Russian military.
   b. the free market.
   c. local governments.
   d. communist party members.
   e. the central government.

7. The likely reason the Soviets required their subject governments in Eastern Europe to impose Stalinist policies during the 1940s was the success of
   a. Jan Masaryk.
   b. Edvard Beneš.
   c. Josip (Tito) Broz.
   d. Imre Nagy.
   e. Wladyslaw Gomulka.

8. During the late 1990s, Serbian aggression against ethnic Albanians drew NATO forces into
   a. Croatia.
   b. Macedonia.
   c. Bosnia.
   d. Kosovo.
   e. Slovenia.

9. All of the following opposed the 2003 U.S. invasion of Iraq *except*
   a. Poland.
   b. France.
   c. Russia.
   d. Germany.
   e. China.

10. The declaration to support "free people who are resisting attempted subjugation by armed minorities or outside pressures" describes
    a. the Eisenhower Plan.
    b. the Marshall Plan.
    c. the Truman Plan.
    d. the Dulles Plan.
    e. containment.

11. In 1948, all of the following invaded Israel except
    a. Iran.
    b. Iraq.
    c. Egypt.
    d. Syria.
    e. Jordan.

12. The Khrushchev era witnessed a retreat from
    a. communism.
    b. Stalinism.
    c. authoritarianism.
    d. militarism.
    e. central planning.

13. The three crises of 1956 included
    a. the Hungarian uprising, Prague Spring, and the Cuban missile crisis.
    b. Polish resistance to Soviet pressure, the Cuban missile crisis, and Prague Spring.
    c. the Suez intervention, Prague Spring, and the Hungarian uprising.
    d. the Suez intervention, Polish resistance to Soviet pressure, and the Hungarian uprising.
    e. the Cuban missile crisis, the Hungarian uprising, and the Suez intervention.

14. The future of the Soviet Union was changed by the 1979 Soviet decision to invade
    a. Chechnya.
    b. Afghanistan.
    c. the Ukraine.
    d. Mongolia.
    e. Pakistan.

15. At the height of U.S. involvement in the war in Vietnam, over _____ U.S. troops were stationed in South Vietnam.
    a. 150,000
    b. 1 million

c. 75,000
d. 500,000
e. 5 million

16. The Cominform describes
    a. an Eastern European military alliance.
    b. reassertion of Stalinists within Eastern European governments.
    c. the Eastern European economic recovery plan.
    d. Khrushchev's Five-Year Plan.
    e. an international Communist Party organization.

17. Putin has contributed to all of the following except
    a. control over oligarchs.
    b. increased availability of consumer goods.
    c. payment of foreign debt.
    d. support for the United States in Afghanistan.
    e. advancing local autonomy.

18. The Balfour Declaration stated that
    a. Britain favored the establishment of a national home for the Jewish people in Palestine.
    b. all former British colonies would eventually gain independence.
    c. European Jews were unwelcome in British colonies.
    d. Britain would respond to attacks on its colonies with force.
    e. Palestine belonged to the Palestinians.

19. Which pairing of colonial independence is incorrect?
    a. Angola gained independence from Portugal.
    b. Congo gained independence from Belgium.
    c. Bangladesh gained independence from Britain.
    d. Indochina gained independence from France.
    e. East Indies gained independence from the Dutch.

20. When Gamal Abdel Nasser nationalized the Suez Canal,
    a. the United States supported British intervention.
    b. the British supported U.S. intervention.
    c. the British and French intervened militarily.
    d. Egypt paid large sums to Britain in compensation.
    e. the Soviet Union intervened militarily.

DOCUMENT-BASED QUESTION

Directions: Construct a valid essay that directly addresses the central issue of the following question. Use facts from the documents provided and from the chapter to prove the position you take in your thesis statement.

What common ideals inspired anticolonialists in the years immediately following World War II? To what extent were anticolonialists inspired by Western notions of freedom and independence?

Document A

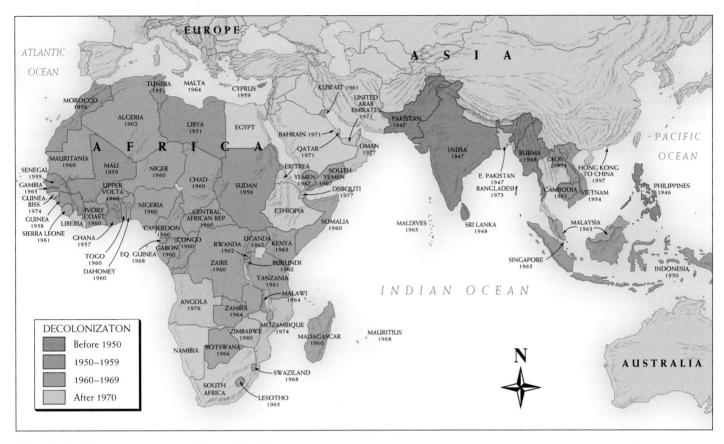

Map 29–6 **DECOLONIZATION SINCE WORLD WAR II.**

Document B

Source: Ho Chi Minh, "Determined to Fight to the Bitter End."

"All men are created equal. They are endowed by their Creator with certain unalienable Rights; among these are Life, Liberty, and the pursuit of Happiness". . . .

The Declaration of the French Revolution made in 1791 on the Rights of Man and the Citizen also states: "All men are born free and with equal rights, and must always remain free and have equal rights."

Those are undeniable truths.

Nevertheless, for more than eighty years, the French imperialists, abusing the standard of Liberty, Equality, and Fraternity, have violated our Fatherland and oppressed our fellow citizens. They have acted contrary to the ideals of humanity and justice. . . .

For these reasons, we solemnly declare to the world that Vietnam has a right to be a free and independent country—and in fact is so already. The entire Vietnamese people are determined to mobilize all their physical and mental strength, to sacrifice their lives and property in order to safeguard their independence and liberty.

Document C

Source: Gamal Abdel Nasser responds to the Suez Crisis, "Those Who Attack Egypt Will Never Leave Egypt Alive."

In these decisive days in the history of mankind, these days in which truth struggles to have itself recognized in international chaos where powers of evil domination and imperialism have prevailed, Egypt stands firmly to preserve her sovereignty. Your country stands solidly and staunchly to preserve her dignity against imperialistic schemes of a number of nations who have uncovered their desires for domination and supremacy. . . .

We shall defend our freedom and independence to the last drop of our blood. This is the staunch feeling of every Egyptian. The whole Arab nation will stand by us in our common fight against aggression and domination. Free peoples, too, people who are really free will stand by us and support us against the forces of tyranny.

Document D

Source: India's first prime minister, Jawaharlal Nehru, explains the ideas that underlay the nonaligned movement.

I speak of India because it is my country, and I have some right to speak for her. But many other countries in

Asia tell the same story, for Asia today is resurgent, and these countries, which long lay under foreign yoke, have won back their independence and are fired by a new spirit and strive toward new ideals. To them, as to us, independence is as vital as the breath they take to sustain life, and colonialism in any form, or anywhere, is abhorrent. . . .

The preservation of peace forms the central aim of India's policy. It is in the pursuit of this policy that we have chosen the path of non-alignment in any military or like pact or alliance. . . .

Through the centuries, India has preached and practiced toleration and understanding. . . . During these millennia of history, India has experienced both good and ill but, throughout her chequered history, she has remembered the message of peace and toleration.

For more on postwar decolonization, see pages 956–962 of this chapter.

The most important accomplishment of the European Community was the launching on January 1, 1999, of the Euro, a single monetary unit that replaced the national currencies of most of its member nations. In Frankfurt, Germany, people crowded around a symbol of the new currency. The world financial crisis that commenced in 2008 has placed many internal pressures on the European Community and upon its currency.   AP Wide World Photos

30

The West at the Dawn of the Twenty-First Century

▼ **The Twentieth-Century Movement of Peoples**
Displacement Through War • External and Internal Migration • The New Muslim Population
• European Population Trends

▼ **Toward a Welfare State Society**
Christian Democratic Parties • The Creation of Welfare States • Resistance to the Expansion of the Welfare State

▼ **New Patterns in Work and Expectations of Women**
Feminism • More Married Women in the Workforce • New Work Patterns • Women in the New Eastern Europe

▼ **Transformations in Knowledge and Culture**
Communism and Western Europe • Existentialism • Expansion of the University Population and Student Rebellion • The Americanization of Europe • A Consumer Society • Environmentalism

▼ **Art Since World War II**
Cultural Divisions and the Cold War • Memory of the Holocaust

▼ **The Christian Heritage**
Neo-Orthodoxy • Liberal Theology • Roman Catholic Reform

▼ **Late-Twentieth-Century Technology: The Arrival of the Computer**
The Demand for Calculating Machines • Early Computer Technology • The Development of Desktop Computers

▼ **The Challenges of European Unification**
Postwar Cooperation • The European Economic Community • The European Union
• Discord over the Union

▼ **New American Leadership and Financial Crisis**

▼ **In Perspective**

THE COLD WAR defined the life of the West during most of the second half of the twentieth century. This conflict affected not only political developments and military alliances, but also the lives of millions of Europeans and Americans. For almost half a century, the easy travel throughout the world that many people take for granted today and that enriches the lives of thousands of American students every year was impossible. Vast areas were closed off. The Iron Curtain separated families. Most of Eastern Europe was cut off from the material and technological as well as cultural advances that marked the second half of the century.

Yet despite these problems, European society, especially in the West, changed remarkably after World War II, as did, of course, the United States. Western Europe enjoyed unprecedented prosperity, peace, and technological advances. During the same years Europe also took unprecedented steps toward economic cooperation and political union.

▼ The Twentieth-Century Movement of Peoples

In the twentieth century, the movement of peoples transformed European society and the character of many European communities. The Soviet communists' forced removal of Russian peasants and the Nazis' deportations and execution of European Jews were only the most dramatic examples of this development. The Second World War and the subsequent economic transformation of the Continent brought further extensive migrations. The most pervasive trend in this movement of peoples was the continuing shift from the countryside to the cities. Today, except for Albania, at least one third of the population of every European nation lives in large cities. In Western Europe, city dwellers are approximately 75 percent of the population.

Other vast forced movements of peoples by governments, however, were little discussed during the Cold War. During the century, millions of Germans, Hungarians, Poles, Ukrainians, Bulgarians, Serbs, Finns, Chechens, Armenians, Greeks, Turks, Balts, and Bosnian Muslims were displaced.

These forced displacements transformed parts of Europe. Stalin literally moved whole nationalities from one area of the Soviet Union to another and killed millions of people in the process. The Nazis first displaced the Jews and then sought to exterminate them. Throughout Eastern Europe, cities that once had large Jewish populations and a vibrant Jewish religious and cultural life lost any Jewish presence. The displacement of Germans from Eastern Europe back into Germany immediately after World War II transformed cities that had been German into places almost wholly populated by Czechs, Poles, or Russians. For example, the present Polish city of Gdansk was once the German city of Danzig, and today's Russian city of Kaliningrad had been the German Königsberg before 1945.

Displacement Through War

World War II created a vast refugee problem. An estimated 46 million people were displaced in central and Eastern Europe and the Soviet Union alone between 1938 and 1948. Many cities in Germany and in central and Eastern Europe had been bombed or overrun by invading armies. The Nazis had moved hundreds of thousands of foreign workers into Germany as slave laborers. Millions more were prisoners of war. Some of these people returned to their homeland willingly; others, particularly Soviet prisoners fearful of being executed by Stalin, had to be forced to go back, and many were executed. Hundreds of thousands of Baltic, Polish, and Yugoslav prisoners found asylum in Western Europe.

Changes in political borders after the war also uprooted many people. For example, Poland, Czechoslovakia, and Hungary forcibly expelled millions of ethnic Germans from their territories to Germany. This transfer of over 12 million Germans in effect "solved" the problem of German minorities living outside of Germany's national boundaries that had been one of Hitler's excuses for aggression against neighboring countries. In another case of forced migration, hundreds of thousands of Poles were transferred to within Poland's new borders from territory the Soviet Union annexed. Other minorities, such as Ukrainians in Poland and Italians on the Yugoslav coast, were driven into their ethnic homelands. As one historian has commented, "War, violence, and massive social dislocation turned Versailles's dream of national homogeneity into realities."[1]

External and Internal Migration

Between 1945 and 1960, approximately half a million Europeans left Europe each year. This was the largest outward migration since the 1920s, when around 700,000 persons had left annually. In the second half of the nineteenth century, most immigrants were from rural areas. After World War II, they often included educated city dwellers. Immediately after the war, some governments encouraged migration because they were afraid that, as in the 1930s, their economies would not be able to provide adequate employment for all their citizens.

Decolonization in the postwar period led many European colonials to return to Europe from overseas. The most dramatic example of this phenomenon was the more than one million French colonials who moved to

---

[1]Mark Mazower, *Dark Continent: Europe's Twentieth Century* (New York: Knopf, 1999), p. 218.

France after the end of the Algerian war in 1962 (see Chapter 29). Britons returned from parts of the British Empire; Dutch returned from Indonesia in the late 1940s; Belgians from the Congo in the 1960s; and Portuguese from Mozambique and Angola in the 1970s.

Decolonization also led non-European inhabitants of the former colonies to migrate to Europe. Great Britain, for example, received thousands of immigrants from its former colonies in the Caribbean, Africa, and the Indian subcontinent. France received many immigrants from its empire in Africa, Indochina, and the Arab world. This influx has proved to be a long-term source of social tension and conflict. In Britain, racial tensions were high during the 1980s. France faced similar difficulties, which contributed to the emergence of the National Front, an extreme right-wing group led by Jean-Marie Le Pen (b. 1928) that sought to exploit the resentment many working-class voters felt toward North African immigrants. In 2002, Le Pen won enough votes to become one of the two candidates in the run-off election for the French presidency, although he lost overwhelmingly to Jacques Chirac (b. 1932) in the final ballot. Similar pressures have arisen in Germany, Austria, Italy, the Netherlands, and even Denmark. Such tension did not result only from immigration from Africa and Asia; internal European migration—from the Balkans, Turkey, and the former Soviet Union, often of people in search of jobs—also changed the social and economic face of the Continent and led to a backlash. In recent years, internal immigration within the European Union has seen the movement of significant numbers of people. However, the growing Muslim presence in Europe has produced some of the most serious ethnic and political tensions.

The New Muslim Population

As recounted earlier in this textbook, well into the twentieth century the European relationship with most of the Muslim world was at arm's length or colonialist. Muslims from the Ottoman Empire, the greatest Muslim state, rarely traveled in Europe, and few Europeans traveled in the empire. Europeans encountered Muslims mainly as subjects, in colonies, such as Algeria, Egypt, the Indian subcontinent, sub-Saharan Africa, and the East Indies. In all these regions from at least the mid-nineteenth century onward, Christian missionaries often clashed with Muslim religious teachers.

At the same time, most Europeans, except for a few communities in the Balkans and the former Soviet Empire, regarded themselves and their national cultures as either Christian or secular. Indeed, until recently most Europeans paid little direct attention to Islam as a domestic matter.

That indifference began to change in the 1960s and had dissolved by the end of the twentieth century as a sizable Muslim population settled in Europe. This highly diverse immigrant community had become an issue in Europe even before the events of September 11, 2001.

The immigration of Muslims into Europe, and particularly Western Europe, arose from two chief sources: European economic growth and decolonization. As the economies of Western Europe began to recover in the quarter century after World War II, a labor shortage developed. To fill this demand, Western Europe imported laborers, many of whom came from Muslim nations. For example, Turkish "guest workers" were invited to move to West Germany—on a temporary basis, it was presumed—in the 1960s, and Britain welcomed Pakistanis. The aftermath of decolonization and the quest for a better life led Muslims from East Africa and the Indian subcontinent to settle in Great Britain. The Algerian war brought many Muslims to France. Today there are approximately 1.3 million Muslims in Great Britain, 3.2 million in Germany, and 4.2 million in France. Smaller but still significant numbers have settled in Italy, Spain, Sweden, Denmark, and the Netherlands, nations that previously had had generally homogeneous populations.

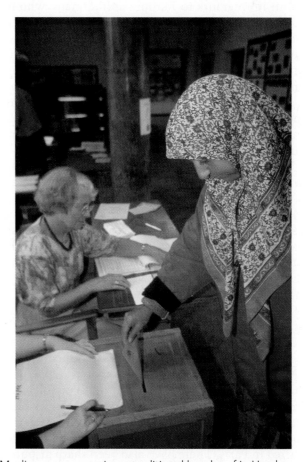

A Muslim woman wearing a traditional headscarf in Hamburg, Germany votes in the Bundestag elections. The presence of foreign-born Muslims whose labor is necessary for the prosperity of the European economy is an important issue in contemporary Europe. Many of these Muslims live in self-contained communities. Peter Arnold, Inc.

These Muslim immigrant communities share certain social and religious characteristics. Originally, many Muslims came to Europe expecting they would eventually return to their homes, an expectation their host countries shared. Neither the immigrants nor the host nations gave much thought to assimilation. Moreover, except for Great Britain, where all immigrants from the Commonwealth may vote immediately upon settling there, European governments made it difficult for Muslim, or any other, immigrants to take part in civic life. Unlike the United States, few European countries had any experience dealing with large-scale immigration. The Muslim communities have, therefore, generally remained unassimilated and self-contained. This apartness has provided internal community support for Muslim immigrants but has also prevented them from fully engaging with the societies in which they live. Many of their children have not learned European languages well, and Muslim women tend to remain confined to their homes.

Yet the world around these communities has changed. Many of the largely unskilled jobs that the immigrants originally filled have disappeared. Most of the Muslim immigrants to Europe, unlike many who have settled in the United States and Canada, were neither highly skilled nor professionally educated. As a result, they and their adult children who may have grown up in Europe find it difficult to get jobs in the modern service economy. Furthermore, as European economic growth has slowed, European Muslims have become the target of politicians, such as Le Pen in France, who seek to blame the immigrants for a host of problems from crime to unemployment.

The radicalization of parts of the Islamic world has also touched the Muslim communities in Europe. Although Turkish Muslims living in Germany come from a nation that has been secularized since the 1920s and thus tend to be less religiously observant than Pakistani Muslims dwelling in Great Britain, Muslims from both countries have been involved in radical Islamic groups, and some belonged to organizations involved in the September 11, 2001, attacks on the United States. The July 7, 2005, suicide bombings in London were carried out by four young Muslims, three of whom had been born in the United Kingdom and one in Jamaica. By contrast, the French government has exerted more control over its Muslim population. However, that policy appeared to have failed badly when in the autumn of 2005 immigrant youth, largely Muslim, carried out riots in various parts of France. These were the most serious civil disturbances in France since 1968. Subsequent riots have occurred in Paris. There have also been sharp disputes in France over attempts by the government to forbid young Muslim women from wearing headscarves while attending secular government schools.

Nonetheless, European Muslims are not a homogeneous group. They come from different countries, have different class backgrounds, and espouse different Islamic traditions. Many European Muslims and Muslim clerics disagree strongly with each other. At the same time, these Muslim communities, so often now marked by deep poverty and unemployment, have become a major concern for European social workers, who disagree among themselves about how their governments should respond to them. What has become clear, however, is that European governments cannot regard their Muslim populations as passive communities; rather European governments and societies must engage them as a permanent fact in the life of early twenty-first-century Europe.

European Population Trends

During the past quarter century, the population of Europe, measured in terms of the European birthrate, has stabilized in a manner that has deeply disturbed many observers. Europeans are having so few children that they are no longer replacing themselves. Whereas in the 1950s European women on average bore 2.1 children, that rate fell to 1.9 in the 1980s and to 1.4 at present, which is below the replacement level. In Mediterranean countries, such as Greece, Spain, and Italy, the rate is even lower. This situation stands in stark contrast to the growth in population in the United States during the past decade when the birthrate reached approximately 2.1. If the current rates more or less hold, by the middle of this century, the United States will have more people than Europe for the first time in history.

There is no consensus on why the European birthrate has declined. One reason often cited is that women are postponing having children until later in their childbearing years. Nonetheless, in response to public opinion, governments have been trying to limit immigration into Europe at a time when it may need new workers.

This falling birthrate means that Europe will face the prospect of an aging population. The energy and drive that youth can provide may shift to the other side of the Atlantic. An aging population is unlikely to give rise to economic innovation. The internal European market, now larger than the internal American market, will shrink. In contrast to the late nineteenth century (see Chapter 23), Europe itself will have fewer Europeans, and Europe's share of the world's population will also decline. Part of Europe's influence on the world in the nineteenth and early twentieth centuries was simply a consequence of the size of its population.

▼ Toward a Welfare State Society

During the decades spanning the Cold War, the U.S. involvement in Vietnam, and the Soviet domination of Eastern Europe, the nations of Western Europe achieved unprecedented economic prosperity and maintained or inaugurated independent, liberal democratic governments. Most of them also confronted problems associated with decolonization and with maintaining economic growth.

The end of the Second World War saw vast constitutional changes in much of Western Europe, except for Portugal and Spain, which remained dictatorships until the mid-1970s. Before or during the war, Germany, Austria, Italy, and France had experienced authoritarian governments. The construction of stable, liberal, democratic political frameworks became a major goal of their postwar political leaders, as well as of the United States. All concerned recognized that the earlier political structures in those nations had failed to resist the rise of right-wing, antidemocratic movements. The Great Depression had shown that democracy requires a social and economic base, as well as a political structure. Most Europeans came to believe that government ought to ensure economic prosperity and social security. Success at doing so, they hoped, would stave off the kind of turmoil that had brought on tyranny and war and could lead to communism.

Christian Democratic Parties

Except for the British Labour Party, the vehicles of the new postwar politics were not, as might have been expected, the democratic socialist parties. Outside Scandinavia, those parties generally did not prosper after the onset of the Cold War. Both communists and conservatives opposed them. Rather, various Christian democratic parties, usually leading coalition governments, introduced the new policies.

These parties were a major new feature of postwar politics. They were largely Roman Catholic in leadership and membership. Catholic parties had existed in Europe since the late nineteenth century. Until the 1930s, however, they had been conservative and had protected the social, political, and educational interests of the church. They had traditionally opposed communism but proposed few positive programs of their own. The postwar Christian democratic parties of Germany, France, Austria, and Italy, however, were progressive and welcomed non-Catholic members. Democracy, social reform, economic growth, and anticommunism were their hallmarks.

The events of the war years largely determined the political leadership of the postwar decade. On the Continent, those groups and parties, including communist parties, that had been active in the resistance against Nazism and fascism held an initial advantage. After 1947, however, in a policy the United States naturally favored, communists were systematically excluded from Western European governments.

The most immediate postwar domestic problems included not only those the physical damage of the conflict created, but often also those that had existed in 1939. The war, however, opened new opportunities to solve those prewar difficulties.

The Creation of Welfare States

The Great Depression, the rise of authoritarian states in the wake of economic dislocation and mass unemployment, and World War II, which involved more people in a war effort than ever before, changed how many Europeans thought about social welfare. Governments began to spend more on social welfare than they did on the military. This reallocation of funds was a reaction to the state violence of the first half of the century and was possible because the NATO defense umbrella, which the United States primarily staffed and funded, protected Western Europe.

The modern European welfare state was broadly similar across the Continent. Before World War II, except in Scandinavia, the two basic models for social legislation were the German and the British. Bismarck had introduced social insurance in Germany during the 1880s to undermine the German Social Democratic Party. In effect, the imperial German government provided workers with social insurance and thus some sense of social security while denying them significant political participation. In early-twentieth-century Britain, where all classes had access to the political system, social insurance was targeted toward the poor. In both the German and British systems, workers were insured only against the risks from disease, injury on the job, and old age. Unemployment was assumed to be only a short-term problem and often one that workers brought on themselves. People higher up in the social structure could look out for themselves and did not need government help.

After World War II, the concept emerged that social insurance against predictable risks was a social right and should be available to all citizens. In Britain, William B. Beveridge (1879–1963) famously set forth this concept in 1942. Paradoxically, making coverage universal, as Beveridge recommended, appealed to conservatives as well as socialists. If medical care, old-age pensions, and other benefits were available to all, they would not become a device to redistribute income from one part of the population to another.

The first major European nation to begin to create a welfare state was Britain, in 1945 to 1951 under the Labour Party ministry of Clement Attlee (1883–1967). The most important element of this early legislation was the creation of the National Health Service. France and Germany did not adopt similar health care legislation until the 1970s, because their governments initially refused to make coverage universal.

The spread of welfare legislation (including unemployment insurance) within Western Europe was related to both the Cold War and domestic political and economic policy. The communist states of Eastern Europe were promising their people social security as well as full employment. The capitalist states came to believe they had to provide similar security for their people, but, in fact, the social security of the communist states was often more rhetoric than reality.

Resistance to the Expansion of the Welfare State

Western European attitudes toward the welfare state have reflected three periods that have marked economic life since the end of the war. The first period was one of reconstruction from 1945 through the early 1950s. It was followed by the second period—almost twenty-five years of generally steady and expanding economic growth. The third period brought first an era of inflation in the late

Margaret Thatcher, a shopkeeper's daughter who became the first female prime minister of Great Britain, served in that office from May 1979 through November 1990. Known as the "Iron Lady" of British politics, she led the Conservative Party to three electoral victories and carried out extensive restructuring of the British government and economy.   AP Wide World Photos

1970s and then one of relatively low growth and high unemployment from the 1990s to the present. During each of the first two periods, a general conviction existed, based on Keynesian economics, that the foundation of economic policy was government involvement in a mixed economy. From the late 1970s, more people came to believe the market should be allowed to regulate itself and that government should be less involved in, though not completely withdraw from, the economy.

The most influential political figure in reasserting the importance of markets and resisting the power of labor unions was Margaret Thatcher (b. 1925) of the British Conservative Party who served as prime minister from 1979 to 1990. She cut taxes and sought to curb inflation. She and her party were determined to roll back many of the socialist policies that Britain had enacted since the war. Her administration privatized many industries that Labour Party governments had nationalized. She also curbed the power of the trade unions in a series of bitter and often violent confrontations. Her goal was to make the British economy more efficient and competitive. Although her administration roused enormous controversy, she was able to push these policies through Parliament. Furthermore, over time the British Labour Party under the leadership of Tony Blair (b. 1953) itself largely came to accept what was at the time known as the Thatcher Revolution. (See "Compare & Connect: Margaret Thatcher and Tony Blair Debate the Government Social Responsibility for Welfare," pages 994–995.)

While Thatcher redirected the British economy, the government-furnished welfare services now found across continental Europe began to encounter resistance. The funding on which they are based assumed a growing population and low unemployment. As the proportion of the population consuming the services of the welfare state—the sick, the injured, the unemployed, and the elderly—increases relative to the number of able-bodied workers who pay for them, the costs of those services have risen.

The leveling off of population growth in Europe discussed in the previous section has thus imperiled the benefits of the welfare state, which Europeans have come to take for granted. Furthermore, during the past two decades, significant levels of unemployment in major Western European nations have increased welfare payments. The low fertility rates across the Continent mean the next working generation will have fewer people to support the retired elderly population. Middle-class taxpayers have also become reluctant to support existing systems.

The general growth of confidence in the ability of market forces rather than government intervention to sustain social cohesion has also spread in the past twenty-five years and has raised questions about the existing welfare structures. Governments across the

Continent, including those normally associated with left-of-center politics, such as the British Labour Party and the German Social Democratic Party, have limited further growth of the welfare state and have reduced benefits. In that respect, Europeans in the next few decades may look at the second half of the twentieth century as the Golden Age of welfare states and may find their own societies dealing with social welfare differently.

▼ New Patterns in Work and Expectations of Women

Since World War II, the work patterns and social expectations of European women have changed enormously. In all social ranks, women have begun to assume larger economic and political roles. More women have entered the "learned professions," and more are filling major managerial positions than ever before in European history. Yet certain more or less traditional patterns continue to describe the position of women in both family and economic life. Despite enormous gains during the second half of the twentieth century, and despite the collapse of those authoritarian governments whose social policies inhibited women from advancing into the mainstream of society, gender inequality remained a major characteristic of the social life of Europe at the opening of the twenty-first century.

Simone de Beauvoir, here with her companion, the philosopher Jean-Paul Sartre, was the major feminist writer in postwar Europe.
Keystone_Paris/Getty Images Inc./Hulton Archive Photos

Feminism

Since World War II, European feminism, although less highly organized than in America, has set forth a new agenda. The most influential postwar work on women's issues was Simone de Beauvoir's (1908–1986) *The Second Sex*, published in 1949. In that work, de Beauvoir explored the difference being a woman had made in her life. (See "Simone de Beauvoir Urges Economic Freedom for Women," page 996.) She was part of the French intellectual establishment and thus wrote from a privileged position. Nonetheless, she and other European feminists argued that, at all levels, European women experienced distinct social and economic disadvantages. Divorce and family laws, for example, favored men. European feminists also called attention to the social problems that women faced, including spousal abuse.

In contrast to earlier feminism, recent feminism has been less a political movement pressing for specific rights than a social movement offering a broader critique of European culture. Several new feminist journals appeared during the 1970s, many of which are still published: *Courage, Emma—Magazine by Women for Women*, and *Spare Rib*. A statement in *Spare Rib*, an English magazine, captures the spirit of these publications:

Spare Rib aims to reflect women's lives in all their diverse situations so that they can recognize themselves in its pages. This is done by making the magazine a vehicle for their writing and their images. Most of all, *Spare Rib* aims to bring women together and support them in taking control of their lives.[2]

This emphasis on women controlling their own lives may be the most important element of recent European feminism. Whereas in the past feminists sought and, in significant measure, gained legal and civil equality with men, they are now pursuing personal independence and issues that are particular to women. In this sense, feminism is an important manifestation of the critical tradition in Western culture.

More Married Women in the Workforce

One of the patterns that seemed firmly established in 1900 has reversed itself. The number of married women in the workforce has risen sharply. Both middle-class and working-class married women have

[2]Quoted in Bonnie S. Anderson and Judith P. Zinsser, *A History of Their Own: Women in Europe from Prehistory to the Present*, Vol. 2 (New York: Harper Perennial, 1988), p. 412.

Margaret Thatcher and Tony Blair Debate Government's Social Responsibility for Welfare

TOWARD THE CLOSE of the twentieth century and the turn of the twenty-first century many of the assumptions that had informed the creation of mid-twentieth-century European welfare states came under criticism and redefinition. Nowhere was the debate sharper than in the United Kingdom where the modern welfare state had essentially been invented through social policies enacted in the aftermath of World War II. Margaret Thatcher's government raised serious questions about the role of government in society. By the turn of the century even the British Labour Party led by Tony Blair had come to modify its own understanding of government social responsibility.

QUESTIONS

1. How and why does Thatcher contend that there is no such thing as society? How does she emphasize the reciprocal character of social relationships?

2. How does Thatcher argue in favor of personal and private charity to aid persons in need? Does she criticize all government aid to citizens?

3. How is it clear in Blair's speech that he is trying to lead a traditional party of the left toward a new understanding of government social responsibility?

4. What does Blair portray as duties of government? How does he seek to mesh government help for individuals with still assigning responsibility to the individuals receiving that help?

5. Though Thatcher and Blair differ in their views of policy, what social and political values do they share despite those differences?

I. Margaret Thatcher Asserts the Need for Individual Responsibility

No single European political figure so challenged and criticized the assumptions of the welfare state and of state intervention in general than Margaret Thatcher, British prime minister from 1979 to 1990. Known as the "Iron Lady," Mrs. Thatcher repeatedly demanded that people take individual responsibility rather than rely on state-sponsored support. Yet her administration did not dismantle the key structures of the British welfare state. The discussion below is from an interview by Mrs. Thatcher in October 1987.

I think we have gone through a period when too many children and people have been given to understand "I have a problem, it is the Government's job to cope with it!" or "I have a problem, I will go and get a grant to cope with it!" "I am homeless, the Government must house me!" and so they are casting their problems on society and who is society? There is no such thing! There are individual men and women . . . there are families and no government can do anything except through people and people look to themselves first. It is our duty to look after ourselves and then also to help look after our neighbour and life is a reciprocal business and people have got the entitlements too much in mind without the obligations, because there is no such thing as an entitlement unless someone has first met an obligation and it is, I think, one of the tragedies in which many of the benefits we give, which were meant to reassure people that if they were sick or ill there was a safety net and there was help, that many of the benefits which were meant to help people who were unfortunate—"It is all right. We joined together and we have these insurance schemes to look after it." That was the objective . . . But it went too far. If children have a problem, it is society that is at fault. There is no such thing as society. There is a living tapestry of men and women and people and the beauty of that tapestry and the quality of our lives will depend upon how much each of us is prepared to take responsibility for ourselves and each of us prepared to turn round and help by our own efforts those who are unfortunate.

Source: This extract derives from a transcript of the original interview rather than the published text. Reprinted with permission from margaretthatcher.org, the official Web site of the Margaret Thatcher Foundation.

One of the most striking and unexpected results of this rising post–World War II population of students and intellectuals was the student rebellion of the 1960s. This development is still not well understood. Student uprisings began in the early 1960s in the United States and grew with opposition to the war in Vietnam. The student rebellion then spread into Europe and other parts of the world. It was almost always associated with a radical political critique of the United States, although Eastern European students resented the Soviet Union even more. The movement was generally antimilitarist. Students also questioned middle-class values and traditional sexual mores and family life.

The student movement peaked in 1968, when American students demonstrated forcibly against U.S. involvement in Vietnam. In the same year, students at the Sorbonne in Paris almost brought down the government of Charles de Gaulle, and in Czechoslovakia, students were in the forefront of the liberal socialist experiment. These protests failed to have an immediate effect on the policies of the governments at which they were directed. The United States stayed in Vietnam until 1973, de Gaulle remained president of France for another year, and the Soviets suppressed the Czech experiment.

By the early 1970s, the era of student rebellion seemed to have passed. Students remained active in European movements against nuclear weapons and particularly against the placement of American nuclear weapons in Germany and elsewhere in Europe. From the mid-1970s, however, although often remaining political radicals, they generally abandoned the disruptive protests that had marked the 1960s.

The Americanization of Europe

During the past half century, through the Marshall Plan, the leadership of NATO, the stationing of huge military bases, student exchanges, popular culture, and tourism, the United States has exerted enormous influence on Europe, especially Western Europe. The word *Americanization*, an often pejorative term in European publications, refers, in part, to this economic and military influence, but also to concerns about cultural loss. Many Europeans feel that American popular entertainment, companies, and business methods threaten to extinguish Europe's unique qualities. Many American firms now have European branches. Large American corporations, such as McDonald's, Starbucks, Apple computers, and the Gap, have outlets in European cities from Dublin to Moscow. American liquor companies

In 1968 a student rebellion in Paris threatened to bring down the government of Charles de Gaulle. This was only one example of the explosion of student activity that rocked the West in the late 1960s. © Bettmann/CORBIS

and distilleries now sell their goods in Europe. Casual American clothing, such as blue jeans and baseball caps, is ubiquitous in Europe. Shopping centers and supermarkets, first pioneered in America, are displacing neighborhood markets in European cities. American television programs, movies, computer games, and rock and rap music are readily available. Furthermore, as Europe moves toward greater economic cooperation, English has become the common language of business, technology, and even some academic fields—and it is American English, not British. (See "Encountering, the Past: Toys from Europe Conquer the United States.")

A Consumer Society

Although European economies came under pressure during the 1990s and experienced high levels of unemployment, the consumer sector has expanded to an extraordinary degree during most of the last half century.

The consumer orientation of the Western European economy emerged as one of the most important characteristics differentiating it from Eastern Europe. Those differences produced political results. In the Soviet Union and the nations it dominated in Eastern Europe, economic planning overwhelmingly favored capital investment and military production. These nations produced inadequate food for their people and few consumer goods. Long lines for staples, such as food and clothing, were common. Automobiles were a luxury. Housing was inadequate. Consumer goods were shoddy.

By contrast, by the early 1950s, Western Europeans enjoyed an excellent food supply that has continued to improve. Also, in a sign of the strength of Western Europe's economy, if not the healthfulness of its diet, fast-food outlets have multiplied.

Western Europe has enjoyed a similar expansion of consumer goods and services. Automobile ownership has soared. Refrigerators, washing machines, electric ranges, televisions, microwaves, videocassette recorders, cameras, computers, CD players, DVD players, and other electronic consumer items are taken for granted. Like their American counterparts, Western Europeans now have a whole gamut of products, such as disposable diapers and prepared baby foods, to help them raise children. They take foreign vacations year round, prompting the expansion of ski resorts in the Alps and beach resorts on the Mediterranean.

This vast expansion of consumerism, which, as we noted in Chapter 15, began in the eighteenth century, became a defining characteristic of Western Europe in the late twentieth century. It stood in marked contrast to the consumer shortages in Eastern Europe. Yet through even the limited number of radios, televisions, movies, and videos available to them, people in the East grew increasingly aware of the discrepancy between their lifestyle and that of the West. They associated Western consumerism with democratic governments, free societies, and economic policies that favored the free market and limited government planning. Thus, the expansion of consumerism in the West, which many intellectuals and moralists deplored, helped generate the discontent that brought down communism in Eastern Europe and the Soviet Union.

Environmentalism

After World War II, shortages of consumer goods created a demand that fueled postwar economic reconstruction and growth into the 1950s and 1960s. In those expansive times, public debate about the ethics of economic expansion and efficiency and their effects on the environment was muted. Concerns about pollution began to grow in the 1970s, and by the 1980s, environmentalists had developed real political clout. Among the most important environmental groups were the German Greens. The Greens formed a political party in 1979 that immediately became an electoral force. During these same years, concern for environmental issues, such as global warming and the pollution of water and the atmosphere, commanded the attention of governments outside Europe and of the United Nations.

Several developments lay behind this new concern for the environment. The Arab oil embargo of 1973 to 1974 pressed home two messages to the industrialized West: Natural resources are limited, and foreign, potentially hostile, countries control critical resources. By the 1970s, too, the environmental consequences of three decades of economic expansion were becoming increasingly apparent. Fish were dying in the Thames River in England. Industrial pollution was destroying life in the Rhine River between Germany and France. Acid rain was killing trees from Sweden to Germany. Finally, long-standing worries about nuclear weapons merged with concerns about their environmental effects, strengthening antinuclear groups and generating opposition to the placement of nuclear weapons in Europe.

The German **Green movement** originated among radical student groups in the late 1960s. Like them, it was anticapitalist, blaming business or pollution. The Greens and other European environmental groups were also strongly antinuclear. Unlike the students of the 1960s, the Greens avoided violence and mass demonstrations, seeking instead to become a significant political presence through the electoral process.

The 1986 disaster at the Chernobyl nuclear reactor in the Soviet Union heightened concern about

TOYS FROM EUROPE CONQUER THE UNITED STATES

TODAY MANY EUROPEANS criticize what they term *Americanization*—the intrusion of popular American products and restaurant chains onto the European scene. Yet over the past half century one European toy—LEGO building blocks manufactured in Denmark—has shaped the experience of childhood for many children in the United States and the rest of the world, entering their lives and imaginations no less powerfully than the cartoon figures associated with the American Disney Corporation.

In 1932, in the midst of the depression, Ole Kirk Christiansen opened a small business in Billund, Denmark, that manufactured household goods and wooden toys. The toys sold so well that two years later the firm renamed itself LEGO from the Danish *LEg GOdt* meaning "Play well." The company remained small, producing only wooden toys, until 1947 when it began to make molded plastic toys. It only sold its products in Denmark.

In 1955, LEGO introduced LEGO Bricks—plastic building blocks of the familiar stud-and-tube type—that it sold in sets under the name LEGO System of Play. That system, which the firm patented in 1958, allowed children to combine LEGO Bricks in an almost endless number of ways, limited only by their own imaginations and that of their parents. The company also extended its market across and began to sell in the United States in 1961.

Thereafter, the success of LEGO as a toy and as a company fed on itself. The company added many new features to the original concept of interlocking building blocks. For example, wheels enabled children to use LEGO kits to build their own trucks, trains, and similar mobile toys.

In 1968, the LEGO Company, no doubt following the example of the Disney Corporation in the United States, opened an amusement park in Billund in which the rides were designed to look like huge LEGO toys. By the end of the century, LEGO had opened similar parks in England, the United States, and Germany.

However, the company remained focused on making toys for children. It designed new toys, such as plastic figures with human heads to ride in LEGO vehicles, and whole LEGO villages, castles, and pirate ships. By the 1990s, LEGO had become the largest toy manufacturer in Europe and a part of modern culture. Museums displayed LEGO products and art built from LEGO blocks. Contests were held to construct the largest or most unusual LEGO structures. In 1999, *Fortune* magazine included the LEGO brick among the "Products of the Century," and in 2002, LEGO persuaded European and American management consultants that working with LEGO blocks would help business executives think more clearly about corporate planning. Perhaps most astonishing is that during a half century of tumultuous change, children around the world have continued to play with these little pieces of plastic.

Source: Factual information derived from the official LEGO Group Web site: www.lego.com/eng/info/history

How has LEGO been an example of the European penetration of popular culture around the world?

Why has the influence of LEGO on children's toys been less controversial than the appearance of American fast-food chains in Europe?

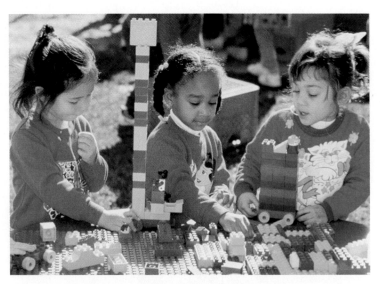

Children across the world play with LEGO toys.   Tom Prettyman/PhotoEdit

environmental issues and raised questions that no European government could ignore. The Soviet government had to confront casualties at the site and relocate tens of thousands of people. Radioactive fallout spread across Europe. Environmentalists had always contended that their issues transcended national borders. The Chernobyl fire proved them right.

After Chernobyl, European governments, East and West, began to respond to environmental concerns. Some observers believe the environment may become a major political issue across the Continent. In Western Europe, environmental groups command many votes. Economic and political integration opens the possibility of transnational cooperation on environmental matters. As the European Economic Community solidifies, it and its member nations will likely impose more environmental regulations on business and industry. The nations of Eastern Europe have been forced to face the cleanup of vast areas of industrial development polluted during the communist era and to try to combine environmental protection with economic growth.

▼ Art Since World War II

It is impossible to cover even briefly the expansive and varied world of Western art since the end of World War II. However, we can note how both the Cold War and the memory of the horrors of the Second World War influenced Western art.

Cultural Divisions and the Cold War

Although they may seem like products from different centuries, the Soviet painter Tatjiana Yablonskaya's (b. 1917) sun-strewn *Bread* (1949) and the American Jackson Pollock's (1912–1956) dizzyingly abstract *One* (Number 31, 1950) were painted only one year apart. The stark differences between these two works mirror the cultural divisions of the early Cold War.

Bread, measuring over six feet high and twelve feet wide, is a monumental example of socialist realism. Established, on Stalin's orders, as the official doctrine of Soviet art and literature in 1934, socialist realism sought to create optimistic and easily intelligible scenes of a bold socialist future, in which prosperity and solidarity would reign. Manual laborers and prominent historical and political figures were painted in a traditional and often rigid figurative manner. Under Soviet control after World War II, socialist realism became the dominant artistic model throughout Eastern Europe, only waning when Nikita Khrushchev liberalized Soviet cultural policy in the late 1950s.

The looping skeins of paint in *One* (Number 31, 1950) may seem completely different from the kind of "realistic" propaganda visible in *Bread*, but Pollock's painting is in fact a central document of postwar American cultural life. Flinging paint from sticks and brushes onto his floor-bound canvas, Pollock freed his lines from representing any figure or outline. The result, in *One* (Number 31, 1950), which is over eight feet high and seventeen feet wide, is a writhing tangle of pure visual

Tatjiana Yablonskaya, *Bread*, 1949. Ria Novosti/Sovfoto/Eastfoto

Jackson Pollock, *One* (Number 31, 1950).   Oil and enamel on unprimed canvas, 8 ft. 10 in. × 17 ft. 5 5/8 in. (269.5 × 530.8 cm). The Museum of Modern Art/Licensed by Scala-Art Resource, NY. Sidney and Harriet Janis Collection Fund (by exchange). Photograph © 2000 The Museum of Modern Art, New York. 00007.68. © 2004 The Pollock-Krasner Foundation/Artists Rights Society (ARS), New York

energy. In the politically charged atmosphere of the early Cold War, critics saw Pollock's exuberant "drip" paintings as the embodiment of American cultural freedom and celebrated the Wyoming-born Pollock as a kind of artist cowboy.

Lurking behind such interpretations was the awareness that the Soviets had imposed socialist realism on Eastern Europe and the Nazis had persecuted avant-garde artists. As skeptical as many viewers might have been about the merits of abstract art (*Time* magazine, for instance, dismissed Pollock as "Jack the dripper" in 1947), many people in the West saw it as the antithesis of socialist, realist totalitarianism.

Indeed, New York City—not Paris—emerged as the international center of modern art after World War II, a position it retains today. As the home of growing collections of twentieth-century art and dozens of European artists who had fled from the Nazis, New York became a fertile training ground for young artists such as Pollock. Just as American political and economic structures became models for the postwar redevelopment of Western Europe, so did American cultural developments. By the time Pollock's first posthumous retrospective toured Europe in 1958, much European painting resembled an elegant imitation of his frenetic lines.

Yablonskaya and Pollock together illustrate the two central poles of twentieth-century art: realism and abstraction. Although artistic style is no longer as closely associated with political programs as it once was, these two poles still frame the work of countless artists today.

Memory of the Holocaust

The British sculptor Rachel Whiteread (b. 1963) is one of the leading artists of today's Europe. Her work illustrates how European art is breaking out of the modernist contours that were set at the beginning of the twentieth century. On one hand, Whiteread's art returns to what seem like familiar forms; on the other, it forces us to view these forms in ways that are as new to us as cubism was to the public in its day.

Whiteread's work is associated with minimalism in contemporary art. This movement, which originated in architecture and interior design, seeks to remove from the object being portrayed as many features as possible while retaining the object's form and the viewer's interest. Minimalist art aims to be as understated as possible. In Whiteread's hands, the minimal becomes the austere, and her work often exudes melancholy and loss.

Whiteread began her career by focusing on objects from everyday life. She would make a plaster cast of an object's interior space. Initially her subjects were small—a hot water bottle, a piece of furniture, or the space under a chair. In 1993, however, she made a cast of the interior space of an entire house that was about

Rachel Whiteread's *Nameless Library* in Vienna commemorates the thousands of Austrian Jews killed in the Nazi Holocaust.   © Reuters NewMedia Inc./CORBIS

to be torn down in London. She left the work untitled, but it became known as *House*. It presents interior space as solid but temporary, subject to the passage of time. Like many of Whiteread's subjects, the object that has been molded—in this case the demolished house—no longer exists, and even the sculpture itself will eventually disappear. *House* stood on the site for only two and a half months before being razed, like the actual house itself, as part of an urban redevelopment plan.

Whiteread's most important public work, and one designed to endure, is *Nameless Library*, the Judenplatz Holocaust Memorial in Vienna, which commemorates the deaths of 65,000 Austrian Jews under the Nazis. This memorial, which resembles a vast haunting tomb, is cast in concrete and embodies the outline of books whose spines are turned inward, thus remaining forever unread and as unopenable as the library's huge concrete doors are. Whiteread has said the molded, unopened books, which have been compared to the ghost of a library, symbolize the loss both of Jewish contributions to culture and of Jewish lives in the Holocaust.

▼ The Christian Heritage

In most ways, Christianity in Europe has continued to be as hard-pressed during the twentieth century as it had been in the late nineteenth. Material prosperity, political ideologies, environmentalism, gender politics, and simple indifference have replaced religious faith for many people. Still, despite the loss of much of their popular support and legal privileges and the low rates of church attendance, the European Christian churches continue to exercise social and political influence. In Germany, the churches were one of the few major institutions that the Nazis did not wholly subdue. Lutheran clergy, such as Martin Niemöller (1892–1984) and Dietrich Bonhoeffer (1906–1945), were leaders of the opposition to Hitler. After the war, in Poland and elsewhere in Eastern Europe, the Roman Catholic Church opposed communism.

In Western Europe, religious affiliation provided much of the initial basis for the Christian Democratic parties. The churches have also raised critical questions about colonialism, nuclear weapons, human rights, war, and other issues. Consequently, even in this most secular of ages, Christian churches have influenced state and society.

Neo-Orthodoxy

Liberal theologians of the nineteenth century often softened the concept of sin and portrayed human nature as close to the divine. The horror of World War I destroyed that optimistic faith. Many Europeans felt that evil had stalked the Continent.

The most important Christian response to World War I appeared in the theology of Karl Barth (1886–1968). In 1919, this Swiss pastor published *A Commentary on the Epistle to the Romans*, which reemphasized the transcendence of God and the dependence of humankind on the divine. Barth portrayed God as wholly other than, and different from, humankind. In a sense, Barth was returning to the Reformation theology of Luther, but the work of Kierkegaard had profoundly influenced his reading of the reformer. Like the Danish writer, Barth regarded the lived experience of men and women as the best testimony to the truth of Luther's theology. Those extreme moments of life Kierkegaard described provided the basis for a knowledge of humanity's need for God.

This view challenged much nineteenth-century writing about human nature. Barth's theology, which came to be known as neo-Orthodoxy, proved influential throughout the West in the wake of new disasters and suffering.

Liberal Theology

Neo-Orthodoxy did not, however, sweep away liberal theology, which had a strong advocate in Paul Tillich (1886–1965). This German-American theologian tended to regard religion as a human, rather than a divine, phenomenon. Whereas Barth saw God as dwelling outside humankind, Tillich believed that evidence of the divine had to be sought in human nature and human culture.

Other liberal theologians, such as Rudolf Bultmann (1884–1976), continued to work on the problems of naturalism and supernaturalism that had troubled earlier writers. Bultmann's major writing took place before World War II but was popularized after the war by the Anglican bishop John Robinson in *Honest to God* (1963). Another liberal Christian writer from Britain, C. S. Lewis (1878–1963), attracted millions of readers during and after World War II. This layman and scholar of medieval literature often expressed his thoughts on theology in the form of letters and short stories. His most famous work is *The Screwtape Letters* (1942). In recent years, however, European religious thought has produced few major Protestant voices.

Roman Catholic Reform

Among Christian denominations, the most significant postwar changes have been in the Roman Catholic Church. Pope John XXIII (r. 1958–1963) initiated these changes, the most extensive in Catholicism for more than a century and, some would say, since the Council of Trent in the sixteenth century. In 1959, Pope John summoned the Twenty-First Ecumenical Council (the Emperor Constantine had called the first council in the fourth century), which came to be called Vatican II. The council finished its work in 1965 under John's successor, Pope Paul VI (r. 1963–1978). Among many changes in Catholic liturgy the council introduced, Mass was now celebrated in the vernacular languages rather than in Latin. The council also encouraged freer relations with other Christian denominations, fostered a new spirit toward Judaism, and gave more power to bishops. In recognition of the growing importance to the church of the world outside Europe and North America, Pope Paul appointed several cardinals from the former colonial nations, transforming the church into a truly world body.

In contrast to these liberal changes, however, Pope Paul and his successors have firmly upheld the celibacy of priests, maintained the church's prohibition on contraception and abortion, and opposed moves to open the priesthood to women. The church's unyielding stand on clerical celibacy has caused many men to leave the priesthood and many men and women to leave religious orders. The laity has widely ignored the prohibition on contraception.

John Paul II, the former Karol Wojtyla, archbishop of Kraków in Poland, was elected in 1978 after the death of John Paul I, whose reign lasted only thirty-four days. The youngest pope since Pius IX (r. 1846–1878), John Paul II (1920–2005) pursued a three-pronged policy during his long pontificate. First, he maintained traditionalist doctrine, stressing the authority of the papacy and attempting to limit doctrinal and liturgical experimentation.

Second, taking a firm stand against communism, he supported the spirit of freedom in Eastern Europe that brought down the communist regimes. As a cardinal in Poland, he had clashed with the communist government. After his election, he visited Poland, lending support to Solidarity. His Polish origins helped make him an important factor in the popular resistance to Eastern Europe's communist governments that developed during the 1980s. He thus opened a new chapter in the relationship between church and state in modern Europe.

Third, John Paul II encouraged the growth of the church in the non-Western world, stressing the need for social justice, but limiting the political activity of priests. The pope's concern for the expansion of Roman

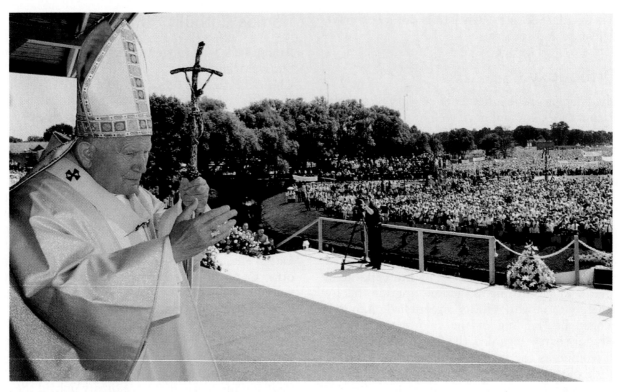

Throughout his pontificate John Paul II continued a close relationship with his native Poland to which he made several visits. The earliest of these was important in demonstrating the authority of the church against Polish communist authorities. Shown here in his Polish visit of June 1999, the pope would celebrate mass before several hundred thousand Poles after the collapse of communism that had occurred a decade earlier. AP Wide World Photos

Catholicism beyond Europe and North America recognized and encouraged what appears to be a transformation in Christianity as a world religion. Whereas in Europe Christian observance whether Roman Catholic, Protestant, or Orthodox had declined sharply during the twentieth century, Christianity has grown rapidly and fervently in Africa and Latin America. Observers estimate that within a few years, over half of the world's Christians will live in those two continents. Recognizing these changes, John Paul II created more cardinals from non-Western nations.

John Paul II died in 2005. His successor was his closest collaborator, the German Cardinal Joseph Ratzinger (b. 1927), who took the name Benedict XVI. The new pope has followed his predecessor in his rigorous defense of orthodoxy. He has pursued what many regard as a more meditative pontificate. However, in September 2006 he delivered a speech in which he quoted a medieval writer criticizing Islam. The speech evoked considerable criticism in Europe and provoked riots in parts of the Islamic world. Since that event, Pope Benedict has sought to take numerous steps to initiate Christian-Muslim dialogue. He has also championed the role of religious freedom for Christians and other religiously observant peoples living in the midst of secular societies. (See "Pope Benedict XVI Calls for the Recognition of Religious Freedom as a Human Right," page 1009.)

▼ Late-Twentieth-Century Technology: The Arrival of the Computer

During the twentieth century, technology crossed international borders the way popular culture did. As with other areas of European life and society, American technology had an unprecedented impact on the Continent, whether in the guise of the first airplanes or Henry Ford's method of producing affordable automobiles. It seems certain, however, that no single American technological achievement of the twentieth century will so influence Western life on both sides of the Atlantic, as well as throughout the rest of the world, as the computer.

POPE BENEDICT XVI CALLS FOR THE RECOGNITION OF RELIGIOUS FREEDOM AS A HUMAN RIGHT

On April 18, 2008, Pope Benedict XVI addressed the United Nations General Assembly in New York City. In the course of a wide-ranging speech the Pope paid special attention to religious freedom as a fundamental human right. He particularly defended religious freedom when its exercise stands in tension or conflict with the values of a surrounding secular society or other surrounding majority values.

How did Pope Benedict XVI define religious freedom as a human right? How did he portray the relationship of the exercise of religious freedom to secular values and secular social institutions? How did he relate religious freedom to human betterment?

Human rights . . . must include the right to religious freedom, understood as the expression of a dimension that is at once individual and communitarian—a vision that brings out the unity of the person while clearly distinguishing between the dimension of the citizen and that of the believer. The activity of the United Nations in recent years has ensured that public debate gives space to viewpoints inspired by a religious vision in all its dimensions, including ritual, worship, education, dissemination of information and the freedom to profess and choose religion. It is inconceivable, then, that believers should have to suppress a part of themselves—their faith—in order to be active citizens. It should never be necessary to deny God in order to enjoy one's rights.

The rights associated with religion are all the more in need of protection if they are considered to clash with a prevailing secular ideology or with majority religious positions of an exclusive nature. The full guarantee of religious liberty cannot be limited to the free exercise of worship, but has to give due consideration to the public dimension of religion, and hence to the possibility of believers playing their part in building the social order. . . .

Refusal to recognize the contribution to society that is rooted in the religious dimension and in the quest for the Absolute—by its nature, expressing communion between persons—would effectively privilege an individualistic approach, and would fragment the unity of the person. . . .

The United Nations remains a privileged setting in which the [Roman Catholic] Church is committed to contributing her experience "of humanity," developed over the centuries among peoples of every race and culture, and placing it at the disposal of all members of the international community. This experience and activity, directed towards attaining freedom for every believer, seeks also to increase the protection given to the rights of the person.

Those rights are grounded and shaped by the transcendent nature of the person, which permits men and women to pursue their journey of faith and their search for God in this world. Recognition of this dimension must be strengthened if we are to sustain humanity's hope for a better world and if we are to create the conditions for peace, development, cooperation, and guarantee of rights for future generations.

Pope Benedict XVI's Address to the United Nations General Assembly, April 18, 2008, as reproduced on the Vatican City Web site: www.vatican.va/holy_father/benedict_xvi/speeches/2008/april/documents/hf_ben-xvi_spe_20080418_un-visit_en.html

The Demand for Calculating Machines

Beginning in the seventeenth century, thinkers associated with the scientific revolution—most famously, the French mathematician and philosopher Blaise Pascal (1623–1662)—attempted to construct machines that would carry out mathematical calculations that human beings would find essentially impossible because of the tedium and the amount of time they involved. Starting in the late nineteenth century, the governments of the consolidating nation-states of Europe and of the United States confronted new administrative tasks that involved collecting and organizing vast amounts of data about national censuses, tax collection, economic statistics, and the administration of pensions and welfare legislation. During the same years, private businesses sought calculating machinery to handle and organize growing amounts of economic and business data. Such machines became technologically possible through the development of complex circuitry for electricity, the most versatile mode of energy in human history. Moreover, inventions that were dependent on electricity, including the telephone, the telegraph, underwater cables, and the wireless, created a new communications industry that in and of itself also required the organization of large databases of customer information to deliver their services. By the late 1920s, companies like National Cash Register, Remington Rand, and International Business Machines Corporation (IBM) had begun to manufacture such business machinery.

Early Computer Technology

As has happened so often in history, warfare was the chief catalyst of change. After World War I and during World War II, the major powers developed new weapons that required exact mathematical ballistic calculations to effectively strike targets with bombs delivered by aircraft or long-range guns.

The first machine genuinely recognizable as a modern digital computer was the Electronic Numerical Integrator and Computer (**ENIAC**), built and designed at Moore Laboratories of the University of Pennsylvania and put into use by the U.S. Army in 1946 for ballistics calculation. The ENIAC was an enormous piece of equipment with 40 panels, 1,500 electric relays, and 18,000 vacuum tubes. It also used thousands of punch cards, and a separate tabulator had to print the data from them. Further computer engineering occurred at the Institute for Advanced Research in Princeton, New Jersey, in laboratories at the Massachusetts Institute of Technology, and in other laboratories the U.S. government and private businesses, especially IBM, ran. The other primary sites for computer development were laboratories in Britain.

The Development of Desktop Computers

During the 1950s, however, the transistor revolutionized electronics, permitting a miniaturization of circuitry that made vacuum tubes obsolete and allowed

The earliest computers were very large. Here in a 1946 photograph J. Presper Eckert and J. W. Mauchly stand by the Electronic Numerical Integrator and Computer (ENIAC), which was dedicated at the University of Pennsylvania Moore School of Electrical Engineering. CORBIS/Bettmann

computers to become smaller. Yet computers still had to be programmed with difficult computer languages by persons expertly trained to use them.

By the late 1960s, however, two innovations transformed computing technology. First, control of the computer was transferred to a bitmap covering the screen of a computer monitor. The mouse, invented in 1964, eased the movement of the cursor around the computer screen. Second, engineers at the Intel Corporation—then a California start-up company—invented the microchip, which became the heart of all future computers.

The bitmap on the screen, operated through the mouse, in effect embedded complicated computer language in the machine, hidden from the user, who simply manipulated images on the screen with the mouse. Almost anyone could thus learn to operate computers. At the same time, the tiny microchip, itself a miniature computer or microprocessor, permitted computer technology to abandon the mainframe and move to still smaller computers. At the Xerox Corporation, engineers devised a small computer using a mouse, but the machine never achieved commercial success. By 1982, IBM had produced a small personal computer but temporarily lost the race for commercialization to a then small company called Apple Computer Corporation. The design features originally developed at Xerox informed the ideas of the Apple engineers, who, in early 1984, produced a small, highly accessible, commercially successful computer, known as the Macintosh, that would fit on a desktop in the home or office. IBM soon adopted the Apple concept with different engineering and marketing approaches and manufactured a product called the Personal Computer, or PC. By the mid-1980s, for a relatively modest cost (and one that has continued to drop), individuals had available for their own personal use in their offices or homes computers with far more power than the old mainframes. The Apple Macintosh and the IBM PC transformed computers into objects of everyday life and, in doing so, began to transform everyday life itself. Nonetheless, the chief contemporary users of computers remain governments followed by the telephone industry, banking and finance, automobile operation, and airline reservation systems.

Despite the potential democratizing character of computer technology, the computer revolution has also introduced new concepts of "haves" and "have-nots" to societies around the world. Computers, whatever their possible shortcomings, enable their users to do things that nonusers cannot do. Whether in poor school districts in the United States or in poor countries of the former Soviet bloc, students who graduate without computer skills will have difficulty making their way in the world's rapidly computerizing economy. Some commentators also fear that boys are more likely than girls to receive technological training in computers. Nations whose governments and businesses become networked into the world of computers will prosper more fully than those whose access to computer technology is deficient. In that regard, the possession of computers and the ability to use them will probably determine future economic competition, just as they have determined recent military competition.

▼ The Challenges of European Unification

The unprecedented steps toward economic cooperation and unity Western European nations took during the second half of the twentieth century were the single most important European success story of that era. The process originated from American encouragement in response to the Soviet domination of Eastern Europe and from the Western European states' own sense that they lacked effective political and economic power. Furthermore, leaders in France and Germany who recoiled from the disastrous peace that followed World War I were determined that something different would arise from the political collapse of Europe after World War II. They understood that cooperation, rather than revenge, must inform the future of Europe.

Postwar Cooperation

The mid-twentieth-century Western European movement toward unity could have occurred in at least three ways: politically, militarily, or economically. Economic cooperation, unlike military and political cooperation, involved little or no immediate loss of sovereignty by the participating nations. Furthermore, it brought material benefits to all the states involved, increasing popular support for their governments. Moreover, the administration of the Marshall Plan and the organization of NATO gave the countries involved new experience in working with each other and demonstrated the productivity and efficiency that mutual cooperation could achieve.

The first effort toward economic cooperation was the formation of the European Coal and Steel Community in 1951 by France, West Germany, Italy, and the Benelux countries (Belgium, the Netherlands, and Luxembourg). The community both benefited from and contributed to the immense growth of material production in Western Europe during this period. Its success reduced the suspicions of government and business groups about coordination and economic integration.

A Closer ▶ LOOK

THE COPENHAGEN OPERA HOUSE

THE NEW OPERA House opened in Copenhagen, Denmark in 2005. The structure has come to symbolize free enterprise in the European Union because its full cost was covered by private, rather than government, funding.

The construction of the Copenhagen Opera House reclaimed areas of decaying dockland in the city. In this respect, it symbolizes similar projects that have been undertaken in other major European ports where docks have been relocated in the late twentieth century.

Henning Larson, a Dane, was the architect. His design, however, has been criticized for being subtly commercial because some observers see the opera house as resembling the grill of an automobile.

AP Wide World Photos

To examine this image in an interactive fashion, please go to www.myhistorylab.com

PEARSON
myhistorylab

The European Economic Community

It took more than the prosperity of the European Coal and Steel Community to draw European leaders toward further unity, however. The unsuccessful Suez intervention of 1956 and the resulting diplomatic isolation of France and Britain persuaded many Europeans that only by acting together could they significantly influence the United States and the Soviet Union or control their own national and regional destinies. So, in 1957, through the Treaty of Rome, the six members of the Coal and Steel Community agreed to form a new organization: the **European Economic Community (EEC)**. The members of the Common Market, as the EEC was soon known, envisioned more than a free-trade union. They sought to achieve the eventual elimination of tariffs, a free flow of capital and labor, and similar wage and social benefits in all their countries.

The Common Market achieved stunning success during its early years. By 1968, well ahead of schedule, the six members had abolished all tariffs among themselves. Trade and labor migration among the members grew steadily. Moreover, nonmember states began to copy the EEC and, later, to seek to join it. In 1959, Britain, Denmark, Norway, Sweden, Switzerland, Austria, and Portugal formed the European Free Trade Area. By 1961, however, Britain had decided to join the Common Market. Twice, in 1963 and 1967, President Charles de Gaulle of France vetoed British membership. He argued that Britain was too closely tied to the United States to support the EEC wholeheartedly. Finally, in 1973, Great Britain, Ireland, and Denmark became members. Throughout the late 1970s, however, and into the 1980s, momentum for expanding EEC membership slowed. Norway and Sweden, with relatively strong economies, declined to join. Although in 1982, Spain, Portugal, and Greece applied for membership and were eventually admitted, sharp disagreements and a sense of stagnation within the EEC continued.

The European Union

In 1988, the leaders of the EEC reached an important decision. By 1992, the EEC was to be a virtual free-trade zone with no trade barriers or other restrictive trade policies among its members. In 1991, the Treaty of Maastricht made a series of specific proposals that led to a unified EEC currency (the Euro) and a strong central bank. The treaty was submitted to referendums in several European states. Denmark initially rejected it, and it passed only narrowly in France and Great Britain, making clear that it needed wider popular support. When the treaty finally took effect in November 1993, the EEC was renamed the **European Union**. Throughout the 1990s, the Union's influence grew. Its most notable achievement was the launching in early 1999 of the **Euro**, which by 2002 had become the common currency in twelve of the member nations.

In May 2004, the European Union added ten new nations, raising the total number of members to twenty-five. (See Map 30–1.) Membership in the European Union indicated that a nation had achieved economic

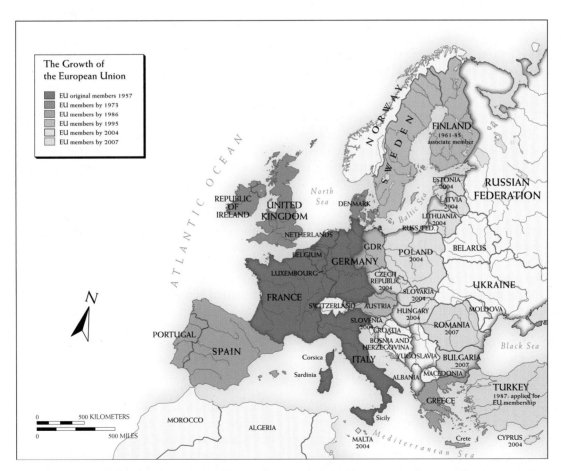

Map 30–1 **THE GROWTH OF THE EUROPEAN UNION** This map traces the growth of membership in the European Union from its founding in 1957 through the introduction of its newest members in 2007. Note that Turkey, though having applied for membership, has not yet been admitted.

stability and genuinely democratic institutions. Nonetheless, several of the new members states from the former Soviet bloc are relatively poor and will require much economic support from the Union.

Discord over the Union

The 2004 expansion of the European Union may mark for some time the high point of European integration. During that year the leaders of the member nations adopted a new constitutional treaty for the Union. This treaty, generally known as the European Constitution, was a long, detailed, and highly complicated document involving a bill of rights and complex economic and political agreements among all the member states. It would have transferred considerable decision-making authority from the governments of the individual states to the central institutions of the European Union, many of which are located in Brussels, Luxembourg, and Strasbourg. To become effective, all the member states had to ratify the constitution either by their parliaments or through national referendums.

To the surprise of many in the European elite, in the spring of 2005, referendums held in France and the Netherlands heavily defeated the new constitutional treaty. Britain, where support for further European integration was lukewarm at best, immediately postponed holding its own referendum. Public opinion in other nations also soured on the constitutional treaty. Furthermore, immediately after these events, discord erupted over the Union's internal budget. These events marked an unprecedented crisis for the European Union and for the project of European integration. A similar crisis erupted in 2008 when a referendum in Ireland failed to support changes in the European Union that would create shared institutions of foreign policy formulation and military policy.

Several factors appear to have brought the European Union to this pass. First, for at least the past fifteen years, a gap has been growing between the European political elites who have led the drive toward unity and the European voting public. The former have either ignored the latter or have moved the project along with only narrow majorities. Second, the general Western European economy has stagnated for the last decade with relatively high rates of unemployment, especially among the young. Voting against the constitution was a way to voice discontent with this situation. Third, many of the smaller member states of the European Union have felt that France and Germany have either ignored them or taken them for granted. Fourth, some nations have come to believe that they were placed at an economic disadvantage when the Euro replaced their former national currencies because the rates of exchange were unfairly calculated. Fifth, many people in

A woman stands between a "yes" and a "no" campaign poster in reference to France's referendum on the EU constitution in a street of Rennes, western France, Friday May 27, 2005, two days before the vote. AP Wide World Photos

the various states, large and small, have become increasingly reluctant to cede national sovereignty and the authority to make economic decisions to the bureaucracy in Brussels. Britain, for example, would like to see less economic regulation. France, on the other hand, is loath to see the European Union gain the power to revise the French labor code with its extensive protections and benefits for workers.

Finally, another large issue has informed the internal skeptics of the current European Union. Over the past several years, the leaders of the major member states have grown more favorable to the eventual admission of Turkey as a member state. If Turkey were admitted, Europe would have to integrate into the Union a state whose population is larger and much poorer than that of any other member state. This would place enormous social and economic burdens on the other states. Furthermore, although the Turkish government has long been seen as adamantly secular, the Turkish people are overwhelmingly Muslim. This "Islamic factor" has become increasingly controversial among those Europeans who, whether they are religiously observant or not, believe European culture to be Christian, and among those secular Europeans who are deeply concerned about the political, economic, and social implications of the Continent's already significant Muslim population. These tensions grew after 2005 when a Danish newspaper published self-consciously irreverent cartoons insulting the Prophet Muhammad. Riots broke out in parts of the Islamic world and in subsequent years Danish businesses and embassies abroad became targets of Islamic attacks.

It seems inconceivable that the effort to unify in Europe will either halt or be reversed. At the present time, however, it also seems certain that all future developments will move much more slowly and will require in-

AN ENGLISH BUSINESS EDITOR CALLS FOR EUROPE TO TAKE CHARGE OF ITS ECONOMIC FUTURE

Richard Lofthouse is the editor of CNBC European Business, *a magazine devoted to contemporary economic and business life. Educated in both Great Britain and the United States, Lofthouse brings a personal global perspective to his analysis. In the summer of 2008 he observed the tendency of Europeans to see their economic life as driven by global forces outside their control. In the face of such challenges, he called upon his readers to recall their cultural heritage and to embrace a spirit of entrepreneurship.*

Why are the challenges facing Europe and the West today international and global in contrast to the domestic political challenges of the third quarter of the twentieth century? What are the forces outside Europe impacting its economic life? What are the cultural qualities to which Lofthouse seeks to rally his readers?

In 1968, rioting across the US followed the assassination of Martin Luther King, while in France students and workers hoped to oust Charles de Gaulle's government. Broadly speaking these tumultuous events concerned generational conflict over prevailing values within the societies where the riots broke out. Forty years later, all the images of civil disobedience such as French fisherman dumping their catches and British hauliers blocking roads illustrate self-interest triggered by global forces rather than local ones, such as rising fuel and food prices.

If globalisation is a bus trip, then, Europe appears to have been steadily reduced in status from driver to conductor to helpless passenger. Almost none of the big issues currently shaping its future are European. In the past six months fear has intensified over China's economic rise and India has become the most seductive destination for entrepreneurial retailers. Most European banks have lost at least half of their value due to wildly misguided risk assessment in the US while most of the rise in the oil price reflects non-Western supply and demand habits.

One might paint Europe as the hapless victim of globalisation. Consideration of energy security suggests that the crunch will worsen as natural gas supplies evaporate (as if high oil prices weren't enough to keep you awake at night). Meanwhile, analysis of the future of retailing suggests that online retailing is set to soar, not least because even Americans are driving less in a bid to keep fuel costs down. Malls might have only just opened their doors in some emerging markets but in the

West they face an uncertain future. The aviation industry believes that if oil remains at $135 a barrel, the world's airlines will lose $6.1bn this year.

It seems as if every business model in town is in the process of being wrecked by OPEC, or China's soaring resource demands, or greedy bankers; in reply, citizens protest that Congress or the European Union Commissioner or big oil companies should fix it and really, you know, it *is* someone else's fault. But that's not our view. In fact, it might be worth remembering Einstein's credo that "the significant problems we have cannot be solved at the same level of thinking with which we created them." This fragment is the basis of most of the entrepreneurship espoused in this publication, and it opens the door to creative solutions to problems that are invariably both global and local.

Europe has a leadership role to play in globalization, providing not just technological solutions to pressing problems such as climate change but perhaps more importantly offering a deep heritage of cultural intelligence and humanity arising from its eighteenth century Enlightenment.

There are hopeful signs to which one may point. A telemetry company is helping hauliers to cut their fuel consumption; an electric car project, backed by both Israel's government and Renault-Nissan, may herald the end of the internal combustion engine as we know it, and a book called *WASTEnomics* bristles with private sector solutions to excessive waste, the product of our extraordinary affluence.

Amended version of editorial published by Richard Lofthouse in *CNBC European Business* (39) (July–August 2008), p. 6. Published with the permission of the author.

creasingly complicated negotiations. Moreover, the future of the European Union has become enmeshed in often bitter and divisive debates within the member states over social policies, the future of their economies, and what role the state should play in economic affairs.

▼ New American Leadership and Financial Crisis

Much of the first decade of the twenty-first century witnessed considerable strain between the new post–Soviet Union Europe and the United States. As noted in Chapter 29, the immediate European reaction to the attacks on the United State on September 11, 2001, were sympathetic. The events leading up to the U.S. Iraq invasion in 2003 and the violence occurring since that invasion caused considerable strain between the United States and Europe, especially in terms of popular opinion. Europeans through their press and to some extent through their governments voiced much criticism over what they regarded as United States unilateral action in its foreign policy.

Three events in 2008 may have begun to change this situation and possibly to lessen those tensions. The first was the Russian invasion of Georgia discussed in Chapter 29. The United States and the European Union agreed in condemning that action. Second, the American presidential election of 2008 saw the strong victory of Barack Obama, the Democratic Party candidate. Obama is the first African American to be elected to the presidency. He ran on a platform critical of the Iraq invasion and American unilateralism. Even though he also voiced strong support for the war in Afghanistan, Obama has generated enormous popular support across Europe. Indeed during the campaign he gave a speech in Berlin that drew a crowd of tens of thousands. Obama's victory in the presidential election and the expansion of Democratic Party majorities in Congress appear to have persuaded at least for the moment many Europeans that their assumptions about American culture were incorrect and that a new era of American foreign and domestic policy is at hand. Only time, of course, can tell whether this change in European public opinion is of a lasting character.

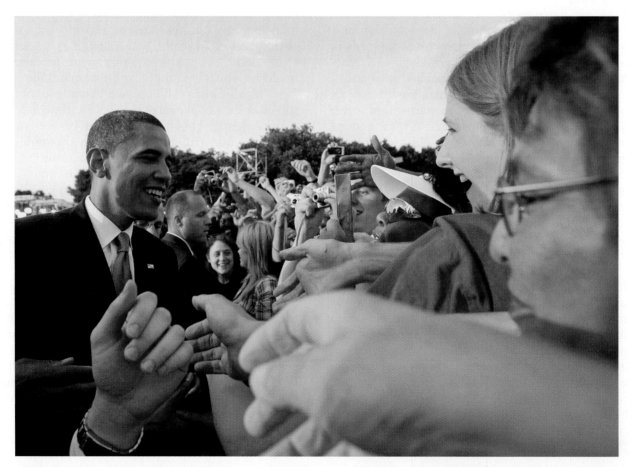

Barack Obama shakes hands with supporters in Berlin, Germany, on July 24, 2008, following a speech he gave before a crowd of tens of thousands at the Victory Column in Tiergarten Park. Reuters/Jim Young/Landov Media

Third, during the second half of 2008 a major international financial crisis potentially of the dimensions of that of the 1930s overwhelmed the American, transatlantic, and world economies. The crisis originated in the United States mortgage market where numerous major banks found themselves holding mortgages which could not be paid. Several major financial institutions in the United States failed as did some banks in Europe. The United States and some European governments intervened deeply in areas of the economy where they had previously generally refrained from intervening. Stock markets around the world lost a third or more of their value. The interconnectedness of world markets demonstrated itself as never before with financial panic displaying itself around the globe.

The financial crisis and its broad fallout even more than the wars in Iraq and Afghanistan will be the major issues confronting the new Obama administration. The financial problems even more than matters of traditional and foreign policy may for the next several years determine the relationship of the United States and Europe and hence the role of the West in the world.

In Perspective

The twentieth century was the most destructive in human history. The wars of the first half of the century killed millions of Europeans and disrupted the fabric of European society. The Bolsheviks, Fascists, and National Socialists sought to remake whole societies according to utopian visions that resulted in repression and death on a massive scale and drove millions of Europeans from their ancestral homes.

With the defeat of National Socialism and Fascism, society in Western Europe developed along more peaceful lines with a powerful economic and cultural influence coming from the United States. Migration and the economic growth of the second half of the century reshaped the society of many Western nations. Welfare systems provided an extensive social safety net. The role and opportunities for women in society expanded. More and more Europeans across the Continent attended universities. The end of Soviet domination began a process in which Eastern Europe increasingly came to participate in the affluence of the West with its myriad consumer goods.

By the close of the century, Europe, like much of the rest of the world, had entered a new technological revolution through the computer and advances in medical care. Economic growth slowed in the 1990s, but most of Europe outside the former communist-dominated regions continued to enjoy some of the highest standards of living in the world, under liberal democratic governments.

The efforts to unify Europe have transformed the Continent and the everyday lives of its citizens. The future of the European Union, however, now stands at a crossroads. The advancing financial crisis will only place new demands on the Union.

AP* TEST PREP

1. In Britain, the most influential opponent of the welfare state was
   a. Churchill.
   b. Thatcher.
   c. Major.
   d. Blair.
   e. Chamberlain.

2. Modern European feminism emphasizes
   a. political equality.
   b. legal equality.
   c. economic equality.
   d. women's control of their own lives.
   e. reproductive rights.

3. The new governments in Eastern Europe have
   a. been hostile to women in politics and public policy.
   b. been hostile to women in the workplace.
   c. shown a great deal of interest in women's issues.
   d. restricted women's access to health care.
   e. shown little interest in women's issues.

4. Existentialism has its roots in the thought of Nietzsche and
   a. Kierkegaard.
   b. Hegel.
   c. Kant.
   d. Locke.
   e. Voltaire.

5. University education is
   a. mandatory throughout Europe.
   b. more common in Europe than in the United States.
   c. less common in Europe than the United States.
   d. only open to the wealthy in Europe.
   e. universal in Europe.

6. The German Green movement originated among
   a. leaders of the Christian Democratic Party.
   b. middle-class socialists.
   c. trade union members.
   d. radical student groups.
   e. leaders of the Communist Party.

7. Karl Barth's theology came to be known as
   a. neo-orthodoxy.
   b. anti-orthodoxy.
   c. Christian minimalism.
   d. neorationalism.
   e. orthodoxy.

8. C. S. Lewis, Rudolf Bultmann, and John Robinson are all considered
   a. proponents of liberation theology.
   b. liberal theologians.
   c. neorationalist theologians.
   d. reactionary theologians.
   e. orthodox theologians.

9. A series of important liberal reforms was enacted by the Catholic Church at
   a. the Council of Milan.
   b. the Second Council of Trent.
   c. the Council of Turin.
   d. the Council of Constantine.
   e. Vatican II.

10. _____ wrote *Being and Time.*
    a. Sartre
    b. Heidegger
    c. Camus
    d. Kierkegaard
    e. Nietzsche

11. All of the following joined the European Union in 2004 except
    a. Turkey.
    b. Poland.
    c. Lithuania.
    d. the Czech Republic.
    e. Hungary.

12. The intellectual movement that best captured the mood of mid-twentieth-century European culture was
    a. intellectualism.
    b. romanticism.
    c. rationalism.
    d. classicism.
    e. existentialism.

13. Simone de Beauvoir is the author of _____, a work that explored the difference being a woman had made in her life.
    a. *Spare Rib*
    b. *Courage, Emma*
    c. *Women for Women*
    d. *The Second Sex*
    e. *The Other Half*

14. Jean-Marie Le Pen's National Front sought to exploit hostility toward
    a. Jews.
    b. Christians.
    c. North African immigrants.
    d. city dwellers.
    e. Belgians.

15. Muslim communities in Europe
    a. generally seek temporary residence in Europe.
    b. are almost uniformly from poor and uneducated backgrounds.
    c. have been quick to assimilate into European culture.
    d. generally have integrated well into the economies of European countries.
    e. reflect diverse Islamic traditions.

16. Which of the following countries remained a dictatorship until the mid-1970s?
    a. Spain
    b. Germany
    c. Italy
    d. Austria
    e. Greece

17. Europeans are having
    a. more children today than they did twenty years ago.
    b. so few children they are no longer replacing themselves.
    c. about 2.5 children per woman.
    d. more children today than they did fifty years ago.
    e. about 3.1 children per woman.

18. The first major European nation to begin to create a welfare state was
    a. France.
    b. West Germany.
    c. the Netherlands.
    d. Britain.
    e. Austria.

19. The disillusionment of European intellectuals with the Soviet Union was prompted by all of the following *except*
    a. Stalin's Five-Year Plans.
    b. the purge trials of the late 1930s.
    c. the Spanish Civil War.
    d. the Nazi-Soviet Pact of 1939.
    e. the Soviet invasion of Hungary.

20. Jackson Pollock's *One* is an example of _____ art.
    a. socialist realist
    b. postimpressionist
    c. abstract
    d. minimalist
    e. expressionist

DOCUMENT-BASED QUESTION

Directions: Construct a valid essay that directly addresses the central issue of the following question. Use facts from the documents provided and from the chapter to prove the position you take in your thesis statement.

Does the movement toward European unification represent a fundamental break with Europe's past? What new challenges to unification have emerged since 1990?

Document A

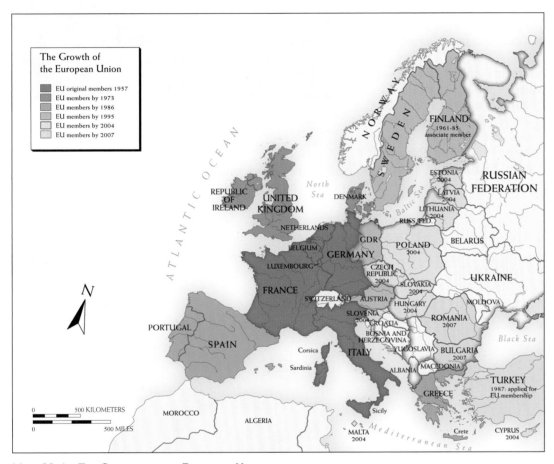

Map 30–1 **THE GROWTH OF THE EUROPEAN UNION.**

Document B

Source: German Chancellor Helmut Khol, "A United Germany in a United Europe" (June 5, 1990).

We Germans are not oblivious of the fact that here and in other countries we are being asked questions as we head for unity:
— What kind of Germany will emerge?
— What will German unity mean for peace and security in the heart of Europe?
— Will this Germany revert to old patterns of behavior; or has it learned the lessons of history? . . .

A future Germany . . . will from the very beginning be a member of the European Community. A united

Germany will take part in 1992 when the large single market with 336 million people is completed. A united Germany will, together with France, be a driving force behind European unification . . .

A future united Germany as a member of the Western defense alliance will increase the security of everyone concerned and thus become a cornerstone of a stable, peaceful, order in Europe.

Document C

Source: French President François Mitterrand, "The Reconciliation of France and Germany" (September 24, 1990).

After destroying each other in three wars in less than a century, France and Germany have sealed their reconciliation, a rare occurrence indeed: They belong to the same community, they meet together, they are forging a genuine friendship. While I speak, on the eve of German unity, instead of harping on the tragic events they experienced in the past because of each other, our two peoples are turned toward the same future. . . .The deep understanding between France and Germany is a reality. As you know, it makes itself felt in the twelve-nation European Community. Can you imagine the trouble and strife, the conflicts of age-old ambitions that were overcome forty years ago by a bold, almost unbelievable undertaking engaged in by first six, nine, then ten, now twelve countries of Europe? . . .

At the beginning of this century and at the end of the previous one, our forbearers expressed their dream of peace with these three words: disarmament, arbitration, collective security. Theirs came to be an era of unrest, dictatorship and war. Let us act in such a way, I beseech you, that through the United Nations, law, solidarity, and peace may finally rule over a new era.

Document D

On January 1, 1999, the European Community launched the Euro, a single monetary unit that replaced the national currencies of most of its member nations.

For more on European unification, see pages 1011–1016 of this chapter.

THE WEST & THE WORLD

Energy and the Modern World

NO SINGLE TECHNOLOGICAL factor so determines the social relationships and standard of living of human beings as energy. The more energy a society can command for each of its members, the stronger and more influential it will be. Throughout recorded human history, those societies that have found ways to improve their access to sources of energy, and have then efficiently applied the energy, have dominated both their immediate environments and much of the world beyond. Indeed, the possession of, or the lack of, efficient, inexpensive sources of energy in large measure determines which nations will be wealthy and which will be poor.

Animals, Wind, and Water

For civilization to advance technologically, energy had to be applied to tasks. The earliest source of such energy was animal power, which was used all over the world except among the peoples on the American continent prior to the arrival of the Europeans. Oxen, water buffalo, and horses were the major draft animals. Of these, horses were the most efficient.

Throughout the world until the eighteenth century, however, wind and water furnished most of the energy for machinery. Sailing ships had been used since ancient times for travel, fishing, and the transport of goods. The wind also worked mills that pumped water and ground grain. Waterwheels proved to be highly flexible machines and by the eighteenth century constituted the major sources of mechanical power in Europe and much of the rest of the world. But wind and water were uncertain sources of energy. The wind could cease; drought could dry up streams. Water-powered machinery had to be located near the stream furnishing the water. Consequently, most of the mills employing such machinery were located in the countryside.

Until the eighteenth century, sailing ships were powered by wind alone. In this fourteenth-century manuscript illustration, sailors navigate with the help of an astrolabe. Ms Fr 2810 f. 188
Navigators using an astrolabe in the Indian Ocean (vellum) by Boucicaut Master (fl. 1390-1430) (and workshop) Livre des Merveilles du Monde (c. 1410-12). Bibliothèque Nationale, Paris, France/Bridgeman Art Library International

Although animals, wind, and water provided energy for relatively complicated machines capable of manufacturing and transporting high-quality goods, the economic and political transformations that have driven the history of the world for the past two and a half centuries could only have occurred through a qualitative as well as quantitative leap in the manner in which human beings commanded energy. The twin sources of this world-transforming energy have been fossil fuels and electricity.

Until the second half of the eighteenth century, fossil fuels—coal, petroleum, and, to a lesser extent, natural gas—contributed only a small portion of human energy requirements. Their use as meaningful sources of energy required a series of inventions that allowed the energy of heat to be changed into mechanical energy.

Steam Power and the Age of Coal

Although peoples living near coal deposits had used it as a household fuel for a very long time, only the invention of the steam engine, patented by James Watt in 1769, established a major industrial demand for coal. The steam engine first permitted the pumping of water from coal mines to increase production. But as the industrial uses for the steam engine grew, the invention itself drove the demand for greater quantities of coal as fuel.

Coal-fueled steam power changed the face of human society during the nineteenth century and continues to provide the energy for the most powerful turbogenerators at the dawn of the twenty-first century. Steam-powered machines could be made larger and more flexible than those powered by wind or water, and as long as coal was available, they could run steadily day and night. Steam engines, in contrast to waterwheels, were transportable. Factories could be moved away from streams in the countryside to urban areas where a ready workforce existed. And goods produced in factories powered by steam engines could be carried around the world by steam-powered locomotives and ships. Those expanding markets in turn called forth more steam-powered factories and even greater use of coal. Furthermore, steam-powered factories could also produce military weapons that could be placed on steam-powered naval vessels constructed of iron and steel in vast coal-fueled blast furnaces. When Theodore Roosevelt sent the U.S. fleet around the world, it was a testimony to the power of coal and steam as well as to the power of the American navy.

The age of steam was the age of coal. The nations possessing large coal deposits dominated much nineteenth-century economic life as the nations that possess oil reserves dominate much contemporary economic life. For many decades, Great Britain dominated the world's production and delivery of coal, which was transported over the entire world. Its domination was challenged only in the late nineteenth century as the United States and later Russia and China began to produce vast quantities of the fuel. Coal remained the chief fuel for the United States until after World War I and for Western Europe until after World War II. It remains the chief fuel for China.

Coal generated a rising standard of living in Europe and the expansion of European and later American power, but coal also generated a number of social problems. The most shocking conditions of exploited labor occurred in coal mines, where parliamentary reports of the 1840s described and illustrated half-clad women and children drawing coal carts from the depths of the mines to the surface. Throughout the nineteenth and twentieth centuries, thousands of miners died in mining disasters. Work in the mines injured the health of miners, as did the pollution sent into the atmosphere by coal fires from both factories and homes. By the early twentieth century, observers had begun to note the damage to the environment caused by strip mining of coal and the later abandonment of the regions.

The Internal Combustion Engine: The Age of Oil

As with coal, the impact of petroleum, the second major fossil fuel, also depended on the invention of machinery to use it. Originally, the use for oil was limited to kerosene, the fuel used for lighting around much of the world by 1900. It was upon the world demand for lamp oil that John D. Rockefeller founded the Standard Oil Company. The invention of the internal combustion engine in 1882 by Rudolf Daimler and the diesel engine in 1892 by Rudolf Diesel transformed the demand for oil. Toward the close of the nineteenth century, extensive oil production had begun in the United States, with Russia, Romania, Sumatra, Mexico, Iran, and Venezuela starting to tap their own oil resources before World War I.

Just as the steam engine had spurred the expansion of the coal industry, the internal combustion engine drove the oil industry. Fuel oil would begin to replace coal, not so much because it was cheaper but rather because it was more efficient, easier to store and transport, and cleaner to burn. Initially, fuel oil tended to be used in those countries where it could be produced relatively near the point of use. Until the end of World War II, the United States was the primary world producer and user of oil. As fuel for the internal combustion engine, oil became the driving force of automobiles, locomotives, airplanes, ships, factory machinery, and electric generators. It revolutionized agricultural machinery and world food production, but as a fuel for transportation, it fostered a social transformation over much of the world.

Until 1924, Henry Ford had disdained national advertising for his cars. But as General Motors gained a competitive edge by making yearly changes in style and technology, Ford was forced to pay more attention to advertising. This ad was directed at "Mrs. Consumer," combining appeals to both female independence and motherly duties.   Ford Motor Company

Starting in the United States and then spreading elsewhere, owning an automobile introduced a new mobility factor into social relationships. People could move easily across long distances to join a new community or to start a new job. Inexpensive gasoline for cars and public transport buses permitted the development of suburbs ever farther removed from traditional urban centers. In turn, retailing moved away from city centers to shopping malls. At the same time, wherever the mechanization of farming through improved farm machinery took place, there usually followed a movement of people from farming communities to urban areas.

Electricity Increases the Demand for Oil

The manufacture of automobiles and other forms of transport using the internal combustion or diesel engine was central to all modern industrial life. As those industries expanded, so did the construction of extensive road systems. These in turn created new demands for fuel oil.

But the greatest demand for fuel oil arose from the application of electricity to the needs of everyday life. Electricity proved to be the most flexible and versatile source of energy for the twentieth century, and its generation provided the single greatest source of demand for both coal and oil. Electricity generation would also employ new modes of water power in the forms of hydroelectric generators.

The scientific basis for the production of electric energy was Michael Faraday's study of electromagnetic induction. In 1831, he demonstrated that mechanical energy under the proper conditions could be converted into electric energy. Even more important, the reverse was also true. Electricity could be generated in one location and applied far away wherever electrical lines could be extended. The applications of electrical power have appeared to be restricted only by the limitations of the inventive imagination.

During the second half of the nineteenth century, a whole host of inventors, such as Thomas Alva Edison, worked through the production and application of electrical power to service large regions. Electricity found applications across the spectrum of human society, actions, and enterprises. Access to electricity in the course of the twentieth century became the key factor for an improved standard of living. A fundamental moment in the decision by Japan to modernize during the late nineteenth century was the construction of the Tokyo Electric Light Company in 1888. The extension of electrical lines into the American countryside was one of the major accomplishments of Franklin Roosevelt's New Deal. Electrical power transformed the workplace, but even more strikingly it transformed homes. Without access to electrical power, domestic households could not make use of any of the growing array of labor-saving appliances such as electric washing machines, electric irons, electric stoves, and electric vacuum cleaners. Electric lights brightened whole cities. Electricity replaced both coal and oil as the source of power for many locomotives; it powered public tram systems and opened the way for the telegraph, the telephone, the wireless, the motion picture camera, and television. It planted the seeds for the computer revolution in communication and information. Electricity allowed manufacturing plants and office complexes to be built wherever electric lines could be carried. Indeed, the spread of access to electrical power has been the single best indication of economic advancement for any nation or region.

Yet within this era of ever-expanding electrification, coal and oil—the fundamental fossil fuels—would still provide the underpinnings of the world's energy. In fact, more oil and coal are used to generate electricity than for any other single purpose. Throughout the twentieth century, the demand for these fuels led to the refinement of their production techniques to permit the extraction of coal from ever-deeper seams and the strip mining of it from regions where previously it would have been economically unproductive to do so. The effort to discover, extract, and transport oil would have major consequences for the world's physical and geopolitical environment far into the twentieth century.

Oil and Global Politics in the Twentieth Century

As the twentieth century began, the United States was by far the largest producer and exporter of petroleum. Yet by the 1920s, the American government began to worry about running out of oil. So, too, did the British, who depended on imported oil for all of their military and industrial needs. During the 1920s and 1930s, both governments encouraged oil companies to forge agreements for the drilling and export of oil from the Middle East. These arrangements fit into the pattern of formal and informal colonialism that still characterized the interwar period.

After World War II, Western Europe, the Soviet Union, and the nations of the Warsaw Pact began to turn from coal to oil as the basis for economic growth. (Japan followed this course during the 1960s.) By 1947, the United States had begun to import more oil than it produced. These two developments—a new dependence on oil by the industrialized nations and the expanded search for oil by the West—formed the basis for the new role that the nations of the Middle East would play in the world economy as the chief oil exporters. Simultaneously, as the world's industrialized economies were growing dependent on Middle East oil production, nationalistic leaders in that region were denouncing former colonial domination and rejecting relationships with the West and with Israel, a country that received strong political support from the United States and Western Europe. The stage was thus set for oil to play a new role in the geopolitical conflicts of the Cold War era.

Playing a major role in those conflicts was the Organization of Petroleum Exporting Nations (OPEC), founded in 1960. Regardless of their differences, OPEC members were united in two things: First, they deeply resented former colonial control of their oil supplies, and second, they were determined that their own governments, not foreign oil companies, would control those vital resources. (Mexico had brought its own petroleum industry under state control before World War II.) In 1973, during the Yom Kippur War, OPEC acted, sharply raising oil prices to nations whose govern-

In 1989, when a supertanker spilled 35,000 tons of crude oil into Alaska's Prince William Sound, rescue workers struggled to save the lives of seabirds and animals. Nevertheless, thousands died. Ron Levy/Global Image Group

ments supported Israel. The action caused severe economic consequences in the West and spurred new efforts to develop local oil reserves in politically safe locations such as in the North Sea. OPEC would attempt similar actions on other occasions, most successfully in 1979. In that year, a revolution in Iran overthrew the government, which had long been supported by the United States. OPEC cut off oil shipments to the West, causing severe dislocations. Concerns about securing oil supplies in the West were again sparked by the Persian Gulf War and other political tensions in the region.

In addition to the political problems associated with Middle East oil production, the industrial world's reliance on oil has had severe environmental consequences. Generally, when the United States dominated oil production, the oil refineries were located near the source of oil production. As the exploitation of oil reserves moved to the Middle East and then later in the century to Alaska and to the North Sea, oil refineries became separated from the drilling locations. Crude oil was shipped to refineries on enormous tankers. More than once, these supertankers have hit shoals or gone aground, causing large oil spills, calamitous to both animals and humans.

The Promise and Danger of Nuclear Energy

Following World War II, nuclear power became a new source for the generation of electrical energy. The power of the atom, first released in the 1940s for military purposes, held the promise of virtually infinite quantities of energy. The world would no longer be dependent on finite supplies of fossil fuel located in politically tense regions of the world. The generation of such energy, however, required the most complex sets of machinery ever devised to produce electrical energy. France and Great Britain began to build nuclear reactors in the 1950s with the United States, the Soviet Union, and various other European nations following in the 1960s. Nations outside the West, such as India and Pakistan, looked to the construction of nuclear power stations as a means of moving more rapidly toward the achievements of industrialization and a rising standard of living through extensive electrification. Nations with limited supplies of fossil fuel, such as Japan, hoped nuclear energy would solve their energy supply problem. The oil shock of the mid-1970s brought new enthusiasm to the adoption of nuclear energy, but the economic downturn of the late 1970s and early 1980s slowed the construction of nuclear-generating stations. The construction of breeder reactors, which would produce their own fuel in the process of generating electrical energy, seemed to promise a world liberated from dependence on a finite supply of fossil fuels. Furthermore, unlike coal and oil, which have many uses besides that of fuel, uranium had no other economic use. The workers in the field of atomic energy were scientists and engineers rather than the kind of industrial labor force that produced coal and oil.

Yet the technology of nuclear energy production proved to be exceedingly dangerous. The atomic reactors produced spent radioactive waste that would remain hazardous for hundreds of years. After many years of warnings of such danger, the Chernobyl nuclear generating plant in the former Soviet Union caused enormous, lasting damage in the spring of 1986. In 1979, the possibility of a similar disaster had occurred at the Three Mile Island plant in Pennsylvania. Both the promise and danger of nuclear power continue to inform the political life of all nations using such power. It is wholly unclear, for example, what will be done with the radioactive spent fuel. Furthermore, the construction of nuclear generating plants has allowed nations that lack atomic weapons to train scientists and other experts who might be able to use that knowledge to develop atomic weapons. Whereas in the United States and Europe the military uses of atomic power came first and were followed by peaceful energy uses, the reverse has been the case in nations such as India and Pakistan. Despite its initial promise, nuclear power has contributed far less to energy production than we originally imagined.

The problem of energy remains with us in the new century. Environmental pollution and all the issues surrounding the nuclear generation of energy will demand increasing attention and expenditure of public funds. Similarly, the political pressures and tensions surrounding the oil supplies of the Middle East will not disappear, as advanced nations seek to secure and protect energy reserves while the nations that possess those reserves seek to secure a rising standard of living for themselves.

Trace the transformation of energy used in the West from wind and water to petroleum. How did coal transform both the industry and the military power of the West? How did inventions, such as the internal combustion engine, change the demands on sources of energy? Why did the rise of electrical power increase the need for petroleum? What opportunities and dangers has nuclear energy posed?

GLOSSARY

absolutism Term applied to strong centralized continental monarchies that attempted to make royal power dominant over aristocracies and other regional authorities.

Acropolis (ACK-row-po-lis) The religious and civic center of Athens. It is the site of the Parthenon.

Act of Supremacy The declaration by Parliament in 1534 that Henry VIII, not the pope, was the head of the church in England.

agape (AG-a-pay) Meaning "love feast." A common meal that was part of the central ritual of early Christian worship.

agora (AG-o-rah) The Greek marketplace and civic center. It was the heart of the social life of the *polis.*

Agricultural Revolution The innovations in farm production that began in the eighteenth century and led to a scientific and mechanized agriculture.

Albigensians (Al-bi-GEN-see-uns) Thirteenth-century advocates of a dualist religion. They took their name from the city of Albi in southern France. Also called *Cathars.*

Anabaptists Protestants who insisted that only adult baptism conformed to Scripture.

anarchism The theory that government and social institutions are oppressive and unnecessary and society should be based on voluntary cooperation among individuals.

Anschluss (AHN-shluz) Meaning "union." The annexation of Austria by Germany in March 1938.

anti-Semitism Prejudice, hostility, or legal discrimination against Jews.

apartheid (a-PAR-tid) An official policy of segregation, assignment of peoples to distinct regions, and other forms of social, political, and economic discrimination based on race associated primarily with South Africa.

apostolic primacy The doctrine that the popes are the direct successors to the Apostle Peter and as such heads of the church.

Apostolic Succession The Christian doctrine that the powers given by Jesus to his original disciples have been handed down from bishop to bishop through ordination.

appeasement The Anglo-French policy of making concessions to Germany in the 1930s to avoid a crisis that would lead to war. It assumed that Germany had real grievances and Hitler's aims were limited and ultimately acceptable.

Areopagus The governing council of Athens, originally open only to the nobility. It was named after the hill on which it met.

arete (AH-ray-tay) Manliness, courage, and the excellence appropriate to a hero. It was considered the highest virtue of Homeric society.

Arianism (AIR-ee-an-ism) The belief formulated by Arius of Alexandria (ca. 280–336 C.E.) that Jesus was a created being, neither fully man nor fully God, but something in between. It did away with the doctrine of the Trinity.

aristocratic resurgence Term applied to the eighteenth-century aristocratic efforts to resist the expanding power of European monarchies.

Asia Minor Modern Turkey. Also called *Anatolia.*

assignats (as-seen-YAHNTS) Government bonds based on the value of confiscated church lands issued during the early French Revolution.

Atomists School of ancient Greek philosophy founded in the fifth century B.C.E. by Leucippus of Miletus and Democritus of Abdera. It held that the world consists of innumerable, tiny, solid, indivisible, and unchangeable particles called *atoms.*

Attica (AT-tick-a) The region of Greece where Athens is located.

Augsburg (AWGS-berg) **Confession** The definitive statement of Lutheran belief made in 1530.

Augustus (AW-gust-us) The title given to Octavian in 27 B.C.E. and borne thereafter by all Roman emperors. It was a semireligious title that implied veneration, majesty, and holiness.

Ausgleich (AWS-glike) Meaning "compromise." The agreement between the Habsburg emperor and the Hungarians to give Hungary considerable administrative autonomy in 1867. It created the Dual Monarchy, or Austria-Hungary.

autocracy (AW-to-kra-see) Government in which the ruler has absolute power.

Axis The alliance between Nazi Germany and fascist Italy. Also called the *Pact of Steel.*

banalities Exactions that the lord of a manor could make on his tenants.

baroque (bah-ROWK) A style of art marked by heavy and dramatic ornamentation and curved rather than straight lines that flourished between 1550 and 1750. It was especially associated with the Catholic Counter-Reformation.

Beguines (bi-GEENS) Lay sisterhoods not bound by the rules of a religious order.

benefice Church offices granted by the ruler of a state or the pope to an individual. It also meant *fief* in the Middle Ages.

bishop Originally a person elected by early Christian congregations to lead them in worship and supervise their funds. In time, bishops became the religious and even political authorities for Christian communities within large geographical areas.

Black Death The bubonic plague that killed millions of Europeans in the fourteenth century.

blitzkrieg (BLITZ-kreeg) Meaning "lightning war." The German tactic early in World War II of employing fast-moving, massed armored columns supported by airpower to overwhelm the enemy.

Bolsheviks Meaning the "majority." Term Lenin applied to his faction of the Russian Social Democratic Party. It became the Communist Party of the Soviet Union after the Russian Revolution.

bourgeois A French word used as an adjective describing something associated with the middle class or as a noun to describe a middle-class person.

boyars The Russian nobility.

Bronze Age The name given to the earliest civilized era, c. 4000 to 1000 B.C.E. The term reflects the importance of the metal bronze, a mixture of tin and copper, for the peoples of this age for use as weapons and tools.

Bundesrat (BUHN-dees-raht) The upper house of the German federal parliament whose members are appointed by the various state governments.

Caesaropapism (SEE-zer-o-PAY-pi-zim) The direct involvement of the ruler in religious doctrine and practice as if he were the head of the church as well as the state.

cahiers de doléances (KAH-hee-ay de dough-LAY-ahnce) Meaning "lists of grievances." Petitions for reforms submitted to the French crown when the Estates General met in 1789.

caliphate (KAH-li-fate) The true line of succession to Muhammad.

capital goods Machines and tools used to produce other goods.

Carbonari (car-buh-NAH-ree) Meaning "charcoal burners." The most famous of the secret republican societies seeking to unify Italy in the 1820s.

categorical imperative According to Emmanuel Kant (1724–1804), the internal sense of moral duty or awareness possessed by all human beings.

catholic Meaning "universal." The body of belief held by most Christians enshrined within the church.

Catholic Emancipation The grant of full political rights to Roman Catholics in Britain in 1829.

censor Official of the Roman republic charged with conducting the census and compiling the lists of citizens and members of the Senate. They could expel senators for financial or moral reasons. Two censors were elected every five years.

Chartism The first large-scale European working-class political movement. It sought political reforms that would favor the interests of skilled British workers in the 1830s and 1840s.

chiaroscuro (kyar-eh-SKEW-row) The use of shading to enhance naturalness in painting and drawing.

civic humanism Education designed to promote humanist leadership of political and cultural life.

civilization A form of human culture marked by urbanism, metallurgy, and writing.

civilizing mission The concept that Western nations could bring advanced science and economic development to non-Western parts of the world that justified imperial administration.

clientage (KLI-ent-age) The custom in ancient Rome whereby men became supporters of more powerful men in return for legal and physical protection and economic benefits.

Cold War The ideological and geographical struggle between the United States and its allies and the USSR and its allies that began after World War II and lasted until the dissolution of the USSR in 1989.

collectivization The bedrock of Stalinist agriculture, which forced Russian peasants to give up their private farms and work as members of collectives, large agricultural units controlled by the state.

coloni (CO-loan-ee) Farmers or sharecroppers on the estates of wealthy Romans.

Commonwealthmen British political writers whose radical republican ideas influenced the American revolutionaries.

concentration camps Camps first established by Great Britain in South Africa during the Boer War to incarcerate noncombatant civilians; later, camps established for political prisoners and other persons deemed dangerous to the state in the Soviet Union and Nazi Germany. The term is now primarily associated with the camps established by the Nazis during the Holocaust.

Concert of Europe Term applied to the European great powers acting together (in "concert") to resolve international disputes between 1815 and the 1850s.

conciliar theory The argument that General Councils were superior in authority to the pope and represented the whole body of the faithful.

condottieri (con-da-TEE-AIR-ee) Military brokers who furnished mercenary forces to the Italian states during the Renaissance.

congregationalist A congregationalist puts a group or assembly above any one individual and prefers an ecclesiastical polity that allows each congregation to be autonomous, or self-governing.

Congress System A series of international meetings among the European great powers to promote mutual cooperation between 1818 and 1822.

conquistadores (kahn-KWIS-teh-door-hez) Meaning "conquerors." The Spanish conquerors of the New World.

conservatism Support for the established order in church and state. In the nineteenth century, it implied support for legitimate monarchies, landed aristocracies, and established churches. Conservatives favored only gradual, or "organic," change.

Consulate French government dominated by Napoleon from 1799 to 1804.

consuls (CON-suls) The two chief magistrates of the Roman state.

Consumer Revolution The vast increase in both the desire and the possibility of consuming goods and services that began in the early eighteenth century and created the demand for sustaining the Industrial Revolution.

containment The U.S. policy during the Cold War of resisting Soviet expansion and influence in the expectation that the USSR would eventually collapse.

Convention French radical legislative body from 1792 to 1794.

Corn Laws British tariffs on imported grain that protected the price of grain grown within the British Isles.

corvée (cor-VAY) A French labor tax requiring peasants to work on roads, bridges, and canals.

Council of Nicaea (NIGH-see-a) The council of Christian bishops at Nicaea in 325 C.E. that formulated the Nicene Creed, a statement of Christian belief that rejected Arianism in favor of the doctrine that Christ is both fully human and fully divine.

Counter-Reformation The sixteenth-century reform movement in the Roman Catholic Church in reaction to the Protestant Reformation.

coup d'état (COO DAY-ta) The sudden violent overthrow of a government by its own army.

creed A brief statement of faith to which true Christians should adhere.

Creoles (KRAY-ol-ez) Persons of Spanish descent born in the Spanish colonies.

Crusades Religious wars directed by the church against infidels and heretics.

culture The ways of living built up by a group and passed on from one generation to another.

cuneiform (Q-nee-i-form) A writing system invented by the Sumerians that used a wedge-shaped stylus, or pointed tool, to write on wet clay tablets that were then baked or dried (*cuneus* means "wedge" in Latin). The writing was also cut into stone.

Curia (CURE-ee-a) The papal government.

Cynic (SIN-ick) **School** A fourth-century philosophical movement that ridiculed all religious observances and turned away from involvement in the affairs of the *polis*. Its most famous exemplar was Diogenes of Sinope (ca. 400–325 B.C.E.).

deacon Meaning "those who serve." In early Christian congregations, deacons assisted the presbyters, or elders.

decolonization The process of European retreat of colonial empires following World War II.

deism A belief in a rational God who had created the universe but then allowed it to function without his interference according to the mechanisms of nature and a belief in rewards and punishments after death for human action.

Delian (DEE-li-an) **League** An alliance of Greek states under the leadership of Athens that was formed in 478–477 B.C.E. to resist the Persians. In time the league was transformed into the Athenian Empire.

deme (DEEM) A small town in Attica or a ward in Athens that became the basic unit of Athenian civic life under the democratic reforms of Clisthenes in 508 B.C.E.

demesne (di-MAIN) The part of a manor that was cultivated directly for the lord of the manor.

divine right of kings The theory that monarchs are appointed by and answerable only to God.

Domesday (DOOMS-day) *Book* A detailed survey of the wealth of England undertaken by William the Conqueror between 1080 and 1086.

domestic system of textile production Method of producing textiles in which agents furnished raw materials to households whose members spun them into thread and then wove cloth, which the agents then sold as finished products.

Donatism The heresy that taught the efficacy of the sacraments depended on the moral character of the clergy who administered them.

Duce (DO-chay) Meaning "leader." Mussolini's title as head of the Fascist Party.

Duma (DOO-ma) The Russian parliament, after the revolution of 1905.

electors Nine German princes who had the right to elect the Holy Roman Emperor.

émigrés (em-ee-GRAYS) French aristocrats who fled France during the Revolution.

empiricism (em-PEER-ih-cism) The use of experiment and observation derived from sensory evidence to construct scientific theory or philosophy of knowledge.

enclosure The consolidation or fencing in of common lands by British landlords to increase production and achieve greater commercial profits. It also involved the reclamation of waste land and the consolidation of strips into block fields.

encomienda (en-co-mee-EN-da) The grant by the Spanish crown to a colonist of the labor of a specific number of Indians for a set period of time.

ENIAC The Electronic Numerical Integrator and Computer. The first genuine modern digital computer, developed in the 1940s.

Enlightenment The eighteenth-century movement led by the *philosophes* that held that change and reform were both desirable through the application of reason and science.

Epicureans (EP-i-cure-ee-ans) School of philosophy founded by Epicurus of Athens (342–271 B.C.E.). It sought to liberate people from fear of death and the supernatural by teaching that the gods took no interest in human affairs and that true happiness consisted in pleasure, which was defined as the absence of pain. This could be achieved by attaining *ataraxia*, freedom from trouble, pain, and responsibility by withdrawing from business and public life.

equestrians (EE-quest-ree-ans) Literally "cavalrymen" or "knights." In the earliest years of the Roman Republic those who could afford to serve as mounted warriors. The equestrians evolved into a social rank of well-to-do businessmen and middle-ranking officials. Many of them supported the Gracchi.

Estates General The medieval French parliament. It consisted of three separate groups, or "estates": clergy, nobility, and commoners. It last met in 1789 at the outbreak of the French Revolution.

Etruscans (EE-trus-cans) A people of central Italy who exerted the most powerful external influence on the early Romans. Etruscan kings ruled Rome until 509 B.C.E.

Eucharist (YOU-ka-rist) Meaning "thanksgiving." The celebration of the Lord's Supper. Considered the central ritual of worship by most Christians. Also called *Holy Communion*.

Euro The common currency created by the EEC in the late 1990s.

European Economic Community (EEC) The economic association formed by France, Germany, Italy, Belgium, the Netherlands, and Luxembourg in 1957. Also known as the *Common Market*.

European Union The new name given to the EEC in 1993. It included most of the states of Western Europe.

excommunication Denial by the church of the right to receive the sacraments.

existentialism The post–World War II Western philosophy that holds human beings are totally responsible for their acts and that this responsibility causes them dread and anguish.

Fabians British socialists in the late nineteenth and early twentieth centuries who sought to achieve socialism through gradual, peaceful, and democratic means.

family economy The basic structure of production and consumption in preindustrial Europe.

fascism Political movements that tend to be antidemocratic, anti-Marxist, antiparliamentary, and often anti-Semitic. Fascists were invariably nationalists and exhalted the nation over the individual. They supported the interests of the middle class and rejected the ideas of the French Revolution and nineteenth-century liberalism. The first fascist regime was founded by Benito Mussolini (1883–1945) in Italy in the 1920s.

fealty An oath of loyalty by a vassal to a lord, promising to perform specified services.

feudal (FEW-dull) **society** The social, political, military, and economic system that prevailed in the Middle Ages and beyond in some parts of Europe.

fief Land granted to a vassal in exchange for services, usually military.

foederati (FAY-der-ah-tee) Barbarian tribes enlisted as special allies of the Roman Empire.

Fourteen Points President Woodrow Wilson's (1856–1924) idealistic war aims.

Fronde (FROHND) A series of rebellions against royal authority in France between 1649 and 1652.

Führer (FYOOR-er) Meaning "leader." The title taken by Hitler when he became dictator of Germany.

gabelle (gah-BELL) The royal tax on salt in France.

Gaul (GAWL) Modern France.

German Confederation Association of German states established at the Congress of Vienna that replaced the Holy Roman Empire from 1815 to 1866.

ghetto Separate communities in which Jews were required by law to live.

glasnost (GLAZ-nohst) Meaning "openness." The policy initiated by Mikhail Gorbachev (MEEK-hail GORE-buh-choff) in the 1980s of permitting open criticism of the policies of the Soviet Communist Party.

Glorious Revolution The largely peaceful replacement of James II by William and Mary as English monarchs in 1688. It marked the beginning of constitutional monarchy in Britain.

gold standard A monetary system in which the value of a unit of a nation's currency is related to a fixed amount of gold.

Golden Bull The agreement in 1356 to establish a seven-member electoral college of German princes to choose the Holy Roman Emperor.

Great Depression A prolonged worldwide economic downturn that began in 1929 with the collapse of the New York Stock Exchange.

Great Purges The imprisonment and execution of millions of Soviet citizens by Stalin between 1934 and 1939.

Great Reform Bill (1832) A limited reform of the British House of Commons and an expansion of the electorate to include a wider variety of the propertied classes. It laid the groundwork for further orderly reforms within the British constitutional system.

Great Schism The appearance of two and at times three rival popes between 1378 and 1415.

Great Trek The migration by Boer (Dutch) farmers during the 1830s and 1840s from regions around Cape Town into the eastern and northeastern regions of South Africa that ultimately resulted in the founding of the Orange Free State and Transvaal.

Green movement A political environmentalist movement that began in West Germany in the 1970s and spread to a number of other Western nations.

grossdeutsch (gross-DOYCH) Meaning "great German." The argument that the German-speaking portions of the Habsburg Empire should be included in a united Germany.

guild An association of merchants or craftsmen that offered protection to its members and set rules for their work and products.

hacienda (ha-SEE-hen-da) A large landed estate in Spanish America.

Hegira (HEJ-ear-a) The flight of Muhammad and his followers from Mecca to Medina in 622 C.E. It marks the beginning of the Islamic calendar.

heliocentric (HE-li-o-cen-trick) **theory** The theory, now universally accepted, that the earth and the other planets revolve around the sun. First proposed by Aristarchos of Samos (310–230 B.C.E.). Its opposite, the geocentric theory, which was dominant until the sixteenth century C.E., held that the sun and the planets revolved around the earth.

Helots (HELL-ots) Hereditary Spartan serfs.

heretic (HAIR-i-tick) A person whose beliefs were contrary to those of the Catholic Church.

hieroglyphics (HI-er-o-gli-phicks) The complicated writing script of ancient Egypt. It combined picture writing with pictographs and sound signs. Hieroglyph means "sacred carvings" in Greek.

Holocaust The Nazi extermination of millions of European Jews between 1940 and 1945. Also called the "final solution to the Jewish problem."

Holy Roman Empire The revival of the old Roman Empire, based mainly in Germany and northern Italy, that endured from 870 to 1806.

home rule The advocacy of a large measure of administrative autonomy for Ireland within the British Empire between the 1880s and 1914.

Homo sapiens (HO-mo say-pee-ans) The scientific name for human beings, from the Latin words meaning "Wise man." *Homo sapiens* emerged some 200,000 years ago.

honestiores (HON-est-ee-or-ez) The Roman term formalized from the beginning of the third century C.E. to denote the privileged classes: senators, equestrians, the municipal aristocracy, and soldiers.

***hoplite* phalanx** (FAY-lanks) The basic unit of Greek warfare in which infantrymen fought in close order, shield to shield, usually eight ranks deep. The phalanx perfectly suited the farmer-soldier-citizen who was the backbone of the *polis*.

hubris (WHO-bris) Arrogance brought on by excessive wealth or good fortune. The Greeks believed it led to moral blindness and divine vengeance.

Huguenots (HYOU-gu-nots) French Calvinists.

humanism The study of the Latin and Greek classics and of the Church Fathers both for their own sake and to promote a rebirth of ancient norms and values.

humanitas (HEW-man-i-tas) The Roman name for a liberal arts education.

humiliores (HEW-mi-lee-orez) The Roman term formalized at the beginning of the third century C.E. for the lower classes.

Hussites (HUS-Its) Followers of John Huss (d. 1415) who questioned Catholic teachings about the Eucharist.

Iconoclasm (i-KON-o-kla-zoom) A heresy in Eastern Christianity that sought to ban the veneration of sacred images, or icons.

id, ego, superego The three entities in Sigmund Freud's model of the internal organization of the human mind. The id consists of the amoral, irrational instincts for self-gratification. The superego embodies the external morality imposed on the personality by society. The ego mediates between the two and allows the personality to cope with the internal and external demands of its existence.

Iliad (ILL-ee-ad) **and the *Odyssey*** (O-dis-see), **The** Epic poems by Homer about the "Dark Age" heroes of Greece who fought at Troy. The poems were written down in the eighth century B.C.E. after centuries of being sung by bards.

imperator (IM-per-a-tor) Under the Roman Republic, it was the title given to a victorious general. Under Augustus and his successors, it became the title of the ruler of Rome meaning "emperor."

imperialism The extension of a nation's authority over other nations or areas through conquest or political or economic hegemony.

Imperialism of Free Trade The advance of European economic and political interests in the nineteenth century by demanding that non-European nations allow European nations, most particularly Great Britain, to introduce their manufactured goods freely into all nations or to introduce other goods, such as opium into China, that allowed those nations to establish economic influence and to determine the terms of trade.

imperium (IM-pear-ee-um) In ancient Rome, the right to issue commands and to enforce them by fines, arrests, and even corporal and capital punishment.

indulgence Remission of the temporal penalty of punishment in purgatory that remained after sins had been forgiven.

Industrial Revolution Mechanization of the European economy that began in Britain in the second half of the eighteenth century.

Inquisition A tribunal created by the Catholic Church in the mid-twelfth century to detect and punish heresy.

insulae (IN-sul-lay) Meaning "islands." The multistoried apartment buildings of Rome in which most of the inhabitants of the city lived.

Intolerable Acts Measures passed by the British Parliament in 1774 to punish the colony of Massachusetts and strengthen Britain's authority in the colonies. The laws provoked colonial opposition, which led immediately to the American Revolution.

investiture controversy The medieval conflict between the church and lay rulers over who would control bishops and abbots, symbolized by the ceremony of "investing" them with the symbols of their authority.

Ionia (I-o-knee-a) The part of western Asia Minor heavily colonized by the Greeks.

Islam (IZ-lahm) Meaning "submission." The religion founded by the prophet Muhammad.

Italia irredenta (ee-TAHL-ee-a ir-REH-dent-a) Meaning "unredeemed Italy." Italian-speaking areas that had been left under Austrian rule at the time of the unification of Italy.

Jacobins (JACK-uh-bins) The radical republican party during the French Revolution that displaced the Girondins.

Jacquerie (jah-KREE) Revolt of the French peasantry.

Jansenism A seventeenth-century movement within the Catholic Church that taught that human beings were so corrupted by original sin that they could do nothing good nor secure their own salvation without divine grace. (It was opposed to the Jesuits.)

Judah (JEW-da) The southern Israelite kingdom established after the death of Solomon in the tenth century B.C.E.

Julian Calendar The reform of the calendar by Julius Caesar in 46 B.C.E. It remained in use throughout Europe until the sixteenth century and in Russia until the Russian Revolution in 1917.

July Monarchy The French regime set up after the overthrow of the Bourbons in July 1830.

Junkers (YOONG-kerz) The noble landlords of Prussia.

jus gentium (YUZ GEN-tee-um) Meaning "law of peoples." The body of Roman law that dealt with foreigners.

jus naturale (YUZ NAH-tu-rah-lay) Meaning "natural law." The Stoic concept of a world ruled by divine reason.

Ka'ba (KAH-bah) A black meteorite in the city of Mecca that became Islam's holiest shrine.

Keynesian economics The theory of John Maynard Keynes (CANES) (1883–1946) that governments could spend their economies out of a depression by running deficits to encourage employment and stimulate the production and consumption of goods.

kleindeutsch (kline-DOYCH) Meaning "small German." The argument that the German-speaking portions of the Habsburg Empire should be excluded from a united Germany.

Kristallnacht (KRIS-tahl-NAHKT) Meaning "crystal night" because of the broken glass that littered German streets after the looting and destruction of Jewish homes, businesses, and synagogues across Germany on the orders of the Nazi Party in November 1938.

kulaks (koo-LAKS) Prosperous Russian peasant farmers.

Kulturkampf (cool-TOOR-cahmff) Meaning the "battle for culture." The conflict between the Roman Catholic Church and the government of the German Empire in the 1870s.

laissez-faire (lay-ZAY-faire) French phrase meaning "allow to do." In economics the doctrine of minimal government interference in the working of the economy.

Late Antiquity The multicultural period between the end of the ancient world and the birth of the Middle Ages, 250–800 C.E.

latifundia (LAT-ee-fun-dee-a) Large plantations for growing cash crops owned by wealthy Romans.

Latium (LAT-ee-um) The region of Italy in which Rome is located. Its inhabitants were called *Latins*.

League of Nations The association of sovereign states set up after World War I to pursue common policies and avert international aggression.

Lebensraum (LAY-benz-rauhm) Meaning "living space." The Nazi plan to colonize and exploit the Slavic areas of Eastern Europe for the benefit of Germany.

levée en masse (le-VAY en MASS) The French revolutionary conscription (1792) of all males into the army and the harnessing of the economy for war production.

liberal arts The medieval university program that consisted of the *trivium* (TRI-vee-um): grammar, rhetoric, and logic, and the *quadrivium* (qua-DRI-vee-um): arithmetic, geometry, astronomy, and music.

liberalism In the nineteenth century, support for representative government dominated by the propertied classes and minimal government interference in the economy.

Logos (LOW-goz) Divine reason, or fire, which according to the Stoics was the guiding principle in nature. Every human had a spark of this divinity, which returned to the eternal divine spirit after death.

Lollards (LALL-erds) Followers of John Wycliffe (d. 1384) who questioned the supremacy and privileges of the pope and the church hierarchy.

Lower Egypt The Nile delta.

Luftwaffe (LUFT-vaff-uh) The German air force in World War II.

Magna Carta (MAG-nuh CAR-tuh) The "Great Charter" limiting royal power that the English nobility forced King John to sign in 1215.

Magna Graecia (MAG-nah GRAY-see-a) Meaning "Great Greece" in Latin, it was the name given by the Romans to southern Italy and Sicily because there were so many Greek colonies in the region.

Magyars (MAH-jars) The majority ethnic group in Hungary.

Mandates The assigning of the former German colonies and Turkish territories in the Middle East to Britain, France, Japan, Belgium, Australia, and South Africa as de facto colonies under the vague supervision of the League of Nations with the hope that the territories would someday advance to independence.

mannerism A style of art in the mid- to late-sixteenth century that permitted artists to express their own "manner" or feelings in contrast to the symmetry and simplicity of the art of the High Renaissance.

manor Village farms owned by a lord.

Marshall Plan The U.S. program named after Secretary of State George C. Marshall of providing economic aid to Europe after World War II.

Marxism The theory of Karl Marx (1818–1883) and Friedrich Engels (FREE-drick ENG-ulz) (1820–1895) that history is the result of class conflict, which will end in the inevitable triumph of the industrial proletariat over the bourgeoisie and the abolition of private property and social class.

Mein Kampf (MINE KAHMFF) Meaning *My Struggle*. Hitler's statement of his political program, published in 1924.

Mensheviks Meaning the "minority." Term Lenin applied to the majority moderate faction of the Russian Social Democratic Party opposed to him and the Bolsheviks.

mercantilism Term used to describe close government control of the economy that sought to maximize exports and accumulate as much precious metals as possible to enable the state to defend its economic and political interests.

Mesopotamia (MEZ-o-po-tay-me-a) Modern Iraq. The land between the Tigris and Euphrates Rivers where the first civilization appeared around 3000 B.C.E.

Messiah (MESS-eye-a) The redeemer whose coming Jews believed would establish the kingdom of God on earth. Christians considered Jesus to be the Messiah (*Christ* means Messiah in Greek).

Methodism An English religious movement begun by John Wesley (1703–1791) that stressed inward, heartfelt religion and the possibility of attaining Christian perfection in this life.

millets Administrative units of the Ottoman Empire that were not geographic but consisted of ethnic or religious minorities to whom particular laws and regulations applied.

Minoans (MIN-o-ans) The Bronze Age civilization that arose in Crete in the third and second millennia B.C.E.

missi dominici (MISS-ee dough-MIN-ee-chee) Meaning "the envoys of the ruler." Royal overseers of the king's law in the Carolingian Empire.

mobilization The placing of a country's military forces on a war footing.

modernism The movement in the arts and literature in the late nineteenth and early twentieth centuries to create new aesthetic forms and to elevate the aesthetic experience of a work of art above the attempt to portray reality as accurately as possible.

moldboard plow A heavy plow introduced in the Middle Ages that cut deep into the soil.

monasticism A movement in the Christian church that arose first in the East in the third and fourth centuries C.E. in which first individual hermits and later organized communities of men and women (monks and nuns) separated themselves from the world to lead lives in imitation of Christ. In the West the Rule of St. Benedict (c. 480–547) became the dominant form of monasticism.

Monophysite (ma-NO-fiz-it) Adherent of the theory that Jesus had only one nature.

monotheism The worship of one universal God.

Mycenaean (MY-cen-a-an) The Bronze Age civilization of mainland Greece that was centered at Mycenae.

"mystery" religions The cults of Isis, Mithra, and Osiris, which promised salvation to those initiated into the secret or "mystery" of their rites. These cults competed with Christianity in the Roman Empire.

nationalism The belief that one is part of a nation, defined as a community with its own language, traditions, customs, and history that distinguish it from other nations and make it the primary focus of a person's loyalty and sense of identity.

natural selection The theory originating with Darwin that organisms evolve through a struggle for existence in which those that have a marginal advantage live long enough to propagate their kind.

naturalism The attempt to portray nature and human life without sentimentality.

Nazis The German Nationalist Socialist Party.

Neolithic (NEE-o-lith-ick) **Revolution** The shift beginning 10,000 years ago from hunter-gatherer societies to settled communities of farmers and artisans. Also called the Age of Agriculture, it witnessed the invention of farming, the domestication of plants and animals, and the development of technologies such as pottery and weaving. The earliest Neolithic societies appeared in the Near East about 8000 B.C.E. "Neolithic" comes from the Greek words for "new stone."

Neoplatonism (KNEE-o-play-ton-ism) A religious philosophy that tried to combine mysticism with classical and rationalist speculation. Its chief formulator was Plotinus (205–270 C.E.).

New Economic Policy (NEP) A limited revival of capitalism, especially in light industry and agriculture, introduced by Lenin in 1921 to repair the damage inflicted on the Russian economy by the Civil War and war communism.

New Imperialism The extension in the late nineteenth and early twentieth centuries of Western political and economic dominance to Asia, the Middle East, and Africa.

nomes Regions or provinces of ancient Egypt governed by officials called *nomarchs*.

oikos (OI-cos) The Greek household, always headed by a male.

Old Believers Those members of the Russian Orthodox Church who refused to accept the reforms of the seventeenth century regarding church texts and ritual.

Old Regime Term applied to the pattern of social, political, and economic relationships and institutions that existed in Europe before the French Revolution.

optimates (OP-tee-ma-tes) Meaning "the best men." Roman politicians who supported the traditional role of the Senate.

orthodox Meaning "holding the right opinions." Applied to the doctrines of the Catholic Church.

Ottoman Empire The imperial Turkish state centered in Constantinople that ruled large parts of the Balkans, North Africa, and the Middle East until 1918.

Paleolithic (PAY-lee-o-lith-ick) **Age, The** The earliest period when stone tools were used, from about 1,000,000 to 10,000 B.C.E. From the Greek meaning "old stone."

Panhellenic (PAN-hell-en-ick) ("all-Greek") The sense of cultural identity that all Greeks felt in common with each other.

Pan-Slavism The movement to create a nation or federation that would embrace all the Slavic peoples of Eastern Europe.

papal infallibility The doctrine that the pope is infallible when pronouncing officially in his capacity as head of the church on matters of faith and morals, enumerated by the First Vatican Council in 1870.

Papal States Territory in central Italy ruled by the pope until 1870.

parlements (par-luh-MAHNS) French regional courts dominated by hereditary nobility. The most important was the *Parlement* of Paris, which claimed the right to register royal decrees before they could become law.

parliamentary monarchy The form of limited or constitutional monarchy set up in Britain after the Glorious Revolution of 1689 in which the monarch was subject to the law and ruled by the consent of parliament.

patricians (PA-tri-she-ans) The hereditary upper class of early Republican Rome.

Peloponnesian (PELL-o-po-knees-ee-an) **Wars** The protracted struggle between Athens and Sparta to dominate Greece between 465 and Athens's final defeat in 404 B.C.E.

Peloponnesus (PELL-o-po-knee-sus) The southern peninsula of Greece where Sparta was located.

peninsulares (pen-in-SUE-la-rez) Persons born in Spain who settled in the Spanish colonies.

perestroika (pare-ess-TROY-ka) Meaning "restructuring." The attempt in the 1980s to reform the Soviet government and economy.

petite bourgeoisie (peh-TEET BOOSH-schwa-zee) The lower middle class.

pharaoh (FAY-row) The god-kings of ancient Egypt. The term originally meant "great house" or palace.

Pharisees (FAIR-i-sees) The group that was most strict in its adherence to Jewish law.

philosophes (fee-lou-SOPHS) The eighteenth-century writers and critics who forged the new attitudes favorable to change. They sought to apply reason and common sense to the institutions and societies of their day.

Phoenicians (FA-nee-shi-ans) The ancient inhabitants of modern Lebanon. A trading people, they established colonies throughout the Mediterranean.

physiocrats Eighteenth-century French thinkers who attacked the mercantilist regulation of the economy, advocated a limited economic role for government, and believed that all economic production depended on sound agriculture.

plantation economy The economic system stretching between Chesapeake Bay and Brazil that produced crops, especially sugar, cotton, and tobacco, using slave labor on large estates.

Platonism Philosophy of Plato that posits preexistent Ideal Forms of which all earthly things are imperfect models.

plebeians (PLEB-bee-ans) The hereditary lower class of early Republican Rome.

plenitude of power The teaching that the popes have power over all other bishops of the church.

pogroms (PO-grohms) Organized riots against Jews in the Russian Empire.

polis (PO-lis) (plural, *poleis*) The basic Greek political unit. Usually, but incompletely, translated as "city-state," the Greeks thought of the *polis* as a community of citizens theoretically descended from a common ancestor.

politique Ruler or person in a position of power who puts the success and well-being of his or her state above all else.

polygyny (po-LIJ-eh-nee) The practice of having two or more wives or concubines at the same time.

polytheism (PAH-lee-thee-ism) The worship of many gods.

pontifex maximus (PON-ti-feks MAK-suh-muss) Meaning "supreme priest." The chief priest of ancient Rome. The title was later assumed by the popes.

Popular Front A government of all left-wing parties that took power in France in 1936 to enact social and economic reforms.

populares (PO-pew-lar-es) Roman politicians who sought to pursue a political career based on the support of the people rather than just the aristocracy.

positivism The philosophy of Auguste Comte that science is the final, or positive, stage of human intellectual development because it involves exact descriptions of phenomena, without recourse to unobservable operative principles, such as gods or spirits.

postimpressionism A term used to describe European painting that followed impressionism; the term actually applies to several styles of art all of which to some extent derived from impression or stood in reaction to impressionism.

Pragmatic Sanction The legal basis negotiated by the Emperor Charles VI (r. 1711–1740) for the Habsburg succession through his daughter Maria Theresa (r. 1740–1780).

predestination The doctrine that God had foreordained all souls to salvation (the "elect") or damnation. It was especially associated with Calvinism.

presbyter (PRESS-bi-ter) Meaning "elder." A person who directed the affairs of early Christian congregations.

Presbyterians Scottish Calvinists and English Protestants who advocated a national church composed of semiautonomous congregations governed by "presbyteries."

proconsulship (PRO-con-sul-ship) In Republican Rome, the extension of a consul's imperium beyond the end of his term of office to allow him to continue to command an army in the field.

protectorate (pro-TEC-tor-ate) A non-Western territory administered by a Western nation without formal conquest or annexation, usually a de facto colony.

Protestant Ethic The theory propounded by Max Weber in 1904 that the religious confidence and self-disciplined activism that were supposedly associated with Protestantism produced an ethic that stimulated the spirit of emergent capitalism.

Ptolemaic (tow-LEM-a-ick) **System** The pre-Copernican explanation of the universe, with the earth at the center of the universe, originated in the ancient world.

Punic (PEW-nick) **Wars** Three wars between Rome and Carthage for dominance of the western Mediterranean that were fought from 264 B.C.E. to 146 B.C.E.

Puritans English Protestants who sought to "purify" the Church of England of any vestiges of Catholicism.

Qur'an (kuh-RAN) Meaning "a reciting." The Islamic bible, which Muslims believe God revealed to the prophet Muhammad.

racism The pseudoscientific theory that biological features of race determine human character and worth.

realism The style of art and literature that seeks to depict the physical world and human life with scientific objectivity and detached observation.

Reformation The sixteenth-century religious movement that sought to reform the Roman Catholic Church and led to the establishment of Protestantism.

regular clergy Monks and nuns who belong to religious orders.

Reichstag (RIKES-stahg) The German parliament, which existed in various forms, until 1945.

Reign of Terror The period between the summer of 1793 and the end of July 1794 when the French revolutionary state used extensive executions and violence to defend the Revolution and suppress its alleged internal enemies.

relativity The scientific theory associated with Einstein that time and space exist not separately but as a combined continuum whose measurement depends as much on the observer as on the entities that are being measured.

Renaissance The revival of ancient learning and the supplanting of traditional religious beliefs by new secular and scientific values that began in Italy in the fourteenth and fifteenth centuries.

reparations The requirement incorporated into the Versailles Treaty that Germany should pay for the cost of World War I.

revisionism The advocacy among nineteenth-century German socialists of achieving a humane socialist society through the evolution of democratic institutions, not revolution.

robot (ROW-boht) The amount of labor landowners demanded from peasants in the Habsburg Monarchy before 1848.

Romanitas (row-MAN-ee-tas) Meaning "Roman-ness." The spread of the Roman way of life and the sense of identifying with Rome across the Roman Empire.

romanticism A reaction in early-nineteenth-century literature, philosophy, and religion against what many considered the excessive rationality and scientific narrowness of the Enlightenment.

SA The Nazi parliamentary forces, or storm troopers.

sans-culottes (SAHN coo-LOTS) Meaning "without knee-breeches." The lower-middle classes and artisans of Paris during the French Revolution.

Schlieffen (SHLEE-fun) **Plan** Germany's plan for achieving a quick victory in the West at the outbreak of World War I by invading France through Belgium and Luxembourg.

Scholasticism Method of study based on logic and dialectic that dominated the medieval schools. It assumed that truth already existed; students had only to organize, elucidate, and defend knowledge learned from authoritative texts, especially those of Aristotle and the Church Fathers.

scientific induction Scientific method in which generalizations are derived from data gained from empirical observations.

scientific revolution The sweeping change in the scientific view of the universe that occurred in the sixteenth and seventeenth centuries. The new scientific concepts and the method of their construction became the standard for assessing the validity of knowledge in the West.

scutage Monetary payments by a vassal to a lord in place of the required military service.

second industrial revolution The emergence of new industries and the spread of industrialization from Britain to other countries, especially Germany and the United States, in the second half of the nineteenth century.

secular clergy Parish clergy who did not belong to a religious order.

seigneur (sane-YOUR) A noble French landlord.

Sejm (SHEM) The legislative assembly of the Polish nobility.

serfs Peasants tied to the land they tilled.

Shi'a (SHE-ah) The minority of Muslims who trace their beliefs from the caliph Ali who was assassinated in 661 C.E.

Sinn Fein (SHIN FAHN) Meaning "ourselves alone." An Irish political movement founded in 1905 that advocated complete political separation from Britain.

Social Darwinism The application of Darwin's concept of "the survival of the fittest" to explain evolution in nature to human social relationships.

Sophists (SO-fists) Professional teachers who emerged in Greece in the mid–fifth century B.C.E. who were paid to teach techniques of rhetoric, dialectic, and argumentation.

soviets Workers and soldiers councils formed in Russia during the Revolution.

spheres of influence A region, city, or territory where a non-Western nation exercised informal administrative influence through economic, diplomatic, or military advisors.

spinning jenny A machine invented in England by James Hargreaves around 1765 to mass-produce thread.

SS The chief security units of the Nazi state.

Stoics (STOW-icks) A philosophical school founded by Zeno of Citium (335–263 B.C.E.) that taught that humans could only be happy with natural law. Human misery was caused by passion, which was a disease of the soul. The wise sought *apatheia*, freedom from passion.

studia humanitatis (STEW-dee-a hew-MAHN-ee tah-tis) During the Renaissance, a liberal arts program of study that embraced grammar, rhetoric, poetry, history, philosophy, and politics.

Sturm und Drang (SHTURM und DRAHNG) Meaning "storm and stress." A movement in German romantic literature and philosophy that emphasized feeling and emotion.

suffragettes British women who lobbied and agitated for the right to vote in the early twentieth century.

Sunna (SOON-ah) Meaning "tradition." The dominant Islamic group.

Sunnis Those who follow the "tradition" (sunna) of the Prophet Muhammad. They are the dominant movement within Islam to which the vast majority of Muslims adhere.

symposium (SIM-po-see-um) The carefully organized drinking party that was the center of Greek aristocratic social life. It featured games, songs, poetry, and even philosophical disputation.

syncretism (SIN-cret-ism) The intermingling of different religions to form an amalgam that contained elements from each.

syndicalism French labor movement that sought to improve workers' conditions through direct action, especially general strikes.

Table of Ranks An official hierarchy established by Peter the Great in imperial Russia that equated a person's social position and privileges with his rank in the state bureaucracy or army.

tabula rasa (tah-BOO-lah RAH-sah) Meaning a "blank page." The philosophical belief associated with John Locke that human beings enter the world with totally unformed characters that are completely shaped by experience.

taille (TIE) The direct tax on the French peasantry.

ten lost tribes The Israelites who were scattered and lost to history when the northern kingdom of Israel fell to the Assyrians in 722 B.C.E.

tertiaries (TER-she-air-ees) Laypeople affiliated with the monastic life who took vows of poverty, chastity, and obedience but remained in the world.

tetrarchy (TET-rar-key) Diocletian's (r. 306–337 C.E.) system for ruling the Roman Empire by four men with power divided territorially.

Thermidorian Reaction The reaction against the radicalism of the French Revolution that began in July 1794. Associated with the end of terror and establishment of the Directory.

thesis, antithesis, and synthesis G. W. F. Hegel's (HAY-gle) (1770–1831) concept of how ideas develop. The *thesis* is a dominant set of ideas. It is challenged by a set of conflicting ideas, the *antithesis*. From the clash of these ideas, a new pattern of thought, the *synthesis*, emerges and eventually becomes the new thesis.

Third Estate The branch of the French Estates General representing all of the kingdom outside the nobility and the clergy.

Third Reich (RIKE) Hitler's regime in Germany, which lasted from 1933 to 1945.

Thirty-Nine Articles (1563) The official statement of the beliefs of the Church of England. They established a moderate form of Protestantism.

three-field system A medieval innovation that increased the amount of land under cultivation by leaving only one third fallow in a given year.

transportation The British policy from the late eighteenth to the mid–nineteenth centuries of shipping persons convicted of the most serious offenses to Australia as an alternative to capital punishment.

transubstantiation The doctrine that the entire substances of the bread and wine are changed in the Eucharist into the body and blood of Christ.

tribunes (TRIB-unes) Roman officials who had to be plebeians and were elected by the plebeian assembly to protect plebeians from the arbitrary power of the magistrates.

ulema (oo-LEE-mah) Meaning "persons with correct knowledge." The Islamic scholarly elite who served a social function similar to the Christian clergy.

Upper Egypt The part of Egypt that runs from the delta to the Sudanese border.

utilitarianism The theory associated with Jeremy Bentham (1748–1832) that the principle of utility, defined as the greatest good for the greatest number of people, should be applied to government, the economy, and the judicial system.

utopian socialism Early-nineteenth-century theories that sought to replace the existing capitalist structure and values with visionary solutions or ideal communities.

vassal A person granted an estate or cash payments in return for accepting the obligation to render services to a lord.

vernacular The everyday language spoken by the people as opposed to Latin.

vingtième (VEN-tee-em) Meaning "one twentieth." A tax on income in France before the Revolution.

Vulgate The Latin translation of the Bible by Jerome (348–420 C.E.) that became the standard bible used by the Catholic Church.

Waldensians (wahl-DEN-see-ens) Medieval heretics who advocated biblical simplicity in reaction to the worldliness of the church.

war communism The economic policy adopted by the Bolsheviks during the Russian Civil War to seize the banks, heavy industry, railroads, and grain.

war guilt clause Clause 231 of the Versailles Treaty, which assigned responsibility for World War I solely to Germany.

water frame A water-powered device invented by Richard Arkwright to produce a more durable cotton fabric. It led to the shift in the production of cotton textiles from households to factories.

Weimar (Why-mar) **Republic** The German democratic regime that existed between the end of World War I and Hitler's coming to power in 1933.

White Russians Those Russians who opposed the Bolsheviks (the "Reds") in the Russian Civil War of 1918–1921.

zemstvos (ZEMPST-vohs) Local governments set up in the Russian Empire in 1864.

Zionism The movement to create a Jewish state in Palestine (the Biblical Zion).

Zollverein (TZOL-fuh-rine) A free-trade union established among the major German states in 1834.

INDEX

Third Dynasty, xxxviii
World War II, 912, 915, *916*
Eiffel Tower, 723, *724*
Einstein, Albert, 764
Eisenhower, Dwight D., 919, 949, 952, 963
Eisenstein, Sergei, 887, 933
Either/Or (Kierkegaard), 999
El Alamein, 915, *916*
El Greco, 294
Electricity, 719, 1023–1024
Electronic Numerical Integrator and Computer, 1010, *1010*
Elegances of the Latin Language (Valla), 291
Elements of the Philosophy of Newton (Voltaire), 513
Eliot, George, 765
Elizabeth I, queen of England, 302, 336, 337, 352, 361, 363, *365*, 366, *366*, 368, 382
Elizabeth of Russia, 494, 540
Elizabeth of York, 301
Emancipation Act (1861), 707
Emancipation Proclamation, 492, 685
Émigrés, 563–564, *565*, 582
Emilie (Rousseau), 528, 529, 531, 598
Eminent Victorians (Strachey), 766
Emma-Magazine by Women for Women (journal), 993
Empiricism, 422–424
Employment
    Chartism, 651, 653–654, *654*
    family of 18th century, 453–454, 456–457
    Industrial Revolution in 18th century and, 460–461
    Industrial Revolution in 19th century and, 650–651, 654, 656
    of women in the 18th century, 453–454
    of women in the 19th century, 656–658, *659*, 728–729
    of women in the 20th century, 993, 997
Enabling Act (1933), 888
Encomienda, 311
Encyclical, 761
Encyclopedia, The (Diderot), 520, *520*, 526, 527, 528
Energy, modern world and, 1021–1026
Enfield rifle, 814
Engels, Friedrich, 666, 668
Enghien, duke of, 583
England. *See also* Britain
    agriculture in, 456
    alliances with Austria and Russia against France, 586
    American Revolution, 495–498
    in Americas, 478, 479–480, 495–496
    aristocracy of 18th century, 447

Austrian Succession, war of (1740-1748), 492–493
enclosures replaces open fields, 456–457
following American Revolution, 500–501
game laws, 451
Hastings, battle of (1066), lxxiii, *lxxiv*
humanism in, 305
Hundred Years' War, 262–267
Industrial Revolution, 461
key events/dates, 499
Magna Carta (1215), lxxiv, lxxv
peasant rebellions in, 260, 450–451
Quadruple Alliance, 594, 596
Reformation in, 334–337
Reformation Parliament, 335–336
relations with Spain, 362–368
revival of monarchy, 301–302, 386–387, lxxiii–lxxiv
romantic literature, 599, 601
social reform, 535
suppression of reforms, following French Revolution, 567
toleration and political stability, 509–510
War of Jenkins's Ear, 492, 630
William the Conqueror, *lxxiv*
England, seventeenth century
    Age of Walpole, *388*, 388–389
    Charles I, 385–386, *386*
    Charles II and restoration of the monarchy, 386–387
    civil war, 385–386
    compared with France, 382
    Cromwell, *386*, 386
    Glorious Revolution, 387–388
    James I, 382–383, 385
    James II, 387–388
    key events/dates, 387
    Long Parliament, 385–386
    parliamentary monarchy, 382
English Factory Act (1833), 656
ENIAC, 1010, *1010*
Enlightened absolutism, 509, 533–543
Enlightenment. *See also under name of author or work*
    absolutism in, 533–543
    defined, 509, 513
    Encyclopedia, The, 520, *520*, 526, 528
    formative influences on, 509–511
    major works of, 527
    philosophes, 511–514, 523–526
    print culture, impact of, 509, *510*, 510–511
    religion and, 514–520
    society and, 520–523
    women and, 527–530

Enquiry into the Obligations of Christians, to use Means for the Conversion of the Heathen, An (Carey), 815
Entente Cordiale, 835
Entertainment
    theater, 17th century, 367
Environmentalism, 1002, 1004
Episteme, xlviii
Erasmus, Desiderius, 293, 298, 304, 305, 319, 324, 328, 342
Erechtheum, xlvi
Erfurt Program, 739–740
Escorial, 359
Essay Concerning Human Understanding, An (Locke), 427, 509
Essay on the Inequality of the Human Races (Gobineau), 773
Essay on the Principles of Population (Malthus), 662
Estates General, French, 263, 548, 550
    becomes the National Assembly, 550–552
    formation of, 265
    Louis XIV calls, into session, 299
    Louis XVI calls, into session, 550
Esterhazy, Prince, 447
Estonia, 861, 970
Ethics (Spinoza), 517
Ethics and science, 756–757
Ethiopia, 955
    Italy attacks, 902–903, 936
Ethiopian Church, 817
Ethnic cleansing, *759*, 974
Euro, *987*, 1013
Europe. *See also under name of country*
    in 1714, *398*
    expansion, 828–829
    territorial changes after World War II, *942*
European Coal and Steel Community, 1011
European Coalition, 594
European Constitution, 1014, *1014*
European Economic Community (EEC), 968, *987*, 1012–1013
European Free Trade Area, 1013
European Union, *1013*, 1013–1016
Evangelicalism, 814–815
Evans, Mary Ann (George Eliot), 765
Evolution and Ethics (Huxley), 758–759
Evolutionary Socialism (Bernstein), 740
Execrabilis, 276
Executions, 467
Existentialism, 999–1000
Explorations, 305–307
    map of, *306*

Exquemelin, Alexander, 481
Exsurge Domine, 324

F

Fabianism, 738–739
Fabius Maximus, Quintus, 738
Factories, 479, 650–653, 659
Falangists, 904
Falkenhayn, Erich von, 847
Falloux Law (1850), 760
Family
    cult of domesticity, 730–731
    economy, 451–455
    Homeric society, xliv
    Nazi Germany, 893
    Reformation and, 343–345
    Soviet Union, 892–893, *893*
    Spartan, xlv
    18th century, 451–455
    19th century, 654, 656, 658, 664, 672, 777
    20th century, 993, 997
Famine in Ireland, 507, 648, 649
Fanaticism, or Mohammed the Prophet (Voltaire), 518
Faraday, Michael, 1024
Farel, Guillaume, 332
Farnese of Parma, Alexander, 362
Fascism, in Italy, 878–881
Fashoda incident, 803
Faust (Goethe), 602
Fawcett, Millicent, 733
Fear and Trembling (Kierkegaard), 999
February Patent, 704
Feisal, prince, *856*
Feltre, Vittorino da, 289
Feminism
    antifeminism in late 19th century, 775–777
    in France (1848), 671–673
    obstacles to equality, 732–733
    rise of political, 732–735
    sexual morality and the family, 732, 777–779
    19th century, 732–735, 775–779
    20th century, 993, 996
    voting rights, *733*, 733–734, 778
Ferdinand, Francis (archduke of Austria), 830, 838, *838*, 840
Ferdinand I, emperor, 358
Ferdinand II, Holy Roman emperor, 371–372, 373, *373*
Ferdinand of Aragon, 297, 298, 300–301, 334, 345
Ferdinand of Austria, 673, 676
Ferdinand VII, king of Spain, 629, 634, 636
Ferrara-Florence, Council of (1439), 289
Ferry, Jules, 760
Festival of the Supreme Being, *575*
Feudal society, lxviii
    fiefs, lxviii
    vassalage, lxviii
Fichte, J.G., 607